AUSTRALIAN

SIGNPOST

Mathematics 9

New South Wales

Stages 5.1–5.3

Alan McSeveny
Rob Conway
Steve Wilkes

AUSTRALIAN CURRICULUM

ALWAYS LEARNING

PEARSON

Train a child in the way he should go, and
when he is old he will not turn from it.

Proverbs 22:6

Pearson Australia
(a division of Pearson Australia Group Pty Ltd)
707 Collins Street, Melbourne, Victoria 3008
PO Box 23360, Melbourne, Victoria 8012
www.pearson.com.au

First published 2014 by Pearson Australia
2019 2018
10 9 8 7 6 5 4

Publisher: Tanya Smith
Editor: Liz Waud
Designer: Glen McClay
Typesetter: Nikki M Group Pty Ltd
Copyright & Pictures Editor: Julia Weaver
Mac Operator: Rob Curulli
Cover art: Glen McClay, David Doyle and Jenny Grigg
Illustrators: Michael Barter and Nikki M Group Pty Ltd
Printed in China (CTPS/04)

National Library of Australia Cataloguing-in-Publication entry
Author: McSeveny, A. (Alan)
Title: Australian Signpost Mathematics New South Wales 9 Stages 5.1–5.3 student book / Alan McSeveny, Rob Conway, Steve Wilkes.
ISBN: 9781486005314 (pbk.)
Target Audience: For secondary school age.
Subjects: Mathematics--Textbooks.
Other Authors/Contributors: Conway, Rob; Wilkes, Steve.
Dewey Number: 510

Pearson Australia Group Pty Ltd ABN 40 004 245 943

Acknowledgements
We would like to thank the following for permission to reproduce copyright material.

The following abbreviations are used in this list: t = top, b = bottom, l = left, r = right, c = centre.

Commonwealth of Australia: © 2013 Australian Taxation Office, p. 231.

Dreamstime: pp. 95, 212.

GeoGebra: Created with GeoGebra (www.geogebra.org), pp. 87, 112, 117, 124, 138, 175, 177, 267, 272, 279, 289, 301, 304, 307, 320, 332, 337, 381, 394, 397.

NASA: p. 14.

Pearson Australia: Alice McBroom, pp. 168, 233b, 237.

Shutterstock: cover, pp. 11, 27, 29, 30, 33, 36, 37, 41, 42t, 42b, 45, 49, 57, 73, 75, 76, 79, 80, 82, 83, 86, 89, 90, 91bl, 91tr, 94, 96, 108tl, 108bl, 108r, 109, 128, 133, 139, 143, 143r, 144, 150, 153, 163, 165, 166, 169t, 169b, 179, 180, 186t, 186b, 200, 214, 221, 224, 228, 232, 233t, 236, 238, 240, 241, 242, 244t, 244b, 246t, 246c, 246b, 247t, 247c, 247b, 250, 252, 267, 285, 293, 294t, 294b, 300, 303, 305, 309, 310, 312, 313t, 313b, 316, 319, 325t, 325b, 340t, 340b, 343, 349t, 349b, 350, 354, 362, 371, 374, 377, 389, 399, 409, 416, 420, 427, 429, 430, 440, 444, 445, 452, 459, 462, 463, 465, 470, 472, 473, 475, 480, 488, 493b, 493t.

Every effort has been made to trace and acknowledge copyright. However, if any infringement has occurred, the publishers tender their apologies and invite the copyright holders to contact them.

CONTENTS

Australian Signpost Mathematics New South Wales 9 Stages 5.1–5.3

The **Australian Signpost Mathematics New South Wales** series has been completely updated to comprehensively cover the NSW Syllabus for the Australian Curriculum. Students and teachers are supported with a Student Book, an eBook, a Homework Program and a Teacher Companion for each stage of development. Features within each component, along with additional resources on the eBook, allow the creation of a personalised learning package for the individual. Improvements in technology, teaching resources and design allow students and teachers to approach the NSW Syllabus with confidence.

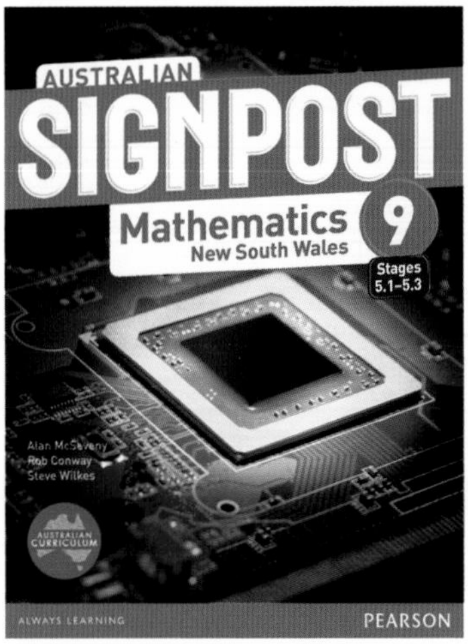

Student Book

The *Australian Signpost Mathematics New South Wales 9 Stages 5.1–5.2* and *Australian Signpost Mathematics New South Wales 9 Stages 5.1–5.3* learning package addresses Stage 5 of the NSW Syllabus for the Australian Curriculum. This new series continues the Signpost tradition of expanding students' ability in a broad range of mathematical skills while emphasising problem-solving and working mathematically.

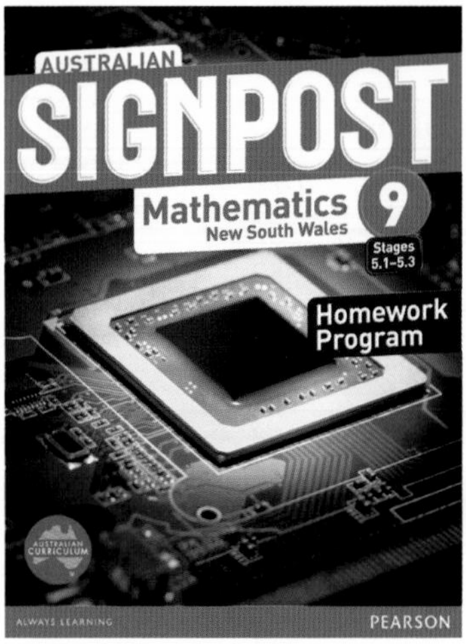

Homework Program

The Homework Program consists of tear-out worksheets that mirror and supplement the content of the student book, providing opportunity for further practice and application of key skills.

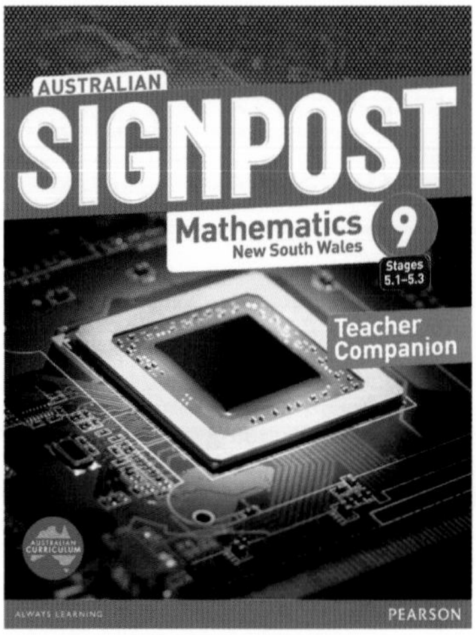

Teacher Companion

The Teacher Companion is an invaluable resource that provides guidance and support to teachers using the **Australian Signpost Mathematics New South Wales** package. It is a practical resource featuring teaching strategies, activities, reference to Stage 5 outcomes and content statements, and links to digital learning materials.

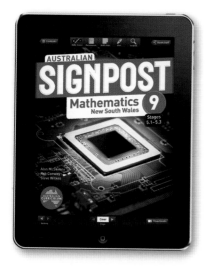

HOW TO USE THE STUDENT BOOK

The **Australian Signpost Mathematics New South Wales 9 Stages 5.1–5.3** learning package covers Stage 5 outcomes of the NSW Syllabus for the Australian Curriculum.

Features of the Student Book

- a complete year's work with full coverage of the NSW Syllabus for the Australian Curriculum
- a flexible structure with carefully graded exercises, colour-coded to indicate level of difficulty
- technological applications with GeoGebra activities and Pearson eBook 3.0 resources
- integration of a broad range of mathematical skills, expanding students' ability to solve problems, work mathematically and investigate
- diagnostic tests, chapter reviews and cumulative revision components for every chapter

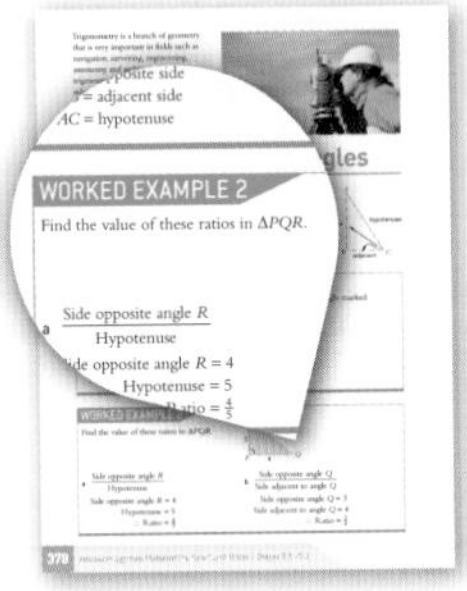

Worked examples

take students through key processes with step-by-step demonstrations of questions similar to those they will encounter.

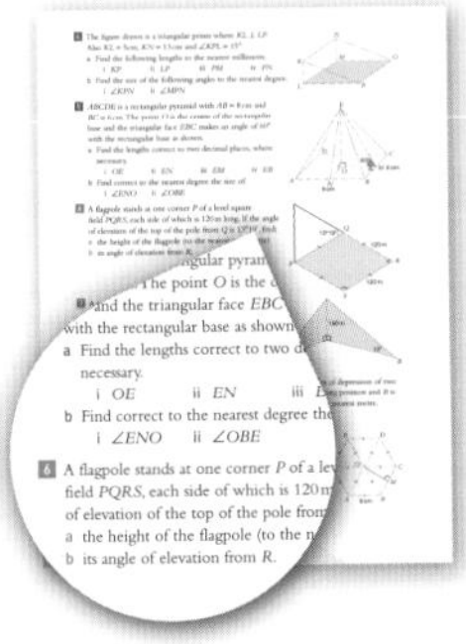

Well-graded exercises

indicate each question's level of difficulty.

2 Foundation
7 Stages 5.1–5.3 level
12 Extension

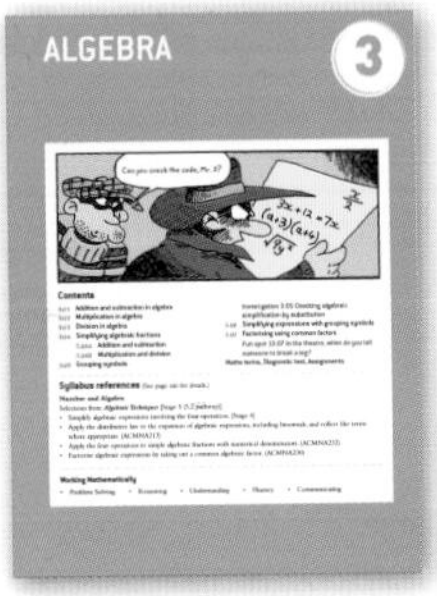

Chapter opener pages

summarise the key content and present the content statements addressed in each chapter. Features within each exercise such as GeoGebra activities, Fun spots and Investigations are listed here.

GeoGebra activities

provide a deeper understanding of concepts covered within the exercise while providing the opportunity to integrate ICT into the classroom.

Prep quizzes

review important skills and knowledge that students will need to complete an exercise.

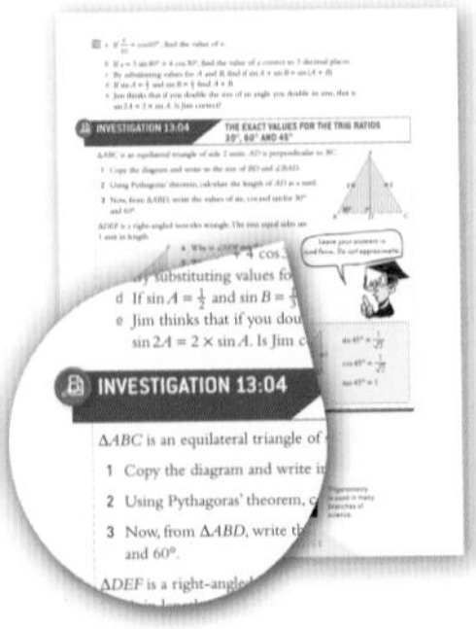

Investigations

encourage students to seek knowledge and develop research skills. The investigative tasks provide opportunities for students to interpret, question, model and communicate mathematically.

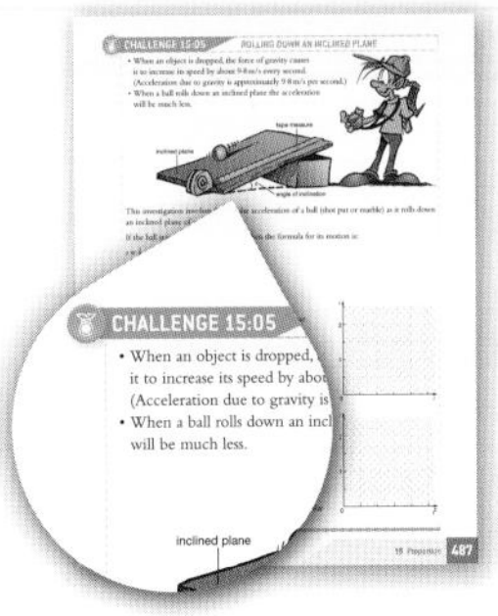

Challenge activities provide more difficult questions and investigations. They can be used to help students with a stronger understanding extend their knowledge.

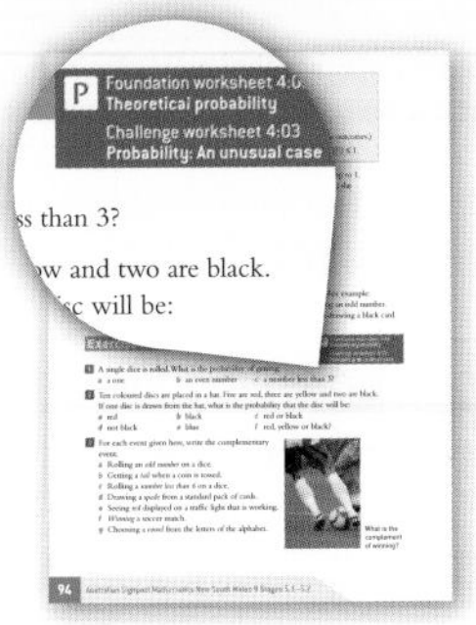

Foundation and Challenge worksheets are indicated in the student book wherever a worksheet is available on the eBook. Foundation worksheets provide alternative exercises for consolidation of the fundamental content of the work being introduced. Challenge worksheets help students apply their learning in more advanced activities.

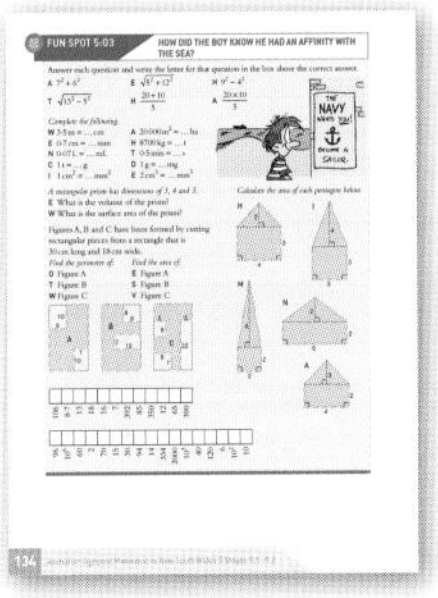

Fun spots provide amusement and interest while reinforcing concepts learnt within the chapter. They encourage creativity and divergent thinking, and show that mathematics is enjoyable.

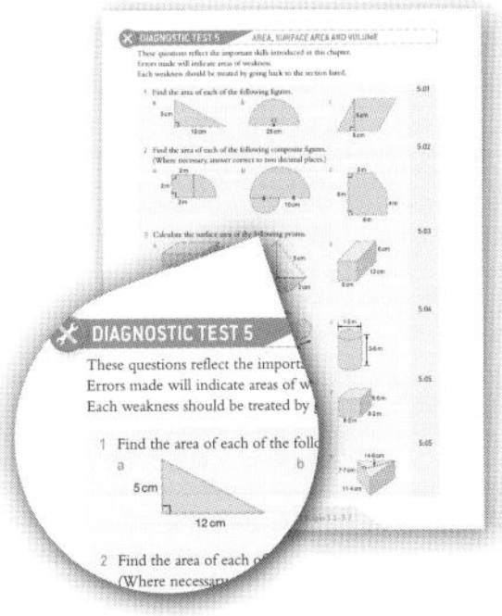

Diagnostic tests at the end of each chapter test students' achievement of outcomes. Importantly, they also indicate student weaknesses that need to be addressed and provide links to the relevant sections in the text or digital resources.

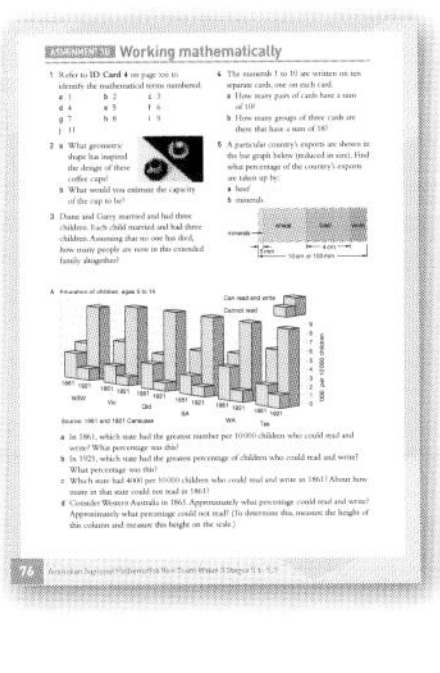

Assignments are provided at the end of each chapter. They concentrate on revising the content of previous chapters and developing students' ability to work mathematically.

Pearson digital resources

A vast range of technology applications are available with the eBook and ProductLink to complement the content presented in the student book. Digital resources include activities, appendices, and Foundation and Challenge worksheets. From the eBook, students can also link directly to the GeoGebra activities referred to in the student book exercises.

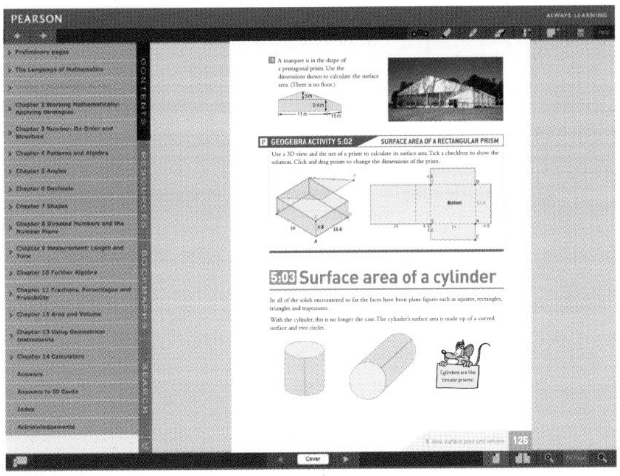

The eBook and ProductLink aim to create a classroom environment that embraces mathematical technologies in a way that consolidates and extends student learning.

TREATMENT OF SYLLABUS CONTENT

The syllabus outcomes and statements relevant to Stages 5.1–5.3 of the NSW Syllabus for the Australian Curriculum are listed below. Chapters where the content is treated are shown.

Working Mathematically (encompassing five components: Communicating, Problem Solving, Reasoning, Understanding and Fluency) is an integral part of the structure of each chapter. Special attention is given to Working Mathematically in Chapter 2 of this Student Book and at the end of each chapter of all Year 9 and 10 Student Books.

Working Mathematically	
A student: > uses appropriate terminology, diagrams and symbols in mathematical contexts	**MA5.1-1WM**
> selects appropriate notations and conventions to communicate mathematical ideas and solutions	**MA5.2-1WM**
> uses and interprets formal definitions and generalisations when explaining solutions and/or conjectures	**MA5.3-1WM**
> selects and uses appropriate strategies to solve problems	**MA5.1-2WM**
> interprets mathematical or real-life situations, systematically applying appropriate strategies to solve problems	**MA5.2-2WM**
> generalises mathematical ideas and techniques to analyse and solve problems efficiently	**MA5.3-2WM**
> provides reasoning to support conclusions that are appropriate to the context	**MA5.1-3WM**
> constructs arguments to prove and justify results	**MA5.2-3WM**
> uses deductive reasoning in presenting arguments and formal proofs	**MA5.3-3WM**
Number and Algebra	
A student: > solves financial problems involving earning, spending and investing money > solves financial problems involving compound interest	**MA5.1-4NA** **MA5.2-4NA**◊
> recognises direct and indirect proportion, and solves problems involving direct proportion > draws, interprets and analyses graphs of physical phenomena	**MA5.2-5NA** **MA5.3-4NA**
> simplifies algebraic fractions, and expands and factorises quadratic expressions > selects and applies appropriate algebraic techniques to operate with algebraic expressions	**MA5.2-6NA** **MA5.3-5NA**§
> operates with algebraic expressions involving positive-integer and zero indices, and establishes the meaning of negative indices for numerical bases > applies index laws to operate with algebraic expressions involving integer indices > performs operations with surds and indices	**MA5.1-5NA** **MA5.2-7NA** **MA5.3-6NA**§
> solves linear and simple quadratic equations, linear inequalities and linear simultaneous equations, using analytical and graphical techniques > solves complex linear, quadratic, simple cubic and simultaneous equations, and rearranges literal equations	**MA5.2-8NA** **MA5.3-7NA**§
> determines the midpoint, gradient and length of an interval, and graphs linear relationships > uses the gradient-intercept form to interpret and graph linear relationships > uses formulas to find midpoint, gradient and distance on the Cartesian plane, and applies standard forms of the equation of a straight line	**MA5.1-6NA** **MA5.2-9NA** **MA5.3-8NA**§
> graphs simple non-linear relationships > connects algebraic and graphical representations of simple non-linear relationships > sketches and interprets a variety of non-linear relationships	**MA5.1-7NA** **MA5.2-10NA**◊ **MA5.3-9NA**§
> recognises, describes and sketches polynomials, and applies the factor and remainder theorems to solve problems	**MA5.3-10NA**#
> uses the definition of a logarithm to establish and apply the laws of logarithms	**MA5.3-11NA**#
> uses function notation to describe and sketch functions	**MA5.3-12NA**#

Measurement and Geometry	
A student: > calculates the areas of composite shapes, and the surface areas of rectangular and triangular prisms > calculates the surface areas of right prisms, cylinders and related compo site solids > applies formulas to find the surface areas of right pyramids, right cones, spheres and related composite solids	 **MA5.1-8MG** **MA5.2-11MG** **MA5.3-13MG**
> applies formulas to calculate the volumes of composite solids composed of right prisms and cylinders > applies formulas to find the volumes of right pyramids, right cones, spheres and related composite solids	**MA5.2-12MG** **MA5.3-14MG**
> interprets very small and very large units of measurement, uses scientific notation, and rounds to significant figures	**MA5.1-9MG**
> applies trigonometry, given diagrams, to solve problems, including problems involving angles of elevation and depression > applies trigonometry to solve problems, including problems involving bearings > applies Pythagoras' theorem, trigonometric relationships, the sine rule, the cosine rule and the area rule, to solve problems, including problems involving three dimensions	**MA5.1-10MG** **MA5.2-13MG◊** **MA5.3-15MG§**
> describes and applies the properties of similar figures and scale drawings > calculates the angle sum of any polygon and uses minimum conditions to prove triangles are congruent or similar > proves triangles are similar, and uses formal geometric reasoning to establish properties of triangles and quadrilaterals	**MA5.1-11MG** **MA5.2-14MG** **MA5.3-16MG§**
> applies deductive reasoning to prove circle theorems and to solve related problems	**MA5.3-17MG#**
Statistics and Probability	
A student: > uses statistical displays to compare sets of data, and evaluates statistical claims made in the media > uses quartiles and box plots to compare sets of data, and evaluates sources of data > uses standard deviation to analyse data	 **MA5.1-12SP** **MA5.2-15SP◊** **MA5.3-18SP**
> investigates relationships between two statistical variables, including their relationship over time > investigates the relationship between numerical variables using lines of best fit, and explores how data is used to inform decision-making processes	**MA5.2-16SP** **MA5.3-19SP**
> calculates relative frequencies to estimate probabilities of simple and compound events > describes and calculates probabilities in multi-step chance experiments	**MA5.1-13SP** **MA5.2-17SP**

The NSW Syllabus for the Australian Curriculum has indicated the minimum achievement of Stage 5 outcomes for students planning to proceed to current Stage 6 Mathematics courses.

◊ Minimum Stage 5 content for students planning to study Preliminary Mathematics General / HSC Mathematics General 2.

§ Minimum Stage 5 content for students planning to study Mathematics ('2 Unit').

Optional Stage 5.3 substrands. Minimum Stage 5 content for students planning to study Mathematics Extension 1.

Stages 5.1–5.3 content

The Stages 5.1–5.3 content is divided into three strands:

- Number and Algebra
- Measurement and Geometry
- Statistics and Probability

Content statements are listed below with their Australian Curriculum code or NSW syllabus reference. The chapters that address each content statement are shown in the right-hand column.

Number and Algebra (5.1)	References	Chapter
Financial Mathematics		
• Solve problems involving earning money.	NSW (Stage 5.1)	Ch 8 (Y9)
• Solve problems involving simple interest.	ACMNA211 (Stage 5.1)	Ch 8 (Y9)
• Connect the compound interest formula to repeated applications of simple interest using appropriate digital technologies.	ACMNA229 (Stages 5.1, 5.2)	Ch 6 (Y10)
Indices		
• Extend and apply the index laws to variables, using positive-integer indices and the zero index.	ACMNA212 (Stage 5.1)	Ch 6 (Y9)
• Simplify algebraic products and quotients using index laws.	ACMNA231 (Stage 5.1)	Ch 6 (Y9)
• Apply index laws to numerical expressions with integer indices.	ACMNA209 (Stage 5.1)	Ch 6 (Y9)
Linear Relationships		
• Find the midpoint and gradient of a line segment (interval) on the Cartesian plane using a range of strategies, including graphing software.	ACMNA294 (Stage 5.1)	Ch 10 (Y9)
• Find the distance between two points located on the Cartesian plane using a range of strategies, including graphing software.	ACMNA214 (Stage 5.1)	Ch 10 (Y9)
• Sketch linear graphs using the coordinates of two points.	ACMNA215 (Stage 5.1)	Ch 7 (Y9), Ch 10 (Y9)
• Solve problems involving parallel and perpendicular lines.	ACMNA238 (Stage 5.1)	Ch 7 (Y10)
Non-linear Relationships		
• Graph simple non-linear relations, with and without the use of digital technologies.	ACMNA296 (Stage 5.1)	Ch 10 (Y9)
• Explore the connection between algebraic and graphical representations of relations such as simple quadratics, circles and exponentials using digital technologies as appropriate.	ACMNA239 (Stage 5.1)	Ch 7 (Y10)

Measurement and Geometry (5.1)	References	Chapters
Area and Surface Area		
• Calculate the areas of composite shapes.	ACMMG216 (Stage 5.1)	Ch 5 (Y9)
• Solve problems involving the surface areas of right prisms.	ACMMG218 (Stage 5.1)	Ch 5 (Y9)
Numbers of Any Magnitude		
• Investigate very small and very large time scales and intervals.	ACMMG219 (Stage 5.1)	Ch 1 (Y9)
• Express numbers in scientific notation.	ACMMG210 (Stage 5.1)	Ch 1 (Y9), Ch 6 (Y9)
Right-angled Triangles (Trigonometry)		
• Use similarity to investigate the constancy of the sine, cosine and tangent ratios for a given angle in right-angled triangles.	ACMMG223 (Stage 5.1)	Ch 13 (Y9)
• Apply trigonometry to solve right-angled triangle problems.	ACMMG224 (Stage 5.1)	Ch 13 (Y9)
• Solve right-angled triangle problems, including those involving angles of elevation and depression.	ACMMG245 (Stage 5.1)	Ch 13 (Y9)
Properties of Geometrical Figures		
• Use the enlargement transformation to explain similarity.	ACMMG220 (Stage 5.1)	Ch 11 (Y9)
• Solve problems using ratio and scale factors in similar figures.	ACMMG221 (Stage 5.1)	Ch 11 (Y9)

Statistics and Probability (5.1)	References	Chapters
Single Variable Data Analysis		
• Identify everyday questions and issues involving at least one numerical and at least one categorical variable, and collect data directly from secondary sources.	ACMSP228 (Stage 5.1)	Ch 9 (Y10)
• Construct back-to-back stem-and-leaf plots and histograms and describe data, using terms including 'skewed', 'symmetric' and 'bi-modal'.	ACMSP282 (Stage 5.1)	Ch 14 (Y9)
• Compare data displays using mean, median and range to describe and interpret numerical data sets in terms of location (centre) and spread.	ACMSP283 (Stage 5.1)	Ch 14 (Y9)
• Evaluate statistical reports in the media and other places by linking claims to displays, statistics and representative data.	ACMSP253 (Stage 5.1)	Ch 9 (Y10)
Probability		
• Calculate relative frequencies from given or collected data to estimate probabilities of events involving 'and' or 'or'.	ACMSP226 (Stage 5.1)	Ch 4 (Y9)

Number and Algebra (5.2)	References	Chapters
Financial Mathematics◊		
• Connect the compound interest formula to repeated applications of simple interest using appropriate digital technologies.	ACMNA229 (Stages 5.1, 5.2)	Ch 6 (Y10)
Ratio and Rates		
• Solve problems involving direct proportion; explore the relationship between graphs and equations corresponding to simple rate problems.	ACMNA208 (Stage 5.2)	Ch 15 (Y9)
Algebraic Techniques		
• Apply the four operations to simple algebraic fractions with numerical denominators.	ACMNA232 (Stage 5.2)	Ch 3 (Y9)
• Apply the four operations to algebraic fractions with pronumerals in the denominator.	NSW (Stage 5.2)	Ch 3 (Y9)
• Apply the distributive law to the expansion of algebraic expressions, including binomials, and collect like terms where appropriate.	ACMNA213 (Stage 5.2)	Ch 3 (Y9)
• Factorise algebraic expressions by taking out a common algebraic factor.	ACMNA230 (Stage 5.2)	Ch 3 (Y9), Ch 12 (Y9)
• Expand binomial products and factorise monic quadratic expressions using a variety of strategies.	ACMNA233 (Stage 5.2)	Ch 12 (Y9)
Indices		
• Apply index laws to algebraic expressions involving integer indices.	NSW (Stage 5.2)	Ch 6 (Y9)
Equations		
• Solve linear equations.	ACMNA215 (Stage 5.2)	Ch 7 (Y9)
• Solve linear equations involving simple algebraic fractions.	ACMNA240 (Stage 5.2)	Ch 7 (Y9)
• Solve simple quadratic equations using a range of strategies.	ACMNA241 (Stage 5.2)	Ch 2 (Y10)
• Substitute values into formulas to determine an unknown.	ACMNA234 (Stage 5.2)	Ch 7 (Y9)
• Solve problems involving linear equations, including those derived from formulas.	ACMNA235 (Stage 5.2)	Ch 7 (Y9)
• Solve linear inequalities and graph their solutions on a number line.	ACMNA236 (Stage 5.2)	Ch 7 (Y9)
• Solve linear simultaneous equations, using algebraic and graphical techniques, including with the use of digital technologies.	ACMNA237 (Stage 5.2)	Ch 9 (Y9)
Linear Relationships		
• Interpret and graph linear relationships using the gradient-intercept form of the equation of a straight line.	NSW (Stage 5.2)	Ch 10 (Y9)
• Solve problems involving parallel and perpendicular lines.	ACMNA238 (Stage 5.2)	Ch 10 (Y9)
Non-linear Relationships◊		
• Graph simple non-linear relationships with and without the use of digital technologies and solve simple related equations.	ACMNA296 (Stage 5.2)	Ch 10 (Y9), Ch 7 (Y10)
• Explore the connection between algebraic and graphical representations of relationships such as simple quadratics, circles and exponentials using digital technologies as appropriate.	ACMNA239 (Stage 5.2)	Ch 7 (Y10)

Measurement and Geometry (5.2)	References	Chapters
Area and Surface Area		
• Calculate the surface areas of cylinders and solve related problems.	ACMMG217 (Stage 5.2)	Ch 5 (Y9)
• Solve problems involving surface area for a range of prisms, cylinders and composite solids.	ACMMG242 (Stage 5.2)	Ch 5 (Y9), Ch 8 (Y10)
Volume		
• Solve problems involving the volumes of right prisms.	ACMMG218 (Stage 5.2)	Ch 5 (Y9)
• Solve problems involving volume for a range of prisms, cylinders and composite solids.	ACMMG242 (Stage 5.2)	Ch 5 (Y9)
Right-angled triangles (Trigonometry)◊		
• Apply trigonometry to solve right-angled triangle problems.	ACMMG224 (Stage 5.2)	Ch 13 (Y9)
• Solve right-angled triangle problems, including those involving direction and angles of elevation and depression.	ACMMG245 (Stage 5.2)	Ch 13 (Y9)
Properties of Geometrical Figures		
• Formulate proofs involving congruent triangles and angle properties.	ACMMG243 (Stage 5.2)	Ch 3 (Y10)
• Use the enlargement transformations to explain similarity and to develop the conditions for triangles to be similar.	ACMMG220 (Stage 5.2)	Ch 11 (Y9)
• Apply logical reasoning, including the use of congruence and similarity, to proofs and numerical exercises involving plane shapes.	ACMMG244 (Stage 5.2)	Ch 3 (Y10), Ch 10 (Y10)

Statistics and Probability (5.2)	References	Chapters
Single Variable Data Analysis◊		
• Determine quartiles and interquartile range.	ACMSP248 (Stage 5.2)	Ch 14 (Y9)
• Construct and interpret box plots and use them to compare data sets.	ACMSP249 (Stage 5.2)	Ch 14 (Y9)
• Compare shapes of box plots to corresponding histograms and dot plots.	ACMSP250 (Stage 5.2)	Ch 14 (Y9)
• Investigate reports of surveys in digital media and elsewhere for information on how data was obtained to estimate population means and medians.	ACMSP227 (Stage 5.2)	Ch 9 (Y10)
Bivariate Data Analysis		
• Investigate and describe bivariate numerical data where the independent variable is time.	ACMSP252 (Stage 5.2)	Ch 9 (Y10)
• Use scatter plots to investigate and comment on relationships between two numerical variables.	ACMSP251 (Stage 5.2)	Ch 9 (Y10)
Probability		
• List all outcomes for two-step chance experiments, with and without replacement, using tree diagrams or arrays; assign probabilities to outcomes and determine probabilities for events.	ACMSP225 (Stage 5.2)	Ch 4 (Y9)
• Describe the results of two- and three-step chance experiments, with and without replacement, assign probabilities to outcomes, and determine probabilities of events; investigate the concept of independence.	ACMSP246 (Stage 5.2)	Ch 4 (Y10)
• Use the language of 'if ... then', 'given', 'of', 'knowing that' to investigate conditional statements and to identify common mistakes in interpreting such language.	ACMSP247 (Stage 5.2)	Ch 4 (Y10)

Number and Algebra (5.3)	References	Chapters
Rates and Ratio		
• Solve problems involving direct proportion; explore the relationship between graphs and equations corresponding to simple rate problems.	ACMNA208 (Stage 5.3)	Ch 15 (Y9)
Algebraic Techniques§		
• Add and subtract algebraic fractions with numerical denominators, including those with binomial numerators.	NSW (Stage 5.3)	Ch 3 (Y9)
• Expand binomial products using a variety of strategies.	ACMNA233 (Stage 5.3)	Ch 3 (Y9), Ch 12 (Y9)
• Factorise monic and non-monic quadratic expressions.	ACMNA269 (Stage 5.3)	Ch 12 (Y9)
Surds and Indices§		
• Define rational and irrational numbers and perform operations with surds and fractional indices.	ACMNA264 (Stage 5.3)	Ch 6 (Y9), Ch 5 (Y10)
Equations§		
• Solve complex linear equations involving algebraic fractions.	NSW (Stage 5.3)	Ch 7 (Y9)
• Solve a wide range of quadratic equations derived from a variety of contexts.	ACMNA269 (Stage 5.3)	Ch 2 (Y10)
• Solve simple cubic equations.	NSW (Stage 5.3)	Ch 12 (Y10)
• Rearrange literal equations.	NSW (Stage 5.3)	Ch 7 (Y9)
• Solve simultaneous equations, where one equation is non-linear, using algebraic and graphical techniques, including the use of digital technologies.	NSW (Stage 5.3)	Ch 12 (Y10)

Linear Relationships§		
• Find the midpoint and gradient of a line segment (interval) on the Cartesian plane.	ACMNA294 (Stage 5.3)	Ch 10 (Y9)
• Find the distance between two points located on a Cartesian plane.	ACMNA214 (Stage 5.3)	Ch 10 (Y9)
• Sketch linear graphs using the coordinates of two points.	ACMNA215 (Stage 5.3)	Ch 10 (Y9)
• Solve problems using various standard forms of the equation of a straight line.	NSW (Stage 5.3)	Ch 7 (Y10)
• Solve problems involving parallel and perpendicular lines.	ACMNA238 (Stage 5.3)	Ch 9 (Y9), Ch 7 (Y10)
Non-linear Relationships§		
• Describe, interpret and sketch parabolas, hyperbolas, circles and exponential functions and their transformations.	ACMNA267 (Stage 5.3)	Ch 7 (Y10)
• Describe, interpret and sketch cubics, other curves and their transformations.	NSW (Stage 5.3)	Ch 7 (Y10)
Polynomials#		
• Investigate the concept of a polynomial and apply the factor and remainder theorems to solve problems.	ACMNA266 (Stage 5.3)	Ch 14 (Y10)
• Apply an understanding of polynomials to sketch a range of curves and describe the features of these curves from their equations.	ACMNA268 (Stage 5.3)	Ch 14 (Y10)
Logarithms#		
• Use the definition of a logarithm to establish and apply the laws of logarithms.	ACMNA265 (Stage 5.3)	Ch 15 (Y10)
• Solve simple exponential equations.	ACMNA270 (Stage 5.3)	Ch 15 (Y10)
Functions and Other Graphs#		
• Describe, interpret and sketch functions.	NSW (Stage 5.3)	Ch 16 (Y10)

Measurement and Geometry (5.3)	References	Chapters
Area and Surface Area		
• Solve problems involving the surface areas of right pyramids, right cones, spheres and related composite solids.	ACMMG271 (Stage 5.3)	Ch 8 (Y10)
Volume		
• Solve problems involving the volumes of right pyramids, right cones, spheres and related composite solids.	ACMMG271 (Stage 5.3)	Ch 8 (Y10)
Trigonometry and Pythagoras' Theorem§		
• Apply Pythagoras' theorem and trigonometry to solve three-dimensional problems in right-angled triangles.	ACMMG276 (Stage 5.3)	Ch 13 (Y9)
• Use the unit circle to define trigonometric functions, and graph them, with and without the use of digital technologies.	ACMMG274 (Stage 5.3)	Ch 11 (Y10)
• Solve simple trigonometric equations.	ACMMG275 (Stage 5.3)	Ch 11 (Y10)
• Establish the sine, cosine and area rules for any triangle and solve related problems.	ACMMG273 (Stage 5.3)	Ch 11 (Y10)
Properties of Geometrical Figures§		
• Formulate proofs involving congruent triangles and angle properties.	ACMMG243 (Stage 5.3)	Ch 3 (Y10)
• Apply logical reasoning, including the use of congruence and similarity, to proofs and numerical exercises involving plane shapes.	ACMMG244 (Stage 5.3)	Ch 10 (Y10)
Circle Geometry#		
• Prove and apply angle and chord properties of circles.	ACMMG272 (Stage 5.3)	Ch 13 (Y10)
• Prove and apply tangent and secant properties of circles.	NSW (Stage 5.3)	Ch 13 (Y10)

Statistics and Probability (5.3)	References	Chapters
Single Variable Data Analysis		
• Calculate and interpret the mean and standard deviation of data and use these to compare data sets.	ACMSP278 (Stage 5.3)	Ch 9 (Y10)
Bivariate Data Analysis		
• Use information technologies to investigate bivariate numerical data sets; where appropriate, students use a straight line to describe the relationship, allowing for variation.	ACMSP279 (Stage 5.3)	Ch 9 (Y10)
• Investigate reports of studies in digital media and elsewhere for information on their planning and implementation.	ACMSP277 (Stage 5.3)	Ch 9 (Y10)

DIGITAL RESOURCES

Chapter	Drag-and-drop activities **ProductLink only**	Technology activities **Excel (E)—ProductLink only** **GeoGebra (G)—eBook and ProductLink**	Worksheets **Foundation worksheets (F)** **Challenge worksheets (C)** **—eBook and ProductLink**
1 Number and measurement	Maths terms 1A Maths terms 1B Significant figures		1:03 Decimals (F) 1:06 Approximation (F) 1:07 Estimation (F)
2 Working mathematically		Sharing the prize (E)	
3 Algebra	Maths terms 3 Addition and subtraction of algebraic fractions Multiplication and division of algebraic fractions Grouping symbols Binomial products Special products		3:02A Simplifying algebraic fractions (F) 3:02B Simplifying algebraic fractions (F) 3:03 Grouping symbols (F) 3:03 Fractions and grouping symbols (C) 3:05 Common factors (F)
4 Probability	Maths terms 4 Two dice Pack of cards	Rolling a single dice a large number of times (G) Rolling a single dice a large number of times (E) Chance experiments (E) Probability (E) Two-step chance experiments (E)	4:02 Experimental probability (F) 4:03 Theoretical probability (F) 4:03 Probability: An unusual case (C)
5 Area, surface area and volume	Maths terms 5 Areas of sectors and composite figures Surface area of a prism Volume	Area formulas (G) Areas of composite figures (G) Surface area of a rectangular prism (G) Volume of a prism (G)	5:01 Area (F) 5:02 Surface area of prisms (F) 5:03 Surface area of a cylinder (F) 5:04 Surface area of composite solids (F) 5:05 Volume (F)
6 Indices	Maths terms 6 Index laws Negative indices Fractional indices		6:01 The index laws (F) 6:02 Negative indices (F) 6:03 Fractional indices (F) 6:03 Algebraic expressions and indices (C) 6:04 Scientific notation (F)
7 Equations, inequalities and formulas	Maths terms 7 Equations with fractions Solving inequalities Formulas Equations from formulas Solving literal equations	Equations with pronumerals on both sides 1 (G) Equations with pronumerals on both sides 2 (G) Flowcharts (E) Equations with grouping symbols 1 (G) Equations with grouping symbols 2 (G) Substituting and transposing formulas (E)	7:01 Equivalent equations (F) 7:02 Equations with grouping symbols (F) 7:03 Equations with fractions I (F) 7:04 Equations with fractions 2 (F) 7:05 Solving problems using equations (F) 7:06 Solving inequalities (F) 7:07 Formulas (F) 7:09 Solving literal equations (F)
8 Financial mathematics	Maths terms 8 Finding the weekly wage Going shopping GST	Gross and net salaries (E)	8:02 Extra payments (F) 8:04 Taxation (F) 8:06 Best buy, shopping lists, change (F)
9 Coordinate geometry	Maths terms 9 x- and y-intercepts and graphs Using $y = mx + b$ to find the gradient General form of a line Parallel and perpendicular lines	The midpoint, gradient and length of an interval (G) Graphing lines using two points (G) Equation grapher (E) Finding the equation of a line (G) Equations of the form $y = mx + b$ (G) Graphing lines using $y = mx + b$ (G) Matching equations of lines to their graphs (G) Graphing parabolas (G) Exponential curves (G) Matching parabolas to their equations (G)	9:01 Distance between points (F) 9:02 Midpoint (F) 9:03 Gradients (F) 9:04 Graphing lines (F) 9:05 Gradient-intercept form (F) 9:06 Point-gradient form (F)

Chapter	Drag-and-drop activities **ProductLink only**	Technology activities **Excel (E)—ProductLink only** **GeoGebra (G)—eBook and ProductLink**	Worksheets **Foundation worksheets (F)** **Challenge worksheets (C)** **—eBook and ProductLink**
10 Simultaneous equations		Simultaneous equations: The graphical method (G) Simultaneous equations: The substitution method (G) Simultaneous equations: The elimination method (G)	10:01 Graphical method of solution (F) 10:02A The substitution method (F) 10:03 Using simultaneous equations to solve problems (F) 10:03 Solving three simultaneous equations (C)
11 Similarity	Maths terms 11 Finding lengths in similar figures Using the scale factor	Similar figures (G) Similar triangles: Equal angles (G) Similar triangles: Matching sides in the same ratio (G) Finding an unknown side in similar triangles (G)	11:02 Similar figures (F) 11:04 Finding unknown sides in similar triangles (F) 11:05B Scale drawing (F)
12 Factorising algebraic expressions	Maths terms 12 Factorising using common factors Grouping in pairs Factorising trinomials 1 Factorising trinomials 2 Mixed factorisations		12:02 Grouping in pairs (F) 12:04 Factorising trinomials (F) 12:08 Addition and subtraction of algebraic fractions (F)
13 Trigonometry	Maths terms 13 The trigonometric ratios Finding sides Finding angles Bearings 1 Bearings 2	Investigating the ratio of sides of similar right-angled triangles (G) Finding an unknown side using the tangent ratio (G) Finding an unknown side using the sine and cosine ratios (G) Finding the hypotenuse using the sine and cosine ratios (G) Using the trigonometric ratios to find an angle (G)	13:03 The range of values of the trigonometric ratios (C) 13:05 Using trigonometry to find side lengths (F) 13:06 Trigonometry and the limit of an area (C) 13:07A Angles of elevation and depression, and bearings (F) 13:07B Problems with more than one triangle (F)
14 Statistics	Maths terms 14 Box-and-whisker plots		14:02 Frequency and cumulative frequency (F) 14:03 Interquartile range (F)
15 Proportion		Filling tanks (E)	

Teachers also have access to other digital resources on the eBook and ProductLink, including:

- syllabus overview document
- editable teaching programs
- answers to all worksheets
- answers to Prep quizzes and Investigations
- answers to the Homework Program.

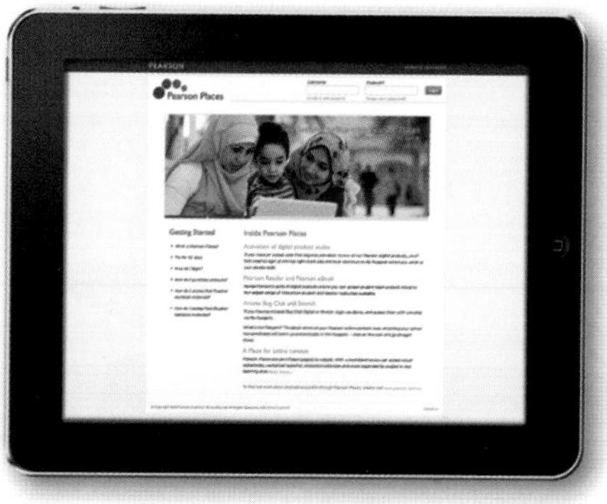

Metric equivalents

Length
$1\,m = 1000\,mm$
$= 100\,cm$
$= 10\,dm$
$1\,cm = 10\,mm$
$1\,km = 1000\,m$
Area
$1\,m^2 = 10\,000\,cm^2$
$1\,ha = 10\,000\,m^2$
$1\,km^2 = 100\,ha$
Mass
$1\,kg = 1000\,g$
$1\,t = 1000\,kg$
$1\,g = 1000\,mg$
Volume
$1\,m^3 = 1\,000\,000\,cm^3$
$= 1000\,dm^3$
$1\,L = 1000\,mL$
$1\,kL = 1000\,L$
$1\,m^3 = 1\,kL$
$1\,cm^3 = 1\,mL$
$1000\,cm^3 = 1\,L$
Time
$1\,min = 60\,s$
$1\,h = 60\,min$
$1\,day = 24\,h$
$1\,year = 365\,days$
$1\,leap\,year = 366\,days$

Months of the year

30 days each has September,
April, June and November.
All the rest have 31, except February alone,
Which has 28 days clear and 29 each leap year.

Seasons

Summer: December, January, February
Autumn: March, April, May
Winter: June, July, August
Spring: September, October, November

It is important that you learn these facts off by heart.

The language of mathematics

You should regularly test your knowledge by identifying the items on each card.

ID Card 1 (Metric units)			
1 m	2 dm	3 cm	4 mm
5 km	6 m^2	7 cm^2	8 km^2
9 ha	10 m^3	11 cm^3	12 s
13 min	14 h	15 m/s	16 km/h
17 g	18 mg	19 kg	20 t
21 L	22 mL	23 kL	24 °C

For answers see page 504.

ID Card 2 (Symbols)			
1 $=$	2 $\doteqdot$ or $\approx$	3 $\neq$	4 $<$
5 $\leq$	6 $\nless$	7 $>$	8 $\geq$
9 4^2	10 4^3	11 $\sqrt{2}$	12 $\sqrt[3]{2}$
13 $\perp$	14 $\parallel$	15 $\equiv$	16 $\vert\vert\vert$
17 %	18 $\therefore$	19 e.g.	20 i.e.
21 π	22 Σ	23 $\bar{x}$	24 $P(E)$

For answers see page 504.

gradient
congruent
converse
volume
See 'Maths Terms' at the end of each chapter.
mean

ID Card 3 (Language)

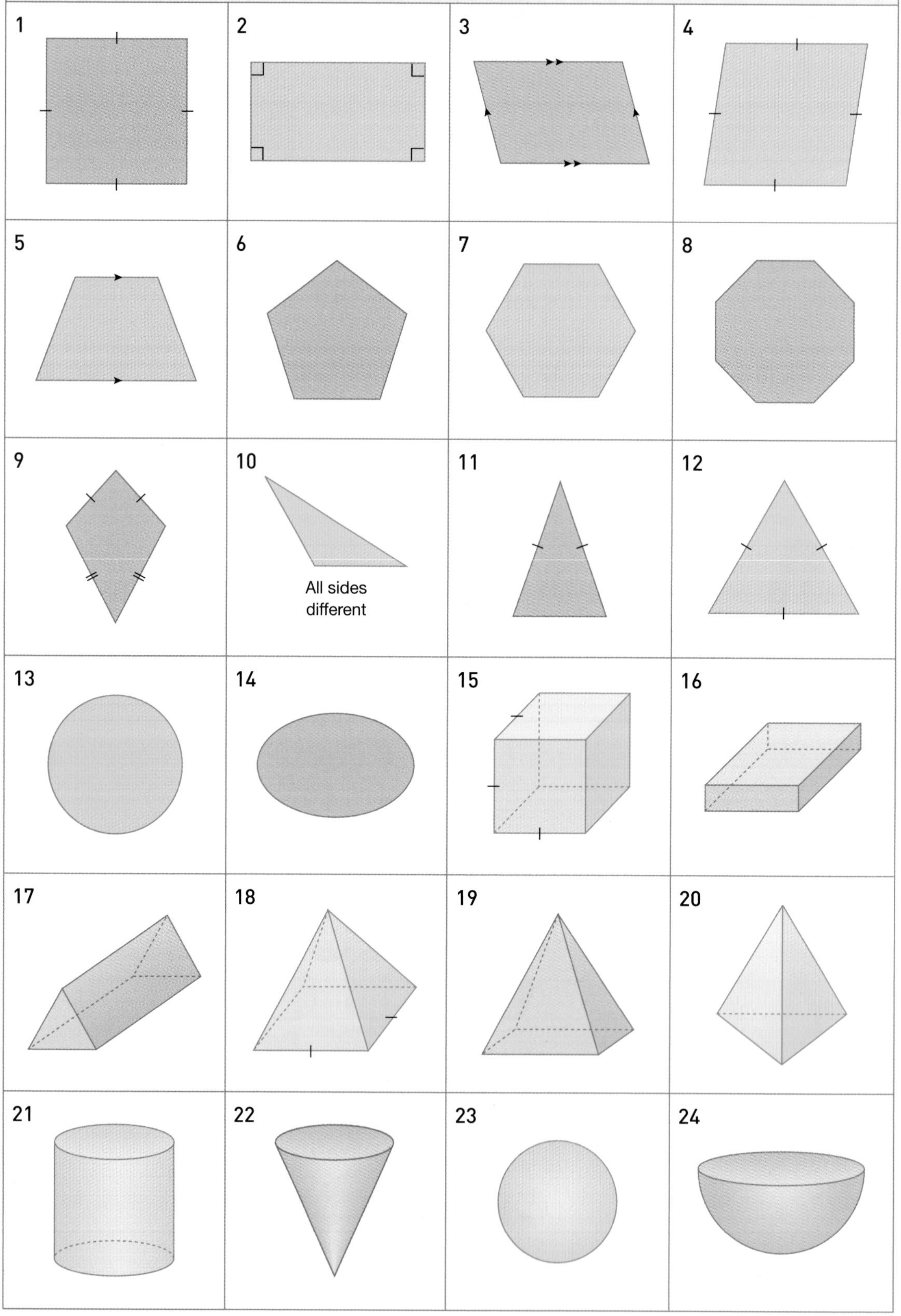

For answers see page 504.

ID Card 4 (Language)

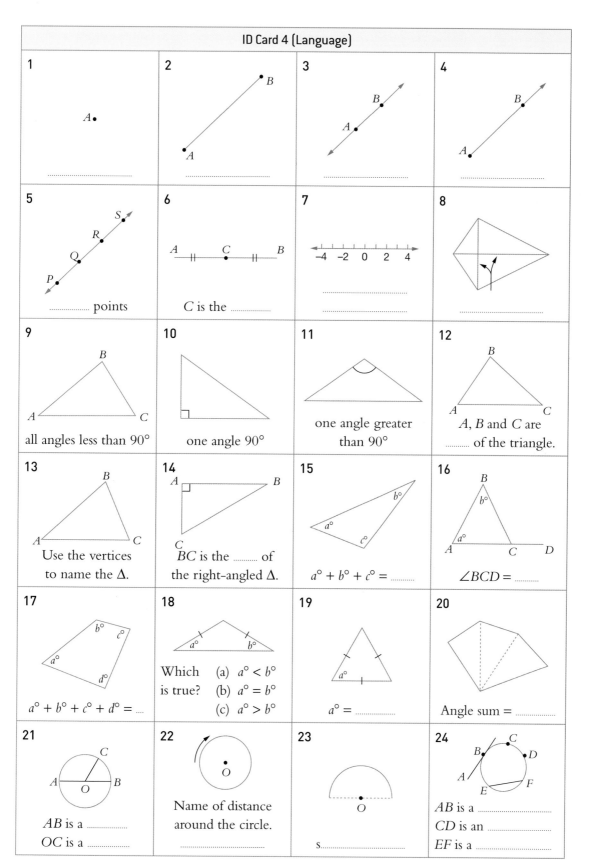

1

....

2

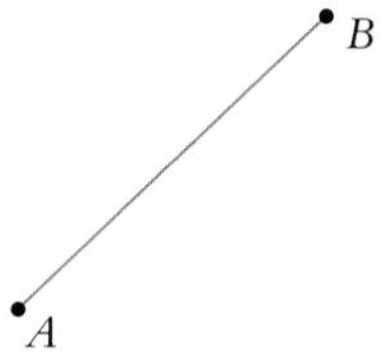

....

3

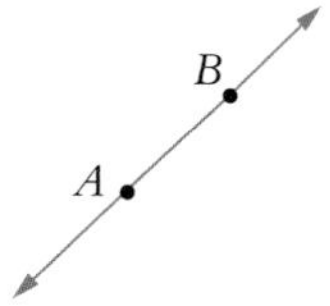

....

4

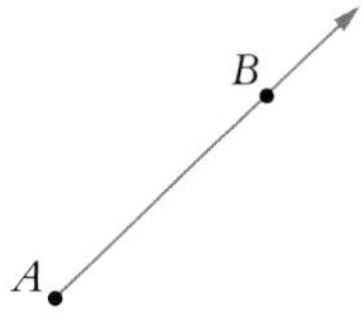

....

5

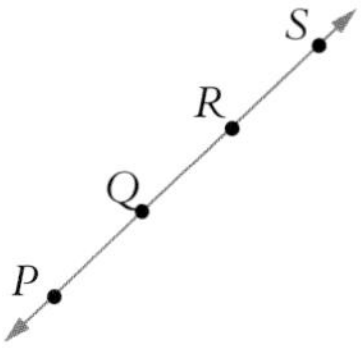

.... points

6

C is the ....

7

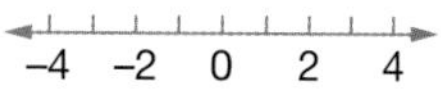

....

....

8

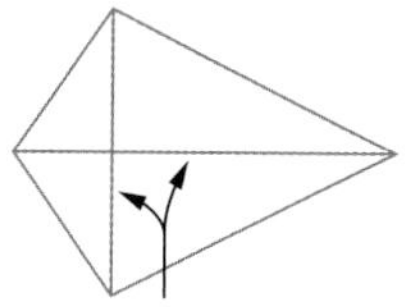

....

9

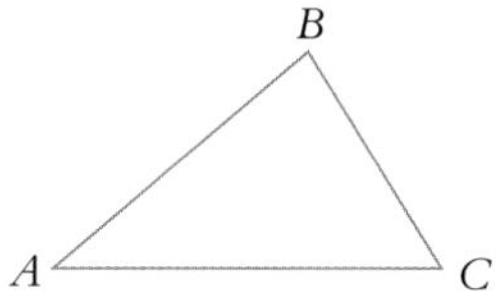

all angles less than 90°

10

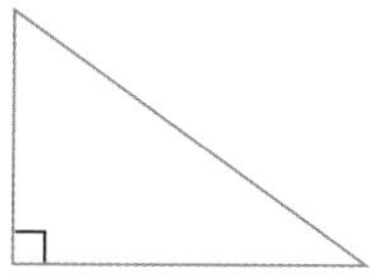

one angle 90°

11

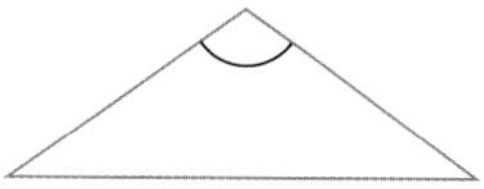

one angle greater than 90°

12

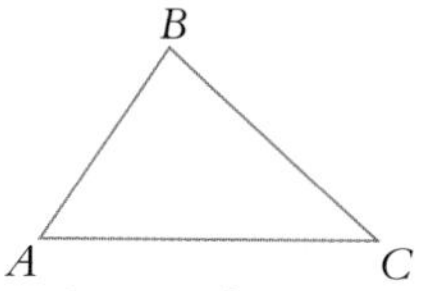

A, *B* and *C* are .... of the triangle.

13

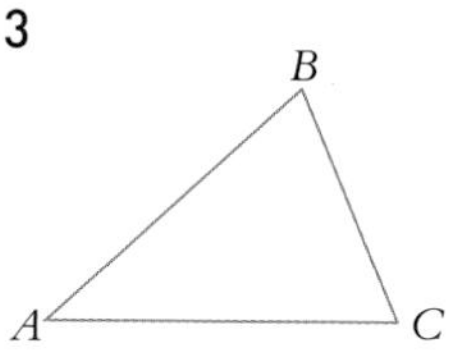

Use the vertices to name the Δ.

14

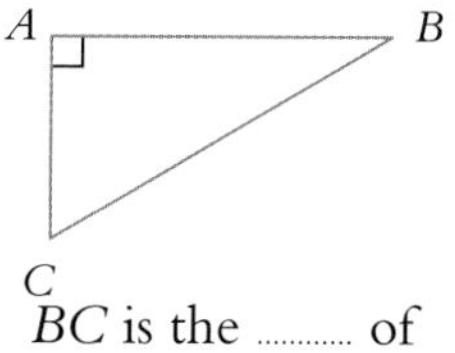

BC is the .... of the right-angled Δ.

15

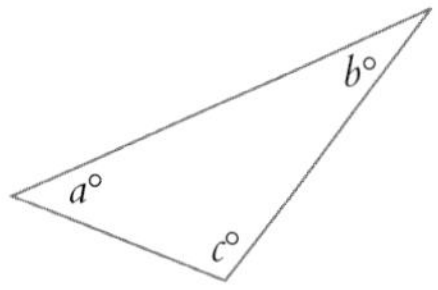

$a° + b° + c° =$ ....

16

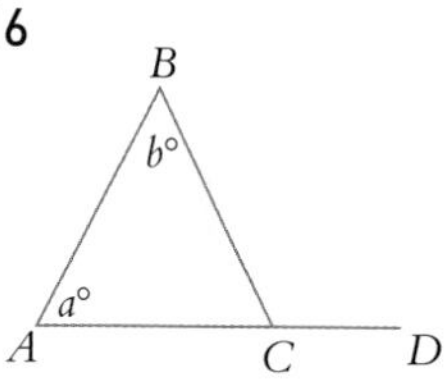

$\angle BCD =$ ....

17

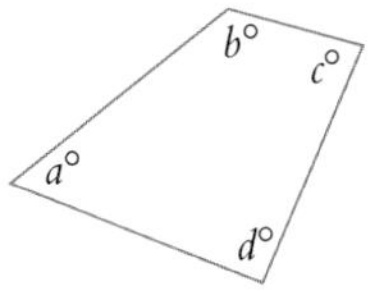

$a° + b° + c° + d° =$ ....

18

Which is true?
(a) $a° < b°$
(b) $a° = b°$
(c) $a° > b°$

19

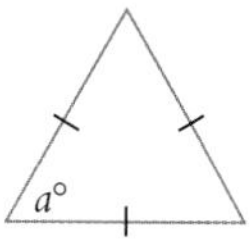

$a° =$ ....

20

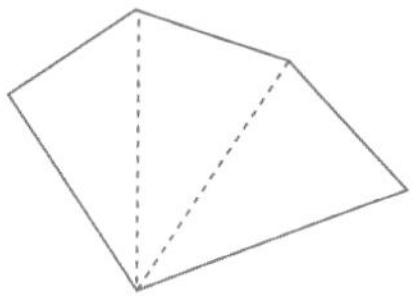

Angle sum = ...

21

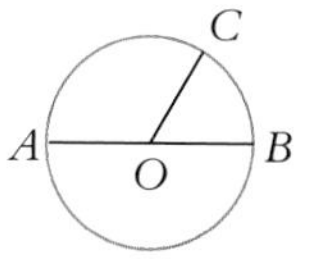

AB is a ....

OC is a ....

22

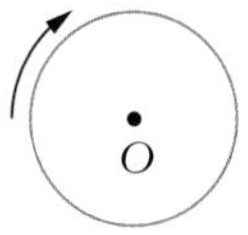

Name of distance around the circle.

....

23

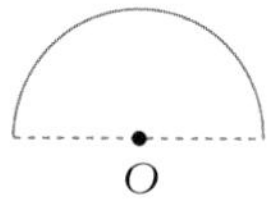

s..

24

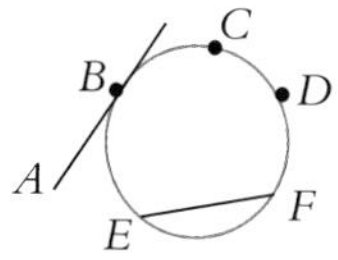

AB is a ....

CD is an ....

EF is a ....

For answers see page 504.

ID Card 5 (Language)

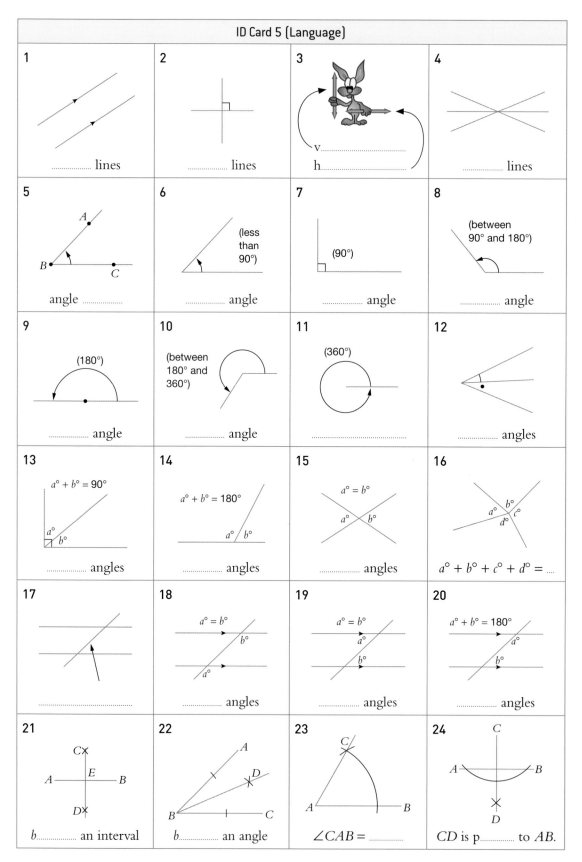

1

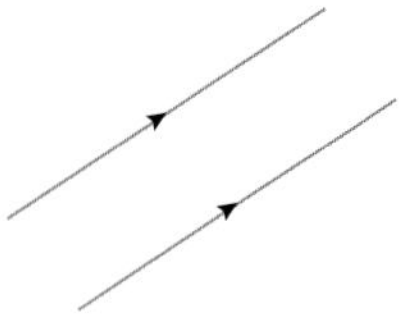

...... lines

2

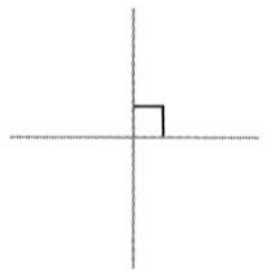

...... lines

3

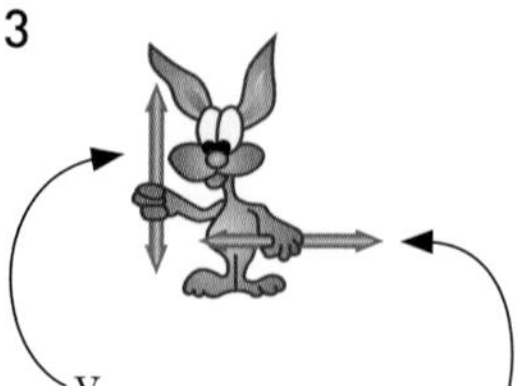

v......

h......

4

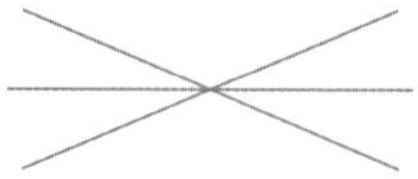

...... lines

5

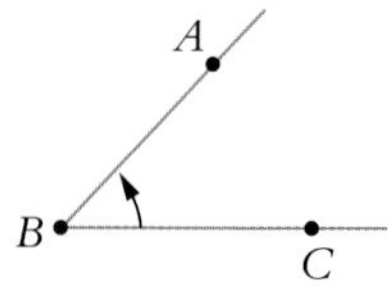

angle ......

6

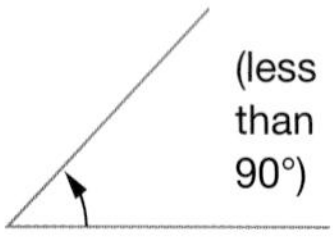

...... angle

7

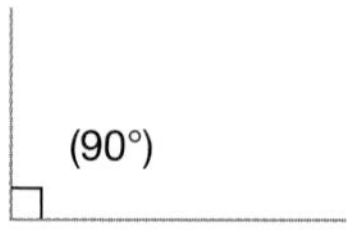

...... angle

8

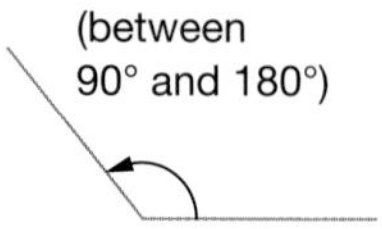

...... angle

9

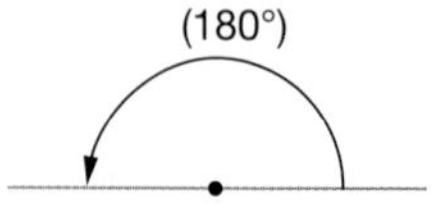

...... angle

10

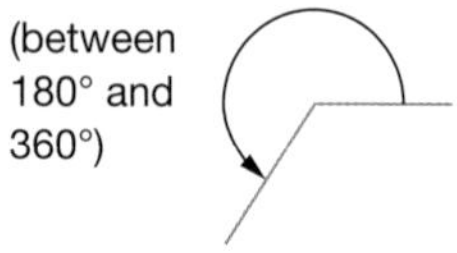

...... angle

11

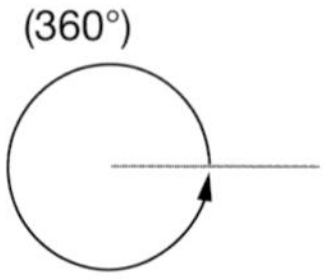

......

12

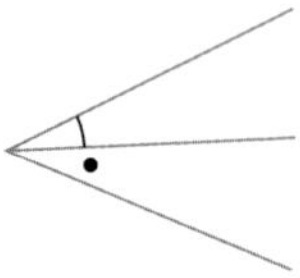

...... angles

13

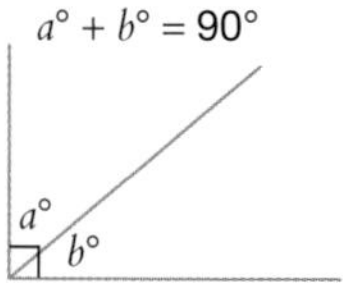

...... angles

14

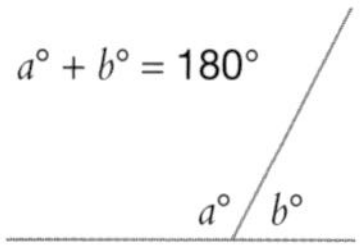

...... angles

15

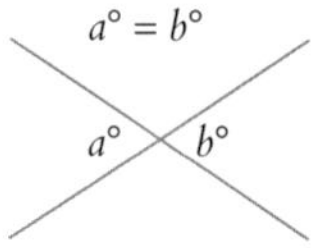

...... angles

16

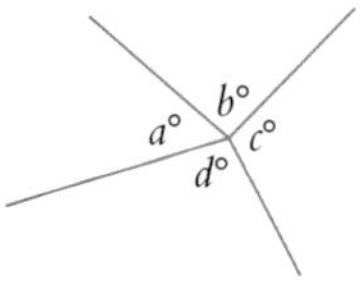

$a° + b° + c° + d° =$ ....

17

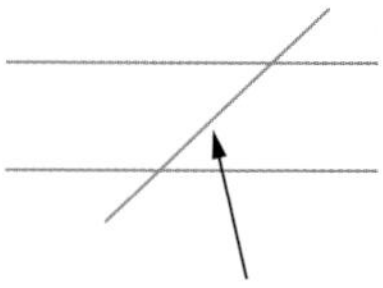

......

18

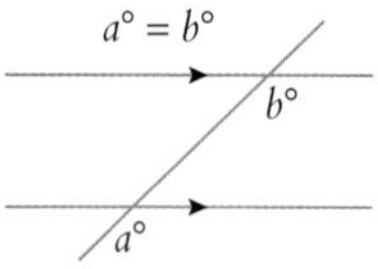

...... angles

19

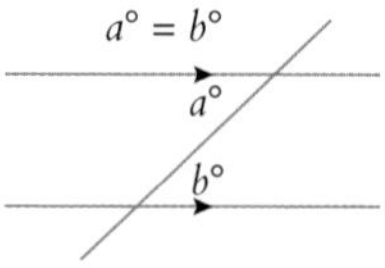

...... angles

20

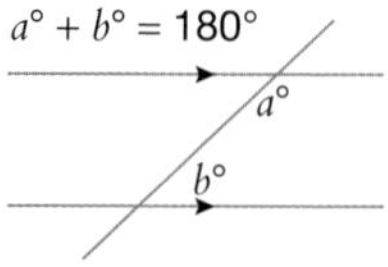

...... angles

21

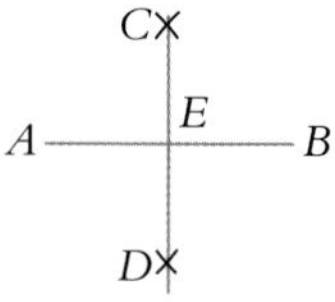

b...... an interval

22

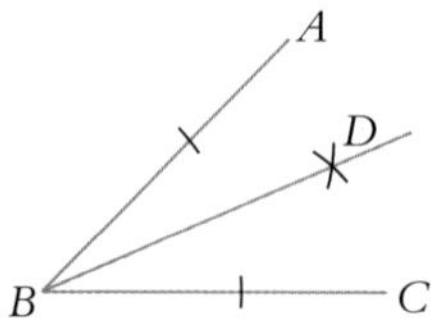

b...... an angle

23

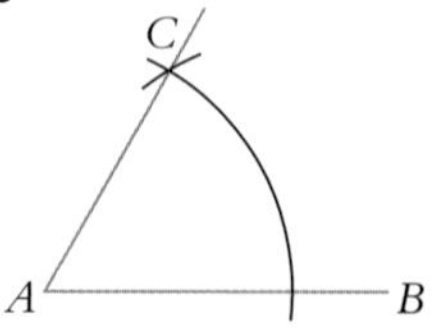

$\angle CAB =$ ......

24

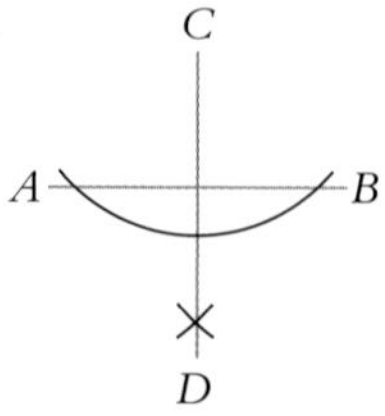

CD is p...... to AB.

For answers see page 504.

ID Card 6 (Language)

1

CE

C........... E...........

AD

A........... D...........

2

BCE

B........... C........... E...........

BC

B........... C...........

3

am

a.................. m..................

means

b.................. m..................

4

pm

p.................. m..................

means

a.................. m..................

5

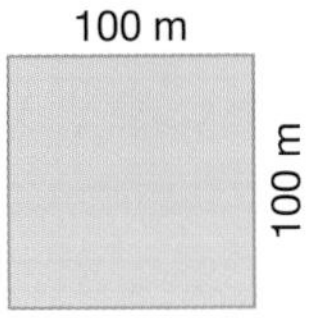

area is 1 ....

6

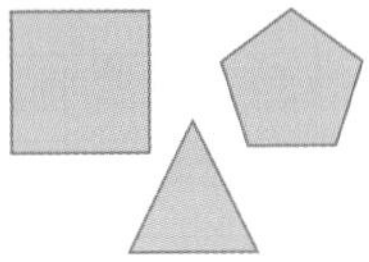

r.................. shapes

7

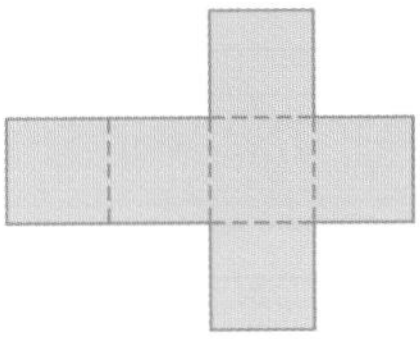

.... of a cube

8

c..................-s..................

9

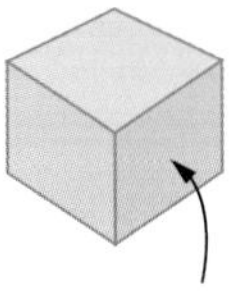

f..................

10

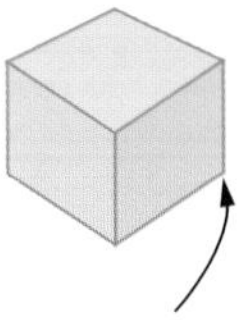

v..................

11

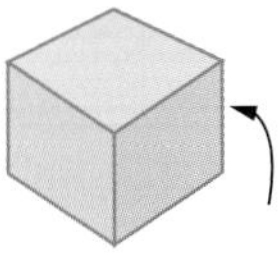

e..................

12

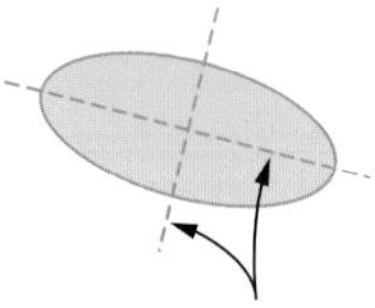

axes of ....

13

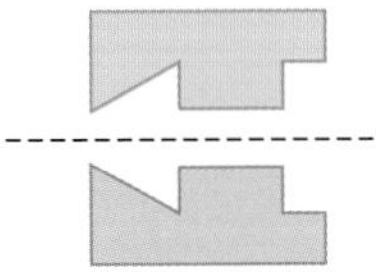

r..................

14

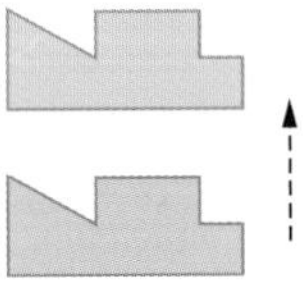

t..................

15

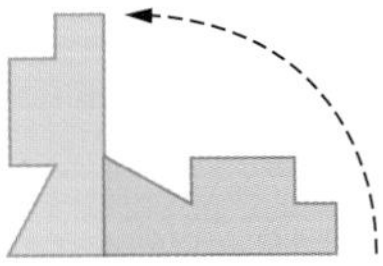

r..................

16

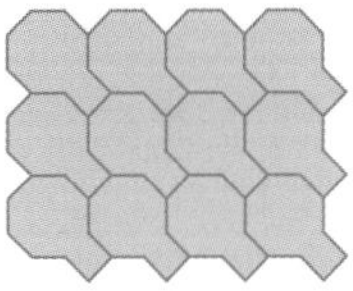

t..................

17

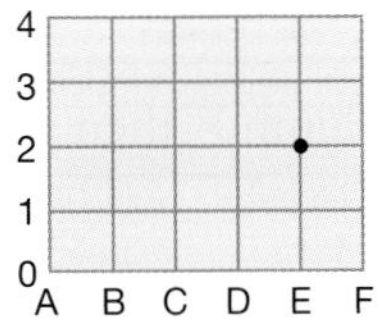

The c..................
of the dot are E2.

18

t..................

19

p.................. graph

20

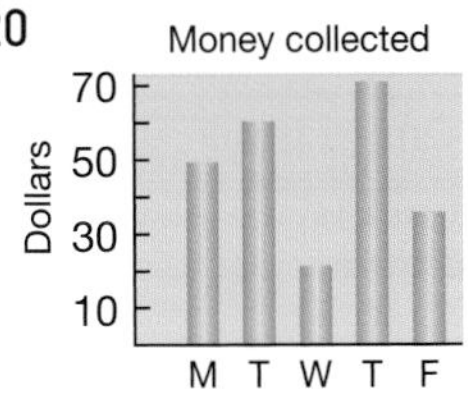

c.................. graph

21

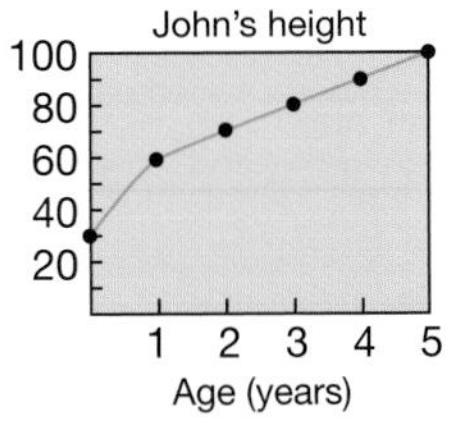

l.................. graph

22

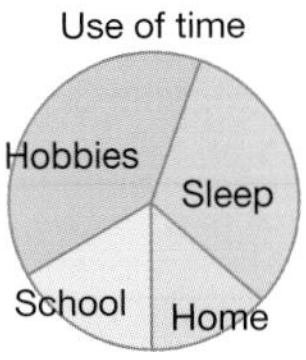

s.................. graph

23

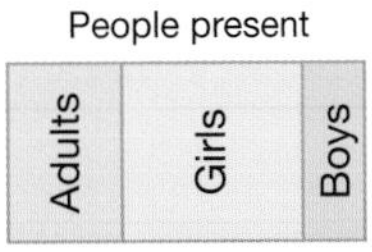

b.................. graph

24

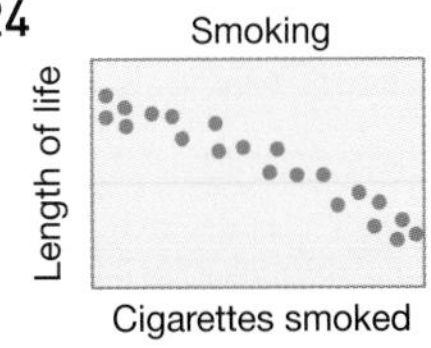

s.................. d..................

For answers see page 505.

Algebra card

	A	B	C	D	E	F	G	H	I	J	K	L	M	N	O
1	3	$2{\cdot}1$	$\frac{1}{4}$	m	$\frac{2m}{3}$	$-3m$	$5m^2$	$-5x$	$\frac{x}{6}$	$-3x$	$-\frac{x}{2}$	$x+2$	$x-3$	$2x+1$	$3x-8$
2	-1	$-0{\cdot}4$	$\frac{1}{8}$	$-4m$	$\frac{m}{4}$	$2m$	$-2m^3$	$3x$	$-\frac{x}{3}$	$5x^2$	$\frac{x}{4}$	$x+7$	$x-6$	$4x+2$	$x-1$
3	5	$0{\cdot}8$	$\frac{1}{3}$	$10m$	$-\frac{m}{4}$	$-5m$	$8m^5$	$10x$	$-\frac{2x}{7}$	$-8x$	$\frac{2x}{5}$	$x+5$	$x+5$	$6x+2$	$x-5$
4	-2	$1{\cdot}5$	$\frac{1}{20}$	$-8m$	$-\frac{3m}{2}$	$7m$	$6m^2$	$-15x$	$\frac{x}{10}$	$-4x^4$	$-\frac{x}{5}$	$x+1$	$x-9$	$3x+3$	$2x+4$
5	-8	$-2{\cdot}5$	$\frac{3}{5}$	$2m$	$-\frac{m}{5}$	$10m$	m^2	$7x$	$\frac{2x}{3}$	$2x^3$	$\frac{x}{3}$	$x+8$	$x+2$	$3x+8$	$3x+1$
6	10	$-0{\cdot}7$	$\frac{2}{7}$	$-5m$	$-\frac{3m}{7}$	$-6m$	$-9m^3$	$9x$	$-\frac{2x}{5}$	x^2	$\frac{3x}{5}$	$x+4$	$x-7$	$3x+1$	$x+7$
7	-6	$-1{\cdot}2$	$\frac{3}{8}$	$8m$	$-\frac{m}{6}$	$9m$	$2m^6$	$-6x$	$\frac{5x}{6}$	$5x^2$	$\frac{2x}{3}$	$x+6$	$x-1$	$x+8$	$2x-5$
8	12	$0{\cdot}5$	$\frac{9}{20}$	$20m$	$\frac{2m}{5}$	$-4m$	$-3m^3$	$-12x$	$\frac{3x}{4}$	$4x^3$	$-\frac{x}{7}$	$x+10$	$x-8$	$5x+2$	$x-10$
9	7	$0{\cdot}1$	$\frac{3}{4}$	$5m$	$\frac{3m}{5}$	$-10m$	m^7	$5x$	$-\frac{3x}{7}$	$-3x^5$	$-\frac{3x}{7}$	$x+2$	$x+5$	$2x+4$	$2x-4$
10	-5	$-0{\cdot}6$	$\frac{7}{10}$	$-9m$	$-\frac{4m}{5}$	$-7m$	$-8m^4$	$-3x$	$-\frac{x}{6}$	$-7x^5$	$\frac{2x}{9}$	$x+1$	$x-7$	$5x+4$	$x+7$
11	-11	$-1{\cdot}8$	$\frac{1}{10}$	$-7m$	$\frac{m}{5}$	$-8m$	$-4m$	$-4x$	$\frac{x}{5}$	$-x^3$	$\frac{x}{3}$	$x+9$	$x+6$	$2x+7$	$x-6$
12	4	$-1{\cdot}4$	$\frac{2}{5}$	$3m$	$\frac{m}{3}$	$12m$	$7m^2$	$-7x$	$-\frac{3x}{4}$	x^{10}	$\frac{x}{6}$	$x+3$	$x-10$	$2x+3$	$2x+3$

How to use this card

As an example, if the instruction given for the Algebra card is 'Column D + Column F' then you would write answers for the following problems.

1 $m + (-3m)$
2 $(-4m) + 2m$
3 $10m + (-5m)$
4 $(-8m) + 7m$
5 $2m + 10m$
6 $(-5m) + (-6m)$
7 $8m + 9m$
8 $20m + (-4m)$
9 $5m + (-10m)$
10 $(-9m) + (-7m)$
11 $(-7m) + (-8m)$
12 $3m + 12m$

NUMBER AND MEASUREMENT

1

Contents

Syllabus references (See pages x–xv for details.)

Measurement and Geometry

Selections from ***Numbers of Any Magnitude*** [Stage 5.1]

- Investigate very small and very large time scales and intervals (ACMMG219)
- Express numbers in scientific notation (ACMNA210)

Working Mathematically

- Communicating
- Problem Solving
- Reasoning
- Understanding
- Fluency

1:01 Review of earlier work

Much of the language met so far is reviewed in the identification cards (ID Cards) found on pages xix to xxiii. These should be referred to throughout the year. Make sure that you can identify every term.

Conversion facts to know

Percentage	1%	5%	10%	$12\frac{1}{2}$%	20%	25%	$33\frac{1}{3}$%	50%	100%
Decimal	0·01	0·05	0·1	0·125	0·2	0·25	$0\cdot\dot{3}$	0·5	1
Fraction	$\frac{1}{100}$	$\frac{1}{20}$	$\frac{1}{10}$	$\frac{1}{8}$	$\frac{1}{5}$	$\frac{1}{4}$	$\frac{1}{3}$	$\frac{1}{2}$	1

Exercise 1:01

P Appendix 1:01A–D

1 Mentally test yourself on ID Cards 1 to 6 (see pages xix–xxiii). Look up the answer to any question that you cannot answer with confidence. Learn the terms you did not know. This can be done by making small cards with questions on one side and the answers on the other. Carry these with you and review them often.

2 a $-7 + 14$ b $2 - 15$ c $3 - (-6)$ d $12 + (-5)$
e -3×2 f -5×6 g $(-15) \div (-3)$ h $63 \div (-9)$
i $14 - 7 \times 10$ j $-3 + 4 \div 4$ k $(4 - 18) \div (-8 + 6)$

3 Write answers in simplest form.
a $\frac{3}{8}+\frac{2}{8}$ b $\frac{9}{10}+\frac{3}{10}$ c $\frac{9}{10}-\frac{7}{10}$ d $\frac{13}{14}-\frac{9}{14}$ e $\frac{3}{4}+\frac{4}{5}$
f $\frac{3}{10}+\frac{2}{5}$ g $\frac{7}{8}-\frac{3}{4}$ h $\frac{9}{10}-\frac{1}{4}$ i $3\frac{1}{2}+4\frac{3}{5}$ j $6\frac{7}{10}+5\frac{3}{4}$
k $4\frac{1}{2}-1\frac{2}{9}$ l $7\frac{1}{2}-\frac{7}{8}$ m $\frac{4}{5}\times\frac{3}{11}$ n $\frac{3}{10}\times\frac{7}{10}$ o $\frac{7}{8}\times\frac{3}{7}$
p $\frac{15}{18}\times\frac{19}{20}$ q $3\frac{1}{2}\times\frac{5}{7}$ r $1\frac{3}{10}\times1\frac{4}{5}$ s $4\times3\frac{4}{5}$ t $2\frac{1}{4}\times3$
u $\frac{8}{10}\div\frac{2}{10}$ v $\frac{3}{5}\div\frac{1}{2}$ w $\frac{8}{9}\div\frac{2}{5}$ x $5\div\frac{1}{4}$ y $7\frac{1}{2}\div3$
z $3\frac{4}{7}\div2\frac{1}{2}$

4 Write answers in simplest form.
a $2\cdot6 + 3\cdot14$ b $18\cdot6 + 3$ c $12\cdot83 - 1\cdot2$ d $9 - 1\cdot824$
e $0\cdot7 \times 6$ f $(0\cdot3)^2$ g $0\cdot02 \times 1\cdot7$ h $0\cdot065 \times 10$
i $3\cdot142 \times 100$ j $0\cdot04 \times 1000$ k $2\cdot1 \times 10^2$ l $1\cdot25 \times 10^3$
m $4\cdot08 \div 2$ n $12\cdot1 \div 5$ o $0\cdot19 \div 4$ p $18\cdot25 \div 100$

5 Convert to fractions in simplest form.
a 18% b 7% c 9·5% d 12·25%

6 Convert to percentages.
a $\frac{11}{20}$ b $1\frac{1}{4}$ c 0·51 d 0·085

7 Convert to decimals.
a 9% b 110% c 23·8% d $4\frac{1}{2}$%

8 Find:

a 35% of 600 m b 7% of 84·3 m

c 7% of my spending money was spent on a watch band that cost $4.20. How much spending money did I have?

d 30% of my weight is 18 kg. How much do I weigh?

e 5 kg of sugar, 8 kg of salt and 7 kg of flour were mixed accidentally. What is the percentage (by weight) of sugar in the mixture?

f Javis scored 24 runs out of the team's total of 60 runs. What percentage of runs did he score?

g Increase $60 by 15%. h Decrease $8 by 35%.

50% of all men play tennis.
This game's only half the fun it used to be . . .

FUN SPOT 1:01 WHAT WAS THE PRIME MINISTER'S NAME IN 1998?

Work out the answer to each part and write the letter for that part in the box that is above the correct answer.

Y Write $\frac{15}{4}$ as a mixed numeral.

M Change $1\frac{3}{4}$ to an improper fraction.

H Write $\frac{2}{5}$ as a percentage.

H Write 0·75 as a fraction.

I Increase 50 kg by 10%.

D 40% of my weight is 26 kg. How much do I weigh?

D What fraction is 125 g of 1 kg?

S Write 4 ÷ 9 as a repeating (recurring) decimal.

S 10 cows, 26 horses and 4 goats are in a paddock. What is the percentage of animals that are horses?

S Increase $5 by 20%.

S 600 kg is divided between Misal and Pratik so that Misal gets $\frac{3}{5}$ of the amount. How much does Pratik get?

Write the basic numeral for:

A −8 + 10 **A** −7 − 3 **A** −6 × 4 **A** 6 − (3 − 4) **A** $(-5)^2$

Write the simplest answer for:

I $\frac{37}{100} - \frac{12}{100}$ **I** $\frac{3}{8} + \frac{1}{3}$ **T** $\frac{4}{5} - \frac{2}{3}$ **T** $\frac{7}{8} \times \frac{8}{7}$

T $(\frac{1}{3})^2$ **T** $4\frac{3}{8} + \frac{5}{8}$ **N** $\frac{1}{2} \div \frac{1}{8}$ **N** 0·05 + 3

O 0·3 − 0·02 **O** 0·3 × 5 **E** $(0 \cdot 3)^2$ **T** 3·142 × 100

E 6·12 ÷ 6 **E** 20·08 ÷ 10 **C** 1·8 ÷ 0·2 **G** $\frac{3}{4}$ of 60 kg

H 5% of 80 kg

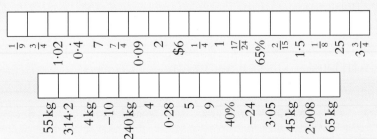

$\frac{1}{9}$	$\frac{3}{4}$	1·02	$0\cdot\dot{4}$	7	$\frac{7}{4}$	0·09	2	$6	$\frac{1}{4}$	1	$\frac{17}{24}$	65%	$\frac{2}{15}$	1·5	$\frac{1}{8}$	25	$3\frac{3}{4}$

55 kg	314·2	4 kg	−10	240 kg	4	0·28	5	9	40%	−24	3·05	45 kg	2·008	65 kg

1:02 Rational numbers

Fractions, decimals, percentages and negative numbers are convenient ways of writing rational numbers.

> A number is *rational* if it can be expressed as the quotient of two integers, $\frac{a}{b}$, where $b \neq 0$.
>
> e.g. $\frac{3}{4}$, 8, 52%, $12\frac{1}{2}$%, 0·186, $0\cdot\dot{3}$, −1·5, −10
>
> An *irrational number* cannot be written as a fraction, $\frac{a}{b}$, where a and b are integers and $b \neq 0$.
>
> e.g. $\sqrt{2}$, $\sqrt{7}$, $\sqrt[3]{4}$, $\sqrt[3]{5}$, π

An integer is a whole number that may be positive, negative or zero.

Real numbers are those that are rational or irrational.

Real numbers	
Rational numbers	Irrational numbers

- Every point on the number line represents either a rational number or an irrational number.
- Any rational number can be expressed as a terminating or recurring decimal.
- Irrational numbers can only be given decimal approximations; however, this does allow us to compare the sizes of real numbers.

Discussion

- How many real numbers are represented by points on the number line between 0 and 2, or between $-\frac{1}{2}$ and 0?

Exercise 1:02

1 From the list on the right, choose two equivalent numbers for:

a $2\frac{1}{2}$ b 130% c 2·8 d $1\frac{1}{4}$

125%	114%	$2\frac{4}{5}$	28%	280%
$2\frac{1}{8}$	1·4	2·5	208%	13
1·25	1·3	$1\frac{3}{10}$	250%	25%

2 Write each list in ascending order (from smallest to largest).

a 0·85, 0·805, 0·9, 1
b 87·5%, 100%, 104%, $12\frac{1}{4}$%
c $\frac{5}{8}$, $\frac{2}{7}$, $\frac{2}{3}$, $\frac{6}{100}$
d $1\frac{3}{4}$, 150%, 1·65, 2
e 1·42, $\sqrt{2}$, 1·41, 140%
f π, $3\frac{1}{4}$, 3·1, $\sqrt{12}$

3 Find the number half-way between:

a 6·8 and 6·9 b $12\frac{1}{2}$% and 20% c $\frac{1}{8}$ and $\frac{1}{5}$ d 6·3 and 6·4.

4 a Write as decimals: $\frac{1}{9}, \frac{2}{9}, \frac{3}{9}, \frac{4}{9}, \frac{5}{9}, \frac{6}{9}, \frac{7}{9}, \frac{8}{9}, \frac{9}{9}$.

b Explain why $0{\cdot}99999\ldots = 1$.

c Write as decimals: $\frac{1}{90}, \frac{2}{90}, \frac{3}{90}, \frac{1}{900}, \frac{2}{900}, \frac{3}{900}$.

d Write as fractions or mixed numbers: $0{\cdot}\dot{4}, 3{\cdot}\dot{1}, -0{\cdot}\dot{5}, -4{\cdot}\dot{5}$.

5 What are the next three numbers in each sequence?

a $0{\cdot}125, 0{\cdot}25, 0{\cdot}5, \ldots$

b $1{\cdot}3, 0{\cdot}65, 0{\cdot}325, \ldots$

6 The average (i.e. mean) of five numbers is 15·8.

a What is the sum of these numbers?

b If four of the numbers are 15s, what is the other number?

7 What is meant by an interest rate of 9·75% p.a.?

8 An advertisement reads: '67% of flats in Tertiary Place already rented. Only one flat remaining for rent.' How many flats would you expect there to be in Tertiary Place?

9 Using a diameter growth rate of 4·3 mm per year, find the number of years it will take for a tree with a diameter of 20 mm to reach a diameter of 50 mm.

10 At the South Pole, the temperature dropped 15°C in 2 hours from −18°C. What was the temperature after that 2 hours?

11 Julius Caesar invaded Britain in 55 BCE and again a year later. What was the date of the second invasion?

12 Chub was playing 'Five Hundred'.

a His score was −150 points. He then gained 520 points. What is his new score?

b His score was 60 points. He then lost 180 points. What is his new score?

c His score was −120 points. He then lost 320 points. What is his new score?

13 What fraction would be displayed on a calculator as:

a 0.3333333

b 0.6666666

c 0.1111111

d 0.5555555

14 To change $\frac{7}{15}$ to a decimal approximation, press 7 ÷ 15 = on a calculator. Use this method to write the following as decimals, correct to five decimal places.

a $\frac{8}{9}$

b $\frac{2}{7}$

c $\frac{7}{13}$

d $\frac{20}{21}$

e $\frac{4}{11}$

f $\frac{5}{18}$

15 Katherine was given a 20% discount followed by a 5% discount.

a What percentage of the original price did she have to pay?

b What overall percentage discount was she given on the original price?

c For what reason might she have been given the second discount?

16 My income was \$21 500 when I started work. If my income has increased by 200%, how much do I earn now?

17 Find the wholesale price of an item that sells for \$650 if the retail price is 130% of the wholesale price.

18 What number when divided by 0·8 gives 16?

19 What information is needed to complete the following questions?

a If Mary scored 40 marks in a test, what was her percentage?

b In a test out of 120, Nandor made only 3 mistakes. What was his percentage score?

c If 53% of cases of cancer occur after the age of 65, what is the chance per 10 000 of developing cancer after the age of 65?

20 In the year 2000, the distance from Australia to Indonesia was 1600 km. If Australia is moving towards Indonesia at a constant rate of 7 cm per year, when (theoretically) will they collide?

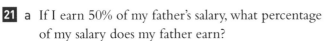

Assume that Indonesia isn't moving in the meantime.
A unit fraction has a numerator of 1.

21 a If I earn 50% of my father's salary, what percentage of my salary does my father earn?

b If X is 80% of Y, express Y as a percentage of X.

c My height is 160% of my child's height. Express my child's height as a percentage of my height.

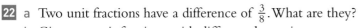

22 a Two unit fractions have a difference of $\frac{3}{8}$. What are they?

b Give two unit fractions with different denominators that subtract to give $\frac{5}{11}$.

23 Let $\frac{a}{b}$ and $\frac{c}{d}$ represent any two rational numbers.

Do we get a rational number if we:

a add them

b subtract them

c multiply them

d divide one by the other?

Explain your answers.

1:03 Recurring decimals

PREP QUIZ 1:03

Write these fractions as decimals.

1 $\frac{1}{4}$ 2 $\frac{2}{5}$ 3 $\frac{1}{3}$ 4 $\frac{5}{6}$

0·639 749 749 74 … is written as $0{\cdot}63\dot{9}7\dot{4}$.

Rewrite these recurring decimals using the 'dot' notation.

5 0·4444… 6 0·631 631 631… 7 0·166 666… 8 0·726 969 69…

Rewrite these decimals in simplest fraction form.

9 0·75 10 0·875

To write fractions in decimal form we simply divide the numerator (top) by the denominator (bottom). This may result in either a terminating or recurring decimal.

This can be checked using your calculator.

For $\frac{3}{8}$: $8\overline{)3\cdot{}^{3}0\,{}^{6}0\,{}^{4}0}$ giving $0\cdot375$

For $\frac{1}{6}$: $6\overline{)1\cdot{}^{1}0\,{}^{4}0\,{}^{4}0\,{}^{4}0}$ giving $0\cdot166\ldots$

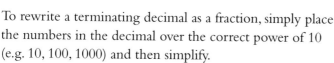

To rewrite a terminating decimal as a fraction, simply place the numbers in the decimal over the correct power of 10 (e.g. 10, 100, 1000) and then simplify.

For example: $0\cdot375 = \frac{375}{1000}\ \begin{matrix}\div 125\\ \div 125\end{matrix}$

$= \frac{3}{8}$

Recurring decimals are sometimes called repeating decimals.

Rewriting a recurring decimal as a fraction is a more difficult process. Carefully examine the two examples below and use the method shown in the following exercise.

WORKED EXAMPLE 1

When each number in the decimal part is repeated.

Write $0\cdot\dot{6}\dot{3}$ as a fraction

Let $x = 0\cdot6363\ldots$

Multiply by 100 because two digits are repeated.

$100x = 63\cdot6363\ldots$

Subtract the two lines.

$100x - x = 63\cdot6363\ldots - 0\cdot6363\ldots$

$99x = 63$

$x = \frac{63}{99}\ \begin{matrix}\div 9\\ \div 9\end{matrix}$

Simplify this fraction.

$\therefore x = \frac{7}{11}$

This answer can be checked by finding $7 \div 11$ using your calculator.

WORKED EXAMPLE 2

When only some digits are repeated.

Write $0\cdot61\dot{7}$ as a fraction

Let $x = 0\cdot61777\ldots$

Multiply by 100 to move the non-repeating digits to the left of the decimal point.

$100x = 61\cdot777\ldots$

Multiply by 1000 to move one set of the repeating digits to the left of the decimal point.

$1000x = 617\cdot777$

Subtract the previous two lines.

$1000x - 100x = 617\cdot777 - 61\cdot777$

$900x = 556$

$x = \frac{556}{900}\ \begin{matrix}\div 4\\ \div 4\end{matrix}$

Simplify this fraction using your calculator.

$\therefore x = \frac{139}{225}$

This answer can be checked by finding $139 \div 225$ using your calculator.

$0\cdot61\dot{7} = \frac{139}{225}$

Exercise 1:03

P Foundation worksheet 1:03
Decimals

1 Write these fractions as terminating decimals.

a $\frac{3}{4}$ b $\frac{4}{5}$ c $\frac{5}{8}$ d $\frac{7}{10}$ e $\frac{7}{100}$

f $\frac{35}{20}$ g $\frac{4}{25}$ h $\frac{17}{50}$ i $\frac{19}{40}$ j $\frac{117}{125}$

2 Write these fractions as recurring decimals.

a $\frac{2}{3}$ b $\frac{5}{9}$ c $\frac{8}{9}$ d $\frac{2}{11}$ e $\frac{1}{7}$

f $\frac{1}{6}$ g $\frac{1}{15}$ h $\frac{7}{15}$ i $\frac{1}{24}$ j $\frac{17}{30}$

3 Write these terminating decimals as fractions.

a 0·47 b 0·16 c 0·125 d 0·85 e 0·035

4 Rewrite these recurring decimals as fractions, following Worked Example 1.

a 0·4444… b 0·575 757… c 0·173 173 173…

d $0{\cdot}\dot{7}$ e $0{\cdot}\dot{3}\dot{6}$ f $0{\cdot}\dot{1}23\dot{4}$

5 Determine the value of $0{\cdot}\dot{3}$.

6 Rewrite these recurring decimals as fractions, following Worked Example 2.

a 0·833 33… b 0·635 353 5… c 0·197 777…

d $0{\cdot}6\dot{4}$ e $0{\cdot}73\dot{6}$ f $0{\cdot}82\dot{4}\dot{9}$

g $0{\cdot}5\dot{1}2\dot{3}$ h $0{\cdot}527\dot{8}$ i $0{\cdot}64\dot{7}3\dot{4}$

1:04 Ratios and rates

PREP QUIZ 1:04

Simplify these fractions.

1 $\frac{50}{60}$ 2 $\frac{16}{20}$ 3 $\frac{72}{84}$ 4 $\frac{125}{625}$

What fraction is:

5 50c of \$1
6 40c of 160c
7 8 kg of 10 kg
8 100 cm of 150 cm
9 1 m of 150 cm
10 \$2 of \$2.50?

A ratio is a comparison of like quantities.
e.g. Comparing 3 km to 5 km we write:
3 to 5 or 3 : 5 or $\frac{3}{5}$

Ratios are just like fractions!
6:10 =3:5
6/10 = 3/5

A rate is a comparison of unlike quantities.
e.g. If 150 kg of flour is used every 10 minutes, the rate of use would be:

$$\frac{150\text{ kg}}{10\text{ min}} \text{ or } \frac{15\text{ kg}}{1\text{ min}} \text{ or } 15\text{ kg/min.}$$

Usually, we write how many of the first quantity correspond to one of the second quantity.

e.g. 46 km in 2 hours is 23 km/h.

WORKED EXAMPLE 1

a Jan's height is 1 m and Dan's is 150 cm. Find the ratio of their heights.

b Of the class, $\frac{3}{5}$ walk to school and $\frac{1}{4}$ ride bicycles. Find the ratio of those who walk to those who ride bicycles.

Solutions

a Jan's height to Dan's height

$= 1\text{ m to }150\text{ cm}$

$= 100\text{ cm to }150\text{ cm}$

$= 100:150$

Divide both terms by 50.

$= 2:3$ or $\frac{2}{3}$

From this ratio we can see that Jan is $\frac{2}{3}$ as tall as Dan.

> Each term is expressed in the same units, then units are left out.

> We may simplify ratios by dividing or multiplying each term by the same number.

b Those walking to those cycling $= \frac{3}{5} : \frac{1}{4}$

Multiply both terms by 20.

$= \frac{3}{{}_1\cancel{5}} \times \frac{\cancel{20}^4}{1} : \frac{1}{{}_1\cancel{4}} \times \frac{\cancel{20}^5}{1}$

$= 12:5$

> To remove fractions, multiply each term by the lowest common denominator.

WORKED EXAMPLE 2

Express the ratio 11 to 4 in the form:

a $X:1$

b $1:Y$

Solutions

a 11 to 4

$= 11:4$

Divide both terms by 4.

$= \frac{11}{4}:1$

$= 2\frac{3}{4}:1$

This is in the form $X:1$.

b 11 to 4

$= 11:4$

Divide both terms by 11.

$= 1:\frac{4}{11}$

This is in the form $1:Y$.

WORKED EXAMPLE 3

It cost me \$36 to purchase 20 kg of potting mix. What is the cost per kilogram?

Solution

$\text{Cost} = \frac{\$36}{20\text{ kg}}$

$= \frac{36}{20}$ dollars per kilogram

$= \$1.80/\text{kg}$

> Units must be shown.

> $\frac{36}{20}$ means $36 \div 20$.

Exercise 1:04

1 Express the first quantity as a fraction of the second.

Simplify the fractions.

a \$5, \$50 b 8 m, 10 m c 10 bags, 100 bags
d 75 g, 80 g e 6 runs, 30 runs f 25 goals, 120 goals

2 Simplify the ratios.

a 6 : 4 b 10 : 5 c 65 : 15
d 14 : 35 e 1000 : 5 f 1100 : 800
g 55 : 20 h 16 : 28 i 10 : 105
j 72 : 2 k 4 : 104 l $10 : \frac{1}{2}$
m $\frac{1}{2} : 2\frac{1}{2}$ n $2\frac{1}{2} : 2$ o $2\frac{3}{4} : 1$
p $2 : 3\frac{1}{4}$

You may use
× or ÷

3 In each, find the ratio of the first quantity to the second, giving your answers in simplest form.

a 7 men, 9 men b 13 kg, 15 kg c 7 cm, 8 cm
d \$8, \$12 e 16 m, 20 m f 15 bags, 85 bags
g 90 g, 100 g h 9 runs, 18 runs i 50 goals, 400 goals

4 Find the ratio of the first quantity to the second. Give answers in simplest form.

Are units the same?

a \$1, 50c b \$5, \$2.50 c \$1.20, \$6
d 1 m, 60 cm e 25 cm, 2 m f 100 m, 1 km
g 600 mL, 1 L h 1 L, 600 mL i 5 L, 1 L 250 mL

5 Write these ratios in the form X:1.

a 13 : 8 b 7 : 4
c 5 : 2 d 110 : 100
e 700 : 500 f 20 : 30
g 2 : 7 h 10 : 9
i 4 : 6 j 15 : 8
k 1 : 3 l $2\frac{1}{2} : \frac{1}{4}$

To change 8 into 1,
we need to divide by 8.

13 : 8
$= \frac{13}{8} : 1$
$= 1\frac{5}{8} : 1$

6 Write these ratios in the form 1 : Y.

a 4 : 5 b 2 : 9 c 8 : 15
d 14 : 6 e 8 : 10 f 1000 : 150
g 100 : 875 h 4 : 22 i 4 : 6

7 a Anne bought a painting for \$600 (cost) and sold the painting for \$800 (selling price). Find the ratio of:

i cost to selling price ii profit to cost iii profit to selling price.

b John, who is 160 cm tall, jumped 180 cm to win the high jump competition. What is the ratio of this jump to his height? Write this ratio in the form X: 1.

c A rectangle has dimensions 96 cm by 60 cm. Find the ratio of:

i its length to breadth
ii its breadth to length.

d 36% of the body's skin is on the legs, whereas 9% is on the head/neck part of the body. Find the ratio of:
  i the skin on the legs to the skin on the head/neck
  ii the skin on the legs to the skin on the rest of the body.

e Joan's normal pulse is 80 beats per minute, while Eric's is only 70. After Joan runs 100 m her pulse rate rises to 120 beats per minute. Find the ratio of:
  i Joan's normal pulse rate to Eric's normal pulse rate
  ii Joan's normal pulse rate to her rate after the run.

f At 60 km/h, a truck takes 58 m to stop (16 m during the driver's reaction time and 42 m braking distance), whereas a car travelling at the same speed takes 38 m to stop (16 m reaction and 22 m braking). Find the ratio of:
  i the truck's stopping distance to the car's stopping distance
  ii the car's reaction distance to the car's braking distance
  iii the truck's braking distance to the car's braking distance.

8 a A recipe recommends the use of two parts sugar to one part flour and one part custard powder. What percentage of the mixture is each part?

b A mix for fixing the ridge-capping on a roof is given as 1 part cement to 5 parts sand and a half part of lime. What fraction of the mixture is each part?

c The ratio of a model to the real thing is called the scale factor. My model of an aeroplane is 40 cm long. If the real plane is 16 m long, what is the scale factor of my model?

9 Write each pair of quantities as a rate in its simplest form.

a 42 kilometres, 7 hours | b $50, 2 tonnes | c 200 grams, $4
d $2500, 10 days | e 12 g, 0·5 L | f 87 boys, 3 teachers

10 a If I walk at 3 km/h, how far can I walk in 3 hours?

b If bananas cost $3.60 per kg, what is the cost of 5 kg of bananas?

c If bananas cost $3.60/kg, how much can I buy for $36?

d Our run rate so far in the cricket match is 17·5 runs per wicket. How many runs have been scored if 4 wickets have been lost?

11 Complete these equivalent rates.

a 25 m/min = ... m/h | b $40/m = ... $/km | c 3 t/min = ... kg/min
d 3000 g/kL = ... g/L | e 3600 g/min = ... g/h | f 120 beats/min = ... beats/s

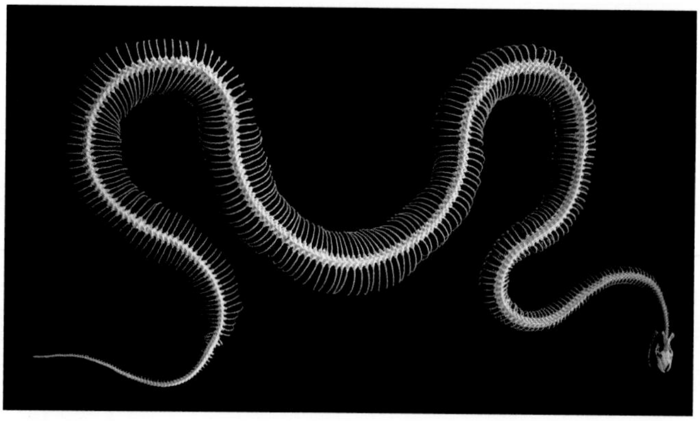

Estimate the number of vertebrae in this python skeleton. The numerous vertebrae, or spinal-column segments, give the backbone great flexibility.

1:05 Significant figures

No matter how accurate measuring instruments are, a quantity such as length cannot be measured exactly. Any measurement is only an approximation.

- A measurement is only useful when one can be confident of its validity. To make sure that a measurement is useful, each digit in the number should be significant. For example, if the height of a person, expressed in significant figures, is written as 2·13 m it is assumed that only the last figure may be in error. Clearly any uncertainty in the first or second figure would remove all significance from the last figure. (If we are not sure of the number of metres, it is pointless to worry about the number of centimetres.)
- It is assumed that in the measurement 2·13 m we have measured the number of metres, the number of tenths of a metre and the number of hundredths of a metre. Three of the figures have been measured so there are three significant figures.
- A significant figure is a number that we believe to be correct within some specific or implied limit of error.
- To calculate the number of significant figures in a measurement we use the rules below.

2·13 m

Rules for determining significant figures

1 Coming from the left, the first non-zero digit is the first significant figure.

2 All figures following the first significant figure are also significant, unless the number is a whole number ending in zeros.

3 Final zeros in a whole number may or may not be significant
e.g. 0·001 20 has three significant figures, 8800 may have two, three or four.

1 Starting from the left, the first significant figure is the first non-zero digit.

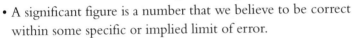

e.g. 0·003 250   865 000   8·007

These are the first non-zero digits.

2 Final zeros in a whole number may or may not be significant.

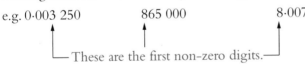

e.g. 56 000 000   73 210   18 000

Unless we are told, we cannot tell whether these zeros are significant.

3 All non-zero digits are significant.

4 Zeros at the end of a decimal are significant.

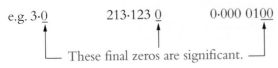

e.g. 3·0   213·123 0   0·000 0100

These final zeros are significant.

Any figure that's been measured is significant.

Method for counting the number of significant figures

> Every figure between the first and last significant figure is significant.

Locate the first and last significant figures, then count the significant figures, including all digits between the first and last significant figures.

WORKED EXAMPLE 1

How many significant figures are in each of the following numbers?

a 316 000 000 (to nearest million)
b 316 000 000 (to nearest thousand)
c 42 007
d 31·0050
e 0·000 130 50

Solutions

a 316 000 000 (to nearest million)
last significant figure: 6; first significant figure: 3
Number of significant figures = 3

b 316 000 000 (to nearest thousand)
last significant figure (thousands); first significant figure
Number of significant figures = 6

c 42 007
last significant figure; first significant figure
Number of significant figures = 5

d 31·0050
last significant figure; first significant figure
Number of significant figures = 6

e 0·000 130 50
last significant figure; first significant figure
Number of significant figures = 5

WORKED EXAMPLE 2

The statements below show examples of rounding to a number of significant figures.

a The distance of the Earth from the Sun is 152 000 000 km.
In this measurement, the distance has been given to the nearest million kilometres. The zeros may or may not be significant but it seems that they are being used only to locate the decimal point. Hence, the measurement has three significant figures.

b An athlete said she ran 5000 m.
The zeros in this measurement may or may not be significant. You would have to decide whether or not they were significant from the context of the statement.

Exercise 1:05

1 How many significant figures are in each of the following numbers?

a 2·1 b 1·76 c 9·05
d 0·62 e 7·305 f 0·104
g 3·6 h 3·60 i 0·002
j 0·056 k 0·04 l 0·40
m 0·00471 n 3·040 o 0·5
p 304 q 7001 r 0·00150
s 0·000 000 125 t 0·000 000 100 u 0·000 000 001

2 How many significant figures are in each of the following numbers?

a 2000 (to the nearest thousand) b 2000 (to the nearest hundred)
c 53 000 (to the nearest thousand) d 530 000 (to the nearest thousand)
e 25 000 (to the nearest ten) f 26 300 (to the nearest hundred)
g 26 000 (to the nearest hundred) h 8 176 530 (to the nearest ten)

3 State the number of significant figures in the following measurements.

a 4·1 L b 12·62 m c 7·08 t
d 0·5 cm e 33·8 °C f 0·070 L
g 0·003 km h 2·5 ML i 0·085 g

4 Give the number of significant figures in each of the following very large measurements. Assume the final zeros are not significant.

a 12 345 678 t b 12 000 000 t
c 25 000 000 000 L d 401 000 000 000 000 km

5 A newspaper article reported that 20 000 people attended Carols in the Domain. How accurate would you expect this number to be? (That is, how many significant figures would the number have?)

The mean radius of Earth is 6370 km, correct to three significant figures. Has this distance been measured to the nearest kilometre, nearest 10 kilometres, nearest 100 kilometres or nearest 1000 kilometres?

INVESTIGATION 1:05 A TRUCK DRIVER'S MEMORIES

- Norm Richardson was a truck driver for 47 years.
- He estimated that he had travelled between 7 and 8 million kilometres driving trucks.
- He would often drive 1000 km in a day. For much of this time he carried coal from the Burragorang Valley to Port Kembla.

Questions

Assume that average values are being calculated.

Give your answers correct to two significant figures.

1 What distance would Norm have travelled each year?

2 If Norm worked 48 weeks each year, how many kilometres per week did he travel?

3 If he drove for 6 days in each week, what distance did he travel each day?

During this time he had two major accidents. The more serious one involved a 44-gallon drum of petrol falling from another truck in front of his truck while he was travelling about 40 km/h around a bend in the road. The drum pushed the engine back into the cabin. He had no control over his vehicle so he jumped from his truck and hurtled into a wire fence. The truck burst into flames and was destroyed.

4 When Norm jumped from the truck, how many metres per second was he travelling?

5 If Norm hit the fence 2 seconds after jumping from his truck, how far was the truck from the fence when he jumped?

6 How many litres of petrol could a 44-gallon drum hold if 1 gallon = 4·546 litres? Round your answer to the nearest litre.

7 How much would the petrol in the drum weigh (to the nearest kg) if 1 litre of petrol weighs 0·711 kg?

1:06 Approximations

PREP QUIZ 1:06

How many significant figures do the following numbers have?

1 3·605 **2** 0·06 **3** 0·1050

Write one more term for each number sequence.

4 3·06, 3·07, … **5** 0·78, 0·79, … **6** 2·408, 2·409, …

7 Is 3·7 closer to 3 or 4?

8 Is 2·327 closer to 2·32 or 2·33?

9 What number is half-way between 3·5 and 3·6?

10 What number is half-way between 0·06 and 0·07?

Discussion

To round a decimal to the nearest whole number, we write the whole number closest to it.

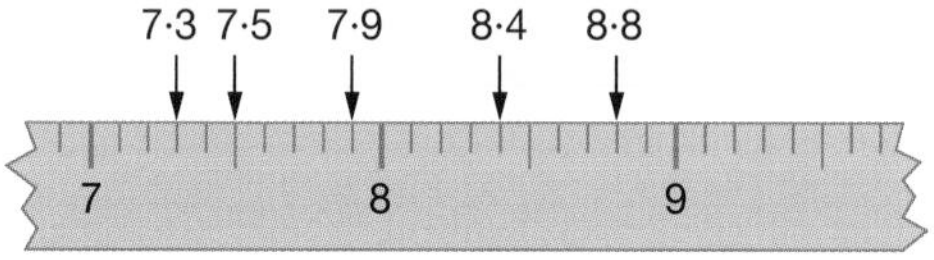

<table>
<tr><td>7·3 is closer to 7</td><td>7·9 is closer to 8</td><td>8·4 is closer to 8</td><td>8·8 is closer to 9</td></tr>
<tr><td colspan="4">7·5 is exactly half-way between 7 and 8. In cases like this we round up.
We say 7·5 = 8, correct to the nearest whole number.</td></tr>
</table>

To round 72 900 to the nearest thousand, we write the thousand closest to it.

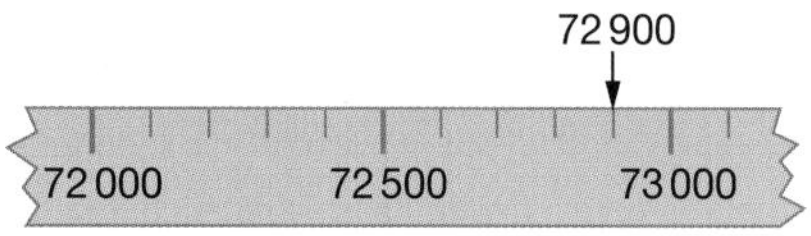

72 900 is closer to 73 000 than to 72 000.
∴ 72 900 = 73 000 (nearest thousand)

To round 0·8134 to the nearest thousandth, we write the thousandth closest to it.

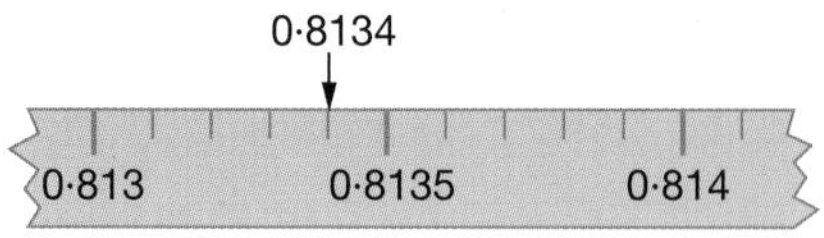

0·8134 is closer to 0·813 than to 0·814.
∴ 0·8134 = 0·813 (nearest thousandth)

> To round (or approximate) a number correct to a given place:
> - round up if the next digit is 5 or more
> - round down if the next digit is less than 5.

WORKED EXAMPLE 1

Round:

a 56 800 000 to the nearest million

b 0·0851 to the nearest hundredth

c 86·149 to one decimal place

d 0·666 15 to four decimal places.

Solutions

a 56 800 000 has a 6 in the millions column.
The number after the 6 is 5 or more (i.e. 8).
∴ 56 800 000 = 57 000 000 (nearest million)

b 0·085 1 has an 8 in the hundredths column.
The number after the 8 is 5 or more (i.e. 5).
∴ 0·0851 = 0·09 (nearest hundredth)

c 86·149 has a 1 in the first decimal place.
The number after the 1 is less than 5 (i.e. 4).
∴ 86·149 = 86·1 (1 dec. pl.)

d 0·666 15 has a 1 in the fourth decimal place.
The number after the 1 is 5 or more (i.e. 5).
∴ 0·666 15 = 0·6662 (4 dec. pl.)

To approximate correct to a certain number of significant figures, we write the number that contains only the required number of significant figures and is closest in value to the given number.

WORKED EXAMPLE 2

Round:

a 507 000 000 to two significant figures

b 1·098 to three significant figures

c 0·006 25 to one significant figure

d 0·080 25 to three significant figures.

Solutions

a The second significant figure is the 0 between the 5 and 7. The number after the zero is 5 or more (i.e. 7).
∴ 507 000 000 = 510 000 000 (2 sig. fig.)

b The third significant figure is the 9. The number after the 9 is 8, so increase the 9 to 10. Put down the 0 and carry the 1.
∴ 1·098 = 1·10 (3 sig. fig.)

c The first significant figure is 6. The number after the 6 is less than 5 (i.e. 2).
∴ 0·006 25 = 0·006 (1 sig. fig.)

d The third significant figure is 2. The number after the 2 is 5 or more (i.e. 5).
∴ 0·080 25 = 0·0803 (3 sig. fig.)

Exercise 1:06

P Foundation worksheet 1:06 Approximation

1 Round these numbers to the nearest hundred.

a 7923	b 1099	c 67 314	d 853·461
e 609·99	f 350	g 74 932	h 7850

2 Round these numbers to the nearest whole number.

a 9·3 b 79·5 c 45·1 d 2·7
e 2·314 f 17·81 g 236·502 h 99·5

When you 'round' you are making an approximation.

3 Round these numbers to the nearest hundredth.

a 243·128 b 79·664 c 91·351 d 9·807
e 0·3046 f 0·0852 g 0·097 h 1·991

I'm supposed to get $496.48, but they gave me $496.50.
$
$

4 Round these numbers, correct to one decimal place.

a 6·70 b 8·45 c 2·119 d 6·092
e 0·05 f 0·035 g 29·88 h 9·99

5 Round these numbers, correct to two significant figures.

a 8170 b 3504 c 655
d 849 e 14580 f 76399
g 49788 h 76500

6 Round the numbers in Question **5**, correct to one significant figure.

7 Round these to three significant figures.

a 694·8 b 35·085 c 320·5 d 0·08154
e 0·66666 f 9·3333 g 10·085 h 9·095

8 To change $1\frac{7}{9}$ to a decimal, Gregory divided 16 by 9 using his calculator. Give the answer correct to:

a 1 dec. pl. b 2 dec. pl.
c 3 dec. pl. d 1 sig. fig.
e 2 sig. fig. f 3 sig. fig.

'sig. fig.' is short for 'significant figures'
'dec. pl.' is short for 'decimal places'

9 Diane cut 60 cm of blue ribbon into 11 equal parts to make a suit for her new baby. After dividing, she got the answer $5{\cdot}\dot{4}\dot{5}$. Give the length of one part correct to:

a the nearest centimetre b the nearest millimetre c 1 dec. pl.
d 2 dec. pl. e 3 dec. pl. f 1 sig. fig.
g 2 sig. fig. h 3 sig. fig.

10 The following calculator display represents an answer in cents. 14059.705
Give this answer correct to:

a the nearest dollar b the nearest cent c 1 dec. pl.
d 2 dec. pl. e 3 dec. pl. f 1 sig. fig.
g 2 sig. fig. h 3 sig. fig.

11 What level of accuracy do you think was used in each of these measurements and what would be the greatest error possible as a result of the approximation?

a The crowd size was 18000.
b The nation's gross domestic product was $62000000000.

Is the level of accuracy to the nearest ten, hundred or thousand?
GO!
NSW

12 What approximation has been made in each of these measurements and what would be the greatest error possible?

a 6·4 cm b 0·007 mg

13 A number is rounded to give 2·15. What could the number have been? What is the smallest the number could have been? Is it possible to write the largest number that can be rounded to give 2·15?

14 Write the measurement 37 648 708 t correct to:

a one significant figure b two significant figures
c three significant figures d five significant figures.
e Which of a to d would you use if you were comparing the steel production of countries?

15 Write the measurement 8·126 m correct to:

a one significant figure b two significant figures
c three significant figures d four significant figures.
e Which of a to d would you use on a building plan?

16 A surveyor measures a length as 42 063 mm.

a How many significant figures does this measurement have?
b Convert the measurement to metres.
c What is this measurement to the nearest metre?
d If this measurement were written to the nearest metre, how many significant figures would be needed?
e Round this number to the nearest centimetre.
f How many significant figures would be needed to write this number to the nearest centimetre?

> 42 063 mm
> = 40 000 mm (1 sig. fig.)
> = 42 000 mm (2 sig. fig.)
> = 42 100 mm (3 sig. fig.)

17 a An answer is given as 3 000 000, correct to one significant figure. What might the exact measure have been?
b Seven people decide to share a bill of $187.45 equally. How much should each person pay? What could be done with the surplus amount?
c The area of a room is needed to order floor tiles. The room dimensions, 2·49 m by 4·31 m, were rounded to 2 m by 4 m to calculate the area. What problems might arise?

18 A 10-digit calculator was used to change fractions into decimals. The truncating of the decimal produced an error. What error is present in the display after entering:

a $\frac{1}{3}$ b $\frac{2}{3}$ c $\frac{5}{9}$?

19 Find an approximation for $345{\cdot}45^2$ by first rounding the 345·45 correct to:

a 1 sig. fig. b 1 dec. pl. c 2 sig. fig.
d What is the difference between the answer to a and the real answer?

20 To find the volume of the tunnel drawn on the right, each measurement was rounded correct to one significant figure before calculation. What error in volume occurred?

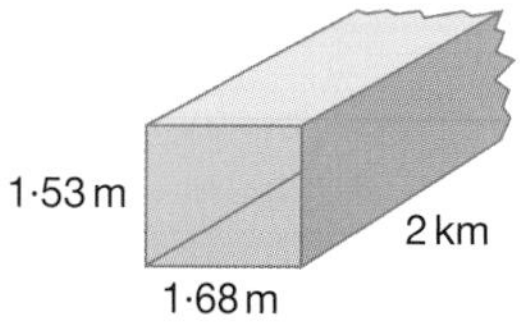

> *Note:* Truncating or rounding numbers before a calculation may produce unwanted errors or inaccuracy.

1:07 Estimation

PREP QUIZ 1:07

1 Write 216 to the nearest hundred.
2 Write 17·68 to the nearest ten.
3 $15{\cdot}61 \times 10$
4 $15{\cdot}61 \times 100$
5 Is $\frac{0{\cdot}716}{3{\cdot}5}$ less than or greater than 1?
6 If $3 < 4$ and $5{\cdot}3 < 7{\cdot}8$, what sign (< or >) can we put in the box? $3 \times 5{\cdot}3 \ \square \ 4 \times 7{\cdot}8$
7 *True* or *false*? $21{\cdot}68 \times 0{\cdot}716 < 21{\cdot}68 \times 1$
8 Which is the best approximation for $0{\cdot}316 \times 0{\cdot}81$?
A 2·5 **B** 0·25 **C** 0·025
9 *True* or *false*? $\frac{7{\cdot}6}{0{\cdot}25} > 7{\cdot}6$
10 *True* or *false*? $\frac{7{\cdot}6}{8{\cdot}3} > 1$

Like all machines, calculators only operate correctly if they are used correctly. Even when doing simple calculations it is still possible to press the wrong button. So it is essential that you learn how to estimate the size of the answer before the calculation is even started.

An estimate is a valuable way to check whether your calculator gives a sensible answer. If your estimate and the actual answer are significantly different, then it tells you that a mistake has been made either in your estimate or your calculation.

The following examples will show you how to estimate the size of an answer.

WORKED EXAMPLES

Estimate the size of each of the following calculations.

1 $14{\cdot}61 - 7{\cdot}15 + 3{\cdot}2$
2 $7{\cdot}56 \times 5{\cdot}173$
3 $0{\cdot}0253 \div 0{\cdot}45$
4 $\frac{21{\cdot}73 \times 0{\cdot}815}{7{\cdot}3}$
5 $\frac{\sqrt{86}}{2{\cdot}8 \times 16{\cdot}18}$

To simplify Question **3**, multiply both numbers by 100.

Solutions

1 $14{\cdot}61 - 7{\cdot}15 + 3{\cdot}2$
$\approx 15 - 7 + 3$
≈ 11

2 $7{\cdot}56 \times 5{\cdot}173$
$\approx 8 \times 5$
≈ 40

3 $0{\cdot}0253 \div 0{\cdot}45$
$= 2{\cdot}53 \div 45$
$\approx 3 \div 45$
$\approx \frac{1}{15}$ or $0{\cdot}07$

$\approx$ or $\doteqdot$ means 'is approximately equal to'.

4 $\frac{21{\cdot}73 \times 0{\cdot}815}{7{\cdot}3}$
$\doteqdot \frac{21 \times 1}{7}$
$\doteqdot 3$

5 $\frac{\sqrt{86}}{2{\cdot}8 \times 16{\cdot}18}$
$\doteqdot \frac{{}^{3}\not{9}}{{}_{1}\not{3} \times 16}$
$\doteqdot \frac{3}{15}$
$\doteqdot \frac{1}{5}$ or $0{\cdot}2$

Where possible, reduce fractions.

- When estimating, look for numbers that are easy to work with, e.g. 1, 10, 100.
- Remember it's an estimate. When you approximate a number you don't have to take the nearest whole number.
- Try thinking of decimals as fractions. It often helps. e.g. $7\cdot6 \times 0\cdot518 \approx 8 \times \frac{1}{2} = 4$
- When dealing with estimates involving fraction bars, look for numbers that nearly cancel out.

  e.g. $\dfrac{\overset{2}{\cancel{17\cdot68}} \times 5\cdot8}{\cancel{8\cdot9}_{1}} \approx \dfrac{2 \times 6}{1} = 12$
- Check that your estimate makes sense.

The golden rule of estimating: Does your answer make sense?

Exercise 1:07

Foundation worksheet 1:07 Estimation

1 Estimate the answers to the following calculations.

a $7\cdot9 + 0\cdot81 + 13\cdot56$
b $42\cdot56 - 15\cdot81 + 9\cdot2$
c $5\cdot6 \times (7\cdot2 + 5\cdot9)$
d $14\cdot31 \times 8\cdot97$
e $73\cdot95 \div 14\cdot2$
f $0\cdot73 \times 0\cdot05 \div 4\cdot53$
g $0\cdot916 \times 0\cdot032 \times 18\cdot34$
h $(15\cdot6 + 6\cdot82) \times 5\cdot31$
i $15\cdot6 + 6\cdot82 \times 5\cdot31$
j $(14\cdot56 + 3\cdot075) \div (0\cdot561 \times 20\cdot52)$

2 Estimate each of the following, giving your answer as an integer (i.e. a whole number).

a $\dfrac{5\cdot6 \times 7\cdot8}{12\cdot9}$
b $\dfrac{21\cdot9 \times 42\cdot6}{68\cdot9}$
c $\dfrac{7\cdot3 \times 9\cdot8}{15\cdot6 \times 3\cdot2}$
d $\dfrac{212 \times 71\cdot5}{15\cdot8 \times 0\cdot89}$
e $\dfrac{19\cdot6 - 5\cdot8}{3\cdot6 \times 1\cdot72}$
f $\dfrac{\sqrt{41\cdot6 + 39\cdot5}}{9\cdot6}$
g $\dfrac{\sqrt{105\cdot6}}{\sqrt{18\cdot85}}$
h $\dfrac{(8\cdot61)^2}{\sqrt{8\cdot61}}$

These are a bit harder, aren't they?

Note:
- The fraction bar acts a little like grouping symbols. You work out the numerator and denominator separately.
- In $\sqrt{41\cdot6+39\cdot5}$ you must work out the addition first. The square root sign also acts like grouping symbols.

3 When estimating the size of a measurement, both the number and the unit must be considered. In each case, choose the most likely answer by estimation.

a The weight of the newborn baby was:
A 350 g　B 7·8 kg　C 3·1 kg　D 50 g

b The length of a mature blue whale is about:
A 27 m　B 3 km　C 32 cm　D 98 m

c 12% discount on a television set marked \$2300 is:
A \$86.60　B \$866　C \$276　D \$27.60

d I just borrowed more than \$80 000 from the bank at a rate of 8·5% p.a. In the next year, the interest on the loan is:
A \$873　B \$6800　C \$185.60　D \$21 140

4 a A pile of paper is 3·2 cm thick. If there are 300 sheets in the pile, estimate the thickness of one sheet of paper.

b Paloma estimated that there were 80 people sitting in an area of 50 m^2 at a Carols by Candlelight concert. She estimated that about 2000 m^2 of area was similarly occupied by the crowd. To the nearest 100, what is her estimate of the crowd size?

c Would 8·6 × 84·4 be between 8 × 80 and 9 × 90? Explain your answer.

5 Two measurements were rounded correct to two significant figures and then multiplied to estimate an area. The working was: 92 m × 0·81 m = 74·52 m^2.
Between which two measurements would the real area lie? How many of the figures in this estimate are useful, given the possible spread of the area?

1:08 Using scientific notation

PREP QUIZ 1:08

Write each number as a basic numeral.

1 3×10^2	**2** 7×10^3	**3** 4×10^6	**4** $7{\cdot}2 \times 100$
5 $7{\cdot}2 \times 10^2$	**6** $1{\cdot}6 \times 10^4$	**7** $2{\cdot}15 \times 10$	**8** $23{\cdot}15 \times 100$

9 (7 × 10 000) + (4 × 1000) + (9 × 100) + (7 × 10) + 6

10 (3 × 1 000 000) + (4 × 100 000)

Powers of 10

When multiplying by a power of 10, move the decimal point to the right.

WORKED EXAMPLE 1

a $2{\cdot}125 \times 10^2 = 2{\cdot}125 \times 100$
$= 212{\cdot}5$

100 has 2 zeros and the power of 10 has an index of 2, so move the decimal point 2 places to the right.

b $8{\cdot}7 \times 10^6 = 8{\cdot}7 \times 1\,000\,000$
$= 8\,700\,000$

1 000 000 has 6 zeros and the power of 10 has an index of 6, so move the decimal point 6 places to the right.

Expanded notation

Questions **9** and **10** of the Prep quiz show numbers written in expanded notation.

Using our knowledge of powers, we can write expanded notation using powers of 10.

1 $(7 \times 10\,000) + (4 \times 1000) + (9 \times 100) + (7 \times 10) + 6$
$= (7 \times 10^4) + (4 \times 10^3) + (9 \times 10^2) + (7 \times 10^1) + 6$
$= 74\,976$
$= 7{\cdot}4976 \times 10^4$ (Here, we moved the decimal point four places.)

We use scientific notation to write large numbers.

2 $(3 \times 1\,000\,000) + (4 \times 100\,000)$
$= (3 \times 10^6) + (4 \times 10^5)$
$= 3\,400\,000$
$= 3{\cdot}4 \times 10^6$ (Here, we moved the decimal point six places.)

$10^3 = 1000$ (one thousand)

$10^6 = 1\,000\,000$ (one million)

$10^9 = 1\,000\,000\,000$ (one billion)

Scientific notation

$7{\cdot}4976 \times 10^4$ and $3{\cdot}4 \times 10^6$ are examples of scientific notation.

> Using scientific notation, we write the number as the product of a number between 1 and 10 and a power of 10.

The number between 1 and 10 shows all the significant figures.

WORKED EXAMPLE 2

Write each number using scientific notation.

a $35\,000 = 3{\cdot}5 \times 10\,000$
$= 3{\cdot}5 \times 10^4$

To get a number between 1 and 10, we move the decimal point 4 places to the left so that 35 000 becomes 3·5. To make up for this, we multiply by 10^4.
(This number has two significant figures.)

b $278\,000\,000 = 2{\cdot}78 \times 100\,000\,000$
$= 2{\cdot}78 \times 10^8$

To get a number between 1 and 10, we move the decimal point 8 places to the left so that 278 000 000 becomes 2·78. To make up for this, we multiply by 10^8.
(This number has three significant figures.)

WORKED EXAMPLE 3

Write each of the numbers (written in scientific notation), as a basic numeral.

a $9{\cdot}03 \times 10^5 = 9{\cdot}03000 \times 100\,000$
$= 903\,000$

To multiply by 10^5, we move the decimal point 5 places to the right.
(This number has three significant figures.)

b $6{\cdot}1 \times 10^7 = 6{\cdot}1000000 \times 10\,000\,000$
$= 61\,000\,000$

To multiply by 10^7, we move the decimal point 7 places to the right.
(This number has two significant figures.)

Exercise 1:08

1 These are written in expanded notation. Write each as a basic numeral.

a $(9 \times 10\,000) + (2 \times 1000) + (3 \times 100) + (6 \times 10) + 5$
b $(7 \times 100\,000) + (4 \times 10\,000) + (3 \times 10)$
c $(3 \times 1\,000\,000) + (4 \times 100\,000) + (8 \times 1000) + 7$
d $(6 \times 10\,000) + (5 \times 1000) + (9 \times 100)$
e $(2 \times 10^4) + (8 \times 10^3) + (4 \times 10^2) + (1 \times 10^1) + 5$
f $(5 \times 10^3) + (9 \times 10^2) + (2 \times 10^1) + 4$
g $(6 \times 10^4) + (9 \times 10^3) + (7 \times 10^2) + (2 \times 10^1) + 7$
h $(3 \times 10^3) + (8 \times 10^2) + (4 \times 10^1) + 1$
i $(7 \times 10^6) + (5 \times 10^5) + (8 \times 10^4)$
j $(2 \times 10^4) + (7 \times 10^3)$

2 Complete each expression to write the number in scientific notation.

a $(1 \times 10^2) + (7 \times 10^1) + 3 = 1{\cdot}73 \times 10^{\cdots}$
b $(9 \times 10^2) + (1 \times 10^1) = 9{\cdot}1 \times 10^{\cdots}$
c $(3 \times 10^6) + (4 \times 10^5) + (5 \times 10^4) = 3{\cdot}45 \times 10^{\cdots}$
d $(6 \times 10^3) + (1 \times 10^2) = 6{\cdot}1 \times 10^{\cdots}$
e $(5 \times 10^7) + (2 \times 10^6) + (2 \times 10^5) = 5{\cdot}22 \times 10^{\cdots}$
f $(4 \times 10^9) + (5 \times 10^8) = 4{\cdot}5 \times 10^{\cdots}$

3 Write each number using scientific notation.

a 8600 b 856 000 c 47 000 d 37 000 000
e 6 000 000 f 230 000 000 g 101 000 000 h 8 125 000 000

4 These are written in scientific notation. Write each number as a basic numeral.

a $6{\cdot}86 \times 10^3$ b $1{\cdot}02 \times 10^2$ c $9{\cdot}5 \times 10^6$ d $4{\cdot}7 \times 10^5$
e $3{\cdot}96 \times 10^6$ f $4{\cdot}55 \times 10^7$ g $8{\cdot}05 \times 10^4$ h $6{\cdot}1 \times 10^9$

5 a Explain the difference between 7×10^3 and 7^3.
b *True* or *false*? There are more than 5×10^9 people on Earth.
c *True* or *false*? $\$5 \times 10^6$ is the same as 5 million dollars.

6 How many significant figures are in each number?

a $4{\cdot}05 \times 10^6$ b $7{\cdot}0 \times 10^4$ c $9{\cdot}3 \times 10^7$ d $8{\cdot}125 \times 10^3$

1:09 Units of measurement

Units of measurement are used to record measurements accurately. The most common units of measurement used in Australia are metric units. In the metric system:

- each measure has a base unit (e.g. for length it is the metre)
- other units are obtained by writing a prefix in front of the base unit (e.g. for length, some are millimetres, centimetres and kilometres).

Prefixes always have the same value as shown in the table below.

Prefix	Symbol	Value
nano	n	one billionth
micro	μ	one millionth
milli	m	one thousandth
centi	c	one hundredth
kilo	k	thousand
mega	M	million
giga	G	billion
tera	T	trillion

A prefix explains the relationship to the base unit.

WORKED EXAMPLES

1 7 micrometres = 7 μm = $\frac{7}{1000000}$ m

2 5 gigabytes = 5 GB = 5 000 000 000 bytes

3 120 terabytes = 120 TB = 120 000 000 000 000 bytes

We must choose the most appropriate unit when measuring. For example, when measuring the distance between Sydney and Melbourne, we use kilometres rather than millimetres. In some situations more than one unit may be appropriate (e.g. the mass of a car can be measured in kilograms or tonnes).

1000 kilobytes (kB) = 1 megabyte (MB)
1000 megabytes (MB) = 1 gigabyte (GB)
1000 gigabytes (GB) = 1 terabyte (TB)
1000 nanoseconds (ns) = 1 microsecond (μs)
1000 microseconds (μs) = 1 milliseconds (ms)
1000 milliseconds (ms) = 1 second (s)

It is also important to be able to convert between different units. To do this we must know the value of the prefixes. This will tell us whether we need to multiply or divide when doing the conversion.

Tm	Gm	Mm	km	m	mm	μm	nm
10^{12} m	10^9 m	10^6 m	10^3 m	1 m	$\frac{1}{10^3}$ m	$\frac{1}{10^6}$ m	$\frac{1}{10^9}$ m

In this table each unit is 1000 times as big as the one on its right.

PREP QUIZ 1:09

Write *true* or *false*.

1 1 μm = 1000 nm
2 1 mm = 1000 μm
3 1 m = 10 mm
4 1 Mm = 1000 km
5 1 GB = 1000 MB
6 1 TB = 1000 GB

Write the following measurements in words.

7 8 GB
8 3 TB
9 4 MB
10 9 kB

WORKED EXAMPLES

1 Convert 5·4 MB (5·4 megabytes) to kilobytes (kB).
2 Convert 500 000 ns (nanoseconds) to microseconds (μs).
3 Convert 25 mm to μm.

Solutions

1 $5{\cdot}4\,\text{MB} = 5{\cdot}4 \times 1000\,\text{kB}$ — $1000\,\text{kB} = 1\,\text{MB}$
$= 5400\,\text{kB}$
OR $5{\cdot}4\,\text{MB} = 5{\cdot}4 \times 10^6\,\text{B}$ — 1 million bytes = 1 megabyte
$= 5{\cdot}4 \times 10^6 \div 10^3\,\text{kB}$ — 1000 bytes = 1 kilobyte
$= 5{\cdot}4 \times 10^3\,\text{kB}$
$= 5400\,\text{kB}$

2 $500\,000\,\text{ns} = 500\,000 \div 1000\,\mu\text{s}$ — $1000\,\text{ns} = 1\,\mu\text{s}$
$= 500\,\mu\text{s}$

3 $25\,\text{mm} = 25 \times 1000\,\mu\text{m}$ — $1000\,\mu\text{m} = 1\,\text{mm}$
$= 2500\,\mu\text{m}$

Note: Some digital devices use different notations to display digital information. e.g. 40 kB could be shown as 40 K or 40 k or 40 KB.

Exercise 1:09

1 Convert the following.

a 7 km to m
b 12 t to kg
c 3 ML to L
d 800 cm to m
e 9·3 m to mm
f 3·45 L to mL
g 7·2 g to mg
h 3845 mL to L
i 500 mm to m

2 Convert the following.

a 5 Mm to m
b 6 Gm to m
c 5 Tm to m
d 6 m to mm
e 9 m to μm
f 3 m to nm
g 17·1 km to m
h 1·8 Gm to m
i 4·8 Mm to m

3 Convert the following.

a 4 MB to B
b 4 MB to kB
c 7 GB to MB
d 3 TB to GB
e 3 μm to nm
f 5000 nm to μm
g 3·2 MB to kB
h 4·1 GB to MB
i 0·6 TB to GB

4 Convert the following.

a 3000 m to km
b 8000 kB to MB
c 11 000 MB to GB
d 6500 GB to TB
e 3500 ns to μs
f 730 ms to μs
g 5 GB to kB
h 2 TB to MB
i 3 TB to kB

5 a How many years, to the nearest year, is the same as 1 gigasecond?
b How many minutes are the same as 1 billion microseconds?
c My computer has a capacity of one terabyte. I have used 100 gigabytes. How much available space do I have on my computer?
d Our computer network server has a capacity of 12 TB (12 terabytes). We have 9000 GB of available space left. How much space have we used?

1:10 Accuracy of measurements

Consider the length of the purple rectangle above. If a group of students were asked to measure its length, how accurately could it be done? Could it be measured exactly or only to a given level of accuracy such as the nearest centimetre?

- It is not possible to give an exact measurement. When measuring, we must record the value for the closest unit mark on the scale.

Therefore, the accuracy of a measuring instrument is limited by its scale. Measuring the interval XY with a ruler marked in millimetres would give a more accurate result than measuring it with a ruler marked only in centimetres.

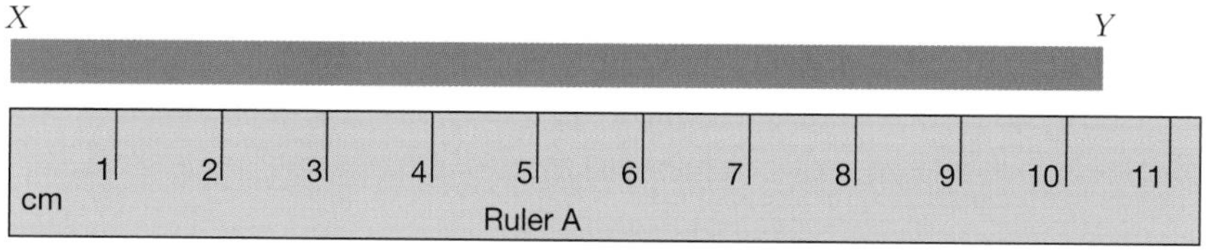

Using ruler A, we measure XY to be 10 cm long.

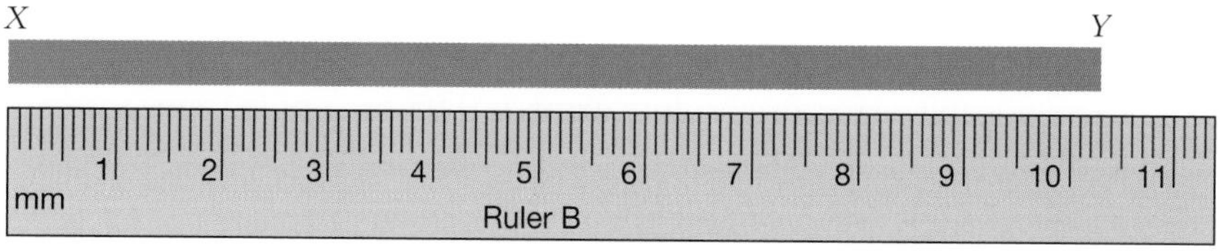

Using ruler B, we measure XY to be 10·3 cm long.

> When using a measuring instrument such as a ruler or a tape measure, the measurement taken cannot be more accurate than the smallest unit on the scale of the instrument. If measured in cm, the measure is correct to the nearest cm.

- Using ruler A we recorded that XY is 10 cm in length. Clearly, any length between 9·5 and 10·5 cm would be recorded as 10 cm. Hence, the greatest possible error when using a ruler marked in centimetres is $\frac{1}{2}$ of a centimetre.

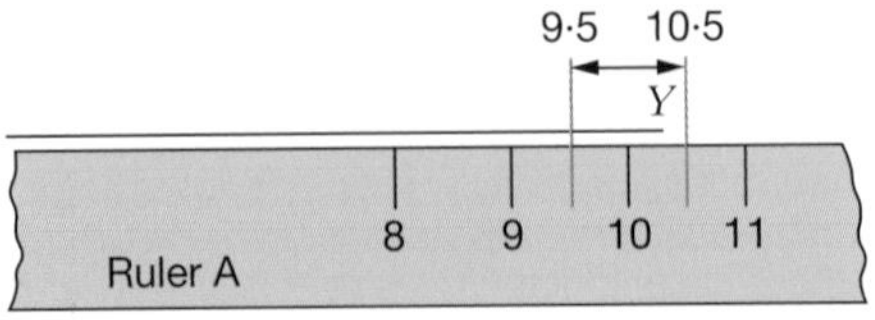

So, if the length XY is recorded as 10 cm, then XY is between 9·5 cm and 10·5 cm or 10 ± 0·5 cm. (The measure could also be 9·5 cm, because this would round up to 10 cm.) The greatest possible error or absolute error is 0·5 cm.

- Using ruler B we recorded that XY is 10·3 cm in length. This means that XY is between 10·25 cm and 10·35 cm as shown. (The measure could also be 10·25 cm, as this would round up to 10·3 cm.)

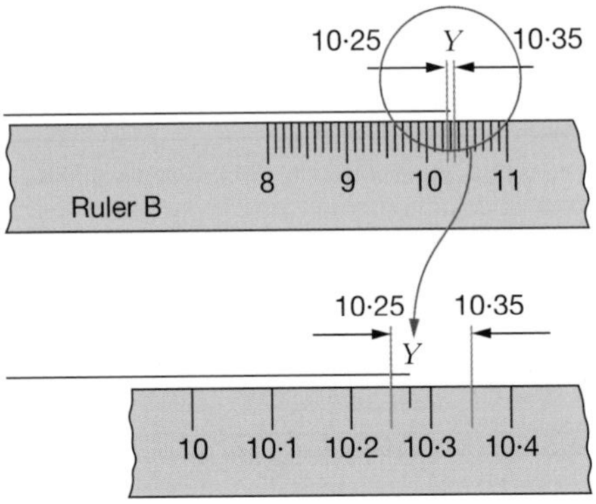

If the length XY is recorded as 10·3 cm, then XY is between 10·25 cm and 10·35 cm or 10·3 ± 0·05 cm. The greatest possible error, or absolute error, is 0·05 or $\frac{1}{2}$ of 0·1 cm.

> The greatest possible error, or absolute error, is equal to half of the smallest unit on the measuring scale.

WORKED EXAMPLE 1

For each of the following, find the absolute error.

a 8 g **b** 17·4 g **c** 27·625 L

Solutions

a 8 g is measured to the nearest gram. The smallest unit used is 1 gram.
The absolute error will be half of 1 g.
∴ Absolute error = 0·5 × 1 g
= 0·5 g

b 17·4 g is measured to the nearest tenth of a gram. The smallest unit used is 0·1 grams.
The absolute error will be half of 0·1 g.
∴ Absolute error = 0·5 × 0·1 g
= 0·05 g

c 27·625 L is measured to the nearest thousandth of a litre. The smallest unit used is 0·001 litres.
The absolute error will be half of 0·001 L.
∴ Absolute error = 0·5 × 0·001 L
= 0·0005 L (or 0·5 mL)

WORKED EXAMPLE 2

Alana's bathroom scales are marked in tenths of a kilogram. She used them to measure her mass to be 63·7 kg. Find the absolute error of the measurement and her smallest and largest possible mass.

Solution

The smallest unit on the bathroom scales is a tenth of a kilogram.
The smallest unit used is 0·1 kilograms. The absolute error will be half of 0·1 kg.

$\therefore$ Absolute error = 0·5 × 0·1 kg
= 0·05 kg

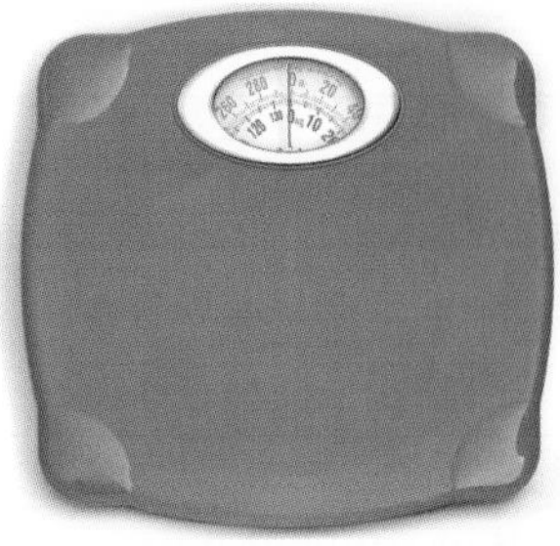

Alana's mass is (63·7 ± 0·05) kg

$\therefore$ Alana's smallest possible mass = (63·7 − 0·05) kg
= 63·65 kg

$\therefore$ Alana's largest possible mass = (63·7 + 0·05) kg
= 63·75 kg

Exercise 1:10

1 Calculate the absolute error (or greatest possible error) for each measurement.

a 37 cm
b 165 g
c 450 L (measured to the nearest 10 L)
d 11·3 cm
e 6·18 m
f 9·0 L (measured to the nearest 0·1 L)
g 285·9 t
h 3·625 s
i 25 000 t (measured to the nearest 1000 t)

2 a A tape measure marked in centimetres was used to measure a length of timber to be 584 cm (or 5·84 m).
  i What is the absolute error of this measurement?
  ii In what range would the actual measurement lie?
b The mass of a silver ingot is 47·29 g when measured on a digital scale.
  i To what accuracy is the scale measuring?
  ii What is the absolute error of the measurement?
  iii In what range would the true mass of the silver lie?
c The mass of a car is listed as 1·4 t.
  i To what degree of accuracy has the mass been measured?
  ii What is the absolute error of the measurement?
  iii In what range will the mass of the car lie?

3 Luke and Jo decided to fill the car's tank with petrol. Luke reported that it took 35 L to fill the tank. Jo reported that it took 34·9 L to fill the tank.
a What is the absolute error of Luke's measurement, and within what range could Luke's measurement lie?
b What is the absolute error of Jo's measurement, and within what range could Jo's measurement lie?

4 Phil and Naomi used a tape marked in centimetres to measure the width and length of a path. Phil measured the width as 1·48 m. Naomi measured the length as 120·36 m.

a What was the absolute error of Phil's measurement? Within what range could Phil's reported measurement fall?

b What was the absolute error of Naomi's measurement? Within what range could Naomi's reported measurement fall?

c Are the absolute errors the same for the two measurements?

d Which measurement would you consider to be the more accurate? Give a reason for your answer.

5 The thickness of a metal slab was measured using various measuring instruments. The results were:

Ruler (marked in cm)	1 cm
Ruler (marked in cm and mm)	1·4 cm
Vernier calipers	1·38 cm
Micrometer screw gauge	1·383 cm

a Which instrument gives the measurement to:

i two significant figures
ii four significant figures?

b What is the absolute error when the thickness was measured with:

i the ruler (marked in cm)
ii the ruler (marked in cm and mm)
iii Vernier calipers
iv the micrometer screw gauge?

c In what range must the thickness of the slab lie if its measurement is recorded as:

i 1·4 cm

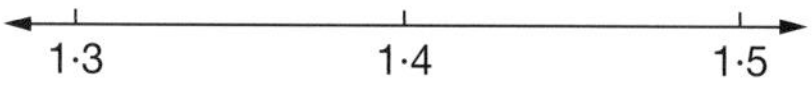

ii 1·38 cm?

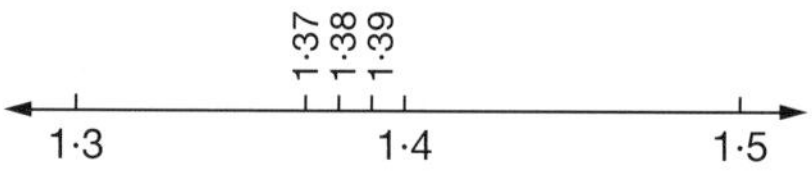

The National Measurement Institute (NMI) ensures the accuracy of measuring instruments under fluctuating environmental conditions such as temperature and electromagnetic interference. Fuel pumps must be accurate to within ±0·3%.

absolute error

- the greatest possible error due to the scale used
- half the smallest unit on the scale used, e.g. the absolute error of 6·2 cm is 0·05 cm

approximate

- to replace a number with a less accurate one, often to make it simpler, e.g. 3·94 m might be approximated to 4 m

decimal place

- the position of a numeral after the decimal point, each position being $\frac{1}{10}$ of the one before it, e.g. 0·639 has three decimal places $0{\cdot}639 = \frac{6}{10} + \frac{3}{100} + \frac{9}{1000}$

estimate

- to calculate roughly (verb)
- a good guess or the result of calculating roughly (noun)

expanded notation

- a way of writing numerals to show the place value of each digit, e.g. 175 000
  $= (1 \times 100\,000) + (7 \times 10\,000) + (5 \times 1000)$
  $= (1 \times 10^5) + (7 \times 10^4) + (5 \times 10^3)$

fraction

- one or more parts of a whole expressed in the form $\frac{a}{b}$, where a and b are integers and $b \neq 0$,
  e.g. $\frac{7}{8}$ 7 ← numerator, 8 ← denominator

integer

- a whole number that may be positive, negative or zero, e.g. 7, −23, 0

percentage

- a fraction that has a denominator of 100, written using the symbol %, e.g. $\frac{27}{100} = 27\%$

rational number

- a number which can be expressed in fraction form; this includes integers, percentages, terminating and recurring decimals, e.g. $\frac{4}{7}, -2\frac{1}{9}, 7, 16\%, -0{\cdot}69, 4{\cdot}6\dot{3}\dot{2}$

recurring decimal (repeating)

- a decimal for which the digits set up a repeating pattern; these numbers can be written as:
  e.g. $0{\cdot}737\,373\ldots = 0{\cdot}\dot{7}\dot{3}$
  $0{\cdot}694\,44\ldots = 0{\cdot}69\dot{4}$

scientific (or standard) notation

- a useful way to write very large or very small numbers
- numbers are written as the product of a number between 1 and 10 and a power of 10, e.g. $76\,000\,000 = 7{\cdot}6 \times 10^7$

significant figure

- a number that we believe to be correct within some limit of error
- to round a number to a number of significant figures is to specify the accuracy required from a calculation, e.g. 16·483 to 3 sig. fig. = 16·5
  0·00475 to 1 sig. fig. = 0·005

terminating decimal

- a decimal number that has a limited number of decimal places, e.g. 0·6, 0·475, 0·0069

DIAGNOSTIC TEST 1 — NUMBER AND MEASUREMENT

These questions reflect some of the important skills introduced in this chapter. Other skills have been covered in diagnostic tests within the chapter or previously in Year 8.
Errors made in this test will indicate areas of weakness.
Each weakness should be treated by going back to the section listed.

	Section
1 Write these fractions as recurring decimals. a $\frac{2}{3}$ b $\frac{1}{6}$ c $\frac{7}{9}$ d $\frac{4}{15}$	1:03
2 Write these recurring decimals in fraction form. a 0·5555... b $0{\cdot}\dot{3}\dot{7}$ c 0·5777... d $0{\cdot}6\dot{8}\dot{9}$	1:03
3 a What is the ratio of 1 m to 150 cm? b Express the ratio of 11 to 4 in the form: i $X:1$ ii $1:Y$ c If it costs $36 to purchase 20 kg of potting mix, what is the cost per kg?	1:04
4 How many significant figures has: a 316 000 000 (nearest thousand) b 42 007 c 0·000 130 50 d 6200	1:07
5 Round: a 56 700 000 to the nearest million b 0·666 15 to 4 dec. pl. c 7·983 to 1 dec. pl. d 4·673 m to the nearest cm e 0·006 25 to 1 sig. fig. f 507 000 000 to 2 sig. fig. g 0·060 75 to 2 sig. fig. h 93 784 231 to 3 sig. fig.	1:05
6 Estimate the size of each calculation to the nearest whole number. a $8{\cdot}73 \times 4{\cdot}132$ b $0{\cdot}0394 \div 0{\cdot}008\,12$ c $\frac{25{\cdot}4 \times 7{\cdot}98}{9{\cdot}93}$ d $\sqrt{65{\cdot}4} \times (4{\cdot}97)^2$	1:07
7 Write each number using scientific notation. a 85 000 b 960 000 000 Write each number as a basic numeral. c $1{\cdot}06 \times 10^6$ d $8{\cdot}4 \times 10^4$	1:08
8 Convert: a 7·2 MB to kB b 40 000 ns to µs	1:09
9 Find the absolute error for: a 6 L b 35·9 kg	1:10
10 a What is the smallest possible mass that could be written as 3·26 g? b In what range will a mass lie if it is recorded as 9·4 kg?	1:10

ASSIGNMENT 1A Chapter review

1 Simplify:

a $15 - 3 \times 2$ b $24 \div 4 + 5 \times 2$

c $-6 \times (-5) \div (-10)$

2 Give the simplest answer to:

a $\frac{7}{10} + \frac{1}{10}$ b $\frac{5}{6} - \frac{2}{3}$

c $\frac{2}{5} \times \frac{1}{4}$ d $\frac{5}{9} \div \frac{2}{3}$

e $2\frac{3}{4} + 3\frac{1}{5}$ f $6\frac{1}{3} - 4\frac{3}{5}$

g $3\frac{1}{2} \times 2\frac{2}{3}$ h $5\frac{1}{4} \div \frac{7}{8}$

3 Simplify:

a $9\cdot2 - 4\cdot73$ b $6\cdot2 \times 0\cdot7$

c $24\cdot3 \div 0\cdot6$ d $(0\cdot3)^2$

4 Write these decimals as fractions.

a 0·35 b 0·875

c $0\cdot\dot{2}\dot{3}$ d $0\cdot\dot{3}4\dot{7}$

5 a Find $7\frac{1}{2}$% of \$350.

b What percentage is \$65 of \$325?

6 Simplify these ratios:

a 25 : 45 b \$6 : \$18

c 50 cm : 2 m d 15 min : $1\frac{1}{2}$ h

7 How many significant figures are there in each of these numbers?

a 5·27

b 0·006 04

c 6·90

d 93 000 (nearest thousand)

e $9\cdot30 \times 10^4$

f $6\cdot02 \times 10^7$

8 Round these numbers as indicated.

a 6·4472	(1 dec. pl.)
b 6·916 73	(nearest hundredth)
c 47 643 908	(nearest thousand)
d 647·542	(nearest whole number)
e 6·3942	(2 sig. fig.)
f 0·005 817	(3 sig. fig.)
g 47 649 503	(3 sig. fig.)
h 0·704 906	(2 sig. fig.)

9 Write each number as a basic numeral.

a $5\cdot82 \times 10^6$

b $9\cdot1 \times 10^3$

10 Write each number using scientific notation.

a 80 000 000 (to the nearest ten million)

b 80 000 000 (to the nearest million)

11 a Convert 2·1 terabytes (2·1 TB) to gigabytes (GB).

b Convert 8·5 gigabytes (8·5 GB) to kilobytes (kB).

c What is the absolute error of the measurement 3·7 km?

d In what range could the measurement 3·7 km lie?

What sort of estimates would organisers of large fun runs have to make?

ASSIGNMENT 1B Working mathematically

1 Refer to **ID Card 1** on page xix to give the mathematical term for:

a 9 b 10 c 15 d 16
e 18 f 19 g 20 h 22
i 23 j 24

2 Refer to **ID Card 2** on page xix to give the mathematical term for:

a 2 b 5 c 10 d 11
e 14 f 15 g 16 h 18
i 19 j 23

3 Twelve schools participate in a knockout competition. How many matches must be played before the winner is decided?

4 How many different counting numbers less than one thousand could be formed if only the digits 5, 6 and 7 could be used? (These could be used more than once in a number.)

5

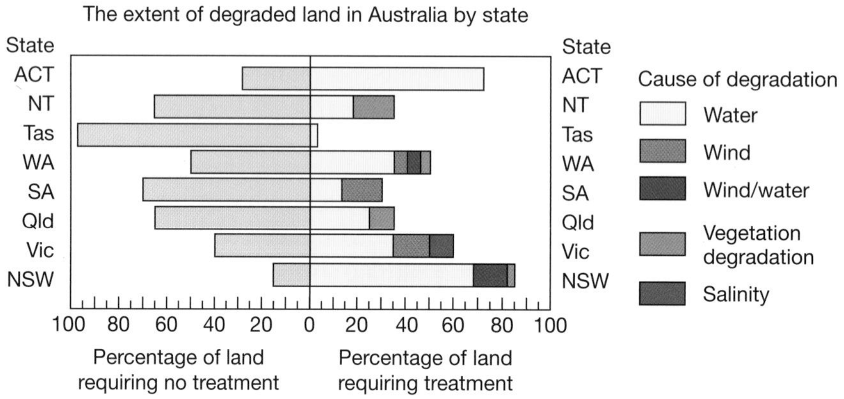

a What percentage of land requires no treatment in:
  i Victoria
  ii Tasmania
  iii Queensland
  iv New South Wales?

b What is the greatest cause of land degradation in Australia?

c Why have water and wind caused so much land degradation in the last 200 years?

d If you wanted to find the percentage of land in Australia requiring no treatment, how would you do it? What additional information would you use?

6

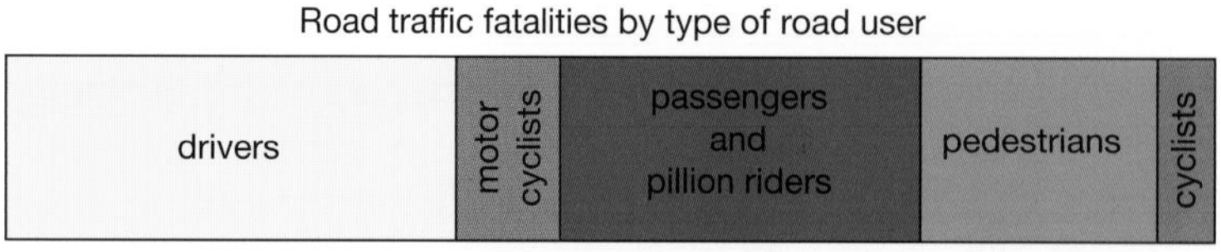

Measure the length of this bar graph. The length represents 100% of road traffic fatalities.

a What percentage of fatalities were drivers?

b What percentage of fatalities were motorcyclists?

c Because fewer motorcyclists were killed than drivers, can you say that it is safer to be a motorcyclist that a driver? Why or why not?

WORKING MATHEMATICALLY

2

Contents

Syllabus references (See pages x–xv for details.)

The Working Mathematically strand is interwoven throughout the content strands **Number and Algebra**, **Measurement and Geometry**, and **Statistics and Probability**.

Aspects of Working Mathematically from Stage 4, Stage 5.1, Stage 5.2 and Stage 5.3 have been covered.

Non-routine problems and problem solving involving work covered in Year 8 will be revised in this chapter. This includes rates, ratios, percentages, measurement and the use of Venn diagrams.

Working Mathematically

- Communicating
- Problem Solving
- Reasoning
- Understanding
- Fluency

2:01 Solving routine problems

In mathematics, the learning of new skills and concepts is usually followed by the use of that newly acquired knowledge to solve problems.

Hence, problems in topics like percentages or measurement are usually routine in that we know what mathematical knowledge we are trying to use.

Steps for solving problems

Step 1 Read the question carefully.
Step 2 Decide what you are asked to find.
Step 3 Look for information that might be helpful.
Step 4 Decide on the method you will use.
Step 5 Set out your solution clearly.
Step 6 Make sure that your answer makes sense.

WORKED EXAMPLE 1

A path 0·8 m wide is to be put around a rectangular garden which is 6·5 m long and 2·8 m wide. If the path is to be 100 mm thick, calculate the volume of concrete in the path and the cost of buying the concrete at $\$140/\text{m}^2$ (to the nearest dollar).

Solution

$$V = Ah$$
$$A = 8{\cdot}1 \times 4{\cdot}4 - 6{\cdot}5 \times 2{\cdot}8$$
$$= 17{\cdot}44\,\text{m}^2$$
$$h = 100\,\text{mm}$$
$$= 0{\cdot}1\,\text{m}$$
$$\therefore V = 17{\cdot}44 \times 0{\cdot}1$$
$$= 1{\cdot}744\,\text{m}^3$$
$$\therefore \text{Cost of concrete} = 1{\cdot}744 \times \$140$$
$$= \$244 \text{ (to the nearest dollar)}$$

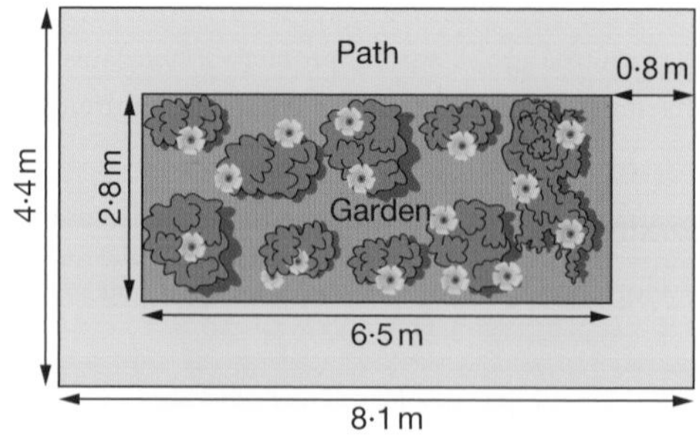

WORKED EXAMPLE 2

a \$9000 is divided between Tom and James in the ratio 4 : 5. How much does each receive?

b The sizes of the angles of a triangle are in the ratio 2 : 3 : 5. Find the size of each angle.

Solutions

a There are 9 parts: 4 for Tom and 5 for James.
$\therefore$ Tom receives $\frac{4}{9}$ of \$9000
= \$4000
James receives $\frac{5}{9}$ of \$9000
= \$5000
(*Note:* The sum of the parts is equal to the whole \$9000.)

b There are 10 parts: 2, 3 and 5.
The angle sum of a triangle is 180°.
10 parts = 180°
1 part = 18°
First angle = $2 \times 18°$
= 36°
Second angle = $3 \times 18°$
= 54°
Third angle = $5 \times 18°$
= 90°
(*Check:* 36° + 54° + 90° = 180°)

Exercise 2:01

1 **a** If the exchange rate for one Australian dollar is 0·9845 American dollars:
- **i** how many American dollars would I get for 500 Australian dollars
- **ii** how many Australian dollars would I get for 500 American dollars? (Hint: Express 1 AUD : 0·9845 USD in the form x AUD : 1 USD).

b On a trip my car usually averages 8·4 L per 100 km. When carrying a heavy load it averages only 11·2 L per 100 km.
- **i** What is the difference in petrol consumption between these two conditions?
- **ii** What is the difference between the distance travelled per litre of petrol used for the two conditions? (Answer to the nearest metre.)

c Toni's average reaction time when driving was measured to be 0·8 seconds. How far would her car travel in this time if its speed was 60 km/h? (Answer correct to the nearest metre.)

d A nurse has to administer medicine at the rate of 4 doses/day to a child. The recommended dosage is 80 mg/kg/day. What is the size of each dose if the child weighs 29 kg?

e Steve and Donald participate in a 45 km charity walk. Steve leaves at 6 am and walks at an average speed of 6 km/h. Donald leaves 1 hour later. At what speed must he walk to meet up with Steve at 1 pm?

2 **a** In a church on Sunday, the ratio of women to men was 5 : 4. How many men were present if 45 women were there?

b At the Entertainment Centre the ratio of basketball players to spectators was 3 : 500. How many spectators were there if there were 30 players?

c Three numbers are in the ratio 1 : 3 : 4. If the difference between the two smaller ones is 10, what are the numbers?

3 a John is paid \$5 an hour and his younger brother Zac is paid \$3 an hour. They worked together for several hours and earned a total of \$56. How much did each earn? How long did they work?

b The lengths of three sides of a triangle are in the ratio 4 : 5 : 3. Find the length of each side if the perimeter of the triangle is 1·08 m.

c Nitrogen (N), phosphorus (P) and potassium (K) are present in a fertiliser in the ratio 23 : 4 : 18. How many grams of each element are present in 1 kg of the fertiliser? (Answer to the nearest gram.)

d Red and blue paint need to be mixed in the ratio 5 : 3 to make a certain colour. If there are 400 L of red paint and 320 L of blue paint, how many litres of the mixed colour can be made?

e A metallurgist knows that a certain alloy has been made by mixing silver, lead and zinc in the ratio 6 : 2 : 7. She takes 600 g of the alloy and melts it and adds 120 g of silver. How much of the other metals must she add to keep the ratio of the metals the same?

4 a Carol's house increased in value from \$260 000 to \$292 000 over a 1-year period, while over the same period Bronte's house increased in value from \$120 000 to \$145 000. By expressing each increase as a percentage of the initial value, state which house has had the larger percentage increase in its value.

b Alan bought some land for \$165 000 and later sold it for \$210 000. Find his profit as a percentage of the selling price (correct to one decimal place).

c A town's population increased by 422 people in a year. If this represented an increase in the population of $2\frac{1}{2}$%, what was the town's population at the start of the year?

d A hardware store has a sale in which it gives a 10% discount off the marked price. For valued customers it gives a further 15% discount off the first discounted price. How much will Larry pay for a saw marked at \$580 if he is a valued customer?

5 a A rectangular area is roped off using a rope 200 m in length. Calculate the area of the rectangle if it is 65 m long.

b A football field is 120 m long and 60 m wide. A fence is to be placed around the field 3 m back from the field. Calculate the length of fencing needed.

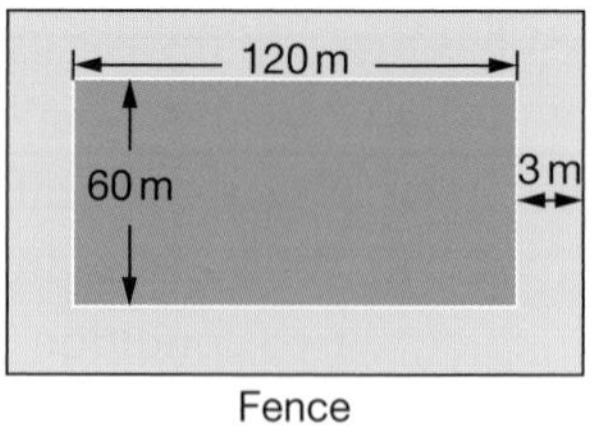

c The diameter of a car wheel is 40 cm. How many complete revolutions will this wheel need to make to travel 1 km? (Hint: $C = \pi d$)

d The area shown here is to be covered in lawn. The area is first enclosed by a concrete border and soil is brought in to cover the area to a depth of 4 cm. Turf rolls are then laid over the soil. Find the cost of:

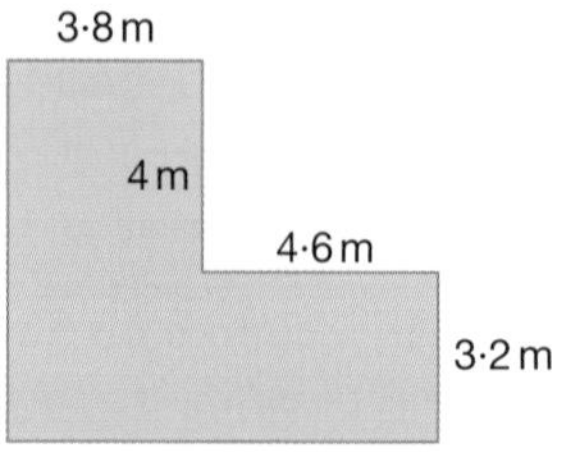

i the concrete edging at \$22/m

ii the turf at \$10/m^2

iii the soil at \$30/m^3.

e Two pieces of wire, each of length 1 m, are bent to form a circle and a square. Which has the larger area, and how much larger is it to the nearest square centimetre?

2:02 Solving non-routine problems

Often in mathematics (as well as in real life), we find a problem that is unlike any we have seen before. We need to reflect on what we already know and see how our existing knowledge can be used. Sometimes we will need to develop new skills to solve the problem, or we might need to look at the problem in a different way.

Applying strategies is one of the processes involved in Working Mathematically.

Problem-solving strategies
- Eliminating possibilities
- Working backwards
- Acting it out
- Looking for patterns
- Solving a simpler problem
- Trial and error
- Making a drawing, diagram or model
- Using algebra
- Using technology

Maybe I can use the computer to help solve some problems.

WORKED EXAMPLE 1

What is the angle between the hands of a clock at 2:25?

Start by drawing a diagram. Add information to the diagram.

Solution

At 2 o'clock the angle between the hands is 60°.

In 60 minutes:
- the minute hand moves through 360°
- the hour hand moves through 30°.

In 25 minutes:
- the minute hand moves through $\frac{25}{60} \times 360° = 150°$
- the hour hand moves through $\frac{25}{60} \times 30° = 12\frac{1}{2}°$.

Hence, from the diagram:

$60° + 12\frac{1}{2}° + \theta = 150°$

$\therefore \theta = 77\frac{1}{2}°$

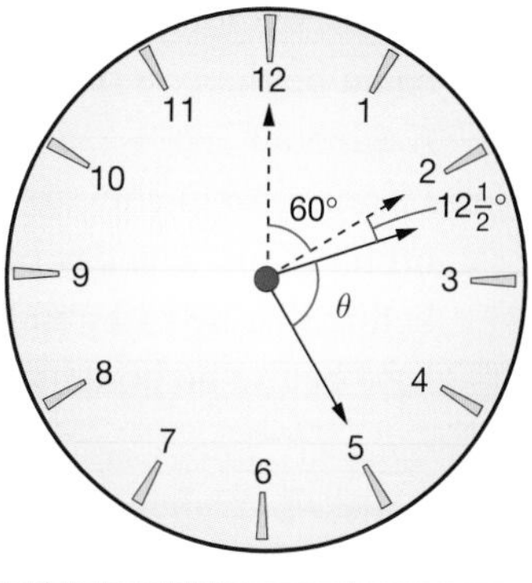

WORKED EXAMPLE 2

Screwdrivers come in four different sizes priced at \$8.90, \$7.80, \$5.40 and \$4.80. I bought seven screwdrivers. Which of the following amounts was the total cost?

A \$48.40 **B** \$34 **C** \$50.65 **D** \$61.40

Solution

Try to eliminate possibilities.

- \$50.65 cannot be the answer as the costs of all screwdrivers are multiples of 10 cents. It's impossible to get the 65 cents.
- Look at the maximum cost.
  $7 \times \$8.90 = \$62.30$
- \$61.40 is less than \$62.30 but close to it.
  $6 \times \$8.90$ and $1 \times \$7.80 = \$61.20$
  Since all other combinations would cost less than \$61.20, \$61.40 cannot be the answer.
- Look at the minimum cost.
  $7 \times \$4.80 = \$33.60$
- \$34 is not much more than \$33.60.
  $6 \times \$4.80$ and $1 \times \$5.40 = \$34.20$
  All other combinations would cost more than \$34.20, so \$34 is not the answer.
- The only possibility remaining is \$48.40, so **A** is the answer.

Note: We could continue to try different combinations of prices but we know that one of the possibilities was correct and we have eliminated the other three.
$(2 \times \$8.90) + (2 \times \$7.80) + (1 \times \$5.40) + (2 \times \$4.80) = \$48.40$

Exercise 2:02

1 Use problem-solving strategies to solve these problems.

a Vickie is expecting a baby. She must pick two given names (in order) for her child from the names she is considering. Girls' names being considered are Rachel, Jessye, Faith and Kate. Boys' names are Jason, Brent and Grant. She is also considering the name Sandy for both a girl or a boy. How many ways of naming the child are being considered?

b If tyres sell for \$96.70, \$113.50, \$125.90 and \$143.30, which of the following amounts could be the cost of five tyres?

A \$483.30 **B** \$592.90 **C** \$610 **D** \$717.50

c Luke has 13 finches now but yesterday he lost $\frac{3}{4}$ of his finches when part of the roof blew off his aviary. The day before that he had given six zebra finches to his cousin and 2 days before that he had purchased two pairs of Gouldian finches. How many finches did Luke have before he bought the Gouldians?

d One 'move' involves turning three coins over. What is the least number of 'moves' needed to change these five 'tails' to five 'heads'?

e The difference of two numbers plus their sum is equal to 1. Write two numbers that satisfy this condition.

f A row of 865 trees was planted. Between the first and second trees, 2 flowers were planted. Between the second and third trees, 1 flower was planted. Between the third and fourth trees, 2 flowers were planted, and so on to the end of the row. How many flowers were planted in total?

g Particular text books have a mass 6 times as great as the summary books. If 5 text books and 10 summary books have a mass of 8 kg in total, what is the mass of 1 text book?

h What is the greatest number of points at which four circles can intersect?

2 For the chessboard on the right, how many squares are there of side length:

a 8 units **b** 7 units
c 6 units **d** 5 units
e 4 units **f** 3 units
g 2 units **h** 1 unit?

Write the total number of squares as the sum of eight square numbers.

3 **a** Which two numbers have a sum of 79 and a product of 1288?

b Which two numbers have a difference of 11 and a product of 5226?

c Which two numbers have a sum of 1200 and a difference of 68?

4 **a** In a basketball competition, each of the six teams must play the other five teams on two occasions. How many games must be played?

b A knockout singles tennis tournament is to be held for 53 players. How many byes must be given in the first round of the competition if the organisers do not want any byes in later rounds?

5 Plastic figures are needed for the doors on the fifth floor of a large hotel. If all of the numbers from 500 to 550 are needed, how many of each of the digits 0, 1, 2, 3, 4, 5, 6, 7, 8 and 9 will be needed?

6 I have 20 Australian bank notes with a value of $720. What could I have? Give at least two solutions.

7 A pentomino is formed by joining five squares together so that each square is joined to another square along an edge. How many different pentominoes are there? (*Note:* They are the same if one can be turned into the other by turning it upside down.)

8 Bill the gardener must buy some native plants. He can choose from waratahs ($8), grevilleas ($3) and banksias ($5). He must choose at least 20 of each type and he must buy at least 300 plants altogether. He also must not exceed his budget of $1200. Find a solution to his problem.

9 a Write the number 81 as the sum of:

i two consecutive integers

ii three consecutive integers.

b Find two other ways in which 81 can be written as the sum of a number of positive consecutive integers.

10 A palindromic number is the same number when its digits are written in reverse order (e.g. 21412). The number 121 is a palindromic square number because $121 = 11^2$.

a How many palindromic squares are there:

i with 1 digit (i.e. less than 10)

ii with 2 digits (i.e. less than 100)

iii with 3 digits (i.e. less than 1000)?

b How many palindromic square numbers are smaller than 1 000 000? (Hint: What could the last digit of a square number be?)

A cheetah can run at 80 km/h. At this rate, how long would it take a cheetah to run 100 km?

2:03 Using Venn diagrams

Drawing Venn diagrams is a useful problem-solving strategy.

- A rectangle is used to stand for the larger group out of which smaller sets are considered.
- Circles are used to represent those smaller sets.
- If the smaller sets have members in common, the circles will overlap.

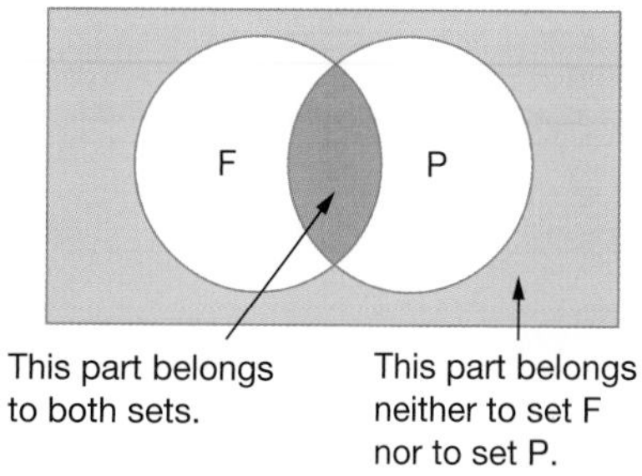
F
P
This part belongs to both sets.
This part belongs neither to set F nor to set P.

WORKED EXAMPLE 1

Of 12 students, 7 play the flute and 8 play the piano. If 2 students play neither instrument, how many students play both instruments?

Solution

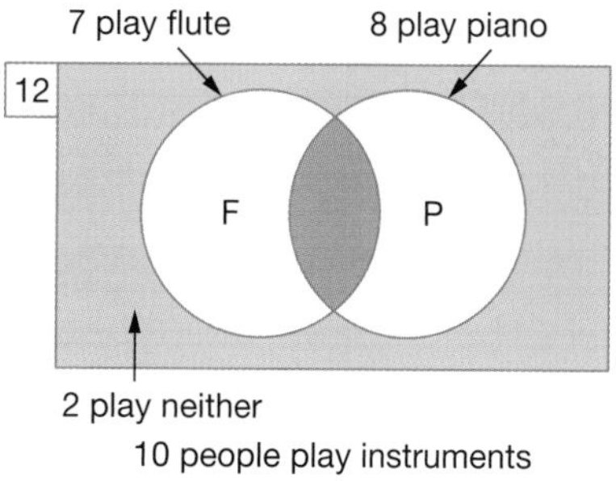
7 play flute
8 play piano
12
F
P
2 play neither
10 people play instruments

A Venn diagram has been drawn on the right.

- As 2 students play neither instrument, 10 students must be placed inside the circles.
- The coloured section is in both circles so, if we add the numbers playing each instrument, the students playing both are counted twice.

  Number inside the circles = (number in F + number in P) − number in overlap

$$10 = (7 + 8) - n$$
$$10 = 15 - n$$
$$n = 15 - 10$$
$$\therefore n = 5$$

Therefore, 5 students play both instruments.

WORKED EXAMPLE 2

Of 30 students, 20 play the piano, 5 the flute and 6 the violin. 3 violinists also play the piano but only 1 of these 3 also play the flute. 5 students play both the piano and the flute. None of the students play any other type of musical instrument. How many students play:

a the piano and the flute but not the violin

b only the piano

c only the flute

d only the violin

e no instrument at all?

Solution

We need to put the information in the question onto the Venn diagram. As we enter this, we can deduce other information.

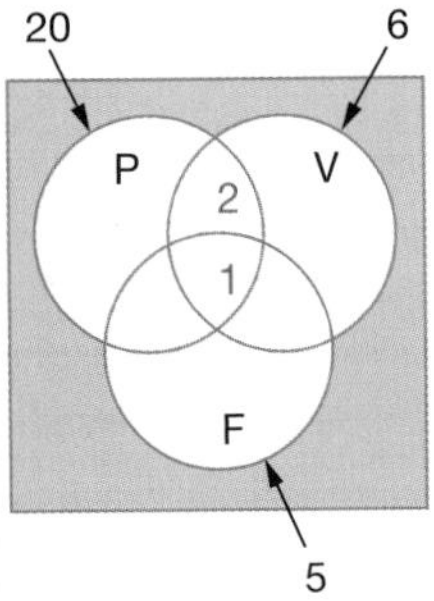

Of the 3 violinists who also play piano, 1 plays the flute. So only 1 person plays all three instruments.

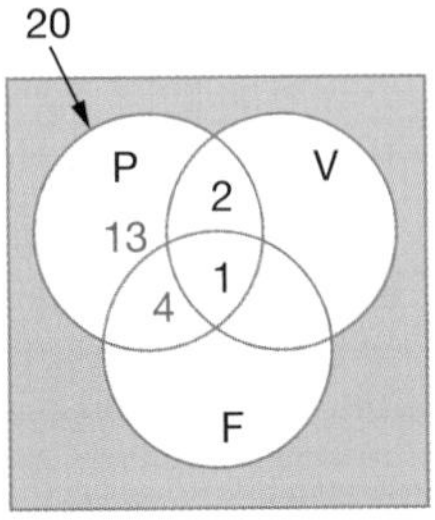

5 students play both piano and flute, so 4 would play only the piano and flute. There are 20 piano players, so 13 must only play the piano.

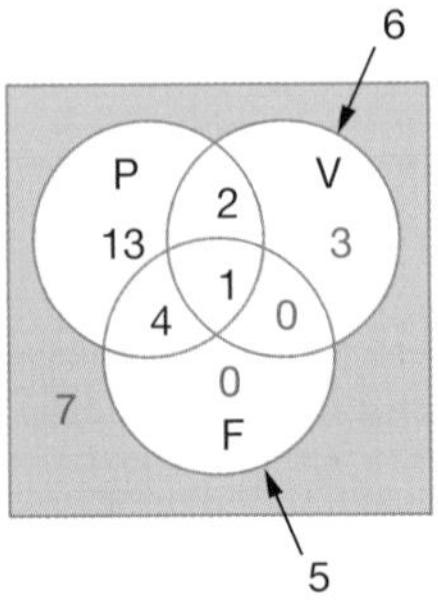

There are only 5 flute players, so the other two sections of that circle will be zero and the remaining section of the violin circle will have 3 members (to make the total of violin players 6). Within the circles there are 23 students, so 7 must be outside. These 7 play no instrument.

The answers can now be read from the final Venn diagram above on the right.

a 4 **b** 13 **c** 0 **d** 3 **e** 7

Exercise 2:03

1 Of 30 people in our class, 9 can catch left-handed, 24 can catch right-handed and 6 can catch with both their left hands and their right hands.

  a How many can catch only with the left hand?
  b How many can catch only with the right hand?
  c How many cannot catch?

2 The *Tribute* was delivered to 75 homes and the *Bugle* was delivered to 68 homes. These papers were delivered to 110 homes.

  a How many homes received both papers?
  b How many homes received only the *Tribute*?
  c How many homes received only the *Bugle*?

3 Of the 30 students in 9M, 13 like surfing, 15 like hiking and 7 like neither.

  a How many students like both surfing and hiking?
  b How many like surfing but not hiking?
  c How many like hiking but not surfing?

4 The Venn diagram on the right shows three intersecting sets: those who play soccer (S), those who play tennis (T) and those who play golf (G). A number in one part of the diagram shows the number of people in that part.

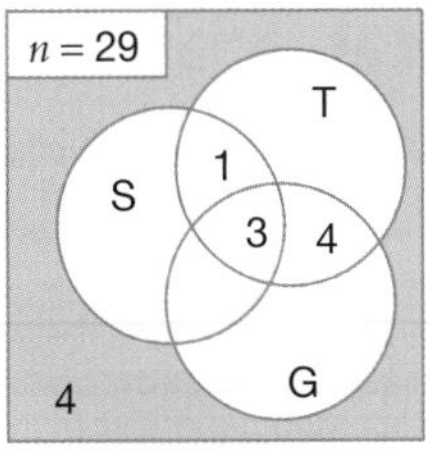

- Our class has 29 students and all but 4 students play at least one of these sports.
- 3 students play all three sports, one plays both soccer and tennis but not golf, 4 play tennis and golf but not soccer, a total of 5 play soccer and golf, a total of 16 play tennis and altogether 11 play soccer. How many play:

a soccer and golf but not tennis

b only tennis

c only soccer

d only golf

e tennis or soccer but not golf?

5 When 24 adults were asked which of Dubbo, Maitland and Terrigal they had visited, the following information was obtained.

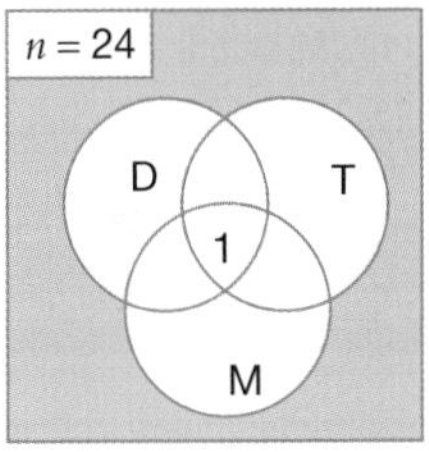

- Only 1 person had visited all three places, 3 had visited Maitland and Dubbo but not Terrigal, 2 had visited Dubbo and Terrigal but not Maitland, 4 had visited Maitland, 16 had visited Dubbo and 3 of the adults had visited none of these places.

a How many people had visited only Dubbo?

b How many people had visited only Maitland?

c How many people had visited only Terrigal?

d How many people had visited Terrigal?

e Are those who have visited Maitland a part of those who have visited Dubbo?

6 This Venn diagram shows three intersecting sets: those friends of Alan that can drive a car (D), those who play tennis (T) and those who are female (F).

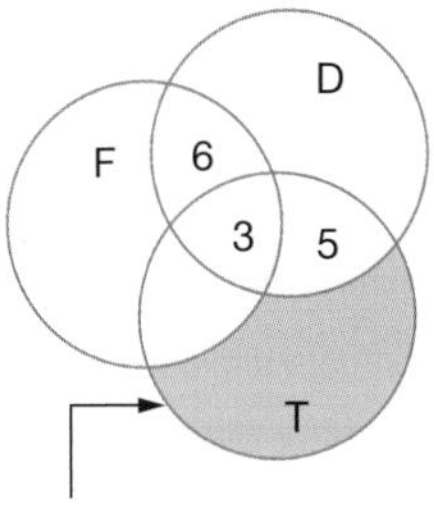

Play tennis but are not female and do not drive (male non-driving tennis players)

- Alan has 40 friends.
- 5 friends fit into none of the three categories, 3 friends fit all three categories, 6 who do not play tennis are females who drive, 5 are male tennis players who drive, 8 are females who play tennis, a total of 20 drive and altogether 17 are female.

Draw a Venn diagram and place numbers in specific sections to find how many friends are:

a male drivers who don't play tennis

b non-driving females who play tennis

c females who neither drive nor play tennis

d male tennis players who don't drive

e tennis players

f females who drive

g either female or drivers

h either drivers or tennis players

i male.

Hi! I'm a female driver who doesn't play tennis. Does Alan have any more friends like me?

FUN SPOT 2:03 WHAT TYPE OF BREAKFAST TAKES AN HOUR TO FINISH?

Haven't you finished yet?
MUNCH! MUNCH!

Work out the answer to each part and write the letter for that part in the box above the correct answer.

E 4 L of paint was divided in the ratio 3 : 7.
What was the smaller share?

I Change 180 km/h into m/s.

10 g of salt is dissolved in 1 L of water.
How much salt would there be in:

I 500 mL **L** 2·5 L **M** 1·8 L
R 200 mL **S** 50 mL **A** 250 mL?

3 L of water drips steadily from a tap in 5 hours.
How much water would be wasted in:

A 1 hour **T** 7 hours
A 4 hours **Y** 30 minutes
D 10 minutes **E** 7 minutes?

2·5 g	100 mL	600 mL	300 mL	4·2 L	50 m/s	18 g	70 mL	0·5 g	1·2 L	2 g	5 g	2·4 L	25 g

INVESTIGATION 2:03 THE SYRACUSE ALGORITHM

Start with any positive integer.

- If it is odd, multiply it by 3 and add 1.
- If it is even, divide it by 2.

Now repeat the process with the resulting number. For example, if you started with 3, the sequence would run:

3–10–5–16–8–4–2–1

Investigate the length of the sequence for different starting numbers. What other properties can you discover?

MATHS TERMS 2

area
- the amount of space inside a 2D shape

percentage
- a fraction with a denominator of 100, written using the symbol %,
  e.g. $7\% = \frac{7}{100}$

perimeter
- the length of the boundary of a figure

rate
- a comparison of unlike quantities, usually expressed by writing how many of the first quantity corresponds to one of the second,
  e.g. 6000 mL in 10 minutes
  = 600 mL per 1 minute
  = 600 mL/min

ratio
- a comparison of like quantities or numbers

volume
- the amount of space inside a 3D shape

Each part of this test has similar items that test a certain question type.
Errors made will indicate areas of weakness.
Each weakness should be treated by going back to the section listed.

1 A 15 kg box of potatoes is sold for $12. — 2:01
a What is the cost per kilogram?
b How much should 20 kg of these potatoes cost?

2 The ratio of Mia's weight to Rex's is 3 : 5. If Rex's weight is 80 kg, how much does Mia weigh? — 2:01

3 The sizes of the angles of a triangle are in the ratio 7 : 2 : 3. Find the size of each angle. — 2:01

4 Ali earns a commission of $5\frac{1}{2}$% on all sales that he makes. What would be his commission on sales of $87 000? — 2:01

5 My salary was increased last week by 5%. This meant an increase of $56 per week. — 2:01
a How much was my weekly salary before the increase?
b What is my new yearly salary if we take one year to be 52·143 weeks?

6 A path 1·2 m wide is to be put around a rectangular garden that is 8·6 m long and 3·5 m wide. What is the area of the path? — 2:01

7 A rectangle has a perimeter of 66 m. If its length is 5 times as long as its breadth, find its dimensions. — 2:02

8 I can buy four different types of plants. The cost of these four types are $17.80, $15.60, $10.80 and $9.60. I bought seven plants. Which of the following amounts could be the total cost? — 2:02
A $108.20 B $68 C $101.35 D $122.80

9 Of 20 students, 8 play tennis and 12 play cricket. If 6 students play neither sport, how many students play both sports? — 2:03

10 Of 50 students, 16 can play the piano, 15 the flute and 6 the violin. All 6 violinists can play the piano, but only 2 of these can also play the flute. 5 students can play both the piano and the flute. No students can play any other type of musical instrument. How many students can play: — 2:03
a the piano and the flute but not the violin
b no instrument at all?

ASSIGNMENT 2A Chapter review

1 A jogger runs at an average rate of 5 km in 20 minutes.

a Express this in:

i km/min ii min/km

b If the jogger were to run 1500 m at this rate, how long would it take?

c If the jogger were to run 100 m at this rate, how long would it take in seconds?

2 In a one-day cricket match against Australia, South Africa scored 286 runs off 50 overs.

a At what rate does Australia have to score to win the match within 50 overs?

b If after 15 overs Australia has scored 72 runs, at what rate will the team now have to score to win the match?

3 Pump A can empty a 1200 L tank in 15 mins, while pump B can empty the tank in 5 mins. How long will it take to empty the tank using both pumps simultaneously?

4 A nurse has to set the drip rate for an IV drip for a patient. The drip has to empty a 500 mL flask in 8 hours. Work out the correct drip rate in drops/minute if it is known that 1 mL = 15 drops.

5 a A discount of 5% was given on a computer priced at \$2750. How much was paid for the computer?

b A salesperson gave a discount of \$120 on a computer with a selling price of \$1890. What was the discount as a percentage of the selling price?

c A discount of 6% on the cost of a new computer saved me \$168.

i What was the original price of the computer?

ii How much did I pay?

6 A photocopier was used to enlarge a drawing by 140%. The copy of the drawing was then enlarged again by 140%. By what percentage has the original now been enlarged?

7 A type of solder is made by mixing lead and tin in the ratio 2 : 3.

a How much lead needs to be mixed with 984 g of tin to make the solder?

b How much of each metal is needed if 2·4 kg of solder is needed?

8 Red and white paint were mixed in the ratio 3 : 1 to make a paint colour. The paint colour should have been made by mixing the paints in the ratio 7 : 2. How many millilitres of red paint needs to be added to 1 litre of the 3 : 1 mix to give the correct ratio of colours?

9 Four non-zero digits are placed in these four squares to make two two-digit numbers across, and two two-digit numbers down.

a Find two different ways in which the digits could be placed to give a total of 237 for the four two-digit numbers.

b If the digits in the squares are all different, the smallest total possible is 83. What is the next smallest total possible?

10 Four identical garden beds are to be made from treated pine sleepers. The sleepers are rectangular prisms 2·4 m long, 20 cm wide and 10 cm high.

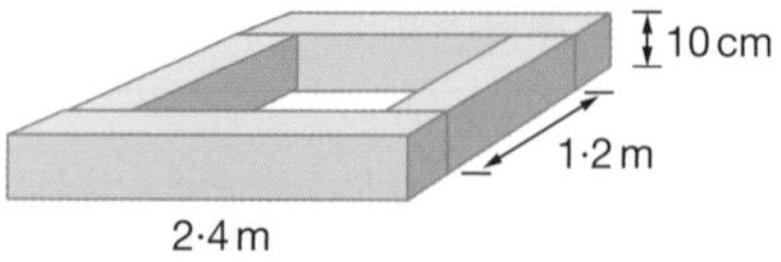

a How many sleepers will be needed to build the four beds?

b What volume of soil is needed to fill the beds?

c How can the pieces shown in the diagram be assembled to give a rectangular bed with the largest volume, and what is that volume?

ASSIGNMENT 2B Working mathematically

1 Refer to **ID Card 4** on page xxi to give the reference numbers of:
   a the solids or 3D shapes
   b the prisms
   c the pyramids
   d the 3D shapes with curved surfaces
   e a triangular prism.

2 Refer to **ID Card 1** on page xix to give the reference numbers of:
   a the units that measure capacity
   b the units that use 'kilo' in their name
   c the units that measure time
   d the symbol for hectares.

3 400 m of fencing encloses a square paddock of area one hectare. If 800 m of fencing were used to enclose a square paddock, how many hectares would be enclosed?

4 Mia is nine years older than Sandra. Alan is twice as old as Mia and Peter is three times as old as Sandra. If the sum of the ages of Alan and Peter is 88, how old is:
   a Sandra b Mia
   c Alan d Peter?

5 This is a diagram of Michelle's model railway. The engine and the two goods wagons are in the positions shown.

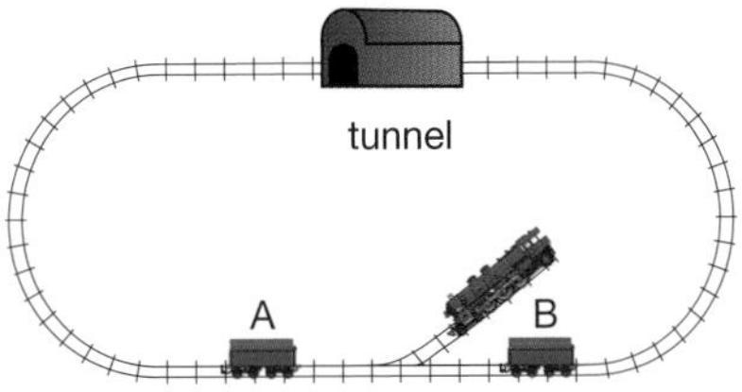

The engine can pass through the tunnel, but the goods wagons are overloaded and cannot pass through the tunnel without losing some of their load.
Explain how you can use the engine to interchange the positions of the two wagons and return the engine to the siding.

6 A plumber must cut 5 m lengths of pipe into the following pieces. How many lengths will the plumber need?
3·2, 1·9, 2·3, 1·8, 3·7, 0·8, 1·3, 2·2, 2·5, 1·2, 1·5, 1·5 (These lengths are in metres.)

In darts, a player can score any number from 1 to 20 or its double or triple. A player can also score 25 for an outer bullseye or 50 for an inner bullseye. In the game '501' each player takes turns to throw three darts. The total of the player's darts is then subtracted from 501 and the aim of the game is to be the first player to finish exactly on 0. The dart that reduces the score to exactly 0 must be a double. What is the least number of darts needed to finish a game of '501'?

ASSIGNMENT 2C Cumulative revision

1 Harry, Lester and Michelle bought a painting. Harry contributed \$2000, Lester \$5000 and Michelle \$3000. They sold the painting 4 years later for \$15 000. If they shared the proceeds in the same ratio as their investments, how much did each receive? 2:01

2 Write *true* or *false*. 1:01

a $200 \times 1{\cdot}5 \neq 100$	b $300 \div 0{\cdot}9 > 300$	c $300 \div 1{\cdot}1 < 300$
d $45 \times 0{\cdot}9 > 45$	e $45 \div 0{\cdot}9 > 45$	f $45 \div 1{\cdot}01 < 45$
g $0{\cdot}05 = 50\%$	h $\pi \doteqdot 3{\cdot}14$	i $0{\cdot}1\% = 0{\cdot}001$
j $0{\cdot}5^2 < 0{\cdot}5$	k $\sqrt{9} > \sqrt[3]{9}$	l $\sqrt{1} > \sqrt[3]{1}$

3 1:01

a $8 - (1 - 5)$	b -24×-3	c $3{\cdot}142 \times 100$
d $3{\cdot}142 \div 100$	e $1{\cdot}05 \times 10^4$	f $1{\cdot}05 \div 10^4$

4 1:01

a Find 15% of \$18.

b The 10% deposit on my bicycle was \$23.50. How much did the bicycle cost?

c Peter scored 27 of his team's total of 60 runs. What percentage of the runs did he score?

d Increase \$38.60 by 10%.

5 1:02

a What fraction would be displayed on a calculator as 0.444444444?

b What is the next term in this pattern?
2·4, 1·2, 0·6, 0·3, …

c 8% p.a. simple interest is paid on \$200 over 2 years. How much interest was paid?

d Find the number half way between 0·05 and 10%.

6 1:04

a Write $\frac{2}{3}$ as a recurring decimal.

b Simplify the ratio 25 : 15.

c Express the ratio 7 : 4 in the form X : 1.

d Write 2500 m/h as km/h.

7 1:05, 1:06

a How many significant figures has 0·020 m?

b Write 80·05 L, correct to three significant figures.

c Round 23 670 000 to the nearest million.

d Round 3·142, correct to two decimal places.

8 1:08

a Write 35 000 000 in scientific notation with two significant figures.

b Write 35 000 000 in scientific notation with three significant figures.

c How many significant figures has $9{\cdot}0 \times 10^9$?

d Write $5{\cdot}08 \times 10^6$ as a basic numeral.

9 1:09

a Convert 2TB (terabytes) to GB (gigabytes).

b Convert 3000 kB (kilobytes) to MB (megabytes).

c Convert 25 000 GB to TB.

d Convert 8·5 MB to kB.

10 Find the absolute error of the measurement: 1:10

a 35 g	b 0·25 m	c 14·128 L

d In what range would a measurement recorded as 6·5 cm lie?

ALGEBRA 3

Contents

Syllabus references (See pages x–xv for details.)

Number and Algebra

Selections from ***Algebraic Techniques*** [Stages 5.2, 5.3§]

- Simplify algebraic expressions involving the four operations [Stage 4]
- Apply the distributive law to the expansion of algebraic expressions, including binomials, and collect like terms where appropriate (ACMNA213)
- Apply the four operations to simple algebraic fractions with numerical denominators (ACMNA232)
- Factorise algebraic expressions by taking out a common algebraic factor (ACMNA230)
- Add and subtract algebraic fractions with numerical denominators, including those with binomial numerators (NSW)
- Expand binomial products using a variety of strategies (ACMNA233)

Working Mathematically

- Problem Solving
- Reasoning
- Understanding
- Fluency
- Communicating

3:01 Simplifying algebraic expressions

PREP QUIZ 3:01

Simplify the following.

1 $7x + 2x$
2 $9x - 8x$
3 $3x \times 2y$
4 $5x \times x$
5 $12x \div 4$
6 $10ab \div 5a$
7 $3a + 2b + 5a + 3b$
8 $6x + 2y - x - y$
9 $3 \times (-2a) \times 4a$
10 $3a \div (-9b)$

WORKED EXAMPLES

Remember that only like terms may be added or subtracted.

1 $5a + 2b - 3a + b = 5a - 3a + 2b + b$
$\quad = 2a + 3b$

2 $5p^2 + 2p - 3p^2 = 5p^2 - 3p^2 + 2p$ (p^2 and p are not like terms.)
$\quad = 2p^2 + 2p$

3 $6ab - 4ba = 6ab - 4ab$
$\quad = 2ab$

4 $-7x \times -3xy^2 = 21x^2y^2$

5 $3pq \times 4qr = 12pqqr$
$\quad = 12pq^2r$

6 $12ac \div 8ab = \dfrac{{}^{3}\cancel{12}\,\cancel{a}c}{{}_{2}\cancel{8}\,\cancel{a}b}$
$\quad = \dfrac{3c}{2b}$

7 $-6x \div 18xy = \dfrac{-{}^{1}\cancel{6}\cancel{x}}{{}_{3}\cancel{18}\,\cancel{x}y}$
$\quad = -\dfrac{1}{3y}$

8 $10a - 3 \times 2a = 10a - 6a$
$\quad = 4a$

9 $(5a + 7a) \times (3b - 2b) = 12a \times b$
$\quad = 12ab$

10 $3m \times 2n \div mn = 6mn \div mn$
$\quad = \dfrac{6\,\cancel{mn}_1}{\cancel{mn}_1}$
$\quad = 6$

11 $\dfrac{7p + 8p - 3p}{2p \times 3q} = \dfrac{{}^{2}\cancel{12}\,\cancel{p}}{{}_{1}\cancel{6}\,\cancel{p}q}$
$\quad = \dfrac{2}{q}$

Remember the order in which operations should be done.
↓
Grouping symbols
↓
× ÷
↓
+ −

Multiply numbers first and then pronumerals.
In $12pq^2r$ only the 'q' is squared.

Exercise 3:01

1 Collect the like terms to simplify these expressions.

a $3x + 2x$ b $8a + 5a$
c $10p + 21p$ d $x + 7x$
e $7a - 4a$ f $9b - 3b$
g $11q - q$ h $12e + 9e$
i $3p + 5p - 6p$ j $4x + 2x + x$
k $10x - 9x + 3x$ l $x + 2x - 3x$
m $2a + p - a + 3p$ n $a + m - a + m$
o $8 + 2x - 5x - 7$ p $8y - 1 - 8y - 1$
q $x^2 + 2x + 2x^2 - x$ r $p^2 + 4p + 3p^2 + p$
s $3q^2 + 8q - 4q - q^2$ t $y^2 + y + y^2 - y$
u $7 - p^2 + p - 5$ v $2a + a^2 + 7 + a$
w $8x - 7 - 7x - 3x^2$ x $5ab - 7 + 3ba - 9$

'Like' terms contain identical pronumeral parts. e.g. 3x + 2x
Did you realise that the + or – sign belongs to the term after it?

2 Simplify these products.

a $8y \times 3$ b $4 \times 4a$ c $3x \times 2y$ d $8p \times 4q$
e $6a \times b$ f $5x \times x$ g $5a \times 3a$ h $ab \times ac$
i $3pq \times 2p$ j $5mn \times mp$ k $4mn \times \frac{1}{2}n$ l $9b \times a^2$
m $6a^2 \times (-7a)$ n $-5x \times -2x$ o $x \times 2y \times 3x$ p $14ab \times (-\frac{1}{2}ab)$
q $(-ab) \times (-bc)$ r $2k \times 3k \times 4k$ s $-2 \times 7x \times -5y$ t $\frac{1}{4}m \times 4n \times (-p)$

3 Simplify:

a $12x \div 4$ b $12x \div 4x$ c $9x^2 \div 3$ d $8x \div 8x$
e $15m \div 10n$ f $32a \div 12b$ g $5 \div 20a$ h $48ab \div 6b$
i $a \div 3a$ j $45ab \div 20ba$ k $-20p \div 4p$ l $-xy \div xz$
m $14a \div (-a)$ n $(-15x) \div (-5xy)$ o $-28mnp \div 7mp$ p $8a^2b \div 16ab^2$

4 Simplify:

a $mn \times np$ b $7 + m + 6 + 3m$ c $14 - 2a + 5$ d $5x^2 \times 0$
e $3xy \times 2yx$ f $8x^2 + 2x + 7x^2 + 3x$ g $3 \times 4y \times 5z$ h $-4x \times 7x$
i $15ab - 9ba + ab$ j $6m - 7m$ k $8b + 3b - 11b$ l $18ab \div 9bc$
m $x \div 3x$ n $2pq \times 9pq$ o $3a + b + 2a - c$ p $-3y \times (-5z)$
q $\frac{1}{2}y + \frac{1}{2}y$ r $m + n - m + n$ s $3a \times 2b \times c$ t $15at \div 10tx$

5 Write the simplest expression for:

a $(2a + 3a) \times 4$ b $(10x - 3x) \div 7$ c $(9b - 3b) \times 2$ d $(3m + 9m) \div 4$
e $12x \div (2x + x)$ f $5a \times (10a + 2a)$ g $3m \times (10m - 9m)$ h $15y \div (9y - 2y)$
i $5a \times 7 \div a$ j $8x \times 4y \div 2xy$ k $10a \div 5 \times 3a$ l $9xy \div 3x \times 2y$
m $2x + 3x \times 4$ n $5x \times 3x + 10x^2$ o $20y - 5 \times 2y$ p $18m - 12m \div 6$
q $3 \times 2n + 5n \times 4$ r $7x + 3 \times 2x - 10x$ s $8x \div 4 - x$ t $11m + 18m \div 2$
u $\dfrac{6 \times 3x}{2x \times 5}$ v $\dfrac{3p + 2p - 1p}{2 \times 2p}$ w $\dfrac{11y - y}{6y + 4y}$ x $\dfrac{5a \times 4b \times 2c}{10c \times b \times 8c}$

3:02 Algebraic fractions

3:02A Addition and subtraction

PREP QUIZ 3:02A

Answer the following:

1 $\frac{3}{5}+\frac{1}{5}$ 2 $\frac{7}{10}-\frac{3}{10}$ 3 $\frac{1}{4}+\frac{1}{3}$

4 $\frac{1}{2}+\frac{3}{8}$ 5 $\frac{2}{5}-\frac{1}{4}$ 6 $\frac{7}{12}-\frac{1}{3}$

Simplify the expressions:

7 $7x + 4x$ 8 $3ab + ab$ 9 $6x - 5x$ 10 $9a - a$

Rewrite each fraction as two equivalent fractions with a common denominator, then add or subtract the numerators.

WORKED EXAMPLES

1 $\frac{3x}{5}+\frac{2x}{5}=\frac{3x+2x}{5}$
$=\frac{{}^{1}\cancel{5}x}{{}_{1}\cancel{5}}$
$=x$

2 $\frac{5}{a}-\frac{3}{a}=\frac{5-3}{a}$
$=\frac{2}{a}$

3 $\frac{x}{3}+\frac{x}{2}=\frac{x\times 2}{3\times 2}+\frac{x\times 3}{2\times 3}$
$=\frac{2x}{6}+\frac{3x}{6}$
$=\frac{5x}{6}$

4 $\frac{4a}{5}-\frac{a}{3}=\frac{4a\times 3}{5\times 3}-\frac{a\times 5}{3\times 5}$
$=\frac{12a}{15}-\frac{5a}{15}$
$=\frac{7a}{15}$

5 $\frac{5m}{8}+\frac{m}{2}=\frac{5m}{8}+\frac{m\times 4}{2\times 4}$
$=\frac{5m}{8}+\frac{4m}{8}$
$=\frac{9m}{8}$

6 $\frac{3x}{4}-\frac{2y}{3}=\frac{9x}{12}-\frac{8y}{12}$
$=\frac{9x-8y}{12}$

7 $\frac{9}{x}+\frac{2}{3x}=\frac{27}{3x}+\frac{2}{3x}$
$=\frac{29}{3x}$

8 $\frac{5a}{2x}-\frac{2a}{3x}=\frac{15a}{6x}-\frac{4a}{6x}$
$=\frac{11a}{6x}$

Exercise 3:02A

P Foundation worksheet 3:02A Simplifying algebraic fractions

1 Simplify the following.

a $\frac{3a}{2}+\frac{a}{2}$ b $\frac{3x}{5}-\frac{2x}{5}$ c $\frac{a}{3}+\frac{4a}{3}$ d $\frac{9m}{10}-\frac{3m}{10}$

e $\frac{x}{4}+\frac{y}{4}$ f $\frac{5a}{3}-\frac{2b}{3}$ g $\frac{2}{a}+\frac{3}{a}$ h $\frac{7}{x}+\frac{1}{x}$

i $\frac{3}{y}-\frac{2}{y}$ j $\frac{9}{m}-\frac{1}{m}$ k $\frac{5a}{x}+\frac{2a}{x}$ l $\frac{2x}{y}-\frac{3x}{y}$

m $\frac{5}{3n}+\frac{7}{3n}$ n $\frac{3}{2x}-\frac{1}{2x}$ o $\frac{8a}{5b}+\frac{2a}{5b}$ p $\frac{7m}{4x}-\frac{3m}{4x}$

2 Reduce each of these expressions to its simplest form.

a $\frac{x}{3}+\frac{x}{5}$ b $\frac{a}{2}+\frac{a}{5}$ c $\frac{y}{3}-\frac{y}{4}$ d $\frac{m}{2}-\frac{m}{4}$

e $\frac{2a}{3}+\frac{a}{2}$ f $\frac{5x}{3}+\frac{2x}{4}$ g $\frac{3n}{8}-\frac{n}{4}$ h $\frac{4p}{5}-\frac{3p}{10}$

i $\frac{x}{4}+\frac{y}{3}$ j $\frac{2a}{3}-\frac{3b}{2}$ k $\frac{3m}{5}+\frac{n}{2}$ l $\frac{k}{6}-\frac{21}{4}$

m $\frac{2}{x}+\frac{4}{3x}$ n $\frac{1}{3a}+\frac{2}{4a}$ o $\frac{7}{2m}-\frac{2}{5m}$ p $\frac{5}{8x}-\frac{1}{2x}$

q $\frac{2a}{3x}+\frac{3a}{2x}$ r $\frac{x}{3m}-\frac{2x}{m}$ s $\frac{5m}{2n}+\frac{3m}{4n}$ t $\frac{2x}{3a}+\frac{y}{4a}$

FUN SPOT 3:02 TRY THIS MATHS-WORD PUZZLE

Hidden in the maze of letters there are many words used in mathematics. Make a list of the words you find and, at the same time, put a line through the letters you use. Words may be written in any direction: up, down, backwards, even diagonally. Also, a letter may be used more than once, but you cannot change direction in order to form a word (i.e. the letters must be in a straight line).

When you have found all the words there should be four letters that have not been used. These four letters can be arranged to form another 'mystery' maths word.

R	E	T	E	M	A	I	D	C
L	E	L	C	R	I	C	G	U
E	T	C	X	R	Y	O	H	B
L	E	I	T	R	A	N	T	E
L	S	Q	U	A	R	E	G	L
A	L	P	L	A	N	E	N	A
R	O	L	A	I	I	G	E	U
A	P	U	L	C	N	A	L	Q
P	E	S	M	M	E	T	R	E

3:02B Multiplication and division

PREP QUIZ 3:02B

Answer the following:

1 $\frac{1}{2} \times \frac{3}{4}$ 2 $\frac{2}{5} \times \frac{3}{4}$ 3 $\frac{4}{9} \times \frac{3}{8}$

4 $\frac{1}{2} \div \frac{3}{4}$ 5 $\frac{3}{5} \div \frac{3}{10}$ 6 $\frac{2}{3} \div \frac{5}{4}$

Simplify these expressions.

7 $5 \times 6x$ 8 $3a \times 2a$ 9 $15a \div 5$ 10 $12ab \div 6b$

When *multiplying*:
- cancel any common factors, then
- multiply the numerators together and multiply the denominators together.

When *dividing*:
- turn the second fraction upside down, then
- multiply as above (invert and multiply).

WORKED EXAMPLES

1 $\frac{2}{a} \times \frac{5}{b} = \frac{2 \times 5}{a \times b}$

$= \frac{10}{ab}$

2 $\frac{5}{x} \times \frac{x}{10} = \frac{{}^{1}\cancel{5}}{{}_{1}\cancel{x}} \times \frac{\cancel{x}^{1}}{\cancel{10}_{2}}$

$= \frac{1 \times 1}{1 \times 2}$

$= \frac{1}{2}$

3 $\frac{3b}{2} \times \frac{4}{5b} = \frac{3\cancel{b}^{1}}{{}_{1}\cancel{2}} \times \frac{\cancel{4}^{2}}{5\cancel{b}_{1}}$

$= \frac{3 \times 2}{1 \times 5}$

$= \frac{6}{5}$ or $1\frac{1}{5}$

4 $\frac{ab}{2} \div \frac{b}{5} = \frac{a\cancel{b}^{1}}{2} \times \frac{5}{\cancel{b}_{1}}$

$= \frac{a \times 5}{2 \times 1}$

$= \frac{5a}{2}$

5 $\frac{8a}{3b} \div \frac{2a}{9b} = \frac{{}^{4}\cancel{8}\cancel{a}}{{}_{1}\cancel{3}\cancel{b}} \times \frac{{}^{3}\cancel{9}\cancel{b}}{{}_{1}\cancel{2}\cancel{a}}$

$= \frac{4 \times 3}{1 \times 1}$

$= 12$

6 $\frac{2a}{3b} \times \frac{b}{4c} \div \frac{10a}{9c} = \frac{4a}{3b} \times \frac{b}{2c} \times \frac{9c}{10a}$

$= \frac{{}^{1}\cancel{2}\,\cancel{4}\,\cancel{a}}{{}_{1}\cancel{3}\,\cancel{b}} \times \frac{{}^{1}\cancel{b}}{{}_{1}\cancel{2}\,\cancel{c}} \times \frac{{}^{3}\cancel{9}\,\cancel{c}}{{}_{5}\cancel{10}\,\cancel{a}}$

$= \frac{1 \times 1 \times 3}{1 \times 1 \times 5}$

$= \frac{3}{5}$

'Invert' means 'turn upside down'.
Don't forget to invert the second fraction when dividing.

Exercise 3:02B

P Foundation worksheet 3:02B **Simplifying algebraic fractions**

1 Simplify these products.

a $\frac{x}{2} \times \frac{y}{3}$ b $\frac{a}{4} \times \frac{b}{3}$ c $\frac{m}{2} \times \frac{m}{5}$ d $\frac{a}{4} \times \frac{a}{10}$

e $\frac{3}{a} \times \frac{4}{m}$ f $\frac{2}{x} \times \frac{1}{y}$ g $\frac{1}{p} \times \frac{4}{p}$ h $\frac{1}{n} \times \frac{1}{3n}$

i $\frac{p}{q} \times \frac{x}{y}$ j $\frac{2}{a} \times \frac{a}{4}$ k $\frac{m}{5} \times \frac{10}{n}$ l $\frac{3x}{5} \times \frac{2}{9x}$

m $\frac{ab}{3} \times \frac{2}{b}$ n $\frac{x}{y} \times \frac{y}{x}$ o $\frac{6m}{5a} \times \frac{15a}{2m}$ p $\frac{8x}{5p} \times \frac{2a}{3x}$

2 Simplify these divisions.

a $\frac{m}{2} \div \frac{m}{4}$ b $\frac{n}{3} \div \frac{n}{5}$ c $\frac{5n}{3} \div \frac{2n}{9}$ d $\frac{x}{5} \div \frac{3x}{10}$

e $\frac{5}{a} \div \frac{2}{a}$ f $\frac{3}{2m} \div \frac{1}{3m}$ g $\frac{a}{b} \div \frac{2a}{b}$ h $\frac{3x}{5y} \div \frac{x}{10y}$

i $\frac{a}{b} \div \frac{x}{y}$ j $\frac{2p}{3q} \div \frac{8p}{9q}$ k $\frac{10k}{3n} \div \frac{2k}{9n}$ l $\frac{a}{2} \div \frac{a}{3}$

m $\frac{xy}{2} \div \frac{y}{4}$ n $\frac{b}{2} \div \frac{ab}{6}$ o $\frac{xy}{c} \div \frac{y}{cx}$ p $\frac{9a}{b} \div \frac{4a}{3b}$

3 Simplify these expressions.

a $\frac{a}{3} \div \frac{12}{5a}$ b $\frac{2}{p} \times \frac{p}{3}$ c $\frac{15}{x} \div 5$ d $3b \div \frac{6}{b}$

e $\frac{xy}{z} \times \frac{2z}{x}$ f $\frac{ab}{c} \div \frac{a}{c}$ g $\frac{9m}{2} \times \frac{4m}{3}$ h $\frac{2x}{y} \div \frac{x}{2y}$

i $\frac{4}{pq} \times \frac{p}{q}$ j $\frac{3}{a} \times \frac{2}{b}$ k $\frac{4ab}{x} \times \frac{xy}{2ac}$ l $\frac{9bc}{2a} \div \frac{6b}{4a}$

m $\frac{2}{x} \times \frac{x}{3} \times \frac{9}{4}$ n $\frac{b}{c} \times \frac{c}{a} \times \frac{a}{b}$ o $\frac{8bc}{3a} \times \frac{9a}{b} \times \frac{1}{4c}$ p $\frac{8}{a} \times \frac{2a}{15} \div \frac{8}{3}$

q $\frac{2m}{3n} \times \frac{5n}{6p} \div \frac{8m}{9p}$ r $\frac{6a}{15} \div \frac{3a}{10b} \times \frac{3}{4b}$ s $\frac{xy}{yz} \times \frac{xz}{ty} \times \frac{tz}{tx}$ t $\frac{2a}{3b} \div \frac{3a}{2b} \div \frac{4a}{9b}$

Algebra is important in the design and construction of buildings.

3:03 Simplifying expressions with grouping symbols

PREP QUIZ 3:03

Simplify:

1 $7x + 3x$
2 $4a^2 - a^2$
3 $4x + 3 + 2x + 5$
4 $2x + 7 - x - 5$
5 $3y^2 + 5y + 2y^2 - y$
6 $7 - 3a + 6 + 5a$

Expand:

7 $3(x - 7)$
8 $9(2 - 5y)$
9 $2a(a + 3)$
10 $-5(x + 7)$

The two most commonly used grouping symbols are:

parentheses	( )
brackets	[ ]

$a(b \pm c) = ab \pm ac$

We are talking about symbols, not cymbals.

To expand an expression, such as $a(b + c)$, each term inside the grouping symbols is multiplied by the term outside the grouping symbols.

WORKED EXAMPLES

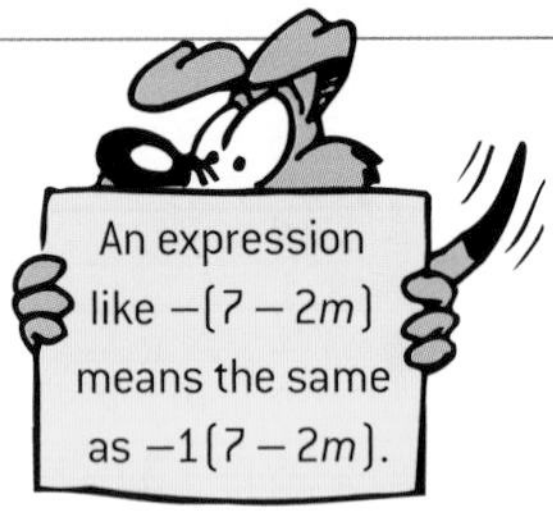

An expression like −[7 − 2m] means the same as −1[7 − 2m].

1 $p(p + 3) = p \times p + p \times 3$
$= p^2 + 3p$

2 $3a(5 - 2a) = 3a \times 5 - 3a \times 2a$
$= 15a - 6a^2$

3 $-5(3x + 4) = (-5) \times 3x + (-5) \times 4$
$= -15x - 20$

4 $-(7 - 2m) = (-1) \times 7 - (-1) \times 2m$
$= -7 + 2m$

5 $x(x - 1) - x^2 + 5 = x^2 - x - x^2 + 5$
$= -x + 5$

6 $2a(a + b) - a(3a - 4b) = 2a^2 + 2ab - 3a^2 + 4ab$
$= 6ab - a^2$

Exercise 3:03

P Foundation worksheet 3:03 **Grouping symbols**
Challenge worksheet 3:03 **Fractions and grouping symbols**

1 The area of rectangle A = $3 \times n = 3n$
The area of rectangle B = $3 \times 4 = 12$
The area of the combined rectangle = $3(n + 4)$
$\therefore 3(n + 4) = 3n + 12$

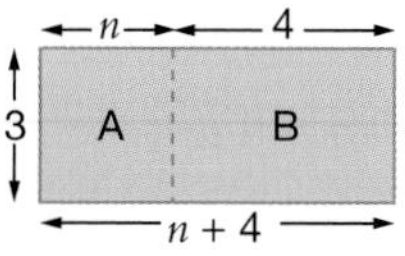

Following the example above, write the area of each of the following rectangles in two ways.

a
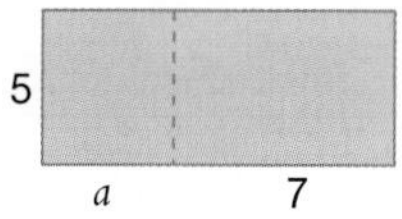

b
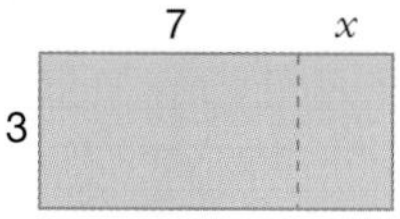

c
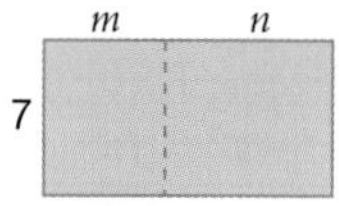

d
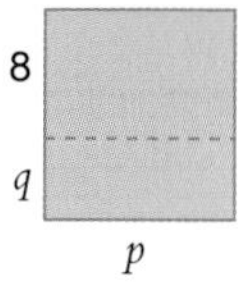

e
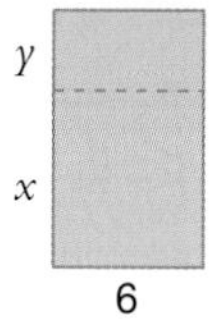

f
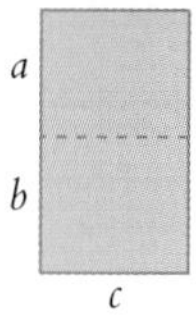

2 Expand:

a $2(x + 3)$ b $3(a + 5)$ c $5(x - 1)$ d $7(m - 3)$
e $2(3a + 2b)$ f $5(x + y)$ g $7(3x - 5y)$ h $6(7m - 8n)$
i $x(x + 7)$ j $a(a - 1)$ k $m(m + 10)$ l $n(n - 3)$
m $3a(2a - 1)$ n $9x(2x + 7)$ o $8p(2 - 5p)$ p $7q(3 + 2q)$
q $x(a + b)$ r $y(2y + x)$ s $2m(m + n)$ t $5a(2a + 3b)$

3 Expand by removing the parentheses.

a $-2(x + 3)$ b $-3(a + 5)$ c $-2(y - 1)$ d $-5(p - 3)$
e $-7(3a + 2)$ f $-5(2x - 1)$ g $-7(3 + 2m)$ h $-4(7 - x)$
i $-(a + 1)$ j $-(3x + 7)$ k $-(8 - 2p)$ l $-(3a + 2b)$
m $-x(x + 10)$ n $-y(5 - y)$ o $-3x(2x + 7)$ p $-10n(8m - n)$

4 Simplify:

a $2(a + 3) + 5a + 2$ b $3(x + 5) + 7x - 8$ c $5(y - 2) + 3y + 7$
d $4(a - 1) + 6a - 5$ e $3(p + 2) - 2p + 4$ f $10(m + 3) - 11m - 15$
g $5a + 6 + 2(a + 7)$ h $2x + 7 + 5(x - 1)$ i $7n - 4 + 3(n - 1)$
j $4h - 1 + 7(h + 2)$ k $6x + 2(x + 1) + 5$ l $4y + 6(y + 2) - 10$
m $3a + 10 - 2(a + 1)$ n $10m + 4 - 5(m + 4)$ o $6 - 2(y - 4) + 4y$
p $20 - 4(x - 2) + 5x$ q $5x + 7 + 2(2x + 7)$ r $4(3a + 1) - 10a + 2$
s $10m + 6 - 3(2m - 1)$ t $8x - 3(1 - 2x) + 10$

5 Simplify each expression by expanding the grouping symbols and then collecting like terms.

a $3(x + 2) + 2(x + 1)$ b $5(y + 2) + 3(y + 4)$ c $2(a + 1) + 5(a - 1)$
d $8(m - 3) + 5(m + 2)$ e $4(3x + 2) + 5(x - 4)$ f $6(x + 7) + 2(2x - 1)$
g $5(x + 7) - 3(x + 4)$ h $6(m + 1) - 3(m + 2)$ i $9(a + 5) - 7(a - 3)$
j $5(n - 5) - 3(n + 7)$ k $x(x + 3) + 3(x + 1)$ l $a(a + 3) + 7(a - 3)$
m $m(m + 3) - 4(m + 3)$ n $t(t - 5) - 4(t - 5)$ o $a(a + 2b) + a(2a + b)$
p $x(x + y) + y(x + y)$

2 Expand these perfect squares and simplify.

a $(x+3)^2$ b $(x+5)^2$ c $(x+1)^2$
d $(x-6)^2$ e $(m-1)^2$ f $(n-5)^2$
g $(x+2)^2$ h $(n-8)^2$ i $(m+11)^2$
j $(a+12)^2$ k $(x+10)^2$ l $(p-9)^2$
m $(x+y)^2$ n $(a+m)^2$ o $(x+t)^2$
p $(a-b)^2$ q $(k-m)^2$ r $(p-q)^2$

3 Expand and simplify:

a $(2x+3)^2$ b $(2x+1)^2$ c $(3x+5)^2$
d $(4a+1)^2$ e $(3a+7)^2$ f $(7t+2)^2$
g $(2x-1)^2$ h $(3a-2)^2$ i $(5m-4)^2$
j $(4t-7)^2$ k $(6q-1)^2$ l $(9n+4)^2$
m $(2x+y)^2$ n $(a+3b)^2$ o $(3t-2x)^2$

3:07B Difference of two squares

PREP QUIZ 3:07B

Evaluate:

1 $7^2 - 3^2$ 2 $(7+3)(7-3)$
3 $4^2 - 2^2$ 4 $(4+2)(4-2)$
5 $5^2 - 1^2$ 6 $(5-1)(5+1)$
7 $6^2 - 3^2$ 8 $(6-3)(6+3)$
9 $10^2 - 9^2$ 10 $(10+9)(10-9)$

This is an investigation of a special relationship.

If the sum of two terms is multiplied by their difference, another special type of product is formed. If $(x+y)$ is multiplied by $(x-y)$ we get:

$$\begin{aligned}(x+y)(x-y) &= x(x-y) + y(x-y)\\ &= x^2 - xy + yx - y^2\\ &= x^2 - y^2\end{aligned}$$

The sum of two terms multiplied by their difference is equal to the square of the first term minus the square of the second term.

$$(x+y)(x-y) = x^2 - y^2$$

WORKED EXAMPLES

1 $(x + 3)(x - 3) = x^2 - 3^2$ (first term squared, second term squared)
$= x^2 - 9$

2 $(2a - 3b)(2a + 3b) = (2a)^2 - (3b)^2$ (first term squared, second term squared)
$= 4a^2 - 9b^2$

3 $(p - 7)(p + 7) = p^2 - 7^2$
$= p^2 - 49$

4 $(5x + y)(5x - y) = (5x)^2 - y^2$
$= 25x^2 - y^2$

Exercise 3:07B

1 Expand these products and simplify.

a $(x + 4)(x - 4)$
b $(a + 1)(a - 1)$
c $(m + 2)(m - 2)$
d $(n + 7)(n - 7)$
e $(p - 5)(p + 5)$
f $(q - 6)(q + 6)$
g $(x - 3)(x + 3)$
h $(y - 9)(y + 9)$
i $(10 + x)(10 - x)$
j $(5 + a)(5 - a)$
k $(8 - x)(8 + x)$
l $(11 - m)(11 + m)$
m $(x + t)(x - t)$
n $(a - b)(a + b)$
o $(m + n)(m - n)$
p $(p - q)(p + q)$

2 Express as the difference of two squares.

a $(2a + 1)(2a - 1)$
b $(3x + 2)(3x - 2)$
c $(5m + 3)(5m - 3)$
d $(9q + 2)(9q - 2)$
e $(4t - 3)(4t + 3)$
f $(7x - 1)(7x + 1)$
g $(8n - 5)(8n + 5)$
h $(10x - 3)(10x + 3)$
i $(2x + y)(2x - y)$
j $(4a + 3b)(4a - 3b)$
k $(5p + 2q)(5p - 2q)$
l $(3m - n)(3m + n)$
m $(2m - 5n)(2m + 5n)$
n $(2p - 3q)(2p + 3q)$
o $(x - 5y)(x + 5y)$
p $(12x - 5y)(12x + 5y)$

3:08 Miscellaneous examples

- It is important that you are able to expand and simplify algebraic expressions readily and accurately, if you are to use algebra in later problem-solving exercises.
- Work through the following miscellaneous questions after examining the following two examples.

Watch out for tricky minus signs.

WORKED EXAMPLES

1 $(x + 3)^2 - (x - 1)(x + 2) = [x^2 + 6x + 9] - [x^2 + x - 2]$
$= x^2 + 6x + 9 - x^2 - x + 2$
$= 5x + 11$

2 $(3x + 5)(x - 1) + (x + 2)^2 - (2x + 1)(2x - 1) = [3x^2 + 2x - 5] + [x^2 + 4x + 4] - [4x^2 - 1]$
$= 3x^2 + 2x - 5 + x^2 + 4x + 4 - 4x^2 + 1$
$= 6x$

Exercise 3:08

Expand and simplify, where possible, each of the following expressions.

1
a $5x + 3(x - 7)$
b $(x + 2)(x - 1)$
c $(2x + 1)(x - 1)$
d $5(x + 2) - x(x + 1)$
e $(3x - 1)^2$
f $(x + 5)(x - 5)$
g $(2x - 7)(3x - 1)$
h $(5x - 1)(5x + 1)$
i $4x + 7 + x(x + 2)$
j $9x - (x + 5) + 5$
k $(x + 10)(x - 3)$
l $(9 - y)(9 + y)$
m $3x(x - 5) - 2x^2$
n $3(x + 2)(x + 1)$
o $(x + y)^2$
p $(x + 2y)(2x + y)$
q $5x - 2(x + y) + 2y$
r $(a + 2b)(a - 2b)$
s $a(x + 2) - x(a + 2)$
t $(3a + 7)(5a - 3)$
u $(2m - 5n)^2$
v $(1 - 5y)(1 + 5y)$
w $3x - 7(x - 3)$
x $(9x - 8y)(9x + 8y)$

2
a $(x + 1)^2 + 5(x + 2)$
b $(a - 3)^2 - 3(a + 1)$
c $(x + 2)(x + 3) - 7(x - 2)$
d $8(x + 2) + (x - 7)(x + 1)$
e $(x + 3)^2 + (x + 1)(x + 2)$
f $(a + 5)(a + 3) - (a + 4)^2$
g $(m + 6)^2 - (m - 1)(m + 1)$
h $(y + 7)(y - 7) - (y + 7)^2$
i $(x + 2)^2 + (x + 1)^2$
j $(a + 3)^2 - (a + 2)^2$
k $(x + 1)(x + 2) + (x + 2)(x + 3)$
l $(a + 1)(a - 2) + (a + 2)(a - 1)$
m $(x + 3)(x - 1) - (x + 2)(x - 5)$
n $(y + 7)(y - 2) - (y + 1)(y + 3)$
o $(2x + 1)^2 - 5(x + 3)$
p $2x(x + 5) + (x + 7)^2$
q $(5x + 1)(x - 3) + (2x + 1)^2$
r $(2x + 1)(3x + 1) - (2x - 1)(3x - 1)$
s $(p + 3)(p - 3) - (q + 3)(q - 3)$
t $(x + y)^2 - (x - y)(x + y)$
u $(a + b)(a + 2b) + (a + b)^2$
v $(m - n)^2 + (m + n)^2$
w $3(x + 1)^2 + 5(x + 1)$
x $2(x - 1)(x + 1) + 3(x + 1)^2$
y $(2x + 3y)^2 - (2x - 3y)(2x + 3y)$
z $(3a + 2b)(2a + 3b) - 6(a + b)^2$

3
a $(x + 1)^2 + (x + 2)^2 + (x + 3)^2$
b $(x + 1)(x + 2) + (x + 2)(x + 3) + (x + 3)(x + 4)$
c $(a - 1)(a + 1) + (a + 1)^2 + (a - 1)^2$
d $(x + 2)^2 + (x + 3)^2 - (x + 2)(x + 3)$
e $(3a + 2b)(2a + 3b) + (3a - 2b)(3a + 2b) + (2a + 3b)(2a - 3b)$
f $(4x + 1)(3x - 1) + (x + 2)^2 - (x - 3)(x + 3)$
g $5(m - 5)^2 - 8(m - 4)^2 + 3(m - 3)^2$
h $(3x + 2y)(3x - 2y) - (2x + y)(2x - y) - (x + 1)(x - 1)$
i $(x + 3y)^2 - (2x + 2y)^2 + (3x + y)^2$
j $2(x - y)(x + y) - (x + y)^2 - (x - y)^2$

CHALLENGE 3:08 PATTERNS IN PRODUCTS

The examples below involve the sum of a series of products. Can you see the patterns involved and, hence, find the simplest expression for each sum?

1 $(x + 1)^2 + (x + 2)^2 \ldots + (x + 9)^2 + (x + 10)^2$
2 $(x + 1)(x + 2) + (x + 2)(x + 3) + \ldots + (x + 9)(x + 10)$
3 $(a - 5)^2 + (a - 4)^2 + \ldots + a^2 + \ldots + (a + 4)^2 + (a + 5)^2$
4 $(5m - n)(5m + n) + (4m - 2n)(4m + 2n) + (3m - 3n)(3m + 3n)$
$+ (2m - 4n)(2m + 4n) + (m - 5n)(m + 5n)$

INVESTIGATION 3:08 USING SPECIAL PRODUCTS IN ARITHMETIC

Perfect squares

Example

Using $(a \pm b)^2 = a^2 \pm 2ab + b^2$, evaluate $(103)^2$.

Solution

Writing 103 as (100 + 3)

$$\begin{aligned}\text{Then}\quad 103^2 &= (100 + 3)^2 \\ &= 100^2 + 2 \times 100 \times 3 + 3^2 \\ &= 10\,000 + 600 + 9 \\ &= 10\,609\end{aligned}$$

Similarly, the square of a number like 98 could be found by writing 98 as (100 − 2).

Exercise

1 Following the example above, evaluate:

a 101^2 b 205^2 c 1004^2 d 72^2

e 98^2 f 199^2 g 995^2 h 67^2

Difference of two squares

Example

Using $(a - b)(a + b) = a^2 - b^2$, evaluate $100^2 - 97^2$.

Solution

$$\begin{aligned}100^2 - 97^2 &= (100 - 97)(100 + 97) \\ &= 3 \times 197 \\ &= 591\end{aligned}$$

This method can be useful when finding a shorter side of a right-angled triangle.

Example

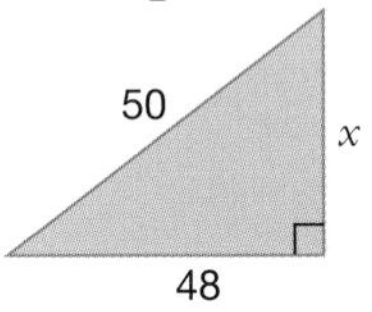

Solution

$$\begin{aligned}x^2 &= 50^2 - 48^2 \\ &= (50 - 48)(50 + 48) \\ &= 2 \times 98 \\ &= 196 \\ \therefore x &= \sqrt{196} \\ &= 14\end{aligned}$$

Exercise

1 Evaluate:

a $100^2 - 98^2$ b $73^2 - 67^2$ c $145^2 - 140^2$ d $651^2 - 641^2$

2 Use the method above to find the value of x for each triangle. (Leave your answer in surd form.)

a

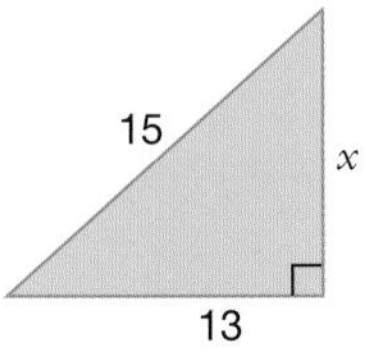

b

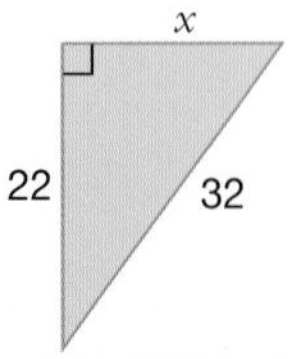

c

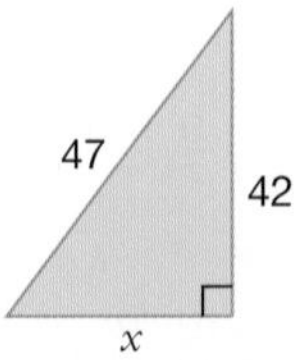

d

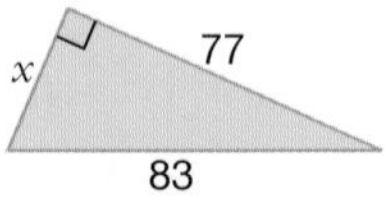

MATHS TERMS 3

algebra
- a branch of mathematics where numbers are represented by symbols

algebraic expression
- a group of terms and numbers that are joined by addition or subtraction signs

binomial
- an algebraic expression consisting of two terms,
  e.g. $2x + 4$, $3x - 2y$

brackets
- the name given to these grouping symbols: [ ]

cancel
- to simplify a fraction by dividing the numerator and denominator by any common factor,
  e.g. $\frac{\overset{7}{\cancel{21}} \div 3}{\underset{10}{\cancel{30}} \div 3}$ so $\frac{21}{30} = \frac{7}{10}$

collect like terms
- to simplify an algebraic expression containing many terms by addition and/or subtraction,
  e.g. $5x + 3 + 7x - 4$
  $= 12x - 1$

difference of two squares
- the result of multiplying two binomials which are the sum and difference of the same terms,
  e.g. $(a + 3)(a - 3) = a^2 - 3^2$
  $= a^2 - 9$

denominator
- the bottom number of a fraction

expand
- to remove grouping symbols by multiplying each term inside the grouping symbols by the term outside

factorise
- to write an expression as a product
- the reverse of expanding

like terms
- terms that have identical pronumeral parts,
  e.g. $7x$ and $10x$, $5a^2b$ and $-3a^2b$

numerator
- the top number of a fraction

parentheses
- the name given to these grouping symbols: ( )

perfect square
- when a binomial is multiplied by itself,
  e.g. $(x + 5)^2$ or $(2a - 3b)^2$

pronumeral
- a symbol, usually a letter, used to represent a number

substitution
- the replacing of a pronumeral with a numeral in an expression,
  e.g. to substitute 3 for a in the expression $4a - 2$ would give:
  $4(3) - 2 = 10$

A machine counts coins by weight. What is the value of a pile of \$M coins that weighs *W* grams if each coin weighs *w* grams?

DIAGNOSTIC TEST 3 ALGEBRA

Each part of this test has similar items that test a certain type of example.
Errors made will indicate areas of weakness.
Each weakness should be treated by going back to the section listed.

1 Simplify: 3:01
a $5a + 2b - 3a + b$
b $5p^2 + 2p - 3p^2$
c $6ab - 4ba$
d $6a - 2x + 5 + x - 2a - 7$

2 Simplify: 3:01
a $8 \times 7m$
b $5a \times 6b$
c $10y \times y$
d $-4n \times 2y$

3 Simplify: 3:01
a $6a \div 2$
b $15xy \div 3x$
c $12ac \div 8ab$
d $-6x \div 18xy$

4 Simplify: 3:02A
a $\frac{3x}{5} + \frac{2x}{5}$
b $\frac{x}{3} - \frac{x}{2}$
c $\frac{4a}{5} - \frac{a}{3}$
d $\frac{5m}{8} + \frac{m}{2}$

5 Simplify: 3:02B
a $\frac{3}{4} \times \frac{n}{3}$
b $\frac{2}{a} \times \frac{5}{b}$
c $\frac{5}{x} \times \frac{x}{10}$
d $\frac{3b}{2} \times \frac{4}{5b}$

6 Simplify completely: 3:04B
a $\frac{3m}{2} \div \frac{1}{4}$
b $\frac{x}{3} \div \frac{x}{6}$
c $\frac{8a}{3b} \div \frac{2a}{9b}$
d $\frac{ab}{2} \div \frac{b}{5}$

7 Expand: 3:03
a $9(x + 7)$
b $6(5a - 2)$
c $p(p + 3)$
d $3a(5 - 2a)$

8 Expand: 3:03
a $-3(x + 2)$
b $-2(m - 8)$
c $-5(3x + 4)$
d $-(7 - 2m)$

9 Expand and simplify: 3:03
a $x(x - 1) - x^2$
b $7n - 4 + 3(n - 1)$
c $2a(a + b) - a(3a - 4b)$

10 Simplify: 3:04
a $\frac{x+4}{2} + \frac{x+3}{5}$
b $\frac{2a-5}{4} + \frac{3a+8}{6}$
c $\frac{3n+1}{4} - \frac{n-2}{3}$

11 Factorise completely: 3:05
a $5m + 10$
b $x^2 - 3x$
c $6ab + 15a$
d $-8y - 12$

12 Expand and simplify: 3:06
a $(x + 3)(x + 4)$
b $(a - 3)(2a - 1)$
c $(2 - y)(3 + y)$
d $(2x + y)(x - 3y)$

13 Expand and simplify: 3:07A
a $(x + 2)^2$
b $(a - 7)^2$
c $(2y + 5)^2$
d $(m - n)^2$

14 Expand and simplify: 3:07B
a $(x + 3)(x - 3)$
b $(y - 7)(y + 7)$
c $(2a + 5)(2a - 5)$
d $(x + y)(x - y)$

ASSIGNMENT 3A Chapter review

1 Simplify the following.

a $6a + a$ b $6x \times 3x$
c $a - 5a$ d $x^2 + x^2$
e $18x \div 3x$ f $12y \div 8$
g $2x + 3y$ h $3ab \times 2b$
i $12a^2b \div 6a$ j $5ab + 7ab$
k $6a^2 - a$ l $4x - 3y - 5x$
m $12 + 6x + 7 - x$ n $6x + 2x \times 3$
o $x^2 - 3x + 2x + 3x^2$ p $12x - 6x \div 3$

2 Simplify:

a $\frac{x}{2} + \frac{x}{3}$ b $\frac{2a}{5} - \frac{a}{10}$
c $\frac{3a}{2} \times \frac{5b}{6}$ d $\frac{10y}{3} \div 5y$
e $\frac{7x}{5} - \frac{x}{3}$ f $\frac{3m}{5} + \frac{m}{3} - \frac{m}{2}$
g $\frac{6n}{5} \times \frac{10}{7n} \div \frac{3}{2n}$ h $\frac{x+3}{2} + \frac{x+1}{3}$
i $\frac{2a-1}{5} + \frac{3a-2}{10}$ j $\frac{2n-1}{6} - \frac{2-n}{9}$

3 Factorise fully:

a $3a + 15$ b $6m + 9$
c $15 - 5y$ d $ax - 3x$
e $2x + 6xy$ f $4x^2 - 2x$
g $9ab - 6bc$ h $6x^2 - 9x + 3xy$

4 Expand and simplify:

a $x(x - 2)$
b $x - 2(x - 2)$
c $(x - 2)(x - 2)$
d $(x - 2)(x + 2)$
e $(x + 2)^2$
f $(2 - x)^2$

5 Expand and simplify where possible.

a $(x - 1)(x + 2)$
b $5x + 3(x - 1)$
c $2(x + 3) - 2x - 3$
d $(2x + 1)(x - 7)$
e $(x + 5)(x - 5)$
f $(3x + 2)^2$
g $x(x - 3) + 2(x + 1)$
h $(2 - x)(3 - x)$
i $(x + y)(y - x)$
j $(2x - y)^2$
k $5[x + 3(x + 1)]$
l $[3x - (x - 2)]^2$

If the width of one figure is x, what is the width of:

a 2 figures
b 4 figures
c half a figure?

ASSIGNMENT 3B Working mathematically

1 Refer to **ID Card 4** on page xxi to identify the mathematical terms numbered:

a 1 b 2 c 3
d 4 e 5 f 6
g 7 h 8 i 9
j 11

2 a What geometric shape has inspired the design of these coffee cups?

b What would you estimate the capacity of the cup to be?

3 Diane and Garry married and had three children. Each child married and had three children. Assuming that no one has died, how many people are now in this extended family altogether?

4 The numerals 1 to 10 are written on ten separate cards, one on each card.

a How many pairs of cards have a sum of 10?

b How many groups of three cards are there that have a sum of 18?

5 A particular country's exports are shown in the bar graph below (reduced in size). Find what percentage of the country's exports are taken up by:

a beef

b minerals.

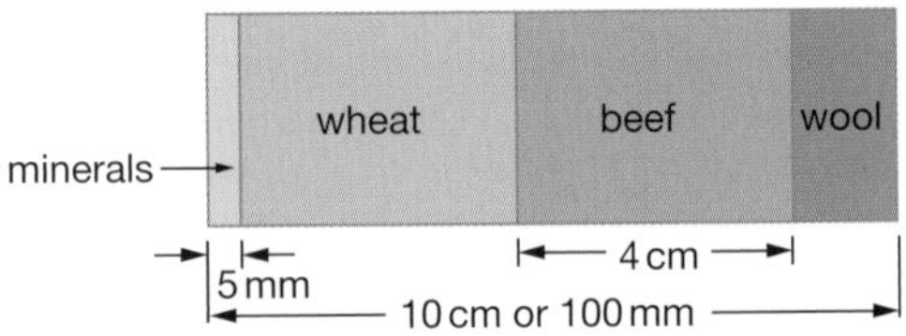

6 Education of children, ages 5 to 14

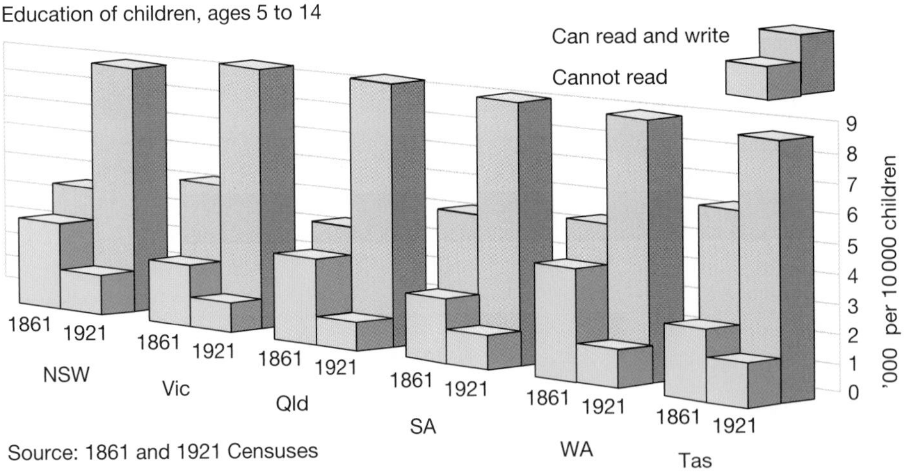

Source: 1861 and 1921 Censuses

a In 1861, which state had the greatest number per 10 000 children who could read and write? What percentage was this?

b In 1921, which state had the greatest percentage of children who could read and write? What percentage was this?

c Which state had 4000 per 10 000 children who could read and write in 1861? About how many in that state could not read in 1861?

d Consider Western Australia in 1861. Approximately what percentage could read and write? Approximately what percentage could not read? (To determine this, measure the height of this column and measure this height on the scale.)

ASSIGNMENT 3C Cumulative revision

1 **a** Increase a wage of $900 by 6·5%. 1:01, 2:01

b In 1980 the population of a town was 42 000. By 2010 the population had decreased by 3·5%. What was the population of the town at that time?

c Which is larger?

i 15% or 20% **ii** $\frac{5}{12}$ or $\frac{2}{5}$ **iii** 0·65 or 0·0655

2 Change the following to decimals. 1:01

a $\frac{7}{8}$ **b** 6·8% **c** $\frac{5}{12}$

3 State the number of significant figures in the following measurements. 1:05

a 8·8 L **b** 123·45 m **c** 6 km **d** 4·0°C

4 In what range would each of the measurements in Question **3** lie? 1:10

5 Estimate the answers to the following calculations. 1:06, 1:07

a $\dfrac{9{\cdot}89 \times 3{\cdot}123}{5{\cdot}089}$ **b** $4{\cdot}95^2 + 2{\cdot}13 \times 5{\cdot}237$

c $\dfrac{212{\cdot}3}{\sqrt{104{\cdot}2}}$ **d** $\dfrac{48{\cdot}24 \times 0{\cdot}888}{(12{\cdot}5 - 7{\cdot}056)^2}$

6 Convert the following. 1:09

a 3·2 ML to L **b** 45 GW to W

c 3TB to MB **d** 15 MHz to kHz

7 Car A uses petrol at the rate of 4·8 L/100 km, whereas car B uses it at a rate of 10 L/100 km. What will the difference in petrol costs be in a year in which both cars travel 30 000 km, if the petrol costs on average $1.45/L? 1:04, 2:01

8 **a** A greengrocer buys 20 cases of oranges at a cost of $15 per case. Each case contains 10 kg of oranges. If he sells the oranges at $4/kg, how many kilograms must he sell before he makes a profit? If he sells all the oranges what will be his profit? 2:01

b Concrete is made by mixing volumes of cement, sand and gravel in the ratio 1 : 4 : 5. Jim calculates that he needs 2 m^3 of concrete to finish a job. How many cubic metres of sand and gravel does he need to order to make the concrete?

9 What is the last digit of the number 2^{2014}? 2:02

10 How many pairs of parallel edges are there in a rectangular prism? 2:02

PROBABILITY

4

Contents

Syllabus references (See pages x–xv for details.)

Statistics and Probability

Selections from ***Probability*** [Stages 5.1, 5.2]

- Calculate relative frequencies from given or collected data to estimate probabilities of events involving 'and' or 'or' (ACMSP226)
- List all outcomes for two-step chance experiments, with and without replacement, using tree diagrams or arrays; assign probabilities to outcomes and determine probabilities for events (ACMSP225)

Working Mathematically

- Communicating
- Problem Solving
- Reasoning
- Understanding
- Fluency

4:01 The language of probability

Terms used in probability

- **Sample space** — The set of all possible outcomes (e.g. 1, 2, 3, 4, 5, 6 on a normal dice).
- **Chance event** — A category in a chance experiment (e.g. rolling a 3 or 4 on a dice).
- **Probability** — The chance of an event happening (e.g. the chance of tossing a tail on a coin is 50%).
- **Trial** — One case of carrying out a chance experiment (e.g. spinning a spinner).
- **Equally likely outcomes** — A situation where each of the outcomes has the same chance of occurring.
- **Subjective probability** — Probabilities based on opinions or judgements.
- **Mutually exclusive events** — These events have no elements in common (e.g. rolling an odd number and rolling an even number on a dice).
- **Non-mutually exclusive** — These events have some elements in common (e.g. rolling an odd number and rolling a number less than 4 on a dice).

The sum of the probabilities of all possible outcomes is always 1 or 100%.

The **complement** of an event happening is that it does not happen.

Understanding the meaning when compound events are described

• Rolling at least 4 on a dice.	This means rolling 4, 5 or 6.
• Rolling at most 4 on a dice.	This means rolling 1, 2, 3 or 4.
• Rolling a number that is not 4 on a dice.	This means rolling 1, 2, 3, 5 or 6.
• Rolling a number that is even and larger than 2.	This means that both attributes must be present (i.e. 4 or 6).
• Choosing someone rich or famous but not both.	The person cannot be both rich and famous.
• Choosing someone rich or famous or both.	The person could be rich or famous or both rich and famous.

Choosing at random

- This is choosing in a way that does not affect the likelihood of any outcome.
- If one student is chosen at random from a class, then each student has the same chance of being chosen. We could put some names in a hat and choose one without looking or we could use two dice of different colours, allotting a different outcome to each student.

For example, rolling two dice provides 36 different outcomes. '1 on Dice A and 6 on Dice B' would be one outcome and may be assigned to Student 1. Each of the students in the class would be assigned a different outcome. When the dice are rolled we select a student at random. (We may have to roll again if one of the outcomes that were not assigned is rolled.)

- Random results can be obtained from coins, dice, spinners or digital generators.

Relative frequency

- The **relative frequency** of an event is the fraction of times that event occurs. (This can also be written as a percentage.) This is the same as the experimental probability of the event occurring.

For example, if two coins were tossed 60 times and two heads occurred 14 times, then the relative frequency is $\frac{14}{60}$. This is called the experimental probability of tossing two heads in this experiment.

> *Note:* If we were to repeat this experiment we may obtain a different relative frequency in the second experiment.

Exercise 4:01

1 Use the labels to the right to describe the chance that a dice, when rolled, will show:

a an odd number b a 6
c a number greater than 6 d a zero
e a number less than 10.

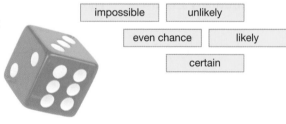

impossible | unlikely | even chance | likely | certain

2 A dice is rolled once. List the outcomes in each of these events.

a A number less than 3 is rolled. b A number less than 3 is not rolled.
c An even number is rolled. d An even number is not rolled.
e A 5 is not rolled. f A 7 is not rolled.

> There are four suits in a standard pack of cards: hearts, diamonds, clubs and spades. Picture cards (or court cards) are the Jack, Queen and King of each suit. There are 13 cards in each suit.

3 Cards from a standard pack can be shown like this: 4H (4 of hearts), JD (Jack of diamonds) or AS (Ace of spades). List the cards from a standard pack that make up each of these events.

a a black Queen b a red card between 4 and 8
c a red Jack d a heart that is between 2 and 5
e a red picture card f a card that is neither black nor a heart

4 Using a standard pack of cards, how many cards are in each event?

a a number higher than 4
b a number that is at least 4
c a number that is a 7
d a number no less than 4
e not a picture card
f not an even number
g black or a number above 7
h a number between 4 and 8
i even or between 4 and 7 but not both
j a number between Ace and 5 or a number greater than 5

5 In a raffle, tickets numbered 1 to 100 are sold. How many tickets are:
a even and higher than 82
b odd and higher than 83
c between 37 and 47
d between 37 and 38
e not between 37 and 47
f not between 37 and 38?

6 **a** What are mutually exclusive events?
b What are non-mutually exclusive events?
c What is the sum of the probabilities of all possible outcomes in a chance experiment?
d What is the complement of an event?
e Explain what it means to choose at random.

7 Two coins were tossed 100 times. The results are shown in the table. Complete the relative frequency column.

Outcome	Frequency	Relative frequency (or experimental probability)
two heads	24	$\frac{24}{100}$ or 24%
head and tail	51	
two tails	25	
Total:	100	

8 A dice was rolled 60 times. The results are shown in the table. Complete the relative frequency column.

Round to the nearest per cent.

Outcome	Frequency	Relative frequency (or experimental probability)
1	8	$\frac{8}{60}$ or about 13%
2	10	
3	9	
4	12	
5	10	
6	11	
Total:	60	

9 Design a four-coloured circular spinner where each sector has a relative frequency of 25%.

10 Design a device where the relative frequency of Alan being chosen is 50%, the relative frequency of Alana being chosen is 25% and the relative frequency of Heather being chosen is 25%.

INVESTIGATION 4:01 ROLLING DICE

Roll two dice and record the result. Carry out this experiment 50 times.

1 Use your results to complete the table below.
(*Note:* One result may be entered against several outcomes.)

2 Choose an expression from those in the list on the right that best describes the probability for each outcome

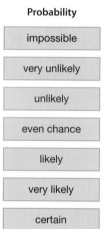

Outcome	Tally	Frequency
12		
2		
less than 12		
less than 6		
even		
1		
less than 10		

Probability

- impossible
- very unlikely
- unlikely
- even chance
- likely
- very likely
- certain

4:02 Experimental probability

PREP QUIZ 4:02

A dice was rolled several times and the following results were obtained.

5, 1, 2, 5, 6, 5, 2, 4, 6, 3

1 How many times was the dice rolled?
2 How many times was the result a 5?
3 What fraction of the rolls were 5s?
4 What fraction of the rolls were 2s?
5 What fraction of the rolls were odd numbers?
6 A coin was tossed 10 times, resulting in 4 heads. How many tails were there?
7 A coin was tossed several times and $\frac{2}{5}$ of the results were tails. What fraction of the tosses were heads?

Simplify:

8 $\frac{4}{12}$ 9 $\frac{16}{20}$ 10 $\frac{24}{50}$

One way of determining the chance of something happening is by observing what occurs in a sample 'experiment'. If simple equipment such as coins, dice, spinners, cards or random numbers are used to represent real events, then the 'experiment' is called a simulation.

The experimental probability is sometimes called the relative frequency.

Experimental probability formula

$$\text{The experimental probability of an event} = \frac{\text{number of times this event occurred}}{\text{total number of trials}}$$
$$= \text{relative frequency}$$

Data (also called empirical evidence) is collected continually, and it can be used to make predictions. Probabilities based on this data are used to determine the cost of insurance, life expectancy and the likelihood of events occurring. These estimates are often called empirical probabilities and are a type of experimental probability. For example, if Australia had beaten England at the SCG four of the last five times they played there, then it would be likely that Australia would win next time.

Experimental probabilities are usually based on an examination of a large number of trials of the activity under examination.

WORKED EXAMPLES

1 A farmer collects 10 eggs and finds that 2 of them are bad. If the farmer collects another egg, what is the chance of getting another bad one?

2 The contents of 20 matchboxes were examined and the results recorded.

Number of matches	48	49	50	51	52	53
Number of boxes	1	5	8	3	2	1

If the contents of a similar box of matches were counted, what would be the experimental probability that it would contain 50 matches or more?

Solutions

1 As 2 of the first 10 eggs were bad, it seems that $\frac{2}{10}$, or $\frac{1}{5}$ of the farmer's eggs might be bad. So, *if* the first 10 eggs were truly representative of all the farmer's eggs *then* the chance of picking another bad one is $\frac{1}{5}$, or 1 out of 5.

2 In the sample, 14 of the 20 boxes had 50 or more matches.
Experimental probability
$$= \frac{\text{number of times this event occurred}}{\text{total number in sample}}$$
$$= \frac{14}{20}$$
The chance of a similar box having 50 or more matches is $\frac{14}{20}$ or $\frac{7}{10}$.

- The probability of an event occurring in an experiment is the same as its 'relative frequency'.
- Relative frequency $= \frac{n(E)}{n(S)}$, where $n(E)$ = number of times this event occurred and $n(S)$ = total number in sample.

Exercise 4:02

P Foundation worksheet 4:02 Experimental probability

1 The first 100 vehicles to pass a checkpoint gave the results in the table. If these figures truly represent the traffic at any time past this checkpoint, determine the experimental probability that the next vehicle will be:

- a a car
- b a motorcycle
- c a bus
- d not a car
- e not a car or truck
- f a car or a truck
- g a bus or a truck
- h a car or a bus.

Type of vehicle	Frequency	Relative frequency
Car	70	$\frac{70}{100}$
Truck	15	$\frac{15}{100}$
Motorcycle	10	$\frac{10}{100}$
Bus	5	$\frac{5}{100}$
Total:	100	1

2 We examined the contents of 37 packets of coloured lollies. The average number of each colour in a packet is shown in the table. One lolly is taken at random from a new packet. Use these results to determine:

- a which colour is most likely to be picked
- b which colour has the least chance of being picked
- c the probability that it is red
- d how many lollies are usually in a packet.

Colour	Frequency	Relative frequency
Brown	10	$\frac{10}{24}$
Green	5	$\frac{5}{24}$
Red	6	$\frac{6}{24}$
Yellow	3	$\frac{3}{24}$
Total:	24	1

3 A factory tested a sample of 100 light bulbs and 5 were found to be faulty. From these results, what is the probability of buying a faulty light bulb? What is the probability of buying a good bulb?

4 Sid Fowler recorded the number of eggs his chickens laid each day, for 6 weeks.

- a If these results are typical for Sid's chickens at any time of the year then find, as a fraction, the probability that on any particular day the number of eggs laid is:
  - i 2
  - ii 4 or 5
  - iii 2 or more.
- b Convert each of your answers to a percentage, correct to the nearest whole per cent.

No. of eggs	Frequency	Relative frequency
0	8	$\frac{8}{42}$
1	13	$\frac{13}{42}$
2	10	$\frac{10}{42}$
3	6	$\frac{6}{42}$
4	3	$\frac{3}{42}$
5	2	$\frac{2}{42}$

5 A survey of 100 households was taken to determine how many used certain washing powders. Based on these results, what is the probability of a household chosen at random:

- a using Foam brand
- b using Supersoap or Pow
- c not using Supersoap or Pow
- d not using any of these four brands?

Brand	Frequency	Relative frequency
Foam	18	$\frac{18}{100}$
Suds-O	27	$\frac{27}{100}$
Supersoap	20	$\frac{20}{100}$
Pow	15	$\frac{15}{100}$

6 Jenny tossed four coins 30 times and the number of heads was recorded each time. The histogram shows the results.

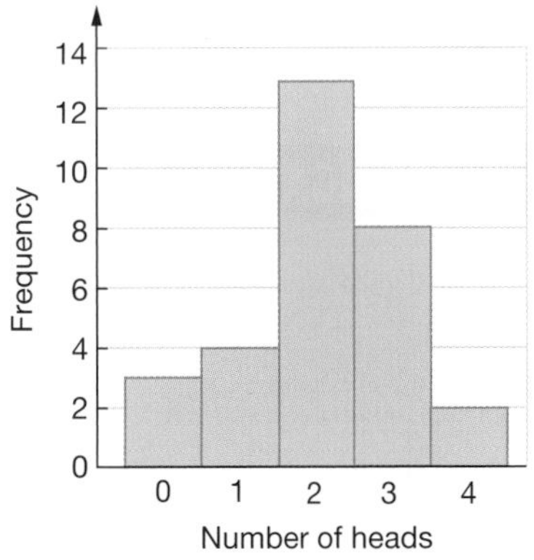

- **a** From this experiment, what is the probability of tossing:
  - **i** no heads
  - **ii** two heads
  - **iii** at least three heads?
- **b** If this experiment were to be repeated, would you expect the same results?
- **c** As the number of trials increases, would the experimental probabilities be more likely to resemble the real probabilities?

7 A dice was rolled 50 times and the results were recorded. The table shows the results.

Number shown	Frequency	Relative frequency
1	7	$\frac{7}{50}$
2	5	$\frac{5}{50}$
3	5	$\frac{5}{50}$
4	10	$\frac{10}{50}$
5	9	$\frac{9}{50}$
6	14	$\frac{14}{50}$

- **a** What is the experimental probability of rolling:
  - **i** a six
  - **ii** a two
  - **iii** an odd number?
- **b** Would you expect to get seven ones every time a dice is rolled 50 times?
- **c** If the dice were rolled 1000 times, how would you expect the experimental probabilities to change?

8 Of Year 9 students, $\frac{4}{20}$ have a shoe size greater than $10\frac{1}{2}$, but $\frac{19}{20}$ have a shoe size less than $11\frac{1}{2}$. What is the chance of a Year 9 student having a shoe size:

- **a** less than or equal to $10\frac{1}{2}$
- **b** $11\frac{1}{2}$ or larger
- **c** between $10\frac{1}{2}$ and $11\frac{1}{2}$?
  (*Note:* This is every size not in **a** and **b**.)

9 **a** Order the following events from least likely to most likely.

- **A** There will be a hail-storm tomorrow.
- **B** The next person to visit my home will be male.
- **C** My next maths teacher will be over 60 years of age.
- **D** I will see the principal of our school next week.
- **E** At least one member of our class will be married within 10 years.

b Estimate the probability of each event listed in part **a**, giving each on the scale 0 to 1.

10 Explain the meaning of a probability of:

a 0   b $\frac{1}{2}$ c 1   d 0·5   e 100%   f 50%

INVESTIGATION 4:02 TOSSING A COIN

When tossing a coin we assume that the probability of getting a head is $\frac{1}{2}$ or 50%, but is this true?

Luke tossed a coin five times and graphed the percentage of heads after each toss. He tossed: head, head, tail, head, tail. His graph is shown below.

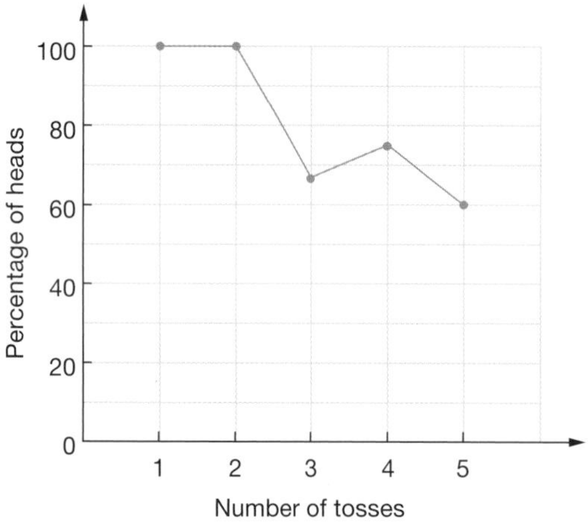

- Percentage of heads after 3 tosses
  $= \frac{2}{3} \times 100\%$
  $= 66\frac{2}{3}\%$
- Percentage of heads after 4 tosses
  $= \frac{3}{4} \times 100\%$
  $= 75\%$

1 Toss a coin 10 times and graph the percentage of heads after each toss. Did the percentage get closer to 50% as the number of tosses increased?

2 Would this experiment be a reasonable simulation for the gender of babies born in a local hospital?

3 If you repeat this investigation, would you obtain the same graph? In what way would the second graph resemble the first?

- Is it reasonable to assume that the probability is $\frac{1}{2}$? Explain.
- Does any bias exist in the design of this experiment?

I often play my son Luke at chess. How could I estimate my chances of beating him in our next game?

P GEOGEBRA ACTIVITY 4:02 ROLLING A SINGLE DICE A LARGE NUMBER OF TIMES

Roll a single dice a large number of times and investigate the probability of each outcome.

Experimental probabilities (%)

	1	2	3	4	5	6
After 12 rolls	8.3	41.7	16.7	8.3	16.7	8.3
After 60 rolls	10	31.7	13.3	13.3	21.7	10
After 120 rolls	10.8	27.5	10	18.3	20.8	12.5
After 300 rolls	12.7	23.7	11	16.3	17.3	19

Results of first 12 rolls

1	2	2	5	6	2	2	3	5	2	4	3

Results of first 60 rolls

1	2	2	5	6	2	2	3	5	2	4	3
5	3	1	3	1	2	5	4	5	6	2	6
4	5	3	1	2	5	4	1	5	1	3	2
2	2	5	2	6	4	5	2	6	5	2	3
2	5	4	2	6	4	4	3	2	2	5	2

4:03 Theoretical probability

PREP QUIZ 4:03

Simplify:

1 $\frac{21}{24}$ **2** $\frac{34}{51}$ **3** $\frac{39}{91}$ **4** $1 - \frac{13}{16}$ **5** $1 - \frac{27}{30}$

A bag contains three white, five red and four black marbles. What fraction are:

6 white **7** black **8** not black?

9 What fraction of the letters of the alphabet are vowels?

10 What fraction of integers from 1 to 50 inclusive are prime?

Performing an experiment will not always give a consistent result, or even a result we may think is most likely to occur.

I tossed a coin 4 times and got 1 head. That means the probability of getting a head must be 1 in 4!
. . . But I got 3 heads when I tried that!
We would have to toss a coin many times to estimate the probability of getting a head.

In many cases we can work out the expected or theoretical probability of an event by considering the possible outcomes. For example, when tossing a coin there are two possible outcomes, a head or a tail.

Since there is only one head, the probability of tossing a head would be 1 out of 2 (i.e. $\frac{1}{2}$).

When calculating the probability of an event we shall assume that each possible outcome is equally likely (i.e. no two-headed coins or loaded dice).
Theoretical probability is the likelihood of outcomes occurring under ideal circumstances.

WORKED EXAMPLE 1

If a dice is rolled, what is the probability of getting:

a a six **b** an odd number **c** a number less than seven?

Solutions

The possible outcomes when rolling a dice are 1, 2, 3, 4, 5, 6. So the number of possible outcomes is 6.

a There is one 6 on a dice. So the probability of rolling a six is 1 out of 6. This can be written as:
$P(6) = \frac{1}{6}$

b There are three odd numbers on a dice. So the probability of rolling an odd number is 3 out of 6.
$P(\text{odd}) = \frac{3}{6}$
$= \frac{1}{2}$

c All six numbers on a dice are less than 7, so the probability of rolling a number less than 7 is 6 out of 6.
$P(< 7) = \frac{6}{6}$
$= 1$

The probability of an event *certain* to happen is 1.
P(sure thing) = 1

WORKED EXAMPLE 2

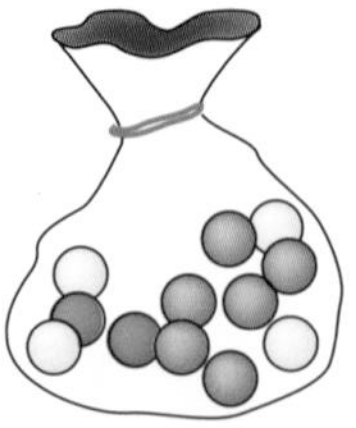

A bag contains six blue marbles, four white marbles and two red marbles.
What is the probability of choosing at random:

a a blue marble **b** a blue or white marble **c** a pink marble?

Solutions

The total number of marbles in the bag is 12. So the number of possible outcomes is 12.

a There are 6 blue marbles.
$\therefore P(\text{blue}) = \frac{6}{12}$
$= \frac{1}{2}$

b There are 10 blue or white marbles.
$\therefore P(\text{blue or white}) = \frac{10}{12}$
$= \frac{5}{6}$

c There are no pink marbles.
$\therefore P(\text{pink}) = \frac{0}{12}$
$= 0$

The probability of an event that *cannot happen* is 0.
P(impossibility) = 0

If each possible outcome is equally likely, then:

$$\text{Probability of an event, } P(E) = \frac{n(E)}{n(S)}$$

where $n(E)$ = number of ways the event can occur
$n(S)$ = number of possible outcomes

(S is used to represent the sample space, which is the set of possible outcomes.)

The probability of any event occurring must lie in the range $0 \leq P(E) \leq 1$.

It should be pointed out that the probabilities of each possible outcome must add up to 1. As a consequence of this, if the probability of an event occurring is $P(E)$, then the probability of E *not* occurring is $1 - P(E)$.

$P(E')$ = Probability of E *not* occurring
$P(E') = 1 - P(E)$

E' is set notation for the 'complement' of E; those outcomes outside of E. For example:

- The complementary event for rolling an even number on a dice is rolling an odd number.
- The complement of drawing a red card from a standard pack of cards is drawing a black card.

Exercise 4:03

P Foundation worksheet 4:03 **Theoretical probability**
Challenge worksheet 4:03 **Probability: An unusual case**

1 A single dice is rolled. What is the probability of getting:
a a one **b** an even number **c** a number less than 3?

2 Ten coloured discs are placed in a hat. Five are red, three are yellow and two are black. If one disc is drawn from the hat, what is the probability that the disc will be:
a red **b** black **c** red or black
d not black **e** blue **f** red, yellow or black?

3 Write the complementary event for each of the following.
a Rolling an *odd number* on a dice.
b Getting a *tail* when a coin is tossed.
c Rolling a *number less than 6* on a dice.
d Drawing a *spade* from a standard pack of cards.
e Seeing *red* displayed on a traffic light that is working.
f *Winning* a soccer match.
g Choosing a *vowel* from the letters of the alphabet.

What is the complement of winning?

4 A card is drawn at random from a standard pack of 52 playing cards. What is the probability that the card is:

a the Ace of diamonds　**b** a King　**c** a red card
d a spade　**e** a black Jack　**f** a 7 or 8
g a picture card (Jack, Queen or King)?

5 The 26 letters of the alphabet are written on cards and placed in a box. If one card is picked at random from the box, what is the chance that the letter on it will be:

a X　**b** a vowel
c M or N　**d** a letter in the word *MATHEMATICS*?

6 Stickers were placed on a dice so that the faces showed three 2s, two 4s and a 6. If the dice is now rolled, what is the probability that the upper surface will be:

a a 2　**b** a 4　**c** a 6
d even　**e** odd　**f** less than 6?

7 Six students, John, Bob, Joan, Helen, Betty and Janet, each wrote their name on a piece of paper and put it in a hat. If one name were drawn at random, what is the probability that the name would:

a be Helen　**b** start with J
c be a girl's name　**d** have four letters in it?

8 A letter is chosen at random from the word *KATOOMBA*. What is the probability that the letter is:

a A　**b** a consonant　**c** one of the first four letters of the alphabet　**d** Z?

9 The numbers from 1 to 25 are written on cards. If one card is chosen at random, what is the probability that the number on the card will be:

a an odd number　**b** a multiple of 5
c a factor of 24　**d** a number that contains the digit 2?

10 A five-digit number is to be formed using the digits 1, 2, 3, 4, 5 (without repetition). What is the probability that the number will:

a be odd (end with 1, 3 or 5)　**b** be even (end with 2 or 4)
c start with 5　**d** be greater than 30 000 (start with 3 or 4)
e be divisible by 3? (Hint: Is the sum of the digits divisible by 3?)

11 If the probability of an event is $\frac{1}{5}$, how many times, on average, would you expect it to occur in 20 trials? Can you say for certain how many times it will occur?

12 A bag contains five red balls numbered 1 to 5 and seven blue balls numbered 1 to 7. If a ball is chosen at random, what is the chance of choosing:

a a red ball　**b** a ball numbered 3　**c** a ball numbered 6
d the blue ball numbered 1　**e** an even-numbered ball?

13 If a dice is rolled 12 times, how many times on average would you expect the result to be:

a a 6　**b** an odd number　**c** a number greater than 2?

14 A survey of Kylie Crescent shows that 20% of the families have 1 child, 45% have 2 children, 15% have 3 children and 10% have more than 3 children. What is the probability that a family chosen at random will have:

a 2 children

b more than 2 children

c at least 2 children

d no children?

15 A roulette wheel is numbered from 0 to 36. Half of the numbers from 1 to 36 are red, the other half are black and the zero slot is green. Find the probability that the result of a spin will be:

a odd

b black

c 0

d not red

e a number from 1 to 6 inclusive

f a number greater than 25.

My interest in this is purely mathematical.

If the result is the green zero, the bank wins all wagers made.

g How often would you expect a zero?

The payout for black or red is 'even money' (i.e. for a successful bet of $1, the payout is $1 plus the original $1 bet).

h If a gambler continued to bet the same amount on black, should he or she eventually win, lose or 'break even'?

In what country did the game of roulette originate?

INVESTIGATION 4:03 CHANCE EXPERIMENTS

1 Carry out an experiment many times, and then estimate the experimental probability of one of the statements below. (In each case, state the number of trials you feel are necessary to get a good estimate.)

a A dice rolled twice will give two consecutive numbers.

b Four cards drawn at random from a standard pack will be of different suits.

c There are ten cards numbered 1 to 10. Three cards drawn at random, one after the other, will all be less than 7 if:

i each time the card is taken it is then replaced

ii each time the card is taken it is not replaced.

2 When two dice are rolled, the upper faces are added.

a Design an experiment to investigate the probability of each possible sum.

b Use a table to record your results. Graph these results as a column graph.

c Use the results of your experiment to estimate the probability of each sum.

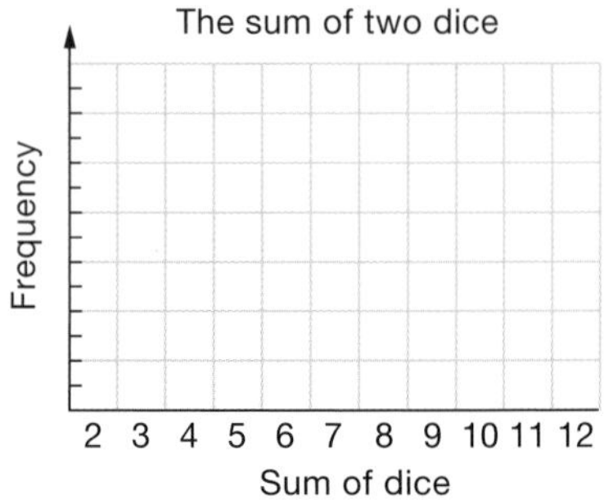

The experiments in Questions **1a** and **1b** can be carried out using Microsoft® Excel® to record and calculate the data. This activity is available on ProductLink.

36 possible outcomes

		2nd throw					
		1	2	3	4	5	6
	1	1, 1	1, 2	1, 3	1, 4	1, 5	1, 6
	2	2, 1	2, 2	2 ,3	2, 4	2, 5	2, 6
1st throw	3	3, 1	3, 2	3 ,3	3, 4	3, 5	3, 6
	4	4, 1	4, 2	4, 3	4, 4	4, 5	4, 6
	5	5, 1	5, 2	5, 3	5, 4	5, 5	5, 6
	6	6, 1	6, 2	6, 3	6, 4	6, 5	6, 6

The favourable outcomes are highlighted.

Theoretical probability = 5/36 ≈ 14%

4:04 Mutually and non-mutually exclusive events

A container holds 30 coloured counters (10 green, 7 blue and 13 of other colours).

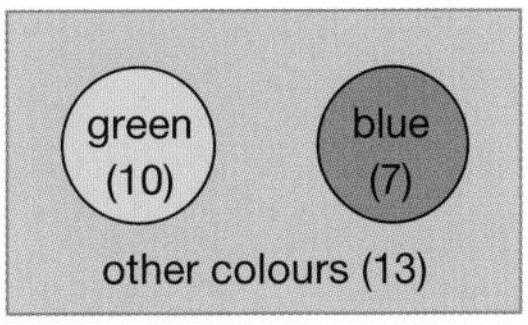

If a counter is drawn at random from the container, what is the probability that it is:

- green
- blue
- green or blue
- neither green nor blue?

It is clear that the probability of drawing either a green or blue counter is equal to the probability of green plus the probability of blue.

$P(\text{green or blue}) = P(\text{green}) + P(\text{blue})$

A counter cannot be both green and blue at the same time so these two events are called mutually exclusive events.

> Mutually exclusive events are events that cannot happen at the same time.
>
> For example:
>
> - Selecting a boy and selecting a girl.
> - Rolling an even number on a dice and rolling a three.
>
> If two events, A and B are mutually exclusive then $P(\text{either } A \text{ or } B) = P(A) + P(B)$.
>
> (If the events were not mutually exclusive, we would need to subtract the probability that both events would happen at the same time.)

WORKED EXAMPLE

A different letter of the alphabet was placed on each of 26 cards. One of these cards was then drawn at random. What is the probability that the card drawn is:

a either a vowel or a consonant

b either a letter of the word *FINAL* or a letter of the word *METHOD*

c either a letter of the word *THICK* or a letter of the word *PICK*?

The vowels are 'a, e, i, o, u'. The rest are consonants.

Solutions

a There are 5 vowels out of 26 letters and there are 21 consonants.

$$\therefore P(\text{either vowel or consonant}) = \frac{5}{26} + \frac{21}{26} = \frac{26}{26} = 1$$

∴ The card is certain to be either a vowel or a consonant.

b $P(\text{letter in the word } FINAL) = \frac{5}{26}$

$P(\text{letter in the word } METHOD) = \frac{6}{26}$

No letters are in both *FINAL* and *METHOD*.

$\therefore P(\text{a letter in either } FINAL \text{ or } METHOD) = \frac{5}{26} + \frac{6}{26}$

$= \frac{11}{26}$

c $P(\text{letter in the word } THICK) = \frac{5}{26}$

$P(\text{letter in the word } PICK) = \frac{4}{26}$

Some letters are in both *THICK* and *PICK*.

These events are not mutually exclusive.

$\therefore P(\text{a letter in either } THICK \text{ or } PICK) \neq \frac{5}{26} + \frac{4}{26}$

The number of different letters in these two words is only 6 (*T*, *H*, *I*, *C*, *K* and *P*).

$\therefore P(\text{a letter in either } THICK \text{ or } PICK) = \frac{6}{26}$

$= \frac{3}{13}$

Exercise 4:04

1 Write 'mutually exclusive' (no outcomes in common) or 'non-mutually exclusive' (at least one outcome in common) for the two events. In each case, the events relate to choosing a card from a standard pack.

a A red card will be chosen. / A picture card will be chosen.

b A King or Queen will be chosen. / An Ace will be chosen.

c A 10 will be chosen. / A heart will be chosen.

2 In a survey on censorship of violence and sex on TV, the following information was collected.

Description	Percentage of total
male adult	20
female adult	22
male teenager	27
female teenager	31

Response selected	Percentage of total
strong censorship needed	57
some censorship needed	25
little censorship needed	13
no censorship needed	5

What is the probability that a person chosen at random from the group surveyed:

a is female **b** is male **c** is an adult **d** is a teenager

e selected either *little censorship needed* or *no censorship needed*

f did not *select strong censorship needed* **g** is not a male adult

h is not a male teenager?

3 A pack of cards has four suits: hearts and diamonds (both red), and spades and clubs (both black). Each suit has 13 cards: Ace, 2, 3, 4, 5, 6, 7, 8, 9, 10, Jack, Queen and King. The Jack, Queen and King are called picture cards.

A card is drawn from a standard pack. What is the probability that the card is:

a red
b not red
c a 6
d not a 6
e a picture card
f a red Ace
g a spade
h a red 13
i either a red 5 or a 10
j either a heart or a black Ace
k either a blue 5 or a 7
l either a heart or a black card

There are 4 suits with 13 cards in each suit, so there are 52 cards in a standard pack. (In some games a Joker is also used.)

In each of the following cases, the events might not be mutually exclusive.

m either a picture card or a diamond
n either a number larger than 2 or a club
o either a heart or a 5
p either a Queen or a black picture card
q either a number between 2 and 8 or an even-numbered heart?

4 Using the results of past tests, I estimated that the probabilities of certain students getting the highest score (assuming no equal firsts) were:

Amy $\frac{3}{10}$, Greg $\frac{1}{4}$, Rachel $\frac{2}{10}$ and Luke $\frac{1}{10}$

The probability that a girl would get the highest score was $\frac{6}{10}$.
Assuming that my assessment is correct, what is the probability that in the next test the person with the highest score will be:

a either Amy or Rachel
b either Amy or Luke
c either Rachel or Luke
d a boy
e someone other than Amy
f someone other than Rachel
g either a boy or a girl
h either Greg or Luke
i a girl other than Amy
j a girl other than Rachel
k a boy other than Luke
l a boy other than Greg
m Amy, Rachel or Luke
n anyone but Amy, Rachel or Luke
o Amy, Rachel, Luke or Greg
p someone other than the four listed?

5 Three coins are tossed. The tree diagram below shows all possible outcomes.

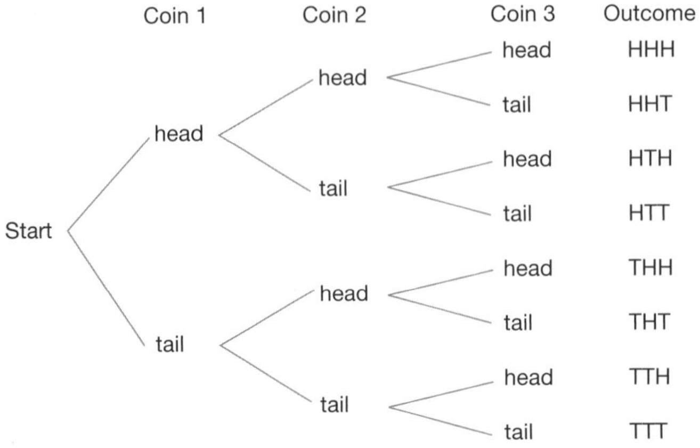

a What is the probability of tossing:
   i exactly 2 heads   ii exactly 2 tails?

b Is it possible that in one toss of the coins we could get 2 heads as well as 2 tails?

c What is the probability that we would get either 2 heads or 2 tails?

d *True* or *false:*
P(either 2 heads or 2 tails) = P(2 heads) + P(2 tails)

e What is the probability of tossing:
   i exactly one tail   ii more than one head?

f Is it possible that in one toss of the coins we could get exactly 1 tail as well as more than 1 head?

g *True* or *false:*
P(either one tail or more than one head) = P(one tail) + P(more than one head)

h *True* or *false:*
If A and B are two mutually exclusive events in the same experiment then
P(either A or B) = $P(A) + P(B)$.

INVESTIGATION 4:04 CHANCE HAPPENINGS

1 **Probability device**
Design and test a probability device to produce results with probabilities of $\frac{1}{5}$, $\frac{2}{3}$ and $\frac{2}{15}$.

2 **Media language**
Investigate the use of chance language in the printed media. Collect examples and organise these in order, from most likely to least likely.

3 **Birthdays**
Investigate the probability of students in your class sharing the same birthday.

4 **Travel**
Investigate which mode of travel is safest.

13 April
Everybody write your birth date on a slip of paper.

4:05 Using diagrams and tables

Venn diagrams and two-way tables can be used to calculate the probability of events.

WORKED EXAMPLE 1

The Venn diagram shows two sports played by 90 Year 9 students.

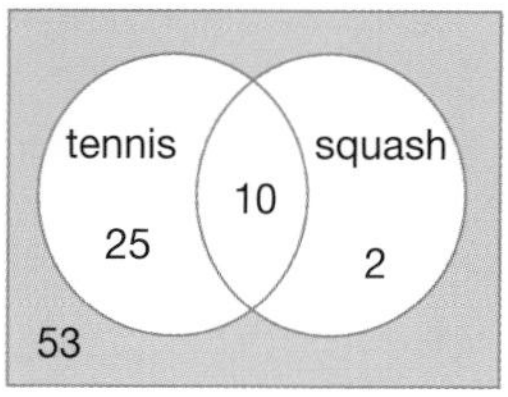

What is the probability that a randomly chosen student plays:

a both tennis and squash
b neither tennis nor squash
c tennis
d tennis or squash but not both?

(Give answers as a fraction and as a percentage, correct to the nearest per cent.)

Solutions

a This is the part where the circles overlap.
10 students play both tennis and squash.
$P(\text{both tennis and squash}) = \frac{10}{90}$ or 11%

b This is the part outside both circles.
53 students play neither tennis nor squash.
$P(\text{neither tennis nor squash}) = \frac{53}{90}$ or 59%

c This is both parts inside the tennis circle.
$25 + 10 = 35$
35 students play tennis.
$P(\text{tennis}) = \frac{35}{90}$ or 39%

d This is the part inside either circle but not in both.
$25 + 2 = 27$
27 students play tennis or squash but not both.
$P(\text{tennis or squash but not both}) = \frac{27}{90}$ or 30%

WORKED EXAMPLE 2

The two-way table shows how many females and males among 85 Year 10 students are right-handed or left-handed. What is the probability that a randomly chosen student is:

a both female and left-handed
b right-handed
c male
d a right-handed male?

	left-handed	right-handed	Total
female	4	41	45
male	7	33	40
Total	11	74	85

(Give answers as a fraction and as a percentage correct to the nearest per cent.)

Solutions

a 4 students are both female and left-handed.
$P(\text{both female and left-handed}) = \frac{4}{85}$ or 5%

b 74 students are right-handed.
$P(\text{right-handed}) = \frac{74}{85}$ or 87%

c 40 students are male.
$P(\text{male}) = \frac{40}{85}$ or 47%

d 33 students are right-handed males.
$P(\text{right-handed male}) = \frac{33}{85}$ or 39%

Exercise 4:05

1 The same information about Year 8 students in KV High School is found in the two-way table and Venn diagram below.

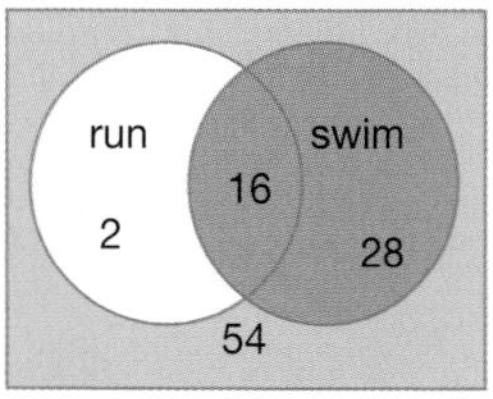

↔

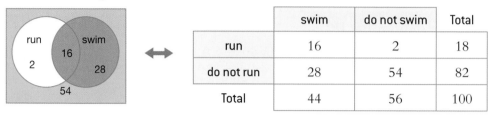

	swim	do not swim	Total
run	16	2	18
do not run	28	54	82
Total	44	56	100

What is the probability that a randomly chosen student:

a runs
b swims
c does not swim
d does not run
e runs and swims
f runs but does not swim
g neither runs nor swims
h swims but does not run
i runs or swims or both?

2 The students of Year 11 were asked whether they played golf and/or bowls. The results are shown in the Venn diagram. What is the probability that a randomly chosen Year 11 student:

a plays golf
b plays bowls
c plays golf or bowls
d does not play golf
e plays neither golf nor bowls
f does not play bowls
g plays both golf and bowls?

Year 11 sport

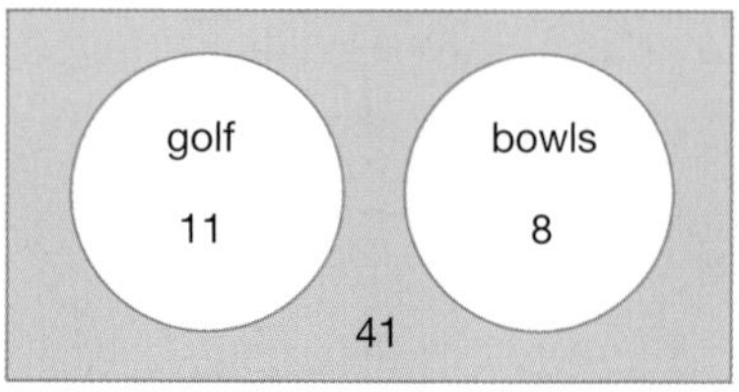

3 We surveyed all children at the concert and asked them their age. The data was used to produce this Venn diagram.

a How many children were at the concert?
b How many children were less than 8 years of age?

If one child is selected at random, what is the chance, written to the nearest per cent, that the child will be:

c less than 8 years of age
d a boy
e a girl younger than 8
f a girl 8 or older
g 8 years of age or older
h a boy 8 or older?

Children at the concert

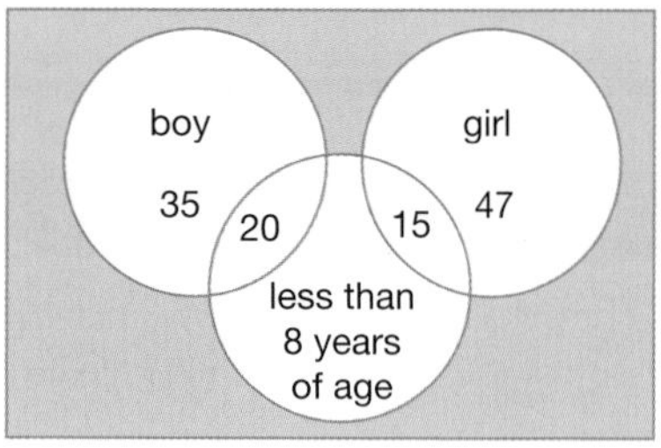

4 We held a census of all students in our school to find out who owned a mobile phone. The results are shown in the two-way table.

	owns a mobile phone	does not own a mobile phone	Total
female	32	25	57
male	29	39	68
Total	61	64	125

If we choose a student at random from our school, what is the probability that the student:

a owns a mobile phone
b does not own a mobile phone
c is a male who owns a mobile phone
d is a male who does not own a mobile phone
e is a female who does not own a mobile phone?

5 50 people were asked which of tea, coffee or hot chocolate they drink. The results are shown in the Venn diagram. If we choose one of these people at random, what is the chance that the person:

a does not drink any of the three drinks
b drinks all three
c drinks tea and coffee but not hot chocolate
d drinks tea but not coffee or hot chocolate
e drinks hot chocolate
f drinks hot chocolate but not tea or coffee?

Drink preferences

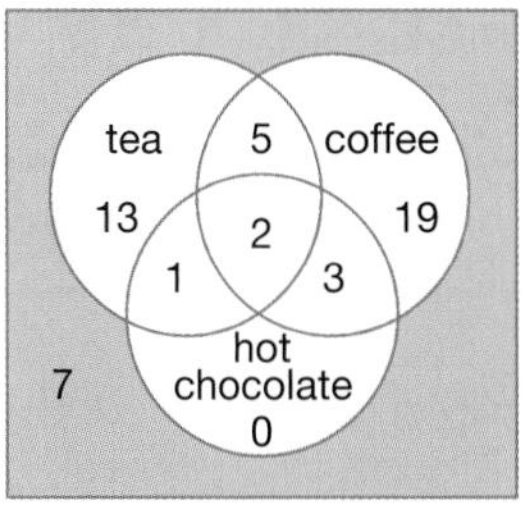

FUN SPOT 4:05 WHAT ARE DEWEY DECIMALS?

Work out the answer to each part and write the letter for that part in any box that is above the correct answer.

One mechanic, six teachers and three nurses are in a waiting room. One of these people is chosen at random. What is the probability that the person chosen is:

A a teacher
B a doctor
D a teacher or a nurse
E not a nurse
F either male or female
G neither a teacher nor a nurse?

One card is taken at random from a standard pack. What is the probability that it is:

H a heart
I black
K not a heart
L the 6 of clubs
M not the 6 of clubs
N a Jack
O not a Jack
R a 4 or 5
S a number between 3 and 10?

The graph shows the number of boys, girls, men and women who purchased sunglasses at our store last week. Use this information to find the experimental probability that the next person to buy sunglasses will be:

T a boy
U a man
V a woman
W not a girl
Y female.

Sales of sunglasses

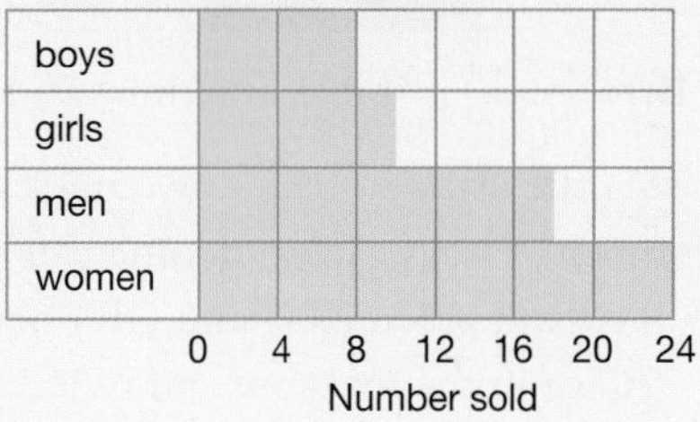

$\frac{5}{6}$	$\frac{1}{4}$	$\frac{3}{5}$	$\frac{2}{15}$	$\frac{17}{30}$	$\frac{12}{13}$	$\frac{3}{10}$	$\frac{1}{10}$	$\frac{7}{10}$	$\frac{2}{15}$	$\frac{5}{6}$	$\frac{1}{4}$	$\frac{7}{10}$	$\frac{1}{13}$	$\frac{17}{30}$	$\frac{12}{13}$	$\frac{3}{10}$	$\frac{2}{13}$

$\frac{51}{52}$	$\frac{3}{5}$	$\frac{2}{15}$	$\frac{1}{4}$	$\frac{6}{13}$	0	$\frac{12}{13}$	$\frac{12}{13}$	$\frac{3}{4}$	$\frac{1}{2}$	$\frac{6}{13}$	$\frac{1}{52}$	$\frac{7}{10}$	1	$\frac{2}{15}$

$\frac{12}{13}$	$\frac{3}{10}$	$\frac{2}{15}$	$\frac{6}{13}$	$\frac{1}{2}$	$\frac{9}{10}$	$\frac{7}{10}$	$\frac{12}{13}$	$\frac{2}{5}$	$\frac{7}{10}$	$\frac{2}{13}$	$\frac{1}{13}$	$\frac{1}{2}$	$\frac{1}{10}$	$\frac{1}{4}$	$\frac{2}{15}$

4:06 Two-step chance experiments

We can use an array or a tree diagram to show all possible outcomes when two events occur at random, one after the other, in a chance experiment.

Random selections without replacement

- 'Without replacement' means that an item taken as the first choice cannot be taken as the second choice.

WORKED EXAMPLE 1

There are one red, two green and three yellow counters in a container. Show all possible outcomes when two counters are taken from the container, one after the other, without replacing the first counter. (This is the same as simply taking two counters together.)

Using an array

There are two green and three yellow counters so we will call the counters red R; green G1 and G2; yellow Y1, Y2 and Y3. Remember that the same counter cannot be chosen in both choices. In the first table, the possible outcomes are coloured.

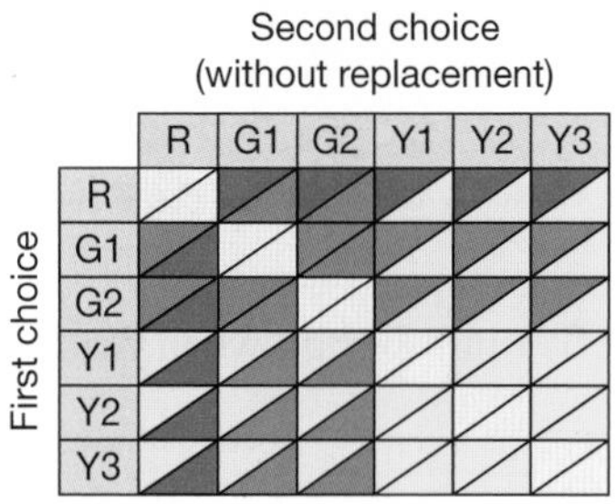

OR

Second choice (without replacement)

First choice	R	G1	G2	Y1	Y2	Y3
R		RG	RG	RY	RY	RY
G1	GR		GG	GY	GY	GY
G2	GR	GG		GY	GY	GY
Y1	YR	YG	YG		YY	YY
Y2	YR	YG	YG	YY		YY
Y3	YR	YG	YG	YY	YY	

There are 30 possible outcomes (6 rows of 5).

Using the array, we can now count the number of ways each outcome can occur.

- Red and green (RG and GR) occurs 4 times (twice in the first row and twice in the first column).
- Red and yellow (RY and YR) occurs 6 times.
- Green and yellow (GY and YG) occurs 12 times.
- Both red is not possible because the first counter is not replaced.
- Both green (GG) occurs 2 times.
- Both yellow (YY) occurs 6 times.

This gives a total of 30 possibilities.

The table shows the probability of each event.

Event	Number of selections	Probability
red and green	4	$\frac{4}{30}$
red and yellow	6	$\frac{6}{30}$
green and yellow	12	$\frac{12}{30}$
both red	0	$\frac{0}{30}$
both green	2	$\frac{2}{30}$
both yellow	6	$\frac{6}{30}$
Total:	30	1

Using a tree diagram

We can also show all possible choices using a tree diagram.

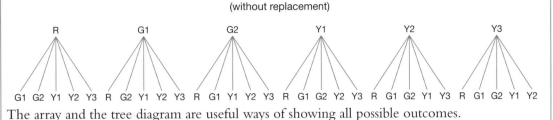

(without replacement)

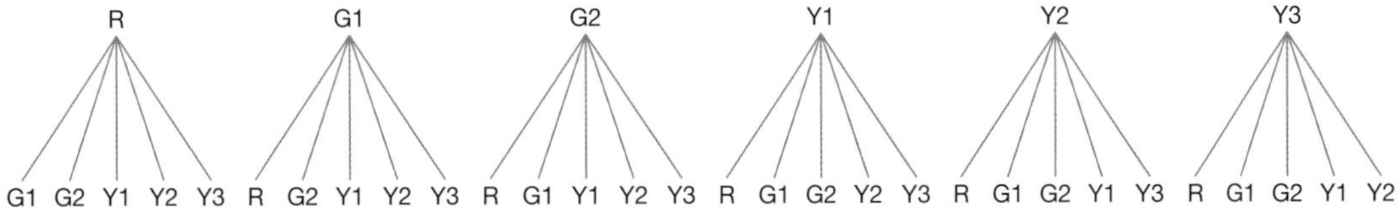

The array and the tree diagram are useful ways of showing all possible outcomes.

In the previous example, if the counter taken as the first choice is returned to the container before the second choice is made, then the array, the tree diagram and the table would be different. This would be called 'choosing two counters *with replacement*'.

Random selections with replacement

- 'With replacement' means that an item taken as the first choice can also be taken as the second choice.

WORKED EXAMPLE 2

Consider a simpler case where we have only three counters: one red and two yellow.

Show all possible outcomes when two counters are taken from the container, one after the other, returning the first choice to the container before making the second choice (i.e. with replacement).

The array and the tree diagram would look like this.

- The number of possible outcomes is 9 (i.e. 3×3).

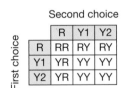

Second choice (columns); First choice (rows)

	R	Y1	Y2
R	RR	RY	RY
Y1	YR	YY	YY
Y2	YR	YY	YY

(with replacement)

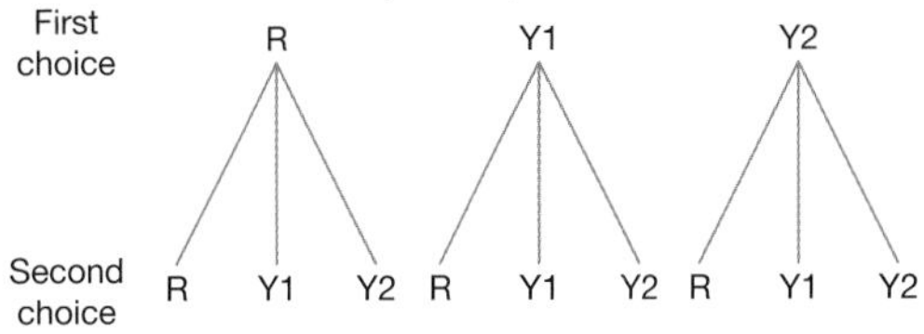

As the first chosen counter is replaced before the second is chosen, it is possible to choose two reds.

Using the array, we can count the number of ways each event could occur.

- Red and yellow could occur in 4 possible ways.
- Both red could occur in 1 possible way.
- Both yellow could occur in 4 possible ways.

This gives a total of 9 possibilities.

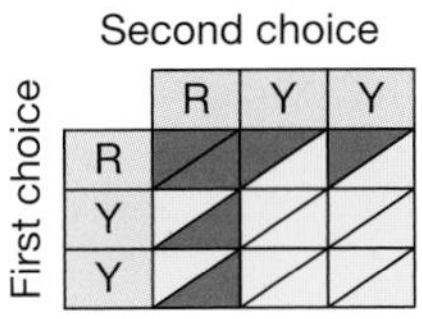

Event	Number of selections	Probability
red and yellow	4	$\frac{4}{9}$
both red	1	$\frac{1}{9}$
both yellow	4	$\frac{4}{9}$
Total:	9	1

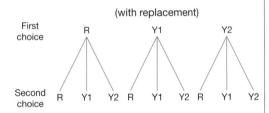

Exercise 4:06

1 A counter is taken at random from this box. It is then returned and another counter is taken at random.

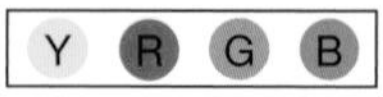

a Complete the tree diagram and the array to show all possible outcomes.

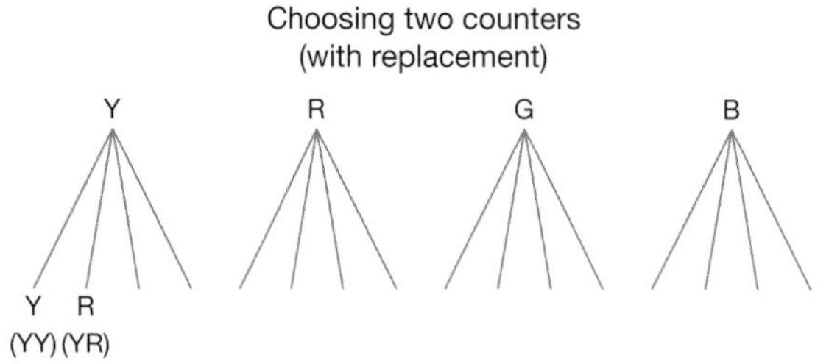

Second choice (with replacement)

First choice	Y	R	G	B
Y	YY			
R	RY			
G				
B				

b How many possible outcomes are shown?

c How many of the outcomes show a red and a yellow?

d What is the probability that a red and a yellow will be taken?

e What is the probability that a red and then a yellow will be taken?

f What is the probability that two yellows will be taken?

g What is the probability that two yellows will not be taken?

2 A counter is taken at random from the box in Question 1. It is not returned. A second counter is then taken at random.

a Complete this tree diagram and this array to show all possible outcomes.

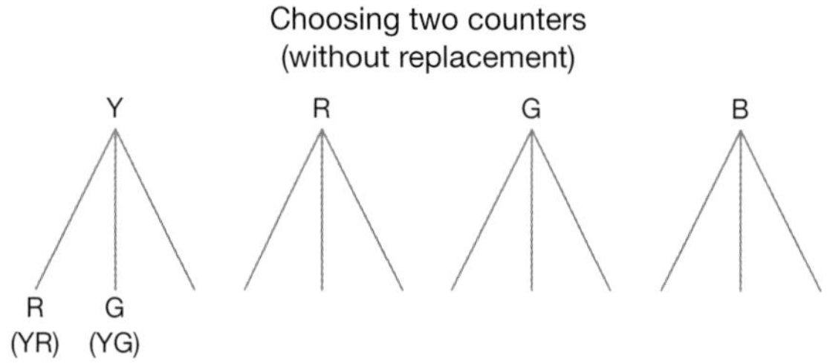

Second choice (without replacement)

First choice	Y	R	G	B
Y		YR	YG	
R				
G				
B				

b How many possible outcomes are shown?

c How many of the outcomes show a red and a yellow?

d What is the probability that a red and a yellow will be taken?

e What is the probability that a red then a yellow will be taken?

f What is the probability that two yellows will be taken?

g What is the probability that two yellows will not be taken?

h Complete this table showing the probability of each event listed.

Event	Number of selections	Probability
yellow and red	2	$\frac{2}{12}$
yellow and green		
yellow and blue		
both yellow		

Event	Number of selections	Probability
red and green		
red and blue		
green and blue		
both red		

3 In a two-step experiment, a coin is tossed and a dice is rolled.

a Use an array and a tree diagram to show all possible outcomes.

b How many possible outcomes are there?

c What is the probability of:

i tossing a head and rolling a 6

ii tossing a head

iii tossing a tail and rolling a number less than 3

iv rolling a 5 or 6

v tossing a head and not rolling a 6

vi not rolling a 6?

d Does the tossing of the coin in any way affect the outcome of rolling the dice?

4 In a two-step experiment, two dice are rolled and the total is calculated.

	⚀	⚁	⚂	⚃	⚄	⚅
⚀	2	3	4	5	6	7
⚁	3	4	5	6	7	8
⚂	4	5	6	7	8	9
⚃	5	6	7	8	9	10
⚄	6	7	8	9	10	11
⚅	7	8	9	10	11	12

a How many outcomes are possible?

b How many different totals are possible?

Use the array to find the probability of rolling a total of:

c 12 d 2 e 7

f 4 g 10 h 9

i 6 j 8 k 5

What is the probability of rolling a total:

l of 7 or 11 m less than 7 n of 2 or 12

o that is even p that is not 7 q that is a prime number?

5 In a two-step experiment, two cards are chosen at random (one after the other) from the five cards shown on the right. The first card is *not replaced* before the second is chosen.

(without replacement)

The suits of playing cards are hearts, diamonds, clubs and spades.

a Make a list of all possible outcomes e.g. (3C, 6H), (3C, 7H), (3C, 8D), …

b How many different outcomes are there?

Use your list to find the probability that the outcome is:

c a 3 and a 6

d a 3 then a 6

e two clubs

f the 3 of clubs followed by a heart

g a heart for the second card

h a club and a heart

i a club then a heart.

What is the probability that the numbers on the two cards have a total:

j of 15 k of 12 l more than 14

m that is even n that is not 15 o less than 12?

6 The experiment in Question 5 is repeated, but this time the first card is *replaced* before the second is chosen.

(with replacement)

a Make a list of all possible outcomes if the first card is replaced before the second card is chosen
e.g. (3C, 3C), (3C, 6H), (3C, 7H), …

b How many different outcomes are there?

Use your list to find the probability that the outcome is:

c a 3 and a 6 d a 3 then a 6 e two clubs

f the 3 of clubs followed by a heart

g a heart for the second card h a club and a heart

i a club then a heart.

What is the probability that the numbers on the two cards have a total:

j of 15 k of 12 l that is more than 14

m that is even n that is not 15 o that is less than 12?

7 In a two-step experiment, two cards are chosen at random (one after the other) from the four cards shown on the right.

a Here, the first card is *not replaced* before the second is chosen. If we have already chosen the 2 of hearts as our first card, what is the probability that we will end up with:

i two hearts ii two even numbers

iii a heart and a diamond iv a total greater than 8

v an even total vi a heart?

b Explain how knowing the result of the first step in part a affected the probability of the events in this two-step chance experiment.

c Here, the first card is *replaced* before the second is chosen. If we have already chosen the 2 of hearts as our first card, what is the probability that we will end up with:

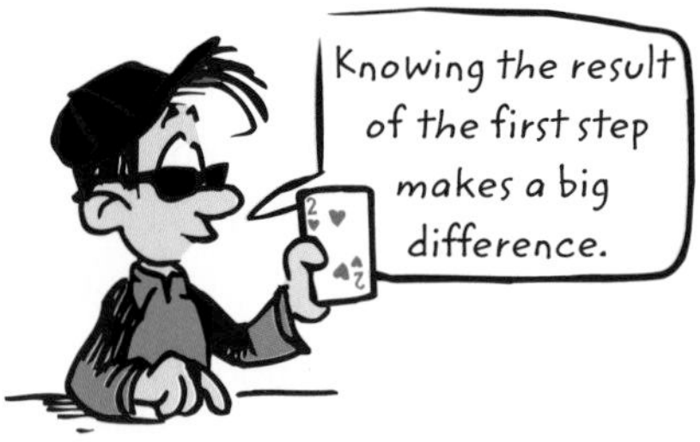
Knowing the result of the first step makes a big difference.

i two hearts ii two even numbers

iii a heart and a diamond iv a total greater than 8

v an even total vi a heart?

d Explain how knowing the result of the first step in part c affected the probability of the events in the two-step chance experiment.

8 A representative of our school is to speak at a Dawn Service in town and at the school Anzac Day service after lunch. The choices must be made from Alan, Luke, Naomi and Rachel.

a A different person is to speak at each service.

i In how many different ways can the speakers be chosen?

ii If the two people are to be chosen at random, what is the probability that the two boys will be chosen?

b In this case, the same person may speak at both services.

i In how many different ways can the speaker be chosen?

ii If the speaker for each is to be chosen at random, what is the probability that there will be a boy speaking at both services?

9 Make up a two-step chance experiment of your own. Describe the experiment and write, and then answer, a set of questions about the probability of events relating to your experiment.

INVESTIGATION 4:06 TWO-STEP CHANCE EXPERIMENTS

1 On four pieces of identical paper or cardboard, write 'red 1', 'red 2', 'green' and 'purple'. Place these in a container and draw out two of them at random, one at a time, without replacement. Use the array below to keep a tally as you repeat this experiment 50 times. Record the results of this experiment by filling in the table, writing the probabilities as percentages.

Second choice (without replacement)

First choice

	R1	R2	G	P
R1				
R2				
G				
P				

Tallies

Event	Number of selections	Experimental probability
2 red		%
red and green		%
red and purple		%
2 green		%
green and purple		%
2 purple		%
Total:		%

2 Repeat the experiment above, but this time replace the first choice before making the second. Use the array below to keep a tally as you repeat this experiment 50 times. Record the results of this experiment by filling in the table, writing the probabilities as percentages.

Second choice (with replacement)

First choice

	R1	R2	G	P
R1				
R2				
G				
P				

Tallies

Event	Number of selections	Experimental probability
2 red		%
red and green		%
red and purple		%
2 green		%
green and purple		%
2 purple		%
Total:		%

3 Compare the results of the two experiments above. What difference does replacing the first choice make? Would you expect there to be a difference? Why? Write a report of at least 100 words on your investigation of these two cases.

The experiments in Investigation 4:06 can be carried out using Microsoft® Excel® to record and calculate the data. This Excel activity can be accessed on ProductLink.

Event	Number of selections	Experimental probability (%)
2 red		
red and green		
red and purple		
2 green		
green and purple		
2 purple		
Total:		100%

MATHS TERMS 4

complementary event

- the complement of an event is all possible outcomes outside that event,
  e.g. the complementary event to 'rolling a six' is 'not rolling a six'
- the probabilities of an event and its complement add up to 1; if $P(E)$ is the probability that E will occur, then the probability that E won't occur is $P(E') = 1 - P(E)$

experimental probability

- the chance of an event occurring as calculated by observing what happens in a sample experiment;
  Experimental probability
  $= \dfrac{\text{no. of times event occurred}}{\text{total number of trials}}$

mutually exclusive events

- events that cannot occur at the same time,
  e.g. rolling an even number and rolling a 3 with a dice

outcomes

- the possible results when calculating a probability,
  e.g. the outcomes when tossing a coin are heads or tails

probability

- the calculated chance of an event happening

random

- without bias
- a way of choosing that does not affect the likelihood of outcomes

sample space

- the list of possible outcomes,
  e.g. when rolling a dice the sample space is 1, 2, 3, 4, 5, 6

simulation

- an experiment which uses simple equipment such as cards or coins to represent a real event,
  e.g. using heads or tails to represent the birth of boys or girls

survey

- to gather data or information from which conclusions might be drawn,
  e.g. to count the number of trucks in a line of traffic or to question a group of students about their favourite music

theoretical probability

- the probability of an event that is determined by considering the possible outcomes,
  e.g. the probability of rolling a 6 with a dice is $\frac{1}{6}$, because there are 6 equally likely outcomes

Venn diagram

- a diagram that uses circles to show the relationship between events

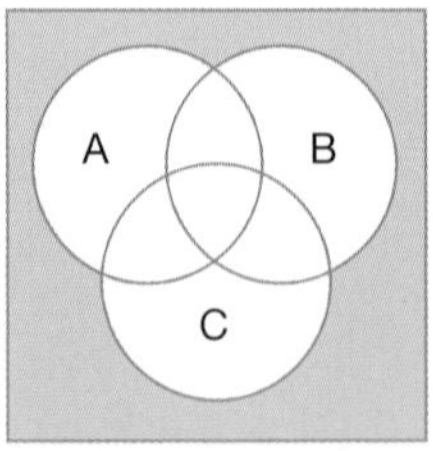

These questions reflect the important skills introduced in this chapter.
Errors made will indicate areas of weakness.
Each weakness should be treated by going back to the section listed.

1 List all possible outcomes of each experiment below. 4:01

a A dice is rolled.

b A coin is tossed.

c The spinner on the right is spun.

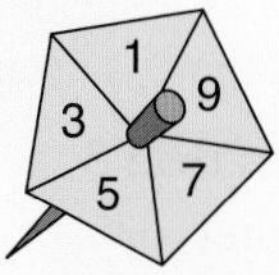

2 My last 44 scores on our golf course have been entered in this table. 4:02

My score	90–93	94–97	98–101	102–105	106–109
Frequency	3	5	7	20	9

I am about to play another game. What is the experimental probability that my score will be:

a lower than 94 b higher than 93 c higher than 109?

Explain why the experimental probability that my score is higher than 109 is zero.

3 A bag contains six blue marbles, four white marbles and two red marbles. A marble is chosen at random. What is the probability of choosing: 4:03

a a blue marble
b a blue or a white marble
c a pink marble
d anything but a white marble?

4 A card is drawn at random from a standard pack. What is the probability that the card is: 4:04

a either a 4 or a 10
b either a red 4 or a 10
c either the 5 of spades or an Ace
d either a heart or a 5
e either a red card or a Jack
f anything except either a red card or a Jack?

5 Use this Venn diagram to find the probability that a randomly chosen student plays: 4:05

a tennis
b neither tennis nor squash
c both tennis and squash
d tennis or squash but not both.

(Give answers as a fraction and as a percentage.)

Sports played by Year 9

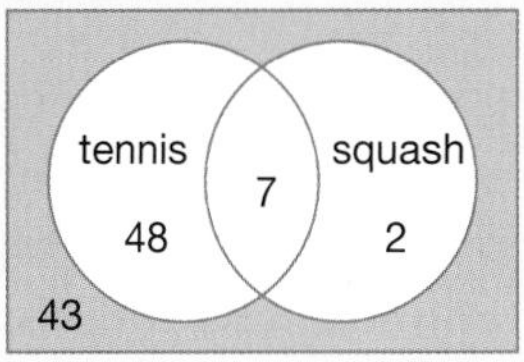

6 Use this table to find the probability that a randomly chosen student is: 4:05

a both female and left-handed
b right-handed
c male
d is a right-handed male.

(Give answers as a fraction and as a percentage.)

Students in Year 12

	left-handed	right-handed	Total
female	3	20	23
male	4	23	27
Total	7	43	50

ASSIGNMENT 4A Chapter review

1 A dice is rolled. What is the probability that it will:

a show a 6
b show a 7
c show a number less than 3
d show an odd number
e show a number less than 7?

2 Presuming that the figures shown in the table are typical of the people in a certain town, what is the probability of a person chosen at random from this town being:

Hair type	Number
Brunette	55
Blonde	35
Red	10

a a blonde
b a red-head
c not a blonde?

3 A box contains ten apples, eight oranges and two lemons. If a piece of fruit is picked at random, what is the chance of getting:
a an orange b a lemon
c an orange or a lemon d a banana?

4 One red (R1), one green (G1) and two yellow counters (Y1 and Y2) are in a container.
a Show all possible outcomes when two counters are taken from the container, one after the other, **without replacing the first counter**. Use your list or diagram to find the probability of randomly choosing 2 counters of the same colour.
b Show all possible outcomes when two counters are take from the container, one after the other, **replacing the first counter before the second is drawn**. Use your list or diagram to find the probability of randomly choosing two counters of the same colour.

5 Bobby Striker played 20 games of tenpin bowls and gained the following scores.

169	148	173	171	156
161	159	183	137	164
152	199	145	168	155
142	175	187	140	167

a Going on his past performances, what is the probability that Bobby's next score will be:
i greater than 170 ii less than 150?
b Bobby did not score over 200. Does this mean that the probability of him scoring a 200 game is zero? Comment on your answer.

6 When two teams play football there are three possible results. Either team could win, or the game could be drawn. Therefore, the probability that a particular team wins is $\frac{1}{3}$. Is this statement correct? Justify your answer.

In poker, the probability of being dealt a royal flush is $\frac{1}{649\,740}$.

ASSIGNMENT 4B Working mathematically

1 Refer to **ID Card 4** on page xxi to identify the mathematical terms numbered:

a 6	b 7
c 8	d 12
e 14	f 15
g 17	h 18
i 19	j 22

2 Use the **Algebra card** on page xxiv to:
   a add column M to column N
   b subtract column M from column N
   c add columns N and O
   d find the value of the term in J if $x = -2$.

3 Through how many degrees does the spoke of a wheel turn in 5 minutes if the wheel is turning at 700 revolutions per minute?

4 Indu is 8 years younger than John, but John is twice her age. How old is Indu?

5 The graph below shows the percentage brand shares of all disposable nappies sold in supermarkets in a year. The scale on the vertical axis has been removed.

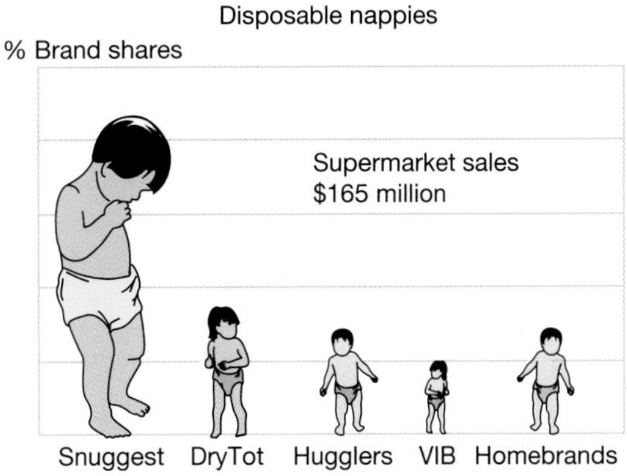

Estimate the percentage of the sales belonging to Snuggest if:
   a the *height* of each picture is the significant measure
   b the *area* of each picture is the significant measure
   c the *volume* of the child represented in each picture is the significant measure.

- One of these keys is the one I want. If I choose one of them at random, what is the probability that it is the one I want?
- If the first one I chose was not the one I wanted, what would be the probability that I will choose the right one on my second choice?
- What would be the probability of choosing the correct key on either my first or second selection?

ASSIGNMENT 4C Cumulative revision

1 Simplify: 1:01

a $3 - (-4 \times 7)$
b $18 - 8 \times 9$
c $(-7)^2 - (-8)^2$

2 a 30% of my wages was taken as tax. This was \$186. What was my wage? 1:01

b I was able to reduce my weight by 4·8 kg. This was 6% of my original weight. What was my original weight?

3 a I scored 7 of our team's 40 points. What percentage of the points did I score? 1:01

b A box of pens contained 16 blue, 8 red and 25 black. What percentage (to 2 dec. pl.) of the pens were red?

4 a Write $\frac{3}{8}$ as a decimal. b Write $\frac{1}{6}$ as a decimal. 1:03

c Write 0·636 363… as a fraction in its simplest form.

5 a Find the ratio of Rob's height (2 m) to Alan's height (180 cm). 1:04, 1:05

b What was my average rate of speed if I travelled 1210 km in 5 h 30 min?

c How many significant figures has 0·0050 m?

6 a Write $6{\cdot}4 \times 10^6$ as a basic numeral. 1:08, 1:09

b Write 95 000 000 in scientific notation using two significant figures.

c Convert 2·3 MB to kB.

7 Simplify: 3:01, 3:02

a $12y - y$
b $8m - 7p + 3p$
c $4a^2 - 2a + 3a^2 + 3a$
d $4a \times 7$
e $3t \times 4t$
f $7a \times 6b \times 10$

8 Simplify: 3:03, 3:04

a $\frac{16a}{4}$
b $8xy \div 2x$
c $-10m \div 20mn$
d $\frac{m}{10} + \frac{3m}{10}$
e $\frac{8m}{5} - \frac{7m}{10}$
f $\frac{5a}{6} + \frac{3a}{5}$
g $\frac{m}{5} \times \frac{m}{4}$
h $\frac{5b}{3} \times \frac{9}{10b}$
i $\frac{xy}{10} \div \frac{y}{5}$

9 Expand and simplify where possible. 3:05, 3:06

a $x(3x + 7)$
b $6y(7 - 2y)$
c $-2(5m - 5)$
d $11m + 15 + 6(m - 9)$
e $4a(a - b) - a(7a - 4b)$

10 Factorise: 3:07

a $8m + 12$
b $4x^2 - 6x$
c $12ab - b$

11 Illustrate each problem using a Venn diagram and then answer the question. 2:03

a Of 15 people, 6 had been to Turkey and 10 had been to China. If 3 people had been to neither country, how many had been to both Turkey and China?

b Of 25 students, 16 had been to Scotland, 9 had been to Wales, and 8 had been to Ireland. 5 had been to both Wales and Scotland but only one of these 5 had been to Ireland as well. Two students had been to Ireland and Wales but not Scotland and 4 students had been to both Scotland and Ireland. How many students had been to none of these countries?

AREA, SURFACE AREA AND VOLUME

5

Contents

Syllabus references (See pages x–xv for details.)

Measurement and Geometry

Selections from ***Area and Surface Area*** [Stages 5.1, 5.2]

- Calculate the areas of composite shapes (ACMMG216)
- Calculate the surface areas of cylinders and solve related problems (ACMMG217)
- Solve problems involving the surface areas of right prisms (ACMMG218)
- Solve problems involving surface area for a range of prisms, cylinders and composite solids (ACMMG242)

Selections from ***Volume*** [Stage 5.2]

- Solve problems involving the volumes of right prisms (ACMMG218)
- Solve problems involving volume for a range of prisms, cylinders and composite solids (ACMMG242)

Working Mathematically

- Communicating
- Problem Solving
- Reasoning
- Understanding
- Fluency

5:01 Area of composite figures

- Composite figures are figures that are made from simpler figures. To calculate their areas you will need to be able to calculate the areas of the basic shapes listed in the following table.

Area formulas

Square $A = s^2$ 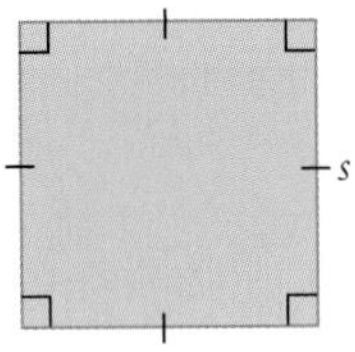 	Rectangle $A = lb$ 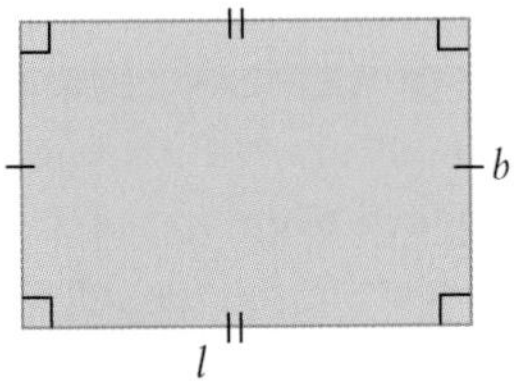 	Triangle $A = \frac{1}{2}bh$ or $A = \frac{bh}{2}$ 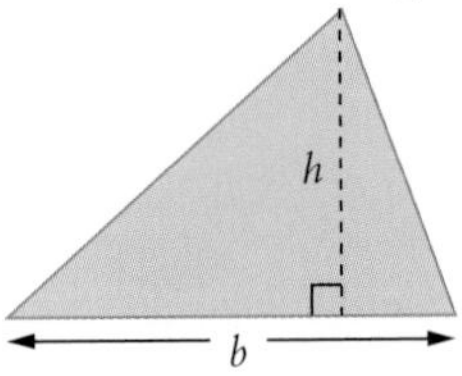
Trapezium $A = \frac{1}{2}h(a+b)$ 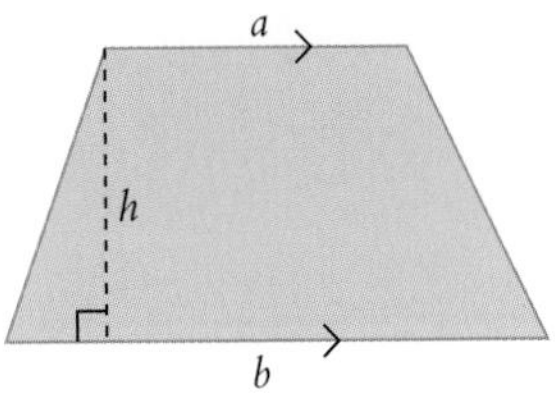 	Parallelogram $A = bh$ 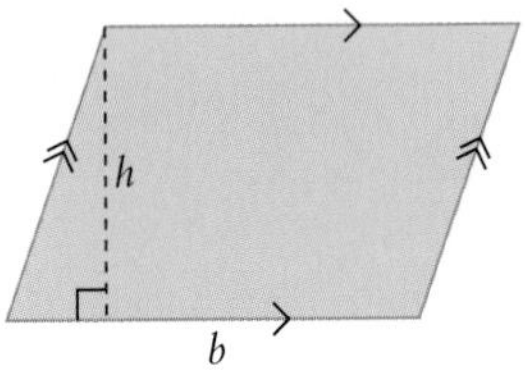 	Rhombus and Kite $A = \frac{1}{2}xy$ 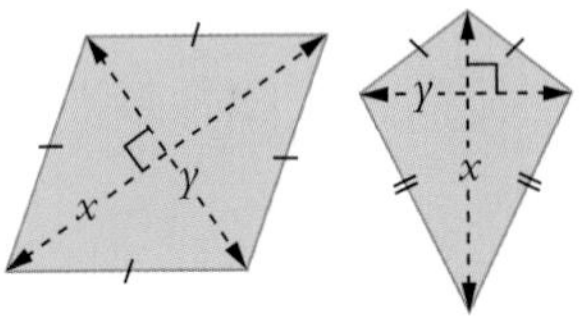 x and y are the lengths of the diagonals
Circle $A = \pi r^2$ 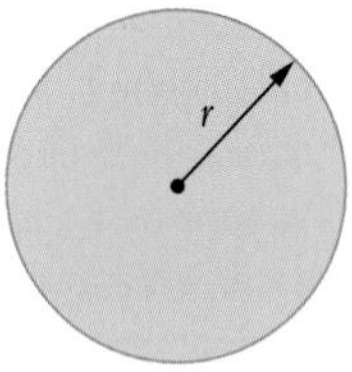 	Sector $A = \frac{\theta}{360} \times \pi r^2$ 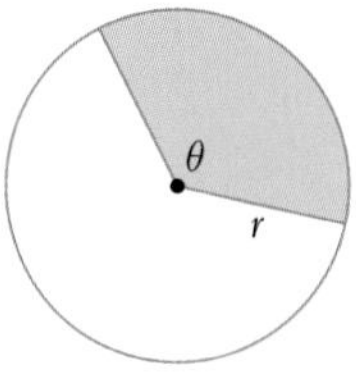 	Quadrilateral 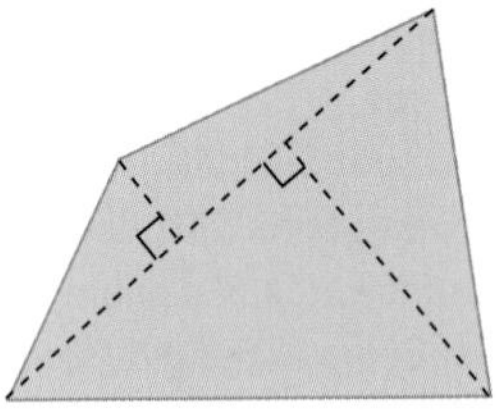 There is no formula. Divide into two triangles and add the areas.

P GEOGEBRA ACTIVITY 5:01A AREA FORMULAS

In this activity you can test your knowledge of the basic area formulas. After calculating the areas of given figures, the figures can be changed. A checkbox is available to show the area calculations.

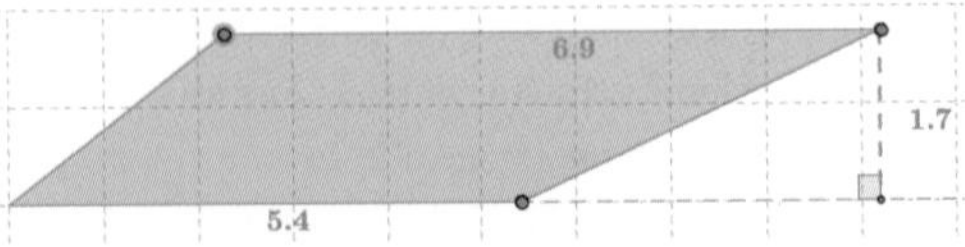

The area of composite figures can be calculated by either of two methods.

Method 1 (by addition of parts)

We imagine that smaller regular figures have been joined to form the figure, as in Figures 1 and 2.

1 Copy the figure.
2 Divide the figure up into simpler parts. Each part is a shape whose area can be calculated directly (e.g. a square or rectangle).
3 Calculate the area of the parts separately.
4 Add the area of the parts to give the area of the figure.

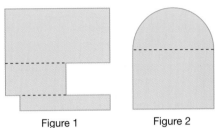

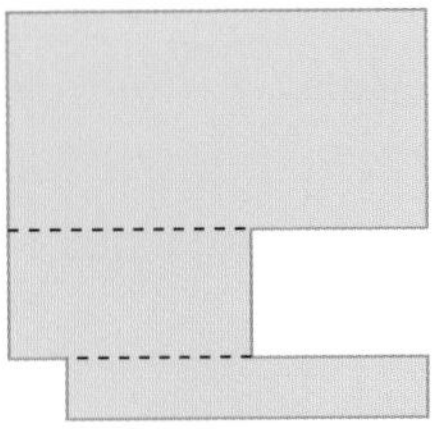
Figure 1

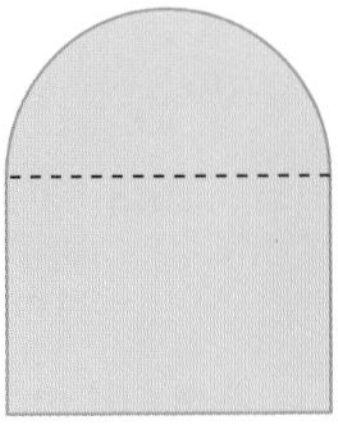
Figure 2

Method 2 (by subtraction)

We imagine the figure is formed by cutting away simple shapes from a larger complete figure, as shown.

1 Copy the figure and mark in the original larger figure from which it has been cut.
2 Calculate the area of the larger original figure.
3 Calculate the area of the parts that have been removed.
4 Area of figure = (area of original figure) − (area of parts that have been removed).

This method is also used when the inside of a figure is removed. The figure shown at right is an **annulus**. To find the area we subtract the area of the small circle from the area of the large circle.

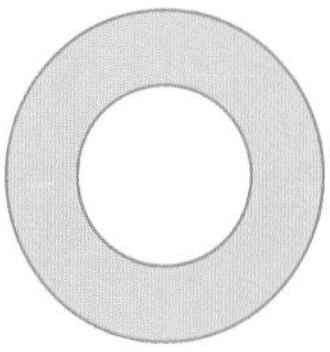

Think carefully before deciding which method to use.

Addition

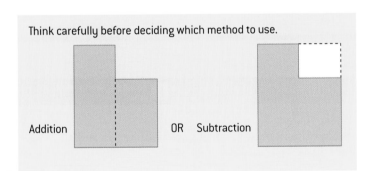

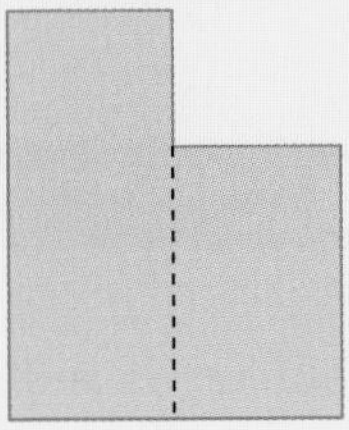

OR Subtraction

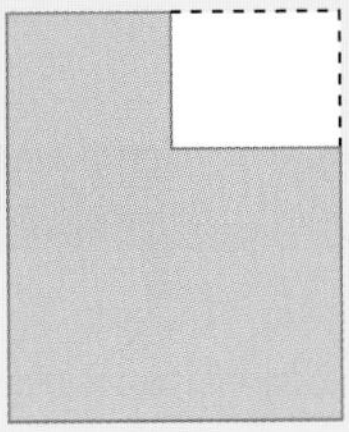

Some questions can be done either way.

WORKED EXAMPLE 1

Calculate the shaded area of each figure.

a

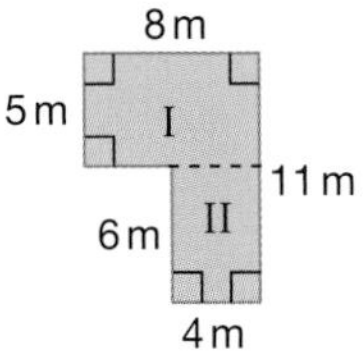

Area of rectangle I
$= 8 \times 5$
$= 40\,\text{m}^2$

Area of rectangle II
$= 6 \times 4$
$= 24\,\text{m}^2$

$\therefore$ Area of figure
$= 40 + 24$
$= 64\,\text{m}^2$

b

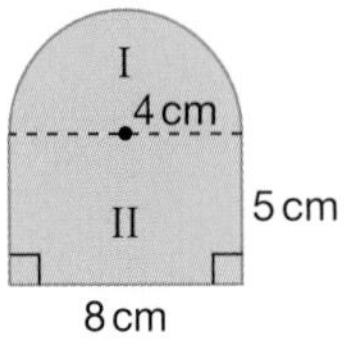

Area of semicircle I
$= \frac{1}{2}\pi r^2$
$= \frac{1}{2} \times \pi \times 16$
$= 25{\cdot}12\,\text{cm}^2$

Area of rectangle II
$= 8 \times 5$
$= 40\,\text{cm}^2$

$\therefore$ Area of figure
$= 40 + 25{\cdot}12$
$= 65{\cdot}12\,\text{cm}^2$ (2 dec. pl.)

c

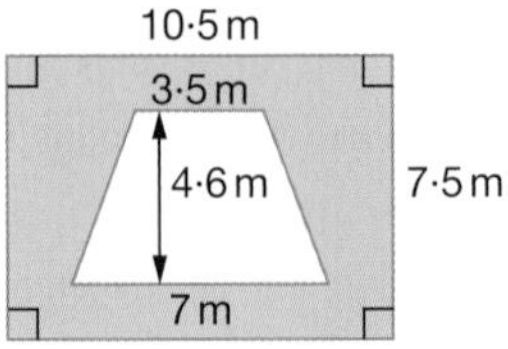

Area of rectangle
$= 10{\cdot}5 \times 7{\cdot}5$
$= 78{\cdot}75\,\text{m}^2$

Area of trapezium
$= \frac{1}{2} \times 4{\cdot}6 \times (3{\cdot}5 + 7)$
$= 24{\cdot}15\,\text{m}^2$

$\therefore$ Shaded area
$= 78{\cdot}75 - 24{\cdot}15$
$= 54{\cdot}6\,\text{m}^2$

d Calculate the shaded area of the figure.

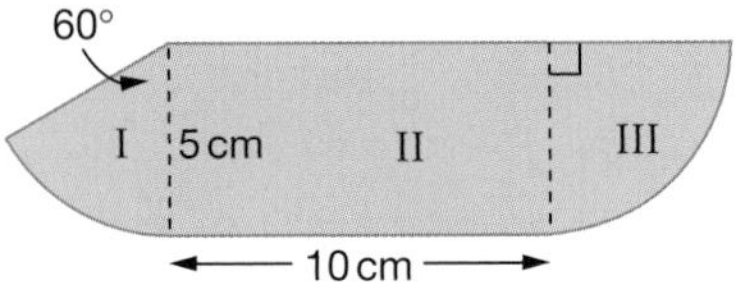

The calculations are all done in one go.

Area of figure = area of sector I + area of rectangle II + area of quadrant III
$= (\frac{60}{360} \times \pi \times 5^2) + (5 \times 10) + (\frac{1}{4} \times \pi \times 5^2)$
$= 82{\cdot}7\,\text{m}^2$ (1 dec. pl.)

Exercise 5:01

Foundation worksheet 5:01
Area

1 Calculate the area of the following composite figures. All angles are right angles and all measurements are in metres.

a

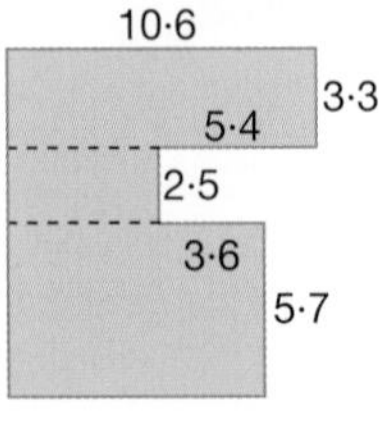

b

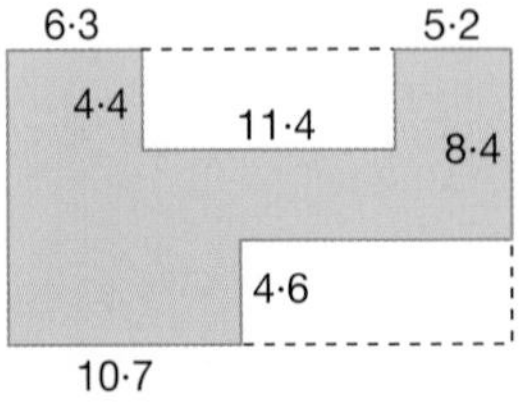

c

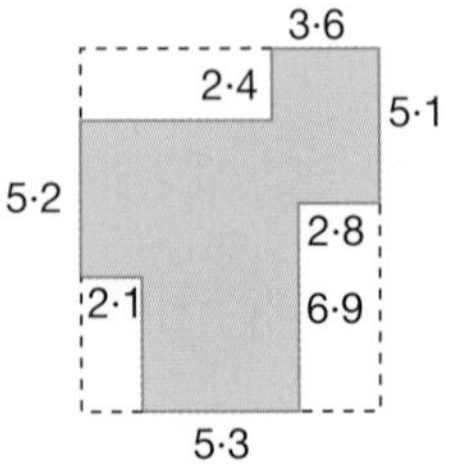

2 Calculate the shaded area of the following figures. All measurements are in metres.

a
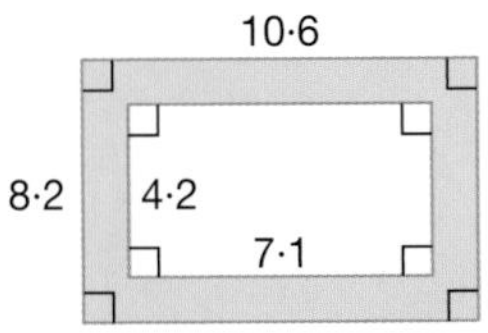

b
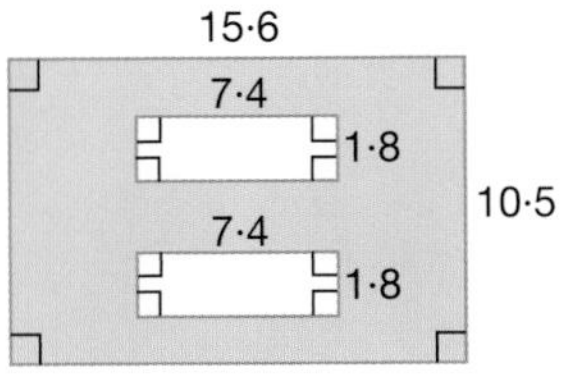

c
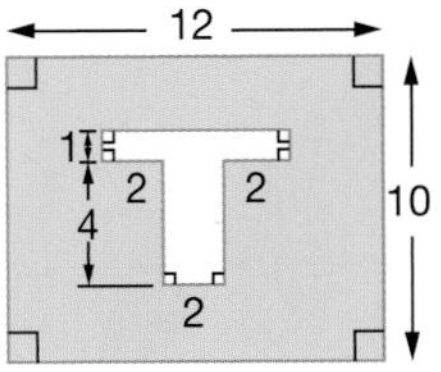

3 Calculate the area of each figure. All measurements are in metres.

a
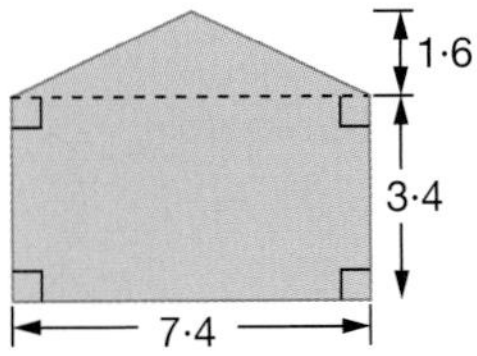

b
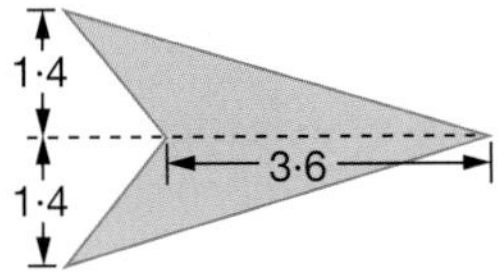

c
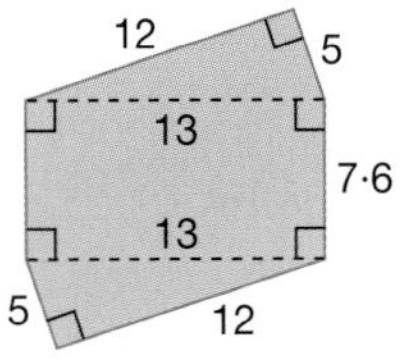

4 Calculate the shaded area of each of the following figures. All measurements are in centimetres. Give answers correct to two decimal places.

a
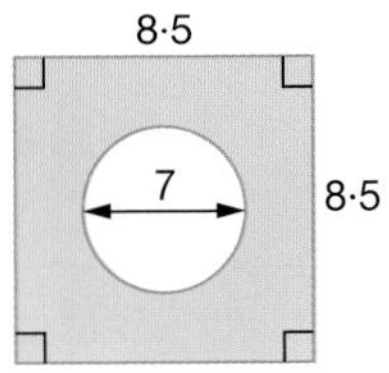

b
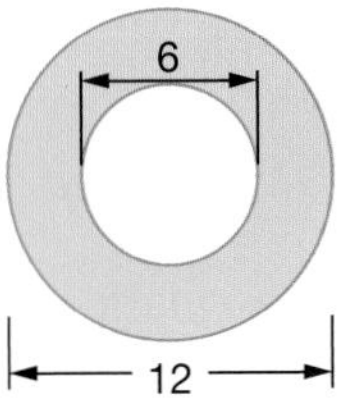

c
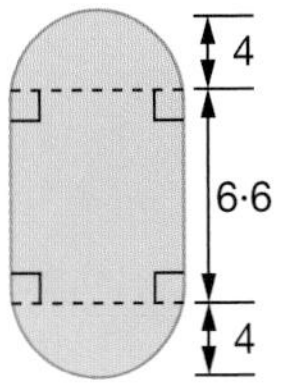

5 Find the area of each of the following composite figures.

a
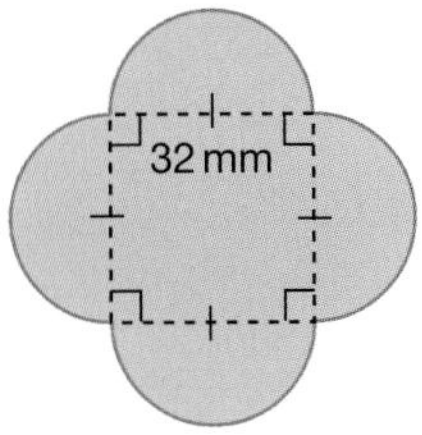

b
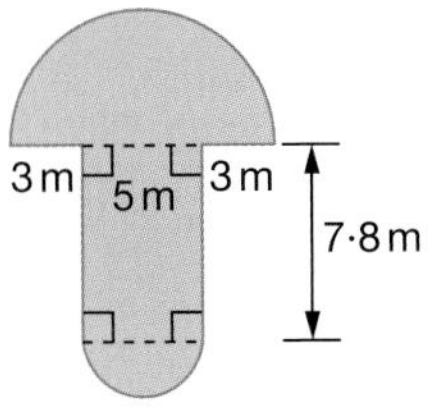

c
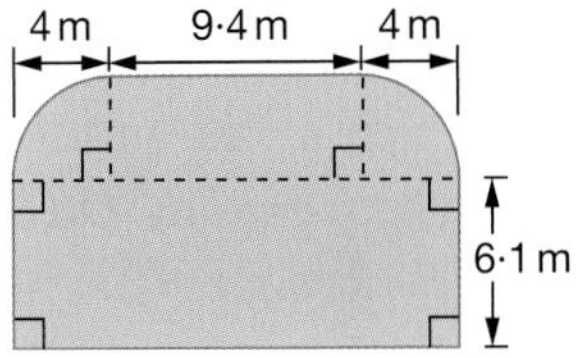

6 Calculate the shaded area of each of the following figures, correct to one decimal place where necessary. All measurements are in metres.

a
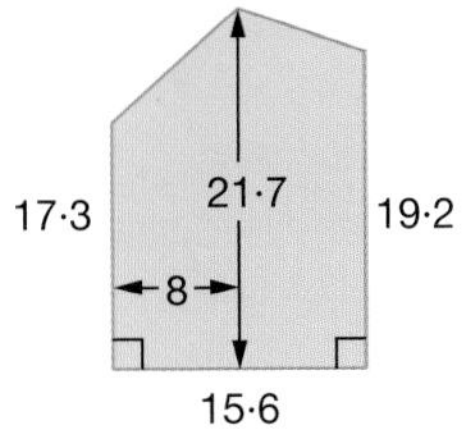

b
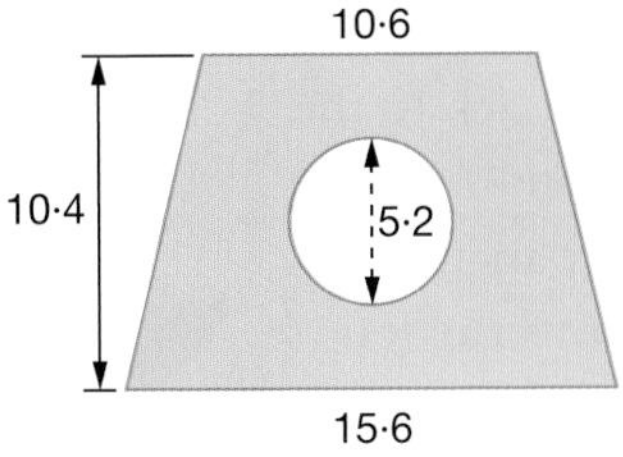

c
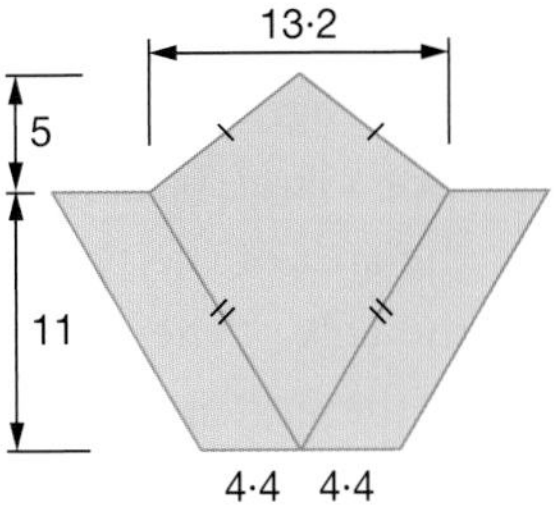

7 Find the shaded area of these figures correct to the nearest square centimetre.

a
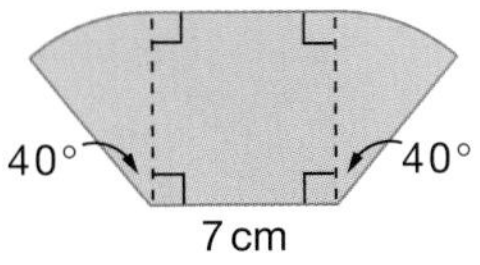

b
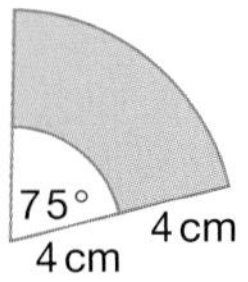

c
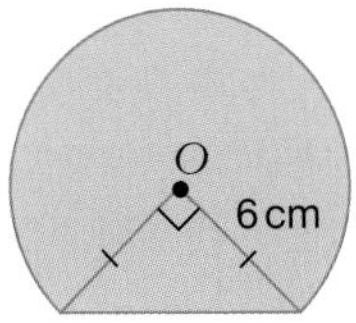

8 Calculate the shaded area in each of the following. All measurements are in centimetres. Give answers correct to one decimal place.

a

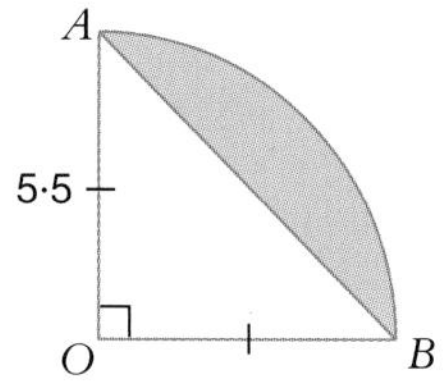

O is the centre of the circle, radius *OA*. Give the answer correct to two significant figures.

b

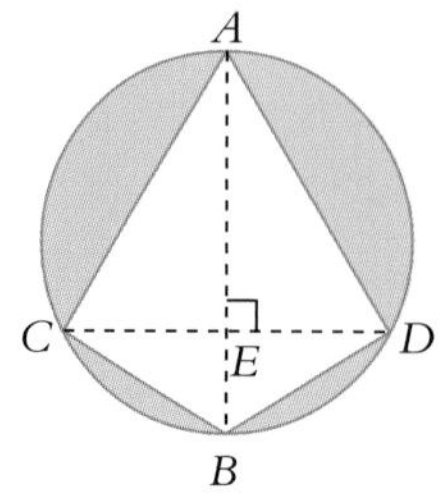

AB is a diameter of the circle. $AB = 26$ and $CD = 22$.

c

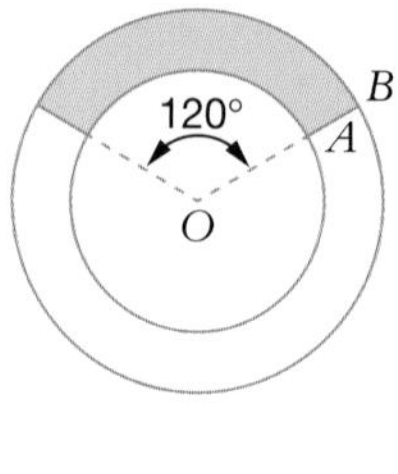

O is the centre. $OA = 10$ and $OB = 20$.

9 Calculate the area of the following figures. All measurements are in metres. In **b** and **c**, all arcs form semicircles. Give answers correct to one decimal place, where necessary.

a

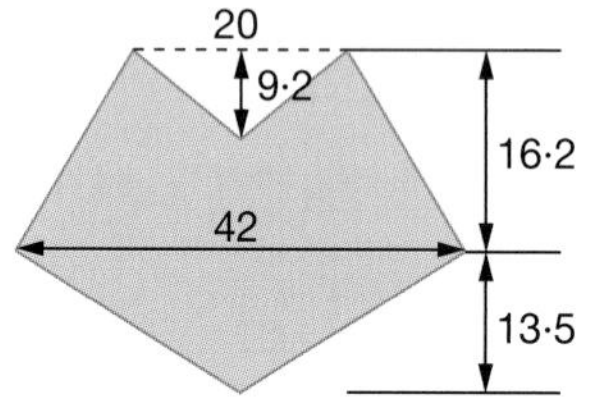

b

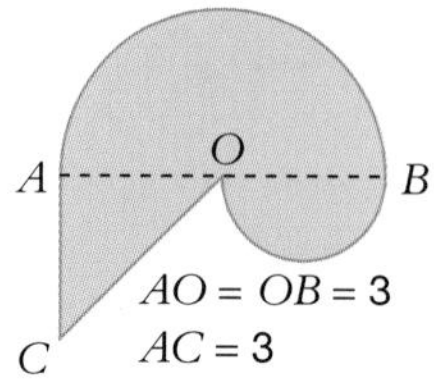

c

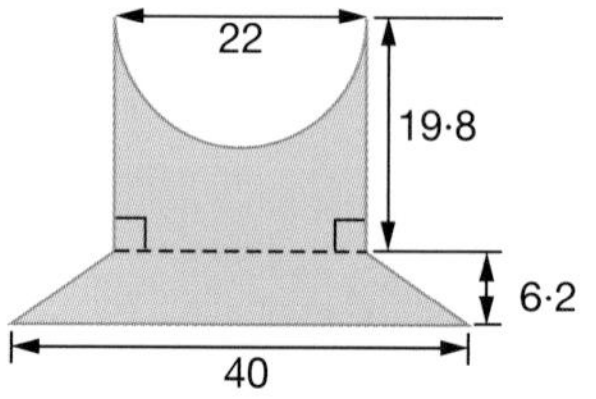

10 In the diagram shown, *BCDEF* is to be covered with tiles at a cost of \$90 per square metre. (All measurements are in metres.)

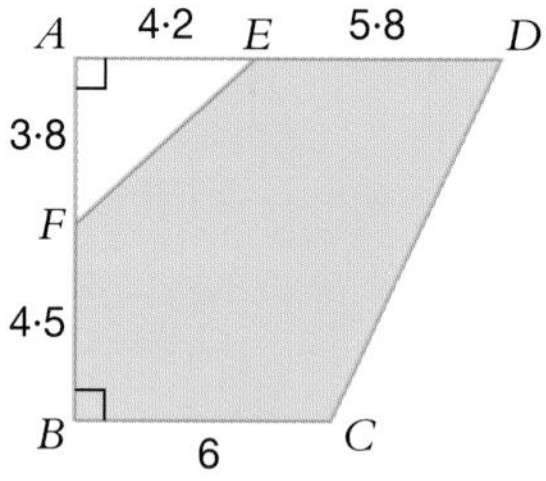

a Calculate the areas of:
   i trapezium *ABCD*
   ii triangle *AEF*.

b Use the answers from part a to find the area of *BCDEF*.

c What is the cost of tiling the floor?

11 The diagram shows a balcony built on the corner of an apartment block. Calculate the area of the balcony.

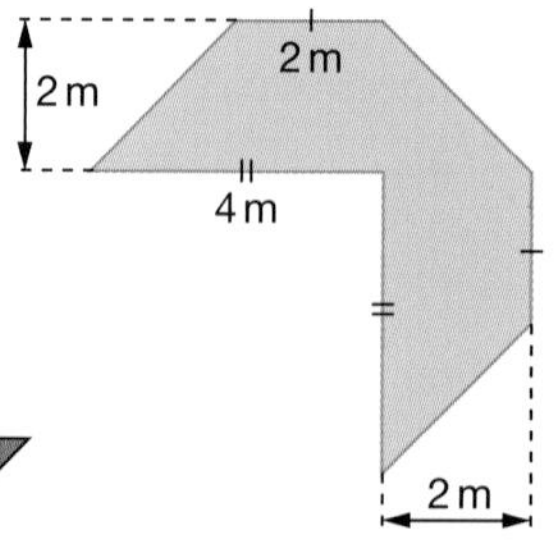

12 A metal sign is being made to attach to the side of a large building. Calculate:

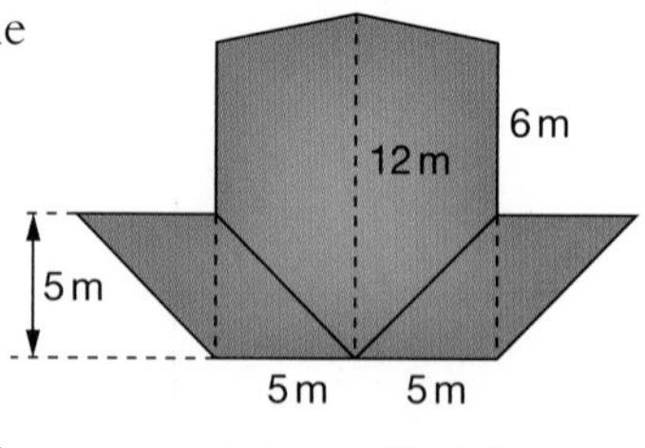

a the area of the sign in square metres

b the cost of the metal and construction of the sign at \$100 per square metre.

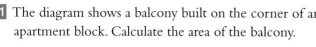

13 A fountain is to be surrounded by a paved area consisting of bricks of two different colours. One colour will form squares, whereas the other will form trapeziums. Calculate:

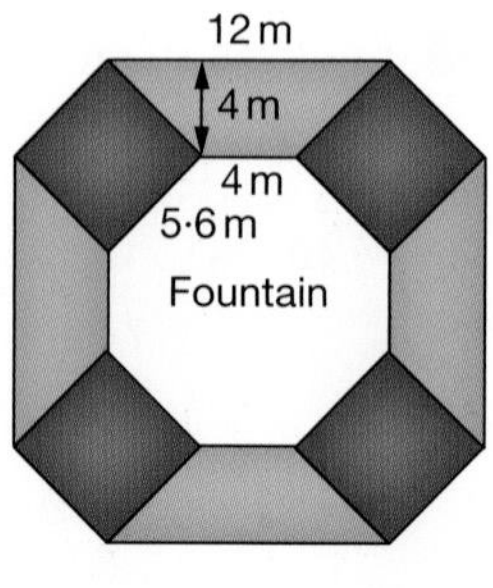

a the area of concrete needed to form the base of the fountain

b the area of bricks needed to make the squares

c the area of bricks needed to make the trapeziums

d the total cost of the job if the paving costs \$60 per m^2 and the concreting costs \$50 per m^2.

14 Find the cost of concreting the paths in the diagram if concreting costs \$50 per m^2. All paths are 0·9 m wide and all measurements are in metres.

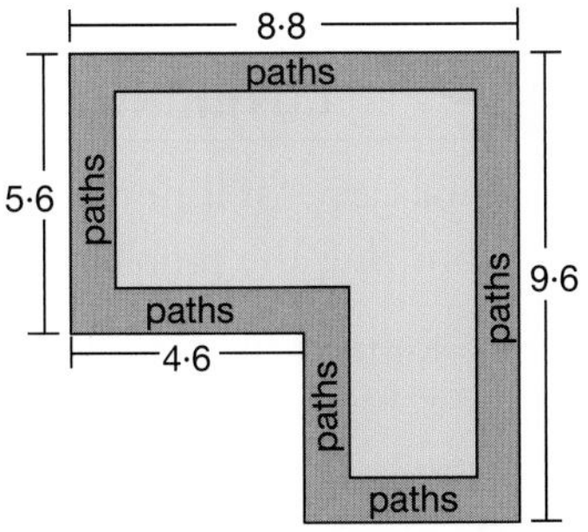

P GEOGEBRA ACTIVITY 5:01B AREAS OF COMPOSITE FIGURES

In this activity you can work through a series of diagrams of increasing complexity. Each of the diagrams can be changed by clicking and dragging points. Work out the area of each figure you have made and then check the answer by ticking a checkbox.

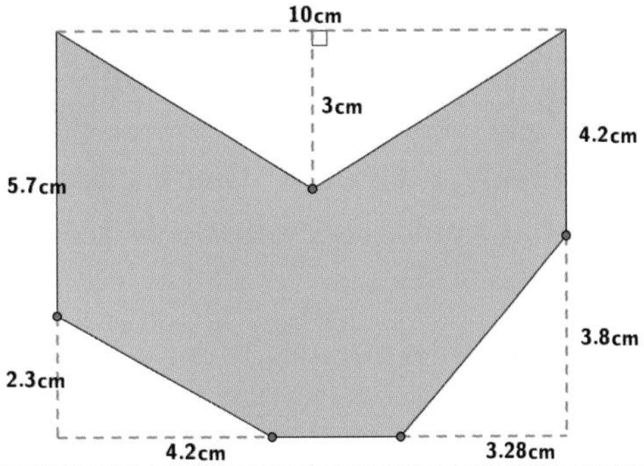

FUN SPOT 5:01 WHY IS IT SO NOISY AT TENNIS?

Answer each equation and write the letter for that question in the box above the correct answer.

A $(0{\cdot}1)^2$ **A** $6 - 1{\cdot}2$ **A** $0{\cdot}4 \div 0{\cdot}1$ **A** 120% of 10

A $\frac{1}{2} + \frac{1}{4}$ **A** $\frac{2}{3} \times 9$ **B** $7 \div \frac{1}{2}$ **C** $3 + 7 \times 2$

C $16 - 5 + 4$ **C** $24 \div (6 \div 2)$ **E** $(10 - 3)^2$ **E** $\frac{1}{2} - 0{\cdot}5$

E $6a + 2a$ **E** $7a - 2a$ **E** $8a - a$ **E** $3 \times 4a$

H $a \times 3^2$ **I** $12a \div 2$

K Evaluate $4x - 5$ if $x = 3$.

L Evaluate a^2 if $a = -3$.

P Simplify $5(2a - 4) + 20$.

R Simplify $6a + 3b - 5a + 3b$.

R Simplify $a(a + 8) - 3(a - 2)$.

R Simplify $a(a + 8) - a(a - 8)$.

S Simplify $\frac{8}{a} \times \frac{a}{8}$.

S Simplify $3 - 2(a - 8)$.

S Simplify $a(a - 1) - a^2$.

T Simplify $\frac{3a}{5} + \frac{2a}{5}$.

Of 15 people, 9 wore sneakers, 8 wore shorts and 3 wore neither sneakers nor shorts.

U How many people wore both sneakers and shorts?

Y How many people wore shorts but not sneakers?

14	$12a$	17	12	5	1	$5a$	$8a$	0·01	15	$9a$	$10a$	9	4·8	3	$7a$	$16a$

$a + 6b$	$\frac{3}{4}$	$6a$	$19 - 2a$	0	$-a$	6	$a^2 + 5a + 6$	4	8	7	49	a

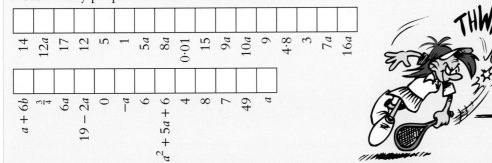

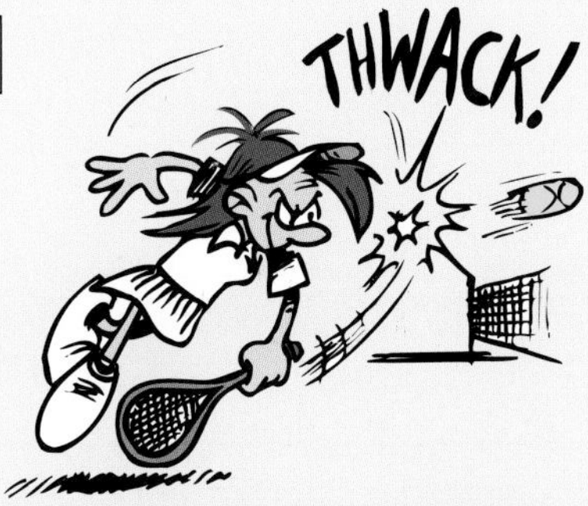

INVESTIGATION 5:01 COVERING FLOORS

When covering a floor with tiles or carpet it is not just a matter of calculating the area of the floor. Other practical considerations alter the problem.

The following examples illustrate some of the factors that need to be considered.

Laying tiles

When laying tiles, an exact number may not cover an area, or a whole number may not lie along each edge. Look at this diagram.

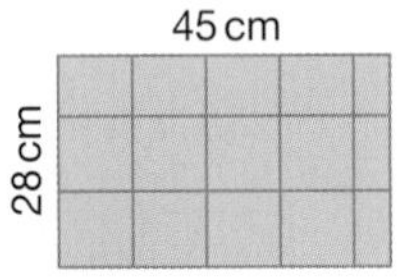

If the tiles are 10 cm by 10 cm, we can see that 15 tiles are needed, presuming that the pieces of tile cut off are not good enough to be used elsewhere. (This is true even though the area is 28 cm × 45 cm, i.e. 1260 cm^2. Divide this by 100 cm^2 (the tile area) and this would suggest that only 12·6 or 13 tiles might be needed.)

I think I've found an easy way to do these!

1 How many tiles 10 cm × 10 cm would be needed to cover an area 3·25 m by 2·17 m?

2 How many tiles 300 mm by 300 mm would be needed to cover an area 2·5 m by 3·8 m?

Laying carpet

Carpet comes in rolls, approximately 3·6 m wide. So when we buy a 'metre of carpet' we are getting a rectangular piece 3·6 m wide by 1 m long. The diagram below represents a room 2·9 m wide and 4·25 m long.

When laying carpet, a carpetlayer can 'run' it *along* the room or *across* the room. The aim is to avoid joins in the carpet and reduce waste. The way the carpet is run will determine how many 'metres of carpet' must be bought.

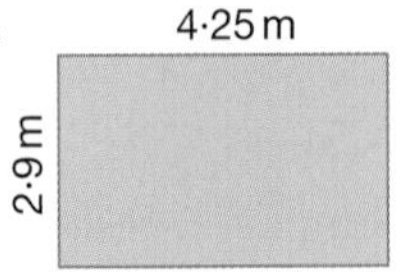

1 How many metres of carpet must be bought if it is run lengthways? How much waste would there be? Would there be any joins?

2 Repeat Question 1 for the carpet if it is run across the room.

5:02 Surface area of a prism

PREP QUIZ 5:02

1 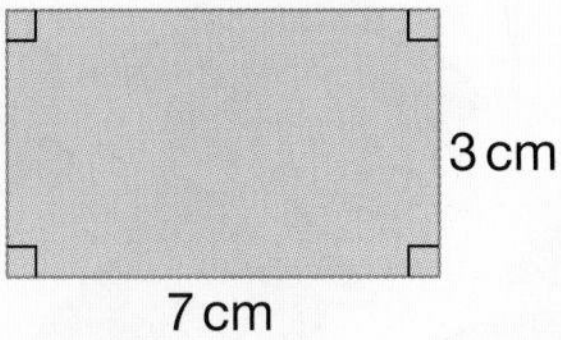

Area = …

2 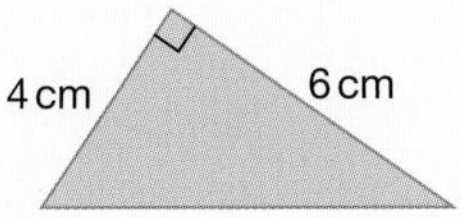

Area = …

3 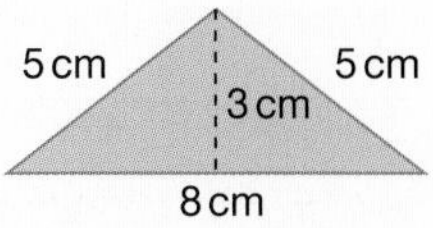

Area = …

For a cube:

4 How many faces are there?

5 What shape are the faces?

For a rectangular prism:

6 How many faces are there?

7 What shape are the faces?

8 Which faces are congruent?

9 How many faces has a triangular prism?

10 Use Pythagoras' theorem to find x in this triangle.

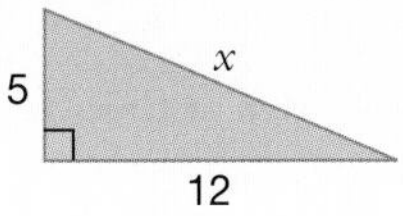

If we look at solid shapes such as those pictured below, we can see that the faces of these solids are plane shapes.

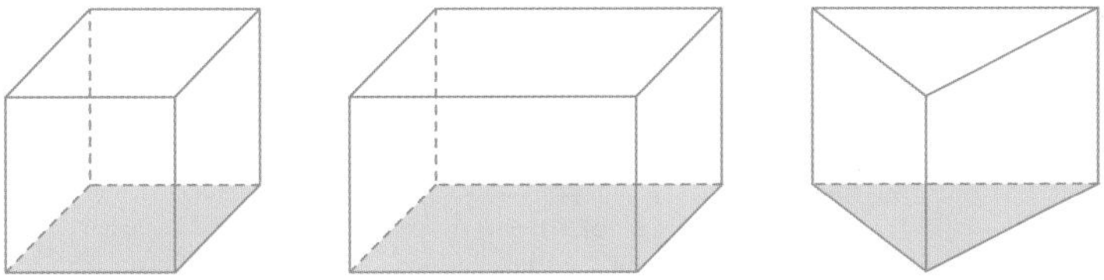

The surface area of a solid is the sum of the areas of its faces.

To calculate the surface area of a solid, you must know the number of faces, the shapes of the faces and whether the solid is *open* or *closed*. A closed solid has a top. An open prism does not have a top. In this section, assume that a solid is closed unless it is stated that it is open.

The net of a solid shows how the faces of the solid appear when the solid is flattened out. As the net consists of all the faces of the solid, the area of the net is equal to the surface area of the solid.

A rectangular prism has three pairs of faces with equal areas. Hence, the surface area can be given by the formula:

$$\text{Surface area} = 2LB + 2LH + 2BH$$
$$= 2(LB + LH + BH)$$

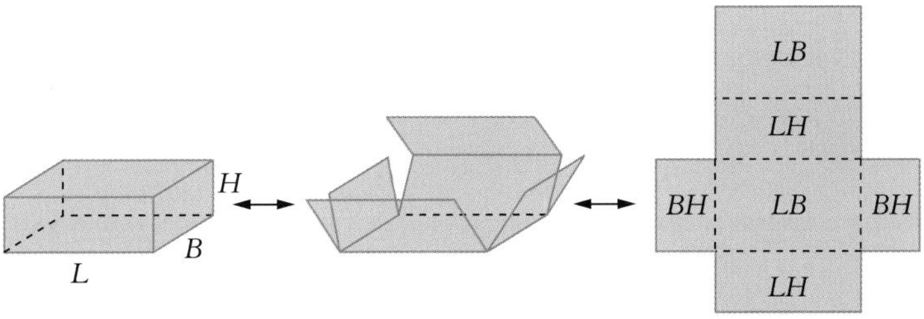

WORKED EXAMPLE 1

Use the nets to find the surface area of the following prisms. (All measurements are in centimetres).

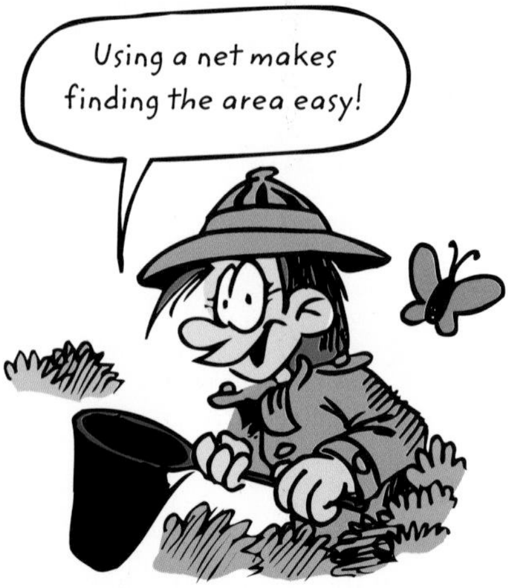

a

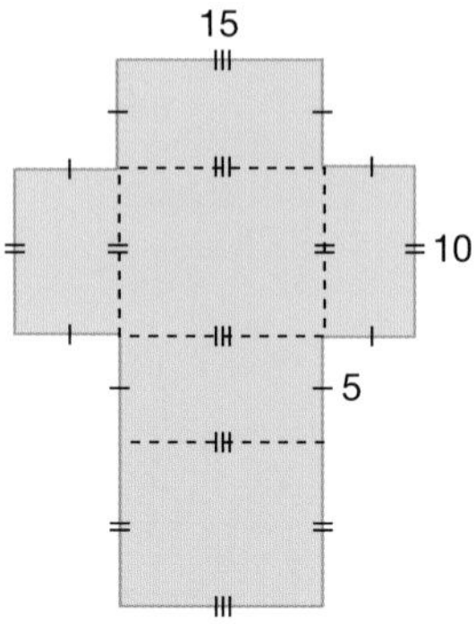

Surface area
= area of net
$= 2 \times (10 \times 5) + 2 \times (15 \times 5) + 2 \times (15 \times 10)$
$= 550\,\text{cm}^2$

The formula can also be used as follows.

Surface area $= 2(LB + LH + BH)$
$= 2(15 \times 10 + 15 \times 5 + 10 \times 5)$
$= 550\,\text{cm}^2$

b

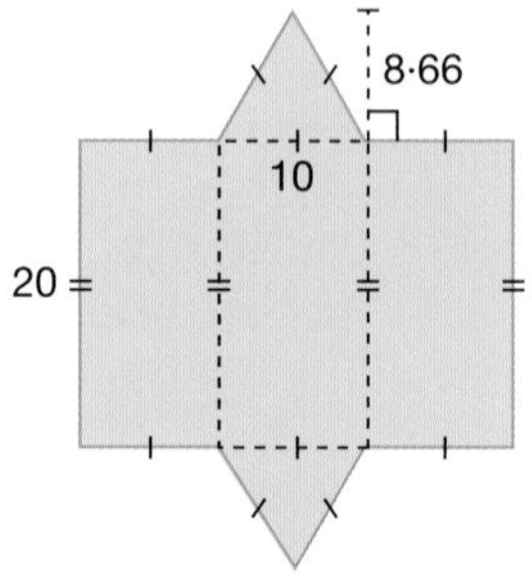

Surface area
= area of net
$= 3 \times (10 \times 20) + 2 \times \frac{1}{2} \times (10 \times 8{\cdot}66)$
$= 686{\cdot}6\,\text{cm}^2$

Note: A formula is generally not used to calculate the surface area of triangular prisms.

WORKED EXAMPLE 2

Find the surface area of the following prisms.

a

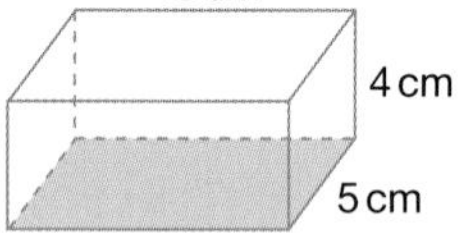

Surface area
$= 2(LB + LH + BH)$
$= 2(10 \times 5) + 10 \times 4 + 5 \times 4)$
$= 220\,\text{cm}^2$

Tips on finding surface area

1 Make a sketch of the solid or its net. Find all necessary dimensions.
2 Check if the solid is open or closed, especially in practical problems.
3 Calculate the areas of the faces (or the net).
4 Different methods can be used. Select a method that suits you.

b

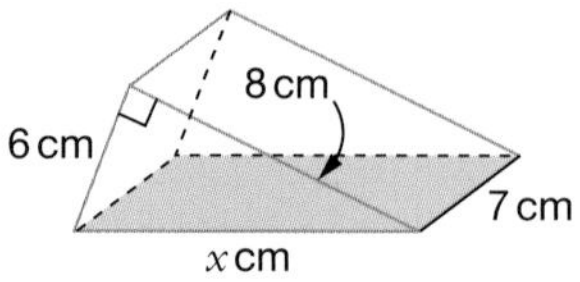

Calculate the width of the bottom using Pythagoras' theorem.

Now $x^2 = 6^2 + 8^2$
$\therefore x^2 = 100$
$\therefore x = 10$

Surface area
= area of triangular faces + area of rectangular faces
$= 2 \times \frac{1}{2} \times 6 \times 8 + (6 + 8 + 10) \times 7$
$= 216\,\text{cm}^2$

WORKED EXAMPLE 3

Find the surface area of this prism.

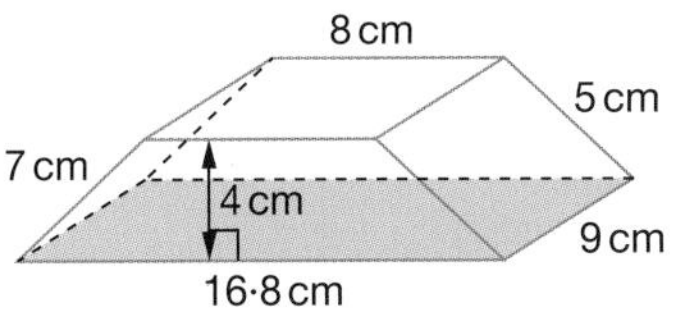

Area of trapezoidal faces

$= 2 \times \frac{1}{2}h(a + b)$

$= 2 \times \frac{1}{2} \times 4 \times (16{\cdot}8 + 8)$

$= 99{\cdot}2\,\text{cm}^2$

Area of rectangular faces

$= (7 + 8 + 5 + 16.8) \times 9$

$= 331{\cdot}2\,\text{cm}^2$

$\therefore$ Surface area $= 331{\cdot}2 + 99{\cdot}2\,\text{cm}^2$

$= 430{\cdot}4\,\text{cm}^2$

Exercise 5:02

Foundation worksheet 5:02
Surface area of prisms

1 For each of the following nets find:

i its area

ii the name of the solid that it produces when folded along the dotted lines

iii whether the prism is open or closed.

a

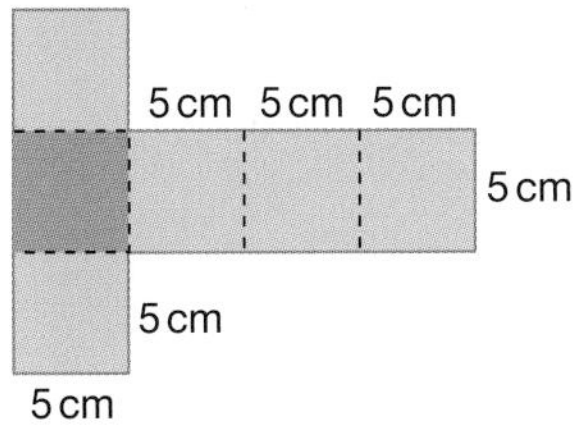

b

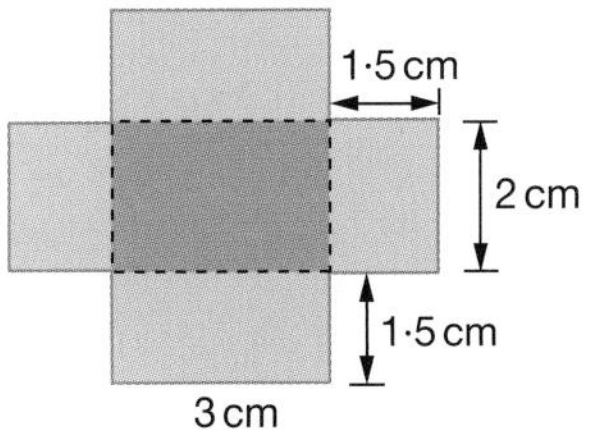

c

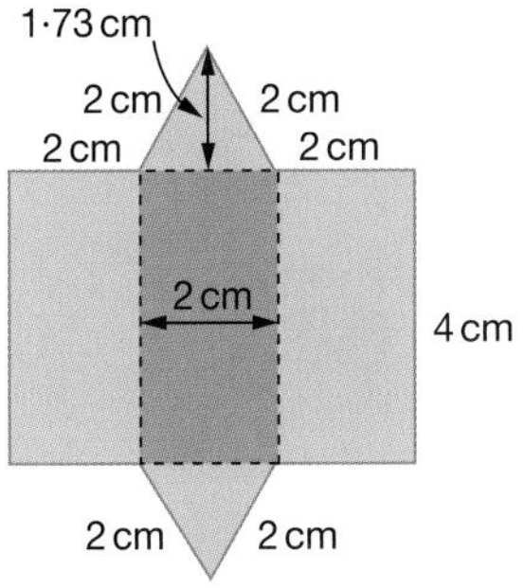

d

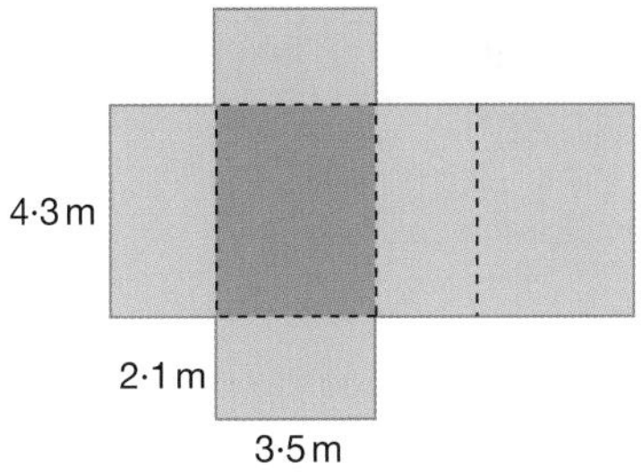

e

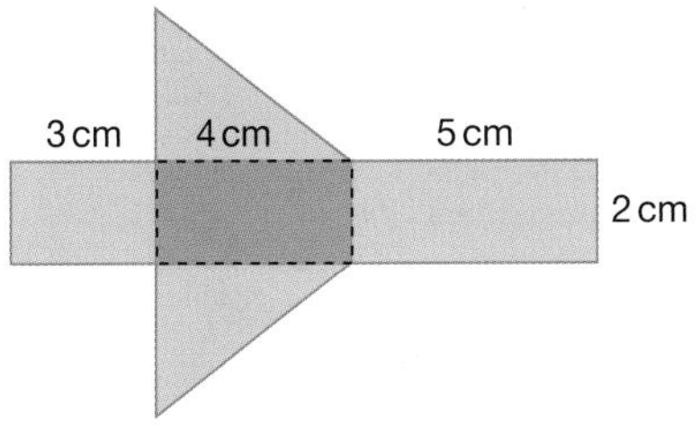

f

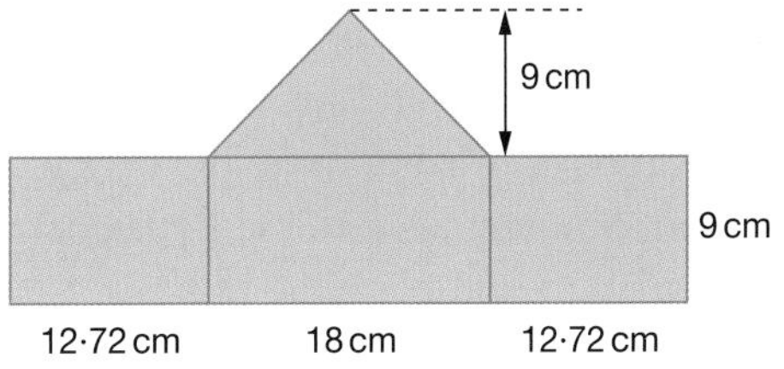

2 Copy and complete the following for the rectangular prism on the right.

Area of top and bottom = …

Area of sides = …

Area of front and back = …

Total surface area = …

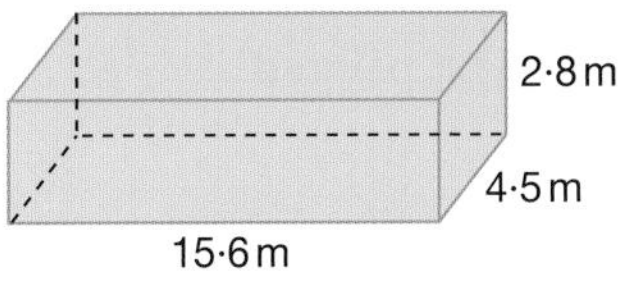

3 Find the surface area of each of these triangular prisms.

a 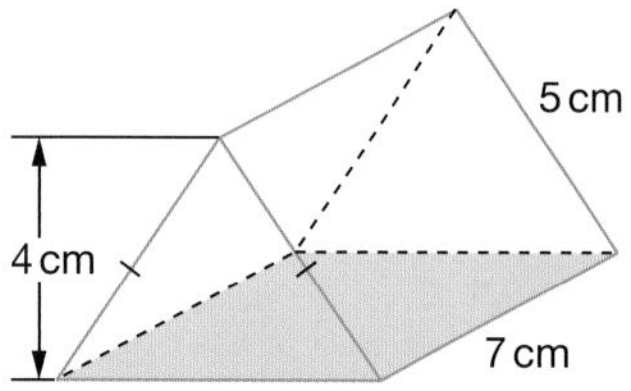

b 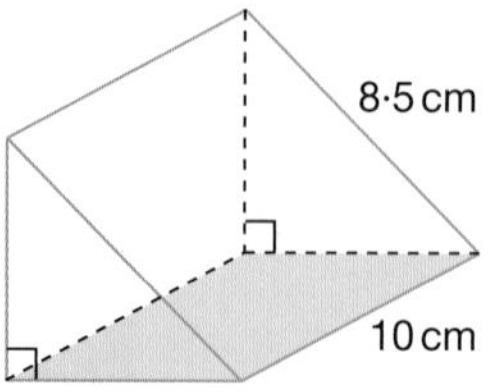

c 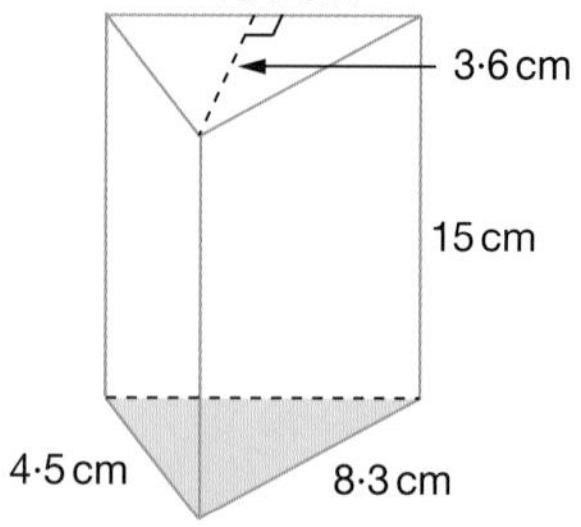

4 Find the surface areas of the following prisms.

a an open cube with an edge length of 10 cm

b a closed rectangular prism 25 cm long, 20 cm wide and 15 cm high

c an open square prism with dimensions 2 m, 2 m and 0·75 m that is missing a rectangular face

Closed prisms have a top.
Open prisms have no top.

5 In each of the following, use Pythagoras' theorem to calculate the unknown length, x, correct to two decimal places, and then calculate the surface area of the solid.

a 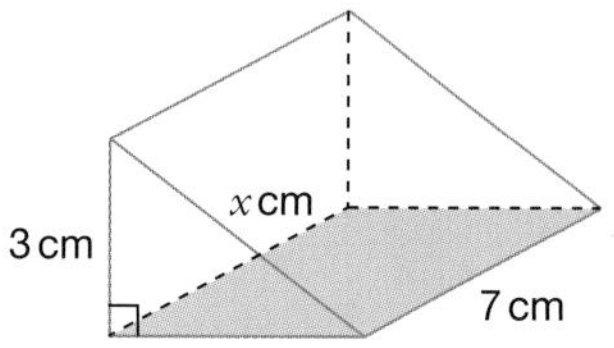

b 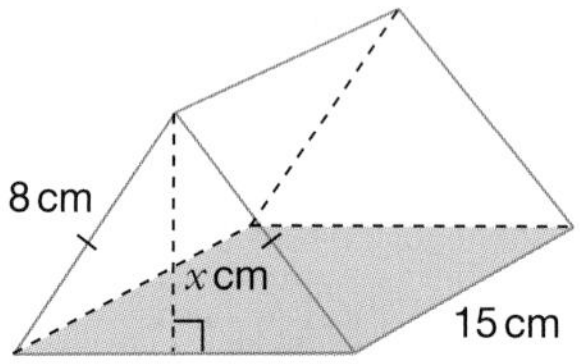

c 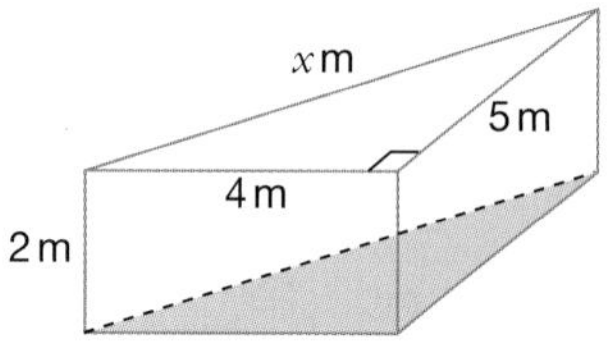

Caution:

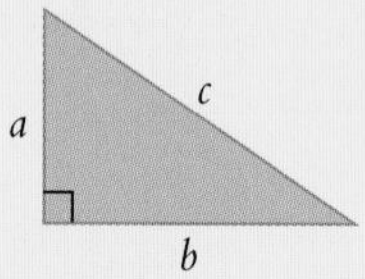

$c^2 = a^2 + b^2$

Right-angled triangles!

6 A chocolate package is in the shape of a triangular prism. The triangle is equilateral with a side edge of 4 cm. What is the area of cardboard used to make the package? (*Note:* You will need to use Pythagoras' theorem to find the value of *h*.)

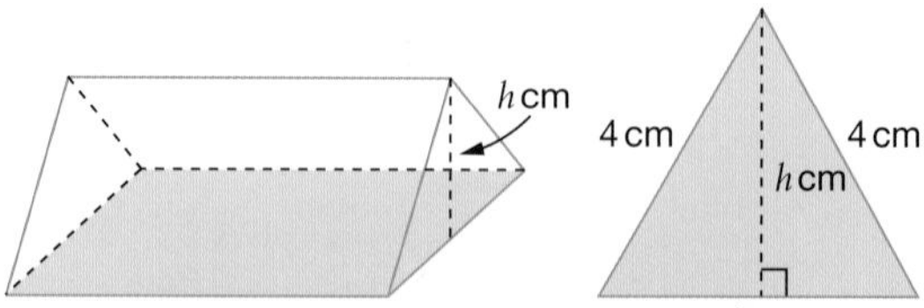

7 The diagram shows a room in the shape of a rectangular prism. The room has two windows and a door that have a combined area of 5·52 m². Calculate the area of the internal walls that need to be painted.

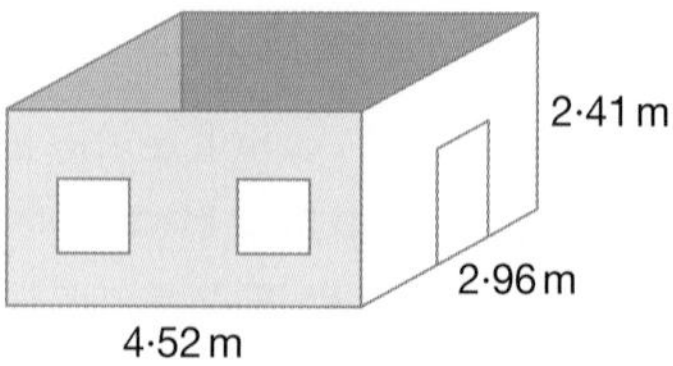

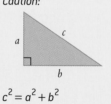

8 Four small cartons are to be stacked and wrapped in cardboard for shipping. The small carton is a square prism with dimensions 20 cm, 20 cm and 10 cm. Which of the two stacks shown will use the smaller amount of cardboard?

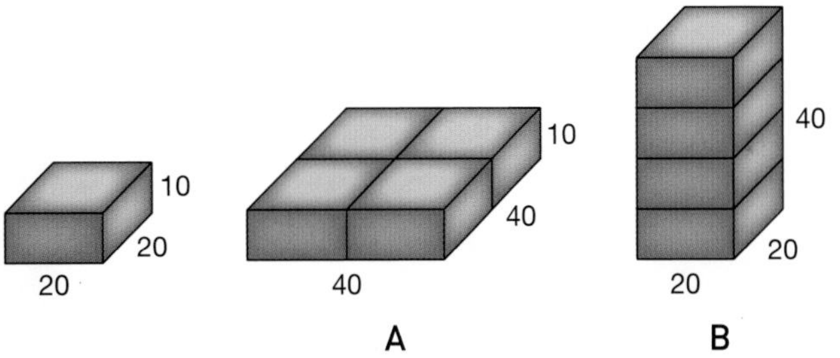

9 A tent has the shape of a triangular prism with dimensions as shown in the diagram.

a Find the area of material needed to make this tent. (Include the floor area.)

b If the material comes in rolls that are 3·7 m wide, what length of material must be purchased so that the tent can be made without any joins except those at the edges? (Hint: Consider the net of the solid.)

c If special joining tape is needed to strengthen each join, what length of tape will be needed?

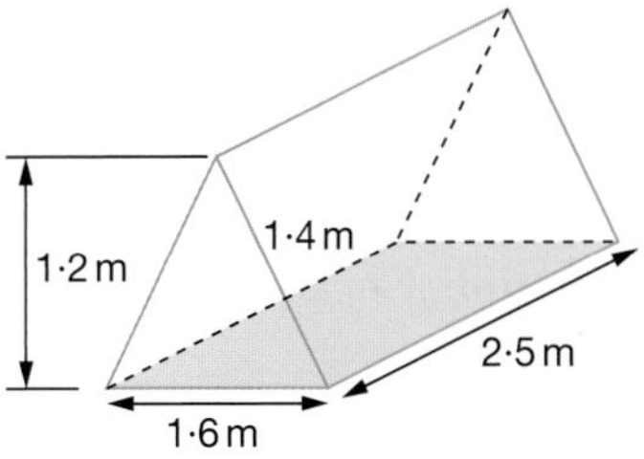

10 Find the surface area of each of the following trapezoidal prisms.

a

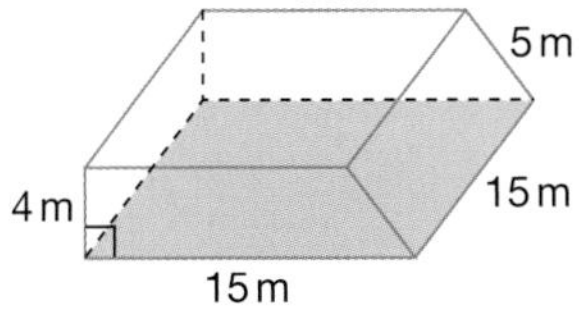

b

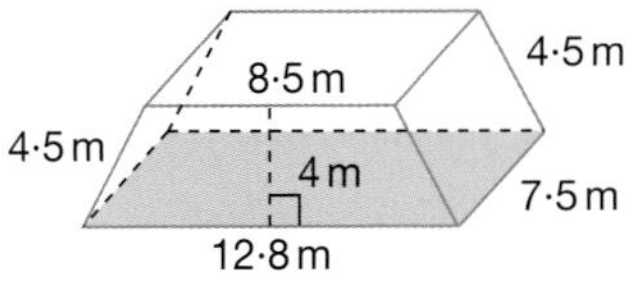

c

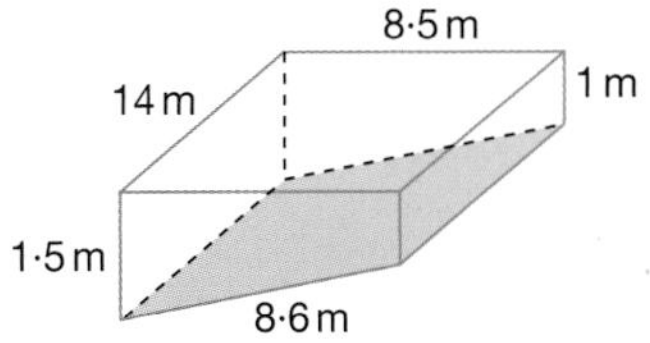

11 In each of the following questions, use Pythagoras' theorem to calculate the unknown length, x, correct to two decimal places, and then calculate the surface area.

a

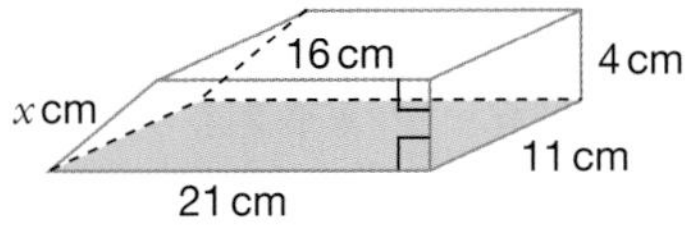

b

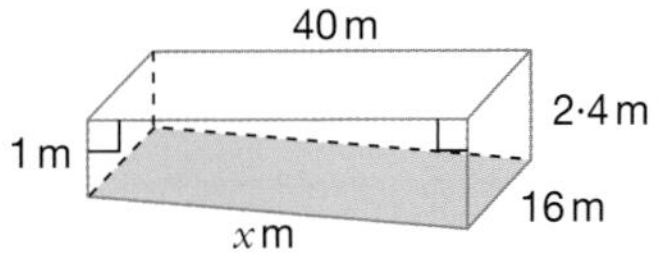

12 A swimming pool has the shape of a trapezoidal prism as shown in the diagram. If this pool is to be tiled, find the cost of tiling it at \$45 per square metre.

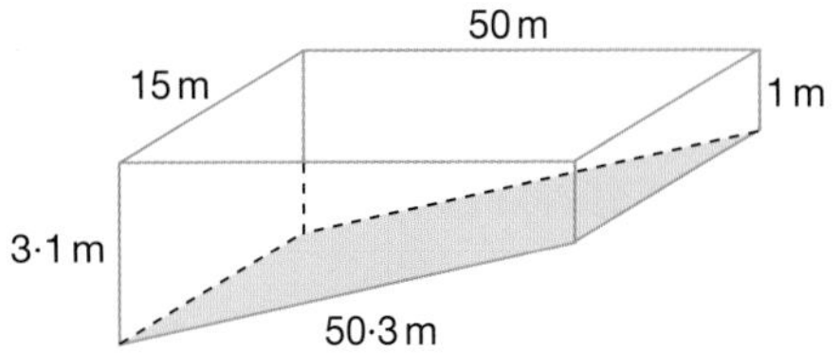

13 Find the surface areas of the following prisms. All measurements are in centimetres.

a

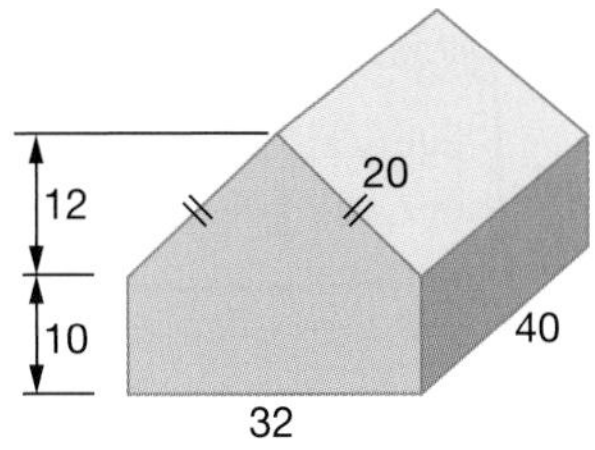

b

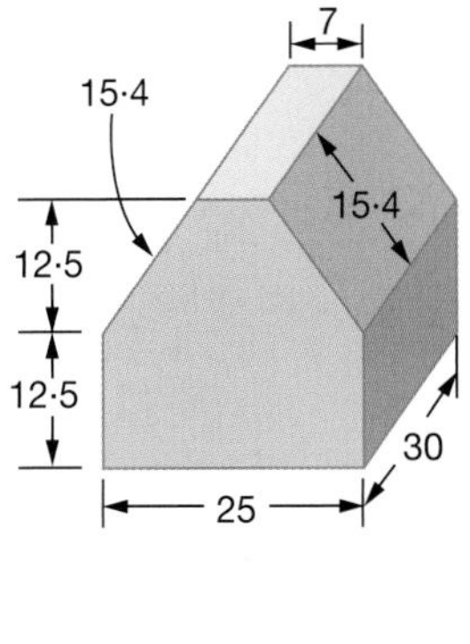

c

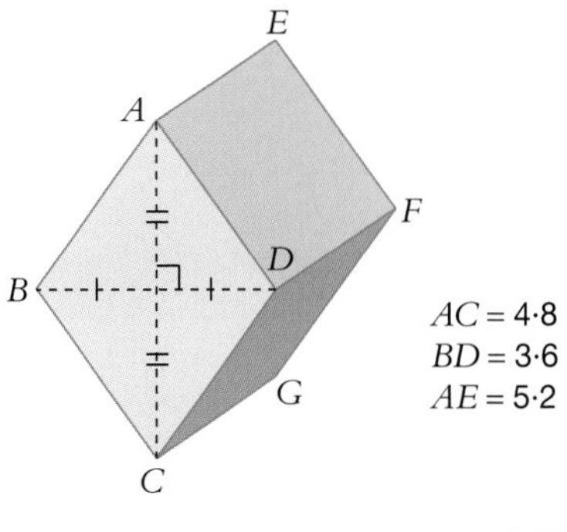

14 A marquee is in the shape of a pentagonal prism. Use the dimensions shown to calculate the surface area. (There is no floor.)

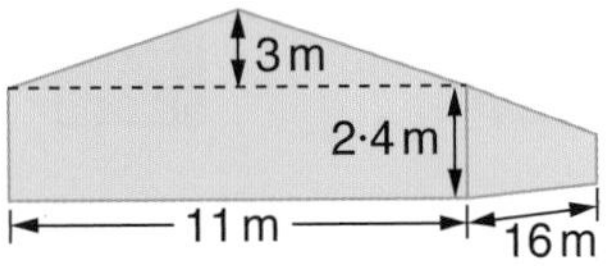

P GEOGEBRA ACTIVITY 5:02 SURFACE AREA OF A RECTANGULAR PRISM

Use a 3D view and the net of a prism to calculate its surface area. Tick a checkbox to show the solution. Click and drag points to change the dimensions of the prism.

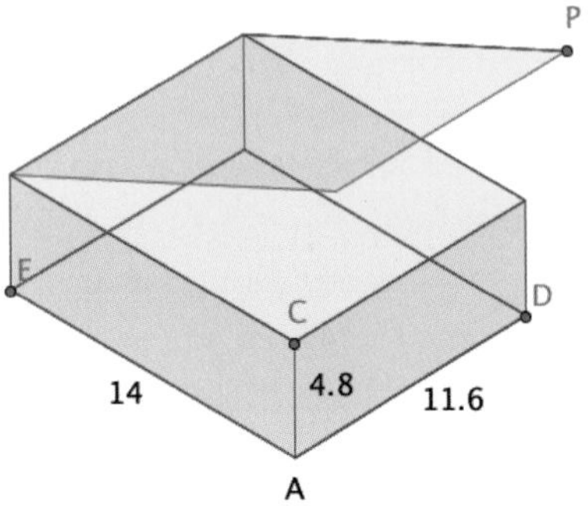

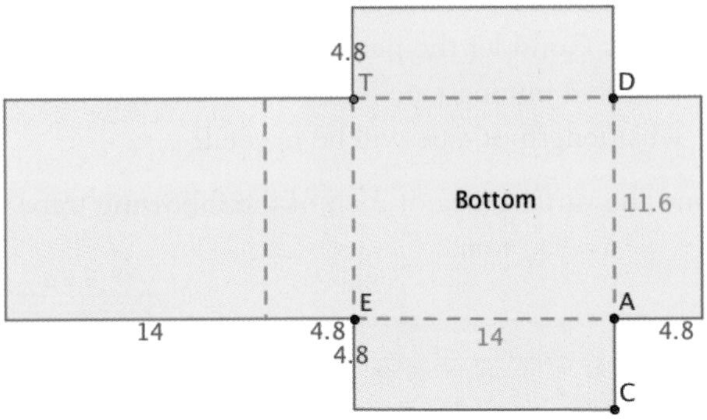

5:03 Surface area of a cylinder

In all of the solids encountered so far the faces have been plane figures such as squares, rectangles, triangles and trapeziums.

With the cylinder, this is no longer the case. The cylinder's surface area is made up of a curved surface and two circles.

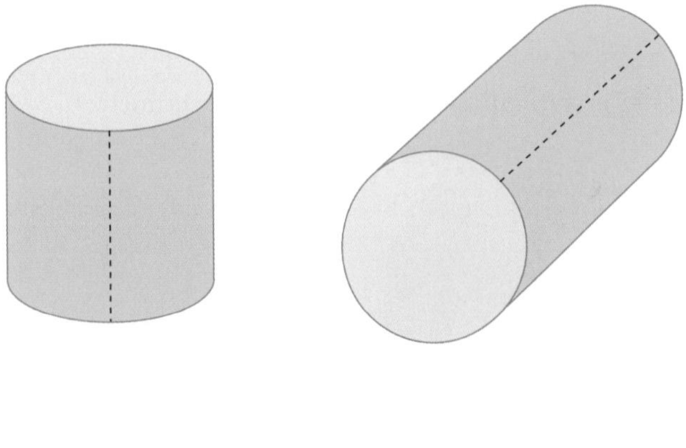

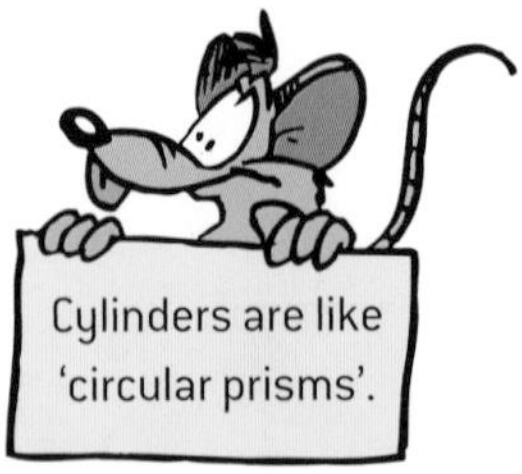

To calculate the area of the curved surface, imagine that the cylinder is hollow. If we cut the curved surface along the dotted line and flattened it out it would form a rectangle.

The area of this rectangle would be the same as the area of the curved surface.

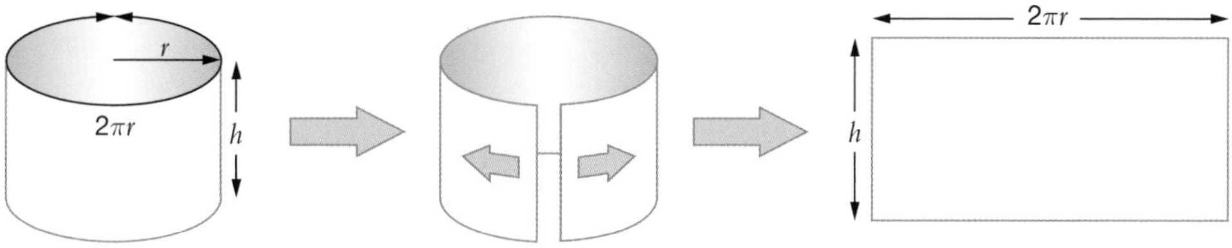

From the series of diagrams above, we see that the curved surface area is equivalent to a rectangle that has a length equal to the circumference of the circle and a width equal to the height of the cylinder. Using the formula for the area of a rectangle we obtain the following formula.

Curved surface area = $2\pi rh$

To find the surface area of the cylinder we add the area of the two circular ends.

Surface area = curved surface area + area of circles
$= 2\pi rh + 2\pi r^2$

PREP QUIZ 5:03

1 Evaluate πr^2, correct to two decimal places, if $r = 1{\cdot}6$.
2 Evaluate $2\pi rh$, correct to three significant figures, if $r = 15{\cdot}6$ and $h = 3{\cdot}8$.
3 If the diameter of a circle is 16 cm, what is the radius?
4 If the radius of a circle is 6·5 cm, what is the diameter?

Questions **5–10** refer to these cylinders.

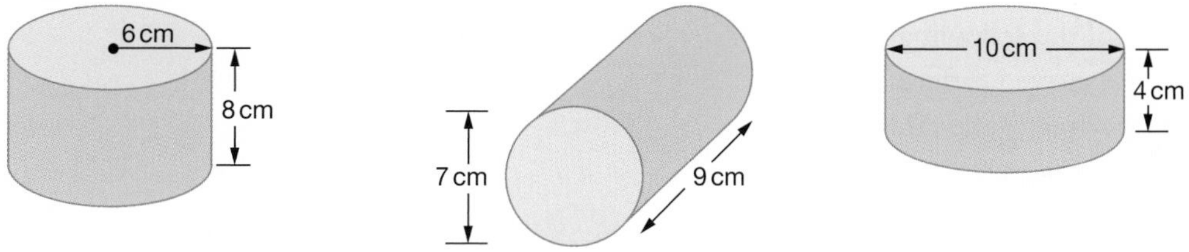

5 Radius = …
6 Height = …
7 Radius = …
8 Height = …
9 $r =$ …
10 $h =$ …

WORKED EXAMPLES

1 Find the surface area of a cylinder that has a radius of 8 cm and a height of 9·5 cm. Give your answer correct to two decimal places.

2 For cylinder A, find:

a the curved surface area

b the area of the circular ends

c the surface area.

Give the answers correct to three significant figures.

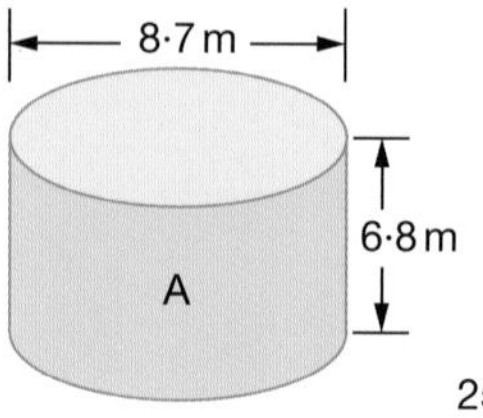

3 Find the curved surface area of cylinder B, correct to one decimal place.

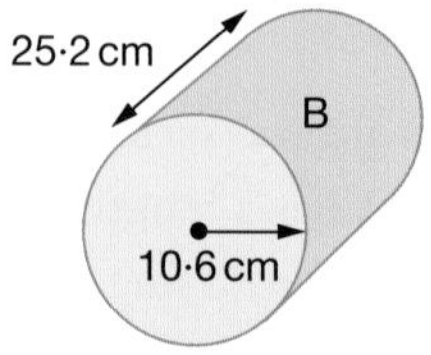

Solutions

1 Surface area $= 2\pi r^2 + 2\pi rh$

$= 2 \times \pi \times 8^2 + 2 \times \pi \times 8 \times 9{\cdot}5$

$= 879{\cdot}65\ \text{cm}^2$ (2 dec. pl.)

2 a Curved surface area

$= 2\pi rh$

$= 2\pi \times 4{\cdot}35 \times 6{\cdot}8$

$= 59{\cdot}16\pi$

$= 186\ \text{m}^2$ (3 sig. fig.)

b Area of circular ends

$= 2\pi r^2$

$= 2\pi \times (4{\cdot}35)^2$

$= 37{\cdot}845\pi$

$= 119\ \text{m}^2$ (3 sig. fig.)

c Surface area

$= 59{\cdot}16\pi + 37{\cdot}845\pi$

$= 305\ \text{m}^2$ (3 sig. fig.)

3 Curved surface area

$= 2\pi rh$

$= 2 \times \pi \times 10{\cdot}6 \times 25{\cdot}2$

$= 1678{\cdot}4\ \text{cm}^2$ (1 dec. pl.)

Exercise 5:03

P Foundation worksheet 5:03
Surface area of a cylinder

1 Find the area of the curved surfaces of the following cylinders. Give your answers correct to two decimal places.

a radius = 8 cm
height = 10 cm

b radius = 4 cm
height = 15 cm

c diameter = 3·6 m
height = 1·8 m

d diameter = 15·7 cm
height = 18·6 cm

2 For each of the following cylinders find, correct to two decimal places:

i the curved surface area

ii the area of the circular ends

iii the total surface area.

a
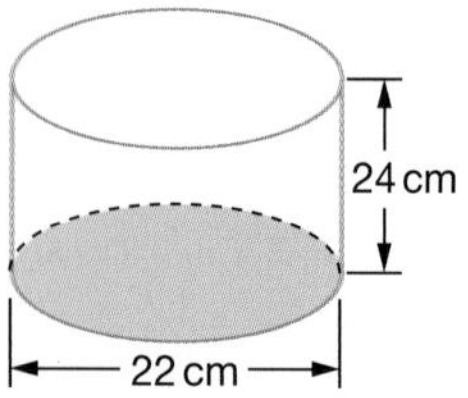

b
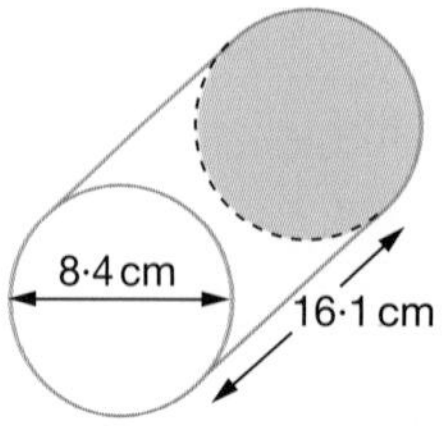

c
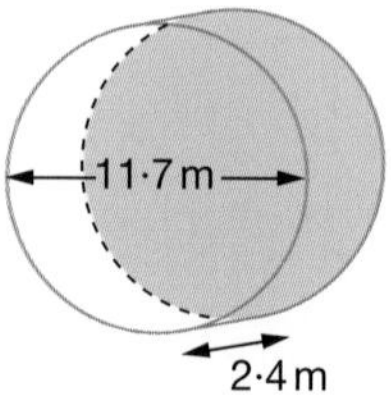

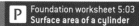

d

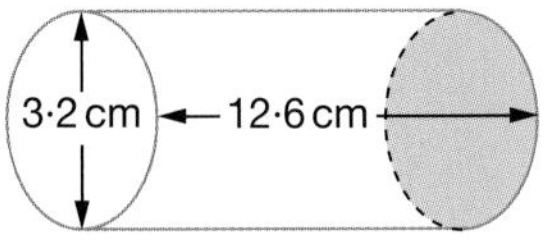

e

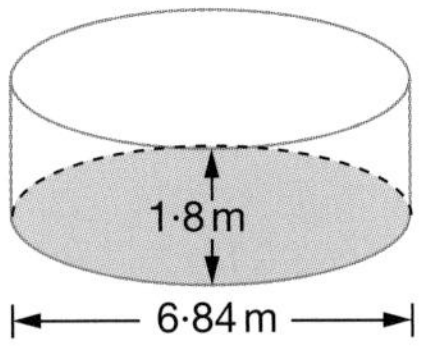

f

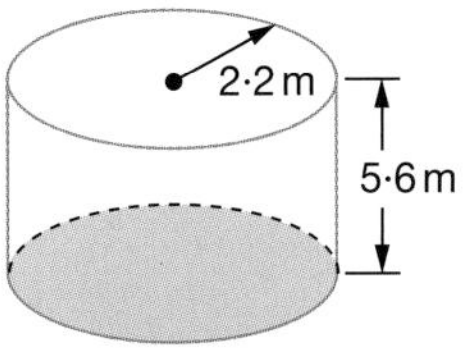

3 Find the surface areas of the following cylinders, giving your answers correct to two significant figures.

a diameter = 14·6 m, height = 95 cm

b radius = 90 cm, height = 3·6 m

c diameter = 2·4 m, height = 750 mm

d radius = 50 mm, height = 75 cm

> *Remember:*
> All measurements must be in the same units.

4 A swimming pool is cylindrical. It has a diameter of 7 m and a depth of 1·2 m. Find the area of the curved surface. Give your answer correct to one decimal place.

5 A cylindrical paint can has a diameter of 25 cm and a height of 30 cm. Calculate the area of metal needed to make the can, including the lid.

6 A silo is cylindrical. It is 25 m high and has a diameter of 7·4 m. Calculate the cost of spraying the curved surface of the silo with a spray-on concrete mixture if it costs $30 per square metre.

7 A cylindrical water tank (with top) has a radius of 2·1 m and a height of 3·2 m. The tank is to be painted inside and outside with rust-preventive paint. Find:

a the total area to be painted, correct to one decimal place

b the cost of the paint, if it is $10.25 per square metre.

8 Ten concrete cylinders are used as fishponds. Each cylinder is 1·5 m high and has an internal diameter of 2 m. The inside of each cylinder is to be treated with a waterproofing paint. Find:

a the total area that needs to be covered to the nearest square metre

b the cost of the treatment if the charge is $70 per square metre.

9 The diagrams show a 1-litre paint can and a 2-litre paint can.

a Calculate the surface area of each can, correct to one decimal place.

b Based on the surface area of metal used, is it cheaper to sell 2 litres of paint in one 2 L can or two 1 L cans?

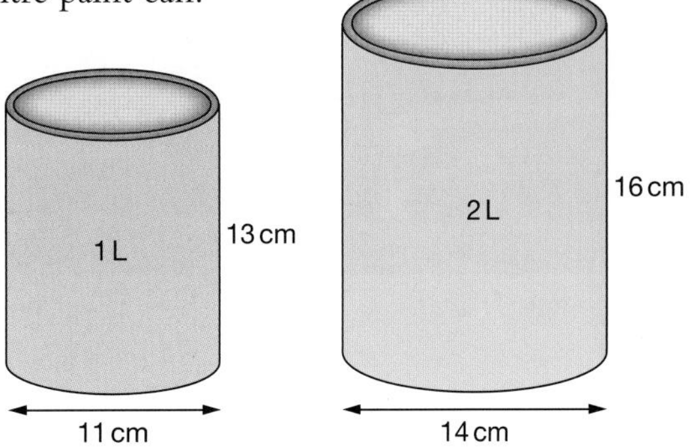

10 The following solids have been formed from a cylinder. Calculate the surface area of each, correct to three significant figures.

a

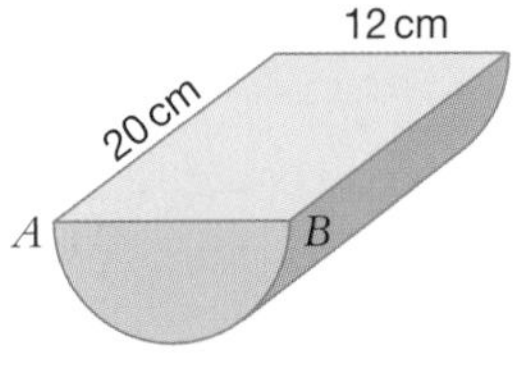

AB is a diameter.

b

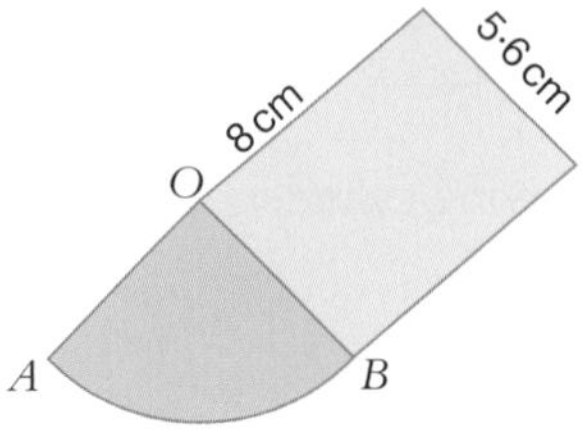

AOB is a quadrant.

11 Calculate the surface area of each of these solids.

a

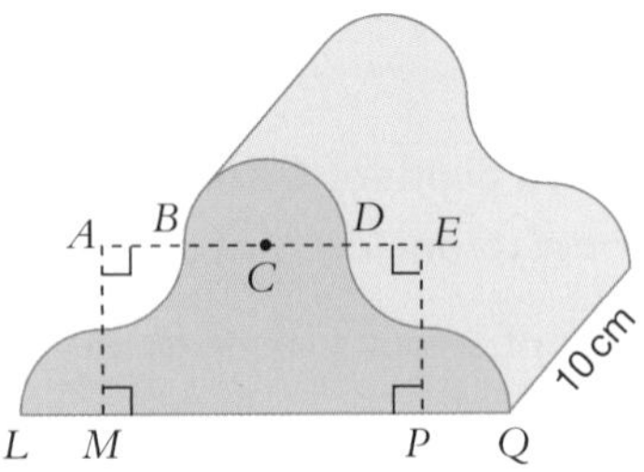

$AB = BC = CD = DE = 5$ cm
$LM = PQ = 5$ cm

b

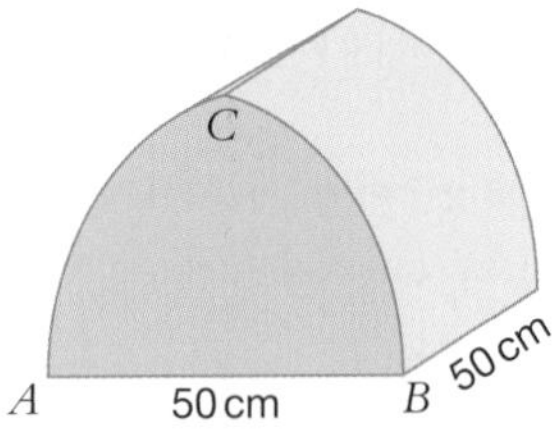

AC is an arc of a circle with centre B.
BC is an arc of a circle with centre A.

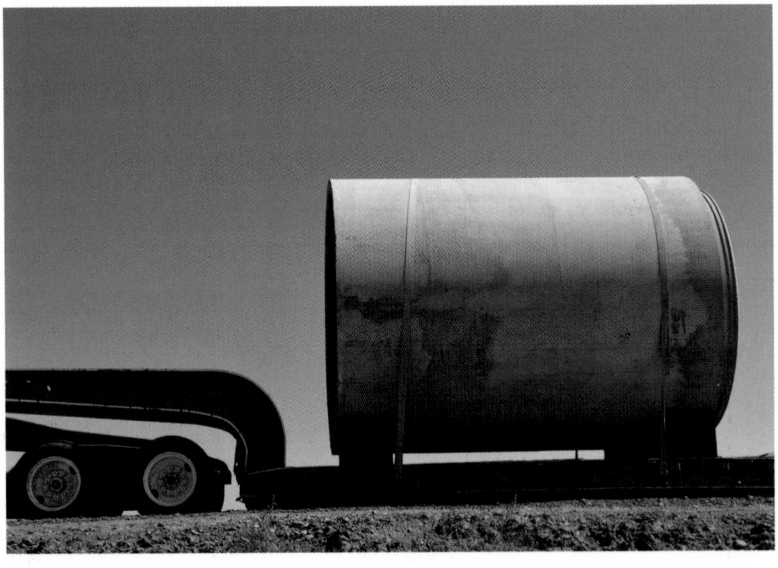

How could the surface area of this large-diameter cylindrical pipe be estimated?

FUN SPOT 5:03

HOW DID THE BOY KNOW HE HAD AN AFFINITY WITH THE SEA?

Answer each question and write the letter for that question in the box above the correct answer.

A $7^2 + 6^2$

E $\sqrt{5^2 + 12^2}$

H $9^2 - 4^2$

T $\sqrt{13^2 - 5^2}$

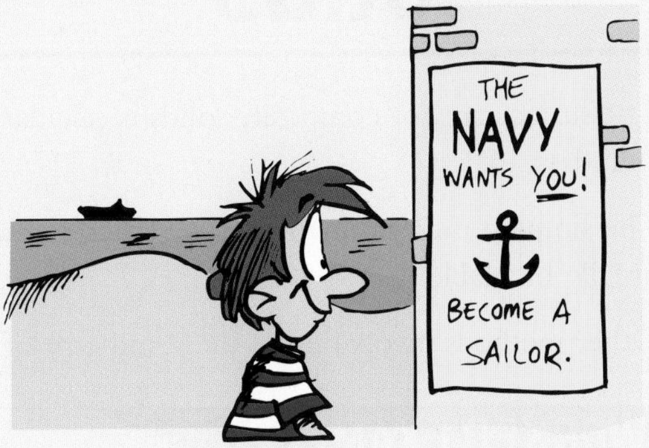

Complete the following.

W 3·5 m = … cm

A 20 000 m^2 = … ha

E 0·7 cm = … mm

H 8700 kg = … t

N 0·07 L = … mL

T 0·5 min = … s

C 1 t = … g

D 1 g = … mg

I 1 cm^2 = … mm^2

E 2 cm^3 = … mm^3

Write the basic numeral for:

A $1·6 \times 10^2$

E $1·6 \times 10^{-2}$

H 7×10^{-3}

W 7×10^3

Figures A, B and C below have been formed by cutting rectangular pieces from a rectangle that is 30 cm long and 18 cm wide.

Find the perimeters of:

O Figure A

T Figure B

W Figure C

Find the areas of:

E Figure A

S Figure B

V Figure C

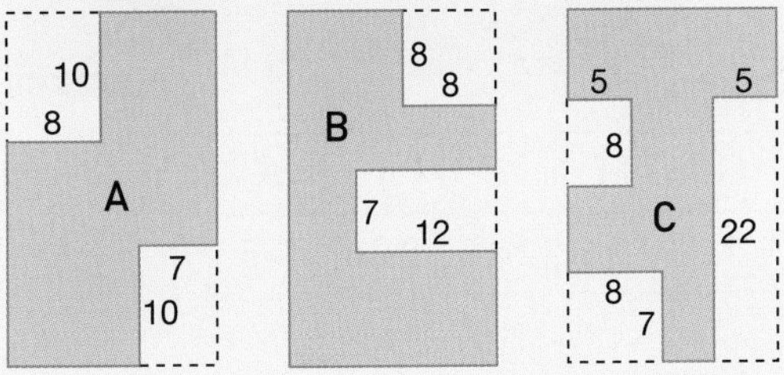

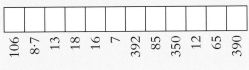

Calculate the area of each pentagon below.

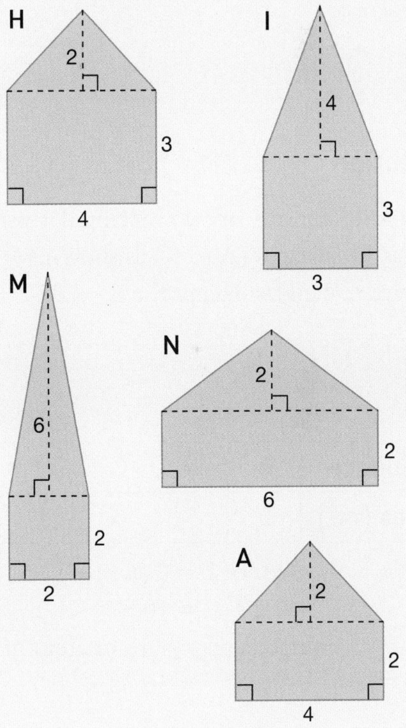

106	8·7	13	18	16	7	392	85	350	12	65	390

96	10^6	0·016	2	70	15	30	7000	12	334	2000	10^3	160	120	0·007	10^2	10

5:04 Surface area of composite solids

The surface area of composite solids is calculated in much the same way as for prisms and cylinders.

The simplest method involves calculating the area of each surface and adding them together, usually in a table.

Other methods involve using the symmetry of the solids to shorten the working.

WORKED EXAMPLE 1

Calculate the surface area of the solid.

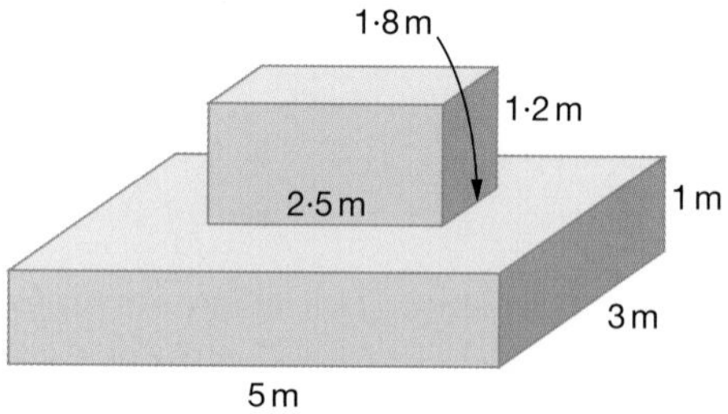

Solution

The solid consists of two rectangular prisms.
It has 11 surfaces (A to K) as shown.
All are rectangles except for F.

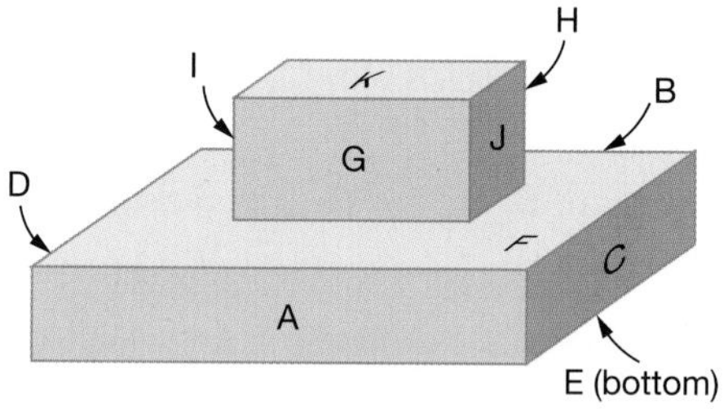

Surface	A	B	C	D	E	F	G	H	I	J	K
Area (m^2)	5	5	3	3	15	10·5	3	3	2·16	2·16	4·5

Note: Area of F = (5 × 3) − (2·5 × 1·8)
= 10·5

∴ Surface area = sum of areas of all surfaces A to K
= 56·32 m^2

Another method is as follows:

Surface area = surface area of top prism + surface area of bottom prism − 2 × common area

Surface area top prism = 2(2·5 × 1·8 + 2·5 × 1·2 + 1·8 × 1·2)
= 19·32 cm^2

Surface area bottom prism = 2(5 × 3 + 3 × 1 + 5 × 1)
= 46 cm^2

Common area = 2·5 × 1·8
= 4·5 cm^2

∴ Surface area = 19·32 + 46 − 2 × 4·5
= 56·32 cm^2

Note: The common area is subtracted twice. It has been included in the SA calculations of both prisms but it is not part of the surface area of the composite solid.

WORKED EXAMPLE 2

Calculate the surface area of the solid.

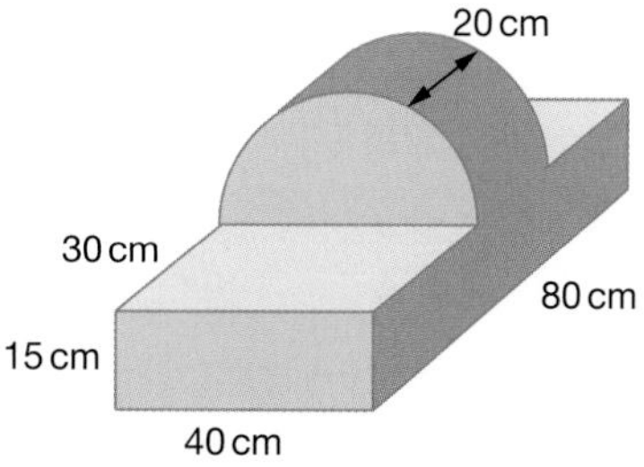

Solution

Surface area = area of curved surface
+ area of semicircles
+ surface area of prism
− common area

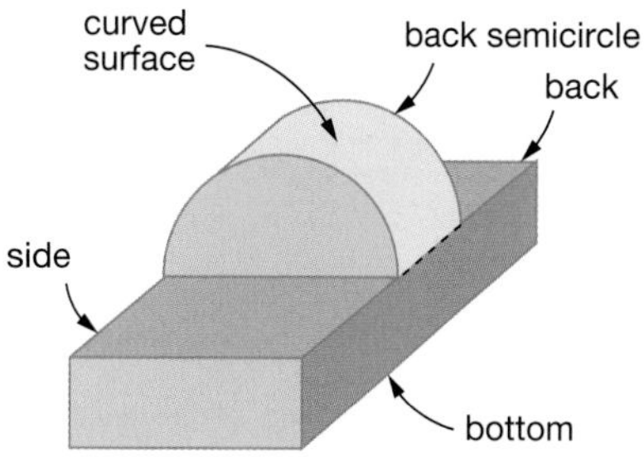

$$\begin{aligned}\text{Area of curved surface} &= 2\pi rh \div 2\\ &= 2 \times \pi \times 20 \times 20 \div 2\\ &= 400\pi\ \text{cm}^2\end{aligned}$$

$$\begin{aligned}\text{Area of semicircles} &= 2 \times \tfrac{1}{2} \times \pi \times r^2\\ &= 2 \times \tfrac{1}{2} \times \pi \times 20^2\\ &= 400\pi\ \text{cm}^2\end{aligned}$$

$$\begin{aligned}\text{Surface area prism} &= 2(40 \times 15 + 80 \times 15 + 40 \times 80)\\ &= 10\,000\ \text{cm}^2\end{aligned}$$

$$\begin{aligned}\text{Common area} &= 40 \times 20\\ &= 800\ \text{cm}^2\end{aligned}$$

$$\begin{aligned}\therefore \text{Surface area} &= 400\pi + 400\pi + 10\,000 - 800\\ &= 11\,713\ \text{cm}^2 \quad (\text{nearest cm}^2)\end{aligned}$$

Exercise 5:04

P Foundation worksheet 5:04
Surface area of composite solids

1 Each of the following solids has been built from 1 cm cubes. What is the surface area of each solid?

a 

b 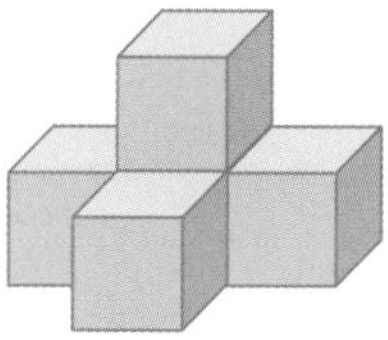

c 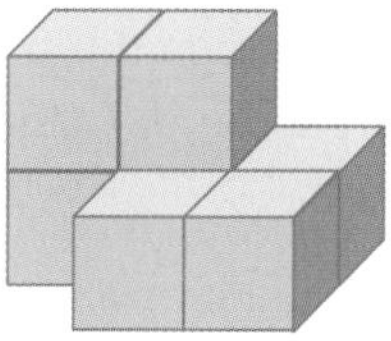

d 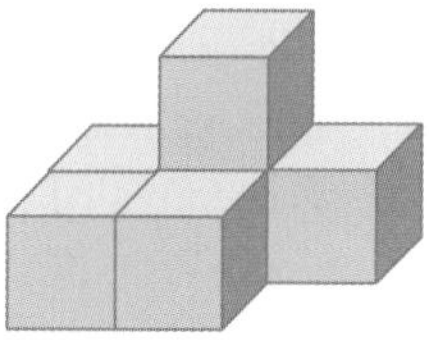

2 The following solids have been built from a 2 cm cube and 1 cm cubes. Calculate the surface area of each solid.

a 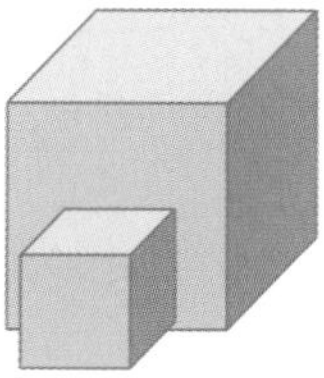

b 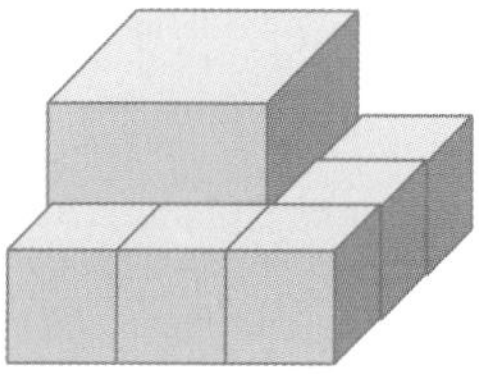

c 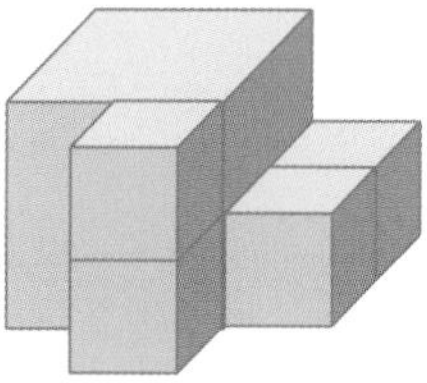

3 Calculate the surface area of the following solids. (All measurements are in centimetres.)

a
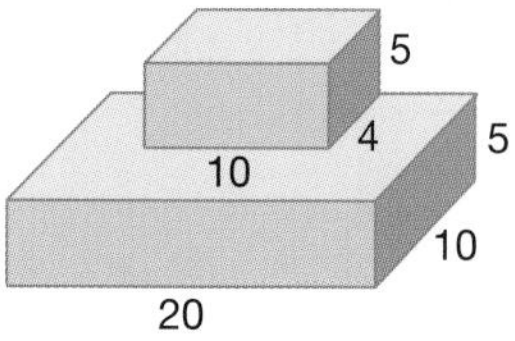

b
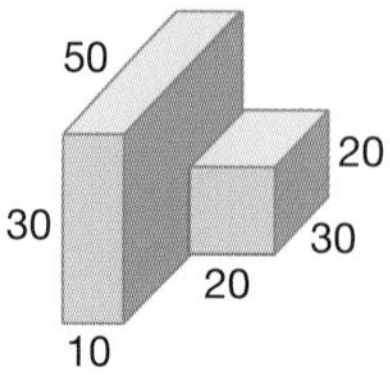

c
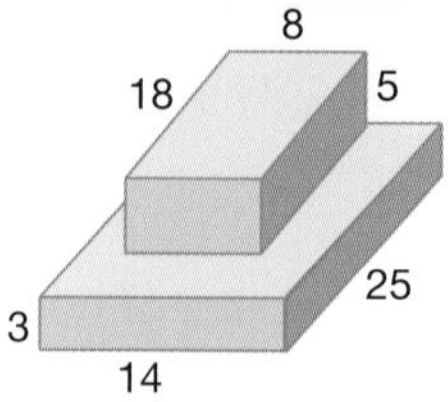

4 Calculate the surface area of the following solids. (All measurements are in centimetres.)

a
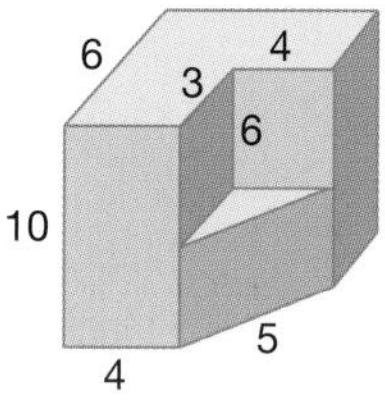

b
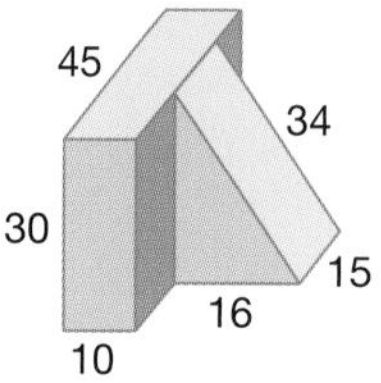

c
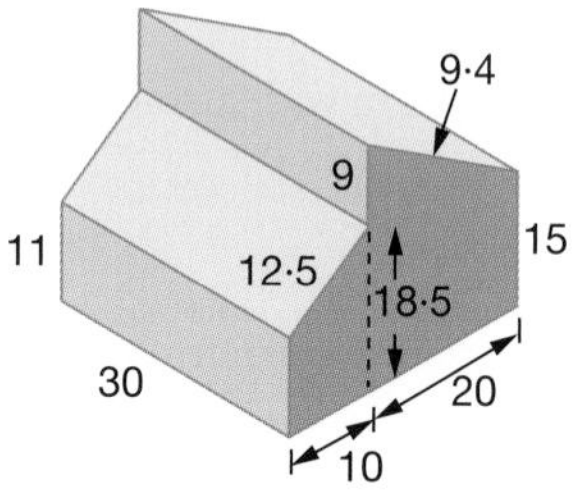

5 Calculate the surface area of the following solids. Give answers correct to one decimal place. (Measurements are in metres.)

a
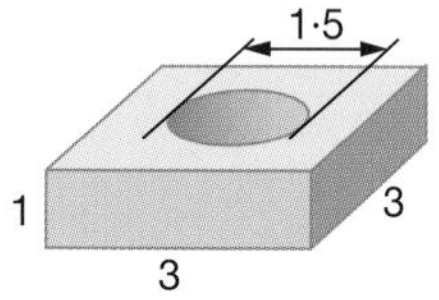

b
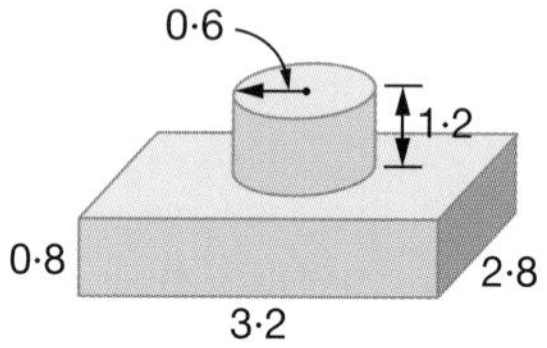

c
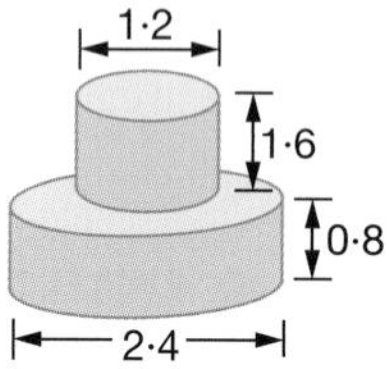

6 Calculate the surface area of the following solids. Give answers correct to one decimal place. (Measurements are in metres.)

a
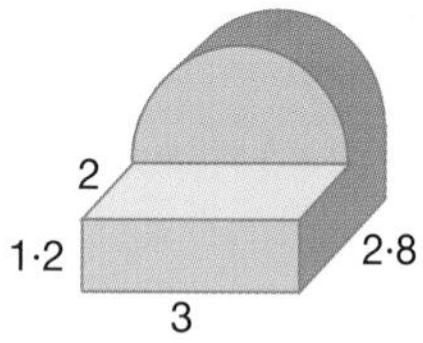

b
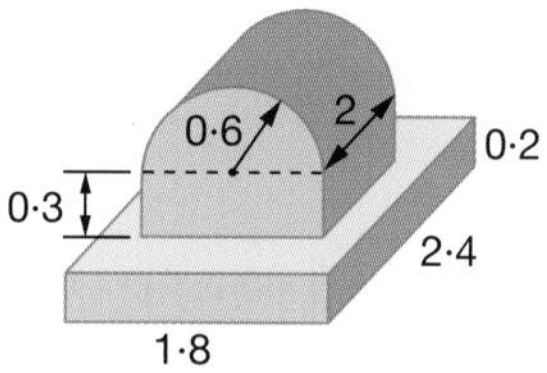

c
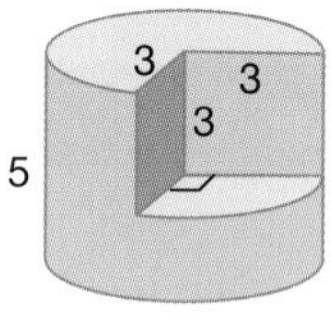

7 The diagram represents a lounge room in a house. The walls and ceiling are to be painted. Find:

a the area of the walls

b the area of the ceiling

c the number of 4 L cans of paint needed to paint the walls and ceiling twice if 1 L of paint covers 16 m^2.

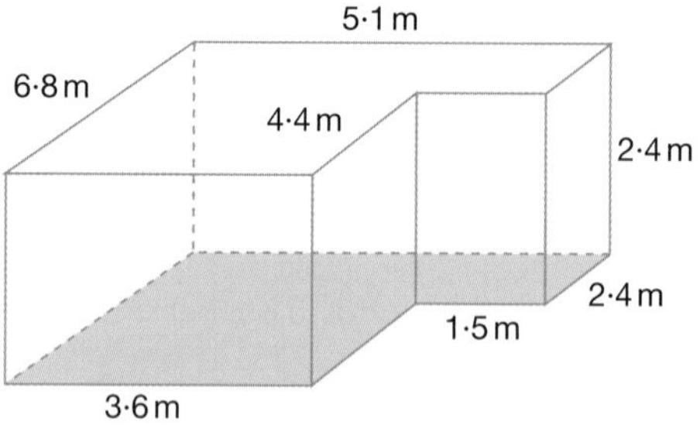

8 Calculate the area of shade cloth needed to cover the walls and roof of this shadehouse, including the door.

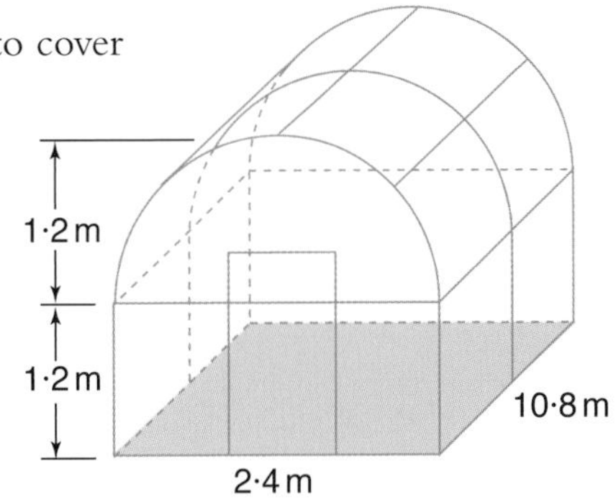

9 The areas visible in this diagram will be covered with sandstone tiles. What is the total cost if the combined cost of materials and labour is $\$120/m^2$?

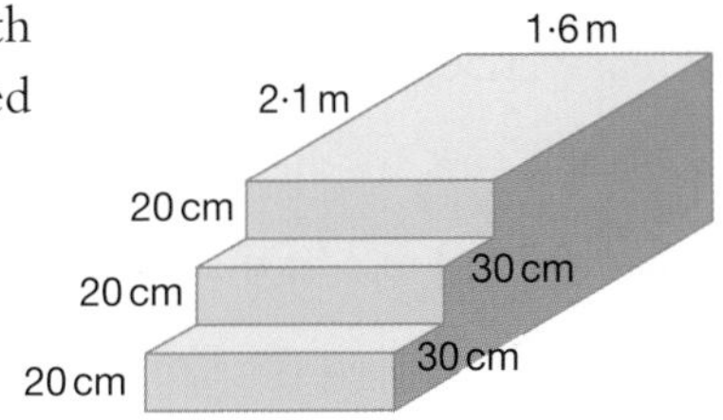

10 A barn is made from aluminium. Calculate the area of metal used in its construction. (Assume it has a total window area of $8·8\,m^2$ and a length of 7.2 m.)

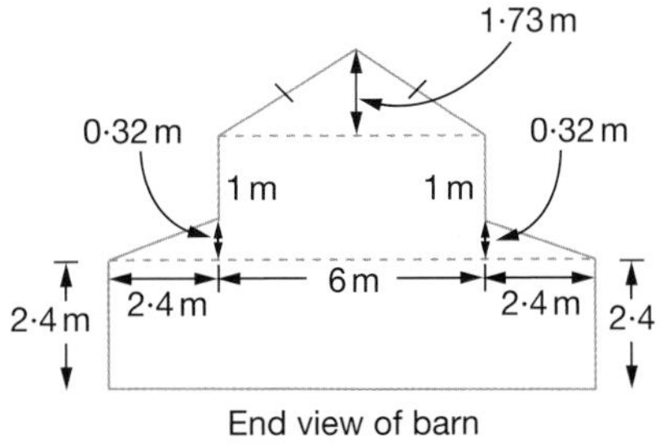

INVESTIGATION 5:04 TRUNCATED CUBES

A truncated cube is one that has had its corners removed. The truncated cube shown in the diagram was formed from a cube of side 3 units. Points were marked on the edges of the cube 1 unit from each vertex and these were joined to form the triangular faces shown. Discuss the mathematical problems that would need to be solved to calculate the surface area of this truncated cube.

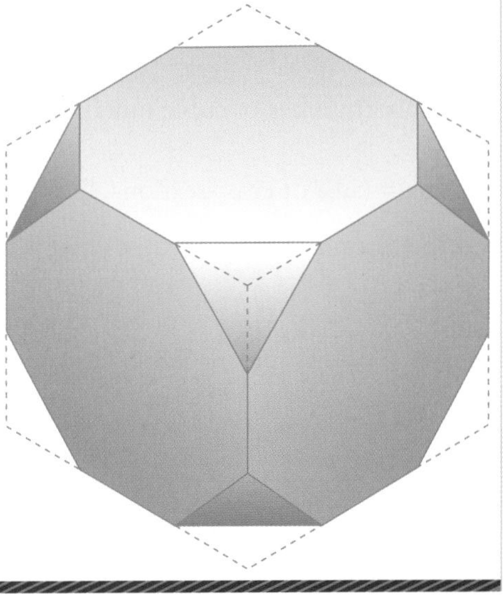

5:05 Volume of prisms, cylinders and composite solids

PREP QUIZ 5:05

The prism shown has been made from layers of cubes.
Each cube has a volume of 1 cm^3.

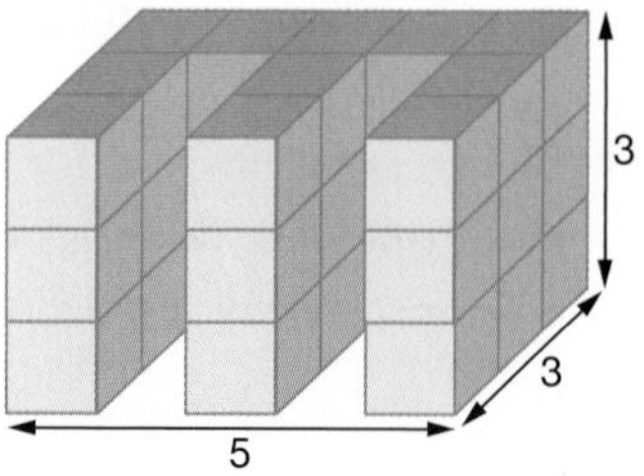

1 How many cubes are there in each layer?

2 How many layers are there?

3 Calculate the volume of the prism by counting cubes.

4 How could the answers to Questions **1** and **2** be used to calculate the volume?

5 The cross-sectional area, A, has been shaded purple. What is the value of A?

6 What is the height, h, of the prism?

7 What is the value of Ah?

8 Are the answers to Questions **1** and **5** the same?

9 Are the answers to Questions **2** and **6** the same?

10 Are the answers to Questions **3** and **7** the same?

This loaf of bread is like a prism. It can be thought of as a series of identical layers of equal volume.

The Prep quiz should have reminded you that for solids with a uniform cross-section, such as prisms and cylinders, the following relationships are true.

- The number of cubic units in each layer is the same as the cross-sectional area, A.
- The number of layers is the same as the height of the prism, h.
- The volume of the prism obtained by counting the cubic units is the same as the product Ah.

The exercise above suggests two ways in which the volume could be calculated.
Volume = (number of cubic units in each layer) × (number of layers)
or
Volume = (area of cross-section, A) × (height of prism, h)

It is the second of these methods that is the most widely applicable.

The volume of all prisms, cylinders and prism-like solids is given by the formula

$$V = Ah$$

where:

V = volume
A = cross-sectional area
h = height of the prism

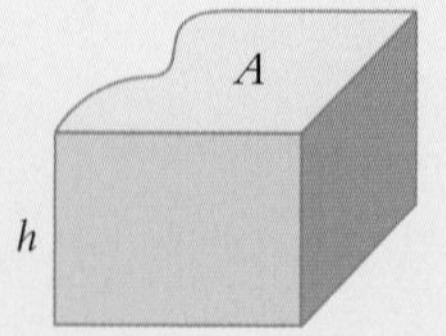

For a cylinder, the cross-section is a circle and $A = \pi r^2$.
The formula is then rewritten as:

$$V = \pi r^2 h$$

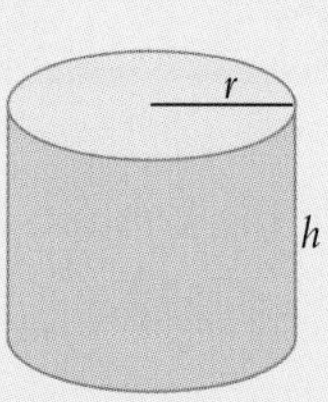

WORKED EXAMPLES

Find the volumes of the following solids.

1

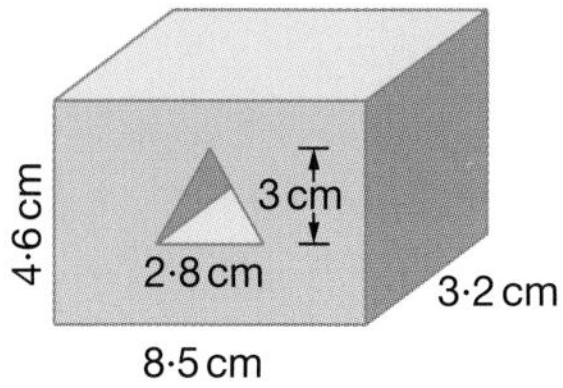

2

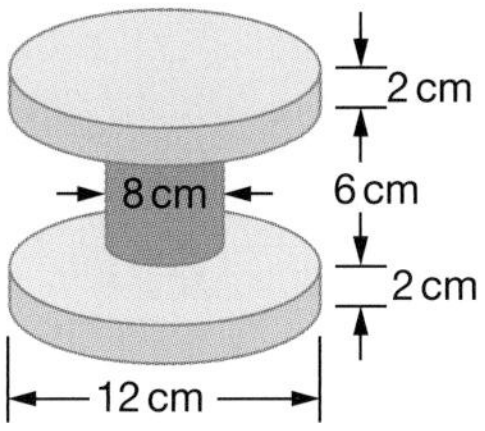

3

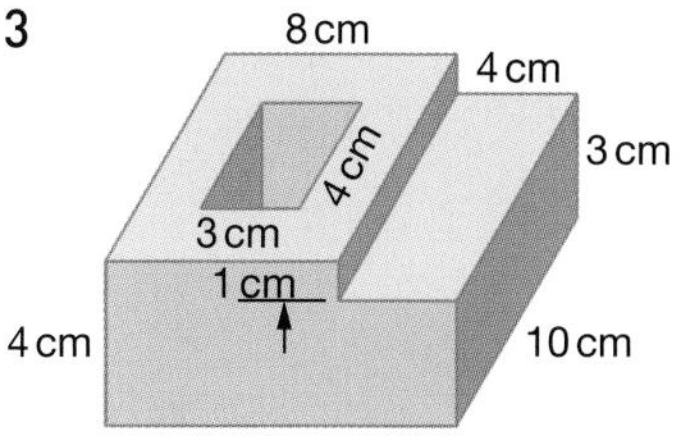

Solutions

1 $V = Ah$

$A = \text{area of rectangle} - \text{area of triangle}$

$= (8{\cdot}5 \times 4{\cdot}6) - \left(\dfrac{2{\cdot}8 \times 3}{2}\right)$

$= 39{\cdot}1 - 4{\cdot}2$

$= 34{\cdot}9\text{ cm}^2$

$h = 3{\cdot}2\text{ cm}$

$\therefore V = 34{\cdot}9 \times 3{\cdot}2$

$= 111{\cdot}68\text{ cm}^3$

In questions that involve π, it's best to leave your answer in terms of π.

2 The solid consists of three cylinders, two of which are identical.

Volume of top cylinder

$V_1 = \pi r^2 h$

$= \pi \times 6^2 \times 2$

$= 72\pi$

Volume of middle cylinder

$V_2 = \pi r^2 h$

$= \pi \times 4^2 \times 6$

$= 96\pi$

$\therefore$ Volume of solid

$= 2V_1 + V_2$

$= 2 \times 72\pi + 96\pi$

$= 240\pi$

$= 754\text{ cm}^3$

(to nearest cm^3)

3 The solid consists of a rectangular prism that has had two rectangular prisms removed. The removal of one prism has formed a hole.

Volume of rectangular hole

$V_1 = A \times h$

$= (3 \times 4) \times 4$

$= 48\text{ cm}^3$

Volume of other removed rectangular prism

$V_2 = A \times h$

$= (4 \times 10) \times 1$

$= 40\text{ cm}^3$

Volume of original rectangular prism

$V_3 = A \times h$

$= (12 \times 10) \times 4$

$= 480\text{ cm}^3$

$\therefore$ Volume of solid

$= V_3 - V_1 - V_2$

$= 480 - 48 - 40$

$= 392\text{ cm}^3$

Exercise 5:05

P Foundation worksheet 5:05 Volume

1 Calculate the volume of the following prisms. (All measurements are in centimetres.)

a
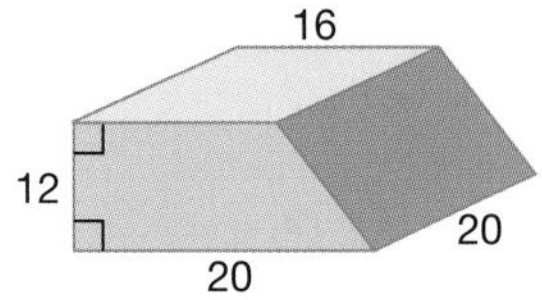

b
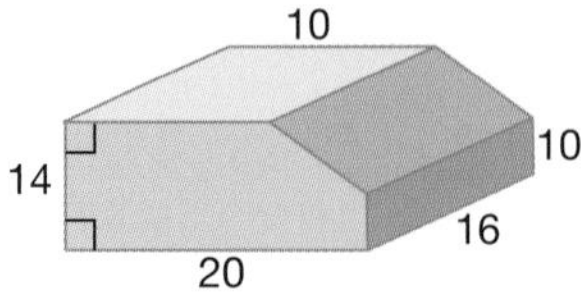

c
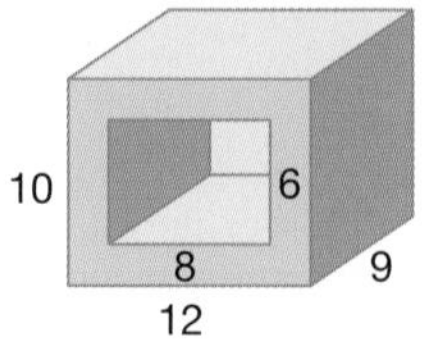

d
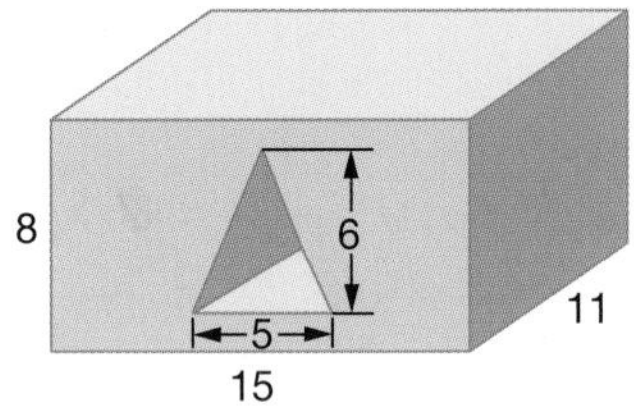

e
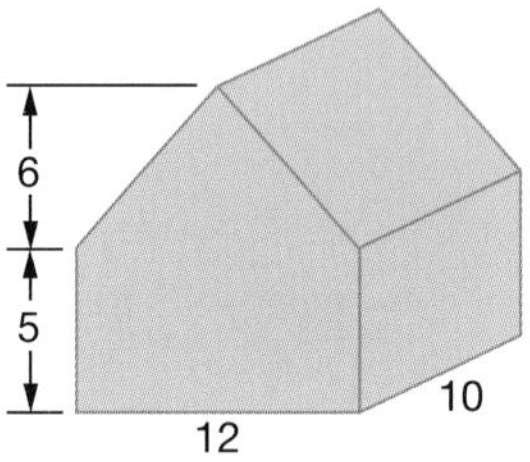

2 Calculate the volume of the following cylinders or parts of cylinders. (Give answers correct to the nearest cubic centimetre.)

a
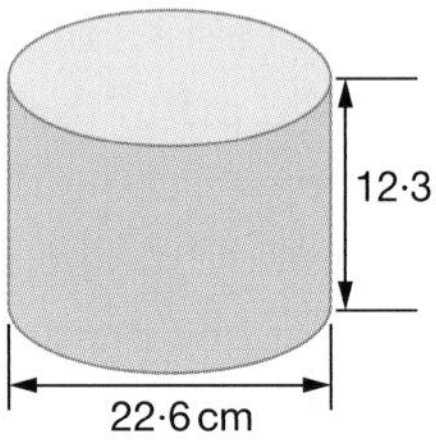

b
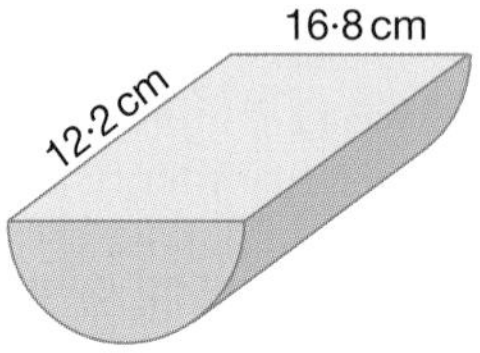

c
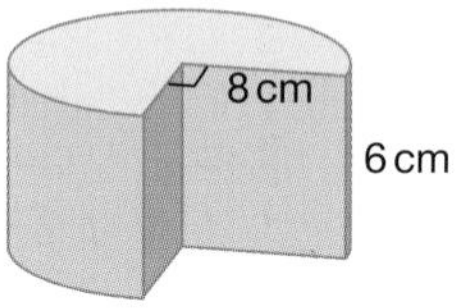

3 Calculate the volume of the following prisms. (All measurements are in cm.)

a
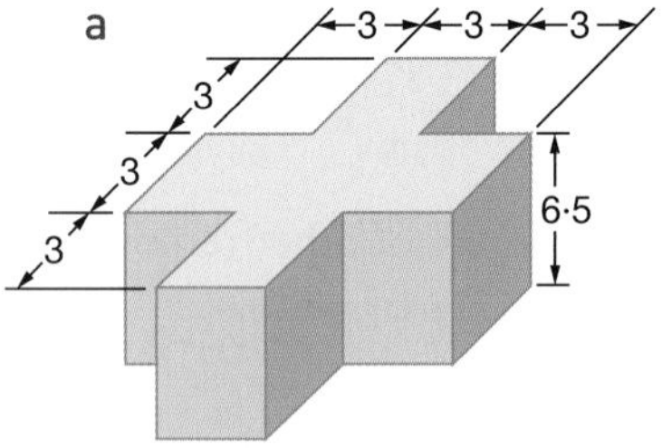

b
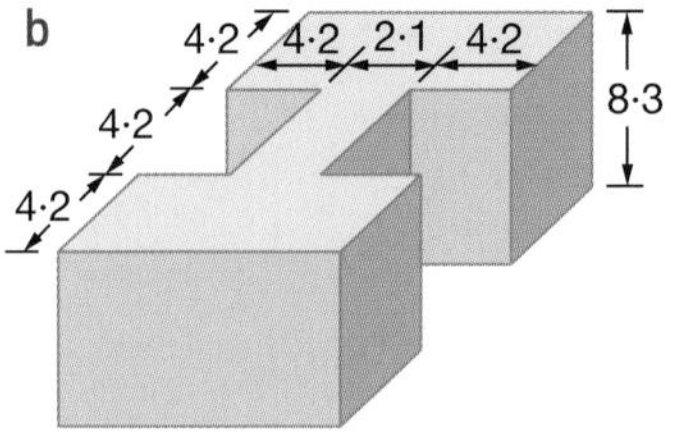

c
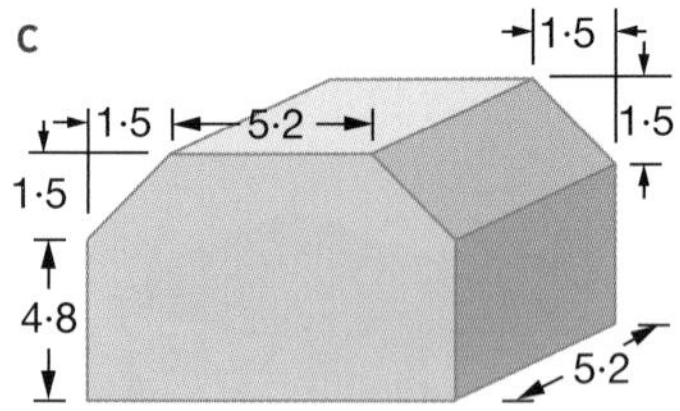

4 Calculate the volume of the following prisms. All measurements are in centimetres. Give answers correct to one decimal place.

a
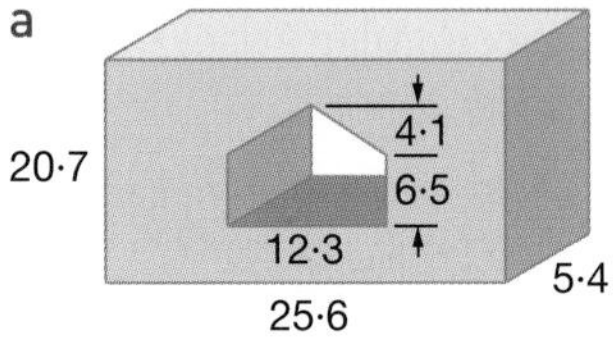

b
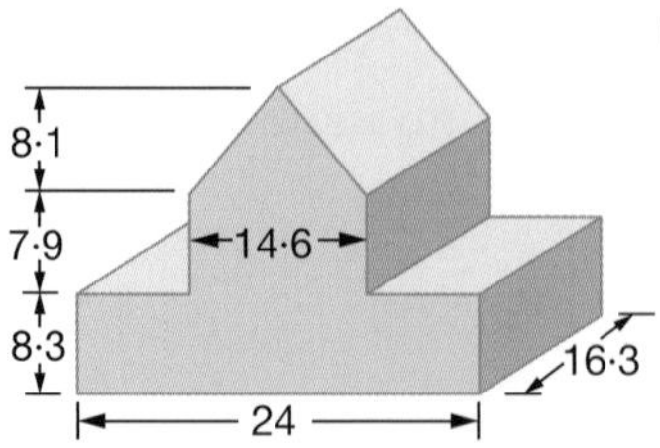

c
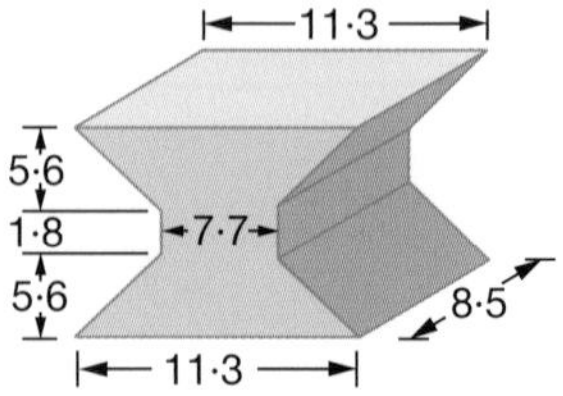

5 Calculate the volume of the following solids, correct to three significant figures.

a
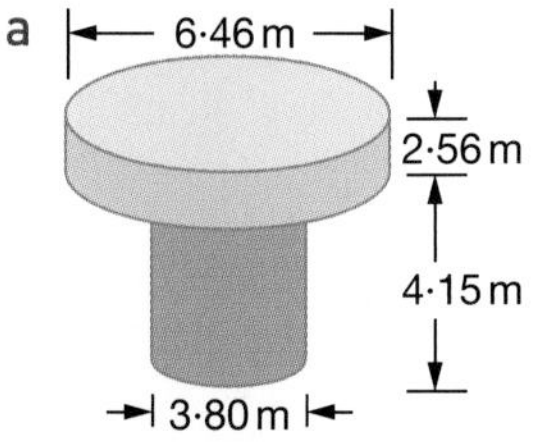

b
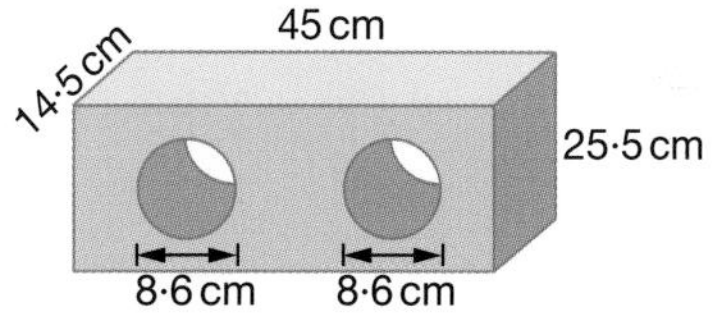

c
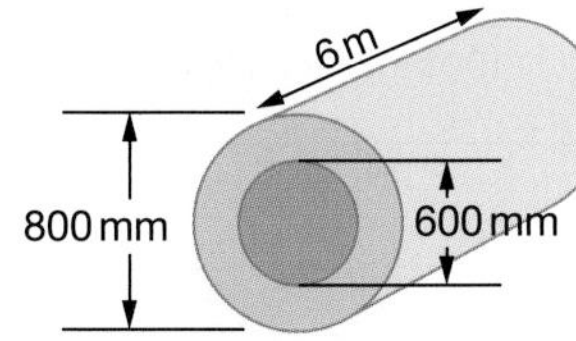

Make sure all measurements are in the same units.

6 Find the volume of the following composite solids.

a
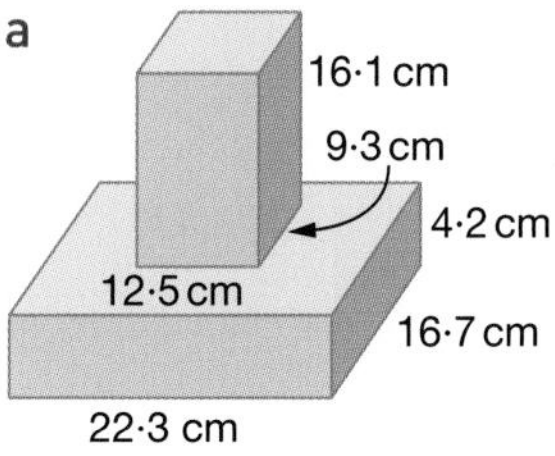

b
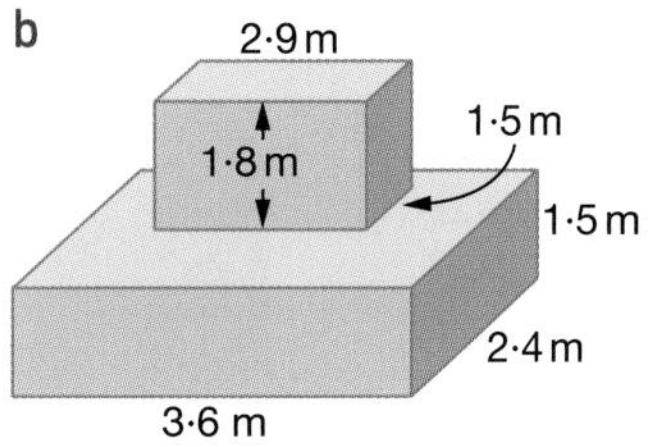

c
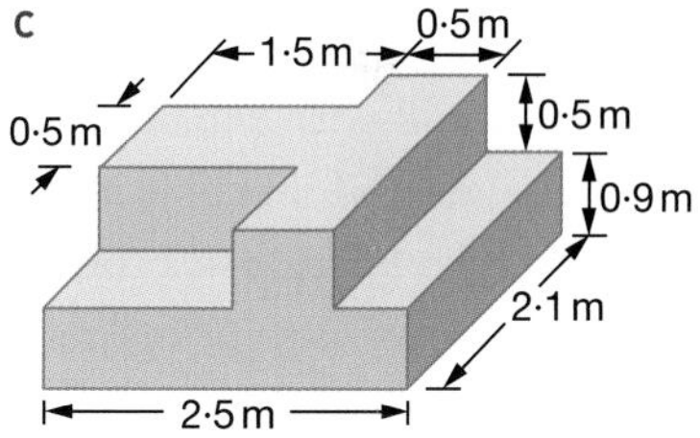

7 Calculate the volume of the following composite solids. All measurements are in centimetres. Give all answers correct to one decimal place.

a
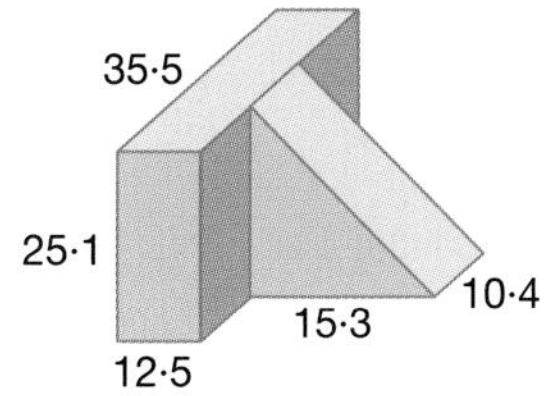

b
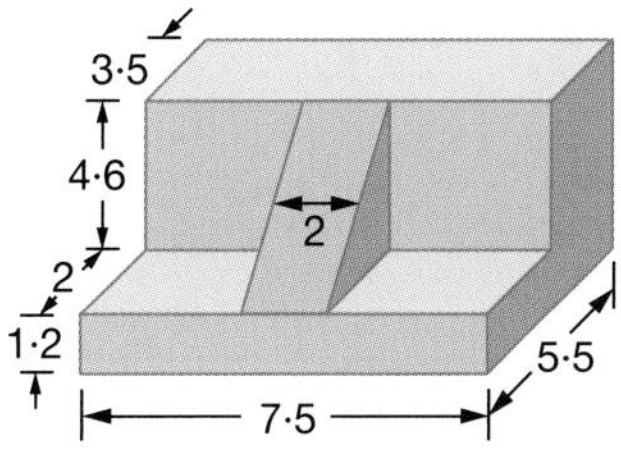

c
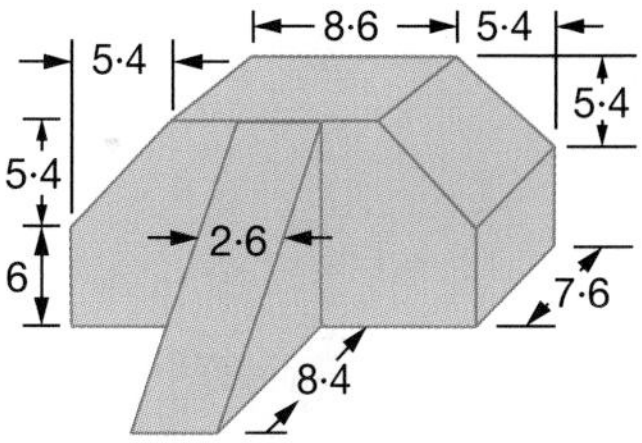

8 Calculate the volume of the following solids. All measurements are in centimetres. Give answers correct to one decimal place.

a
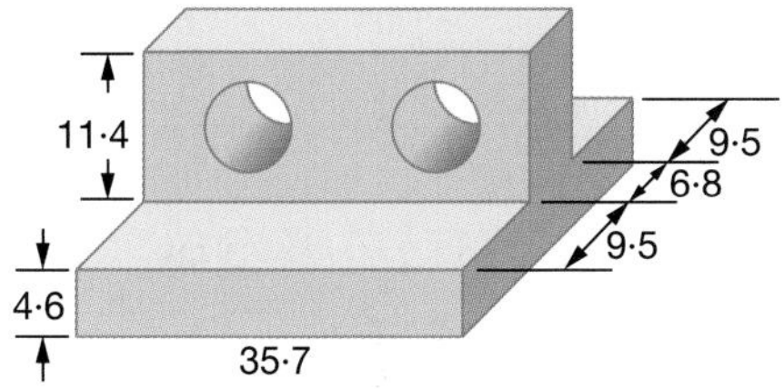

Note: Both circular holes have a diameter of 8·5 cm.

b
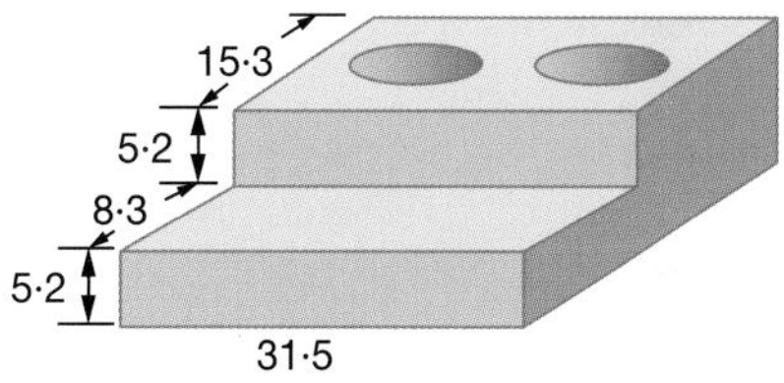

Note: Both circular holes have a diameter of 10·2 cm.

9 A steel tank is given in the diagram. Given that the dimensions are external dimensions and the steel plate is 2 cm thick, calculate the mass of the tank if the density of the steel is 7·8 g/cm^3. Give the answer correct to one decimal place.

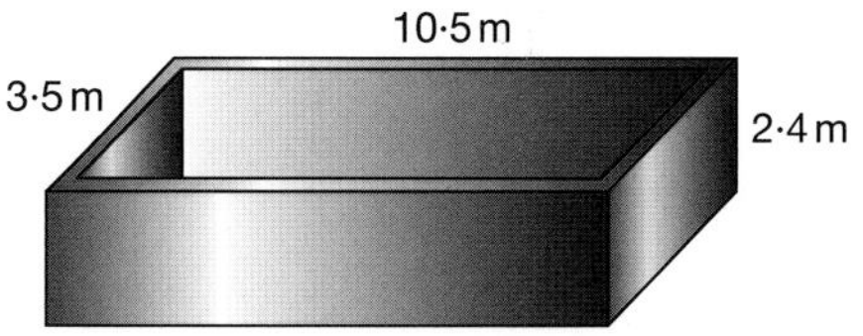

10 Calculate the volume of a concrete beam that has the cross-section shown in the diagram. The beam is 10 m long. Calculate the mass of the beam if 1 m^3 of concrete weighs 2·5 tonnes.

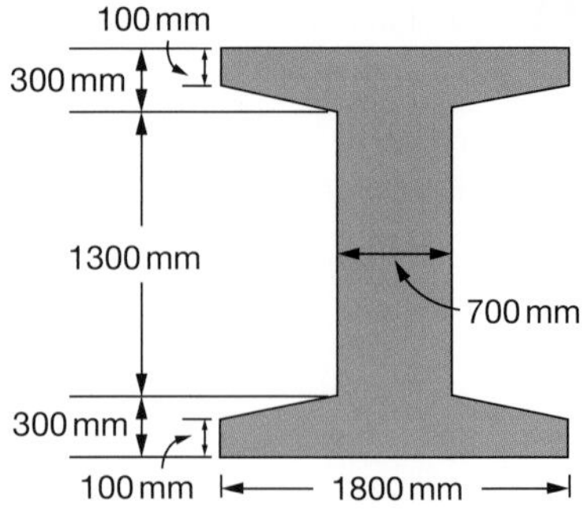

11 A diving pool is shown in the diagram. Calculate the capacity of the pool in kilolitres correct to two significant figures. (Remember that 1 m^3 = 1 kL.)

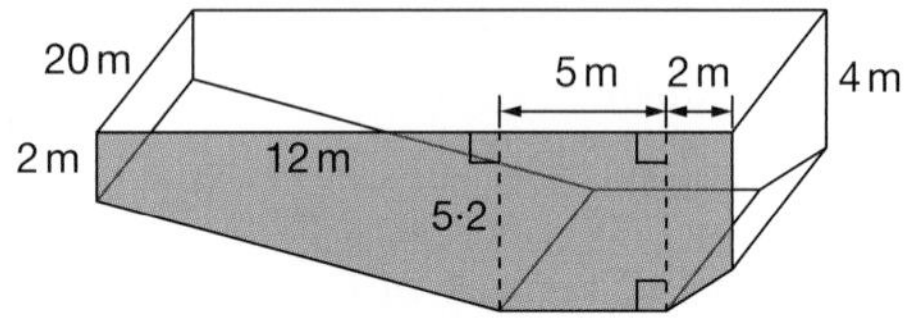

12 The solid pictured is formed by filling a mould with molten metal. Calculate the mass of this object if 1 cm^3 of metal weighs 11·4 g. Give the answer correct to two significant figures.

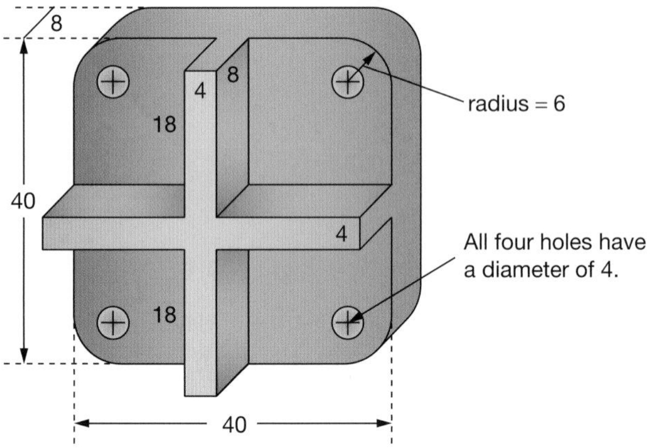

All measurements are in centimetres.

P GEOGEBRA ACTIVITY 5:05 VOLUME OF A PRISM

Click and drag points to change the cross-sectional shape of a prism and then calculate the volume of the prism. Tick a checkbox to check the answer.

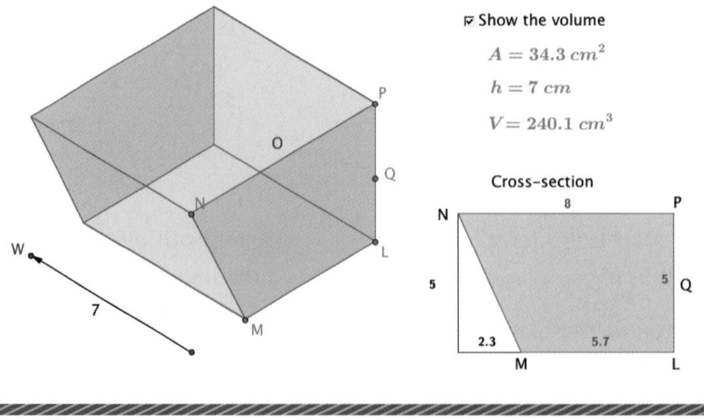

INVESTIGATION 5:05 PERIMETER, AREA AND VOLUME

1 A piece of wire 60 cm long is bent to form a rectangle.

a Give the dimensions of four rectangles that could be formed.

b Use the dimensions for the rectangles in **a** to complete this table.

	Length (L)	Breadth (B)	Area (A)	$L-B$
Rectangle 1				
Rectangle 2				
Rectangle 3				
Rectangle 4				

c What happens to A as $L - B$ becomes smaller?

d Predict the largest area that could be obtained.

e What is the area of the largest rectangle that can be formed from a piece of wire 100 m long?

2 A rectangular piece of cardboard 60 cm long and 20 cm wide is bent to form a hollow rectangular prism with a height of 20 cm.

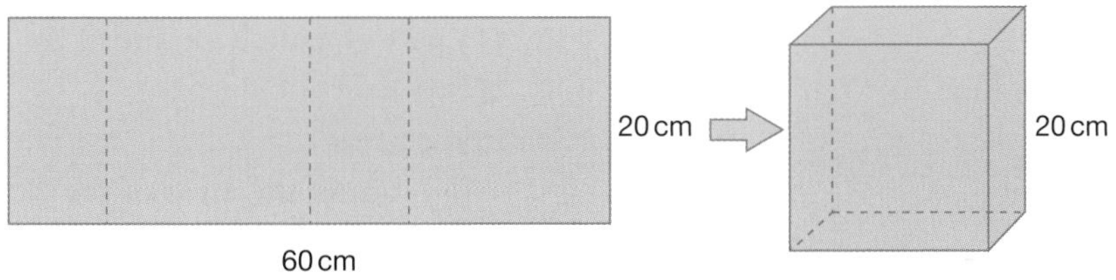

a From the results of Question **1**, predict the maximum volume of a rectangular prism formed from this piece of cardboard.

b If the piece of cardboard were bent to form a cylinder, what would be the volume of the cylinder? Will the volume of the cylinder be greater than the maximum volume obtained in part **a**?

Composite solids of many types are present in these buildings. How would you describe them?

MATHS TERMS 5

area
- the amount of space inside a two-dimensional shape
- units of area:
  square millimetre (mm^2)
  square centimetre (cm^2)
  square metre (m^2)
  hectare (ha)
  square kilometre (km^2)
- formulas are used to calculate the area of the common plane figures

circumference
- the length of a circle's boundary
- the circumference is calculated using either formula: $C = \pi D$ or $C = 2\pi r$

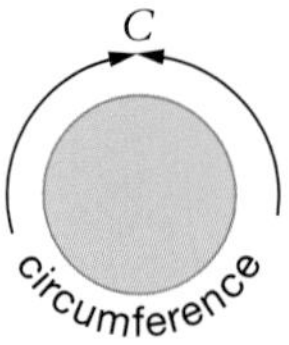

capacity
- the amount of fluid that can be held by a container
- units of capacity:
  litre (L)
  millilitre (mL)
  kilolitre (kL)

composite figure
- a figure that is formed by joining simple figures

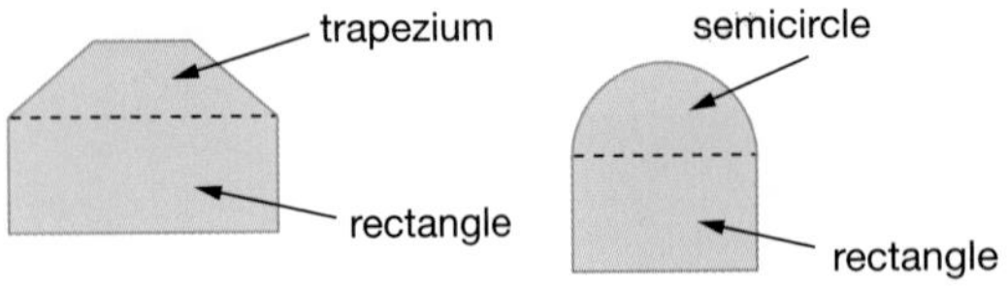

composite solid
- a solid that is formed by joining simple solids

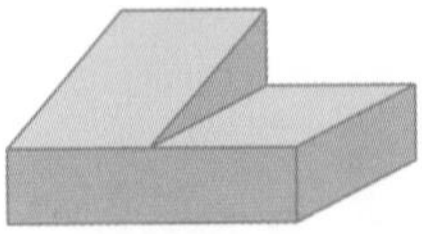

cross-section
- the shape on the face where a solid has been sliced

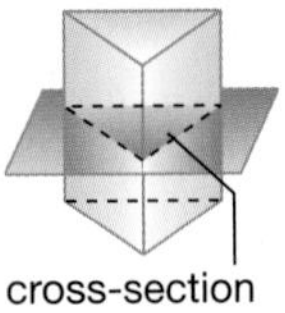

cylinder
- a prism-like solid with a circular cross-section
- it has two circular ends and a curved surface

hectare
- an area of $10\,000\,m^2$
- a square with a side of 100 m

perimeter
- the length of a plane figure's boundary

prism
- a solid that has two identical ends joined by rectangular faces
- cross-sections parallel to the ends are identical to the ends

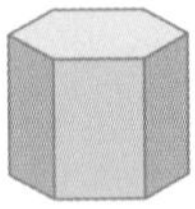

sector
- a part of a circle bounded by two radii and an arc

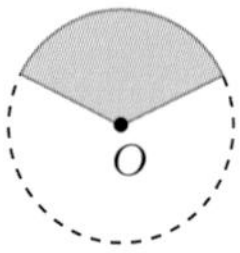

surface area
- the sum of the areas of the faces (or surfaces) of a three-dimensional figure (or solid)

volume
- the amount of space inside a three-dimensional shape
- units of volume:
  cubic centimetre (cm^3)
  cubic metre (m^3)
- formulas are used to calculate the volume of common solids (three-dimensional shapes)

DIAGNOSTIC TEST 5 AREA, SURFACE AREA AND VOLUME

Each part of this test has similar items that test a certain question type.
Errors made will indicate areas of weakness.
Each weakness should be treated by going back to the section listed.

1 Find the area of each of the following composite figures. 5:01
Where necessary, answer correct to two decimal places.

a
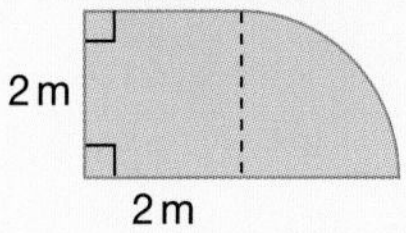

b
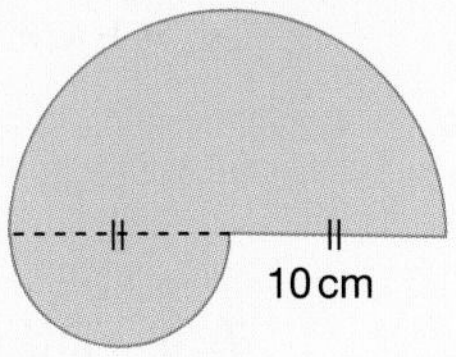

c
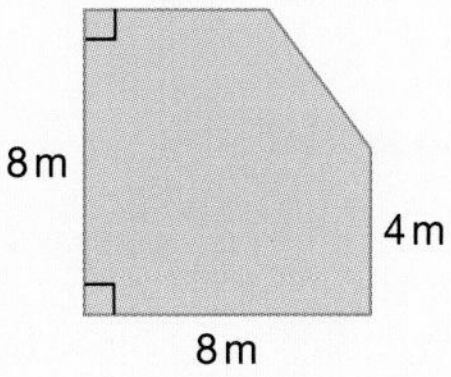

2 Calculate the surface area of the following prisms. 5:02

a
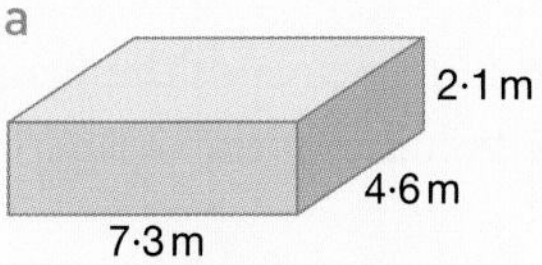

b
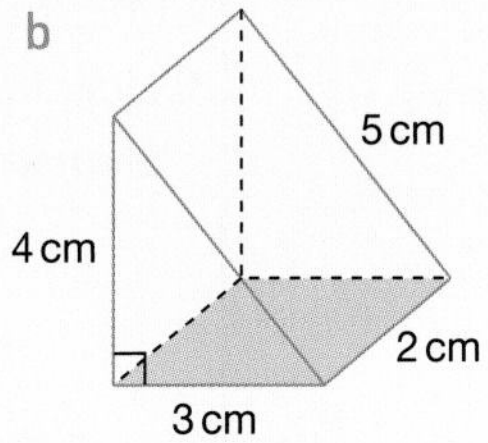

c
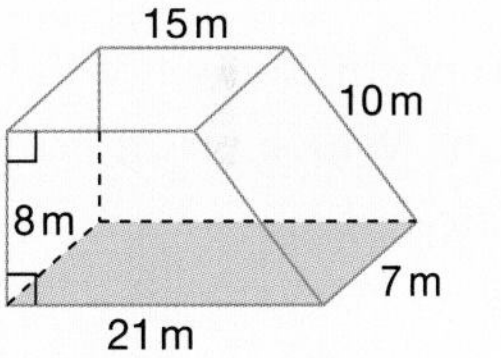

3 Calculate the surface areas of these cylinders. 5:03

a
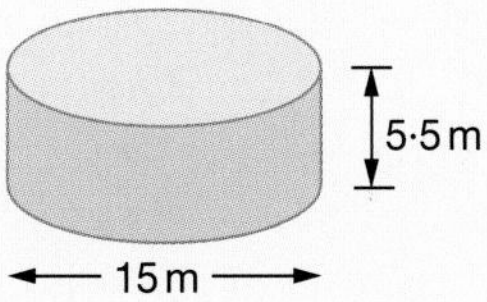

b
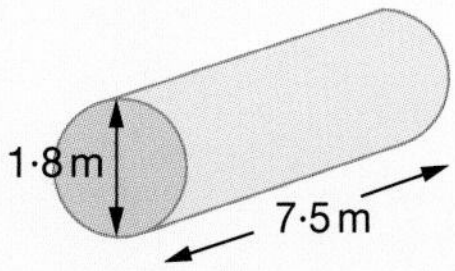

c
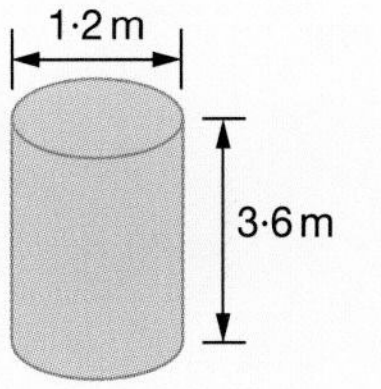

4 Calculate the surface area of these solids. 5:04

a
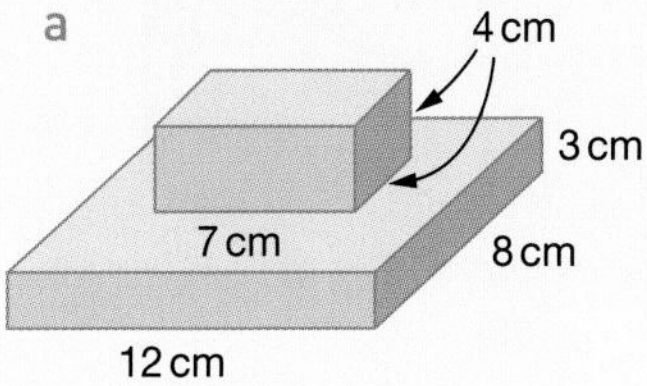

b
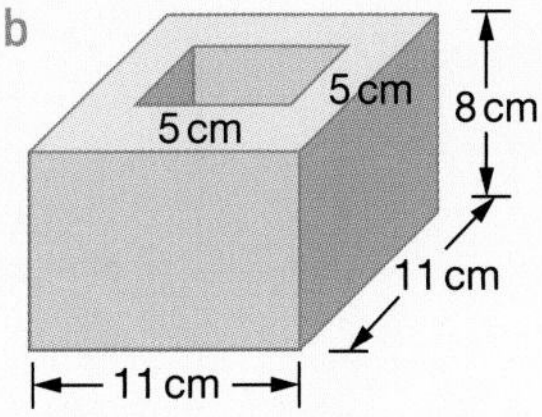

c
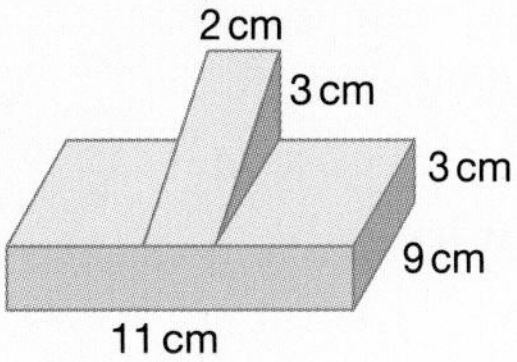

5 Calculate the volumes of the prisms in Question **2**. 5:05

6 Calculate the volumes of the cylinders in Question **3** to the nearest cubic metre. 5:05

7 Calculate the volumes of the solids in Question **4**. 5:05

ASSIGNMENT 5A Chapter review

1 A floor is as shown in the diagram. Find the area of this floor and the cost of covering it with cork tiles if the cost of the tiles is \$40 per m^2.

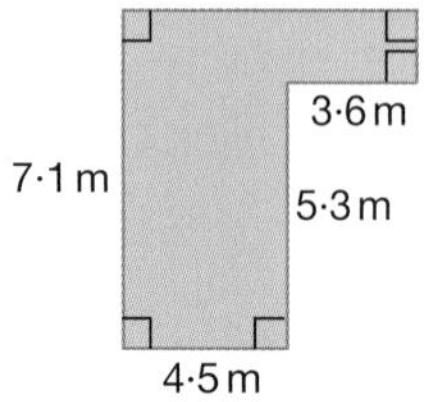

2 A pentagon is made by placing an equilateral triangle on top of a rectangle. What is the area of the pentagon?

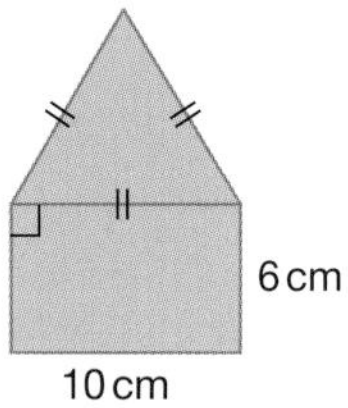

3 The two prisms shown both have a volume of 900 cm^3. Which prism has the smaller surface area?

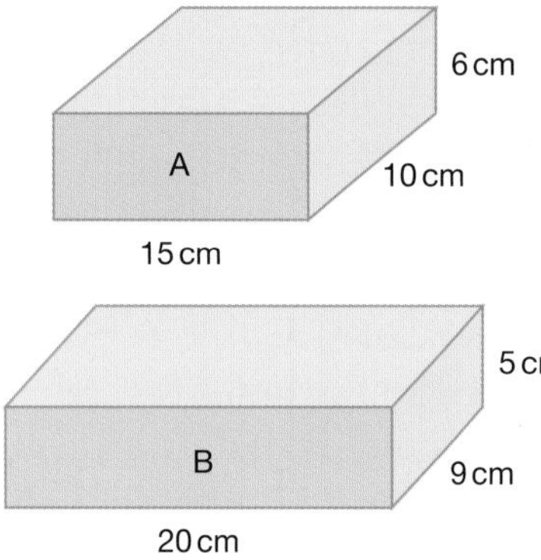

4 The inside and outside of this container are painted. Calculate the area that has to be painted.

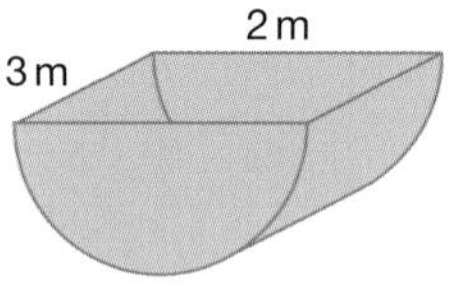

5 Calculate the area of the figure, correct to one decimal place.

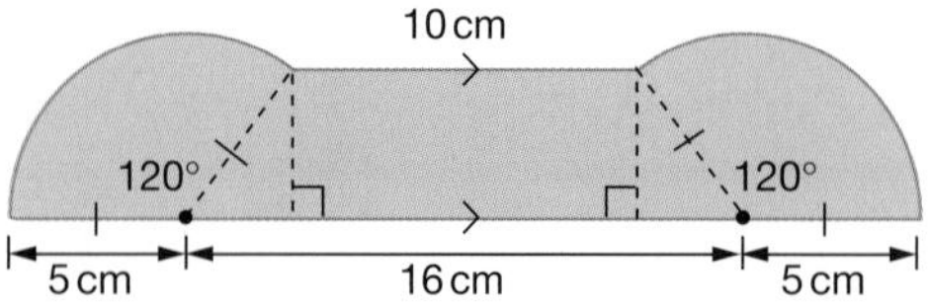

6 **a** Calculate the surface area of the solid below. Measurements are in metres.
b Calculate the volume of the solid.

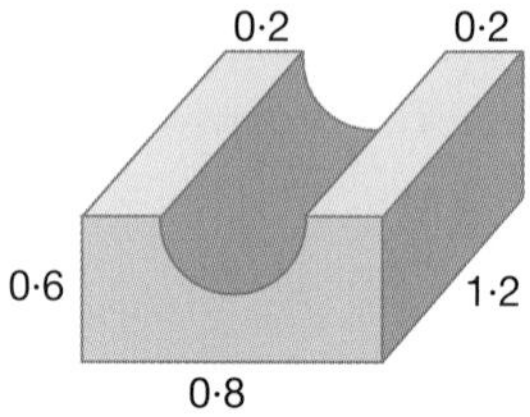

7 **a** Find the value of x in the prism below, correct to one decimal place.
b Calculate the area of the cross-section of the prism.
c Calculate the surface area of the prism.
d Calculate the volume of the prism.

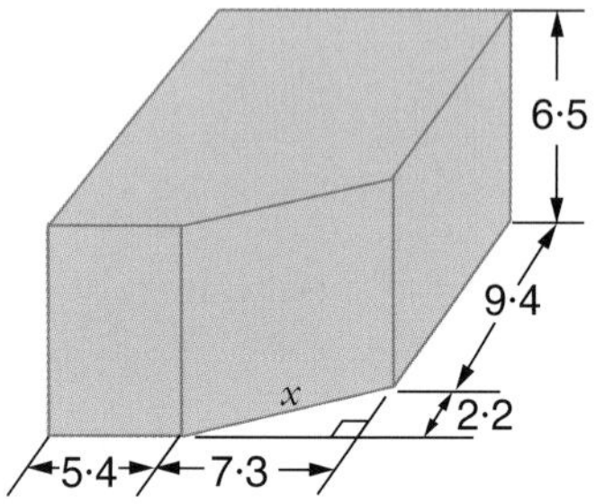

8 **a** Calculate the volume of the solid below.
b Calculate the surface area of the solid.

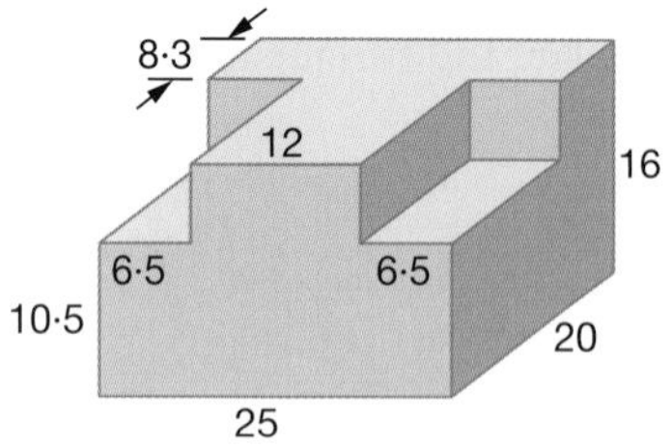

ASSIGNMENT 5B Working mathematically

1 Water is leaking from a tap at a rate of 15 drops/min. If 12 drops = 1 mL, how much water will leak in 1 day?

2 $3! = 3 \times 2 \times 1$ (pronounced 3 factorial)
$5! = 5 \times 4 \times 3 \times 2 \times 1$
$10! = 10 \times 9 \times 8 \times 7 \times 6 \times 5 \times 4 \times 3 \times 2 \times 1$
How many zeros are at the end of 20!?

3 Four different playing cards are dealt into two piles: left first, then right, then left, and then right. The left pile is then placed on top of the right pile. How many times must this process be repeated before the cards return to their original positions? How many times would the process need to be repeated if there had been eight cards?

4 Annabelle asked her grandfather, who was 60 years older than her, how old he was. Her grandfather replied that his age was a number less than 100 and that when he divided his age by 2, 3 and 4, the remainders were 1, 2 and 3 respectively. What possible numbers could Annabelle give as her grandfather's age? Assuming that she knew her own age, could she tell her grandfather how old he was?

5 George Junkiewicz has prepared the timeline below to show when his employees will take their holidays. He has designed it so that no more than two employees are on holidays at the same time. The dots at the end of each line are explained below.

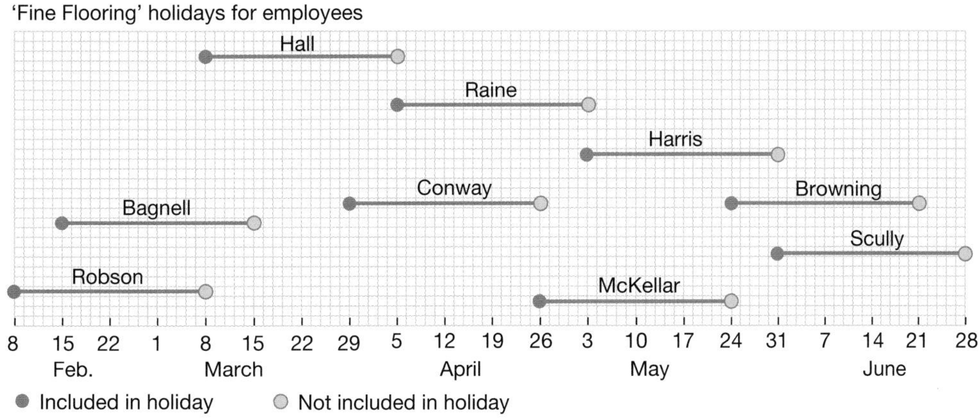

a What is the first day of Conway's holiday?
b On what day does Conway return to work?
c Which two employees are on holidays in the week starting on the 8th of March?
d Which two employees are also on holidays during McKellar's holiday?
e George has to take four weeks of holidays. He is prepared to fit in wherever he can. When must he take his holidays?

ASSIGNMENT 5C Cumulative revision

1 A marathon runner completes a practice run of 30 km in 1 hour 40 minutes. Express this as a rate in: 1:04

a km/h b min/km c s/100 m

2 Simplify: 3:04

a $\frac{x}{3}+\frac{2x}{5}$ b $\frac{x}{3}-\frac{2x}{5}$ c $\frac{x}{3}\times\frac{2x}{5}$ d $\frac{x}{3}\div\frac{2x}{5}$

3 The measurements 6 m, 6·0 m and 6·00 m all have the same numerical value but they have different levels of precision. Between what two numbers would each of these measurements lie? 1:10

4 Give the answer to $\frac{16{\cdot}94\times 32{\cdot}15}{24{\cdot}2}$ correct to: 1:05

a one decimal place
b two decimal places
c one significant figure
d three significant figures.

5 A set of cards is numbered from 1 to 20. The cards are shuffled and one card is chosen at random. Find the probability that the card is: 4:03

a an even number
b a number less than 10
c an even number and a number less than 10
d an even number or a number less than 10
e a number that is odd and greater than 10.

6 Sharon used a random number generator on a computer to investigate how many sixes would appear when three dice were rolled. She repeated the experiment 100 times and her results are shown in the table. 4:02

Number of sixes	Frequency
0	57
1	36
2	7
3	0

a Using these results, find the probability as a percentage of obtaining:
i 0 sixes ii 1 six iii 2 sixes.
b It is possible to obtain 3 sixes. On the basis of these results, what would you estimate the probability of obtaining 3 sixes to be?
c How could you improve the accuracy of these experimental probabilities?

If one dice can land in 6 different ways and two dice can land in 36 different ways, in how many ways can three dice land?

INDICES

6

Contents

Syllabus references (See pages x–xv for details.)

Number and Algebra

Selections from ***Indices*** [Stages 5.1, 5.2] and ***Surds and Indices*** [Stage 5.3§]

- Extend and apply the index laws to variables, using positive-integer indices and the zero index (ACMNA212)
- Simplify algebraic products and quotients using index laws (ACMNA231)
- Apply index laws to numerical expressions with integer indices (ACMNA209)
- Apply index laws to algebraic expressions involving integer indices (NSW)
- Define rational and irrational numbers and perform operations with surds and fractional indices (ACMNA264)

Measurement and Geometry [Stage 5.1]

Selections from ***Numbers of Any Magnitude***

- Express numbers in scientific notation (ACMNA210)

Working Mathematically

- Communicating • Problem Solving • Reasoning • Understanding • Fluency

6:01 Review of indices

$2 \times 2 \times 2 \times 2 = 16$
$2^4 = 16$

- 2 is the base.
- 4 is the index.
- 16 is the basic numeral.

2^4 is the 'index form'
(base 2) of 16

$$x^n = \underbrace{x \times x \times x \times \ldots \times x \times x}_{n \text{ factors}} \text{ (where } n \text{ is a positive integer)}$$

For x^n: x is the base
n is the index

2^4 is called a power of 2.

Multiplication using indices

$3^4 \times 3^2 = (3 \times 3 \times 3 \times 3) \times (3 \times 3)$
$= 3^{4+2} = 3^6$

$x^5 \times x^3 = (x \times x \times x \times x \times x) \times (x \times x \times x)$
$= x^{5+3} = x^8$

Index law 1 When multiplying terms, **add** the indices: $x^m \times x^n = x^{m+n}$

Division using indices

$$3^5 \div 3^2 = \frac{3 \times 3 \times 3 \times \cancel{3} \times \cancel{3}}{\cancel{3} \times \cancel{3}}$$
$= 3^{5-2} = 3^3$

$$x^4 \div x^3 = \frac{x \times \cancel{x} \times \cancel{x} \times \cancel{x}}{\cancel{x} \times \cancel{x} \times \cancel{x}}$$
$= x^{4-3} = x^1$

Index law 2 When dividing terms, **subtract** the indices: $x^m \div x^n = x^{m-n}$

Powers of indices

$(3^3)^2 = 3^3 \times 3^3$
$= 3^{3+3}$ Using index law 1
$= 3^{3 \times 2} = 3^6$

$(x^5)^4 = x^5 \times x^5 \times x^5 \times x^5$
$= x^{5+5+5+5}$ Using index law 1
$= x^{5 \times 4} = x^{20}$

Index law 3 For powers of a power, **multiply** the indices: $(x^m)^n = x^{mn}$

If we simplify the division $x^n \div x^n$, using index law 2:
$x^n \div x^n = x^{n-n} = x^0$

But any expression divided by itself must equal 1.
$x^n \div x^n = 1$

Therefore, x^0 must be equal to 1.
$x^0 = 1$

You should learn these laws.

Index law 4 A term with a zero index is 1: $x^0 = 1$

WORKED EXAMPLES

1 **a** $4^3 = 4 \times 4 \times 4$
$= 64$

b $13^5 = 13 \times 13 \times 13 \times 13 \times 13$

Using the calculator to evaluate 13^5:

Press 13 [$x^{\blacksquare}$] 5 [=]

$13^5 = 371\,293$

c $(-4)^2 = -4 \times -4$
$= 16$

Another name for an index is an exponent.

Remember the index key. Enter the base *x* first, press [$x^{\blacksquare}$], then enter the index 5 and press [=].

2 Using index law 1

a $3^2 \times 3^5 = 3^{2+5}$
$= 3^7$

b $x^3 \times x^2 = x^{3+2}$
$= x^5$

c $6m^2n \times mn^4$
$= 6 \times m^{2+1} \times n^{1+4}$
$= 6m^3n^5$

3 Using index law 2

a $x^7 \div x^2 = x^{7-2}$
$= x^5$

b $15a^5 \div 3a^2 = \dfrac{15a^5}{3a^2}$
$= \dfrac{15}{3} \times \dfrac{a^5}{a^2}$
$= 5 \times a^{5-2}$
$= 5a^3$

c $20a^3b^2 \div 10ab$
$= \dfrac{20a^3b^2}{10ab}$
$= \dfrac{20}{10} \times \dfrac{a^3}{a} \times \dfrac{b^2}{b}$
$= 2a^2b$

4 Using index law 3

a $(a^4)^2 = a^{4 \times 2}$
$= a^8$

b $(2a^4)^3 = 2^3 \times (a^4)^3$
$= 8 \times a^{4 \times 3}$
$= 8a^{12}$

c $(p^4)^3 \div (p^2)^4 = p^{12} \div p^8$
$= p^4$

5 Using index law 4

a $7^0 = 1$

b $18x^3 \div 6x^3$
$= \dfrac{18x^3}{6x^3}$
$= 3 \times x^{3-3}$
$= 3x^0$
$= 3 \times 1$
$= 3$

c $(2y^3)^4 \div (4y^6)^2$
$= \dfrac{2^4 \times (y^3)^4}{4^2 \times (y^6)^2}$
$= \dfrac{16}{16} \times \dfrac{y^{12}}{y^{12}}$
$= 1 \times y^0$
$= 1$

With practice, many of the steps in the above solutions can be left out.

Exercise 6:01

P Foundation worksheet 6:01
The index laws

1 Write each expression in index form.

a $2 \times 2 \times 2 \times 2$ b 3×3 c $5 \times 5 \times 5$
d $7 \times 7 \times 7 \times 7 \times 7$ e $10 \times 10 \times 10$ f $9 \times 9 \times 9 \times 9$
g $x \times x$ h $a \times a \times a \times a$ i $n \times n \times n$
j $m \times m \times m \times m \times m$ k $p \times p \times p \times p \times p \times p$ l $y \times y$
m $4 \times 4 \times 4$ n $t \times t \times t \times t$ o $x \times x \times x \times x \times x$

2 Rewrite in expanded form.

a 2^3 b 4^2 c 6^5 d 10^4
e 7^3 f 3^1 g a^3 h x^4
i y^2 j m^5 k n^7 l p^3

3 Determine the basic numeral.

a 2^5 b 3^4 c 7^2 d 11^2
e 10^4 f 6^3 g 2^8 h 5^7
i 8^5 j 9^5 k 4^{12} l 3^{15}
m $2^6 \times 5^3$ n $3^4 \times 7^3$ o $9^3 \times 5^4$ p $12^3 \times 7^3$

This sure is powerful stuff!

4 Simplify these products, writing answers in index form.

a $10^2 \times 10^3$ b 10×10^2 c $10^3 \times 10^3$
d $5^2 \times 5^4$ e $2^3 \times 2^2$ f $7^5 \times 7$
g $3^2 \times 3^3 \times 3^4$ h $2 \times 2^2 \times 2^5$ i $10^7 \times 10 \times 10^2$

5 Simplify these quotients, writing answers in index form.

a $10^2 \div 10$ b $10^6 \div 10^3$ c $10^5 \div 10^4$
d $5^8 \div 5^4$ e $7^5 \div 7^2$ f $3^{10} \div 3$
g $2^3 \div 2^2$ h $5^3 \div 5^3$ i $2^8 \div 2^2$

6 Simplify these powers, writing answers in index form.

a $(10^2)^3$ b $(10^3)^3$ c $(10^6)^2$ d $(2^3)^4$
e $(2^2)^2$ f $(2^7)^5$ g $(3^4)^2$ h $(5^3)^5$
i $(7^2)^4$ j $(2^3 \times 3^2)^2$ k $(7^3 \times 11^4)^2$ l $(3 \times 2^2)^4$

7 Simplify:

a $x^3 \times x^2$ b $y^4 \times y^2$ c $m^3 \times m^3$ d $m \times m^4$
e $p^5 \times p^5$ f $a \times a$ g $y^3 \times y^4$ h $x^2 \times x$
i $m^2 \times m^5$ j $3y^4 \times y$ k $m^6 \times 3$ l $5x^3 \times 3$

8 Simplify:

a $x^6 \div x^3$ b $x^6 \div x^2$ c $x^6 \div x$ d $m^3 \div m$
e $y^5 \div y^2$ f $m^4 \div m^2$ g $y^6 \div y^6$ h $x^5 \div x^5$
i $y^8 \div y^2$ j $6m^6 \div 3$ k $4y^8 \div 2$ l $20x^5 \div 5$

9 Simplify:

a $(x^2)^3$ b $(y^4)^2$ c $(a^3)^5$ d $(m^2)^0$
e $(x^0)^3$ f $(a^7)^0$ g $(y^3)^2$ h $(a^6)^3$
i $(x^3)^3$ j $(2x)^3$ k $(3x^2)^2$ l $(5m^2)^4$

10 Simplify:

a $8x^4 \times x^3$ b $5a^2 \times a$ c $4m^6 \times m^4$ d $8x^4 \div x^3$ e $5a^2 \div a$
f $4m^6 \div m^4$ g $10y^3 \times 5y$ h $16m^2 \times 2m^2$ i $8a^5 \times 4a^4$ j $10y^3 \div 5y$
k $16m^2 \div 2m^2$ l $8a^5 \div 4a^4$ m $12x^5 \times 6x^3$ n $9a^7 \times 3a^2$ o $18y^6 \times 6y$
p $\frac{12x^5}{6x^3}$ q $\frac{9a^7}{3a^2}$ r $\frac{18y^6}{6y}$ s $\frac{3a^5}{a^3}$ t $\frac{10x^5}{5}$ u $\frac{42a^7}{21a^6}$

11 Simplify:

a $6a^0$ b $6(a^3)^0$ c $(6a^3)^0$
d ab^0 e x^0y^3 f m^5n^0
g $(2m^2)^3$ h $(4n^3)^2$ i $(2p^3)^4$
j $x^2y^3 \times x^3$ k $a^2b^5 \times b^4$ l $xy^3 \times x^4$
m $x^2y^2 \times xy^2$ n $a^3b \times a^2b$ o $m^2n \times mn^3$
p $(x^2y^3)^2$ q $(abc)^2$ r $(pq^3)^3$
s $5x^2y \times 2xy$ t $4a^2b^2 \times 7ab^3$ u $11a^3 \times 4a^2b^2$
v $a \times a \times a \times 3a$ w $3a \times 2a \times -4a$ x $5c^4 \times 4c^2 \div 10c^5$
y $12x^2 - 5x^3 + 10x^2$ z $4x(3x + 2) - (x - 1)$

12 Simplify:

a $5x^2 \times 2x^3 \times 3x$ b $5 \times 2a \times 4a^2$ c $5y \times y^2 \times xy$
d $4x^4 \div 8x$ e $7y^3 \div 49y^2$ f $100x^3 \div 10x^4$
g $(x^2)^3 \times x^2$ h $(a^4)^2 \times a^5$ i $(y^7)^3 \times y^5$
j $(a^2)^3 \div a^4$ k $(m^3)^4 \div m^{10}$ l $n^8 \div (n^2)^3$
m $(y^5)^2 \times (y^3)^3$ n $(2a^4)^3 \times (a^3)^2$ o $(b^4)^3 \div (b^2)^5$
p $(x^4 \times x^7) \div x^9$ q $(4a^3 \times 5a^4) \div 10a^5$ r $7p^7q^5 \div (p^2q)^3$
s $\frac{5x^3 \times 4x^7}{10x^5}$ t $\frac{(3x^3)^2 \times 4x^5}{6x^4 \times x}$ u $\frac{x^2 \times (xy)^3}{(2x)^4}$

13 Expand and simplify:

a $x^2(x^2 - 1)$ b $a^3(5 - a^2)$ c $a^2(5a - a^3)$
d $x(x^2 + y)$ e $m(7 - m^2)$ f $y(y^2 - xy)$
g $3a^2(2a^3 + 3a)$ h $5x(3x^2 - x)$ i $2m^3(n^2 - m^2)$
j $x(5x^2 - 3x + 7)$ k $x^2(2x^2 + 7x - 14)$ l $y(y^2 - 7y - 1)$
m $x^2(x - 7) - x^3$ n $y(4y^3 + 2) - 2y$ o $x(x^2 - 7x + 1) - (x^3 - x^2)$

14 Simplify:

a $3^x \times 3^{x+1}$ b $5^{2y} \div 5^{y+1}$ c $(2^x)^2 \div (2^{1-x})^2$
d $e^{2x+1} \times e^x$ e $e^{2x+1} + e^x$ f $(e^{2x+2})^2 \times e^{x+1}$

INVESTIGATION 6:01 EXPLORING INDEX NOTATION

Searching for patterns is part of mathematics, and being able to explain concepts is important if our ideas are to be shared.

- Find pairs of terms that can be multiplied to give 2^7. Explain the relationship between the members of any pair.
- Find pairs of terms that can be divided to give $3x^2$. Explain the difference between the members of any pair.
- Explain the difference between $7x^0$ and $(7x)^0$.
- Explain why $3^2 \times 3^4 \neq 9^6$.
- List all the pairs of expressions that could be multiplied together to give $10xy^2$. (Use only whole numbers.)
- Fold a sheet of A4 paper in half as many times as you can to create regions with folds. How does the number of regions increase with each new fold? Write a formula for the number of regions R for n folds.

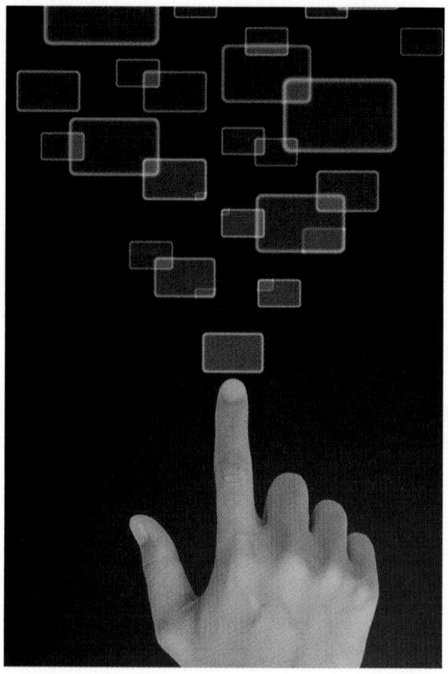

CHALLENGE 6:01 FAMILY TREES

A part of Alan's family tree is drawn below.

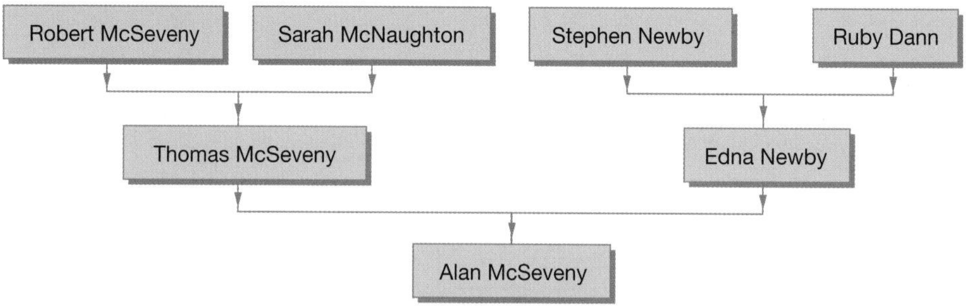

1 How many great-grandparents would Alan have had?

2 Estimate the number of generations you would need to go back so that over one million boxes would be required to show a generation. Would this mean that in that generation there would be over 1 000 000 different ancestors?

3 Estimate Alan's total number of ancestors in the previous 20 generations.

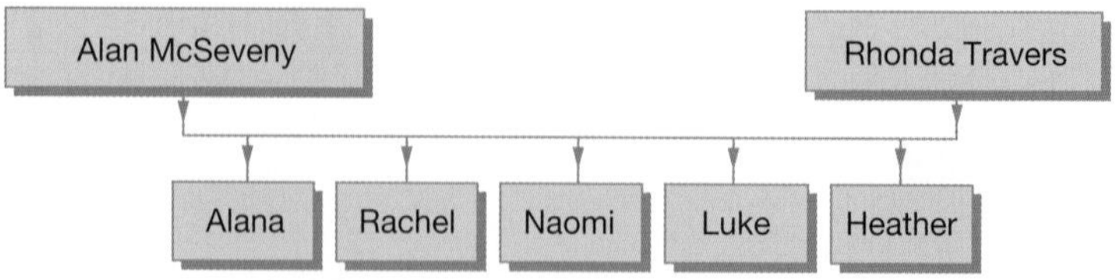

It is much harder to estimate the number of descendants Alan will have in any one generation, as a lot of assumptions will need to be made. Will all of his five children have children of their own? Will there be wars, diseases or population control in the future?

4 Estimate how many generations would be needed before Alan has a total number of descendants in excess of 1 000 000.

6:02 Negative indices

All the indices seen so far have been positive integers or zero.

Using the second index law: $2^3 \div 2^5 = 2^{3-5}$
i.e. $2^3 \div 2^5 = 2^{-2}$

But this could also be written in this way:

$$\frac{2^3}{2^5} = \frac{{}^1\cancel{2} \times {}^1\cancel{2} \times {}^1\cancel{2}}{{}^1\cancel{2} \times {}^1\cancel{2} \times {}^1\cancel{2} \times 2 \times 2}$$
$$= \frac{1}{2 \times 2}$$
$$= \frac{1}{2^2}$$

So $2^{-2} = \dfrac{1}{2^2}$

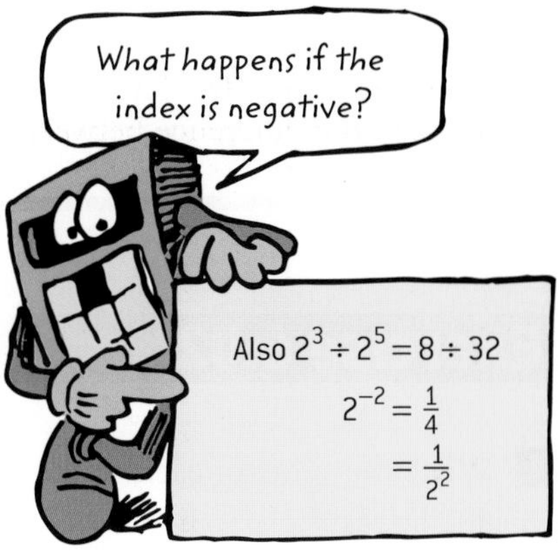

What happens if the index is negative?
Also $2^3 \div 2^5 = 8 \div 32$
$2^{-2} = \frac{1}{4}$
$= \frac{1}{2^2}$

In general, the meaning of a negative index can be summarised by the rule:

$$x^{-m} = \frac{1}{x^m}, \ (x \neq 0)$$

x^{-m} is the reciprocal of x^m, because $x^m \times x^{-m} = 1$

$x^{-3} = \dfrac{1}{x^3}$

$x^3 \times x^{-3} = x^0$
$= 1$

WORKED EXAMPLE 1

Simplify each of the following.

a $3^{-2} = \dfrac{1}{3^2}$
$= \dfrac{1}{9}$

b $5^{-1} = \dfrac{1}{5^1}$
$= \dfrac{1}{5}$

c $x^7 \times x^{-3}$
$= x^{7+(-3)}$
$= x^4$

d $6x^2 \div 3x^4$
$= 2x^{2-4}$
$= 2x^{-2}$
$= \dfrac{2}{x^2}$

e $(\frac{1}{4})^{-2} = \dfrac{1}{(\frac{1}{4})^2}$
$= \dfrac{1}{(\frac{1}{16})}$
$= 16$

$\dfrac{1}{(\frac{1}{16})} = 1 \div \frac{1}{16} = 1 \times \frac{16}{1} = 16$

f $(\frac{2}{3})^{-3} = \dfrac{1}{(\frac{2}{3})^3}$
$= \dfrac{1}{(\frac{8}{27})}$
$= \frac{27}{8}$
$= 3\frac{3}{8}$

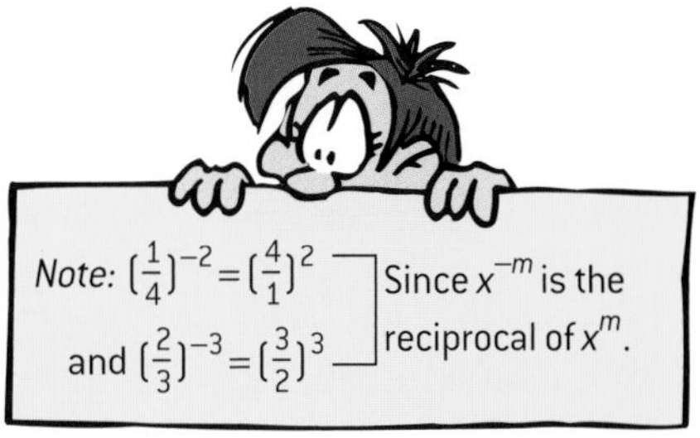

Note: $(\frac{1}{4})^{-2} = (\frac{4}{1})^2$ and $(\frac{2}{3})^{-3} = (\frac{3}{2})^3$
Since x^{-m} is the reciprocal of x^m.

WORKED EXAMPLE 2

Evaluate, using a calculator.

a 2^{-3}　　b $(\frac{1}{3})^{-2}$

Solutions

The key [$x^{\blacksquare}$] can also be used for negative indices. Examine the following:

a Press: 2 [$x^{\blacksquare}$] [(−)] 3 [=]　　Answer: $2^{-3} = \frac{1}{8} = 0{\cdot}125$

b Press: 1 [▤] 3 [▶] [$x^{\blacksquare}$] [(−)] 2 [=]　　Answer: $(\frac{1}{3})^{-2} = (\frac{3}{1})^{2} = 9$

Exercise 6:02

P Foundation worksheet 6:02 **Negative indices**

1 Write the value of each of the following.

a 3^{-1}　b 5^{-1}　c 2^{-1}　d 6^{-2}　e 4^{-2}

f 10^{-3}　g 2^{-4}　h 10^{-4}　i 5^{-2}

2 Write each with a negative index.

a $\frac{1}{11}$　b $\frac{1}{3}$　c $\frac{1}{5}$　d $\frac{1}{7}$　e $\frac{1}{3^3}$　f $\frac{1}{5^4}$

g $\frac{1}{2^8}$　h $\frac{1}{7^2}$　i $\frac{1}{10^2}$　j $\frac{1}{10^3}$　k $\frac{1}{10^6}$　l $\frac{1}{10^5}$

3 Write *true* or *false* for:

a $1024 = 2^{10}$　b $8 = 2^4$　c $3^{-2} = \frac{1}{9}$　d $2(3)^2 = 36$

e $2(3)^{-1} = \frac{1}{6}$　f $4^{-1} = \frac{1}{2}$　g $2^{-1} < 1$　h $-2^8 = (-2)^8$

4 Simplify, leaving answers as powers of ten.

a $10^2 \div 10^5$　b $10^{-2} \times 10^3$　c $10 \div 10^6$　d $10^{-1} \times 10^{-2}$

e $\frac{10^2 \times 10^3}{10^6}$　f $\frac{(10^{-2})^2}{10^2}$　g $\frac{10}{10^2 \div 10^7}$　h $\frac{10^4 \times 10^{-2}}{(10^3)^2}$

5 Write each without a negative index.

a a^{-1}　b x^{-1}　c m^{-1}　d y^{-1}　e x^{-3}　f y^{-2}

g x^{-4}　h m^{-6}　i $2x^{-1}$　j $5a^{-3}$　k $10y^{-2}$　l $36q^{-4}$

6 Rewrite each using a negative index to avoid having a fraction.

a $\frac{1}{x}$　b $\frac{1}{x^2}$　c $\frac{1}{x^3}$　d $\frac{1}{x^4}$　e $\frac{5}{y^2}$　f $\frac{3}{a}$

g $\frac{10}{m^4}$　h $\frac{75}{m^3}$　i $\frac{x}{y^2}$　j $\frac{m}{a^2}$　k $\frac{3a}{b^2}$　l $\frac{4x}{y}$

7 Write each as an integer, fraction or mixed number.

a $\left(\frac{1}{2}\right)^{-1}$ b $\left(\frac{1}{3}\right)^{-1}$ c $\left(\frac{2}{3}\right)^{-1}$ d $\left(\frac{1}{10}\right)^{-1}$

e $\left(\frac{1}{2}\right)^{-2}$ f $\left(\frac{1}{3}\right)^{-2}$ g $\left(\frac{2}{3}\right)^{-2}$ h $\left(\frac{3}{10}\right)^{-2}$

$\left(\frac{a}{b}\right)^{-1} = \frac{b}{a}$

8 Rewrite each expression with a positive index.

a x^{-2} b a^{-5} c $3x^{-1}$ d $5m^{-2}$

e $(x + 1)^{-2}$ f $(3 + a)^{-1}$ g $(6x)^{-2}$ h $4(x + 2)^{-1}$

9 Evaluate the following, using your calculator. Leave your answers in decimal form.

a 2^{-3} b 4^{-2} c 5^{-2} d 8^{-2}

e 2^{-6} f 4^{-3} g $(0{\cdot}5)^{-3}$ h $(0{\cdot}2)^{-2}$

i $(0{\cdot}05)^{-2}$ j $(2{\cdot}5)^{-3}$ k $(0{\cdot}1)^{-5}$ l $(0{\cdot}625)^{-2}$

10 Simplify, writing your answers without negative indices.

a $x^3 \times x^{-2}$ b $a^{-2} \times a^5$ c $m^4 \times m^{-1}$ d $n^5 \times n^{-5}$

e $3a^2 \times a^{-1}$ f $6x^{-2} \times 5x^4$ g $a^{-2} \times 5a^3$ h $15m^{-1} \times 2m^3$

i $x^{-4} \times x$ j $2a^{-2} \times a^{-3}$ k $4y \times 2y^{-2}$ l $15m^{-4} \times 2m^{-1}$

11 Simplify, writing your answers without negative indices.

a $m^4 \div m^{-1}$ b $x^2 \div x^{-2}$ c $y^{-6} \div y^{-8}$ d $x^3 \div x^{-1}$

e $a^{-2} \div a^2$ f $y^{-1} \div y^3$ g $y^{-2} \div y$ h $x^{-3} \div x^{-1}$

i $6x^2 \div 2x^{-1}$ j $10a^3 \div 5a^7$ k $24a^{-2} \div a^3$ l $18n^{-1} \div 9n^{-2}$

12 Simplify, writing your answers without negative indices.

a $(a^{-3})^{-2}$ b $(x^2)^{-1}$ c $(y^{-3})^2$ d $(m^{-2})^{-2}$

e $(2x^2)^{-1}$ f $(3x)^{-2}$ g $(5x^{-1})^2$ h $(7x^{-2})^2$

i $(abc)^{-1}$ j $(a^2b^2c^2)^{-1}$ k $(2a^2b)^{-1}$ l $2(a^2b)^{-1}$

13 If $x = 2$, $y = 3$ and $z = \frac{1}{2}$, evaluate:

a $x^{-1} + y^{-1}$ b $(xy)^{-1}$ c $(xz)^{-1}$ d $x^{-1}y^{-1}z$

14 Simplify:

a $3^x \div 3^{-x}$ b $5^y \div 5^{2-y}$ c $e^{x+1} \div e^{1-x}$ d $(e^x)^2 \div e^{-(x-1)}$

The formula for the volume of a sphere is $V = \frac{4}{3}\pi r^3$, where $\pi \approx 3{\cdot}142$ and r is the radius of the sphere.

6:03 Fractional indices

PREP QUIZ 6:03

Complete:

1 $5^2 = 25$, $\sqrt{25} = \ldots$

2 $7^2 = 49$, $\sqrt{49} = \ldots$

3 $2^3 = 8$, $\sqrt[3]{8} = \ldots$

4 $5^3 = 125$, $\sqrt[3]{125} = \ldots$

Consider the following:

5 $5^a \times 5^a = 5^{2a}$
If $5^n \times 5^n = 5^1$,
what is the value of n?

6 $8^a \times 8^a = 8^{2a}$
If $8^n \times 8^n = 8^1$,
what is the value of n?

7 $x^a \times x^a = x^{2a}$
If $x^n \times x^n = x^1$,
what is the value of n?

8 $y^a \times y^a = y^{2a}$
If $y^n \times y^n = y^1$,
what is the value of n?

9 $5^a \times 5^a \times 5^a = 5^{3a}$
If $5^n \times 5^n \times 5^n = 5^1$,
what is the value of n?

10 $x^a \times x^a \times x^a = x^{3a}$
If $x^n \times x^n \times x^n = x^1$,
what is the value of n?

What is the meaning of a fractional index?

The meaning is shown in the examples below.

1 $$9^{\frac{1}{2}} \times 9^{\frac{1}{2}} = 9^{(\frac{1}{2}+\frac{1}{2})} = 9^1 = 9$$

$$3 \times 3 = 9 \qquad \sqrt{9} \times \sqrt{9} = 9$$

$9^{\frac{1}{2}}$ multiplied by itself gives 9 and $\sqrt{9}$ multiplied by itself gives 9.
So $9^{\frac{1}{2}}$ is the square root of 9.
$\therefore\ 9^{\frac{1}{2}} = \sqrt{9}$

That's neat!
$(5^{\frac{1}{2}})^2 = 5$
That means that
$5^{\frac{1}{2}}$ is the square root of 5.

2 $$5^{\frac{1}{2}} \times 5^{\frac{1}{2}} = 5^{(\frac{1}{2}+\frac{1}{2})} = 5^1 = 5$$

Now $\sqrt{5} \times \sqrt{5} = 5$
So $5^{\frac{1}{2}} = \sqrt{5}$

{ The number that multiplies itself to give 5 (i.e. $5^{\frac{1}{2}}$) is the square root of 5.

3 Similarly:

$$8^{\frac{1}{3}} \times 8^{\frac{1}{3}} \times 8^{\frac{1}{3}} = 8^{(\frac{1}{3}+\frac{1}{3}+\frac{1}{3})} = 8^1 = 8$$

$$2 \times 2 \times 2 = 8 \qquad \sqrt[3]{8} \times \sqrt[3]{8} \times \sqrt[3]{8} = 8$$

Two is the cube root of 8.

So $8^{\frac{1}{3}} = \sqrt[3]{8}$, (the cube root of 8)
$\therefore\ 8^{\frac{1}{3}} = 2$

$(\sqrt[3]{x})^3 = x$ so $\sqrt[3]{x} = x^{\frac{1}{3}}$

$x^{\frac{1}{2}} = \sqrt{x}$,
$x^{\frac{1}{3}} = \sqrt[3]{x}$,
$x^{\frac{1}{n}} = n$th root of x
$x^{\frac{1}{3}}$ is the number that, when multiplied by itself three times, gives x.

WORKED EXAMPLES

1 Simplify the following:

a $25^{\frac{1}{2}}$ b $27^{\frac{1}{3}}$ c $3x^{\frac{1}{2}} \times 4x^{\frac{1}{2}}$

d $(49m^6)^{\frac{1}{2}}$ e $8^{\frac{2}{3}}$ f $9^{-\frac{3}{2}}$

2 Evaluate using your calculator:

a $196^{\frac{1}{2}}$ b $32^{\frac{1}{5}}$ c $256^{-\frac{1}{4}}$ d $125^{-\frac{4}{3}}$

Solutions

1 a $25^{\frac{1}{2}} = \sqrt{25}$
$= 5$

b $27^{\frac{1}{3}} = \sqrt[3]{27}$
$= 3$

c $3x^{\frac{1}{2}} \times 4x^{\frac{1}{2}} = 12x^{\frac{1}{2}\times\frac{1}{2}}$
$= 12x$

d $(49m^6)^{\frac{1}{2}} = 49^{\frac{1}{2}} \times m^{6\times\frac{1}{2}}$
$= \sqrt{49} \times m^3$
$= 7m^3$

e $8^{\frac{2}{3}} = (8^{\frac{1}{3}})^2$
$= (\sqrt[3]{8})^2$
$= 2^2$
$= 4$

f $9^{-\frac{3}{2}} = (9^{\frac{1}{2}})^{-3}$
$= (\sqrt{9})^{-3}$
$= \frac{1}{3^3}$
$= \frac{1}{27}$

From examples **e** and **f**:
$x^{\frac{p}{q}} = \sqrt[q]{x^p}$ or $(\sqrt[q]{x})^p$

2 a $196^{\frac{1}{2}} = \sqrt{196}$
using the square root key
$\sqrt{196} = 14$

b To evaluate $32^{\frac{1}{5}}$
press: 5 [SHIFT] [$\sqrt[\blacksquare]{\square}$] 32 [=]
Answer: $32^{\frac{1}{5}} = 2$

c To evaluate $256^{-\frac{1}{4}}$
Press: 256 [$x^{\blacksquare}$] [(−)] 1 [$\frac{\blacksquare}{\square}$] 4 [=]
Answer: $256^{-\frac{1}{4}} = \frac{1}{4}$ or 0·25

d To evaluate $125^{-\frac{4}{3}}$
Press: 125 [$x^{\blacksquare}$] [(−)] 4 [$\frac{\blacksquare}{\square}$] 3 [=]
Answer: $125^{-\frac{4}{3}} = \frac{1}{625}$ or 0·0016

For roots higher than a square root ($\frac{1}{2}$), use the [$x^{1/y}$] or [$\sqrt[\blacksquare]{\square}$] key.
Some calculators have a cube root ($\frac{1}{3}$) key, [$\sqrt[3]{\ }$] or [$\sqrt[3]{\blacksquare}$].
You may need to use the inverse or [SHIFT] key.
Alternatively, you can use the [$x^{\blacksquare}$] key and enter the power as a fraction.

$(ab)^{\frac{1}{3}} = a^{\frac{1}{3}}b^{\frac{1}{3}}$

Exercise 6:03

P Foundation worksheet 6:03
Fractional indices
Challenge worksheet 6:03
Algebraic expressions and indices

1 Write each of the following using a square root sign.

a $5^{\frac{1}{2}}$ b $10^{\frac{1}{2}}$ c $2^{\frac{1}{2}}$ d $3 \times 2^{\frac{1}{2}}$ e $4 \times 3^{\frac{1}{2}}$ f $7 \times 6^{\frac{1}{2}}$

2 Use a fractional index to write:

a $\sqrt{3}$ b $3\sqrt{2}$ c $\sqrt[3]{11}$ d $7\sqrt{3}$

3 Find the value of the following:

a $4^{\frac{1}{2}}$ b $49^{\frac{1}{2}}$ c $8^{\frac{1}{3}}$ d $16^{\frac{1}{4}}$

e $16^{\frac{1}{2}}$ f $100^{\frac{1}{2}}$ g $144^{\frac{1}{2}}$ h $1^{\frac{1}{2}}$

i $121^{\frac{1}{2}}$ j $32^{\frac{1}{5}}$ k $81^{\frac{1}{2}}$ l $81^{\frac{1}{4}}$

4 Assuming that all pronumerals used are positive, simplify:

a $x^{\frac{1}{2}} \times x^{\frac{1}{2}}$ b $a^{\frac{1}{3}} \times a^{\frac{2}{3}}$ c $m^{\frac{1}{2}} \times m^{\frac{1}{2}}$

d $6x^{\frac{1}{2}} \times 2x^{\frac{1}{2}}$ e $3y^{\frac{1}{4}} \times 2y^{\frac{3}{4}}$ f $9n^{\frac{2}{3}} \times 2n^{\frac{1}{3}}$

g $(x^2)^{\frac{1}{2}}$ h $(y^6)^{\frac{1}{3}}$ i $(4a^6)^{\frac{1}{2}}$

j $(a^2b^4)^{\frac{1}{2}}$ k $(9x^4y^6)^{\frac{1}{2}}$ l $(8x^3y^3)^{\frac{1}{3}}$

$(x^a)^b = x^{ab}$

5 Evaluate:

a $9^{-\frac{1}{2}}$ b $25^{-\frac{1}{2}}$ c $8^{-\frac{1}{3}}$ d $9^{\frac{3}{2}}$ e $4^{\frac{3}{2}}$ f $4^{\frac{5}{2}}$

g $16^{\frac{3}{4}}$ h $125^{\frac{2}{3}}$ i $8^{-\frac{2}{3}}$ j $9^{\frac{5}{2}}$ k $32^{\frac{4}{5}}$ l $16^{-\frac{3}{4}}$

6 Evaluate using your calculator, leaving answers as decimal numbers:

a $225^{\frac{1}{2}}$ b $784^{\frac{1}{2}}$ c $1024^{\frac{1}{2}}$ d $729^{\frac{1}{3}}$ e $3375^{\frac{1}{3}}$ f $3000^{\frac{1}{3}}$

g $225^{\frac{3}{2}}$ h $729^{\frac{2}{3}}$ i $8000^{\frac{5}{3}}$ j $(0 \cdot 125)^{-\frac{2}{3}}$ k $(0 \cdot 25)^{-\frac{5}{2}}$ l $(0 \cdot 01)^{-\frac{3}{2}}$

7 If $a = 4$, $b = 8$ and $c = 9$, evaluate the following:

a $a^{\frac{1}{2}} + b^{\frac{1}{3}}$ b $(ab)^{\frac{1}{5}}$ c $2c^{\frac{3}{2}}$ d $\frac{1}{2}(ac)^{\frac{1}{2}}$

e $a^{-\frac{1}{2}} + b^{-\frac{1}{3}}$ f $(2b)^{-\frac{1}{4}}$ g $(2ab)^{-\frac{1}{6}}$ h $(2bc)^{\frac{1}{2}} - a^{\frac{3}{2}}$

8 Use the fact that $x^{\frac{p}{q}} = \sqrt[q]{x^p}$ to simplify:

a $(27a^3)^{\frac{2}{3}}$ b $(x^6y^{12})^{\frac{2}{3}}$ c $(8m^9)^{\frac{2}{3}}$

d $\left(\frac{a^3}{b^3}\right)^{\frac{2}{3}}$ e $\left(\frac{16}{x^4}\right)^{\frac{3}{4}}$ f $\left(\frac{y^6}{25}\right)^{\frac{3}{2}}$

$x^{\frac{1}{2}} = \sqrt{x}$

$x^{\frac{1}{2}}$ stands for the positive square root of x.

FUN SPOT 6:03 WHY IS A ROOM FULL OF MARRIED PEOPLE ALWAYS EMPTY?

Work out the answer to each part and write the letter for that part in the box that is above the correct answer.

Write in index form.

E 10×10 E $8 \times 8 \times 8$ E $yyyyaa$

Find the value of:

E 3^2 E 2^3 E $5^2 - 5$

A 10^3 A $2^3 - 3^2$

Find the value of x in:

I $2^x = 16$ I $3^x = 9$

Write as a basic numeral.

I $1{\cdot}7 \times 10^2$ I $6{\cdot}04 \div 10$

Evaluate:

O x^0 O $7^0 + 9$ U $11y^0$ N 2^{-2} N 10^{-3}

N $(\frac{2}{3})^{-1}$ N $36^{\frac{1}{2}}$ B $27^{\frac{1}{3}}$ C $7a \times a^{-1}$

H To fill a jar in 6 minutes, Jan doubled the number of peanuts in the jar every minute. After how many minutes was the jar half-full?

Simplify:

S $3x - x$ S $3x \times x$ T $5 \times 5x$ R $10x \div 10$

T $x^2 \times x^3$ T $x^{10} \div x^2$ S $(x^2)^3$ L $60x^3 \div 5x^3$

S $\dfrac{4aab}{ab}$ R $x^{10} \times x^{-3}$ P $x^3 \div x^{-1}$ G $\dfrac{1}{10^2}$

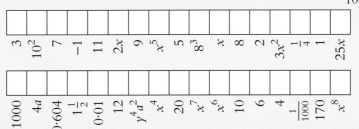

3	10^2	7	−1	11	$2x$	9	x^5	5	8^3	x	8	2	$3x^2$	$\frac{1}{4}$	1	$25x$

1000	$4a$	0·604	$1\frac{1}{2}$	0·01	12	y^4a^2	x^4	20	x^7	x^6	10	6	4	$\frac{1}{1000}$	170	x^8

INVESTIGATION 6:03 REASONING WITH FRACTIONAL INDICES

- Write $\sqrt{x}, \sqrt{x^2}, \sqrt{x^3}, \sqrt{x^4}, \sqrt{x^5}, \ldots$ as expressions with fractional indices and describe the pattern that emerges.
- Find the value of b if $(x^b)^3 = x$.
- Explain why $\sqrt{8} = 2^{\frac{3}{2}} = 2\sqrt{2} = (\sqrt{2})^3$.
- Find some values that x, p and q could take if $x^{\frac{p}{q}} = 2$.

6:04 Scientific (or standard) notation

INVESTIGATION 6:04 MULTIPLYING AND DIVIDING BY POWERS OF 10

Use the $x^{■}$ or the $\times 10^x$ button on your calculator to answer these questions.

Look for a connection between questions and answers and then fill in the rules at the end of the investigation.

Exercises

1 **a** $1{\cdot}8 \times 10^1$ **b** $1{\cdot}8 \times 10^2$ **c** $1{\cdot}8 \times 10^3$
d $4{\cdot}05 \times 10^1$ **e** $4{\cdot}05 \times 10^2$ **f** $4{\cdot}05 \times 10^3$
g $6{\cdot}2 \times 10^4$ **h** $6{\cdot}2 \times 10^5$ **i** $6{\cdot}2 \times 10^6$
j $3{\cdot}1416 \times 10^2$ **k** $3{\cdot}1416 \times 10^3$ **l** $3{\cdot}1416 \times 10^4$

> To multiply by 10^n move the decimal point … places to the …

2 **a** $1{\cdot}8 \div 10^1$ **b** $1{\cdot}8 \div 10^2$ **c** $1{\cdot}8 \div 10^3$
d $968{\cdot}5 \div 10^2$ **e** $968{\cdot}5 \div 10^3$ **f** $968{\cdot}5 \div 10^4$

> To divide by 10^n move the decimal point … places to the …

The investigation above should have reminded you that:
- when we multiply a decimal by 10, 100 or 1000, we move the decimal point 1, 2 or 3 places to the right
- when we divide a decimal by 10, 100 or 1000, we move the decimal point 1, 2 or 3 places to the left.

> When expressing numbers in scientific (or standard) notation, each number is written as the product of a number between 1 and 10, and a power of 10.

$6{\cdot}1 \times 10^5$

- This number is written in scientific notation (or standard form).
- The first part is between 1 and 10.
- The second part is a power of 10.

> 'Scientific notation' is sometimes called 'standard notation' or 'standard form'.

> Scientific notation is useful when writing very large or very small numbers.

Numbers greater than 1

$5970\cdot = 5{\cdot}97 \times 10^3$

To write 5970 in standard form:

- place a decimal point after the first digit
- count the number of places you have to move the decimal point to the left from its original position.

To multiply 5·97 by 10³, we move the decimal point 3 places to the right—which gives 5970.

WORKED EXAMPLE 1

Express the following in scientific notation.

a $243 = 2{\cdot}43 \times 100$
$= 2{\cdot}43 \times 10^2$

b $60\,000 = 6 \times 10\,000$
$= 6 \times 10^4$

c $93\,800\,000 = 9{\cdot}38 \times 10\,000\,000$
$= 9{\cdot}38 \times 10^7$

> $10^6 = 1$ million
> $10^9 = 1$ billion

> If end zeros are significant, write them in your answer.
> e.g. $60\,000 = 6{\cdot}00 \times 10^4$
> (to nearest 100)

> We have moved the decimal point 7 places from its original position.

WORKED EXAMPLE 2

Write each of the following as a basic numeral.

a $1{\cdot}3 \times 10^2 = 1{\cdot}30 \times 100$
$= 130$ (1·3 hundreds)

b $2{\cdot}431 \times 10^2 = 2{\cdot}431 \times 100$
$= 243{\cdot}1$ (2·431 hundreds)

c $4{\cdot}63 \times 10^7 = 4{\cdot}630\,000\,0 \times 10\,000\,000$
$= 46\,300\,000$ (4·63 tens of millions)

> To multiply by 10^7, move the decimal point 7 places right.

Numbers less than 1

$0{\cdot}005\,97 = 5{\cdot}97 \times 10^{-3}$ (5·97 thousandths)

To write 0·005 97 in scientific notation:

- place a decimal point after the first non-zero digit
- count the number of places you have moved the decimal point to the right from its original position.

This will show the negative number needed as the power of 10.

5·97 × 10⁻³ = 0·00597
Multiplying by 10⁻³ is the same as dividing by 10³, so we would move the decimal point 3 places to the left.

> $5{\cdot}97 \times 10^{-3}$ is the same as $5{\cdot}97 \div 10^3$.

WORKED EXAMPLE 1

Express each number in scientific notation.

a $0{\cdot}043 = 4{\cdot}3 \div 100$
$= 4{\cdot}3 \times 10^{-2}$

b $0{\cdot}000\,0597 = 5{\cdot}97 \div 100\,000$
$= 5{\cdot}97 \times 10^{-5}$

c $0{\cdot}004 = 4 \div 1000$
$= 4 \times 10^{-3}$

Shortcut method

- In 0·043, how many places do we move the decimal point for scientific notation? [Answer: 2 places]
- Is 0·043 bigger or smaller than 1? [Answer: smaller]
- So, the power of 10 is −2.
  $\therefore 0{\cdot}043 = 4{\cdot}3 \times 10^{-2}$

WORKED EXAMPLE 2

Write each as a basic numeral.

a $2{\cdot}9 \times 10^{-2} = 002{\cdot}9 \div 100$
$= 0{\cdot}029$

b $9{\cdot}38 \times 10^{-5} = 000\,009{\cdot}38 \div 100\,000$
$= 0{\cdot}000\,093\,8$

c $1{\cdot}004 \times 10^{-3} = 0001{\cdot}004 \div 1000$
$= 0{\cdot}001\,004$

Exercise 6:04

P Foundation worksheet 6:04 Scientific notation

1 a Explain the difference between 2×10^4 and 2^4.
b Explain the difference between 5×10^{-2} and 5^{-2}.
c How many seconds are in 50 000 years?
d Have you lived $8{\cdot}2 \times 10^4$ hours?
e Order the following, from smallest to largest.

$3{\cdot}24 \times 10^3$	6	$9{\cdot}8 \times 10^{-5}$	$5{\cdot}6 \times 10^{-2}$
$1{\cdot}2 \times 10^4$	2·04	$5{\cdot}499 \times 10^2$	0·0034

f Write the thickness of a sheet of paper in scientific notation if 500 sheets of paper have a thickness of 3·8 cm.
g Estimate the thickness of the cover of this book. Write your estimate in scientific notation.

If you're stuck with this exercise, think back to Investigation 6:04 . . .

2 Write as a basic numeral.

a $2{\cdot}1 \times 10^1$	b $2{\cdot}1 \div 10^1$	c $2{\cdot}1 \times 10^{-1}$
d $7{\cdot}04 \times 10^2$	e $7{\cdot}04 \div 10^2$	f $7{\cdot}04 \times 10^{-2}$
g $1{\cdot}375 \times 10^3$	h $1{\cdot}375 \div 10^3$	i $1{\cdot}375 \times 10^{-3}$

3 Express in scientific notation. (Assume that final zeros are not significant.)

a 470	b 2600	c 53 000	d 700	e 50 000
f 700 000	g 65	h 342	i 90	j 4970
k 63 500	l 2 941 000	m 297·1	n 69·3	o 4976·5
p 9 310 000	q 67 000 000	r 190 100	s 600 000	t 501 700
u 100 000				

4 Express in scientific notation.

a 0·075	b 0·0063	c 0·59	d 0·08	e 0·0003
f 0·009	g 0·3	h 0·0301	i 0·000 529	j 0·426
k 0·001	l 0·000 0097	m 0·000 06	n 0·000 907	o 0·000 000 004

5 Write as a basic numeral.

a $2{\cdot}3 \times 10^{2}$	b $9{\cdot}4 \times 10^{4}$	c $3{\cdot}7 \times 10^{3}$	d $2{\cdot}95 \times 10^{2}$
e $8{\cdot}74 \times 10^{1}$	f $7{\cdot}63 \times 10^{5}$	g $1{\cdot}075 \times 10^{3}$	h $2{\cdot}0 \times 10^{4}$
i 8×10^{1}	j $2{\cdot}9 \times 10^{-2}$	k $1{\cdot}9 \times 10^{-3}$	l $9{\cdot}5 \times 10^{-1}$
m $3{\cdot}76 \times 10^{-3}$	n $4{\cdot}63 \times 10^{-4}$	o $1{\cdot}07 \times 10^{-2}$	p 7×10^{-2}
q $8{\cdot}0 \times 10^{-1}$	r 5×10^{-6}	s $9{\cdot}73 \times 10^{5}$	t $6{\cdot}3 \times 10^{-3}$
u $4{\cdot}7 \times 10^{7}$	v $9{\cdot}142 \times 10^{2}$	w $1{\cdot}032 \times 10^{-2}$	x $1{\cdot}0 \times 10^{8}$

6:05 Scientific notation and the calculator

PREP QUIZ 6:05

Write in scientific notation.

1 690 **2** 4000 **3** 963·2 **4** 0·073 **5** 0·0003

Rewrite as basic numerals.

6 $2{\cdot}9 \times 10^{3}$ **7** $8{\cdot}0 \times 10^{5}$ **8** $4{\cdot}6 \times 10^{-2}$ **9** 5×10^{-7} **10** $8{\cdot}14 \times 10^{-1}$

To enter scientific notation, press:

- 5.517 [$\times 10^x$] 12 to enter $5{\cdot}517 \times 10^{12}$
- 3.841 [$\times 10^x$] [(−)] 6 to enter $3{\cdot}841 \times 10^{-6}$

On some calculators the [$\times 10^x$] key is shown as [EXP].

On some calculators:

- $5{\cdot}517 \times 10^{12}$ is shown as [5.517 12]
- $3{\cdot}841 \times 10^{-6}$ is shown as [3.841 -06]

To convert calculator answers into decimal form:

$2{\cdot}16 \times 10^{-3}$

First part ↑ Index ↑

1. Locate the decimal point in the first part of the number (the part between 1 and 10).
2. Look at the sign of the index. This tells you in which direction to move the decimal point. If it is negative the point moves to the left. If it is positive the point moves to the right.
3. Look at the size of the index. This tells you how many places the decimal point has to be moved.
4. Move the decimal point to its new position, filling in any gaps, where necessary, with zeros.

0·002 16

Some scientific calculators give answers in scientific (or standard) notation.

WORKED EXAMPLES

Use a calculator to find the answers.

A calculator may give an answer in scienfitic notation if the number is too large or small to fit on the screen.

1 $630\,000 \times (47\,000)^2$
$= 1{\cdot}391\,67 \times 10^{15}$
$= 1\,391\,670\,000\,000\,000$

2 $45 \div (8614)^3$
$= 7{\cdot}040\,409\,359 \times 10^{-11}$
$= 0{\cdot}000\,000\,000\,070\,404\,093\,59$

The answers to **1** and **2** are too long to fit on the screen.

3 $(8{\cdot}4 \times 10^6) + (3{\cdot}8 \times 10^7)$
Press: *8.4* [×10^x] *6* [+] *3.8* [×10^x] *7*
$= 46\,400\,000$

Note: Not all calculators work the same way.

4 $\sqrt{1{\cdot}44 \times 10^{-6}}$
Press: [√■] *1.44* [×10^x] [(−)] *6* [=]
$= 0{\cdot}0012$

Exercise 6:05

1 Enter each of these on your calculator using the [×10^x] key, and copy the readout.
a $6{\cdot}3 \times 10^4$ b $1{\cdot}4 \times 10^{-3}$ c $9{\cdot}25 \times 10^7$

2 Rewrite these calculator answers in scientific notation using powers of 10.
a *56000* b *43000000* c *763000*
d *0.0004* e *0.0000029* f *0.0000731*
g *1500* h *0.00278* i *6090000*
j Explain why a calculator entry of 2×10^4 has a different value to 2^4.

$1{\cdot}402 \times 10^7$ has four significant figures, as four figures are used in the decimal part.

3 Place the nine answers in Question **2** in order of size from smallest to largest.

4 Give the answers to these in scientific notation, correct to five significant figures.
a 3814^4 b $0{\cdot}0004 \div 8400^2$
c $(0{\cdot}0007)^5$ d $93\,000\,000 \div 0{\cdot}000\,13$
e $(65 \times 847)^3$ f $(0{\cdot}0045)^3 \times (0{\cdot}0038)^2$
g $\dfrac{9865 \times 8380}{0{\cdot}000\,021}$ h $\dfrac{6800}{(0{\cdot}0007)^5}$

Use the index laws to check the size of your answer.

5 Use a calculator to answer correct to four significant figures, and then use the index laws to check your answer.
a $13{\cdot}85 \times (2{\cdot}3 \times 10^4)$ b $(8{\cdot}14 \times 10^{-2})^2$ c $(2{\cdot}1 \times 10^8) \div (8{\cdot}6 \times 10^8)$
d $(3{\cdot}8 \times 10^{-3})^2$ e $468 \times (1{\cdot}8 \times 10^{-5})$ f $(9{\cdot}1 \times 10^4) + (6{\times}8 \times 10^5)$
g $\sqrt{7{\cdot}45 \times 10^9}$ h $\sqrt[3]{9{\cdot}1 \times 10^{-8}}$ i $\sqrt[3]{6{\cdot}714 \times 10^{-12}}$

6 a An American reported that the diameter of the Sun is approximately $8{\cdot}656 \times 10^5$ miles. Write this in kilometres using scientific notation correct to four significant figures. (There are 1·609 km in a mile.) If the Sun's diameter is 109 times that of Earth, what is Earth's diameter, correct to three significant figures?

b The distance to the Sun varies from $1{\cdot}47 \times 10^8$ km in January to $1{\cdot}52 \times 10^8$ km in July. This is because Earth's orbit is an ellipse. What is the difference between these distances?

c If we use the average distance to the Sun ($1{\cdot}50 \times 10^8$ km), how long would it take light travelling at $3{\cdot}0 \times 10^8$ m/s to reach Earth? (Answer correct to the nearest minute.)

d The mass of Earth is approximately 6×10^{21} tonnes. The Sun's mass is about 333 400 times greater than the mass of Earth. What is the mass of the Sun correct to one significant figure?

e We belong to the galaxy known as the Milky Way. It contains about 1×10^{11} stars. If the Sun is taken to have average mass (see part d), what is the total mass, correct to one significant figure, of the stars in the Milky Way?

INVESTIGATION 6:05 USING SCIENTIFIC NOTATION

1 The speed of light is $3{\cdot}0 \times 10^8$ m/s. Use reference materials (such as books or the internet) and your calculator to complete this table for five stars of your choice (e.g. Vega, Polaris, Betelgeuse, Antares, Sirius).

Name of star	Distance from Earth	Time taken for light to travel to Earth
The Sun	$1{\cdot}5 \times 10^8$ km	
Alpha Centauri	$4{\cdot}2 \times 10^{13}$ km	

10^6 is 1 million.
10^9 is 1 billion.

Order the distances of the five stars from Earth, from smallest to largest.

2 Research nanotechnology, which involves the use of very small machine parts. Parts are often measured in micrometres. Make comparisons between the sizes of components.

Distances in astronomy are measured in light years, which is the distance that light travels in a year. A light year is approximately $9{\cdot}5 \times 10^{12}$ km.

6:06 Conversions using scientific notation

Very large and very small units of measurement were introduced in Section 1:09.

In these tables, each unit is 1000 times as big as the one on its right.

Tm	Gm	Mm	km	m	mm	μm	nm
10^{12} m	10^{9} m	10^{6} m	10^{3} m	1 m	10^{-3} m	10^{-6} m	10^{-9} m

1 terabyte = 1000 gigabytes (1 TB = 1000 GB)
1 gigabyte = 1000 megabytes (1 GB = 1000 MB)
1 megabyte = 1000 kilobytes (1 MB = 1000 kB)

TB	GB	MB	kB	B
10^{12} B	10^{9} B	10^{6} B	10^{3} B	1 B

1 second = 1000 milliseconds (1 s = 1000 ms)
1 millisecond = 1000 microseconds (1 ms = 1000 μs)
1 microsecond = 1000 nanoseconds (1 μs = 1000 ns)

s	ms	μs	ns
1 s	10^{-3} s	10^{-6} s	10^{-9} s

- When using scientific notation, all significant figures are shown in the first part of the number.
  e.g. 7×10^{12} B has 1 sig. fig. $\quad$ $7{\cdot}000 \times 10^{-3}$ s has 4 sig. fig.
  $3{\cdot}4 \times 10^{-3}$ s has 2 sig. fig. $\quad$ $3{\cdot}40 \times 10^{-3}$ s has 3 sig. fig.

PREP QUIZ 6:06

Convert:

1 4 terabytes (TB) to gigabytes (GB)
2 7 gigabytes (GB) to megabytes (MB)
3 6 megabytes (MB) to kilobytes (kB)
4 9 kilobytes (kB) to bytes (B)
5 2 metres (m) to millimetres (mm)
6 3 millimetres (mm) to micrometres (μm)
7 5 micrometres (μm) to nanometres (nm)
8 4 megametres (Mm) to metres (m)
9 8 metres (m) to micrometres (μm)
10 7 metres (m) to nanometres (nm)

WORKED EXAMPLES

1 Use scientific notation to write 3·4 terabytes as bytes.
1 TB = 10^{12} B, so
3·4 TB = $3{\cdot}4 \times 10^{12}$ B

2 Use scientific notation to write 7·8 microseconds as seconds.
1 μs = 10^{-6} s, so
7·8 μs = $7{\cdot}8 \times 10^{-6}$ s

3 Use scientific notation to write 850 MB as bytes.
1 MB = 10^{6} B, so
850 MB = 850×10^{6} B
(However, the first part needs to be a number between 1 and 10.)
= $(8{\cdot}5 \times 10^{2}) \times 10^{6}$ B
= $8{\cdot}5 \times 10^{8}$ B

4 Use scientific notation to write 67 ns as seconds.
1 ns = 10^{9} s, so
67 ns = 67×10^{-9} s
(However, the first part needs to be a number between 1 and 10.)
= $(6{\cdot}7 \times 10^{1}) \times 10^{-9}$ s
= $6{\cdot}7 \times 10^{-8}$ s

Exercise 6:06

1 How many significant figures has each of these measurements?

a $9{\cdot}1 \times 10^7$ B　b $4{\cdot}125 \times 10^{-6}$ s　c $3{\cdot}00 \times 10^{-5}$ s　d 9×10^8 L

2 Use scientific notation to write each of these as bytes (B).

a 8000 bytes　b 6 kilobytes　c 4 megabytes　d 8 gigabytes
e 4·7 terabytes　f 2·4 megabytes　g 6·15 kilobytes　h 8·0 gigabytes
i 9·2TB　j 7·70 MB　k 5·15 kB　l 8·0 GB
m 15TB　n 103 MB　o 852 kB　p 605 GB
q 80 000 kB (3 sig. fig.)　r 4000 GB (nearest 100 gigabytes)

3 Use scientific notation to write each of these as seconds (s).

a 8 milliseconds　b 7 microseconds　c 2 nanoseconds
d 9 milliseconds　e 3·60 milliseconds　f 8·4 microseconds
g 7·0 nanoseconds　h 9·56 milliseconds　i 1·25 ns
j 7·7 μs　k 8·125 ms　l 8·0 μs
m 15 ms　n 103 μs　p 605 μs
q 80 000 μs (2 sig. fig.)　r 20 000 ns (nearest 100 nanoseconds)

4 The capacity of Warragamba Dam is $2{\cdot}031 \times 10^{12}$ L. Write this in ML, GL and TL.

5 In biology, the sizes of viruses and bacteria are measured in nanometres (nm) and micrometres (μm). A nanometre is one-thousand-millionth of a metre.
How many nanometres are in:

a a metre
b a millimetre
c a micrometre?

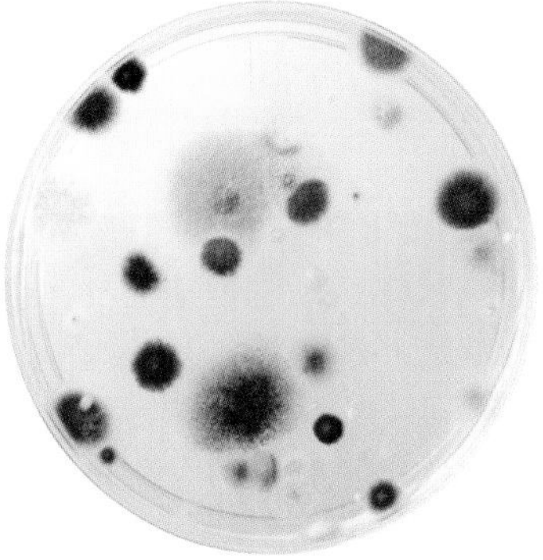

6 In physics, the frequency of electromagnetic radiation is measured in kilohertz (kHz) and gigahertz (GHz).
A gigahertz is one thousand million hertz (Hz).
Convert 1 gigahertz into:

a kilohertz　b megahertz

7 The hard disk of a computer was reported by the manufacturer to have a capacity of about 400 gigabytes. However the operating system of the computer reported that the hard disk had a capacity of 372 GB. This confusion occurs because some operating systems use a binary (base 2) definition of a gigabyte, which is 2^{30} bytes, whereas the disk manufacturers use the base 10 definition, which is 1000 million bytes. So when the computer calculates the size of the hard drive it gives a smaller value than the decimal figure, even though the actual number of bytes is the same.
Find the difference, correct to four significant figures, between 1 GB (base 10) and 1 GB (base 2).

MATHS TERMS 6

base

- the term that is operated on by the index, e.g. for x^n, x is the base
  for 5^3, 5 is the base

exponent

- another term for a power or index
- equations that involve a power are called exponential equations, e.g. $3x = 2^7$

fractional indices

- another way of writing the 'root' of a number or term
- $x^{\frac{1}{2}} = \sqrt{x}$, $x^{\frac{1}{3}} = \sqrt[3]{x}$, $x^{\frac{1}{n}} = \sqrt[n]{x}$

index (plural: **indices**)

- a number indicating how many of a base term need to be multiplied together, e.g. for x^n, n is the index

$$x^n = \underbrace{x \times x \times x \times x \ldots \times x}_{n \text{ factors}}$$

negative indices

- indicate the reciprocal of a term,
  e.g. $x^{-1} = \frac{1}{x}$, $x^{-n} = \frac{1}{x^n}$
  i.e. $5^{-1} = \frac{1}{5}$, $2^{-3} = \frac{1}{2^3} = \frac{1}{8}$

power

- another term for an index or exponent

scientific (standard) notation

- a useful way to write very big or very small numbers
- numbers are written as the product of a number between 1 and 10 and a power of 10,
  e.g. $76\,000\,000 = 7{\cdot}6 \times 10^7$
  $0{\cdot}000\,0054 = 5{\cdot}4 \times 10^{-6}$

zero index

- a term or number with a zero index is equal to 1,
  e.g. $x^0 = 1$, $4^0 = 1$

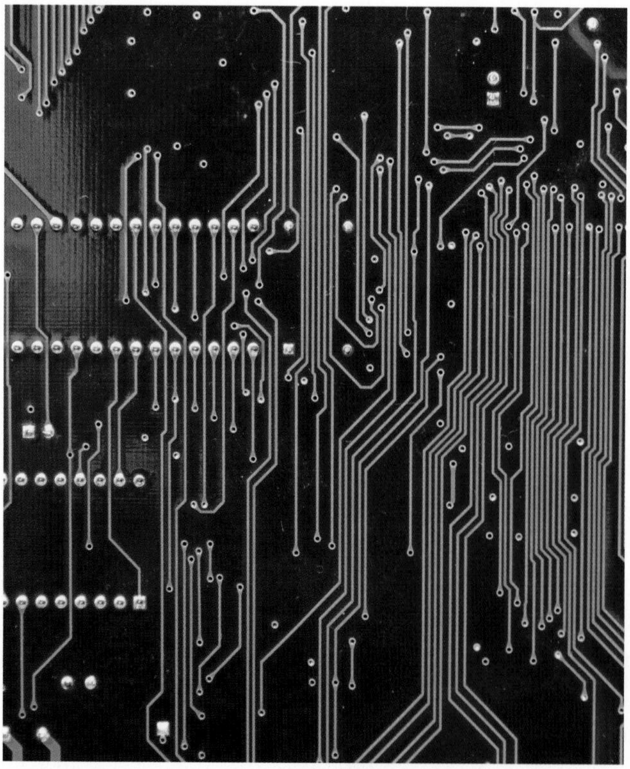

A computer's memory is measured in gigabytes. In computing, a gigabyte is sometimes defined as 2^{30} bytes. Write this number in scientific notation correct to one significant figure.

DIAGNOSTIC TEST 6 INDICES

These questions reflect the important skills introduced in this chapter.
Errors made will indicate areas of weakness.
Each weakness should be treated by going back to the section listed.

1	Evaluate: a 3^2	b 2^4	c 10^3	6:01
2	Simplify: a $3^2 \times 3^5$	b $x^3 \times x^2$	c $6m^2n \times mn^4$	6:01
3	Simplify: a $x^7 \div x^2$	b $15a^5 \div 3a^2$	c $20a^3b^2 \div 10ab$	6:01
4	Simplify: a $(a^4)^2$	b $(x^3)^4$	c $(2a^4)^3$	6:01
5	Simplify: a 7^0	b $5p^0$	c $18x^3 \div 6x^3$	6:01
6	Simplify: a 3^{-2}	b 5^{-1}	c $(\frac{2}{3})^{-3}$	6:02
7	Simplify, writing answers without negative indices. a $x^7 \times x^{-3}$	b $6x^2 \div 3x^4$	c $(3x^{-1})^2$	6:02
8	Simplify: a $25^{\frac{1}{2}}$	b $27^{\frac{1}{3}}$	c $8^{\frac{1}{3}}$	6:03
9	If $x > 0$ and $m > 0$, simplify: a $3x^{\frac{1}{2}} \times 4x^{\frac{1}{2}}$	b $(49m^6)^{\frac{1}{2}}$	c $(8x^3)^{\frac{1}{3}}$	6:03
10	Express in scientific notation. a 243	b 67 000	c 93 800 000	6:04
11	Write as a basic numeral. a $1{\cdot}3 \times 10^2$	b $2{\cdot}431 \times 10^2$	c $4{\cdot}63 \times 10^7$	6:04
12	Express in scientific notation. a 0·043	b 0·000 0597	c 0·004	6:04
13	Write as a basic numeral. a $2{\cdot}9 \times 10^{-2}$	b $9{\cdot}38 \times 10^{-5}$	c $1{\cdot}004 \times 10^{-3}$	6:04
14	Simplify, giving answers in scientific notation. a $(3{\cdot}1 \times 10^8)^2$ c $\sqrt{1{\cdot}96 \times 10^{24}}$	b $(8{\cdot}4 \times 10^6) + (3{\cdot}8 \times 10^7)$ d $\sqrt{1{\cdot}44 \times 10^{-6}}$		6:05
15	Write each of these as bytes (B), using scientific notation. a 270 000 B c 4·3 terabytes (TB)	b 25 kilobytes (kB) d 12 GB		6:06
16	Convert these quantities, giving answers in scientific notation. a 5 s = … µs b 500 g = … mg	c 3 ns = … s	d 5 µg = … g	6:06

ASSIGNMENT 6A Chapter review

1 Simplify, writing the answers in index form:

a $a^2 \times a^3$ b $3a^2 \times 4a^3$

c $a^2b \times ab$ d $3a^2b \times 4ab^2$

e $3^2 \times 3^3$ f $a^6 \div a^3$

g $7m^2 \div m$ h $12y^6 \div 3y^2$

i $20a^4b^3 \div 10a^2b^2$ j $4^7 \div 4^3$

k $(3^2)^4$ l $(x^2)^3$

m $(a^3)^2 \times a^5$ n $m^7 - (m^2)^3$

o $\dfrac{12x^2}{6x}$ p $\dfrac{4a^3}{8a}$

2 Express in simplest form:

a $(2x^2)^0$ b $6x^0$

c $(5x^3)^3$ d $(10a^2)^3$

e $(4x^2)^3 \div 8x^5$

3 Write each of the following in standard form (scientific notation).

a 21 600 b 125

c 0·000 07 d 0·000 156

4 Write each of the following as a basic numeral.

a $8{\cdot}1 \times 10^5$ b $1{\cdot}267 \times 10^3$

c $3{\cdot}5 \times 10^{-2}$ d $1{\cdot}06 \times 10^{-4}$

5 Use your calculator to evaluate:

a 2^{10} b 3^{12}

c $5^5 \times 6^6$ d $7^3 \times 4^5$

6 Find the value of n, if:

a $2^n = 128$ b $3^n = 243$

c $10^n = 100\,000\,000$

7 Simplify and evaluate:

a $3^2 \times 3^5$ b $10^7 \div 10^4$ c $(2^4)^2$

8 Simplify:

a $\dfrac{m^7 \times m^6}{m^{10}}$ b $(2a^3)^3 \times (3a^4)^2$

c $\dfrac{8x^7 \times 9x^4}{6x^6 \times 6x^5}$

9 Evaluate (writing answers in fraction form):

a 5^{-1} b 2^{-4}

c 3^{-2} d 10^{-3}

10 Simplify, giving your answers in scientific notation correct to two significant figures.

a 3579^5

b $(0{\cdot}0075)^{10}$

c $987\,654\,321 \times 123\,456\,789$

d $\dfrac{13\,579 \times 8642}{0{\cdot}000\,456}$

e $(2{\cdot}3 \times 10^7) \times (5{\cdot}6 \times 10^5)$

f $(2{\cdot}3 \times 10^7) + (5{\cdot}6 \times 10^5)$

g $(2{\cdot}3 \times 10^7) \div (5{\cdot}6 \times 10^5)$

h $(2{\cdot}3 \times 10^7) - (5{\cdot}6 \times 10^5)$

11 Noting that $x^{\frac{3}{2}} = (x^3)^{\frac{1}{2}}$, evaluate without using a calculator:

a $4^{\frac{3}{2}}$ b $8^{\frac{2}{3}}$ c $9^{\frac{3}{2}}$ d $1000^{\frac{5}{3}}$

12 Simplify:

a $5x^{\frac{1}{2}} \times 4x^{\frac{1}{2}}$ b $10x^2 \div 5x^4$ c $(36m^4n^6)^{\frac{1}{2}}$

Can you use your calculator to find the value of 2^{500}? What is the largest power of 2 that can be calculated using your calculator?

ASSIGNMENT 6B Working mathematically

1 What is the sum of the numbers on the reverse sides of these regular dice?

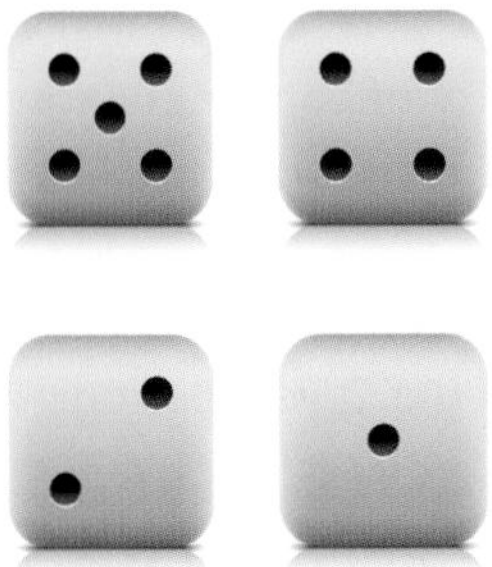

2 A woman spent one quarter of what was in her purse and then a quarter of what remained. If she spent \$42, how much did she originally have in her purse?

3 a A diagonal joins two vertices, and a diagonal cannot be drawn from a vertex to the two adjacent vertices or to itself. How many diagonals can be drawn from one vertex of a regular hexagon? How many vertices has a hexagon?

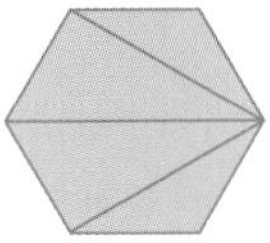

b The number of diagonals of a hexagon is $\frac{6(6-3)}{2}$. How many diagonals has:

i a regular octagon

ii a regular decagon

iii a regular polygon that has 30 sides?

4 Tom was given a cheque for an amount between \$30 and \$31. The bank teller made a mistake and exchanged dollars and cents on the cheque. Tom took the money without examining it and gave \$4 to his son.

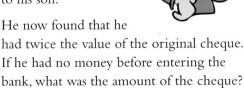

He now found that he had twice the value of the original cheque. If he had no money before entering the bank, what was the amount of the cheque?

5 In the decibel scale for measuring sound, 10 decibels is a sound that is barely audible. A sound 10 times as intense is 20 decibels, and so on up to 140 decibels, which is the threshold of pain. Study the table and answer the questions below.

Noise	Relative intensity	Decibels (dB)
Minimum of audible sound	1	0
Soft wind on leaves	10	10
Whisper at 1 metre	10^2	20
Bush quiet	10^3	30

a If ordinary conversation has a relative intensity of 10^6, what is its loudness in decibels?

b If a lawn mower has a relative intensity of 10^{12}, what is its loudness in decibels?

c By how many times is the relative intensity of the mower greater than that of conversation?

d By how many times is the relative intensity of heavy traffic (loudness 80 dB) greater than that of bush quiet?

e From the above it would appear that heavy traffic (80 dB) is four times as noisy as a whisper at 1 metre (20 dB). However, a rise of 10 dB corresponds to a doubling in the subjective loudness to the human ear. How much louder to the human ear is:

i the average office (50 dB) than bush quiet (30 dB)

ii heavy traffic (80 dB) than a whisper at 1 metre (20 dB)

iii a rock group (110 dB) than a business office (60 dB)?

ASSIGNMENT 6C Cumulative revision

1 Write the following decimals as fractions. 1:03

a $0\cdot8$ **b** $0\cdot125$ **c** $0\cdot002$

d $0\cdot\dot{5}$ **e** $0\cdot\dot{1}\dot{5}$ **f** $0\cdot6\dot{8}$

2 The population of a small town was 9500. After the discovery of copper, the town's population increased in the first year by 20%. In the second year, it increased by another 10%. 2:01

a What was the population of the town at the end of the 2-year period?

b What was the percentage increase in the population over the 2-year period?

3 Simplify: 3:01

a $2a + 3 - a + 3$ **b** $2a + 3 - a - 3$ **c** $2a - 3 + a + 3$ **d** $2a - 3 - a - 3$

4 Simplify: 3:04

a $\frac{a}{5} + \frac{a+1}{3}$ **b** $\frac{2y-1}{5} + \frac{3y-1}{10}$ **c** $\frac{2p-1}{3} - \frac{2p-3}{4}$

5 Simplify: 3:08

a $(a + 4)(a + 6)$ **b** $(x - 1)(x + 1)$ **c** $(m - 4)^2$ **d** $(3y - 5)(2y + 7)$

6 Two big bars of chocolate are offered as prizes by a maths teacher in a quiz contest. Three boys and a girl tie for the highest score, and it is decided to break the tie in true mathematical fashion by drawing two names one after the other from the hat. What is the probability that: 4:04

a the two girls names are chosen

b two boys names are chosen

c at least one of the chocolates is won by a girl?

7 Two trapeziums have been used to form the hexagons shown. What is the area of each hexagon? (All measurements are in centimetres.) 5:01

a

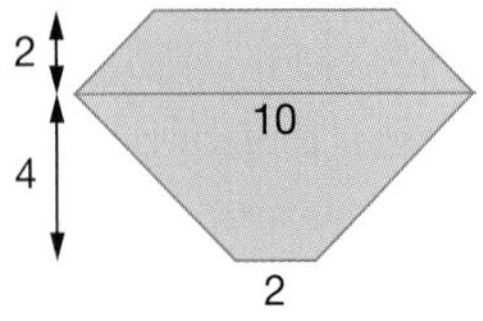

b

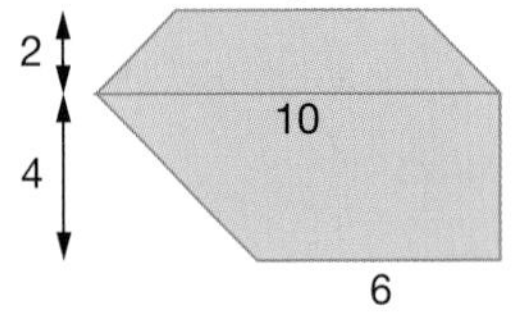

c

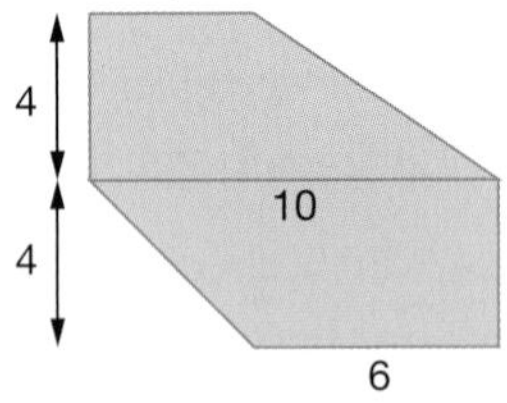

8 The volume of a cylinder is $100\,cm^3$. 5:05

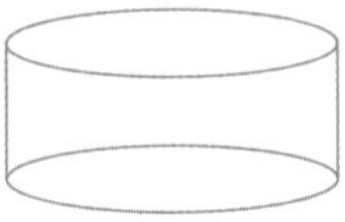

a If the radius of this cylinder is halved and the height is doubled, what would be the volume of the resulting cylinder?

b If the radius of the original cylinder is doubled and the height is halved, what would be the volume of the cylinder now?

EQUATIONS, INEQUALITIES AND FORMULAS

7

Contents

Syllabus references (See pages x–xv for details.)

Number and Algebra

Selections from ***Equations*** [Stages 5.2, 5.3§]

- Solve linear equations (ACMNA215)
- Solve linear equations involving simple algebraic fractions (ACMNA240)
- Substitute values into formulas to determine an unknown (ACMNA234)
- Solve problems involving linear equations, including those derived from formulas (ACMNA235)
- Solve linear inequalities and graph their solutions on a number line (ACMNA236)
- Solve complex linear equations involving algebraic fractions (NSW)
- Rearrange literal equations (NSW)

Working Mathematically

- Communicating • Problem Solving • Reasoning • Understanding • Fluency

7:01 Equivalent equations

- Equations are number sentences where one or more of the numbers is missing or unknown. Because it is unknown, the number is represented by a pronumeral.
- When we solve an equation, we are trying to find the numerical value of the pronumeral that makes the sentence true. With some equations it is easy to find this value or solution. With harder equations more work has to be done before the solution is found.
- A solution is correct if it gives a true number sentence when it replaces the pronumeral in the equation. We say that the solution *satisfies* the equation.

> An equation is a number sentence where one or more of the numbers has been replaced by a pronumeral.

- Solving equations is like balancing scales. With equations we know that one side of the equation is equal to the other side. We could say that the two sides are *balanced*.
- The solution of the equation is the value of the pronumeral that balances the equation.

The sides are balanced.

$x + 10 = 15$

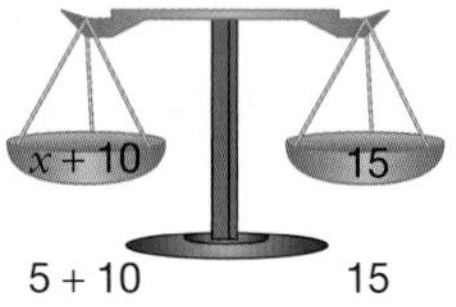

$x = 5$ balances the scale.
$x = 5$ is the solution.

$y - 3 = 8$

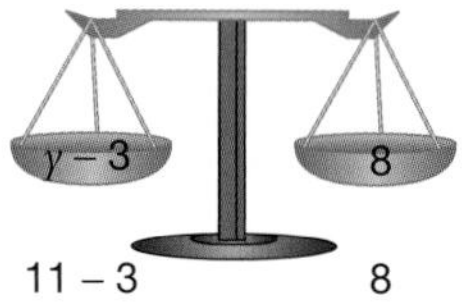

$y = 11$ balances the scale.
$y = 11$ is the solution.

- Solving difficult equations requires us to change the equation into a simpler equation. We change equations into simpler equations by performing the same operation on both sides of the equation.
- We may add (+), subtract (−), multiply (×) or divide (÷) by any number, provided we do the same to both sides of the equation.
- If we do not do the same to both sides of the equation, the equation becomes unbalanced and the sides no longer remain equal.
- If we commence with an equation and do the same thing to both sides of the equation, then the sides will remain equal or balanced and the new equation will have the same solution as the original equation.

> If one equation can be changed into another by performing the same operation on both sides, then the equations are said to be equivalent.

We solve equations by making a series of equivalent equations, each one in the series being simpler than the one before it. In this way we reduce a complicated equation to a simple one. We must remember to perform the same operation on both sides of the equation.

WORKED EXAMPLE 1

a $8a + 6 = 15$ **b** $1 - 3b = 7$ **c** $5a - 7 = a + 2$ **d** $7 - y = 5 - 2y$

Solutions

a
$$8a + 6 = 15$$
$$-6 \quad -6 \qquad \text{subtract 6 from both sides}$$
$$8a = 9$$
$$\div 8 \quad \div 8 \qquad \text{divide both sides by 8}$$
$$\frac{8a}{8} = \frac{9}{8}$$
$$\therefore a = 1\tfrac{1}{8}$$

b
$$1 - 3b = 7$$
$$-1 \quad -1 \qquad \text{subtract 1 from both sides}$$
$$-3b = 6$$
$$\div -3 \quad \div -3 \qquad \text{divide both sides by } -3$$
$$\frac{-3b}{-3} = \frac{6}{-3}$$
$$\therefore b = -2$$

c
$$5a - 7 = a + 2$$
$$-a \quad -a \qquad \text{subtract } a \text{ from both sides}$$
$$4a - 7 = 2$$
$$+7 \quad +7 \qquad \text{add 7 to both sides}$$
$$4a = 9$$
$$\div 4 \quad \div 4 \qquad \text{divide both sides by 4}$$
$$\frac{4a}{4} = \frac{9}{4}$$
$$a = 2\tfrac{1}{4}$$

d
$$7 - y = 5 - 2y$$
$$+2y \quad +2y \qquad \text{add } 2y \text{ to both sides}$$
$$7 + y = 5$$
$$-7 \quad -7 \qquad \text{subtract 7 from both sides}$$
$$y = 5 - 7$$
$$\therefore y = -2$$

WORKED EXAMPLE 2

Check to see whether each given solution is correct by substituting it into the equation.

a $x + 7 = 2x - 5$
$x = 12$

b $5a - 9 = 3 - a$
$a = 5$

Solutions

a LHS $= x + 7$ RHS $= 2x - 5$
$= 12 + 7$ $= 2 \times 12 - 5$
$= 19$ $= 19$

$\therefore$ LHS = RHS

$\therefore x = 12$ is correct

b LHS $= 5a - 9$ RHS $= 3 - a$
$= 5 \times 5 - 9$ $= 3 - 5$
$= 16$ $= -2$

$\therefore$ LHS $\neq$ RHS

$\therefore a = 5$ is incorrect.

Smart people like me always check solutions by substituting.

Exercise 7:01

P Foundation worksheet 7:01 Equivalent equations

1 Solve the following equations.

a $x + 72 = 138$ b $y + 37 = 68$ c $p - 64 = 19$ d $x - 125 = 917$

e $15{\cdot}2 + p = 17{\cdot}1$ f $a + 11{\cdot}3 = 20{\cdot}1$ g $h - 1{\cdot}8 = 6{\cdot}2$ h $b - 3{\cdot}2 = 1{\cdot}7$

i $16 + y = 3$ j $x + 7 = 1$ k $p - 1 = -3$ l $2 - p = 5$

m $7 - a = 1$ n $2{\cdot}1 + y = 1{\cdot}4$ o $-3 + y = 1{\cdot}7$ p $-5 - y = 1$

q $5p = 17$ r $8x = 2{\cdot}4$ s $3{\cdot}5y = 17{\cdot}5$ t $1{\cdot}1p = 0{\cdot}11$

u $\frac{a}{5} = 1$ v $\frac{b}{8} = 12$ w $\frac{x}{7} = -2$ x $\frac{a}{1{\cdot}1} = 3{\cdot}2$

2 Find the value of the variable in each of the following. All solutions are integers.

a $5b + 1 = 26$ b $2m + 9 = 23$

c $5m + 7 = 82$ d $15 = 3p - 57$

e $15 = 3x + 6$ f $1 = 7x - 48$

g $-3 = 7p - 10$ h $12 - 2a = 18$

i $5y + 17 = 2$ j $1 - 3x = 10$

k $8 - 3b = 20$ l $10 - 5b = -30$

Check your answers by substituting into the original equation.
p=−3
2−p=5

3 Solve the following equations.

a $3a + 17 = 28$ b $4p + 6 = 37$

c $9y + 15 = 820$ d $17 + 3x = 88$

e $5m - 13 = 42$ f $11x - 8 = 52$

g $17 = 3y - 3$ h $28 = 7m - 14$

i $15 - 4b = 3$ j $10 - 2a = 1$

k $3a + 15 = 4$ l $10m - 4 = 8$ m $7 = 17 + 7a$ n $44 + 6a = 10$

o $15 - 6a = -10$ p $3a + 5 = -10$ q $2{\cdot}5x + 7 = 10$ r $1{\cdot}2a - 3{\cdot}6 = 4{\cdot}2$

s $2{\cdot}3 - 1{\cdot}4x = 0{\cdot}2$ t $15 + 0{\cdot}9a = 17{\cdot}7$

4 Solve the following equations. (The answers are all integers.)

a $3a + 2 = 2a + 9$ b $5m + 7 = 4m + 8$

c $6q - 3 = 5q + 5$ d $8n = 6n + 12$

e $6x = x + 10$ f $a + 11 = 2a + 5$

g $8x + 3 = x + 31$ h $10x - 5 = x + 4$

i $3x + 9 = 7x + 1$ j $x + 8 = 3x - 10$

k $x + 5 = x - 1$ l $15 - 2m = 6m - 1$

Collect the pronumerals on the side where most are found.

5 Substitute the given solution to see whether it is correct or incorrect.

a $9m - 5 = 4m + 10$, $m = 3$ b $2p + 6 = 9p + 10$, $p = 5$ c $3q + 3 = 2q + 1$, $q = -2$

d $11a + 8 = 5a + 20$, $a = 2$ e $8q - 3 = 5q + 9$, $q = 4$ f $x + 7 = 5x - 4$, $x = 2$

g $2n + 1 = n - 2$, $n = -3$ h $2m + 5 = 8m - 7$, $m = 2$ i $8a + 2 = 3a - 3$, $a = -1$

j $5x = 12x - 14$, $x = 2$ k $11a + 8 = 13a$, $a = 4$ l $27x = 50 + 2x$, $x = 2$

6 Solve these equations.

a $5x + 10 = x + 2$
b $m + 8 = 3m + 5$
c $4p + 7 = p + 11$
d $6m = 2m + 1$
e $4a = a - 1$
f $8n + 6 = n + 6$
g $9a - 2 = 3a + 5$
h $7n - 9 = 9n + 1$
i $7q - 5 = 5q + 4$
j $8n + 7 = 4n + 17$
k $11a + 1 = 5a + 6$
l $4k - 7 = k - 10$
m $2a + 7 = 4a + 15$
n $x + 16 = 7x + 3$
o $3q + 7 = 6q - 1$
p $3m = 7m - 3$
q $4a = 11 - 3a$
r $x - 4 = 7x + 4$
s $2y = 5y + 60$
t $5 - 2x = 3 + x$
u $11 - m = 24 - 4m$

P GEOGEBRA ACTIVITY 7:01 **EQUATIONS WITH PRONUMERALS ON BOTH SIDES**

Select from three different types of equations and then use the sliders to fix the numbers in each equation. Solve the equation and then tick the checkbox to get a worked solution.

$$4x + 5 = 3x + 3$$
$$1x + 5 = 3$$
$$x = -2$$

7:02 Equations with grouping symbols

PREP QUIZ 7:02

Rewrite these expressions without grouping symbols.

1 $7(x + 4)$
2 $2(a - 3)$
3 $5(4a + 9)$
4 $6(2p - 7)$
5 $-3(x - 4)$

Solve these one-step equations.

6 $x + 9 = 4$
7 $x - 8 = -2$
8 $3p = -27$
9 $10p = 5$
10 $6 + x = -1$

If you remember how to expand grouping symbols, then these equations are no harder than those you have already seen.

WORKED EXAMPLE 1

Expand the grouping symbols and then solve the equation.

a
$$2(x + 3) = 8$$
$$2x + 6 = 8$$
$$-6 \quad -6$$
$$2x = 2$$
$$\div 2 \quad \div 2$$
$$\therefore x = 1$$

b
$$5(a - 3) = 3$$
$$5a - 15 = 3$$
$$+15 \quad +15$$
$$5a = 18$$
$$\div 5 \quad \div 5$$
$$\therefore a = \frac{18}{5} \quad \text{or} \quad 3\frac{3}{5}$$

c
$$3(2m - 4) = 4m - 6$$
$$6m - 12 = 4m - 6$$
$$-4m \quad -4m$$
$$2m - 12 = -6$$
$$+12 \quad +12$$
$$2m = 6$$
$$\div 2 \quad \div 2$$
$$\therefore m = 3$$

WORKED EXAMPLE 2

Expand each set of grouping symbols and then solve the equations.

a
$$3(a + 7) = 4(a - 2)$$
$$3a + 21 = 4a - 8$$
$$-3a \quad -3a$$
$$21 = a - 8$$
$$+8 \quad +8$$
$$29 = a$$
$$\therefore a = 29$$

b
$$3(x + 4) + 2(x + 5) = 4$$
$$3x + 12 + 2x + 10 = 4$$
Collect like terms.
$$5x + 22 = 4$$
$$-22 \quad -22$$
$$5x = -18$$
$$\div 5 \quad \div 5$$
$$\therefore x = -3\tfrac{3}{5}$$

Just take it one step at a time.

The solution can be checked by substituting the value back into the original equation.

Exercise 7:02

P Foundation worksheet 7:02
Equations with grouping symbols

1 Expand the grouping symbols and then solve each equation. (Answers are all integers.)

a $3(a + 2) = 18$
b $2(x + 4) = 10$
c $5(6 + m) = 45$
d $6(x - 4) = 6$
e $4(x - 1) = 20$
f $7(x - 3) = 70$
g $5(2y + 1) = 25$
h $3(2p - 7) = 9$
i $10(6 + 5x) = 10$
j $8(1 + x) = 9x + 4$
k $2(5a + 3) = 8a + 10$
l $7(2a + 3) = 10a + 33$
m $9(2x - 1) = x + 42$
n $6(m - 4) = 2m + 8$
o $2(7y - 5) = 15y - 16$
p $2a + 5 = 3(a - 1)$
q $12x + 6 = 6(x + 2)$
r $8 - 2x = 3(x - 4)$

2 Solve each equation.

a $5(a + 1) = 8$
b $2(m - 3) = -3$
c $4(x - 7) = 3$
d $3(3 - x) = 12$
e $5(7 - n) = 15$
f $3(7 - y) = 9$
g $5(2a + 3) = 20$
h $2(5x - 1) = 15$
i $3(4x - 5) = 1$
j $4(x - 2) = x - 2$
k $5(n + 3) = 3n + 11$
l $3(x - 10) = x + 20$
m $2 - x = 3(2x - 1)$
n $8 + 7x = 3(3x - 1)$
o $8n - 16 = 4(3n - 7)$
p $7a = 6(2a - 1)$
q $2n = 3(4n - 10)$
r $5x = 4(2x + 9)$

3 Find the solution to each equation by first expanding all grouping symbols.

a $3(a + 2) = 2(a + 1)$
b $5(x - 1) = 4(x + 2)$
c $5(p - 2) = 4(p + 2)$
d $3(q + 2) = 2(q + 5)$
e $3(m + 1) = 5(m - 1)$
f $6(x + 2) = 4(x + 6)$
g $2(a - 7) = 5(a - 4)$
h $7(t + 2) = 4(t + 5)$
i $3(2a + 1) = 5(a + 2)$
j $4(3p - 1) = 5(2p + 1)$
k $6(t + 7) = 4(t + 10) + 8$
l $5(2a - 1) = 3(a + 6) - 7$
m $3(2 + m) = 5(2 - m) + 6m$
n $6(p + 3) = 5(2 - p) + 7p - 12$

4 Solve each equation. Use Worked Example **2b** (on page 176) as a guide.

a $3(a + 2) + a + 5 = 15$
b $5(m - 1) + 2m = 2$
c $2(m + 3) + 5(m + 2) = 23$
d $3(x + 2) + 2(x - 3) = 10$
e $5(p + 1) + 2(p + 4) = 20$
f $4(t - 2) + 2(t + 5) = 14$
g $4(2a + 3) + 2(a - 5) = 22$
h $2(2m + 3) + 3(m - 5) = 5$
i $5(a - 3) + 3(2 + 3a) = 19$
j $7(a + 5) + 2(6 - 3a) = 1$

5 Try solving these equations, but first read the warning sign.

a $3(a + 2) - 2(a + 1) = 6$
b $5(m + 3) - 4(m + 2) = 10$
c $5(n + 4) - 3(n - 2) = 30$
d $6(a + 2) - 4(a - 1) = 20$
e $4(a + 3) - (a + 2) = 13$
f $4(p + 5) - (p + 3) = 23$
g $5(2a + 1) - 2(a - 4) = 2$
h $6(2x + 5) - 5(3x + 2) = 10$

Warning!
Remember how to expand with a negative term.

$-2(x+4) = -2x - 8$

OR

$-3(a-1) = -3a + 3$

P GEOGEBRA ACTIVITY 7:02 EQUATIONS WITH GROUPING SYMBOLS

Choose from equations with varying degrees of difficulty. Use sliders to fix the numbers in each equation. Solve the equation and then tick the checkbox to get a worked solution.

$$5(3x - 4) = 25$$
$$15x - 20 = 25$$
$$15x = 45$$
$$x = 3$$

FUN SPOT 7:02 IF I HAVE 7 APPLES IN ONE HAND AND 4 IN THE OTHER, WHAT HAVE I GOT?

I $x + 12 = 7$
A $5x = 2$
H $x - 7 = -2$
D $\frac{x}{10} = 5$
N $5x + 30 = 15$
G $15 - 3x = 2x + 5$
B $\frac{5x + 21}{8} = 3$
S $5(3x + 8) + 6(10 - 2x) = 109$

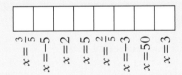

$x = \frac{3}{5}$	$x = -5$	$x = 2$	$x = 5$	$x = \frac{2}{5}$	$x = -3$	$x = 50$	$x = 3$

7:03 Equations with fractions (1)

PREP QUIZ 7:03

Simplify:

1 $-4+4$ 2 -3×-1 3 $-7+4$ 4 $\dfrac{15}{4}$ 5 $16\div-5$

6 $6\times\dfrac{p}{6}$ 7 $\dfrac{12p}{p}$ 8 $4\times\dfrac{(x+7)}{4}$ 9 $4\times\dfrac{5m}{4}$ 10 $4(3-\dfrac{p}{4})$

To remove a fraction, multiply both sides of an equation by the denominator of the fraction.

WORKED EXAMPLES

Find the value of the pronumeral in each of the following equations.

1 $\dfrac{y}{6}-1=3$ 2 $\dfrac{x+7}{4}=8$ 3 $\dfrac{3x-1}{5}=7$

Solutions

1 $\dfrac{y}{6}-1=3$

$\times 6 \quad \times 6$

$6(\dfrac{y}{6}-1)=3\times 6$

$\dfrac{6y}{6}-6=18$

$y-6=18$

$\therefore y=24$

2 $\dfrac{x+7}{4}=8$

$\times 4 \quad \times 4$

$\dfrac{\cancel{4}(x+7)}{\cancel{4}}=8\times 4$

$x+7=32$

$\therefore x=25$

3 $\dfrac{3x-1}{5}=7$

$\times 5 \quad \times 5$

$\dfrac{\cancel{5}(3x-1)}{\cancel{5}}=7\times 5$

$3x-1=35$

$3x=36$

$\therefore x=12$

1 Make sure you multiply both sides of the equation by the same number.

2 Make sure you expand the parentheses correctly.

$4(3+2)=4\times 3+4\times 2$

so

$4(x+2)=4\times x+4\times 2$

$=4x+8$

Exercise 7:03

Foundation worksheet 7:03
Equations with fractions 1

1 Solve the following equations.

a $\frac{y}{4}+3=9$ b $\frac{y}{5}+3=7$ c $4+\frac{p}{6}=10$

d $7=\frac{1}{5}m+4$ e $\frac{1}{4}a-1=2$ f $13-\frac{1}{4}m=6$

g $16=\frac{m}{2}-9$ h $5=8-\frac{p}{6}$ i $\frac{5p}{2}=4$

j $\frac{3m}{4}=6$ k $15=\frac{5p}{3}$ l $\frac{3}{5}m=7$

m $\frac{p+3}{4}=8$ n $\frac{5m+6}{3}=12$ o $\frac{7+x}{4}=2$

p $\frac{15-x}{4}=3$ q $\frac{3m+4}{2}=5$ r $\frac{6+5p}{4}=9$

s $\frac{12a-3}{5}=6$ t $\frac{7-3x}{3}=1$ u $\frac{5a-2}{4}=-3$

v $\frac{-x-2}{4}=5$ w $\frac{1}{7}(10+3p)=9$

The denominator is the bottom number of a fraction.

2 State whether the given solution is correct or incorrect.

a $\frac{x}{4}+7=8$, $x=4$ b $\frac{y}{3}-4=2$, $y=10$ c $6+\frac{m}{4}=9$, $m=12$ d $4=\frac{m}{6}-1$, $m=30$

e $\frac{5m}{4}=3$, $m=3$ f $\frac{m+4}{2}=5$, $m=3$ g $\frac{p-5}{4}=3$, $p=17$ h $\frac{15-p}{4}=-1$, $p=19$

i $\frac{3m+2}{4}=1$, $m=\frac{2}{3}$ j $\frac{4m-6}{3}=8$, $m=6\frac{1}{2}$ k $\frac{1+3p}{2}=-1$, $p=-1$ l $\frac{9-5p}{5}=8$, $p=-8$

3 Solve these equations that have pronumerals on both sides.

a $\frac{2m}{3}-4=m$ b $\frac{x}{5}+3=2x$ c $p-5=\frac{p}{2}$

d $3x-6=\frac{3x}{4}$ e $\frac{x}{4}=3-x$ f $\frac{3n}{2}=2n-5$

g $\frac{a+3}{2}=a$ h $\frac{2x-1}{3}=3x$ i $\frac{1}{3}(2y+3)=4y$

j $\frac{1-3p}{6}=p$ k $\frac{4-x}{5}=x+2$ l $\frac{1}{4}(3b-1)=2-b$

Solve equations one step at a time.

FUN SPOT 7:03 — WHO HOLDS UP SUBMARINES?

Solve each equation and write the letter for that part in the box above the correct answer.

I $\dfrac{m}{4} = 8$ **I** $\dfrac{x}{5} = 4$

U $\dfrac{2n}{3} = 5$ **E** $\dfrac{5y}{3} = 2$

Y $\dfrac{x}{4} + 1 = 5$ **S** $\dfrac{a}{4} + 7 = 8$

L $\dfrac{x}{2} - 8 = 5$ **H** $\dfrac{m}{6} - 5 = 3$

L $\dfrac{a+2}{3} = 4$ **D** $\dfrac{n-3}{5} = 2$

T $\dfrac{3y+1}{5} = 2$ **Q** $\dfrac{7m-4}{2} = 5$

B $\dfrac{12+3x}{4} = 6$

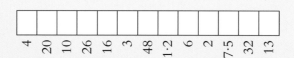

4	20	10	26	16	3	48	1·2	6	2	7·5	32	13

7:04 Equations with fractions (2)

PREP QUIZ 7:04

What are the first three multiples of:

1 2 **2** 5?

What is the lowest common multiple of:

3 2 and 6 **4** 3, 4 and 5 **5** x and $3x$?

Simplify:

6 $5 \times \dfrac{a}{5}$ **7** $10 \times \dfrac{3x}{2}$ **8** $\dfrac{3(2x+1)}{3}$ **9** $\dfrac{4(2x-1)}{2}$ **10** $5 \times 3\left(\dfrac{2x-1}{5}\right)$

In the previous section, the equations involved only one fraction with a single denominator. The equations in this section have more than one denominator. To simplify these equations we must multiply by the lowest common multiple of all the denominators. (In other words, we must multiply by some number that will cancel out every denominator.)

WORKED EXAMPLES

Solve the following equations.

1 $\dfrac{3x}{5}-\dfrac{x}{4}=1$

2 $\dfrac{a}{5}-1=\dfrac{3a-1}{2}+4$

3 $\dfrac{m+2}{3}-\dfrac{m-5}{4}=6$

Solutions

1 $$\frac{3x}{5}-\frac{x}{4}=1$$

Multiply both sides by 20.

$$20\left(\frac{3x}{5}-\frac{x}{4}\right)=1\times 20$$

$$\frac{60x}{5}-\frac{20x}{4}=20$$

$$12x-5x=20$$

$$7x=20$$

$$x=\frac{20}{7}$$

$$\therefore x=2\tfrac{6}{7}$$

2 $$\frac{a}{5}-1=\frac{3a-1}{2}+4$$

$$\frac{a}{5}=\frac{3a-1}{2}+5$$

Multiply both sides by 10.

$$10\left(\frac{a}{5}\right)=10\left(\frac{3a-1}{2}\right)+5\times 10$$

$$2a=5(3a-1)+50$$

$$2a=15a-5+50$$

$$-13a=45$$

$$a=\frac{45}{-13}$$

$$\therefore a=-3\tfrac{6}{13}$$

3 $$\frac{m+2}{3}-\frac{m-5}{4}=6$$

Multiply both sides by 12.

$$12\left(\frac{m+2}{3}-\frac{m-5}{4}\right)=6\times 12$$

$$4(m+2)-3(m-5)=72$$

$$4m+8-3m+15=72$$

$$m+23=72$$

$$\therefore m=49$$

Exercise 7:04

P Foundation worksheet 7:04 **Equations with fractions 2**

1 Solve the following equations. All solutions are integers. Check your solutions by substituting into the equation.

a $\dfrac{x}{2}+\dfrac{x}{3}=5$

b $\dfrac{p}{6}+\dfrac{p}{2}=8$

c $\dfrac{m}{4}+\dfrac{m}{6}=20$

d $\dfrac{y}{2}-\dfrac{y}{4}=3$

e $\dfrac{m}{4}-\dfrac{m}{5}=1$

f $\dfrac{x}{3}-\dfrac{x}{5}=4$

g $\dfrac{3k}{2}+\dfrac{k}{4}=14$

h $\dfrac{5x}{3}+\dfrac{4x}{5}=37$

i $\dfrac{3p}{2}+\dfrac{p}{3}=11$

j $\dfrac{x}{2}-\dfrac{2x}{5}=3$

k $\dfrac{5m}{6}-\dfrac{m}{4}=7$

l $4a-\dfrac{2a}{5}=18$

m $\frac{m}{4} = \frac{m}{3} - 2$ n $\frac{3p}{10} - 4 = \frac{p}{2} - 8$ o $\frac{x}{2} + \frac{x}{10} = \frac{2x}{5} + 4$ p $\frac{b+4}{2} = \frac{b+10}{3}$

q $\frac{m+6}{3} = \frac{2m+4}{4}$ r $\frac{k-1}{4} = \frac{k-5}{2}$

2 Solve:

a $\frac{(x+3)}{2} + \frac{(x+5)}{5} = 8$ b $\frac{(a+1)}{3} + \frac{(a+1)}{4} = 9$

c $\frac{p-3}{3} + \frac{p-2}{4} = 7$ d $\frac{2b-3}{4} + \frac{1+3b}{2} = 6$

e $\frac{2p-3}{2} + \frac{p+4}{3} = 1$ f $1 - p = \frac{p+6}{10}$

g $\frac{1}{3}(x+2) - \frac{1}{5}(2x-1) = 5$ h $\frac{2(a+1)}{3} - \frac{3(1+a)}{4} = a$

i $\frac{2a+3}{2} - \frac{a-2}{3} = \frac{a-1}{4}$

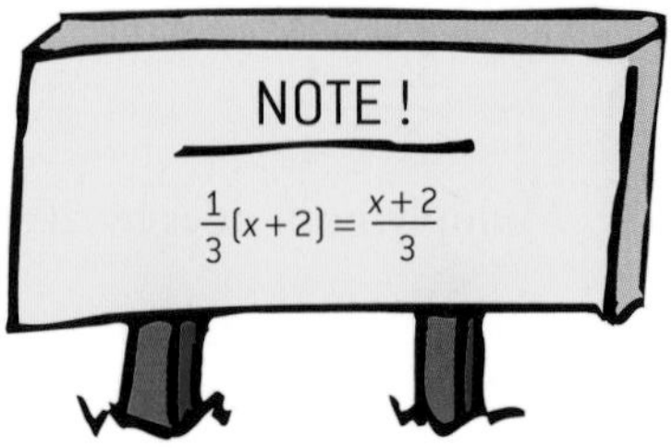

CHALLENGE 7:04 EQUATIONS WITH PRONUMERALS IN THE DENOMINATOR

Some equations may have pronumerals in the denominators. Examine the following examples and then attempt the following questions.

Examples

Solve each equation:

1

$$\frac{3}{2b} + 1 = 4$$
$$\times 2b \quad \times 2b$$
$$2b\left(\frac{3}{2b} + 1\right) = 4 \times 2b$$
$$\frac{6b}{2b} + 2b = 8b$$
$$3 + 2b = 8b$$
$$3 = 6b$$
$$\therefore b = \tfrac{1}{2}$$

2

$$\frac{a}{a-3} = 4$$
$$\times (a-3) \quad \times (a-3)$$
$$\cancel{(a-3)} \times \frac{a}{\cancel{a-3}} = 4 \times (a-3)$$
$$a = 4a - 12$$
$$-3a = -12$$
$$\therefore a = 4$$

3

$$\frac{3}{x+1} = \frac{2}{x+4}$$

Multiply both sides by $(x + 1)(x + 4)$.

$$\frac{3\cancel{(x+1)}(x+4)}{\cancel{(x+1)}} = \frac{2(x+1)\cancel{(x+4)}}{\cancel{(x+4)}}$$
$$3(x + 4) = 2(x + 1)$$
$$3x + 12 = 2x + 2$$
$$x + 12 = 2$$
$$\therefore x = -10$$

Remove the fraction by multiplying by the denominator of the fraction.

Exercises

1 Solve the following equations.

a $\frac{4}{x}=2$
b $\frac{3}{a}=18$
c $\frac{3}{2x}=4$
d $\frac{3}{p}+1=12$
e $\frac{4}{3a}-4=3$
f $5+\frac{3}{x}=2$
g $10-\frac{1}{p}=3$
h $\frac{1}{x-3}=4$
i $\frac{2}{x+5}=6$
j $\frac{4}{y-3}+2=1$
k $\frac{a}{2a+1}-1=6$
l $20-\frac{x}{2x-1}=4$

2 Solve:

a $\frac{1}{x-3}=\frac{1}{2x+1}$
b $\frac{4}{x}+\frac{1}{2x}=\frac{9}{4}$
c $\frac{3}{2k}-\frac{2}{3k}=\frac{5}{18}$
d $\frac{3}{2k-1}=0\cdot 2$
e $\frac{3}{a}-\frac{1}{a-2}=0$
f $2\left(\frac{1}{a}+2\right)=5-\frac{2}{a}$
g $\frac{4}{x}-\frac{1}{2x}=3$
h $\frac{x}{2x+7}=3$
i $\frac{2b-5}{b-2}=5$
j $\frac{3}{2a}+\frac{1}{a}=4-\frac{5}{3a}$
k $\frac{x}{2x+1}-3=1$
l $\frac{1}{1-x}-1=3$

7:05 Solving problems using equations

PREP QUIZ 7:05

What is the sum of:

1 3 and 4
2 x and 3
3 x and y?

What is the product of:

4 3 and 4
5 x and 3
6 x and y?

7 I have \$50. I spend \$$x$. How much do I have left?
8 There are x books and each one costs \$5. What is the total cost of the books?
9 There are x cars with y people in each car. How many people are there altogether?
10 A man is x years old. How old will he be in 5 years time?

Consider the following simple problem.

'I think of a number. If I add 7 to the number the result is 22. What is the number?'

- This problem can be solved by forming an equation. If the missing number is represented by the pronumeral x, then the equation $x + 7 = 22$ represents the information given in the problem. Solving the equation then yields the answer to the original problem.

WORKED EXAMPLES

Translate the following into number sentences.
In all cases use 'x' to represent the unknown number.

We often use 'x' to represent an unknown number.

1 I multiply a number by 2 and the result is 50.
2 If I add 6 to a number the answer is 11.
3 I subtract a number from 6 and the answer is 2.
4 A certain number is multiplied by 3, then 6 is added and the result is 17.

Solutions

1 I multiply a number by 2 and the result is 50.

$2 \times x \qquad = 50$

The equation is $2x = 50$.

2 If I add 6 to a number the answer is 11.

$6 + x \qquad = 11$

The equation is $6 + x = 11$.

3 I subtract a number from 6 and the answer is 2.

$6 - x \qquad = 2$

The equation is $6 - x = 2$.

4 A certain number is multiplied by 3, then 6 is added and the result is 17.

$x \times 3 \qquad + 6 \qquad = 17$

The equation is $3x + 6 = 17$.

To use equations to solve problems we must be able to analyse a written problem, translate it into an equation and then solve it.

Approach

- Read the problem carefully, examining the wording of the question.
- Establish what is to be found and what information is given.
- Ask yourself whether any other information can be assumed (e.g. a pack of cards is a standard pack of 52 cards with no Joker).
- Try to connect the given information to form an equation. This will often require a knowledge of a formula or the meaning of mathematical terms.

WORKED EXAMPLE 1

A rectangle is three times longer than it is wide. If it has a perimeter of 192 m, what are its dimensions?

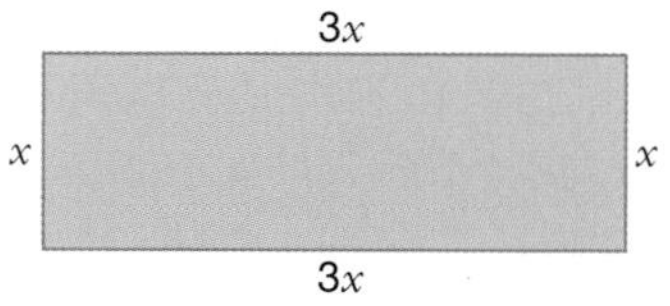

Solution

Let the width be x m.
$\therefore$ The length $= 3 \times x$
$= 3x$ m

Perimeter means the sum of the lengths of the sides (or the distance around the outside of the figure).

$3x + x + 3x + x = 192$
$8x = 192$
$\therefore x = 24$
$\therefore$ The width $= 24$ m
and the length $= 3 \times 24$ m
$= 72$ m

In the first line of each solution, indicate what the pronumeral represents.

WORKED EXAMPLE 2

My father was 28 years old when I was born. If he is now three times as old as I am, what are our present ages?

If he was 28 years older than me when I was born, then he'll always be 28 years older than me, won't he?
FRI
2

Solution

Let my present age be x years.
$\therefore$ My father's present age is $3 \times x$ years.
When I was born my father was 28.
$\therefore$ The difference in our ages is 28 years.
Father's age take away my age always equals 28 years.
$3x - x = 28$
$2x = 28$
$\therefore x = 14$
$3x = 42$
$\therefore$ I am 14 years old and my father is 42 years old.

WORKED EXAMPLE 3

Car A left Sydney for Melbourne at 6:00 am and travelled at an average speed of 80 km/h. At 7:30 am car B left Sydney for Melbourne. If car B travels at an average speed of 100 km/h, at what time will it catch car A?

Solution

Car B will catch car A when both have travelled the same distance *and* distance travelled = average speed × time.

Now let car B catch up to car A t hours after car B starts.

$\therefore$ Car B has been travelling for t hours.

$\therefore$ Car A has been travelling for $(t + 1\frac{1}{2})$ hours (since it started at 6 am).

Distance travelled by car A
$= 80 \times (t + 1\frac{1}{2})$

Distance travelled by car B
$= 100 \times t$

$$\begin{aligned} 80(t + 1\tfrac{1}{2}) &= 100t \\ 80t + 80 \times 1\tfrac{1}{2} &= 100t \\ 120 &= 20t \\ \therefore t &= 6 \end{aligned}$$

$\therefore$ Car B catches car A 6 hours after it starts, i.e. at 1:30 pm.

Car A
Speed = 80 km/h
Starts at 6:00 am
Travels for $(t + 1\frac{1}{2})$ hours
Distance travelled = $80(t + 1\frac{1}{2})$

Car B
Speed = 100 km/h
Starts at 7:30 am
Travels for t hours
Distance travelled = $100t$

Computers are used to solve many equations.

Exercise 7:05

P Foundation worksheet 7:05
Solving problems using equations

1 Translate the following sentences into equations, using the pronumeral 'x' to represent the unknown number. Then solve the equation to find the value of the unknown number.

- a If 5 is added to a number the answer is 22.
- b If I subtract 3 from a certain number the result is 10.
- c I multiply a number by 8 and the result is 32.
- d Dividing a certain number by 8 gives an answer of 7.
- e A number is multiplied by 2, then 6 is added and the result is 14.
- f Three times a certain number is added to 5 and the result is 20.
- g A certain number is multiplied by 5, then 8 is subtracted and the result is 22.
- h If 5 is added to a certain number and the result is multiplied by 4 the answer is 56.
- i When 5 is subtracted from half of a number the result is 3.

'I subtract 3 from a certain number' translates to $x - 3$. 'I subtract a certain number from 3' translates to $3 - x$. Also $x - 3$ is not the same as $3 - x$.

2 For each of the following problems form an equation and then solve it.

- a I think of a number, double it, add 3 and the result is 33. What is the number?
- b I think of a number and multiply it by 4. If I then subtract 3, the answer is 25. Find the number.
- c I think of a number, add 3 and then double that result. If the answer is 22, find the number.
- d I think of a number. After dividing it by 4 and subtracting 7 the result is 1. What is the number?
- e I think of a number. If I add 4 and then divide by 3 the result is 8. Find the number.

3 Solve each of the following problems by first forming an equation.

- a If 5 is added to 3 times a certain number the result is 38. What is the number?
- b If I subtract 6 from 5 times a certain number the result is 29. What is the number?
- c If 5 is subtracted from a certain number and that result is then halved, the answer is 6. What is the number?
- d A number is doubled and then 5 is added. When this is divided by 3 the result is 7. What is the number?

4 **a** My father is three times as old as I am. If he is 26 years older than me, what are our ages?
b Two men have $560 between them. If one man has six times as much money as the other, how much has each man?
c Joan has $7 less than Anne. Together they have $43. How much does each girl have?
d Prize money of $500 is divided between Alan and Jim so that Alan receives $170 more than Jim. How much does each receive?
e If a father is five times as old as his son at present, how old is he if he was 32 years old when his son was born?

5 **a** In a class of 32 students, it is known that there are 6 more boys than girls. How many girls are there in the class?
b A rectangle is 6 cm longer than it is wide. Find its dimensions if its perimeter is 64 cm.
c If a quarter of the weight of a roast is lost in roasting, what weight of roast should be bought in order to have 3 kg of roasted meat?
d A town B is between towns A and C. B is five times as far from C as it is from A. The distance from A to C is 144 km. How far is it from A to B?

6 **a** Six kilograms of an inferior tea is mixed with 3 kilograms of tea that costs $2 a kilogram more. The total price of the mixture is $24. What was the price of the inferior tea?
b Two bike riders X and Y both start at 2 pm riding towards each other from 40 km apart. X rides at 30 km/h, Y at 20 km/h. If they meet after t hours, find when and where they meet.
c A man is twice as old as his son. If 9 years ago the sum of their ages was 66 years, find their present ages.
d A man notices that a tank is half full. After emptying 600 litres from the tank, he observes that it is now one-third full. How much does the tank hold when it is full?

7 **a** Fred is 25 years older than Bill and, in 5 years, he will be twice as old as Bill. Find their present ages.
b A bank teller notices that he has 50 coins all of which are 5c or 10c pieces. He finds that the value of the coins is $4.20. How many of each must he have?
c A tennis player has won 36 out of 54 matches. His sponsor says that he must win 60% of his total number of matches to qualify for a bonus.If there are 26 matches remaining on the tour, how many more must he win to collect this bonus?
d One tank holds 300 litres more than another. If the smaller is two-thirds full, it holds as much as the larger when it is half full. What is the capacity of each?

e A certain journey took 40 min to complete. If half the distance was travelled at an average speed of 100 km/h and the other half at an average speed of 60 km/h, what was the length of the journey?

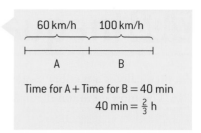

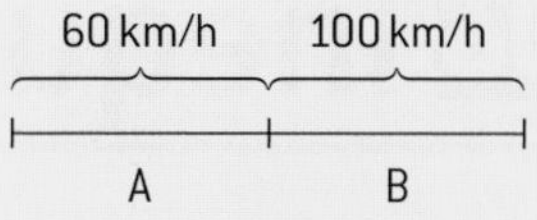

Time for A + Time for B = 40 min

40 min = $\frac{2}{3}$ h

8 a Pump A delivers water at twice the rate of pump B. If both pumps operate together, a tank of 18 000 litres capacity can be filled in 30 minutes. Find the pumping rate of each pump, in litres per minute.

b A car travels between A and B at an average speed of 60 km/h. If the car increased its average speed to 100 km/h it would take 10 minutes less to make the trip. How far is it between the towns?

c Car A is travelling along a freeway at 100 km/h when it is passed by car B. If both cars maintain a constant speed and the end of the freeway is 10 km away, find the speed at which car B must travel to beat car A to the end of the freeway by 1 minute.

d A sum of money is divided between A, B and C in the ratio 1 : 2 : 3. However, before the money is divided C dies and it is decided to divide his share between A and B in the ratio 1 : 3. After C's share is divided B has $2000 more than A. How much money was there altogether?

e Rectangles A and B are both four times as long as they are wide and the length of rectangle A is three times the length of rectangle B. If the difference in the perimeters is 16 cm, find the dimensions of each rectangle.

FUN SPOT 7:05 WHO 'DUNNIT'?

Four boys playing cricket in the park were having a great game when suddenly one of them hit a mighty six, right through Mr Yorker's window. Mr Yorker stormed out and demanded to know who did it. Their responses were:

Bob: 'Steve did it.'

Steve: 'Mark did it.'

Alan: 'I didn't do it.'

Mark: 'Steve lied when he said I did it.'

If only one of the boys is not telling the truth, who hit the ball through the window?

On the other hand, if only one of the four statements is true, who hit the ball?

7:06 Inequalities

An inequality is a number sentence where the 'equals' sign has been replaced by an inequality sign. The most common inequality signs are shown below.

$>$	$<$	$\geq$	$\leq$
'is greater than'	'is less than'	'is greater than or equal to'	'is less than or equal to'

Inequalities, unlike equations, usually have more than one solution.
For example:

- The equation $x + 6 = 10$ has one solution, namely $x = 4$.
- The inequality $x + 6 > 10$ has an infinite number of solutions.

  The numbers $4\frac{1}{2}$, 8, 9·5, 30 are some solutions.
  The full set of solutions is written as $x > 4$.

WORKED EXAMPLES

1 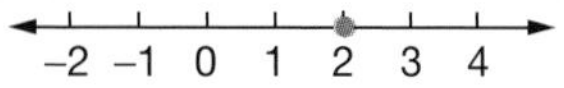

This shows the solution $x = 2$.

2 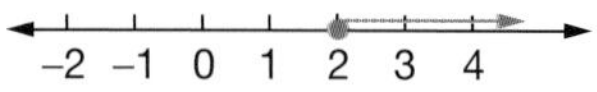

This shows the solution $x \geq 2$.

3 

This shows the solution $x \leq 2$.

4 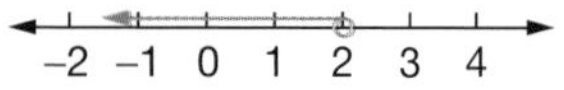

This shows the solution $x < 2$.

5 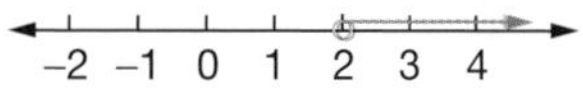

This shows the solution $x > 2$.

INVESTIGATION 7:06 OPERATING ON INEQUALITIES

- When we solved equations we saw that performing the same operation on both sides gave an equivalent equation.
- Use the examples below to investigate what happens with inequalities.

Each of the following inequalities is true. Perform the operation indicated on both sides of each inequality and state if the inequality remains true.

	a	b	c	d
1	$6 > 2$ add 4	$-6 < -4$ add 4	$6 > -4$ add 4	$-2 < 4$ add 4
2	$6 > 2$ subtract 4	$-6 < -4$ subtract 4	$6 > -4$ subtract 4	$-2 < 4$ subtract 4
3	$6 > 2$ multiply by 2	$-6 < -4$ multiply by 2	$6 > -4$ multiply by 2	$-2 < 4$ multiply by 2
4	$6 > 2$ divide by 2	$-6 < -4$ divide by 2	$6 > -4$ divide by 2	$-2 < 4$ divide by 2
5	$6 > 2$ multiply by -3	$-6 < -4$ multiply by -3	$6 > -4$ multiply by -3	$-2 < 4$ multiply by -3
6	$6 > 2$ divide by -2	$-6 < -4$ divide by -2	$6 > -4$ divide by -2	$-2 < 4$ divide by -2

- Write the results of your investigation. Compare these with the results obtained by others in your class.

From the investigation, you should have found that multiplying or dividing a true inequality by a negative number did not produce a true inequality. This is a very important difference between equations and inequalities.

To allow for this, the inequality sign must be reversed when an inequality is multiplied or divided by a negative number.

When multiplying or dividing an inequality by a negative number, the inequality sign must be reversed to obtain an equivalent inequality.
e.g. $<$ is changed to $>$ and $\leq$ is changed to $\geq$.

WORKED EXAMPLES

Solve the following inequalities.

1 $2x + 3 < 6$ **2** $\dfrac{x}{2} - 3 \le 7$ **3** $5 - 3x > 6$

4 $-\frac{1}{3}x < 5$ **5** $2(1 - 2x) \le 6$

Solutions

1
$$\begin{aligned} 2x + 3 &< 6 \\ -3 \quad &\quad -3 \\ 2x &< 3 \\ \div 2 \quad &\quad \div 2 \\ x &< \tfrac{3}{2} \\ \therefore x &< 1\tfrac{1}{2} \end{aligned}$$

2
$$\begin{aligned} \frac{x}{2} - 3 &\le 7 \\ +3 \quad &\quad +3 \\ \frac{x}{2} &\le 10 \\ \times 2 \quad &\quad \times 2 \\ 2 \times \frac{x}{2} &\le 10 \times 2 \\ \therefore x &\le 20 \end{aligned}$$

3
$$\begin{aligned} 5 - 3x &> 6 \\ -5 \quad &\quad -5 \\ -3x &> 1 \\ \div -3 \quad &\quad \div -3 \\ &\text{(reverse sign)} \\ \therefore x &< -\tfrac{1}{3} \end{aligned}$$

4
$$\begin{aligned} -\tfrac{1}{3}x &< 5 \\ \times -3 \quad &\quad \times -3 \\ &\text{(reverse sign)} \\ -\tfrac{1}{3}x \times (-3) &> 5 \times (-3) \\ \therefore x &> -15 \end{aligned}$$

5
$$\begin{aligned} 2(1 - 2x) &\le 6 \\ 2 - 4x &\le 6 \\ -2 \quad &\quad -2 \\ -4x &\le 4 \\ \div -4 \quad &\quad \div -4 \\ &\text{(reverse sign)} \\ \therefore x &\ge -1 \end{aligned}$$

Or
$$\begin{aligned} 2(1 - 2x) &\le 6 \\ 2 - 4x &\le 6 \\ +4x \quad &\quad +4x \\ 2 &\le 6 + 4x \\ -6 \quad &\quad -6 \\ -4 &\le 4x \\ \div 4 \quad &\quad \div 4 \\ -1 &\le x \\ \therefore x &\ge -1 \end{aligned}$$

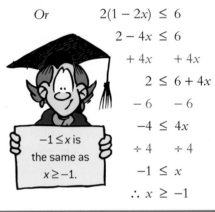

Exercise 7:06

P Foundation worksheet 7:06 **Solving inequalities**

1 State the set of values of x which have been graphed below.

a 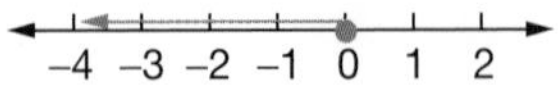

b 

c 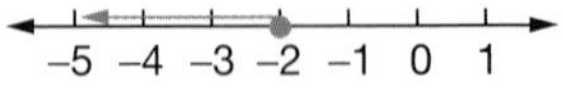

d 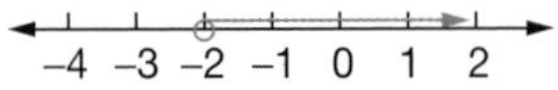

e 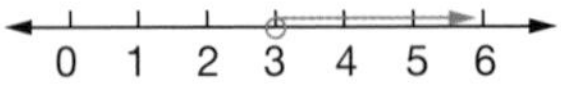

f 

2 The solution to the equation $9 - 2x = 2$ is shown on this number line.

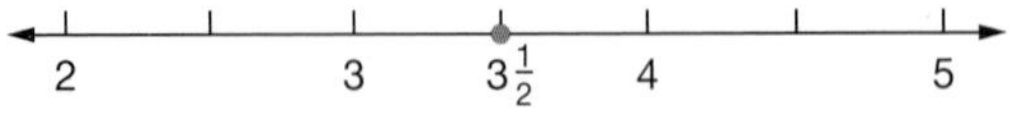

By substituting a value of x from either side of $x = 3\frac{1}{2}$, find which side gives the solution to $9 - 2x < 2$. Use your result to graph the solution to $9 - 2x < 2$.

3 Solve the following inequalities and graph the solution on a number line.

a $x + 6 < 15$ b $y + 7 > 9$ c $m + 6 < 4$

d $m + 10 > 5$ e $5 + p \leq 2$ f $15 \geq m + 6$

g $y - 3 > 2$ h $m - 6 < 1$ i $x - 5 \geq 5$

j $12 < m - 6$ k $3 > p - 2$ l $-1 \leq x - 1$

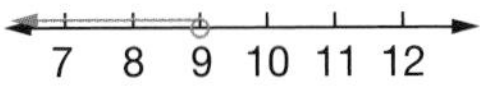

Draw only the part of the line that you need.

4 Solve the following inequalities.

a $3m > 21$ b $6p \leq 42$ c $12m < 24$

d $5y \geq -42$ e $15 > 4x$ f $-20 < 10x$

g $\frac{x}{3} < 5$ h $\frac{y}{2} > 6$ i $\frac{m}{4} \geq 1$

j $\frac{x}{5} < -10$ k $3 > \frac{x}{2}$ l $-4 < \frac{x}{3}$

5 Solve the following inequalities.

a $-3m < 24$ b $-4x > 16$ c $-5p \leq 20$

d $-6x < -12$ e $15 < -6x$ f $10 \geq -3x$

g $-x > 4$ h $-x < 3$ i $5 \geq -x$

j $-\frac{1}{2}x > 3$ k $-\frac{1}{5}x > 1$ l $-\frac{1}{4}x \geq 2$

m $-\frac{x}{2} < 1$ n $-\frac{x}{3} > 2$ o $-\frac{x}{4} > 3$

Remember:
Change < to >, or vice versa, if you multiply or divide by a negative number.

6 Solve:

a $2x + 5 > 11$ b $4m + 3 < 19$

c $2p + 1 \geq 7$ d $10 + 3p \leq 7$

e $4 + 5p \geq 10$ f $13 + 2x < 6$

g $3x - 8 \leq 4$ h $5p - 1 \geq 9$

i $4y - 3 < 2$ j $12 > 5x - 3$

k $3 < 2x - 1$ l $3 \geq 8x - 9$

m $2(x + 3) < 14$ n $3(m + 2) > 15$

o $3(2x - 5) \leq 6$ p $4(x - 3) \geq 5$

q $4 < 2(2m - 3)$ r $2(5p - 4) > 22$

Set them out just like equations!
-x

7 Solve:

a $5 - 3m > 11$ b $10 - 2y < 14$ c $12 \leq 6 - 4x$

d $10 - x \leq 12$ e $2 - m \geq -4$ f $17 - 2m \leq 1$

g $9 - 4p < 7$ h $2(1 - x) < 6$ i $3(4 - y) > 15$

j $3(4 - 2x) \geq 18$ k $2(3 - 5y) \leq -4$ l $2(3 - 2p) > 8$

m $4 \geq 3(1 - 2x)$ n $2(5 - 2a) \leq -5$ o $3(1 - 2x) > 2$

8 Find the solution of each of the following inequalities.

a $5x + 6 > x + 18$
b $3x - 5 < x + 6$
c $m + 3 \geq 2m - 7$
d $3 - a \leq 5 - 2a$
e $12 - b \geq 2b + 21$
f $3(m + 4) < 2(m + 6)$
g $\frac{x}{2} + 1 < 6$
h $\frac{p}{3} - 1 > 4$
i $\frac{3x}{4} - 5 > 1$
j $5 - \frac{2y}{3} < 6$
k $\frac{p-1}{4} < 2$
l $\frac{2p+3}{2} > 7$
m $\frac{4-x}{3} > 1$
n $\frac{x}{2} + \frac{x}{3} > 5$
o $\frac{a}{4} + \frac{a}{2} < 6$
p $3b - \frac{2b}{3} < 5$
q $\frac{x}{2} - \frac{2x}{3} < 3$
r $\frac{y}{2} - 3y > 4$
s $1 - \frac{3a}{2} > -3$
t $\frac{1-2x}{3} < 6$
u $\frac{1-3x}{4} < \frac{2(1-x)}{3}$

9 Write an inequality for each of the following problems, *then* solve it.

a Three times a number is always smaller than eight. What could the number be?
b Four less than twice a number is greater than nine. What values could the number take?
c When four times a number is subtracted from one hundred the answer must be less than twenty five. What is the smallest integer that satisfies this condition?
d Donella has scored 94 points in the last 6 basketball games. If she earns 2 points per basket, how many baskets must she shoot in the next 6 games for her average points per game to be greater than 16?
e Jacky sells ice-creams at the football. If she gets 25 cents for each ice-cream she sells, how many must she sell to have at least \$20, after she has given her brother Aaron the \$5.40 she owes him?

7:07 Formulas: Evaluating the subject

Formulas are special types of equations. A formula represents a relationship between physical quantities. For instance, the formula $A = l \times b$ represents the connection between the area of a rectangle and its length and breadth.

A formula is different from an equation in that it will always have more than one pronumeral. However, to find the value of a pronumeral in a formula we must be told the values of every other pronumeral in the formula.

The 'subject' of a formula is the pronumeral by itself, on the left-hand side.
Did you know that?

PREP QUIZ 7:07

Write the following algebraic expressions in their simplest form.

1 $2 \times a \times b$ **2** $3 \times a \times b \times b$ **3** $3 \times a + 2 \times b$

Write the following expressions in expanded form.

4 $4xy^2$ **5** $(x + y)^2$ **6** $x^2 + y^2$

True or false?

7 $\frac{2a}{3} = \frac{2}{3}a$

If $a = 6$ and $b = 10$, evaluate:

8 $\frac{1}{2}ab^2$ **9** $\frac{a+b}{2}$ **10** $3(a - b)$

WORKED EXAMPLES

1 Given that $I = PRN$, find I when $P = 500$, $R = 0{\cdot}12$ and $N = 4$.

2 If $V = \frac{1}{3}Ah$, find V when $A = 15$ and $h = 4$.

3 Given that $a = 4$ and $b = 3$, find c when $c = \sqrt{a^2 + b^2}$.

4 If $K = \frac{1}{2}mv^2$, find K when $m = 5$ and $v = 6$.

Solutions

1 $P = 500$, $R = 0{\cdot}12$ and $N = 4$

$$\begin{aligned} I &= PRN \\ &= 500 \times 0{\cdot}12 \times 4 \\ \therefore I &= 240 \end{aligned}$$

2 $A = 15$ and $h = 4$

$$\begin{aligned} V &= \tfrac{1}{3}Ah \\ &= \tfrac{1}{3} \times 15 \times 4 \\ &= \frac{1}{\cancel{3}_1} \times \cancel{60}^{20} \\ \therefore V &= 20 \end{aligned}$$

3 $a = 4$ and $b = 3$

$$\begin{aligned} c &= \sqrt{a^2 + b^2} \\ &= \sqrt{4^2 + 3^2} \\ &= \sqrt{16 + 9} \\ &= \sqrt{25} \\ \therefore c &= 5 \end{aligned}$$

4 $m = 5$ and $v = 6$

$$\begin{aligned} K &= \tfrac{1}{2}mv^2 \\ &= \tfrac{1}{2} \times 5 \times 6^2 \\ &= \tfrac{1}{2} \times 5 \times 36 \\ &= \frac{1}{\cancel{2}_1} \times \cancel{180}^{90} \\ \therefore K &= 90 \end{aligned}$$

Remember:
Replace the pronumerals with the given numerals.
To find the value of one of the pronumerals you must be given the value of every other pronumeral.

Exercise 7:07

1 a If $A = lb$, find A when $l = 3\cdot6$ and $b = 2\cdot4$.
b If $A = bh$, find A when $b = 15$ and $h = 3\cdot6$.
c Given that $A = \frac{1}{2}bh$, find A when $b = 15$ and $h = 3\cdot6$.
d Given that $A = s^2$, find A when $s = 3\cdot5$.
e If $A = \frac{1}{2}xy$, find A when $x = 8$ and $y = 11$.
f If $A = \pi r^2$, find A correct to one decimal place if $r = 3\cdot4$.
g Given that $A = \frac{1}{2}h(a + b)$, find A when $h = 8$, $a = 11$ and $b = 9$.
h Given $C = \pi d$, find C correct to one decimal place if $d = 6\cdot8$.
i If $V = lbh$, find V if $l = 8\cdot1$, $b = 7\cdot2$ and $h = 4\cdot5$.
j If $V = Ah$, find V if $A = 341\cdot6$ and $h = 6\cdot15$.
k Given that $P = 2l + 2b$, find P when $l = 3\cdot75$ and $b = 2\cdot45$.
l Given that $c = \sqrt{a^2 + b^2}$, find c when $a = 5$ and $b = 12$.
m If $\alpha = 180° - \beta - \gamma$, find α when $\beta = 30°$ and $\gamma = 45°$.
n If $\alpha = 360° - \beta - \gamma - \delta$, find α when $\beta = 37°$, $\gamma = 51°$ and $\delta = 132°$.
o Given that $E = F + V - 2$, find the number of edges (E) when the number of faces (F) is 7 and the number of vertices (V) is 10.

2 a The formula $C = \frac{5}{9}(F - 32)$ converts degrees Fahrenheit (F) to degrees Celsius (C). Find C when:
i $F = 212$ ii $F = 32$ iii $F = 104$

b The kinetic energy (E) of a particle is given by the formula $E = \frac{1}{2}mv^2$ where m and v are the mass and velocity of the particle respectively. Find E if $m = 6$ and $v = 2\cdot5$.
c The surface area (S) of a cylinder is given by the formula $S = 2\pi r^2 + 2\pi rh$. Evaluate S when $\pi = 3\cdot14$, $r = 1\cdot50$ and $h = 3\cdot25$. Give the answer correct to three significant figures.
d The volume (V) of a cylinder is given by the formula $V = \pi r^2 h$. Find the volume correct to the nearest cubic centimetre if the radius (r) is 8 cm and the height (h) is 10 cm.

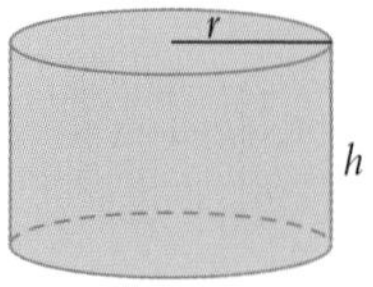

3 a If $P = RI^2$, evaluate P when $R = 2\cdot5$ and $I = 0\cdot6$.
b It is known that $F = \frac{mp}{r^2}$. If $r = 0\cdot2$, $m = 3\cdot6$ and $p = 9\cdot2$, find the value of F.
c $T = 2m\sqrt{\frac{L}{g}}$. Find T if $m = 3\cdot6$, $L = 2\cdot5$ and $g = 0\cdot1$.
d Given the formula $P = \frac{nkT}{V}$, find P when $n = 2\cdot4$, $k = 7\cdot6$, $T = 6$ and $V = 0\cdot15$.
e If $S = \frac{n}{2}[2a + (n - 1)d]$, find S when $n = 20$, $a = -4$ and $d = 0\cdot4$.
f Given the formula $S = ut + \frac{1}{2}at^2$, find S when $u = 8$, $t = 4$ and $a = -10$.
g If $I = PRN$, find I when $P = 450$, $R = 0\cdot12$ and $N = 3\cdot5$.
h If $S = \frac{a(r^n - 1)}{r - 1}$, find S when $a = 5\cdot2$, $r = 1\cdot4$ and $n = 2$.

i If $x = \dfrac{-b + \sqrt{b^2 - 4ac}}{2a}$, find x when $b = 3$, $a = 2$ and $c = -10$. Give the answer correct to two decimal places.

4 The distance D from the top corner of a rectangular box to the opposite bottom corner is given by the formula: $D = \sqrt{x^2 + y^2 + z^2}$, where x, y and z are the dimensions of the box. Find D if the dimensions x, y and z are:

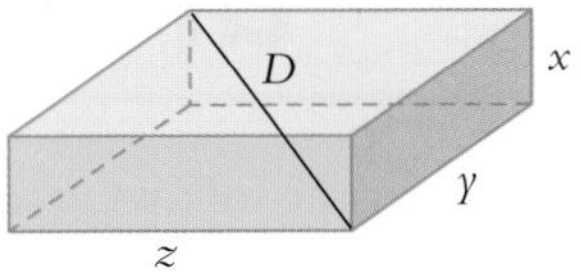

a 3 cm, 4 cm, 5 cm b 7 cm, 11 cm, 15 cm

Answer correct to one decimal place.

5 a Jane works out that the formula for the surface area, S, of the square pyramid shown is: $S = x^2 + x\sqrt{4h^2 + x^2}$

Use Jane's formula to find S when $x = 6$ and $h = 12$.

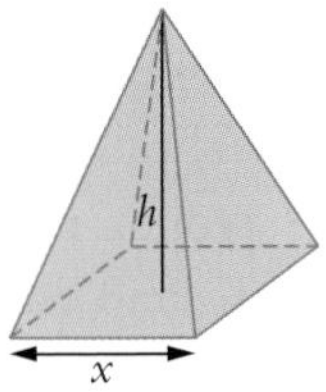

b Heron's formula states that the area of a triangle with sides of lengths a, b and c and semi-perimeter s is $A = \sqrt{s(s-a)(s-b)(s-c)}$

Find A when $a = 7$, $b = 8$, $c = 11$ and $s = 13$.

c Given that $M = (X - Y)(X^2 + XY + Y^2)$ and $N = (X + Y)(X^2 - XY + Y^2)$ find M and N when $X = 8$ and $Y = -3$.

d Given $S = (X + Y + Z)^4 - 3(XY + XZ + YZ)^3 + (XYZ)^2$ find S when $X = -3$, $Y = -4$ and $Z = 5$.

INVESTIGATION 7:07 SPREADSHEET FORMULAS

In spreadsheet programs such as Microsoft® Excel®, a formula can be inserted in the 'formula bar' that will operate on selected 'cells'.

The example below shows a simple example which uses Pythagoras' theorem to find the hypotenuse of a right triangle.

For this triangle, $c = \sqrt{a^2 + b^2}$.

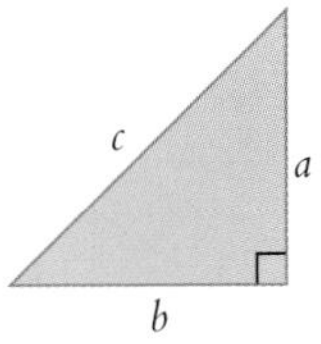

You can see this formula in the formula bar written as:

=SQRT(A2^2+B2^2)

This means that the number in cell C2 will be equal to the square root of (cell A2 squared plus cell B2 squared).

SQRT means 'square root'.
^ means 'to the power of'.

If the numbers in cells A2, B2 are changed, cell C2 will also change automatically.

- Try this example yourself and then experiment with other formulas you know.

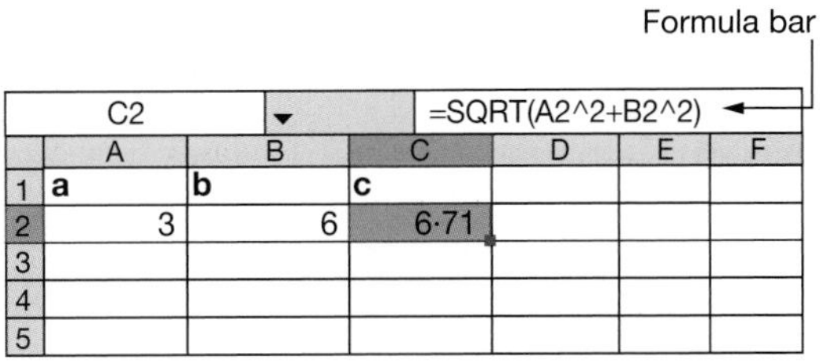

(*Note:* In Excel you can alter the number of decimal places in selected cells by going to 'Number' in the 'Format Cells' option.)

7:08 Formulas: Equations arising from substitution

Consider the following formulas.

$$S = \pi rl \qquad T = 2\pi\sqrt{\frac{l}{g}} \qquad D = \frac{M}{V} \qquad S = ut + \tfrac{1}{2}at^2$$

- The pronumeral that is on the left-hand side of each of these formulas is called the **subject** of the formula. In all the exercises so far, you have been asked to find the subject of the formula.
- We often know the value of the subject and are asked to find the value of one of the other pronumerals.
- To find the value of this pronumeral we will need to solve an equation.

PREP QUIZ 7:08

Solve:

1 $x + 152 = 315$ **2** $y - 73 = 149$ **3** $7x = 343$

4 $\dfrac{x}{10} = 37$ **5** $110 = 14 + x$ **6** $96 = y - 87$

7 $112 = 4p$ **8** $18 = \dfrac{m}{3}$ **9** $2a + 1 = 11$

10 $50 = 16 + 17t$

WORKED EXAMPLE 1

Given that $V = \dfrac{AH}{3}$, find H when $V = 12$ and $A = 5$.

Solution

$V = 12$ and $A = 5$

$$V = \frac{AH}{3}$$

$$\therefore\ 12 = \frac{5H}{3}$$

$$36 = 5H$$

$$\therefore\ H = \frac{36}{5}$$

$$= 7\tfrac{1}{5}$$

Remember: Substitute then solve the equation.
Caution! Equation solving ability needed here.

WORKED EXAMPLE 2

a $A = \frac{1}{2}h(x + y)$. Find the value of x, correct to one decimal place, if $A = 11$, $h = 3{\cdot}6$ and $y = 4{\cdot}5$.

b If $S = \dfrac{a}{1 - r}$, find r when $S = 10$ and $a = 1{\cdot}5$.

Solutions

a $A = 11$, $h = 3{\cdot}6$ and $y = 4{\cdot}5$

$$A = \tfrac{1}{2}h(x + y)$$
$$\therefore\ 11 = \frac{1}{\cancel{2}_1} \times \cancel{3{\cdot}6}^{1{\cdot}8}(x + 4{\cdot}5)$$
$$11 = 1{\cdot}8(x + 4{\cdot}5)$$
$$= 1{\cdot}8x + 1{\cdot}8 \times 4{\cdot}5$$
$$11 = 1{\cdot}8x + 8{\cdot}1$$
$$11 - 8{\cdot}1 = 1{\cdot}8x$$
$$2{\cdot}9 = 1{\cdot}8x$$
$$\frac{2{\cdot}9}{1{\cdot}8} = x$$
$$\therefore\ x = 1{\cdot}6 \text{ (1 dec. pl.)}$$

b $S = 10$ and $a = 1{\cdot}5$

$$S = \frac{a}{1 - r}$$
$$\therefore\ 10 = \frac{1{\cdot}5}{1 - r}$$
$$10(1 - r) = 1{\cdot}5$$
$$10 - 10r = 1{\cdot}5$$
$$-10r = -8{\cdot}5$$
$$\therefore\ r = 0{\cdot}85$$

Exercise 7:08

1 If $v = u + at$, find:

a u when $v = 25$, $a = 3$, $t = 5$

b a when $v = 40$, $u = 10$, $t = 2$

c t when $v = 16$, $u = 4$, $a = 5$

d u when $v = 27{\cdot}2$, $a = 4$, $t = 3{\cdot}5$

e a when $v = 15$, $u = 5$, $t = \frac{1}{4}$

f t when $v = 26$, $u = -16$, $a = 7$

g u when $v = 12{\cdot}68$, $a = 4{\cdot}2$, $t = 1{\cdot}5$

h a when $v = 16$, $u = -4$, $t = 0{\cdot}75$

2 Given that $V = \dfrac{AH}{3}$, find:

a H when $V = 5$ and $A = 3$

b H when $V = 12$ and $A = 9$

c H when $V = 16$ and $A = 10$

d H when $V = 15{\cdot}5$ and $A = 3{\cdot}1$

e A when $V = 6$ and $H = 5$

f A when $V = 15$ and $H = 12$

g A when $V = 7$ and $H = 0{\cdot}7$

h A when $V = 3{\cdot}6$ and $H = 0{\cdot}4$

3 For the formula $K = \frac{1}{2}mv^2$, find:

a m when $K = 60$, $v = 2$

b m when $K = 15$, $v = 3$

c m when $K = 3{\cdot}2$, $v = 4$

d m when $K = 7$, $v = \frac{1}{2}$

e v when $K = 25$, $m = 2$

f v when $K = 36$, $m = 8$

g v when $K = 216$, $m = 3$

h v when $K = \frac{3}{8}$, $m = 3$

4 $A = \frac{1}{2}h(x + y)$. Find:

a x when $A = 10$, $h = 4$, $y = 3$

b x when $A = 20$, $h = 8$, $y = 2$

c y when $A = 6$, $h = 3$, $x = 4$

d y when $A = 45$, $h = 6$, $x = 3$

e h when $A = 3$, $x = 4$, $y = 6$

f h when $A = 18$, $x = 5$, $y = 13$

g h when $A = 7{\cdot}8$, $x = 1{\cdot}7$, $y = 0{\cdot}9$

h h when $A = 5{\cdot}16$, $x = 4{\cdot}6$, $y = 8{\cdot}3$

5 a If $A = lb$, find l when $A = 9{\cdot}6$ and $b = 2{\cdot}4$.
b If $V = RI$, find I when $V = 15$ and $R = 0{\cdot}6$.
c Given that $V = AH$, find H correct to one decimal place, if $V = 12{\cdot}6$ and $A = 4{\cdot}1$.
d It is known that $V = lbh$. Find b correct to two significant figures, if $V = 60$, $l = 3{\cdot}4$ and $h = 2{\cdot}6$.
e Calculate the value of r in the formula $A = 2\pi rh$ if $A = 75$, $\pi = 3{\cdot}14$ and $h = 7{\cdot}6$. (Give your answer correct to one decimal place.)

6 a If $S = \dfrac{a}{1-r}$, find a when $S = 5{\cdot}2$ and $r = 0{\cdot}3$.
b For the formula $S = ut + \frac{1}{2}at^2$ evaluate a, given that $S = 15$, $u = 2$ and $t = 5$.
c $X = \dfrac{x+ky}{1+k}$. Find y when $X = 10$, $k = 2$ and $x = 3$.
d Given that $T = \dfrac{ab}{6} + C$, find b when $T = 15$, $a = 5$, $C = 4$.
e It is known that $F = 32 + \frac{9}{5}C$. Find C if $F = 212$.

7 In each of the following, give your answer correct to two decimal places.
a If $A = lb$, find b given that $A = 15$ and $l = 4{\cdot}8$.
b Given that $A = \pi r^2$, find r when $A = 10$ and $\pi = 3{\cdot}14$.
c If $T = a + (n - 1)d$, find d given $T = 19{\cdot}6$, $a = 3{\cdot}6$, $n = 12$.
d $P = RI^2$. Find R if $P = 100$ and $I = 3{\cdot}6$.
e $F = 32 + \dfrac{9C}{5}$. Find C if $F = 100$.

8 a The area of a circle can be found using the formula $A = \dfrac{\pi d^2}{4}$. Use this formula to find the diameter of a circle that has an area of $100\,\text{cm}^2$.
b It is known that $V = \pi r^2 h$. Find r when $V = 4$ and $h = 1{\cdot}5$.
c Given that $c^2 = a^2 + (c - 1)^2$ find a when $c = 61$.
d If $M = \dfrac{3N+2}{3N-2}$ find N when $M = 0{\cdot}4$.
e If $\dfrac{1}{R} = \dfrac{1}{R_1} + \dfrac{1}{R_2}$ find R when $R_1 = 5$ and $R_2 = 3$.

Formulas are used in many occupations when solving everyday problems.

7:09 Solving literal equations (1)

PREP QUIZ 7:09

Complete the following.

1 $x + 25 = 93$
$\therefore x = 93 - \ldots$

2 $x + a = b$
$\therefore x = b - \ldots$

3 $x - 27 = 53$
$\therefore x = 53 + \ldots$

4 $x - m = n$
$\therefore x = n + \ldots$

5 $5x = 70$
$\therefore x = 70 \div \ldots$

6 $ax = b$
$\therefore x = b \div \ldots$

7 $\dfrac{x}{5} = 3$
$\therefore x = 3 \times \ldots$

8 $\dfrac{x}{m} = n$
$\therefore x = n \times \ldots$

Solve:

9 $2a + 15 = 17$

10 $3(x - 5) = 10$

A formula such as $A = lb$ is written with A as its subject. This means that we can quite easily calculate A if we know the values of l and b. Sometimes, however, we need to rearrange the formula so that one of the other pronumerals is the subject. To do this, the same procedures as for solving equations are used. In the examples, compare the solving of each equation with the changing of the subject of the formula to x, on the right.

Remember:
$+$ is the opposite of $-$
$-$ is the opposite of $+$
$\times$ is the opposite of $\div$
$\div$ is the opposite of $\times$

Another name for a formula is a 'literal equation'.

WORKED EXAMPLE 1

a Solve for x.

i
$3x + 1 = 13$ — $-\,1$ both sides
$3x = 12$ — $\div\,3$ both sides
$\therefore x = 4$

ii
$5 - 2x = 1$ — $+\,2x$ both sides
$5 = 1 + 2x$ — $-\,1$ both sides
$4 = 2x$ — $\div\,2$ both sides
$2 = x$
$\therefore x = 2$

iii
$3(x + 2) = 5$ — expand
$3x + 6 = 5$ — $-\,6$ both sides
$3x = -1$ — $\div\,3$ both sides
$\therefore x = -\frac{1}{3}$

b Make x the subject.

i
$ax + b = c$ — $-\,b$ both sides
$ax = c - b$ — $\div\,a$ both sides
$\therefore x = \dfrac{c - b}{a}$

ii
$m - nx = p$ — $+\,nx$ both sides
$m = p + nx$ — $-\,p$ both sides
$m - p = nx$ — $\div\,n$ both sides
$\dfrac{m - p}{n} = x$
$\therefore x = \dfrac{m - p}{n}$

iii
$a(x + b) = c$ — expand
$ax + ab = c$ — $-\,ab$ both sides
$ax = c - ab$ — $\div\,a$ both sides
$\therefore x = \dfrac{c - ab}{a}$

Note:
Another way of saying 'make x the subject of this formula' is: 'solve this literal equation for x'.

WORKED EXAMPLE 2

Each formula below has been rearranged to make the capital letter pronumeral the subject. The operation done to each side is shown for each step.

a

$v = u + aT$	$-\,u$ both sides
$v - u = aT$	$\div\, a$ both sides
$\dfrac{v-u}{a} = T$	
$\therefore T = \dfrac{v-u}{a}$	

b

$m = \frac{1}{2}(x + Y)$	$\div\, 2$ both sides
$2m = x + Y$	$-\,x$ both sides
$2m - x = Y$	
$\therefore Y = 2m - x$	

c

$t = a + (N - 1)d$	expand
$t = a + Nd - d$	$-\,a$ both sides
$t - a = Nd - d$	$+\,d$ both sides
$t - a + d = Nd$	$\div\, d$ both sides
$\dfrac{t-a+d}{d} = N$	
$\therefore N = \dfrac{t-a+d}{d}$	

d

$a = 2\pi r(r + H)$	expand
$a = 2\pi r^2 + 2\pi rH$	$-\,2\pi r^2$ both sides
$a - 2\pi r^2 = 2\pi rH$	$\div\, 2\pi r$ both sides
$\dfrac{a-2\pi r^2}{2\pi r^2} = H$	
$\therefore H = \dfrac{a-2\pi r^2}{2\pi r^2}$	

To change the subject of a formula (solve a literal equation):
1 Expand parentheses if applicable.
2 By using inverse operations, isolate the pronumeral required to be the subject.

Exercise 7:09

P Foundation worksheet 7:09
Solving literal equations

1 Make x the subject of each formula.

a $p = x + m$
b $m = x + np$
c $n = pq - x$
d $ax = b$
e $3x = y$
f $a^2x = b + c$
g $b - ax = 2d$
h $ax - b = c$
i $c - 2b = ax + b$
j $y = \dfrac{x}{a}$
k $y = \dfrac{a}{x}$
l $\dfrac{x}{y} = b$
m $a = \dfrac{25}{x}$
n $\dfrac{ax}{b} = c$
o $p = \dfrac{2x}{L}$

2 After first expanding the grouping symbols, solve each literal equation for x.

a $a = 2(x + y)$
b $p = 5(t + x)$
c $y = 3(x - 7)$
d $p = q(x - r)$
e $6(a - x) = b$
f $w = t(v - x)$
g $R = 2r(x + 2)$
h $p = 5q(x - y)$
i $A = \pi r(r - x)$

3 Solve each literal equation for the pronumeral shown in the brackets.

a $A = x + y$ $[y]$

b $P = 2l + 2b$ $[L]$

c $C = \pi d$ $[d]$

d $v = u + at$ $[u]$

e $v = u + at$ $[a]$

f $E = mc^2$ $[m]$

g $S = \dfrac{D}{T}$ $[D]$

h $R = \dfrac{V}{I}$ $[V]$

i $I = \dfrac{PRT}{100}$ $[P]$

j $P = RI^2$ $[R]$

k $v^2 = u^2 + 2as$ $[s]$

l $F = ac + p$ $[a]$

m $P = a(m + n)$ $[n]$

n $x = 2a(p + q)$ $[p]$

o $K = \frac{1}{2}mV^2$ $[m]$

p $P = m(v - u)$ $[u]$

q $V = \dfrac{AH}{3}$ $[H]$

r $V = \dfrac{\pi r^2 h}{3}$ $[h]$

s $S = \pi r^2 + \pi rh$ $[h]$

t $E = mgh + \frac{1}{2}mv^2$ $[h]$

u $P = 2ab - 2ak$ $[k]$

v $A = \dfrac{a + b}{2}$ $[a]$

w $A = \dfrac{h(a + b)}{2}$ $[b]$

x $F = \dfrac{q_1 q_2}{r}$ $[r]$

y $T = a + (n - 1)d$ $[d]$

z $S = \dfrac{a(r^n - 1)}{r - 1}$ $[a]$

7:10 Solving literal equations (2)

PREP QUIZ 7:10

Solve the equations:

1 $\dfrac{x}{5} = 3$

2 $\dfrac{x}{8} = \dfrac{3}{4}$

3 $\dfrac{x + 2}{3} = 5$

4 $x^2 = 9$

5 $\sqrt{x} = 5$

6 $(x + 3)^2 = 25$

7 $\sqrt{x - 3} = 2$

Factorise fully:

8 $3x + 12$

9 $x^2 - 2x$

10 $5a^2 + 10ab$

In this section the formulas may also contain a squared term or a square root sign, or the pronumeral that is to become the subject may appear more than once.

Remember!

$\sqrt{}$ is the opposite of $(\ )^2$.

$(\ )^2$ is the opposite of $\sqrt{}$.

WORKED EXAMPLES

Change the subject of the formula to the pronumeral indicated in brackets.

a $E = mc^2$ [c] **b** $v^2 = u^2 - 2as$ [u] **c** $r = \sqrt{\frac{A}{\pi}}$ [A]

d $a = 6 - \frac{12}{R}$ [R] **e** $y = \frac{A}{A+2}$ [A]

Solutions

a
$$E = mc^2 \quad \div m \text{ both sides}$$
$$\frac{E}{m} = c^2 \quad \sqrt{\ } \text{ both sides}$$
$$\therefore c = \pm\sqrt{\frac{E}{m}}$$

b
$$v^2 = u^2 - 2as \quad + 2as \text{ both sides}$$
$$v^2 + 2as = u^2 \quad \sqrt{\ } \text{ both sides}$$
$$\pm\sqrt{v^2 + 2as} = u$$
$$\therefore u = \pm\sqrt{v^2 + 2as}$$

c
$$r = \sqrt{\frac{A}{\pi}} \quad \text{square both sides}$$
$$r^2 = \frac{A}{\pi} \quad \times \pi \text{ both sides}$$
$$\pi r^2 = A$$
$$\therefore A = \pi r^2$$

d
$$a = 6 - \frac{12}{R} \quad \times R \text{ both sides}$$
$$aR = 6R - 12 \quad - 6R \text{ both sides}$$
$$aR - 6R = -12 \quad \text{factorise LHS}$$
$$R(a - 6) = -12 \quad \div (a - 6) \text{ both sides}$$
$$\therefore R = \frac{-12}{a-6}$$

e
$$y = \frac{A}{A+2} \quad \times (A + 2) \text{ both sides}$$
$$y(A + 2) = A \quad \text{expand LHS}$$
$$Ay + 2y = A \quad - Ay \text{ both sides}$$
$$2y = A - Ay \quad \text{factorise RHS}$$
$$2y = A(1 - y) \quad \div (1 - y) \text{ both sides}$$
$$\frac{2y}{1-y} = A$$
$$\therefore A = \frac{2y}{1-y}$$

Remember!
Sometimes formulas are called *literal equations*. When literal equations are 'solved' for a certain pronumeral, it is the same as changing the subject of the formula to that pronumeral.

If the pronumeral that is to be the subject appears in more than one term in the formula, gather the terms together and factorise as in Worked Examples **d** and **e**.

Exercise 7:10

1 Change the subject of each formula to x.

a $mx^2 = n$ **b** $a = bx^2$ **c** $x^2 - a = b$ **d** $h = k - x^2$

e $\frac{x^2}{a} = y$ **f** $m = \frac{nx^2}{3}$ **g** $L = x^2 - y^2$ **h** $A = \frac{B}{x^2}$

2 Make a the subject of each formula.

a $\sqrt{ab} = c$　b $u = \sqrt{3a}$　c $c = \sqrt{a - b}$　d $c = \sqrt{a} - b$

e $P = L + M\sqrt{a}$　f $M - N\sqrt{a} = L$　g $\sqrt{3a - 1} = L$　h $P = \sqrt{b - 2a}$

3 Make N the subject of each formula after first multiplying each term by the lowest common denominator.

a $a = \frac{3N}{2}$　b $a = L - \frac{3N}{2}$　c $\frac{x}{3} = \frac{N}{2} - 1$

d $L = \frac{N}{2} + \frac{M}{3}$　e $x = \frac{N + a}{3}$　f $x = \frac{N - 1}{2} + \frac{M + 1}{3}$

g $\frac{N + u}{3} = \frac{m + u}{4}$　h $\frac{N - a}{b} = \frac{L + b}{a}$

4 Solve each literal equation for x.

a $a + x = b - x$　b $ax = px + q$　c $x + a = ax + b$

d $m - nx = n - mx$　e $px^2 = qx^2 + 2$　f $L = Ax + (1 + B)x$

g $\frac{x}{5} + \frac{x}{3} = a$　h $a = \frac{x}{x + 2}$　i $y = \frac{x}{x - 5}$

j $n = \frac{x + 3}{1 + x}$　k $A = \frac{a + bx}{1 + x}$　l $B = \frac{x + a}{x - a}$

5 Solve each equation for the letter shown in brackets.

	Set A		Set B		Set C	
a	$A = lb$	[b]	$A = X - Y$	[X]	$V = u + at$	[t]
b	$D = \frac{M}{V}$	[V]	$D = \frac{S}{T}$	[S]	$P = RI^2$	[I]
c	$V = \frac{Ah}{3}$	[h]	$V = \frac{1}{3}\pi r^2 h$	[r]	$S = 4\pi r^2$	[r]
d	$M = \frac{a + b}{2}$	[b]	$A = \frac{1}{2}h(x + y)$	[y]	$v^2 = u^2 + 2as$	[s]
e	$x^2 = ay - y^2$	[a]	$S = 2\pi r(r + h)$	[h]	$T = \frac{n}{2}[2a + (n - 1)d]$	[d]
f	$a = \sqrt{bc}$	[c]	$Y = a\sqrt{X}$	[X]	$X = 2\sqrt{a - b}$	[a]
g	$X = \sqrt{\frac{Y}{a}}$	[Y]	$R = \sqrt{\frac{ax}{b}}$	[x]	$m = \sqrt{\frac{a + b}{n}}$	[b]
h	$T = 2\pi\sqrt{\frac{l}{g}}$	[l]	$A = 2x\sqrt{\frac{t}{u}}$	[u]	$u = \sqrt{v^2 - 2as}$	[s]
i	$y = \frac{a}{3} + \frac{b}{2}$	[a]	$Z = \frac{X}{4} + \frac{Y}{3}$	[X]	$A = \frac{b - c}{5}$	[c]
j	$\frac{A + x}{3} = \frac{A + y}{2}$	[A]	$L = \frac{N - 1}{2} + \frac{N + 1}{3}$	[N]	$\frac{X}{a} = \frac{X - a}{b}$	[X]
k	$h = \frac{k}{2k + 1}$	[k]	$y = \frac{a}{a + 2}$	[a]	$z = \frac{x}{x - 3}$	[x]

7:11 Solving problems with formulas

Often the solution of a problem requires the use of a formula. You have met formulas before in other areas of mathematics, such as finding the area and volume of shapes and solids.

In this section you will be asked to solve problems that involve formulas. Sometimes they are given, while at other times you will have to recall the relevant formula yourself.

WORKED EXAMPLES

1 The density of a solid, D, in grams/cm^3 is given by the formula $D = \frac{M}{V}$, where M is the mass in grams and V is the volume in cm^3. Find:

a the density of a 92-gram block of steel if it has a volume of 9·6 cm^3

b the volume of a block of iron that has a density of 7·5 g/cm^3 and a mass of 450 grams.

2 The time, T, taken by a pendulum for one swing is given by $T = 2\pi\sqrt{\frac{l}{g}}$

where $g = 9{\cdot}8\,\text{m/s}^2$ and l is the length of the string in metres.

a Express the formula with l as the subject.

b If the time for one swing is 3·5 s, what must be the length of the pendulum, to the nearest cm?

Solutions

1 $D = \frac{M}{V}$

a $M = 92\,\text{g}$ and $V = 9{\cdot}6\,\text{cm}^3$

$$D = \frac{92}{9{\cdot}6}$$

$$\therefore D = 9{\cdot}58\,\text{g/cm}^3 \text{ (2 dec. pl.)}$$

b $D = 7{\cdot}5\,\text{g/cm}^3$ and $M = 450\,\text{g}$

$$7{\cdot}5 = \frac{450}{V}$$

$$V = \frac{450}{7{\cdot}5}$$

$$\therefore V = 60\,\text{cm}^3$$

2 $T = 2\pi\sqrt{\frac{l}{g}}$

a Rearranging this formula gives:

$$T = 2\pi\sqrt{\frac{l}{g}}$$

$$\frac{T}{2\pi} = \sqrt{\frac{l}{g}}$$

$$\left(\frac{T}{2\pi}\right)^2 = \frac{l}{g}$$

$$\therefore l = g\left(\frac{T}{2\pi}\right)^2$$

b $l = g\left(\frac{T}{2\pi}\right)^2$

$g = 9{\cdot}8$ and $T = 3{\cdot}5$

$$l = 9{\cdot}8\left(\frac{3{\cdot}5}{2\pi}\right)^2$$

Using a calculator:

$l = 3{\cdot}04\,\text{m}$

Note: If the solving of a problem requires the evaluation of a pronumeral that is *not* the subject, we may do it in two ways.

1 Substitute the given values into the formula and solve the resulting equation; or

2 Change the subject of the formula before substituting the given values.

Exercise 7:11

1 a If the perimeter of a square is 16·8 m, what is its area?

b Calculate the area of a rectangle that has a perimeter of 150 cm if its width is 25 cm.

2 a Write the formula for the area of a circle.

b Determine the diameter of a circle, to the nearest cm, if its area is 38·5 cm^2.

3 The temperature in degrees Fahrenheit (F) is related to the Celsius measure (C) by the formula: $F = \frac{9}{5}C + 32$

a If the temperature is 65°C, what is it in degrees Fahrenheit?

b If the temperature is 104°F, what is it in degrees Celsius?

4 The volume of a cube is given by the formula $V = x^3$, where x is the side length of the cube. Find the side length of the cube if the volume is 1728 cm^3.

5 The volume of a cone is given by the formula $V = \dfrac{\pi r^2 h}{3}$, where h is the height of the cone and r is the radius of the cone. If the volume of a cone is 12·6 m^3, find, to the nearest cm:

a the height, if the radius is 1·4 m

b the radius, if the height is 2·2 m.

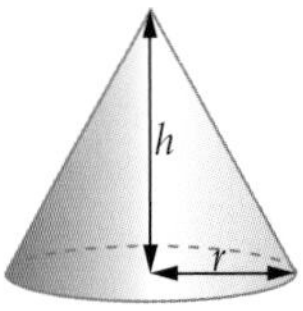

6 Find the radius of a sphere, correct to two significant figures, if its surface area is 45 cm^2. The surface area, S, is given by the formula $S = 4\pi r^2$, where r is the radius.

7 The diagram shows a field made up of a rectangle with two semicircular ends. Calculate a formula for the perimeter, P, in terms of D and x. Calculate the value of D needed to give a perimeter of 400 m if:

a $x = 80$ m

b $x = 100$ m

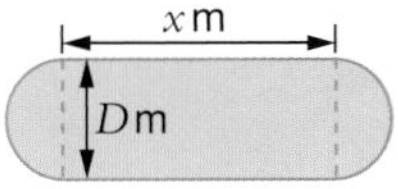

8 If a body has an initial velocity of u m/s and accelerates at a rate of a m/s^2 for t seconds, its velocity v is given by the formula:

$v = u + at$

If the final velocity, v, of a certain body is 25 m/s, find:

a its initial velocity, u, if $a = 5·6$ m/s^2 and $t = 3·2$ seconds

b its acceleration, a, if $u = 13$ m/s and $t = 2·5$ seconds

c the time, t, taken if $u = 14·6$ m/s and $a = 1·6$ m/s^2.

9 The kinetic energy K (in joules) of a particle of mass m kg, moving with a velocity of v m/s, is given by the formula:

$K = \frac{1}{2}mv^2$

If the kinetic energy of a particle is 4·6 joules, find:

a its mass, if the velocity is 1·9 m/s

b its velocity, if the mass is 1·26 kg.

(Give answers correct to one decimal place.)

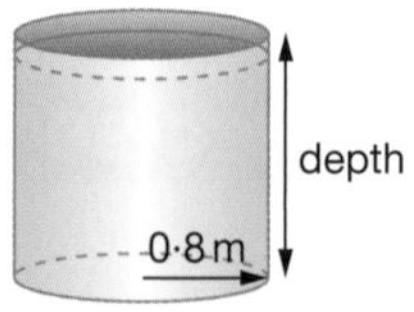

10 A cylindrical tank holds 1200 L of water. If its radius is 0·8 m, what is the depth of the water? (*Note:* 1 cubic metre = 1000 litres.) Give your answer correct to the nearest centimetre.

11 The formula for compound interest is $A = P\left(1 + \frac{r}{100}\right)^n$, where A is the amount accumulated after investing P dollars for n years at a rate of r% p.a.

a Find the amount A after investing \$2000 for 8 years at 11% p.a.

b Find the original investment, P, if it accumulated to \$11 886 in 12 years at $9\frac{1}{2}$% p.a. (Answer correct to the nearest dollar.)

c At what rate must \$10 000 be invested to accumulate to \$19 254 in 5 years? Answer correct to two significant figures.

12 a Construct a formula for the area of this annulus.

b If R = 6·9 cm and r = 4·1 cm, find its area.

c If its area is 45 cm^2 and R = 5·2 cm, find r.

d If its area is 75 cm^2 and r = 3·9 cm, find R.

(Give answers correct to one decimal place.)

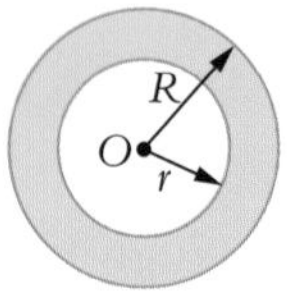

13 a Construct a formula for the volume of this solid.

b Find its volume if r = 2·6 m and h = 5·1 m.

c Find h if its volume is 290 m^2 and r = 3·2 m.

(Give answers correct to three significant figures.)

(Volume of sphere = $\frac{4}{3}\pi r^3$)

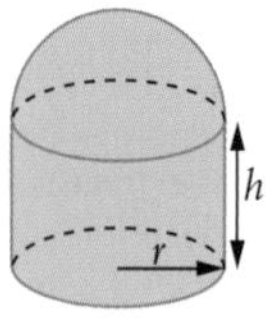

14 The formula $V = \frac{q}{4\pi\varepsilon_0 r}$ gives the potential V volts, at a distance r metres from a point charge of q coulombs.

a Find V if $q = 1{\cdot}0 \times 10^{-8}$ coulombs, r = 0·2 m and $4\pi\varepsilon_0 = 9{\cdot}0 \times 10^9$.

b Find r if $q = 3{\cdot}0 \times 10^{-7}$ coulombs, V = 54 000 volts and $4\pi\varepsilon_0 = 9{\cdot}0 \times 10^9$.

15 The formula $F = \frac{Kq_1q_2}{r^2}$ gives the force, in newtons, between two point charges of q_1 and q_2 coulombs that are r metres apart. If two equally charged balls are placed 0·1 m apart and the force between the balls is $9{\cdot}8 \times 10^{-4}$ newtons, calculate the charge on each ball. ($K = 9{\cdot}0 \times 10^9$)

FUN SPOT 7:11 WHY ARE COOKS CRUEL?

Work out the answer to each part and put the letter for that part in the box that is above the correct answer.

Simplify:

E $9a - 5a$

E $10x - x$

E $4 \times 2y$

E $18m \div 2$

E $-3a + 9a$

E $(-3a)^2$

E $-a - 5a$

A $9x + x$

A $7x + a + x$

A $20m \div m$

A $-8 \times \frac{1}{2}x$

A $5x^2 - x - x$

I $ax \times 5a$

I $\frac{3}{a} \times \frac{a}{3}$

U $25x^2 \div 5x - 3x$

T $6a^2 - a^2 - 5$

T $16a^2 \div (-2a^2)$

T $8x^2 \div 4x \times 2x$

Write an expression for:

T one more than x

B the product of a and b

B the average of x and a

B the difference between x and a

Find the value of $x^2 - 4x + 4$ if:

S $x = 7$

S $x = 10$

S $x = 9$

C $x = -1$

Solve these equations:

H $x + 8 = 5$

H $x - 9 = 4$

F $\frac{-13}{x} = 1$

C $\frac{x}{3} = 1$

$l = 6$, $b = 8$, $h = 10$, $a = 5$, $b = 9$ and $s = 7$, find A if:

R $A = lb$

M $A = \frac{1}{2}bh$

N $A = S^2$

D $A = \frac{1}{2}h(a + b)$

Evaluate:

Y $\frac{a}{2}$ if $a = \frac{1}{2}$

G $\frac{1}{M}$ if $M = \frac{1}{2}$

G $90° - \theta$ if $\theta = 17°$

H $3{\cdot}14r^2$ if $r = 10$

R $\frac{8}{1-r}$ if $r = 0{\cdot}5$

P $\frac{9C}{5}$ if $C = 20$

W $ut + \frac{1}{2}at^2$ if $u = 12$, $a = 9{\cdot}8$ and $t = 10$

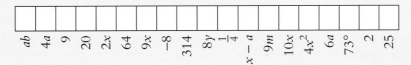

ab	$4a$	9	20	$2x$	64	$9x$	−8	314	$8y$	$\frac{1}{4}$	$x - a$	$9m$	$10x$	$4x^2$	$6a$	73°	2	25

610	$x = 13$	$5a^2x$	36	$x = 3$	$A = 48$	$-6a$	$-4x$	$A = 40$	$5x^2 - 2x$	$A = 49$	$A = 70$	$\frac{x+a}{2}$	$8x + a$	$5a^2 - 5$	$x + 1$	$9a^2$	16	$x = -13$	1	49	$x = -3$

MATHS TERMS 7

equation

- a number sentence where one or more of the numbers is missing or unknown
- the unknown number is represented by a pronumeral,
  e.g. $x + 5 = 8$, $\frac{3x+1}{7} = \frac{x-5}{2}$

expression

- an algebraic expression consists of one or more terms joined together by operation signs,
  e.g. $a + 5$, $x^2 - x + 4$, $\frac{3m-1}{7}$
- an expression does not have an 'equals' sign like an equation

formula (plural: **formulas**)

- represents a relationship between physical quantities
- always has more than one pronumeral,
  e.g. $A = l \times b$ represents the relationship between the area (A) of a rectangle and its length (l) and breadth (b)

grouping symbols

- the most common types are:
  parentheses ( )
  brackets [ ]
  braces { }
- used to 'group' a number of terms together in an expression,
  e.g. $5(x + 3)$

inequality signs

- > greater than, < less than
- ≥ greater than or equal to,
  ≤ less than or equal to,
  e.g. $x + 3 < 4$ means that
  $x + 3$ is less than 4

inequality

- an equation where an inequality sign is used instead of an equals sign,
  e.g. $4x - 1 > 5$ or $\frac{x}{3} \le 4$

inverse operation

- the operation that will reverse or 'undo' a previous operation,
  e.g. addition is the inverse operation of subtraction,
  division is the inverse operation of multiplication

pronumeral

- a symbol used to represent a number
- usually a letter such as x

solution

- method of finding the answer to a problem
- the solution to an equation is the number or numbers that satisfy the equation or make it a true sentence,
  e.g. $x = 3$ is the solution to $x + 2 = 5$

solve

- find the solution or answer to a problem or equation

subject

- the subject of a formula is the pronumeral by itself, on the left-hand side,
  e.g. in the formula $v = u + at$ the subject is v

substitute

- to replace a pronumeral with a numeral,
  e.g. Substitute 3 for a in the expression
  $4a - 2$:
  $4(3) - 2$
  $= 12 - 2$
  $= 10$

DIAGNOSTIC TEST 7 EQUATIONS, INEQUALITIES AND FORMULAS

Each part of this test has similar items that test a certain type of question.
Failure in more than one item will identify an area of weakness.
Each weakness should be treated by going back to the section listed.

1 Solve: 7:01

a $4p + 3 = 31$ b $2m - 7 = 17$ c $25 = 5 - 2m$

2 Solve: 7:01

a $3x + 5 = 2x + 1$ b $5a - 7 = 3a - 1$ c $4b + 7 = b - 8$

3 Solve: 7:02

a $3(x + 1) = 9$ b $4(a - 3) = 24$ c $6(x - 3) + 4x = 8$

4 Solve: 7:02

a $3(x + 4) = 2(x - 3)$ b $3(a - 1) + 5(a + 3) = 20$
c $2(2m + 3) - 3(m - 5) = 7$

5 Solve: 7:03

a $\frac{y}{2} + 1 = 7$ b $\frac{m}{2} - 1 = 5$ c $4 = 13 - \frac{p}{2}$ d $\frac{3m}{5} = 6$

6 Solve: 7:03

a $\frac{m+3}{4} = 2$ b $\frac{m-6}{3} = 1$ c $\frac{3p-7}{2} = 7$ d $\frac{5+3x}{5} = 5$

7 Solve: 7:03

a $\frac{m}{5} + 2 = m$ b $2x + 1 = \frac{3x}{2}$ c $\frac{n+7}{4} = 2n$ d $\frac{5a-2}{3} = 3 - a$

8 Solve: 7:04

a $\frac{a}{3} + \frac{a}{2} = 10$ b $\frac{2m}{3} - \frac{m}{2} = 4$ c $\frac{x}{4} = \frac{x}{5} - 3$ d $\frac{2y+1}{4} = \frac{3y-4}{3}$

9 Form an equation from the given data for each of these. 7:05
(In each case let a represent the unknown number.)

a I think of a number, multiply it by 2, add 7 and the result is 10.
b I think of a number, divide it by 3, subtract 4 and the result is 4.
c I think of a number, add 6, then multiply by 3 and the result is 32.

10 Form an equation for each question. (Let the unknown quantity be x.) 7:05

a The sum of a brother's and sister's ages is 57 years. If the brother is 5 years older than his sister, find their ages.
b A rectangle is three times longer than it is wide. If its perimeter is 48 cm, find its length and width.
c A father is presently three times as old as his son. In 10 years he will be twice as old as his son. Find their present ages.

11 Graph the following on a number line. 7:06

a $x > 3$ b $x \le -1$ c $x \ge 0$ d $x < 5$

12 Solve: 7:06

a $2x + 5 \geq 6$ b $\dfrac{2x-1}{3} < 6$ c $3x - 7 > x + 3$

13 Solve: 7:06

a $5 - 3x > 11$ b $-\dfrac{1}{3}x > 21$ c $3 - 4a > 2 - a$

14 a If $v = u + at$, find v when $u = 6{\cdot}8$, $a = 9{\cdot}8$ and $t = 3$. 7:07

b If $C = 2\pi r^2$, find C when $\pi = \frac{22}{7}$ and $r = 0{\cdot}77$.

c Given $A = \frac{1}{2}h(a + b)$, find A when $h = 2{\cdot}6$, $a = 9{\cdot}4$ and $b = 16{\cdot}4$.

15 a If $M = 2m + 3n$, find m when $M = 17{\cdot}5$ and $n = 0{\cdot}5$. 7:08

b If $V = \dfrac{Ah}{3}$, find h when $V = 6{\cdot}03$ and $A = 1{\cdot}2$.

c Given that $V = 4\pi r^2$, find r when $\pi = 3{\cdot}14$ and $V = 153{\cdot}86$.

16 Change the subject of each formula to a. 7:09

a $x = 3a - 2b$ b $V^2 = u^2 + 2as$ c $A = \dfrac{D(a+b)}{h}$

17 Change the subject of each formula to y. 7:10

a $ay^2 = x$ b $T = A\sqrt{\dfrac{B}{y}}$ c $P = \dfrac{y}{1+y}$

Many equations need to be solved in the design and construction of aircraft.

ASSIGNMENT 7A Chapter review

1 Solve:

a $5m - 7 = 8$
b $3y + 7 = 4$
c $6m - 1 = 17$
d $4n + 10 = 2$
e $3x + 7 = 5x - 4$
f $12 - 5x = 10 - 3x$

2 Solve these equations that involve grouping symbols.

a $5(x + 7) = 30$
b $7(a - 3) = 21$
c $8(m - 1) = 4$
d $4(x + 3) = 3(x + 2)$
e $5(n - 2) = 3(n + 4)$
f $10(x - 7) = 7(x - 10)$
g $4(2a + 3) + 3(a - 3) = 5$
h $5(3n + 4) + 2(5 - 2n) = 7$
i $6(m + 4) - 5(m + 3) = 6$
j $7(4x + 3) - 3(8x - 5) = 0$

3 Solve:

a $\frac{x}{4} + 3 = 5$
b $\frac{m}{5} - 2 = 1$
c $\frac{2x}{3} - 4 = 2$
d $\frac{a+7}{4} = 6$
e $\frac{y-5}{3} = 1$
f $\frac{3p+1}{5} = 2$
g $\frac{2m}{3} - 1 = m$
h $\frac{5m-1}{4} = 2m$
i $2n + 5 = \frac{n-1}{3}$
j $\frac{x+5}{2} = \frac{x-3}{4}$
k $\frac{a}{5} - \frac{a}{2} = 7$
l $\frac{5q+1}{2} = \frac{q}{3} - \frac{q}{4}$

4 Solve and graph each solution on a number line.

a $m + 7 \geq 5$
b $2x - 1 < 7$
c $5n + 1 \leq 3$
d $3x + 7 \leq x + 10$
e $y - 5 > 3y - 8$
f $4n + 7 \geq 7n - 4$
g $6 - 2x > 14$
h $-\frac{2x}{3} \geq 6$
i $10 - 3a \leq 7 - a$

5 Write an equation for each of the following and then solve it.

a A number is multiplied by 3, then 7 is added and the result is 15.
b Nine is subtracted from a number and the result is multiplied by five to equal thirty.
c Eight times a certain number plus ten is equal to twelve times the same number minus seven.
d A boy is 12 years older than his sister. If in 4 years time he will be twice her age, what are their present ages?
e Two sisters are presently 2 years old and 12 years old. How many years will have to pass before the elder sister is $1\frac{1}{2}$ times the age of the younger sister?

6 a Given that $S = ut + \frac{1}{2}at^2$, find S when $u = 7, t = 3, a = 10$.
b If $C = 2mr$, find m when $C = 17{\cdot}6$ and $r = 1{\cdot}1$.
c If $P = \frac{1}{a} + \frac{1}{b}$, find P when $a = 0{\cdot}4$ and $b = 0{\cdot}625$.

7 a If $D = \frac{M}{V}$, find V when $D = 1{\cdot}5$ and $M = 0{\cdot}5$.
b If $E = \frac{Ab}{A+b}$, find b when $E = 15$ and $A = 0{\cdot}4$.
c Given that $M = \frac{X}{a} + \frac{X}{b}$, find a when $M = 27{\cdot}5, X = 15, b = 3$.

8 Rearrange each formula to make P the subject.

a $A = \frac{PRT}{100}$
b $V = RP^2$
c $T = \sqrt{\frac{3P}{R}}$
d $X = \frac{1}{P} - \frac{1}{Q}$

9 Challenge question: Solve the following equations.

a $\frac{3}{x} = 5$
b $\frac{2}{x-1} = 3$
c $\frac{x}{x+1} = 4$
d $\frac{4}{3x} - \frac{2}{x} = 5$
e $\frac{x}{2x-1} - 3 = \frac{1}{4}$
f $\frac{1}{3} - \frac{1}{p-1} = 3$

ASSIGNMENT 7B Working mathematically

1 Four digits placed in these squares will form two numbers across and two numbers down. The four numbers add to give 140. What are the four digits and how are they placed in the squares? (None of the digits is zero.)

2 Find the algebraic rule for these tables of values.

a

x	0	1	2	3
y	12	9	6	3

b

t	−1	1	3	5
s	2	2	10	26

3 Ten students lined up at a tap for a drink of water. Each person took 1 minute.

a How long did it take for all students to have a drink?

b What was the total time spent waiting and drinking by all 10 students?

4 Find the basic numeral for:

$$(1-\tfrac{1}{2})+(\tfrac{1}{2}-\tfrac{1}{3})+(\tfrac{1}{3}-\tfrac{1}{4})$$
$$+(\tfrac{1}{4}-\tfrac{1}{5})+(\tfrac{1}{5}-\tfrac{1}{6})+(\tfrac{1}{6}-\tfrac{1}{7})$$
$$+(\tfrac{1}{7}-\tfrac{1}{8})+(\tfrac{1}{8}-\tfrac{1}{9})+(\tfrac{1}{9}-\tfrac{1}{10})$$

5 In computing, the units kilobyte, megabyte and gigabyte are used. Because computers use the binary system, which is based on powers of 2, each prefix is given the value of the power of 2 nearest to its true value. For example:

kilo = 1000

$2^{10} = 1024$

This is the power of 2 nearest to 1000.
So 1 kilobyte = 1024 bytes.

a Find what power of 2 is closest in value to:

i 1 000 000

ii 1 000 000 000

b How many bytes are there in:

i a megabyte

ii a gigabyte?

6

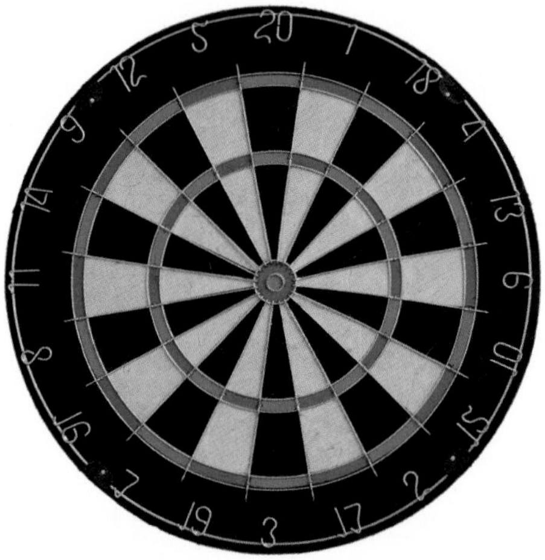

a Three darts are thrown and all land in the '20' sector. What are the possible total scores for the three darts if all darts can land on either the 20, double 20 or triple 20?

b Three darts are thrown and all land in the 'x' sector. Write an algebraic expression for the possible total scores.

c Three darts are thrown and all land in the same sector. The total score is 102. In what sector did the darts land?

ASSIGNMENT 7C Cumulative revision

1 a A business estimates that its expenses will rise next year by 4·8%. If its expenses this year were \$110 500, what do they estimate that they will be next year? 2:01

b Wages are the largest part of a company's expenses. If their expenses were \$110 500 and they paid \$54 000 in wages, what percentage were the wages of the expenses?

2 An athlete runs 21 km in 63 min. 1:04, 2:01

a Express this rate as a rate in:

i km/min ii km/h iii min/km

b At this rate how long does it take to run 100 m?

3 Expand and simplify these expressions. 3:08

a $a(a + 3) - 2(a + 3)$ b $(a - 2)(a + 3)$

c $(a - 2)(a + 2)$ d $(a - 2)^2$

4 A company interested in starting up a gym surveyed people in the local area and obtained the following results. 4:05

	Exercises regularly	No regular exercise	Totals
Male	85	115	200
Female	82	68	150
Totals	167	183	350

Based on these results, find the probability (to the nearest whole precentage) that a person chosen at random:

a exercises regularly

b is female and exercises regularly

c exercises regularly, if we know that the person chosen is male

d is male, if we know that the person chosen exercises regularly.

5 Each of the following boxes is a rectangular prism with the same volume. Calculate the area of cardboard needed to make each box. Which one uses less cardboard? 5:02

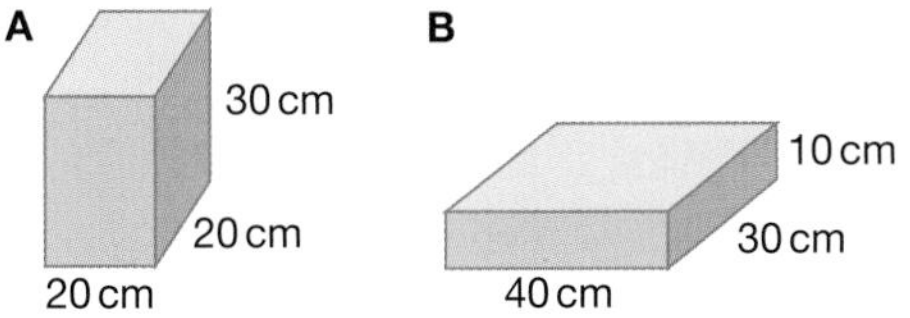

6 Simplify each of the following, writing your answer as a power of 10. 6:02, 6:03

a $10^4 \times 10^6$ b $10^4 \div 10^6$ c $(10^3)^{\frac{2}{3}}$ d $(10^{-2})^3 \div (10^6)^{-2}$

7 Evaluate the following. 6:02, 6:03

a 4^{-2} b $4^{\frac{1}{2}}$ c $8^{\frac{2}{3}}$ d $8^{-\frac{2}{3}}$

8 Simplify the following, writing each answer in scientific notation. 6:05

a $0{\cdot}000\,000\,25 \times 0{\cdot}000\,0046$ b $(1{\cdot}52 \times 10^7) \div (2{\cdot}64 \times 10^{-6})$

FINANCIAL MATHEMATICS

8

Contents

Syllabus references (See pages x–xv for details.)

Number and Algebra

Selections from ***Financial Mathematics*** [Stage 5.1]

- Solve problems involving earning money (NSW)
- Solve problems involving simple interest (ACMNA211)

Working Mathematically

- Communicating
- Problem Solving
- Reasoning
- Understanding
- Fluency

8:01 Earning money

Some people work for themselves and charge a fee for their services or sell for a profit, but most people work for others to obtain an income. In the chart below, the main ways of earning an income from an employer are introduced.

Employment				
Salary	**Wages**	**Casual**	**Commission**	**Piece work**
Meaning				
A fixed amount is paid for the year's work even though it may be paid weekly or fortnightly.	Usually paid weekly to a permanent employee and based on an hourly rate, for an agreed number of hours per week.	A fixed rate is paid per hour. The worker is not employed permanently, and works only when needed.	This payment is usually a percentage of the value of goods sold.	The worker is paid a fixed amount for each piece of work completed.
Advantages				
Permanent employment. Holiday and sick pay. Superannuation. A bonus may be given as an incentive, or time off for working outside normal working hours.	Permanent employment. Holiday and sick pay. Superannuation. If additional hours are worked, additional money is earned, sometimes at a higher hourly rate of pay.	A higher rate of pay is given as a compensation for other benefits lost. Part-time work may suit some, or casual work may be a second job. Superannuation.	The more you sell the more you are paid. Some firms pay a low wage plus a commission to act as an incentive.	The harder you work, the more you earn. You can choose how much work you do, and in some cases the work may be done in your own home.
Disadvantages				
During busy periods, additional hours might be worked without additional pay. Very little flexibility in working times e.g. 9 am–5 pm	There is little incentive to work harder, since your pay is fixed to time, not effort. Little flexibility in working times, e.g. 9 am–5 pm	No holiday or sick pay. No permanency of employment. Few fringe benefits.	There may be no holiday or sick pay. If you sell nothing you are paid nothing. Your security depends on the popularity of your product.	No holiday or sick pay. No fringe benefits. No permanency of employment in most piece work.
Salary	**Wages**	**Casual**	**Commission**	**Piece work**
 teachers	 mechanics	 swimming instructors	 sales people	 dressmakers

WORKED EXAMPLES

1 Use the information on the right to answer these questions.

POSITIONS VACANT

5 people required to promote our nationally known building product in the suburbs.

Pay: \$500 p.w. and 2% commission.

Please phone YRU-POOR during business hours.

a How much would an employee earn in a week if no sales were made?

b If Jane sold \$18 000 worth of building products in a week, how much would she earn?

c If Peter sold \$24 000 worth of materials in a week and \$5000 worth in the next, find his average weekly income for the 2 weeks.

2 Luke has a casual job from 4:00 pm until 5:30 pm Monday to Friday. He also works from 9 am until 12:30 pm on Saturdays. Find his weekly income if his casual rate is \$18.80 per hour Monday to Friday, and \$28.20 an hour on Saturdays.

Solutions

1 a Week's earnings = \$500 + 2% of \$0
= \$500 + \$0

∴ Employee making no sales is paid \$500.

b Jane's earnings = \$500 + 2% of \$18 000
= \$500 + 0·02 × \$18 000
= \$860 in the week

c Week 1

Peter's earnings = \$500 + 2% of \$24 000
= \$500 + 0·02 × \$24 000

∴ Earnings week 1 = \$980

Week 2

Peter's earnings = \$500 + 2% of \$5000
= \$500 + 0·02 × \$5000

∴ Earnings week 2 = \$600

∴ Peter's average weekly wage = (\$980 + \$600) ÷ 2
= \$790

2 Luke's weekly income = (hours, Mon–Fri) × \$18.80 + (hours, Sat) × \$28.20

$= (1\frac{1}{2} \times 5) \times \$18.80 + 3\frac{1}{2} \times \$28.20$

$= 1{\cdot}5 \times 5 \times \$18.80 + 3{\cdot}5 \times \$28.20$

$= \$239.70$

Exercise 8:01

1 Write answers in your own words.

a What are the advantages of working for a wage?

b What is piece work?

c What is a salary?

d What form of payment gives the worker a percentage of the value of goods sold?

e What advantages are there in casual work?

f What are the disadvantages of being on a salary?

g What is a wage?

h Which forms of payment depend on success or the amount of work completed?

i What are the disadvantages of casual work?

j Which two forms of payment are often combined in determining a worker's pay?

2 a A man is paid \$28.50 an hour for a 35-hour week. What is his normal weekly wage?

b A boy is paid a wage based on \$16.15 an hour. How much is he paid for an 8-hour day of work?

c For a 38-hour working week a woman is paid \$1079.20. Find her hourly rate of pay.

d Adam is paid \$16.05 an hour for a 35-hour week. Luke receives \$15.75 an hour for a 38-hour week. Who has the higher weekly wage and by how much?

e Irene is paid \$999.70 for a 38-hour week, whereas Shireen is paid \$906.50 for a 35-hour week. Who has the higher rate of pay and by how much?

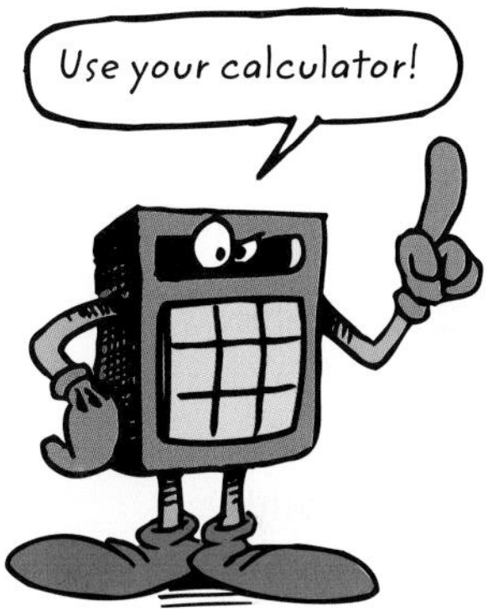

f A painter works a 38-hour week for an hourly rate of \$29.65. An extra height allowance of \$1.95 per hour is paid. Find his total weekly wage.

g A woman is paid a salary of \$46 089 per year. How much would she receive each week if it is calculated on 52·178 weeks in a year? (Answer to nearest dollar.)

h Find the weekly income (assuming there are 52·178 weeks in the year) for a salary of:

i \$43 000 ii \$76 400 iii \$138 950 iv \$58 200

(Give answers to the nearest cent.)

> It is assumed that each day of the year, the salaried person earns $\frac{1}{365\frac{1}{4}}$ of their annual salary.
> There are $365\frac{1}{4}$ days, on average, in a year.
> ∴ On average 52·178 (approximately) weeks are in each year.

i Find the yearly salary of a person whose monthly income is:

i \$4600 ii \$3150.50 iii \$5305 iv \$8950

j Two jobs are advertised: one with a salary of \$55 000, the other a salary with a fortnightly payment of \$2165.60. Which is the greater weekly salary and by how much? Use '1 year = 52·178 weeks.' (Give your answer correct to the nearest cent.)

k Two jobs are advertised. One is based on 37 hours per week at $30.15 an hour, the other is a yearly salary of $59 400. If 1 year is taken to be 52·178 weeks, which weekly income is higher and by how much? (Answer to the nearest cent.)

3 a i Does this job guarantee an income?

ii If you have never heard of the products of this company, is it likely that you will sell much of their product?

iii Is any compensation mentioned for petrol used or provision of a vehicle?

iv Find the commission paid on sales of:

1 $3000 2 $7430

3 $16 580 4 $920

CLEAN-U-UP PTY LTD
Selling cleaning machinery equipment and chemicals.
Sales people required to sell on total commission of 23% of sales.
Great potential!
Excellent reward.
Ring: Ugo Broke. YRU-000.

b Janice is offered a sales position with a retainer (guaranteed wage) of $740 plus a commission of 7% on sales.

i How much could she make in a week for the following weekly sales?

1 $800 2 $3500 3 $4865 4 $5213

ii She is told that the average weekly sales per person is $6300. What is the average weekly income?

c John works as a sales assistant receiving $800 per week plus 10% commission on sales in excess of $5000 for the week. Find his income for the following weekly sales.

i $3400 ii $5700 iii $8424 iv $6129.50

4 a Heather works in a supermarket on a casual basis. She is paid $16.60 an hour from Monday to Friday and $20.85 an hour on Saturdays. Find her week's income if she works from 3:30 pm until 5:30 pm, Monday to Friday, and from 8:30 am until 1:00 pm on Saturday.

b Edward works as a waiter from 6:00 pm until 1:30 am for 4 days in 1 week. His hourly rate of pay is $18.35 and he gets an average of $6.50 as tips per working night. Find his income for the week. (A 'tip' is a payment in appreciation of good service.)

c An electrician charged $54 per hour for labour. Find the charge for labour if he works from 11:20 am until 1:50 pm.

5 a A factory worker was paid $4.16 for each garment completed. How much would be earned if 240 garments were completed?

b A doctor charges each patient $65 for a consultation. If she works for 5 hours during one day and sees an average of six patients per hour, find the amount of money received that day. Her costs per day are $730. What was her profit for the day?

c Smokey and Smiley were two shearers who were paid $5.40 for each sheep shorn. By how much was Smokey's pay greater than Smiley's, if Smokey sheared 673 sheep and Smiley sheared only 489?

d Flo works at home altering dresses for a dress shop. She is paid $24.95 for a major alteration and $16.80 for a small alteration. In the week before Christmas, she completed 13 major alterations and 27 small alterations. Find her income for the week. If she spent 39 hours working on the alterations, what was her hourly rate of pay? (Answer to the nearest cent.)

8:02 Extra payments

There are several additional payments that may add to a person's income. Terms needed are listed below.

1 **Overtime:** This is time worked in excess of a standard day or week. Often rates of $1\frac{1}{2}$ or 2 times the normal rate of pay are paid for overtime.

2 **Bonus:** This is money, or an equivalent, given in addition to an employee's usual income.

3 **Holiday loading:** A payment calculated as a fixed percentage of the normal pay over a fixed number of weeks. It may be paid at the beginning of annual holidays to meet the increased expenses often occurring then.

4 **Superannuation:** This is a payment made by an employer into an investment fund nominated by the employee which provides benefits for the employee upon retirement. Employees are eligible for superannuation payments if they are between the ages of 18 and 69 inclusive and earn at least \$450 per month. These payments must be at least 9·25% of the employee's 'ordinary time' earnings. Extra contributions may also be made by the employee.

Time cards or time sheets

These can be used to record the number of hours worked in a week. A time clock can be used to stamp times on to the card. Therefore an employee 'clocks on' at the beginning of a shift and 'clocks off' at the end. The record of hours worked will also indicate any overtime hours worked.

No. 53 Name: Tom McSeveny				TIME CARD						Whit. Pty Ltd
Week ending	**Fri 21 Jan**		**Fri 28 Jan**		**Fri 4 Feb**		**Fri 11 Feb**		**Fri 18 Feb**	
Day	**IN**	**OUT**	**IN**	**OUT**	**IN**	**OUT**	**IN**	**OUT**	**IN**	**OUT**
Sat	–	–	–	–	8:00	10:02	8:00	12:00	8:02	11:30
Sun	–	–	–	–	–	–	–	–	–	–
Mon	7:57	4:00	8:00	4:04	7:59	4:00	8:00	4:02	7:57	3:59
Tues	7:58	4:02	7:55	3:59	7:56	4:02	8:00	4:05	8:00	4:05
Wed	8:00	4:01	8:00	4:02	8:03	4:01	7:56	3:02	7:58	4:07
Thu	8:02	4:05	7:58	7:00	7:58	4:03	8:01	4:02	7:55	6:00
Fri	8:00	4:00	8:00	4:00	8:00	4:01	8:02	6:31	7:59	6:30

Hourly rate: \$26.20
Lunch: 12 noon until 1:00 pm (unpaid)
Normal hours: Mon-Fri, 8:00 am – 4:00 pm
Overtime: 'Time-and-a-half' is paid and 'double-time' for overtime in excess of 3 hours (on any one day)

Note:

1 In the week ending 21 Jan, no overtime was worked.
Total of hours worked = (8 hours × 5) − 5 hours for lunch
= 35 hours

2 In the week ending 11 Feb, only 34 normal hours were worked, as Tom left work 1 hour early on Wednesday. However, $2\frac{1}{2}$ hours overtime was worked on Friday and 4 hours on the Saturday. Of the 4 hours worked on Saturday, the first 3 hours were time-and-a-half and the final hour was at double-time.

A few minutes variation from the hour or half-hour will not be considered in determining hours worked.

WORKED EXAMPLE 1

a During one week Peter worked 35 hours at the normal rate of \$17.60 per hour. He also worked 6 hours overtime: 4 at 'time-and-a-half' and 2 at 'double-time'. How much did he earn?

b Use the time card on the previous page to calculate Tom McSeveny's wage for the week ending Friday, 18 February.

c Calculate Diane's holiday loading if she is given $17\frac{1}{2}\%$ of 4 weeks' salary and she earns \$2980 per fortnight.

I don't get paid for lunch...
DONUTS

Solutions

a Peter's earnings = (35 h at \$17.60) + (4 h at \$17.60 × $1\frac{1}{2}$) + (2 h at \$17.60 × 2) [time-and-a-half ↓, double-time ↓]
= (35 × 17·6) + (4 × 17·6 × 1·5) + (2 × 17·6 × 2) dollars
= \$792 (using a calculator)

b For the week ending Friday, 18 February, Tom worked:

Normal hours: 35 hours (8–4, Mon–Fri with 1 hour lunch)

Time-and-a-half: $7\frac{1}{2}$ hours (8–11 on Sat, 4–6 on Thur, 4–6:30 on Fri)

Double-time: $\frac{1}{2}$ hour (11–11:30 on Sat as double-time is paid only after 3 hours)

∴ Tom's earnings = (35 h at \$26.20) + ($7\frac{1}{2}$ h at \$26.20 × $1\frac{1}{2}$) + ($\frac{1}{2}$ h at \$26.20 × 2)
= (35 × 26·2) + (7·5 × 26·2 × 1·5) + (0·5 × 26·2 × 2) dollars
= \$1237.95 (using a calculator)

c Diane's holiday loading = $17\frac{1}{2}\%$ of 4 weeks' salary
= $17\frac{1}{2}\%$ of (\$2980 × 2)
= 0·175 × (2980 × 2) dollars
= \$1043

$17\frac{1}{2}\% = \frac{17\cdot5}{100}$
$= 17\cdot5 \div 100$
$= 0\cdot175$

WORKED EXAMPLE 2

For each of the 4 weeks in June, Paul's gross wage was \$1375. What amount did Paul's employer have to contribute to his superannuation fund for the month if it is 9·25% of his monthly earnings?

Solution

Paul's earnings for the month = \$1375 × 4
= \$5500

∴ Superannuation payment = 9·25% of \$5500
= 0·925 × \$5500
= \$508.75

Superannuation = 9·25% of earnings
This will increase to 12% by 2019.

Exercise 8:02

P Foundation worksheet 8:02
Extra payments

1 a Bill earns \$9.60 per hour. Calculate his wages for the week if he worked 35 hours at the normal rate and 5 hours overtime at 'time-and-a-half'.

b At Bigfoot Enterprises a wage rate of \$12.70 per hour is paid on the first 37 hours and 'time-and-a-half' after that. What is the wage for a 42-hour week?

c Each day Pauline receives \$18.10 per hour for the first 7 hours, 'time-and-a-half' for the next 2 hours, and 'double-time' thereafter. Find her wage for:

i a 6-hour day ii a 9-hour day iii an $8\frac{1}{2}$-hour day iv an 11-hour day

d An electrician earns a wage of \$22.40 per hour for a 35-hour week and 'time-and-a-half' after that. Find the wage for a working week of:

i 30 hours ii 37 hours iii $41\frac{1}{2}$ hours iv $45\frac{1}{2}$ hours

e A pipe factory asks a labourer to work 8 hours on Saturday at 'time-and-a-half' for the first 3 hours and 'double-time' after that. If his normal rate of pay is \$20.40, how much is he paid for the day's work?

f Brian earns \$17.60 an hour, whereas his boss earns \$23.20 an hour. How much more than Brian is the boss paid for a 7-hour day? If Brian gets time-and-a-half for overtime, how many additional hours would he need to work in a day to get the same wage as his boss?

g By referring to the time card on page 221, complete the summary below.

The tricky parts of the time card on page 221 are shaded.

No. 53 Name: Tom McSeveny	Time card summary			Whit. Pty Ltd. Rate: \$26.20 p/h
Week ending	Number of hours at:			Wage
	normal rates	time-and-a-half	double-time	
21 Jan				
28 Jan				
4 Feb				
11 Feb				
18 Feb				

2 a If $17\frac{1}{2}\%$ holiday loading is given on 4 weeks' normal pay, find the holiday loading for:

i John, who earns \$4000 in 4 weeks
ii Mary, who earns \$2820 in a fortnight
iii Wilkes, who earns \$1495 a week
iv McNally, who earns \$29.80 an hour (for a 35-hour week).
(Assume that in each case no extra payments are included.)

b When June was given her holiday pay she received 4 weeks' pay and a $17\frac{1}{2}\%$ holiday loading. If her normal wage is \$1427 per week, how much holiday pay did she receive?

c Fred works a 35-hour week at a rate of \$27.60 per hour. Calculate his holiday loading if $17\frac{1}{2}\%$ is given on 4 weeks' wage.

d Mr Bigsuccess earns a salary of \$96 000 per year. At the end of the year he is given a bonus equal to 80% of one month's pay. How much did he earn in the year?

e Alana managed a small business for a salary of \$56 400. At the end of a successful year in which the business made a profit of \$211 000, she was given a bonus of 1·2% of the profits. What was her bonus and what was her income for the year?

f Luke works for a mining company at a wage rate of \$42.80 per hour. If he works underground he is paid a penalty rate of \$13.65 per hour in addition to his normal pay. Find his weekly wage if during the normal 38 hours he works underground for 16 hours.

g Mary works in a food-processing plant at a wage rate of \$25.95 per hour. From time to time she is required to work beside ovens where the temperature is uncomfortable. When this is necessary, she is paid an additional \$2.95 an hour. Calculate her wage for a normal working week of 36 hours where 5 hours were beside the ovens.

h Lyn received a $17\frac{1}{2}\%$ holiday loading on 4 weeks' normal wages. (She works a 36-hour week.) Find her normal weekly wage if the total of 4 weeks' wages and the holiday loading was:

i \$4700 ii \$6298

i Sundeep received a holiday-loading payment of \$868 that represented $17\frac{1}{2}\%$ on 4 weeks' wages. What is his weekly wage? What percentage of his total income for the year (containing 52 weeks) does the holiday loading represent? (Answer correct to two decimal places.)

3 a Calculate the 9·25% superannuation contribution owing for the following monthly earnings.

i \$3200 ii \$1260 iii \$5340 iv \$7335

b For a month in which there are four weekly wage payments, calculate the employer superannuation contribution 9·25% for these weekly wages.

i \$765 ii \$1170 iii \$1520 iv \$2136

c Libby works 40 hours a week for \$27.40 per hour. For a month in which there are five wage payments, calculate Libby's superannuation contribution at 9·25%.

d Jo works occasionally at the local cafe when they need her. For the last 6 months her monthly earnings were: \$580, \$390, \$760, \$1020, \$350 and \$840. What would have been the total amount in superannuation payments at 9·25% the employer would have had to pay for this 6 months?

Note: No super payment is required if monthly earnings are less than \$450.

e Find the total monthly earnings corresponding to superannuation contributions of:
i \$370 ii \$536.50 iii \$320.05 iv \$654.16

4 Ayse's salary is \$47 300, but she expects it to rise 2% at the beginning of each year to keep pace with inflation. What would her salary be at the beginning of:
a the second year b the third year c the sixth year d the eleventh year?

8:03 Wage deductions

A person's weekly wage or salary is referred to as the weekly gross pay. After deductions have been made the amount actually received is called the weekly net pay.

Possible deductions

Income tax The Commonwealth government takes a part of all incomes earned to finance federal, state and local government activities. Employers deduct this tax on the government's behalf at the end of each pay period. It is called PAYG (pay-as-you-go). The rate of tax varies according to the amount of money earned and the number of dependants.

Superannuation This is a form of insurance or investment. Often the employee, as well as the employer, contributes to this fund. It provides for an income or lump-sum payment upon retirement, and in the event of the employee's death it provides a pension for the family.

Miscellaneous Other deductions could be for medical insurance, life insurance, home payments, credit union savings and union membership fees.

Here is a pay advice slip representing 2 weeks' pay.

	Serial No.	Dept.	Location	Gross Salary or Wage Rate (1)	Super Units		Fortnight Ended	Net Pay (5)	Pay Advice No.
					Entld.	Held			
Peter Newby	6552750	AA	8436	76880	113	113	4/11/13	1998.70	12381

* Reasons for Adjustments
A – increment B – award agreement C – national wage D – promotion
E – L.W.O.P. F – allowance G – termination H – resumed duty
I – reduction in salary Z – combination of reasons

Deductions this fortnight				Pay this fortnight			
Taxation (7)	S'annuation (8)	M'laneous	Total (6)	Normal Pay (2)	Adjustments (3)	Overtime (3)	Gross Earnings (4)
636.80	147.50	163.80	948.10	2946.80	–	–	2946.80

Peter Newby has a gross yearly salary or wage (1) of $76 880, earns $2946.80 (2) per fortnight and in the fortnight ending 4/11/13 had no adjustments or overtime (3). This means that his gross earnings were $2946.80 (4). His net pay (5) was only $1998.70 because his total deductions (6) were $948.10.

Peter paid $636.80 in tax (7) on an income of $2946.80. This is about 22%. His contribution to superannuation (8) was $147.50.

WORKED EXAMPLE

a Find the net pay for the week if John earns $923.60, is taxed $138.50, pays $36.90 for superannuation and has miscellaneous deductions totalling $76.30.

b What percentage of his gross pay did he pay in tax?

Solution

a Total deductions = Tax + Superannuation + Miscellaneous
= $138.50 + $36.90 + $76.30
= $251.70

∴ John's net pay = $923.60 − $251.70
= $671.90

I've just collected my net pay.

b John's tax payment = $138.50

$$\text{Tax as a percentage of gross pay} = \frac{\text{tax}}{\text{gross pay}} \times 100\%$$

$$= \frac{\$138.50}{\$923.60} \times 100\%$$

$$= 15\%$$

Exercise 8:03

1 Find the net pay if:

a gross pay is $315.60 and total deductions are $115

b gross pay is $810.20, tax is $99.70, superannuation is $20.70 and miscellaneous is $94.80

c gross pay is $461.55, tax is $22.20, superannuation is $4.80 and union fees are $2.60

d gross pay (for a fortnight) is $1930.40, superannuation is $48.50, miscellaneous is $174.70 and tax is $303.55

e gross salary is $902.10, superannuation is $31.90, medical insurance is $21.60, life insurance is $4.10, house payment is $76.50, credit union savings are $11.00, union fees are $2.45 and tax is $131.60.

Wow! You must have some fishing spot! Where'd you net this stuff?
At the river bank!
GROAN!

2 a Vicki Turner receives a yearly salary of $72 096, pays 21% of her weekly gross salary (calculated on 52·18 weeks in the year) in income tax, pays 5% of her weekly gross to her superannuation fund and has $86 in miscellaneous deductions each week. Find her:

- i weekly gross salary
- ii weekly tax deductions
- iii weekly superannuation payment
- iv weekly net pay.

'Net pay' is what you take home.

b Use Question **2a** to complete this pay advice slip.

Turner, Vicki	Serial No.	Gross Salary or Wage Rate	Super Units		Week Ended	Net Pay	Pay Advice No.
			Entld.	Held			
	6841672		98	98	29/11/13		11364

*** Reasons for Adjustments**

A – increment	**B** – award agreement	**C** – national wage	**D** – promotion
E – L.W.O.P.	**F** – allowance	**G** – termination	**H** – resumed duty
I – reduction in salary		**Z** – combination of reasons	

Deductions this week				Pay this week			
Taxation	S'annuation	M'laneous	Total	Normal Pay	Adjustments	Overtime	Gross Earnings
					–	–	

3 Find the net pay and the tax as a percentage of the gross pay for each person.

	Name	Gross Pay	Tax	Net Pay	Tax as % of Gross Pay
a	R. Collison	$385.70	$6.90		
b	G. Foster	$1450.00	$308.70		
c	B. Jones	$947.50	$145.40		
d	R. Sinclair	$2591.60	$727.10		

4 a Upon retirement, Joe Simmons received annual superannuation payments of 68% of his final year's salary. If his salary at that time was $62 600, how much is his annual superannuation (before tax)?

b Ellen's annual superannuation is 63% of her finishing wage of $52 186. What is her monthly income? (Answer correct to the nearest cent.)

c John earns $82 490 a year. If he were to die, his widow would receive 65% of this figure in superannuation payments each year. What would be her weekly income from the superannuation payments (before tax) taking 1 year to be 52·18 weeks?

d Jim has just retired. He has the option of receiving a monthly payment of $2450 or $330 000 as a 'lump sum' (a final single payment).
   i Find the yearly superannuation payment.
   ii What yearly income would result if the lump sum could be invested at 7% p.a.?
   iii Which option seems most attractive and why?
   iv What would his yearly income be if he elected to receive 30% of the monthly payment, and 70% of the lump sum of which he invested 40% at 7% p.a.?

Challenge

1 Expected returns in superannuation, based on average life span, could be calculated.
2 Effects of inflation (with or without indexation) on these expected returns could be considered.

e Janice retired in 1995 on a fixed income of $2400 per month. How many toothbrushes costing $1.80 could she buy with a month's income? One year later, inflation had caused the cost of toothbrushes to rise by 8%. How many toothbrushes could she buy with a month's income after the rise? (As years pass, inflation greatly affects the purchasing power of people on fixed incomes.)

5 Maryanne's gross pay for a week is $874.20. Her employer must pay an additional 9·25% of this amount into her superannuation fund. Maryanne chooses to make additional voluntary payments of 5% of her weekly pay into this fund.
   a How much is being paid into the superannuation fund each week?
   b What is the total cost to the employer each week of employing Maryanne?
   c Maryanne receives a 4% pay rise. By how much will the superannuation contributions increase?

8:04 Income tax

- The annual Income Tax Return is a form, filled out each year, to determine the exact amount of tax that has to be paid for the preceding 12 months. Since most people have been paying tax as they have earned their income, this exercise may mean that a *tax rebate* is given.
- Some expenses, such as those necessary for earning an income, are classified as tax deductions, and the tax we have paid on this money will be returned to us. On the other hand, if we have additional income (such as interest on savings) that has not yet been taxed, additional taxes will have to be paid. The tax deductions are subtracted from the total income to derive the *taxable income*.
- The tax to be paid on the *taxable income* can be calculated from the table below (2013 scale).
- If your taxable income is more than $22 828, your Medicare levy is 1·5% of that taxable income. This covers you for basic medical costs and is a separate payment in addition to tax.

Taxable income	Tax on this income
$0–$18 200	Nil
$18 201–$37 000	19c for each $1 over $18 200
$37 001–$80 000	$3572 plus 32.5c for each $1 over $37 000
$80 001–$180 000	$17 547 plus 37c for each $1 over $80 000
$180 001 and over	$54 547 plus 45c for each $1 over $180 000

The above rates do not include the Medicare levy of 1·5%.

WORKED EXAMPLE

Albert received a salary of \$47 542 and a total from other income (investments) of \$496. His total tax deductions were \$1150. During the year he had already paid tax instalments amounting to \$10 710.75. Find:

a his total income

b his taxable income

c how much Albert must pay as his Medicare levy

d the tax payable on his taxable income

e his refund due or balance payable when the Medicare levy is included

f how much extra Albert would receive each week if he is given a wage rise of \$10 per week.

Solutions

a Albert's total income
= \$47 542 + \$496
= \$48 038

b Albert's taxable income
= total income − tax deductions
= \$48 038 − \$1150
= \$46 888

c Medicare levy
= 1·5% of the taxable income
= 1·5% of \$46 888
= \$703.32

d Taxable income = \$46 888 (or \$37 000 + \$9888)
Tax on \$37 000 = \$3572 (from the tax table) Ⓐ
Tax on \$9888 at 32.5 cents = \$3213.60 (32.5c/\$ for amount over \$37 000) Ⓑ
∴ Tax on \$46 888 = Ⓐ + Ⓑ
= \$3572 + \$3213.60
= \$6785.60

e Tax on \$46 888 + Medicare levy
= \$6785.60 + \$703.32
= \$7488.92
Tax instalments paid = \$10 710.75
∴ Refund = \$10 710.75 − \$7488.92
= \$3221.82

f For salaries over \$37 000 and less than \$80 001, for each additional \$1 earned you pay 32.5 cents tax and a Medicare levy of 1·5%.
∴ Tax on an extra \$10 per week = 10 × \$0.325 + 1·5% of \$10
= \$3.25 + \$0.15
∴ Amount left after tax = \$10 − \$3.40
= \$6.60 per week

Exercise 8:04

P Foundation worksheet 8:04 Taxation

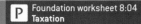

1 Use the tax table on page 228 to determine the tax payable, not including the Medicare levy, on a taxable income of:

a $13 963 b $22 587 c $41 460 d $97 346 e $284 914

2 Sally has a salary of $33 600, receives income from other sources of $342, has tax deductions of $655, and has paid PAYG tax instalments throughout the year of $6570.

Find:

a her total income
b her taxable income
c tax payable on her taxable income
d her refund or balance payable after the Medicare levy of 1·5% is paid.

PAYG stands for:
'Pay As You Go'
i.e. you pay tax instalments as you earn your income

3 When Joy left school she had a weekly wage of $988. During the financial year there were 52 weeks of pay received. (*Note:* In a normal year of 52 weeks and one day, there could be 53 paydays.) She had no extra income and calculated her tax deductions to be $217. Find the tax payable on her taxable income.

4 Karl earned $82 850 as a tiler. His employer deducted tax payments of $18 650. However, Karl earned a further $4156 on weekends and during his holidays. His tax deductions came to $2096 for expenses in earning the additional income. Find:

a Karl's total income
b Karl's taxable income
c the tax on his taxable income
d additional tax payable or refund, including the Medicare levy of 1·5%.

5 Eight workers in a factory were each given a pay rise of $2000 per annum. How much of the $2000 would each have received after tax and the Medicare levy of $30? Their yearly taxable incomes are listed below. (Use the tax table on page 228.)

a M. Callow $13 900
b A. Smith $25 500
c P. Farmer $45 200
d M. Awad $83 720
e R. Sissi $193 000
f P. Mifsud $36 000
g R. Ringe $79 500
h S. Sze $179 200

Note:
The Medicare levy is not paid if your taxable income is less than $22 829.

INVESTIGATION 8:04 INCOME TAX RETURNS

1 a Obtain copies of an Income Tax Return form.
  b Choose an occupation, an income figure and a number of dependants.
  c Make a list of tax deductions (money spent to produce the income). Estimate an amount for each of these, trying to be as realistic as possible.
  d Complete the Income Tax Return form using the estimates above.

2 a Using class data, investigate rates of pay from students' part-time jobs, or jobs advertised.
  b Calculate the tax to be paid on five of these jobs.

Australian Government
Australian Taxation Office

Individual tax return **2012**

1 July 2011 to 30 June 2012

Print neatly in BLOCK LETTERS with a black or blue ballpoint pen only.

Your tax file number (TFN) [ ]

See the **Privacy** note in the *Taxpayer's declaration* on page 14 of this tax return.

Are you an Australian resident? [ ] Print **Y** for yes or **N** for no.

Have you included any attachments? [ ] Print **Y** for yes or **N** for no.

Your name Title – for example, Mr, Mrs, Ms, Miss [ ]

Your sex Print **X** in the relevant box. Male [ ] Female [ ]

Surname or family name [ ]

Given names [ ]

Has any part of your name changed since completing your last tax return? [ ] Print **Y** for yes or **N** for no. If you answered yes, print previous surname. [ ]

Your postal address

Has your postal address changed since completing your last tax return? [ ] Print **Y** for yes or **N** for no.

Suburb or town — State — Postcode

Country – if not Australia

Your home address

If the same as your current postal address, print **AS ABOVE**.

Suburb or town — State — Postcode

Country – if not Australia

Your date of birth

If you were under 18 years of age on 30 June 2012 you must complete item **A1** on page 5 of this tax return.

Day Month Year

Final tax return

If you know this is your final tax return, print **FINAL**. [ ]

Your daytime phone number Area code [ ] Phone number [ ]

Electronic funds transfer (EFT)

Provide your financial institution details.

Write the BSB number, account number and account name below.

BSB number (must be six digits) [ ] Account number [ ]

Account name (for example, JQ Citizen. Do not show the account type, such as cheque, savings, mortgage offset) **F**

[ ]

NAT 1371-6.2012 **IN-CONFIDENCE – when completed** PAGE 1

FUN SPOT 8:04 WHAT IS BROUGHT TO THE TABLE, CUT, BUT NEVER EATEN?

Work out the answer to each question and write the letter for that part in the box that is above the correct answer.

Express as a percentage:

A 0·76 **A** 0·125 **A** $\frac{3}{5}$

O 12% of $81 250 **C** $13.50 × 38 + $20.25 × 6

C Sid is paid $22.80 an hour for a 40-hour week. What is his normal weekly wage?

D For a 38-hour week Naomi is paid $744.80. Find her hourly rate of pay.

F My salary is $31 306.80 per year. How much would I receive each week if it is calculated on 52·178 weeks in a year?

S Alana has a casual job from 4:00 pm until 5:30 pm Monday to Friday. What is her weekly income if her casual rate is $9.20 per hour?

P A tiler charges $28.50 per square metre to lay tiles. How much would he charge to lay an area of 8 square metres?

K Find the net pay for a week if Anna earns $520.50, is taxed $104.10, pays $8 for superannuation and has miscellaneous deductions totalling $77.40.

R In the previous question, what percentage of Anna's gross pay was paid in tax?

60%	$228	76%	$634.50	$331	$9750	$600	$912	12.5%	20%	$19.60	$69

It is important to balance your budget.

8:05 Spending money

PREP QUIZ 8:05

Find:

1 10% of \$60 **2** 10% of \$31 **3** 10% of \$43.50 **4** 10% of \$6.73

Calculate the following:

5 \$55 ÷ 11 **6** \$67.10 ÷ 11 **7** \$93.50 ÷ 11

Find the price per kg if:

8 4 kg costs \$10 **9** 7 kg costs \$32.90 **10** 15 kg costs \$43.20

This section is a review of work covered in Year 8. This included determining 'best buys', calculating discounts, finding the GST included in prices and determining a percentage profit or loss. The worked examples below will remind you of the skills involved.

Best buys

When we know the cost of a certain amount of a product we usually find the cost of 1 unit so we can compare prices. This is called the **unitary method**.

WORKED EXAMPLES

1 A bag of 12 apples costs \$3.60 and a bag of 20 costs \$5.00.
What is the price per apple for each bag?
Which is the better buy?

2 A 130 mL can of spaghetti costs 55 cents and a 420 mL can costs \$1.60.
Which is the better buy?

Solutions

1 To find the 'unit' price of one apple in each bag we divide by the number in each bag.

For the bag of 12, the unit cost = \$3.60 ÷ 12
= 0.30c

For the bag of 20, the unit cost = \$5.00 ÷ 20
= 0.25c

The bag of 20 is the better buy.

2 For this example we need to use a calculator.
We can divide the cost of the 130 mL can by 130 to find the cost of 1 mL (1 unit) and then multiply this figure by 420 to find the cost of 420 mL at this price.

Press: 0.55 [÷] 130 [×] 420 [=]

The answer is \$1.78, to the nearest cent. This is more expensive than the cost of the 420 mL can at \$1.60. So the 420 mL can is the better buy.

Discounts

Often when selling goods a retailer will offer a discount on the advertised price to encourage a buyer to purchase. Sometimes a discount might be given to favoured or regular customers.

WORKED EXAMPLES

1 a Greg was given $12\frac{1}{2}$% discount on a rug with a marked price of $248. How much did he pay?

b A television marked at $2240 was eventually sold for $2128. What was the discount and what was the percentage discount given on the marked price?

c After a discount of 14% was given, I paid $5848 for my yellow Holden. What was the original marked price?

2 Brenda bought a TV priced at $1200 after it was discounted by 10%. Brenda received a further 5% discount because she was a member of staff. How much did she pay for the TV?

Solutions

1 a Discount on rug = 12·5% of $248
= 0·125 × $248
= $31
Amount paid = $248 − $31
= $217

b Discount on TV = $2240 − $2128
= $112
Percentage discount = ($112 ÷ $2240) × 100%
= 5%

c Price paid = (100 − 14)% of marked price
= 86% of marked price
1% of marked price = $5848 ÷ 86
= $68
100% of marked price = $6800

2 Price after original 10% discount = (100 − 10)% of $1200
= 90% of $1200
= $1080

This is an example of successive discounts.

Price after a further 5% discount = (100 − 5)% of $1080
= 95% of $1080
= $1026

(*Note:* This is not the same as a 15% discount off the original price i.e. 85% of $1200 = $1020)

GST (Goods and Services Tax)

The GST is a tax of 10% on most goods and services. It is included in the price you pay. It is simple, however, to calculate the GST included in any price by dividing by 11, since the base price has been increased by 10% or $\frac{1}{10}$. This means that the price that includes the GST is $\frac{11}{10}$ times the original price.

To calculate the GST to add on to a price, simply find 10% of the price.

To find the GST included in a price, divide the price by 11.

WORKED EXAMPLES

1 Find the GST that needs to be applied to a price of \$325.

2 What is the retail price of a DVD player worth \$325 after the GST has been applied?

3 How much GST is contained in a price of \$357.50?

4 What was the price of an item retailing at \$357.50 before the GST was applied?

Solutions

1 The GST is 10% of the price.

$\therefore$ GST = \$325 × 10%
= \$32.50

2 The GST is added on to get the retail price.

$\therefore$ Retail price = \$325 + \$32.50
= \$357.50

Note: The retail price can also be calculated by multiplying the original price by 110% (or 1·1) since 10% is added on.

Retail price = \$325 × 1·1
= \$357.50

3 To find the GST contained in a price, we divide it by 11. (If the original price is increased by $\frac{1}{10}$, then the retail price, including the GST, is $\frac{11}{10}$ of the original price.)

$\therefore$ GST = \$357.50 ÷ 11
= \$32.50

4 To find the original price, simply subtract the GST from the retail price.

$\therefore$ Original price = \$357.50 − \$32.50
= \$325

Note: The original price can also be found by multiplying the retail price by $\frac{10}{11}$.

Original price = \$357.50 × $\frac{10}{11}$
= \$325

Profit and loss

Sometimes we need to consider whether our purchases, or sales, have been worthwhile.

We may do this by calculating and comparing the percentage profit or loss we may have made on a given transaction.

- When buying and selling:

  Selling price = Cost price + Profit

  Profit = Selling price − Cost price

  If the profit is *negative*, then we have made a *loss*.
- When calculating money made:

  Profit = Money received − Expenses

WORKED EXAMPLES

1 A book was bought online for \$16 and sold for \$20. Find the profit as a percentage of the:

a cost price

b selling price.

2 The cost price of a car is \$7800. If the dealer wants to make a profit of 15% on the cost price, what must be the selling price of the car?

3 A selling price of \$392 includes a 12% profit margin on the original cost price. What was the cost price?

Solutions

1 Profit = Selling price − Cost price
= \$20 − \$16
= \$4

∴ Percentage profit on:

a Cost price = $\frac{\$4}{\$16} \times 100\%$
= 25%

b Selling price = $\frac{\$4}{\$20} \times 100\%$
= 20%

2 Profit = Cost price × 15%
= \$7800 × 15%
= \$1170

∴ Selling price = Cost price + Profit
= \$7800 + \$1170
= \$8970

3 Selling price = Cost price + 12% of Cost price
= 112% of Cost price
= $\frac{112}{100}$ × Cost price

∴ Cost price = Selling price × $\frac{100}{112}$
= 392 × $\frac{100}{112}$
= \$350

Exercise 8:05

1 a If 3 books cost \$5, find the cost of 12 books.
b If 5 bananas cost \$2, find the cost of 8 bananas.
c If 4 cakes cost \$10, find the cost of 7 cakes.
d If 8 stamps cost \$4.80, find the cost of 15 stamps.
e If 15 bolts cost \$5.25, find the cost of 24 bolts.
f If 24 lollies cost \$3.60, find the cost of 75 lollies.

2 Find the cost of 1 'unit' in each of the examples below and then determine the best buy.

Use the unitary method

a i 3 apples cost \$1.20 ii 5 apples cost \$1.50
b i 4 bags cost \$3.00 ii 7 bags cost \$5.60
c i 8 kg cost \$10.40 ii 12 kg cost \$15.00
d i 10 comics cost \$26 ii 8 comics cost \$22.40
e i 12 litres cost \$15.60 ii 15 litres cost \$19.95
f i 24 plants cost \$105.60 ii 32 plants cost \$134.40

3 Find the discount on the following prices at the given percentages. Also find the discounted price.

a \$50, 10% b \$20, 20% c \$100, 8%
d \$24, 25% e \$40, 50% f \$50, 15%
g \$30, 40% h \$28, 75% i \$200, 90%
j \$25, 12% k \$45, 60% l \$80, 35%

4 For each marked price below, find the discount that was given to arrive at the final selling price. Also find what percentage this discount was of the marked price.

a Marked price = \$40, Selling price = \$30 b Marked price = \$50, Selling price = \$45
c Marked price = \$100, Selling price = \$75 d Marked price = \$60, Selling price = \$48
e Marked price = \$36, Selling price = \$18 f Marked price = \$25, Selling price = \$23
g Marked price = \$24, Selling price = \$21 h Marked price = \$36, Selling price = \$24

5 Find the GST that must be added to the following prices. Also state the final retail price.

GST = 10%

a \$50 b \$20 c \$100
d \$25 e \$8 f \$12
g \$56 h \$37 i \$83
j \$5.50 k \$9.60 l \$16.40
m \$5.26 n \$23.42 o \$71.96

6 Find the GST that is contained in the following retail prices. (Answer to the nearest cent, when necessary.)

Divide by 11!

a \$44 b \$77 c \$132
d \$24.20 e \$92.40 f \$12.65
g \$8.14 h \$21.34 i \$81.73
j \$50 k \$24 l \$145
m \$9.50 n \$21.90 o \$67.45

7 Complete the table, filling in the missing cost price, profit or selling price.

	Cost price	Profit	Selling price
a	\$400	\$100	
b	\$240		\$300
c		\$70	\$420
d	\$840	\$42	
e	\$750		\$1000

8 For each of the examples in the table in Question **7**, find the profit as a percentage of:

a the cost price b the selling price.

Answer to the nearest whole percentage, when necessary.

9 Find the best buy for each of the alternatives below.

a 4 tyres for \$450 or 5 tyres for \$550
b 6 ice-creams for \$20.40 or 10 ice-creams for \$35
c 2 litres of paint for \$43.60 or 5 litres for \$92.50
d 250 mL soft drink for \$2.30 or 600 mL soft drink for \$5.20
e 375 g can for \$4.20 or 650 g can for \$7.50
f 4 lollies for \$4.40 or 5 lollies for \$5.70
g 250 mL shampoo for \$5.20 or 375 mL shampoo for \$7.65
h 2.5 kg of potatoes for \$3.40 or 20 kg of potatoes for \$25

10 Find the best buy for each of the following.

a 250 g for \$4.20 or 420 g for \$6.60 or 600 g for \$9.20
b 3 litres for \$44 or 5 litres for \$72 or 8 litres for \$120
c 275 mL bottle for \$3.75 or 450 mL bottle for \$6.30 or 1 L bottle for \$12.90

11 a Rachel was given a discount of 45% on a T-shirt with a marked price of \$32. How much did she pay?

b Katherine was given a 7% discount on all purchases because she was a store employee. If the total of her purchases came to \$85, how much did she pay?

c After bargaining, I purchased a chess set for \$240 that was originally advertised for \$320. What discount was I given and what is this as a percentage of the advertised price?

d My airline ticket was to cost me \$550 but, because I booked more than 6 weeks ahead, I was given a discount price of \$385. What percentage discount was I given?

e After a discount of 10% was given, Luke paid \$585 for an additional hard disk drive for his computer. What was the original price of this hard disk drive?

f My mother paid \$21.70 to attend an exhibit. She had been given a discount of 65% because she was a pensioner. What was the original price?

g Because Helen was prepared to pay cash for a yellow car with a marked price of \$9200, she was given a discount of \$1012. What percentage was the discount of the marked price?

h Greg was given a discount of 10% on the marked price of a kitchen table. If the discount was \$22, how much did he pay?

12 Calculate the final price if successive discounts of 20% and 10% were applied to a price of \$100.

13 A bookstore discounted all its books by 15%. A further discount of 10% was given to the local school. How much did they pay for books that originally sold for a total of $1750?

14 Apply the following successive discounts to the given prices.

a 10%, 10%, $500

b 15%, 25%, $720

c 5%, 20%, $260

d $12\frac{1}{2}\%$, 15%, $965

e $7\frac{1}{2}\%$, $17\frac{1}{2}\%$, $2230

Does it matter in which order the discounts are applied?

15 When retailers sell a mixture of goods where the GST is only applied to some, they normally indicate which items on the bill include the GST. This bill indicates the items that include the GST with an asterisk (*). Determine the amount of GST that would be included in the total on this bill.

SHOPQUICK	
Sauce	$ 1.20
Biscuits*	$ 1.35
Bread	$ 3.60
Toothbrush*	$ 3.10
Soap*	$ 1.93
Total	$ 11.18
GST incl. = ?	

16 A retailer indicates the GST items with a percentage sign (%). Determine the GST included in these bills.

a

% Magazine	$ 2.85
% Deodorant	$ 4.00
Milk	$ 5.60
Muffins	$ 2.60
% Biscuits	$ 2.17
Total	$ 17.22
GST incl. = ?	

b

Bread	$ 2.70
Flour	$ 0.90
% Ice-cream	$ 4.48
% Soap	$ 0.98
% Tissues	$ 5.10
Total	$ 14.16
GST incl. = ?	

c

Bananas	$ 3.50
% Soap	$ 3.92
% Detergent	$ 3.31
Tea bags	$ 4.46
Eggs	$ 2.89
% Bath salts	$ 6.05
Rice	$ 1.54
% Biscuits	$ 2.56
Total	$ 28.23
GST incl. = ?	

17 What was the original price before the GST of 10% was added to each of these retail prices?

a $77 b $132 c $198

d $275 e $15.40 f $28.60

g $106.70 h $126.50 i $13.86

j $41.25 k $237.05 l $1238.38

18 a The prices of three items were $10.56, $10.30 and $21.00. The total of the GST included in the bill was $0.96. Which was the only price that included a 10% GST?

b Four prices on a bill were $5.60, $7.70, $9.30 and $10.56. The total of the bill, excluding GST, was $31.50. Which of the four prices did not include GST?

c Five articles cost $20.90, $37.40, $52.80, $61.60 and $45.10. GST of 10% was then added to some of these prices. The total bill was then $230.56. Which prices had GST added to them?

19 Luke bought a microphone for \$28 and sold it for \$50. Find:

a his profit from the sale

b the profit as a percentage of the cost price

c the profit as a percentage of the selling price.

20 When selling products in a store, a percentage mark-up is added to the cost price to obtain the marked (or selling) price. If sporting gear has a mark-up of 60%, toys 40% and clothing 45%, what will be the marked price of:

a a baseball bat with a cost price of \$24

b a doll with a cost price of \$15

c a T-shirt with a cost price of \$8.60?

21 A store marks up everything by 40%. If the selling price of a tennis racquet is \$308, what is the cost price and the profit on the racquet?

22 A travelling salesman marks up each item by 110%. Find the cost price and the profit on an item with a selling price of:

a \$630 b \$8.40 c \$127.05

23 John travelled to a factory for a 'direct buy' purchase of 60 litres of paint for \$690. He noticed that the same paint was being sold at a local store for a 'sale' price of \$46.60 for 4 litres. Which was the less expensive and by how much? If John spent an hour travelling and used \$4.60 worth of petrol, which do you think was the better buy? Why?

24 Jane bought a new tyre for \$160, Robyn bought one for \$130 and Diane bought a retread for \$76. If Jane's tyre lasted 32 000 km, Robyn's 27 500 km, and Diane's 16 000 km, which was the best buy? (Assume that safety and performance for the tyres are the same.)

25 A radio on sale for \$50 is reduced in price by 30%. Later the discounted price is increased by 30%. What is the final price? By what percentage (to the nearest per cent) must the first discounted price be increased to give the original price?

26 Stephen bought a computer that had a marked price of \$960. He received a discount of 15%. He paid a deposit of \$81.60 and monthly repayments of \$67.30 for 1 year. Find the interest paid, expressed as a percentage of the money borrowed.

27 John had to pay interest on his credit card balance. He pays 1·7% per month on the greatest amount owing during each month. The greatest amount owing in April was \$166, in May \$294 and in June \$408. Find the total interest charged for the three months.

28 Heather works for a toy store where the percentage mark-up is 40% of the cost price. She is offered 10% discount on any item and can have this on the cost price before mark-up occurs, or on the marked price. Use each method to find the discount price Heather would have to pay on a game that has a cost price of \$32. What do you notice?

29 The ratio Cost price : Profit : Selling price is 100 : 30 : 130. If the profit is \$24 what is the selling price?

30 The ratio Cost price : Profit : Selling price is 8 : 3 : 11. If the cost price is \$74.20 what will be the selling price?

31 Michael bought DVD players for $320 each. He wants to make a profit of 30% after passing on a 10% GST to the government. How much should he charge for each DVD player?

32 Lounge suites initially bought for $1100 each are to be sold at a loss of 40%. However, GST must still be charged and passed on to the government. What must be the sale price of each suite?

33 A machine was sold for a 25% profit of $270 on the cost price.
a What was the selling price if an additional GST of 10% has to be added?
b What was the cost price?
c What percentage was the selling price, including the GST, of the cost price?

34 A hardware store offered multiple discounts of 12% and 15% on a chain saw with a list price of $480. The first discount is given on the list price, the second on the first net price.
a What is the final purchase price?
b What is the final purchase price, if the 15% discount is applied first?
c Are the answers to a and b the same?
d Is the multiple discount equivalent to a single discount of 27%?
e What single discount is equivalent to multiple discounts of 12% and 15%?
f What single discount is equivalent to multiple discounts of 10% and 20%?

35 The following formula converts multiple discounts to a single discount.
Single discount rate $= [1 - (1 - d_1)(1 - d_2)(1 - d_3)\ldots] \times 100\%$,
where $d_1, d_2 \ldots$ are successive discounts expressed as decimals. Use the formula to find a single discount equal to the multiple discounts of:
a 11% and 8%
b 16%, 12% and 7%
c 10%, 9% and 5%
d $12\frac{1}{2}\%$, $4\frac{1}{4}\%$ and 2·1%

We shop online!

8:06 Ways of paying

When buying the things we need, we can pay cash (by cheque or by electronic fund transfer), buy on terms or use credit cards.

EFTPOS stands for electronic funds transfer at point of sale.

Using money		
Paying cash or transferring funds	Buying with credit card	Buying on terms
Meaning		
A payment with cheque, electronic funds transfer (EFTPOS) card or money.	A readily acceptable method of making credit purchases. 'Buy now pay later'.	A way of having the item and spreading the payment over a period of time. (Hire purchase)
Advantages		
Paying cash may help you get a discount. Money is accepted anywhere. You own the item. You keep out of debt. It doesn't encourage impulse buying. With cheque or EFTPOS card you don't have to carry a lot of money.	Convenient. Safer than carrying large sums of money. Useful in meeting unexpected costs. If payment is made promptly the charge is small. Many stores accept credit cards.	You can buy essential items and make use of them as you pay. Buying a house on terms saves rent. The item bought may be used to generate income. Little immediate cost.
Disadvantages		
Carrying large sums of money can be dangerous (risk of loss) and some shops won't accept cheques or EFTPOS cards. You may miss out on a good buy if you don't carry much money with you.	There is a tendency to overspend, buying on impulse and not out of need. The interest charged on the debt is high. Hidden costs (bank charges on stores) generally lift prices.	Relies on a regular income and, if you cannot continue payments, the item can be repossessed, sold and, if its value has depreciated (dropped), you still may owe money. High interest rates. You are in debt.

When transferring funds a 'Debit Card' can be used. The money comes from an account in which you have sufficient funds.

When we buy on terms (hire purchase), or we don't 'pay off' a credit card each month, we are charged interest that is calculated as a percentage of the amount we owe. For the examples in this exercise, we will be using simple interest, which is calculated as an annual percentage of the amount borrowed multiplied by the number of years taken to repay the amount.

For example, if \$5000 is borrowed at an interest rate of 7% p.a. and the loan is repaid over 3 years, the amount of interest charged would be calculated as:

> Amount borrowed is called the **principal.**
> **p.a.** stands for 'per annum' (or per year)

$$\begin{aligned}\text{Interest} &= \text{Principal} \times \text{Rate of interest} \times \text{No. of years}\\ &= \$5000 \times 7\% \times 3\\ &= \$5000 \times 0.07 \times 3\\ &= \$1050\end{aligned}$$

> $I = PRN$
>
> **I**nterest = **P**rincipal × **R**ate of interest × **N**umber of terms

Therefore, the total amount that will have to be paid will be the original amount borrowed (the principal) plus the interest.

$$\begin{aligned}\text{Amount to be repaid} &= \text{Principal} + \text{Interest}\\ &= \$5000 + \$1050\\ &= \$6050\end{aligned}$$

> Amount paid may be divided into weekly or fortnighly repayments.

So if payments are to be made weekly, then:

$$\begin{aligned}\text{Weekly repayment} &= \$6050 \div 52\\ &= \$116.35\end{aligned}$$

WORKED EXAMPLE 1

Bryn bought a car on terms of \$100 deposit and 60 monthly repayments of \$179.80. The price of the car was \$5000.

a How much did she pay for the car?

b How much interest did she pay on the money borrowed?

c How much money did she borrow?

Solutions

a $\begin{aligned}\text{Total payments for car} &= \text{Deposit} + \text{Payments}\\ &= \$100 + 60 \times \$179.80\\ &= \$10\,888\end{aligned}$

b $\begin{aligned}\text{Interest} &= \text{Extra money paid}\\ &= \$10\,888 - \$5000\\ &= \$5888\end{aligned}$

c $\begin{aligned}\text{Amount borrowed} &= \text{Price of car} - \text{Deposit}\\ &= \$5000 - \$100\\ &= \$4900\end{aligned}$

WORKED EXAMPLE 2

Malak bought a home theatre package for \$3000 by paying a 10% deposit and the balance over 2 years at an interest rate of 8% p.a.

a How much was the deposit?
b How much was the balance owing after paying the deposit?
c How much interest was charged on this balance?
d What was the total owing over the 2 years?
e If the repayments were monthly, how much was each repayment?
f How much more did Malak pay for the package than if he had paid by cash?

Solutions

a Deposit = \$3000 × 10%
= \$300

b Balance owing = Price − Deposit
= \$3000 − \$300
= \$2700

c Interest = Balance owing × Interest rate × No. of years
= \$2700 × 8% × 2
= \$2700 × 0.08 × 2
= \$432

d Total amount owing = Balance owing + Interest
= \$2700 + \$432
= \$3132

e Repayment = Total amount owing ÷ No. of weeks
= \$3132 ÷ (52 × 2)
= \$3132 ÷ 104
= \$30.12 (to the nearest cent)

f Total amount paid for the package = Deposit + Repayments
= \$300 + \$30.12 × 104
= \$3432.48

∴ Amount Malak paid more than cash = \$3432.48 − \$3000
= \$432.48

> The slight difference between the extra amount Malak paid and the interest calculation is due to the rounding of the repayment amount to the nearest cent.

WORKED EXAMPLE 3

Sylvia's bank charges 1.5% per month interest on balances owing on her credit card. At the end of May, Sylvia has a balance of \$960 on her credit card. If she makes a repayment of \$200, how much interest will she be charged next month?

Solutions

Amount owing on Sylvia's credit card after May payment = \$960 − \$200
= \$760

∴ Interest charged in June on amount owing from May = \$760 × 1.5%
= \$760 × 0.015
= \$11.40

Exercise 8:06

Foundation worksheet 8:06
Best buy, shopping lists, change

1 Use the table on page 242 to answer these questions in your own words.

a What are the advantages of paying cash?

b What are the advantages of buying on terms?

c What are the disadvantages of buying on terms?

d What are the disadvantages of buying with credit cards?

2 a Find the amount John will pay for a fishing line worth \$87 if he pays \$7 deposit and \$5.70 per month for 24 months. How much extra will he pay in interest charges?

b How much will Ingrid pay for her wedding dress worth \$1290 if she pays \$90 deposit and \$74 per month for 2 years? How much interest will she pay on the money borrowed?

c When Robyn said that she could buy an item marked at \$640 for \$610 at another store, the salesperson offered her the item for \$601.60 if she bought it immediately. She bought it on terms, paying a deposit of \$20 and monthly repayments of \$23.30 for 4 years. How much did she pay all together? How much extra did she pay in interest charges?

d Joshua wants to buy a tent with a marked price of \$730. He wants to pay it off on terms. For each of the following, work out how much he pays altogether and the interest charged.

- i Deposit of \$100 and monthly payments of \$64.50 for 1 year.
- ii Deposit of \$100 and monthly payments of \$38.30 for 2 years.
- iii Deposit of \$100 and monthly payments of \$29.60 for 3 years.
- iv Deposit of \$100 and monthly payments of \$25.20 for 4 years.
- v Deposit of \$100 and monthly payments of \$22.60 for 5 years.
- vi Deposit of \$100 and monthly payments of \$17.35 for 10 years.

e A man bought a car for \$8250 paying a deposit of \$250, \$130 in extra charges, and paying \$280 per month over 5 years. How much would he have to pay altogether? After paying four payments he found it was too expensive. The car was repossessed and sold for \$6400. The finance company then sent him a bill for \$1066.70, being the difference between what he owed and what they received for the car. He paid the bill and had no car. How much money had he paid altogether?

When borrowing money:
1 Read the terms
2 Work out the costs
3 Be prepared to say NO!

3 Find the amount of interest charged on the following principal amounts for the given interest rate and time period.

a \$1000, 5% p.a., 4 years
b \$2500, 7% p.a., 3 years
c \$5600, 6% p.a., 2 years
d \$900, 8% p.a., 3 years
e \$2000, 7·5% p.a., 2 years
f \$2500, 8·5% p.a., 4 years
g \$10 000, 9% p.a., 2 years
h \$12 500, 7·25% p.a., 15 months

4 For each example in Question **3** find the balance owing by adding the interest to the principal. Then divide the balance owing by the number of weeks in each example to calculate the correct weekly repayment. (Assume there are 52 weeks in a year.)

5 A racing bicycle priced at \$8600 was bought on hire purchase over 3 years, paying an interest rate of 9% p.a. No deposit was paid and repayments were made monthly.

a Find the amount of interest charged.
b What is the total amount paid for the bicycle?
c Find the amount of each monthly repayment.

6 Peggy wanted to buy a sports car worth \$55 900. The car dealer gave her \$12 400 for her old car as a trade-in. She used this as a deposit. She agreed to pay the balance to pay off over 5 years at an interest rate of 7·9% p.a.

a Find the balance owing after paying the deposit.
b How much interest is charged on the balance owing?
c What is the total amount that has to be repaid over the 5 years?
d Find the amount of each monthly repayment.

7 Ivan and Ivy bought a furniture package deal. The value of the furniture was \$12 400. They agreed to pay a 10% deposit and the balance off over 4 years via fortnightly repayments. The interest rate charged was 8·6% p.a.

a Find the amount of the deposit.
b What is the balance owing after paying the deposit?
c How much interest is charged on the balance owing?
d What is the total amount that has to be paid over the 4 years?
e Find the amount of each fortnightly repayment. (Assume there are 26 fortnights in a year.)

8 Find the amount of monthly interest charged on the following credit card balances at the given interest rate. Where daily interest is given, assume the month has 30 days.

a \$100, 2% per month
b \$250, 1·8% per month
c \$560, 1·78% per month
d \$978, 1·92% per month
e \$200, 18% p.a.
f \$2500, 20·24% p.a.
g \$1000, 0·06% per day
h \$1250, 0·055 45% per day

9 Terry's bank charges 1·7% per month interest on balances owing on his credit card. At the end of April Terry has a balance of \$680 on his credit card. If he makes a repayment of \$180, how much interest will he be charged next month?

10 Wendy's bank charges 21% per annum interest on balances owing on her credit card. At the end of June Wendy has a balance of \$1450 on her credit card.

a If she forgets to make a payment for the month, how much interest will she be charged next month?
b Wendy is also charged a penalty of \$25 for not making a payment. If she makes no further purchases in July, what will be the balance owing at the end of July on her credit card?
c Wendy does make a payment of \$500 at the end of July. What will be the amount of interest charged on the remaining balance?

11 Meryl bought a second-hand caravan, priced at \$10 050, on terms of \$300 deposit and 60 monthly repayments of \$260.

a Find the total amount paid for the caravan.

b What amount of interest was paid?

c What was the amount of interest paid each year?

d What percentage of the amount borrowed was this yearly interest? (This is the annual simple interest rate that was charged on the money borrowed.)

12 Ken bought a motor bike on hire purchase. He paid a 20% deposit and monthly repayments of \$331.52 for 4 years. The price of the bike was \$14 800.

a Find the balance owing on the bike after the deposit had been paid.

b How much did Ken pay in repayments?

c How much interest was charged?

d Determine the annual rate of interest charged on the amount borrowed.

13 Allyson's credit card charges a daily interest rate of 0·049% on balances owing at the end of each month. At the end of the month Allyson has a balance of \$840 and she makes a payment of \$200.

a What is the yearly interest rate as a percentage, correct to one decimal place?

b At the end of the next month (which has 30 days) how much interest will be charged on the balance owing from the previous month?

c If Allyson makes a further payment of \$400 after 10 days into the next month, how much interest will she save herself from paying at the end of the month?

FUN SPOT 8:06 THE PUZZLE OF THE MISSING DOLLAR

Three men had lunch in a busy restaurant. When it came time to pay their bill, each of the men gave the waiter \$30. So, the waiter received \$90 altogether.

When the waiter added up the bill, he found it only came to \$85. Knowing that \$5 would not divide among the three men evenly, the waiter decided to give each of the men \$1 change and put the remaining \$2 in his pocket.

It now appears that each man has paid \$29 for the meal, and the waiter has \$2; a total of \$89.

Where is the missing dollar?

MATHS TERMS 8

commission
- income usually calculated as a percentage of the value of the goods sold

discount (noun)
- the amount or percentage a price is reduced by

discount (verb)
- to reduce the price of goods sold

GST
- Goods and Services Tax
- 10% of a base price is added on to the cost of most goods and services and included in the advertised retail price

gross pay
- the amount of pay before any deductions such as income tax are subtracted

income tax
- tax paid to the government which is based on the amount of income received

interest
- fee charged on borrowed money
- usually charged as a percentage of the amount borrowed

net pay
- the amount of pay an employee receives after deductions such as income tax have been subtracted

overtime
- time worked by an employee in excess of a standard day or week
- usually rates of pay $1\frac{1}{2}$ or 2 times the normal rate of pay are paid for overtime

profit
- the gain when a good is sold for a higher price than its cost price
- if the selling price is lower a negative profit, or loss, is made

salary
- a fixed amount paid for a year's employment. It may be paid weekly or fortnightly

simple interest
- interest charged at a given rate on the original amount borrowed (principal), multiplied by the length of time of the loan
  $I = PRN$, where I = Interest,
  P = Principal, R = Rate of interest,
  N = Number of terms

superannuation
- an investment fund usually contributed to by both employer and employee on the employee's behalf
- it provides benefits for employees upon retirement, or for relatives if the employee dies

taxable income
- amount after allowable deductions are subtracted from the gross pay
- the income tax payable is calculated on this amount

wage
- pay given to an employee, often based on an agreed hourly rate
- usually paid weekly or fortnightly

DIAGNOSTIC TEST 8 FINANCIAL MATHEMATICS

These questions reflect the important skills introduced in this chapter.
Errors made will indicate areas of weakness.
Each weakness should be treated by going back to the section listed.

1 a John sells cars for a living. He is paid a retainer (a base wage) of $550 a week as well as 2% commission on sales made. Find his income for the week, if in one week he sells cars to the value of: — 8:01

i $80 000 ii $96 500

b Luke has a casual job from 4:00 pm until 5:30 pm Monday to Friday. He also works from 9 am until 12:30 pm on Saturdays. Find his weekly income if his casual rate is $19.80 per hour Monday to Friday, and $24.70 an hour on Saturdays.

2 a During one week Petra worked 35 hours at the normal rate of $22.60 per hour. She also worked 6 hours overtime: 4 at 'time-and-a-half' and 2 at 'double-time'. How much did she earn? — 8:02

b Calculate Diane's holiday loading if she is given $17\frac{1}{2}$% of 4 weeks' salary and she earns $1860 per fortnight.

3 a Find the net pay for the week if John earns $1586.80, is taxed $365.20, pays $73.50 into his superannuation and has miscellaneous deductions totalling $79.40. — 8:03

b What percentage of John's gross pay did he pay in tax?

4 Alana received a salary of $73 465 and other income (investments) of $965 during the year. Her total tax deductions were $2804. She had already paid tax instalments amounting to $15 634 for the year. — 8:04

a What is her total income for the year?

b What is her taxable income for the year?

c Calculate her Medicare levy (1·5%).

d Find her tax payable on her taxable income using the table on page 228.

e Find her refund due or balance payable after the Medicare levy is included.

f How much extra would Alana receive each week if she is given a wage rise of $100 per week? (Don't forget to subtract $1.50 for Medicare payments.)

5 a A lawn fertiliser comes in three sizes: 20 kg (for $11.60), 50 kg (for $24.80) and 110 kg (for $56.60). Which size is the best buy? — 8:06

b Rich Red strawberry flavouring can be purchased at 240 mL for $1.70, 660 mL for $3.75, or 1 L for $6.25. Which buy represents the best value?

6 a Determine the GST that needs to be added to a base price of $73.70. — 8:05

b Determine the retail price after 10% GST is added to a base price of $53.90.

c How much GST is contained in a retail price of $32.45?

d What was the base price before 10% GST was added to give a retail price of $21.45?

7 a Naomi was given $12\frac{1}{2}$% discount on a rug with a marked price of $460. How much did she pay? 8:05

b A television marked at $4200 was eventually sold for $3612. What was the discount and what was the percentage discount given on the marked price?

c After a discount of 13% was given, I paid $27 840 for my yellow Holden. What was the original marked price?

8 a Jane bought a desk with a marked price of $650. She was given a discount of 10% for paying cash, and then received a further 10% off the discounted price because the desk was scratched. How much did she pay? 8:05

b What is the final price if successive discounts of 15% and 20% are applied to a retail price of $1250?

9 a Rachel bought a painting for $250 and sold it for $575. Find the profit as a percentage of the cost. 8:05

b We held a games night to raise money for The House with No Steps. We charged each of the 287 people who came an entrance fee of $17.50. Hire of the hall cost $110, decorations cost $63, prizes $185.60, food $687, cleaning $96 and advertising $240.
How much money did we make and what percentage is this of the money received?

10 a Jim bought a car with a marked price of $3000. He paid a deposit of $100 and 36 monthly payments of $136.20. How much did he pay? How much more than the marked price did he pay? 8:06

b Peta installed a new kitchen that cost $14 350. She agreed to pay for it by paying monthly instalments for 2 years. She was charged 9% p.a. interest. Find:

i the amount of interest charged
ii the total amount paid over the 2 years
iii the amount of each instalment.

c Bhupesh bought a truck worth $82 000 by paying 20% deposit and the balance off over 5 years at an interest rate of 7.8%. Find:

i the amount of the deposit
ii the balance owing after the deposit was paid
iii the amount of interest charged
iv the amount of each repayment if paid monthly.

ASSIGNMENT 8A Chapter review

1 a A woman works for a wage of $16.80 per hour. How much will she earn in a week in which she works:

i 40 hours at normal time

ii 40 hours of normal time and 5 hours of overtime if overtime is paid at $1\frac{1}{2}$ times the normal rate of pay?

b A salesman works for a wage of $500 per week plus 3% commission. How much will he earn in a week if he sells $4500 worth of goods?

c A factory worker is paid a wage of $540 a week. The factory has a special bonus system which enables a worker to be paid an extra 25c per article for every article in excess of the weekly quota of 5000. How much will the worker earn in a week in which 7200 articles are made?

d How much holiday pay will a girl receive if she is to be paid 4 weeks' holiday pay plus a holiday loading of $17\frac{1}{2}$% of 4 weeks' pay? Her weekly wage is $452.

2 a Fibreglass resin comes in the following sizes: 1 kg for $9.80, 5 kg for $26.80, and 21 kg for $59.60.

i What is the best value for money?

ii What is the most economical way of buying 17 kg?

b A TV set with a cash price of $680 is bought for a deposit of $68 and 48 monthly payments of $15.68. Find the difference between the cash price and the price paid.

c Calculate the amount of GST included in items that retailed for $736, $245 and $579.

3 Mary-Ann is paid an annual salary of $53 350. Her allowable tax deductions total $1340. During the year her employer paid income tax instalments on her behalf of $12 732.

a What is Mary-Ann's taxable income?

b How much income tax should she pay for the year?

c What is the amount of her refund from the tax office?

4 Jeremy added 10% GST onto the price of a book valued at $29.90 to get its retail price. He then discounted the retail price by 10% to get a sales price.

a What is the retail price?

b What is the sales price?

c Is the sales price the same as the original value of the book?

d By what percentage should Jeremy have discounted the retail price to get back to the original value of the book?

5 a Vicki sold azaleas in her nursery for $15.90. She bought them for $11.35. What percentage profit does she make?

b Michael sold a bike he bought for $350 to a friend 2 years later for $230. What percentage loss is this?

6 A boat priced at $17 300 was bought by paying 15% deposit with the balance being paid off over 3 years at 8·5% p.a. interest, by fortnightly repayments. Find:

a the amount of the deposit

b the balance owing after the deposit was paid

c the amount of interest charged

d the amount of each repayment

e the total amount paid for the boat.

ASSIGNMENT 8B Working mathematically

1 At a meeting each person who arrived shook the hand of every other person present. How many handshakes would have occurred if:

a three people were present

b five people were present

c eight people were present?

2 Two ladders are standing in a passageway, as shown, leaning against each wall with the foot of each ladder against the opposite wall. If the ladders reach 5 m and 10 m up each wall, how high above the ground is the point P where they meet?

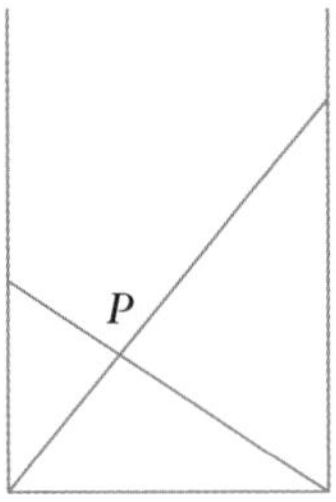

3

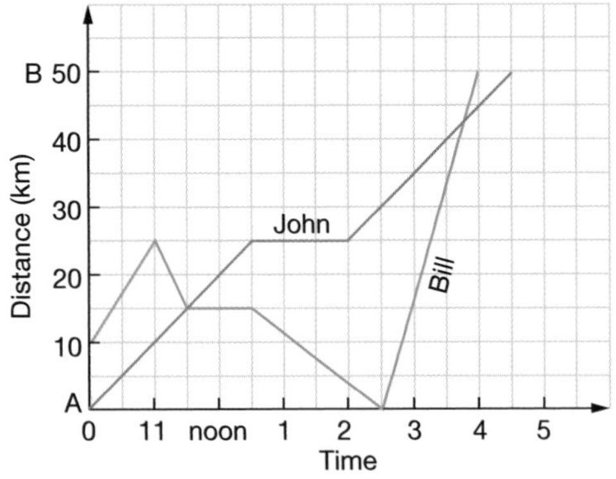

This travel graph shows the journeys of John and Bill between town A and town B. (they travel on the same road.)

a How far from A is Bill when he commences his journey?

b How far is John from B at 2:30 pm?

c When do John and Bill first meet?

d Who reaches town B first?

e At what time does Bill stop to rest?

f How far does John travel?

g How far apart are John and Bill when Bill is at town A?

h How far does Bill travel?

4 Through how many degrees does the hour hand of a clock turn in half an hour?

5 A loan of \$1000 is to be repaid at an interest rate of 20% p.a. The faster the loan is repaid, the less interest is charged. The graph shows how the amount to be repaid varies according to the time taken to repay the loan.

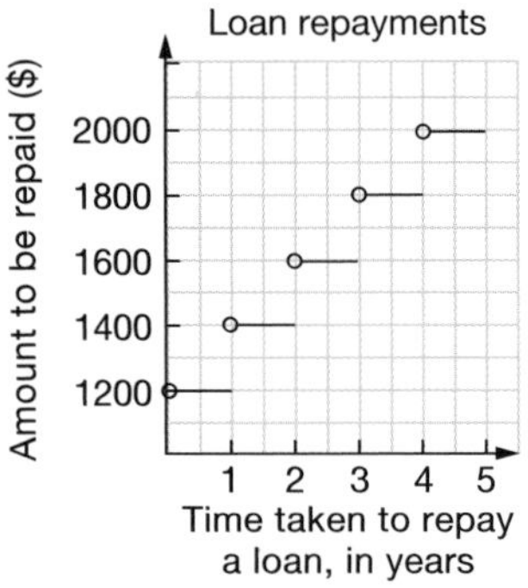

a How much has to be repaid if $3\frac{1}{2}$ years is taken to repay the loan?

b If a person wished to repay the loan in 2 years what amount would have to be repaid?

c How much must be paid monthly if this loan is to be repaid in 4 years?

ASSIGNMENT 8C Cumulative revision

1 What is the absolute error in a measurement of: 1:10

a 5 cm b 8·5 cm c 5·254 m

2 a Write correct to two significant figures. 1:05–1:07

i 27·1608 ii 0·0716

b Estimate the answers to the following questions. Then use a calculator to evaluate each answer correct to two significant figures.

i $\dfrac{21{\cdot}7 \times \sqrt{47{\cdot}62}}{6{\cdot}9}$ ii $\sqrt{\dfrac{23{\cdot}5 \times 6{\cdot}73}{(3{\cdot}2 + 1{\cdot}967)}}$

3 a What percentage is 25 g of 0·45 kg? 2:01

b My wage increases from \$850 per week to \$900 per week. What is the percentage increase?

c A woman buys 500 shares for \$1.55 each. She sells them later for \$2.10 each. What profit does she make, and what is the profit as a percentage of the purchase price?

4 Simplify: 3:02

a $\dfrac{m-3}{4} + \dfrac{m}{6}$ b $\dfrac{m}{4} - \dfrac{m-3}{6}$ c $\dfrac{m}{4} \times \dfrac{m}{6}$ d $\dfrac{m}{4} \div \dfrac{m}{6}$

5 Find the area of the following figure, which is formed from two quadrants and a rectangle. Measurements are in metres. Give your answer correct to one decimal place. 5:01

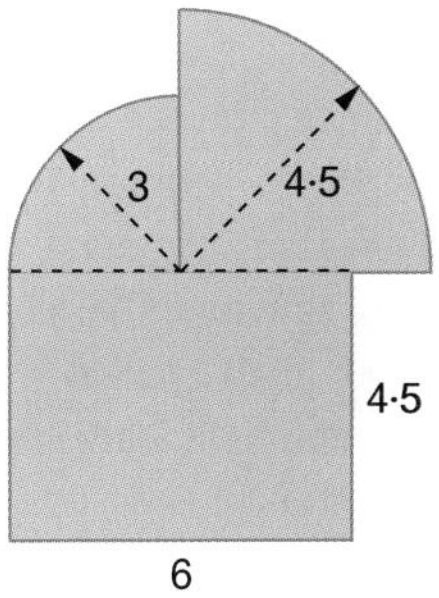

6 Write the following numbers in scientific notation. 6:04

a 213 000 b 215 000 000

c 0·005 67 d 0·000 000 12

7 Solve: 7:03, 7:04

a $\dfrac{a}{4} - 6 = 8$ b $\dfrac{3a}{5} + \dfrac{a}{2} = 22$ c $\dfrac{3a+5}{8} = \dfrac{a-4}{6}$

8 Make x the subject of each formula. 7:10

a $y = 5x - 7$ b $ax + by = c$ c $v^2 = u^2 - 2ax$

COORDINATE GEOMETRY

9

Contents

Syllabus references (See pages x–xv for details.)

Number and Algebra

Selections from ***Linear Relationships*** [Stages 5.1, 5.2]

- Find the midpoint and gradient of a line segment (interval) on the Cartesian plane using a range of strategies, including graphing software (ACMNA294)
- Find the distance between two points located on the Cartesian plane using a range of strategies, including graphing software (ACMNA214)
- Sketch linear graphs using the coordinates of two points (ACMNA215)
- Interpret and graph linear relationships using the gradient-intercept form of the equation of a straight line (NSW)
- Solve problems using various standard forms of the equation of a straight line (NSW)

Selections from ***Non-linear Relationships*** [Stages 5.1, $5.2^{\Diamond}$]

- Graph simple non-linear relations, with and without the use of digital technologies (ACMNA296)

Working Mathematically

- Communicating • Problem Solving • Reasoning • Understanding • Fluency

Coordinate geometry is a powerful mathematical technique that allows algebraic methods to be used in the solution of geometrical problems.

In this chapter we will look at the basic ideas of:

- the distance between two points or the length of an interval
- the midpoint of an interval
- gradient (or slope) of an interval or line
- the relationship between a straight line and its equation.

We will then see how these can be used to solve problems.

9:01 The distance between two points

To calculate the distance between two points on a number plane, form a right-angled triangle and apply Pythagoras' theorem. This is shown in the following examples.

WORKED EXAMPLES

1 Find the distance between the points (1, 2) and (4, 6).

2 If A is (−2, 2) and B is (4, 5) find the length of AB.

Solutions

1

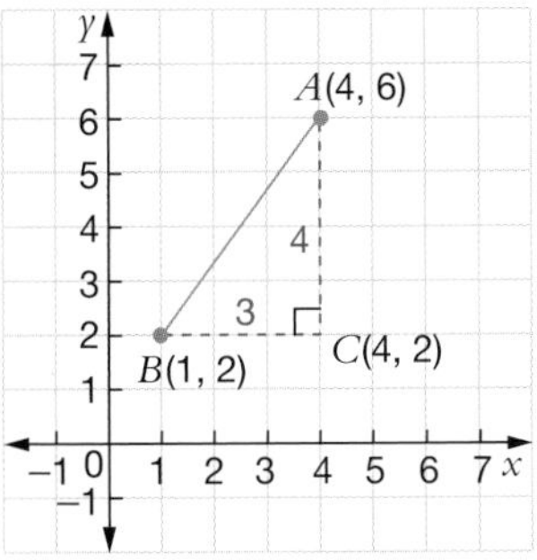

$$c^2 = a^2 + b^2$$
$$AB^2 = AC^2 + BC^2$$
$$= 4^2 + 3^2$$
$$= 16 + 9$$
$$= 25$$
$$\therefore\ AB = \sqrt{25}$$

$\therefore$ the length of AB is 5 units.

2

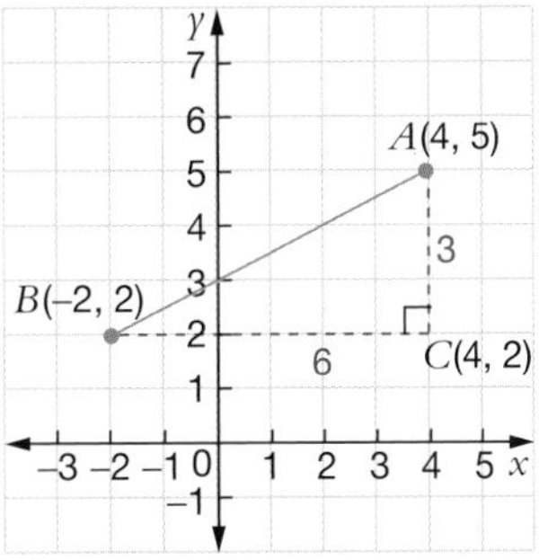

$$c^2 = a^2 + b^2$$
$$AB^2 = AC^2 + BC^2$$
$$= 3^2 + 6^2$$
$$= 9 + 36$$
$$= 45$$
$$\therefore\ AB = \sqrt{45}$$

$\therefore$ the length of AB is $\sqrt{45}$ unit.

√45 is a surd.
It is the exact length of AB.

By drawing a right-angled triangle, we can use Pythagoras' theorem to find the distance between any two points on the number plane.

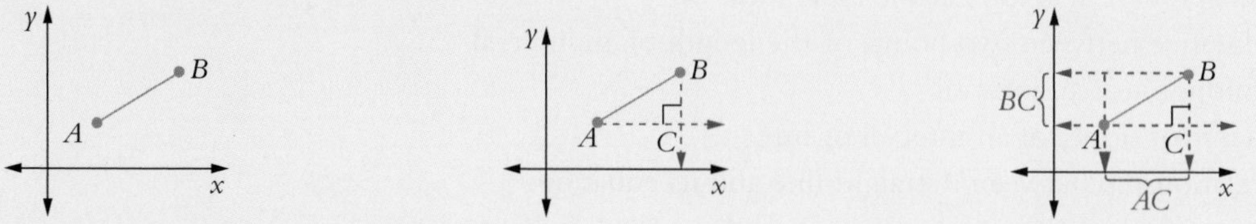

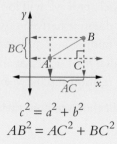

$$c^2 = a^2 + b^2$$
$$AB^2 = AC^2 + BC^2$$

Distance formula

A formula for finding the distance between two points, $A(x_1, y_1)$ and $B(x_2, y_2)$, can be found using Pythagoras' theorem. We wish to find the length of interval AB.

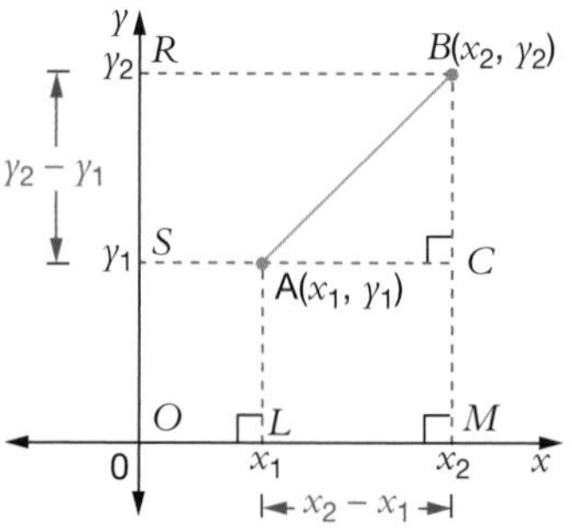

Now $LM = x_2 - x_1$ $(LM = MO - LO)$

$\therefore$ $\boxed{AC = x_2 - x_1}$ ($ACML$ is a rectangle)

and $RS = y_2 - y_1$ $(RS = RO - SO)$

$\therefore$ $\boxed{BC = y_2 - y_1}$ ($BCSR$ is a rectangle)

Now $AB^2 = AC^2 + BC^2$ (Pythagoras' theorem)

$= (x_2 - x_1)^2 + (y_2 - y_1)^2$

$\therefore AB = \sqrt{(x_2 - x_1)^2 + (y_2 - y_1)^2}$

The distance AB between $A(x_1, y_1)$ and $B(x_2, y_2)$ is given by:

$$d = \sqrt{(x_2 - x_1)^2 + (y_2 - y_1)^2}$$

If A is renamed (x_2, y_2) and B is renamed (x_1, y_1) the formula becomes:

$$d = \sqrt{(x_1 - x_2)^2 + (y_1 - y_2)^2}$$

Using either formula will give the same result.

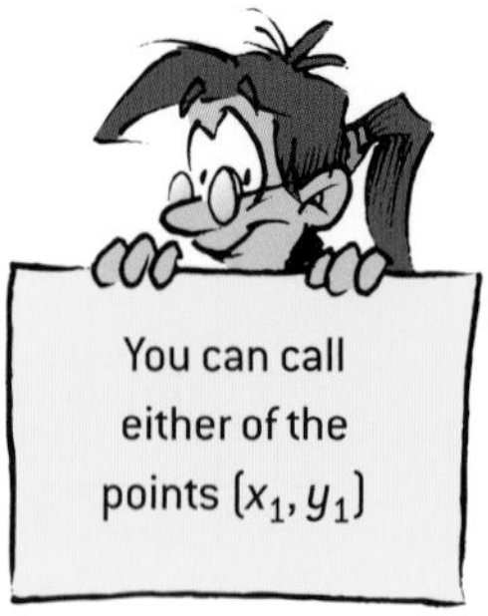

You can call either of the points (x_1, y_1)

WORKED EXAMPLES

1 Find the distance between the points (3, 8) and (5, 4).

2 Find the distance between the points (−2, 0) and (8, −5)

Solutions

1 Distance $= \sqrt{(x_2 - x_1)^2 + (y_2 - y_1)^2}$

$(x_1, y_1) = (3, 8)$ and $(x_2, y_2) = (5, 4)$

$$\therefore\ d = \sqrt{(5-3)^2 + (4-8)^2}$$
$$= \sqrt{(2)^2 + (-4)^2}$$
$$= \sqrt{4 + 16}$$
$$= \sqrt{20}$$

∴ Distance = 4·47 (2 dec. pl.)

2 Distance $= \sqrt{(x_2 - x_1)^2 + (y_2 - y_1)^2}$

$(x_1, y_1) = (-2, 0)$ and $(x_2, y_2) = (8, -5)$

$$\therefore\ d = \sqrt{(8 - -2)^2 + (-5-0)^2}$$
$$= \sqrt{(10)^2 + (-5)^2}$$
$$= \sqrt{100 + 25}$$
$$= \sqrt{125}$$

∴ Distance = 11·18 (2 dec. pl.)

- If the coordinates are reversed, the formula still gives the same answer. Hence, in Worked Example **1**, if we make $(x_1, y_1) = (5, 4)$ and $(x_2, y_2) = (3, 8)$, we would produce the same answer.

Exercise 9:01

P Foundation worksheet 9:01 **Distance between points**

1 Use Pythagoras' theorem to find the length of each of the following. (Leave your answer as a surd, where necessary.)

a

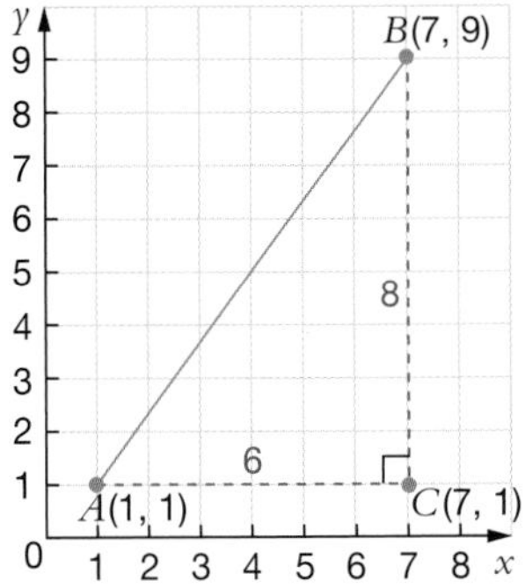

b

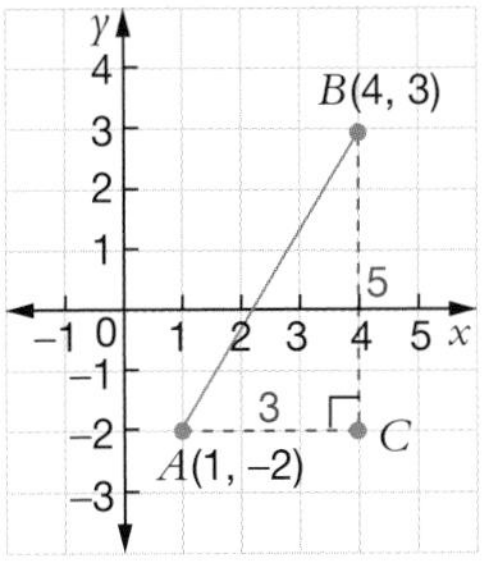

c

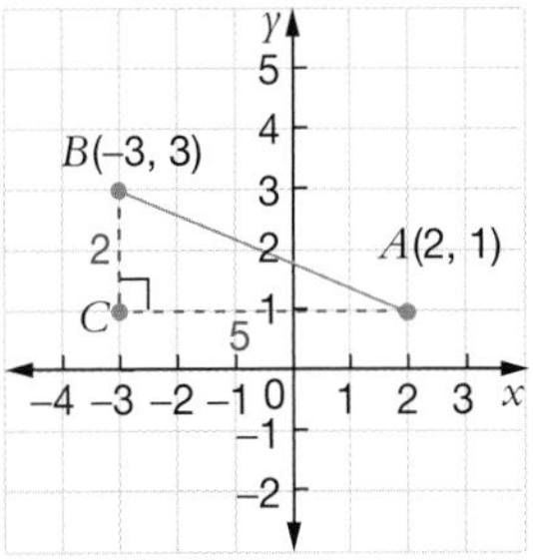

2 Find the lengths BC and AC and use these to find the lengths of AB. (Leave your answers in surd form.)

a

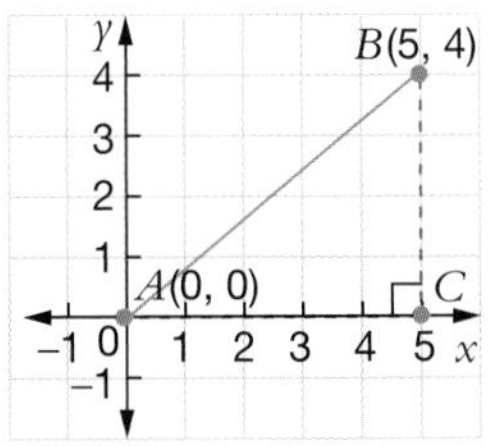

b

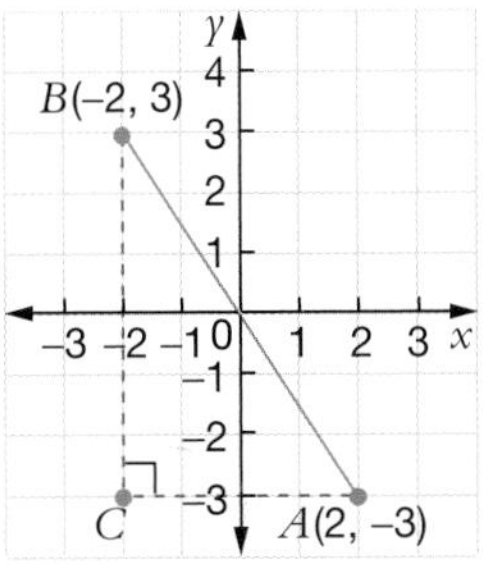

c

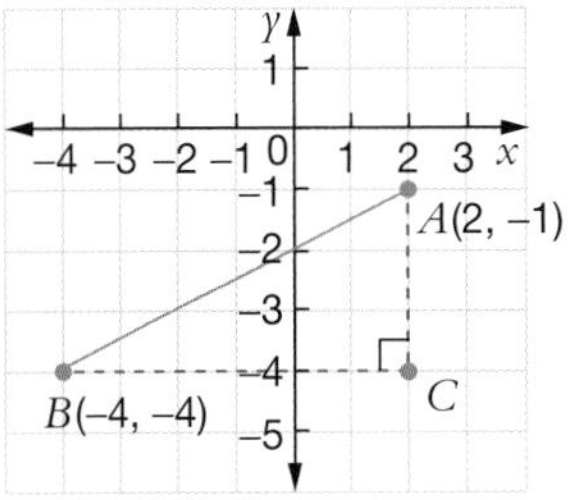

3 Use Pythagoras' theorem to find the length of interval AB in each of the following. (Leave answers in surd form.)

a
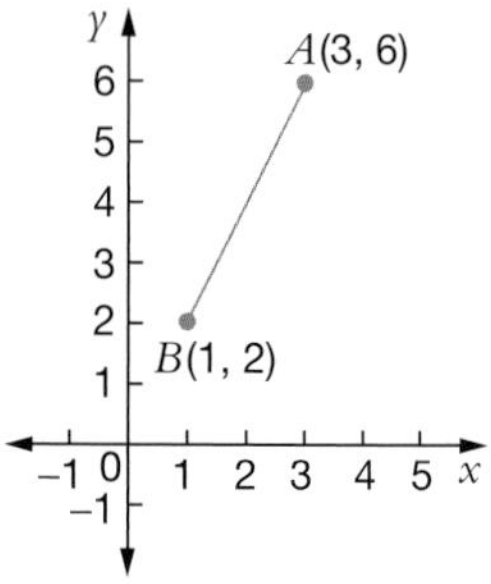

b
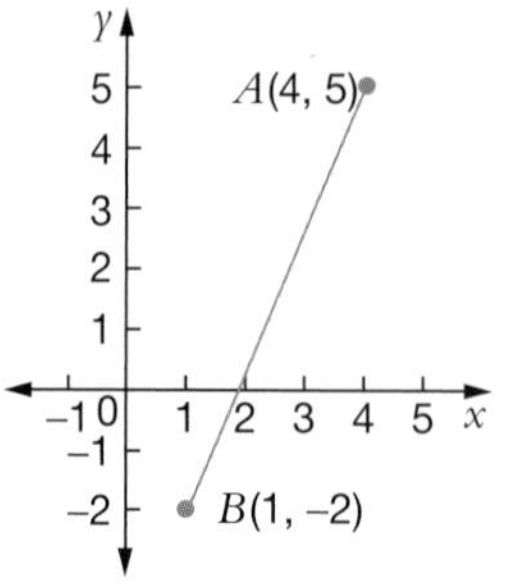

c
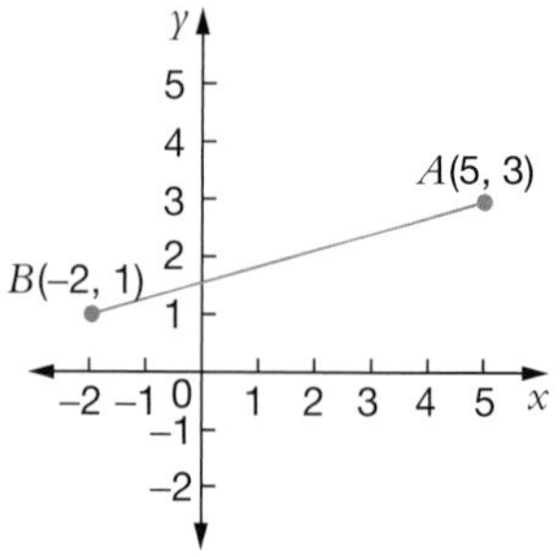

d
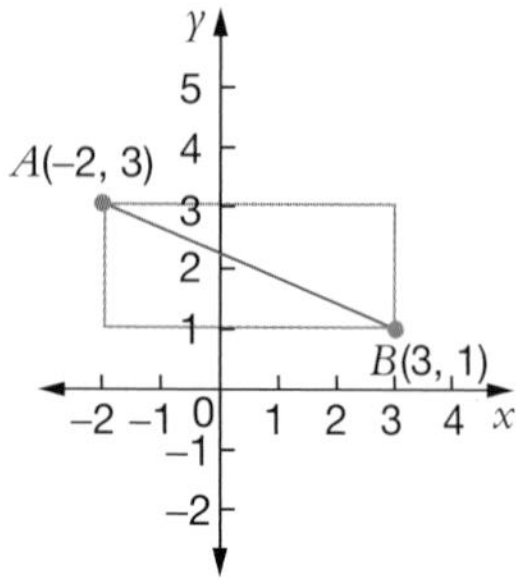

e
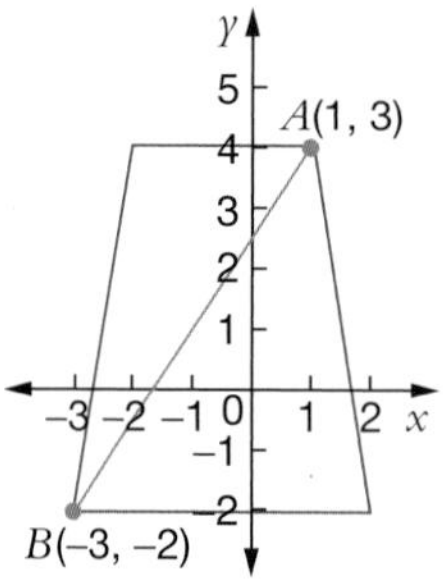

f
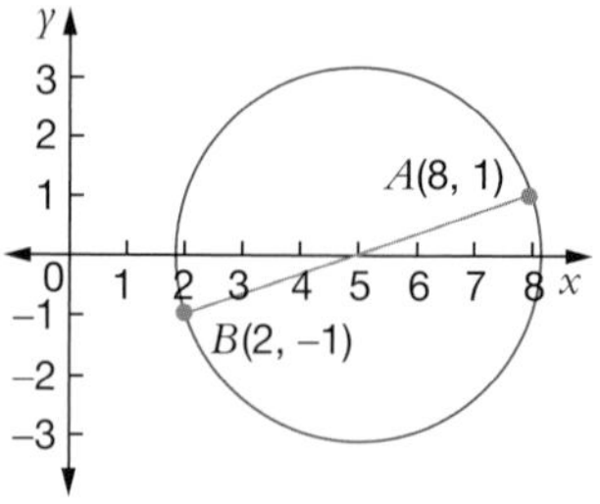

4 Use the formula $\sqrt{(x_2 - x_1)^2 + (y_2 - y_1)^2}$ to find the distance between the points:

a $(4, 2)$ and $(7, 6)$ b $(0, 1)$ and $(8, 7)$ c $(-6, 4)$ and $(-2, 1)$
d $(-2, -4)$ and $(4, 4)$ e $(-6, 2)$ and $(6, 7)$ f $(4, 9)$ and $(-1, -3)$
g $(3, 0)$ and $(5, -4)$ h $(8, 2)$ and $(7, 0)$ i $(6, -1)$ and $(-2, 4)$
j $(-3, 2)$ and $(-7, 3)$ k $(6, 2)$ and $(1, 1)$ l $(4, 4)$ and $(3, 3)$

5 a Find the distance from the point $(4, 2)$ to the origin.
b Which of the points $(-1, 2)$ or $(3, 5)$ is closer to the point $(3, 0)$?
c Find the distance from the point $(-2, 4)$ to the point $(3, -5)$.
d Which of the points $(7, 2)$ or $(-4, -4)$ is further from $(0, 0)$?

6 a The vertices of a triangle are $A(0, 0)$, $B(3, 4)$ and $C(-4, 5)$. Find the length of each side.
b $ABCD$ is a parallelogram where A is the point $(2, 3)$, B is $(5, 5)$, C is $(4, 3)$ and D is $(1, 1)$. Show that the opposite sides of the parallelogram are equal.
c Find the length of the two diagonals of the parallelogram in part **b**.
d $EFGH$ is a quadrilateral, where E is the point $(0, 1)$, F is $(3, 2)$, G is $(2, -1)$ and H is $(-1, -2)$. Prove that $EFGH$ is a rhombus. (The sides of a rhombus are equal.)
e $(3, 2)$ is the centre of a circle. $(6, 6)$ is a point on the circumference. What is the radius of the circle?
f Prove that the triangle ABC is isosceles if A is $(-2, -1)$, B is $(4, 1)$ and C is $(2, -5)$. (Isosceles triangles have two sides equal.)
g A is the point $(-13, 7)$ and B is $(11, -3)$. M is half-way between A and B. How far is M from B?

9:02 The midpoint of an interval

PREP QUIZ 9:02

1 $\frac{4+10}{2} = ?$

2 $\frac{-2+4}{2} = ?$

3 What is the average of 4 and 10?

4 What is the average of −2 and 4?

5 What number is half-way between 4 and 10?

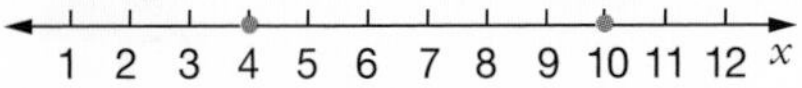

6 What number is half-way between −2 and 4?

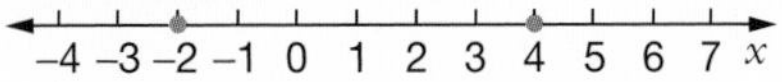

7 What number is half-way between 1 and 5?

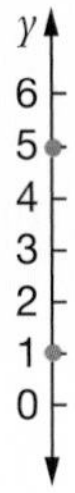

8 What number is half-way between −1 and 3?

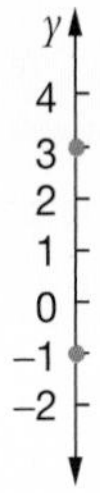

9 $\frac{1+5}{2} = ?$

10 $\frac{-1+3}{2} = ?$

- The midpoint of an interval is the half-way position. If M is the midpoint of AB then it is half-way between A and B.

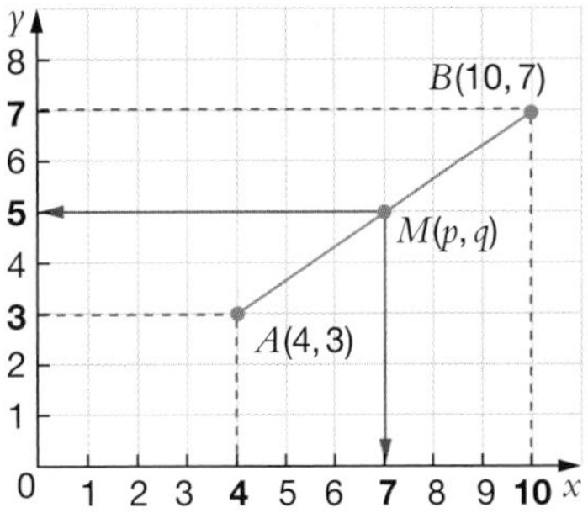

Consider the x-coordinates.

7 is half-way between 4 and 10. → The average of 4 and 10 is 7. → $\frac{4+10}{2} = 7$ → $p = \frac{x_1 + x_2}{2}$

Consider the y-coordinates.

5 is half-way between 3 and 7. → The average of 3 and 7 is 5. → $\frac{3+7}{2} = 5$ → $q = \frac{y_1 + y_2}{2}$

Hence, M is the point (7, 5).

Midpoint formula

The midpoint M of AB, where A is (x_1, y_1) and B is (x_2, y_2), is given by:

$$M = \left(\frac{x_1 + x_2}{2}, \frac{y_1 + y_2}{2}\right)$$

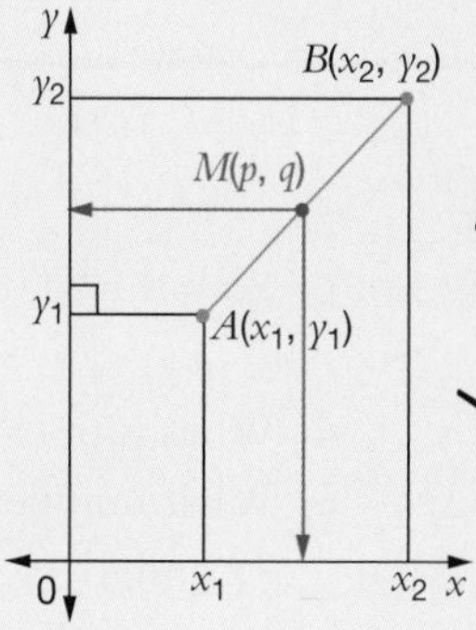

$M = \left(\frac{x_1 + x_2}{2}, \frac{y_1 + y_2}{2}\right)$
Could you please say that in English, Miss?

WORKED EXAMPLES

1 Find the midpoint of the interval joining (2, 6) and (8, 10).

2 Find the midpoint of interval AB, if A is the point (−3, 5) and B is (4, −2).

Solutions

1 Midpoint $= \left(\frac{x_1 + x_2}{2}, \frac{y_1 + y_2}{2}\right)$

$= \left(\frac{2 + 8}{2}, \frac{6 + 10}{2}\right)$

$= (5, 8)$

2 Midpoint $= \left(\frac{x_1 + x_2}{2}, \frac{y_1 + y_2}{2}\right)$

$= \left(\frac{-3 + 4}{2}, \frac{5 + -2}{2}\right)$

$= (\frac{1}{2}, \frac{3}{2})$ or $(\frac{1}{2}, 1\frac{1}{2})$

Exercise 9:02

P Foundation worksheet 9:02 Midpoint

1 Use the graph to find the midpoint of each interval.

a

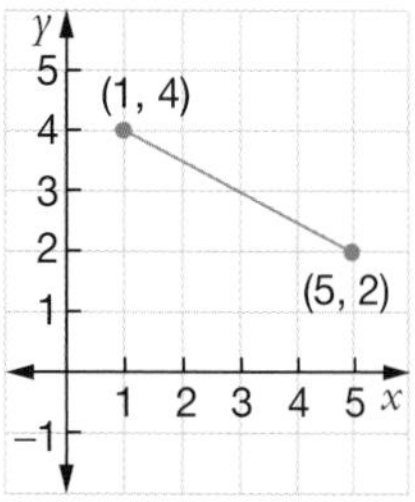

b

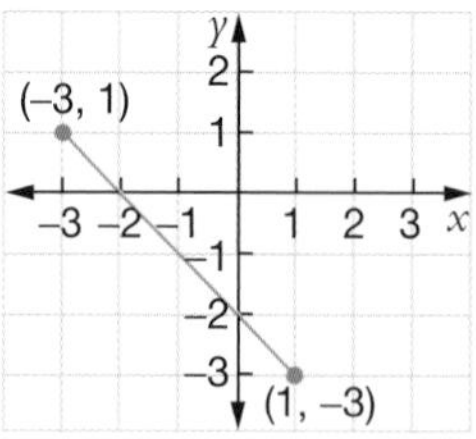

c

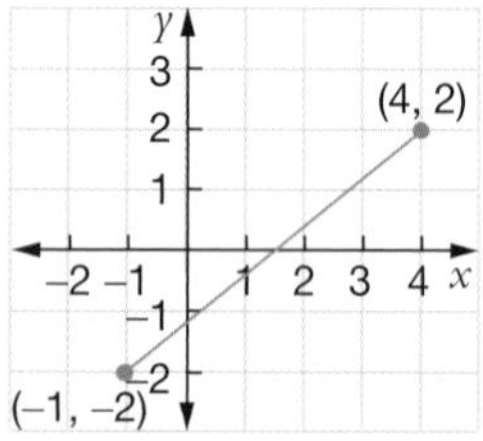

2 Use the graph to find the midpoints of the intervals:

a AB b CD c GH

d EF e LM f PQ

g RS h TU i VW

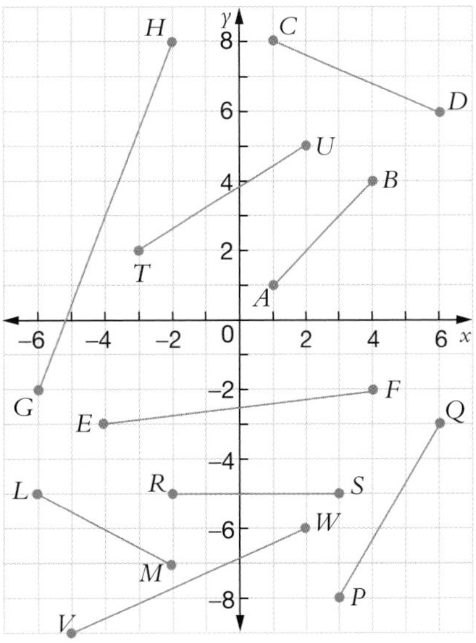

3 Find the midpoint of each interval AB if:

a A is $(2, 4)$, B is $(6, 10)$
b A is $(1, 8)$, B is $(5, 6)$
c A is $(4, 1)$, B is $(8, 7)$
d A is $(0, 0)$, B is $(-4, 2)$
e A is $(-1, 0)$, B is $(5, 4)$
f A is $(-2, -6)$, B is $(4, 2)$
g A is $(-8, -6)$, B is $(0, -10)$
h A is $(-2, 4)$, B is $(-4, -6)$
i A is $(-2, -4)$, B is $(-6, -7)$

4 Find the midpoint of the interval joining:

a $(-3, -3)$ and $(2, -3)$
b $(8, -1)$ and $(7, -1)$
c $(5, 5)$ and $(5, -5)$
d $(6, -7)$ and $(-7, 6)$
e $(0, -4)$ and $(-4, 0)$
f $(6, -6)$ and $(5, -5)$
g $(111, 98)$ and $(63, 42)$
h $(68, -23)$ and $(72, -29)$
i $(400, 52)$ and $(124, 100)$

5 a i Find the midpoint of AC.
ii Find the midpoint of BD.
iii Are the answers for **i** and **ii** the same?
iv What property of a rectangle does this result demonstrate?

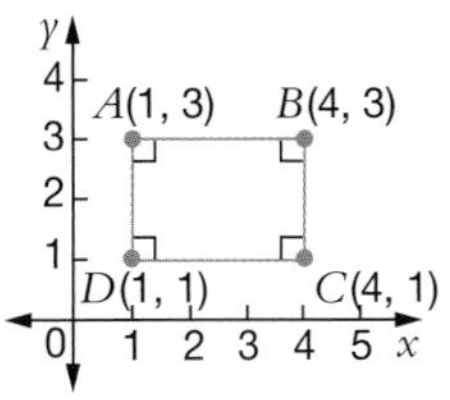

b If $(4, 6)$ and $(2, 10)$ are points at opposite ends of a diameter of a circle, what are the coordinates of the centre?

c i Find the midpoint of AC.
ii Find the midpoint of BD.
iii Are the answers for **i** and **ii** the same?
iv What property of a parallelogram does this result demonstrate?

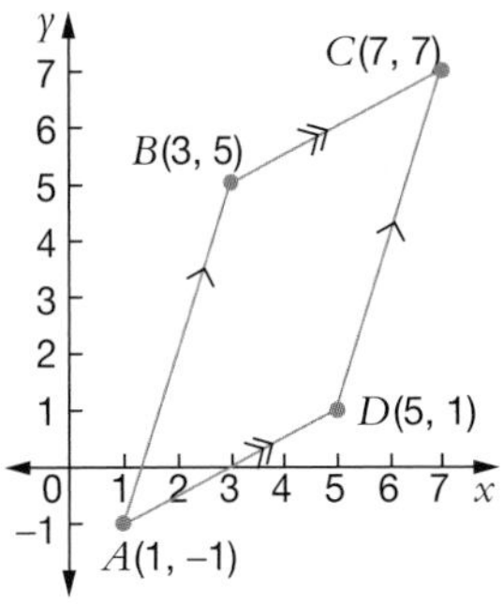

6 a If the midpoint of $(3, k)$ and $(13, 6)$ is $(8, 3)$, find the value of k.
b The midpoint of AB is $(7, -3)$. Find the value of d and e if A is the point $(d, 0)$ and B is $(-1, e)$.
c The midpoint of AB is $(-6, 2)$. If A is the point $(4, 4)$, what are the coordinates of B?
d A circle with centre $(3, 4)$ has a diameter of AB. If A is the point $(-1, 6)$ what are the coordinates of B?

7 a If A is the point $(1, 4)$ and B is the point $(15, 10)$, what are the coordinates of the points C, D and E?
b If A is the point $(1, 4)$ and D is the point $(15, 10)$, what are the coordinates of the points B, C and E?

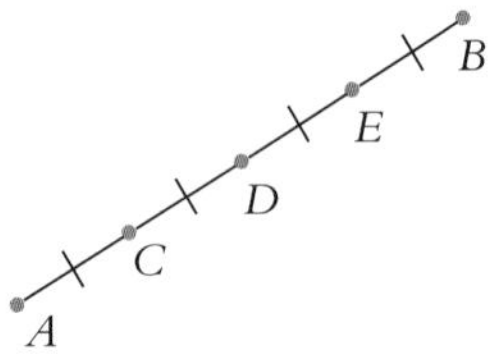

8 a Use coordinate geometry to show that the points $A(-12, 10)$, $B(8, 0)$, $C(4, -6)$ and $D(-16, 4)$ form a parallelogram.
b Use coordinate geometry to show that the points $(-3, 2)$, $(5, -2)$, $(4, -4)$ and $(-4, 0)$ form a rectangle.

9:03 The gradient of an interval

PREP QUIZ 9:03

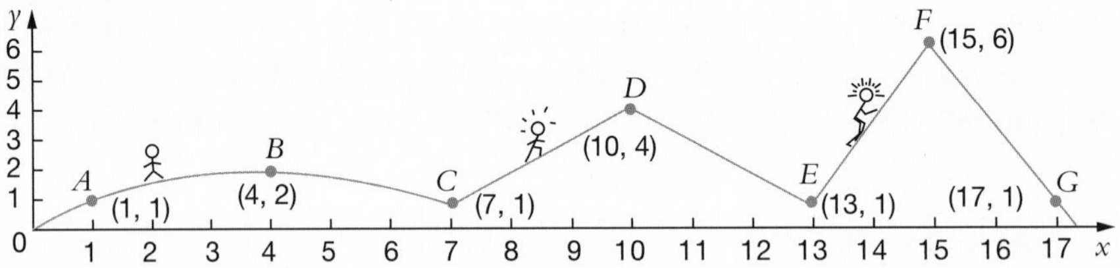

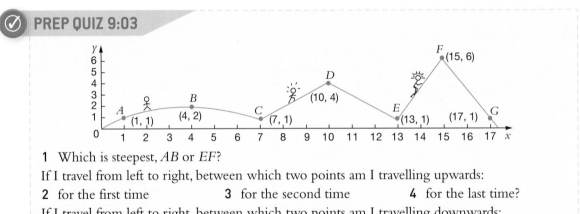

1 Which is steepest, AB or EF?

If I travel from left to right, between which two points am I travelling upwards:

2 for the first time 3 for the second time 4 for the last time?

If I travel from left to right, between which two points am I travelling downwards:

5 for the first time 6 for the second time 7 for the last time?

Is the hill sloping up, down, or not at all, at these points?

8 A 9 G 10 F

The gradient or slope of an interval (or line) is a measure of *how steep* it is.

Negative gradient

Steep (positive gradient)

Steeper

If we move from left to right:

- an interval going down is said to have a negative gradient (or slope)
- an interval going up is said to have a positive gradient (or slope)
- a horizontal interval (not going up or down) has zero gradient.

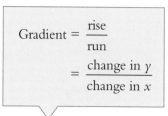

$$\text{Gradient} = \frac{\text{rise}}{\text{run}} = \frac{\text{change in } y}{\text{change in } x}$$

We find the gradient of an interval by comparing its rise (change in y) with its run (change in x).

- So, a gradient of $\frac{1}{2}$ means that for every run of 2 there is a rise of 1 (or for every 2 you go across, you go up 1).

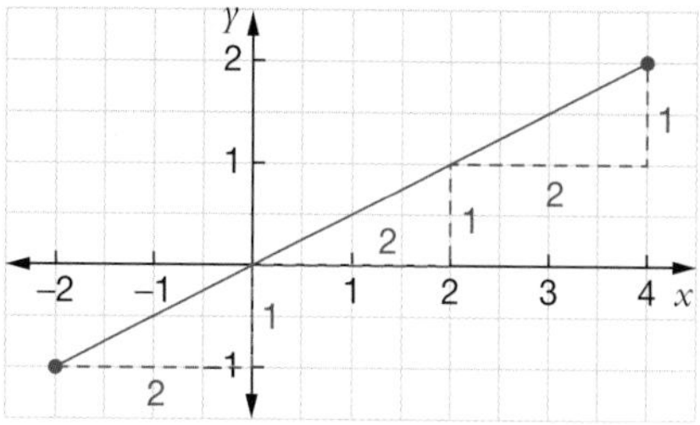

Finding the gradient of a line

1 Select any two points on the line.
2 Join the points and form a right-angled triangle by drawing a vertical line from the higher point and a horizontal side from the lower point.
3 Find the change in the y-coordinates (rise) and the change in the x-coordinates (run).
4 Use the formula above to find the gradient.

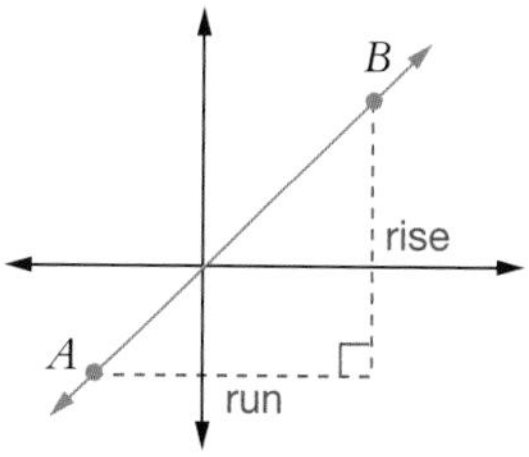

WORKED EXAMPLES

Use the points A and B to find the gradient of the interval AB in each case.

1

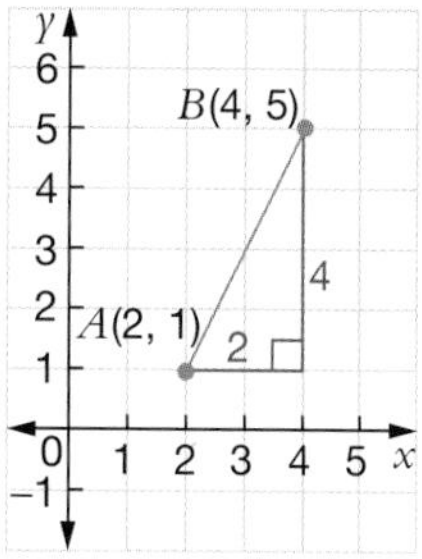

2

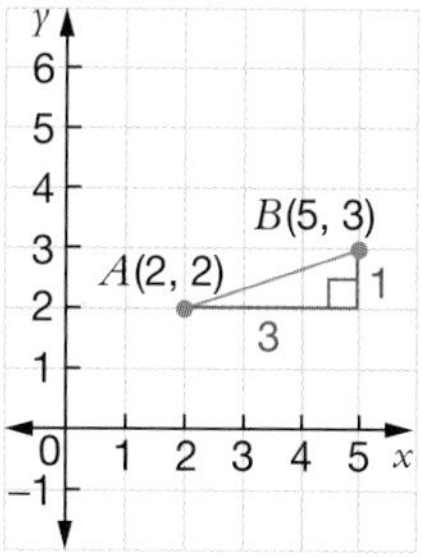

3

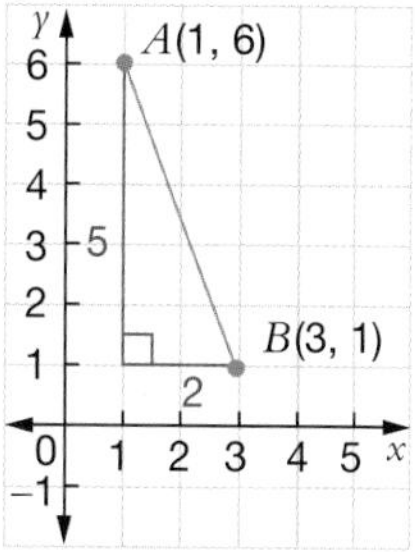

Solutions

1 Gradient

$$= \frac{\text{change in } y}{\text{change in } x}$$

$$= \frac{\text{up } 4}{\text{across } 2}$$

$$= \frac{4}{2}$$

$$= 2$$

2 $$m = \frac{\text{change in } y}{\text{change in } x}$$

$$= \frac{\text{up } 1}{\text{across } 3}$$

$$= \frac{1}{3}$$

m is used for 'gradient'

3 $$m = \frac{\text{change in } y}{\text{change in } x}$$

$$= \frac{\text{down } 5}{\text{across } 2}$$

$$= \frac{-5}{2}$$

$$= -2\tfrac{1}{2}$$

Gradient formula

We wish to find a formula for the gradient of a line AB where A is (x_1, y_1) and B is (x_2, y_2).

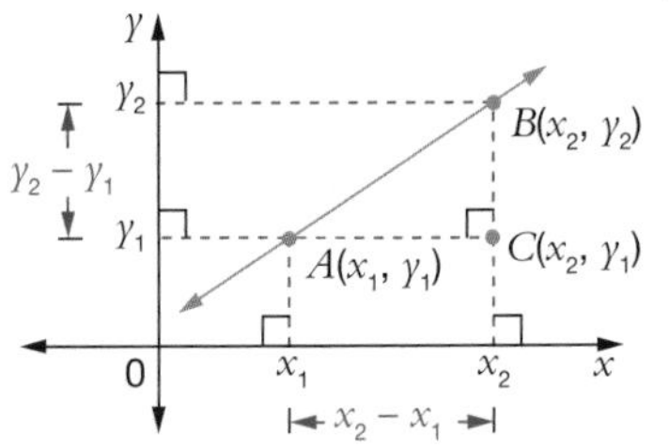

$$\text{Gradient of } AB = \frac{\text{rise}}{\text{run}}$$

$$= \frac{\text{change in } y}{\text{change in } x}$$

$$= \frac{BC}{AC}$$

$$\therefore\ m = \frac{y_2 - y_1}{x_2 - x_1} \quad \text{(opposite sides of a rectangle are equal)}$$

The gradient of the line that passes through the points $A(x_1, y_1)$ and $B(x_2, y_2)$ is given by the formula:

$$m = \frac{y_2 - y_1}{x_2 - x_1} \qquad \left(\textit{Note:} \text{ The formula } m = \frac{y_1 - y_2}{x_1 - x_2} \text{ can also be used.}\right)$$

WORKED EXAMPLES

Find the gradient of the straight line passing through the following points.

1 (1, 3) and (4, 7)

2 (6, –2) and (2, –1)

It doesn't matter which point is called (x_1, y_1).

Solutions

1 Let (x_1, y_1) be (1, 3) and (x_2, y_2) be (4, 7).

$$\text{Gradient} = \frac{y_2 - y_1}{x_2 - x_1}$$

$$= \frac{7-3}{4-1}$$

$$= \frac{4}{3}$$

$\therefore$ The gradient is $1\frac{1}{3}$.

2 Let (x_1, y_1) be (6, –2) and (x_2, y_2) be (2, –1).

$$m = \frac{y_2 - y_1}{x_2 - x_1}$$

$$= \frac{-1-(-2)}{2-6}$$

$$= \frac{1}{-4}$$

$\therefore$ The gradient is $-\frac{1}{4}$.

Architectural design often requires an understanding of gradients (slopes).

Exercise 9:03

P Foundation worksheet 9:03
Gradients

1 State whether each interval or line below has a positive or negative gradient.

a 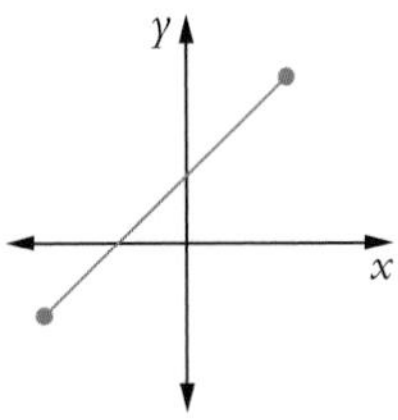

b 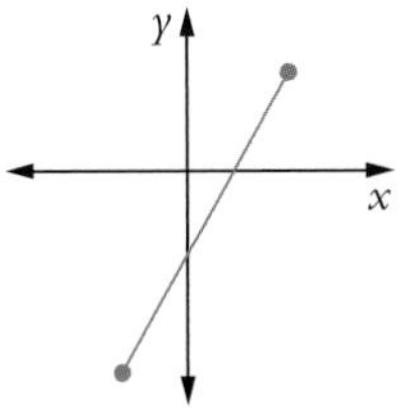

c 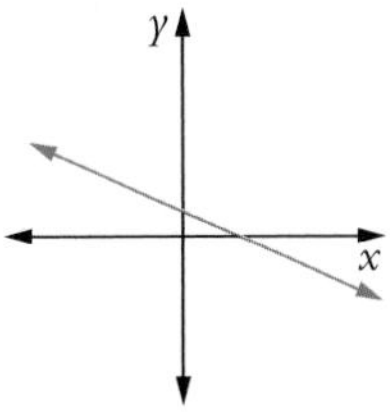

d 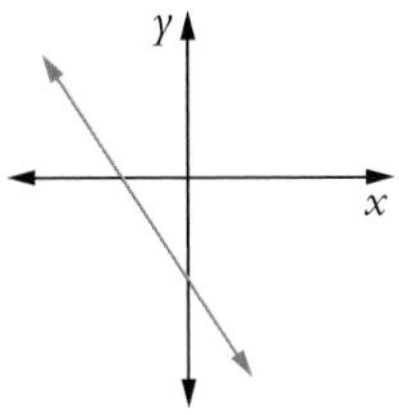

e 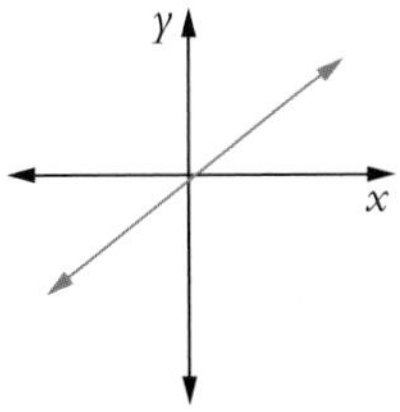

f 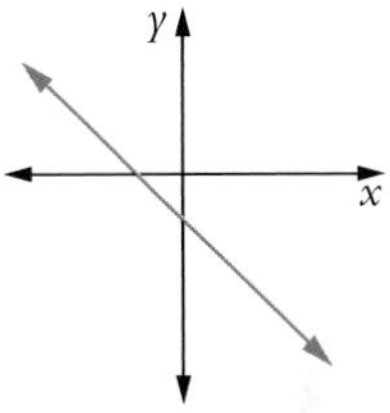

2 Find the gradient of the interval *AB*.

a 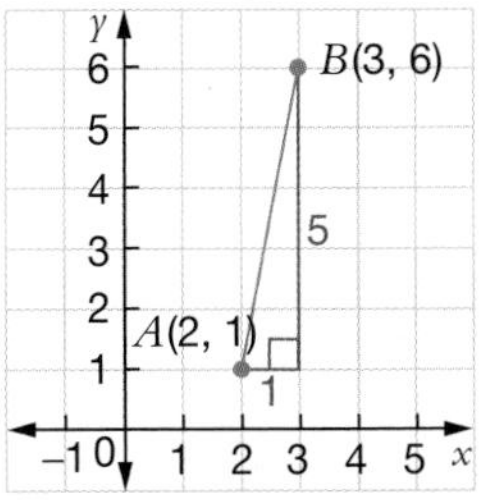

b 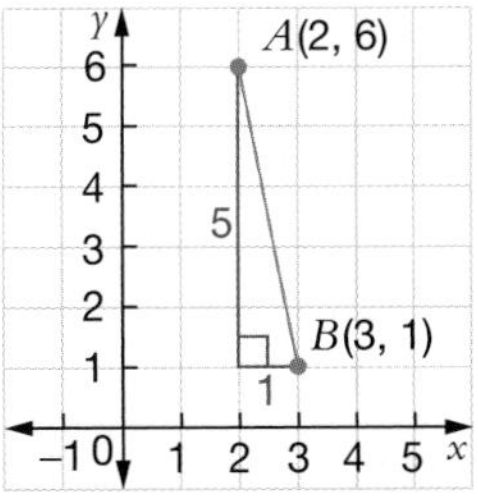

c 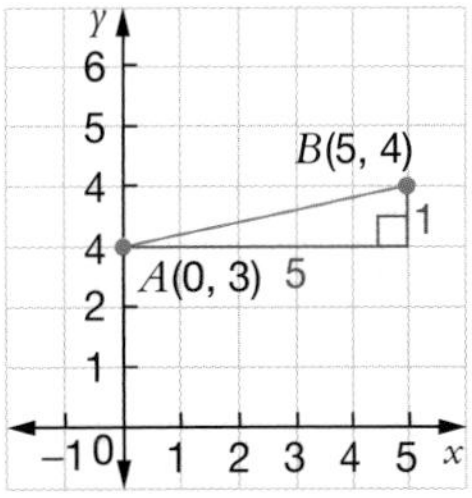

3 Find the gradient of the interval *AB*.

a 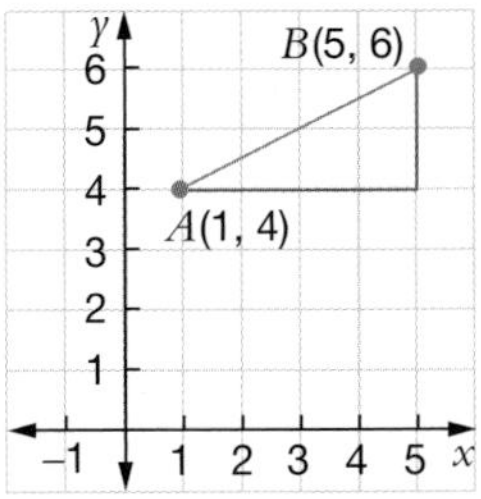

b 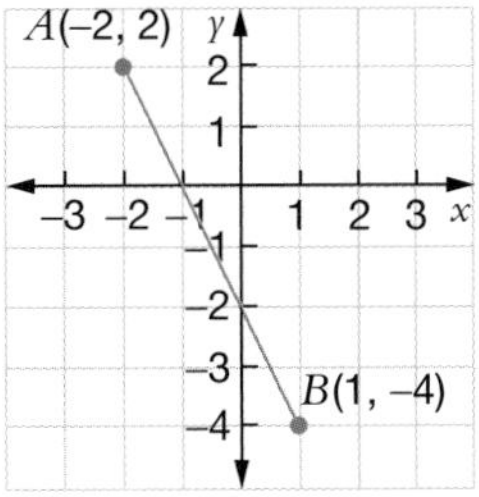

c 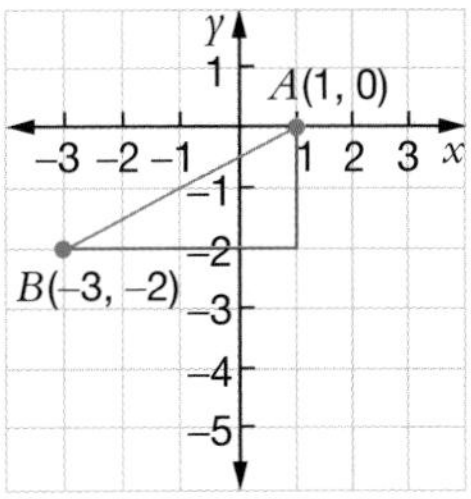

4 Use the points *C* and *D* to find the slope of the line.

a 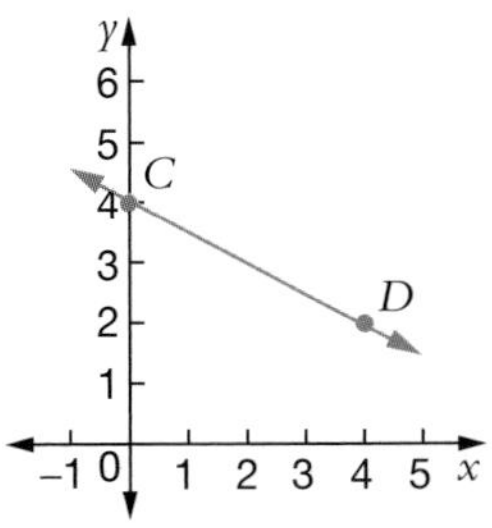

b 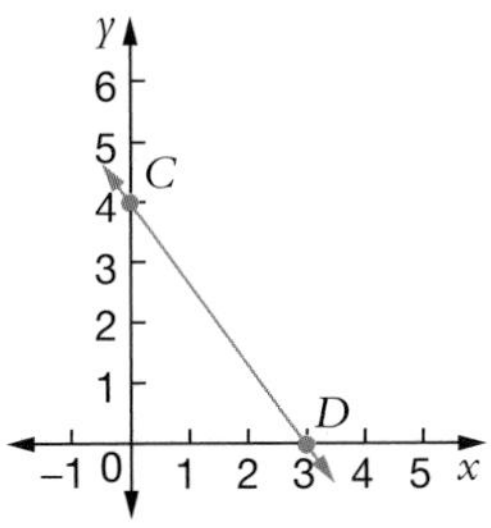

c 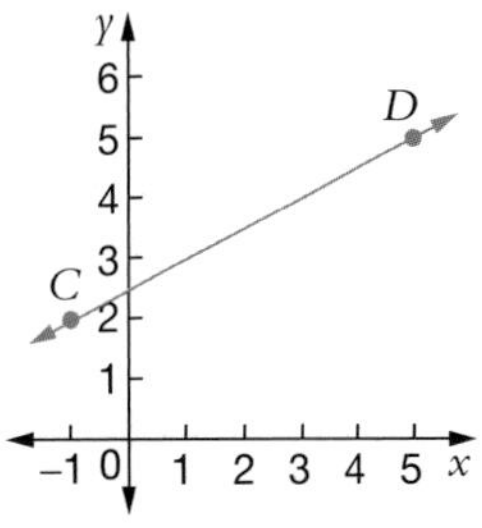

5 Use the formula $m = \dfrac{y_2 - y_1}{x_2 - x_1}$ to find the gradient of the straight line passing through the points:

a $(2, 6)$ and $(5, 7)$ b $(4, 2)$ and $(5, 6)$
c $(3, 1)$ and $(7, 3)$ d $(0, 0)$ and $(5, 2)$
e $(0, 5)$ and $(6, 6)$ f $(3, 0)$ and $(5, 6)$
g $(-3, -2)$ and $(0, 6)$ h $(4, -1)$ and $(3, 3)$
i $(2, 3)$ and $(-4, 9)$ j $(-4, 1)$ and $(-2, -4)$
k $(5, 2)$ and $(7, -6)$ l $(-3, -1)$ and $(-6, -7)$

6 a Find the gradient of the line that passes through $A(3, 1)$ and $B(5, 11)$.
b Find the slope of the line that passes through $O(0, 0)$ and $B(-1, -2)$.
c On the graph shown, all of the points A, B, C and D lie on the same straight line, $x + 2y = 6$.
Find the gradient of the line using the points:
i A and B ii C and D iii A and D iv B and C
Conclusion: Any two points on a straight line can be used to find the gradient of that line. A straight line has only one gradient.
d Use the gradient of an interval to show that the points $(-2, 5)$, $(2, 13)$ and $(6, 21)$ are collinear (lie on the same straight line).

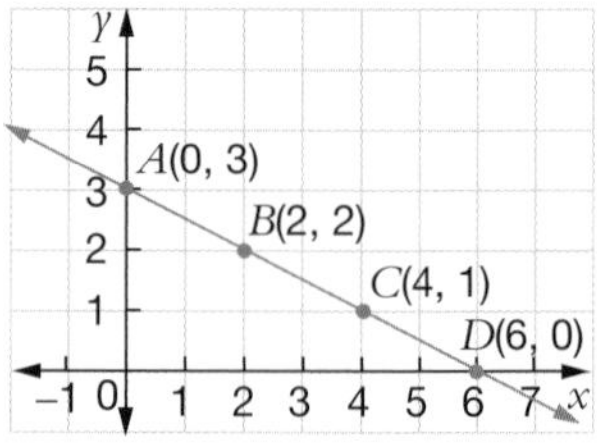

7 a Calculate the gradients of the four lines shown on the right.
b Which lines have the same gradients?
c Which lines are parallel?

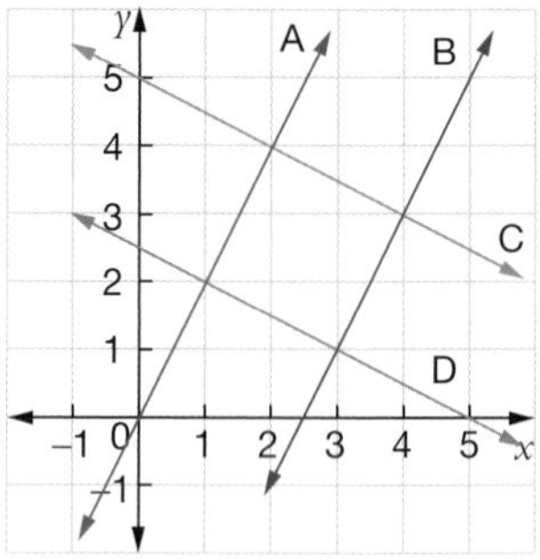

8 a On the same number plane, draw:
i line through $(0, 0)$ with a gradient of -2
ii a line through $(1, 1)$ which is parallel to the line in i.
b Do the lines in i and ii have the same gradient?

If two lines have the same gradient they are *parallel*.

9 a i Find the gradient of BC and of AD.
ii Find the gradient of AB and of DC.
iii What kind of quadrilateral is $ABCD$? Give a reason for your answer.
b Prove that a quadrilateral that has vertices $A(2, 3)$, $B(9, 5)$, $C(4, 0)$ and $D(-3, -2)$ is a parallelogram. (It will be necessary to prove that opposite sides are parallel.)

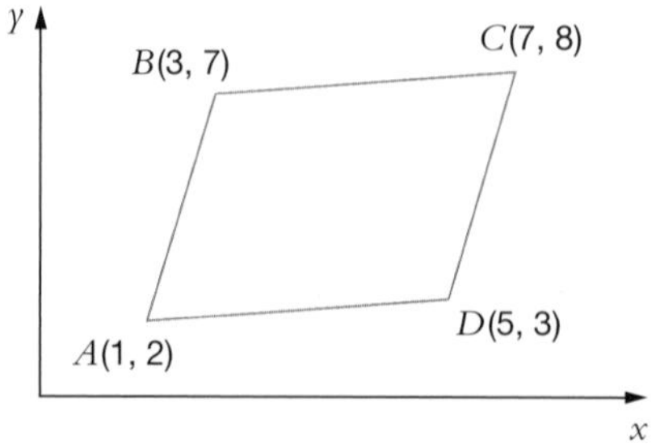

10 Use the fact that *a rhombus is a parallelogram with a pair of adjacent sides equal* to prove that the points $A(-1, 1)$, $B(11, 4)$, $C(8, -8)$ and $D(-4, -11)$ form the vertices of a rhombus.

P GEOGEBRA ACTIVITY 9:03 — THE MIDPOINT, GRADIENT AND LENGTH OF AN INTERVAL

In this activity you can click and drag points to change the length and gradient of an interval. Calculate the midpoint, gradient and length of the interval, and then tick the checkbox to see the solution.

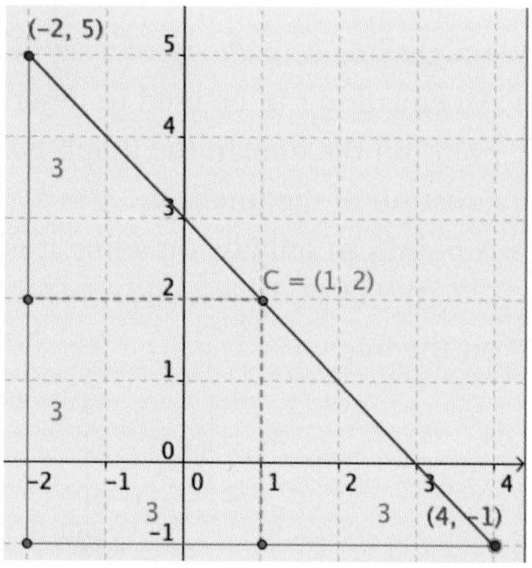

INVESTIGATION 9:03 — GRADIENTS AND BUILDING

- Engineers, architects and builders need to understand and calculate gradients when designing and constructing ramps, driveways and roads.
- They usually refer to a gradient in ratio form.
  e.g. A driveway can have a maximum gradient of 1 in 4 (1 : 4). This means a run of 4 units will produce a rise (or fall) of 1 unit. We would say the gradient is $\frac{1}{4}$.

1 The graph below shows three slopes. Which of the slopes A, B or C is:

a 1 in 4 **b** 1 in 6 **c** 1 in 12?

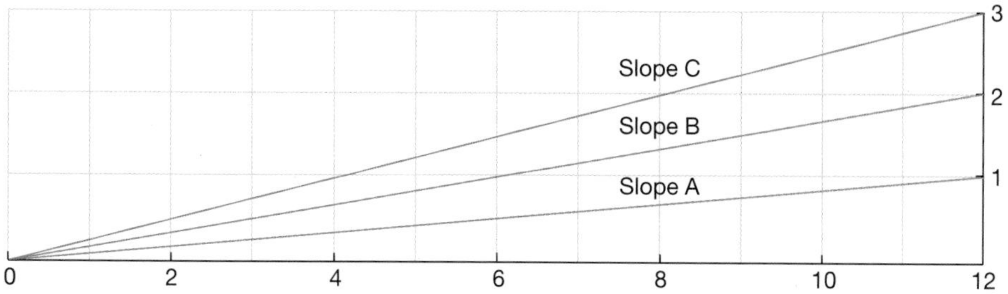

2 A slope is to be 1 in 4 (1 : 4). What would the run have to be if the rise is:

a 2 m **b** 1·4 m **c** 3·2 m?

3 Use the graph above (or ratio) to find the rise for a:

a 1 in 6 slope, if the run is 9 m **b** 1 in 12 slope, if the run is 6 m.

4 A builder has to construct a wheelchair ramp from the front of the house to the front of the property, a run of 10 m. He calculates the fall to be 0·8 m. Building regulations state that the maximum gradient of a ramp is 1 in 14. Is it possible for the builder to build a straight ramp? If not, how can he build it and satisfy the regulations?

9:04 Graphing straight lines

A straight line is made up of a set of points, each with its own pair of coordinates.

- An equation can be used to describe the relationship between the x- and y-coordinates of any point on the line. In the graph below, the sum of the coordinates at each point is 3, so the equation of the line is $x + y = 3$.
- A point can only lie on a line if its coordinates satisfy the equation of the line. For the points (−3, 2) and (2, 3), it is clear that the sum of the coordinates is not equal to 3. So they do not lie on the line.

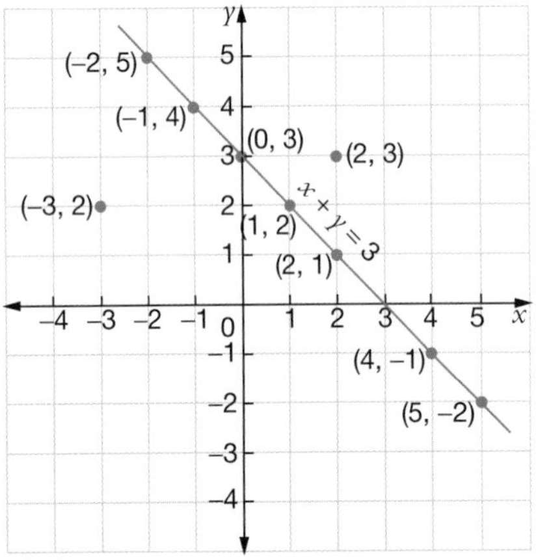

The x and y in the equation are the point's coordinates.
x + y = 3

To graph a straight line we need:

- an equation to allow us to calculate the x- and y-coordinates for each point on the line
- a table to store at least two sets of coordinates
- a number plane on which to plot the points.

Two important points on a line are:

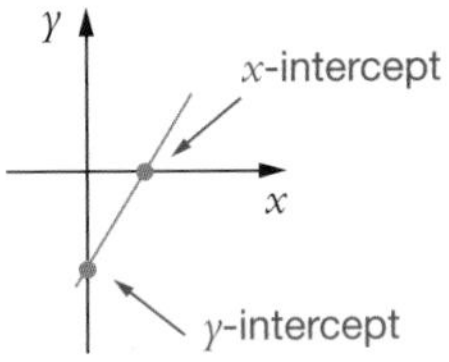

- the x-intercept (where the line crosses the x-axis)
  This is found by substituting $y = 0$ into the line's equation and then solving for x.
- the y-intercept (where the line crosses the y-axis)
  This is found by substituting $x = 0$ into the line's equation and then solving for y.
  Because they are easily found the x- and y-intercepts are commonly used to graph a line.

Horizontal and vertical lines

The line on the right is vertical.

- The following table of values shows the points marked on the line.

x	2	2	2	2	2	2
y	−2	−1	0	1	2	3

- There seems to be no connection between x and y.
  However, x is always 2. So the equation is $x = 2$.

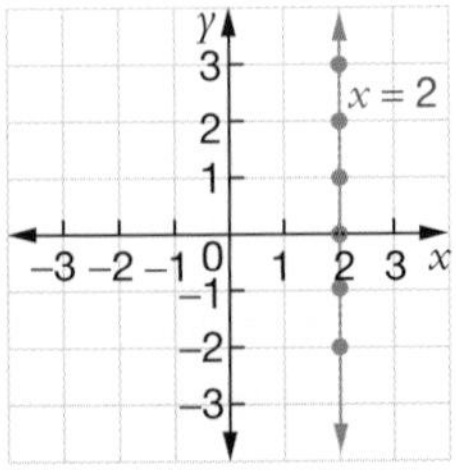

Vertical lines have equations of the form $x = a$, where a is the x-intercept.

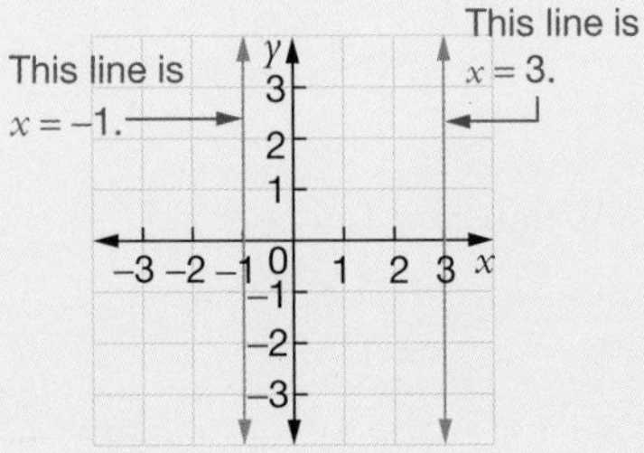

This line is $x = -1$.
This line is $x = 3$.

They cut the x-axis at −1 and 3.

The line on the right is horizontal.

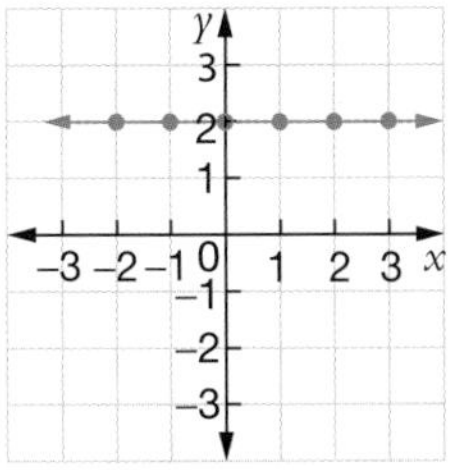

- The following table of values shows the points marked on the line.

x	−2	−1	0	1	2	3
y	2	2	2	2	2	2

- There seems to be no connection between x and y.
  However, y is always 2. So the equation is $y = 2$.

Horizontal lines have equations of the form $y = b$, where b is the y-intercept.

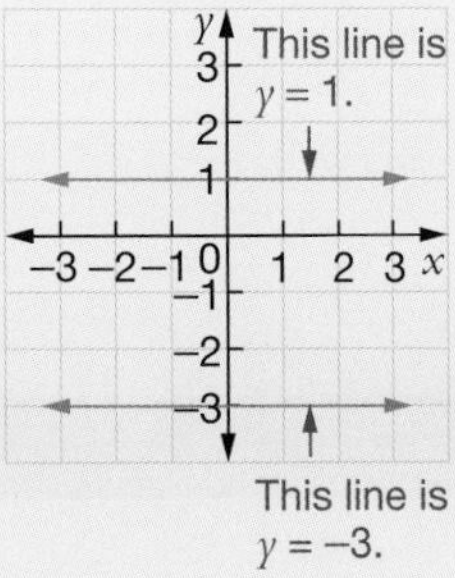

This line is $y = 1$.
This line is $y = -3$.

They cut the y-axis at −3 and 1.

WORKED EXAMPLES

Draw the graph of each straight line. In Question **3** calculate the x- and y-intercepts.

1 $x + y = 5$ **2** $y = 3x - 2$ **3** $4x + y = 2$

Solutions

1 $x + y = 5$

x	0	1	2
y	5	4	−3

2 $y = 3x - 2$

x	0	1	2
y	−2	1	4

3 $4x + y = 2$

x	0	$\frac{1}{2}$
y	2	0

When $x = 0$,
$0 + y = 5$
$\therefore y = 5$

When $x = 1$,
$1 + y = 5$
$\therefore y = 4$

When $x = 2$,
$2 + y = 5$
$\therefore y = 3$

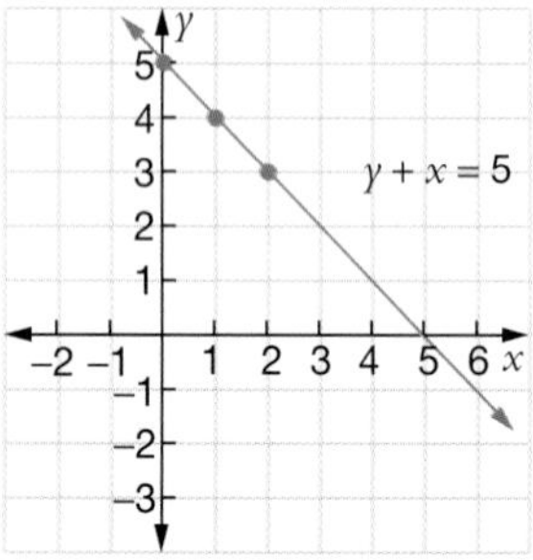

When $x = 0$,
$y = 3 \times 0 - 2$
$= -2$

When $x = 1$,
$y = 3 \times 1 - 2$
$\therefore y = 1$

When $x = 2$,
$y = 3 \times 2 - 2$
$\therefore y = 4$

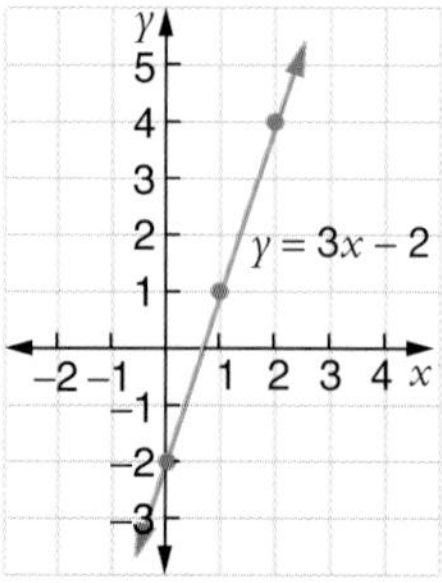

When $x = 0$,
$4 \times 0 + y = 2$
$0 + y = 2$
$\therefore y = 2$

When $y = 0$,
$4\,x + 0 = 2$
$4x = 2$
$x = \frac{1}{2}$

$\therefore x$-intercept $= \frac{1}{2}$
$\therefore y$-intercept $= 2$

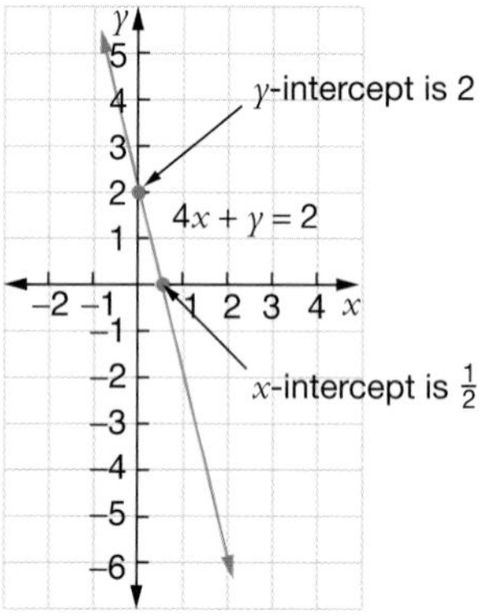

Exercise 9:04

P Foundation worksheet 9:04 Graphing lines

1 Complete the table for each equation.

a $y = x + 1$

x	0	1	2
y			

b $y = 2x$

x	0	1	2
y			

c $y = 3x + 1$

x	0	1	2
y			

d $y = 6 - 2x$

x	0	1	2
y			

e $y = x + 3$

x	0	1	2
y			

f $y = 7x + 2$

x	2	3	4
y			

g $y = x - 7$

x	0	1	2
y			

h $y = 1 - x$

x	0	1	2
y			

i $y = 3$

x	0	1	2
y			

2 Graph the lines described by these equations.

a $x + y = 3$ b $x + y = 5$ c $x + y = 2$
d $y = x + 1$ e $y = x + 4$ f $y = x + 2$
g $y = 2x - 1$ h $y = 3x - 1$ i $y = 2x - 2$
j $y = x + 3$ k $y = 2x$ l $y = 6 - 2x$

3 Draw the graphs of these equations on the same number plane. What do these lines have in common?

a $y = 2x - 1$ b $y = 2x$ c $y = 2x + 3$

4 Draw the graphs of these equations on the same number plane. What do these lines have in common?

a $y = x$ b $y = 2x$ c $y = 3x$

5 Draw the graphs of these equations on the same number plane. What do these lines have in common?

a $y = 2x - 1$ b $x + y = 2$ c $y = x$

6 On which of the following lines does the point (6, 7) lie?

A $y = x + 1$ B $x + 2y = 20$ C $y = 3x - 4$
D $4x - 3y = 3$ E $x - y = 1$ F $y = x - 1$

7 a Does (4, 0) lie on the line $4x + 3y = 16$?
b Does the line $y = 2x - 3$ pass through the point (7, 11)?
c Which of the points (7, 2) and (7, −2) lie on the line $y = x - 9$?
d Which of the points (5, 0) and (0, 5) lie on the line $x + 2y = 5$?

8 For each number plane write the equations of the lines A to F.

a
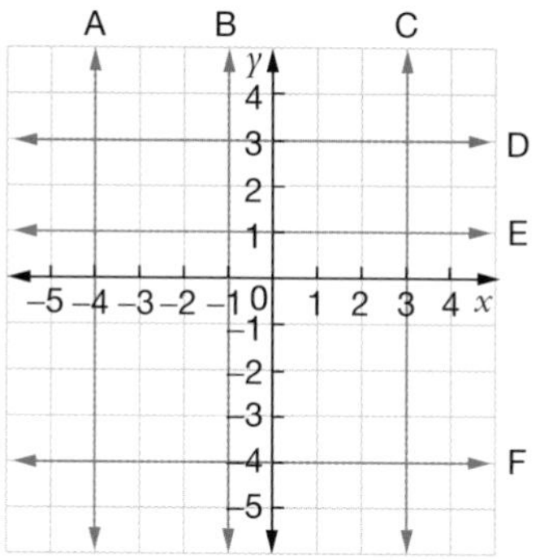

b
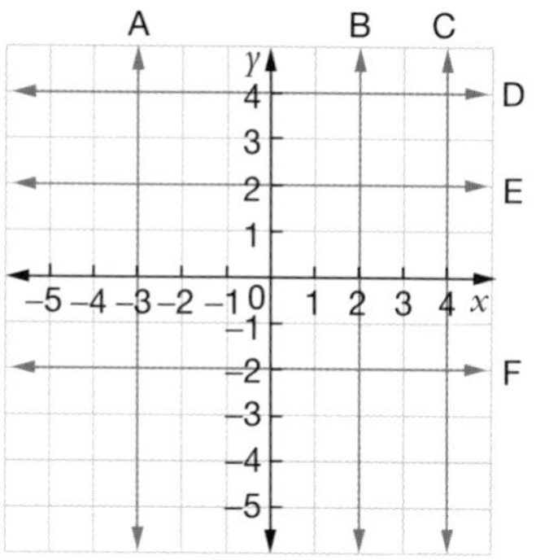

9 Using values from −5 to 5 on each axis, draw the graphs of the following straight lines. Use a new diagram for each part.

a $y = 4$, $x = 5$, $y = -1$, $x = 0$ b $x = 1$, $y = 0$, $x = 2$, $y = 3$
c $y = 4$, $x = 2$, $y = -2$, $x = -4$ d $x = 5$, $y = -5$, $x = 2$, $y = 2$
e $y = -2$, $y = 0$, $x = 0$, $x = 3$

Which of these encloses a square region?

Is THAT all?
Hey, no problem!
I can do that!

10 Match each of the lines A to F with one of the following equations.

a $y = 2x$ b $y = x - 2$ c $2x + y = 0$

d $y = x$ e $x + y = 3$ f $2x + y = 2$

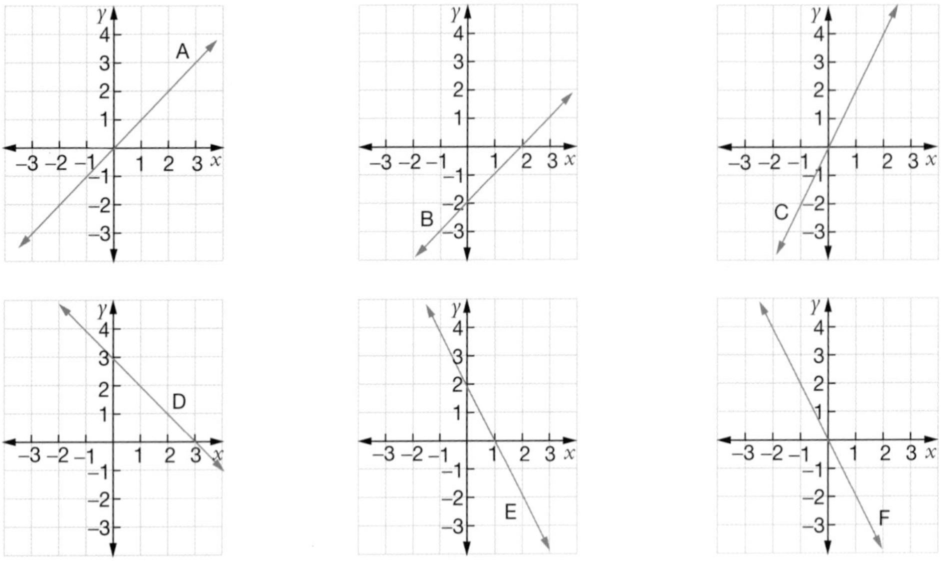

11 Which of the lines A, B, C or D at right could be described by the following equation?

a $x - y = 2$ b $x + y = 4$

c $2x + y + 2 = 0$ d $x - 2y + 2 = 0$

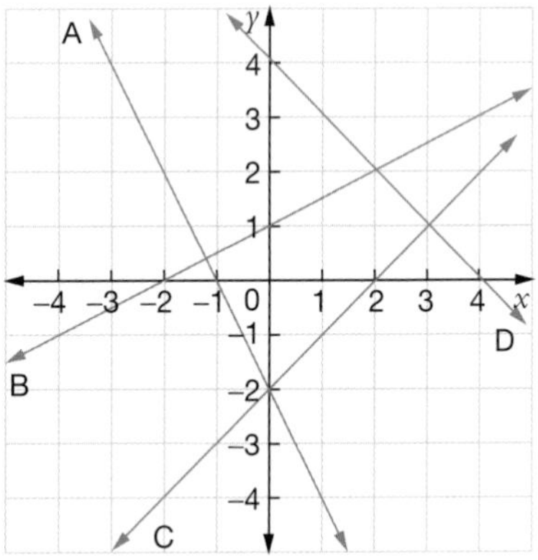

12 Find the x- and y-intercepts and use them to graph the following lines.

a $2x + y = 2$ b $3x + y = 6$

c $2x + y = 4$ d $2x - y = 4$

e $3x - y = 3$ f $4x - y = 2$

13 Use a suitable method to graph each of these lines.

a $3x + 2y = 7$ b $5x - 2y - 6 = 0$ c $2x - 3y - 5 = 0$

P GEOGEBRA ACTIVITY 9:04 GRAPHING LINES USING TWO POINTS

Choose one of the three sets of equations and work out the coordinates of two points on the line. Then click and drag two given points to these positions. If you have calculated correctly, the given line will appear. You can then repeat the process with the other two lines. The degree of difficulty of calculating the points varies from line to line.

New sets of three equations can be generated randomly.

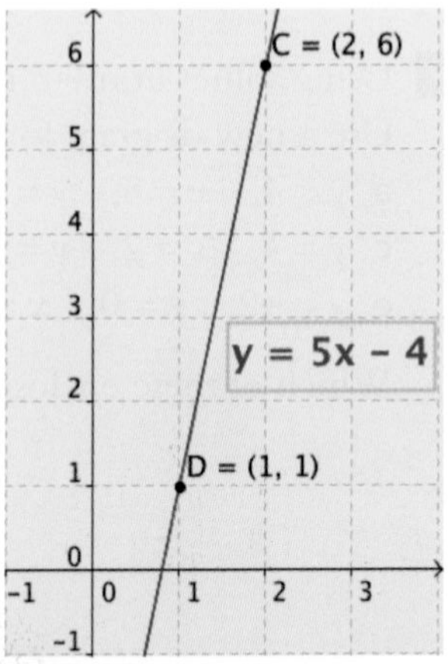

WHAT IS THE EASIEST JOB IN A WATCH FACTORY?

Answer each question and write the letter for that question in the box above the correct answer.

A The length of $AC = \square$ units.
N The length of $BC = \square$ units.
D The length of $AB = \square$ units.
(Use Pythagoras' theorem.)

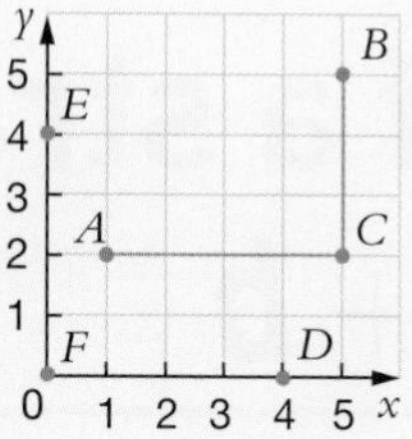

Find the coordinates of:

A D **N** E **S** F

T Which quadrant is shown here?

Find the equation of:

A AC **O** BC **C** the x-axis

D the y-axis

If $y = 4x - 10$ find the value of y when:

A $x = 5$ **E** $x = 2$ **F** $x = 0$ **G** $x = 1$

Which of the equations $y = x + 3$, $y = 2x + 1$, $y = 3x$ has produced the table?

I

x	0	1	2	3
y	0	3	6	9

K

x	0	1	2	3
y	3	4	5	6

M

x	3	4	5	6
y	7	9	11	13

Solve:

N $2x = x + 8$ **O** $3y - 8 = 10$ **R** $11x = 5x + 12$

S $\dfrac{x-1}{3} = 2$ **T** $x^3 = 1$ **U** $y^3 = -1$

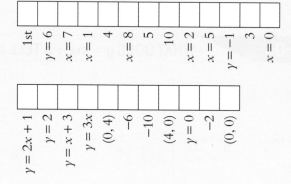

1st	$y = 6$	$x = 7$	$x = 1$	4	$x = 8$	5	10	$x = 2$	$x = 5$	$y = -1$	3	$x = 0$

$y = 2x + 1$	$y = 2$	$y = x + 3$	$y = 3x$	(0, 4)	−6	−10	(4, 0)	$y = 0$	−2	(0, 0)

9:05 The gradient–intercept form of a straight line: $y = mx + b$

PREP QUIZ 9:05

If $x = 0$, what is the value of:

1 $2x$ 2 $mx + b$?

If $x = 0$, what is the value of y when:

3 $y = 3x + 2$ 4 $y = 4x - 1$?

What is the gradient of:

5 line A 6 line B?

What are the coordinates of the y-intercept of:

7 line A 8 line B?

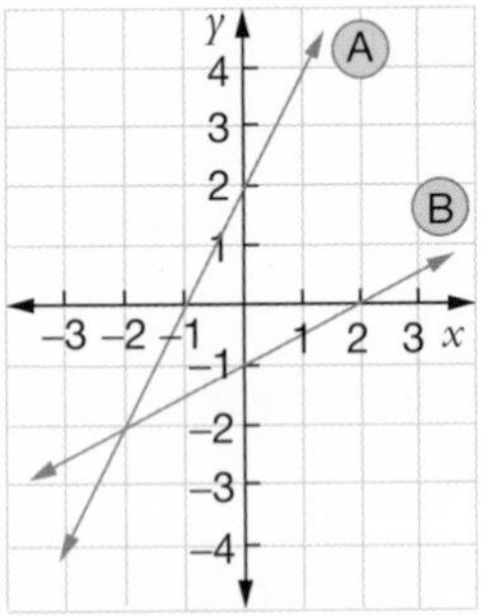

9 Does every point on the y-axis have an x-coordinate of 0?

10 Can the y-intercept of a line be found by substituting $x = 0$?

- The equation of a line can be written in several ways. For example:
  $x - y - 4 = 0$, $y = x - 4$ and $x - y = 4$ are different ways of writing the same equation.
- $x - y - 4 = 0$ is said to be in *general form*.
  It is common for the equation of a line to be written in general form. We must be able to convert an equation from the gradient-intercept form to the general form and vice-versa.
- $y = x - 4$ allows us to get information about the line directly from the equation.

INVESTIGATION 9:05 WHAT DOES $y = mx + b$ TELL US?

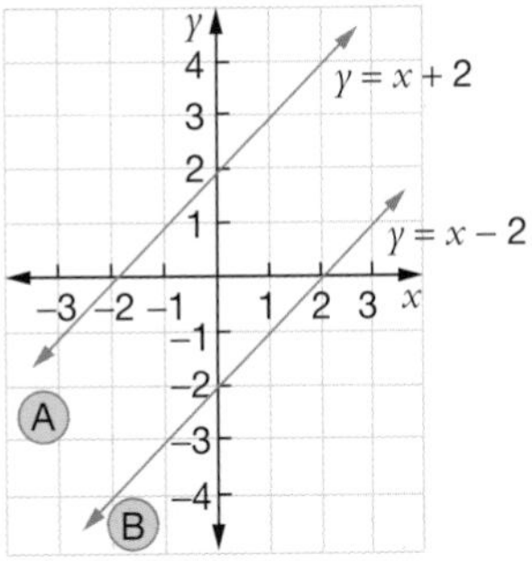

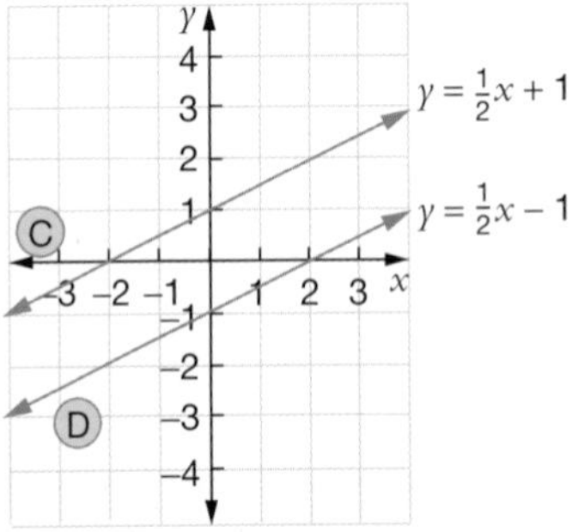

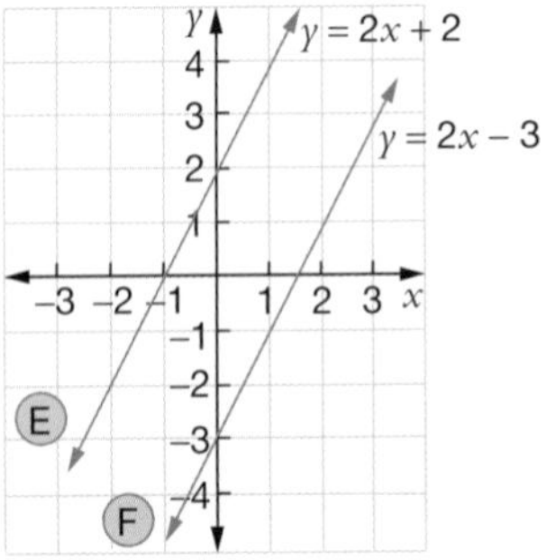

1 Use the graphs above to complete the table on the following page.

Line	Equation	Gradient	y-intercept
A	$y = x + 2$		
B	$y = x - 2$		
C	$y = \frac{1}{2}x + 1$		
D	$y = \frac{1}{2}x - 1$		
E	$y = 2x + 2$		
F	$y = 2x - 3$		

In an equation like $y = 3x - 5$:

- the number 3, in front of x, tells us how many of x we have and is called the coefficient of x
- similarly, the number in front of y is called the coefficient of y. In this case the coefficient of y is 1
- the number -5 is called the constant.

3 is the coefficient of x.
y = 3x − 5

2 Complete the table below.

Line	Equation	Coefficient of x	Constant
A	$y = x + 2$		
B	$y = x - 2$		
C	$y = \frac{1}{2}x + 1$		
D	$y = \frac{1}{2}x - 1$		
E	$y = 2x + 2$		
F	$y = 2x - 3$		

3 From the tables in Questions **1** and **2**, state how the gradient and y-intercept of a line are related to its equation.

4 The graphs of equations $2x + y - 3 = 0$ and $y = -2x + 3$ are the same line. The gradient is -2 and the y-intercept is 3. Which form of the equation gives this information directly?

5 What does the form $y = mx + b$ tell us about a line?

- When an equation of a line is written in the form $y = mx + b$:
  m gives the gradient
  b gives the y-intercept
- Clearly, lines with the same gradient are parallel.
  (See the pairs of lines in Investigation 9:05.)
- When an equation of a line is written in the form $ax + by + c = 0$, where a, b and c are integers and $a > 0$, it is said to be in general form.

WORKED EXAMPLE 1

Write the gradient and y-intercept of these lines.

a $y = 3x - 5$

Here, $m = 3$, $b = -5$.
The gradient is 3 and the y-intercept is -5.

b $y = -2x$

Here, $m = -2$, $b = 0$.
The gradient is -2 and the y-intercept is 0.

c $y = 4 - 3x$

Here $m = -3$, $b = 4$.
The gradient is -3 and the y-intercept is 4.

WORKED EXAMPLE 2

Find the gradient and y-intercept from the graph and write the equation of the line.

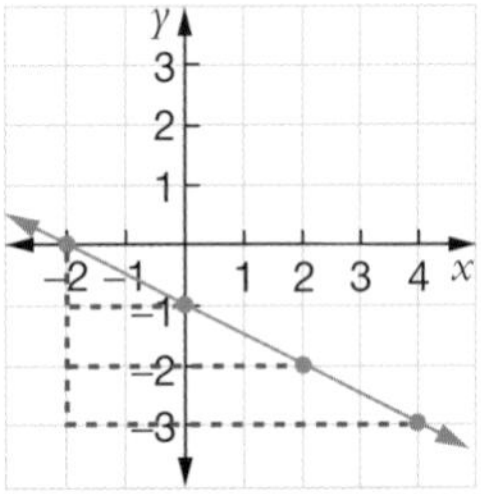

This line is 'falling', so, the gradient is negative.

From the graph:
For every run of 2 there is a fall of 1,
gradient $= -\frac{1}{2}$
y-intercept $= -1$
$\therefore$ Equation of the line is $y = -\frac{1}{2}x - 1$.

WORKED EXAMPLE 3

Change the equation into the form $y = mx + b$ to find the gradient and y-intercept of the following.

a $2y = 4x + 3$

$2y = 4x + 3$
$\div 2 \quad \div 2 \quad \div 2$
$y = 2x + 1\frac{1}{2}$

$\therefore$ gradient $= 2$
y-intercept $= 1\frac{1}{2}$

b $3x + y = 1$

$3x + y = 1$
$-3x \qquad -3x$
$y = 1 - 3x$

$\therefore$ gradient $= -3$
y-intercept $= 1$

c $2x - 3y + 6 = 0$

$2x - 3y + 6 = 0$
$+3y \qquad +3y$
$2x + 6 = 3y$
$\div 3 \quad \div 3 \quad \div 3$
$\frac{2}{3}x + 2 = y$

$\therefore$ gradient $= \frac{2}{3}$
y-intercept $= 2$

WORKED EXAMPLE 4

Use the y-intercept and gradient to graph the line $y = 3x - 2$.

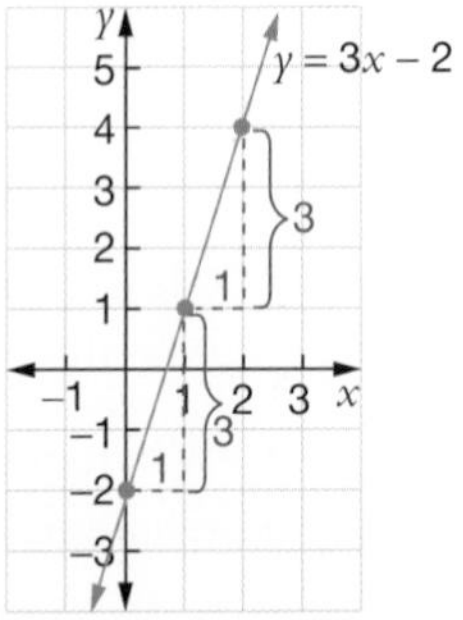

Start at the y-intercept of -2.

Now gradient $= \frac{\text{rise}}{\text{run}} = 3 = \frac{3}{1}$

$\therefore$ For every run of 1 there is a rise of 3.

WORKED EXAMPLE 5

Use the y-intercept and gradient to graph the line $4x + y = 2$.
First, rearrange the equation.

$$4x + y = 2$$
$$\quad -4x \quad -4x$$
$$y = -4x + 2$$

Then graph the line using the y-intercept of 2 and gradient of -4.

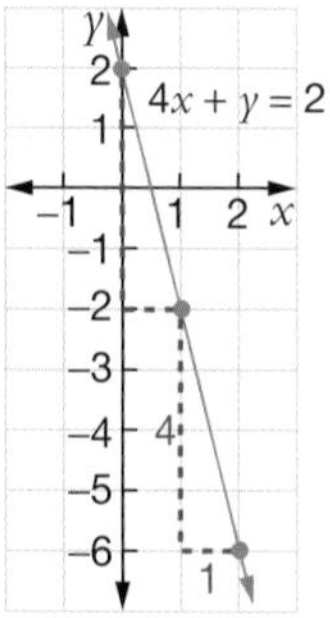

Remember! A negative gradient always slopes down to the right.

Exercise 9:05

P Foundation worksheet 9:05 Gradient–intercept form

1 What are the gradient and y-intercept of each of the following lines?

a $y = 2x + 3$	b $y = 5x + 1$	c $y = 3x + 2$	d $y = 1x + 6$
e $y = 4x + 0$	f $y = x$	g $y = x - 2$	h $y = 5x - 1$
i $y = 6x - 4$	j $y = -2x + 3$	k $y = -x - 2$	l $y = -3x + 1$
m $y = \frac{1}{2}x + 4$	n $y = \frac{3}{4}x - 2$	o $y = \dfrac{x}{3} + 5$	p $y = 4 - 3x$
q $y = -2 + 4x$	r $y = 3 - \frac{1}{2}x$		

2 Find the equation of the line that has:

a a gradient of 4 and a y-intercept of 9
b a gradient of -2 and a y-intercept of 3
c a gradient of 7 and a y-intercept of -1
d a gradient of -5 and a y-intercept of -2
e a gradient of $\frac{1}{2}$ and a y-intercept of 5
f a gradient of $\frac{2}{3}$ and a y-intercept of -4
g a y-intercept of 1 and a gradient of 3
h a y-intercept of -3 and a gradient of 2
i a y-intercept of $\frac{1}{2}$ and a gradient of 5
j a gradient of 1 and a y-intercept of $1\frac{1}{2}$

y = mx + b
½x + 5 = x/2 + 5

3 For each diagram find the gradient and the y-intercept and use these to write the equation of each line.

a
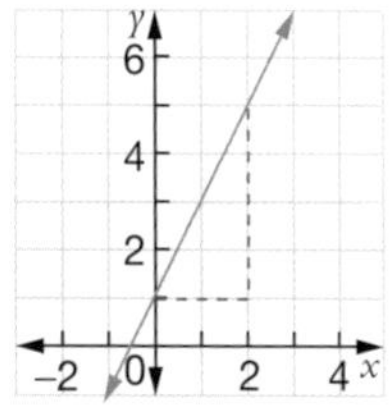

b
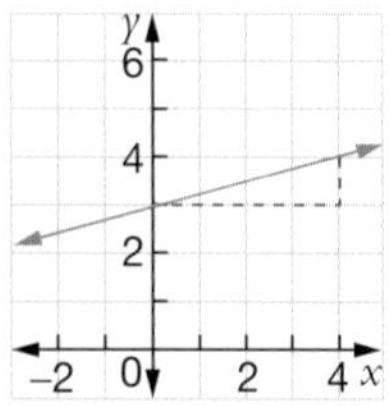

c
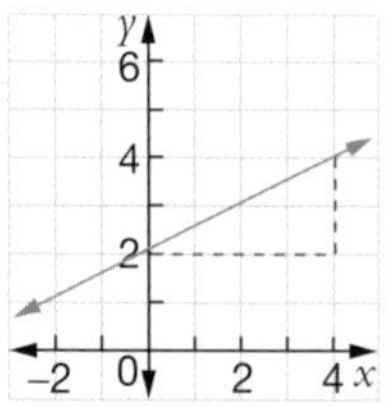

d
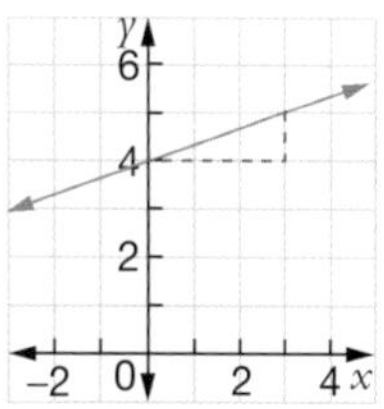

e

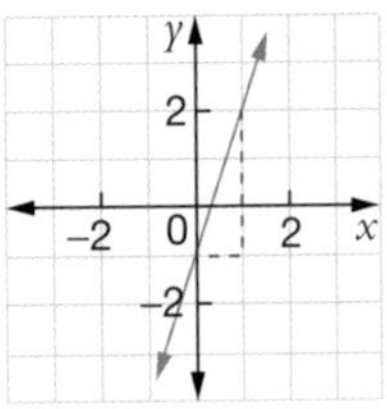

f

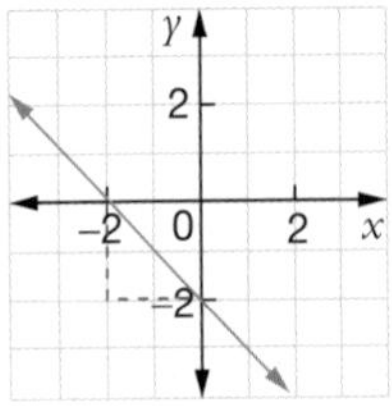

g

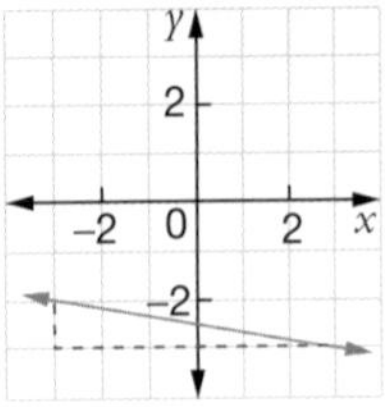

h

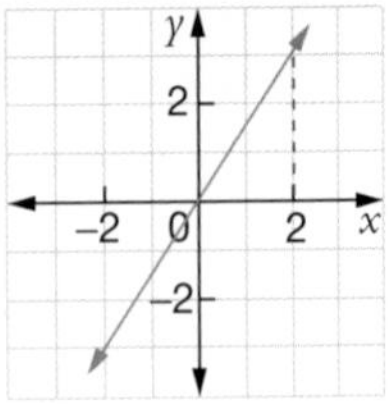

4 Match the graphs A to G with the equations below.

a $y = x$

b $y = 6 - 2x$

c $y = x + 2$

d $y = -2$

e $y = \frac{1}{2}x - 3$

f $y = -2x + 2$

g $y = 2x + 2$

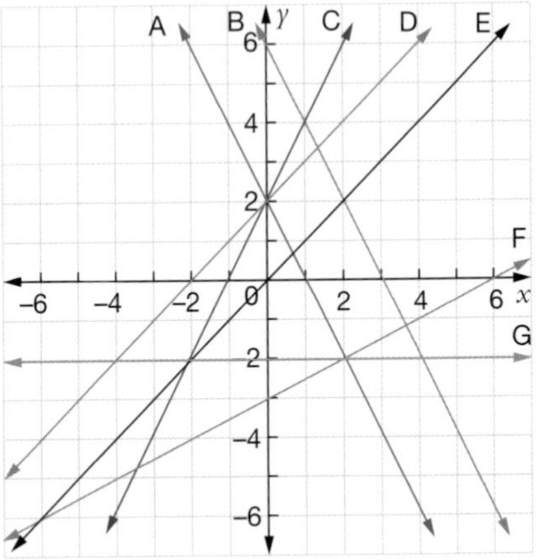

5 By first changing the equation into the form $y = mx + b$, find the gradient and y-intercept of the following.

a $2y = 4x + 10$

$\div 2 \qquad \div 2$

$y = \ldots$

$\therefore$ gradient is …

y-intercept is …

b $y + 3 = 3x$

$-3 \qquad -3$

$y = \ldots$

$\therefore$ gradient is …

y-intercept is …

c $\frac{y}{2} = x + 2$

$\times 2 \qquad \times 2$

$y = \ldots$

$\therefore$ gradient is …

y-intercept is …

d $3y = 6x - 3$

e $y - 8 = 5x$

f $\frac{y}{3} = 2x - 4$

g $4y = 12x - 8$

h $y + 4 = -2x$

i $y - 2x = 7$

j $x + y = 4$

k $2y = x + 3$

l $3x + y = 5$

m $6x + 2y = 4$

$-6x \qquad -6x$

$2y = \ldots$

$\div 2 \qquad \div 2$

$y = \ldots$

$\therefore$ gradient is …

y-intercept is …

n $3x + 2y = 6$

$-3x \qquad -3x$

$2y = \ldots$

$\div 2 \qquad \div 2$

$y = \ldots$

$\therefore$ gradient is …

y-intercept is …

o $2x - 5y + 1 = 0$

$+5y \qquad +5y$

$\ldots = 5y$

$\div 5 \qquad \div 5$

$\ldots = y$

$\therefore$ gradient is …

y-intercept is …

6 Lines with the same gradient are parallel. Are the following pairs of lines parallel or not?

a $y = 3x + 2$ and $y = 3x - 1$

b $y = 5x - 2$ and $y = 2x - 5$

c $y = x + 7$ and $y = x + 1$

d $y = x - 3$ and $y = 1x + 2$

7 a Which of the following lines are parallel to $y = 2x + 3$?

$y = 3x + 2$ $\qquad$ $2x - y + 6 = 0$

$2y = x + 3$ $\qquad$ $y = 2x - 3$

b Two of the following lines are parallel. Which are they?

$y = x - 3 \qquad x + y = 3 \qquad y = 3x \qquad 3y = x \qquad y = -x + 8$

If two lines are parallel, they have the same gradient.

8 Draw the graph of each line on a separate number plane by following these steps. (Look at Worked Example 4.)

- Mark the y-intercept (the value of b) on the y-axis.
- 'Count' the gradient (the value of m) from this point, and mark a second point.
- Draw a line through this second point and the y-intercept.

a $y = 2x + 1$ b $y = x + 2$ c $y = 3x - 1$
d $y = -2x - 1$ e $y = -x + 1$ f $y = -3x - 3$
g $y = \frac{1}{2}x + 2$ h $y = \frac{1}{3}x - 1$ i $y = \frac{3}{2}x$
j $y = -\frac{1}{2}x + 1$ k $y = -\frac{1}{3}x$ l $y = -\frac{3}{2}x - 1$

9 a Graph lines with a y-intercept of 1 and a gradient of 0, 1, 2 and −1 on the same number plane.
b Graph lines with a slope of −1 and y-intercepts of −2, 0, 1 and 2 on the same number plane.

10 The equation of each line has been given in general form. Find the gradient of each line by rearranging the equation into gradient–intercept form.

a $2x + y + 6 = 0$ b $4x - 2y + 5 = 0$ c $x + 2y + 1 = 0$
d $4x - 3y + 6 = 0$ e $4x - y + 3 = 0$ f $x + 3y - 6 = 0$

P GEOGEBRA ACTIVITY 9:05 EQUATIONS OF A LINE

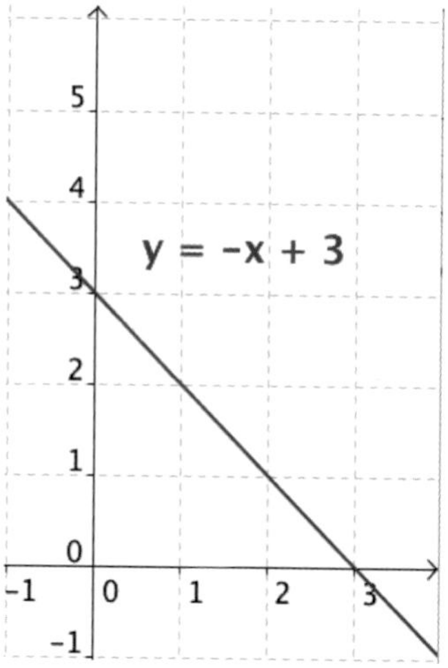

1 **Finding the equation of a line**
In this activity a line is generated randomly. Find the gradient and y-intercept of the line and use these to write its equation in the form $y = mx + b$. Tick a checkbox to see if the equation is correct.

2 **Equations of the form $y = mx + b$**
Use sliders to vary the values of m and b on a blue line. As these values are varied you can analyse the effect that each has on the shape of the graph. You can then find the equation of a randomly produced red line. Use the sliders to change the values of m and b on the blue line until it coincides with the red line.

3 **Graphing lines using $y = mx + b$**
In this activity you are given an equation and asked to graph the line by first dragging a point to the y-intercept. A gradient triangle and a line appears when this is done correctly. The gradient triangle is used to find another point on the line. When this is successful, the line changes colour.

4 **Matching equations of lines to their graphs**
The graphs and equations of four different lines are given for you to match each equation to its graph. You can then check the solutions and generate a new set of lines and equations.

9:06 The equation of a straight line, given point and gradient

PREP QUIZ 9:06

A line has the equation $y = 3x + 5$. Find:

1 its gradient
2 its y-intercept
3 the value of y when $x = 2$
4 the value of x when $y = 5$.

If $y = mx + c$, find the value of c if:

5 $m = 2, x = 0, y = 4$
6 $m = -2, x = 1, y = 3$
7 $m = 3, x = -1, y = -2$
8 $m = -2, x = -4, y = 10$
9 $m = 0, x = 2, y = 3$
10 $m = 1, x = 2, y = 2$

Any number of lines can be drawn through a given point. Each of these lines has a different gradient, so the equation of a straight line can be found if we know its gradient and a point through which it passes.

The equation of a line that passes through the point $(1, 2)$ and has a gradient of 3 can be found using the equation $y = mx + b$. We know that $m = 3$, but we must also find the value of b. To do this, we substitute the coordinates of $(1, 2)$ into the equation, as a point on the line must satisfy its equation.

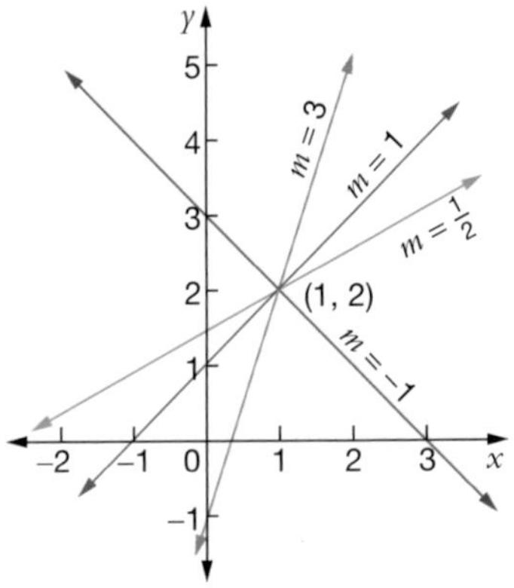

$y = mx + b$

$\therefore\ y = 3x + b$ $\quad$ $m = 3$ is given

$2 = 3(1) + b$ $\quad$ $(1, 2)$ lies on the line

$2 = 3 + b$

$\therefore\ b = -1$

$\therefore$ The equation of the line is $y = 3x - 1$.

> To find the equation of a straight line that has a gradient of 2 and passes through $(7, 5)$:
> **1** Substitute $m = 2$, $x = 7$ and $y = 5$ into the formula $y = mx + b$ to find the value of b.
> **2** Rewrite $y = mx + b$, replacing m and b with their numerical values.

We can use the method above to discover a formula that could be used instead.

The equation of a line that has a gradient m and passes through the point (x_1, y_1) can be found using the equation $y = mx + b$.

$y = mx + b$ $\quad$ gradient is m

$\therefore\ y_1 = mx_1 + b$ $\quad$ (x_1, y_1) lies on the line

$\therefore\ b = y_1 - mx_1$

$\therefore$ The equation of the line is

$y = mx + (y_1 - mx_1)$

$y - y_1 = mx - mx_1$

$\therefore\ y - y_1 = m(x - x_1)$

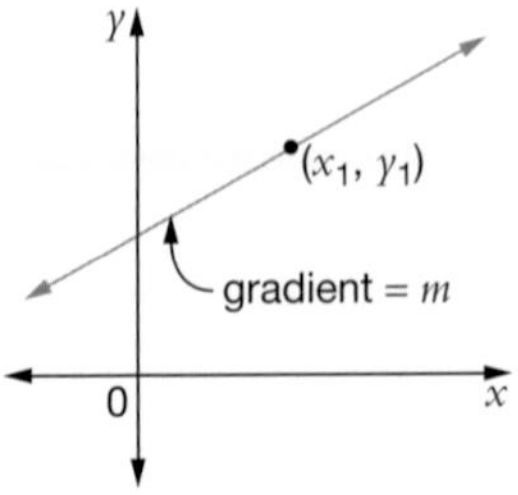

This last form of the answer is the easiest to remember as it could be written as $\dfrac{y-y_1}{x-x_1}=m$.

The equation of a line with gradient m that passes through the point (x_1, y_1) is given by:

$y-y_1=m(x-x_1)$ or $\dfrac{y-y_1}{x-x_1}=m$.

WORKED EXAMPLES

1 Find the equation of the line that passes through (1, 4) and has gradient 2.

2 A straight line has gradient $-\frac{1}{2}$ and passes through the point (1, 3). Find the equation of this line.

You can use either formula.
y − y1 = m(x − x1) or y = mx + b

Solutions

1 Let the equation of the line be:

$y = mx + b$

$\therefore y = 2x + b$ $m = 2$ is given

$4 = 2(1) + b$ (1, 4) lies on the line

$4 = 2 + b$

$\therefore b = 2$

$\therefore$ The equation is $y = 2x + 2$.

Or 1 $y-y_1=m(x-x_1)$

(x_1, y_1) is (1, 4), $m = 2$

$\therefore y-4=2(x-1)$

$y-4=2x-2$

$\therefore y=2x+2$ is the equation of the line.

2 Let the equation be:

$y = mx + b$

$\therefore y=-\frac{1}{2}x+b$ $m=-\frac{1}{2}$ is given

$3=-\frac{1}{2}(1)+b$ (1, 3) is on the line

$3=-\frac{1}{2}+b$

$\therefore b=3\frac{1}{2}$

$\therefore$ The equation is $y=-\frac{1}{2}x+3\frac{1}{2}$.

Or 2 $y-y_1=m(x-x_1)$

(x_1, y_1) is (1, 3), $m=-\frac{1}{2}$

$\therefore y-3=-\frac{1}{2}(x-1)$

$y-3=-\frac{1}{2}x+\frac{1}{2}$

$\therefore y=-\frac{1}{2}x+3\frac{1}{2}$ is the equation of the line.

Exercise 9:06

P Foundation worksheet 9:06 Point–gradient form

1 For each part, find b if the given point lies on the given line.

a $(1, 3)$, $y = 2x + b$ b $(2, 10)$, $y = 4x + b$ c $(-1, 3)$, $y = 2x + b$

d $(5, 5)$, $y = 2x + b$ e $(3, 1)$, $y = x + b$ f $(-1, -9)$, $y = -2x + b$

2 Find the equation of the straight line (giving answers in the form $y = mx + b$) if it has:

a gradient 2 and passes through the point (1, 3)
b gradient 5 and passes through the point (0, 0)
c gradient 3 and passes through the point (2, 2)
d slope 4 and passes through the point (−1, 6)
e gradient −1 and passes through the point (−2, 8)
f gradient −2 and passes through the point (0, 7)
g slope −5 and passes through the point (1, 0)
h gradient $\frac{1}{2}$ and passes through the point (4, 5)
i gradient $\frac{1}{4}$ and passes through the point $(6, 3\frac{1}{2})$
j slope $-\frac{1}{2}$ and passes through the point (−4, −1).

'Slope' is another name for 'gradient'.

3 a A straight line has a gradient of 2 and passes through the point (3, 2). Find the equation of the line.
b A straight line has a gradient of −1. If the line passes through the point (2, 1), find the equation of the line.
c What is the equation of a straight line that passes through the point (−2, 0) and has a gradient of 3?
d A straight line that passes through the point (1, −2) has a gradient of −3. What is the equation of this line?
e A straight line that has a gradient of 3 passes through the origin. What is the equation of this line?
f Find the equation of the straight line that has a gradient of 4 and passes through the point (−1, −2).
g (2, 8) is on a line that has a gradient of 4. Find the equation of this line.
h The point (−6, 4) lies on a straight line that has a gradient of −2. What is the equation of this line?
i Find the equation of the straight line that has a gradient of 2 and passes through the midpoint of the interval joining (1, 3) and (5, 5).
j A straight line passes through the midpoint of the interval joining (0, 0) and (−6, 4). Find the equation of the line if its gradient is $\frac{1}{2}$.

9:07 The equation of a straight line, given two points

Only one straight line can be drawn through two points. Given two points on a straight line, we can always find the equation of that line.

Consider the line passing through (1, 1) and (2, 4). Let the equation of the line be:
$y = mx + b$ (formula)

First find the gradient using the two points.

$$m = \frac{y_2 - y_1}{x_2 - x_1} \qquad (x_1, y_1) = (1, 1)$$
$$= \frac{4-1}{2-1} \qquad (x_2, y_2) = (2, 4)$$
$$= 3$$

$\therefore\ y = 3x + b \qquad m = 3$

$4 = 3(2 + b) \qquad$ (2, 4) lies on the line

$\therefore\ b = -2$

$\therefore$ The equation of the line is $y = 3x - 2$.

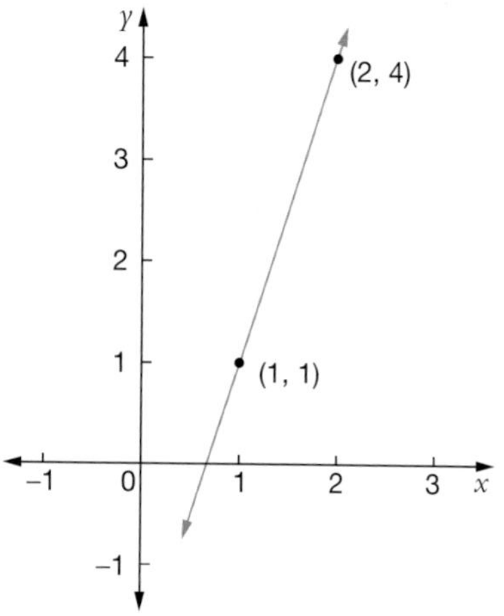

To find the equation of a straight line that passes through the two points (1, 2) and (3, 6):

1. Find the value of the gradient m, using the given points.
2. For $y = mx + b$, find the value of b by substituting the value of m and the coordinates of one of the given points.
3. Rewrite $y = mx + b$ replacing m and b with their numerical values.

Another method is to use the formula: $y - y_1 = \frac{y_2 - y_1}{x_2 - x_1}(x - x_1)$, where (x_1, y_1) and (x_2, y_2) are points on the line.

WORKED EXAMPLE

Find the equation of the line that passes through the points (−1, 2) and (2, 8).

Solution

Let the equation of the line be:

$y = mx + b$

Now $m = \frac{y_2 - y_1}{x_2 - x_1} \qquad (x_1, y_1) = (-1, 2)$

$= \frac{8-2}{2-(-1)} \qquad (x_2, y_2) = (2, 8)$

$= \frac{6}{3}$

$\therefore\ m = 2$

$\therefore\ y = 2x + b \qquad m = 2$

(2, 8) lies on the line.

$\therefore\ 8 = 2(2) + b$

$\therefore\ b = 4$

$\therefore$ The equation is $y = 2x + 4$.

Or

$y - y_1 = \frac{y_2 - y_1}{x_2 - x_1}(x - x_1)$

(x_1, y_1) is (−1, 2), (x_2, y_2) is (2, 8)

$\therefore\ y - 2 = \frac{8-2}{2-(-1)}[x - (-1)]$

$y - 2 = \frac{6}{3}(x + 1)$

$y - 2 = 2(x + 1)$

$y - 2 = 2x + 2$

$\therefore\ y = 2x + 4$ is the equation of the line.

Exercise 9:07

1 Find the gradient of the line that passes through the points:

a (2, 0) and (3, 4)
b (−1, 3) and (2, 6)
c (3, 1) and (1, 5)
d (−2, −1) and (0, 9)
e (−2, 1) and (2, 2)
f (5, 2) and (4, 3)
g (0, 0) and (1, 3)
h (1, 1) and (4, 4)
i (−1, 8) and (1, −2)
j (0, 0) and (1, −3)

2 Find the equations of the lines that pass through each pair of points in Question 1.

3 a Find the equation of the line that passes through the points (−2, −2) and (1, 4).
b The points $A(4, 3)$ and $B(5, 0)$ lie on the line AB. What is the equation of AB?
c What is the equation of the line AB if A is the point (−2, −4) and B is (2, 12)?
d Find the equation of the line that passes through the points (1, 6) and (2, 8). By substitution in this equation, show that (3, 10) also lies on this line.
e What is the equation of the line CD if C is the point (2, 3) and D is the point (4, 5)?

4 A is the point (−2, 1), B is the point (1, 4) and C is the point (3, −2).
a Find the gradient of each side of ΔABC.
b Find the equation of each of the lines AB, BC and AC.
c Find the y-intercept of each of the lines AB, BC and AC.
d Find the equation of the line passing through point A and the midpoint of interval BC.
e Find the gradient and y-intercept of the line passing through point A and the midpoint of interval BC.

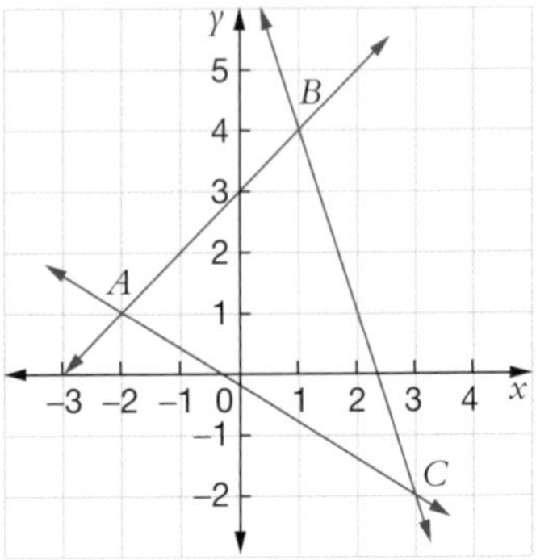

5 a Find the equation of the line joining $A(1, 2)$ and $B(5, -6)$. Hence, show that $C(3, -2)$ also lies on this line.
b $A(-2, 2)$, $B(1, -4)$ and $C(3, -8)$ are points on the number plane. Show that they are collinear.
c Show that the points (−2, −11), (3, 4) and (4, 7) are collinear.

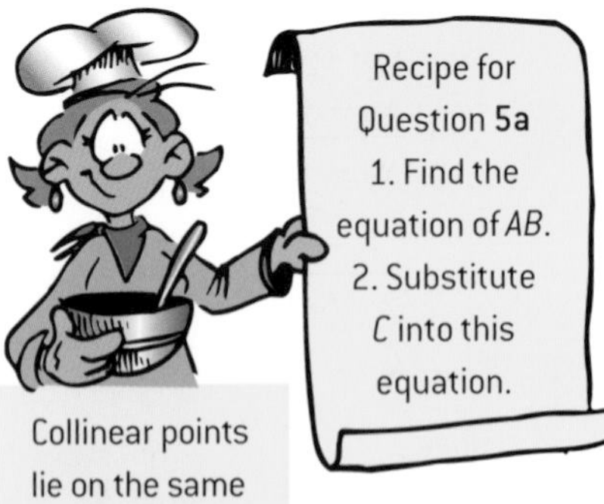

Recipe for Question 5a
1. Find the equation of AB.
2. Substitute C into this equation.

Collinear points lie on the same straight line.

6 Find the equation in general form of the lines that pass through the points:
a (3, −2) and (−4, 1)
b (−2, −4) and (3, 2)
c (1·3, −2·6) and (4, −7·3)
d $(1\frac{1}{2}, -\frac{2}{3})$ and $(-2\frac{1}{3}, \frac{1}{2})$

FUN SPOT 9:07 WHY DID THE BANANA GO OUT WITH A FIG?

Answer each question and write the letter for that question in the box above the correct answer.

For the points $A(2, 5)$, $B(-1, 3)$, $C(4, 2)$, $D(0, 6)$, find:

E distance AC
E distance CD
E distance BD
A slope of AB
A slope of AD
T slope of BC
T midpoint of DC
N midpoint of AC
I midpoint of AB

Find the gradient of the following lines.

C $y = 2x - 1$
U $2y = x - 5$
G $2x + y + 1 = 0$

Find the y-intercept of the following lines.

D $y = 2x - 1$
T $2y = x - 5$
L $2x + y - 1 = 0$

Find the equation of the line with:

C gradient of 2 and a y-intercept of -1
O slope of 3 and a y-intercept of 5
T y-intercept of 4 and a slope of -2
S y-intercept of -2 and a slope of 4.

Write in the form $y = mx + b$.

B $2x - y - 5 = 0$
E $2x - y + 5 = 0$
A $x = \frac{1}{2}y - 2$

In the diagram, find:

D the slope of AB
U coordinates of C.

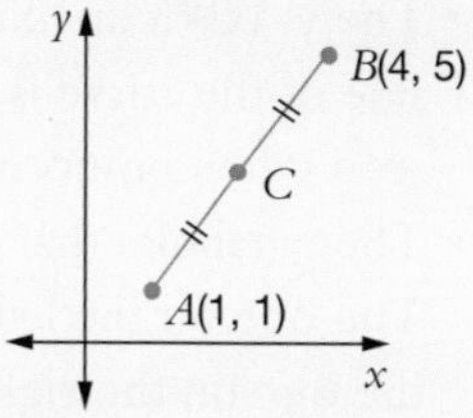

$y = 2x - 5$	$y = 2x + 5$	2	$-\frac{1}{2}$	$\frac{1}{2}$	$y = 4x - 2$	$\sqrt{13}$	$(\frac{1}{2}, 4)$	$(2, 4)$	$y = 2x - 1$	$y = 3x + 5$	$(2\frac{1}{2}, 3)$	1	-1	$(3, 3\frac{1}{2})$	$-\frac{1}{5}$	-2	$\sqrt{10}$	$-2\frac{1}{2}$	$\frac{2}{3}$	$\frac{4}{3}$	$y = 2x + 4$	$y = 4 - 2x$	$\sqrt{32}$

How many times in a day are the minute and hour hands of the clock at right angles?

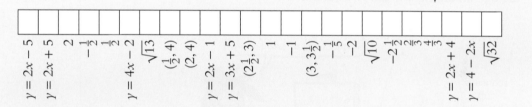

9:08 Non-linear graphs

Up to this point, all the graphs have been straight lines. There are many types of mathematical curves and in this section we will look at two of them, the parabola and the exponential curve.

Parabolas

- The equations of parabolas can be identified because they have x^2 as the highest power of x.
  The simplest equation of a parabola is $y = x^2$.
- As with the straight line, the equation is used to find the points on the curve. Some of these are shown in the table.

$y = x^2$

x	−3	−2	−1	0	1	2	3
y	9	4	1	0	1	4	9

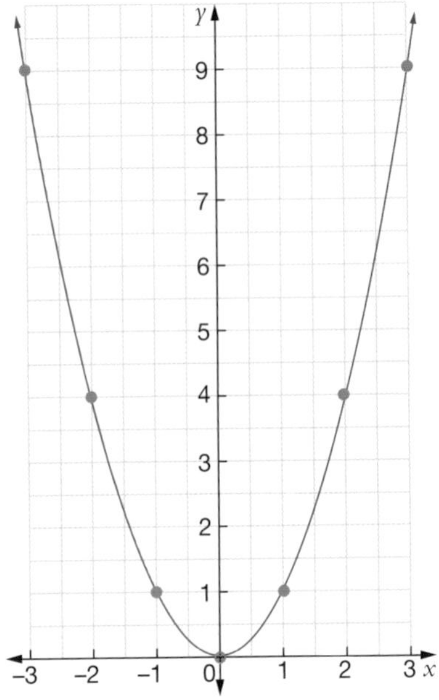

For an accurate graph, many points would have to be plotted.

- From the graph, we can see that the parabola has a turning point, or vertex, which is the minimum value of y on $y = x^2$.
- The y-axis is an axis of symmetry of the curve, so the right side of the curve is a reflection of the left side. This can be seen when points on either side of the axis are compared.
- The parabolas that we will consider have two basic shapes. The one on the left below is said to be concave up, whereas the one on the right is said to be concave down.

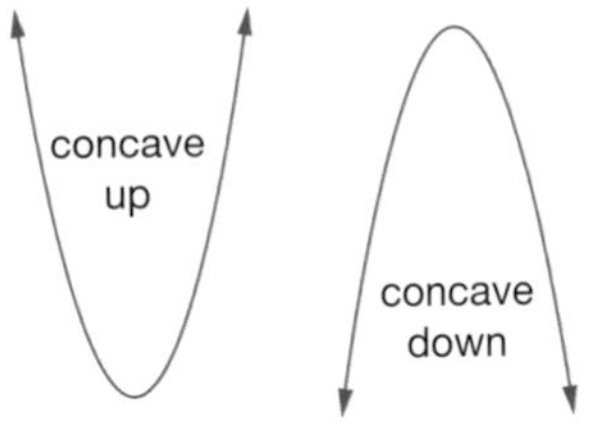

Parabolas can be happy (up) or sad (down)

Exponential graphs

- The simplest exponential equation is $y = 2^x$.
  Notice that in this equation x is a power, and hence there is a connection with the topic of Indices (see Chapter 6).
  Again, a table of values is used to find points that lie on the curve.

$y = 2^x$

x	−3	−2	−1	0	1	2	3
y	0·125	0·25	0·5	1	2	4	8

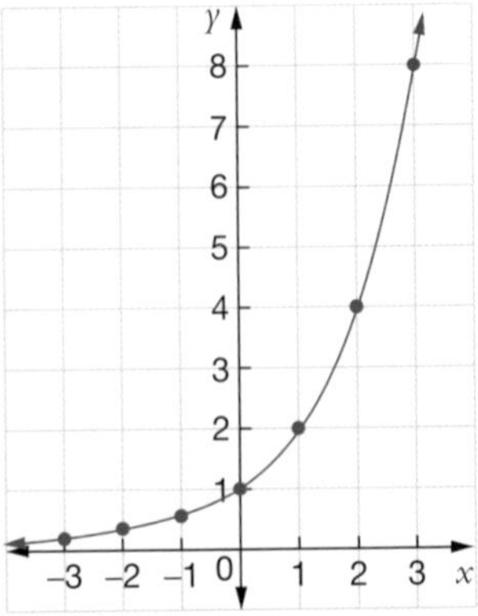

- When plotting points it is often necessary to round the y-values to one decimal place.
- Notice what happens to the y-values of the points as the x-values increase and decrease.

Exercise 9:08

1 Copy and complete the following tables. By comparing the values obtained with the given graphs, find which of the graphs A to C would result from plotting each set of points.

a $y = x^2 + 1$

x	−3	−2	−1	0	1	2	3
y							

b $y = x^2 - 1$

x	−3	−2	−1	0	1	2	3
y							

c $y = x^2 + 2$

x	−3	−2	−1	0	1	2	3
y							

A
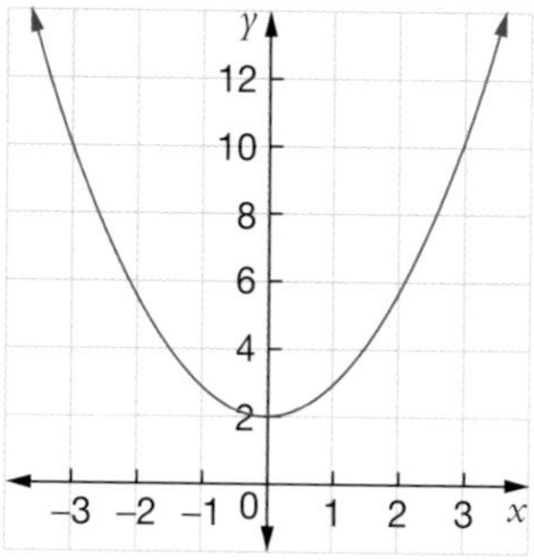

B
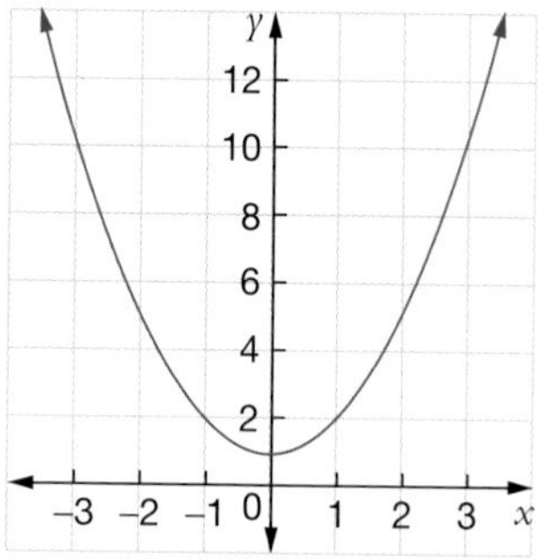

C
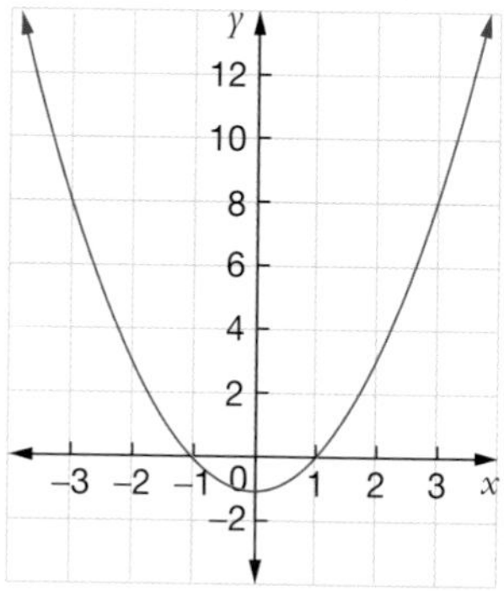

2 Complete a table of values ranging from $x = -3$ to $x = 3$ for the parabola $y = x^2 - 2$ and use the values obtained to graph the equation.

3 a What are the coordinates of the vertex for each of the parabolas in question 1?
b Is the vertex also the y-intercept of the parabola?
c Are the parabolas symmetrical?
d Does the vertex lie on the axis of symmetry?

4 Complete a table of values ranging from $x = -3$ to $x = 3$ for each of the following equations. State which of the graphs E, F or G would be obtained by plotting those points.

a $y = -x^2$ b $y = -x^2 + 1$ c $y = -x^2 - 2$

E
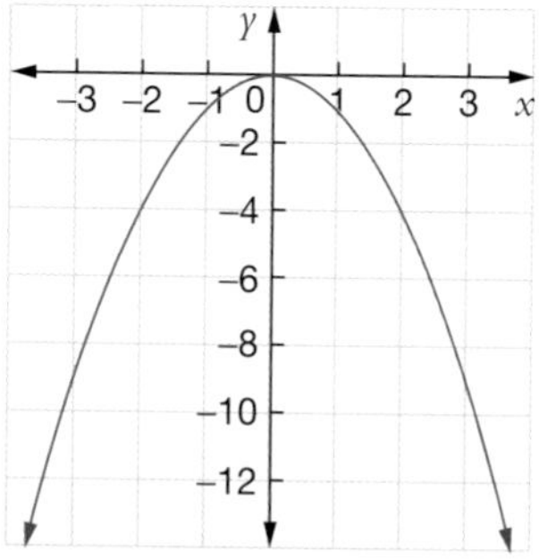

F
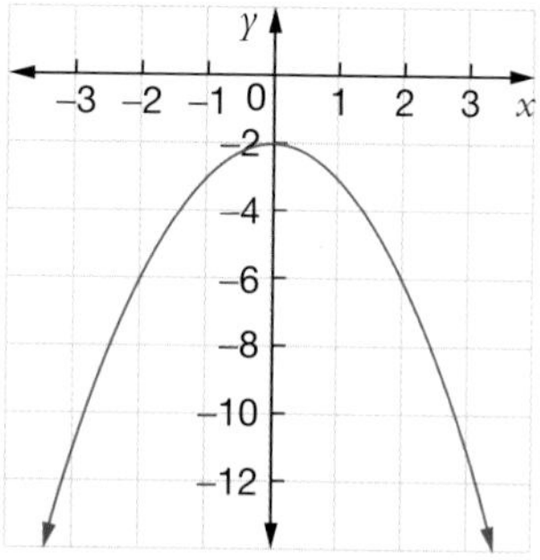

G
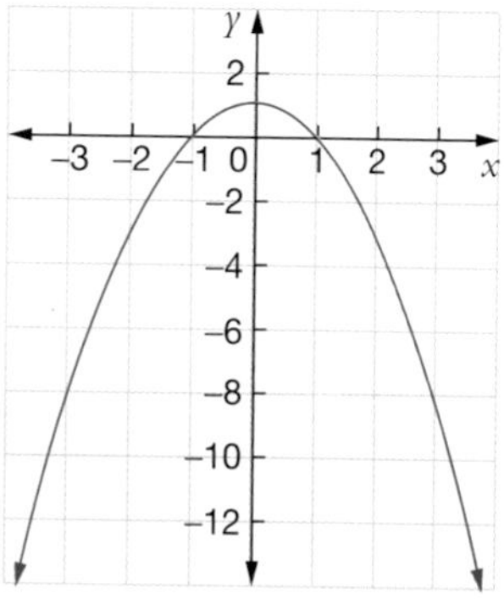

5 a Write the coordinates of the vertex for each of the parabolas in question **4**.
b Is the vertex also the y-intercept of the parabola?
c Are the parabolas symmetrical?
d Does the vertex lie on the axis of symmetry?

6 For each of the following, complete a table of values and use it to state the graph (A, B, C or D) that matches the equation.
a $y = x^2 + 3$
b $y = 1 - x^2$
c $y = x^2 - 4$
d $y = -x^2 + 4$

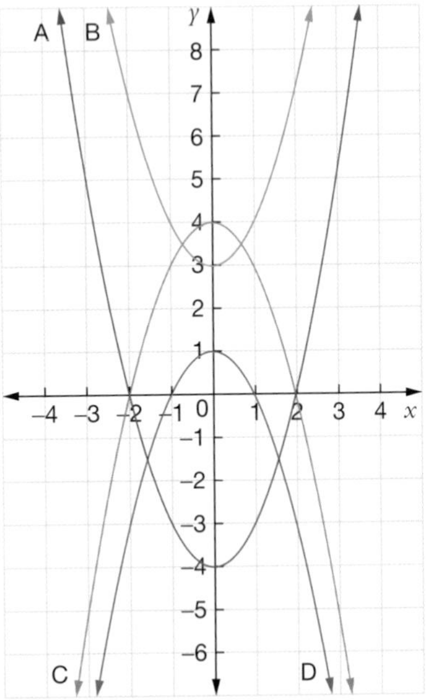

7 Using the results from Questions **1** to **6**, how can you use the equation of a parabola to tell if the parabola is concave up or concave down?

8 Using a table of values ranging from −3 to 3, graph each of the following equations.
a $y = 3 - x^2$
b $y = x^2 + 4$
c $y = -x^2 - 1$

9 Copy and complete each of the following table of values. Which of the exponential graphs E, F, G or H would result from plotting that set of points?

a $y = 2^x$

x	−3	−2	−1	0	1	2	3
y							

b $y = 2^{-x}$

x	−3	−2	−1	0	1	2	3
y							

c $y = -2^x$

x	−3	−2	−1	0	1	2	3
y							

d $y = -2^{-x}$

x	−3	−2	−1	0	1	2	3
y							

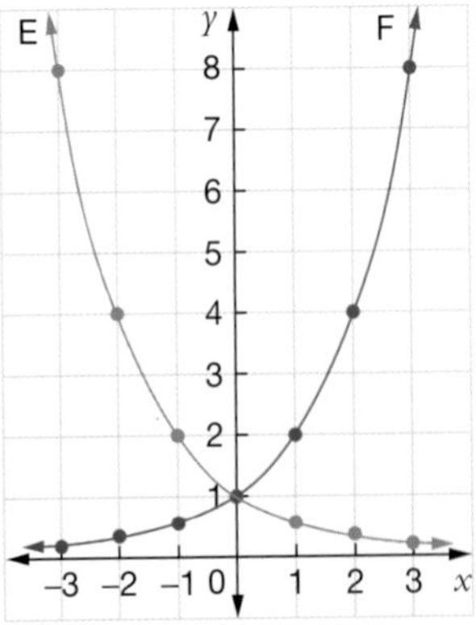

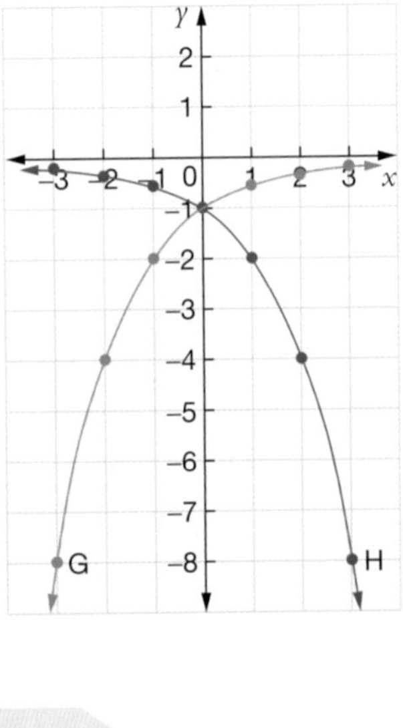

10 By finding suitable points, match each equation with one of the exponential curves A to D.

a $y = -1 + 2^x$

b $y = 4 + 2^{-x}$

c $y = -2^x + 2$

d $y = 2 - 2^{-x}$

Hint: Use the equations to find the y-intercept for each curve. If these are the same, find another point.

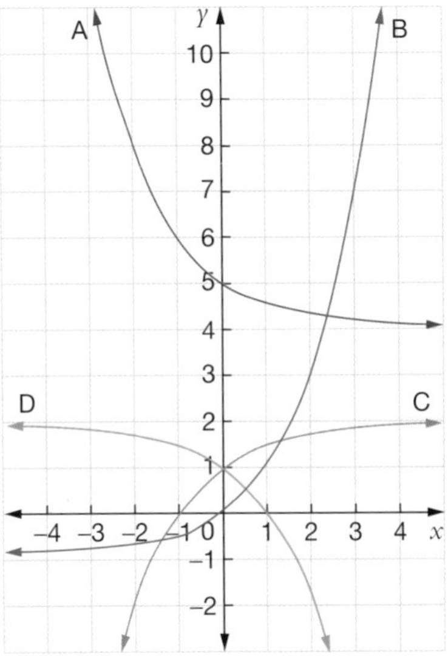

P GEOGEBRA ACTIVITY 9:08 NON-LINEAR GRAPHS

1 **Graphing parabolas**

The equations of two parabolas that are given can be varied by using sliders. After completing a table of values the points can be plotted via the Input bar. Tick the checkbox to reveal the graph and show whether the points have been plotted accurately.

2 **Exponential curves**

This is similar to Activity 1 but uses exponential curves rather than parabolas.

3 **Matching parabolas to their equations**

The equations of five parabolas and their graphs are given and you are asked to match each parabola to its equation. Tick a checkbox to show the correct answer. A new set of equations and parabolas can be randomly generated.

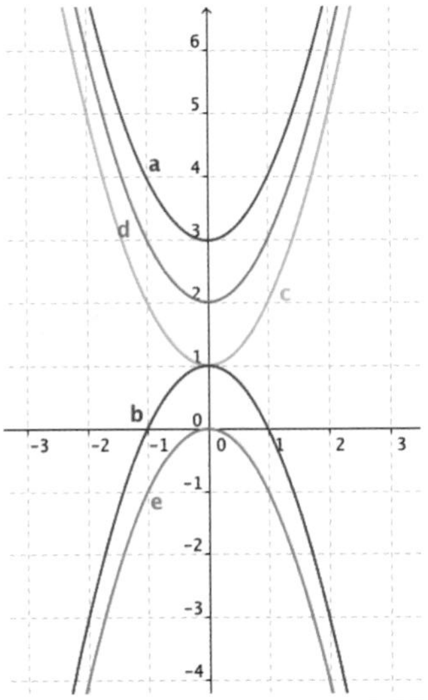

MATHS TERMS 9

coefficient

- the number that multiplies a pronumeral in an equation,
  e.g. $3x - 5y = 6$
  coefficient of x is 3
  coefficient of y is -5

coordinates

- a pair of numbers that gives the position of a point in a number plane relative to the origin
- the first of the coordinates is the x-coordinate. It tells how far right (or left) the point is from the origin
- the second of the coordinates is called the y-coordinate. It tells how far the point is above (or below) the origin

constant
- the number part of an equation or expression,
  e.g. $3x - 5y = 6$
  The constant is 6

distance formula
- gives the distance between the points (x_1, y_1) and (x_2, y_2)

$$d = \sqrt{(x_2 - x_1)^2 + (y_2 - y_1)^2}$$

general form
- a way of writing the equation of a line
- the equation is written in the form $ax + by + c = 0$, where a, b, c are integers and $a > 0$

gradient
- the slope of a line or interval; it can be measured using the formula:

$$\text{Gradient} = \frac{\text{rise}}{\text{run}}$$

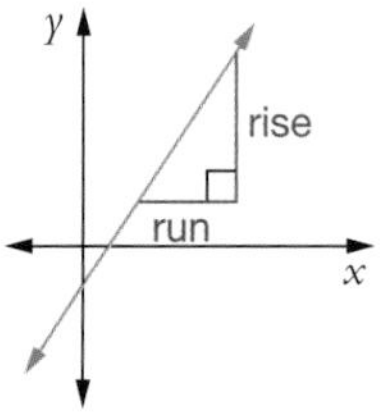

gradient formula
- gives the gradient of the interval joining (x_1, y_1) to (x_2, y_2)

$$m = \frac{y_2 - y_1}{x_2 - x_1}$$

gradient-intercept form
- a way of writing the equation of a line, e.g. $y = 2x - 5$, $y = \frac{1}{2}x + 2$
  when an equation is rearranged and written in the form $y = mx + b$ then m is the gradient and b is the y-intercept

graph (noun)
- a diagram showing the relationship between two variable quantities, usually shown on a number plane

graph (verb)
- to plot the points that lie on a line or curve

interval
- the part of a line between two points

midpoint
- point marking the middle of an interval

midpoint formula
- gives the midpoint of the interval joining (x_1, y_1) to (x_2, y_2)

$$\text{Midpoint} = \left(\frac{x_1 + x_2}{2}, \frac{y_1 + y_2}{2}\right)$$

number plane
- a rectangular grid that allows the position of points to be identified by an ordered pair of numbers

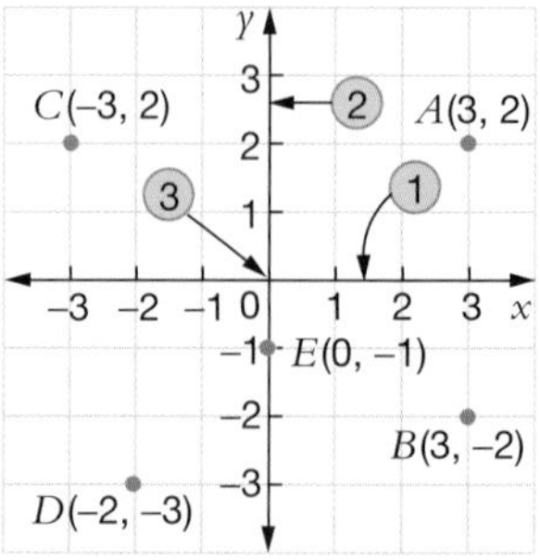

origin
- the point where the x-axis and y-axis intersect, (0, 0); see ③ in *number plane*

plot
- to mark the position of a point on the number plane

quadrants
- the four quarters that the number plane is divided into by the x- and y-axes

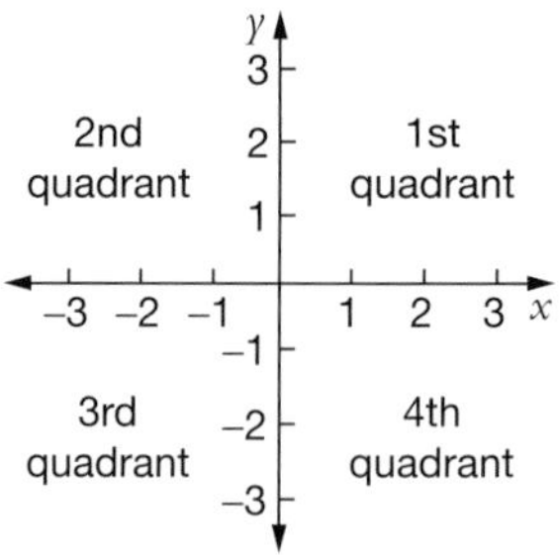

x-axis
- the horizontal number line in a number plane; see ① in *number plane*

x-intercept
- the point where a line or curve crosses the x-axis

y-axis
- the vertical number line in a number plane; see ② in *number plane*

y-intercept
- the point where a line or curve crosses the y-axis

DIAGNOSTIC TEST 9 COORDINATE GEOMETRY

These questions reflect the important skills introduced in this chapter.
Errors made will indicate areas of weakness.
Each weakness should be treated by going back to the section listed.

1 Find the length of the interval AB in each of the following. (Leave answers in surd form.) 9:01

a
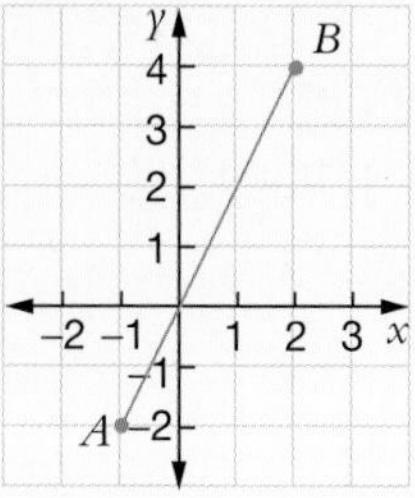

b
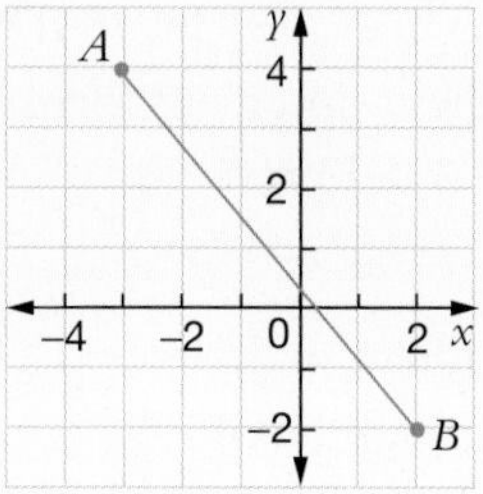

c
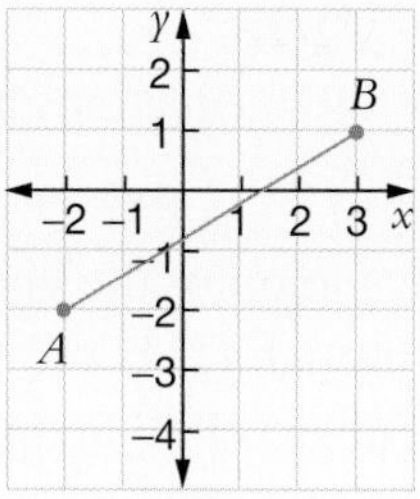

2 Use the distance formula to find the distance between each pair of points. 9:01

a (1, 2) and (7, 10) b (3, 0) and (5, 3) c (−3, −2) and (1, −3)

3 Find the midpoint of the interval joining each pair of points. 9:02

a (1, 2) and (7, 10) b (3, 0) and (5, 3) c (−3, −2) and (1, −3)

4 What is the gradient of each line? 9:03

a
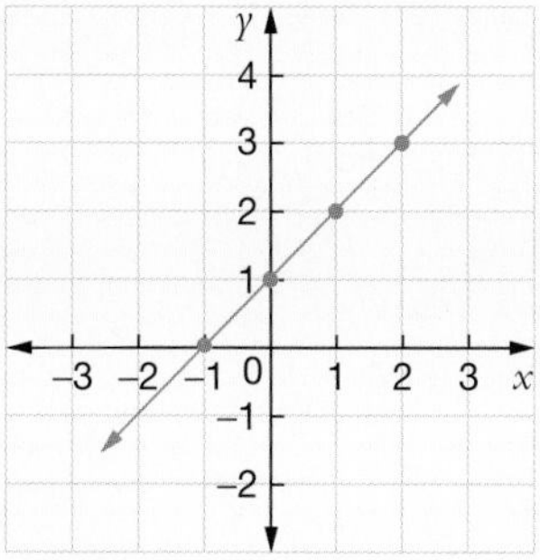

b
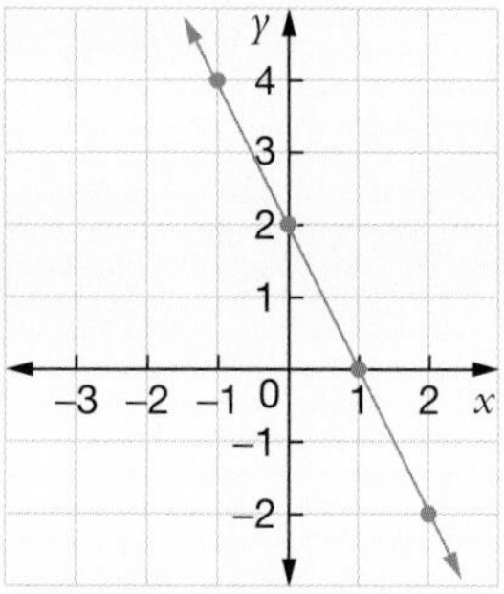

c
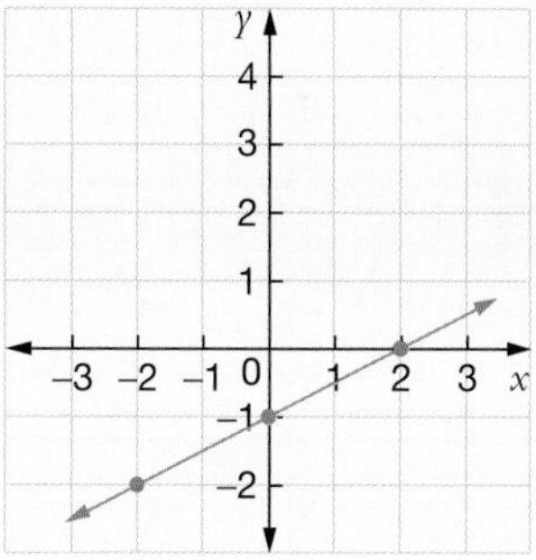

5 Find the gradient of the line that passes through: 9:03

a (1, 3), (2, 7) b (−2, 8), (4, 5) c (0, 3), (3, 5)

6 a Does the point (3, 2) lie on the line $x + y = 5$? 9:04

b Does the point (−1, 3) lie on the line $y = x + 2$?

c Does the point (2, −2) lie on the line $y = x - 4$?

7 Graph the lines with the following equations. 9:04

a $y = 2x + 1$ b $2x - y = 3$ c $3x + 2y = 6$

8 State the x- and y-intercepts of the lines. 9:04

a $2x - y = 3$ b $x + 3y = 6$ c $x + 2y = 4$

9 Graph these lines. 9:04

a $x = 2$ b $y = -1$ c $x = -2$

10 Write the equation of the line that has: 9:05

a a gradient of 3 and a y-intercept of 2

b a gradient of $\frac{1}{2}$ and a y-intercept of -3

c a y-intercept of 3 and a gradient of -1

11 Write each of the answers to Question 10 in general form. 9:05

12 What is the gradient and y-intercept of these lines? 9:05

a $y = 2x + 3$ b $y = 3 - 2x$ c $y = -x + 4$

13 Rearrange these equations into gradient–intercept form. 9:05

a $4x - y + 6 = 0$ b $2x + 3y - 3 = 0$ c $5x + 2y + 1 = 0$

14 Find the equation of the line that: 9:06

a passes through (1, 4) and has a gradient of 2

b has a gradient of -3 and passes through (1, 3)

c has a gradient of $\frac{1}{2}$ and passes through $(-2, 0)$.

15 Find the equation of the line that: 9:07

a passes through the points (1, 1) and (2, 3)

b passes through the points $(-1, 2)$ and $(1, -4)$

c passes through the origin and (3, 4).

16 Match each equation with the corresponding parabola in the diagram.

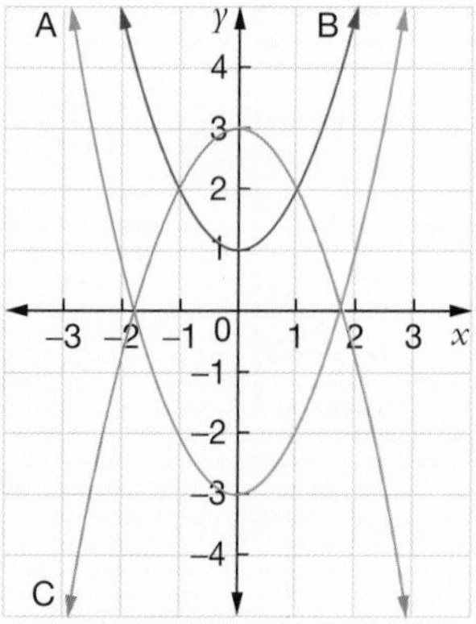

a $y = -x^2 + 3$

b $y = x^2 + 1$

c $y = x^2 - 3$

17 Match each equation with the corresponding exponential curve in the diagram. 9:08

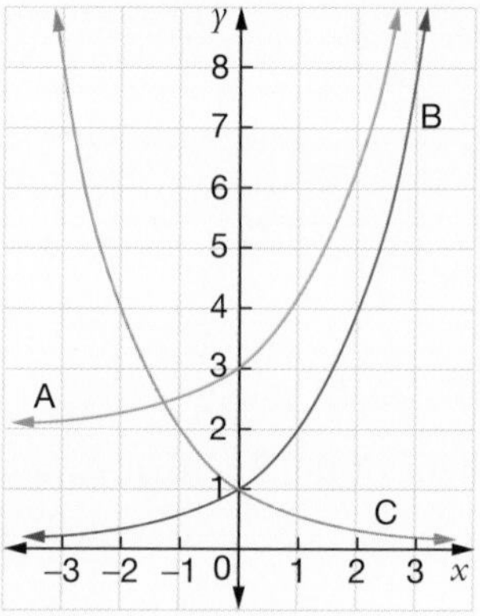

a $y = 2^x$

b $y = 2^{-x}$

c $y = 2 + 2^x$

ASSIGNMENT 9A Chapter review

1 Find:

a the length AB as a surd

b the slope of AB

c the midpoint of AB.

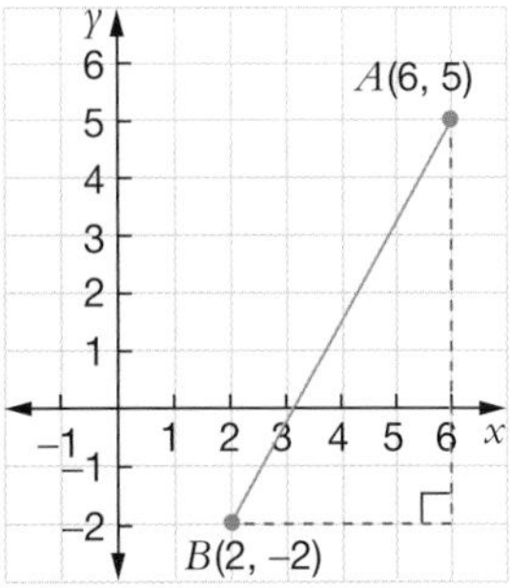

2 A is the point (2, 5) and B is the point (7, 17).

a What is the length AB (as a surd)?

b What is the slope of AB?

c What is the midpoint of AB?

3 A is the point (6, 5) and B is the point (2, −2).

a What is the equation of the line AB?

b The line AB passes through the point (100, b). What is the value of b?

4 a A line has an x-intercept of 3 and a gradient of 1. Find where the line crosses the y-axis and hence, write its equation.

b A line has a slope of $-\frac{1}{2}$ and a y-intercept of 6. What is its equation? What is its x-intercept?

c A line has an x-intercept of 3 and a y-intercept of 6. What is its equation?

5 The points $X(2, 2)$, $Y(-2, 4)$ and $Z(-4, 0)$ form a triangle. Show that the triangle is both isosceles and right-angled.

6 A median of a triangle is a line drawn from a vertex to the midpoint of the opposite side. Find the equation of the median through A of the triangle formed by the points $A(3, 4)$, $B(-2, -4)$ and $C(-6, 8)$.

7 Show that the points $A(5, 21)$, $B(30, 41)$ and $C(100, 97)$ are collinear (they all lie on the same straight line).

8 $OABC$ is a parallelogram. D is the point where BC meets the y-axis. Find:

a the coordinates of B and its distance from the origin

b the distance OD

c the area of ΔODC.

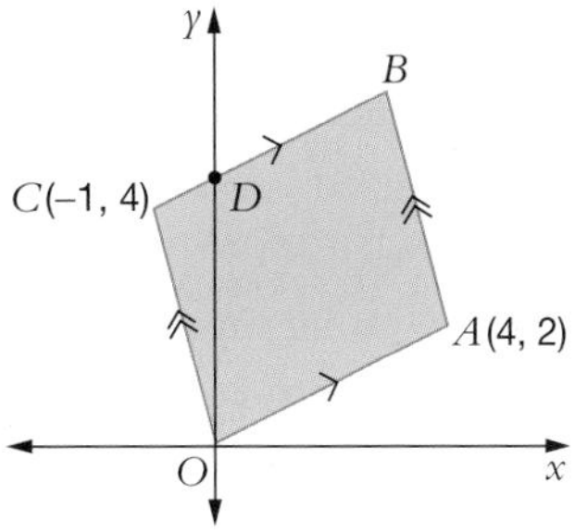

The coordinate system for locating points on Earth is based on circles.

ASSIGNMENT 9B Working mathematically

1 The diagram shows a 4-minute timer.

a If this timer was started with the pointer on zero, what number would it be pointing to after 17 minutes?

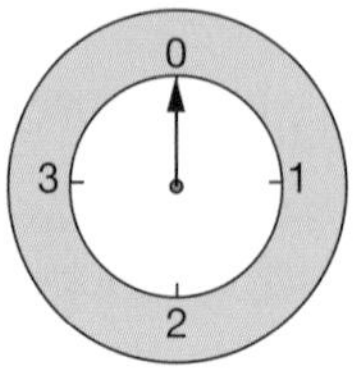

b At what times between 30 minutes and 1 hour will the pointer be pointing at number 3?

2 The faces of a cube are divided into 4 squares. If each square on each face is to be painted, what is the minimum number of colours needed if no squares that share an edge can be the same colour?

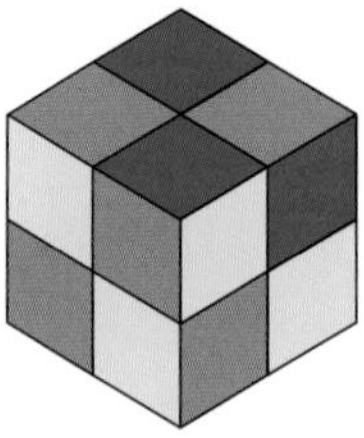

3 Brendan and Warwick wish to use a photocopier to reduce drawings.

a Brendan's drawing is 15 cm high but must be reduced to 8 cm to fit into the space he has left for his project. What percentage setting must he choose on the photocopier to achieve the required reduction?

b Warwick thinks the machine is malfunctioning so he decides to check it by reducing his drawing, which is 20 cm long. He chooses the 60% setting. If the machine is functioning properly, what would you expect the length of his picture to be?

c The setting button jams on 68%. What size copies are possible by repeated use of this button? (Give all answers above 20%)

4 Four friends decide to play tennis. Find out how many different:

a singles matches can be played (a singles match is one player against another player)

b doubles matches can be played (a doubles match is two players against two players).

5 What is the smallest whole number that, if you multiply by 7, will give you an answer consisting entirely of 8s?

6 A 4×4 grid is drawn and the numbers 1, 2, 3 and 4 are placed in the grid so that every number occurs only once in each row and only once in each column.

1	2	3	
	4		2
4			

a Find the missing numbers in the grid shown.

b Now place the numbers in a 4×4 grid, following the rules above, so that the sums of the diagonals are 16 and 4.

ASSIGNMENT 9C Cumulative revision

1 Expand and simplify each of the following. 3:06, 3:07

a $(5a - 2)(2 - 5a)$ b $(5a - 2)(2 + 5a)$ c $(5a - 2)^2$

2 A 2009–10 survey produced the following figures on the involvement of people aged 15 years and over in organised and non-organised sporting and physical recreational activities. If a person over 15 is chosen at random, what is the chance that they: 4:05

a do not participate in sport or physical recreation

b participate only in organised activities

c participate in only non-organised activities

d participate in an organised activity

e participate in both organised and non-organised activites?

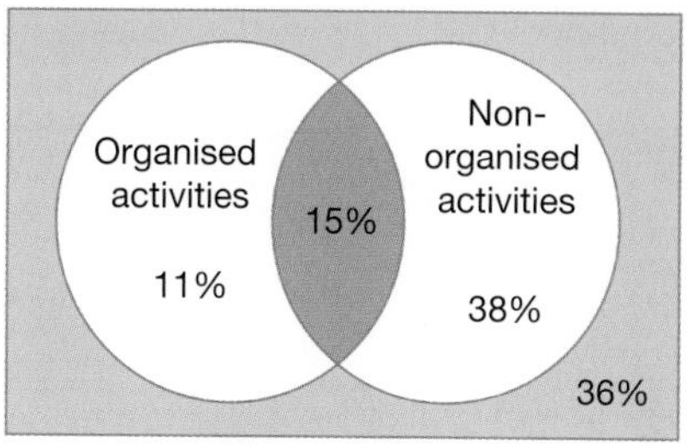

3 The composite solid shown has been formed from a rectangular prism by removing a triangular prism. Calculate the volume and surface area of the solid. 5:05, 5:06

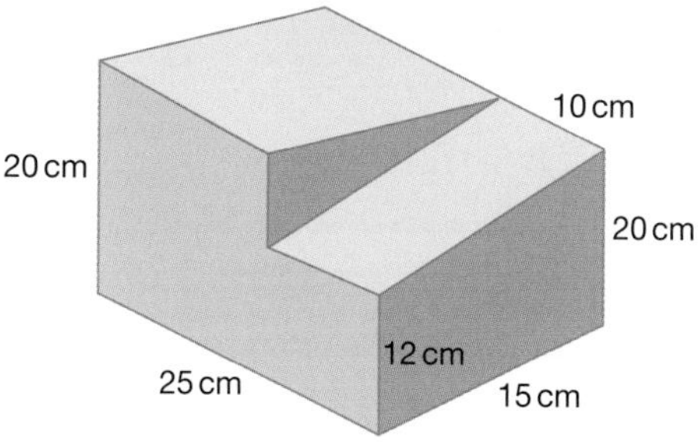

4 a In a supermarket, the normal rate of pay is \$18 per hour and overtime is paid at one-and-a-half times the normal rate. How much will be earned by a person who works 38 hours at normal rates and 6 hours of overtime? 8:02, 8:08

b A shop is having a sale. The original ticket prices are reduced by 50% to give the sale price. Loyalty members of the shop are then given a further 25% discount off the sale price. How much will a loyalty member pay for a coat with an original ticket price of \$250? What was the overall percentage discount?

5 Solve: 7:03, 7:04

a $\dfrac{3m - 4}{6} = 8$ b $\dfrac{5m}{2} - \dfrac{(2m - 7)}{3} = 8$

6 a Write each of the following as a fraction. 6:02, 6:03

i a^{-2} ii $6a^{-2}$ iii $(6a)^{-2}$

b Evaluate:

i $4^{\frac{1}{2}}$ ii $9^{-\frac{3}{2}}$ iii $4^{-\frac{1}{2}} \times 9^{\frac{3}{2}}$

SIMULTANEOUS EQUATIONS

10

Contents

Syllabus references (See pages x–xv for details.)

Number and Algebra

Sections from ***Equations*** [Stage 5.2]

- Solve linear simultaneous equations, using algebraic and graphical techniques, including with the use of digital technologies (ACMNA237)

Working Mathematically

- Communicating
- Problem Solving
- Reasoning
- Understanding
- Fluency

10:01 The graphical method of solution

PREP QUIZ 10:01

If $y = 2x - 1$, find y when:

1 $x = 1$ 2 $x = 0$ 3 $x = -1$ 4 $x = -5$

If $x - 2y = 5$, find y when:

5 $x = 0$ 6 $x = 1$ 7 $x = 2$ 8 $x = -4$

9 If $3x - y = 2$, complete the table below.

x	0	1	2
y			

10 Copy this number plane and graph the line $3x - y = 2$.

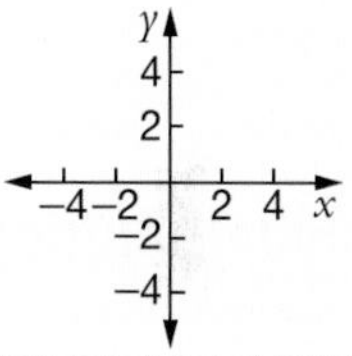

There are many situations in which we need to find when or where two conditions occur together. The following example illustrates this.

WORKED EXAMPLE 1

The sum of two numbers is 16. Their difference is 4. What are the numbers?

Graphical solution

We are looking for two numbers, which we will call x and y, that satisfy both conditions.

We write the two conditions as equations.

1 'The sum is 16' becomes $x + y = 16$.

2 'The difference is 4' becomes $x - y = 4$.

If we graph these two equations, we can find the point where the graphs cross.

The value of x and y at the point of intersection satisfies both conditions, as it lies on both lines.

These values of x and y are the two numbers we have been asked to find.

- From the graph, we can see that the lines cross at (10, 6), so the simultaneous solution is $x = 10$ and $y = 6$.
- Therefore the two numbers are 10 and 6.

$x + y = 16$

x	4	8	12
y	12	8	4

$x - y = 4$

x	4	8	12
y	0	4	8

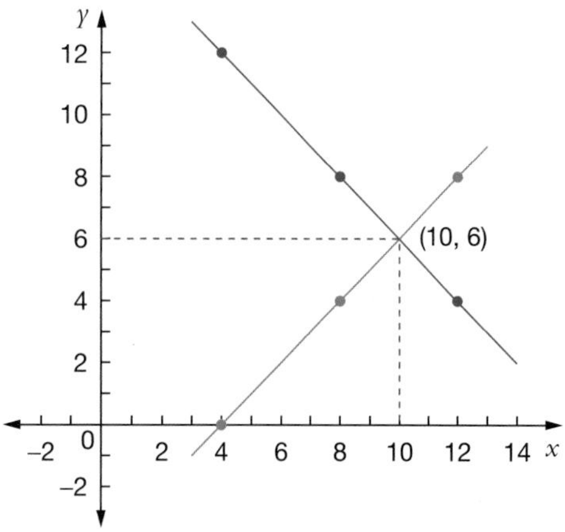

To solve problems involving two conditions, the given information has to be written in the form of two equations. The equations are then graphed using a table of values (as shown in the previous example). The point of intersection of the graphs tells us where the two conditions occur together.

WORKED EXAMPLE 2

Solve the following equations simultaneously.

$x + y = 5$

$2x - y = 4$

Graphical solution

You will remember from your earlier work on coordinate geometry that when the solutions to an equation such as $x + y = 5$ are graphed on a number plane, they form a straight line.

Hence, to solve the equations $x + y = 5$ and $2x - y = 4$ simultaneously, we could simply graph each line and find the point of intersection. Since this point lies on both lines, its coordinates give the solution.

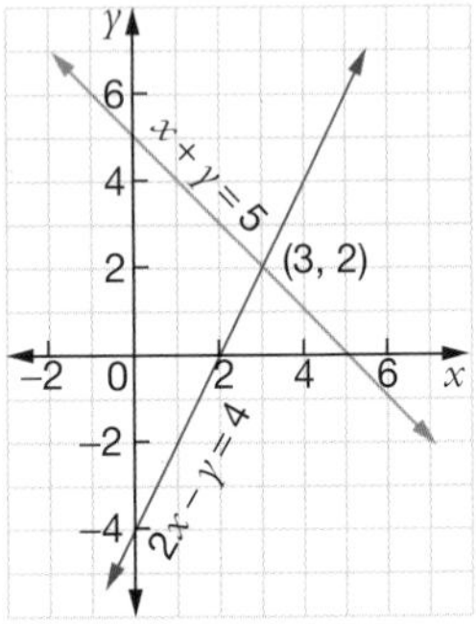

$x + y = 5$

x	0	1	2
y	5	4	3

$2x - y = 4$

x	0	1	2
y	−4	−2	0

- The lines $x + y = 5$ and $2x - y = 4$ intersect at (3, 2).
  Therefore the solution is:
  $x = 3$
  $y = 2$

> To solve a pair of simultaneous equations graphically, we graph each line.
> The solution is given by the coordinates of the point of intersection of the lines.

It is sometimes difficult to graph lines accurately and it is often difficult to read the coordinates of the point of intersection.

Despite these problems, the graphical method remains an extremely useful technique for solving simultaneous equations.

Exercise 10:01

P Foundation worksheet 10:01
Graphical method of solution

1 Use the graph to write the solutions to the following pairs of simultaneous equations.

a $y = x + 1$
$x + y = 3$

b $y = x + 1$
$x + 2y = -4$

c $y = x + 3$
$3x + 5y = 7$

d $y = x + 3$
$x + y = 3$

e $x + y = 3$
$3x + 5y = 7$

f $3x - 2y = 9$
$x + y = 3$

g $y = x + 3$
$y = x + 1$

h $y = x + 1$
$2y = 2x + 2$

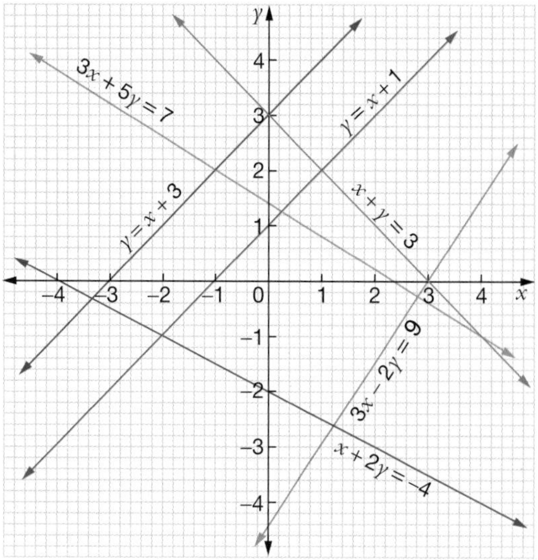

2 Use the graph in Question 1 to estimate, correct to one decimal place, the solutions of the following simultaneous equations.

a $y = x + 1$
$3x + 5y = 7$

b $y = x + 3$
$x + 2y = -4$

c $3x - 2y = 9$
$x + 2y = -4$

d $3x - 2y = 9$
$3x + 5y = 7$

3 Solve each of the following pairs of equations by graphical means. All solutions are integral (i.e. they are whole numbers).

a $x + y = 1$
$2x - y = 5$

b $2x + y = 3$
$x + y = 1$

c $x - y = 3$
$2x + y = 0$

d $3x - y - 2 = 0$
$x - y + 2 = 0$

e $3a - 2b = 1$
$a - b = 1$

f $p + 2q = 2$
$p - q = -4$

g $3a + 2b = 5$
$a = 1$

h $p = 6$
$p - q = 4$

4 Solve each pair of simultaneous equations by the graphical method. (Use a scale of 1 cm to 1 unit on each axis.)

a $y = 4x$
$x + y = 3$

b $3x - y = 1$
$x - y = 2$

c $x = 4y$
$x + y = 1$

5 Estimate the solution to each of the following pairs of simultaneous equations by graphing each, using a scale of 1 cm to 1 unit on each axis. Give the answers correct to one decimal place.

a $4x + 3y = 3$
$x - 2y = 1$

b $x - y = 2$
$8x + 4y = 7$

c $4a - 6b = 1$
$4a + 3b = 4$

6 The sum of two numbers is 15. Their difference is 3.
Use the graphical method of solving simultaneous equations to find the two numbers.

WORKED EXAMPLE 3 (EXTENSION)

A runner set off from a point and maintained a speed of 9 km/h. Another runner left the same point 10 minutes later, followed the same course, and maintained a speed of 12 km/h. When, and after what distance travelled, would the second runner have caught up to the first runner?

We have chosen to solve this question graphically.

First runner

t	0	30	40	60
d	0	4·5	6	9

Second runner

t	10	30	40	70
d	0	4	6	12

From these tables we can see that the runners meet after 6 km and 40 minutes.

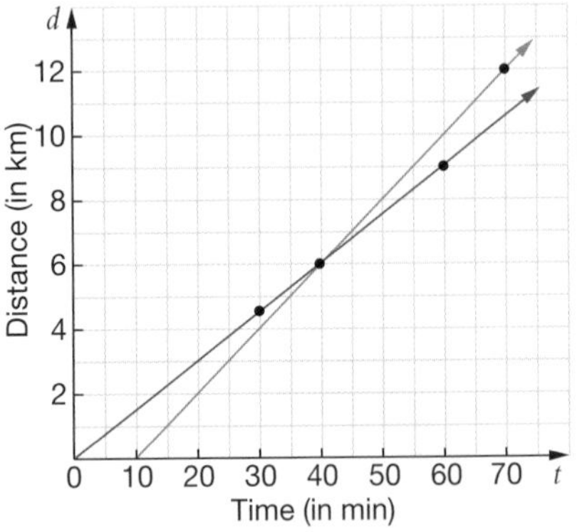

t = time in minutes after the first runner begins
d = distance travelled in kilometres

- From the graph, we can see that the lines cross at (40, 6).
- The simultaneous solution is $t = 40$, $d = 6$.
- The second runner caught the first runner 40 min after the first runner had started and when both runners had travelled 6 km.

After the second runner has run for 30 minutes, t=40.

7 A car passed a point on a course at exactly 12 noon and maintained a speed of 60 km/h. A second car passed the same point 1 hour later, followed the same course, and maintained a speed of 100 km/h. When, and after what distance from this point, would the second car have caught up to the first car? (Hint: Use the method shown in Worked Example 3 but leave the time in hours.)

8 Mary's salary consisted of a retainer of $480 a week plus $100 for each machine sold in that week. Bob had no retainer, but was paid $180 for each machine sold. Study the tables below, graph the lines, and use them to find the number, N, of machines Bob would have to sell to have a wage equal to Mary (assuming they both sell the same number of machines). What salary, S, would each receive for this number of sales?

Mary

N	0	4	8
S	480	880	1280

Bob

N	0	4	8
S	0	720	1440

N = number of machines S = salary

9 No Frills Car Rental offers new cars for rent at \$38 per day and 50c for every 10 km travelled in excess of 100 km per day. Prestige Car Rental offers the same type of car for \$30 per day plus \$1 for every 10 km travelled in excess of 100 km per day. Draw a graph of each case on axes like those shown, and determine what distance would need to be travelled in a day so that the rentals charged by each company would be the same.

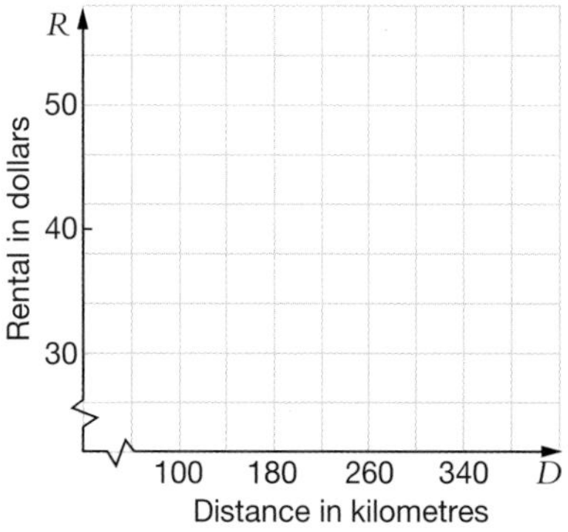

10 Star Car Rental offers new cars for rent at \$38 per day and \$1 for every 10 km travelled in excess of 100 km per day. Safety Car Rental offers the same type of car for \$30 per day plus 50c for every 10 km travelled in excess of 100 km per day.
Draw a graph of each on axes like those in Question 9, and discuss the results.

P GEOGEBRA ACTIVITY 10:01 SIMULTANEOUS EQUATIONS: THE GRAPHICAL METHOD

Two different activities explore the graphical solution.

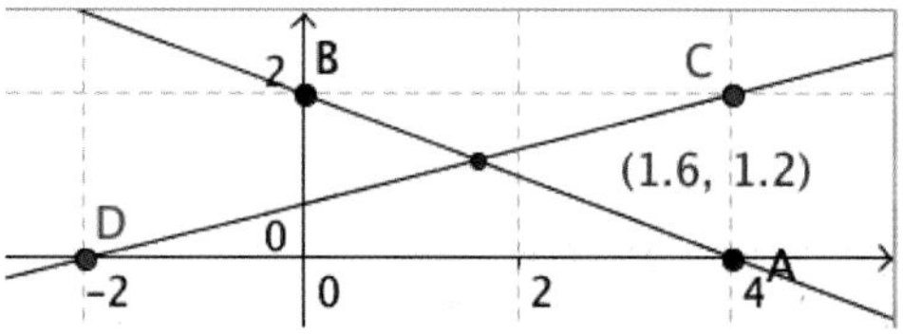

FUN SPOT 10:01 WHAT DID THE BOOK SAY TO THE LIBRARIAN?

Work out the answer to each part and write the letter for that part in the box that is above the correct answer.

Write the equation of:

A line AB

U line BF

I the y-axis

U line OF

E line CB

T line EF

Y line CD

C line OB

A line EB

O line AF

K line AE

T the x-axis

N line OD

O line OA

$y = \frac{5}{3}x$	$y = \frac{4}{3}x + 1$	$y = x$	$x = 0$	$y = 0$	$y = 5$	$x = -3$	$y = \frac{1}{3}x + 4$	$y = 3$	$y = -\frac{5}{3}x$	$x = 3$	$y = -\frac{4}{3}x + 1$	$y = -x$	$y = -3$

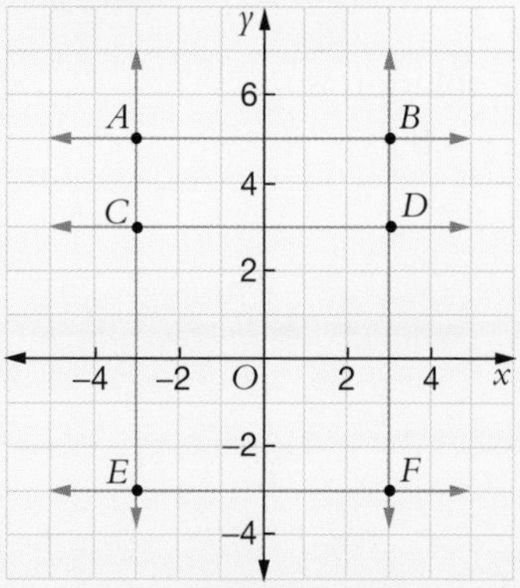

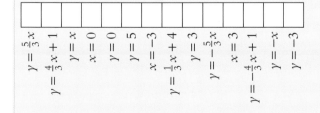

10:02 The algebraic method of solution

In the previous section we found that some graphical solutions lacked accuracy. Because of this, we need a method that gives the exact solution. There are two such algebraic methods: the substitution method and the elimination method.

10:02A Substitution method

WORKED EXAMPLE 1

Solve the simultaneous equations:

$2x + y = 12$ and $y = 5x - 2$

In this method one pronumeral is replaced by an equivalent expression involving the other pronumeral.

Solution

When solving simultaneous equations, first 'number' the equations involved.

$2x + y = 12$ 1

$y = 5x - 2$ 2

Now from 2 we can see that $5x - 2$ is equal to y.
If we substitute this for y in equation 1, we have:

$$\begin{aligned} 2x + (5x - 2) &= 12 \\ 7x - 2 &= 12 \\ 7x &= 14 \\ x &= 2 \end{aligned}$$

So the value of x is 2. This value for x can now be substituted into either equation 1 or equation 2 to find the value for y.

In 1:

$$\begin{aligned} 2(2) + y &= 12 \\ 4 + y &= 12 \\ y &= 8 \end{aligned}$$

In 2:

$$\begin{aligned} y &= 5(2) - 2 \\ &= 10 - 2 \\ &= 8 \end{aligned}$$

So, the solution is:

$x = 2, y = 8$

To check this answer substitute into equations 1 and 2.

WORKED EXAMPLE 2

Solve the simultaneous equations:

$3a + 2b = 7$ and $4a - 3b = 2$

Solution

$3a + 2b = 7$ 1

$4a - 3b = 2$ 2

Making a the subject of 2 gives:

$$a = \frac{2 + 3b}{4}$$

If we substitute this expression for a into equation 1, we get:

$$3\left(\frac{2+3b}{4}\right) + 2b = 7$$

$$3(2 + 3b) + 8b = 28$$

$$6 + 9b + 8b = 28$$

$$17b = 22$$

$$b = \frac{22}{17}$$

Multiply both sides by 4.

Substituting this value for b into equation 2 gives:

$$4a - 3\left(\tfrac{22}{17}\right) = 2$$

$$4a - \frac{66}{17} = \frac{34}{17}$$

$$4a = \frac{100}{17}$$

$$a = \frac{25}{17}$$

So, the solution is:

$a = \frac{25}{17}$, $b = \frac{22}{17}$

To check your answer, substitute $a = \frac{25}{17}$, $b = \frac{22}{17}$ in equations 1 and 2.

Exercise 10:02A

P Foundation worksheet 10:02A
The substitution method

1 Solve the following pairs of equations using the substitution method. Check all solutions.

a $x + y = 3$ and $y = 4$

b $x + y = 7$ and $y = x + 3$

c $x + y = -3$ and $y = x + 1$

d $x - y = 5$ and $y = 1 - x$

e $2x + y = 9$ and $y = x - 3$

f $2x + y = 8$ and $y = x - 4$

g $2x - y = 10$ and $y = 10 - 3x$

h $x + 2y = 9$ and $y = 2x - 3$

i $2x + y = 14$ and $x = 6$

j $2x + y = 7$ and $x = y - 4$

2 Use one of each pair of equations to express y in terms of x. Then use the method of substitution to solve the equations. Check all solutions.

a $x + 2y = 4$
$x - y = 7$

b $2x - 3y = 4$
$2x + y = 6$

c $x + 2y = 8$
$x + y = -2$

d $x - y = 2$
$x + 2y = 11$

e $2x - y = -8$
$2x + y = 0$

f $x + y = 5$
$2x + y = 7$

g $x + 2y = 11$
$2x - y = 2$

h $3x + y = 13$
$x + 2y = 1$

i $3x + 2y = 2$
$2x - y = -8$

3 Solve the following simultaneous equations using the substitution method.

a $2x - y = 1$
$4x + 2y = 5$

b $3a + b = 6$
$9a + 2b = 1$

c $m - 2n = 3$
$5m + 2n = 2$

d $4x - 2y = 1$
$x + 3y = -1$

Questions 3 and 4 involve harder substitutions and arithmetic.

4 Solve the following pairs of simultaneous equations.

a $2a - 3b = 1$
$4a + 2b = 5$

b $7x - 2y = 2$
$3x + 4y = 8$

c $3m - 4n = 1$
$2m + 3n = 4$

d $2x - 3y = 10$
$5x - 3y = 3$

P GEOGEBRA ACTIVITY 10:02A SIMULTANEOUS EQUATIONS: THE SUBSTITUTION METHOD

This activity explores the substitution method of solution.

$x - y = 2$ (1)

$x - 5y = 26$ (2)

$x = 2 + y$ (3)

$(2 + y) - 5y = 26$ Substitute (3) in (2)

$2 + y - 5y = 26$

$-4y = 24$

$y = -6$

$x = 2 + -6$ Substitute in (3)

$x = -4$

10:02B Elimination method

WORKED EXAMPLE 1

Solve the pair of simultaneous equations.

$5x - 3y = 20$

$2x + 3y = 15$

In this method, one of the pronumerals is eliminated by adding or subtracting the equations.

Solution

You add or subtract the equations, depending upon which operation will eliminate one of the pronumerals.

First, number each equation.

$5x - 3y = 20 \quad 1$

$2x + 3y = 15 \quad 2$

Now if these equations are 'added', the y terms will be eliminated, giving:

$7x = 35$

$x = 5$

Substituting this value into equation 1 gives:

$5(5) - 3y = 20$

$25 - 3y = 20$

$3y = 5$

$y = \frac{5}{3}$ or $1\frac{2}{3}$

$\therefore$ The solution is $x = 5$, $y = 1\frac{2}{3}$.

Check in 1: $5(5) - 3(1\frac{2}{3}) = 20$ (true)

Check in 2: $2(5) + 3(1\frac{2}{3}) = 15$ (true)

Check that the values satisfy both original equations.
x
y

WORKED EXAMPLE 2

Solve the pair of simultaneous equations.

$x + 5y = 14$

$x - 3y = 6$

Take one step at a time.

Solution

First, number each equation.

$x + 5y = 14 \quad 1$

$x - 3y = 6 \quad 2$

Now, if equation 2 is 'subtracted' from equation 1, the x terms are eliminated.

$8y = 8$

$y = 1$

Substituting this value into 1 gives:

$x + 5(1) = 14$

$x + 5 = 14$

$x = 9$

$\therefore$ The solution is $x = 9$, $y = 1$.

Check in 1: $9 + 5(1) = 14$ (true)

Check in 2: $9 - 3(1) = 6$ (true)

WORKED EXAMPLE 3

Solve the pair of simultaneous equations.

$2x + 3y = 21$

$5x + 2y = 3$

To eliminate a pronumeral, the size of the coefficients in each equation must be made the same by multiplying one or both equations by a constant.

Solution

First, number each equation.

$2x + 3y = 21 \quad 1$

$5x + 2y = 3 \quad 2$

Multiply equation 1 by 2 and equation 2 by 3.

$4x + 6y = 42 \quad 1^\star$

$15x + 6y = 9 \quad 2^\star$

Now, $2^\star$ is subtracted from $1^\star$, so the y terms are eliminated.

$-11x = 33$

$x = -3$

Substituting this value into 1 gives:

$2(-3) + 3y = 21$

$-6 + 3y = 21$

$3y = 27$

$y = 9$

$\therefore$ The solution is $x = -3$, $y = 9$.

Check in 1: $2(-3) + 3(9) = 21$ (true)

Check in 2: $5(-3) + 2(9) = 3$ (true)

Note: x could have been eliminated instead of y, by multiplying 1 by 5 and 2 by 2.

Exercise 10:02B

1 Add the equations to solve each pair of equations using the elimination method.

a $x + y = 9$, $x - y = 1$
b $x + y = 14$, $2x - y = 1$
c $2x + y = 7$, $x - y = 2$
d $x + 2y = 3$, $x - 2y = 7$
e $3x - 2y = 5$, $x + 2y = 7$
f $5x - 2y = 1$, $3x + 2y = 7$
g $x + 3y = 10$, $-x + y = 6$
h $-x + 2y = 12$, $x + 2y = -4$
i $3x + y = 11$, $-3x + 2y = 10$
j $2x + 7y = 5$, $x - 7y = 16$
k $5x - 2y = 0$, $4x + 2y = 9$
l $7x + 5y = -3$, $2x - 5y = 21$

2 Subtract the equations to solve each pair of equations using the elimination method.

a $2x + y = 5$, $x + y = 3$
b $5x + y = 7$, $3x + y = 1$
c $10x + 2y = 2$, $7x + 2y = -1$
d $3x - 2y = 0$, $x - 2y = 4$
e $5x - y = 14$, $2x - y = 2$
f $x - 3y = 1$, $2x - 3y = 5$

g $2x + y = 10$
$x + y = 7$

h $2x + 5y = 7$
$2x + y = 5$

i $5x - y = 16$
$5x - 3y = 8$

j $6x + y = 13$
$6x - y = 11$

k $2x + 5y = 20$
$3x + 5y = 17$

l $7x - 2y = 1$
$4x - 2y = 4$

3 Solve these simultaneous equations using the elimination method.

a $2x + y = 7$
$x - y = -4$

b $x + y = 5$
$2x - y = 1$

c $x - y = 12$
$2x + y = 3$

d $3x + 2y = 2$
$x - 2y = -10$

e $2x + 3y = 13$
$4x - 3y = -1$

f $3x + 4y = -1$
$3x - 2y = -10$

g $5x + 2y = 1$
$3x - 2y = 7$

h $7x - 3y = 31$
$7x + y = -1$

i $8x - 2y = 34$
$8x + 4y = 4$

4 After multiplying either or both of the equations by a constant, use the elimination method to solve each pair of equations.

a $x + y = 7$
$2x + 3y = 17$

b $2x + y = 7$
$x + 2y = 11$

c $5x + y = 12$
$3x + 2y = 10$

d $4x - y = 10$
$x + 3y = 9$

e $4x - y = 6$
$3x + 2y = -1$

f $5x - 2y = -16$
$x + 3y = 7$

g $12x - 3y = 18$
$4x + 2y = 0$

h $3x - 7y = 2$
$9x + 5y = 32$

i $2x + 3y = 8$
$3x + 2y = 7$

j $5x + 2y = 10$
$4x + 3y = 15$

k $5x + 2y = 28$
$3x + 5y = 51$

l $2x + 2y = -2$
$3x - 5y = -19$

m $7x + 3y = 4$
$5x + 2y = 3$

n $2x - 4y = -2$
$3x + 5y = 45$

Use the same setting out as in the examples.
x + y = 7 1
2x + 3y = 17 2
1 × 2
2x + 2y = 14 1*

P GEOGEBRA ACTIVITY 10:02B SIMULTANEOUS EQUATIONS: THE ELIMINATION METHOD

This activity explores the elimination method of solution.

$5x - 2y = 6$ (1)
$5x + 2y = 12$ (2)

(1) + (2) $10x = 18$
$x = 1.8$

The y-coefficients are equal in value but opposite signs so add the two equations to eliminate y.

Substitute in (2) $5 \times 1.8 + 2y = 12$
$9 + 2y = 12$
$2y = 3$
$y = 1.5$

10:03 Using simultaneous equations to solve problems

Simultaneous equations can be used to solve problems that involve two conditions, often in a easier way than with only one equation. The same techniques we use to solve single equations are used here.

These clues will help you solve the problem!

Remember:
- Read the question carefully.
- Work out what the problem wants you to find.
- Use pronumerals to represent the unknown quantities.
- Translate the words of the question into mathematical expressions.
- Form equations by showing how different mathematical expressions are related.
- Solve the equations.
- Finish off with a sentence stating the value of the quantity or quantities that were found.

WORKED EXAMPLE

Adam is 6 years older than his sister, Bronwyn.
If the sum of their ages is 56 years, find their ages.

This is a fairly easy problem, but you must set it out just like the harder ones.

Solution

Let Adam's age be x years.
Let Bronwyn's age be y years.
Adam is 6 years older than Bronwyn.
$\therefore\ x = y + 6$ 1
The sum of their ages is 56 years.
$\therefore\ x + y = 56$ 2
Solving these simultaneously gives:
$x = 31$ and $y = 25$.
$\therefore$ Adam is 31 years old and Bronwyn is 25 years old.

Exercise 10:03

P Foundation worksheet 10:03
Using simultaneous equations to solve problems
Challenge worksheet 10:03
Solving three simultaneous equations

1 Form pairs of simultaneous equations and solve the following problems. Let the numbers be x and y.

a The sum of two numbers is 25 and their difference is 11. Find the numbers.
b The sum of two numbers is 97 and their difference is 33. Find the numbers.

c The sum of two numbers is 12, and one of the numbers is three times the other. Find the numbers.

d The difference between two numbers is 9 and the smaller number plus twice the larger number is equal to 24. Find the numbers.

e The larger of two numbers is equal to 3 times the smaller number plus 7. Also, twice the larger number plus 5 times the smaller is equal to 69. Find the numbers.

2 Each of the following problems has two unknown quantities and two pieces of information. Form two simultaneous equations and solve each problem.

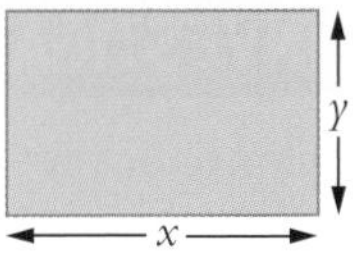

a The length of a rectangle is 5 cm more than the width. If the perimeter of the rectangle is 22 cm, find the length and the width.

b One pen and one pencil cost \$2. Two pens and three pencils cost \$4.70. Find the cost of each.

c If a student's maths mark exceeded her science mark by 15, and the total marks for both tests was 129, find each mark.

d Six chocolates and three drinks cost \$14.70, whereas three chocolates and two drinks cost \$8.60. Find the price of each.

e Bill has twice as much money as Jim. If I give Jim \$2.50, he will have three times as much as Bill. How much did Bill and Jim have originally?

3 Form two equations from the information on each figure to find values for x and y.

a

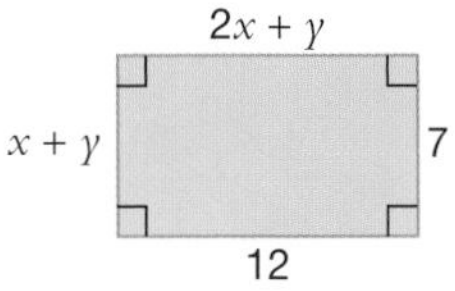

b

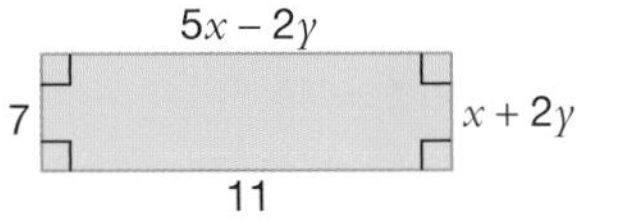

c

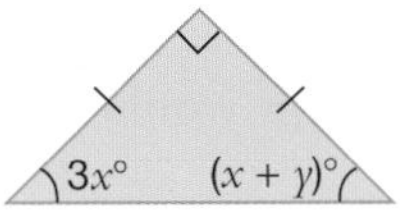

d

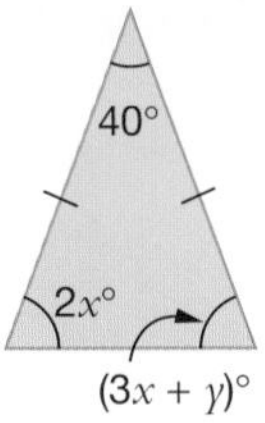

e

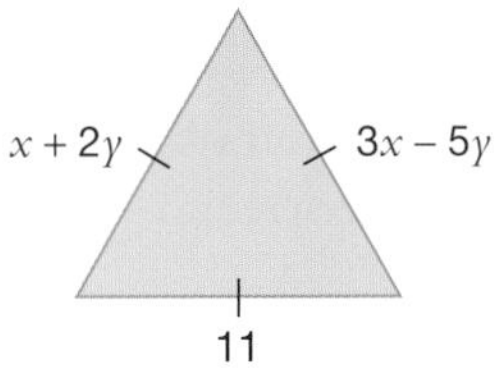

f

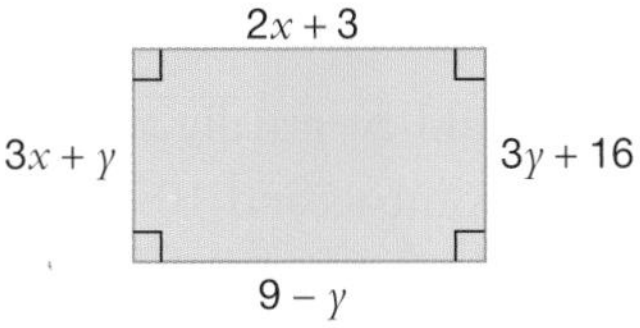

4 a A rectangle is 4 cm longer than it is wide. If both the length and breadth are increased by 1 cm, the area would be increased by 18 cm^2. Find the length and breadth of the rectangle.

b A truck is loaded with two different types of boxes. If 150 of box A and 115 of box B are loaded onto the truck, its capacity of 10 tonnes is reached. If 300 of box A are loaded, then the truck can only take 30 of box B before the capacity of 10 tonnes is reached. Find the weight of each box.

c A theatre has 2100 seats. All of the rows of seats in the theatre have either 45 seats or 40 seats. If there are three times as many rows with 45 seats than those with 40 seats, how many rows are there?

d A firm has five times as many junior workers as it does senior workers. If the weekly wage for a senior is \$620 and for a junior is \$460, find how many of each are employed when the total weekly wage bill is \$43 800.

5 Use graphical methods to solve the following problems.

a Esther can buy scarves for \$6 each. She bought a roll of material for \$20 and gave it to a dressmaker, who then charged \$3.50 to make each scarf. How many scarves would Esther need to have made for the cost to be the same as buying them for \$6 each?

b Star Bicycles had produced 3000 bicycles and were producing 200 more per week. Prince Bicycles had produced 2500 bicycles and were producing 300 more each week. After how many weeks would they have produced the same number of bicycles?

INVESTIGATION 10:03 SOLVING PROBLEMS BY 'GUESS AND CHECK'

Consider the following problem.

> A zoo enclosure contains wombats and emus. If there are 50 eyes and 80 legs, find the number of each type of animal.

We know that each animal has two eyes. A wombat has four legs and an emu has two legs. We could try to solve this problem by guessing a solution and then checking it.

Solution

If each animal has two eyes, then, because there are 50 eyes, I know there must be 25 animals.

If my first guess is 13 wombats and 12 emus, then the number of legs would be $13 \times 4 + 12 \times 2 = 76$.

Since there are more legs than 76, I need to increase the number of wombats to increase the number of legs to 80.

I would eventually arrive at the correct solution of 15 wombats and 10 emus, which gives the correct number of legs ($15 \times 4 + 10 \times 2 = 80$).

Try solving these problems by guessing and then checking various solutions.

1 Two numbers add to give 86 and subtract to give 18. What are the numbers?

2 At the school disco, there were 52 more girls than boys. If the total attendance was 420, how many boys and how many girls attended?

3 In scoring 200 runs, Max hit a total of 128 runs as boundaries. (A boundary is either 4 runs or 6 runs.) If he scored 29 boundaries in total, how many boundaries of each type did he score?

4 Sharon spent \$5158 buying either Company A shares or Company B shares. These were valued at \$10.50 and \$6.80 respectively. If she bought 641 shares in total, how many of each did she buy?

- In this chapter you have learned to solve questions like this using simultaneous equations. Solve each of these problems using simultaneous equations.

MATHS TERMS 10

elimination method

- solving simultaneous equations by adding or subtracting the equations together to 'eliminate' one pronumeral

graphical solution

- the solution obtained by graphing two equations in the number plane and observing the point of intersection
- if the point of intersection is (3, −2), then the solution is $x = 3$ and $y = -2$

guess and check

- a method of solving problems by guessing a solution and then checking to see if it works. Solutions are modified until the correct solution is found

simultaneous equations

- when two (or more) pieces of information about a problem can be represented by two (or more) equations
- these are then solved to find the common or simultaneous solution, e.g. the equations $x + y = 10$ and $x - y = 6$ have many solutions but the only simultaneous solution is $x = 8$ and $y = 2$

substitution method

- solving simultaneous equations by substituting an equivalent expression for one pronumeral in terms of another, obtained from another equation, e.g. if $y = x + 3$ and $x + y = 7$, then the second equation could be written as $x + (x + 3) = 7$ by substituting for y using the first equation

DIAGNOSTIC TEST 10 SIMULTANEOUS EQUATIONS

These questions reflect the important skills introduced in this chapter.
Errors made will indicate areas of weakness.
Each weakness should be treated by going back to the section listed.

1 Use the graph to solve the following simultaneous equations. **10:01**

a $x + y = -3$
$y = x + 1$

b $y = x + 1$
$3y - x = 7$

c $3y - x = 7$
$x + y = -3$

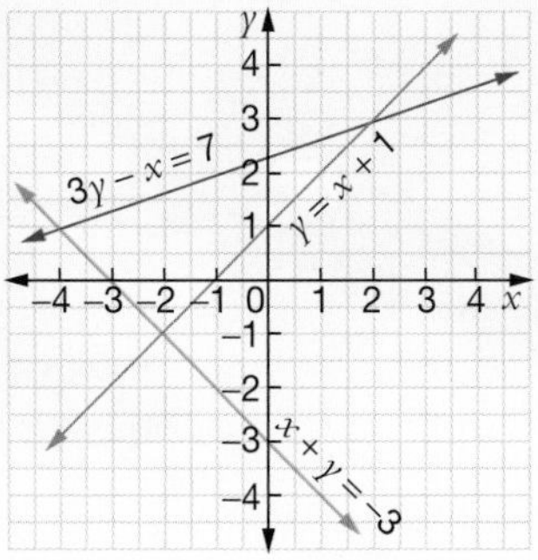

2 Solve the following simultaneous equations using the substitution method. **10:02A**

a $y = x - 2$
$2x + y = 7$

b $x - y = 5$
$2x + 3y = 2$

c $4a - b = 3$
$2a + 3b = 11$

3 Solve the following simultaneous equations using the elimination method. **10:02B**

a $2x - y = 3$
$3x + y = 7$

b $4x - 3y = 11$
$2x + y = 5$

c $2a - 3b = 4$
$3a - 2b = 6$

ASSIGNMENT 10A Chapter review

1 Solve the following simultaneous equations using the most suitable method.

a $x + y = 3$
$2x - y = 6$

b $4x - y = 3$
$2x + y = 5$

c $4a + b = 6$
$5a - 7b = 9$

d $6a - 3b = 4$
$4a - 3b = 8$

e $a - 3b = 5$
$5a + b = 6$

f $2x - 3y = 6$
$3x - 2y = 5$

g $p = 2q - 7$
$4p + 3q = 5$

h $4x - y = 3$
$4x - 3y = 7$

i $7m - 4n - 6 = 0$
$3m + n = 4$

2 A man is three times as old as his daughter. If the difference in their ages is 36 years, find the ages of father and daughter.

3 A theatre can hold 200 people. If the price of admission was \$5 per adult and \$2 per child, find the number of each present if the theatre was full and takings were \$577.

4 A man has 100 shares of stock A and 200 shares of stock B. The total value of the stocks is \$420. If he sells 50 shares of stock A and buys 60 shares of stock B, the value of his stocks is \$402. Find the price of each share.

5 Rectangle A is three times longer than rectangle B and twice as wide. If the perimeters are 50 cm and 20 cm respectively, find the dimensions of the larger rectangle.

6 A rectangle has a perimeter of 40 cm. If the length is reduced by 5 cm and 5 cm is added to the width, it becomes a square. Find the dimensions of the rectangle.

7 A kayaker paddles at 16 km/h with the current and 8 km/h against the current. Find the speed of the current.

ASSIGNMENT 10B Working mathematically

1 You need to replace the wire in your clothesline. Discuss how you would estimate the length of wire required.

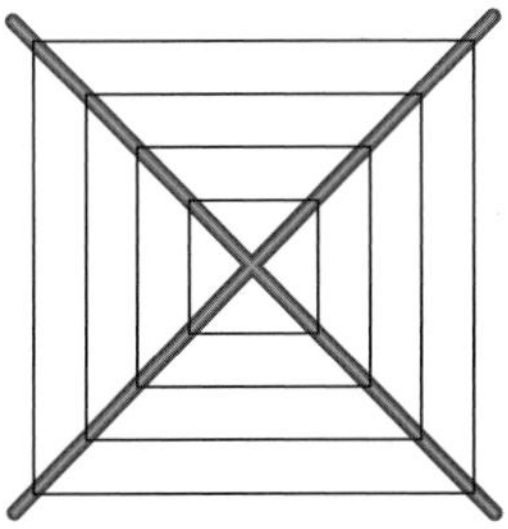

a On what measurements would you base your estimate?

b Is it better to overestimate or underestimate?

c What level of accuracy do you feel is necessary? The diagram shows the arrangement of the wire.

2 What is the last digit of the number 3^{2004}?

3 Two smaller isosceles triangles are joined to form a larger isosceles triangle as shown in the diagram. What is the value of x?

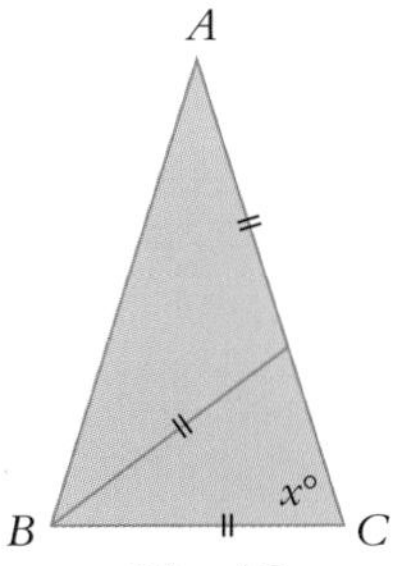

$AB = AC$

4 In a round-robin competition each team plays every other team. How many games would be played in a round-robin competition that had:

a three teams
b four teams
c five teams
d eight teams?

5 In how many different ways can you select three chocolates from five?

6 A school swimming coach has to pick a medley relay team. The team must have four swimmers, each of whom must swim one of the four strokes. From the information in the table choose the fastest combination of swimmers.

Name	Back	Breast	Fly	Free
Dixon	37·00	44·91	34·66	30·18
Wynn	37·17	41·98	36·59	31·10
Goad	38·88			
Nguyen	41·15	49·05	39·07	34·13
McCully		43·01		32·70
Grover		43·17		
Harris			37·34	34·44

What is the fastest medley relay?

ASSIGNMENT 10C Cumulative revision

1 a $-8 - (-16)$ b $(-4)^2$ c $64 \div (4 - 8)$ 1:01
d $-1 - 1 - 1$ e $1{\cdot}25 \times 100$ f $30 \times 0{\cdot}2$
g 7% of 300 h 125% of 10 i $\frac{3}{4}$ of (-60)
j $\frac{4}{5} \times 1\frac{1}{4}$ k $\frac{3}{4} + \frac{7}{10}$ l $1\frac{1}{4} - \frac{7}{10}$

2 a Petrol and oil are mixed in the ratio 50 : 1 to produce 2-stroke fuel. 1:04
i How much petrol needs to be mixed with 20 mL of oil?
ii What quantity of oil needs to be added to 5 L of petrol to make the 2-stroke fuel?

b Max swims laps in a 50 m Olympic pool. He completes 400 m in 7 mins 12 s. 1:04
i What is his average lap time in seconds/lap?
ii At this rate, how long would it take him to swim 1 km?

c An answer is given as 25 000 km, correct to two significant figures. What might the exact measurement have been? 1:06

d Write the basic numeral for $4{\cdot}65 \times 10^6$. 1:08

e Convert 6·5 GB to MB. 1:09

3 Simplify: 3:01, 3:02, 3:03
a $3m + 8m^2 - 5m$ b $-8x \times 4y$ c $8a \div 4ab$
d $\dfrac{x}{5} - \dfrac{x}{8}$ e $\dfrac{4x}{5} + \dfrac{7x+1}{10}$ f $\dfrac{3}{a} \times \dfrac{5a}{9}$
g $9(x + 5) - 5$ h $3a(7 - 2a) + 6a^2$ i $-(3 - 4m)$

4 Use this Venn diagram to find the probability that a student, chosen randomly from those surveyed, studied: 4:05
a Indonesian
b French or Indonesian but not both.

Languages studied

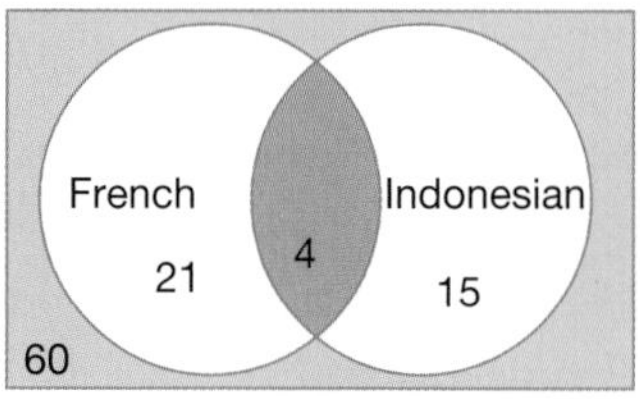

5 Simplify: 6:02, 6:03,
a $(p^2)^3 + 5p^0$ b $(\frac{3}{4})^{-2}$ c $27^{\frac{1}{3}}$

6 Write 2·5 GB as bytes (B), using scientific notation. 6:06

7 Solve. 7:03, 7:04
a $\dfrac{x}{4} - 5 = 14$ b $\dfrac{x-10}{3} = 2x + 1$ c $\dfrac{y}{2} + \dfrac{y}{5} = 6$

8 Ali bought land for \$160 000 and sold it for \$185 600. Find the profit as a percentage of the cost. 8:05

SIMILARITY

11

Contents

Syllabus references (See pages x–xv for details.)

Measurement and Geometry

Selections from ***Properties of Geometrical Figures*** [Stages 5.1, 5.2]

- Use the enlargement transformation to explain similarity (ACMMG220)
- Solve problems using ratio and scale factors in similar figures (ACMMG221)
- Use the enlargement transformations to explain similarity and to develop the conditions for triangles to be similar (ACMMG220)

Working Mathematically

- Communicating
- Problem Solving
- Reasoning
- Understanding
- Fluency

11:01 Similar figures

In mathematics, the word **similar** does not mean 'almost equal' or 'nearly the same' but actually means 'the same shape'.

- Two figures are similar when one figure can be enlarged and superimposed on the other so that they coincide exactly.
- Similar figures have the same shape, but different size.

We use similar figures in house plans, when enlarging photographs, when using projectors, when making models, in scale drawings, and when using maps.

If two figures are similar, one can be thought of as the enlargement or reduction of the other. The amount of the enlargement or reduction is determined by the scale factor. The scale factor can be found by dividing any pair of matching sides.

- Figure 2 is an enlargement of Figure 1.

  The scale factor $= \frac{6}{2} = 3$.

  Each length in Figure 2 is 3 times the matching length in Figure 1.

- Figure 1 is a reduction of Figure 2.

  The scale factor $= \frac{2}{6} = \frac{1}{3}$.

  Each length in Figure 1 is $\frac{1}{3}$ the matching length in Figure 2.

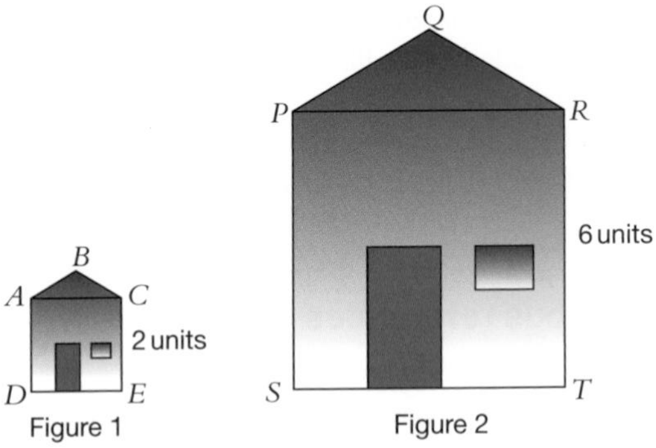

When a figure is enlarged or reduced, the sizes of matching angles do not change.

When naming similar figures, the vertices should be listed in matching order.
In the figures shown, we would write $ABCED \,|||\, PQRTS$.
The symbol ||| means 'is similar to'.

Exercise 11:01

1 The figures drawn on the right are similar. If the smaller figure were traced and cut out it could be moved around to show all of the matching angles, as shown in the examples below.

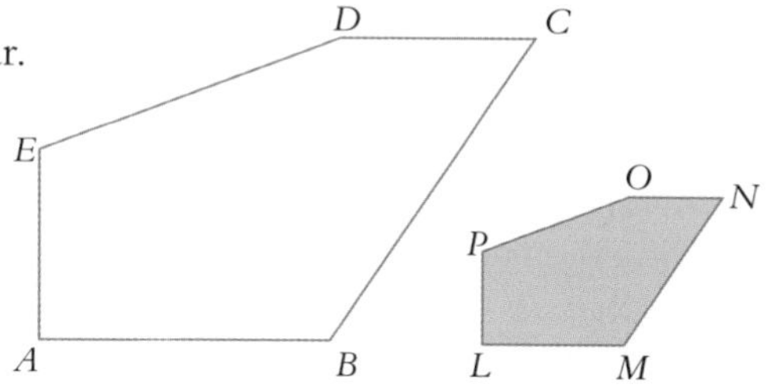

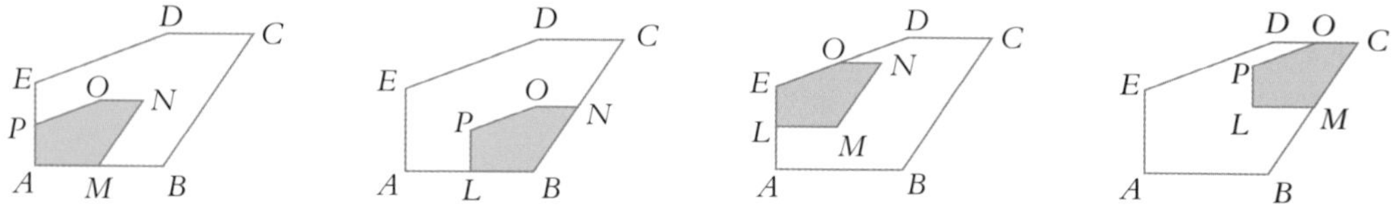

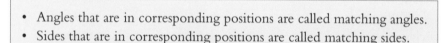

a Which angle in the figure *PLMNO* is in the same position as:

i $\angle A$ ii $\angle B$ iii $\angle C$ iv $\angle D$ v $\angle E$?

b Which side in the figure *PLMNO* is in the same position as:

i *AE* ii *DC* iii *CB* iv *ED* v *AB*?

- Angles that are in corresponding positions are called matching angles.
- Sides that are in corresponding positions are called matching sides.

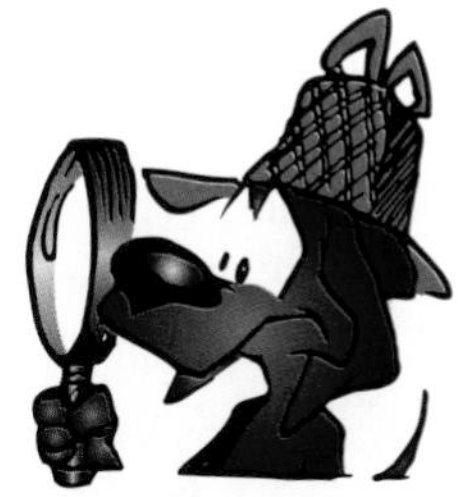

2 For each of the following pairs of similar figures, list the pairs of matching angles and write a similarity statement like *ABCD* ||| *LMNP*.

a
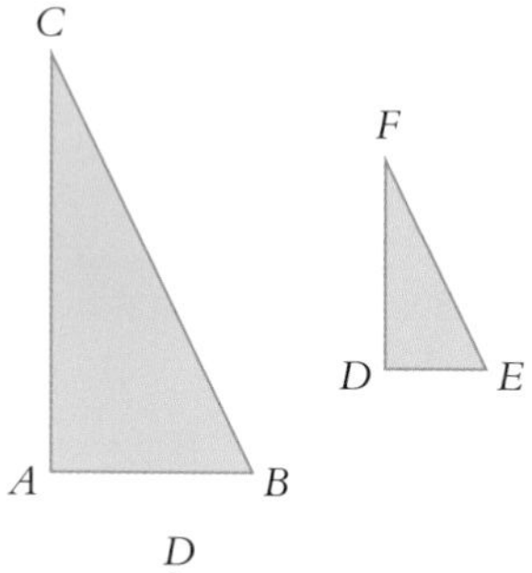

b
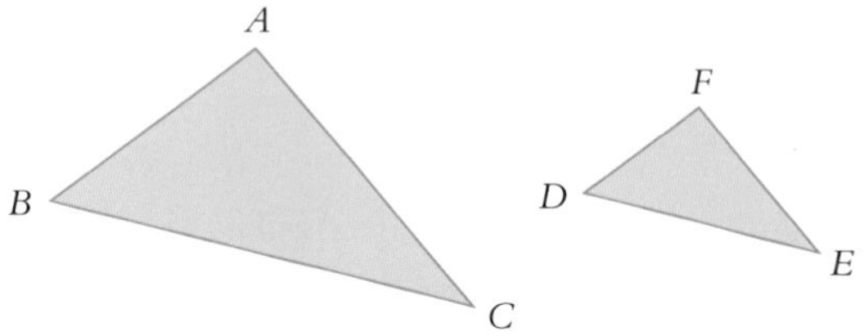

c
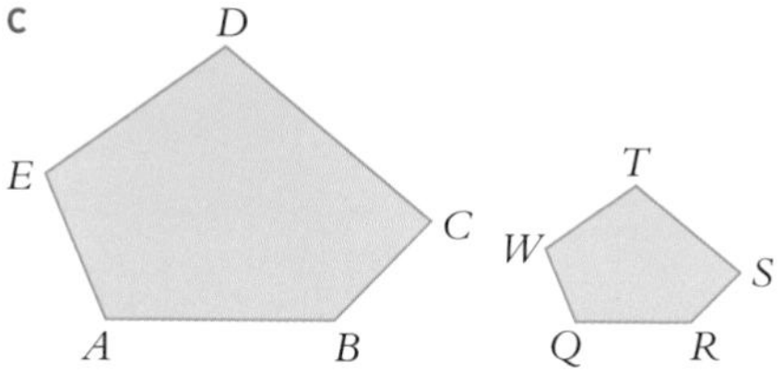

d
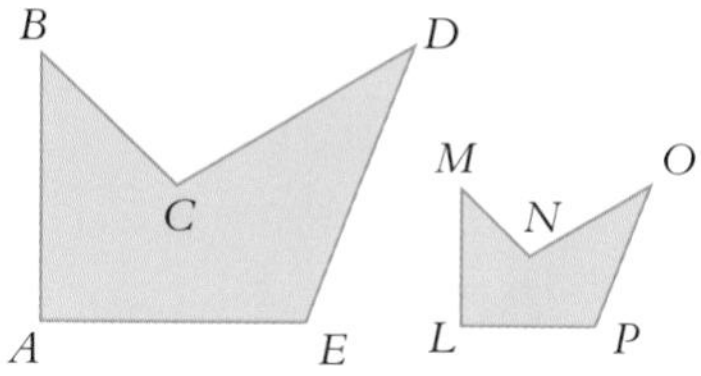

For two figures to be similar, all matching angles must be equal.

List the vertices of similar figures in matching order.

3 For each pair of figures in Question 2, write the pairs of matching sides.

4 a A photograph is 8 cm long and 4 cm wide. If the photograph is to be enlarged so that the length is 16 cm, what will the width be?

b A photograph is enlarged. If the length is tripled, what happens to its width?

c When a photograph is enlarged, is it possible to increase the length without changing the width?

d Could rectangle A be enlarged to give rectangle B?

When enlarging, if you double the length, you must double the width also.

5 Write *true* or *false* for the following, and give a reason for each answer.

a Any two circles are similar.

b Any two equilateral triangles are similar.

c Any two isosceles triangles are similar.

6 a Are all of these circles similar?

b If all the other circles are copies of circle A, what is the enlargement factor for:

i B　　ii C

iii D　　iv E?

c If all the other circles are copies of C, what is the reduction factor for:

i D　　ii A

iii B　　iv E?

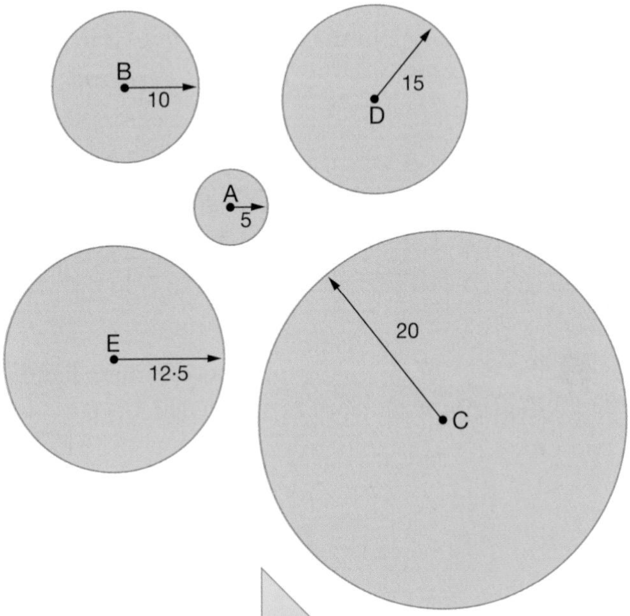

7 The four figures shown are similar.
What is the scale factor that changes:

a A to C

b C to A

c A to B

d B to C

e A to D

f D to B?

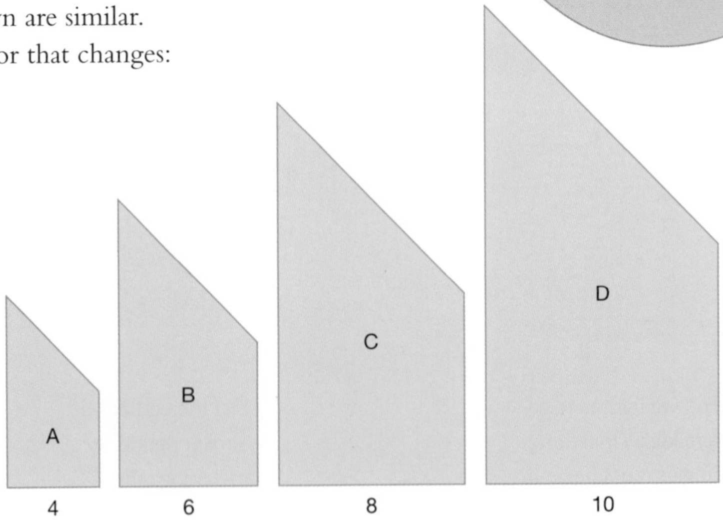

8 Each of the rectangles shown is similar to one of the other rectangles. Find the pairs of rectangles that are similar.

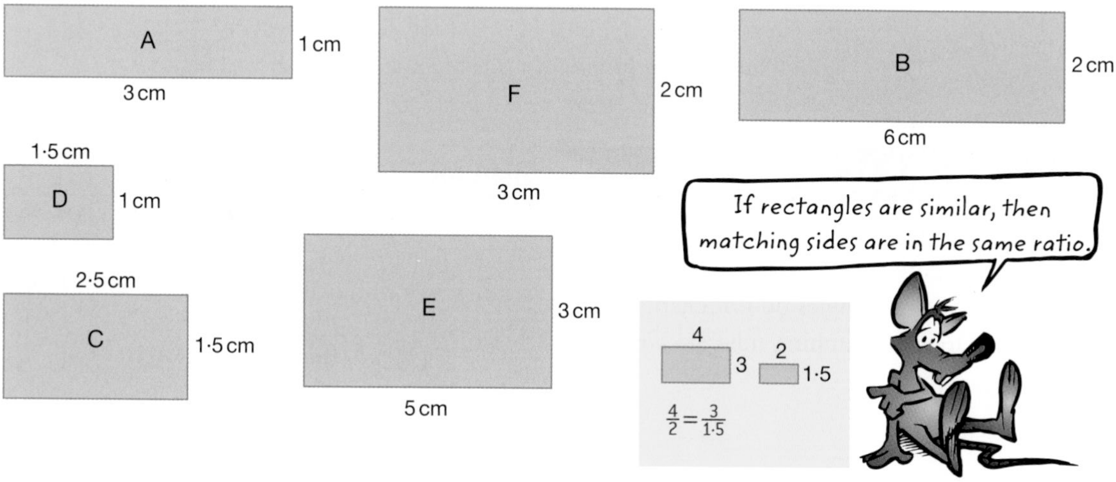

9 Calculate the dimensions of the quadrilateral shown if it is:

a enlarged using a scale factor of 2

b enlarged using a scale factor of 3·2

c reduced using a scale factor of 0·8

d reduced using a scale factor of 0·45.

In each case, list the sides from smallest to largest.

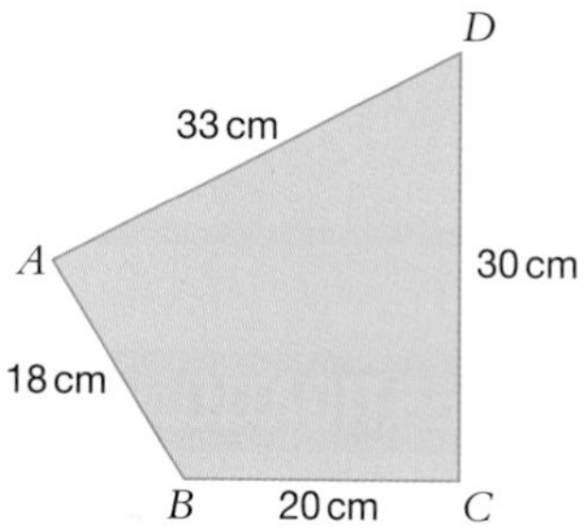

10 The diagram shows the construction for the enlargement of quadrilateral *ABCD* using an enlargement factor of 3. What are the lengths of the sides of the quadrilateral *PQRS*? (*Note: OR* is three times the length of *OC*.)

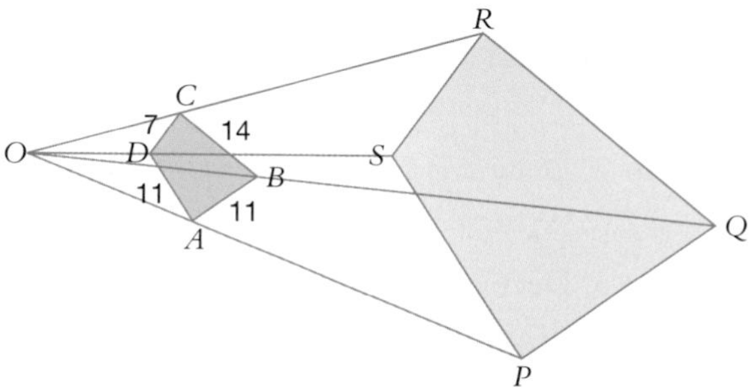

11 On a photocopier, a document can be enlarged or reduced using the zoom function. On most photocopiers the scale factor has to be entered as a percentage.

a What percentage would be used for a scale factor of:

i 2   ii $\frac{1}{2}$?

b What percentage would need to be entered for a scale factor of:

i $2\frac{1}{4}$ ii $\frac{3}{4}$?

c A rectangle that is 10 cm long and 6 cm wide is to be copied on a photocopier. What would the dimensions of the copied rectangle be if it is copied using a scale factor of:

i 160%   ii 80%?

In similar figures:
- matching angles are equal
- the ratio of the lengths of matching sides is constant.

The ratio of matching lengths is the **scale factor**.

P GEOGEBRA ACTIVITY 11:01 SIMILAR FIGURES

This activity allows you to see that when a figure is enlarged or reduced:
- the matching angles do not change
- the ratios of matching sides are equal.

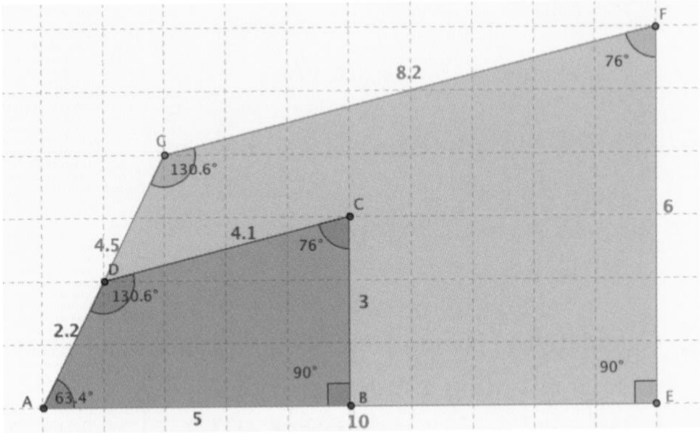

INVESTIGATION 11:01 DRAWING ENLARGEMENTS AND REDUCTIONS

- To draw a figure similar to *ABCD* by enlargement, follow these steps.

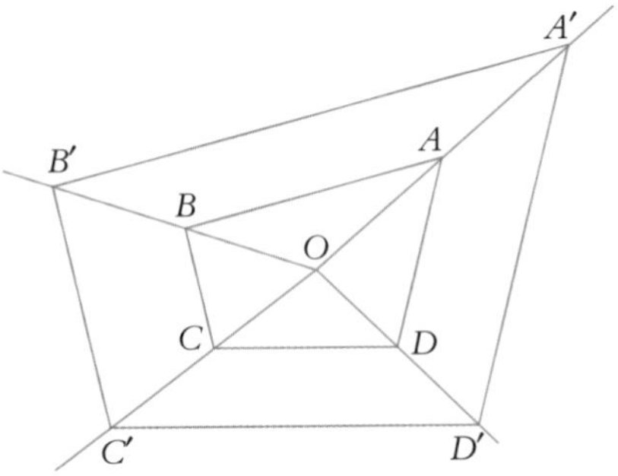

Step 1 Select a point *O* to be the centre of enlargement.

Step 2 Draw rays from *O* through each of the vertices *A*, *B*, *C* and *D*.

Step 3 Decide on an enlargement factor, say 2.

Step 4 Move each vertex to a new position on its ray, which is twice its present distance from *O*. For example, if *A* is 18 mm from *O*, then the new position is 36 mm from *O*.

- Draw a figure like those below and then make a similar figure using the method above. Try using different scale factors.

a

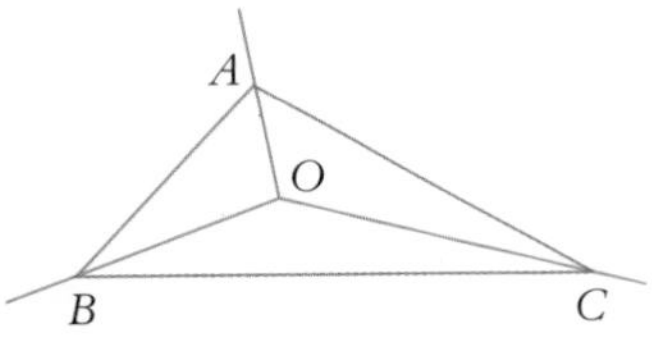

b

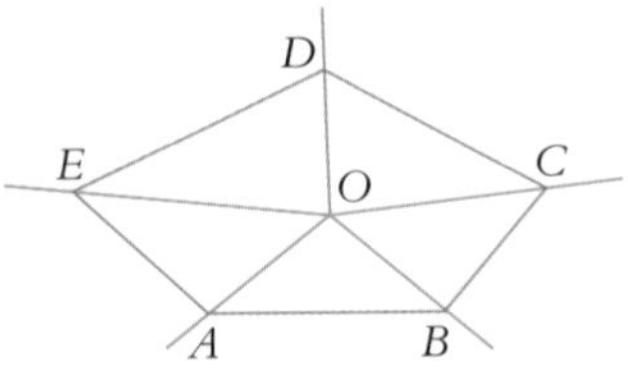

c

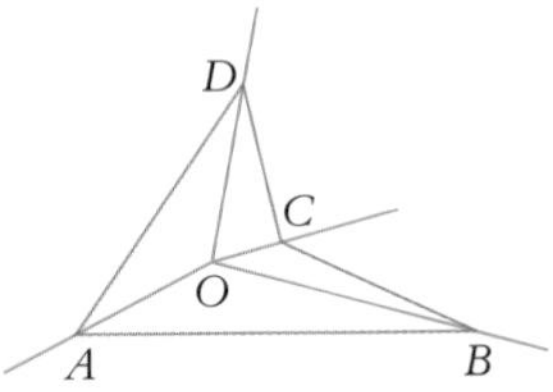

- Measure the angles of each figure and check that matching angles are equal. Measure the sides of each figure and find the ratio of each pair of matching sides. These should be equal.
- If your construction is accurate you should also find that each pair of matching sides is parallel.

11:02 Finding unknown sides of similar figures

PREP QUIZ 11:02

The two triangles are similar.
What side matches:

1 AB **2** AC **3** BC?

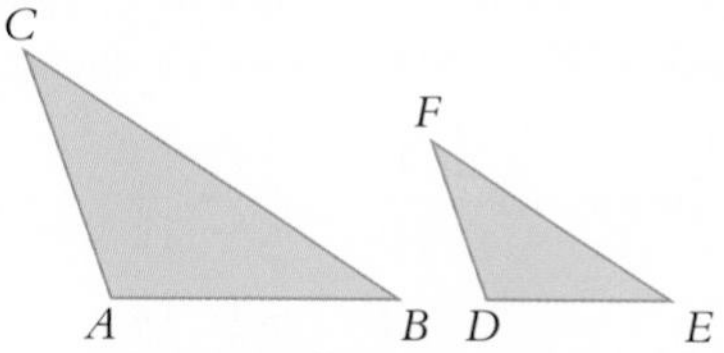

What is the scale factor that changes:

4 A to B **5** A to C
6 B to C **7** C to B
8 C to A **9** B to A?

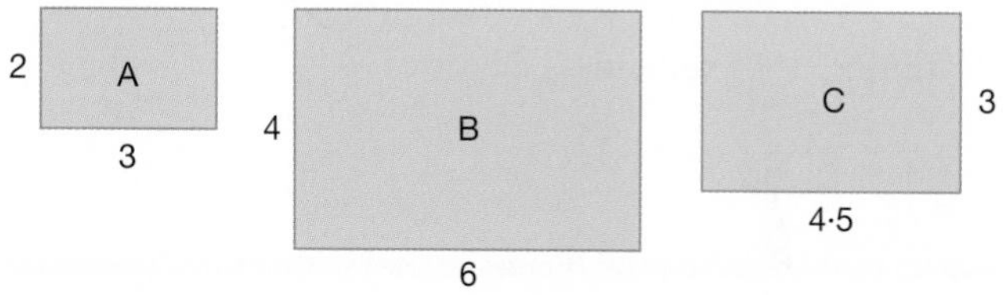

10 A triangle with sides of 3 cm, 4 cm and 5 cm is enlarged using a scale factor of 3. In the enlarged triangle, what will be the length of the:
a longest side **b** shortest side?

WORKED EXAMPLE 1

The two figures shown are similar. Calculate the enlargement factor and use it to find the value of the pronumerals.

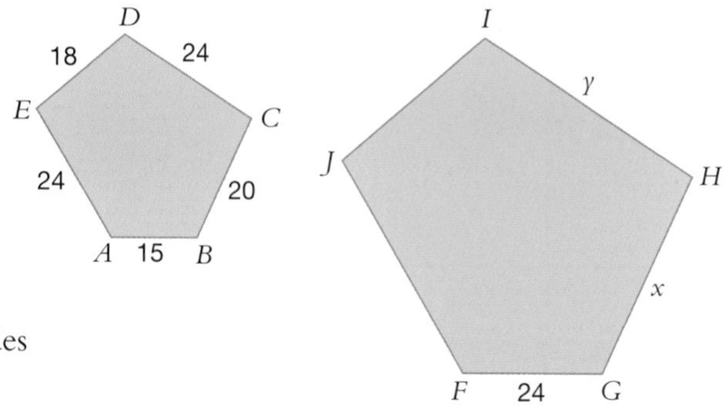

Solution

Enlargement factor = ratio of matching sides

$$= \frac{FG}{AB} = \frac{24}{15} = 1·6$$

$x = 1·6 \times 20$
$= 32$

$y = 1·6 \times 24$
$= 38·4$

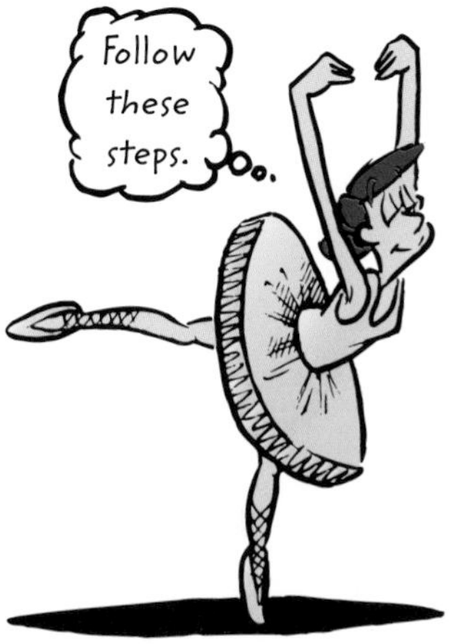

Follow these steps:

Step 1 Use a pair of known matching sides to calculate the enlargement or reduction factor.

Step 2 Find the unknown side and its matching side.

Step 3 Multiply the known side by the scale factor.

WORKED EXAMPLE 2

ABCD is similar to *EFGH*.
Find the values of x and y.

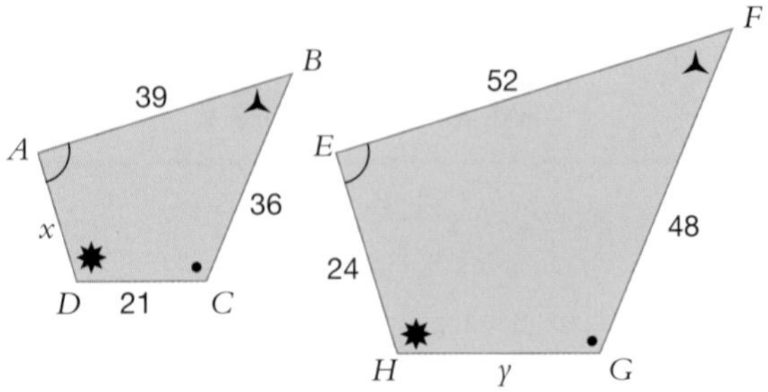

Solution

The scale factor can be found by dividing any pair of matching sides.

$\therefore$ Reduction factor: $\frac{AB}{EF} = \frac{39}{52} = \frac{3}{4}$

$\therefore$ Enlargement factor: $\frac{EF}{AB} = \frac{52}{39} = \frac{4}{3}$

To find x, use a reduction factor of $\frac{3}{4}$.

$x = \frac{3}{4} \times 24$
$= 18$

To find y, use and enlargement factor of $\frac{4}{3}$.

$y = \frac{4}{3} \times 21$
$= 28$

If the scale factor of similar figures is $2:3$, then:
- the *reduction factor* is $\frac{2}{3}$
- the *enlargement factor* is $\frac{3}{2}$

e.g. In these triangles the scale factor is $20:30$ or $2:3$.

$\therefore x = \frac{2}{3} \times 24$

$y = \frac{3}{2} \times 28$

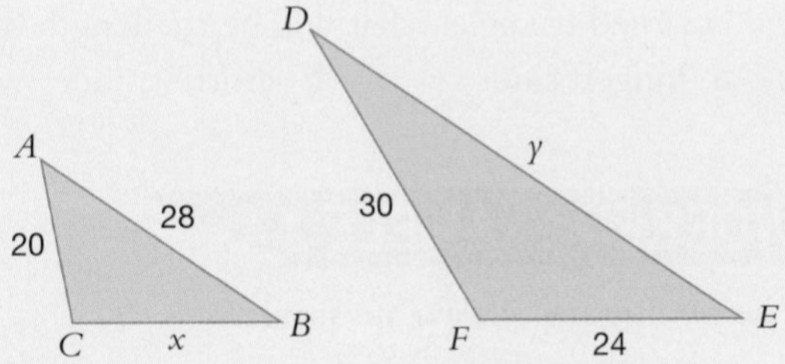

ΔABC is similar to ΔDEF is written as:

$\Delta ABC \,|||\, \Delta DEF$

Exercise 11:02

P Foundation worksheet 11:02
Similar figures

1 In each case, give the reduction factor and the enlargement factor of these similar figures.

a

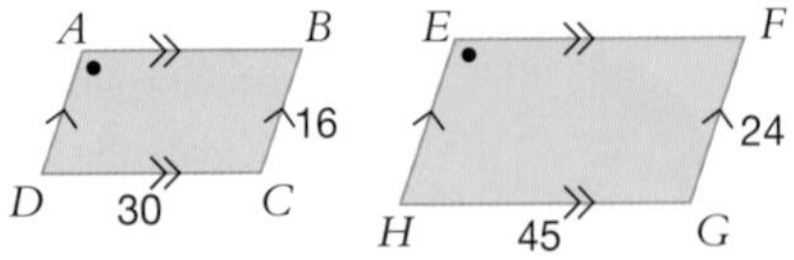

Scale factor = $30:45 = 2:3$

Reduction factor = $\frac{\square}{\square}$

Enlargement factor = $\frac{\square}{\square}$

b

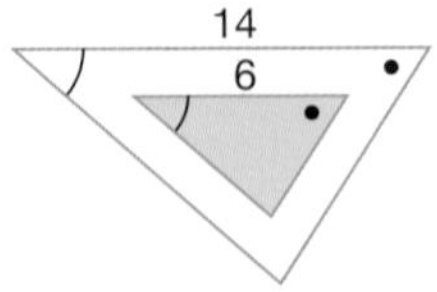

Scale factor = $14:6 = 7:3$

Reduction factor = $\frac{\square}{\square}$

Enlargement factor = $\frac{\square}{\square}$

c

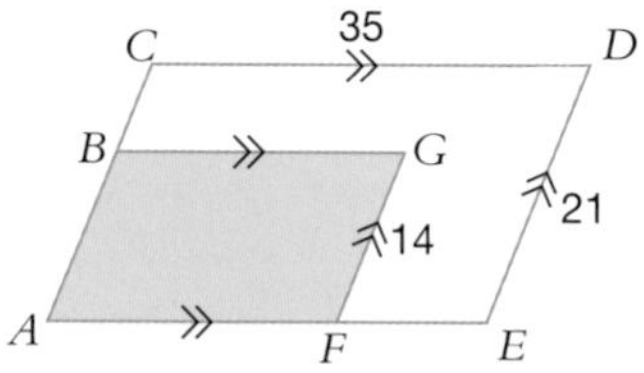

Scale factor = 21 : 14 = 3 : 2

Reduction factor = $\frac{\square}{\square}$

Enlargement factor = $\frac{\square}{\square}$

d

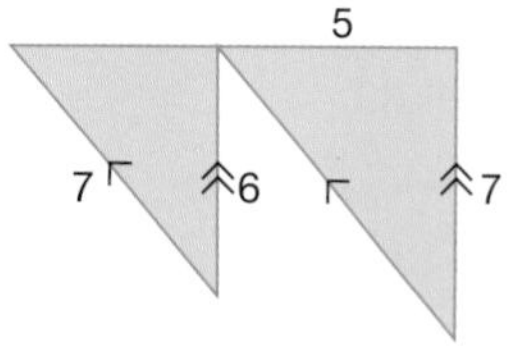

Scale factor = 6 : 7

Reduction factor = $\frac{\square}{\square}$

Enlargement factor = $\frac{\square}{\square}$

2 In each part, the figures are similar. Find the value of each pronumeral.

a

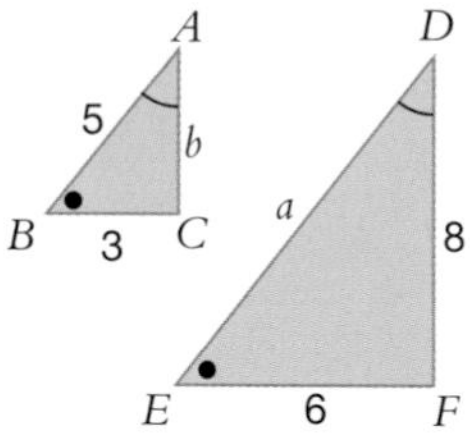

Scale factor = 3 : 6 = 1 : 2

Enlargement factor = 2

Reduction factor = $\frac{1}{2}$

$a = \ldots \times 5$ $\quad b = \ldots \times 8$

$\therefore a = \ldots$ $\quad \therefore b = \ldots$

b

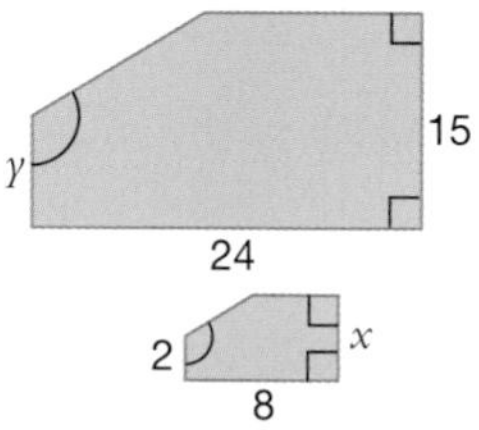

Scale factor = 24 : 8 = 3 : 1

Enlargement factor = 3

Reduction factor = $\frac{1}{3}$

$x = \ldots \times 15$ $\quad y = \ldots \times 2$

$\therefore x = \ldots$ $\quad \therefore y = \ldots$

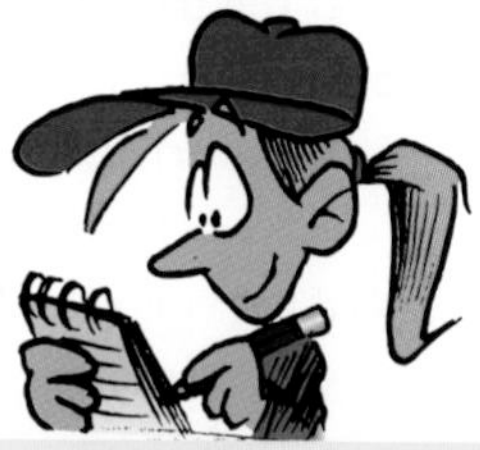

c

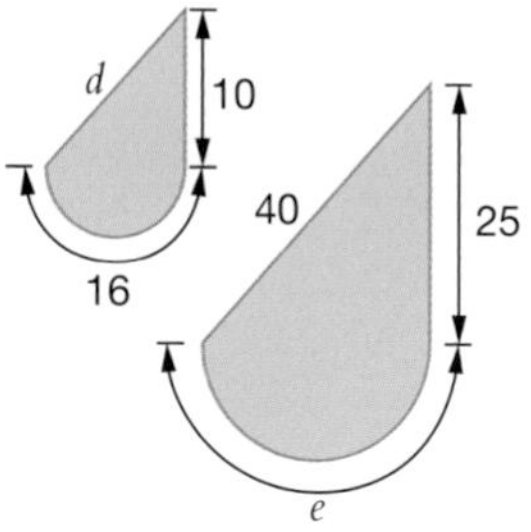

Scale factor = 10 : 25 = 2 : 5

Enlargement factor = $\frac{5}{2}$

Reduction factor = $\frac{2}{5}$

$d = \ldots \times 40$ $\quad e = \ldots \times 16$

$\therefore d = \ldots$ $\quad \therefore e = \ldots$

||| means 'is similar to'
e.g. $\Delta ABC \, ||| \, \Delta DEF$

3 Each of the following pairs of figures are similar. Find the enlargement factor and use it to find the value of each pronumeral.

a

b

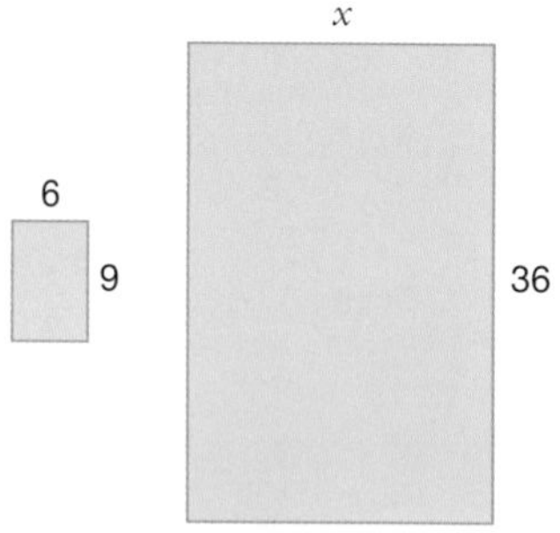

c

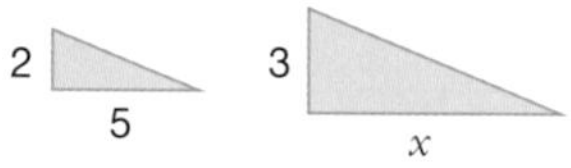

d

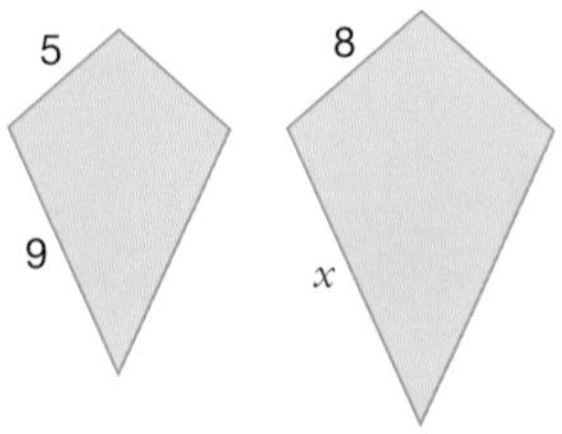

4 Each of the following pairs of figures are similar. Find the reduction factor and use it to find the value of each pronumeral.

a
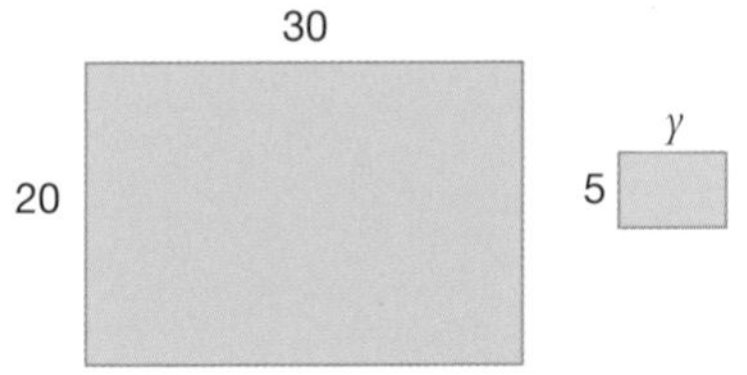

b
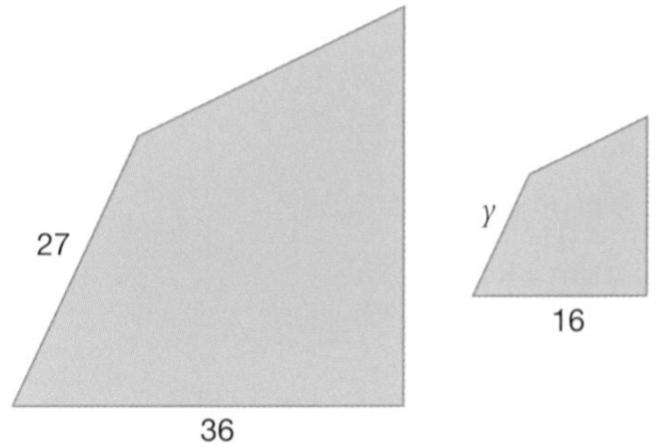

c
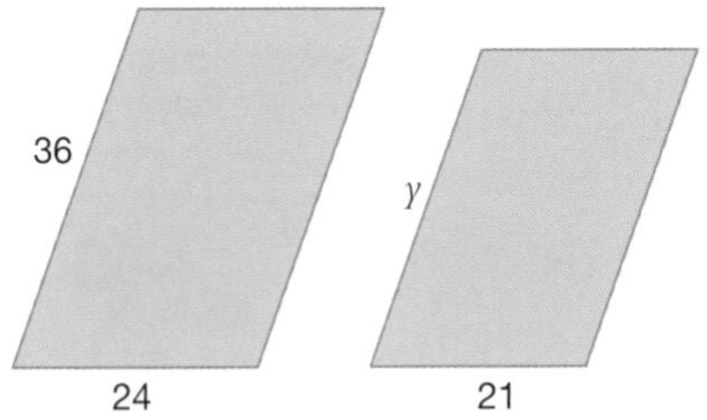

d
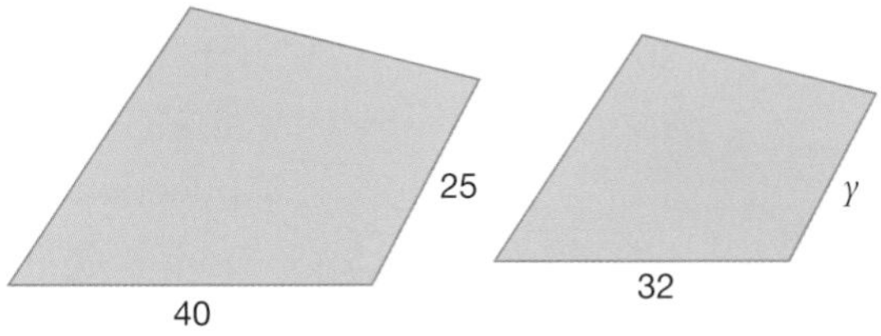

5 A triangle has sides of length 9 cm, 12 cm and 15 cm.

a If the triangle is enlarged using a scale factor of 4, what will be the length of the shortest side?

b If the triangle is reduced using a scale factor of $\frac{2}{3}$, what will be the length of the longest side?

c If the triangle is enlarged so that the longest side becomes 21 cm long, what would the scale factor be? How long would the shortest side of the enlarged triangle be?

d A rectangular photograph is 15 cm long and 10 cm wide. If this is enlarged on a photocopier so that the length becomes 18 cm, what would the width become?

6 The figures in each part are similar. Find the scale factor and the value of the pronumeral for each part.

a
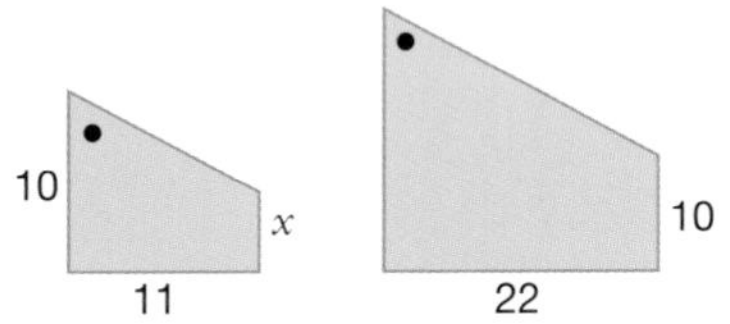

b
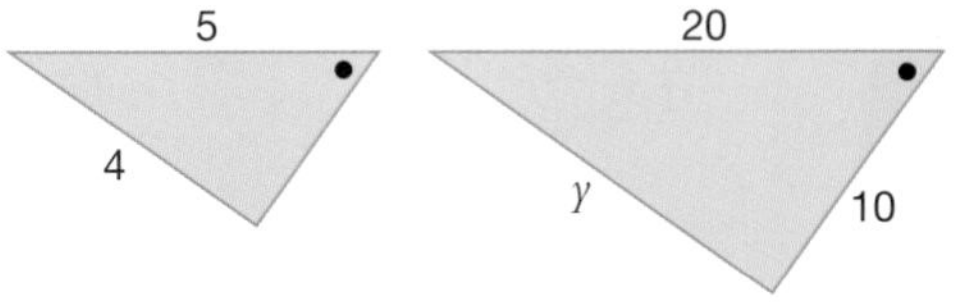

c
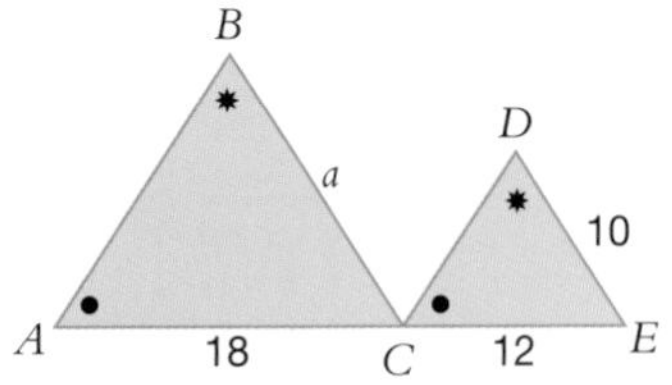

d
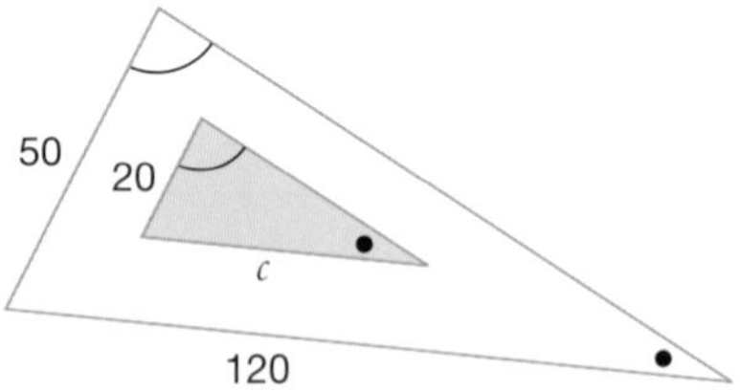

e
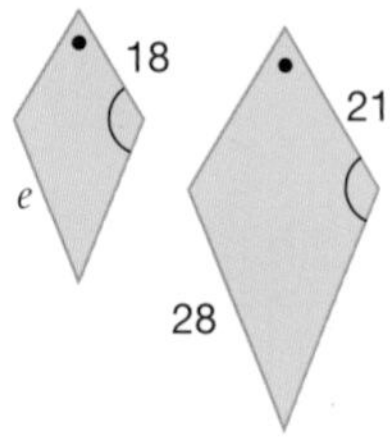

f
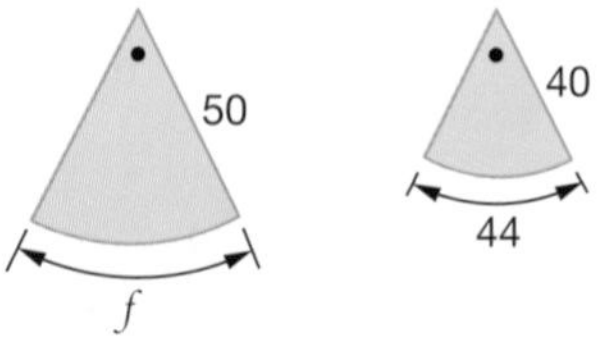

7 For these similar figures, write each scale factor and find the value of the pronumerals, correct to one decimal place.

a

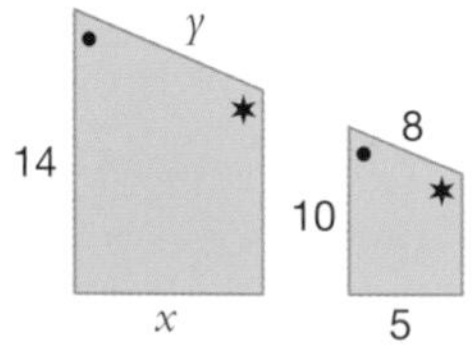

b

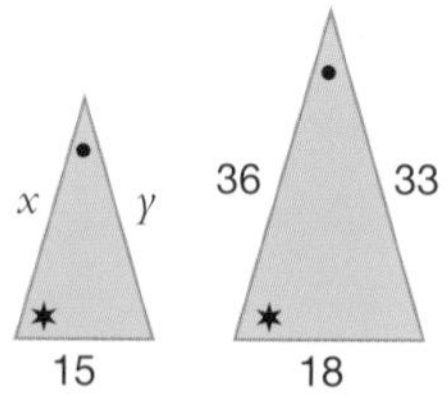

c

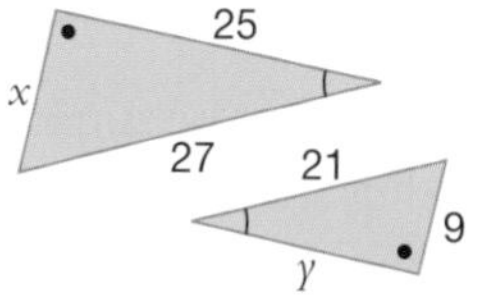

d

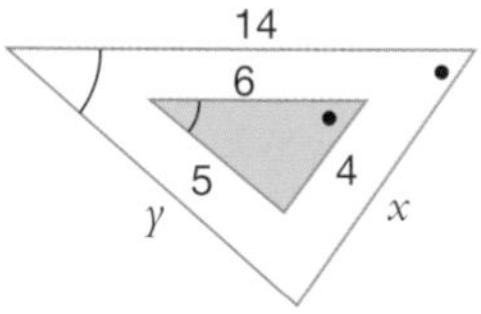

e

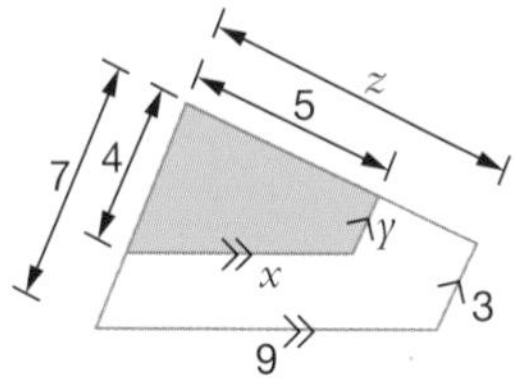

From the scale factor you can write the reduction or enlargement factor.

INVESTIGATION 11:02 PHOTO ENLARGEMENTS

A photographic store offers to print any combination of three sizes of the same photo on a single sheet of paper that is 30·5 cm by 21 cm. The different sizes are used in the combination below. The sizes are all similar and have lengths of 25 cm, 18 cm and 12 cm. The width of the largest photo is 20 cm.

1 Calculate the widths of each of the two smaller photo sizes.

2 Investigate what combinations of the three photo sizes are possible on the 30·5 cm by 21 cm sheet. Describe how you could arrange the photos.

The mathematics of similar figures is used in building models.

11:03 Similar triangles

For two *figures* to be similar you need to show that:

- matching angles are equal **and**
- matching sides are in the same ratio.

The following exercises investigate the conditions that are necessary for two *triangles* to be similar.

11:03A Matching angles

Similar triangles have matching angles that are equal.

Exercise 11:03A

1 The two triangles have the same-sized angles.

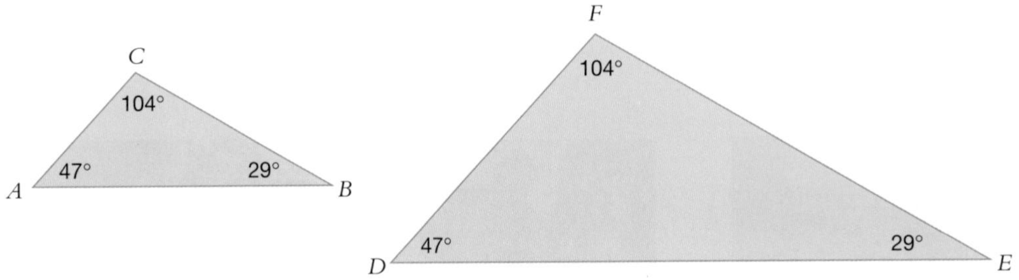

a Measure the side lengths to the nearest millimetre and complete the table below.

Side	AB	AC	BC	DE	DF	EF
Length						

b Use your answers above to calculate each of the following side ratios, correct to one decimal place.

i $\dfrac{DE}{AB}$ ii $\dfrac{DF}{AC}$ iii $\dfrac{EF}{BC}$

c *True* or *false?* $\dfrac{DE}{AB} = \dfrac{DF}{AC} = \dfrac{EF}{BC}$

> If the ratios of matching sides are equal, we say that the three sides of one triangle are proportional to the three sides of the other triangle. More simply, the sides of the triangles are proportional.

2 a Measure the lengths of the sides of ΔABC and ΔDEF to the nearest millimetre.

b Calculate the value of the following ratios, correct to one decimal place:

i $\frac{DE}{AB}$ ii $\frac{EF}{BC}$ iii $\frac{DF}{AC}$

c Are the sides of the triangles proportional?

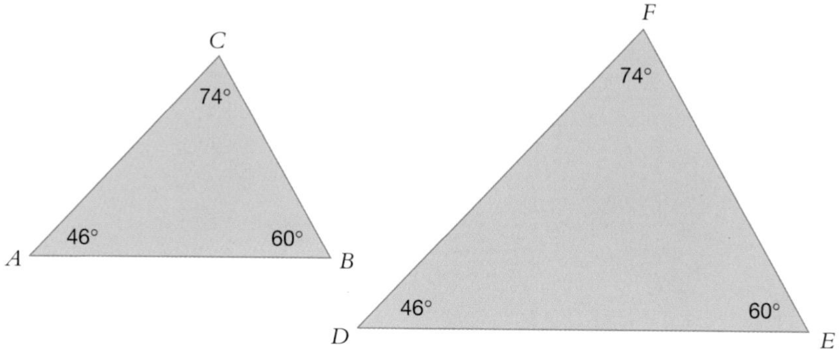

3 The three triangles shown are drawn on a grid of parallel lines. All of the small triangles are congruent.

a Consider ΔABC and ΔDEF.

i Are the matching angles equal?

ii What is the value of each of the matching side ratios $\frac{DE}{AB}, \frac{EF}{BC}, \frac{DF}{AC}$?

iii Are the sides of the two triangles proportional?

b Consider ΔGHI and ΔDEF.

i Name the pairs of matching angles. Are the matching angles equal?

ii What is the value of each of the following ratios: $\frac{DE}{GH}, \frac{EF}{HI}, \frac{DF}{IG}$?

iii Are the triangles similar?

Congruent figures are the same shape and size. When one is placed on top of the other they coincide exactly.

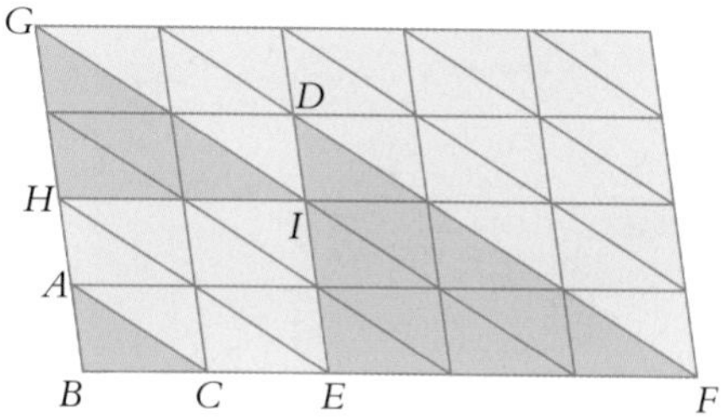

Questions 1 to 3 illustrate the following result.

Test 1
If two angles of one triangle are equal to two angles of another triangle, then the two triangles are similar.

4 Identify the triangles that are similar in each of the following.

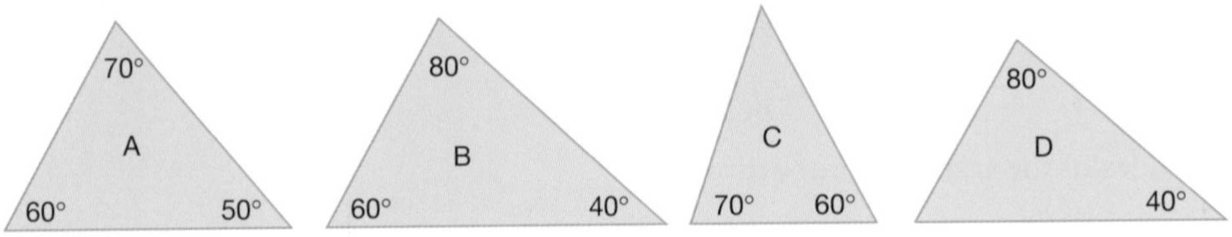

5 Below are five pairs of similar triangles. Each of the triangles A to E is similar to one of the triangles F to J. Select the triangle that is similar to triangle:

a A **b** B **c** C **d** D **e** E

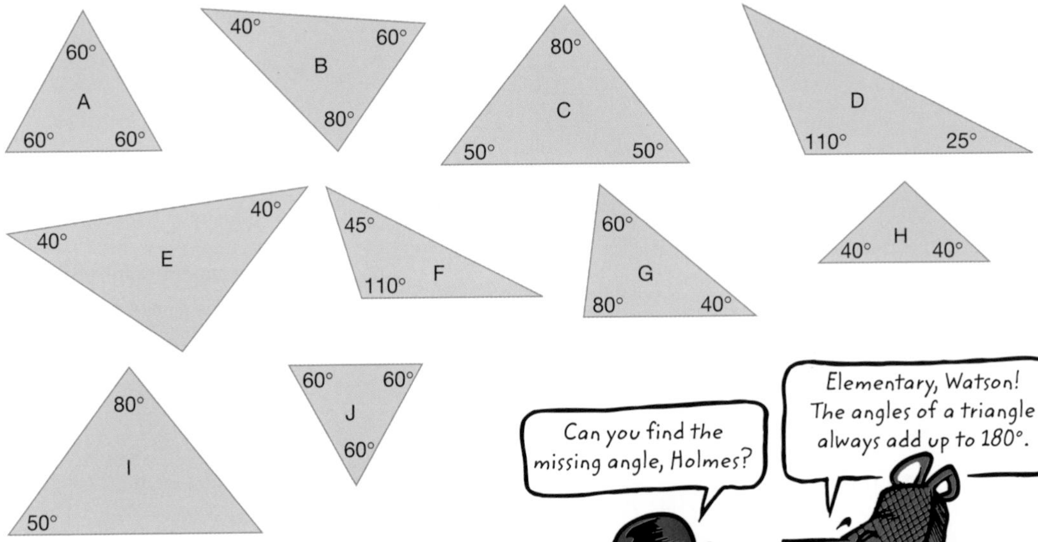

Can you find the missing angle, Holmes?
Elementary, Watson! The angles of a triangle always add up to 180°.

11:03B Ratios of matching sides

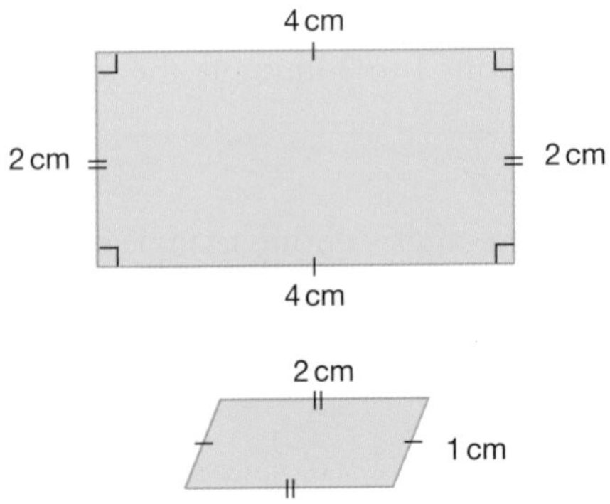

The rectangle and parallelogram shown here are a reminder that if the ratios of matching sides are equal, then the figures are not necessarily similar. The matching angles must also be equal.

In this exercise we investigate pairs of triangles that have matching sides in the same ratio.

Exercise 11:03B

1 Triangle ABC has been used to form a grid that has three sets of parallel lines.

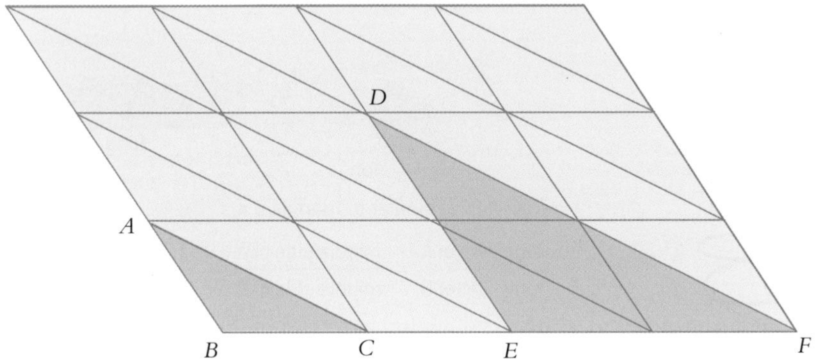

a Are all the sides of ΔDEF twice as long as the sides of ΔABC?

b What is the value of each of the following ratios?

i $\dfrac{DF}{AC}$ ii $\dfrac{DE}{AB}$ iii $\dfrac{EF}{BC}$

c Are the sides of the triangles proportional?

d Are the matching angles equal?

e Are the triangles similar?

2 a Evaluate the ratios $\dfrac{BC}{YZ}$, $\dfrac{AC}{XZ}$ and $\dfrac{AB}{XY}$.

Are the three sides of ΔABC proportional to the three sides of ΔXYZ?

b Are the matching angles equal?

c Are the two triangles similar?

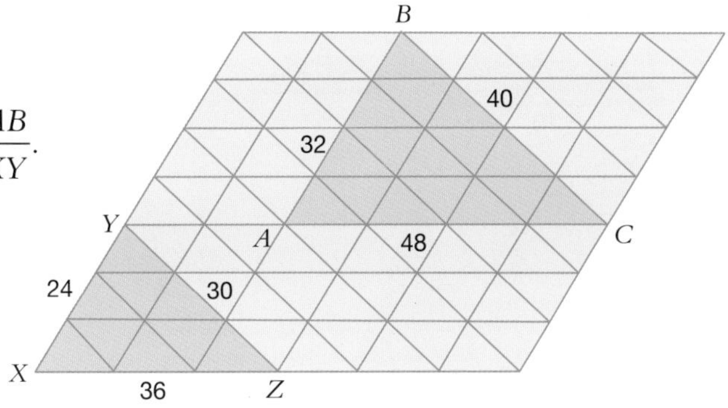

Questions 1 and 2 illustrate the following result.

> **Test 2**
> If the three sides of one triangle are proportional to the three sides of another triangle, then the triangles are similar. This means that matching angles are also equal.

3 Identify the triangles that are similar in each of the following.

a

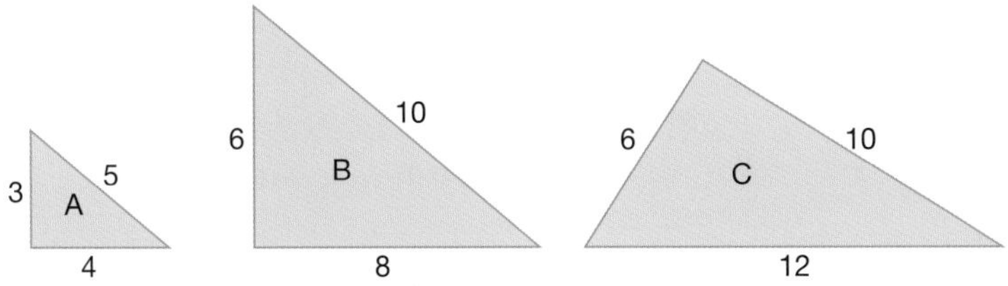

b

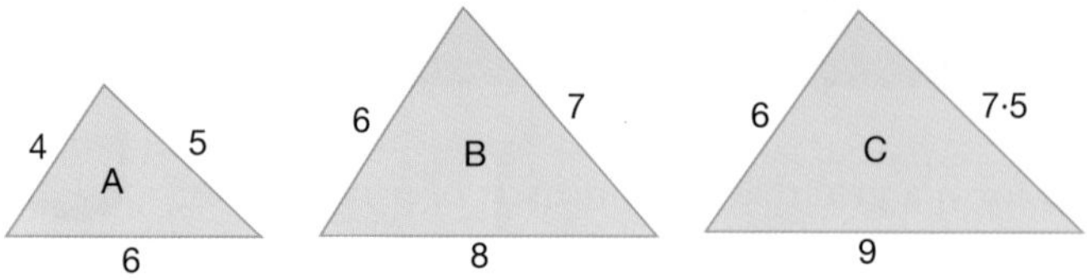

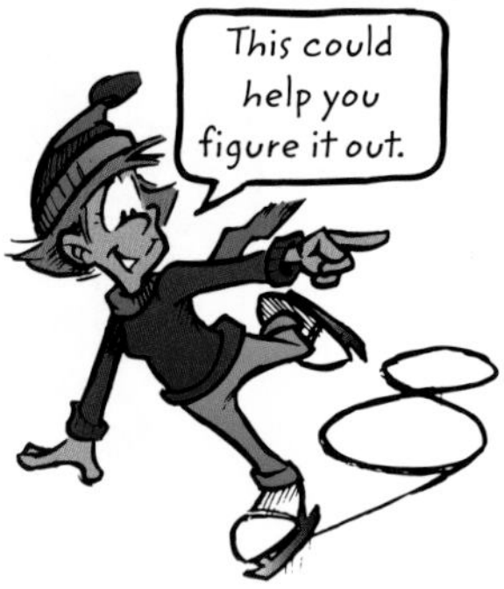

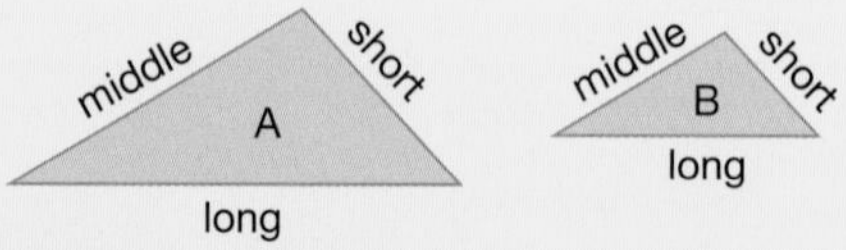

Triangle A is similar to triangle B if:

$$\frac{\text{long side of A}}{\text{long side of B}} = \frac{\text{middle side of A}}{\text{middle side of B}} = \frac{\text{short side of A}}{\text{short side of B}}$$

If these ratios are equal the sides of the triangles are said to be in proportion (or proportional).

4 Below are five pairs of similar triangles. Each of the triangles A to E is similar to one of the triangles F to J. By checking the ratios of matching sides, find the triangle that is similar to:

a A **b** B **c** C **d** D **e** E

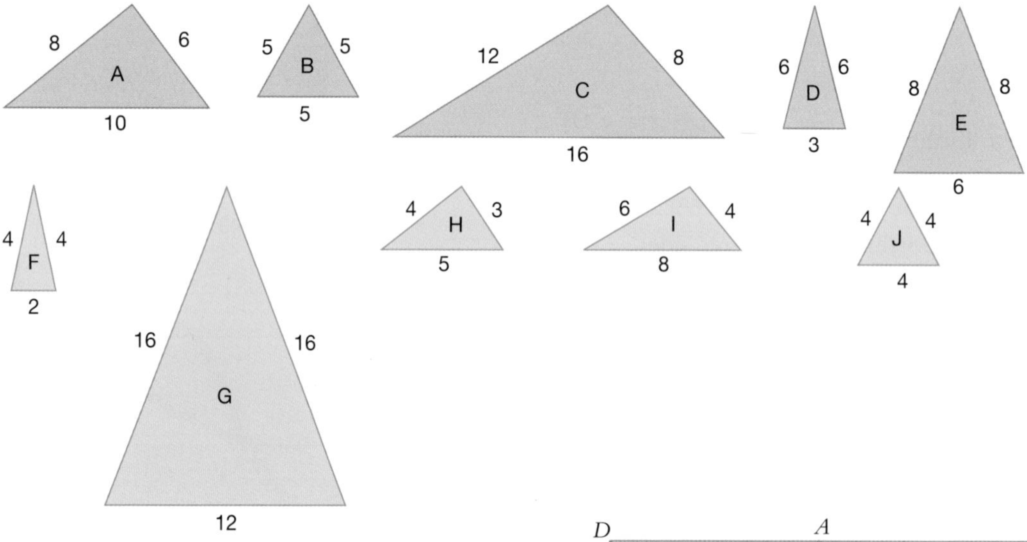

5 In ΔABC and ΔDEF:

$$\frac{DE}{AB} = \frac{EF}{BC} = 2 \text{ and } \angle B = \angle E.$$

a Does $\dfrac{DF}{AC} = 2$?

b Are the two triangles similar?

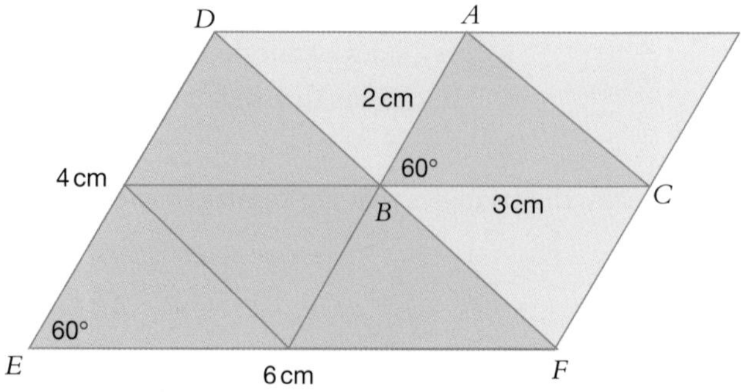

Question **5** illustrates the third condition for two triangles to be similar.

> **Test 3**
> If two sides of one triangle are proportional to two sides of another triangle, and the included angles are equal, then the two triangles are similar.

6 Identify the pair of similar triangles in each of the following.

a

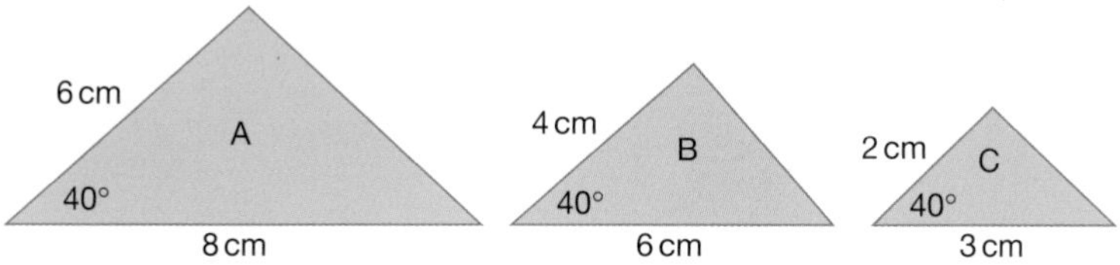

b

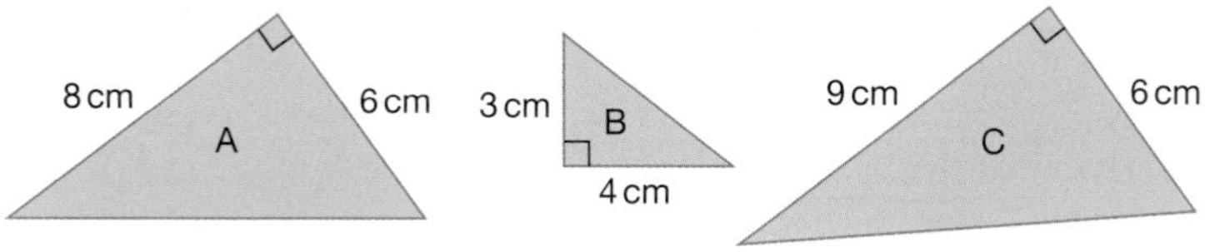

7 In ΔABC and ΔDEF:

$$\frac{DF}{AC} = \frac{DE}{AB} = 3 \text{ and}$$

$\angle ABC$ and $\angle DEF$ are both right angles.

a Does $\dfrac{EF}{BC} = 3$? **b** Are the two triangles similar?

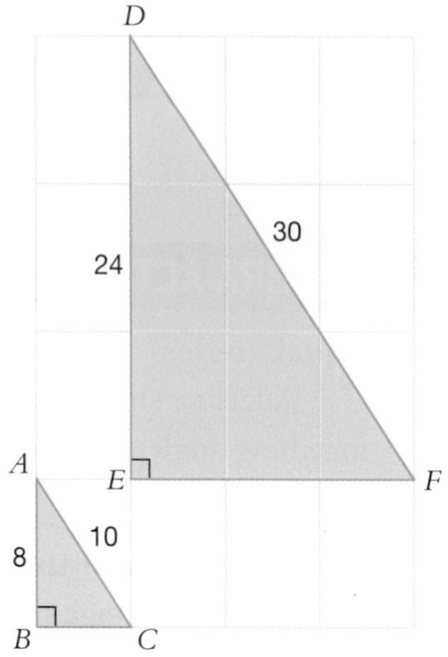

Question **7** illustrates the fourth condition for two triangles to be similar.

> **Test 4**
> If the hypotenuse and a second side of a right-angled triangle are proportional to the hypotenuse and a second side of another right-angled triangle, then the two triangles are similar.

8 Identify the pair of similar triangles in each of the following.

a

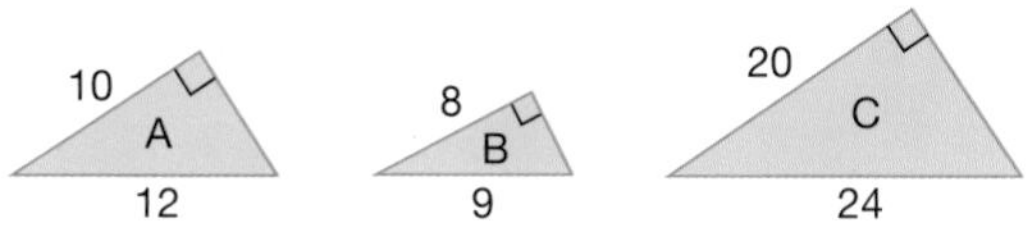

b

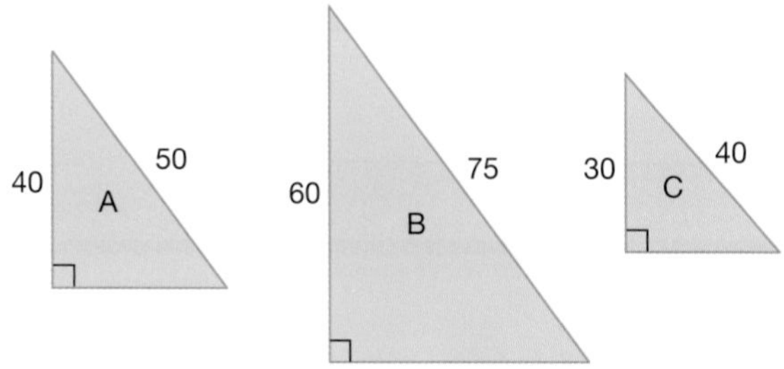

c

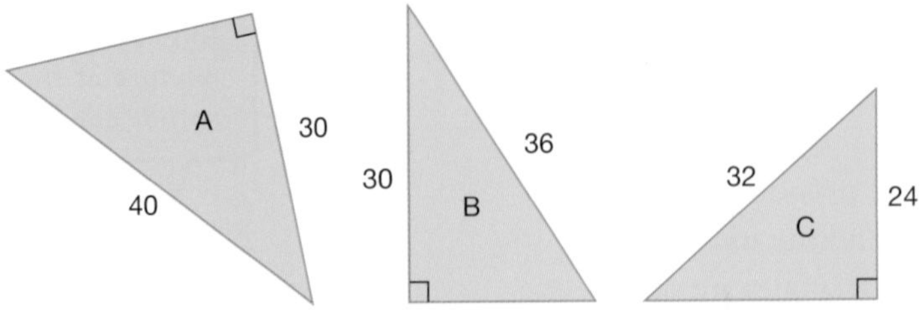

9 Find two similar triangles in each of the following. State which condition could be used to show that the triangles are similar. (Triangles may overlap.)

a

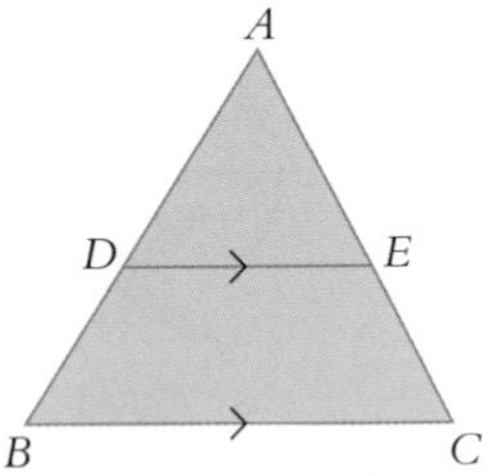

b

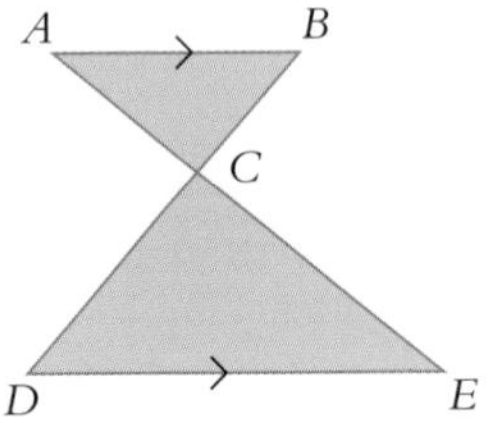

c

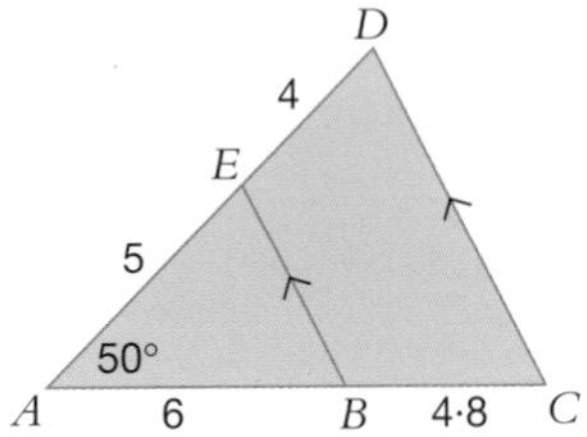

d

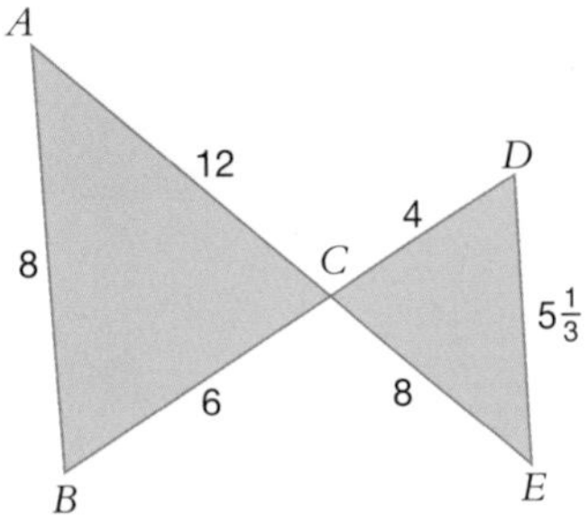

e

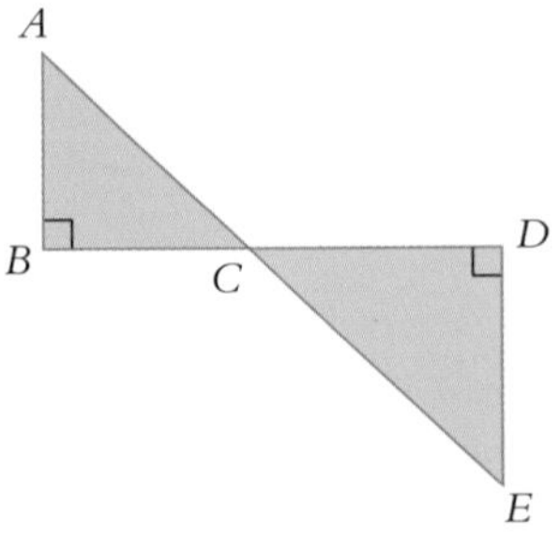

You'll need to remember your angle geometry in a, b and e.

P GEOGEBRA ACTIVITY 11:03 SIMILAR TRIANGLES

1 **Equal angles**

Use sliders to change the sizes of the angles in a pair of triangles. You can see that when matching angles are equal, the ratios of matching sides are also equal. Hence, the two triangles are similar.

2 **Matching sides in the same ratio**

Use sliders to change the lengths of the sides. As the side lengths change, the ratios of the matching sides also change. You can see that when the ratios of matching sides are equal, the matching angles are also equal. Hence, the triangles are similar.

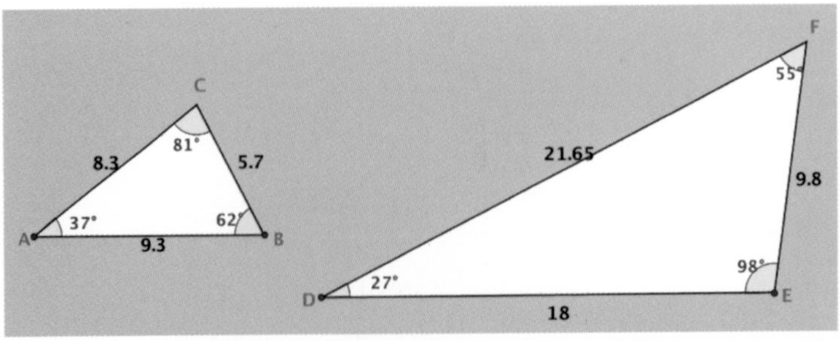

11:04 Using proportion to find unknown sides

PREP QUIZ 11:04

Complete the following.

1 In any triangle, the longest side is opposite the …… angle.

2 In any triangle, the smallest side is opposite the …… angle.

3 If two triangles are similar, the two longest sides are matching. *True* or *false*?

4 If two triangles are similar, the two shortest sides are matching. *True* or *false*?

5 Matching sides are opposite matching angles. *True* or *false*?

The triangles on the right are similar.

6 Which is the matching side to *AB*?

7 Complete the proportion statement:

$$\frac{1\cdot5}{2} = \frac{2\cdot25}{?} = \frac{3}{?}$$

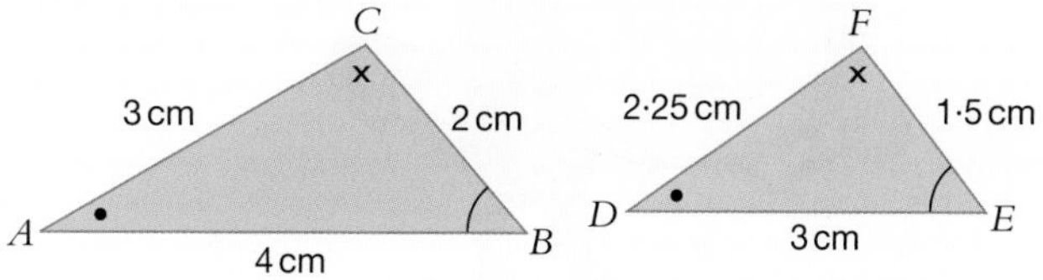

In the triangles on the right, which side in ΔEDF is in a matching position to:

8 *BC*

9 *AC*?

10 Complete the proportion statement:

$$\frac{8}{6} = \frac{16}{?} = \frac{20}{?}$$

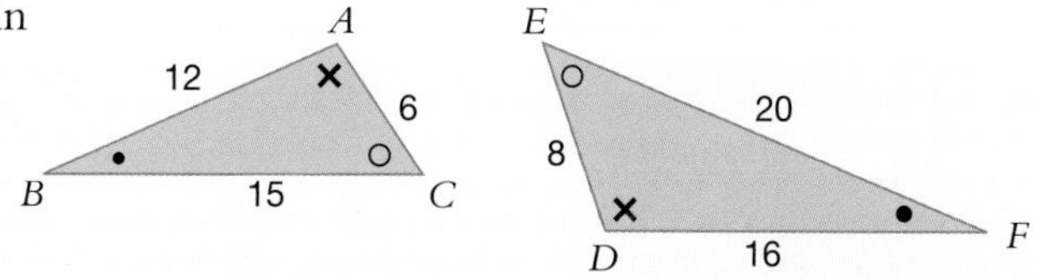

The unknown sides in similar triangles can be found using the scale factor method (see Section 11:02) or by using a proportion statement (i.e. a statement that matching sides are in the same ratio).

WORKED EXAMPLE 1

Find the value of the pronumeral.

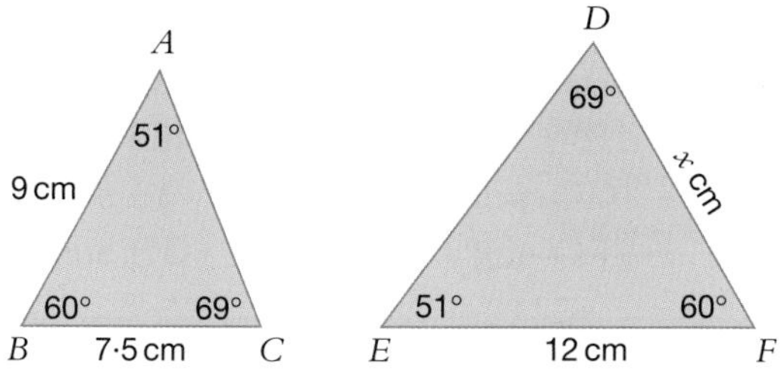

The symbol ||| means 'is similar to'.

Solution

$\Delta ABC ||| \Delta EFD$ (matching angles are equal)

The matching sides are:

x and 7·5 (both opposite 51° angle)

12 and 9 (both opposite the 69° angle)

$$\frac{x}{7\cdot5} = \frac{12}{9} \quad \text{(sides are in proportion)}$$

$$x = 7\cdot5 \times \frac{12}{9}$$

$$x = 10 \text{ cm}$$

WORKED EXAMPLE 2

a Find the value of the pronumeral.

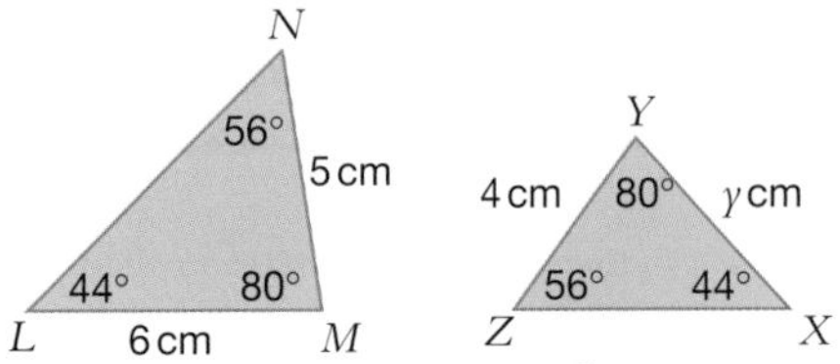

Solution

$\Delta LMN \,|||\, XYZ$ (matching angles are equal)

The matching sides are:

y and 6 (both opposite 56° angle)

4 and 5 (both opposite the 44° angle)

$$\frac{y}{6} = \frac{4}{5} \quad \text{(sides are in proportion)}$$

$$y = 6 \times \frac{4}{5}$$

$$y = 4{\cdot}8\text{ cm}$$

The symbol ||| means 'is similar to'.

b Find the value of the pronumeral.

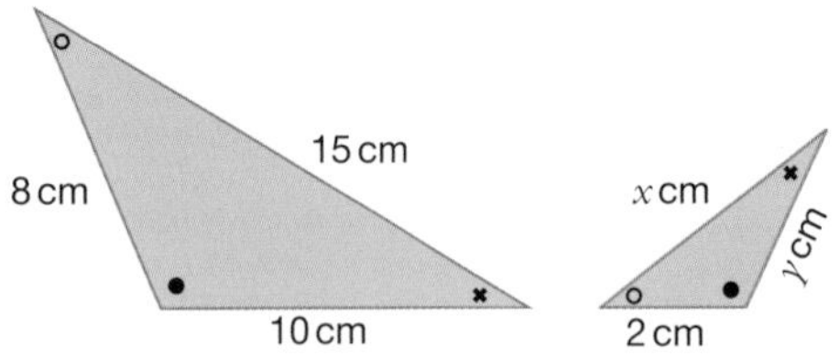

In any proportion statement such as this:

$$\frac{x}{15} = \frac{y}{10} = \frac{2}{8}$$

- the sides on the top all come from the same triangle
- the matching sides underneath these all come from the other triangle.

When finding an unknown side, check your answer by asking yourself: 'Should the unknown side be bigger or smaller than its matching side?'

Solution

The triangles are similar as the matching angles are equal. As matching sides are opposite matching angles, the matching pairs are:

x and 15, y and 10 and 2 and 8

$$\therefore \frac{x}{15} = \frac{y}{10} = \frac{2}{8} \quad \text{(sides are in proportion)}$$

$\frac{x}{15} = \frac{2}{8}$ and $\frac{y}{10} = \frac{2}{8}$

$x = 15 \times \frac{2}{8}$ $\qquad$ $y = 10 \times \frac{2}{8}$

$= 3{\cdot}75$ $\qquad$ $= 2{\cdot}5$

Exercise 11:04

P Foundation worksheet 11:04
Finding unknown sides in similar triangles

1 For each of the following, copy and complete the working.

a

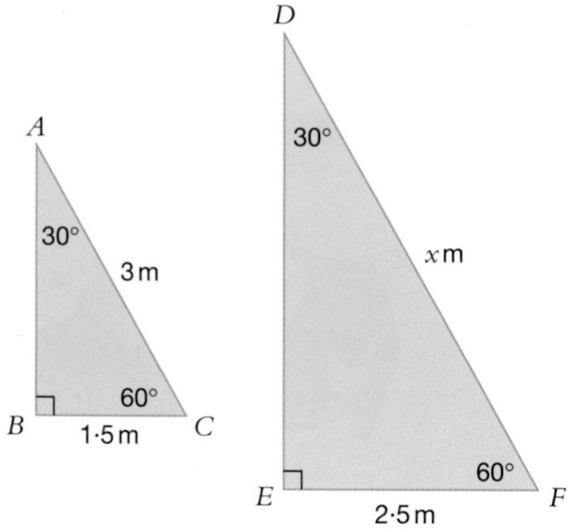

$\Delta ABC \,|||\, \Delta DEF$

AB matches with …

BC matches with …

AC matches with …

$\therefore \dfrac{DF}{\ldots} = \dfrac{EF}{\ldots}$

$\therefore \dfrac{x}{\ldots} = \dfrac{2{\cdot}5}{\ldots}$

$\therefore x = \ldots \times \dfrac{2{\cdot}5}{\ldots}$

$\therefore x = \ldots$

b

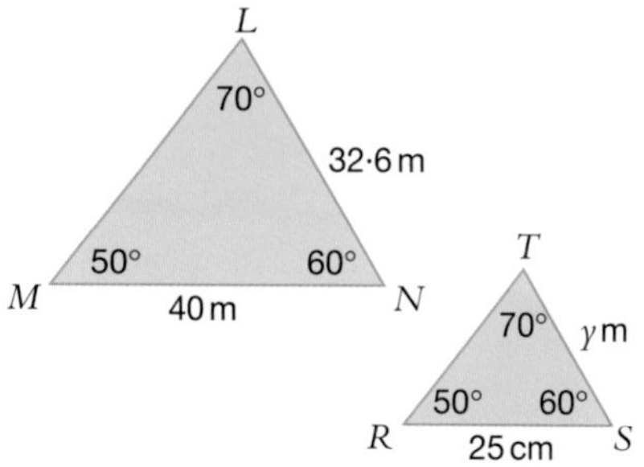

$\Delta LMN \,|||\, \Delta TRS$

LM matches with …

LN matches with …

MN matches with …

$\therefore \dfrac{TS}{\ldots} = \dfrac{RS}{\ldots}$

$\therefore \dfrac{y}{\ldots} = \dfrac{25}{\ldots}$

$\therefore y = \ldots \times \dfrac{25}{\ldots}$

$\therefore y = \ldots$

2 Find the values of the pronumerals, correct to one decimal place where necessary.

a

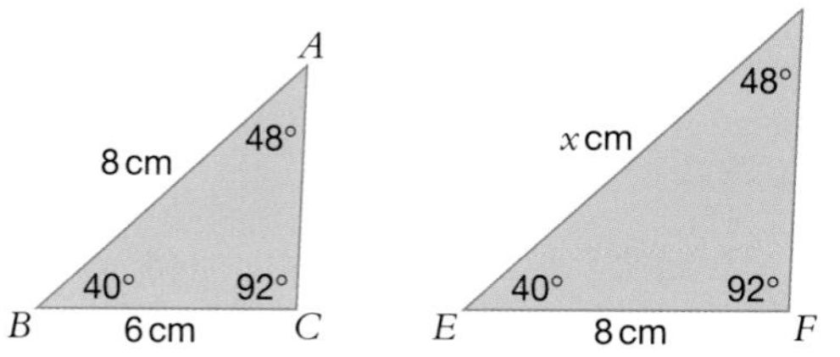

b

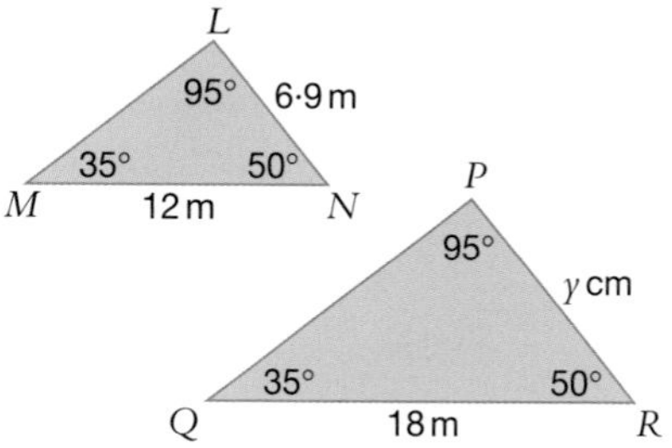

c

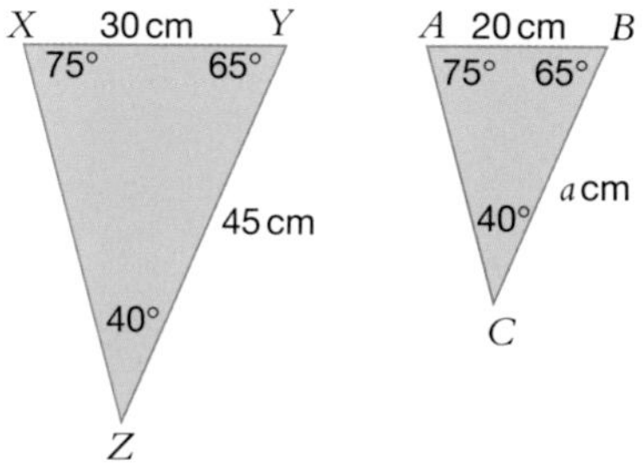

d

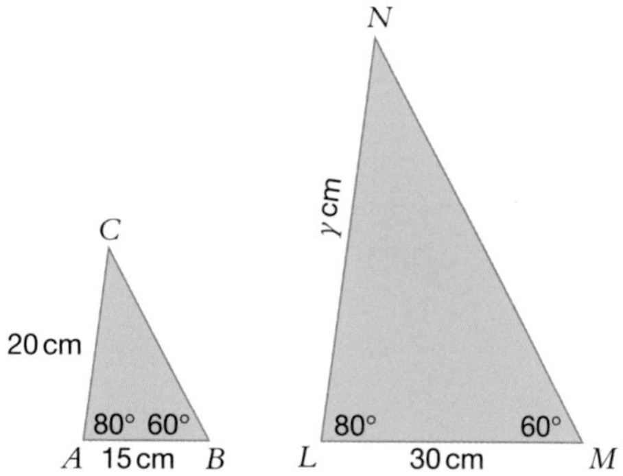

3 Find the values of the pronumerals, correct to one decimal place where necessary.

a

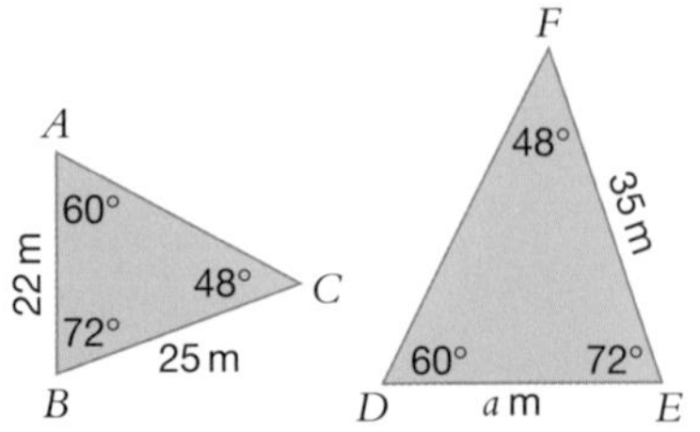

b

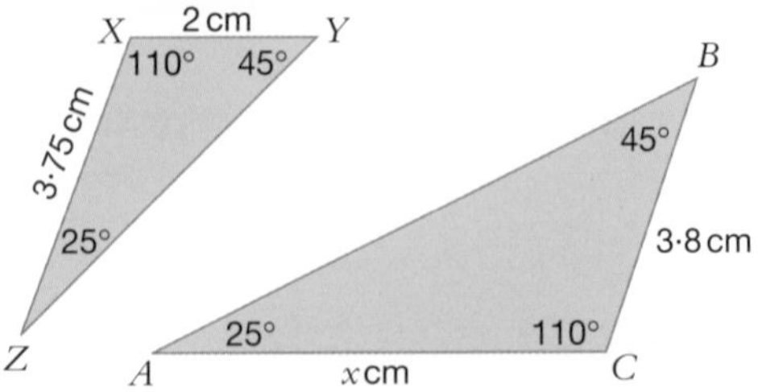

c

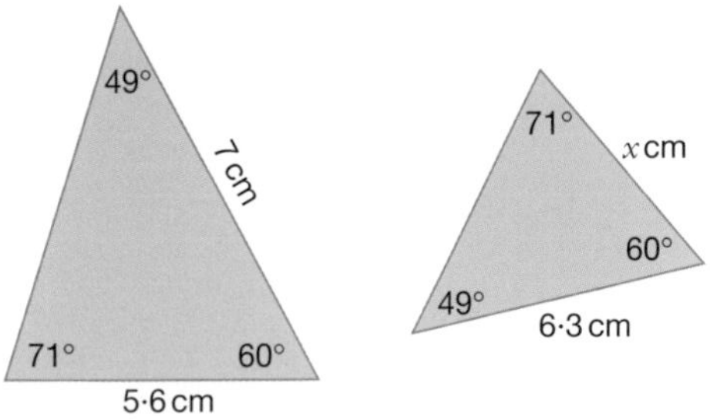

Don't forget this!
Matching sides are opposite equal angles.

4 Find the value of the pronumeral in each of the following.

a

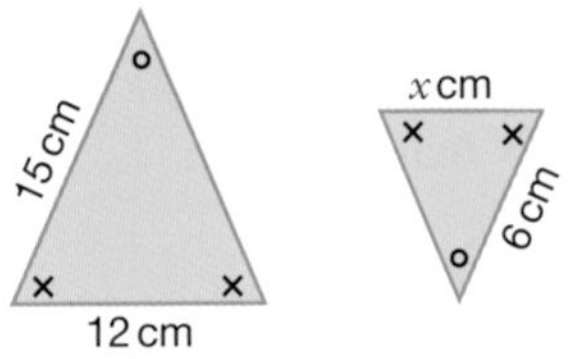

b

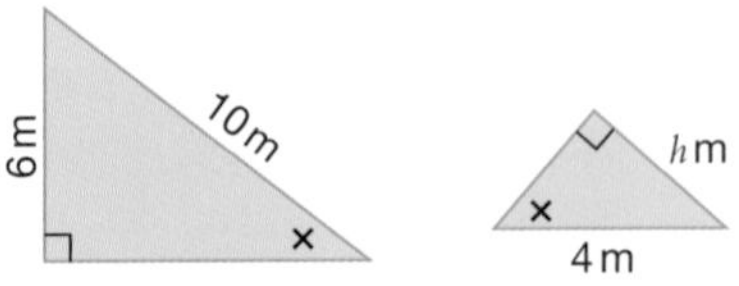

c

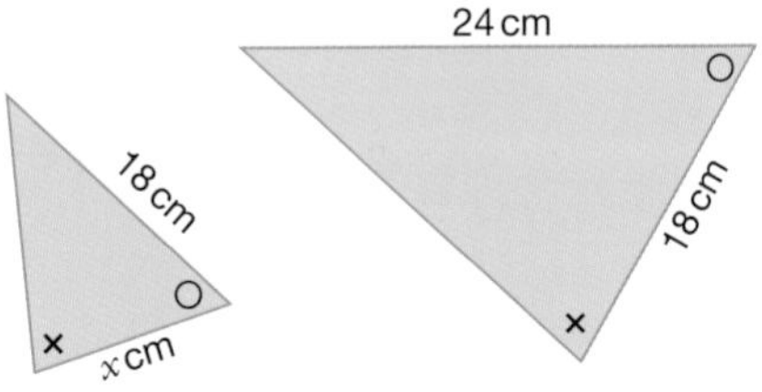

d

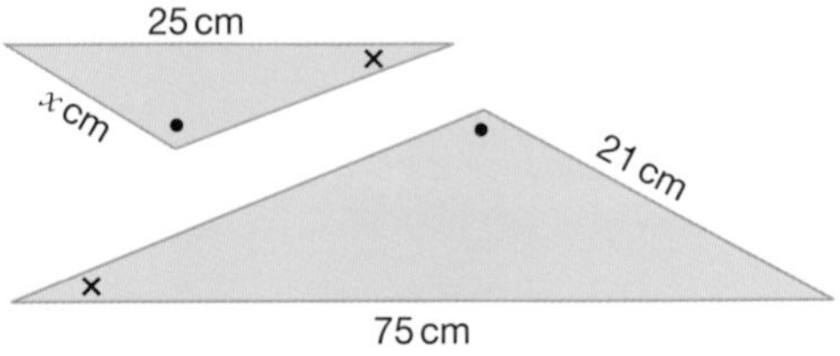

5 Find the values of the pronumerals in each of the following.

a

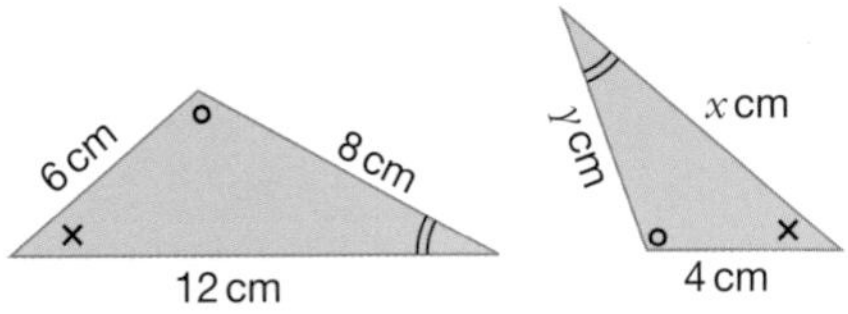

b

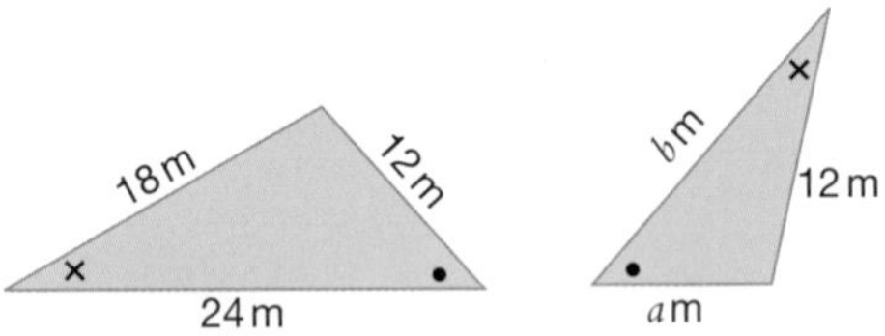

c

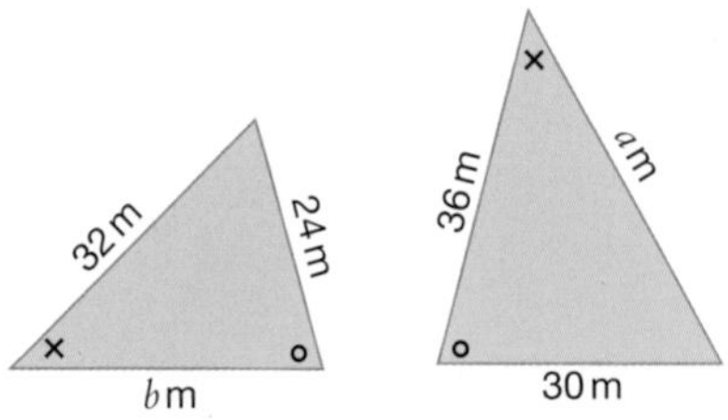

d

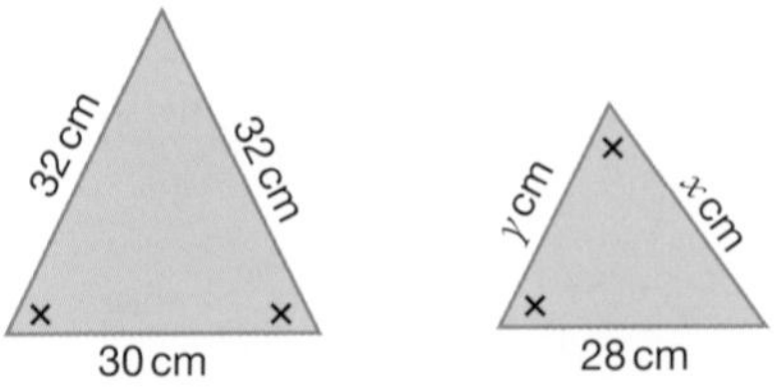

6 **a** A girl found that her shadow was 4 m long when the shadow of a flagpole was 12 m long. If her height is 1·5 m, what is the height of the flagpole?

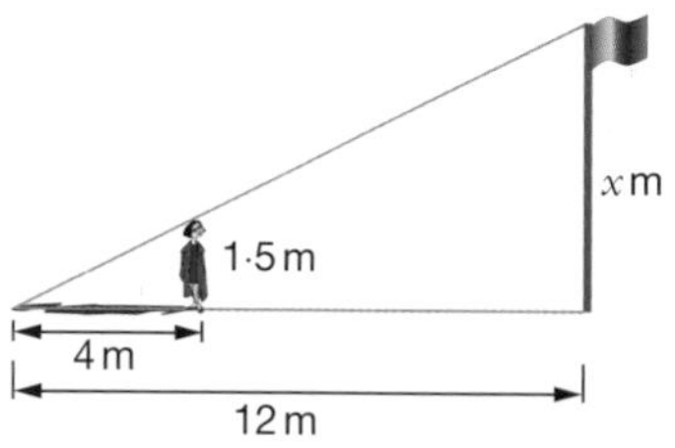

b To find the height of a tree, Greg used a mirror placed on the ground. He moved it until he could see the top of the tree in the mirror. At this point, his eye was 1·4 m from the ground and the mirror was 2 m from him, whereas the tree was 6 m from the mirror. Find the height of the tree.

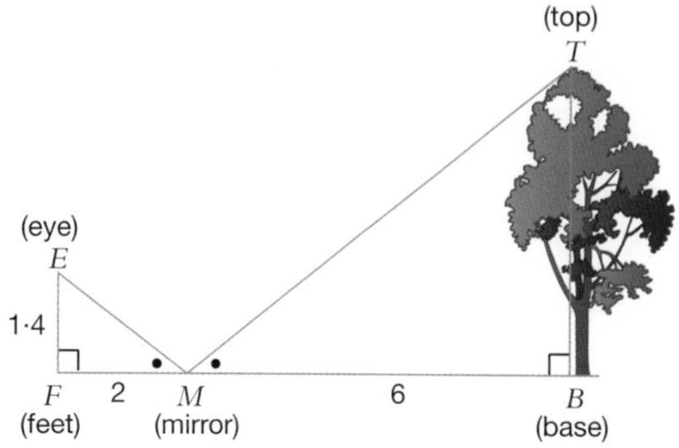

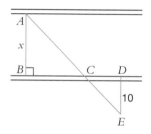

c The distance across a storm channel was discovered by choosing a point A on the opposite bank and finding the point B that was directly opposite A. Point E was chosen so that it was 10 m from the bank D, and by sighting from E to A, the point C was found. The distances DC and CB were measured to be 9 m and 18 m, respectively. How wide was the channel?

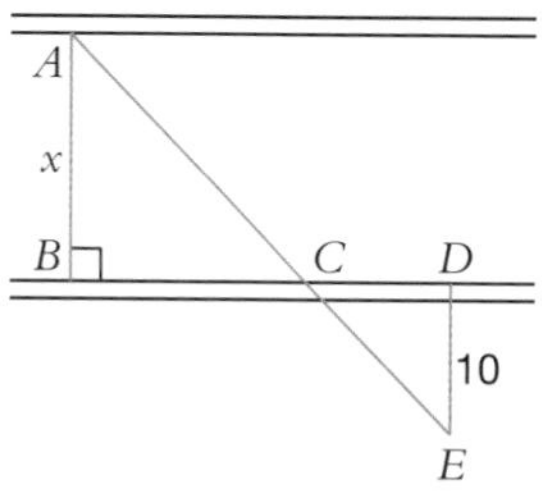

P GEOGEBRA ACTIVITY 11:04 — FINDING AN UNKNOWN SIDE IN SIMILAR TRIANGLES

Click and drag the vertices of two triangles to change the shape of the triangles as well as their size and orientation. Then complete the matching sides ratio and calculate the length of the missing side. Tick a checkbox to check your answer.

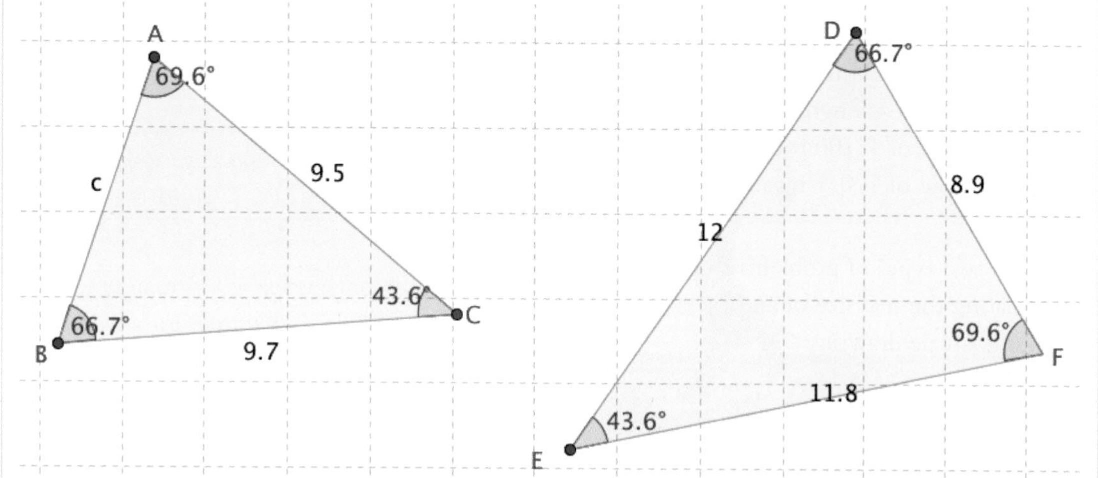

11:05 Scale drawings

PREP QUIZ 11:05

Complete the following:

1 1 m = … cm

2 1 m = … mm

Convert:

3 20 m to cm

4 25 000 mm to m

Simplify the ratios:

5 1 cm : 1 m

6 1 mm : 1 m

A line is 6 cm long. How long would it be if it was:

7 reduced using a reduction factor of $\frac{1}{10}$

8 enlarged using an enlargement factor of 10?

Complete the following:

9 1 : 100 = 5 : …

10 1 : 100 = … : 400

A scale drawing is the same shape as the object it represents but it has a different size.

1 : 10 gives a bigger drawing than 1 : 100.

- A scale of 1 : 100 means that one unit on the drawing represents 100 units on the original object.
- A scale of 1 : 100 gives a drawing that is smaller than the original object.
  The lengths on the drawing are $\frac{1}{100}$ the lengths on the original.
- A scale of 100 : 1 gives a drawing that is larger than the original.
  The lengths on the drawing are 100 times longer than the original lengths.
- The scale determines the size of the drawing. So a 1 : 10 scale drawing would be bigger than a 1 : 100 scale drawing of the same object.

> A scale drawing of an object is the same shape as the object but a different size.
> Scale = length on drawing : length on the real object
> A scale of 1 : 100 means the drawing is smaller than the real object.
> A scale of 100 : 1 means the drawing is larger than the real object.

There are two types of problems that involve scale drawings:
- calculating the real size of an object from a scale drawing
- making a scale drawing.

11:05A Calculating real sizes from scale drawings

WORKED EXAMPLES

A landscape gardener has made this scale drawing of a formal garden.

a What real distance is represented by a distance of 1 cm on the drawing?

b What is the length of the square that forms the outer boundary of the garden?

c What is the diameter of the circular pond in the middle of the garden?

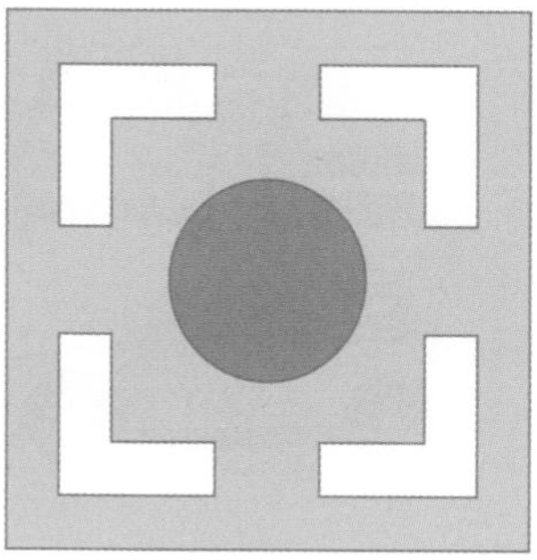

Scale 1 : 400

Solutions

a As the scale is 1 : 400, the real length is 400 times bigger than the length on the drawing.

$\therefore$ Real length $= 1\text{ cm} \times 400$
$= 400\text{ cm}$
$= 4\text{ m}$

b The length of the side of the square is 4 cm on the drawing.

$\therefore$ Real length $= 4 \times 4\text{ m}$
$= 16\text{ m}$

c Diameter of pond is 1·5 cm on drawing.

$\therefore$ Real diameter $= 1{\cdot}5 \times 4\text{ m}$
$= 6\text{ m}$

Exercise 11:05A

1 Copy and complete each of the following:

a 1 cm : 1 m = 1 : □ b 1 m : 1 km = 1 : □ c 1 mm : 1 m = 1 : □

2 The scale on a map is 1 : 1000. Calculate the real distance between two points if they are the following distance apart on the map.

a 3 cm b 4·6 cm c 23 mm

3 The scale on a drawing is 1 cm to 5 m. Calculate the real distance between two points if they are the following distance apart on the drawing.

a 7 cm b 1 mm c 2·4 cm

4 A scale drawing of a badminton court is shown.

a Measure the length and width of the court on the drawing in millimetres.

b Use the scale to calculate the length and width of the court in millimetres.

c Convert the length and width into metres.

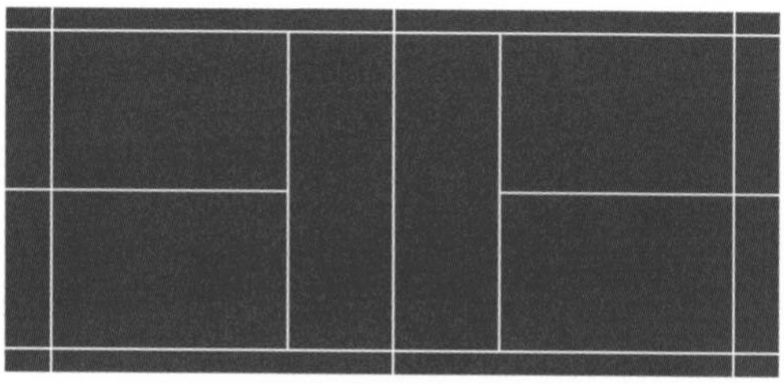

Scale 1 : 200

5 A scale drawing of an insect is shown.

a Measure the length and width of the body of the insect.

b Convert the measurements in part **a** into real measurements if the scale of the drawing is:

i 10 : 1 ii 20 : 1

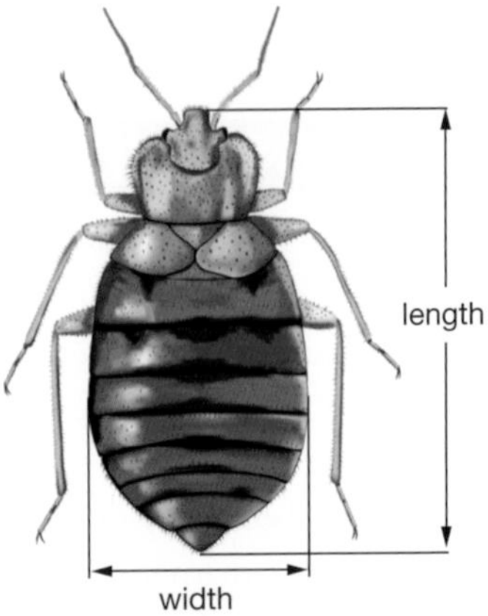

6 The diagram shows a set of scale drawings of a car. The real length of the car is 3700 mm.

a What is the length of the car on the drawing?

b Use the real length and your answer to **a** to find the scale of the drawing.

c By measurement and calculation find:

i the real width of the car excluding mirrors

ii the real height of the car.

7 a What real distance is represented by 1 cm on this map?

b What is the length of Wilga St?

c What is the length of Douglas Road from Tallawong Avenue to Walters Road?

d Calculate the cost of repairing this section of Douglas Road at \$15 000 per 100 metres.

e Estimate the area of land occupied by Evans High School.

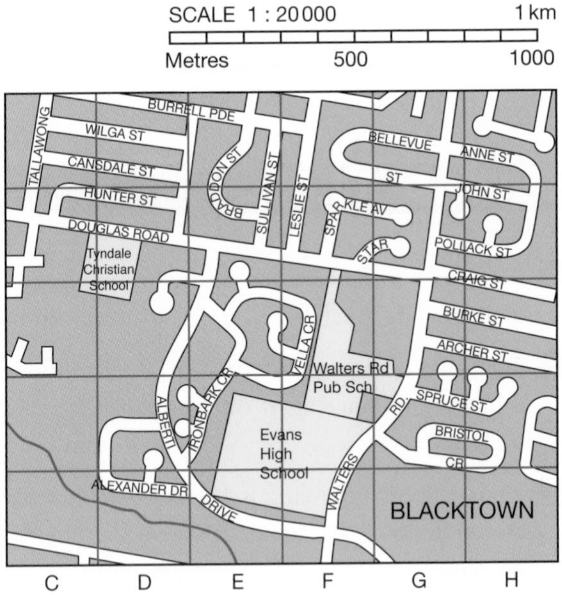

8 The measurements on this plan are in millimetres.

a What length on the plan stands for 5500 mm?

b What distance would be represented by 1 mm on the plan?

c What is the scale of the plan?

d Calculate the distance from one corner of the family room to the opposite corner.

e What is the distance between the window in the kitchen and the adjacent window in the meals area?

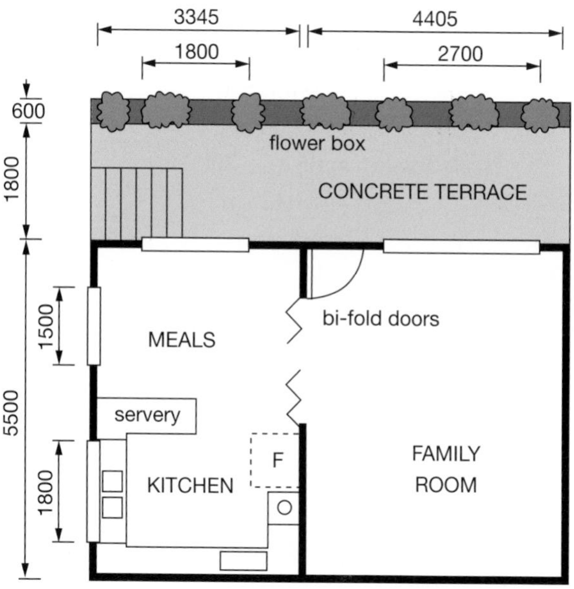

11:05B Making a scale drawing

To make a scale drawing we need to:

1 find the real lengths involved

2 decide how large the drawing will be

3 choose an appropriate scale

4 transfer the real lengths into scale lengths using the scale.

> To decide on a scale, find the ratio of the length available for the drawing to the length of the real object.
> Scale = length of drawing : length of object

Discussion

A scale drawing of a particular soccer field is to be drawn. The finished drawing must fit inside a rectangle that is 7·5 cm long and 5·5 cm wide. Carefully examine the steps used to do this.

- By measurement or research, we discover that the dimensions of the soccer field are 115 m by 85 m.
- We choose a length that will fit the available space (a rectangle 7·5 cm by 5·5 cm).

  Let's make the length about 6 cm.

  Scale = length of drawing : length of field
  = 6 cm : 115 m
  = 6 : 11 500
  ≑ 1 : 1917

  Let the scale be 1 : 2000.

• Find the dimensions of the diagram.

Scaled length = 115 m ÷ 2000
= 0·0575 m
= 5·75 cm

Scaled width = 85 m ÷ 2000
= 0·0425 m
= 4·25 cm

• Draw the soccer field.

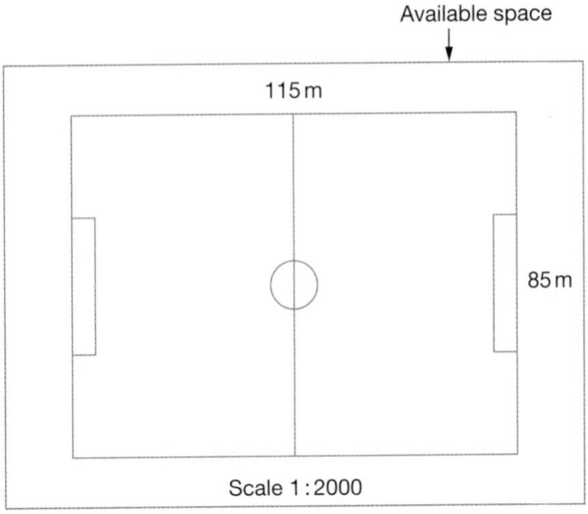

Exercise 11:05B

P Foundation worksheet 11:05B Scale drawing

1 A scale drawing is to be made using a scale of 1 : 4. This means that the distance on the drawing is $\frac{1}{4}$ of the real distance. What length on the drawing would represent a real distance of:

a 100 cm b 80 cm c 1·2 m d 68 mm e 668 mm?

2 The scale of a drawing is 4 : 1. This means that the distance on the drawing is 4 times greater than the real distance. What length on the drawing represents a real distance of:

a 4 cm b 8 mm c 3·5 mm d 0·8 mm e 1·3 cm?

3 A scale drawing uses a scale of 1 : 100. What length on the drawing would represent a distance of:

a 100 cm b 200 cm c 800 cm
d 8 m e 3·5 m f 2000 mm?

Holmes, the scale is 1 : b.
Elementary! Divide the distance by b to find the scaled length.

4 What is the scale of a diagram that represents a real length of 20 m by a length of:

a 20 cm b 10 cm c 2 cm
d 20 mm e 50 cm f 5 mm?

5 A field is 40 m long and 20 m wide. What would these dimensions be on a scale drawing if the scale is:

a 1 : 40 b 1 : 200 c 1 : 500 d 1 : 1000?

6 The sketch on the right shows a block of land that has the shape of a trapezium. Use the sketch to make a scale drawing of the block of land using a scale of:

a 1 : 1000 b 1 : 2000 c 1 : 5000

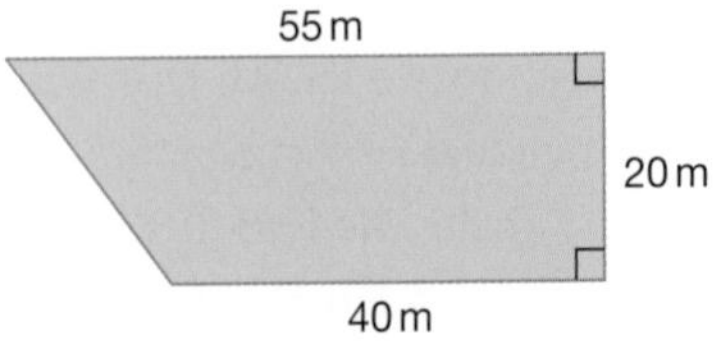

7 A scale drawing is to be made of a soccer field that is 110 m long and 80 m wide. What would be an appropriate scale for a scale drawing if it had to fit inside a rectangle with dimensions:

a 24 cm by 18 cm b 30 cm by 21 cm c 70 mm by 45 mm?

8 Make a scale drawing of a tennis court, choosing a scale that will allow the drawing to fit comfortably on your page. (*Note:* The outside dimensions of a tennis court are 23·77 m by 10·97 m.)

9 Make a scale drawing of one of your hands so that the drawing fits into a square of side length 10 cm.

10 a A house is 21 500 mm long and 14 800 mm wide. What lengths on a scale drawing would you use to represent these dimensions if the scale is 1 : 100?

b A 1 : 30 scale model of a tower is to be built. If the tower is 90 m high, how high will the model be?

c A company is asked to make a model of a shower block that has dimensions 8000 mm by 4200 mm. What would be the dimensions of the model if the scale is 1 : 20?

d A plan of a house is drawn using a scale of 1 : 100. What would be the scaled dimensions of the kitchen if its real dimensions are 4800 mm by 3600 mm? Calculate the scaled length of the sink top if the real length is 120 cm.

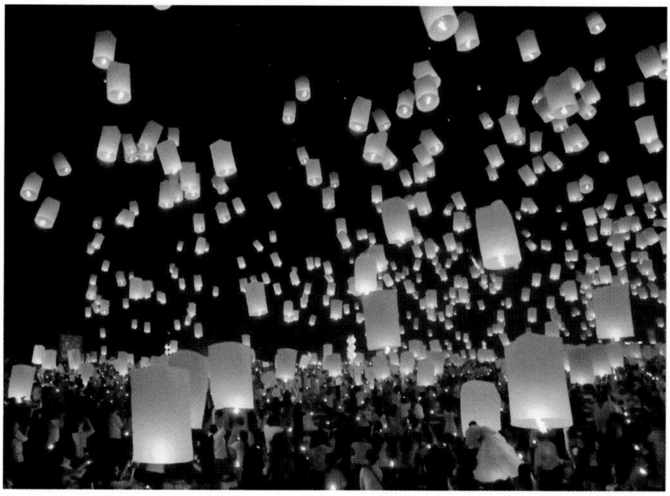

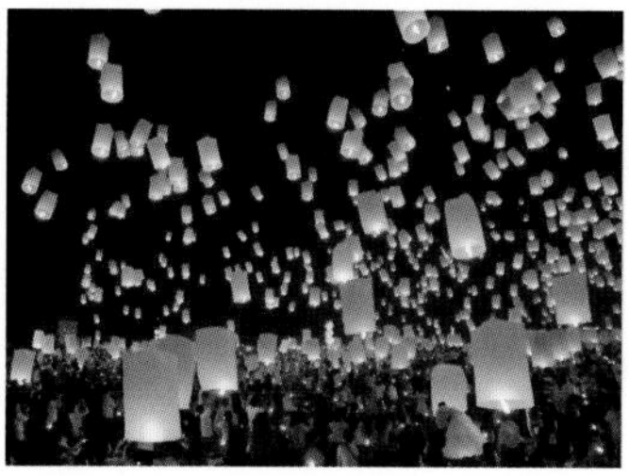

The larger photo is twice as long and twice as wide as the original photo. Could you say it is twice as big? Explain your answer.

FUN SPOT 11:05 WHAT HAPPENED TO THE MUSHROOM THAT WAS DOUBLE PARKED?

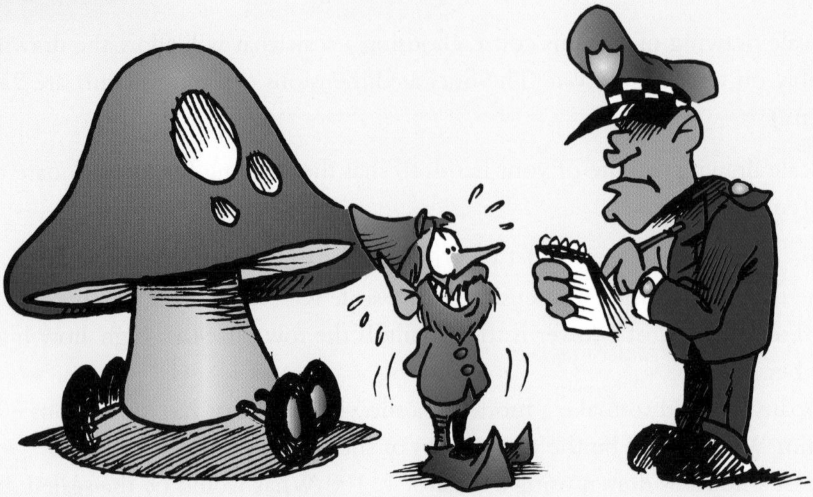

Work out the answer to each part and write the letter for that part in the box that is above the correct answer.

Simplify each ratio:

A 20 : 4 **A** 8 : 16 **B** 8 : 6 **C** 1 : 0·5 **D** $\frac{8}{10}$ **E** $\frac{9}{6}$

Solve:

E $\frac{x}{2} = \frac{3}{2}$ **E** $\frac{x}{3} = \frac{1}{3}$ **I** $\frac{x}{3} = 9$ **L** $\frac{x}{2} = \frac{3}{5}$

Find the values below for each pair of triangles:

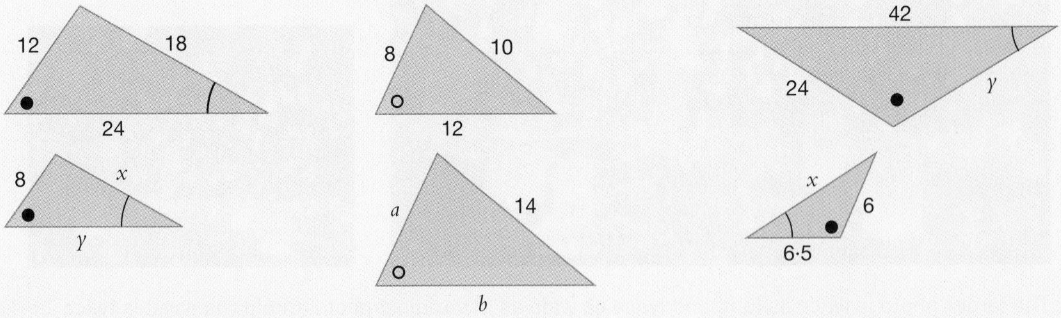

M Reduction factor =
S x =
W y =

O Enlargement factor =
T a =
O b =

O Enlargement factor =
T x =
T y =

$x = 27$	26

4 : 3	$\frac{3}{2}$	2 : 1	5 : 1	$\frac{2}{3}$	$x = 1$

1 : 2

11 : 2	16 : 8	16	$x = 3$	$\frac{4}{5}$

$x = 12$	10 : 5	1 : 4	4	$x = 1·2$

MATHS TERMS 11

dimensions

- size measured in particular directions, usually length, breadth and height

enlargement

- a bigger version of the original

enlargement factor

- the factor by which each length of the original has been enlarged to produce a similar figure

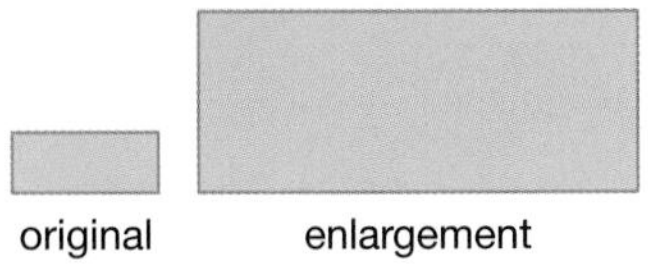

matching

- in the same (or corresponding) position
- matching sides and angles

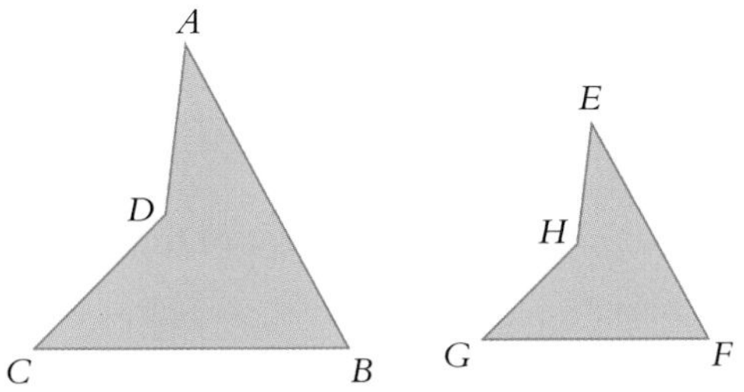

matching sides	matching angles
• *AB* and *EF*	• $\angle A$ and $\angle E$
• *BC* and *FG*	• $\angle B$ and $\angle F$
• *CD* and *GH*	• $\angle C$ and $\angle G$
• *DA* and *HE*	• $\angle D$ and $\angle H$

ratio

- a comparison of two like quantities or numbers written in a definite order,
  e.g. 1 cm to 1 m = 1 cm : 100 cm
  = 1 : 100

reduction

- a smaller version of the original

reduction factor

- the factor by which each length of the original has been reduced to produce the similar figure

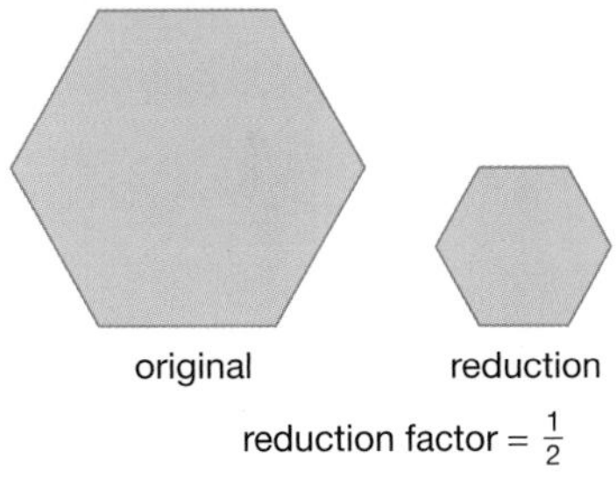

scale (scale factor)

- the ratio of distance on a map or drawing to the real or original distance,
  e.g. a scale of 1 : 10 000 means that lengths on the drawing are $\frac{1}{10\,000}$ of the length of the original

scale drawing

- a drawing of an object in which all dimensions have been enlarged or reduced by the same factor

similar figures

- figures that have the same shape but a different size
- matching angles are equal
- the enlargement or reduction factor gives us the ratio of matching sides

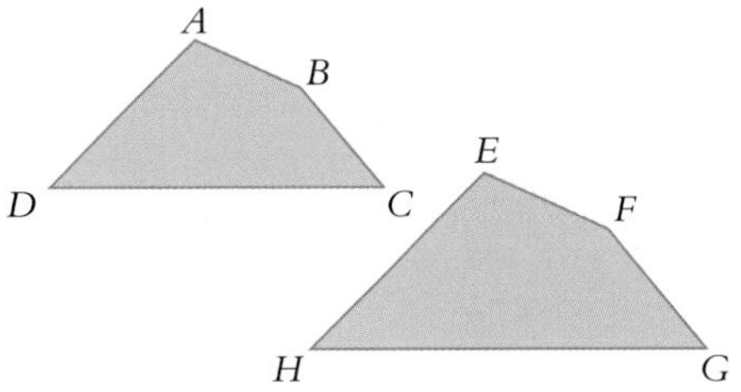

- *ABCD* is similar to *EFGH*,
  i.e. $ABCD \,|||\, EFGH$
  $\angle A = \angle E$, $\angle B = \angle F$, $\angle C = \angle G$, $\angle D = \angle H$
- the enlargement factor = $\dfrac{EH}{AD}$

superimpose

- to place one figure upon another in such a way that the parts of one coincide with the parts of the other

DIAGNOSTIC TEST 11 SIMILARITY

Each section of the test has similar items that test a certain type of question.
Errors made will indicate areas of weakness.
Each weakness should be treated by going back to the section listed.

1 State whether each pair of figures below are similar. 11:01

a 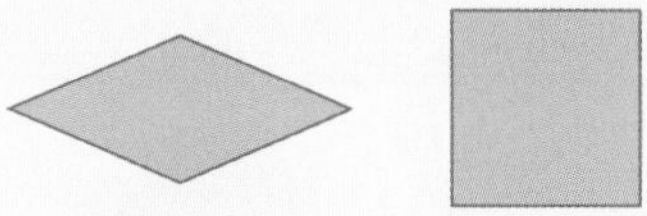

b 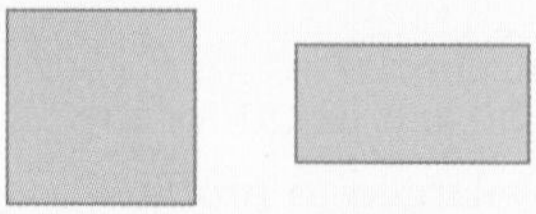

c 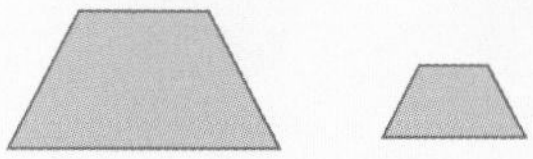

d 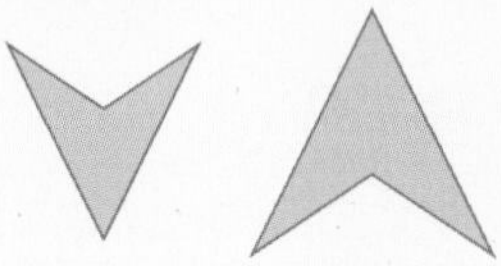

2 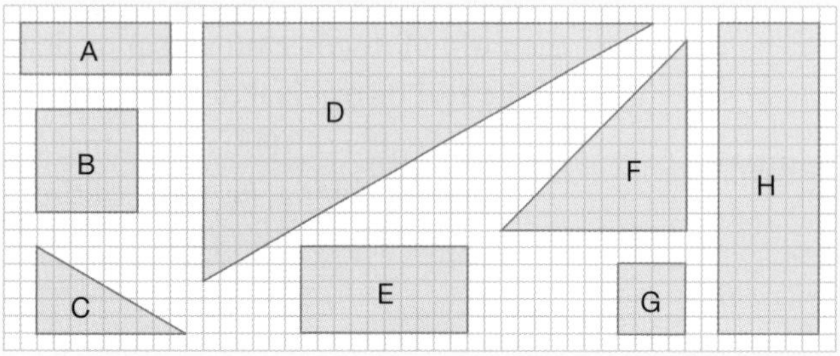

11:01

a Name three pairs of similar figures from those shown above.

b For each pair of similar figures, assume that the larger is an enlargement of the smaller. In each case, write the enlargement factor.

3 Are the rectangles in the following pairs similar? 11:01

a 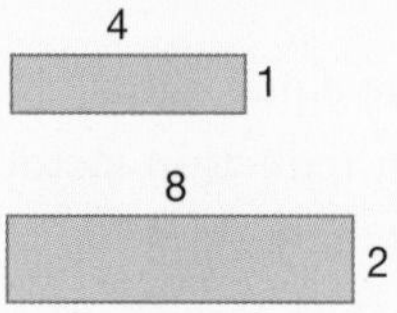

b 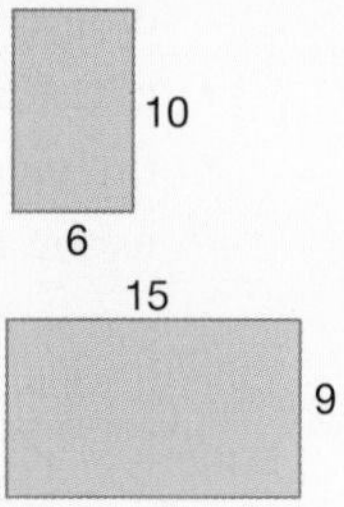

c 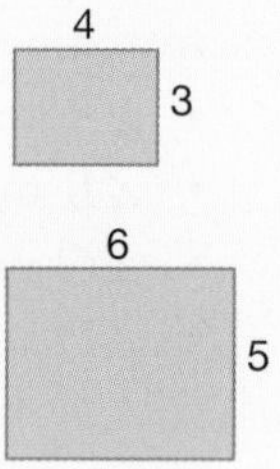

4 Each pair of figures is similar. Find the value of each pronumeral. 11:02

a 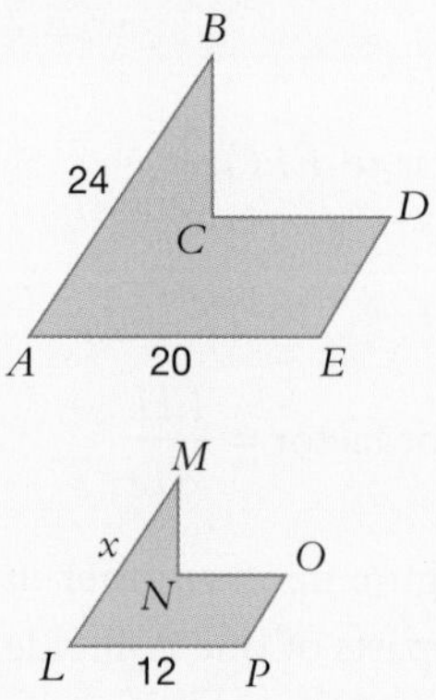

b 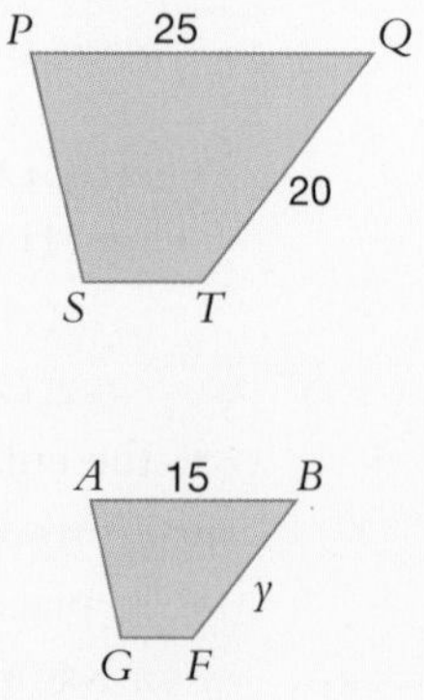

c 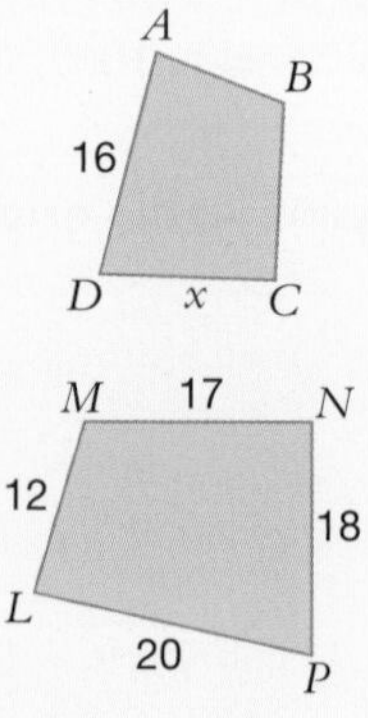

5 Are the following pairs of triangles similar? 11:03

a
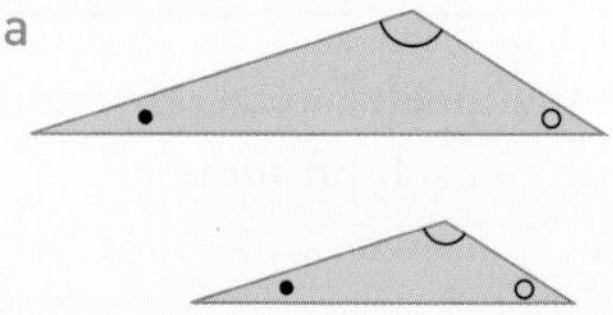

b
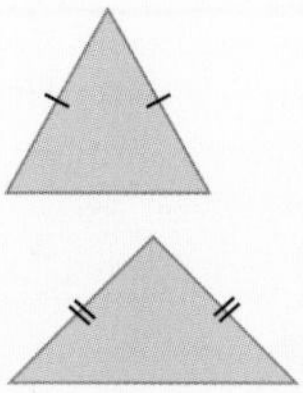

c
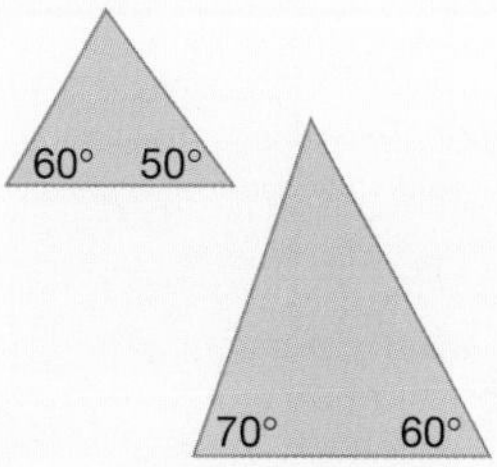

6 Are the following pairs of triangles similar? 11:03

a
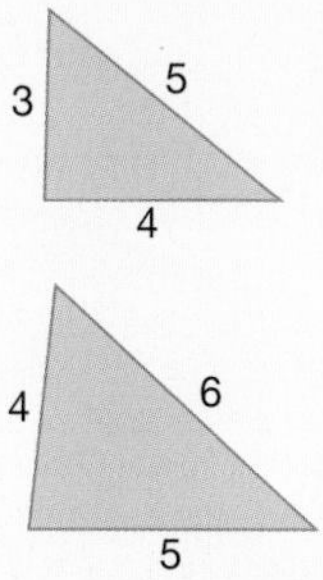

b
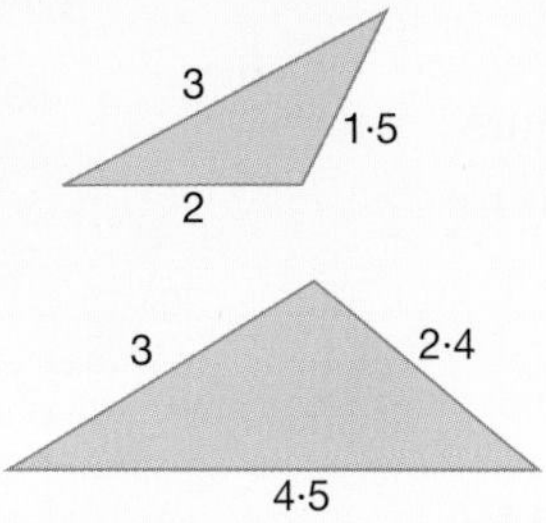

c
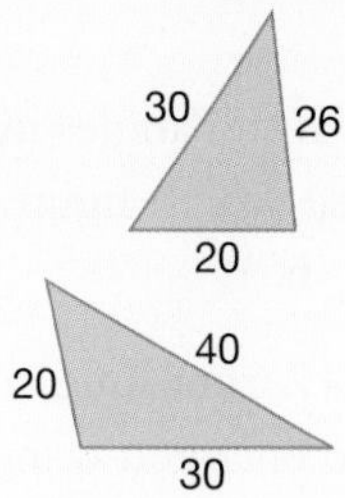

7 Are the following pairs of triangles similar? 11:03

a
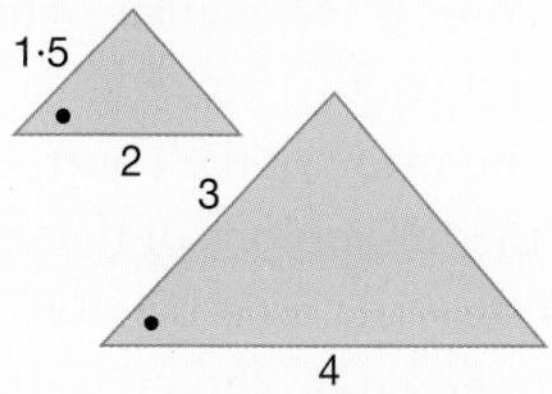

b
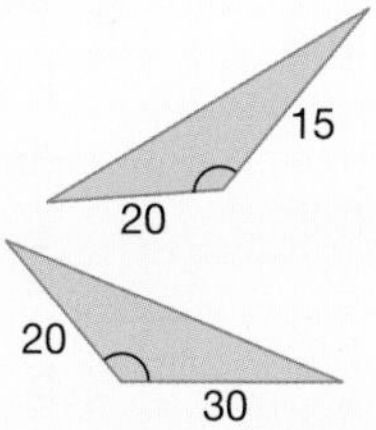

c
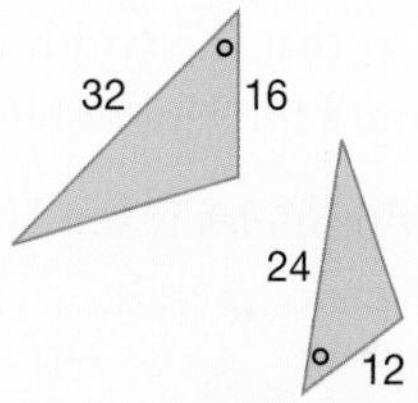

8 Find the value of the pronumeral in each of the following. 11:04

a
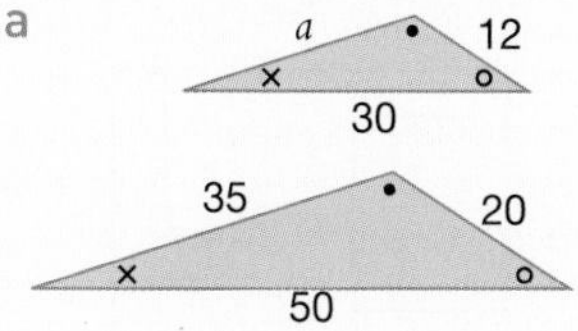

b
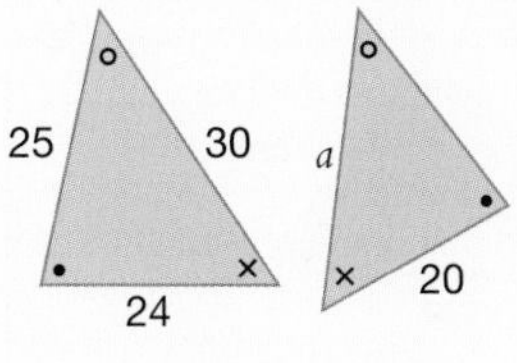

c
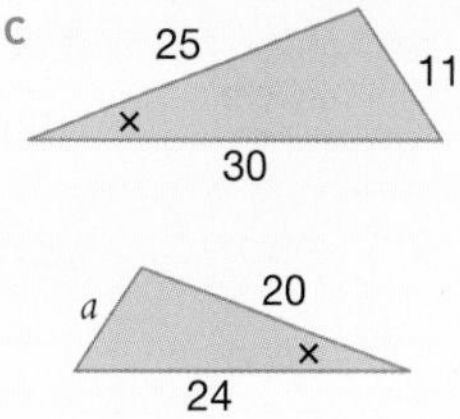

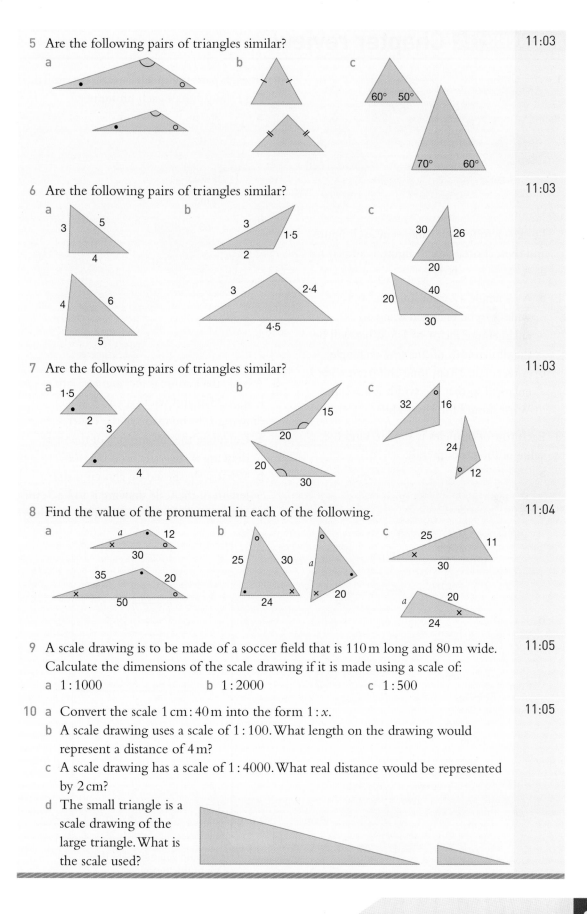

9 A scale drawing is to be made of a soccer field that is 110 m long and 80 m wide. Calculate the dimensions of the scale drawing if it is made using a scale of: 11:05

a 1 : 1000
b 1 : 2000
c 1 : 500

10 a Convert the scale 1 cm : 40 m into the form 1 : x. 11:05

b A scale drawing uses a scale of 1 : 100. What length on the drawing would represent a distance of 4 m?

c A scale drawing has a scale of 1 : 4000. What real distance would be represented by 2 cm?

d The small triangle is a scale drawing of the large triangle. What is the scale used?

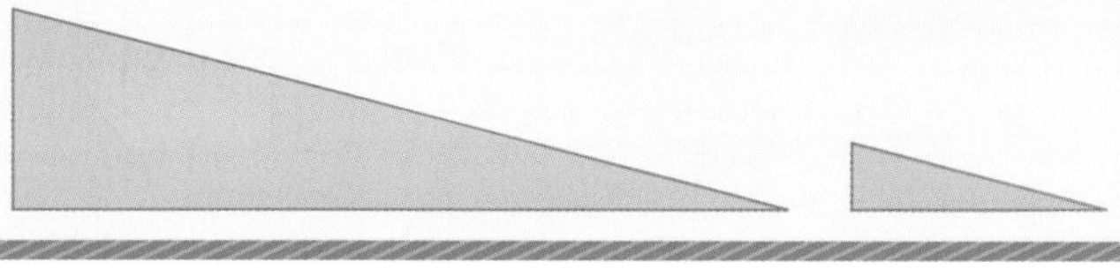

ASSIGNMENT 11A Chapter review

1 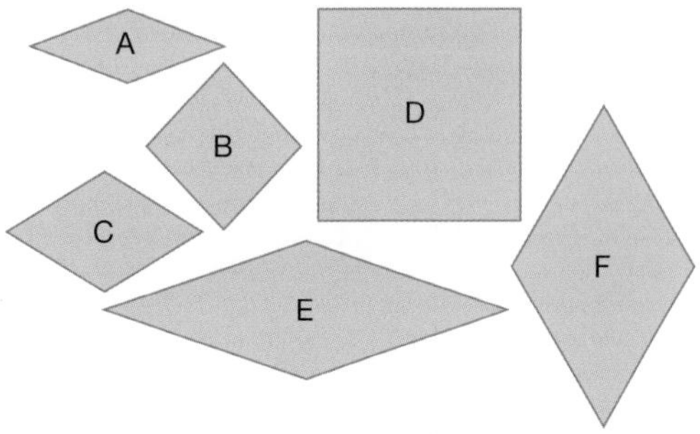

Look carefully at the angles in each figure and then choose which figure is similar to:

a A **b** B **c** C

2 **a** A rectangle 12·6 cm long and 6·8 cm wide is to be enlarged using an enlargement factor of 1·5. What will be the dimensions of the new rectangle?

b A rectangle 15 cm long and 6 cm wide is enlarged so that the width is 13·2 cm. What should the length be?

3 Each pair of triangles is similar. Find the value of the pronumerals.

a

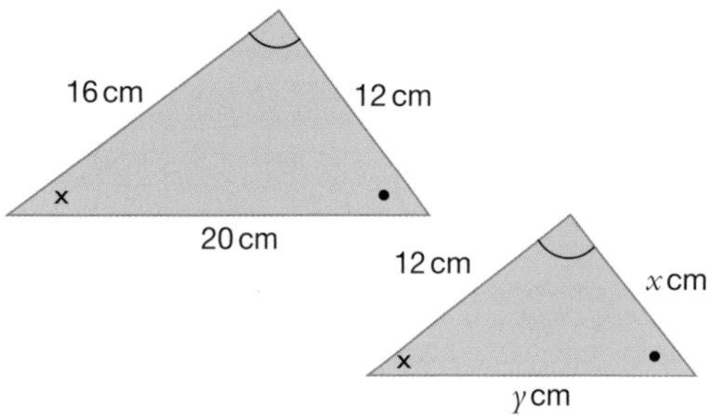

b

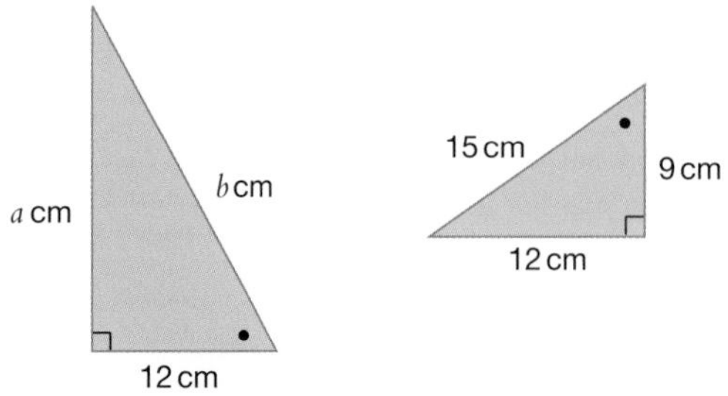

c

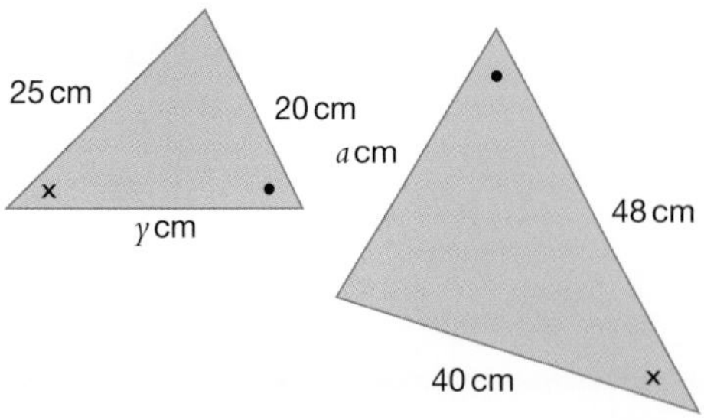

4 In each part, the quadrilaterals are similar. Find the value of each pronumeral.

a

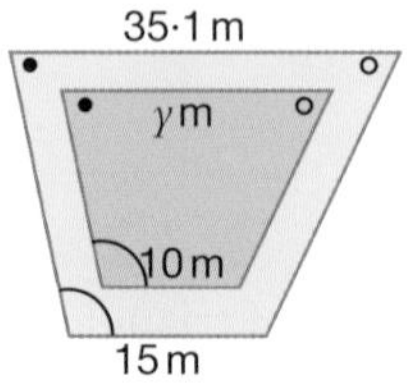

b

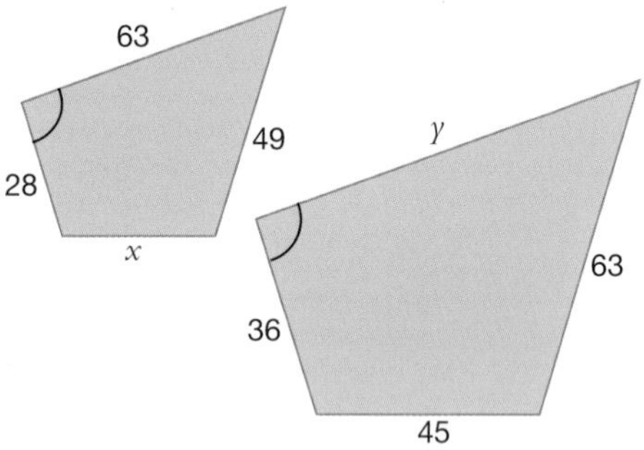

5 A basketball court is rectangular with length 28 m and width 15 m. A scale drawing is to be made of the court.

a Calculate the dimensions of the scale drawing if the scale used is 1:100.

b What scale should be chosen if the length of the scale drawing is to be 7 cm? What would be the width of the drawing?

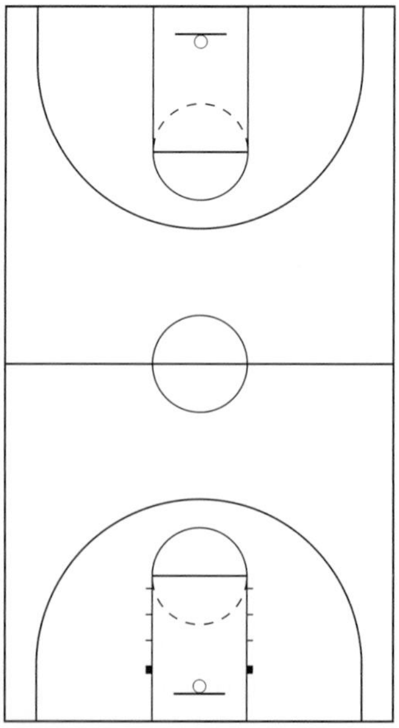

How could you estimate the scale of this drawing?

ASSIGNMENT 11B Working mathematically

1 On a dartboard, it is possible with one dart to score:
- a number from 1 to 20
- the double or triple of a number from 1 to 20
- 25 or 50 for an outer or inner bullseye.

Hence, the largest score possible with one dart is 60 and the smallest is 1. What scores between 1 and 60 are impossible?

2 In a recent class test, the average was 74·5%. If the 11 girls in the class averaged 80%, what was the boys' average mark if there were 28 students in the class?

3 When a glass of juice is full, the total weight of the glass and juice is 400 g. When the glass is one-third full of juice, its weight is 280 g. How much does the glass weigh?

4 The following diagram shows the roads that run between Alpha, Beta and Gamma. How many ways are there to travel from:

a Alpha to Beta directly
b Beta to Gamma
c Gamma to Beta and back again
d Gamma to Beta and back again, without using any road twice?

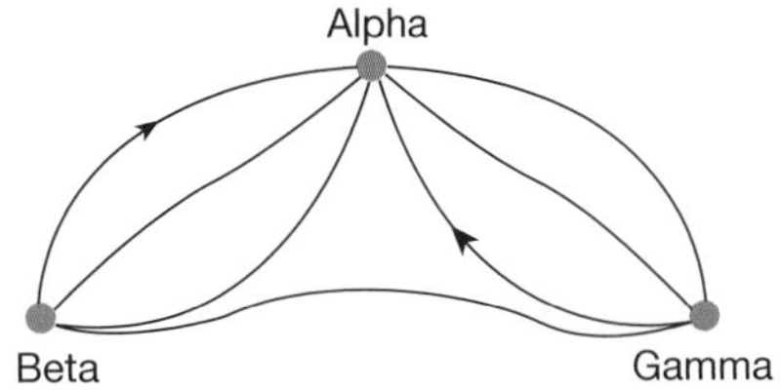

Arrows indicate one way only

5 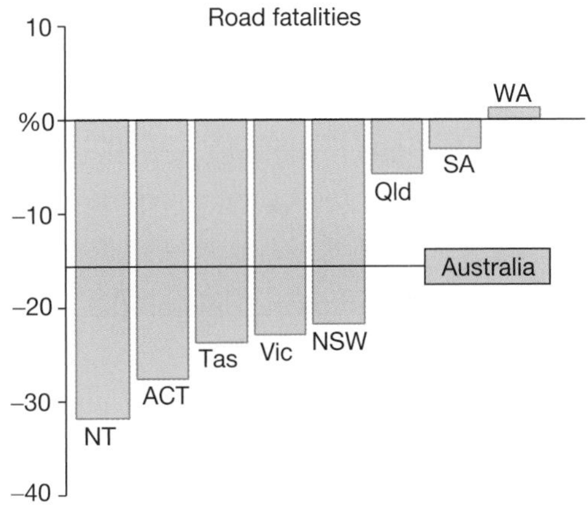

This graph shows the percentage change in road fatalities in Australian regions for a 12-month period compared with the previous 5-year average.

a What does the dark line labelled 'Australia' refer to?
b What percentage change has occurred in:
 i WA ii Vic iii NT?
c How would you describe this year's statistics compared with those of the previous 5 years?

ASSIGNMENT 11C Cumulative revision

1 Simplify: 6:03

a $12x^3 \div 4x^2$ **b** $12x^3 \div 4x^{-2}$ **c** $12x^{-3} \div 4x^2$ **d** $4x^{-2} \div 12x^3$

2 Use a power of 10 to complete each of the following. 6:06

a 1 km = … m **b** 1 mm = … m **c** 1 GL = … L **d** 1 μm = … m

3 Simplify: 3:02

a $\frac{a}{4} + \frac{a}{5}$ **b** $\frac{a}{4} - \frac{a}{5}$ **c** $\frac{a}{4} \times \frac{a}{5}$ **d** $\frac{a}{4} \div \frac{a}{5}$

4 Calculate the area of these figures, correct to one decimal place. They have been formed from a rectangle by subtracting quadrants of different sizes. (All measurements are in centimetres.) 5:02

a

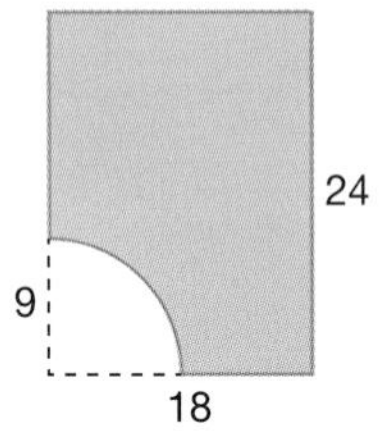

b

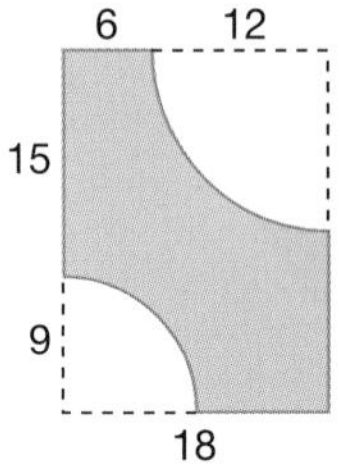

5 A salesperson earns \$600 per week plus a commission of 5·5% on their sales. 8:01

a How much will they earn in a week when they sell \$10 000 worth of goods?

b Calculate their annual income based on average weekly sales of \$8000. (Assume that there are 52 weeks in a year.)

6 Graph the following lines on the same number plane. 9:04

$x + y = 6$, $y = 4$, $y = 2x - 3$

7 Bag A contains 2 red balls and 1 white ball. Bag B contains 1 red and 1 white ball. One ball is selected from each bag. 4:06

a Use a list, table or tree diagram to record the possible outcomes.

b Use your answer in part **a** to find the probability that the balls are:

i both red **ii** both white **iii** different colours.

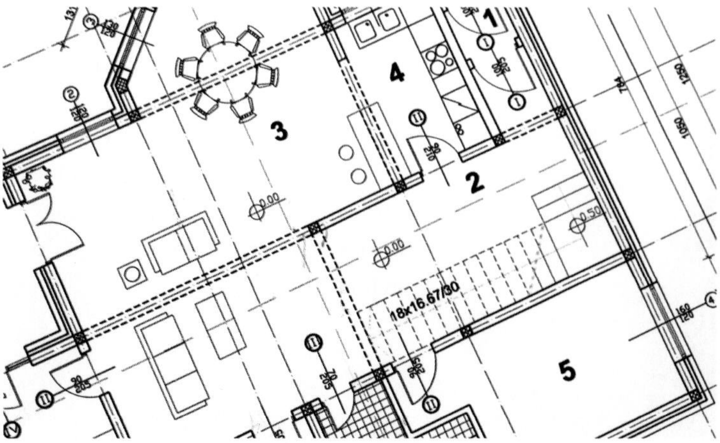

The plans and drawings made by architects and engineers are scale drawings.

FACTORISING ALGEBRAIC EXPRESSIONS

12

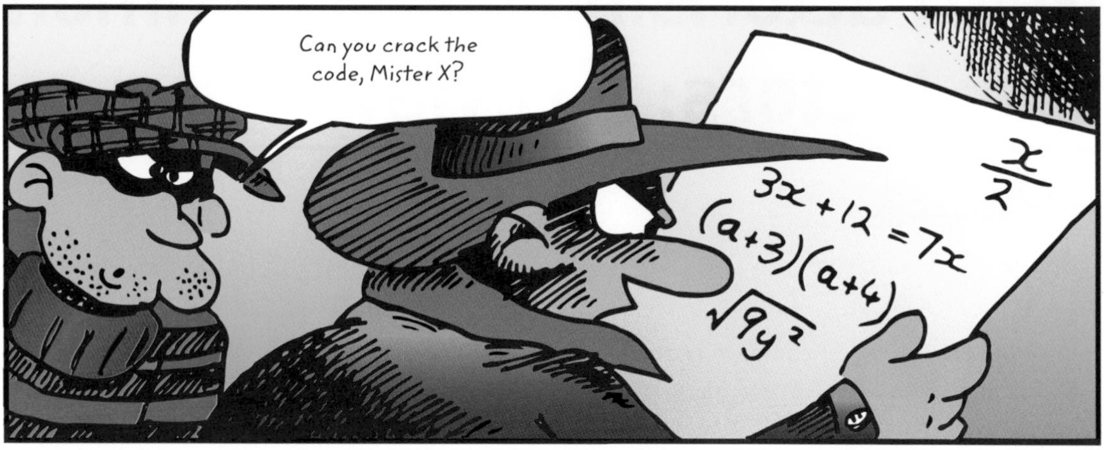

Contents

Syllabus references (See pages x–xv for details.)

Number and Algebra

Selections from ***Algebraic Techniques*** [Stages 5.2, 5.3§]

- Factorise algebraic expressions by taking out a common algebraic factor (ACMNA230)
- Factorise monic and non-monic quadratic expressions (ACMNA269)

Working Mathematically

- Communicating
- Problem Solving
- Reasoning
- Understanding
- Fluency

In Chapter 3, you expanded algebraic expressions that were written as products in factorised form. As shown in the following examples, each product was written without grouping symbols.

$$3a(5 - 2a) = 15a - 6a^2$$
$$(a - 2)(a + 7) = a^2 + 5a - 14$$
$$(x + 5)^2 = x^2 + 10x + 25$$
$$(m + 2)(m - 2) = m^2 - 4$$

Now you will reverse this process and factorise algebraic expressions.

12:01 Factorising using common factors: A review

PREP QUIZ 12:01

Expand:

1 $3(x + 7)$ **2** $a(a - 1)$ **3** $4p(2p - 3q)$ **4** $-5m(3 - 2n)$

Write the HCF (highest common factor) of:

5 $10x$ and $15x$ **6** $8x^2$ and $6xy$

Factorise by taking out a common factor:

7 $4n + 8$ **8** $w^2 - 6w$ **9** $ab + bc$ **10** $-6y - 9$

The simplest method of factorising is 'taking out' a common factor. This method was met in Chapter 3.

This is an important skill because it is the first method that should be considered when factorising any expression. It is also sometimes used in conjunction with other methods.

See Section 3:05.

Check your competence with this skill by completing the short exercise below.

Exercise 12:01

1 Factorise the following by taking out the highest common factor.

a $2x + 8$ b $10m + 5$ c $9a + 6$ d $4 + 6y$
e $7w - 21$ f $15n - 20$ g $12 - 18t$ h $16 - 8z$
i $x^2 + 5x$ j $am + an$ k $6p - p^2$ l $ab - a$

2 Factorise fully.

a $2ax + 6ay$ b $5m^2 + 5mn$ c $9ab + 6bc$ d $4yz + 6xy$
e $7tw - 14t^2$ f $15n - 10n^2$ g $12p - 8pq$ h $6fg - 8gh$
i $x^2y + xy^2$ j $am^2 + amn$ k $6p - 6p^2$ l $abc - bc$

3 Factorise by taking out a negative common factor.

a $-2x-8$　b $-5m+5$　c $-9a+12$　d $-4-8y$
e $-7w^2-w$　f $-mn-np$　g $-12t^2+8t$　h $-16xy+24yz$

4 Factorise:

a $3x+x^2-ax$　b $ax+ay+az$　c $4m-8n+6p$
d $5ab-15ac+10ad$　e $x^2-7x+xy$　f $10ab-5bc-15b^2$

5 Remembering that $a(b+2)+4(b+2)=(b+2)(a+4)$, factorise the following.

a $2(a+x)+b(a+x)$　b $x(3+b)+2(3+b)$　c $a(a+3)-2(a+3)$
d $3m(m-1)+5(m-1)$　e $x(2x+5)-(2x+5)$　f $7(7-z)-z(7-z)$

12:02 Factorising by grouping in pairs

PREP QUIZ 12:02

Factorise these expressions.

1 $3a+18$　2 $5x+ax$　3 $pq-px$　4 $3ax-9bx$
5 x^2-2x　6 a^3+a^2　7 $9-3a$　8 $-5m-10$
9 $9(a+1)+x(a+1)$　10 $x(x+y)-1(x+y)$

For some algebraic expressions, there may not be a factor common in every term. Consider the expression $3x+3+mx+m$.

There is no factor common in every term, but:

- the first two terms have a common factor of 3
- the last two terms have a common factor of m.

$$3x+3+mx+m=3(x+1)+m(x+1)$$

Now it can be seen that $(x+1)$ is a common factor for each term.

$$3(x+1)+m(x+1)=(x+1)(3+m)$$

Therefore:

$$3x+3+mx+m=(x+1)(3+m)$$

The original expression has been factorised by grouping the terms in pairs.

WORKED EXAMPLE 1

a $2x+2y+ax+ay=2(x+y)+a(x+y)$
$\quad=(x+y)(2+a)$

b $a^2+3a+ax+3x=a(a+3)+x(a+3)$
$\quad=(a+3)(a+x)$

WORKED EXAMPLE 2

a $ax - bx + am - bm = x(a - b) + m(a - b)$
$= (a - b)(x + m)$

b $ab + b^2 - a - b = b(a + b) - 1(a + b)$
$= (a + b)(b - 1)$

c $5x + 2y + xy + 10 = 5x + 10 + 2y + xy$
$= 5(x + 2) + y(2 + x)$
$= (x + 2)(5 + y)$

Note: Terms had to be rearranged to pair those with common factors.

$$ab + ac + bd + cd = a(b + c) + d(b + c)$$
$$= (b + c)(a + d)$$

Exercise 12:02

P Foundation worksheet 12:02 **Grouping in pairs**

1 Complete the factorisation of each expression below.

a $2(a + b) + x(a + b)$
b $a(x + 7) + p(x + 7)$
c $m(x - y) + n(x - y)$
d $x(m + n) - y(m + n)$
e $a^2(2 - x) + 7(2 - x)$
f $q(q - 2) - 2(q - 2)$
g $(x + y) + a(x + y)$
h $x(1 - 3y) - 2(1 - 3y)$

2 Factorise these expressions.

a $pa + pb + qa + qb$
b $3a + 3b + ax + bx$
c $mn + 3np + 5m + 15p$
d $a^2 + ab + ac + bc$
e $9x^2 - 12x + 3xy - 4y$
f $12p^2 - 16p + 3pq - 4q$
g $ab + 3c + 3a + bc$
h $xy + y + 4x + 4$
i $a^3 + a^2 + a + 1$
j $pq + 5r + 5p + qr$
k $xy - x + y - 1$
l $8a - 2 + 4ay - y$
m $mn + m + n + 1$
n $x^2 + my + xy + mx$
o $x^2 - xy + xw - yw$
p $x^2 + yz + xz + xy$
q $11a + 4c + 44 + ac$
r $a^3 - a^2 + a - 1$

3 Factorise the following.

a $xy + xz - wy - wz$
b $ab + bc - ad - cd$
c $5a + 15 - ab - 3b$
d $6x - 24 - xy + 4y$
e $11y + 22 - xy - 2x$
f $ax^2 - ax - x + 1$

Can you find a formula that calculates the day of the week for any given date?
How many different calendars are needed to describe any given year?

12:03 Factorising using the difference of two squares

PREP QUIZ 12.03

Simplify: 1 $\sqrt{16}$ 2 $\sqrt{49}$ 3 $\sqrt{121}$

If x is positive, simplify: 4 $\sqrt{x^2}$ 5 $\sqrt{9x^2}$ 6 $\sqrt{64x^2}$

Expand and simplify. 7 $(x-2)(x+2)$ 8 $(x+5)(x-5)$ 9 $(7-a)(7+a)$ 10 $(3m+2n)(3m-2n)$

If the expression we want to factorise is the difference of two squares, we can simply reverse the procedure seen in Section 3:07B.

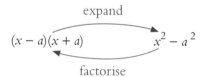

expand

$(x-a)(x+a)$ → $x^2 - a^2$

factorise

WORKED EXAMPLE 1

a $x^2 - 9 = x^2 - 3^2$
$\quad = (x-3)(x+3)$

b $25a^2 - b^2 = (5a)^2 - b^2$
$\quad = (5a-b)(5a+b)$

c $a^4 - 64 = (a^2)^2 - 8^2$
$\quad = (a^2-8)(a^2+8)$

c $36m^2 - 49n^2 = (6m)^2 - (7n)^2$
$\quad = (6m-7n)(6m+7n)$

$$x^2 - y^2 = (x-y)(x+y)$$

Note: $(x-y)(x+y) = (x+y)(x-y)$

Exercise 12.03

1 Factorise each of these expressions.

a $x^2 - 4$	b $a^2 - 16$	c $m^2 - 25$	d $p^2 - 81$
e $y^2 - 100$	f $x^2 - 121$	g $9 - x^2$	h $1 - n^2$
i $49 - y^2$	j $a^2 - b^2$	k $x^2 - a^2$	l $y^2 - a^2$
m $9a^2 - 4$	n $16x^2 - 1$	o $25p^2 - 9$	p $49 - 4a^2$
q $25p^2 - a^2$	r $m^2 - 81n^2$	s $100a^2 - 9b^2$	t $81x^2 - 121y^2$

2 Factorise by first taking out a common factor.

a $2x^2 - 32$
b $3x^2 - 108$
c $4a^2 - 100$
d $5y^2 - 20$
e $24a^2 - 6b^2$
f $3x^2 - 27y^2$
g $8y^2 - 128$
h $80p^2 - 5q^2$
i $4x^2 - 64$
j $3x^2 - 3$
k $72p^2 - 2$
l $2 - 18x^2$
m $8a^2 - 18m^2$
n $125 - 20a^2$
o $200x^2 - 18y^2$
p $98m^2 - 8n^2$

WORKED EXAMPLE 2

$$18x^2 - 50 = 2(9x^2 - 25)$$
$$= 2([3x]^2 - 5^2)$$
$$= 2(3x - 5)(3x + 5)$$

CHALLENGE 12:03 THE DIFFERENCE OF TWO CUBES (EXTENSION)

- The large cube has a volume of a^3 cubic units
It is made up of four smaller parts
(a cube and three rectangular prisms).
Our aim is to find an expression for the difference of two cubes $(a^3 - b^3)$.

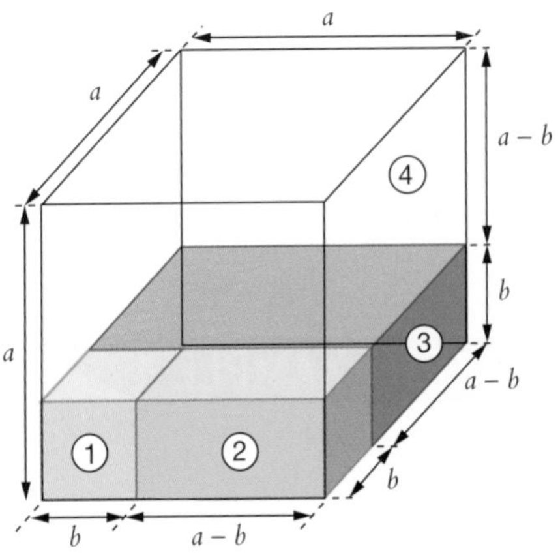

1 Complete the table below.

2 Write an expression for the volume of the large cube (a^3) in terms of the volumes of the four smaller parts.
$a^3 = V_{①} + V_{②} + V_{③} + V_{④}$

3 Use your answer to Question **2** to write an expression for $a^3 - b^3$.

Volume ①	Volume ②	Volume ③	Volume ④
$b \times b \times b$			

Express each volume as a product of its factors.

> Difference of two cubes
> $a^3 - b^3 = (a - b)(a^2 + ab + b^2)$

Applying this to algebraic expressions, we could factorise a difference of two cubes.

e.g. $x^3 - 8 = x^3 - 2^3$
$= (x - 2)(x^2 + 2x + 4)$

Exercises

Factorise these expressions using the difference of two cubes rule.

1 $m^3 - n^3$
2 $x^3 - y^3$
3 $a^3 - 8$
4 $m^3 - 27$
5 $x^3 - 1000$
6 $y^3 - 125$
7 $64 - n^3$
8 $27 - k^3$
9 $8m^3 - 27$
10 $64x^3 - 125y^3$
11 $125x^3 - 8y^3$
12 $27m^3 - 343n^3$

12:04 Factorising quadratic trinomials

PREP QUIZ 12:04

Expand:

1 $(x + 2)(x + 3)$
2 $(a - 1)(a + 3)$
3 $(m - 7)(m - 2)$
4 $(x + 5)^2$
5 $(a - 2)^2$

Find two numbers a and b where:

6 $a + b = 5$ and $ab = 6$
7 $a + b = 9$ and $ab = 20$
8 $a + b = -2$ and $ab = -15$
9 $a + b = 3$ and $ab = -4$
10 $a + b = 7$ and $ab = -18$

- An expression with three terms is called a *trinomial.*
- Expressions like $x^2 + 3x - 4$ are called *quadratic trinomials.* The highest power of the variable is 2.
- Factorising is the reverse of expanding.

$$(x + a)(x + b) = x^2 + ax + bx + ab$$
$$= x^2 + (a + b)x + ab$$

Using this result, to factorise $x^2 + 5x + 6$ we look for two values a and b, where $a + b = 5$ and $ab = 6$.
These numbers are 2 and 3, so:
$x^2 + 5x + 6 = (x + 2)(x + 3)$

2 and 3 add to give 5 and multiply to give 6.

WORKED EXAMPLES

Factorise:

1 $x^2 + 7x + 10$
2 $m^2 - 6m + 8$
3 $y^2 + y - 12$
4 $x^2 - 9x - 36$
5 $3y^2 + 15y - 72$

If $x^2 + 7x + 10 = (x + a)(x + b)$ then $a + b = 7$ and $ab = 10$.

Solutions

1 $2 + 5 = 7$
$2 \times 5 = 10$

$\therefore x^2 + 7x + 10$
$= (x + 2)(x + 5)$

2 $(-2) + (-4) = -6$
$(-2) \times (-4) = 8$

$\therefore m^2 - 6m + 8$
$= (m - 2)(m - 4)$

3 $(-3) + 4 = 1$
$(-3) \times 4 = -12$

$\therefore y^2 + y - 12$
$= (y - 3)(y + 4)$

4 $3 + (-12) = -9$
$3 \times (-12) = -36$

$\therefore x^2 - 9x - 36$
$= (x + 3)(x - 12)$

5 $(-3) + 8 = 5$
$(-3) \times 8 = -24$

$3y^2 + 15y - 72$
$= 3(y^2 + 5y - 24)$
$= 3(y - 3)(y + 8)$

Step 1:
Take out any common factor.

Exercise 12:04

Foundation worksheet 12:04 Factorising trinomials

1 Factorise each of these trinomials.

a $x^2 + 4x + 3$ b $x^2 + 3x + 2$ c $x^2 + 6x + 5$
d $x^2 + 7x + 6$ e $x^2 + 9x + 20$ f $x^2 + 10x + 25$
g $x^2 + 12x + 36$ h $x^2 + 10x + 21$ i $x^2 + 9x + 18$
j $x^2 + 14x + 40$ k $x^2 + 15x + 54$ l $x^2 + 13x + 36$
m $x^2 - 4x + 4$ n $x^2 - 12x + 36$ o $x^2 - 7x + 12$
p $x^2 - 9x + 20$ q $x^2 + 2x - 3$ r $x^2 + x - 12$
s $x^2 + 4x - 12$ t $x^2 + 7x - 30$ u $x^2 - x - 2$
v $x^2 - 10x - 24$ w $x^2 - 7x - 30$ x $x^2 - x - 56$

2 Factorise:

a $a^2 + 6a + 8$ b $m^2 + 9m + 18$ c $y^2 + 13y + 42$
d $p^2 + 7p + 12$ e $x^2 + 12x + 20$ f $n^2 + 17n + 42$
g $s^2 + 21s + 54$ h $a^2 + 18a + 56$ i $x^2 - 3x - 4$
j $a^2 - 2a - 8$ k $p^2 - 5p - 24$ l $y^2 + y - 6$
m $x^2 + 7x - 8$ n $q^2 + 5q - 24$ o $m^2 + 12m - 45$
p $a^2 + 18a - 63$ q $y^2 + 6y - 55$ r $x^2 - 2x + 1$
s $k^2 - 5k + 6$ t $x^2 - 13x + 36$ u $a^2 - 22a + 72$
v $p^2 + 22p + 96$ w $q^2 - 12q - 45$ x $m^2 - 4m - 77$

3 Factorise by first taking out a common factor (see Worked Example **5** on page 357).

a $2x^2 + 6x + 4$ b $3x^2 - 6x - 9$ c $5x^2 - 10x - 40$
d $2x^2 + 16x + 32$ e $3x^2 - 30x - 33$ f $3x^2 + 21x + 36$
g $4a^2 - 12a - 40$ h $2n^2 + 8n + 6$ i $5x^2 - 30x + 40$
j $3x^2 - 21x + 36$ k $3a^2 - 15a - 108$ l $5x^2 + 15x - 350$

FUN SPOT 12:04 HOW MUCH LOGIC DO YOU HAVE?

See if you can solve the three problems below.

1 What is the next letter in this sequence?
O, T, T, F, F, S, S, ...?

2 A man passing a pilot in an airport exclaimed, 'I am that pilot's father!' But the pilot was not the man's son. How can this be?

3 Two guards are guarding two sacks. One guard always tells the truth, but the other guard always lies, but you do not know which guard is which. One of the sacks is full of gold; the other is full of peanuts. You are permitted to take one of the sacks but you are not sure which one contains the gold.
You are also allowed to ask one of the guards just one question. What question should you ask to ensure you get the sack of gold?

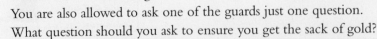

12:05 Factorising further quadratic trinomials

- In all quadratic trinomials factorised so far, the *coefficient* of x^2 has been 1. We will now consider cases where the *coefficient* of x^2 is not 1.

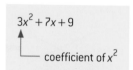

$3x^2 + 7x + 9$

↑ coefficient of x^2

To expand $(5x - 1)(x + 3)$ we can use a cross diagram.

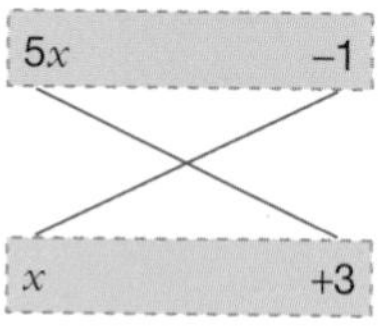

$5x^2$ is the product of the two left terms.
-3 is the product of the two right terms.
$14x$ is the sum of the products along the cross.
i.e. $15x + (-x)$

$\therefore (5x - 1)(x + 3) = 5x^2 + 14x - 3$

- One method used to factorise trinomials like $5x^2 + 14x - 3$ is called the cross method.

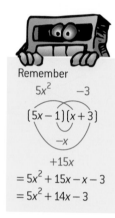

Remember

$5x^2 \quad -3$

$(5x - 1)(x + 3)$

$-x$

$+15x$

$= 5x^2 + 15x - x - 3$

$= 5x^2 + 14x - 3$

Cross method

To factorise $5x^2 + 14x - 3$, we need to reverse the expanding process. We need to choose two factors of $5x^2$ and two factors of -3 to write on the cross.

Try:

$\begin{cases} 5x \\ x \end{cases}$ and $\begin{cases} -3 \\ +1 \end{cases}$

- If $(5x - 3)$ and $(x + 1)$ are the factors of $5x^2 + 14x - 3$, then the products of numbers on the ends of each arm will have a sum of $+14x$.

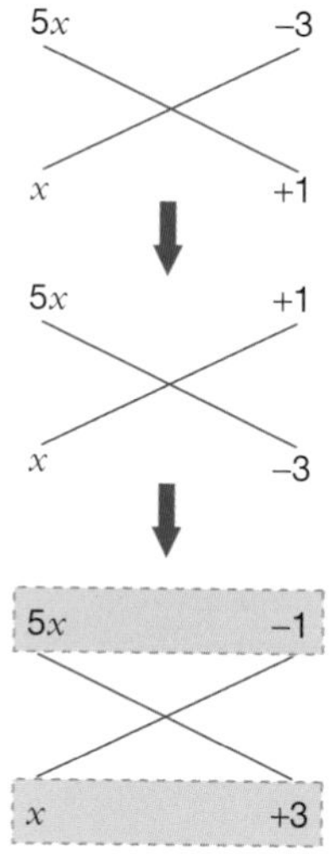

- When we add the cross-products here, we get: $(5x) + (-3x) = 2x$
  This does not give the correct middle term of $14x$, so $(5x - 3)$ and $(x + 1)$ are **not** factors.

- Vary the terms on the cross.

  Try: $\begin{cases} 5x \\ x \end{cases}$ and $\begin{cases} +1 \\ -3 \end{cases}$

Cross-product $= (-15x) + (x) = -14x$

Try: $\begin{cases} 5x \\ x \end{cases}$ and $\begin{cases} -1 \\ +3 \end{cases}$

Cross-product $= (15x) + (-x) = 14x$

$\therefore$ This must be the correct combination.

$\therefore 5x^2 + 14x - 3 = (5x - 1)(x + 3)$

Examine the examples on the next page. Make sure you understand the method.

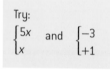

WORKED EXAMPLES

Find the factors of:

1 $3x^2 - 19x + 6$ 2 $4x^2 - x - 3$ 3 $2x^2 + 25x + 12$

Solutions

1
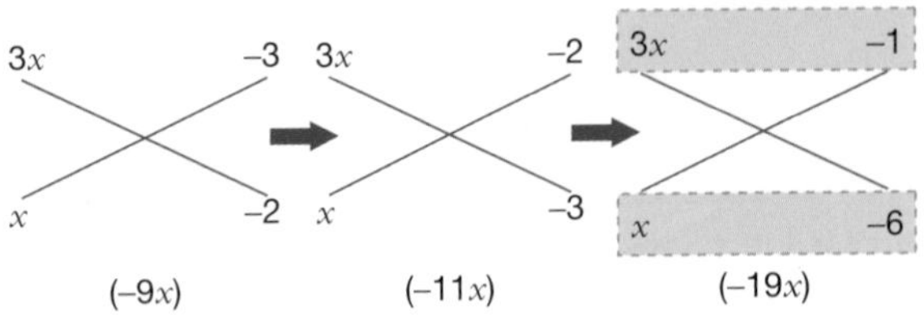

This cross-product gives the correct middle term of $-19x$.

$3x^2 - 19x + 6 = (3x - 1)(x - 6)$

Note: The factors of +6 had to be both negative to give a negative middle term.

2
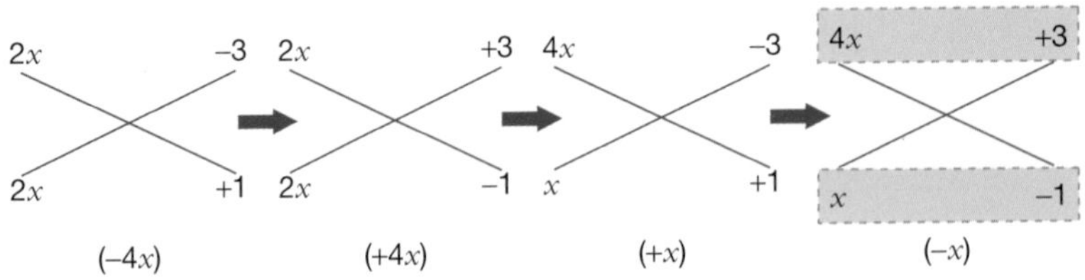

$\therefore 4x^2 - x - 3$
$= (4x + 3)(x - 1)$

3 In practice, we would not draw a separate cross for each new set of factors. We simply cross out the factors that don't work and try a new set.

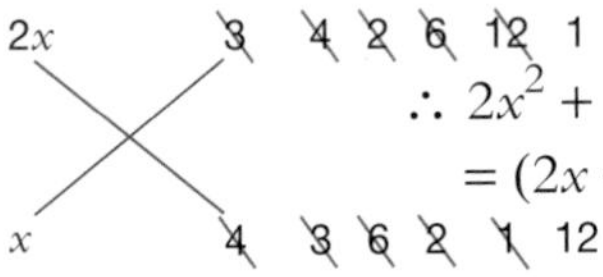

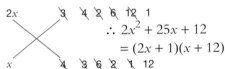

$\therefore 2x^2 + 25x + 12$
$= (2x + 1)(x + 12)$

To factorise a quadratic trinomial, $ax^2 + bx + c$, when a (the coefficient of x^2) is not 1, use the cross method.

Alternative method: Splitting the middle term

To factorise $5x^2 + 14x - 3$ we first multiply the two 'outer' numbers together and note it above the last number.

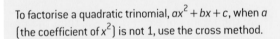

$5 \times -3 = -15$

i.e. $5x^2 + 14x - 3$

We then find two numbers that multiply to give -15 and add to give $+14$. The only possible numbers are $+15$ and -1.

$15 \times -1 = -15$ and $15 + -1 = 14$

We now 'split' the middle term, $+14x$ using these numbers, i.e. $+15x$, $-1x$ and rewrite the trinomial with four terms.

i.e. $5x^2 + 14x - 3 = 5x^2 + 15x - 1x - 3$

This expression we now factorise by grouping in pairs:

$$5x^2 + 15x - 1x - 3 = 5x(x + 3) - 1(x + 3)$$
$$= (x + 3)(5x - 1)$$
$$\therefore 5x^2 + 14x - 3 = (x + 3)(5x - 1)$$

WORKED EXAMPLES

Factorise:

1 $2x^2 - 5x - 12$

2 $12a^2 - 29a + 15$

Solutions

1 $2x^2 - 5x - 12 = 2x^2 - 5x - 12$ (−24) $(-8 \times 3 = -24 \text{ and } -8 + 3 = -5)$

$= 2x^2 - 8x + 3x - 12$

$= 2x(x - 4) + 3(x - 4)$

$= (x - 4)(2x + 3)$

With this method, sometimes the product can be a big number.

2 $12a^2 - 29a + 15 = 12a^2 - 29a + 15$ (180) $(-9 \times -20 = 180 \text{ and } -9 + -20 = -29)$

$= 12a^2 - 9a - 20a + 15$

$= 3a(4a - 3) - 5(4a - 3)$

$= (4a - 3)(3a - 5)$

Exercise 12:05

1 a Which diagram will give the factors of $2x^2 + 13x + 6$?

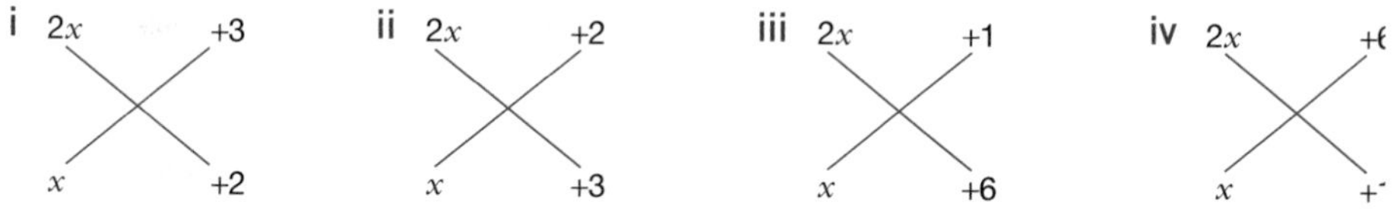

b Which diagram will give the factors of $9x^2 - 9x - 4$?

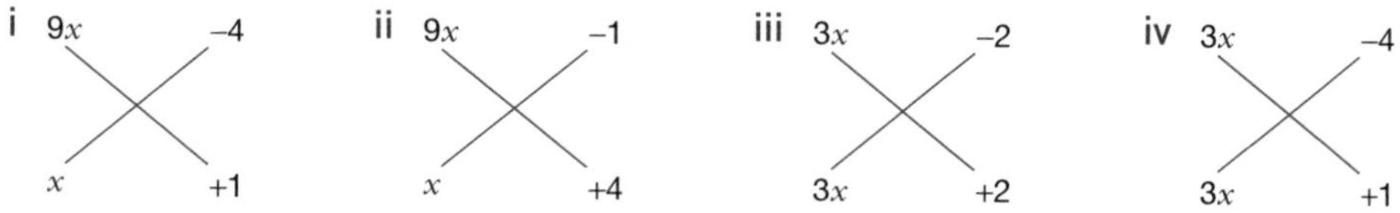

c Which diagram will give the factors of $5x^2 - 19x + 12$?

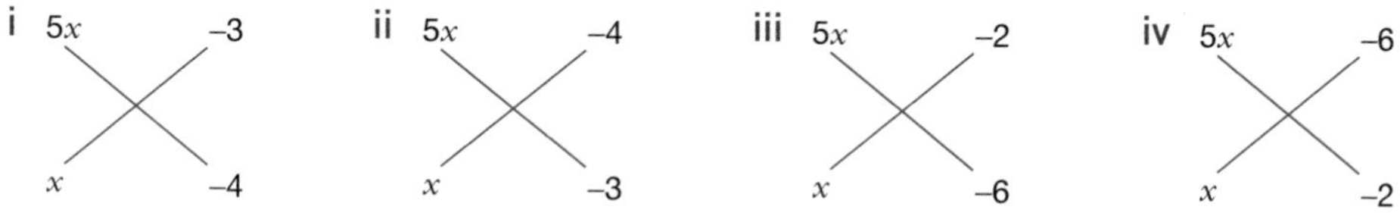

d Which diagram will give the factors of $12x^2 + 7x - 10$?

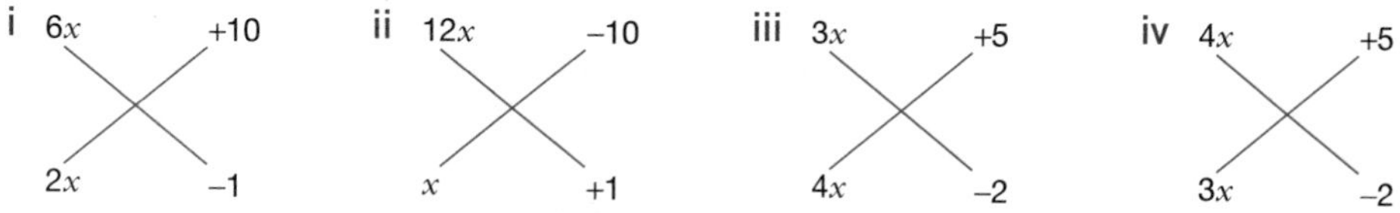

2 Factorise these expressions.

a $2x^2 + 7x + 3$ b $3x^2 + 8x + 4$ c $2x^2 + 7x + 6$
d $2x^2 + 11x + 5$ e $3x^2 + 5x + 2$ f $2x^2 + 11x + 15$
g $4x^2 + 13x + 3$ h $5x^2 + 17x + 6$ i $2x^2 + 13x + 15$
j $2x^2 - 5x + 2$ k $3x^2 - 11x + 6$ l $5x^2 - 17x + 6$
m $4x^2 - 11x + 6$ n $10x^2 - 21x + 9$ o $5x^2 - 22x + 21$
p $2x^2 + x - 10$ q $3x^2 + 4x - 15$ r $4x^2 + 11x - 3$
s $2x^2 - x - 6$ t $2x^2 - 5x - 3$ u $3x^2 - x - 30$
v $6x^2 - 5x - 21$ w $2x^2 - 5x - 12$ x $4x^2 - x - 18$

3 Find the factors of the following.

a $12x^2 + 7x + 1$ b $6a^2 + 5a + 1$ c $6p^2 + 7p + 2$
d $10y^2 - 9y + 2$ e $12x^2 - 7x + 1$ f $9a^2 - 21a + 10$
g $8m^2 + 18m - 5$ h $6n^2 - 7n - 3$ i $21q^2 - 20q + 4$
j $20x^2 - x - 1$ k $8m^2 - 2m - 15$ l $18y^2 - 3y - 10$
m $6a^2 + 5a - 6$ n $15k^2 + 26k + 8$ o $8x^2 + 18x + 9$
p $4 - 3a - a^2$ q $2 + m - 10m^2$ r $6 + 7x - 3x^2$
s $6 - 7x - 3x^2$ t $15 - x - 28x^2$ u $2 + 9n - 35n^2$
v $3x^2 + 10xy + 8y^2$ w $2x^2 - 5xy + 2y^2$ x $5m^2 - 2mn - 7n^2$

4 Factorise by first taking out the common factor.

a $6x^2 + 10x - 4$ b $6a^2 - 2a - 4$ c $6a^2 + 9a - 27$
d $8x^2 + 12x - 36$ e $6x^2 + 28x + 16$ f $12p^2 + 12p - 9$
g $30q^2 + 55q - 35$ h $10m^2 - 46m + 24$ i $50a^2 + 15a - 5$
j $4 - 6x - 10x^2$ k $36 - 3t - 3t^2$ l $9 + 24x + 12x^2$

5 Complete each in as many ways as possible by writing positive whole numbers in the boxes and inserting operation signs.

a $(x \ldots \square)(x \ldots \square) = x^2 \ldots \square x \ldots 15$
b $(x \ldots \square)(x \ldots \square) = x^2 \ldots \square x - 12$
c $(x \ldots \square)(x \ldots \square) = x^2 \ldots 5x + \square$
d $(5x \ldots \square)(x \ldots \square) = 5x^2 \ldots \square x \ldots 2$

This is an exercise you can sink your teeth into!

12:06 Factorising: Miscellaneous types

When factorising any algebraic expressions, remember this checklist . . .

1. Take out any common factors.
2. If there are two terms, is it a difference of two squares: $a^2 - b^2$?
3. If there are three terms, is it a quadratic trinomial: $ax^2 + bx + c$?
4. If there are four terms, can it be factorised by grouping in pairs?

WORKED EXAMPLES

1 $4x^2 - 36$
$= 4(x^2 - 9)$ common factor
$= 4(x - 3)(x + 3)$ difference of two squares

2 $15x^2y - 20xy + 10xy^2$
$= 5xy(3x - 4 + 2y)$ common factor

3 $8x^2 - 40x + 32$
$= 8(x^2 - 5x + 4)$ common factor
$= 8(x - 4)(x - 1)$ quadratic trinomial

4 $12 - a - 6a^2$
$= (3 + 2a)(4 - 3a)$ quadratic trinomial

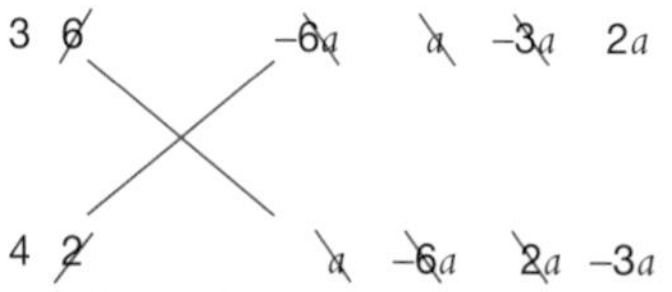

5 $ap - aq - 3p + 3q$
$= a(p - q) - 3(p - q)$ grouping in pairs
$= (p - q)(a - 3)$

Exercise 12:06

1 Factorise each of these expressions.

a $x^2 - 6x + 5$
b $x^2 - 9$
c $xy + 2y + 9x + 18$
d $a^2 - 9a$
e $a^2 - 6a + 9$
f $4x^2 - 1$
g $12x^2 - x - 35$
h $a^2 - 13a + 40$
i $5a^2b - 10ab^3$
j $p^2 - q^2$
k $pq - 3p + 10q - 30$
l $7x^2 + 11x - 6$
m $a^2 + 3a - ab$
n $16 - 25a^2$
o $1 - 2a - 24a^2$
p $4m + 4n - am - an$
q $5ay - 10y + 15xy$
r $15x^2 - x - 28$
s $x^2y^2 - 1$
t $x^2 - x - 56$
u $2mn + 3np + 4m + 6p$
v $100a^2 - 49x^2$
w $2 - 5x - 3x^2$
x $k^2 + 2k - 48$

2 Factorise completely.

a $2 - 8x^2$
b $5x^2 - 10x - 5xy + 10y$
c $2a^2 - 22a + 48$
d $3m^2 - 18m + 27$
e $x^4 - 1$
f $p^3 - 4p^2 - p + 4$
g $4x^2 - 36$
h $a^3 - a$
i $3a^2 - 39a + 120$
j $9 - 9p^2$
k $3k^2 + 3k - 18$
l $24a^2 - 42a + 9$
m $ax^2 + axy + 3ax + 3ay$
n $(x + y)^2 + 3(x + y)$
o $5xy^2 - 20xz^2$
p $6ax^2 + 5ax - 6a$
q $x^2 - y^2 + 5x - 5y$
r $3x^2 - 12x + 12$
s $63x^2 - 28y^2$
t $a^4 - 16$
u $(a - 2)^2 - 4$
v $1 + p + p^2 + p^3$
w $8t^2 - 28t - 60$
x $8 - 8x - 6x^2$

FUN SPOT 12:06 WHAT DID THE CATERPILLAR SAY WHEN IT SAW THE BUTTERFLY?

Answer each question and write the letter for that question in the box above the correct answer.

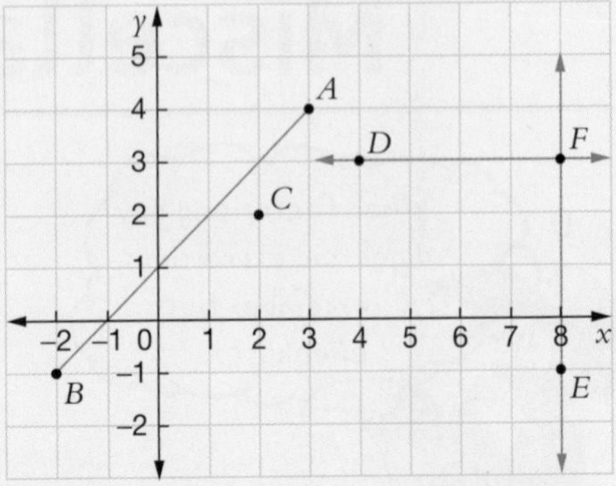

For the number plane on the right, find:

E the equation of the x-axis
E the distance BC
E the midpoint of AB
E the equation of AB
F the gradient of DF
H the intersection of DF and EF
I the distance of F from the origin
G the equation of the y-axis
E the distance AB
G the gradient of AB
E the y-intercept of DF
H the equation of DF
I the intersection of AB and BC.

Simplify:

I $10x^2 + x^2$ **L** $10x^2 - x^2$ **L** $10x^2 \times x^2$
M $10x^2 \div x^2$ **N** $\frac{1}{4}$ of $8x^4$ **N** 5% of $40x$
N $(2x^2)^3$ **N** $\frac{x}{2} + \frac{x}{2}$

A playing card is chosen at random from a standard pack.
Find the probability that it is:

O the Ace of spades **P** a heart
R a King **S** a picture card
T a red card greater than 3 but less than 9.

Expand and simplify:

O $(x + 1)(x + 7)$ **O** $(a - b)(a + b)$
S $(a + b)^2$ **T** $(a - b)^2$

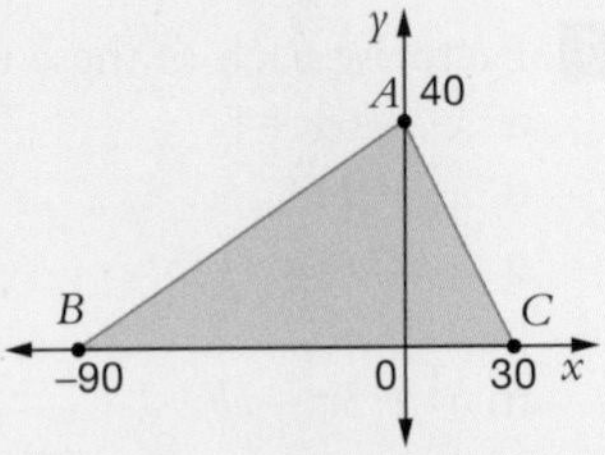

On this number plane, find the length of:

T OC **U** OA **U** AC
V BC **W** OB **Y** AB
O What is the area of ΔABC?

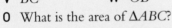

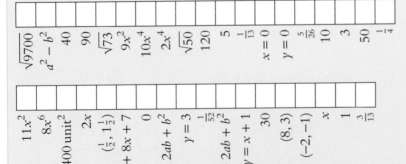

$\sqrt{9700}$	$a^2 - b^2$	40	90	$\sqrt{73}$	$9x^2$	$10x^4$	$2x^4$	$\sqrt{50}$	120	5	$\frac{1}{13}$	$x = 0$	$y = 0$	$\frac{5}{26}$	10	3	50	$\frac{1}{4}$

$11x^2$	$8x^6$	2400 unit^2	$2x$	$(\frac{1}{2}, 1\frac{1}{2})$	$x^2 + 8x + 7$	0	$a^2 - 2ab + b^2$	$y = 3$	$\frac{1}{52}$	$a^2 + 2ab + b^2$	$y = x + 1$	30	$(8, 3)$	$(-2, -1)$	x	1	$\frac{3}{13}$

12:07 Simplifying algebraic fractions: Multiplication and division

PREP QUIZ 12:07

Simplify the following:

1 $\dfrac{5a^2}{10a}$ **2** $\dfrac{12xy^2}{8x^2y}$ **3** $\dfrac{2x}{3} \times \dfrac{6}{x}$ **4** $\dfrac{2x}{3} \div \dfrac{4x}{9}$

Factorise:

5 $6x^2 + 9x$ **6** $x^2 + 7x + 12$ **7** $x^2 - 49$

8 $3x^2 + 6x + 3$ **9** $3x + 3y + ax + ay$ **10** $2x^2 + 9x - 5$

Just as numerical fractions can be simplified by cancelling common factors in the numerator and the denominator, so algebraic fractions can often be simplified in the same way after first factorising where possible.

WORKED EXAMPLE 1

Simplifying looks simple.

a $\dfrac{2x-2}{3x-3} = \dfrac{2\cancel{(x-1)}^1}{3\cancel{(x-1)}_1}$

$= \dfrac{2}{3}$

b $\dfrac{x^2+7x+12}{x^2-9} = \dfrac{(x+4)\cancel{(x+3)}^1}{(x-3)\cancel{(x+3)}_1}$

$= \dfrac{x+4}{x-3}$

c $\dfrac{6-6a^2}{3+3a+x+ax} = \dfrac{6(1-a)\cancel{(1+a)}^1}{(3+x)\cancel{(1+a)}_1}$

$= \dfrac{6(1-a)}{3+x}$

d $\dfrac{3x^2-9x}{3x^2-27} = \dfrac{\cancel{3}x\cancel{(x-3)}^1}{\cancel{3}\cancel{(x-3)}_1(x+3)}$

$= \dfrac{x}{x+3}$

Algebraic fractions should also be factorised before completing a multiplication or a division because the cancelling of common factors often simplifies these processes.

WORKED EXAMPLE 2

a $\dfrac{5x+15}{x+1} \times \dfrac{2x+2}{5} = \dfrac{{}^{1}\cancel{5}(x+3)}{{}_{1}\cancel{(x+1)}} \times \dfrac{2\cancel{(x+1)}^{1}}{\cancel{5}_{1}}$

$= 2(x+3)$

b $\dfrac{x^2-9}{x^2+5x+6} \times \dfrac{3x+6}{x^2-2x-3} = \dfrac{{}^{1}\cancel{(x-3)}\,\cancel{(x+3)}^{1}}{{}_{1}\cancel{(x+2)}\,\cancel{(x+3)}_{1}} \times \dfrac{3\cancel{(x+2)}^{1}}{{}_{1}\cancel{(x-3)}(x+1)}$

$= \dfrac{3}{x+1}$

c $\dfrac{6x-14}{3x-9} \div \dfrac{3x-7}{5x-15} = \dfrac{2\cancel{(3x-7)}^{1}}{3\cancel{(x-3)}^{1}} \times \dfrac{5\cancel{(x-3)}^{1}}{\cancel{(3x-7)}^{1}}$

$= \dfrac{10}{3}$ or $3\dfrac{1}{3}$

d $\dfrac{a^2-16}{a^2-25} \div \dfrac{a^2-2a-8}{a^2+10a+25} = \dfrac{{}^{1}\cancel{(a-4)}(a+4)}{(a-5)\cancel{(a+5)}_{1}} \times \dfrac{(a+5)\cancel{(a+5)}^{1}}{{}_{1}\cancel{(a-4)}(a+2)}$

$= \dfrac{(a+4)(a+5)}{(a-5)(a+2)}$

To simplify algebraic fractions, factorise both numerator and denominator where possible, and then cancel.

Exercise 12:07

1 Factorise and simplify.

a $\dfrac{5x+10}{5}$ b $\dfrac{4}{2x+6}$ c $\dfrac{12}{3x-9}$

d $\dfrac{2x-10}{x-5}$ e $\dfrac{x+7}{3x+21}$ f $\dfrac{5a-5}{8a-8}$

g $\dfrac{3a+9}{6a+18}$ h $\dfrac{7m-28}{3m-12}$ i $\dfrac{x^2+x}{x^2-x}$

j $\dfrac{x^2-4}{x-2}$ k $\dfrac{a+1}{a^2-1}$ l $\dfrac{4y^2-9}{4y+6}$

m $\dfrac{a^2-4a}{3a-a^2}$ n $\dfrac{2x^2-2}{2x-2}$ o $\dfrac{x^2-36}{3x-18}$

p $\dfrac{a^2-3a-4}{a+1}$ q $\dfrac{x^2-6x+9}{x-3}$ r $\dfrac{x^2-4}{x^2+3x+2}$

s $\dfrac{x^2+3x+2}{x^2+5x+6}$

t $\dfrac{m^2+5m-24}{m^2-7m+12}$

u $\dfrac{t^2+7t+12}{t^2-9}$

v $\dfrac{a^2-x^2}{a^2+3a+ax+3x}$

w $\dfrac{2x^2-x-1}{4x^2-1}$

x $\dfrac{18a^2-8}{6a^2+a-2}$

2 Simplify the following.

a $\dfrac{2x+4}{3}\times\dfrac{6x}{x+2}$

b $\dfrac{5y-15}{2y+8}\times\dfrac{y+4}{10}$

c $\dfrac{2x-4}{3x-9}\times\dfrac{5x-15}{7x-14}$

d $\dfrac{5n+10}{n+3}\times\dfrac{6n+18}{4n+8}$

e $\dfrac{7y+28}{21}\times\dfrac{6}{6y+24}$

f $\dfrac{1+2a}{10+30a}\times\dfrac{6+18a}{1-2a}$

g $\dfrac{y^2+y}{2y+8}\times\dfrac{4y+6}{3y+3}$

h $\dfrac{x^2-3x}{x^2}\times\dfrac{2x^2+5x}{9x-27}$

i $\dfrac{x+3}{x^2-9}\times\dfrac{x-3}{x+1}$

j $\dfrac{3x+15}{x^2-25}\times\dfrac{x^2-49}{3x-21}$

k $\dfrac{a^2+5a+6}{a^2-4}\times\dfrac{a^2-a-2}{a^2-1}$

l $\dfrac{y^2+3y+2}{y^2+5y+6}\times\dfrac{y^2+7y+12}{y^2+5y+4}$

m $\dfrac{x^2+6x+5}{x^2+5x+4}\times\dfrac{x^2+7x+12}{x^2+12x+35}$

n $\dfrac{m^2-1}{m^2-6m+5}\times\dfrac{m^2-10m+25}{m^2-25}$

o $\dfrac{a^2-4}{a^2+3a-4}\times\dfrac{a^2-16}{a^2+2a-8}$

p $\dfrac{2x^2+4x+2}{x^2-1}\times\dfrac{x^2+3x-4}{4x+4}$

q $\dfrac{3x^2+5x+2}{x^2-x-2}\times\dfrac{x^2+x-6}{3x^2+11x+6}$

r $\dfrac{5a^2+16a+3}{25a^2-1}\times\dfrac{5a^2-a}{2a^2+5a-3}$

s $\dfrac{x^2-y^2+x-y}{x^2-2xy+y^2}\times\dfrac{10x-10y}{5x+5y+5}$

t $\dfrac{(a+b)^2-c^2}{a^2+ab+ac+bc}\times\dfrac{a^2+ab-ac-bc}{a+b+c}$

3 Simplify:

a $\dfrac{3a+6}{2}\div\dfrac{a+2}{4}$

b $\dfrac{x+2}{5x}\div\dfrac{7x+14}{10x}$

c $\dfrac{5m-10}{m+1}\div\dfrac{3m-6}{3m+3}$

d $\dfrac{6m+9}{2m-8}\div\dfrac{2m+3}{3m-12}$

e $\dfrac{3x}{5x+15}\div\dfrac{x^2+x}{x+3}$

f $\dfrac{24y-16}{4y+6}\div\dfrac{3y-2}{8y+12}$

g $\dfrac{5m-20}{4m+6}\div\dfrac{5m-20}{2m^2+3m}$

h $\dfrac{25k+15}{3k-3}\div\dfrac{5k+3}{3k}$

i $\dfrac{n^2-9}{2n+4}\div\dfrac{n+3}{2}$

j $\dfrac{y+7}{y-7}\div\dfrac{y^2-49}{y^2-7y}$

k $\dfrac{a^2+5a+4}{a^2-16}\div\dfrac{a^2-9}{a^2-a-12}$

l $\dfrac{x^2+6x+9}{x^2+8x+15}\div\dfrac{x^2+5x+6}{x^2+7x+10}$

m $\dfrac{x^2-4}{x^2-7x+10} \div \dfrac{x^2-x-6}{x^2-3x-10}$

n $\dfrac{p^2+7p+10}{p^2-2p-8} \div \dfrac{p^2+2p-15}{p^2+p-12}$

o $\dfrac{n^2-49}{n^2-9} \div \dfrac{n^2+14n+49}{n^2-6n+9}$

p $\dfrac{2x^2-8x-42}{x^2+6x+9} \div \dfrac{x^2-9x+14}{x^2+x-6}$

q $\dfrac{3x^2-48}{x^2-3x-4} \div \dfrac{x^2+4x}{x^3-x}$

r $\dfrac{2a^2-a-1}{a^2-1} \div \dfrac{6a^2+a-1}{3a^2+2a-1}$

s $\dfrac{x+y+x^2-y^2}{x^2+2xy+y^2} \div \dfrac{1+x-y}{2x+2y}$

t $\dfrac{p^2-(q+r)^2}{p^2+pq-pr-qr} \div \dfrac{p-q-r}{p^2-pq-pr+qr}$

12:08 Addition and subtraction of algebraic fractions

PREP QUIZ 12:08

Simplify:

1 $\dfrac{1}{2}+\dfrac{3}{5}$ 2 $\dfrac{3}{4}+\dfrac{3}{8}$ 3 $\dfrac{9}{10}-\dfrac{3}{5}$ 4 $\dfrac{7}{15}-\dfrac{3}{20}$ 5 $\dfrac{5}{2x}+\dfrac{7}{x}$

6 $\dfrac{2}{a}+\dfrac{1}{2a}$ 7 $\dfrac{2}{3a}+\dfrac{3}{2a}$ 8 $\dfrac{1}{x}-\dfrac{1}{4x}$ 9 $\dfrac{a}{2x}+\dfrac{2a}{x}$ 10 $\dfrac{5m}{2n}-\dfrac{4m}{3n}$

The Prep quiz above should have reminded you that the lowest common denominator needs to be found when adding or subtracting fractions. If the denominators involve two or more terms, factorising first may help in finding the lowest common denominator.
For example:

$$\begin{aligned}\frac{2}{x^2-9}+\frac{5}{x^2+5x+6} &= \frac{2}{(x-3)(x+3)}+\frac{5}{(x+3)(x+2)}\\ &= \frac{2(x+2)+5(x-3)}{(x-3)(x+3)(x+2)}\\ &= \frac{2x+4+5x-15}{(x-3)(x+3)(x+2)}\\ &= \frac{7x-11}{(x-3)(x+3)(x+2)}\end{aligned}$$

LCD
stands for
lowest
common
denominator.

Here, LCD = $(x-3)(x+3)(x+2)$.
Note that the factors of each denominator are present without repeating any factor common to both. Each numerator is then multiplied by each factor not present in its original denominator.

When adding or subtracting fractions:

- factorise the denominator of each fraction
- find the lowest common denominator
- rewrite each fraction with this common denominator and simplify.

WORKED EXAMPLES

1 $$\frac{2}{x+2}+\frac{1}{x+3}=\frac{2(x+3)+1(x+2)}{(x-3)(x+3)}$$
$$=\frac{2x+6+x+2}{(x+2)(x+3)}$$
$$=\frac{3x+8}{(x+2)(x+3)}$$

2 $$\frac{3}{2x+1}-\frac{4}{3x-1}=\frac{3(3x-1)-4(2x+1)}{(2x+1)(3x-1)}$$
$$=\frac{9x-3-8x-4}{(2x+1)(3x-1)}$$
$$=\frac{x-7}{(2x+1)(3x-1)}$$

No factorising was needed in these first two examples.

3 $$\frac{1}{x^2+5x+6}+\frac{2}{x+3}$$
$$=\frac{1}{(x+2)(x+3)}+\frac{2}{(x+3)}$$
$$=\frac{1+2(x+2)}{(x+2)(x+3)}$$
$$=\frac{1+2x+4}{(x+2)(x+3)}$$
$$=\frac{2x+5}{(x+2)(x+3)}$$

4 $$\frac{4}{x^2+x}-\frac{3}{x^2-1}$$
$$=\frac{4}{x(x+1)}+\frac{2}{(x-1)(x+1)}$$
$$=\frac{4(x-1)-3x}{x(x+1)(x-1)}$$
$$=\frac{4x-4-3x}{x(x+1)(x-1)}$$
$$=\frac{x-4}{x(x+1)(x-1)}$$

5 $$\frac{x+3}{x^2+2x+1}-\frac{x-1}{x^2-x-2}$$
$$=\frac{x+3}{(x+1)(x+1)}-\frac{x-1}{(x+1)(x-2)}$$
$$=\frac{(x+3)(x-2)-(x-1)(x+1)}{(x+1)(x+1)(x-2)}$$
$$=\frac{x^2+x-6-(x^2-1)}{(x+1)(x+1)(x-2)}$$
$$=\frac{x-5}{(x+1)^2(x-2)}$$

Exercise 12:08

P Foundation worksheet 12:08
Addition and subtraction of algebraic fractions

1 Simplify each of the following. (*Note:* No factorising is needed.)

a $\dfrac{1}{x+1}+\dfrac{1}{x-1}$ b $\dfrac{1}{a+5}+\dfrac{1}{a+3}$ c $\dfrac{1}{y-7}-\dfrac{1}{y+1}$

d $\dfrac{2}{x+3}+\dfrac{3}{x+5}$ e $\dfrac{5}{m+1}-\dfrac{3}{m-2}$ f $\dfrac{6}{t+10}-\dfrac{3}{t+2}$

g $\dfrac{1}{2x-1}+\dfrac{3}{x-1}$ h $\dfrac{9}{3x+2}-\dfrac{7}{2x+5}$ i $\dfrac{8}{5x-1}+\dfrac{7}{3x+1}$

j $\dfrac{3}{2x}+\dfrac{5}{x+7}$ k $\dfrac{9}{2x+5}-\dfrac{5}{3x}$ l $\dfrac{1}{2a}-\dfrac{3}{2a+1}$

m $\dfrac{x}{x+3}+\dfrac{x}{x+1}$ n $\dfrac{a}{2a+1}-\dfrac{2a}{4a-1}$ o $\dfrac{x+1}{x+2}+\dfrac{x+2}{x+1}$

2 Simplify. (*Note:* The denominators are already factorised.)

a $\dfrac{1}{(x+1)(x+2)}+\dfrac{1}{x+1}$ b $\dfrac{1}{x(x+2)}+\dfrac{1}{x+2}$

c $\dfrac{1}{x+3}-\dfrac{1}{x(x+3)}$ d $\dfrac{1}{x-5}-\dfrac{1}{(x-5)(x+2)}$

e $\dfrac{3}{(x+2)(x+3)}+\dfrac{4}{x+2}$ f $\dfrac{5}{x+4}-\dfrac{3}{(x+1)(x+4)}$

g $\dfrac{1}{(x+1)(x+2)}+\dfrac{1}{(x+2)(x+3)}$ h $\dfrac{2}{(x-3)(x+3)}+\dfrac{4}{(x+3)(x+1)}$

i $\dfrac{3}{(x+7)(x-1)}+\dfrac{5}{(x+7)(x+1)}$ j $\dfrac{9}{(x+9)(x+3)}-\dfrac{7}{(x+3)(x-1)}$

k $\dfrac{1}{(2x+1)(x+5)}+\dfrac{3}{(x+5)(x+2)}$ l $\dfrac{5}{(2x-1)(3x+2)}-\dfrac{6}{x(2x-1)}$

m $\dfrac{x-1}{(x+3)(x+1)}+\dfrac{x+1}{(x+3)(x-1)}$ n $\dfrac{x+2}{x(x+3)}-\dfrac{x-1}{x(x+2)}$

3 Simplify, by first factorising each denominator where possible.

a $\dfrac{1}{x^2+x}+\dfrac{1}{x+1}$ b $\dfrac{1}{3x+9}-\dfrac{1}{x+3}$

c $\dfrac{2}{2x+3}+\dfrac{3}{4x+6}$ d $\dfrac{5}{x^2-1}+\dfrac{3}{x-1}$

e $\dfrac{1}{x^2-9}+\dfrac{1}{2x-6}$ f $\dfrac{1}{x^2+x}-\dfrac{1}{x^2-1}$

g $\dfrac{1}{x^2+2x+1}+\dfrac{1}{x^2-1}$ h $\dfrac{1}{x^2+7x+12}+\dfrac{1}{x^2+8x+16}$

i $\dfrac{2}{x^2+6x+8}+\dfrac{4}{x^2+5x+6}$ j $\dfrac{2}{x^2+7x+12}+\dfrac{4}{x^2+5x+4}$

k $\dfrac{3}{x^2-x-2}-\dfrac{4}{x^2-2x-3}$ l $\dfrac{3}{x^2-x-6}-\dfrac{2}{x^2-2x-3}$

m $\dfrac{5}{x^2 - 3x - 4} - \dfrac{3}{x^2 - x - 2}$

n $\dfrac{3}{2x^2 + 7x - 4} - \dfrac{4}{3x^2 + 14x + 8}$

o $\dfrac{2}{x^2 - 49} + \dfrac{4}{x^2 - 4x - 21}$

p $\dfrac{4}{2x^2 + x - 1} - \dfrac{1}{x^2 - 1}$

q $\dfrac{x+1}{x^2 + 5x + 6} + \dfrac{x-1}{x^2 - 9}$

r $\dfrac{x+3}{x^2 - 16} - \dfrac{x+2}{x^2 - 4x}$

s $\dfrac{2x}{5x^2 - 20} + \dfrac{x+1}{x^2 + 4x + 4}$

t $\dfrac{5x+2}{2x^2 - 5x - 3} + \dfrac{3x-1}{4x^2 - 1}$

MATHS TERMS 12

binomial
- an algebraic expression consisting of two terms,
  e.g. $2x + 4$, $3x - 2y$

coefficient
- the number that multiplies a pronumeral in an algebraic expression,
  e.g. in $3x - 5y$:
  - the coefficient of x is 3
  - the coefficient of y is -5

expand
- to remove grouping symbols by multiplying each term inside grouping symbols by the term or terms outside

factorise
- to write an expression as a product of its factors
- the reverse of expanding

product
- the result of multiplying terms or expressions together

quadratic trinomial
- expressions such as $x^2 + 4x + 3$
- the highest power of the variable is 2

trinomial
- an algebraic expression consisting of three terms

This spiral or helix is a mathematical shape.
Discover how it can be drawn.
Investigate its links to the golden rectangle.

DIAGNOSTIC TEST 12 FACTORISING ALGEBRAIC EXPRESSIONS

Each part of this test has similar items that test a particular skill.
Errors made will indicate areas of weakness.
Each weakness should be treated by going back to the section listed.

1 Factorise by taking out a common factor. 12:01

a $3x - 12$ b $ax + ay$ c $-2x - 6$ d $ax + bx - cx$

2 Factorise by grouping in pairs. 12:02

a $ax + bx + 2a + 2b$ b $6m + 6n + am + an$

c $xy - x + y - 1$ d $ab + 4c + 4a + bc$

3 Factorise these differences of two squares. 12:03

a $x^2 - 25$ b $a^2 - x^2$ c $4 - m^2$ d $9x^2 - 1$

4 Factorise these trinomials. 12:04

a $x^2 + 7x + 12$ b $x^2 - 5x + 6$ c $x^2 - 3x - 10$ d $x^2 + x - 20$

5 Factorise: 12:05

a $2x^2 + 11x + 5$ b $3x^2 - 11x + 6$ c $4x^2 - x - 18$ d $6x^2 + 5x + 1$

6 Simplify, by first factorising where possible. 12:07

a $\dfrac{6x+12}{6}$ b $\dfrac{12a-18}{14a-21}$ c $\dfrac{x^2+5x}{ax+5a}$ d $\dfrac{x^2+3x-10}{x^2-4}$

7 Simplify: 12:07

a $\dfrac{3x+6}{4} \times \dfrac{8x}{x+2}$ b $\dfrac{a^2+5a+6}{a^2-9} \times \dfrac{a^2-1}{a^2+3a+2}$

c $\dfrac{3m-6}{m+3} \div \dfrac{5m-10}{3m+9}$ d $\dfrac{x^2-3x-10}{x^2-x-6} \div \dfrac{x^2-7x+10}{x^2-4}$

8 Simplify: 12:08

a $\dfrac{2}{x+3} + \dfrac{1}{x-1}$ b $\dfrac{1}{x(x+2)} - \dfrac{1}{(x+2)(x+1)}$

c $\dfrac{5}{x^2-9} + \dfrac{3}{2x-6}$ d $\dfrac{x}{x^2+7x+12} - \dfrac{x+2}{x^2+2x-3}$

ASSIGNMENT 12A Chapter review

1 Factorise the following expressions.

a $a^2 + 9a + 20$
b $2p - 4q$
c $m^2 - 4m - 45$
d $5x^3 + 10x^2 + x + 2$
e $4x^2 - 1$
f $x^2y - xy$
g $6a^2 - 13a + 5$
h $x^2 + x - 30$
i $3a^2 - 4a - 15$
j $xy + xz + py + pz$
k $2x^2 + x - 1$
l $x^3 - 3x^2 + 2x - 6$
m $-5ab - 10a^2b^2$
n $x^2 - y^2 + 2x - 2y$
o $2 - 3x - 9x^2$

2 Factorise each expression fully.

a $2y^2 - 18$
b $3r^2 + 9r - 84$
c $4x^3 + 6x + 4x^2 + 6$
d $2 - 18x^2$
e $a^3 + a^2 - 72a$
f $33 + 36a + 3a^2$
g $(x - y)^2 + x - y$
h $(x - 2)^2 - 4$

3 Simplify each of the following.

a $\dfrac{x^2 + 9x - 36}{x^2 - 9}$

b $\dfrac{20x^2 - 5}{2x^2 + 5x - 3}$

c $\dfrac{3}{x+2} + \dfrac{2}{x+3}$

d $\dfrac{x}{x-1} - \dfrac{2x}{x-2}$

e $\dfrac{x^2 - 1}{5x} \times \dfrac{x^2 + x}{x^2 + 2x + 1}$

f $\dfrac{x-1}{x^2 - 4} \div \dfrac{x^2 - 4x + 3}{x^2 - x - 6}$

g $\dfrac{x+1}{x+2} - \dfrac{x+2}{x+1}$

h $\dfrac{2}{3x-1} + \dfrac{1}{(3x-1)^2}$

i $\dfrac{4}{3+2x} - \dfrac{3}{2x+3}$

j $\dfrac{x^2 + 5x - 14}{5x^2 - 20} \times \dfrac{x^2 + 4x + 4}{x^2 - 49}$

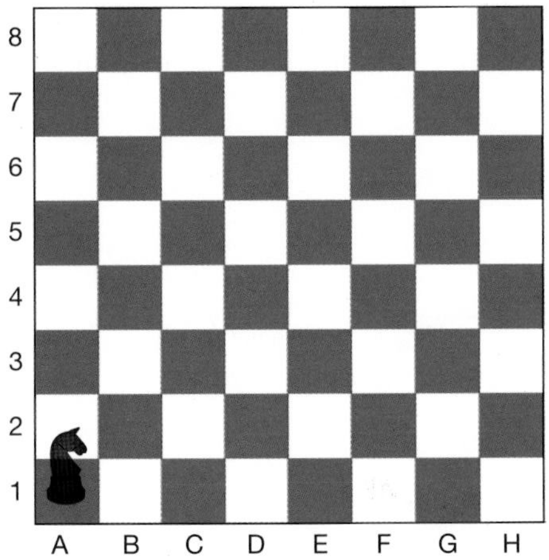

Chess is played on an 8 by 8 square grid. Each square is named using a letter and a number. The Knight pictured is standing on the square A1.

A Knight can move 3 squares from its starting position to its finishing position. The squares must form an 'L' shape in any direction. Some possible moves are shown below.

Which squares can the Knight move to from square A1?

If the Knight was standing on the square C1, what squares could it move to?

Give a sequence of squares showing how the Knight could move from A1 to B1 to C1 to ... H1.

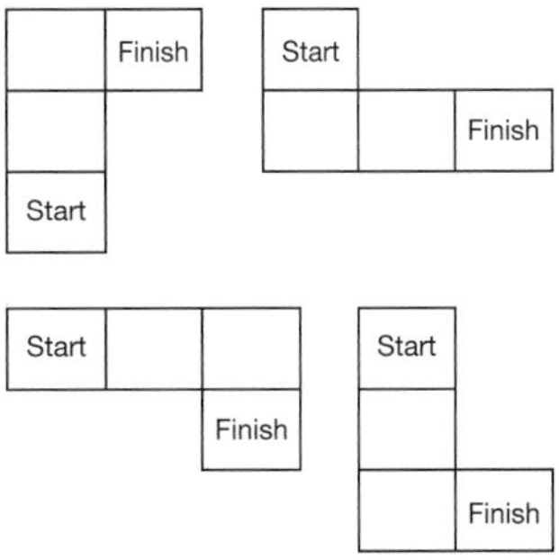

ASSIGNMENT 12B Working mathematically

1 What is the smallest possible number of children in a family if each child has:

a at least one brother and at least one sister

b at least two brothers and at least two sisters?

2 If you turn a right-handed glove inside out, is it still a right-handed glove or has it become a left-handed glove?

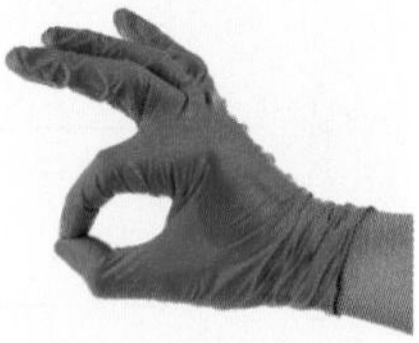

3 If the exterior angles x, y and z of a triangle are in the ratio $4:5:6$, what is the ratio of the interior angles a, b and c?

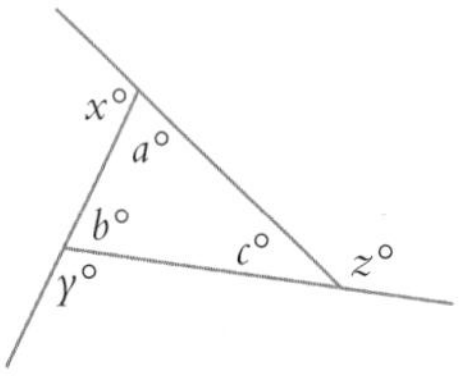

4 The average of five numbers is 11. A sixth number is added and the new average is 12. What is the sixth number?

5 This sector graph shows the method of travelling to work for all persons.

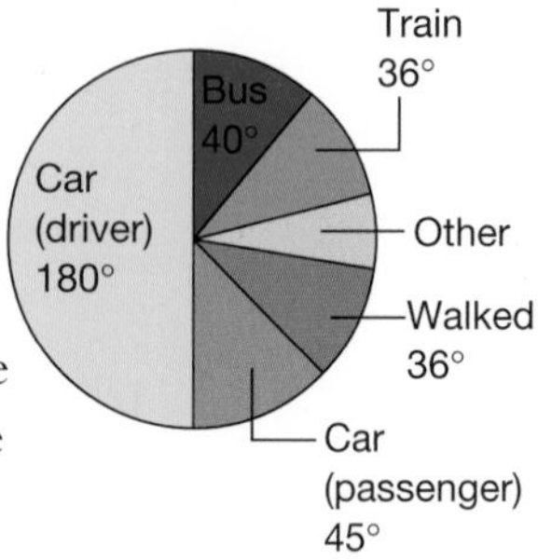

a What percentage of the workforce caught a train to work?

b What percentage of the workforce was driven to work?

c What is the size of the sector angle for 'other' means of transport? Do not use a protractor.

d What percentage of the workforce used a car to get to work?

6 Use the graph below to answer the following questions.

a Who has the greater chance of having heart disease: a 60-year-old woman or a 60-year-old man?

b Who has the greater chance of having cancer: a 50-year-old woman or a 50-year-old man?

c Which of the three diseases reveals the greatest gender difference for the 20-to-50-year-old range?

d Would the number of 80-year-old men suffering from heart disease be greater or less than the number of 80-year-old women suffering from heart disease? Give a reason for your answer.

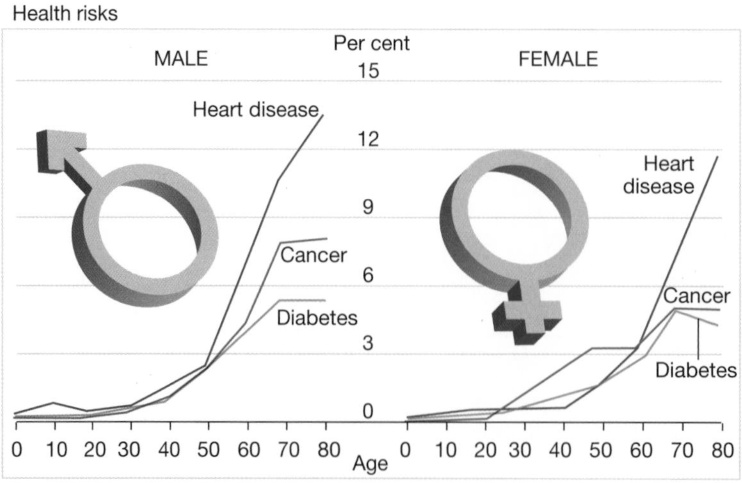

Source: Australian Institute of Health and Welfare

ASSIGNMENT 12C Cumulative revision

1 Solve the inequalities. 7:06

a $2a - 7 > 10$ b $-3x > 12$ c $-\frac{3m}{5} \geq 12$

2 Under a fringe benefits tax agreement an employee can reduce their taxable income by putting 30% of their salary into an expense account. If their salary is \$55 200 per annum, find: 2:01

a how much can be paid into the expense account

b the tax saving if every dollar that goes into the expense account reduces the tax payable by 32·5 cents.

3 a Find the length of the interval joining the point $(1, -1)$ to the point $(-3, 2)$. 9:01, 9:04, 9:03

b Find the x- and y- intercepts of the line $3x + 2y = 9$.

c What is the slope of the line that has an x-intercept of -2 and a y-intercept of -4?

4 Calculate the volume of the following prism. (Measurements are in centimetres.) 5:05

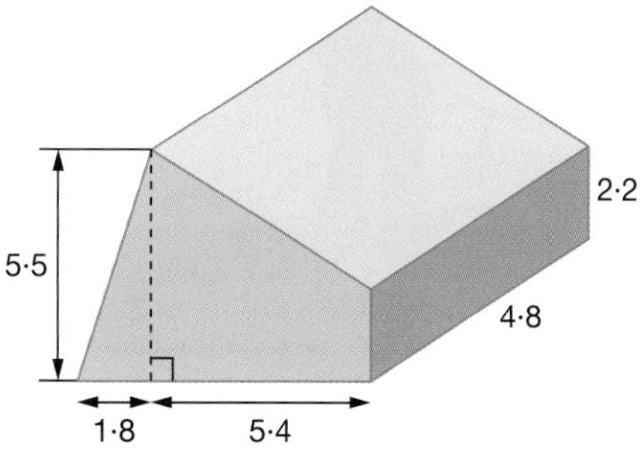

5 Jim buys 2000 shares in the WeDiGiT mining company at a cost of \$2.10 per share. After 3 months he sells 500 shares at \$2.50 per share. He then waits for the market to improve and then sells another 750 shares for \$3.20 per share. Find Jim's profit and the percentage return on the original cost of those 1250 shares. 8:05

6 Hannah earns \$34.75 per hour. Find: 8:03

a her gross weekly wage if she works a 38 hour week

b her net weekly wage if she has the following deductions: PAYG \$287, Superannuation \$223, Union membership \$5.20, Health insurance \$69.75, Credit Union deduction (savings) \$200.

7 Find the equation of a line in the number plane which: 9:05, 9:06, 9:07

a has a gradient of 3 and a y-intercept at $(0, 4)$

b has a gradient of -2 and passes through the point $(3, -1)$

c passes through the two points $(-2, 5)$ and $(4, -7)$.

8 Solve these pairs of simultaneous equations. 10:02

a $3x + 4y = 6$ and $5x - 3y = 39$

b $y = 7 - 3x$ and $5x - 2y + 25 = 0$

TRIGONOMETRY 13

Contents

Syllabus references (See pages x–xv for details.)

Measurement and Geometry

Selection from ***Right-Angled Triangles (Trigonometry)*** [Stages 5.1, 5.2◊]

- Use similarity to investigate the constancy of the sine, cosine and tangent ratios for a given angle in right-angled triangles (ACMMG223)
- Apply trigonometry to solve right-angled triangle problems (ACMMG224)
- Solve right-angled triangle problems, including those involving direction and angles of elevation and depression (ACMMG245)

Selections from ***Trigonometry and Pythagoras' Theorem*** [Stage 5.3§]

- Apply Pythagoras' theorem and trigonometry to solve three-dimensional problems in right-angled triangles (ACMMG276)

Working Mathematically

- Communicating • Problem Solving • Reasoning • Understanding • Fluency

Trigonometry is a branch of geometry that is very important in fields such as navigation, surveying, engineering, astronomy and architecture. Basic trigonometry is used to find unknown sides and angles in right-angled triangles. 'The word 'trigonometry' is derived from *trigonometria* meaning 'a system for measuring triangles'.

13:01 Right-angled triangles

Before introducing trigonometry, we need to be aware of some further information concerning right-angled triangles.

From Pythagoras' theorem, we know that the longest side in a right-angled triangle is called the hypotenuse. The other two sides also have names that refer to one of the acute angles in the triangle. The side farthest from the angle is the opposite side, and the side next to the angle is the adjacent side.

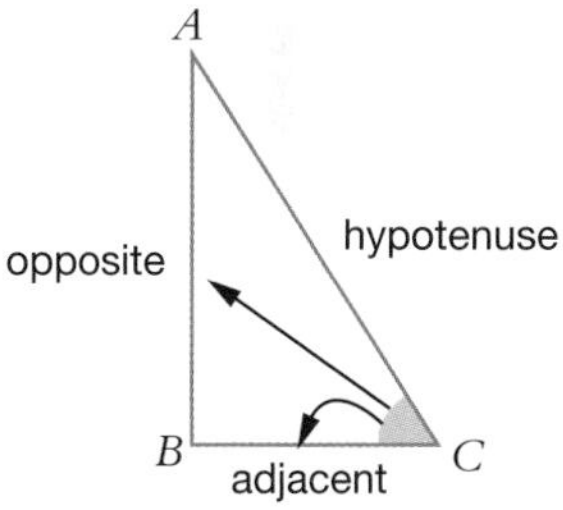

WORKED EXAMPLE 1

Name the sides in these two right-angled triangles with reference to the angle marked.

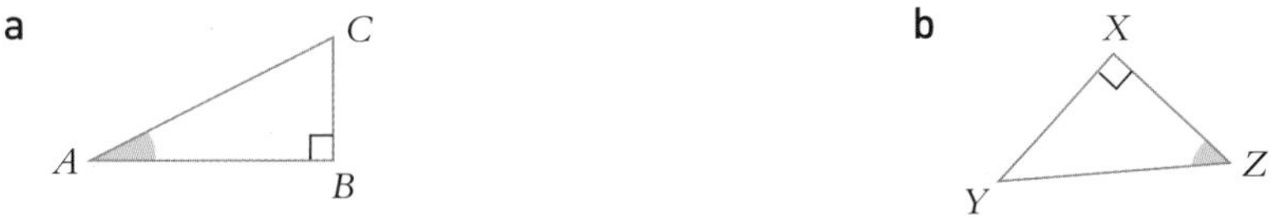

a

BC = opposite side
AB = adjacent side
AC = hypotenuse

b

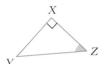

XY = opposite side
XZ = adjacent side
YZ = hypotenuse

WORKED EXAMPLE 2

Find the value of these ratios in ΔPQR.

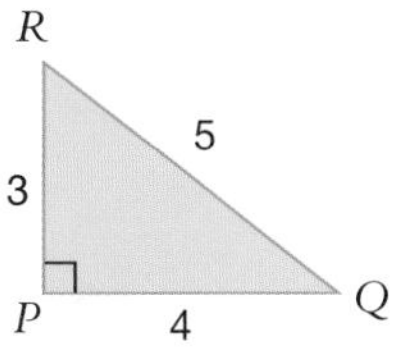

a $\dfrac{\text{Side opposite angle } R}{\text{Hypotenuse}}$

Side opposite angle $R = 4$
Hypotenuse $= 5$
$\therefore$ Ratio $= \frac{4}{5}$

b $\dfrac{\text{Side opposite angle } Q}{\text{Side adjacent to angle } Q}$

Side opposite angle $Q = 3$
Side adjacent to angle $Q = 4$
$\therefore$ Ratio $= \frac{3}{4}$

Exercise 13:01

1 Name the side opposite the marked angle in each triangle.

a
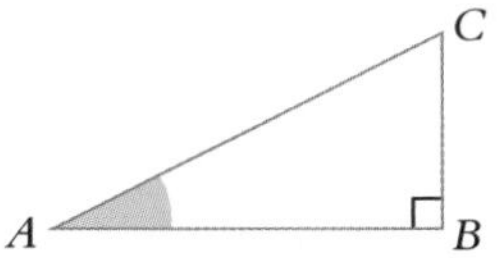

b
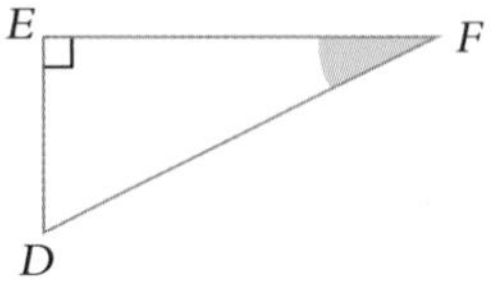

c
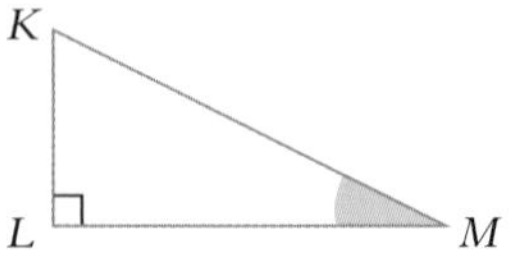

d
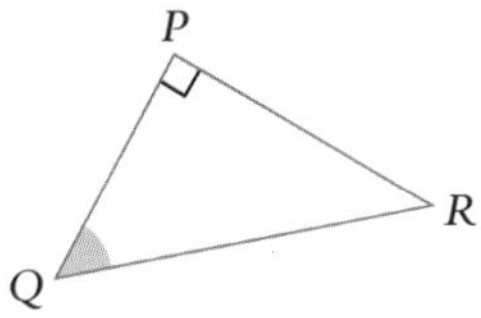

e
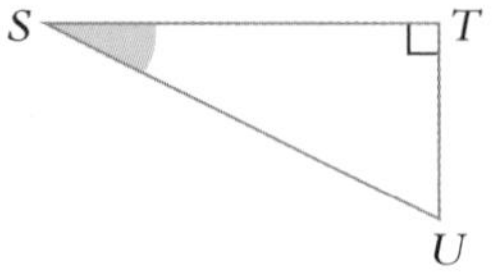

f
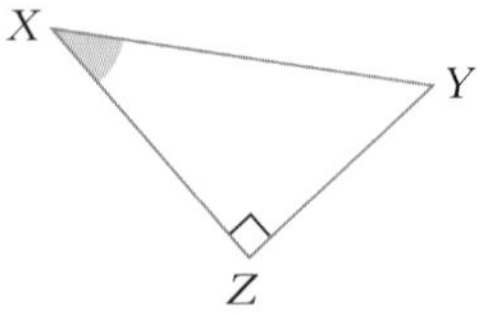

2 Name the adjacent side in each of the triangles in Question 1.

3 Name the hypotenuse in each triangle in Question 1.

4 In triangle ABC:

a which side is opposite angle B

b which side is adjacent to angle C

c which angle is opposite side AB

d which angle is adjacent to side AC?

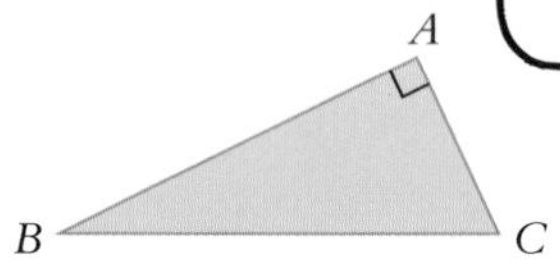

5 Find the value of the ratio $\dfrac{\text{Side opposite angle } P}{\text{Side adjacent to angle } P}$ in these triangles.

a
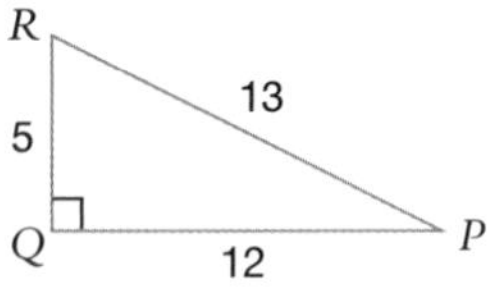

b
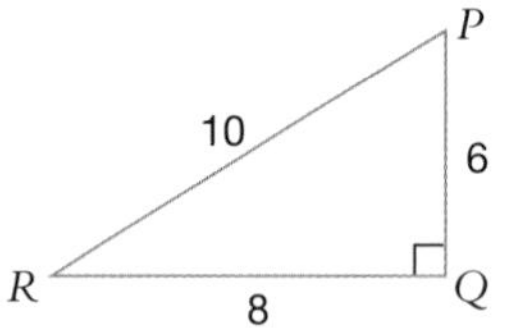

c
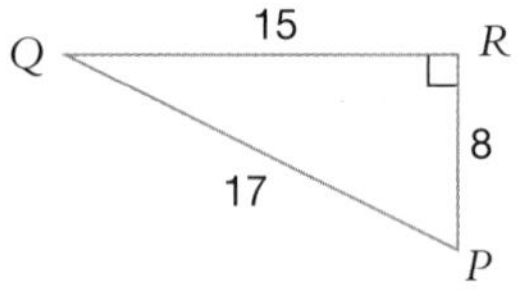

6 Find the value of the ratio $\dfrac{\text{Side adjacent to angle } P}{\text{Hypotenuse}}$ for each triangle in Question 5.

7 Find the value of each of the following ratios for the triangle shown.

a $\dfrac{\text{Side opposite angle } A}{\text{Hypotenuse}}$

b $\dfrac{\text{Side opposite angle } B}{\text{Hypotenuse}}$

c $\dfrac{\text{Side adjacent to angle } A}{\text{Hypotenuse}}$

d $\dfrac{\text{Side opposite angle } B}{\text{Side adjacent to angle } B}$

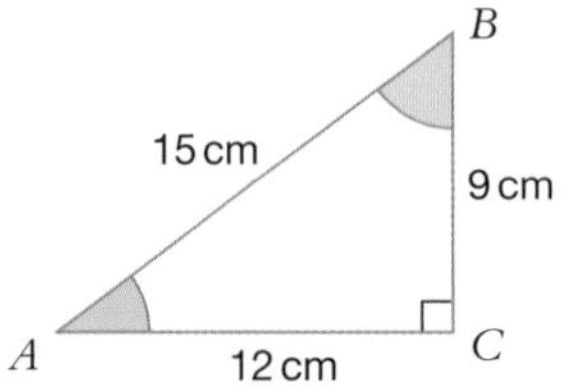

13:02 Similar right-angled triangles: The ratio of sides

PREP QUIZ 13:02

For each triangle state whether AB is opposite the angle marked, adjacent to the angle marked, or is the hypotenuse.

1 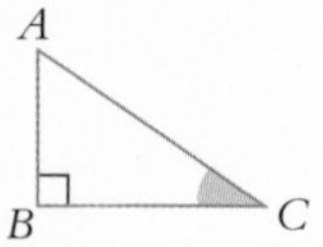

2 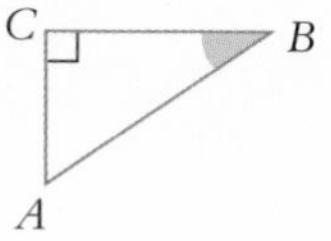

3 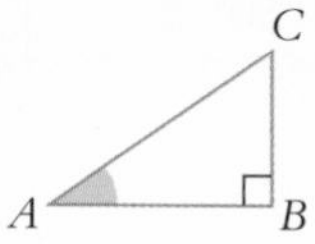

Complete the following statements.

4 If a triangle is enlarged, the original triangle and the enlarged triangle are said to be …
5 When a triangle is enlarged, the angles do not …
6 When a triangle is enlarged, the ratios of matching sides are …
7 If a 4 cm side is enlarged using a scale factor of 3, the length of the enlarged side is …

In the pairs of triangles below, find x.

8 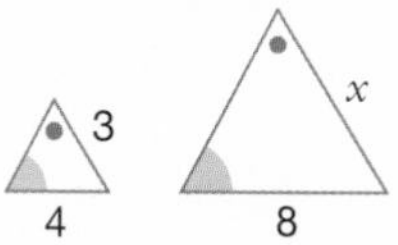

9 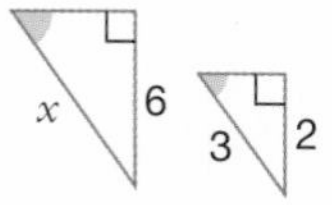

10 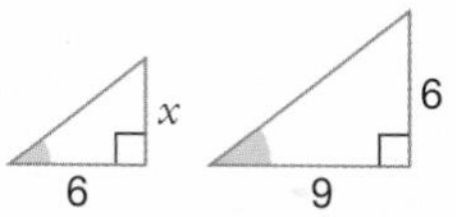

Exercise 13:02

1 a Three similar right-angled triangles are shown. Measure the lengths of the sides to the nearest millimetre and then copy and complete the following table.

	θ	$\frac{o}{h}$	$\frac{a}{h}$	$\frac{o}{a}$
1	30°			
2	30°			
3	30°			

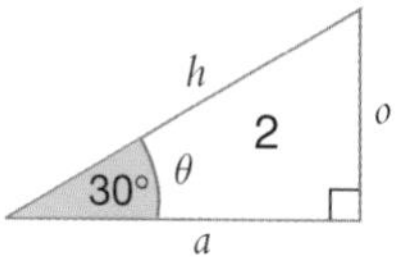

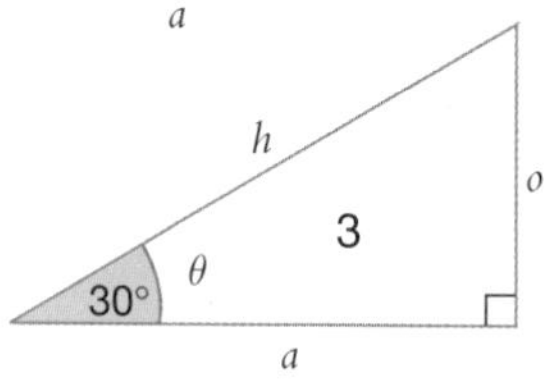

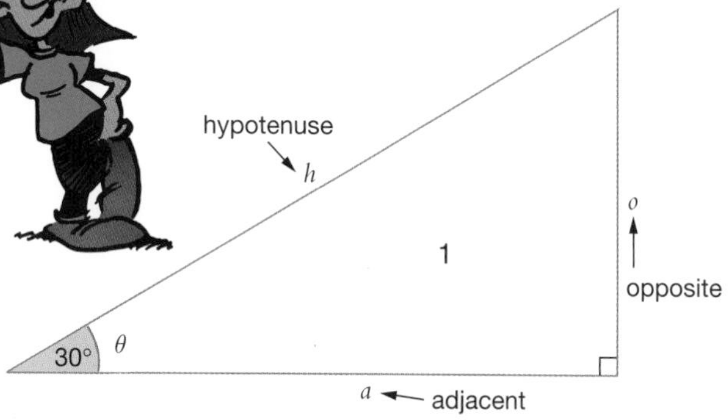

b What conclusion can you draw from the ratios $\frac{o}{h}$, $\frac{a}{h}$, $\frac{o}{a}$ in each triangle?

2 **a** Copy and complete the following table using the three similar triangles below. (Give your answers correct to one decimal place.)

(triangle)	θ	$\frac{o}{h}$	$\frac{a}{h}$	$\frac{o}{a}$
1	50°			
2	50°			
3	50°			

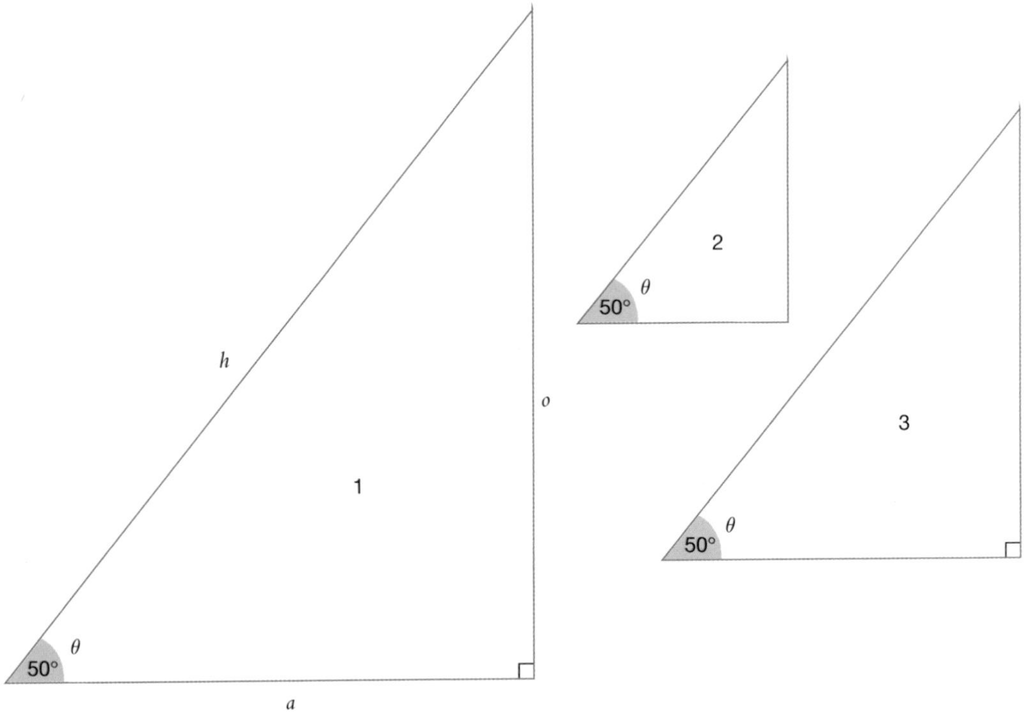

b What conclusion can you draw from the ratios $\frac{o}{h}, \frac{a}{h}, \frac{o}{a}$ in each triangle?

3

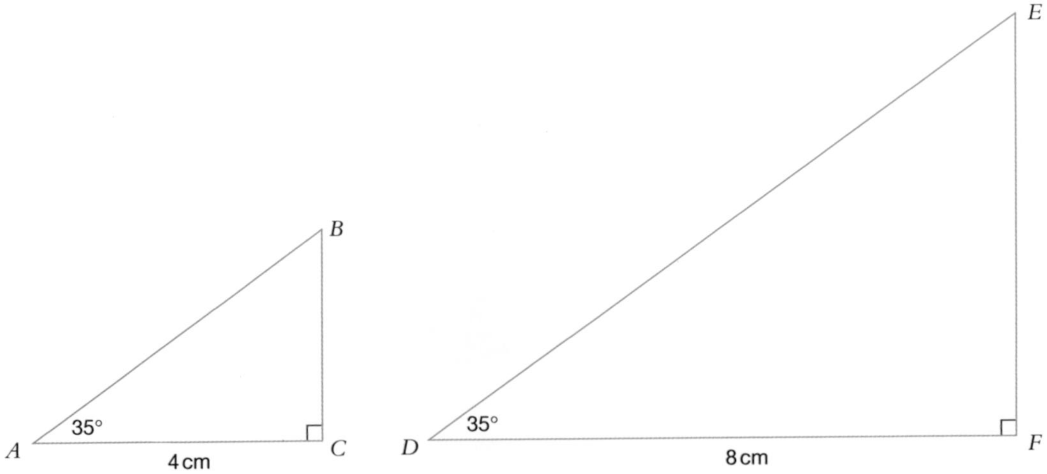

a Measure the sides of ΔABC on the previous page and then calculate the value of the following ratios, correct to one decimal place.

i $\frac{o}{h}$ ii $\frac{a}{h}$ iii $\frac{o}{a}$

b Measure the sides of ΔDEF on the previous page and calculate the value of each ratio, correct to one decimal place.

i $\frac{o}{h}$ ii $\frac{a}{h}$ iii $\frac{o}{a}$

c What conclusions can you draw from the results in parts **a** and **b**?

4 Triangle ABC is similar to triangle DEF (they have two pairs of matching angles equal).

a What enlargement factor has been used to change ΔABC into ΔDEF?

b Use the fact that the ratios of matching sides are equal to find the values of x and y.

c For ΔABC, write the values of the ratios:

i $\frac{o}{h}$ ii $\frac{a}{h}$ iii $\frac{o}{a}$

d For ΔDEF, write the values of the ratios:

i $\frac{o}{h}$ ii $\frac{a}{h}$ iii $\frac{o}{a}$

e Compare the values of the ratios in the two triangles. What conclusions can you draw?

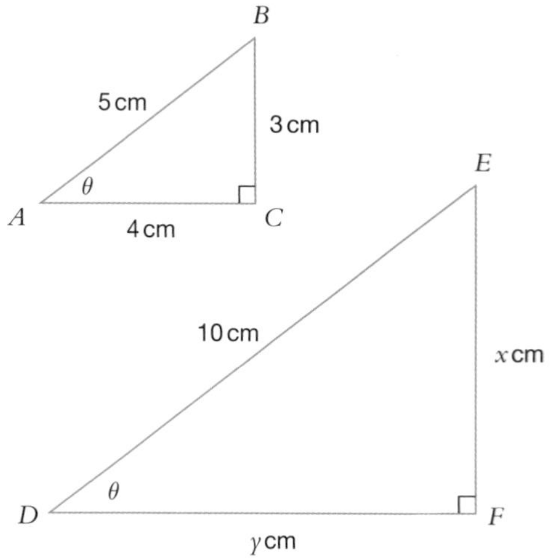

P GEOGEBRA ACTIVITY 13:02 INVESTIGATING THE RATIO OF SIDES OF SIMILAR RIGHT-ANGLED TRIANGLES

In this activity you can see that the values of the ratios $\frac{o}{h}$, $\frac{a}{h}$ and $\frac{o}{a}$ for a given angle in a right-angled triangle are constant, regardless of the size of the triangle.

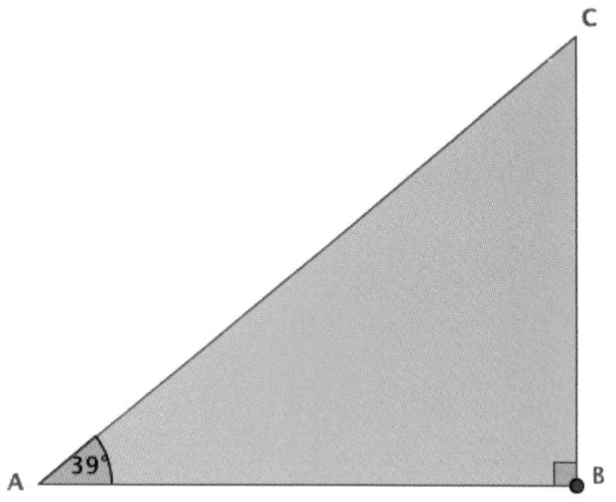

13:03 Trigonometric ratios

In Chapter 11 we saw that two triangles are similar if one triangle is the enlargement of the other. When two triangles are similar they have three pairs of equal angles and the ratios of their matching sides are equal. (We say the sides are in proportion.)

Similar triangles can always be superimposed to produce a diagram like the one below. Measure the sides and check the results in the table. (Answers are correct to one decimal place.)

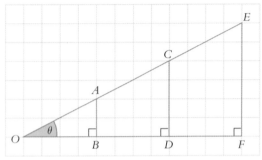

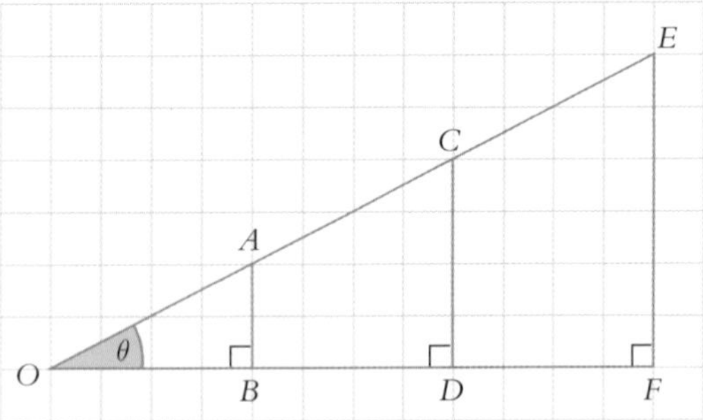

	θ	$\frac{o}{h}$	$\frac{a}{h}$	$\frac{o}{a}$
ΔAOB	27°	0·4	0·9	0·5
ΔCOD	27°	0·4	0·9	0·5
ΔEOF	27°	0·4	0·9	0·5

- The answers in the table suggest that, in a series of similar right-angled triangles, the ratios $\frac{o}{h}$, $\frac{a}{h}$ and $\frac{o}{a}$ are equal for a particular angle. This is, in fact, true and can be proved in the following way.

In the diagram, ΔCOD and ΔEOF are enlargements of ΔAOB.
The enlargement factors are 2 and 3 respectively.

It seems that $\frac{o}{h}$, $\frac{a}{h}$ and $\frac{o}{a}$ are the same for each triangle.

Hence:

$OD = 2OB$, $CD = 2AB$ and $OC = 2OA$
$OE = 3OA$, $EF = 3AB$ and $OF = 3OB$

Now in ΔAOB: $\frac{o}{h} = \frac{AB}{OA}$

ΔCOD: $\frac{o}{h} = \frac{CD}{OD} = \frac{2AB}{2OA} = \frac{AB}{OA}$

ΔEOF: $\frac{o}{h} = \frac{CD}{OD} = \frac{3AB}{3OA} = \frac{AB}{OA}$

$\therefore \frac{o}{h}$ has the same value in all three triangles.

- This method can also be used to show that the ratios $\frac{a}{h}$ and $\frac{o}{a}$ also have the same values in all three triangles.

- The ratios $\frac{o}{h}$, $\frac{a}{h}$, $\frac{o}{a}$ are called the trigonometric ratios (abbreviated to 'trig ratios') and are given special titles.

The ratio $\frac{o}{h}$ $\left(\frac{\text{side opposite angle } \theta}{\text{hypotenuse}}\right)$ is called the *sine ratio*. It is abbreviated to $\sin\theta$.

The ratio $\frac{a}{h}$ $\left(\frac{\text{side adjacent angle } \theta}{\text{hypotenuse}}\right)$ is called the *cosine ratio*. It is abbreviated to $\cos\theta$.

The ratio $\frac{o}{a}$ $\left(\frac{\text{side opposite angle } \theta}{\text{side adjacent angle } \theta}\right)$ is called the *tangent ratio*. It is abbreviated to $\tan\theta$.

Similar triangles can be used to prove that the three ratios above have constant values for any particular angle, regardless of how big the right-angled triangle may be.

This can be shown as follows.

ΔABC has been enlarged using a scale factor of m to produce ΔDEF. If the sides of ΔABC are of length a, b and c units then the matching sides of ΔDEF have lengths of ma, mb and mc units.

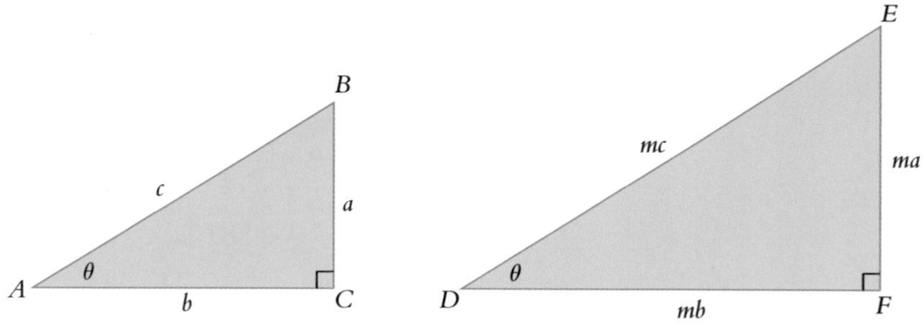

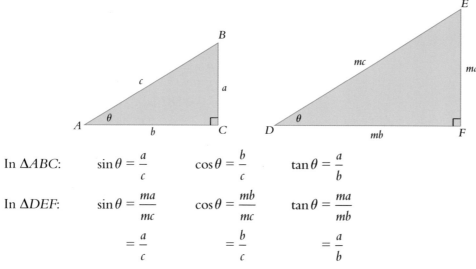

In ΔABC: $\sin\theta = \frac{a}{c}$ $\cos\theta = \frac{b}{c}$ $\tan\theta = \frac{a}{b}$

In ΔDEF: $\sin\theta = \frac{ma}{mc} = \frac{a}{c}$ $\cos\theta = \frac{mb}{mc} = \frac{b}{c}$ $\tan\theta = \frac{ma}{mb} = \frac{a}{b}$

Hence, the ratios have the same values in both triangles.

The sine, cosine and tangent ratios have the same values for any particular angle, regardless of the size of the right-angled triangle.

- The lengths of right-angled triangles can often be surds, so values of the trig ratios obtained with a calculator may not be exact.

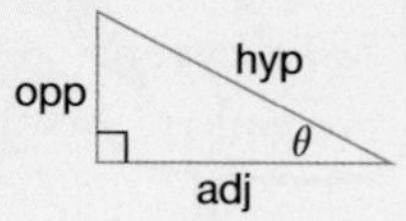

$\sin\theta = \frac{\text{opposite}}{\text{hypotenuse}}$ $\cos\theta = \frac{\text{adjacent}}{\text{hypotenuse}}$ $\tan\theta = \frac{\text{opposite}}{\text{adjacent}}$

- Because $\frac{o}{h} \div \frac{a}{h} = \frac{o}{h}$, then:

$\sin\theta \div \cos\theta = \tan\theta$ or $\tan\theta = \frac{\sin\theta}{\cos\theta}$

WORKED EXAMPLE 1

Find $\sin\theta$, $\cos\theta$ and $\tan\theta$ for each triangle, as a decimal correct to three decimal places.

a

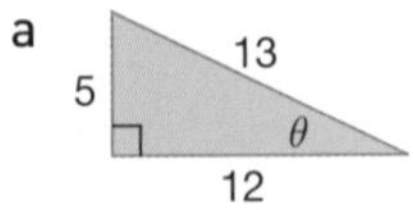

b

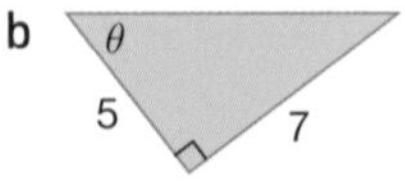

Solutions

a $\sin\theta = \dfrac{\text{opp}}{\text{hyp}}$

$= \frac{5}{13}$

$\doteqdot 0{\cdot}385$

$\cos\theta = \dfrac{\text{adj}}{\text{hyp}}$

$= \frac{12}{13}$

$\doteqdot 0{\cdot}923$

$\tan\theta = \dfrac{\text{opp}}{\text{adj}}$

$= \frac{5}{12}$

$\doteqdot 0{\cdot}417$

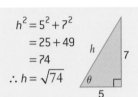

$h^2 = 5^2 + 7^2$
$= 25 + 49$
$= 74$
$\therefore h = \sqrt{74}$

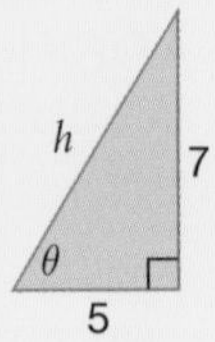

b First the hypotenuse must be calculated using Pythagoras' theorem. So, then:

$\sin\theta = \dfrac{7}{\sqrt{74}}$

$\doteqdot 0{\cdot}814$

$\tan\theta = \dfrac{7}{5}$

$\doteqdot 1{\cdot}400$

$\cos\theta = \dfrac{5}{\sqrt{74}}$

$\doteqdot 0{\cdot}581$

Exact trig values often involve surds.

WORKED EXAMPLE 2

Find $\sin\theta$, $\cos\theta$ and $\tan\theta$ as exact values.

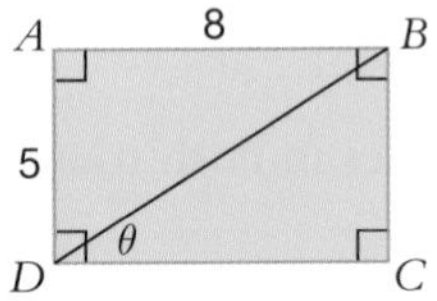

Solution

$ABCD$ is a rectangle.
Hence, $DC = 8$, $BC = 5$
Also $BD = \sqrt{89}$ (Pythagoras' theorem)

$\therefore \sin\theta = \dfrac{BC}{BD} = \dfrac{5}{\sqrt{89}}$ $\quad \cos\theta = \dfrac{CD}{BD} = \dfrac{8}{\sqrt{89}}$ $\quad \tan\theta = \dfrac{BC}{CD} = \dfrac{5}{8}$

sin	=	opp	/	hyp	cos	=	adj	/	hyp	tan	=	opp	/	adj
↓		↓		↓	↓		↓		↓	↓		↓		↓
S		O		H	C		A		H	T		O		A
↓		↓		↓	↓		↓		↓	↓		↓		↓
Some		Old		Hare	Came		A		Hopping	Through		Our		Area

Exercise 13:03

P Challenge worksheet 13:03
The range of values of the trigonometric ratios

1 Find $\sin\theta$, $\cos\theta$ and $\tan\theta$ in these triangles (as simple fractions).

a
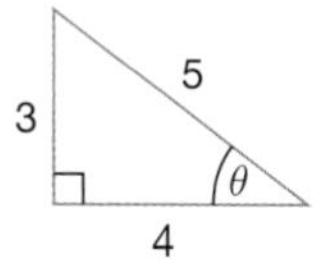

b
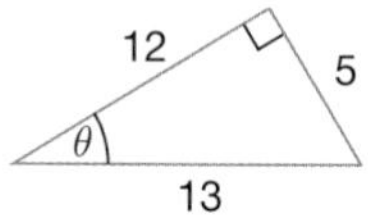

c
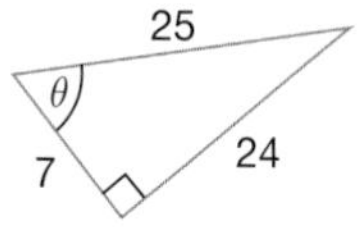

2 Find the unknown side using Pythagoras' theorem and then find $\sin\theta$, $\cos\theta$ and $\tan\theta$ in decimal form, correct to three decimal places.

a
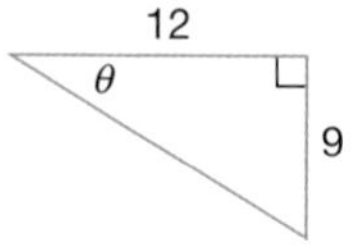

b
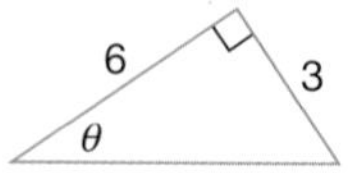

c
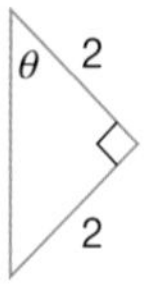

3 Use Pythagoras' theorem to find side YZ, then state the value of $\tan X$.

a
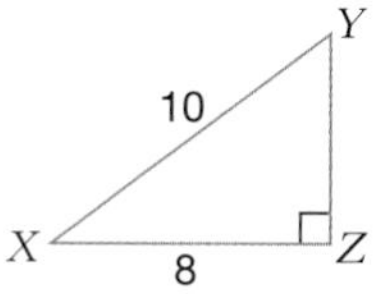

b
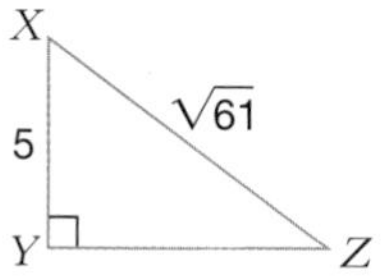

c
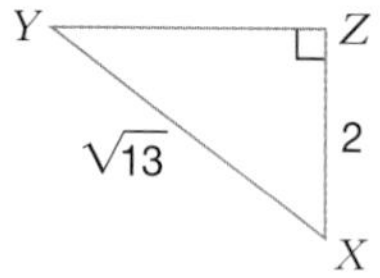

4 Complete the statements below using the side lengths for each triangle.

a
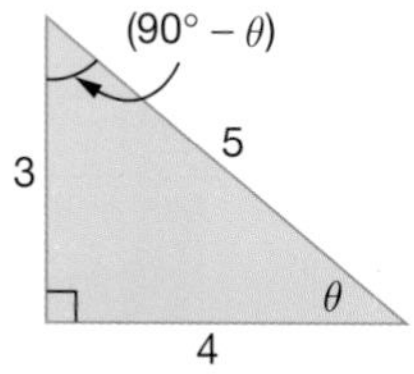

$\sin\theta = \ldots$

$\cos(90° - \theta) = \ldots$

b
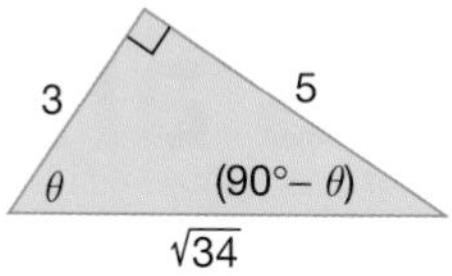

$\cos\theta = \ldots$

$\sin(90° - \theta) = \ldots$

c
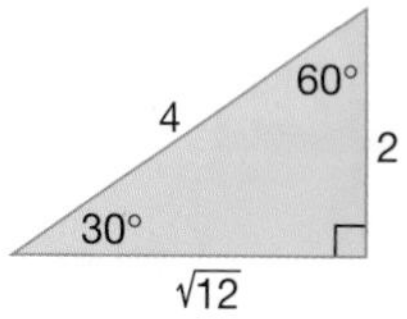

$\sin 60° = \ldots$

$\cos 30° = \ldots$

5 Complete these statements using the side lengths in the triangle shown.

a $\sin\theta = \ldots$

$\cos(90° - \theta) = \ldots$

b $\cos\theta = \ldots$

$\sin(90° - \theta) = \ldots$

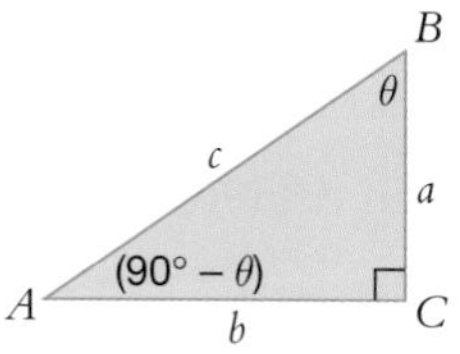

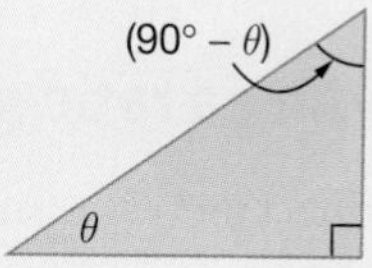

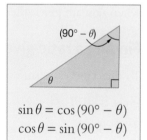

$\sin\theta = \cos(90° - \theta)$

$\cos\theta = \sin(90° - \theta)$

6 Find the value of x, given that:

a $\cos 25° = \sin x°$ b $\sin 60° = \cos x°$ c $\cos 10° = \sin x°$

7 a For the triangle shown at right, write the value of:

i $\sin A$ ii $\cos A$

iii $\tan A$ iv $\sin A \div \cos A$

b Does $\tan A = \dfrac{\sin A}{\cos A}$?

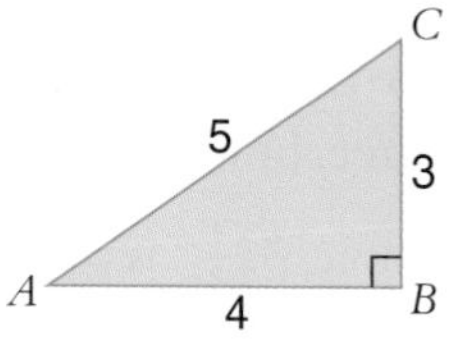

8 a Use Pythagoras' theorem to find the value of the missing side as a surd. Hence find the value of $\sin 30°$, $\cos 30°$ and $\tan 30°$. (Leave your answer as a surd.)

b Evaluate the answers in part **a** using a calculator and arrange the values for $\sin 30°$, $\cos 30°$ and $\tan 30°$ in ascending order.

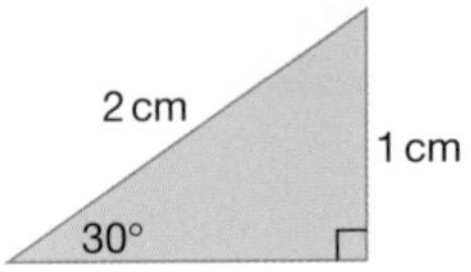

9 a If $\sin A = \frac{1}{4}$, find the values of $\cos A$ and $\tan A$.

b It is known that $\cos\theta = \frac{3}{4}$. What is the value of $\sin\theta$?

10 a Find:

i $\sin A$

ii $\sin C$

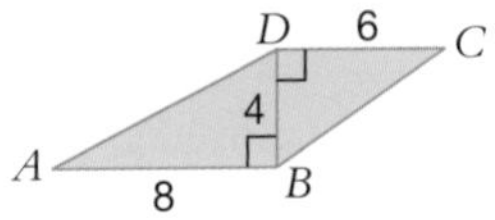

b Find:

i $\sin\theta$

ii $\cos\alpha$

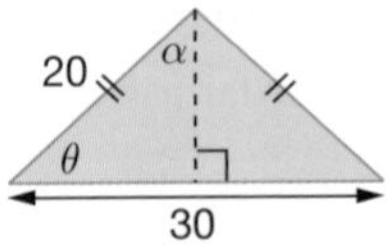

11 a By finding $\tan\theta$ in two different triangles, find the value of m.

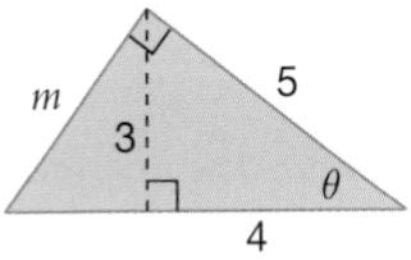

b Find x and y. (*Note:* $DE = x$ and $CE = y$)

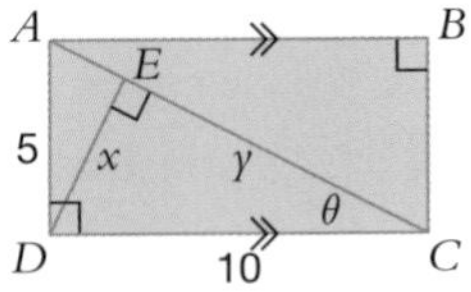

c Find:

i $\sin\theta$ ii $\cos\theta$ iii m

iv n v $\sin 2\theta$

vi Show that $\sin 2\theta = 2 \times \sin\theta \times \cos\theta$

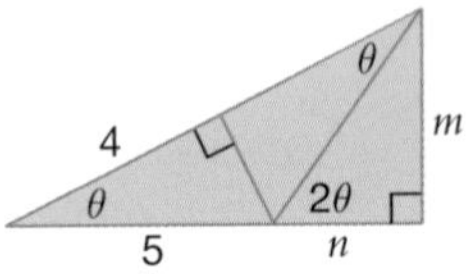

13:04 Trig ratios and the calculator

As shown in the previous section, the values of the trig ratios are constant for any particular angle and these values can be found using a calculator. You can also use the calculator to find a ratio when you are given the angle, or vice versa.

Finding a ratio given the angle

To find $\tan 31°$, ensure your calculator is operating in degrees.

Press: tan 31 =

The calculator should give $\tan 31° = 0{\cdot}600\,860\,6$, correct to seven decimal places.

Degrees and minutes

So far the angles have all been in whole degrees. One degree, however, can be divided into 60 minutes.

For example, $31\frac{1}{2}°$ is 31 degrees and 30 minutes. This would be written as $31°30'$.

We can now find the trigonometric ratios of angles given to the nearest minute by using the calculator as shown in the examples below.

WORKED EXAMPLES

Find, correct to four decimal places: **1** $\sin 25°41'$ **2** $\tan 79°05'$

Solutions

Two methods are shown, one for each solution. Choose the one that best suits your calculator.

Method 1

1 For calculators with a Degrees/Minutes/Seconds key [° ' "].
Press: [sin] 25 [° ' "] 41 [° ' "] [=]
The calculator gives 0·433 396 953.

Method 2

2 We convert 79°05′ into decimal degrees by realising that 05′ is $\frac{5}{60}$ of one degree.
Press: [tan] 79 [+] 5 [÷] 60 [)] [=]
The calculator gives 5·184 803 521.

Warning:
The keying instructions shown here are for the Casio fx-82AU PLUS. Other calculators may operate differently.

Finding an angle given the ratio

If the value of the trigonometric ratio is known and you want to find the size of the angle to the nearest minute, follow the steps in the examples below.

WORKED EXAMPLES

1 If $\sin\theta = 0{\cdot}632$, find θ to the nearest minute.
2 If $\cos\theta = 0{\cdot}2954$, find θ to the nearest minute.

What if I want to find the angle?

Solutions

Note: One minute may be divided further, into 60 seconds, and this fact will be used to round answers to the nearest minute.

Again two methods are shown. Choose the one that best suits your calculator.

Method 1

1 If $\sin\theta = 0{\cdot}632$, press: [SHIFT] [sin⁻¹] 0.632 [=]
The calculator now displays 39·197 833 53°. To convert this to degrees/minutes/seconds mode, press [° ' "]. The calculator gives 39°11′52·2″.
$\therefore\ \theta = 39°12'$ (nearest minute)

Warning:
Your calculator may work differently to the one used here.

Method 2

2 If $\cos\theta = 0{\cdot}2954$, press: [SHIFT] [sin⁻¹] 0.2954 [=]
The answer on the screen is 72·818 475 degrees. The alternative method of converting this to degrees and minutes is to find what 0·818 475 of one degree is in minutes (i.e. 0·818 475 × 60). This gives an answer of 49·1085 minutes or 49′ correct to the nearest minute.
$\therefore\ \theta = 72°49'$

Exercise 13:04

1 Using the degrees/minutes/seconds key on your calculator, write each of the following in degrees and minutes, giving answers correct to the nearest minute.

a $16 \cdot 5°$ b $38 \cdot 25°$ c $73 \cdot 9°$ d $305 \cdot 75°$
e $40 \cdot 23°$ f $100 \cdot 66°$ g $12 \cdot 016°$ h $238 \cdot 845°$

2 Write in degrees, correct to three decimal places where necessary.

a $17°45'$ b $48°16'$ c $125°43'$ d $88°37'$
e $320°15'$ f $70°54'$ g $241°29'$ h $36°53'$

3 Use your calculator to find the value of the following, correct to four decimal places.

a $\sin 30°$ b $\cos 30°$ c $\tan 30°$ d $\sin 71°$
e $\cos 58°$ f $\tan 63°$ g $\sin 7°$ h $\cos 85°$

4 Find the size of θ (to the nearest degree) where θ is acute.

a $\sin\theta = 0 \cdot 259$ b $\sin\theta = 0 \cdot 934$ c $\sin\theta = 0 \cdot 619$
d $\cos\theta = 0 \cdot 222$ e $\cos\theta = 0 \cdot 317$ f $\cos\theta = 0 \cdot 9$
g $\tan\theta = 1 \cdot 2$ h $\tan\theta = 0 \cdot 816$ i $\tan\theta = 3$

5 Find, correct to three decimal places, the following ratios.

a $\sin 30°10'$ b $\sin 62°45'$ c $\cos 52°30'$ d $\cos 83°03'$
e $\tan 61 \cdot 25°$ f $\tan 79 \cdot 36°$ g $\sin 17 \cdot 8°$ h $\tan 72 \cdot 57°$

6 Find θ to the nearest minute, given that θ is acute.

a $\sin\theta = 0 \cdot 6$ b $\sin\theta = 0 \cdot 43$ c $\sin\theta = 0 \cdot 645$
d $\cos\theta = 0 \cdot 2$ e $\cos\theta = 0 \cdot 031$ f $\cos\theta = 0 \cdot 5216$
g $\tan\theta = 1 \cdot 3$ h $\tan\theta = 0 \cdot 625$ i $\tan\theta = 2 \cdot 67$

7 Redo Question **6**, this time giving answers in degrees correct to two decimal places.

8 What are the values of $\frac{o}{a}$, $\frac{o}{h}$ and $\frac{a}{h}$ for each of the following triangles, correct to three decimal places?

a
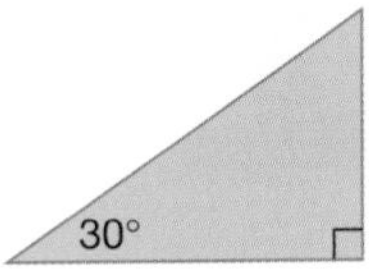

b
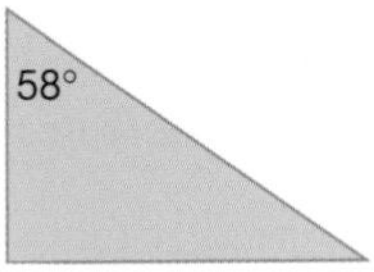

c
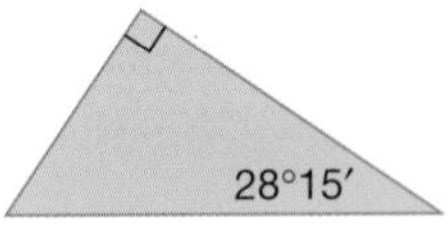

9 Find the value of $\frac{x}{10}$ for each of the following, correct to three decimal places.

a
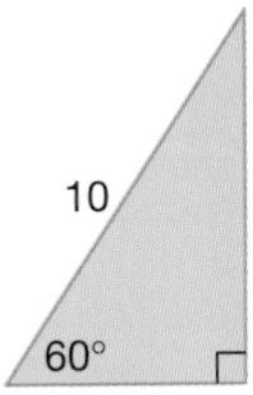

b
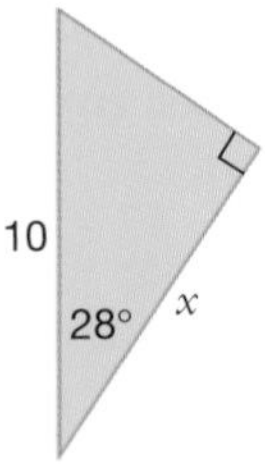

c
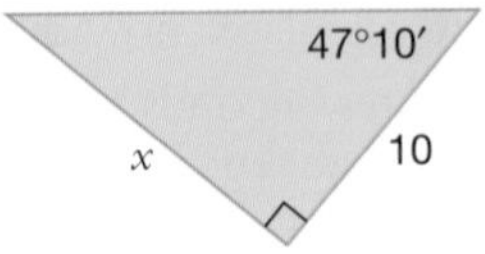

10 a If $\frac{x}{10} = \cos 60°$, find the value of x.

b If $a = 3\sin 40° + 4\cos 30°$, find the value of a correct to three decimal places.

c By substituting values for A and B, find whether $\sin A + \sin B = \sin(A + B)$.

d If $\sin A = \frac{1}{2}$ and $\sin B = \frac{1}{3}$ find $A + B$.

e Jim thinks that if you double the size of an angle you double its sine; that is, $\sin 2A = 2 \times \sin A$. Is Jim correct?

INVESTIGATION 13:04 THE EXACT VALUES FOR THE TRIG RATIOS 30°, 60° AND 45°

ΔABC is an equilateral triangle of side 2 units. AD is perpendicular to BC.

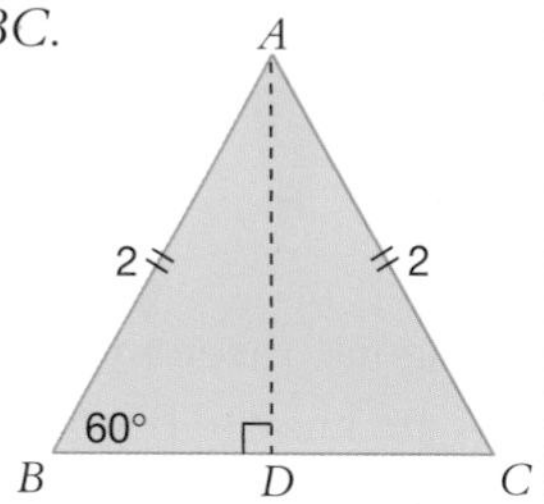

1 Copy the diagram and write in the size of BD and $\angle BAD$.

2 Using Pythagoras' theorem, calculate the length of AD as a surd.

3 Now, from ΔABD, write the values of sin, cos and tan for 30° and 60°.

ΔDEF is a right-angled isosceles triangle. The two equal sides are 1 unit in length.

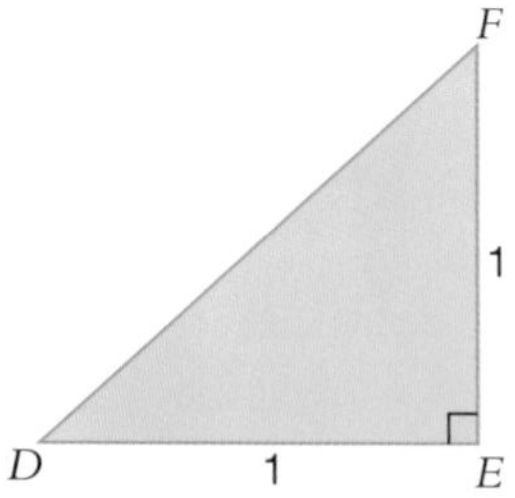

4 Why is $\angle EDF$ equal to 45°?

5 What is the length of DF as a surd?

6 Write the values of sin 45°, cos 45° and tan 45°.

Leave your answers in surd form. Do not approximate.

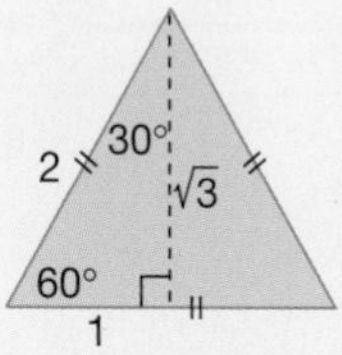

$\sin 60° = \frac{\sqrt{3}}{2}$, $\sin 30° = \frac{1}{2}$

$\cos 60° = \frac{1}{2}$, $\cos 30° = \frac{\sqrt{3}}{2}$

$\tan 60° = \sqrt{3}$, $\tan 30° = \frac{1}{\sqrt{3}}$

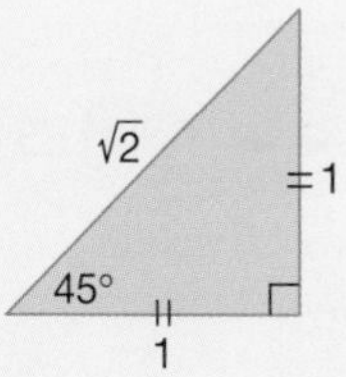

$\sin 45° = \frac{1}{\sqrt{2}}$

$\cos 45° = \frac{1}{\sqrt{2}}$

$\tan 45° = 1$

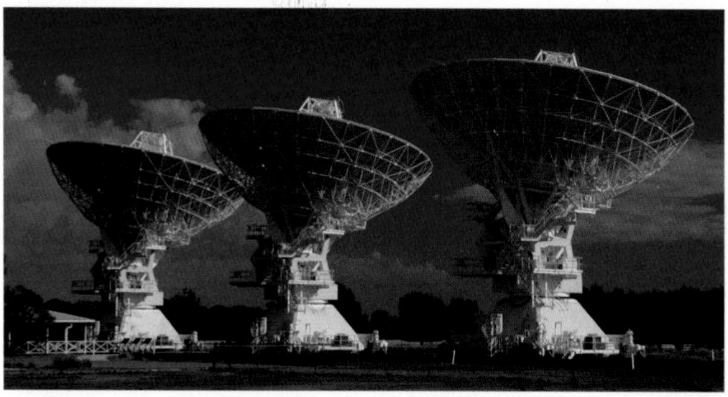

Trigonometry is used in many branches of science.

13:05 Finding an unknown side

PREP QUIZ 13:05

For the triangle given,
state the length of the:

1 hypotenuse
2 side opposite $\angle A$
3 side adjacent to $\angle A$;

state the value of:

4 $\sin A$
5 $\cos A$
6 $\tan C$.

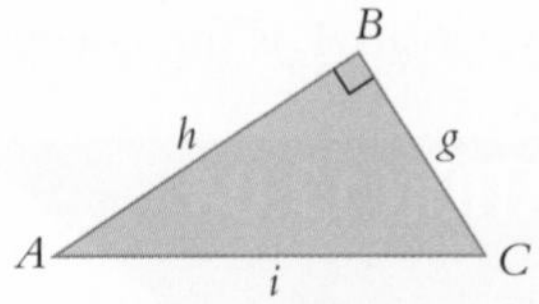

Find correct to three decimal places:

7 $\sin 75°$
8 $\tan 25°30'$
9 If $\tan 25° = \dfrac{x}{4}$ then $x = \ldots$
10 If $\tan 25° = \dfrac{4}{x}$ then $x = \ldots$

Pythagoras' theorem is used to find an unknown side in a right-angled triangle when the other two sides are known. Trigonometry is used when only one side and one of the acute angles are known.

WORKED EXAMPLE 1

Find the values of the pronumerals correct to one decimal place.

a
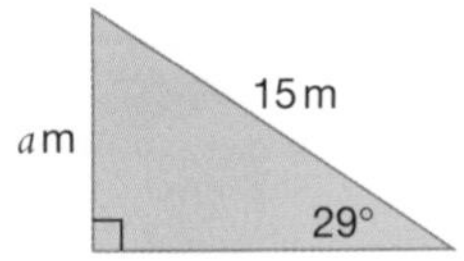

b
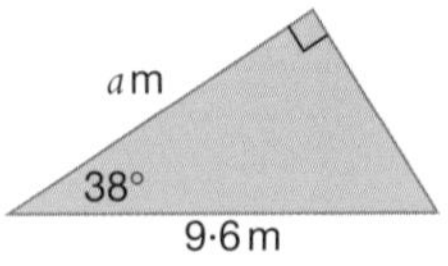

c
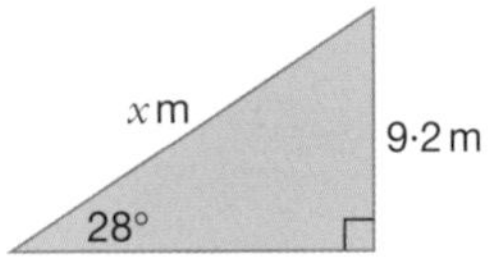

Solutions

Use the trig keys on your calculator.

a $\dfrac{a}{15} = \sin 29°$

$\therefore a = (\sin 29°) \times 15$ ↔ sin 29) × 15 =

$= 7{\cdot}272\,144\,3$

So $a = 7{\cdot}3$ (1 dec. pl.)

b $\dfrac{a}{9{\cdot}6} = \cos 38°$

$\therefore a = (\cos 38°) \times 9{\cdot}6$ ↔ cos 38) × 9.6 =

$= 7{\cdot}564\,903\,2$

$= 7{\cdot}6$ (1 dec. pl.)

c $\dfrac{9{\cdot}2}{x} = \sin 28°$ (Note that x is the denominator of the fraction, not the numerator.)

$\dfrac{x}{9{\cdot}2} = \dfrac{1}{\sin 28°}$

$\therefore x = \dfrac{9{\cdot}2}{\sin 28°}$ ↔ 9.2 ÷ sin 28 =

$= 19{\cdot}6$ (1 dec. pl.)

If x is the hypotenuse you'll need to invert each side of the equation.
x
9·2
28°

WORKED EXAMPLE 2

Find the length of a guy rope that must be used to secure a pole 12·5 m high, if the angle the guy rope makes with the ground is 56°.

Make sure your calculator is operating in 'degrees' mode.

Solutions

Let the length of the rope be x metres.

$$\frac{12\cdot5}{x} = \sin 56°$$

$$\therefore \frac{x}{12\cdot5} = \frac{1}{\sin 56°}$$

$$x = \frac{12\cdot5}{\sin 56°}$$

$$\doteqdot 15\cdot08$$

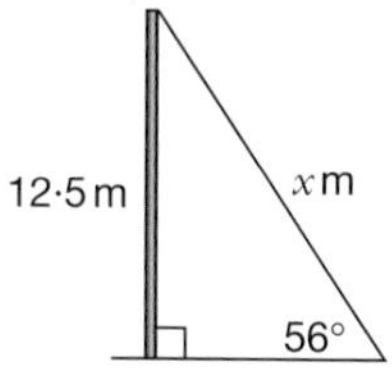

∴ The rope is 15·08 m long (nearest centimetre).

Exercise 13:05

P Foundation worksheet 13:05
Using trigonometry to find side lengths

1 Find the values of the pronumeral in each triangle, correct to one decimal place.

a
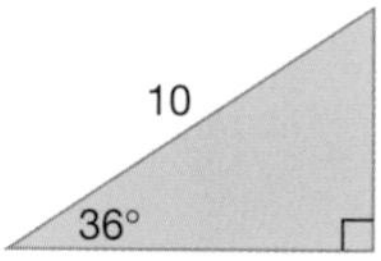

b
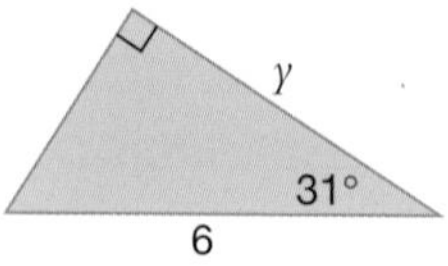

c
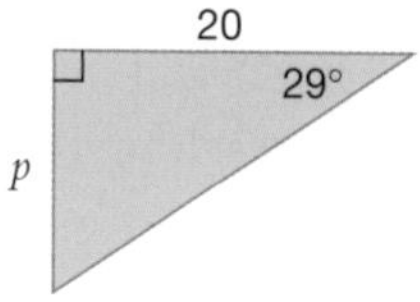

d
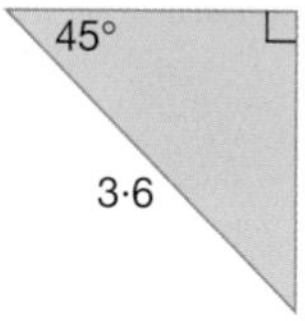

e
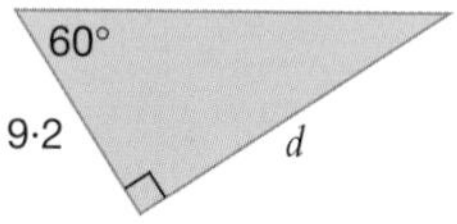

f
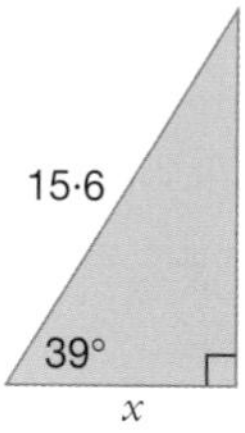

g
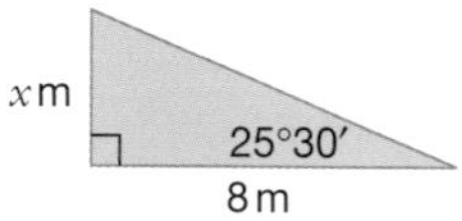

h
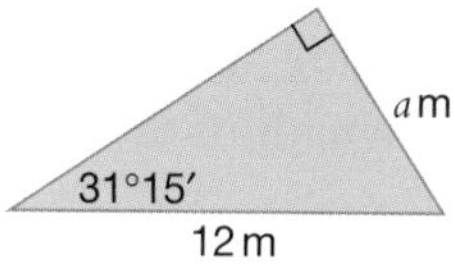

i
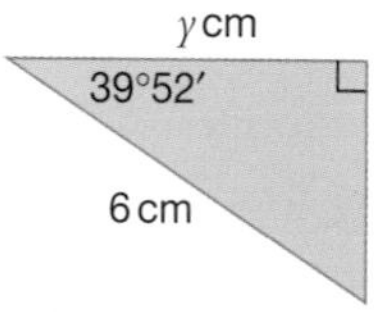

j
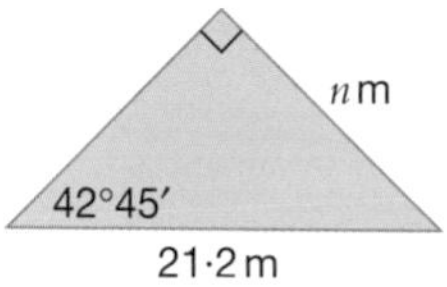

k
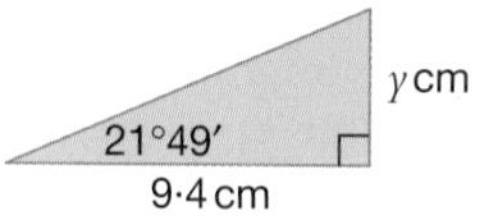

l
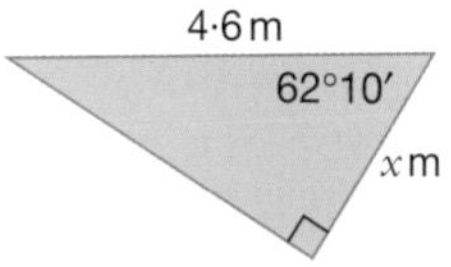

2 Determine the values of each pronumeral, correct to one decimal place.

a
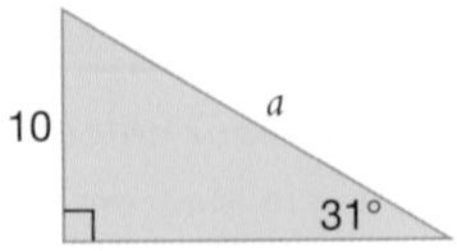

b
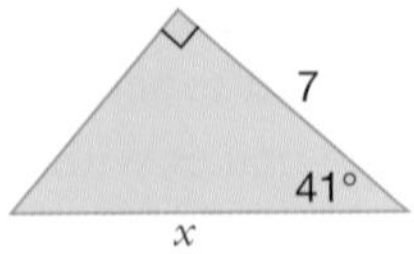

c
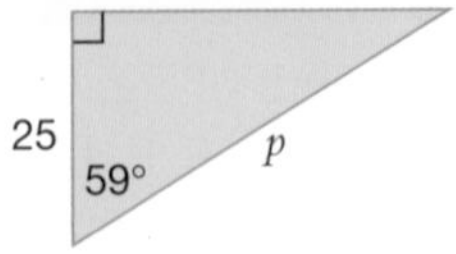

d
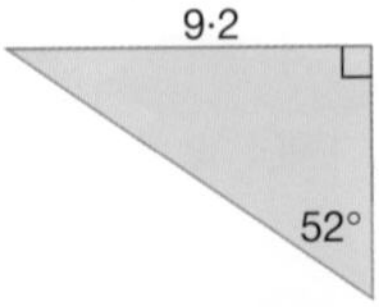

e
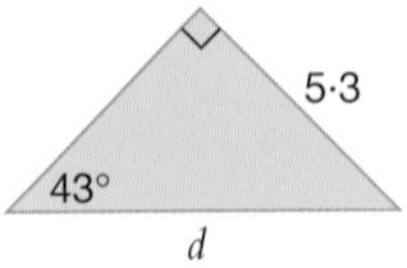

f
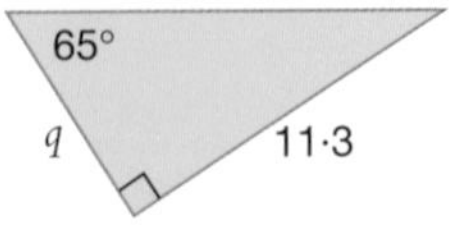

g
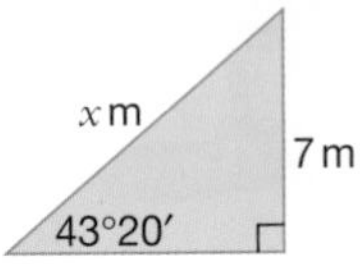

h
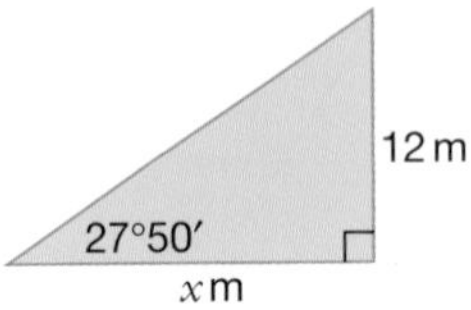

i
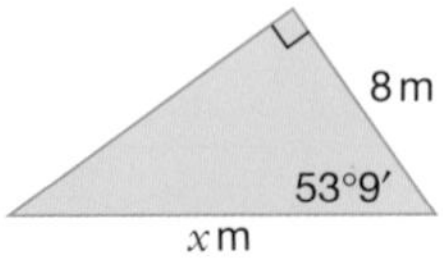

j
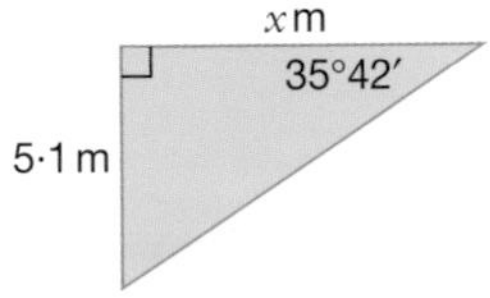

k
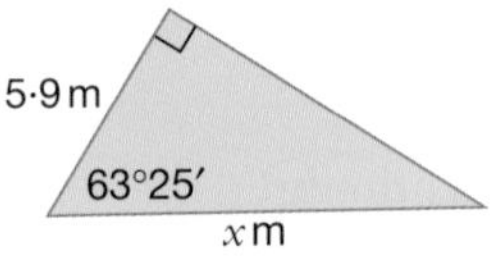

l
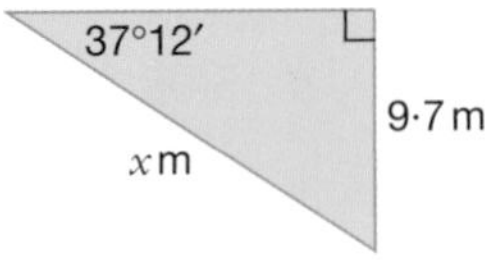

3 Find out everything you can about the triangle.

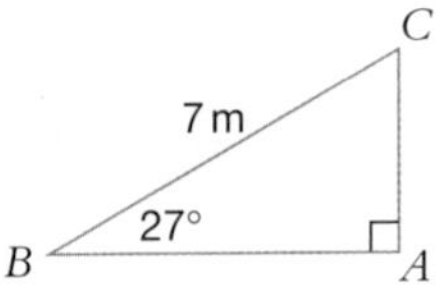

4 A ladder leans against a wall so that the angle it makes with the ground is 52° and its base is 4 m from the wall. How far does the ladder reach up the wall (to the nearest centimetre)?

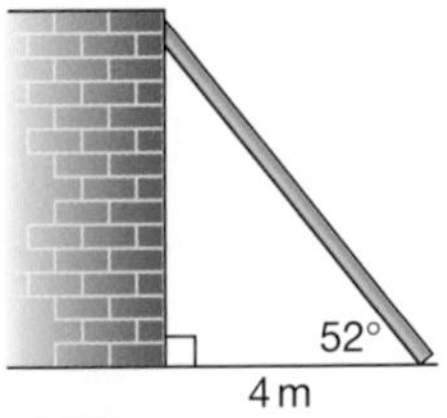

5 A ladder leaning against a wall reaches 5·3 m up the wall when the angle between the ground and the ladder is 73°. How long, to the nearest centimetre, is the ladder?

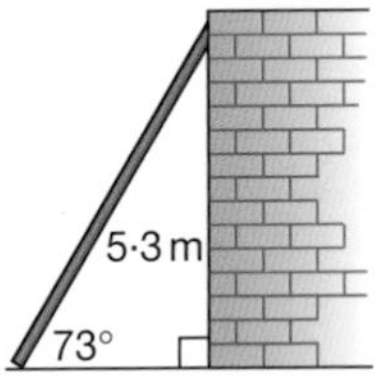

6 The diagonal of a rectangle is 16·3 cm long and makes an angle with the longest side of 37°. Find the length of the rectangle, to the nearest centimetre.

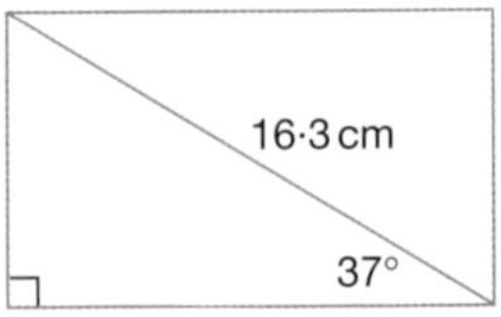

7 A person on the deck of a ship observes a lighthouse on the top of a 70 m cliff at an angle of 3°. How far out to sea is the ship (to the nearest metre)?

8 A boat is anchored in a river that is 3·2 m deep. If the anchor rope makes an angle of 52° with the surface of the water, how long is the rope from the surface of the water? (Answer to the nearest centimetre.)

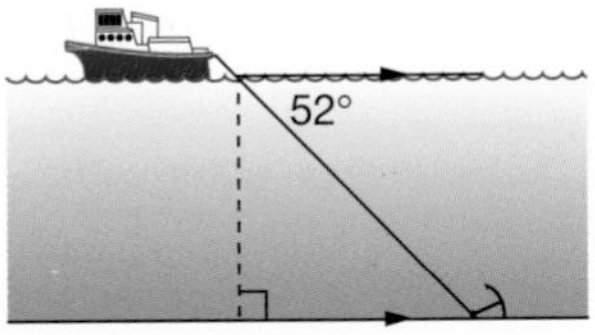

9 The equal sides of an isosceles triangle are 16 m long and the apex angle is 80°. Find, to the nearest centimetre, the length of the base.

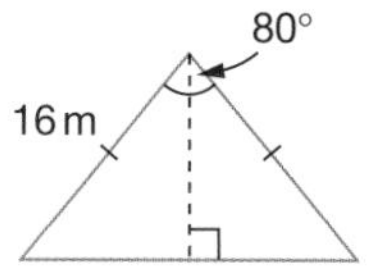

10 The base of an isosceles triangle is 9·6 cm long and each of the base angles is 38°42′. Find the length of each of the equal sides. (Answer correct to three significant figures.)

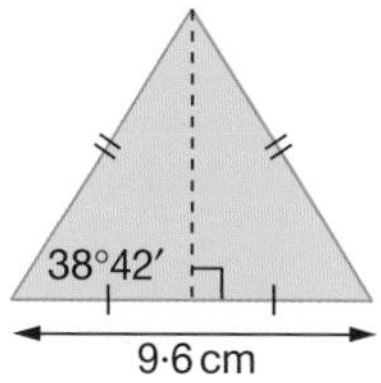

11 If the length of a child's slippery-dip is 3·4 m and one end makes an angle of 38°42′ with the ground, how high above the ground is the other end? (Answer to the nearest centimetre.)

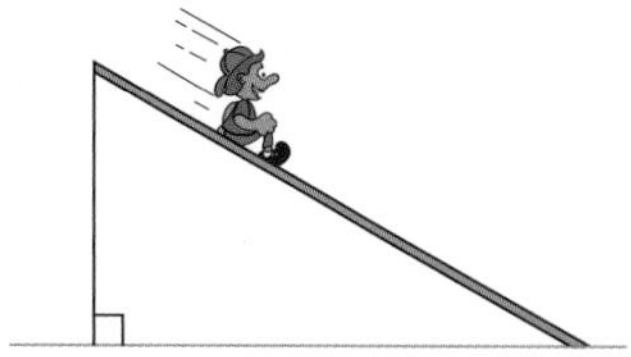

For questions **12** to **20**, draw a diagram first!

12 **a** In ΔABC, $\angle A = 90°$, $\angle B = 63°25'$ and $BC = 6$ m. Find AC, correct to the nearest centimetre.
b In ΔXYZ, $\angle Z = 90°$, $\angle X = 42°34'$ and $XZ = 9{\cdot}2$ m. Find YZ, correct to the nearest centimetre.
c In ΔABC, $\angle B = 90°$, $\angle A = 52°$ and $AB = 2{\cdot}7$ cm. Find AC, to one decimal place.
d In ΔXYZ, $\angle X = 90°$, $\angle Y = 31°20'$ and $XZ = 10{\cdot}3$ cm. Find XY, to one decimal place.

13 The diagonal of a square is 21·2 cm. Find the length of each side (to the nearest millimetre).

14 Find the length of the diagonal of a rectangle if the length of the rectangle is 7·5 cm and the diagonal makes an angle of 25° with each of the longer sides. (Answer correct to the nearest millimetre.)

15 Find the length of a rectangle if its diagonal is 34 cm long and the angle the diagonal makes with the length is 27°50′. (Answer correct to the nearest centimetre.)

16 Find the base of an isosceles triangle if the height is 8·2 cm and the base angles are each 39°. (Answer correct to the nearest millimetre.)

17 When the altitude of the sun is 51°47′, a vertical stick casts a shadow 45 cm long. How high, to the nearest millimetre, is the stick?

18 A painting is hung symmetrically by means of a string passing over a nail with its ends attached to the upper corners of the painting. If the distance between the corners is 55 cm and the angle between the two halves of the string is 105°, find the length of the string, correct to the nearest millimetre.

19 The vertical rise from the bottom to the top of a track that slopes uniformly at 6°54′ with the horizontal is 36 m. Find, to one decimal place, the length of the track.

20 A road rises steadily at an angle of 6°45′. What will be the vertical rise of the road for a horizontal distance of 300 m? (Answer correct to the nearest metre.)

21 At noon a factory chimney casts a shadow when the sun's altitude is 85°24′. If the chimney is 65 m high, what is the length of the shadow, to the nearest centimetre?

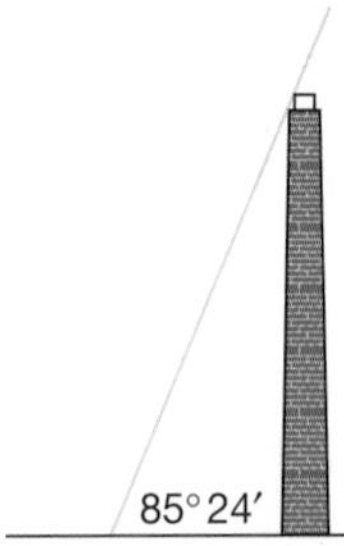

22 Calculate the sloping area of this roof that needs to be tiled, given that the width of the roof is 5·4 m and its length is 9·2 m. Each roof section is pitched at an angle of 23°. (Answer correct to the nearest square metre.)

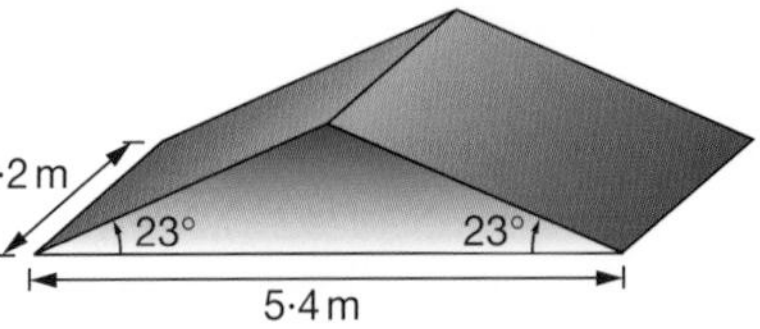

23 A plane is flying at an altitude (height) of 750 m. A boy on the ground first observes the plane when it is directly overhead. Thirty seconds later, the angle of elevation of the plane from the boy is 24°14′.

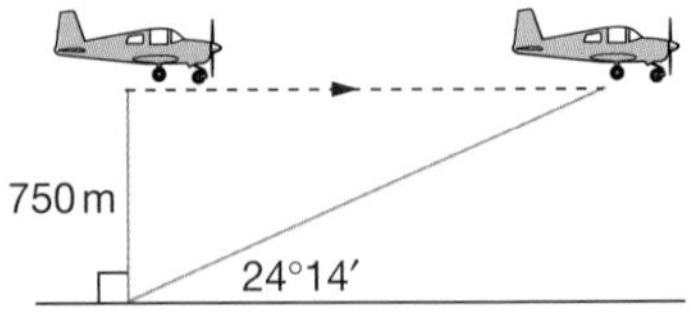

a Through what distance did the plane fly in 30 seconds, to the nearest metre?

b Calculate the speed of the plane in km/h, correct to three significant figures.

24 Calculate the area of a right-angled triangle that has a hypotenuse 8 cm long and an angle of 50°.

25 A regular hexagon of side a units is made by joining six equilateral triangles together, as shown in the diagram.
We want to find a formula for the area of the hexagon in terms of its side length, a.
Consider the area of *one* of the equilateral triangles.

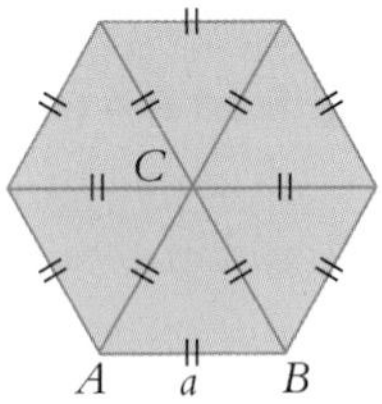

a Using the exact trig ratios on page 389, find the exact length of DC.

b What is the area of ΔABC?

c What is the area of a hexagon of side a units?

d Find the area of a hexagon with a side length of:

i 2 cm   ii 5 cm   iii 10 cm

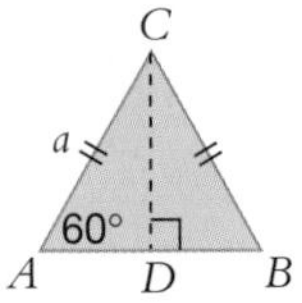

P GEOGEBRA ACTIVITY 13:05 USING THE TRIG RATIOS TO FIND A SIDE

In these three activities you can alter the shape of the right-angled triangle and calculate the length of an unknown side. Check your answer by ticking a checkbox.

1 Finding unknown sides using the tangent ratio.

2 Finding unknown sides using the sine and cosine ratios.

3 Finding the hypotenuse using the sine and cosine ratios.

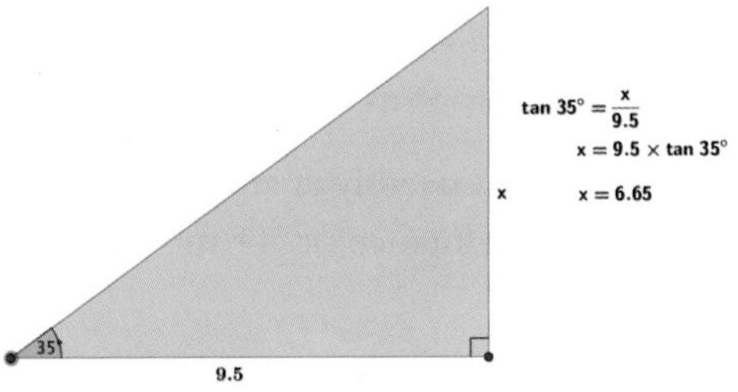

13:06 Finding an unknown angle

PREP QUIZ 13:06

Complete the ratios below for each triangle.

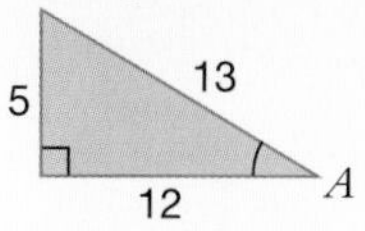

1 $\sin A =$
2 $\cos A =$

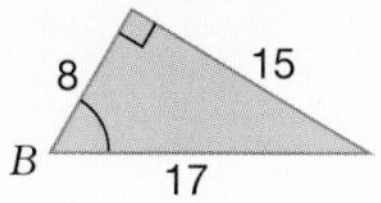

3 $\tan B =$
4 $\sin B =$

Given that θ is acute, find θ to the nearest degree, if:

5 $\tan\theta = 0{\cdot}635$ 6 $\sin\theta = 0{\cdot}2135$ 7 $\cos\theta = 0{\cdot}0926$

If $0° < A < 90°$, find A to the nearest minute if:

8 $\sin A = 0{\cdot}52$ 9 $\tan A = 2{\cdot}673$ 10 $\cos A = 0{\cdot}7231$

In Section 13:04 we saw that a calculator can be used to find the size of an angle if the value of the trigonometric ratio is known.

WORKED EXAMPLES

1 Find the size of angle θ.
Answer to the nearest degree.

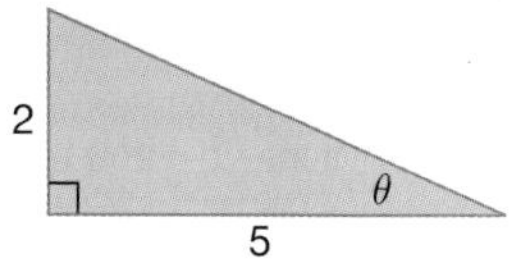

2 What angle, to the nearest minute, does the diagonal of a rectangle make with its length, if the dimensions of the rectangle are 12·6 cm by 8·9 cm?

Remember 'SHIFT' may be called '2nd F' on some calculators.

Solutions

1 In this triangle, $\tan\theta = \frac{2}{5}$

$= 0{\cdot}4$ ↔ SHIFT tan⁻¹ 0.4 =

$\theta = 21{\cdot}80\ldots$

$= 22°$ (nearest degree)

2

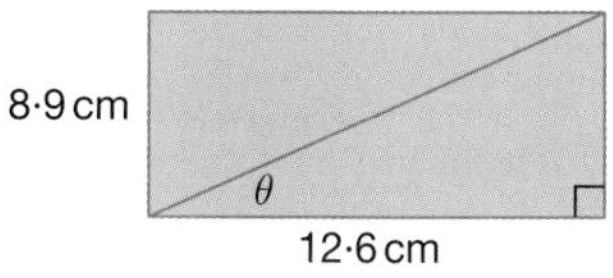

Let the required angle be θ. Then:

$\tan\theta = \dfrac{8{\cdot}9}{12{\cdot}6}$ ↔ SHIFT tan⁻¹ 8.9 ÷ 12.6) = ° ' "

$\therefore\ \theta = 35°14'7{\cdot}59''$

$\therefore\ \theta = 35°14'$ (to the nearest minute)

Exercise 13:06

P Challenge worksheet 13:06 Trigonometry and the limit of an area

1 Find the size of the angle marked θ in each triangle. Give your answers correct to the nearest degree.

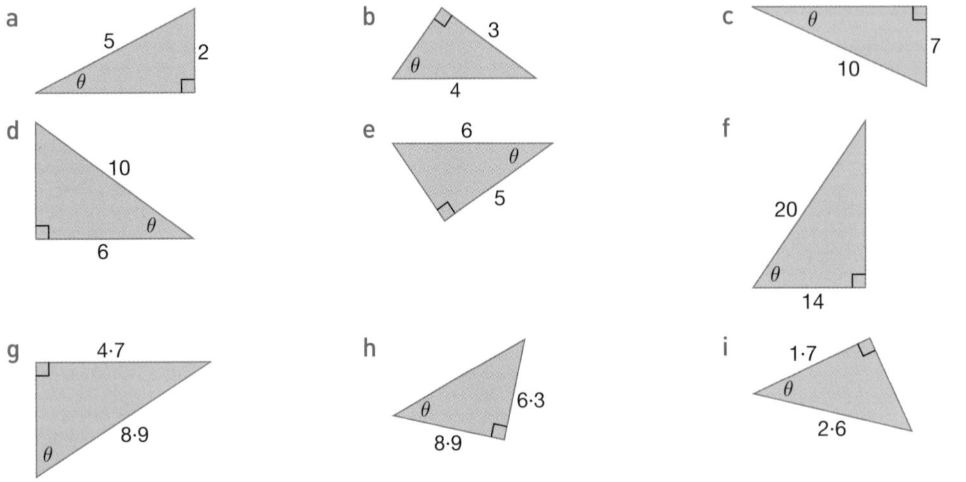

2 For each, find the size of θ correct to the nearest minute.

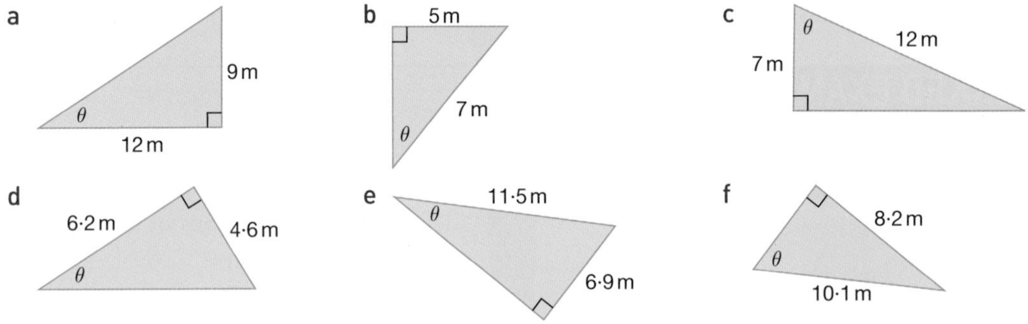

3 Use trigonometry to find x in three different ways.

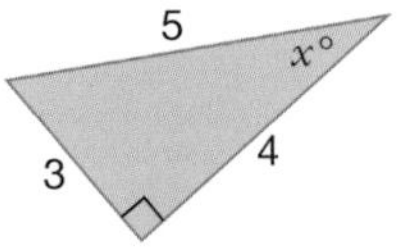

4 **a** In ΔLMN, $\angle M = 90°$, $LN = 9{\cdot}2$ m and $LM = 8{\cdot}2$ m. Find $\angle L$, to the nearest degree.

b In ΔPQR, $\angle R = 90°$, $PR = 6{\cdot}9$ m and $QR = 5{\cdot}1$ m. Find $\angle P$, to the nearest minute.

5 **a** A ladder reaches 9 m up a wall and the foot of the ladder is 2 m from the base of the wall. What angle does the ladder make with the ground? Answer correct to the nearest degree.

b What angle will a 5 m ladder make with the ground if it is to reach 4·4 m up a wall? Answer correct to the nearest degree.

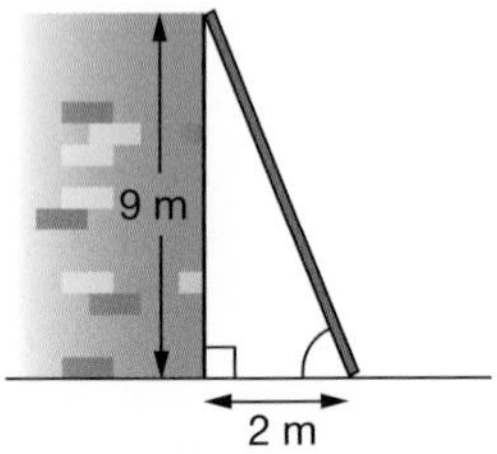

6 The beam of a seesaw is 4·2 m long. If one end is 1·2 m above the ground when the other end is resting on the ground, find the angle the beam makes with the ground, correct to the nearest degree.

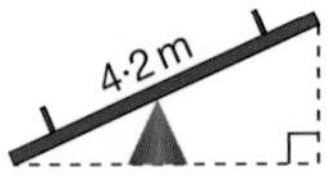

7 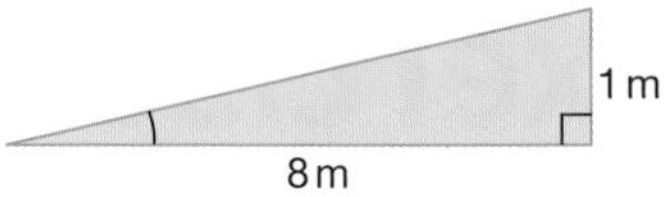

A road is inclined so that it rises 1 m for each horizontal distance of 8 m. What angle does the road make with the horizontal? Answer correct to the nearest minute.

8 At a certain time of the day, a tree 25 m high casts a shadow 32 m long. At this time of day, what angle do the rays of sunlight make with the ground? Answer correct to the nearest minute.

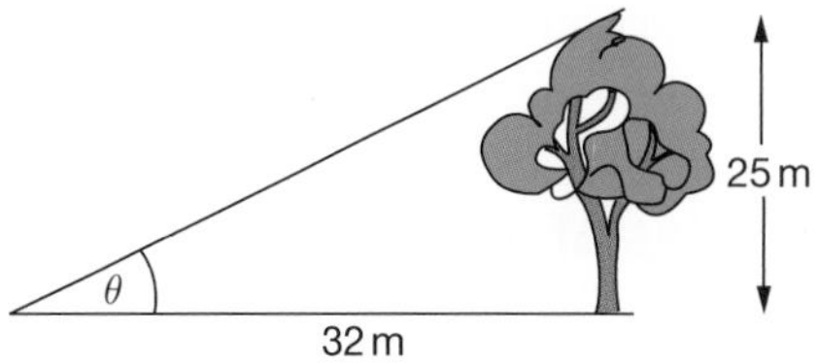

9 What angle does a diagonal of a rectangle make with each of the sides if the dimensions of the rectangle are 4·7 m by 3·2 m? Answer correct to the nearest minute.

10 Find the angle θ in each of the following. Answer correct to the nearest minute.

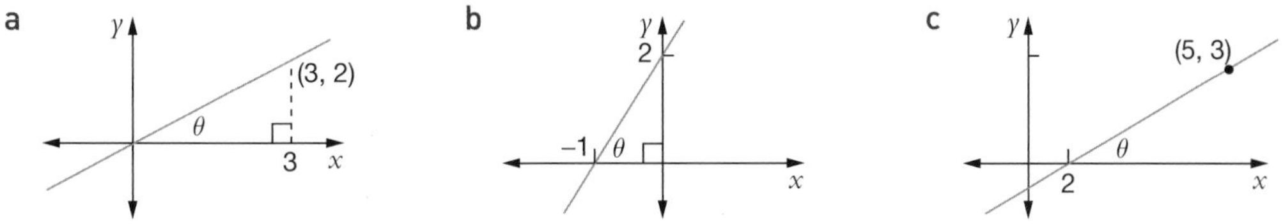

11 The cross-section of a roof is an isosceles triangle. Find the pitch of the roof (the angle it makes with the horizontal) if the width of the roof is 9·6 m and the length of one of the pitched sections is 5·1 m. Give your answer correct to the nearest minute.

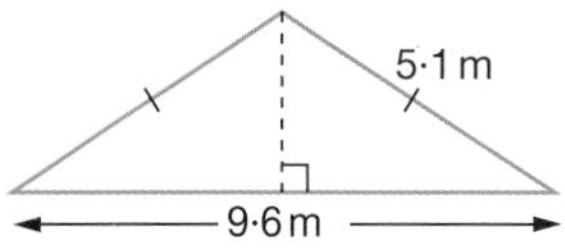

12 Find the size of the base angles of an isosceles triangle if the length of the base is 10 cm and the height is 8·4 cm. (Answer to the nearest minute.)

13 Find the apex angle of an isosceles triangle if the length of each of the equal sides is 14·3 cm and the length of the base is 20·8 cm. Give your answer to the nearest minute.

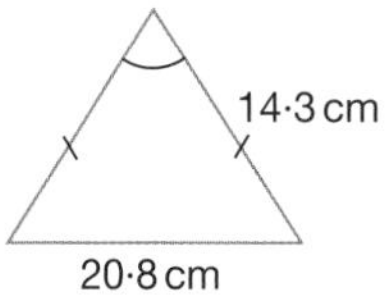

14 The diagram shows a trapezium.

a If $BC = 8$, find θ.

b If $CE = 8$, find θ.

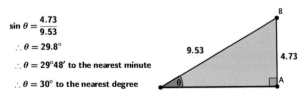

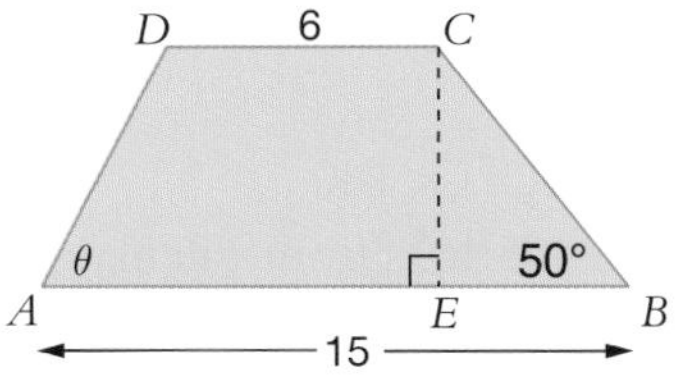

P GEOGEBRA ACTIVITY 13:06 USING THE TRIG RATIOS TO FIND AN ANGLE

In this activity the lengths of two sides of a right-angled triangle are given and you have to determine the correct ratio to find the required angle. The given side lengths are chosen randomly so that you can practise using all three ratios. A checkbox can be used to show the solution.

$\sin \theta = \frac{4.73}{9.53}$

$\therefore \theta = 29.8°$

$\therefore \theta = 29°48'$ to the nearest minute

$\therefore \theta = 30°$ to the nearest degree

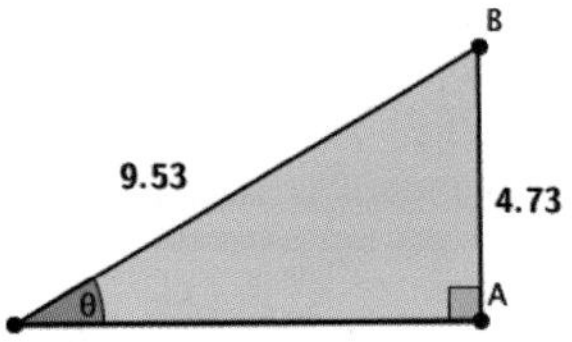

13:07 Miscellaneous exercises

Before continuing with further trigonometric examples there is some general information that should be mentioned.

Angles of elevation and depression

When looking upwards towards an object, the **angle of elevation** is defined as the angle between the line of sight and the horizontal.

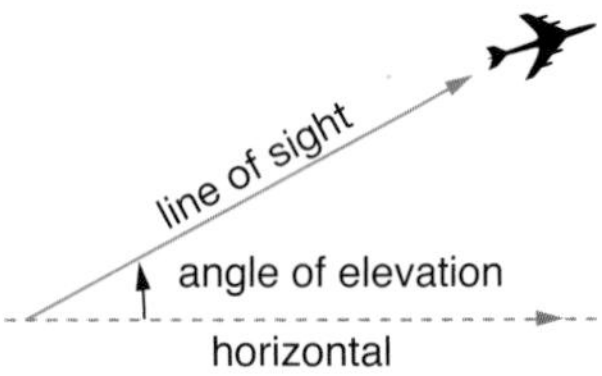

When looking downwards towards an object, the **angle of depression** is defined as the angle between the line of sight and the horizontal.

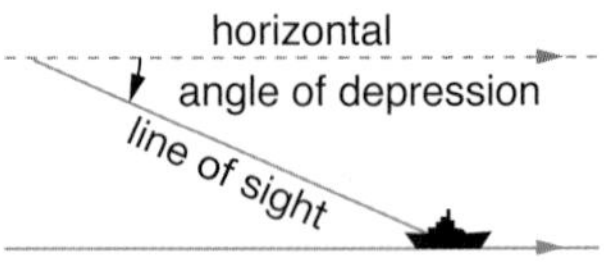

WORKED EXAMPLES

1 The angle of elevation of the top of a vertical cliff is observed to be 23° from a boat 180 m from the base of the cliff. What is the height of the cliff? Answer correct to one decimal place.

2 An observer stands on the top of a 40 m cliff to observe a boat that is 650 m out from the base of the cliff. What is the angle of depression from the observer to the boat? (Answer to the nearest minute.)

Solutions

1 Let the height of the cliff be h m.

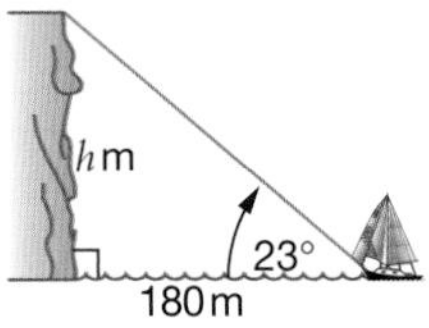

$$\frac{h}{180} = \tan 23°$$
$$h = (\tan 23°) \times 180$$
$$= 76{\cdot}405\,467 \text{ (from calculator)}$$

∴ Height of cliff is 76·4 m (1 dec. pl.).

2

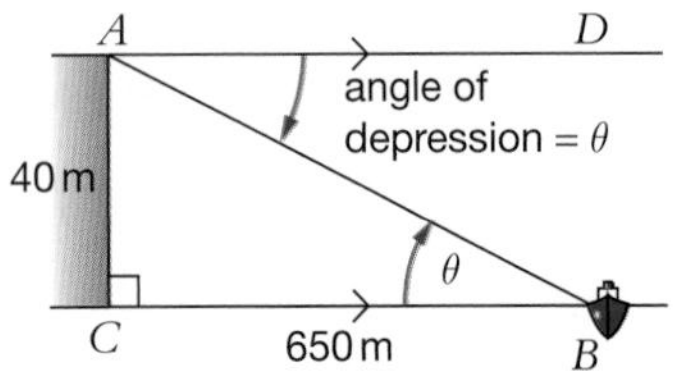

Note: The angle of depression ∠DAB = ∠ABC (alternate angles and parallel lines).

$\tan\theta = \frac{40}{650}$ ↔ SHIFT tan⁻¹ 40 ÷ 650) = ° ' "

$\theta = 3°31'17{\cdot}23''$

∴ Angle of depression is 3°31′ (to the nearest minute).

Compass bearings

- The direction of a point Y from point X is called the bearing of Y from X.
- A bearing is usually expressed in one of two ways. These are illustrated in the examples below.

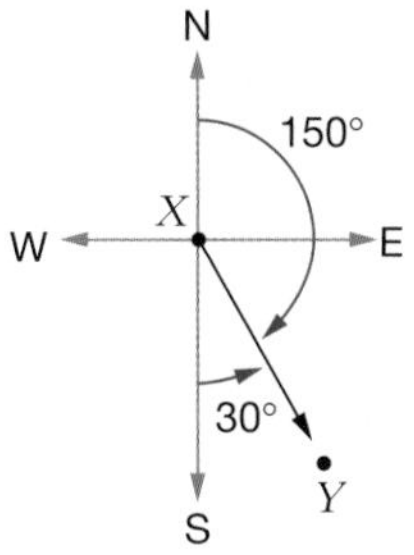

Method 1:

This method measures the size of the angle between the line XY and north. The angle is always measured in a clockwise direction. This is the method used in geography and navigation. These are called three-figure bearings.

The bearing of Y from X is 150°.

Method 2:

This method measures how far the line XY has rotated to the east or west of the north-south line. In this example, it has rotated 30° to the east from south.

∴ The bearing of Y from X is S30°E.

Sometimes only letters are used. So SE (or south-east) is halfway between south (180°) and east (90°); that is, 135° or S45°E.

Other examples would look like these.

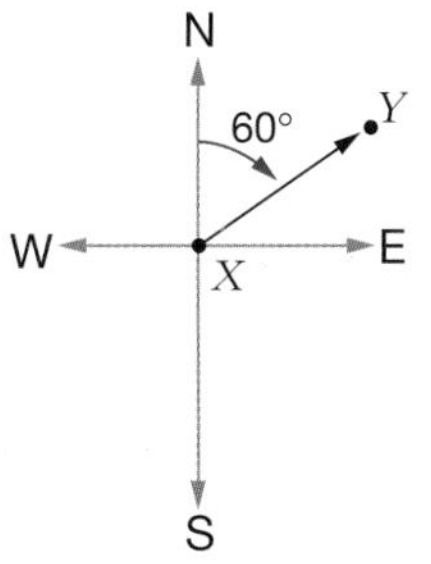

060° or N60°E

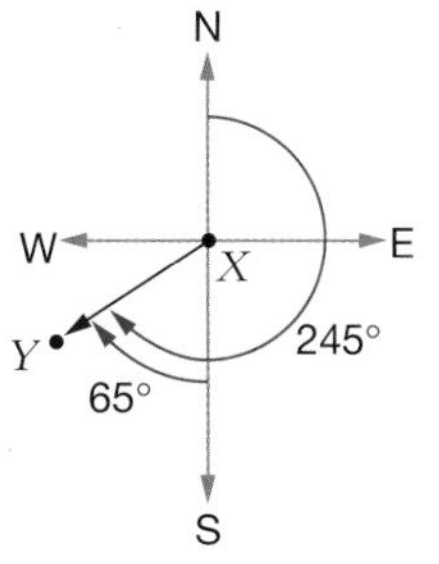

245° or S65°W

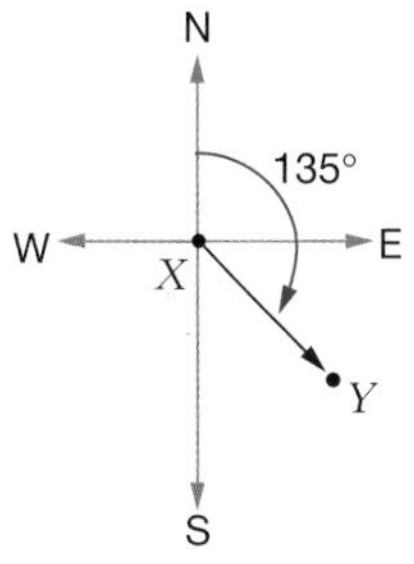

135° or SE

WORKED EXAMPLE 1

If the town of Bartley is 5 km north and 3 km west of Kelly Valley, find the bearing of Bartley from Kelly Valley.

Solutions

The diagram shows the positions of Bartley and Kelly Valley.

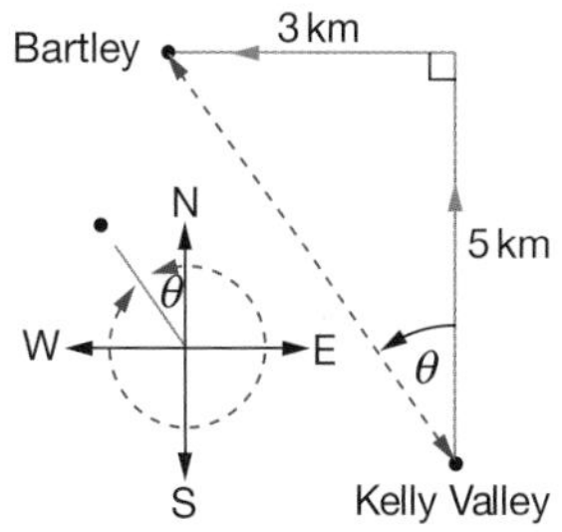

Let the angle indicated in the diagram be θ.

$$\begin{aligned}\tan\theta &= \tfrac{3}{5}\\ &= 0{\cdot}6\\ \theta &= 31° \text{ (nearest degree)}\end{aligned}$$

∴ The bearing of Bartley from Kelly Valley is 329° or N31°W.

WORKED EXAMPLE 2

Two people start walking from the same point. The first walks due east for 3·5 km and the second walks in the direction 123° until the second person is due south of the first person. How far did the second person walk (to the nearest metre)?

Solution

This diagram shows the information in the question above.

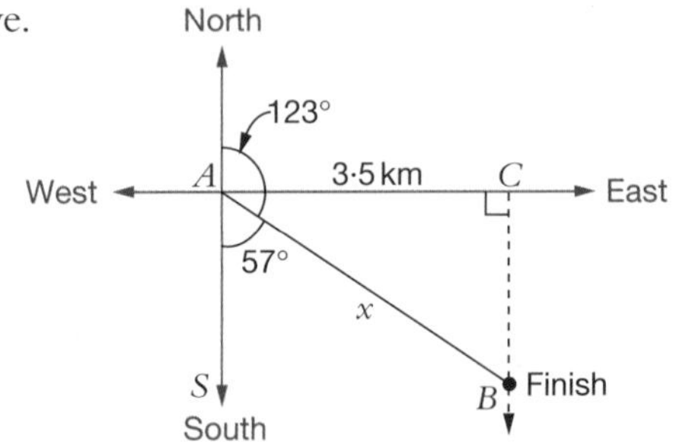

$\angle SAB = \angle CBA$ (alternate angles, $AS \parallel CB$)

$\angle CBA = 57°$

$\dfrac{3{\cdot}5}{x} = \sin 57°$

$\dfrac{x}{3{\cdot}5} = \dfrac{1}{\sin 57°}$

$x = \dfrac{3{\cdot}5}{\sin 57°}$

$= 4{\cdot}173\text{ km}$

Press: 3.5 [÷] [sin] 57 [=]

Other solutions are possible.

Exercise 13:07

P Foundation worksheet 13:07A
Angles of elevation and depression, and bearings
Foundation worksheet 13:07B
Problems with more than one triangle

1 The angle of elevation of the top of a tower from a point 35 m from the centre of the base of the tower was measured with a clinometer and found to be 63°. Find the height of the tower, correct to one decimal place.

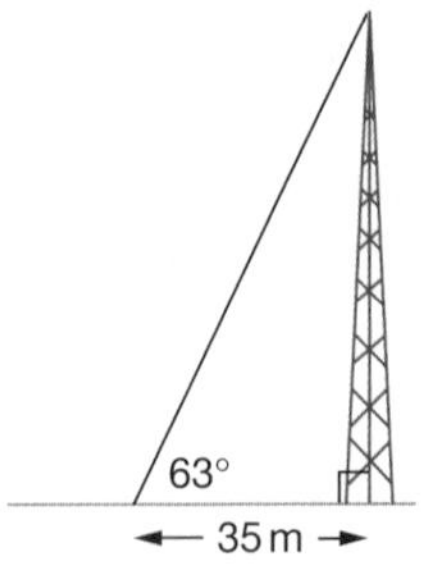

2 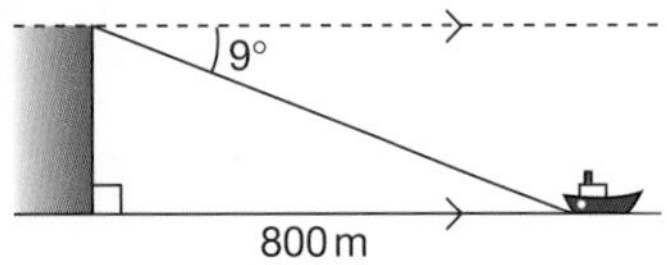

The angle of depression of a boat 800 m out to sea from the top of a vertical cliff is 9°. Find the height of the cliff, to the nearest metre.

3 From the top of a cliff 72 m high, the angle of depression of a boat is 12°47′. How far is the boat from the base of the cliff? (Answer to the nearest metre.)

4 A vertical shadow stick has a height of 1·8 m. If the angle of elevation of the Sun is 42°, what is the length of the shadow at that time, correct to one decimal place?

5 Find the angle of elevation of the top of a vertical tower from a point 25 m from its base, if the height of the tower is 40 m. (Answer to the nearest degree.)

6 From a lighthouse 70 m above sea level a ship, 1·2 km out to sea, is observed. What is the angle of depression from the lighthouse to the ship? (Answer to the nearest minute.)

7 A kite is on the end of a string 80 m long. If the vertical height of the kite, above the ground, is 69 m, find the angle of elevation of the kite from the person holding the string. (Assume the string is a straight line, and answer to the nearest minute.)

8 A cyclist travels 15 km in the direction N15°27′E. How far has he travelled in a northerly direction (to the nearest metre)?

9 A ship sails from P to Q, a distance of 150 km on a course of 120°30′. How far is P north of Q? Also, how far is Q east of P? (Answer to the nearest kilometre.)

10 Two towns, A and B, are 9 km apart and the bearing of B from A is 320°. Find how far B is west of A (to the nearest kilometre).

11 Two cars leave from the same starting point, one in a direction due west, the second in a direction with a bearing of 195°. After travelling 15 km, the first car is due north of the second. How far has the second car travelled (to the nearest kilometre)?

12 An aircraft flew 10 km south and then 6 km west. What is its bearing from its starting point? (Answer to the nearest degree.)

13 A, B and C are three towns. A lies 7 km north-east of B, and B lies 12·5 km north-west of C. Find the bearing of A from C. Also, how far is A from C? (Answer to the nearest metre.)

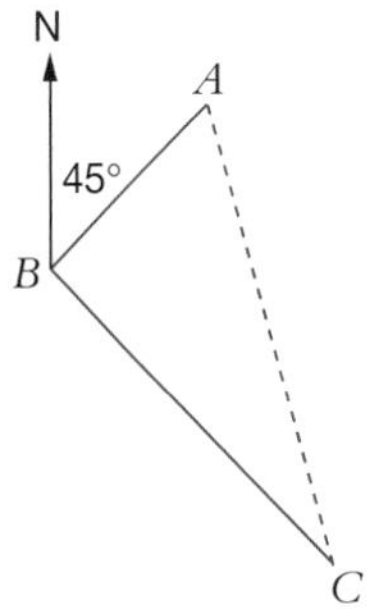

14 A ship is 5 nautical miles from a wharf on a bearing of 321°, and a lighthouse is 11·5 nautical miles from the wharf on a bearing of 231°. Find the bearing of the ship from the lighthouse. (Answer correct to the nearest minute.)

15 The bearings from a point P of two landmarks X and Y are 35° and 125° and their distances from P are 420 m and 950 m respectively. Find the bearing of Y from X (to the nearest minute).

16 X is due north of Y and 2 km distant. Z is due east of Y and has a bearing of S35°12′E from X. How far, to the nearest metre, is Z from X?

17 A wire is stretched from point A on the top of a building, 21·3 m high, to point B on the top of a shorter building, 15·6 m high. The angle of depression from A to B is 20°15′.

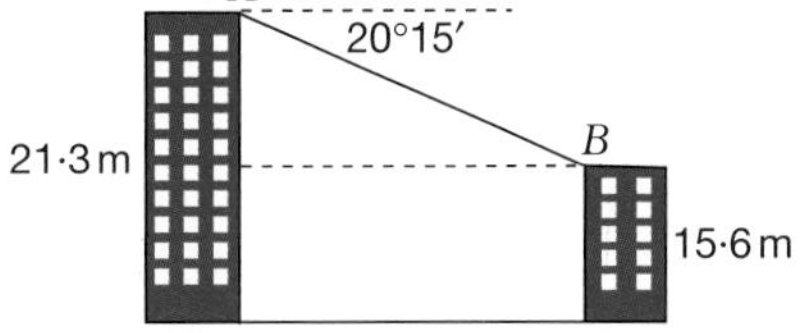

a What is the horizontal distance between the buildings (to the nearest centimetre)?

b How long is the wire (to the nearest centimetre)?

18 PQ is a diameter of the circle with centre O, with $\angle PRQ = 90°$. If the radius of the circle is 6 cm find, to the nearest millimetre, the length of the chord PR, given that $\angle PQR = 40°$.

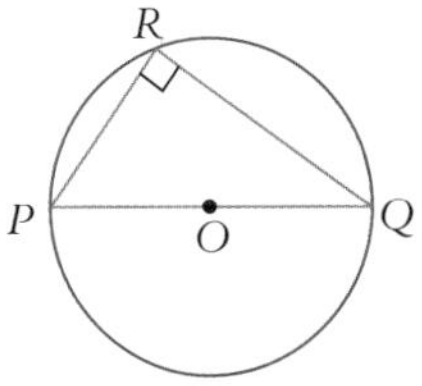

19 A tangent of length 16 cm is drawn to a circle of radius 7·5 cm from an external point T. What is the angle, marked θ in the diagram, that this tangent subtends at the centre of the circle?

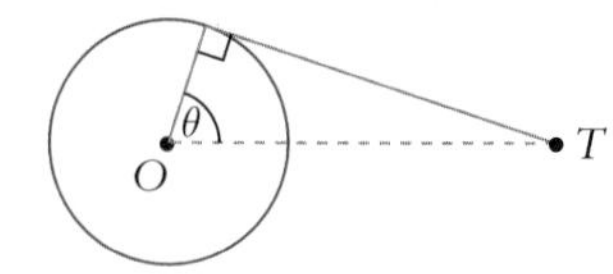

20 The diagonals of a rhombus are 11 cm and 7·6 cm. Find the angles, to the nearest degree, of the rhombus.

21 Find the acute angle, to the nearest minute, between the diagonals of a rectangle that has sides of 8 cm and 14 cm.

22 The eaves of a roof sloping at 23° overhang the walls, the edge of the roof being 75 cm from the top of the wall. The top of the wall is 5·4 m above the ground. What is the height above the ground of the edge of the roof, to the nearest centimetre?

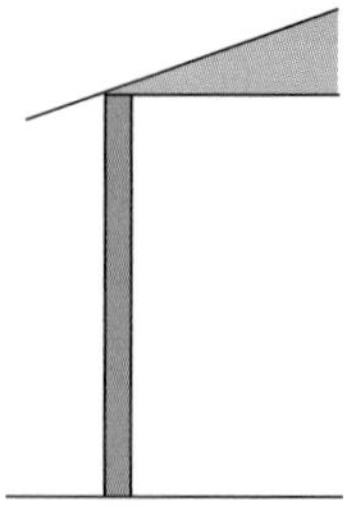

23 The arms of a pair of compasses are each 12 cm long. To what angle (to the nearest minute) must they be opened to draw a circle of 4 cm radius? How far from the paper will the joint be, if the compasses are held upright? (Answer to the nearest millimetre.)

24 Find the *exact* value of x in each of the following.

a

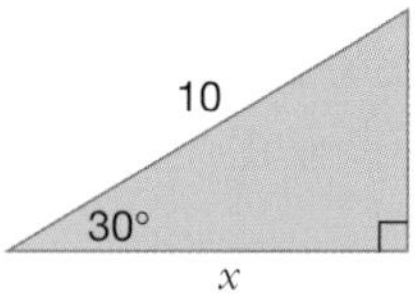

b

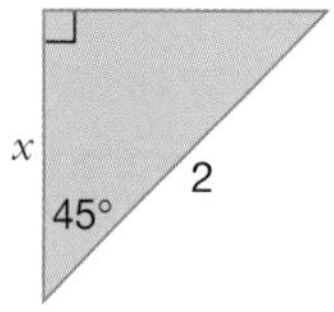

c

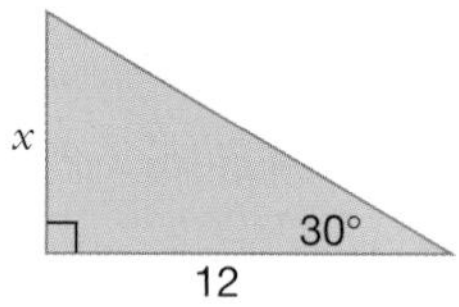

25 **a** A rectangle is 10 cm long. The angle between the diagonal and the length is 30°. What is the exact area of the rectangle?

b A pole is to be secured by three guy wires. The wires are to be fixed 10 m from the base of the pole and must form an angle of 60° with the ground (which is horizontal). What will be the exact length of each guy wire?

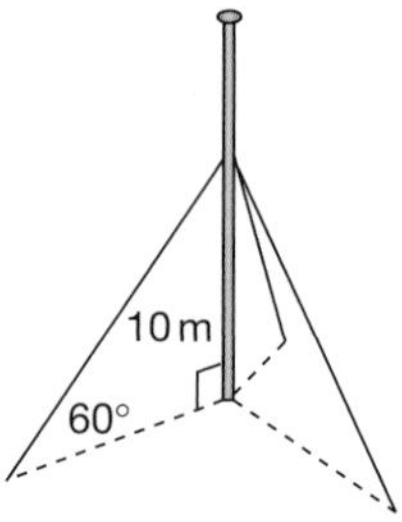

c Find the exact value of x in the diagram.

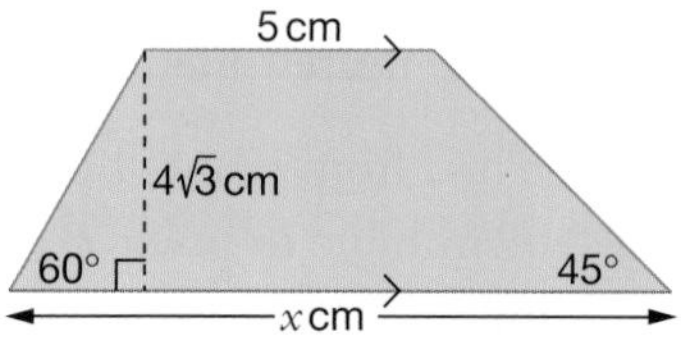

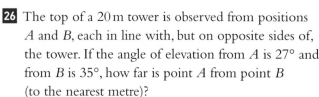

26 The top of a 20 m tower is observed from positions A and B, each in line with, but on opposite sides of, the tower. If the angle of elevation from A is 27° and from B is 35°, how far is point A from point B (to the nearest metre)?

two

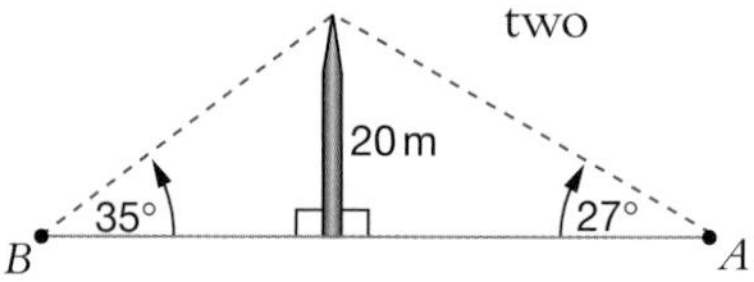

27 In triangle ABC, BD is perpendicular to AC. Given that $AB = 13$ m, $BD = 11$ m and $DC = 10$ m, find, to the nearest degree, the size of angle ABC.

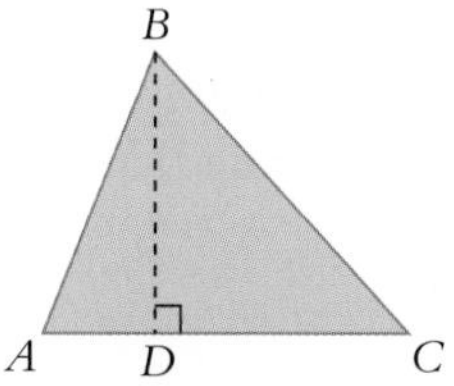

28 Two points, P and Q, are in line with the foot of a tower 25 m high. The angle of depression from the top of the tower to P is 43° and to Q is 57°. How far apart are the points? (Answer to the nearest metre.)

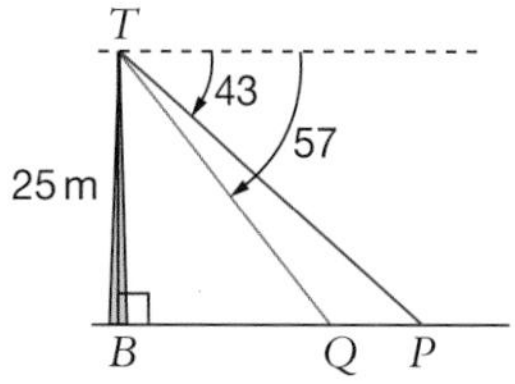

29 A plane is flying at an altitude of 900 m. From a point P on the ground the angle of elevation to the plane was 68°30′, and 20 seconds later the angle of elevation from P had changed to 25°12′. How far had the plane flown in that time, and what was its speed, to the nearest kilometre per hour? (Find the distance to the nearest metre.)

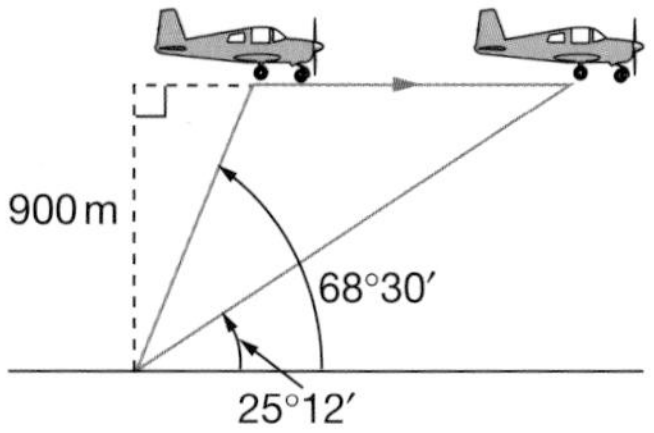

30 Two ladders are the same distance from the base of a wall. The longer ladder is 15 m long and makes an angle of 58° with the ground. If the shorter ladder is 12·6 m long, what angle does it make with the ground? (Answer to the nearest degree.)

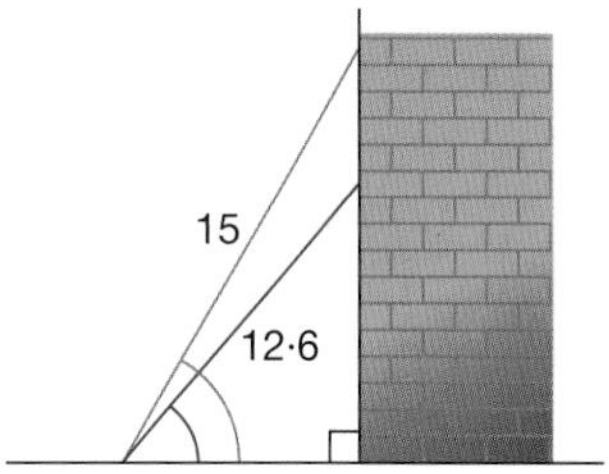

13:08 Three-dimensional problems

Right-angled triangles can be found in many three-dimensional objects. Pythagoras' theorem can be used to calculate the length of sides, while trigonometric methods can be used to calculate the lengths of sides and the sizes of angles.

WORKED EXAMPLE 1

For the rectangular prism shown, find:

a the length of EC

b $\angle CEG$

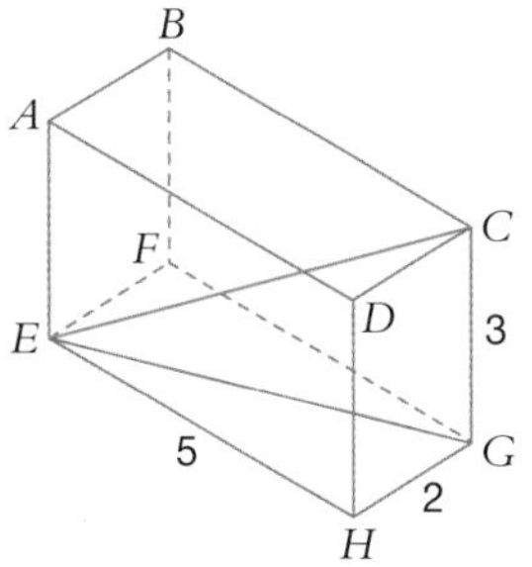

Solution

Triangles EGC and EHG are both right-angled.

a In ΔEHG,

$EG^2 = 5^2 + 2^2$

$= 29$

$EG = \sqrt{29}$ cm

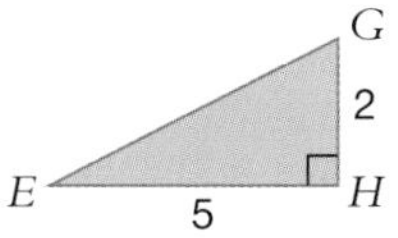

In ΔEGC,

$EC^2 = (\sqrt{29})^2 + 3^2$

$= 38$

$EC = \sqrt{38}$ cm

$= 6{\cdot}16$ cm (2 dec. pl.)

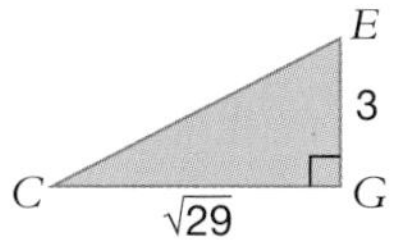

b In ΔEGC,

$\tan(\angle CEG) = \dfrac{3}{\sqrt{29}}$

$\doteqdot 0{\cdot}5571$

$\angle CEG = \tan^{-1}(0{\cdot}5571)$

$\therefore \angle CEG = 29°7'$

(nearest minute)

WORKED EXAMPLE 2

The diagram shows a right square pyramid that has base edges 4 cm in length. If $\angle EMF = 63°$, find, correct to two decimal places:

a the length EF

b the length EB.

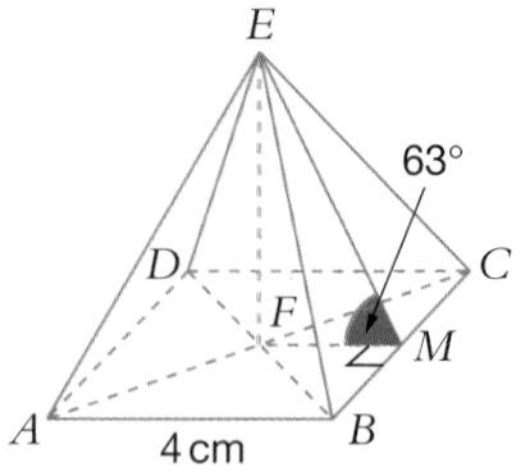

Solutions

a In ΔEFM,

$$\tan 63° = \frac{EF}{2}$$

$$\therefore EF = 2 \tan 63°$$

$$= 3{\cdot}93 \text{ cm}$$

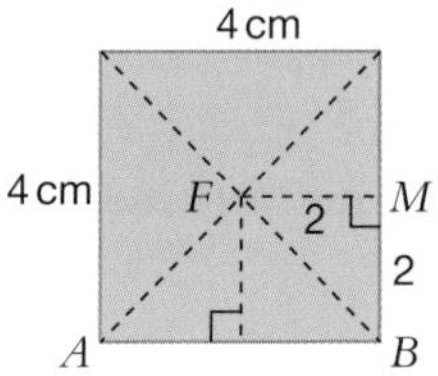

b F is the centre of the square base.

$$FB^2 = 2^2 + 2^2$$

$$= 8$$

$$FB = \sqrt{8} \text{ cm}$$

In ΔEFB

$$EB^2 = FB^2 + EF^2$$

$$= 8 + (2 \tan 63°)^2$$

$$EB^2 = 23{\cdot}407$$

$$EB = 4{\cdot}84 \text{ cm}$$

(2 dec. pl.)

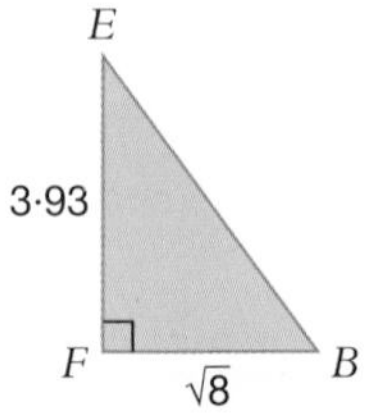

Exercise 13:08

1 The figure shows a rectangular prism.

a Calculate the lengths:

i HA **ii** BD **iii** BH

b Calculate the size of the angles:

i $\angle HAD$ **ii** $\angle HBD$ **iii** $\angle HBA$

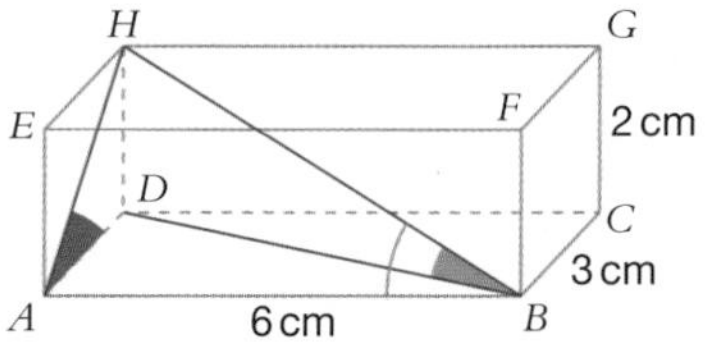

2 The figure shown is a right square pyramid with base edges of 8 cm and slant edges of 12 cm. Calculate:

a the length of PR (3 sig. fig.)

b the height OT (3 sig. fig.)

c the size of $\angle TPQ$

d the size of $\angle TPO$

e the size of $\angle TMO$ where M, is the midpoint of QR.

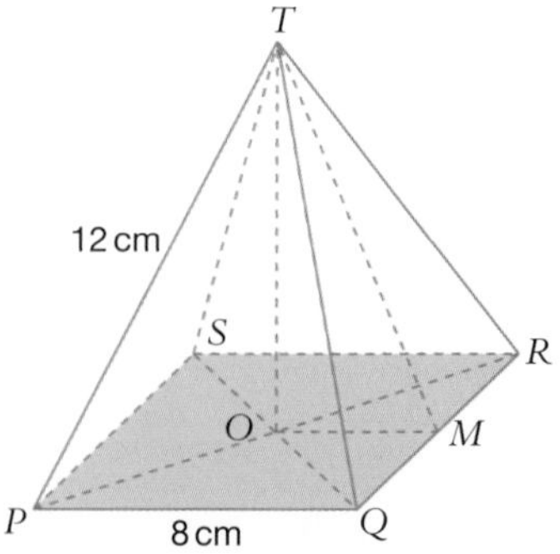

3

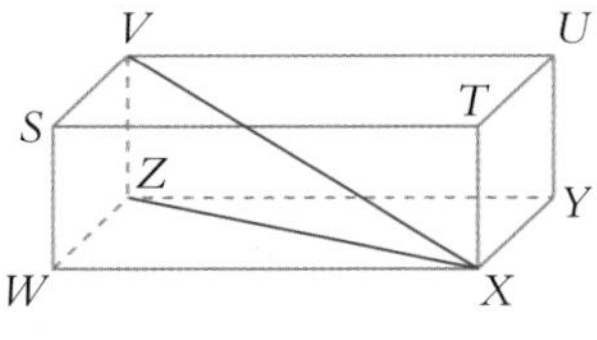

The figure drawn is a rectangular prism, where $WX = 7$ cm and $WZ = 5$ cm. Given that $\angle VXZ = 21°43'$, calculate the height of the prism, VZ, to the nearest millimetre.

4 The figure drawn is a triangular prism where $KL \perp LP$. Also $KL = 5$cm, $KN = 13$ cm and $\angle KPL = 15°$.

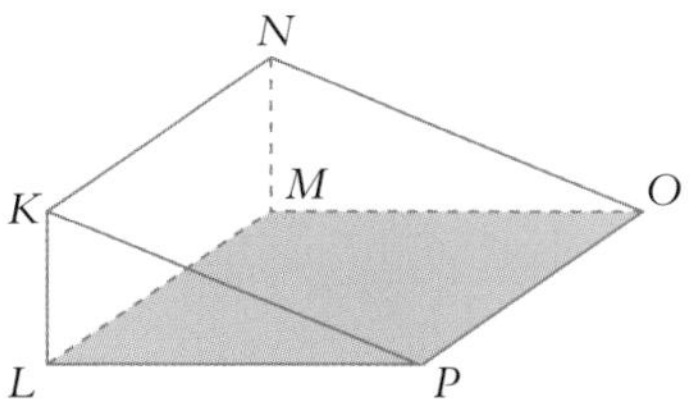

a Find the following lengths to the nearest millimetre.

i KP **ii** LP **iii** PM **iv** PN

b Find the size of the following angles to the nearest degree.

i $\angle KPN$ **ii** $\angle MPN$

5 $ABCDE$ is a rectangular pyramid with $AB = 8$ cm and $BC = 6$ cm. The point O is the centre of the rectangular base and the triangular face EBC makes an angle of 60° with the rectangular base as shown.

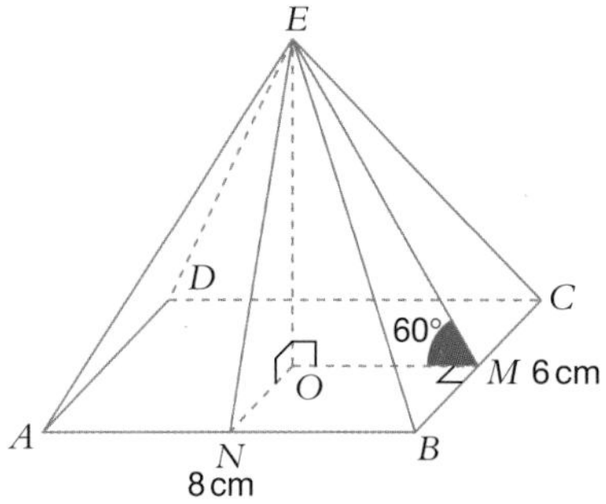

a Find the lengths correct to two decimal places, where necessary.

i OE **ii** EN **iii** EM **iv** EB

b Find, correct to the nearest degree, the size of:

i $\angle ENO$ **ii** $\angle OBE$

6 A flagpole stands at one corner P of a level square field $PQRS$, each side of which is 120 m long. If the angle of elevation of the top of the pole from Q is 13°19′, find:

a the height of the flagpole (to the nearest centimetre)

b its angle of elevation from R.

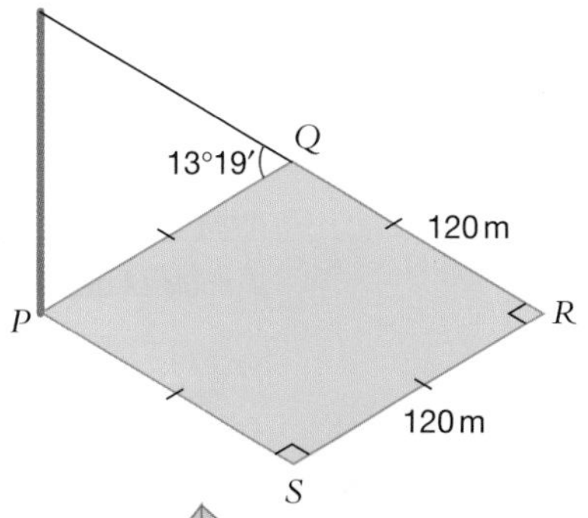

7 A monument is erected on top of a building. The top of the monument is 150 m above the ground. From a point A due south of the monument, the angle of elevation of the top of the monument is 16°. From a point B that is due east of the monument, the angle of elevation is 10°. If A and B are on level ground, find the distance from A to B to the nearest metre.

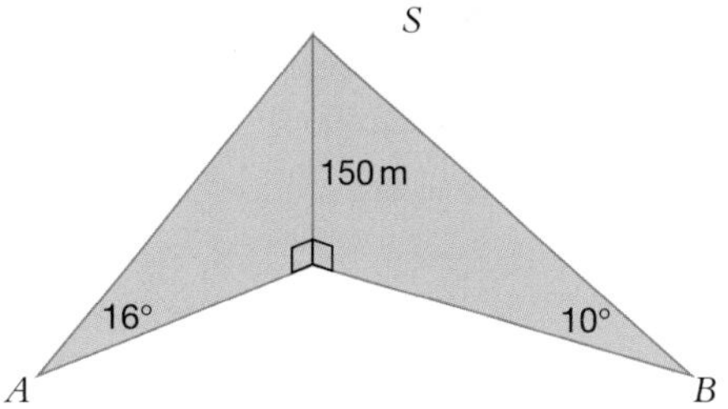

8 From a viewing platform at the top of a building 110 m high the angles of depression of two points A and B are 28° and 17° respectively. If A is due east of the viewing position and B is due south of it and both are on level ground, find the distance AB to the nearest metre.

9 A right hexagonal pyramid has base edges of 9 cm and a height of 12 cm. Find, to the nearest minute:

a the angle one of the slant edges makes with the base (e.g. $\angle OAP$)

b the angle one of the triangular faces makes with the base (e.g. $\angle OMP$).

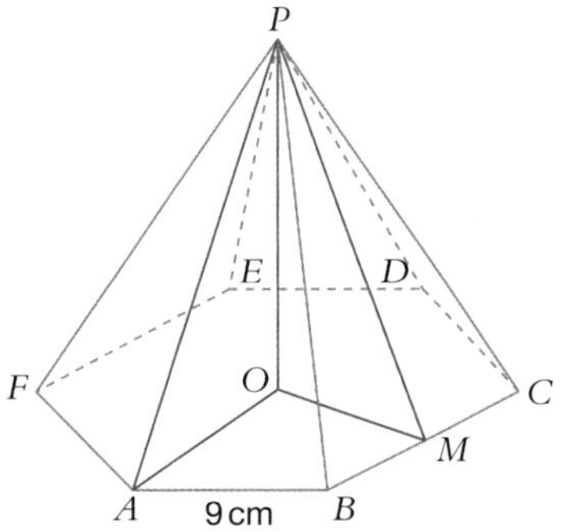

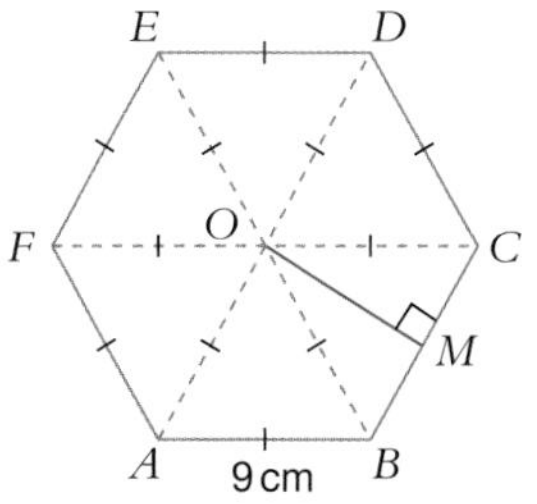

10 The diagram shows part of a roof construction. Triangles ACE, FCE and DCE are all right-angled at E. The points A, F, B, D and E are all in the same plane and F is the midpoint of AB. C is directly above E and $\angle EDC = 30°$. $BF = BD$.

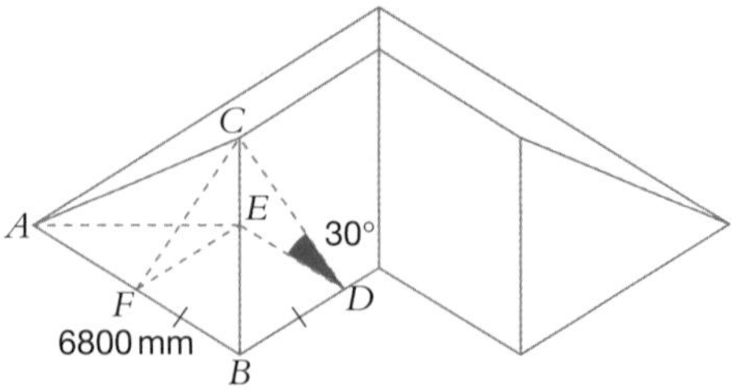

a Find to the nearest millimetre, the lengths:

i CE ii CD iii AC

b Calculate the size of $\angle EAC$ to the nearest degree.

MATHS TERMS 13

adjacent side (to a given angle)

- the side of a triangle that together with the hypotenuse forms the arms of a given angle

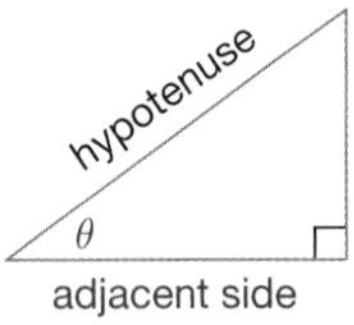

angle of depression

- when looking down, the angle between the line of sight and the horizontal

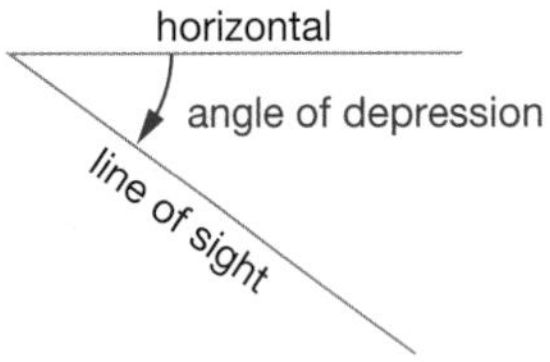

angle of elevation

- when looking up, the angle between the line of sight and the horizontal

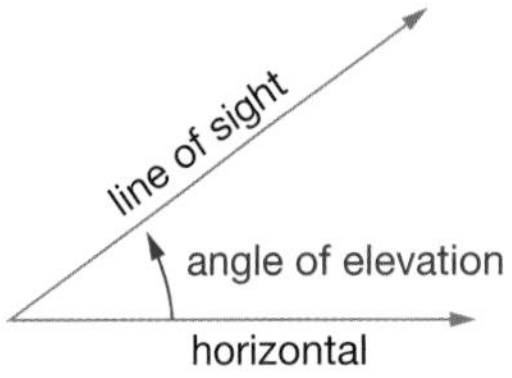

bearing

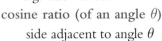

- an angle used to measure the direction of a line from north
- bearings can be recorded in two different ways, e.g. 120° or S60°E

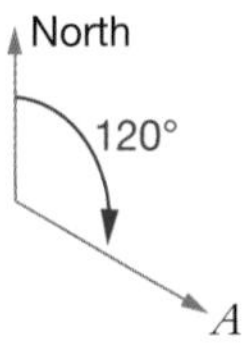

cosine ratio (of an angle θ)

- $\dfrac{\text{side adjacent to angle } \theta}{\text{hypotenuse}}$
- abbreviated to $\cos\theta$

hypotenuse

- the longest side in a right-angled triangle
- the side that is not one of the arms of the right angle in a right-angled triangle

opposite side (to a given angle)

- the side of a triangle that is not one of the arms of the given angle

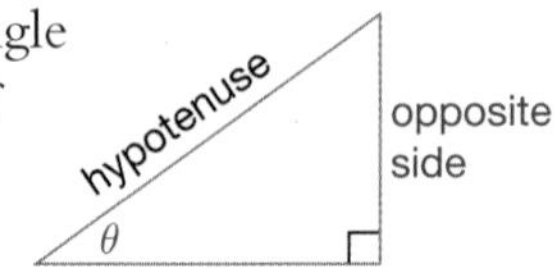

similar triangles

- two triangles that have the same shape but a different size
- triangles that can be changed into each other by either an enlargement or reduction
- triangles that have matching angles equal
- triangles where the ratio of matching sides is constant

sine ratio (of an angle θ)

- $\dfrac{\text{side opposite angle } \theta}{\text{hypotenuse}}$
- abbreviated to $\sin\theta$

tangent ratio (of an angle θ)

- $\dfrac{\text{side opposite angle } \theta}{\text{side adjacent to angle } \theta}$
- abbreviated to $\tan\theta$

trigonometric (trig) ratios

- a collective name for different ratios of the side lengths of right-angled triangles
- the ratios have constant values for any particular angle

trigonometry

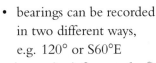

- a branch of mathematics, part of which deals with the calculation of the sides and angles of triangles

DIAGNOSTIC TEST 13 TRIGONOMETRY

These questions reflect the important skills introduced in this chapter.
Errors made will indicate areas of weakness.
Each weakness should be treated by going back to the section listed.

1 Evaluate, correct to four decimal places: 13:04
a $\tan 75°$ b $\sin 23°$ c $\cos 68{\cdot}3°$ d $\tan 48{\cdot}25°$

2 Evaluate, correct to three decimal places: 13:04
a $\sin 25°30'$ b $\tan 59°09'$ c $\cos 173°21'$ d $\sin 342°12'$

3 If $0° < \theta < 90°$, find θ, to the nearest minute, given that: 13:04
a $\cos\theta = 0{\cdot}639$ b $\sin\theta = 0{\cdot}741$ c $\tan\theta = 0{\cdot}071$ d $\tan\theta = 3{\cdot}46$

4 Name the side asked for in each triangle with respect to θ. 13:01

a
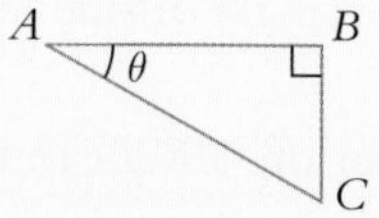

adjacent side

b
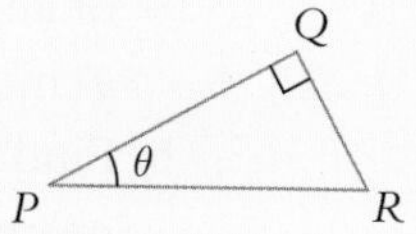

hypotenuse

c
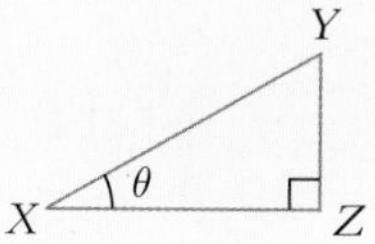

opposite side

5 State, as a fraction, the value of each given trig ratio. 13:03

a
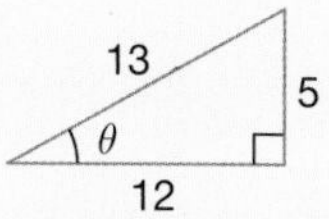

sin θ

b
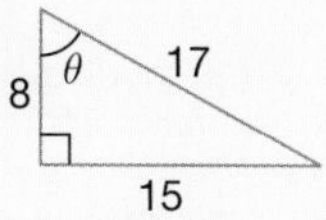

tan θ

c
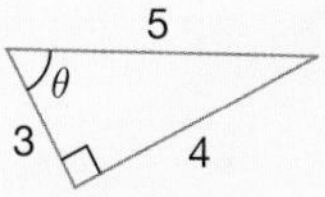

cos θ

6 Find x, correct to one decimal place. 13:05

a
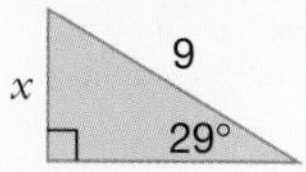

b
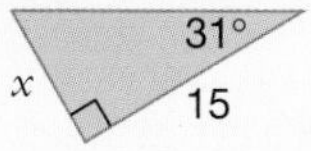

c
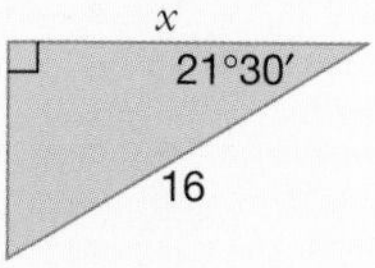

d
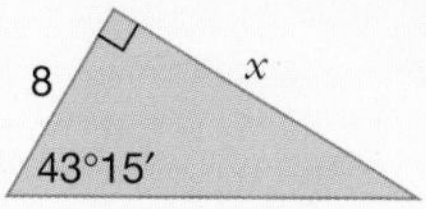

7 Find a, correct to one decimal place. 13:05

a
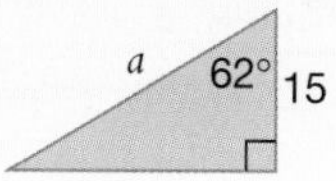

b
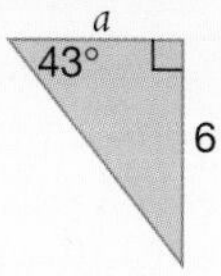

c
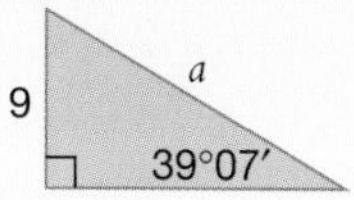

d
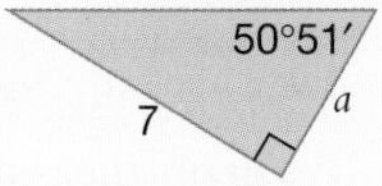

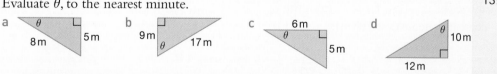

8 Evaluate θ, to the nearest minute. 13:06

a
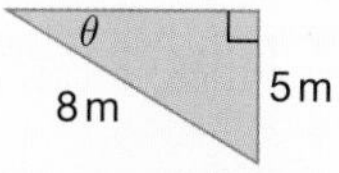

b
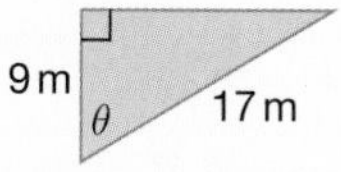

c
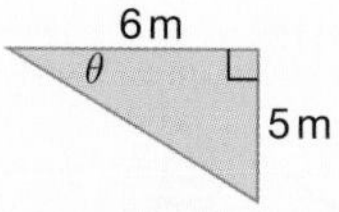

d
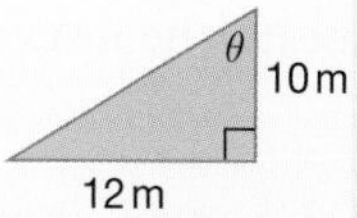

ASSIGNMENT 13A Chapter review

1 Find the value of the pronumerals, correct to two significant figures.

a

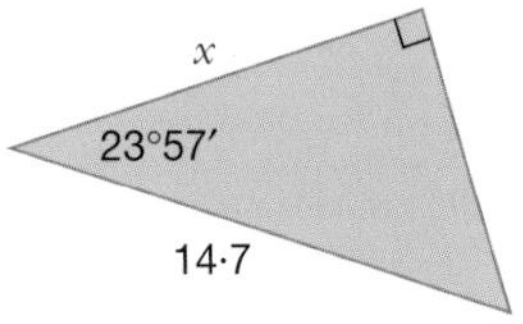

b

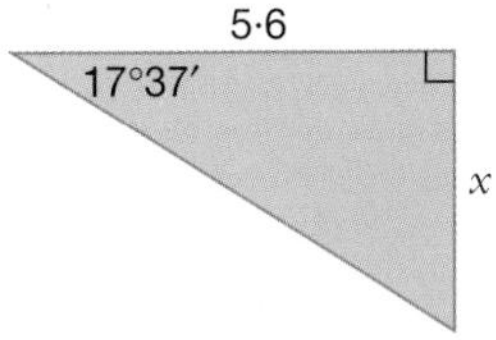

c

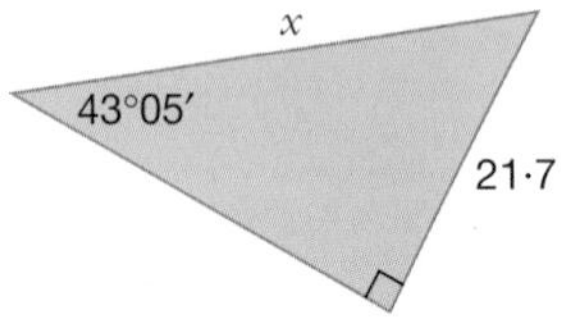

2 Find the value of θ, to the nearest minute.

a

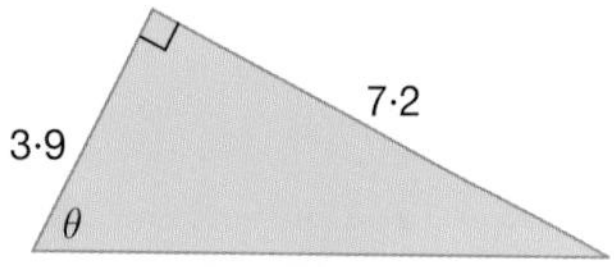

b

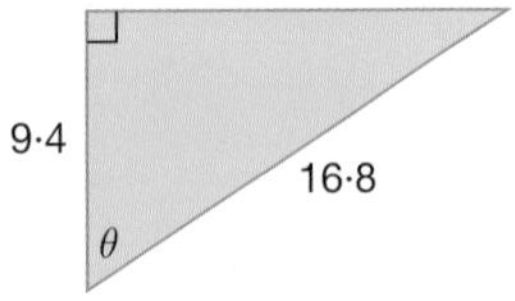

c

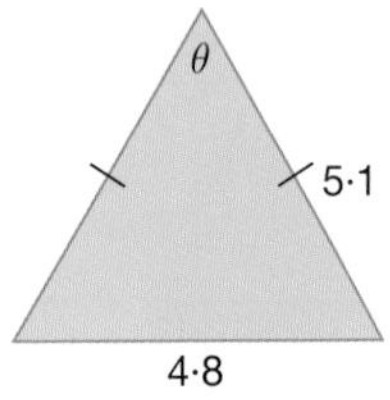

3 a A ship's captain measures the angle of elevation of a lighthouse as 4°. If he knows that the lighthouse is 105 m above the sea, how far is he from the coast (to the nearest 100 m)?

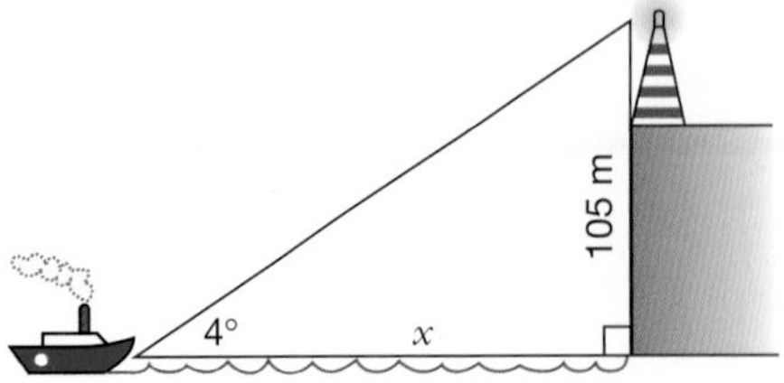

b A plane flies at a speed of 650 km/h. It starts from point A and flies on a bearing of 120° for 3 hours. At that time, how far is it:

- **i** south of A
- **ii** east of A?

4 a Use the fact that the exact value of $\sin 60^\circ = \dfrac{\sqrt{3}}{2}$ to find the perpendicular height of an equilateral triangle of side a cm. Hence, find a formula for the area of an equilateral triangle of side length a cm.

b Find the perimeter of $ABCD$, to the nearest metre.

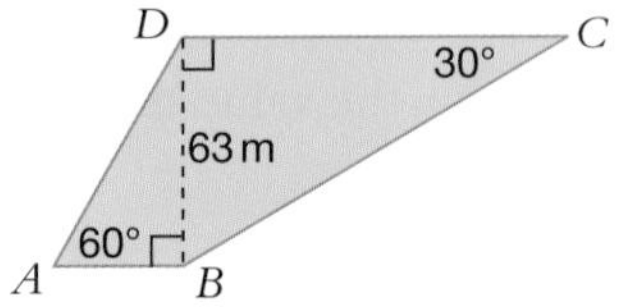

5 The triangular prism shown represents part of a roof. Find the values of AB and AC, correct to the nearest millimetre.

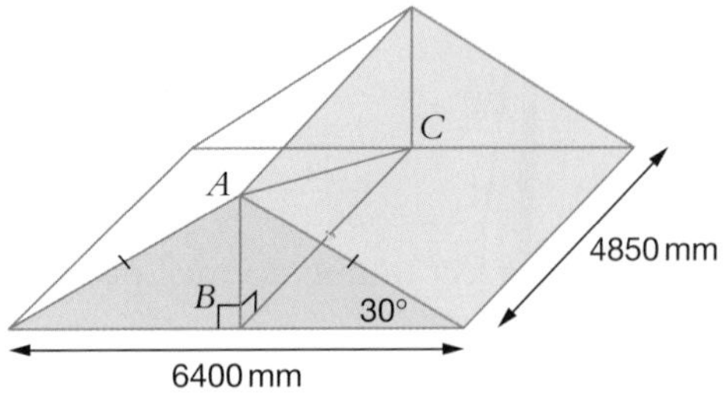

ASSIGNMENT 13B Working mathematically

1 How many numbers greater than 4000 can be formed from each of the set of cards below?

a 1 2 3 4

b 1 2 3 4 5

2 The line passing through $A(0, 4)$ and $B(6, 0)$ intersects the line $y = \frac{2x}{5}$ at C. Find the area of ΔOBC.

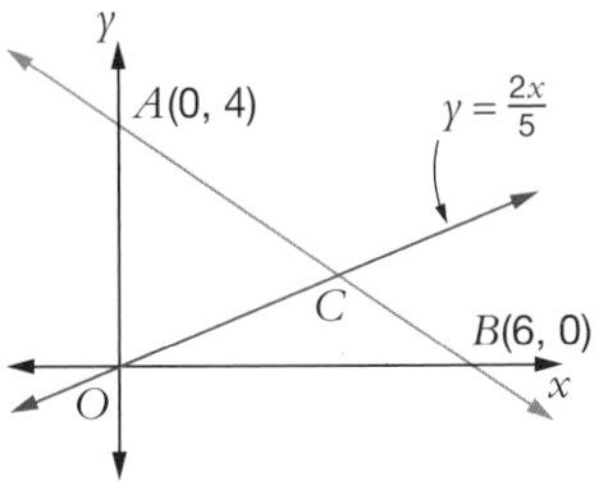

3 Every male bee has only one parent, a female. Every female bee has two parents, a male and a female. In the 8th generation back, how many ancestors has a male bee? (Assume that no ancestor occurs more than once.)

4 A builder is asked to make the window shown. What is the value of θ, a and b?

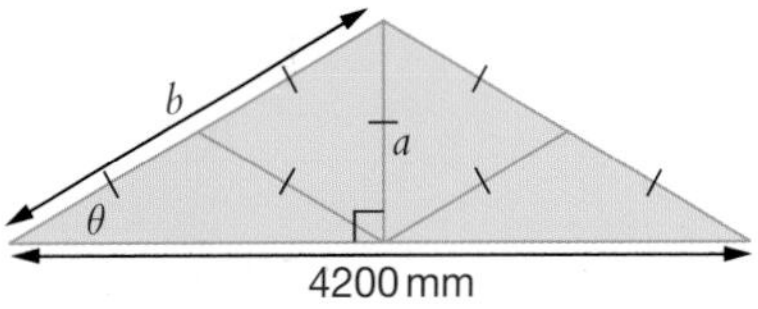

5 A solid is formed from a cube by cutting off the corners in such a way that the vertices of the new solid will be at the midpoints of the edges of the original cube. If each of the new edges is a units long, what is the surface area of the solid?

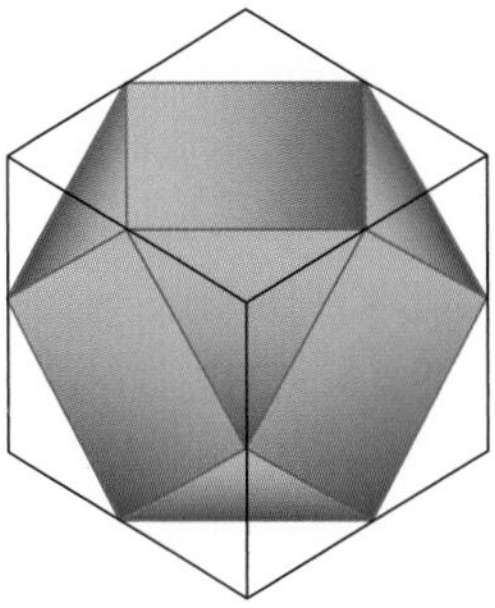

6 Two shops sell the same drink for the same price per bottle. Shop A offers a 10% discount, while shop B offers 13 bottles for the price of 12. Which shop offers the better discount if 12 bottles are bought?

Trigonometry is used in the building industry to determine the length of sides and the size of angles.

ASSIGNMENT 13C Cumulative revision

1 Factorise: 12:06

a $a^2 - 9a$ b $a^2 - 9$ c $a^3 - 9a$

2 Simplify: 3:02, 3:04, 12:07

a $\frac{5}{3a} - \frac{2}{5a}$ b $\frac{x+3}{4} - \frac{x-2}{3}$ c $\frac{4m+12}{3} \div \frac{m+3}{6}$

3 The equation of the line AB is $y = 2x + 5$. Ch 9

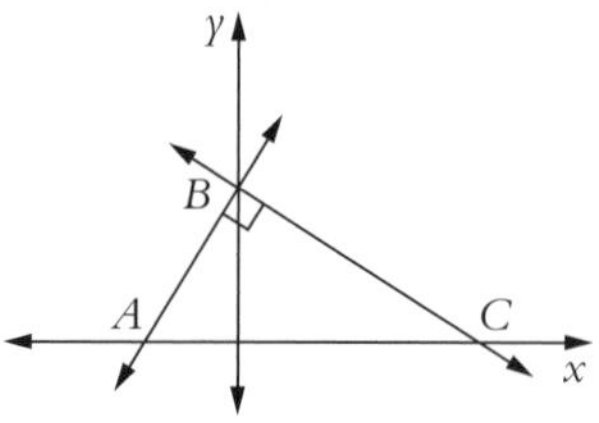

a Find the coordinates of B.

b Find the coordinates of A.

c What is the gradient of AB?

d What is the gradient of BC?

e Find the equation of the line BC.

f What is the equation of the line parallel to AB that passes through the origin?

g What is the equation of the line passing through the midpoint of interval AB, parallel to the x-axis?

4 Expand the given products and collect like terms. 3:06–3:08

a $(x - y)^2$ b $(2a - 3)(a - 3)$ c $(a + 1)(a^2 - a + 1)$

d $(a + 2)^2$ e $(a + 2)^3$

5 Simplify: 6:02

a $a^{-2} \div a$ b $4a^3b \div 2a^2b^2$ c $2a^2b \div 4a^3b$

d $(a^2b^{-3})^{-1}$ e $(2a^3)^{-1} \div a^{-2}$

6 Solve: 7:06

a $7 - 3x \geq 6$ b $\frac{2a}{5} - 3 \geq a$ c $4(1 - x) < \frac{2x}{3}$

7 Solve the following pairs of simultaneous equations. 10:02

a $2a - b = 6$, $a - b = 4$ b $4x - 3y = 2$, $x + 2y = 6$ c $3p - 4q = 6$, $2p - 3q = 10$

8 Rearrange each formula to make P the subject. 7:09, 7:10

a $A = \frac{PRT}{100}$ b $V = RP^2$ c $T = \sqrt{\frac{3P}{R}}$ d $X = \frac{1}{P} - \frac{1}{Q}$

Roger has four different pizza toppings. How many different pizzas could be made using:

- one topping
- two toppings
- any number of toppings?

STATISTICS

14

Contents

Syllabus references (See pages x–xv for details.)

Statistics and Probability

Selections from ***Single Variable Data Analysis*** [Stages 5.1, 5.2$^{\Diamond}$]

- Construct back-to-back stem-and-leaf plots and histograms and describe data, using terms including 'skewed', 'symmetric' and 'bi-modal' (ACMSP282)
- Compare data displays using mean, median and range to describe and interpret numerical data sets in terms of location (centre) and spread (ACMSP283)
- Determine quartiles and interquartile range (ACMSP248)
- Construct and interpret box plots and use them to compare data sets (ACMSP249)
- Compare shapes of box plots to corresponding histograms and dot plots (ACMSP250)

Working Mathematically

- Communicating
- Problem Solving
- Reasoning
- Understanding
- Fluency

14:01 Review of statistics

In Years 7 and 8 the work in statistics concentrated on the classification, collection, organisation and analysis of data.

The topics covered included:

- types of data: categorical and numerical (discrete or continuous)
- frequency tables and their graphs
- analysing data: range, mode, mean, median
- stem-and-leaf plots and dot plots
- sources of data: primary and secondary sources
- sampling a population: random, systematic and stratified sampling
- grouped data.

Here is a reminder of the statistical measures used and their definitions.

The **range** = highest score − lowest score.
The **mode** is the outcome that occurs the most.
The **median** is the middle score for an odd number of scores.
The **median** is the average of the middle two scores for an even number of scores.
The **mean** is the arithmetic average.

$$\text{Mean} = \frac{\text{sum of the scores}}{\text{total number of scores}}$$
$$= \frac{\text{sum of } fx \text{ column}}{\text{sum of } f \text{ column}}$$

The Greek letter Σ (sigma) is used for 'the sum of'.
The symbol $\overline{x}$ (x bar) is used for 'the mean'.
So, a compact definition of the mean is $\overline{x} = \frac{\Sigma x}{\Sigma f}$.

WORKED EXAMPLE 1

Find the range, mode, median and mean of each set of scores.

a 4 4 4 12 9 6 10

b 15 36 40 23 18 46 21 28 32 36

Solutions

a Range = highest score − lowest score
= 12 − 4
= 8

Mode = score occurring most
= 4

Median = middle score
= 6

$$\text{Mean} = \frac{\text{sum of the scores}}{\text{total number of scores}}$$
$$= \frac{4+4+4+12+9+6+10}{7}$$
$$= 7$$

b Range = highest score − lowest score
= 46 − 15
= 31

Mode = score occurring most
= 36

Median = average of two middle scores
$$= \frac{28+32}{2}$$
= 30

$$\text{Mean} = \frac{295}{10}$$
= 29·5

WORKED EXAMPLE 2

The following marks out of ten were obtained in a class quiz.

5 3 8 6 7 5 7 3 4 5 7 8 5 5 4 6 6 6 3 6 6 3 6 4 5 3 7 5 6

- Organise these scores into a frequency distribution table.
- Use the table to calculate the mode, median and mean mark for the quiz.

Solution

Mark (x)	Tally	Frequency (f)	fx
3	𝍸	5	15
4	|||	3	12
5	𝍸 ||	7	35
6	𝍸 |||	8	48
7	||||	4	28
8	||	2	16
	Total:	29	154

- The mode is the score that occurs the most. Here, the mode is 6.
- The median is the middle score when the scores are arranged in order. As there are 29 scores, the 15th score will be the middle score. Counting down the frequency column, it can be seen that the 15th score is a 5. Hence, the median is 5.
- The mean $= \dfrac{\text{sum of } fx \text{ column}}{\text{sum of } f \text{ column}} = \dfrac{\Sigma fx}{\Sigma f}$

  $= \dfrac{154}{29}$

  $= 5{\cdot}3$ (1 dec. pl.)

WORKED EXAMPLE 3

Draw a frequency histogram and polygon for the data in Worked Example 2.

Solution

- The frequency histogram is a column graph.
- The graph has a title and the axes are labelled.
- The first column begins one-half of a column width in from the vertical axis.
- The frequency polygon is a line graph.
- The first non-zero dot is one unit in from the vertical axis.
- The dots showing the data are joined by straight lines and joined to the horizontal axis as shown.

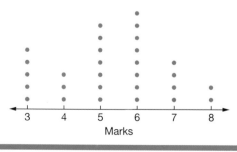

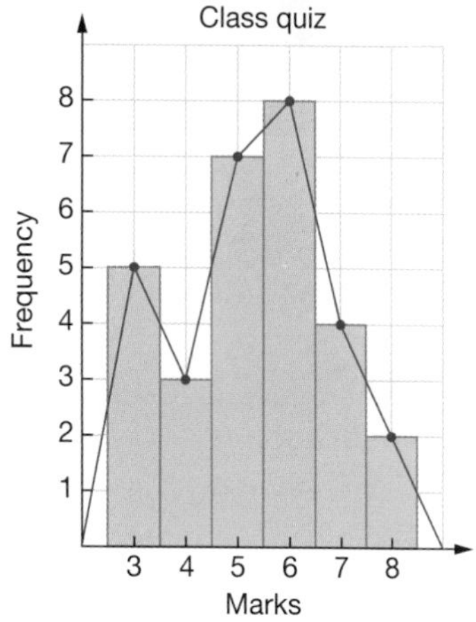

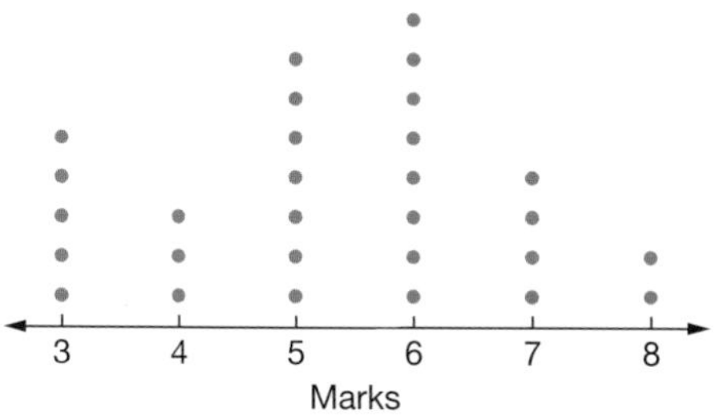

WORKED EXAMPLE 4

The scores for a group of 45 students on a spelling test out of 60 were:

50	41	34	25	18	8	35	45	54	14	59	28	39	42	53
34	51	38	47	21	50	9	54	57	46	10	48	34	11	40
52	8	23	42	52	46	37	27	55	17	32	41	30	25	11

a Sort this set of data into a grouped frequency distribution table with groupings of 0–9, 10–19 etc.

b Find the modal class, median class and an estimate for the mean using the class centres for each group.

c Construct a stem-and-leaf plot and use this to find the mode, median and mean. Compare these measures with those for the grouped data.

Solutions

a

Class	Class centre (*c.c.*)	Tally	Frequency (f)	$f \times c.c.$
0–9	4·5	|||	3	13·5
10–19	14·5	~~||||~~ |	6	87
20–29	24·5	~~||||~~ |	6	147
30–39	34·5	~~||||~~ ||||	9	310·5
40–49	44·5	~~||||~~ ~~||||~~	10	445
50–59	54·5	~~||||~~ ~~||||~~ |	11	599·5
		Total:	$\Sigma f = 45$	$\Sigma(f \times c.c.) = 1602{\cdot}5$

b Modal class = 50–59 (highest frequency of 11)

Median class = 30–39 (count down the frequency column to the middle score; 23rd out of 45)

$$\text{Mean} = \frac{\Sigma f \times c.c.}{\Sigma f} = \frac{1602{\cdot}5}{45} = 35{\cdot}6 \text{ (1 dec. pl.)}$$

c The stem-and-leaf plot looks like this:

Stem	Leaf
0	8 8 9
1	0 1 1 4 7 8
2	1 3 5 5 7 8
3	0 2 4 4 4 5 7 8 9
4	0 1 1 2 2 5 6 6 7 8
5	0 0 1 2 2 3 4 4 5 7 9

This is an 'ordered' stem-and-leaf plot as the data has been arranged in order.

The mode is 34 as it is the score that occurs the most.

The median is 38, the 23rd score (middle score of 45 scores).

$$\text{The mean} = \frac{\Sigma x}{\Sigma f} = \frac{1593}{45} = 35{\cdot}4$$

Comparing these measures with those of the grouped table shows the mode and modal class to be very different. However, the median lies within the median class and the mean is only slightly different.

If this data is compared with the group's results for a previous test using a back-to-back stem-and-leaf plot, simple comparisons can be made.

Previous test | **Latest test**

Leaf	Stem	Leaf
9 7 6 5 4	0	8 8 9
9 8 6 5 5 4 3 3 2 1	1	0 1 1 4 7 8
9 8 6 5 4 4 4 2 1 0 0	2	1 3 5 5 7 8
9 9 8 6 6 5 3 3 2 1	3	0 2 4 4 4 5 7 8 9
9 8 7 5 3 2 2 0	4	0 1 1 2 2 5 6 6 7 8
8	5	0 0 1 2 2 3 4 4 5 7 9

The mode for the previous test was 24.

The median was 22.

The mean $= \frac{\Sigma x}{\Sigma f} = \frac{1206}{45} = 26{\cdot}8$.

There also appeared to be an outlier score of 58.

In particular, the median and mean indicated significant overall improvement in the scores. This can also be seen by comparing the distribution of the scores in the back-to-back plot.

***Reminder:* How to use a calculator to find the mean**

- For sets of individual scores, simply add the scores in the calculator and then divide this sum by the number of scores.

The following instructions are for a Casio fx-82AU PLUS. Consult your calculator's manual if you have a different model. Most calculators have a statistics mode that enables the use of various statistical functions. The 'mean' function, which is usually labelled as $\bar{x}$, is used here.

To find the mean for grouped scores:

- Firstly press SHIFT then SET UP and toggle to the second screen of functions. Select 3:STAT. Then select 1:ON to choose a frequency column.
- Press MODE then select 2:STAT to enter statistics mode.
- Select 1:1-VAR and two columns should appear on the screen.
- Enter the scores in the 'Outcome' column labelled 'x' using the = key.
- Toggle across to the second column labelled 'FREQ' and up to the top of the column and enter the frequency for each score.

Outcome	Frequency
0	2
1	3
2	4
3	7
4	3
5	1

Now this step is IMPORTANT!

Press the AC (All Clear) key to remove the table from the screen.

- Press SHIFT then STAT (located above the 1 key).
- Select 4: VAR. You will be presented with four choices.
- Select 2: $\bar{x}$ and then press the = key. This gives you the mean of 2·45.

Note: If you don't enter any numbers in the frequency column, the calculator assumes there is only one of each score.

Exercise 14:01

1 Determine the: i range, ii mode, iii median and iv mean for each set of scores.

a 5, 9, 2, 7, 5, 8, 4

b 5, 8, 5, 7, 8, 5, 9, 7

c 21, 24, 19, 25, 24

d 1·3, 1·5, 1·1, 1·5, 1·6, 1·4, 1·7, 1·9

2 Use your calculator to evaluate $\bar{x}$ for each set of scores.

a 6, 9, 7, 8, 5
4, 9, 6, 5, 4
3, 8, 8, 5, 7
6, 5, 7, 5, 4

b 61, 47, 56, 87, 91
44, 59, 65, 77, 73
49, 39, 82, 60, 51
84, 73, 67, 65, 55

c 8, 8, 8, 8, 8, 8
6, 6, 6, 6, 6, 6
7, 7, 7, 7, 7, 7
9, 9, 9, 9, 3, 3

d

Outcome	Frequency
1	6
2	9
3	11
4	7
5	2

e

Outcome	Frequency
48	6
49	11
50	27
51	15
52	8
53	3

f

Outcome	Frequency
12	2
13	15
14	43
15	67
16	27
17	8

3 a Barbara's bowling average after 9 games is 178. If her next three games are 190, 164 and 216, what is her new average (mean) based on the 12 games she has bowled?

b Rob bowls in a competition where 4 games are bowled in each night of competition. His average (mean) is 187. In his first two games he scores 191 and 163. What must he total in the last two games if he wants his average to stay at 187?

4 a Copy and complete this table and then determine the mode, mean and median for this set of data.

b How many scores were greater than the mean? How many were less than the mean?

c What is the range of the scores?

d Draw a frequency histogram and polygon for this data.

Outcome	Frequency	fx
5	1	
6	4	
7	6	
8	7	
9	5	
10	2	

Total:

5 This table shows the number of each type of car that passed by Jenny's house in an hour. This is an example of **categorical data**. (The other questions in this exercise involve **numerical data**.)

Type of car	Frequency
Ford	12
Holden	15
Hyundai	13
Mazda	20
Nissan	9
Toyota	17

This data is from a primary source as Jenny collected it herself.

a What type of car is the 'mode', i.e. the one that had the highest frequency?
b Can you determine the mean type of car?
c Can you determine the median?
d What type of graph would best represent this data?

6 This frequency polygon represents a survey of all families in Allyson Street.

a Using this data, complete the table.

Children	Frequency	*fx*
0		
1		
2		
3		
4		
5		
6		

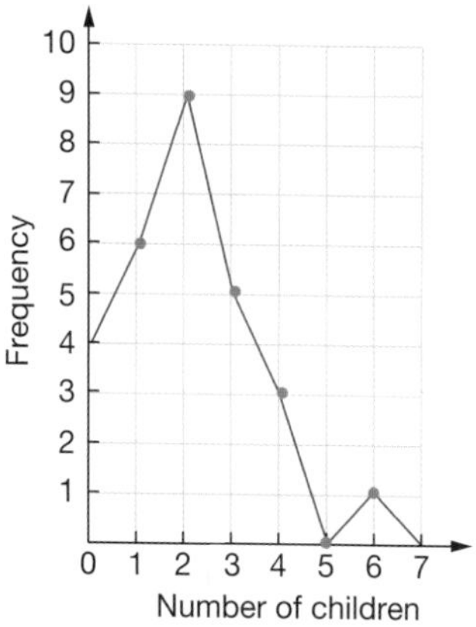

b How many families were surveyed in Allyson Street?
c How many children lived in Allyson Street?
d What was the most common number of children per family (mode)?
e If the national average number of children per family is 2·0, is the average number of children per family in Allyson Street above or below this national average?

7 For each set of data below determine the:

i range ii mode iii median iv mean

a

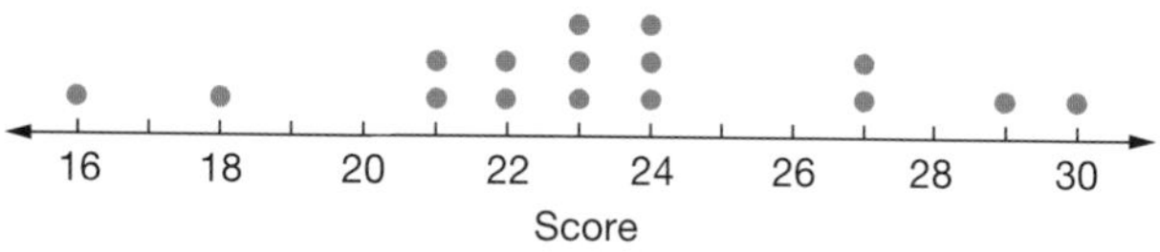

b Time taken (minutes) to complete a bicycle race:

Stem	Leaf
3	8
4	2 6 9
5	3 3 6 7
6	0 1 3 3 4 7 8
7	4 6 6 8 9
8	3 4 8 9

It's cycle-logical!

8 Each golfer in a tournament completed three rounds of golf. The scores for each round were tabulated in this grouped frequency distribution table.

a Copy and complete this table.

b How many golfers competed in this tournament?

c What was the maximum possible range?

d What is the modal class?

e Use the class centres to find an approximation for the mean.

f Determine the median class.

g Construct a frequency histogram.

Class	Class centre (*c.c.*)	Frequency (f)	$f \times c.c.$
64–66	65	25	
67–69		74	
70–72		73	
73–75		24	
76–78		2	
	Total:	...	...

9 A test of 20 spelling words was given to one hundred students. These marks are the results.

a Tabulate this data in a frequency distribution table.

b Draw a frequency histogram.

c Determine the mean number of spelling words answered correctly.

d If Kylie spelt 17 words correctly, was she above or below the mean?

e If this information is to be displayed as a grouped frequency distribution, would it be best to use a class interval of 2, 5 or 10?

f Display the information above as a grouped frequency distribution using class intervals of:
i 2 (9–10, 11–12, ..., 19–20) ii 5 (6–10, 11–15, 16–20) iii 10 (1–10, 11–20)
Explain how changing the grouping of the data has changed the shape of the display.

Number correct

17	19	15	13	20	19	15	16	14	20
18	19	15	17	19	12	9	20	19	16
12	14	14	18	16	19	20	19	18	14
10	9	18	16	15	11	15	16	19	20
20	13	14	17	17	19	18	14	15	17
18	20	20	17	19	12	11	17	16	19
17	20	19	16	13	17	15	15	20	20
12	14	20	19	17	18	14	18	18	12
9	16	17	19	20	17	19	17	20	19
17	15	14	20	18	13	14	15	19	18

10 Year 9 students decided to sell chocolates to earn sufficient money to buy a Christmas present for each patient in the local nursing home. The list on the right shows the number of chocolates sold by each student.

a Prepare a grouped frequency table using a class interval of:
i 2 ii 5 iii 10

b Draw a frequency histogram using the table with class interval:
i 2 ii 5 iii 10

c From your results so far, choose the most appropriate class interval to display these scores. Give reasons for your choice.

Number sold

7	0	35	14	22
17	30	11	5	29
26	20	12	24	15
10	16	32	39	28
19	28	11	24	30
21	32	18	21	4
30	19	6	20	35
38	26	23	8	37

11 Mario took a systematic sample of students from Year 9. He identified every tenth student on the alphabetical roll and recorded their English and Maths percentage test results.

Maths: 72, 63, 87, 94, 55, 46, 66, 81, 62, 84, 97, 59, 75, 77, 49, 57, 68, 77, 51, 70

English: 61, 39, 52, 45, 79, 59, 51, 63, 71, 75, 66, 60, 53, 48, 59, 68, 61, 72, 46, 59

The Maths marks have already been entered into this ordered back-to-back stem-and-leaf plot.

a Copy the plot and enter the English marks. (Remember to order them first.)

b For each set of marks, determine the:

i range ii median iii mean

c One particular student scored 77 for Maths but only 75 for English. Can you say this student is better at Maths than English? Justify your answer.

(Maths) Leaf	Stem	Leaf (English)
	3	
9 6	4	
9 7 5 1	5	
8 6 3 2	6	
7 7 5 2 0	7	
7 4 1	8	
7 4	9	

12 Year 9's exam results have been organised into an ordered stem-and-leaf plot using a class size of 5 as shown.

a Complete the frequency column and use it to determine the modal class.

b Complete the 'class centre' and 'frequency times class centre' columns. Use the totals to calculate an approximation for the mean.

c Determine the actual median for these results using the leaf column.

d Determine the median class using the frequency column. How does this compare with the answer to part c?

Stem	Leaf	f	*c.c.*	$f \times$ *c.c.*
$6^{(5)}$	8 8 9 9 9		67	
$7^{(0)}$	0 0 0 0 1 2 2 3 4			
$7^{(5)}$	5 5 5 5 6 6 7 7 7 7 8 8			
$8^{(0)}$	0 0 0 1 1 1 1 2 3 4 4			
$8^{(5)}$	5 8			
$9^{(0)}$	0 0 0 1 2 3 3 4			
$9^{(5)}$	7 8 9			
	Totals:	...		...

13 For this question you will generate the data yourself by using the random number generator on your calculator. Each element of data will be a random number squared.

a Press the following keys:

SHIFT Ran# = x^2 =

This will give a 6-digit decimal such as 0·283 024.

Now take the first two decimal places and record this as a number between 00 and 99 in the table. Do this a total of 100 times.

b Determine:

i the modal class

ii the median class

iii an approximate value for the mean using the class centres.

c Construct a frequency polygon.

d Compare the shape of your graph with others in the class. Do you notice any consistent pattern? What reasons are there for any pattern in the data?

Class	*c.c.*	Tally	f	$f \times$ *c.c.*
0–9	4·5			
10–19	14·5			
20–29	24·5			
30–39	34·5			
40–49	44·5			
50–59	54·5			
60–69	64·5			
70–79	74·5			
80–89	84·5			
90–99	94·5			
		Total:	...	...

B10 = =SUM(B2:B8)

	A	B	C	D	E	F	G	H	I	J	K	L	M	N	O
1	***DAY***	***TAKINGS***		***DAY***	***TAKINGS***		***DAY***	***TAKINGS***		***DAY***	***TAKINGS***		***DAY***	***TAKINGS***	
2	27-Oct	$2,490		3-Nov	$3,260		10-Nov	$2,800		17-Nov	$2,570		24-Nov	$2,170	
3	28-Oct	$4,360		4-Nov	$4,040		11-Nov	$4,690		18-Nov	$2,920		25-Nov	$3,640	
4	29-Oct	$1,440		5-Nov	$1,420		12-Nov	$1,520		19-Nov	$2,360		26-Nov	$1,420	
5	30-Oct	$1,660		6-Nov	$1,960		13-Nov	$1,340		20-Nov	$1,100		27-Nov	$1,350	
6	31-Oct	$1,370		7-Nov	$1,180		14-Nov	$1,900		21-Nov	$1,170		28-Nov	$1,480	
7	1-Nov	$1,430		8-Nov	$1,230		15-Nov	$1,440		22-Nov	$1,700		29-Nov	$1,350	
8	2-Nov	$1,860		9-Nov	$1,510		16-Nov	$1,660		23-Nov	$1,550		30-Nov	$1,440	
9															
10		$14,610													
11															
12															

The calculating power of a spreadsheet makes it an extremely useful statistical tool.

Part of a spreadsheet is shown above. It shows the daily takings for the Lazy Lizard Café for the 5-week period from 27 October until 30 November.

- Enter this information into a spreadsheet.

Note the formula =SUM(B2:B8) has been entered in cell B10. This gives the weekly takings by adding the numbers in cells B2 to B8.

1 Write formulas to give the weekly takings for the other 4 weeks.

2 Now write a formula that could give you the total takings for the 5-week period.

Each row of the spreadsheet gives the takings for the same day of the week. For example, the days are all Saturdays in row 2 and all Sundays in row 3.

The formula =AVERAGE(B2,E2,H2,K2,N2) will calculate the mean of the numbers in cells B2, E2, H2, K2 and N2. Typing this formula into cell O2 will give the average sales for Saturday.

- Copy this formula into cells O3 to O8 using 'Fill Down'. Use the results to find the average sales for each day of the week from Saturday to Friday.

3 Which day of the week has the highest average takings?

4 Which day has the lowest average takings?

14:02 Cumulative frequency

The previous section reminded you how to sort data into a frequency distribution table, and how to analyse the data using various statistical measures. The data could also be displayed in the form of a frequency histogram or polygon.

A further column that may be attached to the frequency distribution table is the 'cumulative frequency' or *c.f.* column. This column gives the progressive total of the outcomes.

This column has been added to the frequency distribution table below.

WORKED EXAMPLE

Outcome (x)	Tally	Frequency (f)	Cumulative frequency ($c.f.$)
3	|||	3	3
4	|||	3	6
5	||||	4	10
6	~~||||~~	5	15
7	||||	4	19
8	||	2	21
9	|||	3	24
10	||	2	26
	Total:	26	

For a class of 26 students the following marks out of 10 were obtained in a test.

- 15 students scored 6 or less. Since 4 students scored 7, the cumulative frequency of 7 is 15 + 4 or 19.
- The last figure in the *c.f.* column must be equal to the sum of the frequencies, as all students are on or below the highest outcome.

The cumulative frequency can also be displayed in the form of a histogram or polygon. However, there are some differences, as noted below.

- The histogram progressively steps upwards to the right.
- The polygon is obtained by joining the top right-hand corner of each column. (Why is it drawn this way?)
- Imagine that the column before the '3' column has zero height.

Another name for the cumulative frequency polygon is the 'ogive'.

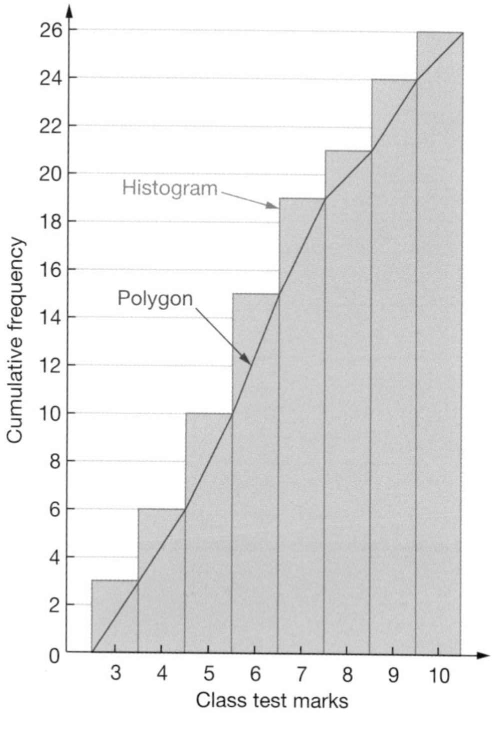

Finding the median from a frequency distribution table

The cumulative frequency can be used to find the median of a set of scores.

WORKED EXAMPLES

1

Outcome (x)	Frequency (f)	Cumulative frequency
3	5	5
4	3	8
5	7	15
6	8	23
7	4	27
8	2	29

The middle score is the 15th score (14 above it and 14 below it).
The 15th score is a 5.
∴ Median = 5

2

Outcome (x)	Frequency (f)	*c.f.*
5	2	2
6	4	6
7	3	9
8	7	16
9	5	21
10	1	22

Here, there is an even number of scores (22) so the middle two scores are the 11th and 12th scores.
From the *c.f.* column it can be seen that each of these scores is 8.
∴ Median = 8

3

Outcome (x)	Frequency (f)	*c.f.*
5	6	6
6	9	15
7	5	20
8	4	24
9	3	27
10	3	30

Here, there is also an even number of scores (30) so the middle two scores are the 15th and 16th scores.
In this example, the 15th score is 6 and the 16th score is 7. The median is the average of these two scores.
∴ Median = 6·5 (or $6\frac{1}{2}$)

Finding the median from an ogive

The cumulative frequency polygon, or ogive, can be used to find the median. Note that the method used is different from the method used for the frequency table.

WORKED EXAMPLE 1

To find the median, follow these steps.

- Find the half-way point ($\frac{1}{2} \times 26 = 13$).
- Draw a horizontal line from this point to the ogive.
- Then draw a vertical line to meet the horizontal axis.
- This meets the horizontal axis within the '6' column.

$\therefore$ The median is 6.

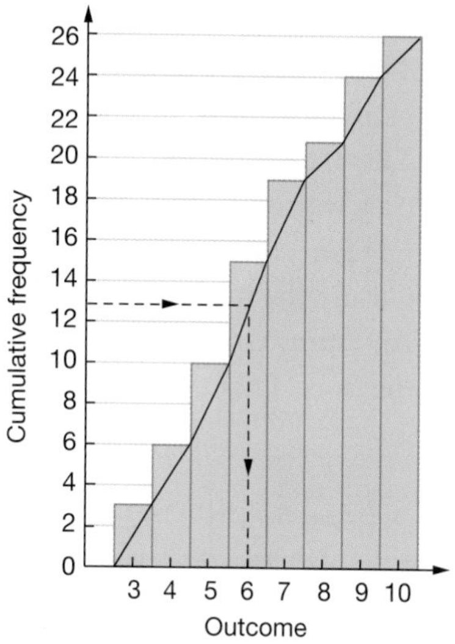

For **grouped data**, the outcomes are grouped into classes with a representative class centre (*c.c.*). The horizontal axis usually shows these class centres and the median class is found as above. Alternatively, an estimate for a median could be read from the horizontal axis, as shown below.

WORKED EXAMPLE 2

The percentage results for sixty students in an examination are given in this table.

Class	Class centre (*c.c.*)	Tally	Frequency (*f*)	$f \times c.c.$	*c.f.*
29–37	33	||	2	66	2
38–46	42	卌	5	210	7
47–55	51	卌 |||	8	408	15
56–64	60	卌 卌 ||	12	720	27
65–73	69	卌 卌 ||||	14	966	41
74–82	78	卌 ||||	9	702	50
83–91	87	卌 ||	7	609	57
92–100	96	|||	3	288	60
		Total:	60	3969	

When constructing frequency diagrams for grouped data, the only point to note is that the columns are indicated on the horizontal axis by the class centres. The diagram for the worked example above would look like this.

- The cumulative frequency polygon can be drawn by joining the top right corners of each column.
- There are 60 scores altogether, so to find the median class we come across from 30 until we meet the polygon and then down to the horizontal axis.
- Clearly the median class is 65–73.
- An estimate of the median mark can be read from the horizontal axis, i.e. 67.

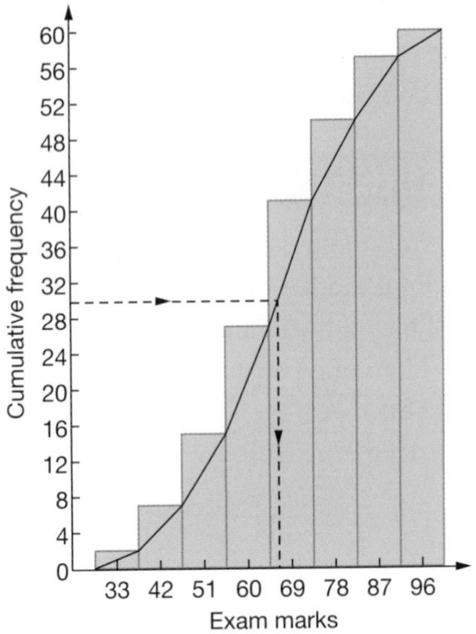

The cumulative frequency of an outcome gives the number of outcomes equal to, or less than, that particular outcome.

Exercise 14:02

P Foundation worksheet 14:02
Frequency and cumulative frequency

1 Calculate the total of the frequency column and complete the cumulative frequency column in each of these tables.

a

Outcome (x)	f	*c.f.*
0	3	3
1	8	11
2	11	22
3	17	
4	9	
5	2	

Total:

b

Outcome (x)	f	*c.f.*
9	1	
10	13	
11	22	
12	30	
13	21	
14	13	

Total:

c

Outcome (x)	f	$c.f.$
0	1	
1	0	
2	3	
3	8	
4	14	
5	20	
6	31	
7	32	
8	28	
9	11	
10	5	

Total:

d

Outcome (x)	f	$c.f.$
15	4	
20	8	
25	3	
30	9	
35	7	
40	10	
45	15	
50	8	
55	10	
60	2	
65	4	

Total:

x is the 'outcome', f is the 'frequency'.

2 Use the cumulative frequency histogram shown to complete the table below.

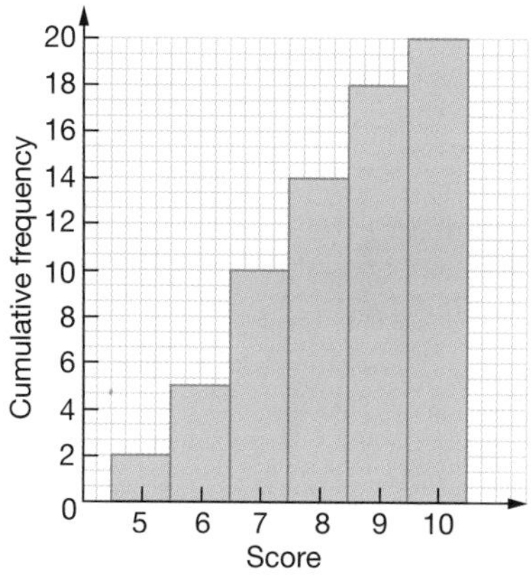

Outcome	Frequency (f)	fx	$c.f.$
5			
6			
7			
8			
9			
10			

Total: $\Sigma f =$ $\Sigma fx =$

From the table, determine the:

a mode

b mean

c median

d range

To find the: mode use the f column median use the c.f. column mean use the fx and f columns.

3 Five coins were tossed many times and the number of heads recorded. The cumulative frequency for each number of heads was calculated and a cumulative frequency graph was drawn.

a How many times did zero heads occur?
b How many times did 1 or less heads occur?
c How many times did 2 or less heads occur?
d How many times did 3 or less heads occur?
e Think about your answers to **c** and **d**. How many times did 3 heads occur?
f How many times were the 5 coins tossed?

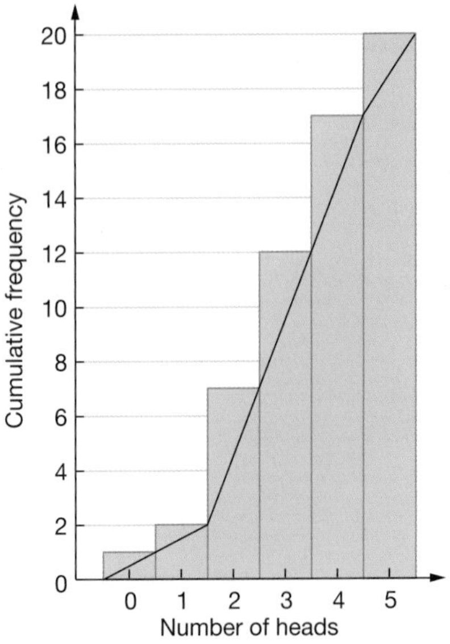

4 Sharon organises her family's football tipping competition. Each week Dad, Sharon, Adam and Bron have to pick the results of the 7 rugby league matches played. The table below shows the results for rounds 1 to 5.

	Sharon		Adam		Dad		Bron	
	Score	Prog. Total	Score	Prog. Total	Score	Prog. Total	Score	Prog. Total
Round 1	4	4	6	6	4		4	4
Round 2	3	7	3	9	4		3	7
Round 3	6	13	4	13	6		5	12
Round 4	4	17	4	17	2		3	15
Round 5	5	22	4	21	5		4	19

a 'Prog. Total' is short for 'Progressive Total'. It is like a cumulative frequency column. Complete Dad's Prog. Total column.
b Who was leading the competition at the end of:
i round 1 ii round 3 iii round 5?
c What has been the highest score achieved in a round? How many times has this happened?
d Who has had the lowest score in a round?
e In round 6 the scores were: Sharon 6, Adam 6, Dad 7, Bron 5. Use these results to add the next line in the table.

5 Two dice were rolled one hundred times and the total showing on the two upper faces was recorded to obtain this set of scores.

5	7	6	12	10	2	4	5	7	9	7	6	4	3	5	8	6	3	5	6
5	8	7	9	6	8	9	4	8	7	8	4	8	4	8	7	6	7	10	5
9	5	6	5	2	9	5	9	11	10	6	7	7	7	10	6	11	10	7	8
8	3	9	3	5	8	7	12	10	9	7	8	7	5	6	4	5	8	9	11
10	6	9	6	7	8	9	10	11	3	6	4	7	2	4	8	8	4	6	7

a By completing a frequency distribution table, determine the mode and mean of the set of scores.

b Complete a cumulative frequency column and use it to find the median.

c Look at the cumulative frequency column to determine how many scores were less than the median.

6 In the game of golf, a par is the number of strokes allocated to complete a given hole. Holes can only have a par of 3, 4 or 5 strokes. If a par is not scored, the score is said to be either under or over par. Different holes can be rated for difficulty by analysing players' scores on the hole.

The tables below show the scores achieved by all the players in a recent British Open on two holes.

5th Hole Par 4

Player's score	Frequency	Cumulative frequency
3	54	
4	314	
5	85	
6	3	

7th Hole Par 5

Player's score	Frequency	Cumulative frequency
3	20	
4	211	
5	198	
6	23	
7	4	

a Complete the cumulative frequency for each hole.

b For the 5th hole:

  i how many players scored par or better (4 or under)?

  ii how many players scored above par?

c For the 7th hole:

  i how many players scored par or better (5 or under)?

  ii how many players scored above par?

d What percentage of players scored above par on the 5th and 7th holes respectively? What does this indicate about the difficulty of the respective holes?

e Draw a cumulative frequency polygon for both sets of data. How does the shape of the polygon indicate the degree of difficulty of the hole?

7 The table below shows the players' scores for the second round in the same British Open golf tournament. The par for the course (sum of the pars for all 18 holes) is 71.

Score	68	69	70	71	72	73	74	75	76	77	78	79
Frequency	1	0	6	9	13	16	8	8	8	3	0	1
Cumulative frequency												

Complete the cumulative frequency column and use it (or some other method) to answer the following questions.

a How many players scored under par (lower than 71)?

b How many players scored par or better (71 or lower)?

c How many players scored worse that par (higher that 71)?

8 Use the ogive to find the median from each graph.

a

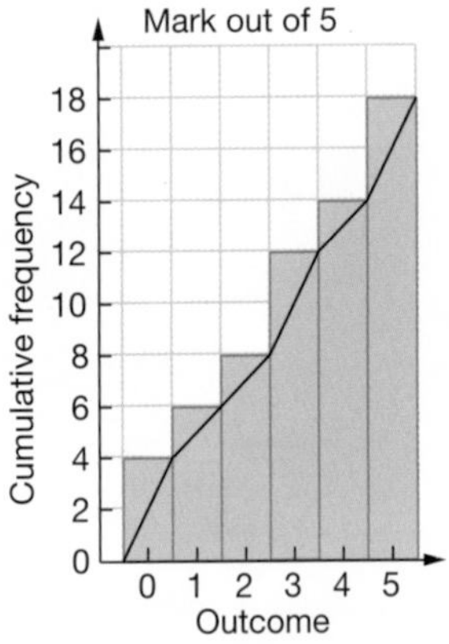

b

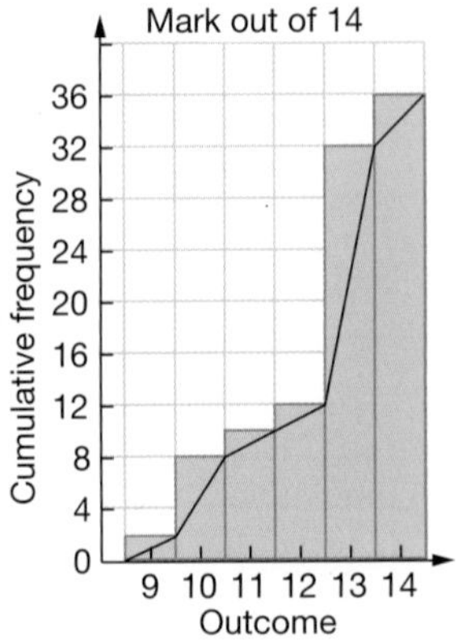

c

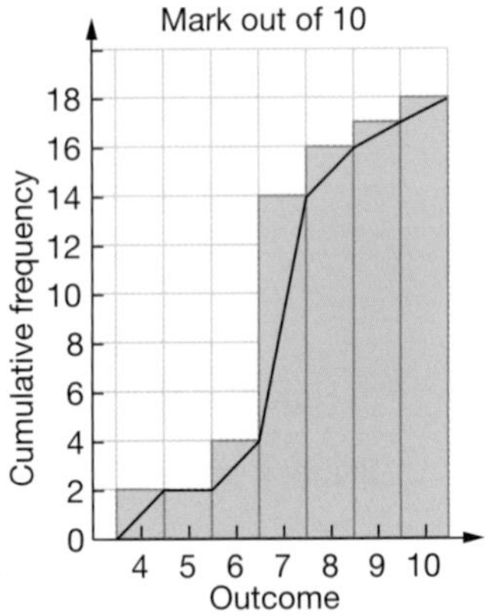

d

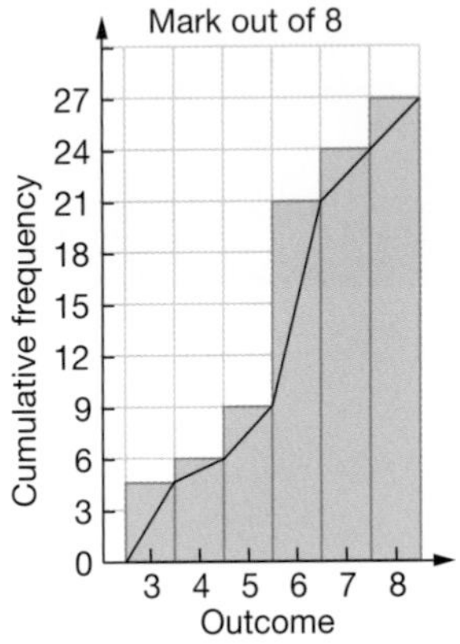

e

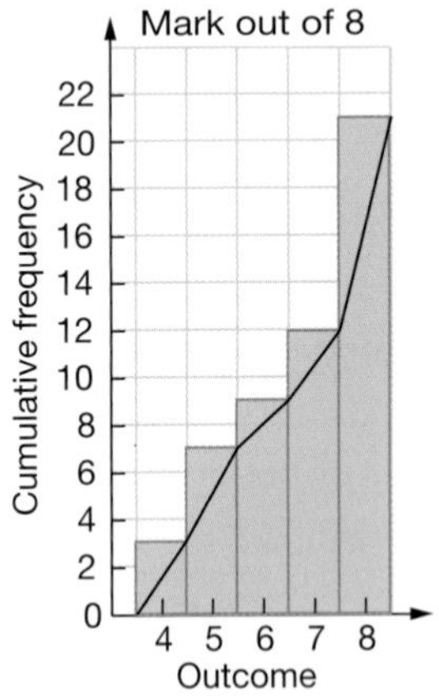

f

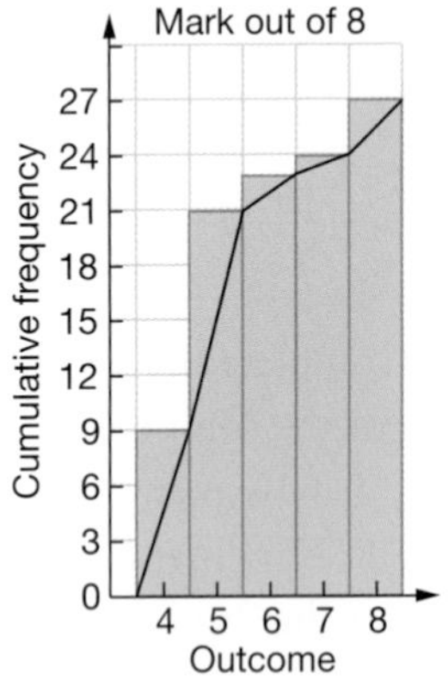

9 The number of cans of drink sold by a shop each day is shown in this table of grouped data.

a Construct a cumulative frequency histogram and ogive.

b Determine the median class.

No. of cans sold (x)	*c.c.*	Frequency (f)	*c.f.*
16–22	19	7	7
23–29	26	18	25
30–36	33	18	43
37–43	40	15	58
44–50	47	8	66
51–57	54	4	70

10 From this frequency histogram:

a determine what the class groupings must have been if the data are discrete whole numbers

b construct a cumulative frequency histogram and ogive

c determine the median class.

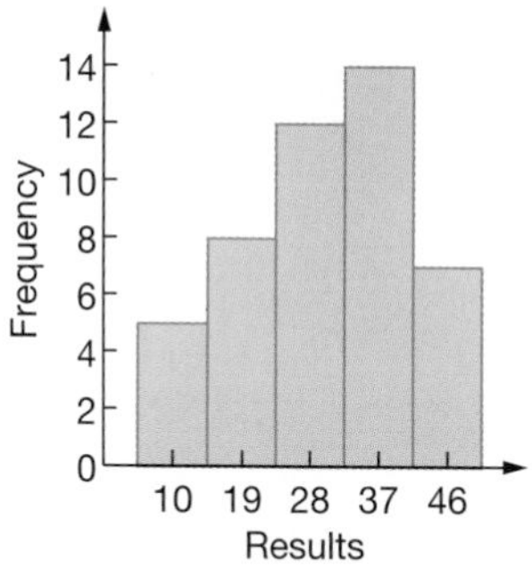

11 From this cumulative frequency diagram:

a determine the median class

b complete the table below to show the frequency of each class

c.c.	2	7	12	17	22	27	32
f							

c determine the modal class

d calculate the mean.

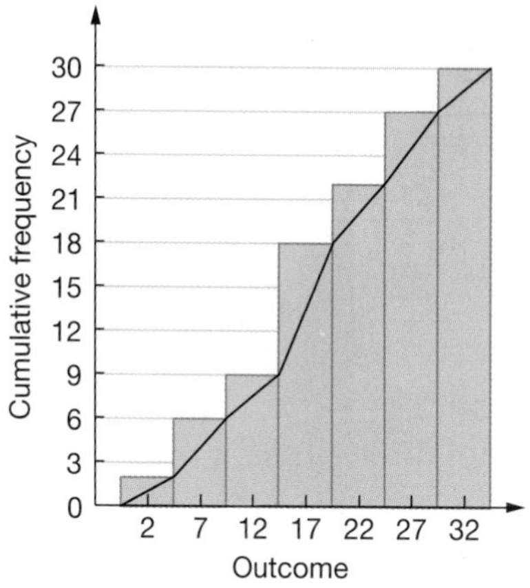

12 The exam results for Year 9 students have been collated in this grouped frequency distribution table.

Class	*c.c.*	Tally	Frequency (f)	$f \times c.c.$	*c.f.*
1–10	5·5	卌 ||||	9	49·5	9
11–20	15·5	卌 卌 卌	15	232·5	24
21–30	25·5	卌 卌 卌 ||||	19	484·5	43
31–40	35·5	卌 卌 卌 ||	17	603·5	60
41–50	45·5	卌 卌 卌 卌	20	910	80
51–60	55·5	卌 卌 卌 ||	17	943·5	97
61–70	65·5	卌 卌 卌 卌 |	21	1375·5	118
71–80	75·5	卌 卌 卌 |	16	1208	134
81–90	85·5	卌 卌 卌 |||	18	1539	152
91–100	95·5	卌 |||	8	764	160

Total: $\Sigma f = 160$ $\Sigma(f \times c.c.) = 8110$

a What is the greatest possible range for this data?
b What is the modal class?
c Calculate a value for the mean.
d Construct a cumulative frequency histogram and ogive.
e From your graph, determine the median class.
f Considering part e, what would be a reasonable single numerical value for the median?
g What percentage of students obtained: i more than 80 ii 20 or less iii more than 50?

Weather bureaus around the world keep statistics on many aspects of weather. Average rainfall and average temperature are often quoted in weather broadcasts.

14:03 Measures of spread: Interquartile range

PREP QUIZ 14:03

Set A: 8, 8, 8, 8, 8	Set D: 8, 8, 8, 8, 8
Set B: 7, 8, 8, 8, 8	Set E: 7, 8, 8, 8, 9
Set C: 1, 8, 8, 8, 8	Set F: 6, 7, 8, 9, 10

Find the range of the scores in:

1 Set A **2** Set B **3** Set C

4 Which set contains an outlier?

5 Is the range affected by an outlier?

Find the mean in:

6 Set D **7** Set E **8** Set F

9 Which set of scores is the least spread out?

10 Which set of scores is the most spread out?

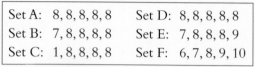

- So far we have concentrated on finding the measures of central tendency: mode, mean and median. These values tell us how the scores tend to cluster.
- We have used the range as a measure of spread. But, as seen in the Prep quiz above, the range is easily affected by an outlier.
- A much better measure of spread than the range is the interquartile range (IQR). This is the range of the middle 50% of scores.

WORKED EXAMPLE 1

Find the interquartile range of the scores:
1, 2, 2, 5, 7, 9, 10, 10, 11, 11, 11, 11

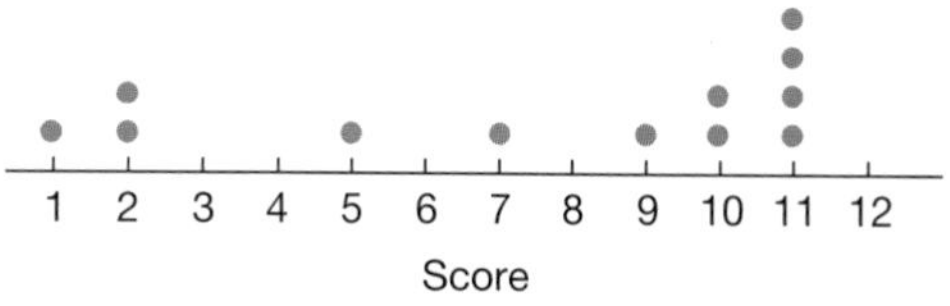

Method 1

- Make sure that the scores are in ascending order.
- Divide the scores into four equal groups. (This is not always possible. See Worked Example 2.)

1, 2, 2, ↑ 5, 7, 9, ↑ 10, 10, 11, ↑ 11, 11, 11,

1st quartile (25th percentile): $Q_1 = \dfrac{2+5}{2} = 3{\cdot}5$

Median (50th percentile): $Q_2 = \dfrac{9+10}{2} = 9{\cdot}5$

3rd quartile (75th percentile): $Q_3 = \dfrac{11+11}{2} = 11$

The 1st quartile (Q_1) is 3·5, which lies half-way between 2 and 5.
The 2nd quartile (median) is 9·5, which lies half-way between 9 and 10.
The 3rd quartile (Q_3) is 11.

- The interquartile range is the difference between the 3rd and 1st quartiles.

$$\begin{aligned}\text{Interquartile range} &= Q_3 - Q_1\\ &= 11 - 3{\cdot}5\\ &= 7{\cdot}5\end{aligned}$$

Method 2

- Construct a cumulative frequency polygon.
- Come across from the vertical axis to the polygon from positions representing 25%, 50% and 75% of the scores. Take the readings on the horizontal axis to obtain the 1st quartile, median and 3rd quartile.

x	f	$c.f.$
1	1	1
2	2	3
3	0	3
4	0	3
5	1	4
6	0	4
7	1	5
8	0	5
9	1	6
10	2	8
11	4	12

$\Sigma f = 12$

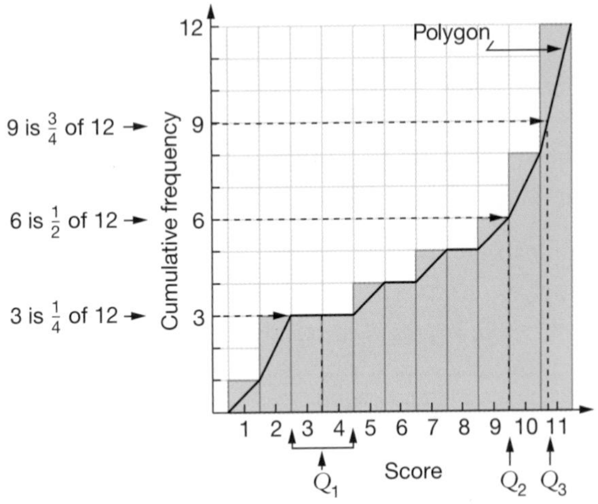

The 1st quartile (Q_1) is somewhere in the range 2·5 to 4·5, as the polygon has the height 3 for those values. We resolve this problem by taking the average of 2·5 and 4·5.

$$\therefore\ Q_1 = \frac{2{\cdot}5 + 4{\cdot}5}{2}$$
$$= 3{\cdot}5$$

Quartile is similar to the word quarter. Quartiles divide the data into four equal groups.

The median (Q_2) is seen to be 9·5.

The 3rd quartile (Q_3) is seen to be 11 (or 10·75 if we consider the horizontal scale to be continuous rather than discrete).

The interquartile range $= Q_3 - Q_1$
$= 11 - 3{\cdot}5$
$= 7{\cdot}5$

The interquartile range is more useful when the number of scores is large. When the number of scores is small (e.g. 7), it is hard to define 'the middle half of the scores'.

The **interquartile range** is:
- the range of the middle 50% of the scores
- the difference between the points below which 75% and 25% of scores fall (the difference between the third and first quartiles)
- the median of the upper half of the scores minus the median of the lower half.

WORKED EXAMPLE 2

Find the interquartile range for the following sets of scores.

Set A: 1, 2, 2, 5, 7, 9, 10, 10, 11, 11, 11

Set B: 1, 2, 2, 5, 7, 9, 10, 10, 11, 11

Solution

When the number of scores in a set is not a multiple of 4, they cannot be divided into 4 equal groups.

Set A has 11 scores. Hence, the middle score, 9, is the median (Q_2).

The middle score of the bottom 5 scores is Q_1.

The middle score of the top 5 scores is Q_3.

1, 2, (2), 5, 7, (9), 10, 10, (11), 11, 11

1st quartile $Q_1 = 2$ | Median $Q_2 = 9$ | 3rd quartile $Q_3 = 11$

$$\begin{aligned}\text{The interquartile range} &= Q_3 - Q_1\\ &= 11 - 2\\ &= 9\end{aligned}$$

Set B has 10 scores. Hence, the median is between the 5th and 6th scores.

This divides the scores into two groups of 5 scores.

The middle scores of the bottom and top groups are Q_1 and Q_3 respectively.

1, 2, (2), 5, 7, (8) 9, 10, (10), 11, 11

1st quartile $Q_1 = 2$ | Median $Q_2 = \frac{7+9}{2} = 8$ | 3rd quartile $Q_3 = 10$

$$\begin{aligned}\text{The interquartile range} &= Q_3 - Q_1\\ &= 10 - 2\\ &= 8\end{aligned}$$

Exercise 14:03

P Foundation worksheet 14:03 Interquartile range

1 Use Method 1 (Worked Example 1 on page 431) to find the interquartile range of each set of scores. (Rewrite the scores in order as the first step in each case.)

a 6, 4, 3, 8, 5, 4, 2, 7

b 1, 5, 2, 6, 3, 8, 7, 5, 4, 5, 7, 9

c 60, 84, 79, 83, 94, 88, 92, 99, 80, 90, 95, 78

d 15, 43, 30, 22, 41, 30, 27, 25, 28, 20, 19, 22, 25, 24, 33, 31, 41, 40, 49, 37

e 56, 83, 60, 72, 61, 52, 73, 24, 88, 70, 57, 63, 60, 48, 36, 53, 65, 49, 62, 65

2 The scores of 32 students have been used to graph this cumulative frequency histogram and polygon. Use the graph to find:

- **a** the median, Q_2
- **b** the 1st quartile, Q_1
- **c** the 3rd quartile, Q_3
- **d** the interquartile range, $Q_3 - Q_1$.

(*Note:* Here the answers are whole numbers.)

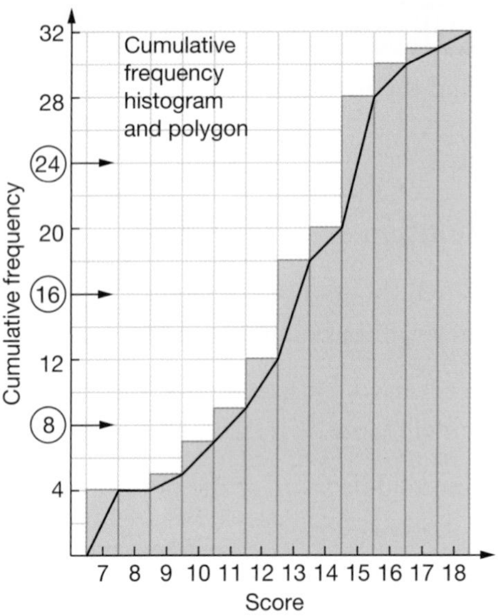

3 The same 32 students sat for a second test. The results have been used to draw this graph. Use the graph to find:

- **a** the median, Q_2
- **b** the 1st quartile, Q_1
- **c** the 3rd quartile, Q_3
- **d** the interquartile range, $Q_3 - Q_1$.

(*Note:* Here some answers will involve decimals.)

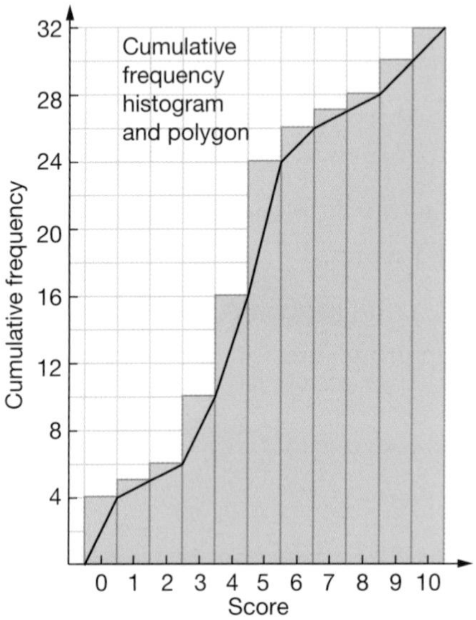

4 Make up a frequency distribution table for these scores.

7 8 6 9 4 6 5 5 4 2 3 7 6 6 5 8 4 5 6 4
7 6 8 5 3 4 8 9 6 5 4 5 7 3 6 6 5 5 5 6

Use your frequency distribution table to find:

- **a** the interquartile range using Method 1
- **b** the interquartile range using Method 2.

5 Use a cumulative frequency polygon to find the interquartile range for each of the following.

a

Marks	Frequency
16	3
17	4
18	5
19	5
20	3

b

Times	Frequency
35	3
36	4
37	7
38	10
39	18
40	18

6 Find the interquartile ranges of the following sets of scores.

a 25, 45, 46, 50, 58, 58, 65, 66, 70, 90

b 25, 25, 26, 26, 26, 28, 29, 30, 30, 32, 32

c 45, 45, 56, 56, 58, 59, 59, 59, 80

7 Use the cumulative frequency polygons to find the interquartile range of each set of scores.

a

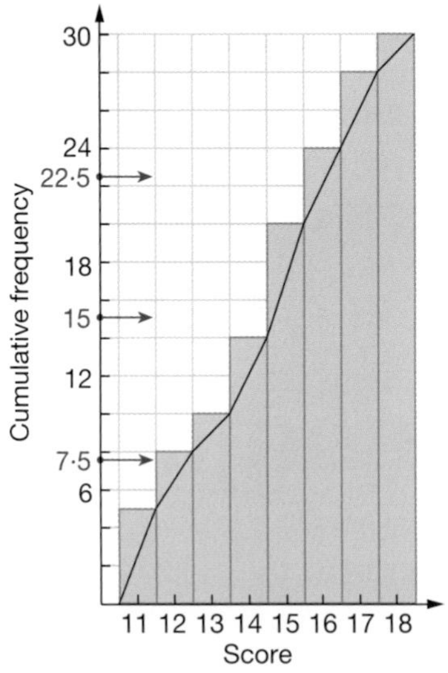

b

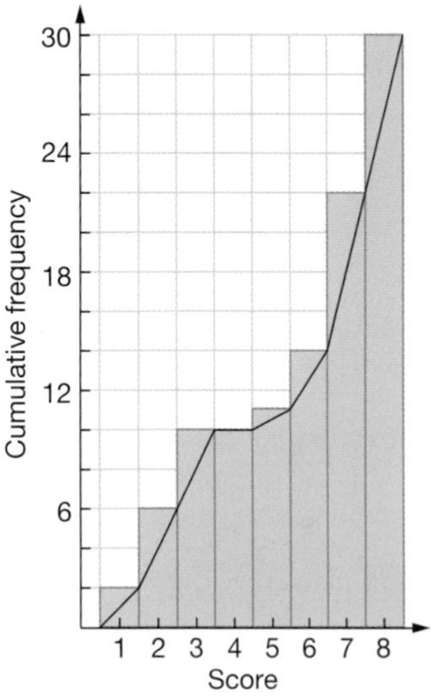

8 A cumulative frequency polygon (ogive) can also be used to obtain the interquartile range for grouped data. The weights of 128 boys were measured to the nearest kilogram and grouped in classes of 50–54 kg, 55–59 kg and so on up to 85–89 kg.

Use the ogive to estimate the following.

a 1st quartile

b 3rd quartile

c interquartile range.

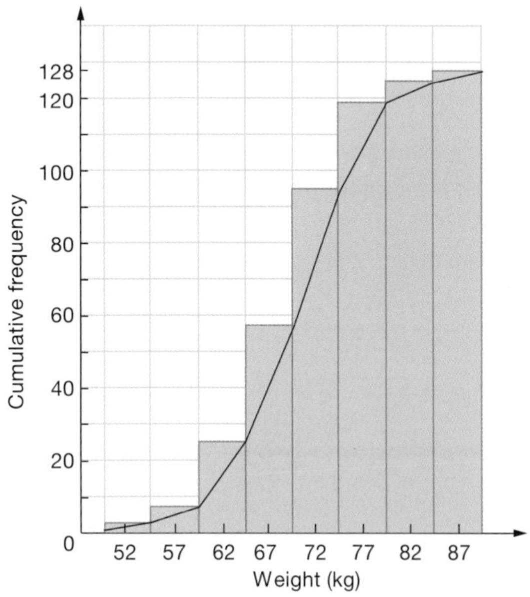

9 Find the quartiles for each of the following sets of data and then find the interquartile range. (Note that in both the dot plot and the stem-and-leaf plot, the scores have already been arranged in order.)

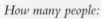

a

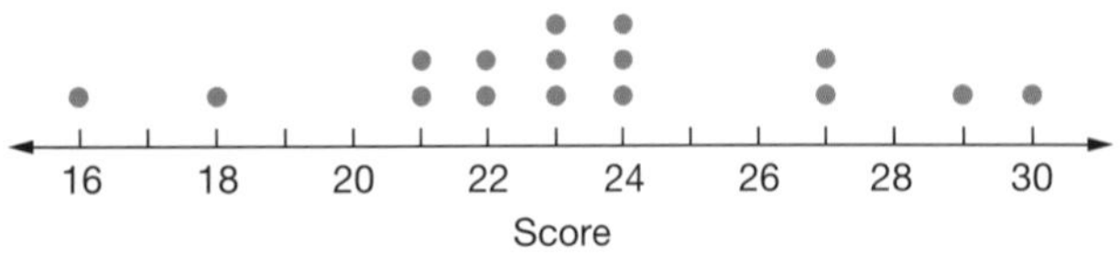

b

Stem	Leaf
3	8
4	2 6 9
5	3 3 6 7
6	0 1 3 3 4 7 8
7	4 6 6 8 9
8	3 4 8 9

FUN SPOT 14:03 WHY DID THE ROBBER FLEE FROM THE MUSIC STORE?

Work out the answer to each part and write the letter for that part in any box that is above the correct answer.

In a coordination test, 12 students were rated 1 (poor) to 6 (outstanding).
The results are shown in the frequency table.

x	f	*c.f.*
1	4	
2	2	
3	1	
4	2	
5	1	
6	2	

What is:

A the mode
E the range
F the mean
F the cumulative frequency of 5
E the median
E the highest score
R the fraction of scores that are 6
H the cumulative frequency of 6?

How many people:

H were rated as outstanding
H were rated higher than 6
I were rated less than 4
L were rated poor?

One of these students is selected at random.
What is the probability that the student's rating is:

N 3
T less than 3
W anything but 3?
O 1
U less than 5

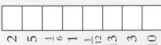

2	5	$\frac{1}{6}$	1	$\frac{1}{12}$	13	3	10

$\frac{11}{12}$	7	$\frac{1}{2}$	12	$\frac{1}{2}$	0	2.5	4	$\frac{3}{4}$	$\frac{1}{2}$	6

14:04 Box plots

In Stage 4, the dot plot and stem-and-leaf plot were used to illustrate certain aspects of a set of scores or distribution.

Another type of display is the box-and-whisker plot, or more simply, box plot. This is drawn using a **five-point summary** of the data as shown below.

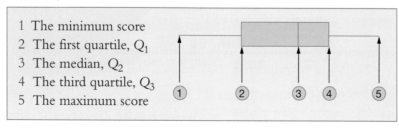

1 The minimum score
2 The first quartile, Q_1
3 The median, Q_2
4 The third quartile, Q_3
5 The maximum score

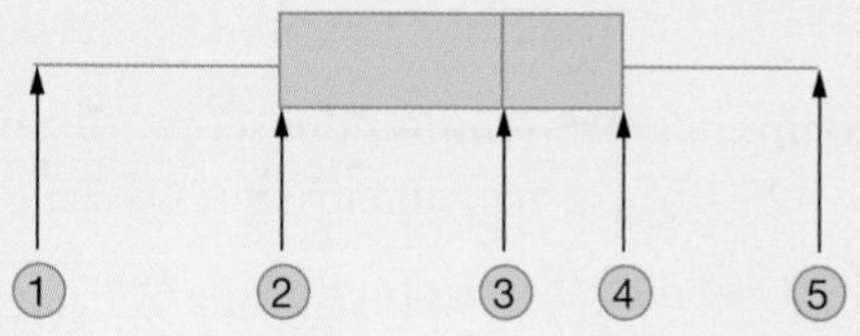

In a box plot:

- the box shows the middle 50% (the interquartile range) between Q_1 and Q_3
- the whiskers extend from the box to the highest and lowest scores
- the whiskers show the range of the scores.

WORKED EXAMPLE 1

The scores in an assessment task for a class were as follows.

40 71 74 20 43 63 83 57 63 26 43 87 74 89 66 63

Find the five-point summary of these marks and use it to construct a box plot.

Solution

Rearrange the scores in order and find Q_2, then Q_1 and Q_3.

20 26 40 43 43 57 63 63 63 66 71 74 74 83 87 89

(Q_1 between 43 and 43; Q_2 between 63 and 63; Q_3 between 74 and 74)

The five-point summary is (20, 43, 63, 74, 89).

Use the five-point summary and a suitable scale (1 mark = 1 mm) to construct the box-and-whisker diagram or box plot.

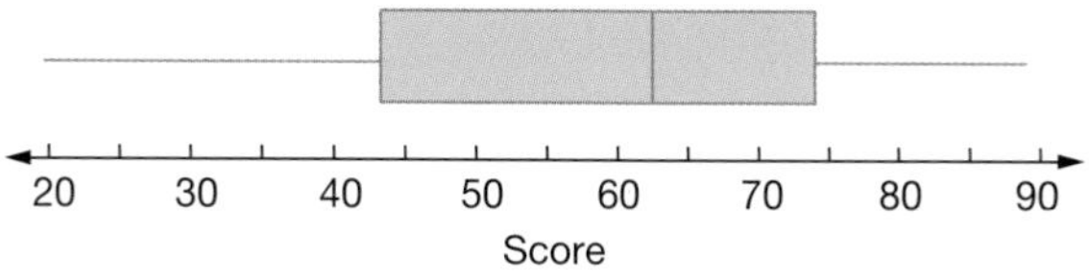

WORKED EXAMPLE 2

Use the box plot to find the:

a range
b interquartile range
c median
d percentage of scores above 60
e percentage of scores below 36.

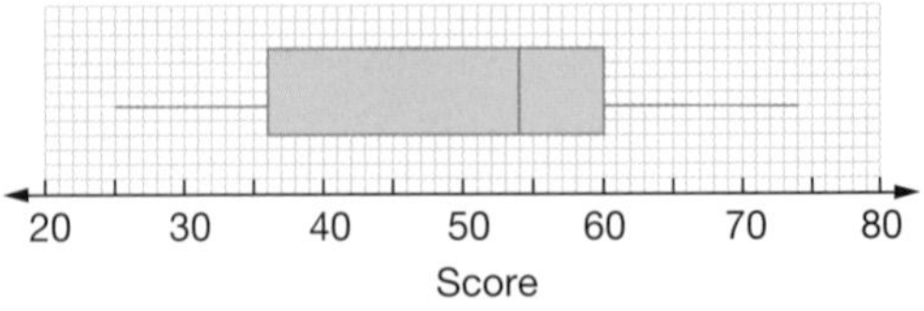

Solution

a Range = maximum score − minimum score
$= 74 - 25$
$= 49$

b Interquartile range $= Q_3 - Q_1$
$= 60 - 36$
$= 24$

c Median = 54

d As $Q_3 = 60$, 25% of the scores are above 60.

e As $Q_1 = 36$, 25% of the scores are below 36.

Exercise 14:04

1 Use each box plot to find the:
i median ii range iii interquartile range.

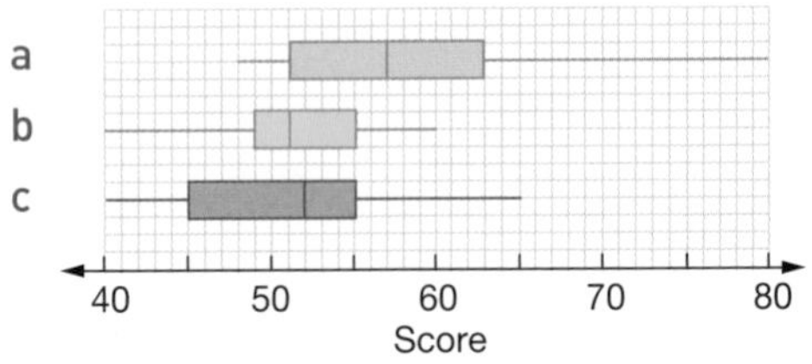

2 Find the five-point summary for each of the following sets of data and use it to construct a box plot.
a 7, 7, 8, 8, 8, 9, 9, 9, 10, 12, 12, 12
b 16, 24, 25, 25, 26, 28, 28, 28, 28, 30, 32, 33, 34, 34, 37, 38
c 14, 19, 29, 36, 40, 43, 43, 44, 46, 46, 47, 49

3 Find the five-point summary for each of the following sets of data and use it to construct a box plot.
a 43, 37, 42, 48, 39, 39, 40, 40, 44, 47, 45, 44
b 75, 78, 63, 59, 68, 72, 74, 83, 87, 86, 59, 75, 82, 82, 84, 85, 77, 76, 70, 83

A dot plot or stem-and-leaf plot is helpful when you have to sort unordered data.

4 These double box plots represent the distance travelled to school by members of Year 9 and Year 10.

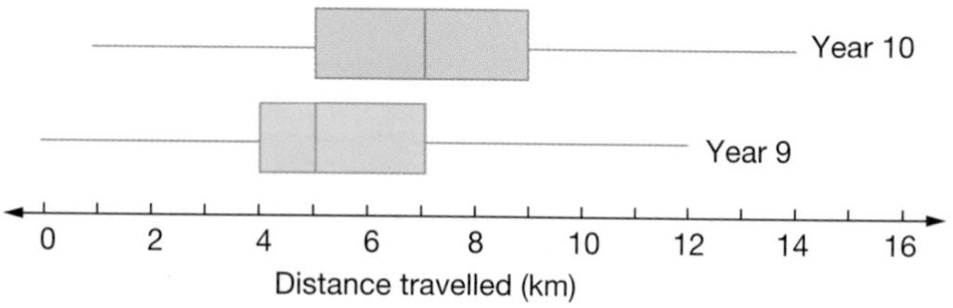

a What percentage of Year 9 students travel:
 i farther than 7 km ii farther than 5 km?
b What percentage of Year 10 students travel:
 i farther than 7 km ii farther than 5 km?
c Find the interquartile range for:
 i Year 9 ii Year 10
d Which group does more travelling?

5 a Use the dot plot to find the five-point summary for the scores.
b Construct a box plot for the scores.

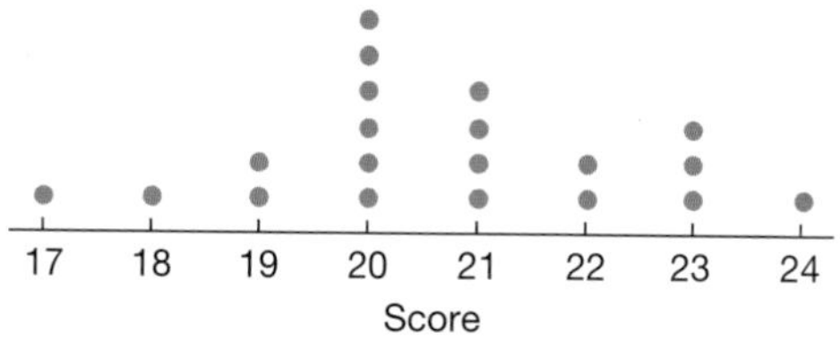

6 The marks of 24 students in a half-yearly test are recorded in the stem-and-leaf plot.
a Find the five-point summary for these marks.
b Construct a box plot for the marks.

Test scores

Stem	Leaf
2	6 7 8
3	5 8 8 9
4	0 1 3 8 9
5	2 5 6 7 7
6	7 9 9
7	5 5
8	2 2

7 Ray and Ken play 40 games of golf over a 1-year period. Their scores are shown on the double box plots below.

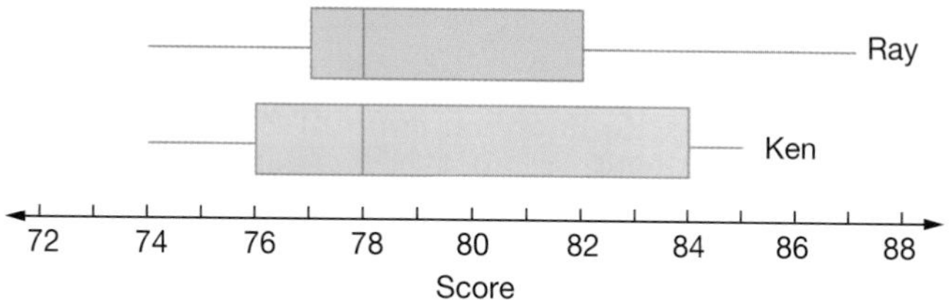

a What is the five-point summary for Ken's scores?
b Which golfer's scores have the smaller range?
c Which golfer's scores have the smaller interquartile range?
d Given your answers to **b** and **c**, which golfer do you think is the most consistent? Give a reason for your answer.

8 Rick recorded how long it took him to drive to work over 28 consecutive days. The times taken to the nearest minute are shown in the frequency table.

Time (minutes)	38	39	40	41	42	43	44	52
Frequency	1	2	6	7	5	4	2	1

One year later, after the addition of traffic lights and other traffic management measures, Rick repeated the process and obtained the following results.

Time (minutes)	38	39	40	41	42	43	45
Frequency	1	4	8	9	4	1	1

Draw double box plots to illustrate the before and after results and use them to comment on the effectiveness of the traffic changes.

INVESTIGATION 14:04 CODE BREAKING AND STATISTICS

Codebreakers use statistics to help decipher codes. They use the facts that certain letters are more common than others. What letter of the alphabet appears most often? What is the most common vowel? What consonant occurs most often?

1 Write what you think the answers are to the three questions above.

2 Use the statements above to do an alphabetic analysis. Were your answers in **1** supported by the statistics?

As well as deciphering codes, mathematicians are often employed to devise security codes to prevent access by unauthorised users. In particular, cryptographers are employed to stop computer hackers from accessing computer records.

On one side we have mathematicians trying to break codes, and on the other side we have mathematicians trying to design codes that cannot be broken.

14:05 Comparing sets of data

Statistics are often used to look at the similarities and differences between sets of data. Here are some examples.

- Teachers are often interested in comparing the marks of a class on different topics or comparing the marks of different classes on the same topic.
- Medical researchers could compare the heart rates of different groups of people after exercise.
- Coaches might compare the performances of different players over a season or the same player over different seasons.
- Managing directors of companies could compare sales and profits over different periods.

As well as calculating the measures of cluster (the mean, median and mode) and the measures of spread (the range and interquartile range), a comparison would usually involve using graphical methods. Back-to-back stem-and-leaf plots, double-column graphs, double box plots and histograms are useful ways of comparing sets of data.

Shape of a distribution

A significant feature of a set of data is its shape. This is most easily seen using a histogram or stem-and-leaf plot. For some data sets with many scores and a large range, the graph is often shown as a curve.

The graphs below show the results of 120 students on four different problem-solving tests.

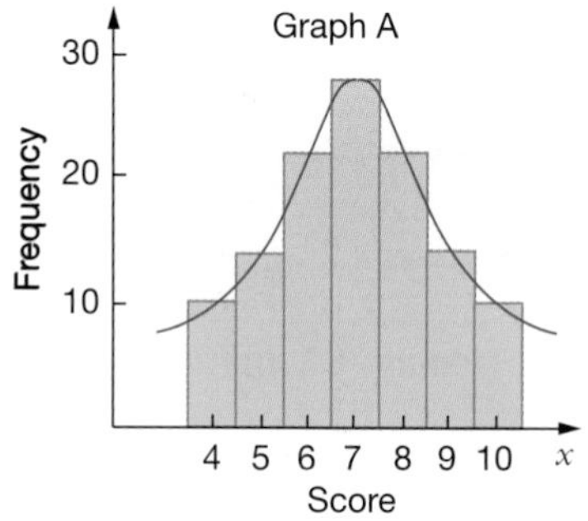

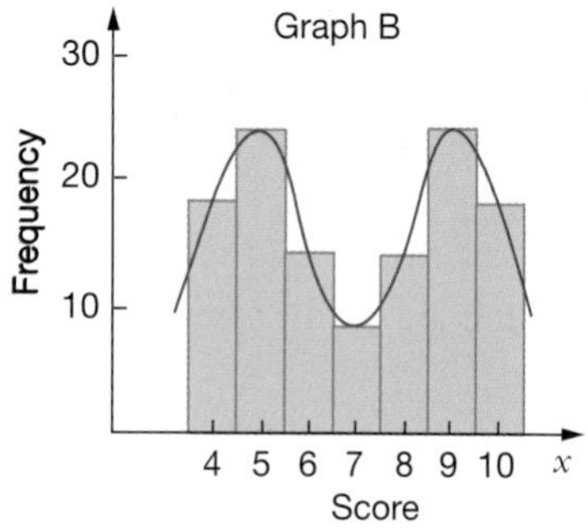

- Graphs A and B are examples of **symmetric distributions**.
- Graph A has one mode; it is said to be unimodal.
- Graph B has two modes; it is **bi-modal**.
- A unimodal symmetric distribution is quite common in statistics and is called a **normal distribution**.
- Symmetric distributions are evenly distributed about the mean.

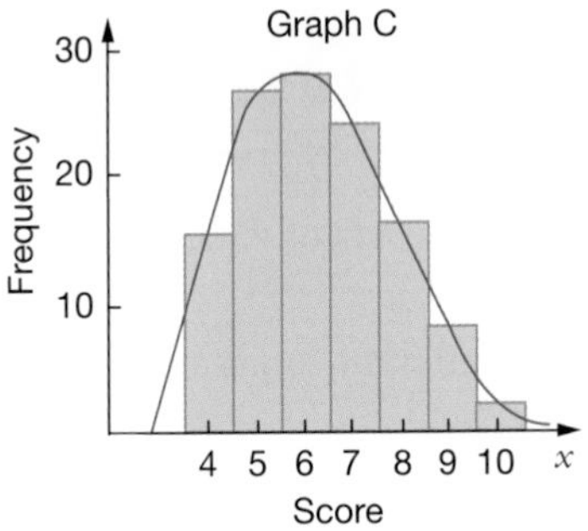

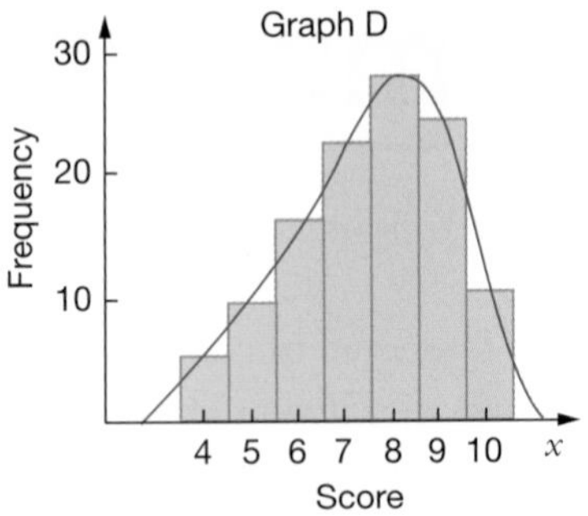

- Graphs C and D are examples of **skewed distributions**.
- If most of the scores are at the low end, the skew is said to be positive.
- If most of the scores are at the high end, the skew is said to be negative.

WORKED EXAMPLE

Our class was given a topic test in which we performed poorly. Our teacher decided to give a similar test one week later, after a thorough revision of the topic. The results are shown on this back-to-back stem-and-leaf plot. (This is an ordered display.)

Compare the results of the class on the two tests. Note that two students were absent during Test 1.

Test scores (4|1 represents 41)

Test 1	Stem	Test 2
9 8 6 6 0	3	
9 7 7 3 1 1 1	4	3 6 6 8 8
8 8 5 3 3 0	5	1 7 9 9
9 8 7 5 3	6	3 8 9
	7	0 5 5 5 8 9
	8	2 6 7 7
0	9	0 0 1 3

Solution

- The improvement in the second test is clear to see. The medians, which are easily found, verify this, as do the means.

	Test 1	Test 2
Median	49·5	72·5
Mean	51·5	69·8

Test 1 IQR = 60·5 – 41 = 19·5
Test 2 IQR = 86 – 57 = 29

- The spread of the scores in Test 1 is smaller than in Test 2. The interquartile range confirms this.

	Test 1	Test 2
Interquartile range	19·5	29
Range	60	50

The presence of the outlier in Test 1 had made the range an unreliable measure of spread.

The double box plots clearly show these features.

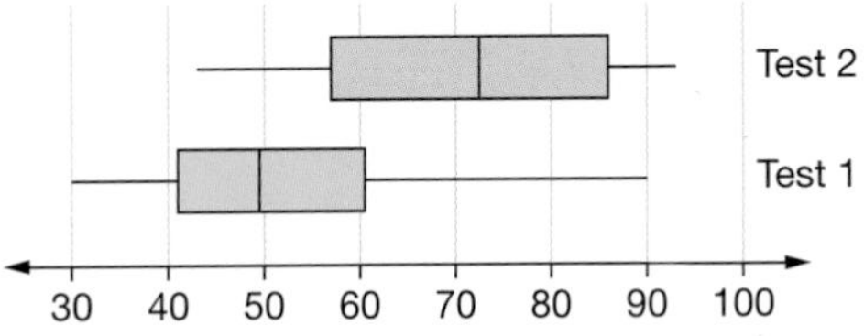

Test 1 is positively skewed as more scores are at the 'low end' indicated by the median being lower than the mean.
Test 2 is negatively skewed as more scores are at the 'high end', indicated by the median being greater than the mean.

Exercise 14:05

1 The age distributions of students in four high schools are shown below.

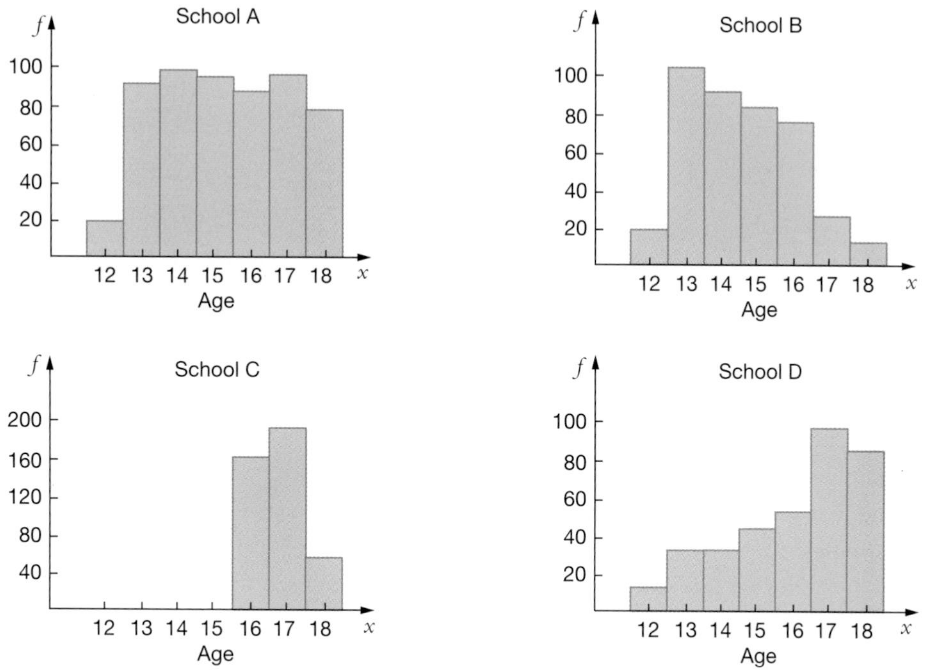

a Which schools' age distributions are skewed? What causes the skew?
b Which schools' age distribution is closest to being distributed evenly?
c In which school would the mean age of a student be:
  i closest to 15   ii below 15   iii over 15   iv the largest?

2 The marks for two classes on the same test are shown in the dot plots below.

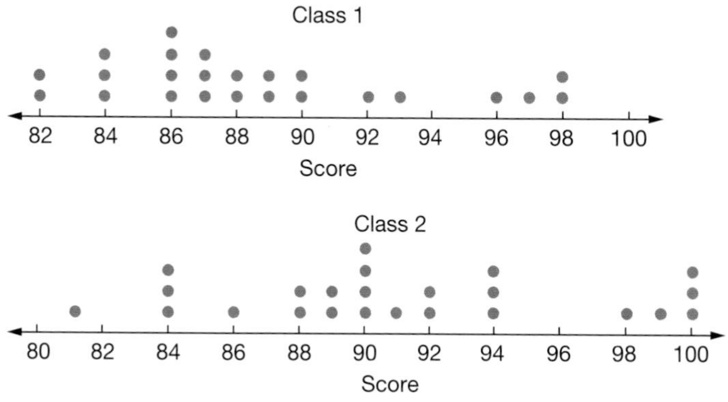

a Which set of results is more skewed?
b By just looking at the dot plots, estimate which class has:
  i the higher mean   ii the greater spread of scores.
c Check your answer to part **b** by calculating the mean and range for each set of scores.

3 A school librarian was interested in comparing the number of books borrowed by boys and girls. At the end of the year, she looked at the number of books borrowed by each child and prepared the following graphs.

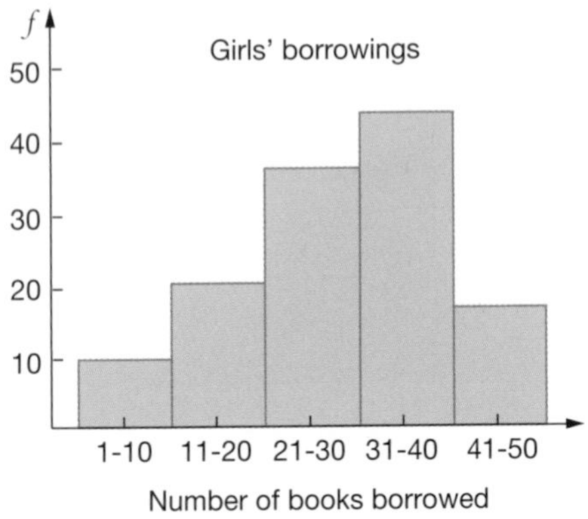

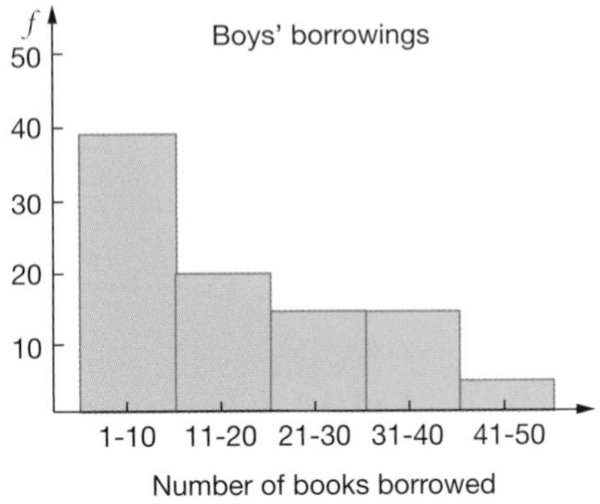

a Describe the shape of the distribution for:
  i the girls' borrowings
  ii the boys' borrowings.

b What is the first impression that the shapes of the distributions give about the boys' and girls' borrowings?

c Why do you think two grouped frequency histograms were used to display the results instead of a back-to-back stem-and-leaf plot?

d What sort of distribution would result if the librarian combined the boys' and girls' results?

4 The stem-and-leaf plot shows the marks of a class on two different topic tests.

a Which set of marks is nearly symmetric?

b Which set of marks has the smaller spread? What measures of spread can you use to support your answer?

c Calculate the median and mean for each set of marks. What do they suggest about the class performance on the two tests?

To check the shape of the distribution turn the stem-and-leaf plot side on.

Class tests

Topic 1	Stem	Topic 2
6 5	3	
9 3 0	4	4 6 7 9
9 8 4 3 0	5	4
9 8 8 6 0	6	2 3 7
9 8 4 4	7	0 8 8 9
6 5	8	3 5 8 8 8 9 9
	9	5

5 Thirty students entered a swimming program hoping to improve their swimming. Before and after the program, students were rated as non-swimmer (N), weak swimmer (W), competent swimmer (C), good swimmer (G) or excellent swimmer (E).

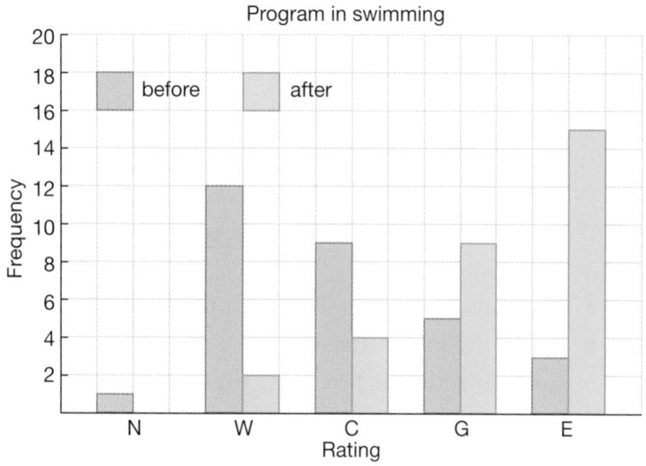

a What was the mode rating before the program?

b What was the mode rating after the program?

c Before the program, what percentage of students were rated either non-swimmers or weak swimmers?

d After the program, what percentage of students were rated good or excellent swimmers?

e How would you describe the success of the program?

6 In two problem-solving tests, 5 questions were given to a class. The scores are shown below.

Problem test 1

5 1 3 4 3 4 1 1 2 2 5 3 3 1 1 2 4 3 2 4 4 3 2

Problem test 2

0 2 4 4 2 2 3 0 0 2 4 4 1 3 3 2 2 3 2 2 0 2 2

a Arrange the scores into a frequency distribution table and use frequency histograms to display the data.

b Calculate the mean and median for each test. What do they suggest about the difficulty of the tests?

c Both sets of scores have a range of 4. Which set of scores has the greater spread? Give a reason for your answer.

7 This box plot represents the heights of 30 Year 10 students. The histogram also represents the heights of 30 students.

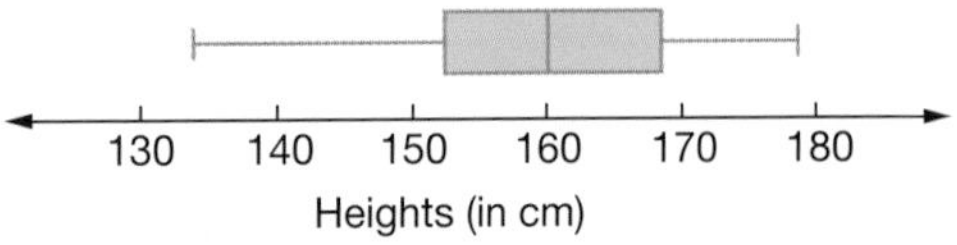

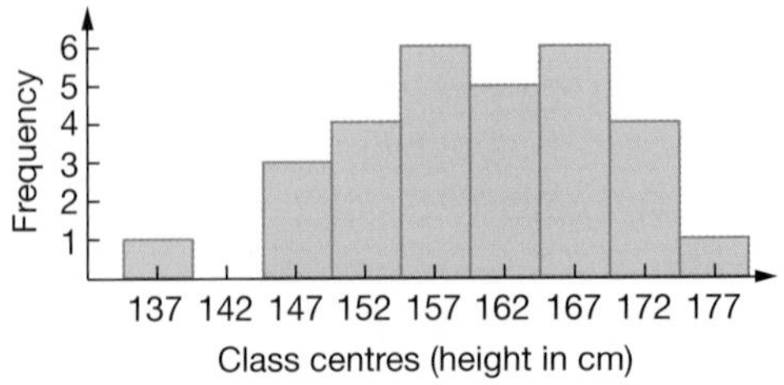

a What information is shown on the box plot?

b Could the information in the histogram represent the same 30 Year 10 students who are represented in the box plot? Explain.

8 A researcher tested two different brands of batteries to see how long they lasted. Her results are shown in the double box plots below.

Use the double box plots to compare the performance of Brand X and Brand Y.

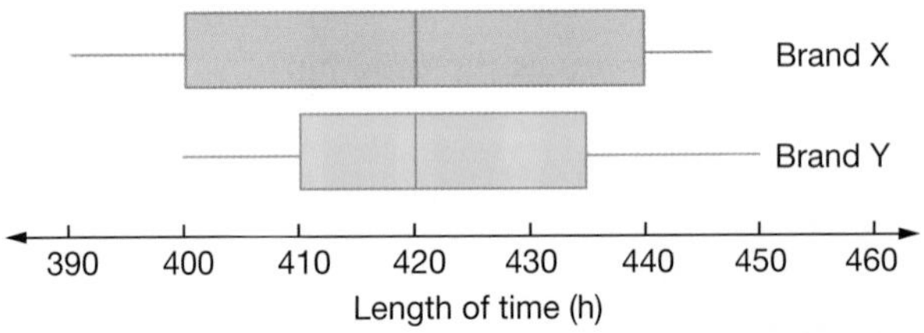

9 Two groups of adults underwent a simple fitness test. One minute after undergoing a period of strenuous exercise, their heart rates were measured.

The results are shown in the back-to-back stem-and-leaf plot.

a What does the shape of the stem-and-leaf plot suggest about the data?

b Calculate the median and interquartile range for each group and use them to compare the results for each group.

Heart rates

Group 1	Stem	Group 2
7 5 5	11	
9 9 9 9 8 8 7 7 6	12	5 5 6
6 6 4 4 0	13	4 6 8 8
4 2 0	14	2 3 6 6 7 8 8
	15	3 5 5 7
	16	2 4

10 A local council was interested in speeding up the time it took to approve applications to build a house. It looked at the time taken in days to process 40 applications. After reviewing its procedures and monitoring processes, it then looked at another 40 applications. The results are shown below.

Before

44	53	38	39	52	41	40	41
43	43	42	57	47	45	50	50
68	50	45	42	58	48	40	39
44	46	52	45	46	53	54	40
48	47	43	38	43	42	54	55

After

40	39	43	42	54	48	46	44
51	52	44	38	40	40	51	52
39	46	46	49	52	51	42	43
40	45	44	39	50	43	48	40
52	53	38	40	47	44	47	42

a Discuss an appropriate way to organise and display the data.

b What measures of cluster and spread would you use to describe the data?

c How effective have the council's review procedures been in reducing the approval time?

INVESTIGATION 14:05 THE AGEING POPULATION

The Australian Bureau of Statistics collects information on a wide variety of topics. This information is used by governments to help formulate social policy.

The gradual ageing of Australia's population has caused a rethinking of the government's policy towards pensions, superannuation and caring for the aged.

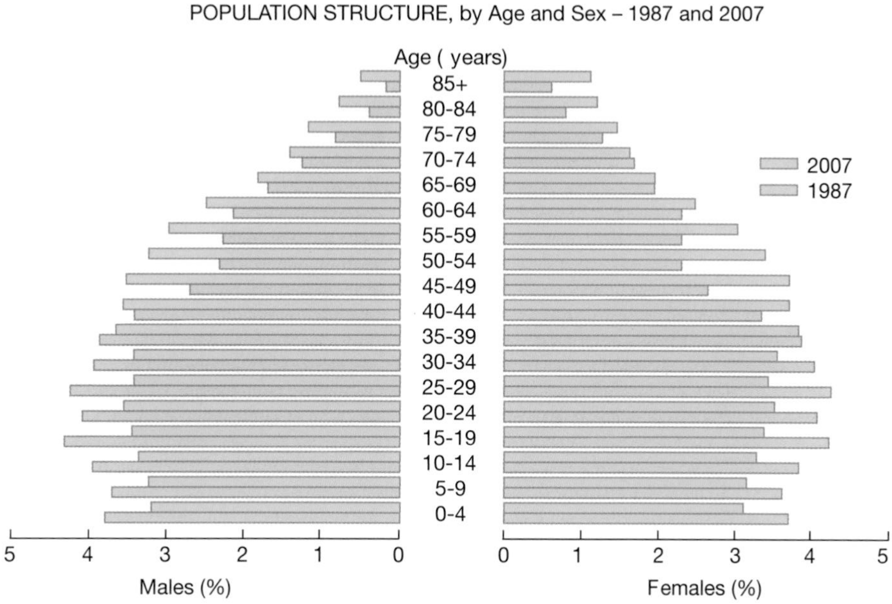

Where your answers are percentages, give them correct to one decimal place.

1 In 1987, what percentage of Australians were males aged:
   a 10–14 b 40–44 c 70–74?

2 In 2007, what percentage of Australians were males aged:
   a 10–14 b 40–44 c 70–74?

3 What do your answers to Questions **1** and **2** suggest about the changes in the male population over the 20 years from 1987 to 2007? Does this trend also occur in the female population?

4 a What percentage of Australians were aged 70 and over in:
   i 1987 ii 2007?
   b If there were 1 920 200 people aged over 70 in 2007, calculate the total population of Australia in that year. Give your answer to the nearest thousand.

5 The approximate number of Australian females aged 65–69 was 300 100 in 1987 and 401 200 in 2007 and yet, looking at the diagram, the percentage of females in the 65–69 age group was relatively similar in 1987 and 2007. How is this possible?

MATHS TERMS 14

box-and-whisker plot (box plot)
- a diagram obtained from the five-point summary
- the box shows the middle 50% of scores (the interquartile range)
- the whiskers show us the extent of the bottom and top quartiles as well as the range

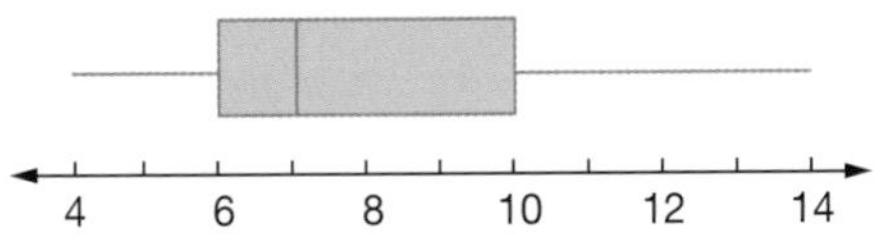

class centre
- the middle outcome of a class,
  e.g. the class 1–5 has a class centre of 3

class interval
- the size of the groups into which the data is organised,
  e.g. 1–5 (5 scores); 11–20 (10 scores)

cumulative frequency histogram (and polygon)
- these show the outcomes and their cumulative frequencies

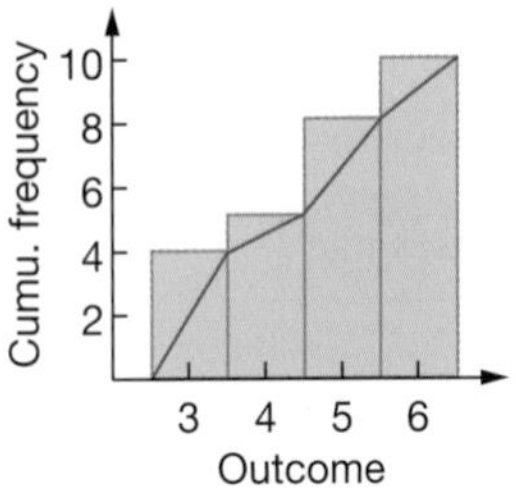

dot plot
- a graph that uses one axis and a number of dots above the axis

five-point summary
- a set of numbers consisting of the minimum score, the three quartiles and the maximum score

frequency
- the number of times an outcome occurs in the data,
  e.g. for the data 3, 6, 5, 3, 5, 5, 4, 3, 3, 6 the outcome 5 has a frequency of 3

frequency distribution table
- a table that shows all the possible outcomes and their frequencies (it usually is extended by adding other columns such as the cumulative frequency),

e.g.

Outcome	Frequency	Cumulative frequency
3	4	4
4	1	5
5	3	8
6	2	10

frequency histogram
- a type of column graph showing the outcomes and their frequencies,

e.g.

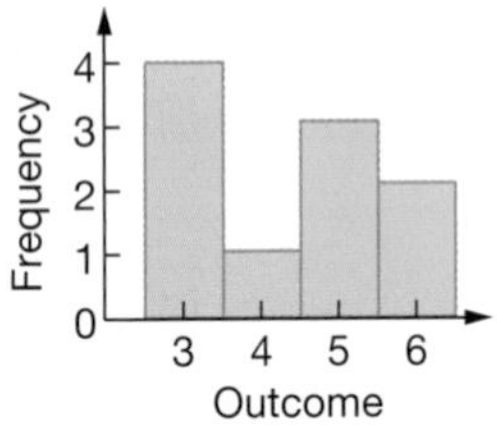

frequency polygon
- a line graph formed by joining the midpoints of the top of each column; to complete the polygon the outcomes immediately above and below those present are used (the heights of these columns is zero)

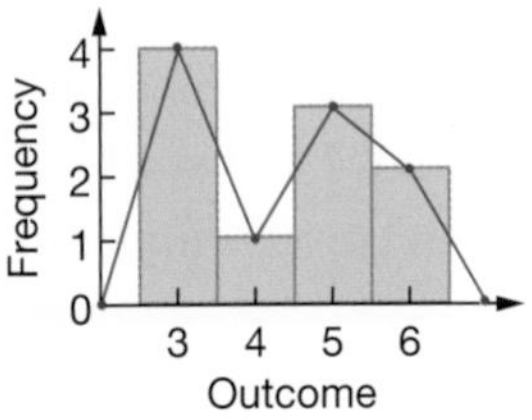

grouped data
- the organisation of data into groups or classes

interquartile range
- $IQR = Q_3 - Q_1$
- the range of the middle 50% of scores
- the median of the upper half of scores minus the median of the lower half of scores

mean
- the number obtained by 'evening out' all the scores until they are equal,
  e.g. if the scores 3, 6, 5, 3, 5, 5, 4, 3, 3, 6 were 'evened out', the number obtained would be 4·3
- to obtain the mean, use the formula:

$$\text{Mean} = \frac{\text{sum of the scores}}{\text{total number of scores}}$$

median
- the middle score for an odd number of scores, or the mean of the middle two scores for an even number of scores

median class
- in grouped data, the class that contains the median

mode (modal class)
- the outcome or class that contains the most scores

ogive
- this is another name for the cumulative frequency polygon

outcome
- a possible value of the data

outlier
- a score that is separated from the main body of scores

quartiles
- the points that divide the scores up into quarters
- the second quartile, Q_2, divides the scores into halves (Q_2 = median)
- the first quartile, Q_1, is the median of the lower half of scores
- the third quartile, Q_3, is the median of the upper half of scores

4 5 6 | 6 7 7 | 7 9 9 | 11 12 15

$Q_1 = 6 \quad Q_2 = 7 \quad Q_3 = 10$

range
- the difference between the highest and lowest scores

shape (of a distribution)
- a set of scores can be symmetric or skewed (see pages 441 and 442)

statistics
- the collection, organisation and interpretation of numerical data

stem-and-leaf plot
- a graph that shows the spread of scores without losing the identity of the data

Spreadsheets can be used to analyse data and display information. Statistical formulas can be entered in cells to add data or to calculate the mean.

DIAGNOSTIC TEST 14 STATISTICS

These questions reflect the important skills introduced in this chapter.
Errors made will indicate areas of weakness.
Each weakness should be treated by going back to the section listed.

1 The students of class 9M were given a reading test and rated from 0 (a poor reader) to 5 (an excellent reader). The results are given below. 14:01, 14:02

4	1	0	2	3	3	3	2	2	1
0	2	2	4	3	5	3	2	1	3
2	0	3	1	3	4	5	1	0	2

a Complete this frequency distribution table.

Outcome (x)	Tally	f	$c.f.$
0			
1			
2			
3			
4			
5			

Total:

b What is the frequency of 5?

c How many students were given a rating less than 4?

d On the same diagram, draw the frequency histogram and the frequency polygon.

e On the same diagram draw the cumulative frequency histogram and the cumulative frequency polygon.

f What is the range of these scores?

g Find the mode, median and mean for these scores.

2 Use your calculator to evaluate the mean for the scores in the following frequency tables. Give your answer correct to two decimal places. 14:01

a

Outcome	Freq.
27	18
28	50
29	23
30	9

b

Outcome	4·1	4·2	4·3	4·4	4·5	4·6	4·7
Freq.	7	11	16	8	12	7	3

3 These are the scores gained by each team competing in the Lithgow car rally this year. 14:01, 14:02

27	18	0	45	63	49	50	31	9	26
4	41	38	20	69	38	17	43	16	37
28	14	58	52	37	43	38	51	44	33
25	38	11	43	40	56	62	48	53	22

a Draw a grouped frequency table using classes 0–9, 10–19 etc. Use the columns: class, class centre, tally, frequency and cumulative frequency.

b Prepare a stem-and-leaf plot for the scores above.

4 Find the median for each of the following.

a

Outcome (x)	*c.f.*
4	3
5	7
6	10
7	16
8	23

b

Outcome (x)	*c.f.*
11	7
12	15
13	33
14	53
15	62

c

Outcome(x)	*c.f.*
1	24
2	37
3	44
4	47
5	50

5 Use the following graphs to calculate the median for each set of data. 14:02

a
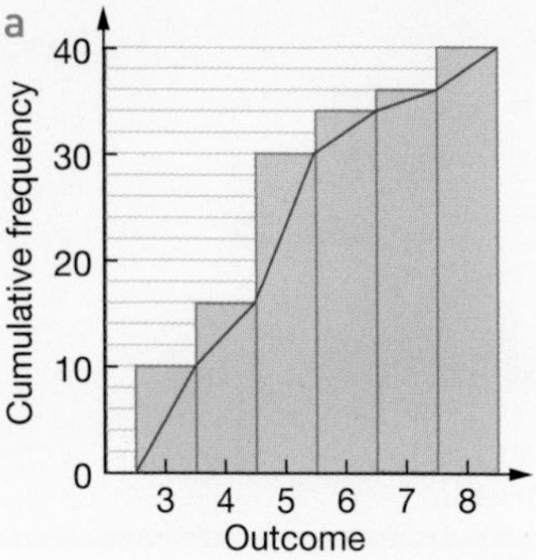

b
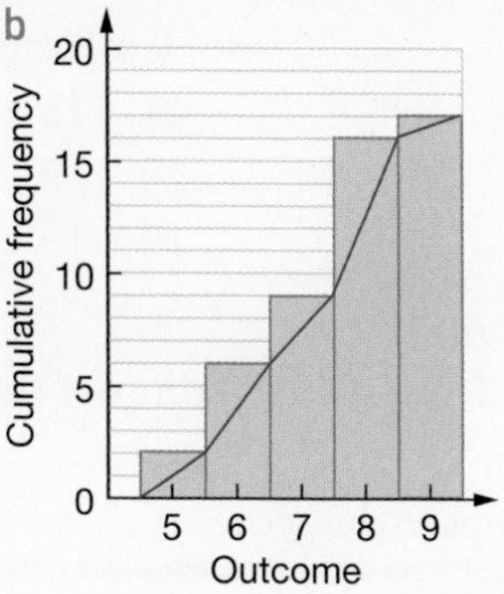

c
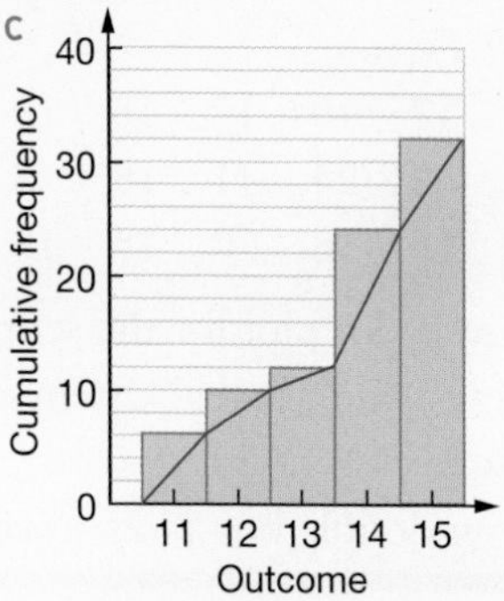

6 a Find the interquartile range of the scores: 14:03

1, 2, 2, 5, 7, 9, 10, 10, 11, 11, 11, 11

b Draw a cumulative frequency polygon using the frequency distribution table below and use it to find the interquartile range of the scores.

x	10	11	12	13	14	15	16	17	18	19
f	2	0	5	4	5	6	5	6	3	4

c The lengths of 16 fish caught were measured. The results are shown on this dot plot. What is the interquartile range?

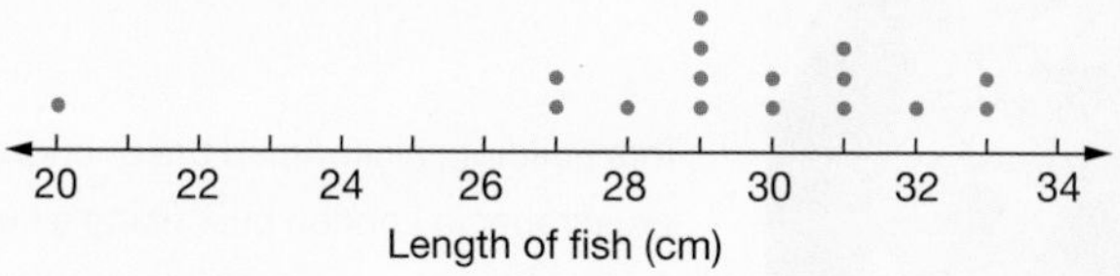

d What is the interquartile range of the times shown in the stem-and-leaf plot?

Time	
Stem	Leaf
3	8 8
4	0 3 4 5 8
5	1 3 4 4
6	0

7 Find the five-point summary for each set of data in Question 6. 14:04

8 Draw box plots for the data in Question 6 a, b and c. 14:04

9 These double box plots were drawn to compare the results of Year 10 in two tests. 14:05

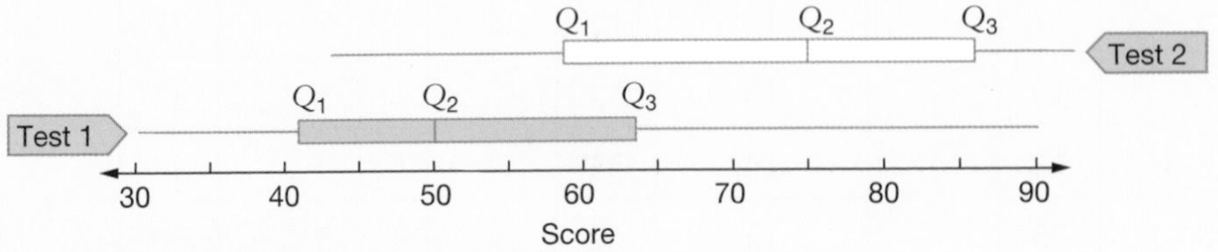

a By how much was the median for Test 2 higher than the median of Test 1?

b What was the range and interquartile range of Test 1?

10 *Test 1 scores*

12	17	19	12	15	10
9	22	24	11	18	8
25	15	18	20	18	18

Test 2 scores

21	15	18	7	11	16
20	12	23	12	10	13
12	19	12	14	20	9

a Draw a dot plot for the scores on Test 1.

b Draw a back-to-back stem-and-leaf plot to compare the scores on Test 1 and Test 2.

c Draw double box plots to compare the scores on Tests 1 and 2.

This building, nicknamed the Gherkin, is the first skyscraper in London built using a sustainable design. Sensors on the building collect data that is used to control the lighting, ventilation and heating, which reduces energy usage.

ASSIGNMENT 14A Chapter review

1 The average length of the two index fingers of 24 teachers was recorded. The results are shown on this dot plot.

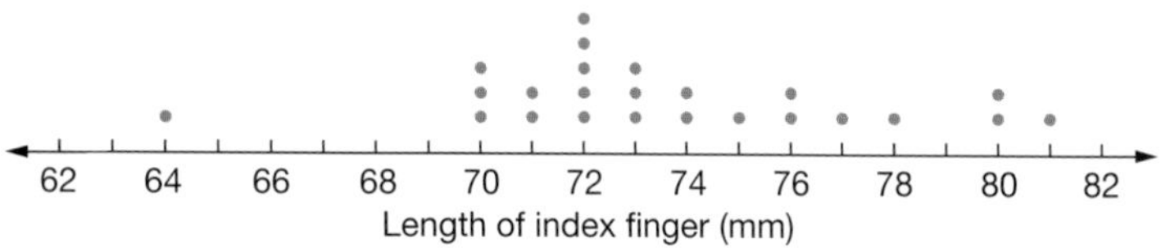

a Are any outliers present in this data?

b Find the five-point summary for the data if the outlier is:

i included ii omitted.

c What is the interquartile range if the outlier is:

i included ii omitted?

d Comment on the shape of the distribution (ignore the outlier in this case).

2 A group of Year 9 students sat for a college reading test and the results were entered in this stem-and-leaf plot.

a How many scored in the 50s?

b What was the mode of the results?

c How many students scored less than 50?

d How many students were tested?

e What was the median of the results?

f If 65 and above is considered to be a passing grade, how many passed?

g Make a grouped frequency table for this data using classes of 30–39, 40–49, …

Test results, Year 9 (7|3 represents 73)	
Stem	Leaf
3	1 8 2
4	6 3 3 1 3
5	4 1 1 5
6	2 2 8 4 7 7 1
7	6 3 4 6 5 5 1 4
8	2 6 6 7 3 3 1
9	2 9 9 1 0 0

3 Year 3 and Year 4 students were tested on their knowledge of multiplication tables. The results are shown in this back-to-back stem-and-leaf plot.

Compare the results of Year 3 and Year 4 on this test. (You will need to refer to at least one measure of cluster and one measure of spread.)

Test scores (5|1 represents 51)		
Year 3 results	Stem	Year 4 results
9 8 3 0	3	5
8 8 7 4 2 2 2	4	
8 7 7 4 0	5	1 4 6 6 9
7 6 3	6	0 2 2 5 8
1	7	3 6 8 8 9 9 9
	8	0 0

4 a For the data shown in this histogram, determine the:

i range

ii median

iii interquartile range

iv five-point summary.

b Use this information to construct a box plot.

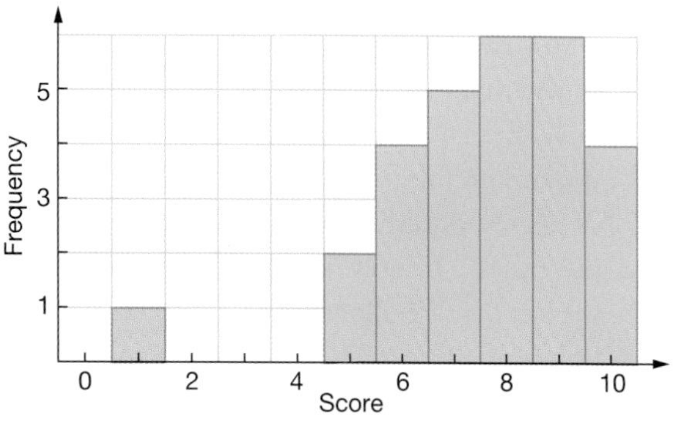

5 After the Year 8 semester exam the maths staff organised the 99 marks into a grouped frequency distribution. The results are shown in the table.

a Copy and complete the grouped frequency distribution table. Use it to find:
i the modal class ii the mean.

b Construct an ogive and use it to find the median class.

Class	Class centre ($c.c.$)	f	$c.f.$	$f \times c.c.$
10–19		2		
20–29		9		
30–39		10		
40–49		8		
50–59		16		
60–69		20		
70–79		13		
80–89		14		
90–99		7		

ASSIGNMENT 14B Working mathematically

1 Peter is now twice as old as Paul was when Peter was as old as Paul is now. How old is Peter if their ages add to 91?

2 Find the perimeter and area of this figure.

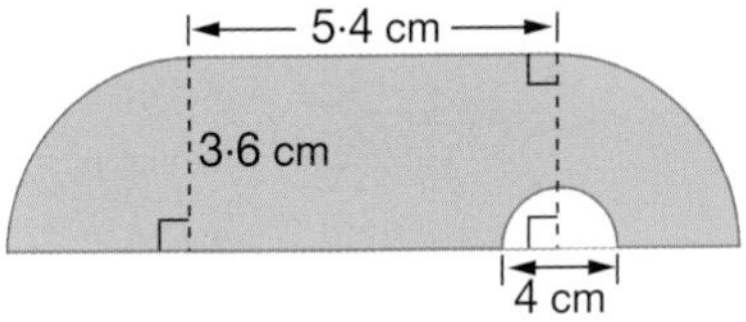

3 When this net is folded to form a cube, the numbers on the three faces that meet at each vertex are multiplied together. What is the smallest product possible?

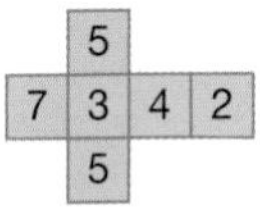

4 In a 360-minute tennis match, 4 players were always on the court. There were 12 players (6 from each team), and they were each on the court for the same amount of time. How many minutes did each player spend on the court?

5 The scores of all players in a recent golf tournament are recorded in the following table. Explain what calculations you would use to rate the holes and list them in order of degree of difficulty (1 the hardest to 4 the easiest). In golf, 'par' is the number of strokes that are allocated to complete a hole and a lower score is better than a higher score.

Hole	Par	Golfer's scores					
		2	3	4	5	6	7
2	4	1	51	310	85	9	–
7	5	–	20	211	198	23	4
11	3	25	269	156	4	–	–
16	3	50	292	99	13	–	–

6 Choose the heading from the list below that would best fit each graph.

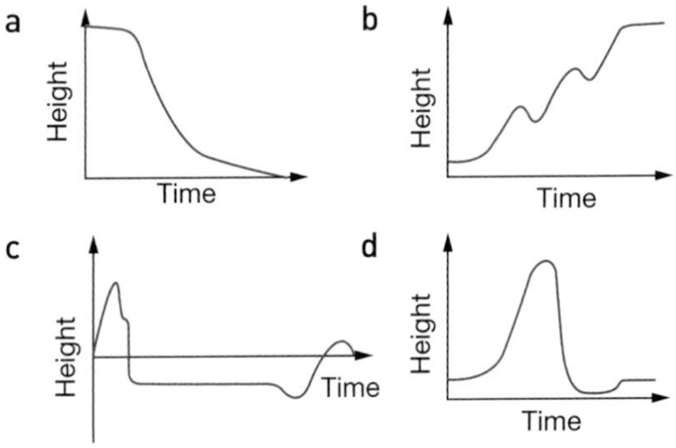

A The hook of a fishing line while fishing.
B An arrow fired into the air.
C Flying a kite.
D Position of my head while pole vaulting.
E A parachute jump.
F Position of my foot as I kick a ball.

ASSIGNMENT 14C Cumulative revision

1 a Find the value of x, correct to one decimal place.
b The two short sides of a right-angled triangle are 5 m and 8 m in length. Find the sizes of the angles in the triangle to the nearest degree.

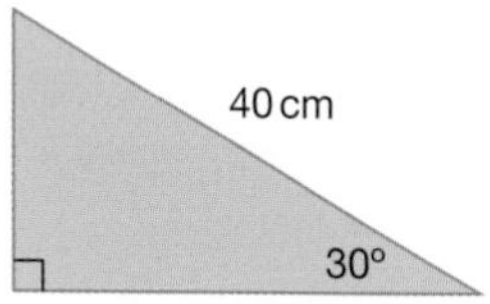

13:05

2 On a photocopier the enlargement and reduction factors are given as percentages. Find the enlargement and reduction factor for the following. 11:01

a Enlarge a photograph that is 18 cm long and 13 cm wide so that it is 28·8 cm long and 20·8 cm wide.
b Reduce a drawing that is a square of side 16 cm to a square of side 12 cm.

3 a Find the gradient and y-intercept of the line AB and use it to write its equation.
b Find the equation of the line DC and use it to find the x-intercept of the line.
c Use simultaneous equations to find the point of intersection of line AB with the line $2x + y = 4$.

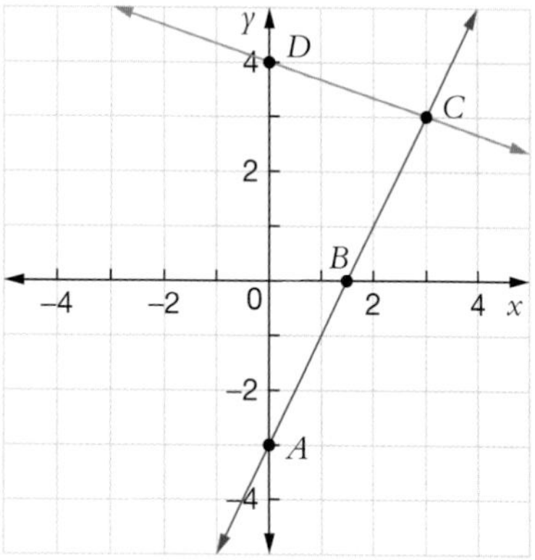

9:05, 9:06, 10:02A

4 Factorise these expressions: 12:06

a $x^2 + 3x - 10$
b $a^2 - a - 56$
c $4y^2 - 9$
d $x^2 - 3x + ax - 3a$
e $15n^2 - n - 2$

5 Simplify these expressions involving algebraic fractions. 12:07, 12:08

a $\dfrac{x^2 - 2x - 3}{x^2 - 5x + 6}$
b $\dfrac{x^2 - 9}{x + 5} \times \dfrac{x^2 + 7x + 10}{x^2 + 5x + 6}$
c $\dfrac{5}{x^2 - 4} - \dfrac{4}{x^2 + 2x - 8}$

6 Bag A contains 32 red and 48 green marbles. Bag B contains 18 red and 26 green marbles. 4:03

a Calculate the probability of choosing a red marble from Bag A.
b What is the probability of choosing a red marble from Bag B?
c Which bag gives the best chance of choosing a red marble?

7 At the end of the financial year Hannah's total income is \$71 325. She has allowable tax deductions of \$3327 and throughout the year she has made PAYG deductions totalling \$14 924. Calculate: 8:04

a her taxable income
b the tax payable on her taxable income if she has to pay \$4650 plus 30c for each dollar over \$37 000
c the Medicare levy, which is 1·5% of her taxable income
d the refund due or the amount of tax still payable.

PROPORTION

15

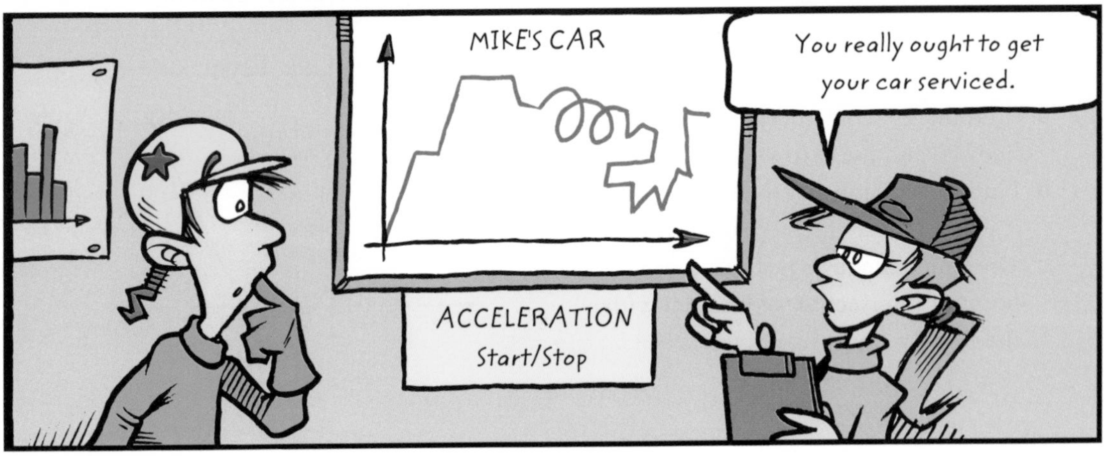

Contents

Syllabus references (See pages x–xv for details.)

Number and Algebra

Selections from ***Ratios and Rates*** [Stages 5.2, 5.3]

- Solve problems involving direct proportion; explore the relationship between graphs and equations corresponding to simple rate problems (ACMNA208)

Working Mathematically

- Communicating
- Problem Solving
- Reasoning
- Understanding
- Fluency

15:01 Review of rates

PREP QUIZ 15:01

If Wendy earns \$16 per hour, how much would she earn in:

1 2 hours **2** 3 hours **3** 5 hours **4** half an hour?

Complete:

5 1 kg = … g **6** 1 tonne = … kg **7** 1 hour = … min
8 1 cm = … mm **9** $1\ \text{m}^2 = \ldots\ \text{cm}^2$ **10** 1·5 litres = … millilitres

> A rate is a comparison of unlike quantities.
> e.g. If I travel 180 km in 3 hours my average rate of speed is $\frac{180\ \text{km}}{3\ \text{h}}$ or 60 km/h or 60 km per hour.

We usually write how many of the first quantity correspond to one of the second quantity.
e.g. 60 kilometres per one hour = 60 km/h

WORKED EXAMPLE 1

a 84 km in 2 hours
Divide each term by 2.
= 42 km in 1 hour
= 42 km/h

Or

84 km in 2 hours

$= \frac{84\ \text{km}}{2\ \text{h}}$

$= \frac{84}{2}\frac{\text{km}}{\text{h}}$

$= 42\ \text{km/h}$

Units must be shown.

Worked Example **1a** is an average rate, because when you travel, your speed may vary from moment to moment. Example **b** is a constant rate, because each kg will cost the same.

b 16 kg of tomatoes are sold for \$10.
What is the cost per kilogram?

Cost $= \frac{\$10}{16\ \text{kg}}$

$= \frac{1000}{16}\frac{\text{cents}}{\text{kg}}$

$= \frac{125}{2}\frac{\text{cents}}{\text{kg}}$

$= 62{\cdot}5$ cents/kg

cents/kg is the same as c/kg.
kg

c A plumber charges a householder \$64 per hour to fix the plumbing in a house.
Find the cost if it takes the plumber $4\frac{1}{2}$ hours.

Rate = \$64 per 1 hour
$= \$64 \times 4\frac{1}{2}$ hours   Multiply both terms by $4\frac{1}{2}$.
∴ Cost = \$288

WORKED EXAMPLE 2

a Change 1·5 km/min into km/h

1·5 km/min = (1·5 × 60) km/h
= 90 km/h

b Change 25 000 mL/h into L/h

25 000 mL/h = (25 000 ÷ 1000) L/h
= 25 L/h

c Convert 72 litres per hour into cm^3 per second

$$72\text{ L per h} = \frac{72\text{ L}}{1\text{ h}} = \frac{(72 \times 1000)\text{ mL}}{(60 \times 60)\text{ s}} = \frac{72\,000\text{ cm}^3}{3600\text{ s}} = 20\text{ cm}^3/\text{s}$$

Remember: 1 mL = 1 cm^3

d Convert 10 m/s into km/h

$$10\text{ m per s} = \frac{10\text{ m}}{1\text{ s}} = \frac{10\text{ m} \times 60 \times 60}{1\text{ h}} = \frac{36\,000\text{ m}}{1\text{ h}} = \frac{(36\,000 \div 1000)\text{ km}}{1\text{ h}} = 36\text{ km/h}$$

Exercise 15:01

1 Write each pair of quantities as a rate in its simplest form.

a 6 km, 2 h
b 10 kg, \$5
c 500c, 10 kg
d 100 mL, 100 cm^3
e 160 L, 4 h
f \$100, 5 h
g \$315, 7 days
h 70 km, 10 L
i 20 degrees, 5 min
j 7000 g, 100 cm
k 50 t, 2 blocks
l 60 km, $\frac{1}{2}$ h
m 88 runs, 8 wickets
n 18 children, 6 mothers
o 75 g, 10 cm^3

2 a I walk at 5 km/h. How far can I walk in 3 hours?

b Nails cost \$2.45 per kg. What is the cost of 20 kg?

c I can buy four exercise books for \$5. How many books can I buy for \$20?

d I earn \$8.45 per hour. How much am I paid for 12 hours work?

e The run rate per wicket in a cricket match has been 37·5 runs per wicket. How many runs have been scored if 6 wickets have been lost?

f The energy value of milk is measured as 670 kilojoules per cup. What is the energy value of 3 cups of milk?

g If the rate of exchange for one British pound is 1·60 American dollars, find the value of 10 British pounds in American currency.

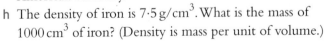

h The density of iron is 7·5 g/cm^3. What is the mass of 1000 cm^3 of iron? (Density is mass per unit of volume.)

i If light travels at 300 000 km/s, how far would it travel in one minute?

j If I am taxed 1·6c for every \$1 on the value of my \$50 000 block of land, how much must I pay?

3 Complete these equivalent rates.

a $1\,km/min = \ldots\ km/h$
b $25\,cents/g = \ldots\ cents/kg$
c $40\,000\ m/h = \ldots\ km/h$
d $\$5/kg = \ldots\ c/kg$
e $3\,m/s = \ldots\ m/min$
f $7\,m/s = \ldots\ mm/s$
g $6{\cdot}5\,km/L = \ldots\ m/L$
h $7200\,m/L = \ldots\ m/mL$
i $120\,beats/min = \ldots\ beats/s$
j $\$70/day = \ldots\ \$/week$
k $30\,c/m^2 = \ldots\ c/ha$
l $8500\,kg/day = \ldots\ t/day$

4 Complete these conversions that involve changing both quantities to smaller units.

a $60\,km/h = \ldots\ m/min$
b $72\,km/h = \ldots\ m/s$
c $24\,m/min = \ldots\ cm/s$
d $1{\cdot}2\,m/min = \ldots\ mm/s$
e $\$50/kg = \ldots\ c/g$
f $144\,L/h = \ldots\ mL/s$
g $60\,km/h = \ldots\ m/s$
h $7\,km/L = \ldots\ m/mL$
i $3\,t/h = \ldots\ kg/min$
j $\$50/m^2 = \ldots\ c/cm^2$

How many cubic cm in a cubic metre?

5 Complete these conversions that involve changing both quantities to larger units.

a $100\,m/min = \ldots\ km/h$
b $25\,m/s = \ldots\ km/h$
c $5\,mm/s = \ldots\ cm/min$
d $150\,cm/s = \ldots\ km/h$
e $30\,mm/s = \ldots\ km/h$
f $95\,c/h = \ldots\ \$/week$ (40 hours)
g $800\,kg/h = \ldots\ t/day$
h $50\,c/m^2 = \ldots\ \$/ha$
i $20\,mL/m = \ldots\ L/km$
j $5\,g/cm^3 = \ldots\ kg/m^3$

6 In 1999, Noah Ngeny of Kenya ran 1000 m in 2 minutes, 11·96 seconds. What was his average speed in km/h?

7 Usain Bolt of Jamaica set a new record for running 100 m in 9·58 seconds. What average speed is this in km/h, correct to one decimal place?

VTB
Bolt

8 In 1998, Takahiro Sunada of Japan ran 100 km in 6 hours, 13 minutes and 33 seconds. What was his average speed in km/h, correct to one decimal place?

9 A car is approaching a pedestrian crossing at 108 km/h. If it is 90 m from the crossing, how much time do you have to cross before the car reaches the crossing, assuming the car does not slow down?

15:02 Direct proportion

PREP QUIZ 15:02

Complete:

1 20 m/s = ... m/min
2 7000 m/h = ... km/h
3 360 g/min = ... g/s
4 200 m in 10 s = ... m/s
5 12 L in 1 hour = ... mL/min
6 $24 for 10 kg = ... $/kg
7 What will 20 pencils cost if 4 pencils cost $1.36?
8 If 3 folders cost $2.40, how much will 8 cost?
9 Jenny measures 23 heart beats in 12 seconds. How many beats per minute is this?
10 Rob jogs at an average speed of 5 minutes and 35 seconds per km. How long will it take him to complete a fun run with a distance of 14 km?

If all parts of a shape or object are increased or decreased by the same ratio or fraction, then lengths on the original shape or object and lengths on the new shape or object are said to be in *direct proportion*. Any increase or decrease in one variable will result in a proportional change in the other variable (they will vary at the same rate).

For example, if a photo and its enlargement are in direct proportion, then we could determine unknown measurements using the enlargement factor. If the original photo measures 15 cm by 12 cm and the length of the enlargement is 25 cm, then its width w can be found using the following ratio statement.

$$\frac{w}{12} = \frac{25}{15}$$

$$w = \frac{25}{15} \times 12$$

$$\therefore w = 20\,\text{cm}$$

Ratio of the lengths = Ratio of the widths

We can approach this problem in a different way.

If any length (L) on the enlargement is proportional to the corresponding length (l) on the original photo, we can write this as:

$$L \propto l$$

The symbol $\propto$ means 'is proportional to'.

To be in direct proportion, all lengths are multiplied by the same factor, so we can write:

$L = kl$ where k is the **constant of proportionality** (or the proportional constant)

Now substitute corresponding values that are known. In this case, $L = 25$ cm and $l = 15$ cm.

$$L = kl$$

$$25 = k \times 15$$

$$\therefore k = \frac{25}{15} \text{ or } \frac{5}{3}$$

We know that for any length on the photo (l), the corresponding length on the enlargement (L) is given by:

$$L = \frac{5l}{3}$$

You can see the same ratio appearing in both methods.
5/3
5/3

So if the width of the photo is 12 cm, then the corresponding width on the enlargement is given by:

$$L = \frac{5}{3} \times 12$$
$$= 20\,\text{cm}$$

$$\frac{w}{12} = \frac{25}{15}$$
$$w = \frac{5}{3} \times 12$$
$$= 20\,\text{cm}$$

$$L = kl$$
$$w = \frac{5}{3} \times 12$$
$$= 20\,\text{cm}$$

WORKED EXAMPLE 1

10 litres of paint covers 75 m^2 of wall. The area of wall covered is directly proportional to the amount of paint used.

a Write an equation expressing this relationship and find the constant of proportionality.

b Use this to find the area of wall covered by 7 litres of paint.

c How many litres of paint would be needed to cover 180 m^2 of wall?

Solutions

a $A \propto p$ where A is the area of wall covered and p is the amount of paint used.

So $A = kp$

$\therefore 75 = k \times 10$ (Substituting the corresponding known values.)

$k = \frac{75}{10}$ or 7·5

$\therefore$ The equation expressing this direct proportion is $A = 7{\cdot}5p$.

b To find the area covered by 7 litres of paint, substitute $p = 7$ into the equation to find the corresponding value of A.

$A = 7{\cdot}5p$

$= 7{\cdot}5 \times 7$

$= 52{\cdot}5$

So, 7 litres of paint covers 52·5 m^2.

c Similarly, by substituting $A = 180$ into the equation, we can find the corresponding value of p.

$A = 7{\cdot}5p$

$180 = 7{\cdot}5p$

$p = \frac{180}{7{\cdot}5}$

$= 24$

So, 24 litres of paint covers 180 m^2.

WORKED EXAMPLE 2

A 36 000 kJ survival pack is enough to sustain 5 hikers for a period of 4 days.

a How many kilojoules would be needed for 7 hikers to last 3 days?

b How many days would a 129 600 kJ pack last 4 hikers?

c How many hikers could survive on a 108 000 kJ pack for 3 days?

Solutions

Consider the supply needed by 5 hikers (h) for 4 days (d) as 20 rations (5×4).

Then a 36 000 kJ pack (P) will supply 20 rations ($h \times d$).

So, $P = k(hd)$

Finding k: $36\,000 = k \times 20$

$k = 1800$

$\therefore P = 1800hd$

a To supply 7 hikers for 3 days

$P = 1800 \times 7 \times 3$

$= 37\,800$

So, 7 people for 3 days would need 37 800 kJ.

b If $P = 129\,600$, then $129\,600 = 1800hd$

$hd = 129\,600 \div 1800$

$= 72$

Now $h = 4$, so $4d = 72$

$d = 18$

So, 129 600 kJ divided among 4 people would last 18 days.

c Similarly, if $P = 108\,000$, then $108\,000 = 1800hd$

$hd = 60$

Now $d = 3$, so $3h = 60$

$h = 20$

So, 108 000 kJ divided over 3 days would sustain 20 people.

Exercise 15:02

1 A is directly proportional to m.

a Write an equation relating A to m.

b If $A = 15$ when $m = 6$, find the constant of proportionality.

c What will be the value of A if $m = 10$?

d If $A = 50$ what is the corresponding value of m?

2 Y is directly proportional to x.

a Write an equation relating Y and x.

b If $Y = 20$ when $x = 25$, find the constant of proportionality.

c What will be the value of Y when $x = 10$?

d If $Y = 52$ what is the corresponding value of x?

3 The height (H) of a plant is directly proportional to the number of days (d) it has been growing.

a Write a proportional statement linking H and d.

b Find the proportional constant if after 4 days the height of the plant is 30 cm.

c What will be the height of the plant after 7 days?

d After how many days will the height of the plant reach 75 cm?

4 The quantity of paint (p) required for a job is directly proportional to the area (a) that is to be painted.

a Write an equation expressing this proportional relationship.

b If 4 litres of paint will cover 35 m^2, find the proportional constant.

c How many litres of paint will be needed to cover an area of 60 m^2. Answer to the nearest litre.

d What area will 15 litres of paint cover? Answer to the 'next' whole square metre.

5 P is directly proportional to m. When $m = 8{\cdot}6$, $P = 15{\cdot}05$.

a Find an equation relating P and m.

b What is the value of P when m is 1·8?

c What is the value of m when P is 20·65?

6 Y is directly proportional to x^2. When $x = 7$, $Y = 24{\cdot}5$.

a Find an equation relating Y and x^2.

b What is the value of Y when $x = 9$?

c What is the positive value of x when $Y = 8$?

7 The velocity V (in m/s) of a falling object is directly proportional to the time t (in seconds) after release. After 2 seconds the velocity is 19·6 m/s.

a Find an equation relating velocity and time.

b What will be the velocity after 3 seconds?

c When will the velocity be 10 m/s? Give your answer correct to two decimal places.

8 As a general rule, a minimum of 50 m^2 is required for every 4 people working in an office.

a How much space would be needed for 10 people?

b What would be the maximum number of people that could work in an office space of 180 m^2?

9 A mobile phone call lasting 5 minutes and 20 seconds costs $3.50. If the cost is proportional to the length of the call:

a What would be the cost of an 8-minute call? (Hint: Express the time in seconds.)

b How long a call could be made for $8? Give your answer to the nearest second.

10 In a gas fire, the amount X of oxygen used is directly proportional to the amount G of natural gas burned. The burning of 35 kg of natural gas uses 56 kg of oxygen. How many kilograms of oxygen are needed to burn 21 kg of natural gas?

11 Fourteen cans of food can feed 10 cats for 3 days.

a Find an equation relating the number of cans of food (F) to the number of cats (c) and number of days (y).

b For how many days would 21 cans of food feed 10 cats?

c How many cans would be needed to feed 10 cats for 9 days?

d How many cans would be needed to feed 15 cats for 3 days?

e How many cans would be needed to feed 15 cats for 9 days?

For Questions 11 to 13, look at Worked Example 2.

12 The length of a ditch is directly proportional to the number of men and the amount of time they spend digging.

a Find an equation relating the length of the ditch (D) to the number of men (n) and the number of hours (h) they spend digging it.

b If it takes 6 men 4 hours to dig a ditch 10 m long, find the constant of proportionality for this equation.

c What length of ditch could 9 men dig in 4 hours?

d What length of ditch could 6 men dig in 6 hours?

e What length of ditch could 9 men dig in 6 hours?

f How many men would it take to dig a ditch 25 m long in 5 hours?

13 For a certain species of tree, 10 mature trees can produce the same amount of oxygen inhaled by 500 people over a 4-year period.

a Over a 4-year period, how many people inhale the the amount of oxygen produced by 16 mature trees?

b How many trees would be needed to produce the same amount of oxygen used by 200 people, over a 4-year period?

c How many trees would be needed to produce the oxygen used by 800 people over a 10-year period?

14 The force F needed to stretch a spring is directly proportional to the amount y the spring is stretched. A force of 7·5 newtons stretches a spring by 3 cm. Find the amount the spring will be stretched by a force of 8 newtons.

15 The distance D that an object falls is directly proportional to the square of the time t of the fall. That is, $D \propto t^2$. If an object falls 19·6 m in 2 seconds, find:

a an equation relating D and t

b how far will it fall in 4 seconds.

16 The volume V of a sphere and the cube of its radius are directly proportional. For a sphere of radius 1 cm, the volume is 4·189 cm^3.

a Find an equation relating V and r.

b What is the volume of a sphere of radius 3 cm?

c If the volume is 4189 cm^3, what is the radius?

17 The period of a simple pendulum is the time it takes to swing through one complete cycle. The period T (in seconds) of a simple pendulum is directly proportional to the square root of its length l (in metres). It is known that the period is 2·7 s when the length of the pendulum is 1·8 m.

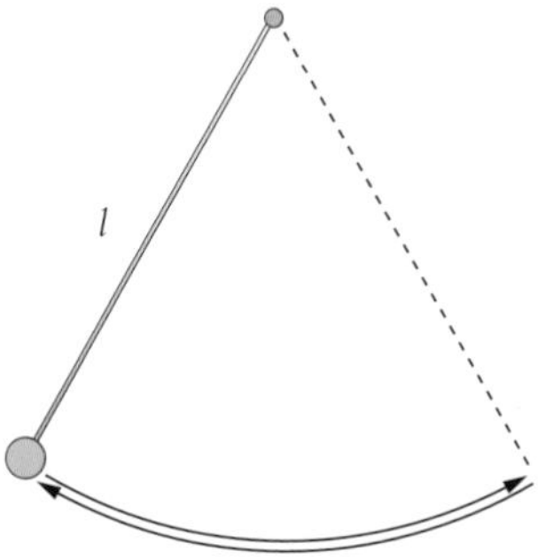

a Find an equation relating T and l, writing the value of the proportional constant correct to three decimal places.

b What is the period of a pendulum of length 0·9 m? (Answer correct to one decimal place.)

c What is the length of a pendulum that has a period of 1 second? (Answer correct to the nearest centimetre.)

15:03 Graphing direct proportion

PREP QUIZ 15:03

These equations represent straight lines in the number plane. What is the gradient of each line?

1 $y = 3x$

2 $y = x$

3 $y = \frac{x}{2}$

4 $y = \frac{5x}{3}$

5 $y = 0{\cdot}25x$

6 If $y = 5x$, find y if $x = 7$.

7 If $y = \frac{x}{3}$, find y if $x = 1{\cdot}26$.

8 If $y = \frac{7x}{9}$, find y if $x = 4\frac{1}{2}$.

9 If $y = 3x$, find x if $y = 27$.

10 If $y = 0{\cdot}4x$, find x if $y = 1$.

In Chapter 9 we saw that equations like those in the Prep quiz represent straight lines, when graphed on the number plane. Also, they all pass through the origin because $x = 0$ when $y = 0$. Each line has a constant gradient. The measure of this gradient (or slope) is given by the coefficient of x.

For the line $y = mx$, m is the gradient.

This equation is of the same form as the equation for direct proportion: $y = kx$, where x and y are the quantities in proportion and k is the constant of proportionality.

So, if we graphed the relationship between two quantities that are in direct proportion we would expect to see a straight line that passes through the origin with a gradient equal to the proportional constant k.

WORKED EXAMPLE 1

If 10 litres of paint (p) covers an area (A) of $75\,\text{m}^2$, this gives an equation of direct proportion: $A = 7{\cdot}5p$ (See Worked Example **1** in Section 15:02.)
Graph this equation and use it to find:

a the area covered by 14 litres of paint

b the paint required to cover $30\,\text{m}^2$.

Solution

The graph can be simply drawn by plotting the two known pairs of values (i.e. when $p = 10$, $A = 75$ and of course, when $p = 0$, $A = 0$). This is shown by the red dots on the graph. A straight line is then drawn from (0, 0) passing through (10, 75). The gradient of the line can be measured as 7·5; that is, the value of the constant of proportionality. Any other values required can now be read from the graph.

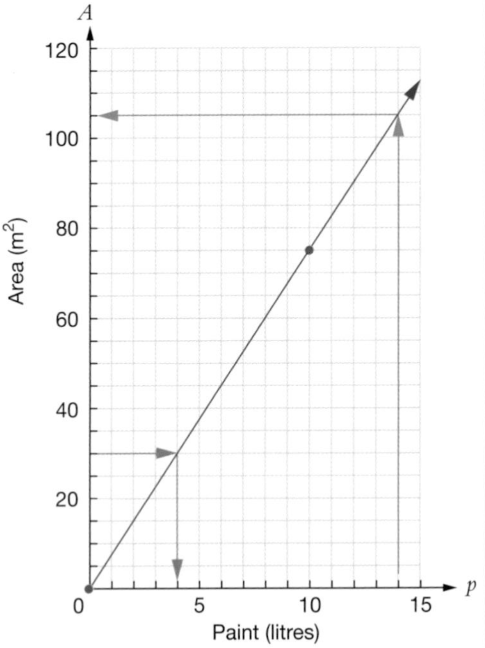

a So, if $p = 14$, reading from 14 on the horizontal axis up to the line and across to the vertical axis, we find $A = 105$. Therefore, 14 litres of paint will cover $105\,\text{m}^2$.

b If we read from $A = 30$ on the vertical axis, across and down to the horizontal axis, we find the corresponding value for p is $p = 4$. So, to cover an area of $30\,\text{m}^2$ we need 4 litres of paint.

WORKED EXAMPLE 2

The currency exchange rate says that 1 Australian dollar will buy 1·3 New Zealand dollars.

a Use this fact to draw a graph showing this proportional relationship.

b What is the gradient of this linear graph and hence, the constant of proportionality?

c How many \$NZ will \$A50 buy?

d How many \$A will \$NZ50 buy?

Solutions

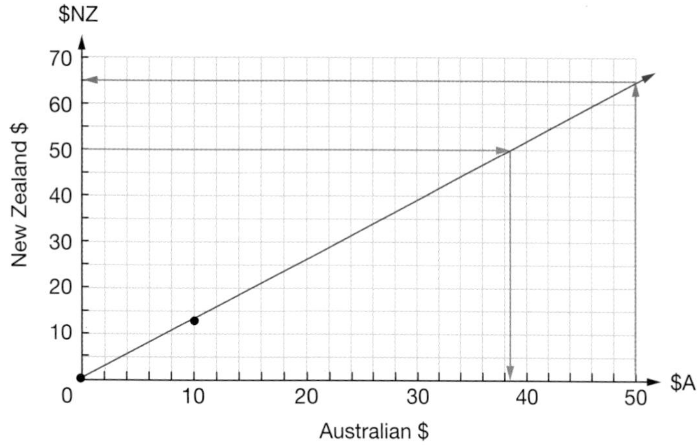

a If \$A1 = \$NZ1.30, then \$A10 = \$NZ13. This is a more convenient pair of values to graph. Plotting (0, 0) and (10, 13) and drawing the line gives the graph shown here.

b The gradient (and the value of the constant of proportionality) is 1·3.

c Following the purple arrows on the graph, we see that \$A50 will buy \$NZ65.

d Following the green arrows shows that \$NZ50 will buy slightly more than \$A38. A more exact answer is difficult to read from the graph, but by using the equation:

\$NZ = 1·3\$A

50 = 1·3\$A (substituting \$NZ = 50)

So, \$A = 50 ÷ 1·3

= \$38.46 to the nearest cent

Therefore, \$50 will buy \$A38.46.

Exercise 15:03

1 This graph shows the market for apples. The cost (C) is directly proportional to the number (n) of boxes bought.

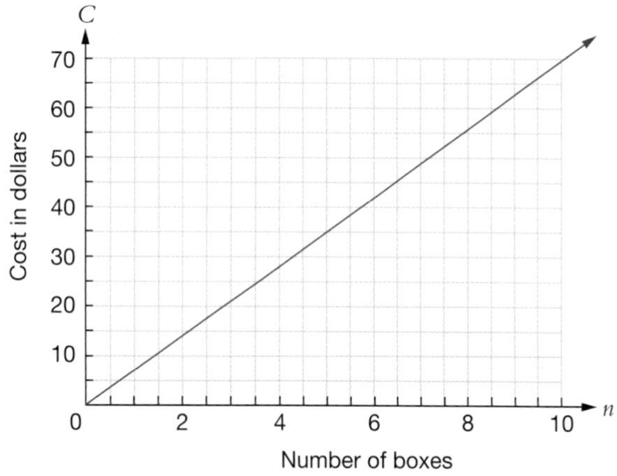

a Determine the cost per box of apples.

b Hence, determine the value of the constant of proportionality k in the equation: $C = kn$

c What would be the cost of 50 boxes?

d How many whole boxes could be bought for \$100?

2 If a car travels at a constant speed then the distance travelled (D) is directly proportional to the time taken (t). This graph shows this relationship.

a How far has the car travelled in 5 hours?

b Therefore, what is the speed in km/h?

c Hence, what is the value of the proportional constant in the equation $D = kt$?

d How far would the car travel, at the same speed, in 7 hours?

e How long would it take to travel 200 km at the same speed? (Answer in hours and minutes.)

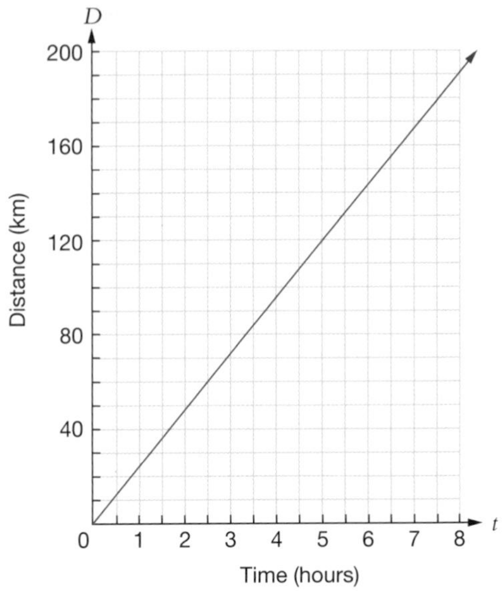

3 The exchange rate between Australian and British currency is \$A1 = £0.65 (or 65 British pence).

a How many British pounds (£) would 100 Australian dollars buy?

b Construct a line graph with Australian dollars on the horizontal axis, up to \$A100, and British pounds, up to £65, on the vertical axis.

c The equation for this straight line would be of the form $B = k$A. What is the value of k?

d How many British pounds would 500 Australian dollars buy?

e How many Australian dollars would 500 British pounds buy?

4 A casual worker earns \$22.50 per hour.

a How much would be earned by working 4 hours?

b Use your answer to part **a** to draw a graph with the horizontal axis showing the hours worked and the vertical axis showing the amount earned.

c Write an equation that relates the amount earned (A) to the number of hours worked (h).

d How many whole hours must be worked to earn \$200?

5 A mix of petrol and oil is used for some lawn mowers. Every 5 L of petrol requires 100 mL of oil.

a If $O = kP$, where P = litres of petrol and O = millilitres of oil, find the value of k.

b Draw the graph of this relationship with the volume of petrol on the horizontal axis.

c How many litres of oil would be required to mix with 50 L of petrol?

d If $P = KL$, where P = litres of petrol and L = litres of oil, find the value of K. (Hint: Use your answer to part **c**.)

e Now draw the graph of the equation in part **d**, with the volume of oil on the horizontal axis.

6 Two trucks, A and B, are travelling at two different constant speeds. Therefore, the distance travelled and the time taken are in direct proportion.

a Given the equation $d = kt$, find the value of k for each truck.

b How much farther has truck B travelled than truck A after 4 hours?

c After what time period are the two trucks 50 km apart?

d After 5 hours, truck A increased its speed so that it caught up to truck B after another 5 hours. To what speed did it increase?

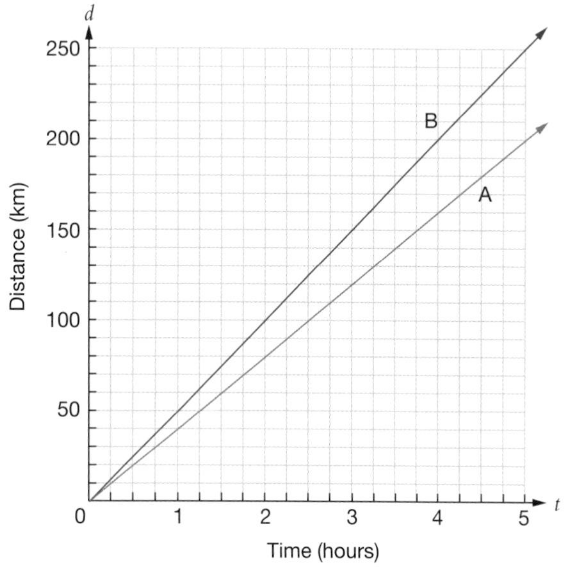

INVESTIGATION 15:03 PROPORTIONAL UPS AND DOWNS!

Consider the following examples and write your answers in the table below.

1 If 4 men take 12 hours to build a brick fence, how long would it take:
a 1 man
b 6 men?

2 If 3 women can paint a wall in 4 hours, how long would it take:
a 1 woman
b 4 women?

3 For 6 days, 12 cans of dog food will feed 3 dogs. For how long will the same amount of dog food feed:
a 1 dog
b 9 dogs?

4 It takes 3 men 4 hours to dig a hole. To dig a hole the same size, how long would it take:
a 1 man
b 5 men?

1	Time for 4 men	Time for 1 man	Time for 6 men
	12 hours		
2	Time for 3 women	Time for 1 woman	Time for 4 women
	4 hours		
3	Time for 3 dogs	Time for 1 dog	Time for 9 dogs
	6 days		
4	Time for 3 men	Time for 1 man	Time for 5 men
	4 hours		

5 What do you notice about the answers for the time in each case as the number of men, women or dogs:
a decreases
b increases?

15:04 Inverse proportion

In Investigation 15:03, you should have seen that as one quantity increased, the other decreased. This is the reverse of what happens with examples of direct proportion.

For example, if 5 painters take 6 days to paint a house, it should obviously take 3 painters longer to do the same job. That is, if the number of painters decreases, the time taken increases. Likewise, more painters would take less time.

Logically, if it takes 5 painters 6 days to do the job, it should take 1 painter 5 times as long.

So 1 painter should take 5 × 6 days, which is 30 days.

Likewise, if it takes 1 painter 30 days to do the job, then 3 painters should divide the time taken by 3.

So 3 painters should take 30 days ÷ 3, which is 10 days.

This is an example of **inverse proportion**, sometimes called **indirect proportion**.

We say that the time taken (T) is inversely proportional to the number of painters (p).

We write this as: $T \propto \frac{1}{p}$

or $T = \frac{k}{p}$ where k is the **constant of proportionality** (or the proportional constant)

If we know 5 painters take 6 days, then substituting these values will determine the value of k.

$$T = \frac{k}{p}$$

So $6 = \frac{k}{5}$

$\therefore$ $k = 30$ (6×5)

The equation $T = \frac{30}{p}$ represents the relationship between the number of painters used to paint the house and the time taken to complete the job.

Now consider the following worked examples.

WORKED EXAMPLE 1

If 10 harvesters take 12 days to complete the harvesting, how long would it take 15 harvesters?

Solution

There are two methods for solving these problems involving inverse proportion.

Method 1 Unitary method

We know that 10 harvesters take 12 days.

We then find how long it takes 1 harvester.

1 harvester would take 10 times as long.

$12 \times 10 = 120$

1 harvester would take 120 days.

15 harvesters would divide the time by 15.

$120 \div 15 = 8$

So, 15 harvesters would take 8 days.

Method 2 Inverse proportion equation

$T = \frac{k}{H}$ where T = time in days and H = no. of harvesters

When $H = 10$, $T = 12$

$12 = \frac{k}{10}$ $\therefore k = 120\ (12 \times 10)$

$T = \frac{120}{H}$

When $H = 15$, $T = \frac{120}{15} = 8$

So, 15 harvesters would take 8 days.

WORKED EXAMPLE 2

If I travel at 50 km/h it will take me 4 hours to get home. How long will it take if I travel at an average speed of 60 km/h?

Solution

Method 1 Unitary method

A speed of 50 km/h takes 4 hours.

A speed of 1 km/h will take 50 times as long.

Time taken for the trip at 1 km/h

$= 4 \times 50$

$= 200$ hours

A speed of 60 km/h will take $\frac{1}{60}$ of the time.

So, 200 hours would be divided by 60.

Time taken for the trip at 60 km/h

$= 200 \div 60$

$= 3\frac{1}{3}$ hours or 3 hours, 20 minutes.

Method 2 Inverse proportion equation

$T = \frac{k}{S}$, where T = time in hours and S = speed in km/h

When $S = 50$, $T = 4$

$4 = \frac{k}{50}$ $\therefore k = 4 \times 50$
$= 200$

So, $T = \frac{200}{S}$

When $S = 60$, $T = \frac{200}{60}$
$= 3\frac{1}{3}$

So, the time taken at 60 km/h is 3 hours, 20 minutes.

Exercise 15:04

1 Four boys can mow a paddock in 3 hours.

a How long would it take 1 boy?

b How long would it take 6 boys?

2 Five people can eat 3 large pizzas in 20 minutes.

a How long would it take 1 person to eat the 3 pizzas?

b How long would it take 4 people?

3 Three people can survive on the provisions in a raft for 16 days. For how long could 8 people survive on the same provisions?

4 A team of 15 fruit pickers can clear 6 hectares of fruit in a week.

a How many days would it take 21 fruit pickers?

b If the 6 hectares had to be cleared in 2 days, how many fruit pickers would be needed?

5 A swimmer covers a distance of 300 m in 5 minutes.

a What is the average speed of the swimmer in metres per second?

b At what speed would the distance be covered in 4 minutes?

c How long would it take for the distance to be covered at a speed of 1·5 m/s?

6 N is inversely proportional to P. When $N = 25$, $P = 12$.

a Determine an equation relating N and P.

b When $P = 10$, what is the value of N?

c What is the value of P when $N = 100$?

7 X and Y are inversely proportional. When $X = 20$, $Y = 10$.

a Find an equation showing the relationship between X and Y.

b What is the value of Y when $X = 5$?

c what is the value of X when $Y = 5$?

8 The time T taken to empty a water tank is inversely proportional to the cross-sectional area A of the drainage pipe. A drainage pipe with a cross-sectional area of 40 cm^2 takes 16 minutes to empty a full tank.

a Find an equation relating T and A.

b How long would it take to empty the full tank if the drainage pipe has a cross-sectional area of 30 cm^2?

c What must be the cross-sectional area of the pipe if the tank is emptied in 10 minutes?

9 The rate of vibration R of a string under constant tension is inversely proportional to the length L of the string. The string vibrates 120 times per second when the string has a length of 124 cm.

a Find an equation relating R and L.

b What is the rate of vibration when the length is 80 cm?

c What is the length of string that vibrates 480 times per second?

10 At a given temperature, the pressure P of a gas is inversely proportional to the volume V. In a container of volume 2·3 L, a gas exerts a pressure of 130 units. How much pressure would the gas exert if the volume were 0·7 L? (Answer to the nearest whole unit.)

11 X is inversely proportional to the square of Y. When $Y = 8$, $X = 100$.

a Find an equation relating X and Y.

b What is the value of X when Y is 5?

c Find the value of Y when X is 4.

12 The mass M of an object is inversely proportional to the square of its distance D from the centre of the Earth. A man has a mass of 70 kg on the surface of the Earth. Take the radius of the Earth to be 6400 km.

a Find an equation relating M and D.

b What is the mass of the man when 200 km above the surface of the Earth? Give your answer correct to two decimal places.

13 If it takes 5 cats 2 days to catch 6 mice, how many days will it take 3 cats to catch 9 mice? (Hint: It might be useful to set up a table with the headings as shown here.)

Cats	Days	Mice

14 If 3 boys take 2 hours to mow 3 lawns, how many boys can mow 6 lawns in 3 hours?

15 A 60 piece orchestra takes 12 minutes to play the Radetsky March. How long would it take an 80 piece orchestra?

Gymnasts often find themselves in inverse positions.

INVESTIGATION 15:04 GRAPHING INVERSE PROPORTION

If two quantities are in inverse proportion, then as one quantity increases, the other decreases. So if we graphed an equation representing an inverse proportion relationship we would expect the graph to slope downwards to the right in the number plane. That is, we would expect it to have a negative gradient.

This is true but, unlike the graph of a direct proportion, it is not a straight line.

Consider the example on page 470 about painting a house.

The equation was $T = \frac{30}{P}$.

A table of values for this equation would be:

P	1	2	3	5	10	15	30
T	30	15	10	6	3	2	1

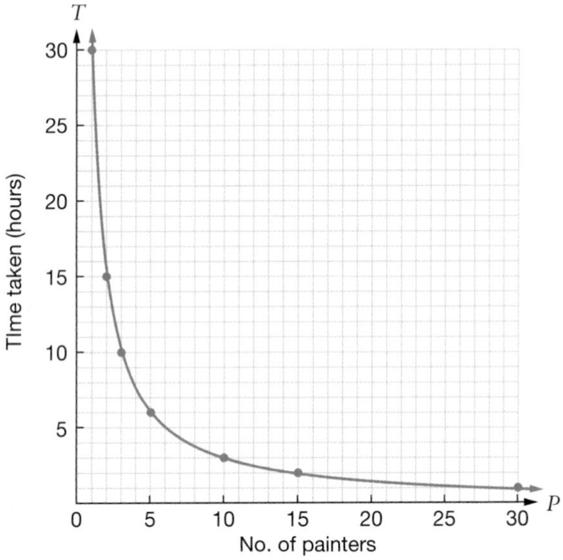

Plotting these points produces the pattern shown by the dots in this graph. Connecting the points results in a curve called a **hyperbola**. [The graph is said to be hyperbolic.]

Of course not all the points on the curve in this example have meaning, because you can't have a fraction of a painter.

Exercises

1 Complete the table of values for the equation $y = \frac{12}{x}$ and sketch its graph in the number plane.

x	1	2	3	4	6	12
y						

2 Using a table of values, or otherwise, draw a graph for each of these equations.

a $y = \frac{20}{x}$ **b** $b = \frac{50}{n}$ **c** $S = \frac{100}{t}$

3 Determine the equation of each graph by considering points that lie along the line.

a

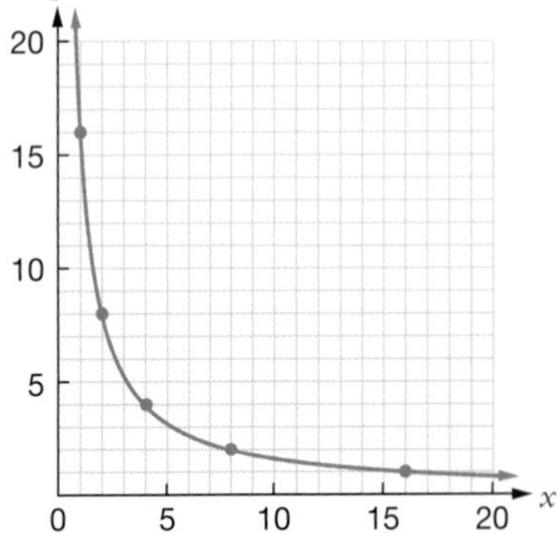

b

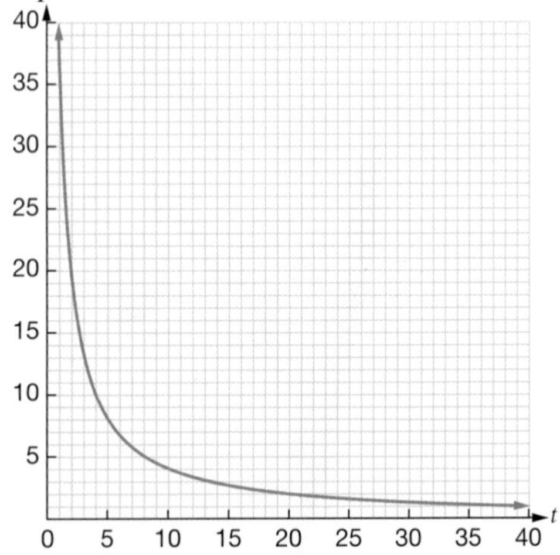

FUN SPOT 15:04 — HOW DO POETS WRITE UPSIDE DOWN?

Answer each question and write the letter for that question in the box above the correct answer.

E 15 kg of potatoes costs \$10. How many kilograms of potatoes can I buy for \$12?

S Baking cakes for 8 people needs 12 eggs. How many eggs are needed to bake cakes for 20 people?

N 20 litres of petrol costs \$28. How many litres can I buy for \$63?

E A tap leaks 2·25 L of water in 30 minutes. How many millilitres of water will leak in 1 minute?

R A car travelling at 60 km/h takes 2 hours to complete a journey. At what speed, in km/h, will a car take 3 hours to complete the same journey?

I If 5 bricklayers take 6 hours to build a wall, how many bricklayers would build the wall in two hours?

V If 4 boys can eat 16 pies in 10 minutes, how many minutes would it take 6 boys to eat 24 pies?

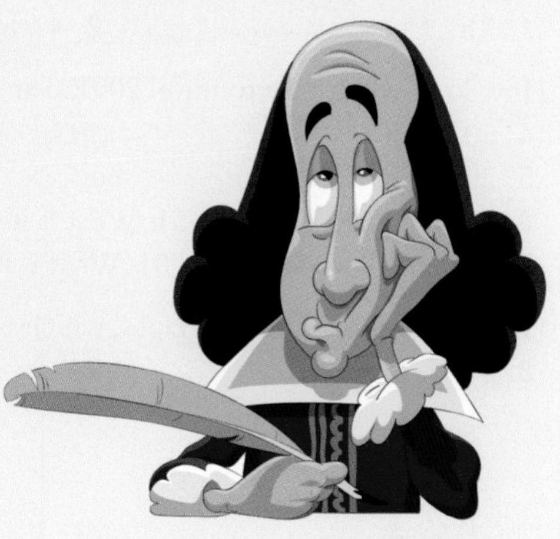

		–					
15	45		10	18	40	30	75

15:05 Distance–time graphs

15:05A Linear graphs: A review

- A distance–time graph (or travel graph) can be a type of line graph used to describe one or more trips or journeys.
- The vertical axis represents distance from a certain point, while the horizontal axis represents time.
- The formulas that connect distance travelled (D), time taken (T) and average speed (S) are given below.

Distance
Time
A steep line means a fast trip.

$$D = S \times T \qquad S = \frac{D}{T} \qquad T = \frac{D}{S}$$

PREP QUIZ 15:05A

A car is travelling at an average speed of 100 km/h. How far will it travel in:

1 2 h **2** $4\frac{1}{2}$ h **3** 15 min?

How long will it take to travel 200 km at an average speed of:

4 50 km/h

5 20 km/h?

6 A car travels 350 km in 5 h. What is its average speed?

7 A plane flies 1500 km in 3 h. What is its average speed?

For each of the following graphs, which is the steepest, A or B?

8

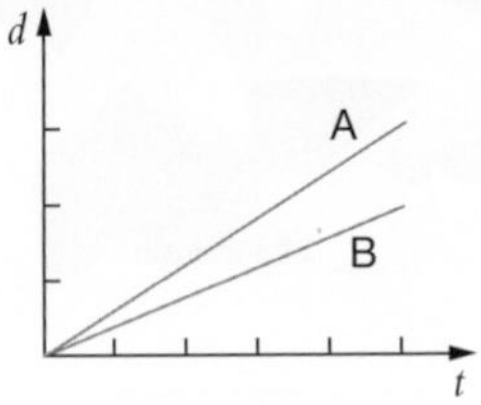

9

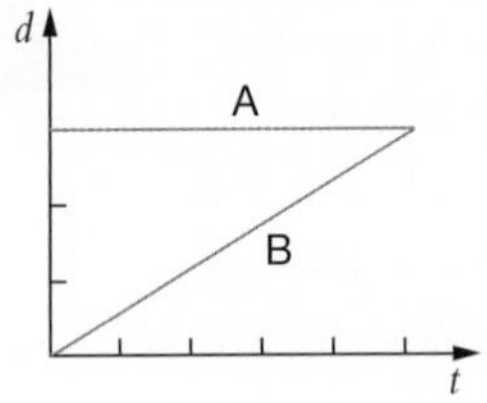

10

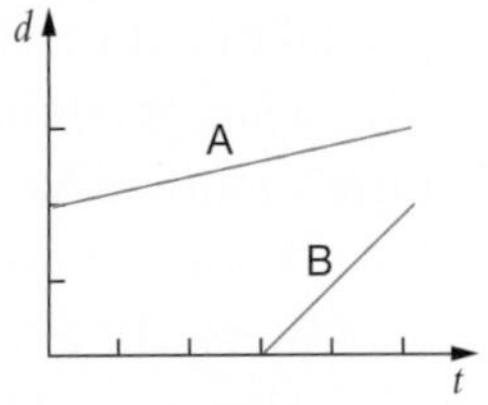

Don and Jim are travelling along the same straight road. The graph gives the distance of each person from town A at different times.

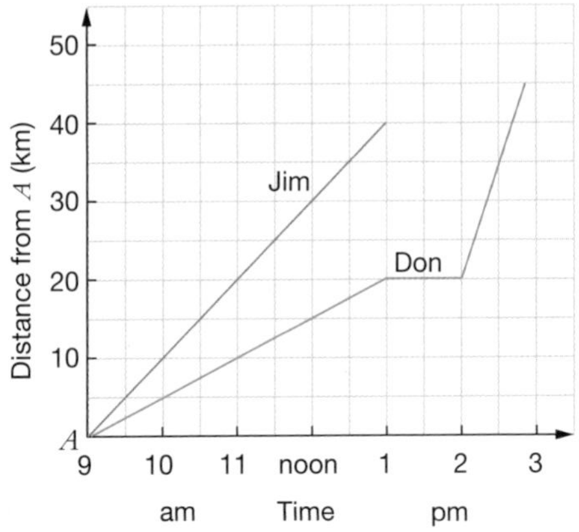

- From our knowledge of line graphs we can work out what distances correspond to what times. For example, at 1:00 pm Jim is 40 km from A.
- The straight lines give us information about speeds. From 9:00 am to 1:00 pm Jim travelled a greater distance than Don. Because Jim travelled a greater distance in the same time, he must have travelled at a greater speed.
- From 9:00 am to 1:00 pm the line representing Jim's trip is steeper than the line representing Don's trip. From this we can see that the steeper the line, the greater the speed. From the graph we can also see that Jim's trip finishes at 1:00 pm when he is 40 km from A. However, Don's trip continues.
- From 1:00 pm to 2:00 pm we notice that Don's distance from A has not changed. He has remained the same distance from A and so would have stopped.
- At 2:00 pm Don's journey continues. He travelled at a faster speed from 2:00 pm to 3:00 pm than he did from 9:00 am to 1:00 pm.
- A change in speed is indicated by a change in steepness. The graph shows us that Jim's speed is unchanged.

> - A change in steepness means a change in speed.
> - The steeper the line, the faster the journey.
> - The flatter the line, the slower the journey.
> - A horizontal line indicates that the person or object is stationary.

WORKED EXAMPLE 1

This travel graph shows the journeys of John and Bill between town A and town B. (They travel on the same road.)

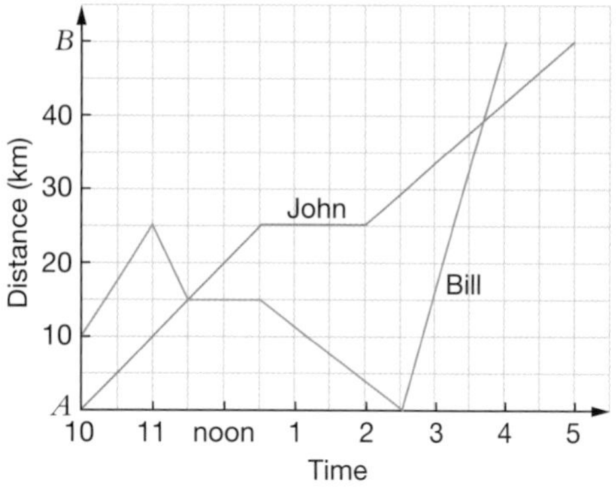

a How far from A is Bill when he commences his journey?

b How far is John from B at 2:30 pm?

c When do John and Bill first meet?

d Who reaches town B first?

e At what time does Bill stop to rest?

f How far does John travel?

g How far apart are John and Bill when Bill is at town A?

h How far does Bill travel?

Solution

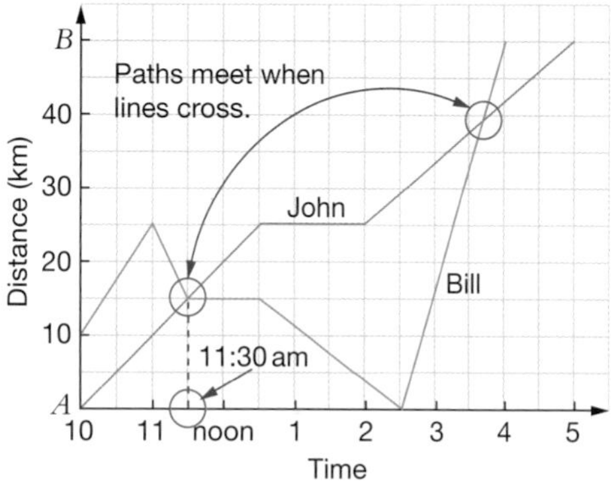

a Bill commences his journey at 10:00 am.
At that time he is 10 km from town A.

b At 2:30 pm John is 20 km from B (because he is 30 km from A).

c John and Bill first meet at 11:30 am.

d Bill reaches town B at 4:00 pm. John reaches town B at 5:00 pm.
∴ Bill reaches town B first.

e The horizontal section indicates a rest.
∴ Bill stops at 11:30 am.

f John travels from town A to town B without backtracking.
∴ John travels 50 km.

g Bill is at town A at 2:30 pm. At that time John is about 30 km from A.
∴ They are about 30 km apart when Bill is at A.

h Bill's journey involves backtracking.
He moves towards B, then returns to A and then moves to B.
Distance travelled (10:00 am–11:00 am)
$= 25 - 10$
$= 15$ km
Distance travelled (11:00 am–2:30 pm)
$= 25 - 0$
$= 25$ km
Distance travelled (2:30 pm–4:00 pm)
$= 50 - 0$
$= 50$ km
Total distance travelled
$= (15 + 25 + 50)$ km
$= 90$ km

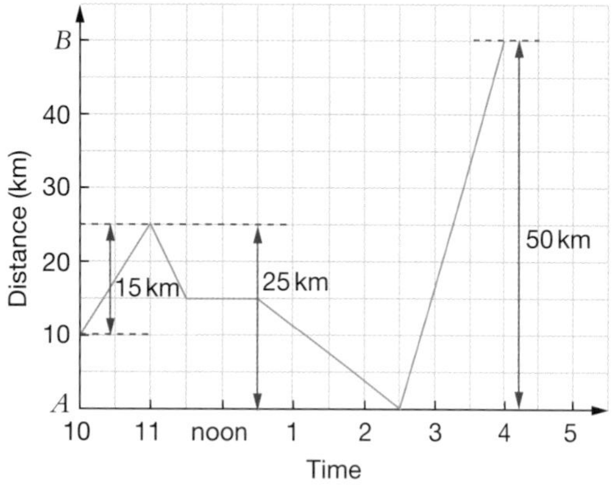

WORKED EXAMPLE 2

Use the following information to construct a travel graph.

A motorist left home at 9:00 am to drive to a country town. He drove 180 km in 2 hours. After resting for an hour, he drove 200 km in 2 hours. He then spent 2 hours in the town before starting his return journey. On the return journey he drove 180 km in 2 hours, rested for half an hour and then reached home, taking another 2 hours.

Solution

Before drawing the graph, tabulate the distances and times, and then decide on a suitable scale.

Left home at 9:00 am:
(Drove 180 km in 2 h.)
∴ 180 km from home at 11:00 am.
(Rested for 1 h.)
∴ 180 km from home at 12:00 pm.
(Drove 200 km in 2 h.)
∴ 380 km from home at 2:00 pm.
(Spent 2 h in town.)
∴ 380 km from home at 4:00 pm.

The return journey:
(Drove 180 km in $1\frac{1}{2}$ h.)
∴ 200 km from home at 5:30 pm.
(Rested for $\frac{1}{2}$ h.)
∴ 200 km from home at 6:00 pm.
(Reached home after another 2 h.)
∴ 0 km from home at 8:00 pm.

Distance ranges from 0 to 380 km.
∴ A suitable scale is 1 cm : 40 km.
Time ranges from 9:00 am to 8:00 pm.
∴ A suitable scale is 1 cm : 2 h.

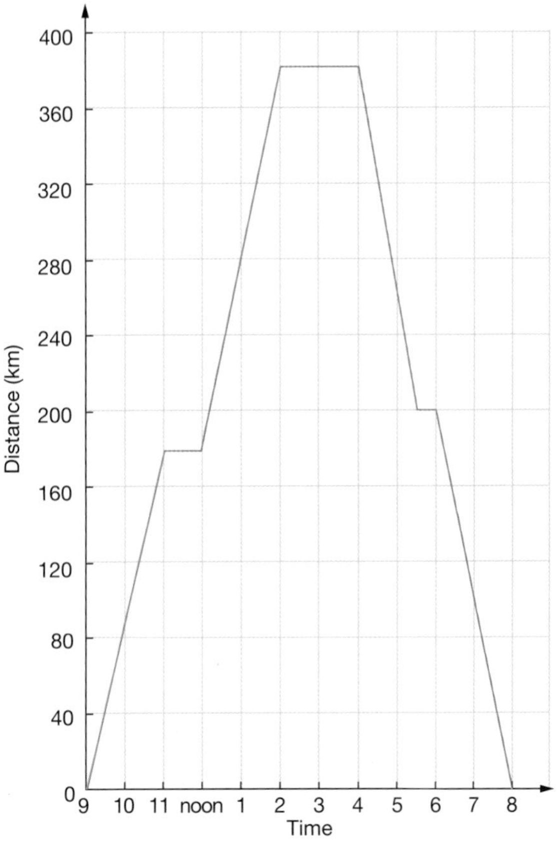

Exercise 15:05A

1 The graph shows the trip of a boy who travels from his home.

a How far from home is he at 11:00 am?

b When is he 40 km from home?

c How far from home is he at the end of his trip?

d How far does he travel between 11:00 am and 4:00 pm?

e Does his speed change during the journey? If so, at what time?

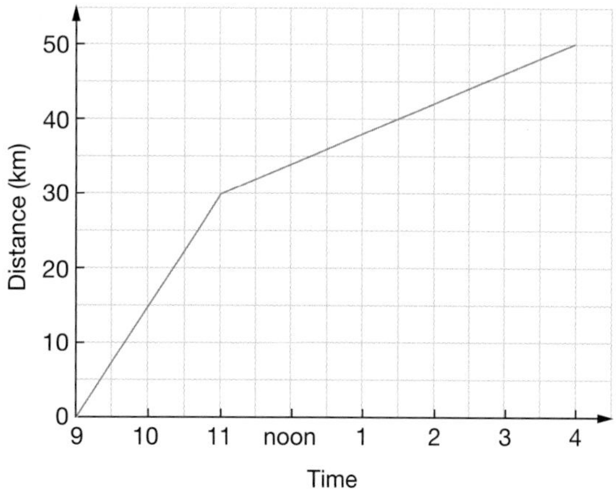

2 The graph gives the distance of a woman from her home at different times.

a How far from home is she at 10:00 am?

b At what time does she stop to rest?

c What is the total distance travelled?

d It is known that the woman completes her journey by riding in a car, walking, and riding a bike (not necessarily in that order). Between which times was she riding in the car?

e What is her average speed from 9:00 am to 11:00 am?

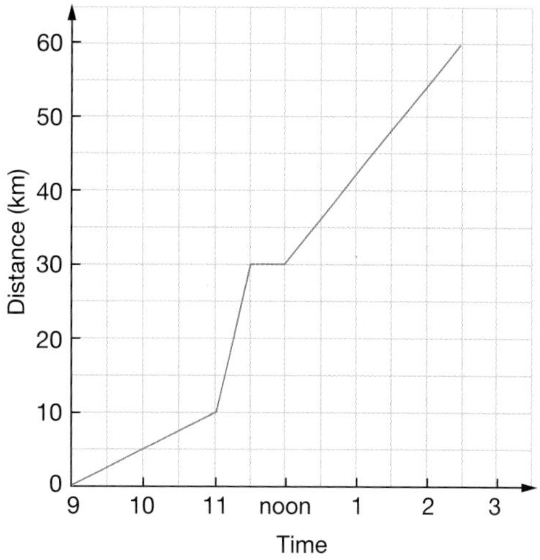

3 The travel graph shows the distance of a cyclist from her home between 10:00 am and 4:00 pm.

a How far does the cyclist travel in the first 2 hours?

b How far from home is she when she stops to rest?

c At what time does she commence the return journey?

d At 3:00 pm her speed changes. Does it increase or decrease? How can you tell without calculating the actual speeds?

e How far does she travel?

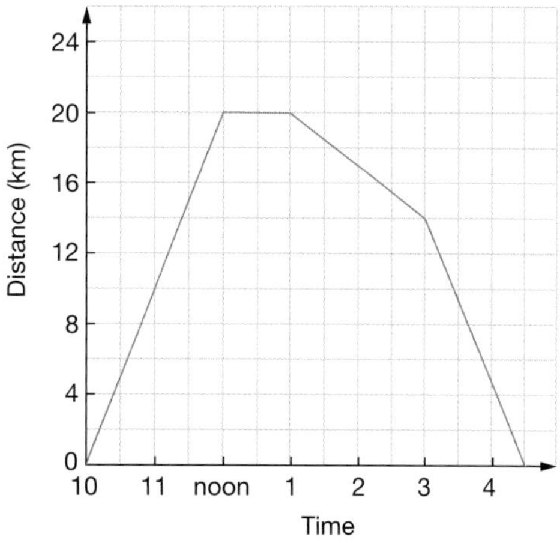

4 The graph shows the distance of a man from town *A* between noon and 6:00 pm.

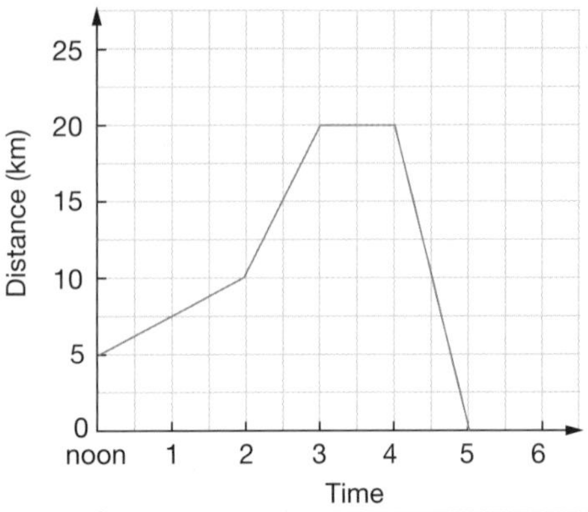

a How far from *A* is the man when he starts his trip?

b What is the farthest distance from *A* that he reaches?

c How far does he travel on his trip?

d At 2:00 pm his speed changes. Does it increase or decrease?

e Between what times is his speed greatest?

5 The graph shows the journeys of two motorists, Conway and Bartley. They are travelling on the same road and in the same direction, leaving town *A* at 9:00 am.

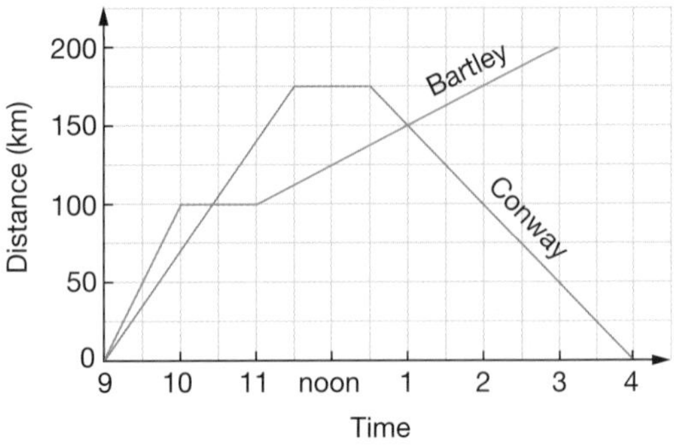

a Who travels the fastest in the first hour?

b How many times do they pass each other?

c At what time do they pass the second time?

d How far apart are they at 3:00 pm?

e How far does each man travel altogether?

6 Two towns *A* and *B* are 300 km apart. One motorist travels from *A* to *B* while the other travels from *B* to *A*. Their journeys are shown on the graph.

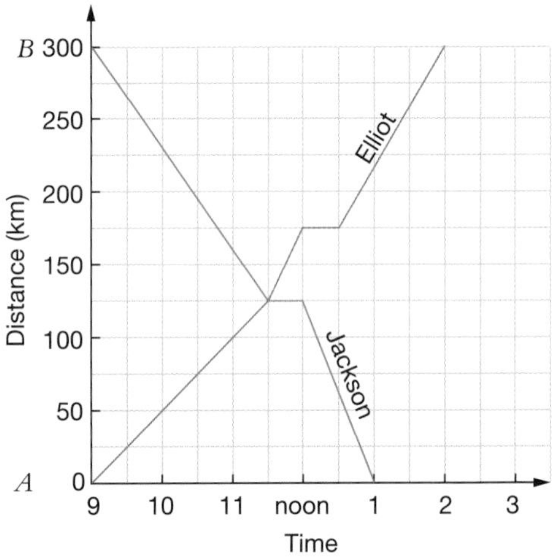

a Who completes the trip in the shortest time?

b What is Jackson's average speed for the trip?

c At 11:30 am does Elliot increase or decrease speed?

d Which period of Jackson's trip is the slower: from 10 to 11 am or from noon to 1 pm?

e How far from town *B* is Elliot when she stops to rest?

7 Noel cycled to his friend's place. He started at 8:00 am and covered 15 km in the first hour. After resting for half an hour he then covered the next 20 km to his friend's place in 2 hours.

a At what time did he reach his friend's place?

b How far was it from his home to his friend's place?

c Using a scale of 1 cm : 5 km on the distance axis and 1 cm : $\frac{1}{2}$ h on the time axis, make a travel graph for Noel's trip.

8 A family leaves Sydney by car at 10:00 am. They drive 160 km in 2 hours and then stop for lunch. After 1 hour they continue on, driving 200 km in the next 2 hours. The speed is then reduced and 90 km is covered in $1\frac{1}{2}$ hours. After stopping to rest for half an hour they then complete the last 60 km of their trip in 45 minutes.

a When did they complete their journey?
b How far did they drive?
c At what time did they stop for lunch?
d When did they make their second stop?
e Make a travel graph to illustrate this journey.

15:05B Non-linear graphs

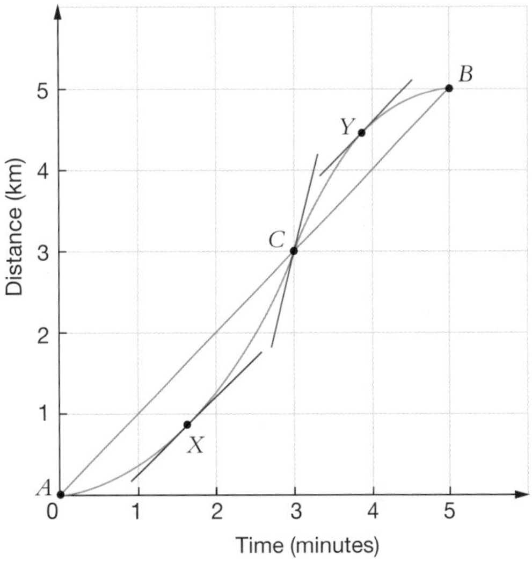

- The distance–time graphs in 15:05A were all composed of straight-line segments. In reality, these might only be an average representation of the motion.
- Consider this simple graph that shows a car's journey from A to B.
- The straight purple line shows the car arriving at B, 5 km away, in 5 minutes. The average speed of 1 km/min is shown by this line.
- The green curve would more accurately represent the motion of the car during its journey.
- At A and B the curve is flat, or horizontal, showing that its speed is zero, since the car has stopped at these points.
- At point C the car would be going fastest as the curve is steepest at this point.
- An indication of the speed at any point on the curve can be worked out by noting the slope of the tangent to the curve at this point. Three tangents have been drawn in blue at points X, Y and C. Since the slope of the tangents at X and Y is the same as the purple line, the speed of the car at X and Y would be 1 km/min.
- Can you see that the speed of the car between X and Y would be greater than 1 km/min since the curve is steeper in this section?
- Can you see that from A to X and from Y to B the car's speed would be less than 1 km/min?
- From the tangent to the curve at point C, what might you deduce about the car in this example?

WORKED EXAMPLE 1

A football is kicked from ground level and lands on a roof.

a To what height did the ball rise, and how high was the roof?

b What was the average speed of the ball until it reached its maximum height?

c What was the speed of the ball at its maximum height?

d When was the ball travelling at its fastest speed?

e When was the height decreasing?

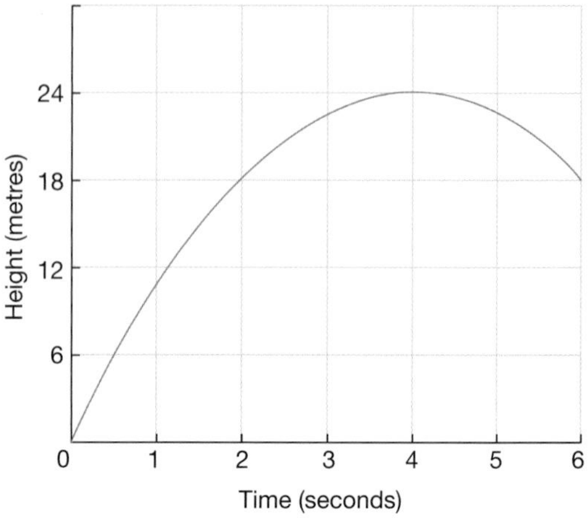

Solution

a The maximum height (H) is 24 m. The height of the roof (R) is 18 m.

b The average speed from the ground G to H is indicated by the straight green line. The ball travelled 24 m in 4 seconds, so the average speed was 6 m/s.

c The speed of the ball at H is zero because the graph is flat at this point. That is, the slope of the tangent to the curve is zero.

d The fastest speed was at G, when the ball was first kicked. After that, the ball was slowing down. Its height was increasing, but at a decreasing rate. (It goes up, but the same increase will take a longer time.)

e The height was obviously decreasing after 4 seconds. This is shown on the graph by the line going down or decreasing. The slope of the tangent at any point between H and R would be negative.

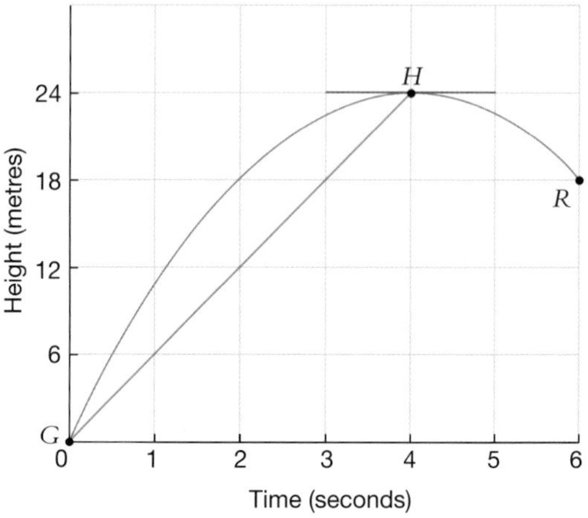

The height of the ball 'increases' at a decreasing rate!
and then it 'decreases' at an increasing rate!

WORKED EXAMPLE 2

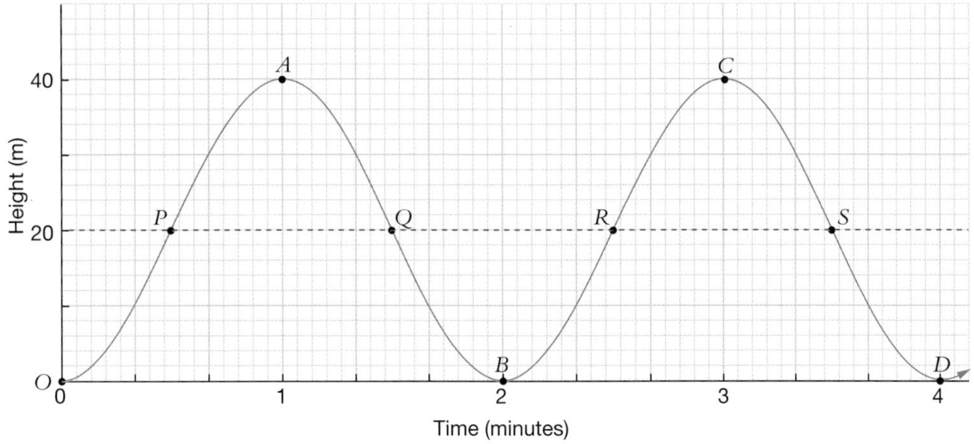

This graph shows the height of a particular seat on a Ferris wheel as it rotates to a height of 40 m.

a At what point is the rate of change in the height zero?

b When is the seat rising at its fastest speed?

c When is the seat falling at its fastest speed?

d Describe the rate of change in height of the seat from O to A.

Solution

a At the top and bottom of each rotation, the rate of change in height is zero; i.e. at points O, A, B, C, D on the graph.

b The seat is rising its fastest when the graph is increasing at the greatest rate. This is at points P and R, where the slope of the curve is steepest; i.e. at a height of 20 m.

c The seat is also falling at its fastest rate when the height is 20 m, but at points Q and S, where the slope of the curve is negative.

d The height of the seat increases from zero at O at an increasing rate until it reaches point P. The height continues to increase, but at a decreasing rate, until it reaches its maximum height at point A, where the rate of change is zero.

Exercise 15:05B

1 Amanda cycled from her home (H) to her friend's house (F), 30 km away. The black curved line shows her actual distance from H at any time.

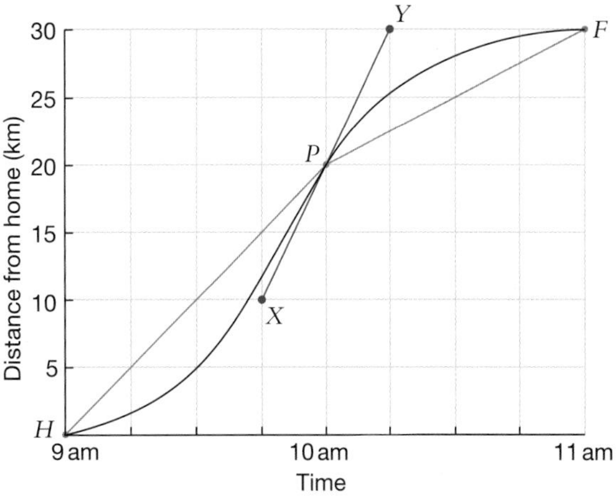

a What is her average speed for the whole ride?

b What is the average speed from H to point P?

c What is the average speed from P to F?

d If the blue line XY is the tangent to the curve at point P, what is Amanda's actual speed at P?

2 Jono drove from O to S in $3\frac{1}{2}$ hours. His speed varied due to traffic conditions.

a What was Jono's average speed from O to Q?

b Was Jono driving faster at point P or point Q?

c Was Jono driving faster at point Q or point R?

d Use the blue tangent drawn through point P to determine the speed at which Jono was travelling at this time.

e Similarly, calculate Jono's speed at point R.

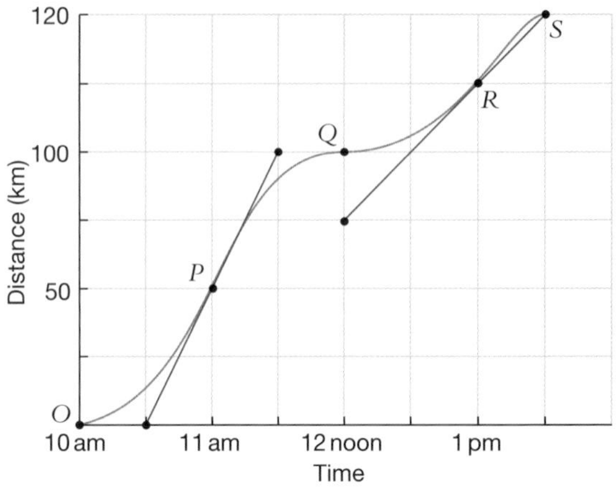

3 This graph shows Benny's journey in blue and Robyn's journey in purple as they made their way from A to B via different routes. They both arrived at the same time.

a What was their average speed?

b At 2 pm they were both 40 km from A, but who was travelling at the greater speed at this point?

c When they were each 10 km from B, who was travelling at the greater speed?

d At approximately what two times during their journeys was Benny's and Robyn's speed the same?

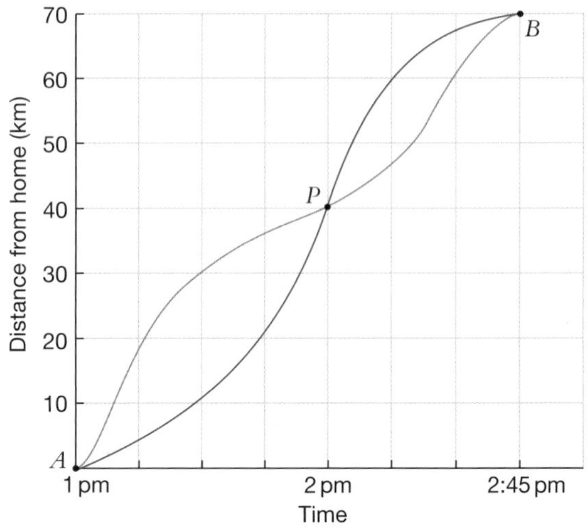

4 Briony drove from home to a friend's house 100 km away. After staying a short while, she then drove home.

a What was Briony's average speed from home to her friend's house?

b Is Briony's speed greater or less than this average speed at:

i point A ii point B?

c After point D, the slope of the graph is negative, indicating that Briony is travelling in the opposite direction towards home. At what point on the journey home does Briony's speed appear the greatest?

d Between which two points on the journey to Briony's friend's house was Briony's distance from home increasing at a decreasing rate?

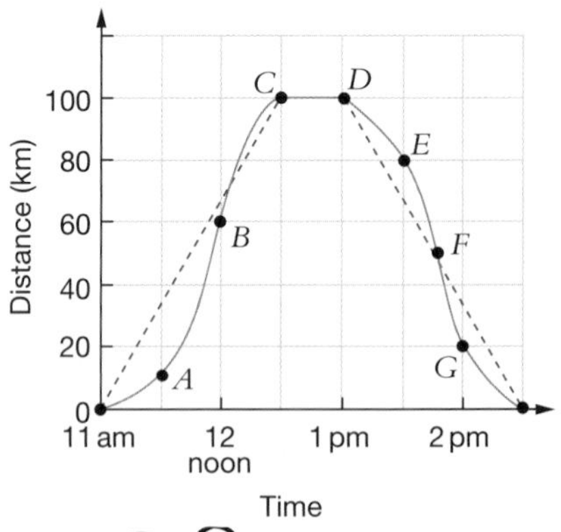

5 A projectile was fired 90 m into the air and returned to the ground after 6 seconds.

a What was the average speed of the projectile from the start to its maximum height H?

b Determine the speed of the projectile at point P, when the height was 80 m.

c Determine the speed at point Q, when the projectile was at a height of 50 m on its return journey.

d The projectile's height increased for the first 3 seconds. Did it do so at an increasing or decreasing rate?

e The height then decreased until the projectile reached the ground. Did it do so at an increasing or decreasing rate?

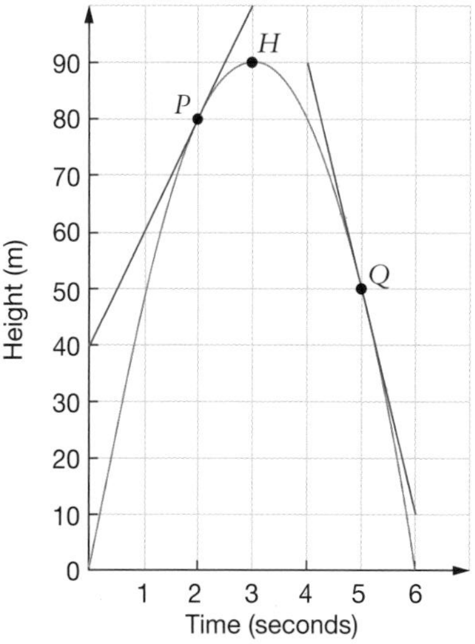

6 Grain is poured into a conical silo. The graph shows the height of grain as the grain is poured in after t minutes. The equation for this graph is $h = 1{\cdot}56\sqrt[3]{100\,t}$ (that is, $1{\cdot}56 \times \sqrt[3]{100\,t}$).

a Determine the height of grain in the silo when the elapsed time is:

i 10 min   ii 2 min

b Describe the rate of change of the height as the silo is filled.

c By drawing tangents to the curve, estimate the rate of change in the height of the grain in metres/min when:

i $t = 1$ ii $t = 2$

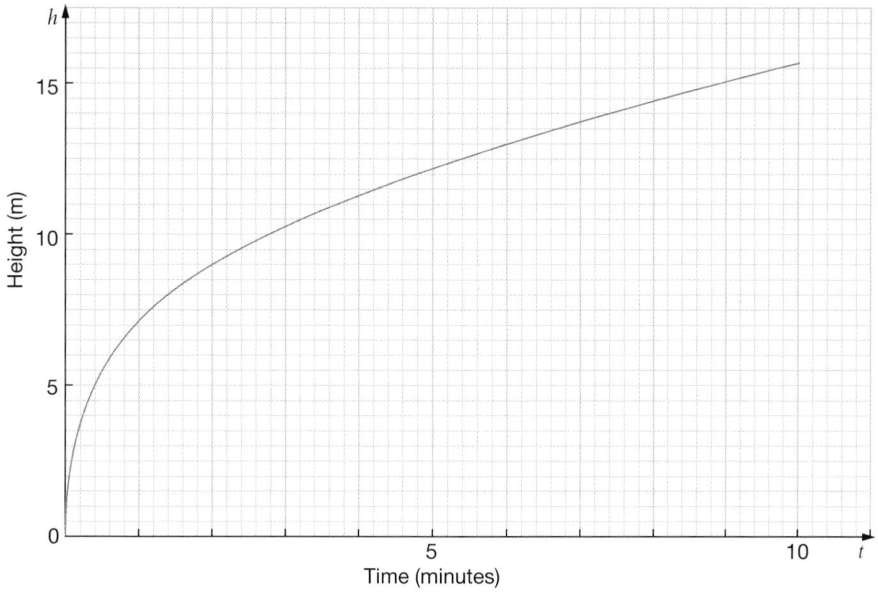

CHALLENGE 15:05 ROLLING DOWN AN INCLINED PLANE

- When an object is dropped, the force of gravity causes it to increase its speed by about 9·8 m/s every second. (Acceleration due to gravity is approximately 9·8 m/s per second.)
- When a ball rolls down an inclined plane the acceleration will be much less.

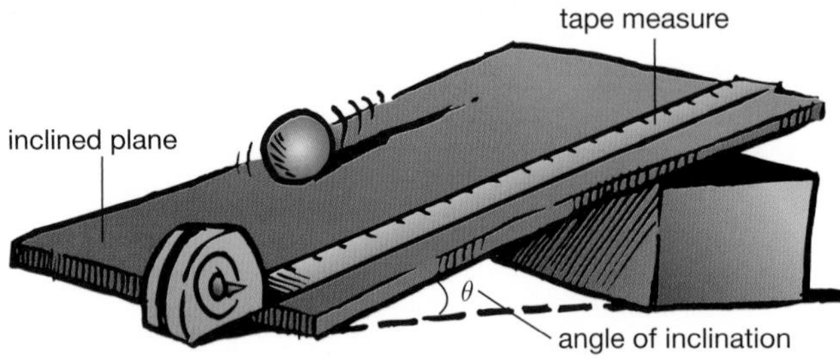

This investigation involves finding the acceleration of a ball (e.g. shot put or marble) as it rolls down an inclined plane of your choice.

If the ball starts from rest (speed = 0), then the formula for its motion is:

$s = \frac{1}{2}at^2$

where s = distance travelled

t = time taken

a = acceleration

Steps

1 Make a long inclined plane (over 2 m long) with an angle of inclination of about 10°.

2 Use a stopwatch to time the ball as it rolls 0·5, 1, 1·5 and 2 m down the inclined plane. Complete the table below as you go.

s	0·5	1	1·5	2
t				
t^2				

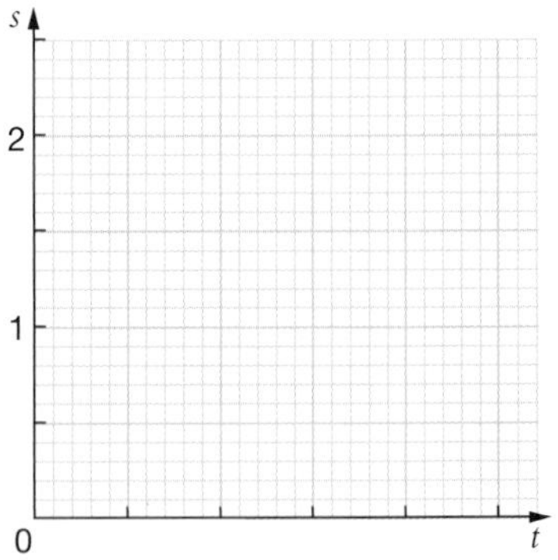

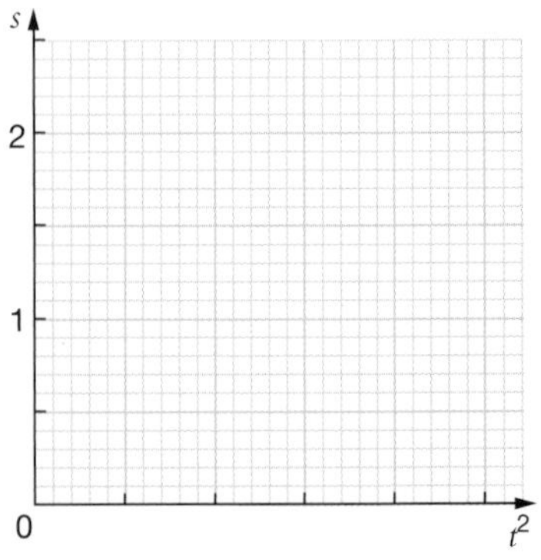

3 Plot s against t and draw the curve of best fit.

4 Plot s against t^2 (s on the vertical axis and t^2 on the horizontal axis).

5 Draw the line of best fit. The gradient of this line (rise divided by run) will be an approximation to $\frac{1}{2}a$. Double the gradient to find a. (If friction were not present, the acceleration of the ball would be $9{\cdot}8 \sin\theta$, where θ is the angle of inclination of the inclined plane.)

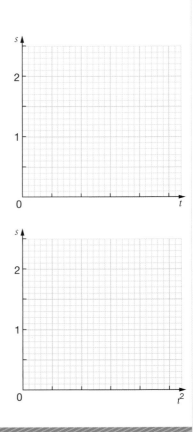

15:06 Relating graphs to physical phenomena

Much of a mathematician's work is concerned with finding a relationship between two quantities that can change or vary their values. For example, we could study a person's height at different times of their life. As one quantity changes (e.g. time), the other changes or varies (e.g. height). The features that change, and the pronumerals used to represent them, are called *variables*.

Graphs provide an excellent means of exploring the relationship between variables. They give an immediate 'picture' of the relationship, from which we can see such things as:

- whether a variable is increasing or decreasing with respect to the other variable
- when a variable has its highest or lowest value
- whether a variable is increasing quickly or slowly with respect to the other variable.

Graphs can be used to show relationships between data such as:

- temperature and time of day (or year)
- height and weight
- water level before, during and after a bath
- distance and speed
- light brightness and proximity
- tidal movements over time.

PREP QUIZ 15:06

In which of the following graphs does:

1 M increase as t increases
2 M decrease as t increases
3 M stay unchanged?

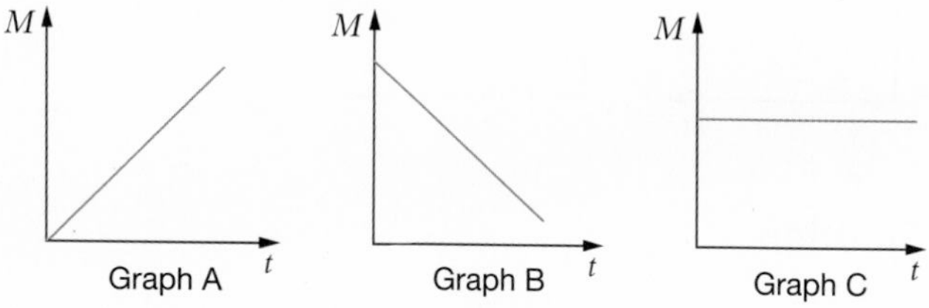

In the following graphs, for which line is the mass increasing more quickly, I or II?

4
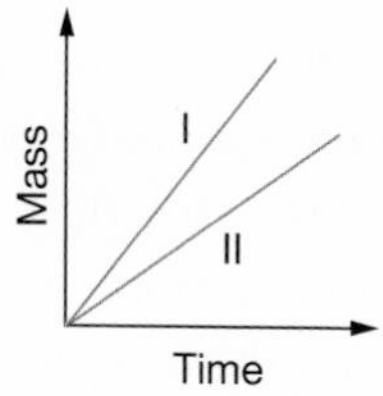

5
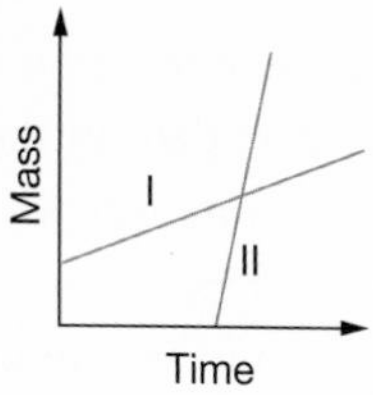

In which part of this graph does:

6 the height increase slowly
7 the height increase quickly?

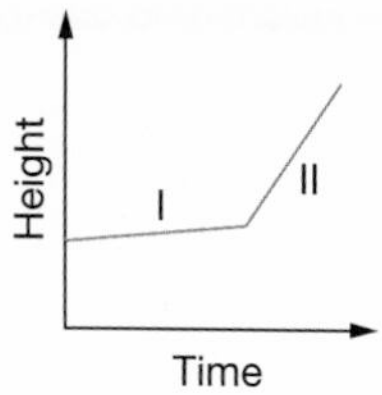

In which of the graphs does:

8 M increase slowly at first and then quickly
9 M increase quickly at first, then slowly
10 M increase at the same rate?

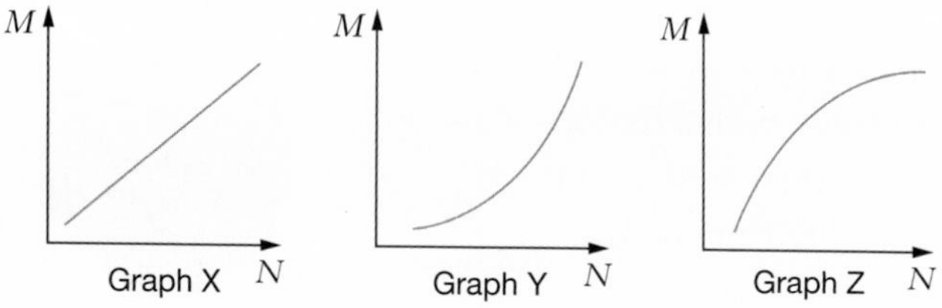

WORKED EXAMPLE 1

A person is driving a car at a certain speed and then increases that speed. Which graph represents this?

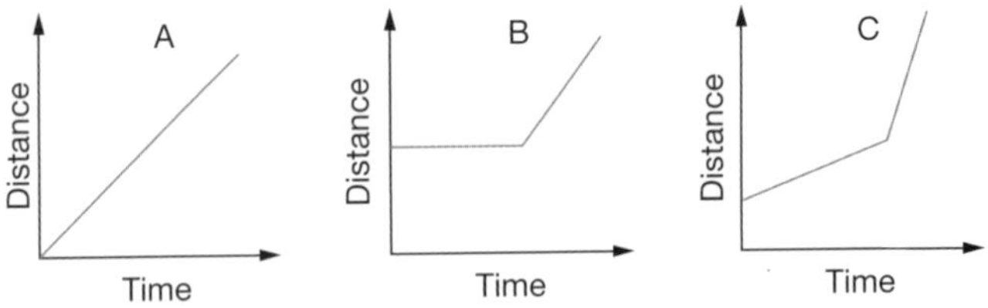

Solution

Since two speeds are involved, the second one greater than the first, the graph must have two sections, one for each speed. Graph A is unsuitable because it consists of only one section. Graph B is unsuitable because the first section is a horizontal section, which indicates that the car was not moving. But the question indicates that the car was moving and then changed its speed. Graph C best illustrates the information given.

WORKED EXAMPLE 2

Water is added to the tank shown at a steady rate. Which graph best represents the increase in the water level *h*?

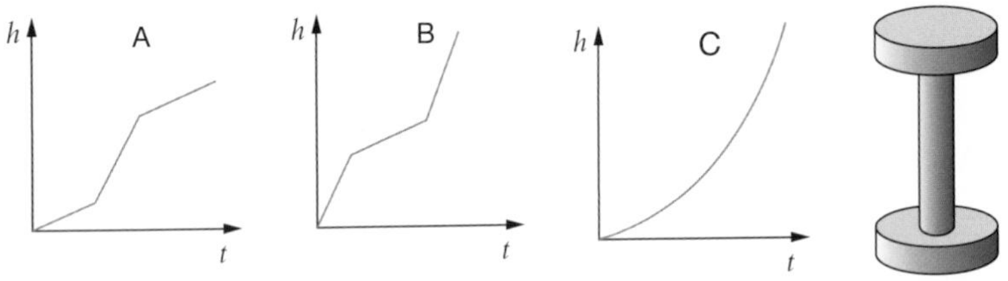

The skinny one will fill up faster than the wide one.

Solution

The middle part of the tank is skinnier than the bottom and the top. Therefore, if water is poured in at a steady rate it will rise faster in the middle part than in the other two sections. The water level, *h*, will increase more quickly for this section of the tank than for the others. The correct graph must consist of three sections, with the steepest section in the middle. Hence, graph A is the best representation.

WORKED EXAMPLE 3

Describe what this graph is showing.

Solution

A flat basketball was inflated, probably with a motorised pump. It was then used until it was punctured and deflated.

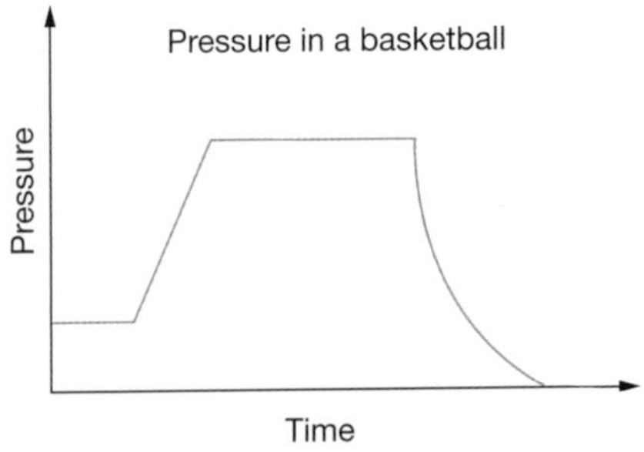

WORKED EXAMPLE 4

A point A is on the circumference of a wheel. If this wheel is rolled, make a graph to show the height of this point above the ground.

Solution

The highest point on the wheel above the ground is when it is at the top of the wheel. Therefore the greatest height above the ground is the diameter of the wheel.

The smallest height above the ground is zero, which occurs when the point is actually on the ground.

Because the wheel is rolling, the height of point A will oscillate between these positions.

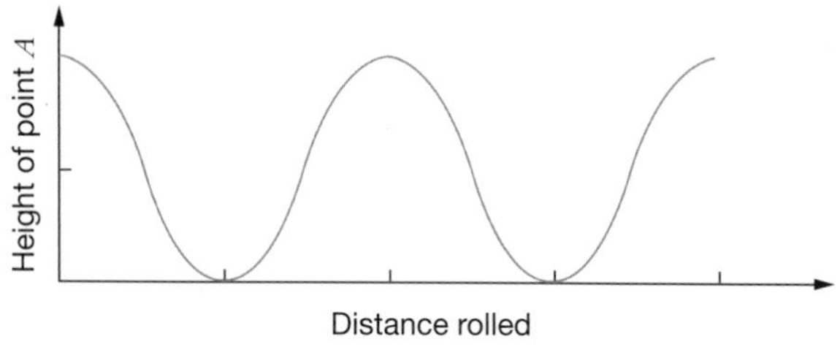

WORKED EXAMPLE 5

An automatic pump is used to fill a cylindrical tank. The tank, which is empty at the start, is filled at a steady rate.

The tank remains full for a period before it is emptied at a steady rate. If it is emptied faster than it is filled, make a sketch that shows the variation in water level in the tank for one complete pumping cycle.

Solution

At the start of the cycle the tank is empty and so the water level is zero.

The tank is then filled at a steady rate, which means that the water level will rise at a steady rate.

After it is filled, the tank remains full for a period. For this period, the water level remains the same.

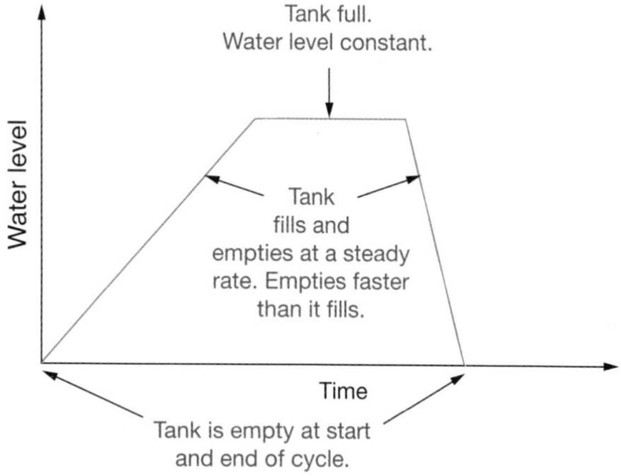

The tank is then emptied at a steady rate but faster than the rate at which it was filled. This means that the line in this section of the graph must be steeper than the line in the first section.

It is also important to be able to describe and interpret information presented in graphs.

Exercise 15:06

1 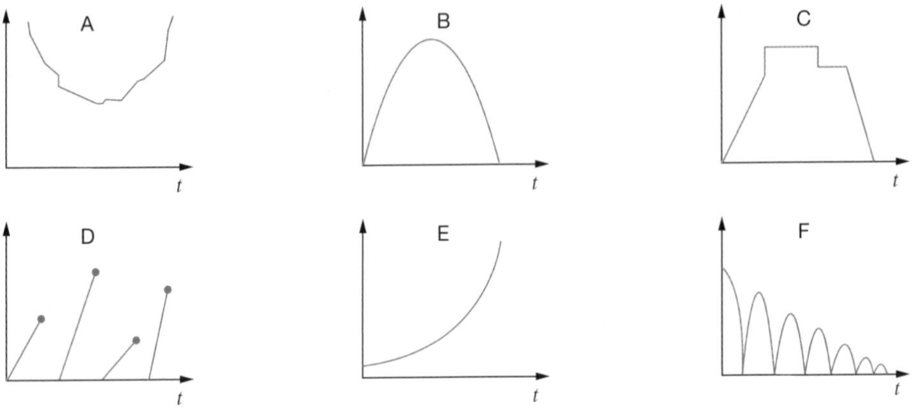

Choose the graph above that best represents each situation below.

- **a** Population growth as time passes.
- **b** The number of people waiting for a train on a station as time passes.
- **c** The maximum daily temperature in Sydney throughout a year.
- **d** The depth of water in a bath as time passes as it is filled, a person gets in, has a bath, the person gets out and then the water is let out.
- **e** The height of a ball as time passes as it is dropped from a window and continues to bounce.
- **f** The height of a stone as time passes if the stone is thrown into the air.

2 A motorist drives for three hours averaging 80 km/h, 60 km/h and 90 km/h respectively in each hour. Which graph best represents the trip?

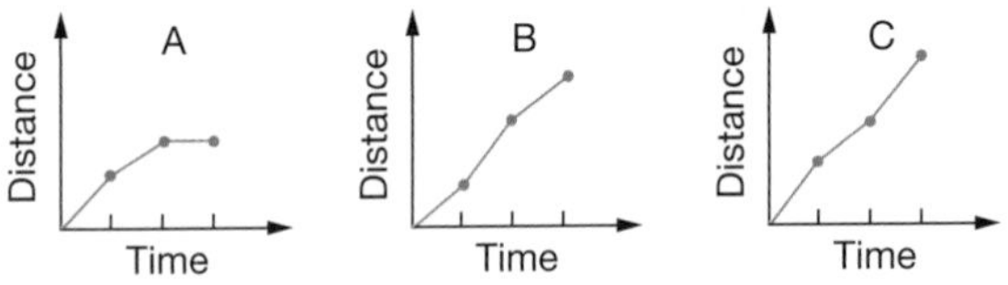

3 A boy rode his bike down the road. He rode quickly at the start and then slowed down. Which graph best represents his journey?

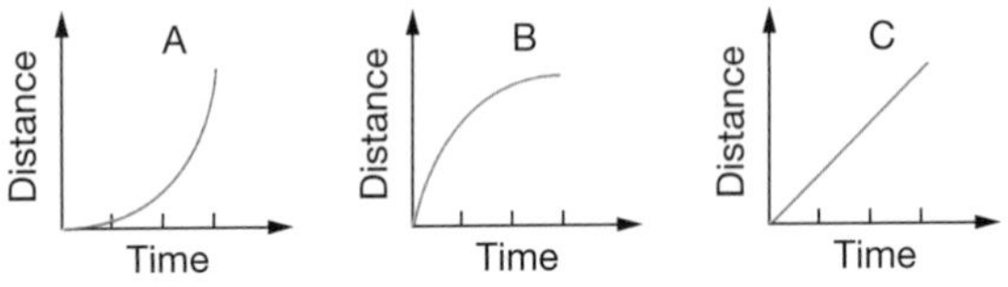

4 The diagram on the right shows the water level in a tank that is filled and emptied periodically. Give an interpretation of this graph by describing what happens in the first 120 minutes.

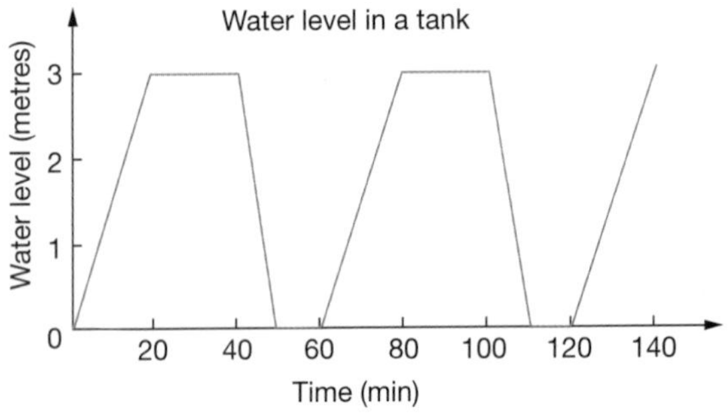

5 Give a reasonable story or explanation for the information shown in each graph below.

a
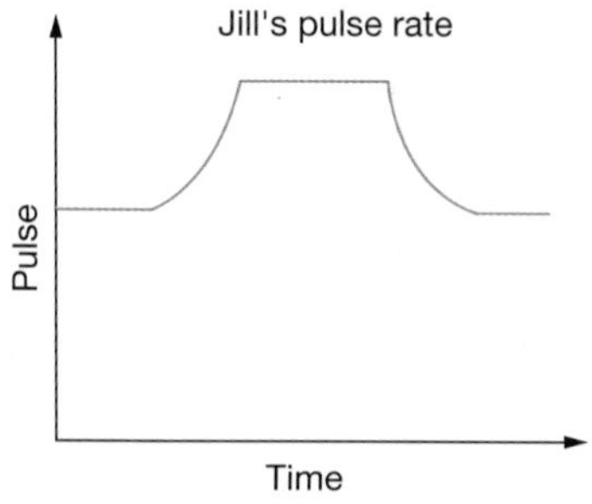

b
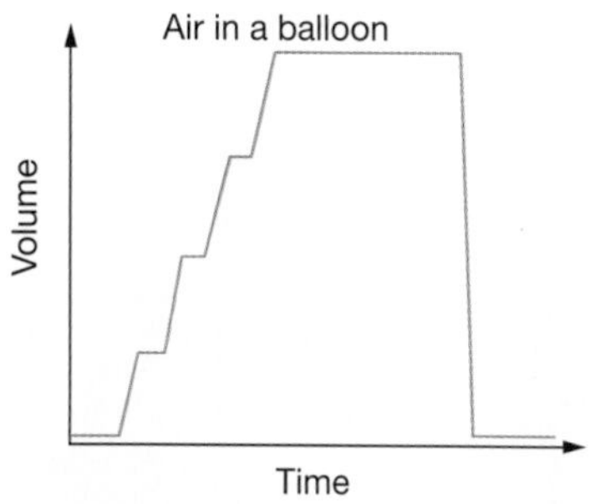

c
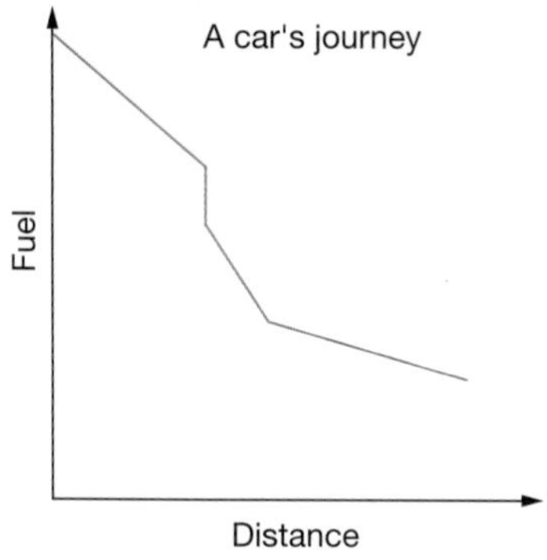

d
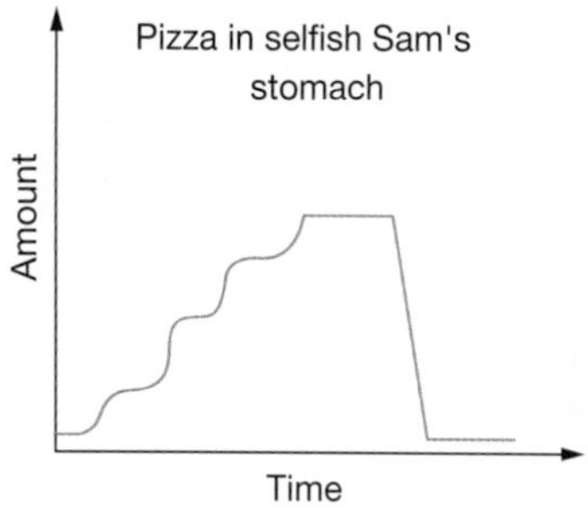

6 X is a point on the circumference of a roller, as shown in the diagram. The roller can be moved in either a clockwise or an anticlockwise direction.
The graphs below give the height of X above the ground. Which graph represents the clockwise rotation?

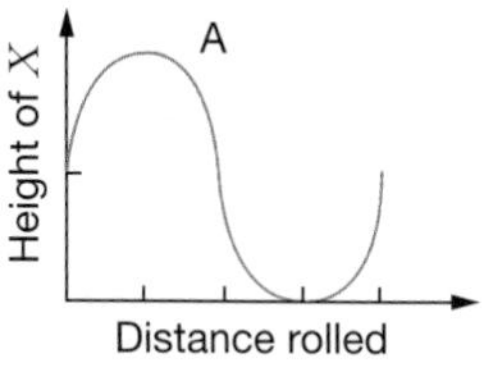

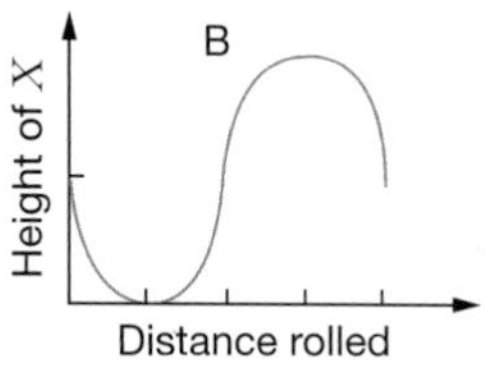

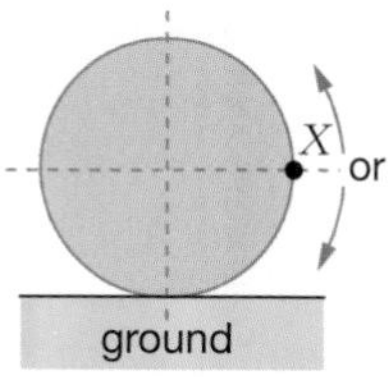

7 Shock absorbers in a car are designed to reduce the bouncing up and down that is caused when the car hits a bump in the road. The following three graphs show the vertical distance moved by a point on the front bonnet of the car, after hitting a bump. Which graph best represents a well-designed shock absorber?

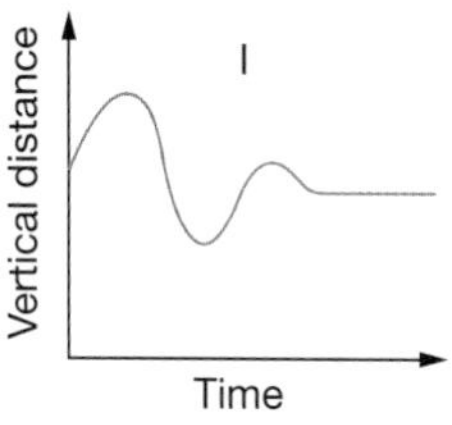

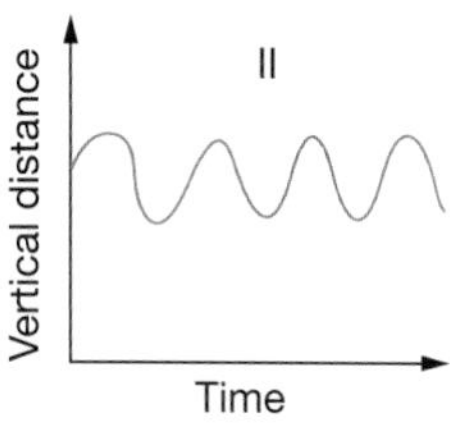

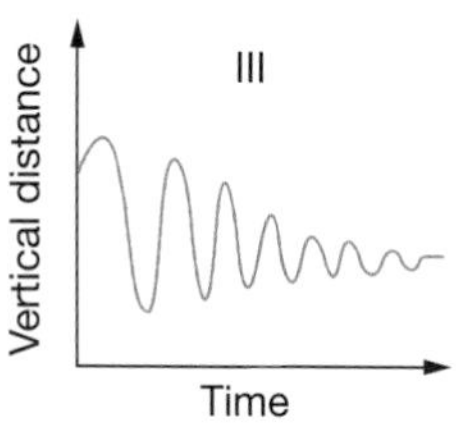

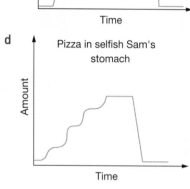

8 Each of the four containers pictured is filled with water at a steady rate. When the level of water in each container was plotted, the graphs **a** to **d** were obtained. Match each container to its graph.

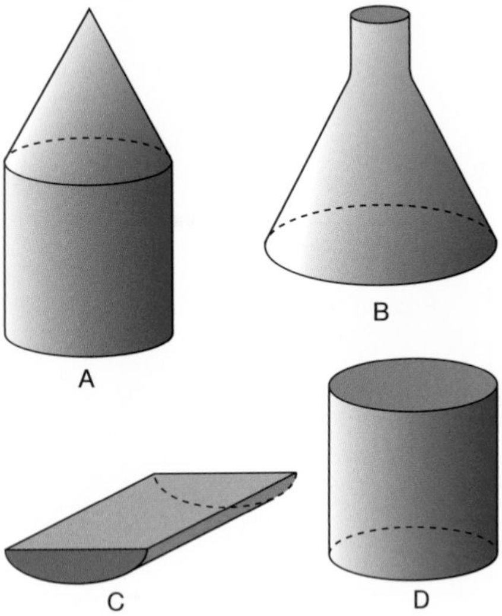

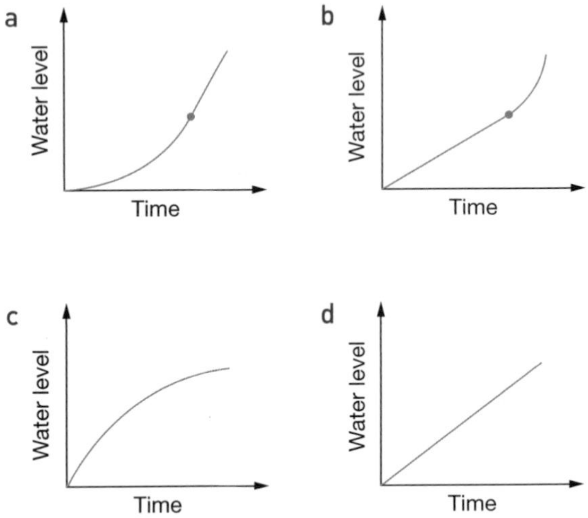

9 The following is known about the solubility of four chemical salts.

Salt A: As the temperature increases the solubility increases, slowly at first and then at a much faster rate.

Salt B: Shows very little increase in solubility as the temperature increases.

Salt C: Increases its solubility at a steady rate as the temperature increases.

Salt D: As the temperature increases the solubility decreases and then increases.

Match each salt to the graphs **a** to **d**.

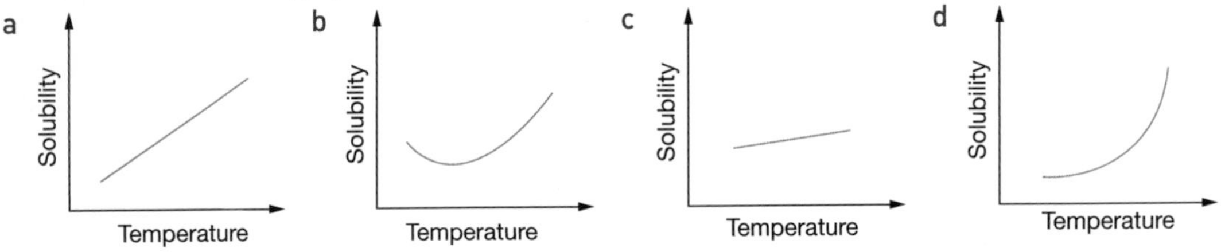

10 A point A is on the circumference of a wheel. The wheel completes one revolution where the starting position of A can be at any of the points 1, 2, 3 or 4 marked on the diagram on the right.

If the wheel is rolled from left to right, which graph best represents the height of A above the ground when A starts at:

a position 1 **b** position 3 **c** position 2?

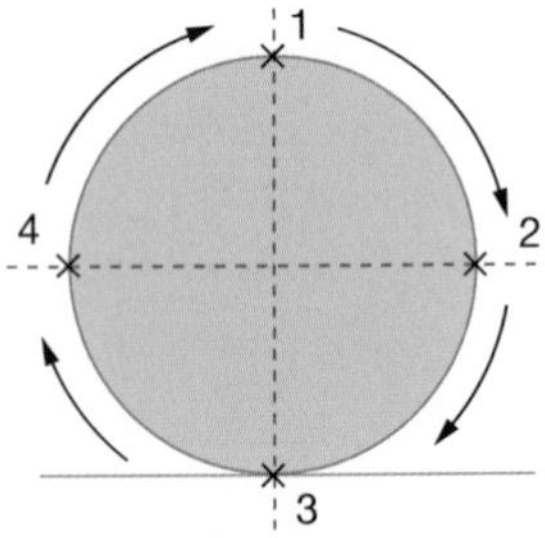

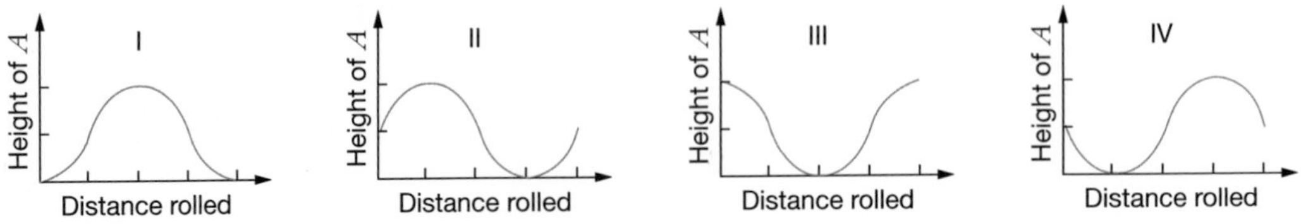

11 Two boys are riding on a seesaw. Make a sketch representing the height of a boy above the ground as time passes if he starts on the ground and goes up and down twice.

12 When boiling water is allowed to cool, it is known that it loses heat quickly at the start and, as time goes on, it loses heat at a slower rate.
Make a sketch to show the shape of a graph that would support this information. Show water temperature on the vertical axis and time on the horizontal axis.

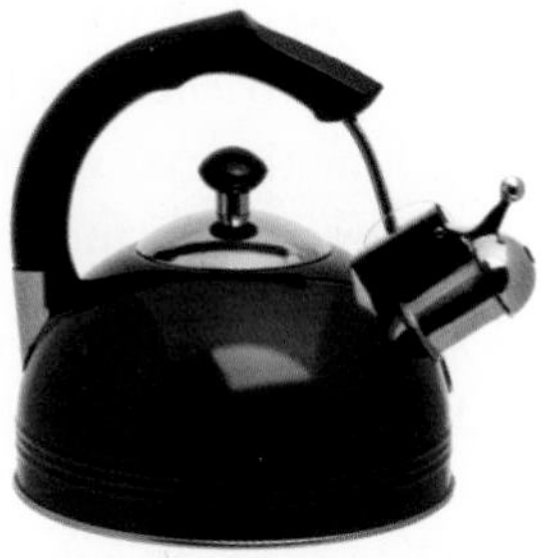

13 A mass of 1 kg is hanging from a vertical spring as shown in the diagram. If this mass is pulled downwards and then released, the mass will move.
Make a sketch to show how the position of the mass will vary from its equilibrium position as time passes.

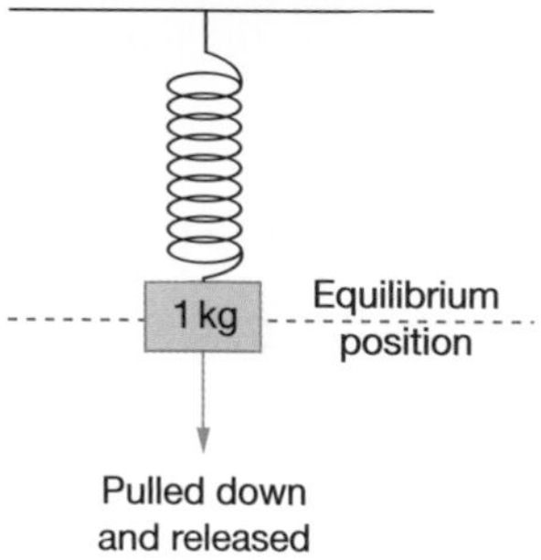

14 Sketch a line graph to represent each of the following situations. Choose axis labels wisely. Time, when mentioned, should always appear on the horizontal axis.

a how water level varies in a bath as it is being filled
b the relationship between speed and time when a car travels at a constant speed
c the relationship between speed and time when a car travelling at a constant speed brakes slowly before coming to a halt
d a similar relationship as in part c, but the car brakes quickly
e how the brightness of a red traffic light varies against time
f how the water level in a bath varies against time when you take a bath
g how the water level in a leaking tank varies against time just after the leak starts
h how the temperature of boiled water varies against time as it cools
i how the fluid level in a cup of tea varies against time as it is consumed
j how the level of fuel in a fuel tank varies against the number of kilometres travelled by a car
k how the water level in a glass containing water and floating ice changes as the ice melts
l how your excitement level changes as you work through this exercise

15 A parachutist jumps from a plane. Before she opens her chute, her speed increases at a constant rate. On opening her chute her speed falls rapidly, approaching a constant terminal value. Make a sketch showing how her speed varies with time.

16 A car is approaching a set of traffic lights at a constant speed when the driver sees the lights change and immediately applies the brakes. The car comes to a stop. After waiting for the lights to change the car accelerates away until it reaches the same constant speed at which it had approached the lights. Make a sketch showing:

a how the car's speed relates to time

b how the distance travelled by the car relates to time.

17 A person walking in the desert attempts to walk in a straight line. However, her legs are not exactly the same length and so she walks in a circle.

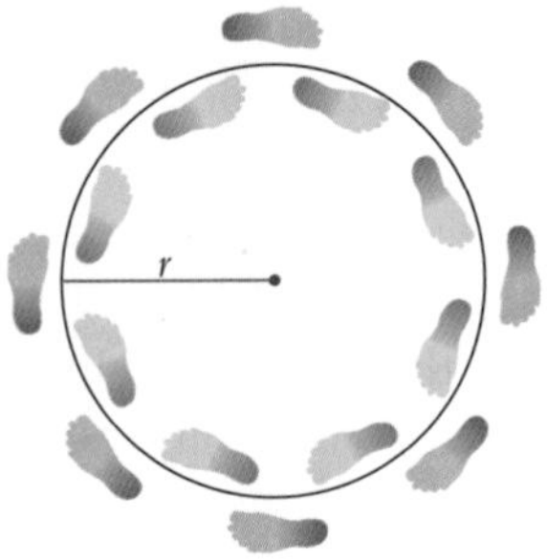

The table below shows the relationship between the difference (d) between the length of the step of the left and right legs and the radius (r) of the circle in which the person walks.

Difference d (mm)	1	2	3	4	5
Radius of circle r (m)	180	90	60	45	36

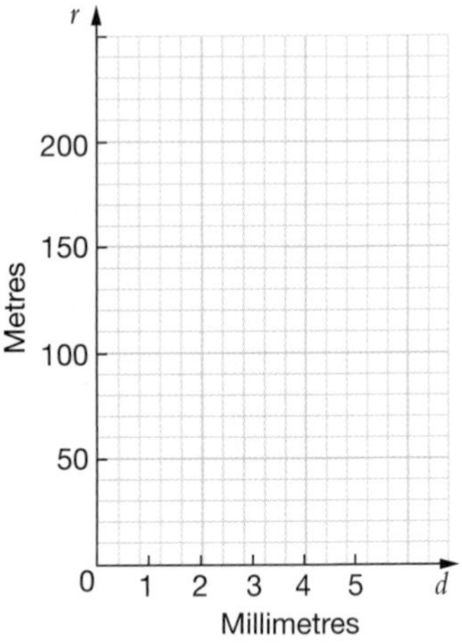

a If her left leg is longer than her right leg, would she turn to the left or to the right?

b As the difference between the lengths of steps increases, what happens to the radius of the circle?

c Plot the information in the table onto the number plane to the right. Draw a curve joining these points.

d Write a formula to describe this relationship.

e If the difference in steps is 1·5 mm, what would be the radius of the circle in which she walked?

f What happens when there is no difference in steps?

18 Gary discovered that, when draining his pool, the volume of water (V litres) remaining in the pool is related to the time (t minutes) that the water has been draining. The formula relating V and t is:

$$V = 20(30 - t)^2$$

a When $t = 0$ (initially), the pool was full. What volume of water can the pool hold?

b Copy and complete this table using the formula.

t	0	5	10	20	25	30
V	18 000					

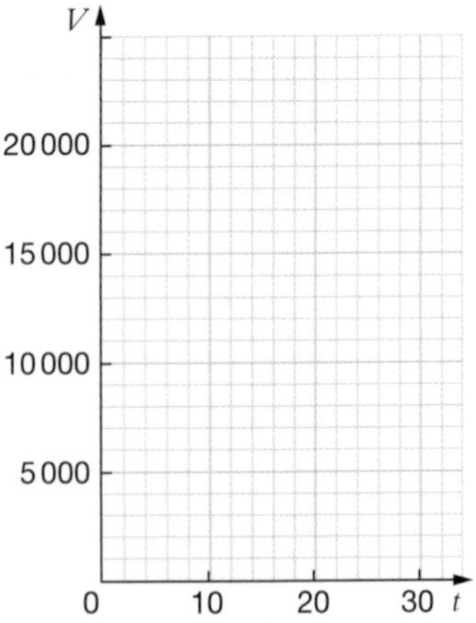

c Graph the relationship using the axes shown.

d How long does it take to drain 9000 L from the pool?

e Does the water drain from the pool at a steady rate? Explain your answer.

CHALLENGE 15:06 CURVES AND STOPPING DISTANCES

The approximate stopping distance of a car is given by the formula:
$d = v + 0{\cdot}073v^2$

The approximate stopping distance of a truck is given by the formula:
$d = v + 0{\cdot}146v^2$

- For both formulas, d is measured in metres and v is measured in metres per second.
- This table relates stopping distance and the speed of a **car** for various speeds.
  $d = v + 0{\cdot}073v^2$

v	0 km/h (0 m/s)	30 km/h (8·3 m/s)	60 km/h (16·7 m/s)	80 km/h (22·2 m/s)	100 km/h (27·8 m/s)
d	0 m	13·4 m	36·9 m	58·3 m	84·1 m

1 Complete the table below, which relates stopping distance and the speed of a **truck** for various speeds.
$d = v + 0{\cdot}146v^2$

v	0 km/h (0 m/s)	30 km/h (8·3 m/s)	60 km/h (16·7 m/s)	80 km/h (22·2 m/s)	100 km/h (27·8 m/s)
d					

2 The graph below is a model of the distance between cars after stopping. The cars are 100 m apart, heading towards one another, when the drivers sense danger. The drivers brake at the same instant.

- The green axes and graph refer to the car coming from the right. The purple axes and graph refer to the car coming from the left.
- In the first table above, the reading on the vertical axis (speed) is mentioned first.

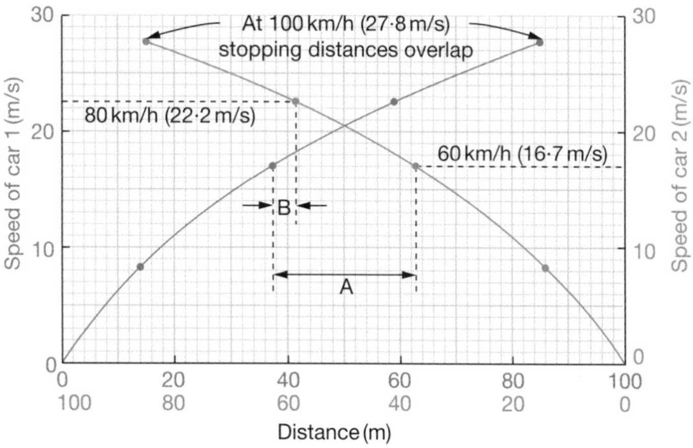

Examples

- If both cars are travelling at 60 km/h (16·7 m/s), the interval *A* gives the distance apart when they stop. From the graph, this is 26 m.
- If the stopping distances of the cars have overlapped, then a collision has occurred. At 100 km/h (27·8 m/s) the readings on the distance axis have overlapped, indicating a collision.
- If the purple car is travelling at 60 km/h (16·7 m/s) and the green car at 80 km/h (22·2 m/s), the interval *B* gives the distance apart when they stop. From the graph, this is about 4 m.

Questions

1 a Do the cars collide if they are both travelling at 80 km/h? At what speed (in m/s) would a collision just be avoided if the cars are travelling at the same speed?

b What would be the distance between the cars after stopping, if they had both been travelling at:

i 10 m/s ii 20 m/s?

c At what speed would both cars be travelling if they stop:

i 20 m apart ii 60 m apart?

d What would be the distance between the cars after stopping, if the speeds of the cars were:

i purple, 10 m/s; green, 27 m/s ii purple, 23 m/s; green, 12 m/s?

2 Draw a graph, similar to the one above, to model the distance between vehicles after stopping if the vehicles are the car and the truck referred to in the tables on page 495.

Use the questions in **1** above as a guide to list similar findings using your new graph.

FUN SPOT 15:06 — WHAT DO YOU CALL A SNOWMAN IN THE SUN?

Answer each question and write the letter for the correct answer in the box above the question number.

Match each distance/time graph with the correct description of the motion shown by the graph.

1
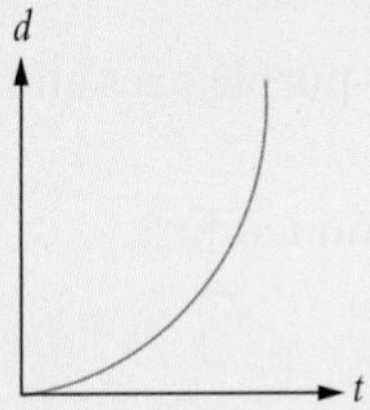

2
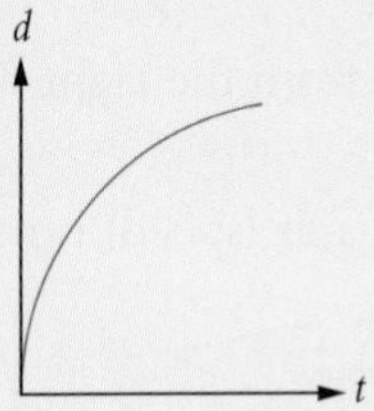

3
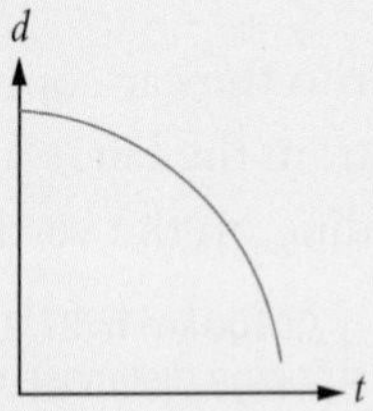

4
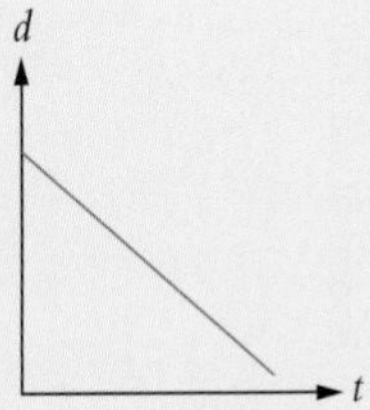

5
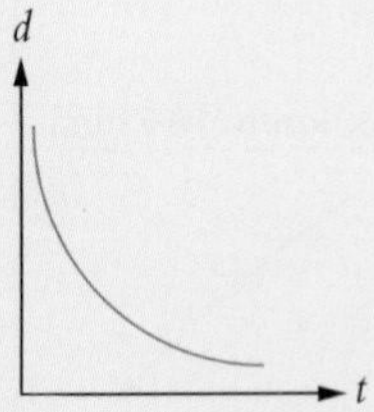

6
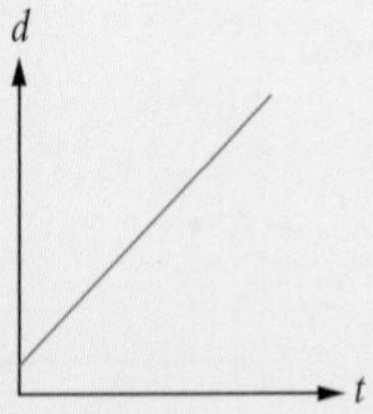

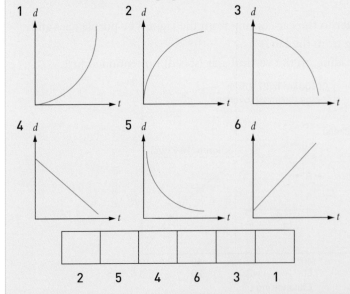

L decreasing at an increasing rate
U decreasing at an decreasing rate
D decreasing at an constant rate
E increasing at an increasing rate
P increasing at an decreasing rate
D increasing at an constant rate

2	5	4	6	3	1

MATHS TERMS 15

axis (plural: **axes**)
- each graph has two axes, a horizontal axis and a vertical axis, which show the two quantities that are being compared on the graph

constant of proportionality
- the numerical factor by which both quantities are increased or decreased in a given ratio

direct proportion
- when both related quantities are increased (or decreased) in a given ratio, i.e. both quantities are multiplied by the same value
- two quantities Y and X in direct proportion are related by the equation $Y = kX$, where k is the constant of proportionality

graph
- a representation of numerical data in the form of a diagram
- a graph provides a quick way of analysing patterns in numerical data

inverse proportion
- when one related quantity increases as the other decreases in a given ratio
- two quantities Y and X in inverse proportion are related by the equation $Y = \frac{k}{X}$, where k is the constant of proportionality

phenomenon (plural: **phenomena**)
- an object or occurrence that is observed
- a physical phenomenon is one that can be measured

proportion
- when all measures of an object or shape are increased, or decreased, by the same factor

rate
- a comparison of unlike quantities written in a definite order, e.g. 100 km in 5 hours or 20 km/h
- units are used in this comparison, e.g. 8 people per car

scale
- set of marks at measured distances on an axis
- used in measuring or making proportional reductions or enlargements

speed
- relative rate of motion or action
- defined as: $\frac{\text{distance}}{\text{time}}$
- measured in units such as km/h or m/s

travel graph (distance–time graph)
- a line graph in which distance travelled is plotted against time taken
- the gradient (or slope) of the line is an indication of the speed of the motion

DIAGNOSTIC TEST 15 PROPORTION

These questions reflect some of the important skills introduced in this chapter.
Errors made in this test will indicate areas of weakness.
Each weakness should be treated by going back to the section listed.

1 Write each rate in its simplest terms. 15:01

a 200 km in 4 hours = … km/h

b \$56 for 7 kg = \$… /kg

c 60 litres in $2\frac{1}{2}$ hours = … L/h

d 250 g per 10 cm^3 = … g/cm^3

2 Convert these rates. 15:01

a 6 km/h = … m/min

b 120 000 mL/min = … L/s

c 15 000 kg/day = … t /day

d \$100 per hectare = … c/m^2

3 For each example below, state whether it is an example of direct or indirect proportion. 15:02, 15:04

a The ingredients for making pizzas and the number of people who are going to eat them.

b The number of people eating pizzas and the time taken to eat them.

c The speed at which a car travels and the distance covered in a given time.

d The speed at which a car travels and the time taken to cover a certain distance.

4 M is directly proportional to t, and when $t = 6$, $M = 30$. 15:02

a Given that $M = kt$, find the value of k.

b Find the value of M when $t = 17$.

c Find the value of t when $M = 174$.

5 Travelling at a constant average speed I can travel a distance D in a certain time T. 15:02
If I travel 120 km in 5 hours:

a Determine an equation for this relationship in the form $D = kT$.

b What is the constant of proportionality?

c How far can I travel in 8 hours?

d How long would it take me to travel 228 km?

6 This graph shows the number of cartons a factory can produce in a given time. 15:03

a By determining the gradient of the line, find the constant of proportionality for this example of direct proportion.

b How many cartons could be produced in 22 hours?

c How many hours would be needed to produce 200 cartons? Give your answer in hours and minutes.

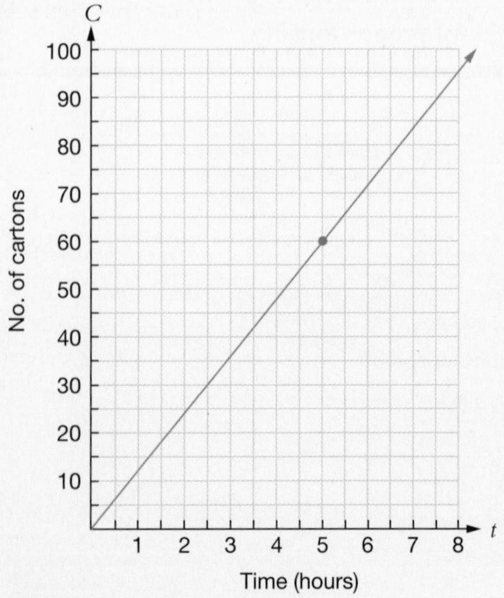

7 The time taken (t) to clean the windows of a building is inversely proportional to the number of cleaners employed (n). It takes 8 hours for 6 cleaners to clean the windows. 15:04

a Find an equation in the form $t = \frac{k}{n}$ for this relationship.

b What is the constant of proportionality?

c How long would it take 12 cleaners to do the same job?

d How many cleaners are needed to do the job in 3 hours?

8 The time taken (T) for Henry to drive home is inversely proportional to the average speed (S) at which he drives. If his speed is 40 km/h he gets home in 3 hours. 15:04

a What is the proportional constant for this relationship?

b How long does he take if he increases his average speed to 50 km/h? (Give your answer in hours and minutes.)

c At what speed must he travel to get home in 2 hours?

9 The frequency of a note produced on a string is inversely proportional to the length of the string. A string of length 50 cm produces a frequency of 600 Hz. 15:04

a What frequency is produced by a string of length 40 cm?

b What length of string would produce a frequency of 800 Hz?

10 Which section of each graph represents the greatest speed? 15:05A

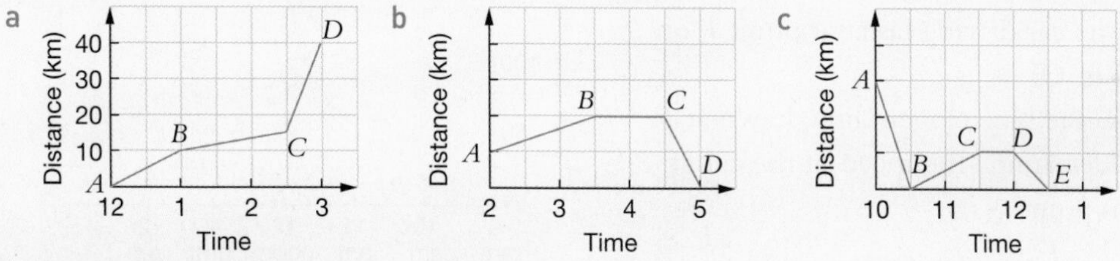

11 Which section of each of the graphs in Question 10 represents the slowest speed? 15:05A

12 This graph shows the distance of two brothers, Joe and Jacky, from home. 15:05A

a How far does Joe start from home?

b What is Jacky's average speed from:

  i 10 am to 12 noon

  ii 12 noon to 1:30 pm

  iii 2 pm to 3 pm?

c What is Joe's average speed for the entire journey from 10 am to 3 pm?

d What is Joe's greatest speed and between which times is it recorded?

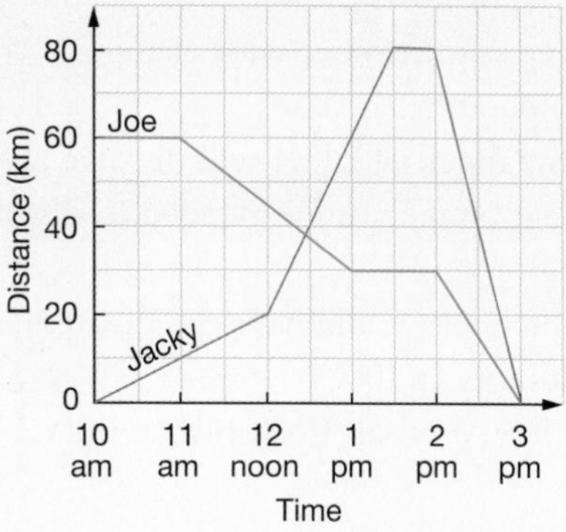

13 a How long does it take the water to reach a temperature of 80°C?
b What is the temperature of the water after 10 min?
c What is the temperature of the water after 20 min?
d From the graph it can be seen that the water doesn't cool at a constant rate. The dotted line represents a constant cooling rate. If the water had cooled at a constant rate, what would its temperature have been after 10 min?

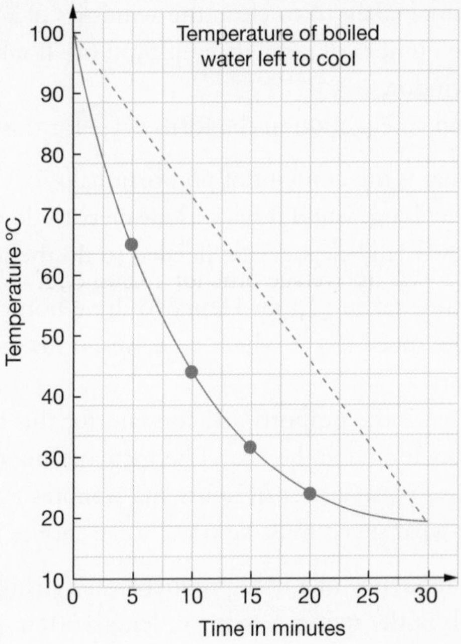

15:06

14 This graph shows the journey of a car from A to B, 200 km away.
a What is the average speed from A to B?
b Is the car driving faster at point P or point Q?
c Use the blue tangent line drawn at R to determine the speed of the car at this point.

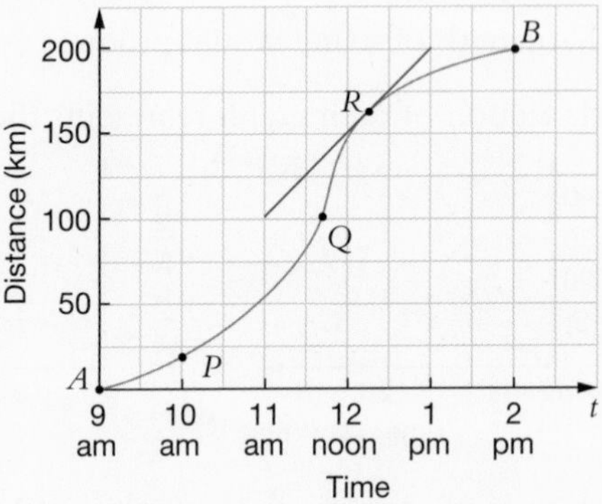

15:05B

15 The graph shows the variation in solubility of three salts in water with change in temperature.
a How much of salt II will dissolve at 40°C?
b What temperature is needed to dissolve 40 g of salt III?
c Which salt would have the greatest solubility at 40°C?
d Will 50 g of salt II dissolve at 30°C?

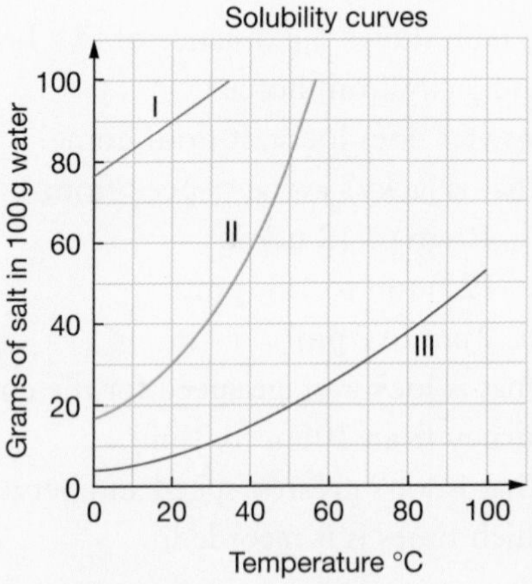

15:06

16 Draw a line graph to represent:
a how the water level in a cylindrical tank varies against time as it is being constantly filled
b how the intensity of light changes as the sun rises and falls during the day
c the average temperature each month for a year in Sydney.

15:06

ASSIGNMENT 15A Chapter review

1 Convert this rate: 1 mL/s = … L/h

2 British athlete Mohamed Farah won the gold medal at the 2012 Olympic Games for the men's 10 000 m in a time of just over 27 minutes and 30 seconds.
  a What was his average time for 1 kilometre?
  b What average speed is this in km/h? (Answer correct to one decimal place.)

3 If the exchange rate between Australian dollars ($A) and European euros (€) is $A1 = €0.85, find:
  a how many euros could be exchanged for $A400
  b how many whole $A could be bought for €400.

4 In a compound, 7 kg of chemical x must be mixed with 4 kg of chemical y.
  a How much of chemical y is needed if 59·5 kg of chemical x is used?
  b How much of chemical x is needed if 59·5 kg of chemical y is used?

5 The diagonals of any square intersect at the middle of the square. The perimeter (P) of a square is directly proportional to the distance d from the middle to one of the corners. When the perimeter is 16 cm, the distance from the middle to a corner is 2·83 cm.

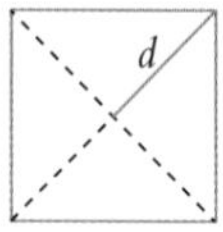

  a Find the distance from the middle to a corner, correct to two decimal places, if the perimeter is 25 cm.
  b Find the perimeter if the distance from the middle to a corner is 15 cm. Give your answer to the nearest centimetre.

6 If 36 men can do a job in 8 days:
  a how long should it take 12 men to do the same job
  b how many men should it take to do the job in 6 days?

7 It was found that a 3 m length of timber (L) can support a maximum weight (W) of 230 kg.
  a Find an equation relating W and L.
  b Find the weight that can be supported safely when the length of the timber is 3·5 m. (Give your answer in kg, correct to one decimal place.)
  c Find the longest length of timber that can safely support a weight of 180 kg. (Give your answer correct to the nearest cm.)

8 In a stadium 1500 seats are possible when 60 cm is allowed for each person.
  a If 1800 seats were needed at 60 cm per person, how much more length of seating would be required?
  b If 1800 seats were needed, without being able to extend the stadium, how much would be allowed for each person? Is this reasonable?

9 Draw a travel graph that shows the information given.
Briony left home at 9 am, walking at 5 km/h until 11 am when she accepted a lift from a friend. The car travelled at an average speed of 40 km/h for 2 hours. Briony then stopped for lunch until 1:30 pm. She then caught a train and arrived home at 3 pm. The horizontal axis should show the time and the vertical axis the distance from home.

10 Give a reasonable story or explanation for the information shown on this graph.

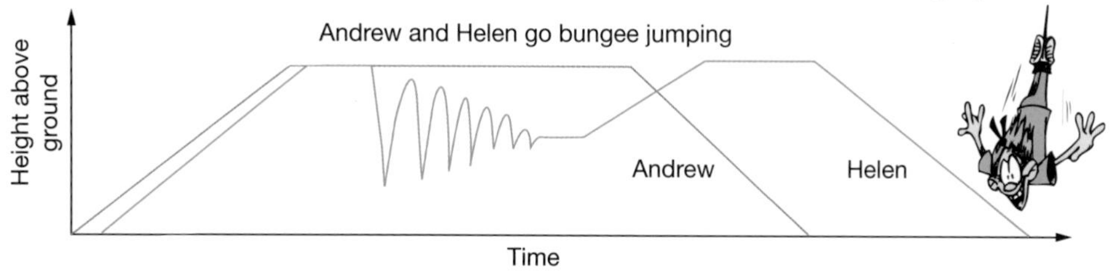

ASSIGNMENT 15B Working mathematically

1 Naomi bought a computer system for Luke. The marked price was \$2300. She paid a deposit of \$1200 and 12 monthly payments of \$115.

a How much did she pay?

b How much more than the marked price did she pay?

c What percentage was the extra money paid of the amount owing after the deposit was paid? (Give the percentage correct to one decimal place.)

2 For this cylinder find:

a the area of the base

b the curved surface area

c the total surface area.

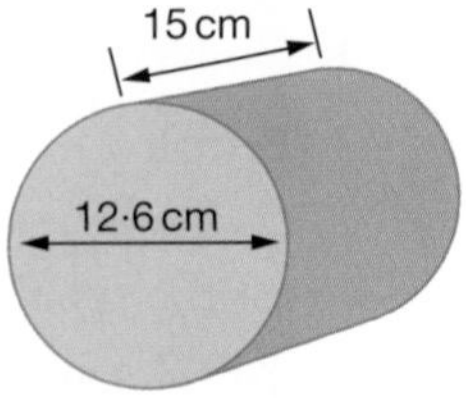

3 A salesman's wages are \$230 per week plus a commission of $4\frac{1}{2}\%$ on his sales. How much will he earn in a week when he sells \$7000 worth of goods?

4 The graph below shows the 'normal' weight for girls aged 0 to 3 years. The numbers on the right side of the graph are percentages. (Only 3% of 3-year-old girls have a weight less than 11·3 kg.)

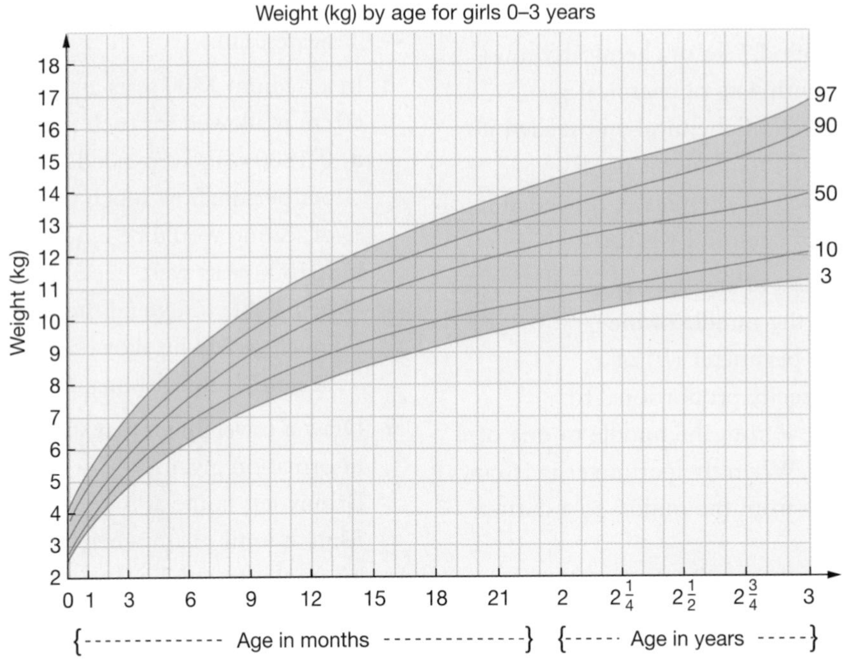

a Why are there two 3s on the horizontal axis?

b What is the median weight for girls of age:

i 3 months ii 1 year iii 19 months

iv 2 years 3 months v 1 year 2 months?

c What percentage of 3-year-old girls have a weight between 13·9 kg and 16 kg?

d What weights would be considered 'normal' for a girl of age 2 months?

e What weights would be considered 'normal' at birth for a girl?

ASSIGNMENT 15C Cumulative revision

1 Find the value of the pronumeral in each of the following, correct to one decimal place. 13:05

a

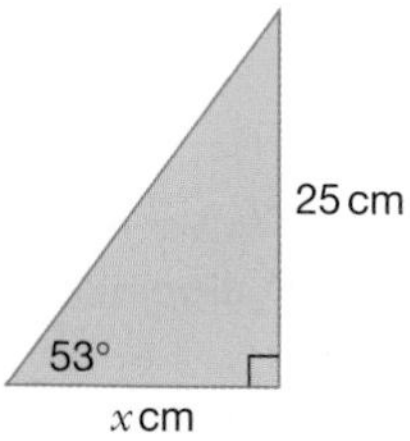

b

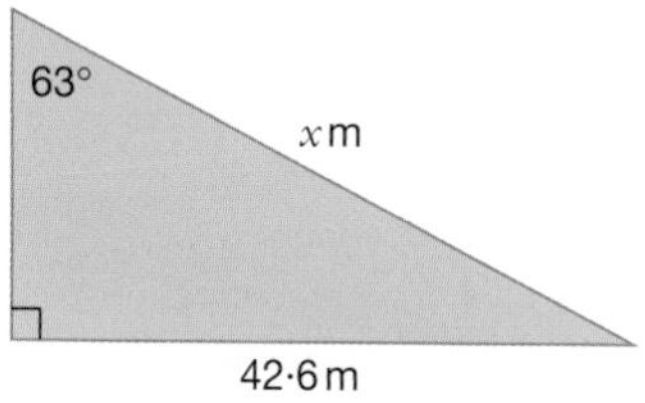

2 A swimming pool is in the shape of a prism. Its cross-section is formed from two trapeziums. Calculate the volume of the pool in cubic metres and its capacity in litres. (All measurements are in metres.) 5:05

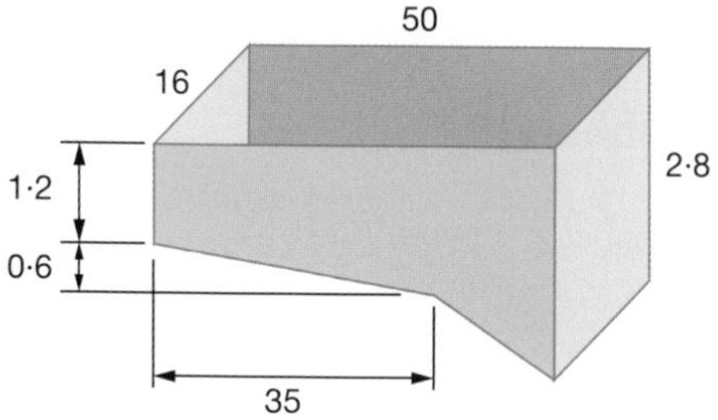

3 The points $A(-4, 0)$, $B(6, 0)$ and $C(0, 6)$ form a triangle. D and E are the midpoints of AC and BC respectively. Find: 9:01, 9:02

a the length of AB **b** the coordinates of D and E **c** the length of DE.

4 The formula $S = \dfrac{n + n^2}{2}$ can be used to find the sum (S) of a long series of numbers like $S = 1 + 2 + 3 + 4 + \ldots + n$. 7:08, 7:09

a Find the value of S when $n = 4$. Check your answer by adding $1 + 2 + 3 + 4$.

b Find the value of S when $n = 100$.

c Use the formula twice to find the sum $101 + 102 + 103 + 104 + \ldots + 200$.

d Use guess-and-check to find the value of n for which $S = 131\,328$.

5 Two normal dice are taken and the numbers are changed. On dice A the 1 is replaced by a 6. On dice B the numbers 5 and 6 are replaced by the number 3. 4:06

a Use a list, array or tree diagram to write all the possible outcomes when the two dice are rolled.

b What is the probability that a 3 will appear when the two dice are rolled?

c When the two dice are rolled is it more likely to get a 6 to appear or a 4 to appear?

6 **a** Use the stem-and-leaf plot to find: 14:03, 14:04

i the range **ii** the mode

iii the median **iv** the interquartile range.

b Draw a box plot for this set of data.

Stem	Leaf
0	7 9
1	3 5 6 6 8
2	0 2 5 8 8 9
3	1 3 3 3 7 9
4	3 4 6 6 8
5	0 0 3 5

ANSWERS

ID Cards

ID Card 1 (Metric units)

1 metres
2 decimetres
3 centimetres
4 millimetres
5 kilometres
6 square metres
7 square centimetres
8 square kilometres
9 hectares
10 cubic metres
11 cubic centimetres
12 seconds
13 minutes
14 hours
15 metres per second
16 kilometres per hour
17 grams
18 milligrams
19 kilograms
20 tonnes
21 litres
22 millilitres
23 kilolitres
24 degrees Celsius

ID Card 2 (Symbols)

1 is equal to
2 is approximately equal to
3 is not equal to
4 is less than
5 is less than or equal to
6 is not less than
7 is greater than
8 is greater than or equal to
9 4 squared
10 4 cubed
11 the square root of 2
12 the cube root of 2
13 is perpendicular to
14 is parallel to
15 is congruent to
16 is similar to
17 per cent
18 therefore
19 for example
20 that is
21 pi
22 the sum of
23 the mean
24 probability of event E

ID Card 3 (Language)

1 square
2 rectangle
3 parallelogram
4 rhombus (or diamond)
5 trapezium
6 regular pentagon
7 regular hexagon
8 regular octagon
9 kite
10 scalene triangle
11 isosceles triangle
12 equilateral triangle
13 circle
14 oval (or ellipse)
15 cube
16 rectangular prism
17 triangular prism
18 square pyramid
19 rectangular pyramid
20 triangular pyramid
21 cylinder
22 cone
23 sphere
24 hemisphere

ID Card 4 (Language)

1 point A
2 interval AB
3 line AB
4 ray AB
5 collinear points
6 midpoint
7 number line
8 diagonals
9 acute-angled triangle
10 right-angled triangle
11 obtuse-angled triangle
12 vertices
13 ΔABC
14 hypotenuse
15 180°
16 $a° + b°$
17 360°
18 (b) $a° = b°$
19 $a° = 60°$
20 $3 \times 180° = 540°$
21 AB is a diameter, OC is a radius
22 circumference
23 semicircle
24 AB is a tangent, CD is an arc, EF is a chord

ID Card 5 (Language)

1 parallel lines
2 perpendicular lines
3 vertical, horizontal
4 concurrent lines
5 angle ABC or CBA
6 acute angle
7 right angle
8 obtuse angle
9 straight angle
10 reflex angle
11 revolution
12 adjacent angles
13 complementary angles
14 supplementary angles
15 vertically opposite angles
16 360°
17 transversal
18 corresponding angles
19 alternate angles
20 co-interior angles
21 bisecting an interval
22 bisecting an angle
23 $\angle CAB = 60°$
24 CD is perpendicular to AB

ID Card 6 (Language)

1 Common Era, Anno Domini
2 Before Common Era, Before Christ
3 ante meridiem (before midday)
4 post meridiem (after midday)
5 hectare
6 regular shapes
7 net of a cube
8 cross-section
9 face
10 vertex
11 edge
12 axes of symmetry
13 reflection (or flip)
14 translation (or slide)
15 rotation (or turn)
16 tessellation
17 coordinates
18 tally
19 picture graph
20 column graph
21 line graph
22 sector (or pie) graph
23 bar graph
24 scatter diagram

Chapter 1

Exercise 1:01

1 See answers to ID cards.

2 a 7 b −13 c 9 d 7
e −6 f −30 g 5 h −7
i −56 j −2 k 7

3 a $\frac{5}{8}$ b $1\frac{1}{5}$ c $\frac{1}{5}$ d $\frac{2}{7}$
e $1\frac{11}{20}$ f $\frac{7}{10}$ g $\frac{1}{8}$ h $\frac{13}{20}$
i $8\frac{1}{10}$ j $12\frac{9}{20}$ k $3\frac{5}{18}$ l $6\frac{5}{8}$
m $\frac{12}{55}$ n $\frac{21}{100}$ o $\frac{3}{8}$ p $\frac{57}{72}$
q $2\frac{1}{2}$ r $2\frac{17}{50}$ s $15\frac{1}{5}$ t $6\frac{3}{4}$
u 4 v $1\frac{1}{5}$ w $2\frac{2}{9}$ x 20
y $2\frac{1}{2}$ z $1\frac{3}{7}$

4 a 5·74 b 21·6 c 11·63 d 7·176
e 4·2 f 0·09 g 0·034 h 0·65
i 314·2 j 40 k 210 l 1250
m 2·04 n 2·42 o 0·475 p 0·1825

5 a $\frac{9}{50}$ b $\frac{7}{100}$ c $\frac{19}{200}$ d $\frac{49}{400}$

6 a 55% b 125% c 51% d 8·5%

7 a 0·09 b 1·1 c 0·238 d 0·045

8 a 210 m b 5·901 m c $60 d 60 kg
e 25% f 40% g $69 h $5.20

Exercise 1:02

1 a 250%, 2·5 b 1·3, $1\frac{3}{10}$
c 280%, $2\frac{4}{5}$ d 125%, 1·25

2 a 0·805, 0·85, 0·9, 1
b $12\frac{1}{4}$%, 87·5%, 100%, 104%
c $\frac{6}{100}, \frac{2}{7}, \frac{5}{8}, \frac{2}{3}$
d 150%, 1·65, $1\frac{3}{4}$, 2
e 140%, 1·41, $\sqrt{2}$, 1·42
f 3·1, π, $3\frac{1}{4}$, $\sqrt{12}$

3 a 6·85 b $16\frac{1}{4}$
c $\frac{13}{80}$ or 0·1625 d 6·375

4 a $0{\cdot}\dot{1}, 0{\cdot}\dot{2}, 0{\cdot}\dot{3}, 0{\cdot}\dot{4}, 0{\cdot}\dot{5}, 0{\cdot}\dot{6}, 0{\cdot}\dot{7}, 0{\cdot}\dot{8}, 0{\cdot}\dot{9}$
b $\frac{1}{9} = 0{\cdot}\dot{1}, \frac{9}{9} = 0{\cdot}\dot{9}$. However, $\frac{9}{9} = 1$.
c $0{\cdot}0\dot{1}, 0{\cdot}0\dot{2}, 0{\cdot}0\dot{3}, 0{\cdot}00\dot{1}, 0{\cdot}00\dot{2}, 0{\cdot}00\dot{3}$
d $\frac{4}{9}, 3\frac{1}{9}, -\frac{5}{9}, -4\frac{5}{9}$

5 a 1, 2, 4 b 0·1625, 0·08125, 0·040625

6 a 79 b 19

7 Each year, $9.75 is paid in interest for every $100 invested.

8 The building can house three tenants.

9 7 years 10 −33° 11 54 BC

12 a 370 b −120 c −440

13 a $\frac{1}{3}$ b $\frac{2}{3}$ c $\frac{1}{9}$ d $\frac{5}{9}$

14 a 0·888 89 b 0·285 71 c 0·538 46
d 0·952 38 e 0·363 64 f 0·277 78

15 a 76% b 24%
c Answers may vary. She may have been an employee of the store.

16 $64 500 17 $500 18 12·8

19 a The number of possible marks she could have scored.
b The number of marks each mistake cost him.
c The number who have cancer and the number over 65.

20 In about 23 million years.

21 a 200% b 125% c 62·5%

22 a $\frac{1}{2}, \frac{1}{8}$ b $\frac{1}{2}, \frac{1}{22}$

23 a Yes, $\frac{ad + bc}{bd}$ is rational.
b Yes, $\frac{ad - bc}{bd}$ is rational.
c Yes, $\frac{ac}{bd}$ is rational.
d Yes, $\frac{ad}{bc}$ is rational.

Prep quiz 1:03

1 0·25 2 0·4 3 $0{\cdot}\dot{3}$ 4 $0{\cdot}8\dot{3}$
5 $0{\cdot}\dot{4}$ 6 $0{\cdot}\dot{6}3\dot{1}$ 7 $0{\cdot}1\dot{6}$ 8 $0{\cdot}72\dot{6}\dot{9}$
9 $\frac{3}{4}$ 10 $\frac{7}{8}$

Exercise 1:03

1 a 0·75 b 0·8 c 0·625 d 0·7
e 0·07 f 1·75 g 0·16 h 0·34
i 0·475 j 0·936

2 a $0{\cdot}\dot{6}$ b $0{\cdot}\dot{5}$ c $0{\cdot}\dot{8}$ d $0{\cdot}\dot{1}\dot{8}$
e $0{\cdot}\dot{1}4285\dot{7}$ f $0{\cdot}1\dot{6}$ g $0{\cdot}0\dot{6}$ h $0{\cdot}4\dot{6}$

i $0{\cdot}041\dot{6}$ j $0{\cdot}5\dot{6}$

3 a $\frac{47}{100}$ b $\frac{4}{25}$ c $\frac{1}{8}$ d $\frac{17}{20}$
e $\frac{7}{200}$

4 a $\frac{4}{9}$ b $\frac{19}{33}$ c $\frac{173}{999}$ d $\frac{7}{9}$
e $\frac{4}{11}$ f $\frac{1234}{9999}$

5 $\frac{1}{3}$

6 a $\frac{5}{6}$ b $\frac{629}{990}$ c $\frac{89}{450}$ d $\frac{29}{45}$
e $\frac{221}{300}$ f $\frac{8167}{9900}$ g $\frac{853}{1665}$ h $\frac{4751}{9000}$
i $\frac{6467}{9990}$

Prep quiz 1:04

1 $\frac{5}{6}$ 2 $\frac{4}{5}$ 3 $\frac{6}{7}$ 4 $\frac{1}{5}$ 5 $\frac{1}{2}$
6 $\frac{1}{4}$ 7 $\frac{4}{5}$ 8 $\frac{2}{3}$ 9 $\frac{2}{3}$ 10 $\frac{4}{5}$

Exercise 1:04

1 a $\frac{1}{10}$ b $\frac{4}{5}$ c $\frac{1}{10}$ d $\frac{15}{16}$
e $\frac{1}{5}$ f $\frac{5}{24}$

2 a 3:2 b 2:1 c 13:3 d 2:5
e 200:1 f 11:8 g 11:4 h 4:7
i 2:21 j 36:1 k 1:26 l 20:1
m 1:5 n 5:4 o 11:4 p 8:13

3 a 7:9 b 13:15 c 7:8 d 2:3
e 4:5 f 3:17 g 9:10 h 1:2
i 1:8

4 a 2:1 b 2:1 c 1:5 d 5:3
e 1:8 f 1:10 g 3:5 h 5:3
i 20:4:1

5 a $1\frac{5}{8}:1$ b $1\frac{3}{4}:1$ c $2\frac{1}{2}:1$ d $1\frac{1}{10}:1$
e $1\frac{2}{5}:1$ f $\frac{2}{3}:1$ g $\frac{2}{7}:1$ h $1\frac{1}{9}:1$
i $\frac{2}{3}:1$ j $1\frac{7}{8}:1$ k $\frac{1}{3}:1$ l 10:1

6 a $1:1\frac{1}{4}$ b $1:4\frac{1}{2}$ c $1:1\frac{7}{8}$ d $1:\frac{3}{7}$
e $1:1\frac{1}{4}$ f $1:\frac{3}{20}$ g $1:8\frac{3}{4}$ h $1:5\frac{1}{2}$
i $1:1\frac{1}{2}$

7 a i 3:4 ii 1:3 iii 1:4
b $1\frac{1}{8}:1$
c i 8:5 ii 5:8
d i 4:1 ii 9:16
e i 8:7 ii 2:3
f i 29:19 ii 8:11 iii 21:11

8 a The mixture would be 50% sugar, 25% flour and 25% custard powder.
b The mixture would be $\frac{2}{13}$ cement, $\frac{10}{13}$ sand and $\frac{1}{13}$ lime.
c 1:40

9 a 6 km/h b $25/t c 50 g/$
d $250/day e 24 g/L f 29 boys/teacher

10 a 9 km b $18 c 10 kg d 70 runs

11 a 1500 m/h b $40 000/km c 3000 kg/min
d 3 g/L e 216 000 g/h f 2 beats/s

Exercise 1:05

1 a 2 b 3 c 3 d 2 e 4
f 3 g 2 h 3 i 1 j 2
k 1 l 2 m 3 n 4 o 1
p 3 q 4 r 3 s 3 t 3
u 1

2 a 1 b 2 c 2 d 3 e 4
f 3 g 3 h 6

3 a 2 b 4 c 3 d 1 e 3
f 2 g 1 h 2 i 2

4 a 8 b 2 c 2 d 3

5 1 or 2 significant figures (i.e. to the nearest 10 000 or the nearest 1000)

Investigation 1:05

Answers are correct to two significant figures.

1 between 150 000 km/year and 170 000 km/year
2 between 3100 km/week and 3500 km/week
3 between 520 km/day and 590 (or 580) km/day
4 11 m/s 5 22 m 6 200 L 7 142 kg

Prep quiz 1:06

1 4 2 1 3 4 4 3·08 5 0·80
6 2·410 7 4 8 2·33 9 3·55 10 0·065

Exercise 1:06

1 a 7900 b 1100 c 67 300 d 900
e 600 f 400 g 74 900 h 7900

2 a 9 b 80 c 45 d 3
e 2 f 18 g 237 h 100

3 a 243·13 b 79·66 c 91·35 d 9·81
e 0·30 f 0·09 g 0·10 h 1·99

4 a 6·7 b 8·5 c 2·1 d 6·1
e 0·1 f 0·0 g 29·9 h 10·0

5 a 8200 b 3500 c 660 d 850
e 15 000 f 76 000 g 50 000 h 77 000

6 a 8000 b 4000 c 700 d 800
e 10 000 f 80 000 g 50 000 h 80 000

7 a 695 b 35·1 c 321 d 0·0815
e 0·667 f 9·33 g 10·1 h 9·10

8 a 1·8 b 1·78 c 1·778 d 2
e 1·8 f 1·78

9 a 5 cm b 55 mm c 5·5 cm d 5·45 cm
e 5·455 cm f 5 cm g 5·5 cm h 5·45 cm

10 a $141 b $140·60
c 14 059·7 cents d 14 059·71 cents
e 14 059·705 cents f $100
g $140 h $141

11 a nearest thousand, 500
b nearest billion (i.e. $1 000 000 000), 500 000 000

12 a nearest tenth, 0·05 cm
b nearest thousandth, 0·0005 mg

13 Any number between 2·145 and 2·155 or equal to 2·145. No, because the number can have any number of decimal places and must be less than 2·155.

14 a 40 000 000 t b 38 000 000 t
c 37 600 000 t d 37 649 000 t
e Answers will vary. Most people would choose part **b** or part **a**.

15 a 8 m b 8·1 m c 8·13 d 8·126 m
e Parts **d** or **c**, as builders use mm on building plans.

16 a 5 b 42·063 m c 42 m
d 2 e 4206 cm f 4

17 a Any number between 2 500 000 and 3 500 000 or equal to 2 500 000
b $26.80, Answers will vary but the 15c over could be given as a tip.
c There will be insufficient tiles. Because parts of tiles are required in some places, you must round up, so that the entire floor can be covered using parts of tiles and you must also allow for breakages as the tiles are cut.

18 a $0{\cdot}000\,000\,000\,\dot{3}$ b $0{\cdot}000\,000\,000\,\dot{6}$
c $0{\cdot}000\,000\,000\,\dot{5}$

19 a 90 000 b 119 370·25
c 122 500 d 29 335·7025

20 2859·2 m^3

Prep quiz 1:07

1 200 2 20 3 156·1 4 1561 5 < 1
6 < 7 true 8 B 9 true 10 false

Exercise 1:07

The answers given below for exercise 1:07 are examples of estimations. Students' answers may differ.

1 a 22 b 36 c 70 d 126 e 5
f 0·01 g 0·6 h 115 i 50 j 1·8

2 a about 4 b about 12 c about 1·6
d about 1000 e about 2 f about 1
g about 2 h about 27

3 a C 3·1 kg b A 27 m
c C $276 d B $6800

4 a 0·01 cm or 0·1 mm b 3200
c Yes, because in 8 × 80 both numbers have been rounded down and in 9 × 90 both have been rounded up.

5 73·6575 and 75·3875
The first 2 or possibly 3 figures could be used to establish the boundaries of the exact area.
(i.e. 73·6575 ≤ the measurement < 75·3875)

Prep quiz 1:08

1 300 2 7000 3 4 000 000 4 720
5 720 6 16 000 7 21·5 8 2315
9 74 976 10 3 400 000

Exercise 1:08

1 a 92 365 b 740 030 c 3 408 007
d 65 900 e 28 415 f 5924
g 69 727 h 3841 i 7 580 000
j 27 000

2 a $1{\cdot}73 \times 10^2$ b $9{\cdot}1 \times 10^2$ c $3{\cdot}45 \times 10^6$
d $6{\cdot}1 \times 10^3$ e $5{\cdot}22 \times 10^7$ f $4{\cdot}5 \times 10^9$

3 a $8{\cdot}6 \times 10^3$ b $8{\cdot}56 \times 10^5$ c $4{\cdot}7 \times 10^4$
d $3{\cdot}7 \times 10^7$ e 6×10^6 f $2{\cdot}3 \times 10^8$
g $1{\cdot}01 \times 10^8$ h $8{\cdot}125 \times 10^9$

4 a 6860 b 102 c 9 500 000
d 470 000 e 3 960 000 f 45 500 000
g 80 500 h 6 100 000 000

5 a 7×10^3 means $7 \times 10 \times 10 \times 10$ and 7^3 means $7 \times 7 \times 7$
b true c true

6 a 3 b 2 c 2 d 4

Prep quiz 1:09

1 true 2 true 3 false 4 true
5 true 6 true
7 eight gigabytes 8 three terabytes
9 four megabytes 10 nine kilobytes

Exercise 1:09

1 a 7000 m b 12 000 kg c 3 000 000 L
d 8 m e 9300 mm f 3450 mL
g 7200 mg h 3·845 L i 0·5 m

2 a 5 000 000 m b 6 000 000 000 m
c 5 000 000 000 000 m d 6000 mm
e 9 000 000 μm f 3 000 000 000 nm
g 17 100 m h 1 800 000 000
i 4 800 000 m

3 a 4 000 000 B b 4000 kB c 7000 MB
d 3000 GB e 3000 nm f 5 μm
g 3200 kB h 4100 MB i 600 GB

4 a 3 km b 8 MB
c 11 GB d 6·5 TB
e 3·5 μs f 730 000 μs
g 5 000 000 kB h 2 000 000 MB
i 3 000 000 000 kB

5 a 32 years b 17 min
c 900 gigabytes (i.e. 900 GB)
d 3000 GB (or 3TB)

Exercise 1:10

1 a 0·5 cm b 0·5 g c 5 L
d 0·05 cm e 0·005 m f 0·05 L
g 0·05 t h 0·0005 s i 500 t

2 a i 0·5 cm (or 5 mm)
ii 583·5 cm up to 584·5 cm (but excluding 584·5 cm)
b i to the nearest hundredth of a gram (i.e. 0·01 g)
ii 0·005 g
iii 47·285 g up to 47·295 g (but excluding 47·295 g)
c i to the nearest tenth of a tonne (i.e. 0·1 t)
ii 0·05 t (or 50 kg)
iii 1·35 t up to 1·45 t (but excluding 1·45 t)

3 a 0·5 L, 34·5 L up to 35·5 L (but excluding 35·5 L)
  b 0·05 L, 34·85 L up to 34·95 L (but excluding 34·95 L)
4 a 0·005 m (or 5 mm), 1·475 m up to 1·485 m (but excluding 1·485 m)
  b 0·005 m (or 5 mm), 120·355 m up to 120·365 m (but excluding 120·365 m)
  c yes
  d Generally, Naomi's measurement would be considered more accurate, as her greatest possible error (0·005 m) is approximately 0·0042% of her measurement. Phil's greatest possible error (0·005 m) is approximately 0·34% of his measurement.
5 a i ruler (marked in cm and mm)
    ii micrometer screw gauge
  b i 0·5 cm (or 5 mm) ii 0·05 cm
    iii 0·005 cm iv 0·0005 cm
  c i 1·35 cm up to 1·45 cm (but excluding 1·45 cm)
    ii 1·375 cm to 1·385 cm (but excluding 1·385 cm)

Diagnostic test 1

1 a $0\cdot\dot{6}$ b $0\cdot1\dot{6}$ c $0\cdot\dot{7}$ d $0\cdot2\dot{6}$
2 a $\frac{5}{9}$ b $\frac{37}{99}$ c $\frac{26}{45}$ d $\frac{683}{990}$
3 a 2:3
  b i $2\frac{3}{4}:1$ ii $1:\frac{4}{11}$
  c $1.80 (per kilogram)
4 a 6 b 5 c 5
  d can't tell, may be 2, 3 or 4
5 a 57 000 000 b 0·6662 c 8·0
  d 4·67 m e 0·006 f 510 000 000
  g 0·061 h 93 800 000
6 Answers may vary slightly.
  a 36 b 5 c 20 d 200
7 a $8{\cdot}5 \times 10^4$ b $9{\cdot}6 \times 10^8$
  c 1 060 000 d 84 000
8 a 7200 kB b 40 µs
9 a 0·5 L b 0·05 kg
10 a 3·255 g
  b 9·35 kg up to 9·45 kg (but excluding 9·45 kg)

ASSIGNMENT 1A

1 a 9 b 16 c −3
2 a $\frac{4}{5}$ b $\frac{1}{6}$ c $\frac{1}{10}$ d $\frac{5}{6}$
  e $5\frac{19}{20}$ f $1\frac{11}{15}$ g $9\frac{1}{3}$ h 6
3 a 4·47 b 4·34 c 40·5 d 0·09
4 a $\frac{7}{20}$ b $\frac{7}{8}$ c $\frac{23}{99}$ d $\frac{172}{495}$
5 a $26.25 b 20%
6 a 5:9 b 1:3 c 1:4 d 1:6
7 a 3 b 3 c 3 d 2
  e 3 f 3
8 a 6·4 b 6·92 c 47 644 000
  d 648 e 6·4 f 0·005 82
  g 47 600 000 h 0·70
9 a 5 820 000 b 9100
10 a 8×10^7 b 80×10^6

11 a 2100 GB b 8 500 000 kB
  c 0·05 km (or 50 m)
  d 3·65 km up to 3·75 km (but excluding 3·75 km)

ASSIGNMENT 1B

1 a hectares b cubic metres
  c metres per second d kilometres per hour
  e milligrams f kilograms
  g tonnes h millilitres
  i kilolitres j degrees Celsius
2 a is approximately equal to
  b is less than or equal to
  c 4 cubed d the square root of 2
  e is parallel to f is congruent to
  g is similar to h therefore
  i for example j the mean
3 11 4 39
5 a i 40% ii 97% iii 66% iv 15%
  b water
  c Removal of trees allowing erosion.
  d You require the percentage of Australia's total area taken up by each state (or territory). For each state (or territory), you would multiply the percentage of Australia's area by the percentage of land requiring no treatment for that state. Total these answers and you have the percentage of land in Australia requiring no treatment.
6 a 37% b 9%
  c No, because there are many more car drivers than motorcyclists. The rate of fatalities is much higher for motorcyclists.

Chapter 2

Exercise 2:01

1 a i US$492.25 ii AU$507.87 (to nearest cent)
  b i 2·8 L/100 km ii 2·976 km or 2976 m
  c 13 m d 580 mg e 7 km/h
2 a 36 (men) b 5000 (spectators)
  c 5, 15 and 20
3 a John earned $35. Zac earned $21. They worked for 7 hours.
  b 0·36 m, 0·45 m and 0·27 m
  c 511 g of nitrogen, 89 g of phosphorus, 400 g of potassium.
  d If 400 L of the red paint is used, 240 L of blue paint would be used, so 640 L of the mixed colour can be made.
  e 40 g of lead and 140 g of zinc
4 a Bronte's house (20·8% to 1 dec. pl.)
  b 21·4% c 16 880 people d $443.70
5 a 2275 m^2 b 384 m c 796 revolutions
  d i $686.40 ii $420.80 iii $50.50
  e The circle has the larger area by 171 cm^2.

Exercise 2:02

1 a 32 b B c 54 d 3
e One number must be $\frac{1}{2}$. The other can be any number.
f 1296 g 1·2 kg h 12

2 a 1 b 4 c 9 d 16
e 25 f 36 g 49 h 64
Total = $1^2 + 2^2 + 3^2 + 4^2 + 5^2 + 6^2 + 7^2 + 8^2$

3 a 56, 23 b 67, 78 c 634, 566

4 a 15 b 11

5 sixteen 0s; fifteen each of 1, 2, 3 and 4; fifty-seven 5s or five each of 6, 7, 8 and 9

6 2 × \$100, 7 × \$50, 6 × \$20, 5 × \$10;
6 × \$ 100, 10 × \$10, 4 × \$5

7 12

8 There are many solutions. One solution is:
40 waratahs, 210 grevilleas and 50 banksias.
This gives 300 plants at a cost of \$1200.

9 a i 40 + 41 ii 26 + 27 + 28
b 11, 12, 13, 14, 15, 16 (six consecutive integers) or 5, 6, 7, 8, 9, 10, 11, 12, 13 (9 consecutive integers)

10 a i 3 ii 0 iii 3
b 13

Exercise 2:03

1 a 3 b 18 c 3
2 a 33 b 42 c 35
3 a 5 b 8 c 10
4 a 5 b 8 c 2 d 2 e 11
5 a 10 b 0 c 5 d 8 e yes
6 a 6 b 5 c 3 d 7 e 20
f 9 g 28 h 32 i 23

Diagnostic test 2

1 a 80c/kg b \$16
2 48 kg 3 105°, 30°, 45° 4 \$4785
5 a \$1120 b \$58 400.16
6 34·8 m^2
7 length = 27·5 m, breadth = 5·5 m
8 \$108.20 9 6 play both sports.
10 a 3 b 24

ASSIGNMENT 2A

1 a i 0·25 km/min ii 4 min/km
b 6 min c 24 s

2 a 287 runs/50 overs = 5·74 runs/over
b 6·12 runs/over (rounded up to 2 dec. pl.)

3 3 min 45 s

4 16 drops/min

5 a \$2612.50 b 6·35% (2 dec. pl.)
c i \$2800 ii \$2632

6 196%

7 a 656 g b lead 0·96 kg, tin 1·44 kg

8 125 mL

9 a

9	3
2	1

9	4
1	1

(other solutions do exist)

b 85

10 a 12 b 0·96 m^3
c

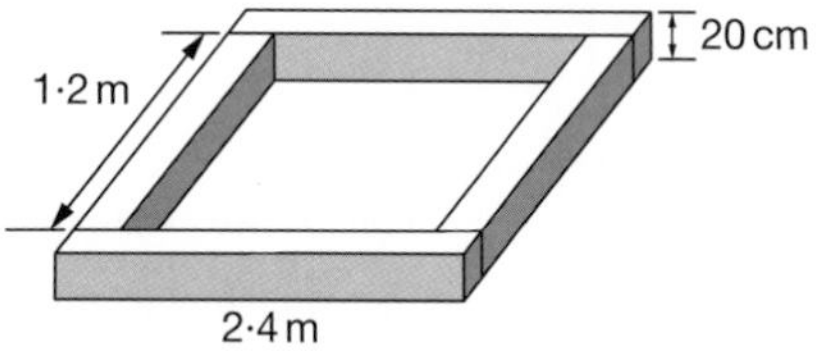

Turning the sleepers on edge gives a volume of 0·528 m^3.

ASSIGNMENT 2B

1 a 15 to 24 b 15, 16, 17 c 18, 19, 20
d 21, 22, 23, 24 e 17

2 a 21, 22, 23 b 5, 8, 16, 19, 23
c 12, 13, 14 d 9

3 4 hectares

4 a 14 b 23 c 46 d 42

5 The engine leaves the siding and reverses to couple with B. Then both return to siding and B is unhooked. The engine leaves the siding and then goes anticlockwise around the track and picks up A and pushes it into the siding and picks up B again. The engine then pulls out of the siding and then reverses to uncouple B in its original position. A is then returned to the siding and uncoupled. The engine then travels clockwise around the track and pushes B to A's original position and is then uncoupled. The engine then picks up A from the siding and shunts it into B's original position. The engine then returns to the siding.

6 5 lengths are needed. Pieces taken from each length: (3·2 + 1·5), (1·8 + 2·3 + 0·8), (3·7 + 1·2), (2·5 + 2·2), (1·9 + 1·5 + 1·3)

ASSIGNMENT 2C

1 Harry would receive \$3000, Lester would receive \$7500 and Michelle would receive \$4500.

2 a true b true c true d false
e true f true g false h true
i true j true k true l false

3 a 12 b 72 c 314·2 d 0·031 42
e 10 500 f 0·000 105

4 a \$2.70 b \$235 c 45% d \$42.46

5 a $\frac{4}{9}$ b 0·15
c \$32 d 0·075 (or 7·5%)

6 a $0 \cdot \dot{6}$ b 5 : 3
c 1·75 : 1 (or $1\frac{3}{4}$: 1) d 2·5 km/h

7 a 2 b 80·1 L
c 24 000 000 d 3·14

8 a $3·5 \times 10^7$ b $3·50 \times 10^7$
c 2 d 5 080 000

9 a 2000 GB b 3 MB c 25 TB d 8500 kB
10 a 0·5 g b 0·005 m c 0·0005 L
d 6·45 up to 6·55 (but not including 6·55)

Chapter 3

Prep quiz 3:01

1 $9x$ 2 x 3 $6xy$ 4 $5x^2$
5 $3x$ 6 $2b$ 7 $8a + 5b$ 8 $5x + y$
9 $-24a^2$ 10 $-\frac{a}{3b}$

Exercise 3:01

1 a $5x$ b $13a$ c $31p$
d $8x$ e $3a$ f $6b$
g $10q$ h $21e$ i $2p$
j $7x$ k $4x$ l 0
m $a + 4p$ n $2m$ o $1 - 3x$
p -2 q $3x^2 + x$ r $4p^2 + 5p$
s $2q^2 + 4q$ t $2y^2$ u $2 - p^2 + p$
v $3a + a^2 + 7$ w $x - 7 - 3x^2$ x $8ab - 16$

2 a $24y$ b $16a$ c $6xy$
d $32pq$ e $6ab$ f $5x^2$
g $15a^2$ h a^2bc i $6p^2q$
j $5m^2np$ k $2mn^2$ l $9a^2b$
m $-42a^3$ n $10x^2$ o $6x^2y$
p $-7a^2b^2$ q ab^2c r $24k^3$
s $70xy$ t $-mnp$

3 a $3x$ b 3 c $3x^2$ d 1
e $\frac{3m}{2n}$ f $\frac{8a}{3b}$ g $\frac{1}{4a}$ h $8a$
i $\frac{1}{3}$ j $\frac{9}{4}$ k -5 l $-\frac{y}{z}$
m -14 n $\frac{3}{y}$ o $-4n$ p $\frac{a}{2b}$

4 a mn^2p b $4m + 13$ c $19 - 2a$
d 0 e $6x^2y^2$ f $15x^2 + 5x$
g $60yz$ h $-28x^2$ i $7ab$
j $-m$ k 0 l $\frac{2a}{c}$
m $\frac{1}{3}$ n $18p^2q^2$ o $5a + b - c$
p $15yz$ q y r $2n$
s $6abc$ t $\frac{3a}{2x}$

5 a $20a$ b x c $12b$ d $3m$
e 4 f $60a^2$ g $3m^2$ h $\frac{15}{7}$
i 35 j 16 k $6a^2$ l $6y^2$
m $14x$ n $25x^2$ o $10y$ p $16m$
q $26n$ r $3x$ s x t $20m$
u $\frac{9}{5}$ v 1 w 1 x $\frac{a}{2c}$

Prep quiz 3:02A

1 $\frac{4}{5}$ 2 $\frac{2}{5}$ 3 $\frac{7}{12}$ 4 $\frac{7}{8}$ 5 $\frac{3}{20}$
6 $\frac{1}{4}$ 7 $11x$ 8 $4ab$ 9 x 10 $8a$

Exercise 3:02A

1 a $2a$ b $\frac{x}{5}$ c $\frac{5a}{3}$ d $\frac{3m}{5}$
e $\frac{x+y}{4}$ f $\frac{5a-2b}{3}$ g $\frac{5}{a}$ h $\frac{8}{x}$
i $\frac{1}{y}$ j $\frac{8}{m}$ k $\frac{7a}{x}$ l $\frac{-x}{y}$
m $\frac{4}{n}$ n $\frac{1}{x}$ o $\frac{2a}{b}$ p $\frac{m}{x}$

2 a $\frac{8x}{15}$ b $\frac{7a}{10}$ c $\frac{y}{12}$ d $\frac{m}{4}$
e $\frac{7a}{6}$ f $\frac{13x}{6}$ g $\frac{n}{8}$ h $\frac{p}{2}$
i $\frac{3x+4y}{12}$ j $\frac{4a-9b}{6}$ k $\frac{6m+5n}{10}$ l $\frac{2k-63}{12}$
m $\frac{10}{3x}$ n $\frac{5}{6a}$ o $\frac{31}{10m}$ p $\frac{1}{8x}$
q $\frac{13a}{6x}$ r $\frac{-5x}{3m}$ s $\frac{13m}{4n}$ t $\frac{8x+3y}{12a}$

Prep quiz 3:02B

1 $\frac{3}{8}$ 2 $\frac{3}{10}$ 3 $\frac{1}{6}$ 4 $\frac{2}{3}$ 5 2
6 $\frac{8}{15}$ 7 $30x$ 8 $6a^2$ 9 $3a$ 10 $2a$

Exercise 3:02B

1 a $\frac{xy}{6}$ b $\frac{ab}{12}$ c $\frac{m^2}{10}$ d $\frac{a^2}{40}$
e $\frac{12}{am}$ f $\frac{2}{xy}$ g $\frac{4}{p^2}$ h $\frac{1}{3n^2}$
i $\frac{px}{qy}$ j $\frac{1}{2}$ k $\frac{2m}{n}$ l $\frac{2}{15}$
m $\frac{2a}{3}$ n 1 o 9 p $\frac{16a}{15p}$

2 a 2 b $\frac{5}{3}$ c $\frac{15}{2}$ d $\frac{2}{3}$
e $\frac{5}{2}$ f $\frac{9}{2}$ g $\frac{1}{2}$ h 6
i $\frac{ay}{bx}$ j $\frac{3}{4}$ k 15 l $\frac{3}{2}$
m $2x$ n $\frac{3}{a}$ o x^2 p $\frac{27}{4}$

3 a $\frac{5a^2}{36}$ b $\frac{2}{3}$ c $\frac{3}{x}$ d $\frac{b^2}{2}$
e $2y$ f b g $6m^2$ h 4
i $\frac{4}{q^2}$ j $\frac{6}{ab}$ k $\frac{2by}{c}$ l $3c$
m $\frac{3}{2}$ n 1 o 6 p $\frac{2}{5}$
q $\frac{5}{8}$ r 1 s $\frac{xz}{ty}$ t $\frac{b}{a}$

Prep quiz 3:03

1 $10x$ 2 $3a^2$ 3 $6x + 8$ 4 $x + 2$
5 $5x^2 + 4y$ 6 $13 + 2a$ 7 $3x - 21$ 8 $18 - 45y$
9 $2a^2 + 6a$ 10 $-5x - 35$

Exercise 3:03

1 a $5a + 35, 5(a + 7)$ b $21 + 3x, 3(7 + x)$
c $7m + 7n, 7(m + n)$ d $pq + 8p, p(q + 8)$
e $6x + 6y, 6(x + y)$ f $bc + ac, c(b + a)$

2 a $2x + 6$ b $3a + 15$ c $5x - 5$
d $7m - 21$ e $6a + 4b$ f $5x + 5y$
g $21x - 35y$ h $42m - 48n$ i $x^2 + 7x$
j $a^2 - a$ k $m^2 + 10m$ l $n^2 - 3n$
m $6a^2 - 3a$ n $18x^2 + 63x$ o $16p - 40p^2$
p $21q + 14q^2$ q $ax + bx$ r $2y^2 + xy$
s $2m^2 + 2mn$ t $10a^2 + 15ab$

3 a $-2x - 6$ b $-3a - 15$ c $-2y + 2$
d $-5p + 15$ e $-21a - 14$ f $-10x + 5$
g $-21 - 14m$ h $-28 + 4x$ i $-a - 1$
j $-3x - 7$ k $-8 + 2p$ l $-3a - 2b$
m $-x^2 - 10x$ n $-5y + y^2$ o $-6x^2 - 21x$
p $-80mn + 10n^2$

4 a $7a + 8$ b $10x + 7$ c $8y - 3$
d $10a - 9$ e $p + 10$ f $15 - m$
g $7a + 20$ h $7x + 2$ i $10n - 7$
j $11h + 13$ k $8x + 7$ l $10y + 2$
m $a + 8$ n $5m - 16$ o $2y + 14$
p $x + 28$ q $9x + 21$ r $2a + 6$
s $4m + 9$ t $14x + 7$

5 a $5x + 8$ b $8y + 22$ c $7a - 3$
d $13m - 14$ e $17x - 12$ f $10x + 40$
g $2x + 23$ h $3m$ i $2a + 66$
j $2n - 46$ k $x^2 + 6x + 3$ l $a^2 + 10a - 21$
m $m^2 - m - 12$ n $t^2 - 9t + 20$ o $3a^2 + 3ab$
p $x^2 + 2xy + y^2$

Prep quiz 3:04

1 $3x + 15$ 2 $5m - 35$ 3 $12y + 2$
4 $18p - 27q$ 5 20 6 12
7 8 8 $\frac{9x}{20}$ 9 $\frac{a}{12}$
10 $\frac{m+2n}{8}$

Exercise 3:04

1 a $\frac{5x+12}{6}$ b $\frac{7a+15}{10}$ c $\frac{13n-7}{21}$
d $\frac{8x+17}{15}$ e $\frac{12m+13}{35}$ f $\frac{p+4}{12}$

2 a $\frac{3a+4}{4}$ b $\frac{3w+2}{10}$ c $\frac{7d-2}{6}$
d $\frac{5x+13}{12}$ e $\frac{7m+2}{24}$ f $\frac{q+3}{18}$

3 a $\frac{8x+17}{6}$ b $\frac{22a+25}{20}$ c $\frac{32n+5}{12}$
d $\frac{27t-17}{15}$ e $\frac{37u-30}{24}$ f $\frac{65q+8}{90}$
g $\frac{4a+5}{6}$ h $\frac{5n+3}{8}$ i $\frac{19g}{9}$
j $\frac{25y-7}{24}$ k $\frac{8-2x}{15}$ l $\frac{13-14a}{40}$

4 a $\frac{x-2}{6}$ b $\frac{y-15}{10}$ c $\frac{2n-1}{15}$
d $\frac{x+29}{30}$ e $\frac{2m+8}{35}$ f $\frac{5p+8}{12}$
g $\frac{1}{6}$ h $\frac{t+4}{8}$ i $\frac{11w}{9}$
j $\frac{19-2y}{24}$ k $\frac{-1-x}{30}$ l $\frac{7+2z}{40}$

5 a $\frac{31x+91}{30}$ b $\frac{86a+35}{60}$ c $\frac{14m+13}{6}$
d $\frac{12y+29}{20}$ e $\frac{5x-3}{4}$ f $\frac{4z+13}{20}$

Challenge 3:04

1 $\frac{2x^2+5x+12}{6x}$ 2 $\frac{5x+14}{6x}$
3 $\frac{7a}{10x}$ 4 $\frac{10a+7ax+5x}{10ax}$
5 $\frac{2x-2}{15x}$ 6 $\frac{7n+2}{12n}$
7 $\frac{a^2+b^2}{ab}$ 8 $\frac{5xy-2x^2-15y^2}{6xy}$

Prep quiz 3:05

1 $2x + 10$ 2 $4x^2 - x$
3 $6a^2 + 21a$ 4 $2m^2 + 6mn$
5 $\{1, 2, 3, 4, 6, 12\}$ 6 $\{1, 2, 4, 5, 10, 20\}$
7 $\{1, 2, 3, 5, 6, 10, 15, 30\}$ 8 4
9 6 10 10

Exercise 3:05

1 a $4(x + 2)$ b $6(a + 3)$ c $4(2a - 3)$
d $5(x + 2y)$ e $7(3x - 2y)$ f $3(4pq - 5x)$
g $n(m - p)$ h $a(b - c)$ i $2a(x + 2y)$
j $y(y - 5)$ k $at(5 - 3a)$ l $mn(7 - n)$

2 a $2(x + 5)$ b $2(3a + 2)$ c $7(y + 3)$
d $4(7 + x)$ e $3(9 - y)$ f $6(4x + 1)$
g $9(x - 5)$ h $4(4 - 3a)$ i $3(3x + y)$
j $5(a + 2b)$ k $5(3m - 4n)$ l $2(2b - 3a)$
m $m(p + n)$ n $a(x + y)$ o $x(x + y)$
p $p(p - q)$ q $a(p + 3)$ r $x(5 + a)$
s $m(4 - n)$ t $t(x - 1)$

3 a $3a(x + 2y)$ b $5m(n - 2p)$ c $2b(2a - 3c)$
d $3q(3p - 2r)$ e $5x(x - 2y)$ f $3a(b + 2a)$
g $2m(5m - 2n)$ h $4x(3x + y)$ i $bc(a + d)$

j $pq(a-b)$	k $xy(z+1)$	l $mn(1-p)$
m $xa(x-y)$	n $5x(a-2y)$	o $ap(a-5)$
p $xy(y+z)$	q $5b(2a-3c)$	r $xy(5x-3y)$
s $ap(p-a)$	t $ab(5-ab)$	

4 a $-2(a+3)$ b $-5(x+3)$ c $-4(2m+3)$
d $-5(2x+1)$ e $-4(2x-1)$ f $-3(n-3)$
g $-7(y-5)$ h $-2(3a-2)$ i $-x(x+3)$
j $-m(m+1)$ k $-x(3x-2)$ l $-5y(y-2)$
m $-p(4+p)$ n $-x(3+2x)$ o $-m(1-7m)$
p $-2a(2-9a)$

5 a $a(b+c+d)$ b $x(3+y+z)$
c $m(m-3+n)$ d $a(7-b+a)$
e $p(p+q-5)$ f $2(x+2y-3z)$
g $5(2a-b+3c)$ h $3(3x^2+2x-4)$
i $2(4-2x+3x^2)$ j $5(5+3y-4y^2)$
k $x(xy-3y+1)$ l $2a(b-2c+5)$
m $3x(x+2y-3)$ n $xy(x+1+y)$
o $ab(ab+3a+2b)$ p $mn(1+4m-8n)$

6 a $(a+2)(a+3)$ b $(m+2)(m+4)$
c $(x-1)(x+5)$ d $(b+1)(b-5)$
e $(y-2)(7-y)$ f $(t-7)(t-9)$
g $(2m-3)(4+3m)$ h $(7x+1)(2x-5)$
i $(a+3)(x-1)$ j $(2y-1)(y-1)$
k $(p-3)(p-3)$ l $(5x+3)(1-x)$

Prep quiz 3:06

1 $12x$ 2 a 3 x^2-2x+3
4 $2x+10$ 5 x^2-2x 6 $-3a-3$
7 $-5y+y^2$ 8 x^2+4x+3 9 $25-a^2$
10 $6x^2-19x-10$

Exercise 3:06

1 a $ab+3a+2b+6$ b $xy+4x+y+4$
c $mn+5m+7n+35$ d $ax+2a+3x+6$
e $pq+4p+5q+20$ f $2xy+6x+y+3$
g $3ap+2a+18p+12$ h $8xy+12x+2y+3$
i $6ab-21a+2b-7$ j $14px+7x+10p+5$
k $5px-20p+3x-12$ l $2ax+4bx+ay+2by$

2 a a^2+5a+6 b x^2+6x+5
c $n^2+7n+12$ d $p^2+7p+10$
e m^2-2m-3 f $y^2+5y-14$
g x^2-5x-6 h t^2-2t-8
i x^2-6x+8 j n^2-8n+7
k $a^2-9a+18$ l $x^2-19x+90$
m $y^2-4y-77$ n a^2-a-2
o $x^2-16x+64$ p $m^2-11m+18$
q a^2-9 r $x^2-4x-21$
s $y^2+17y+60$ t a^2-64
u $q^2+10q+25$ v $x^2-10x+9$
w $t^2+13t+30$ x $k^2+3k-88$

3 a $2a^2+7a+3$ b $2x^2+5x+2$
c $3m^2+17m+10$ d $4y^2+13y+3$
e $4x^2+8x+3$ f $6n^2+7n+2$
g $8x^2+18x+9$ h $10t^2+19t+6$
i $10x^2-12x+2$ j $24p^2-13p-2$
k $10m^2-29m+10$ l $21q^2+q-2$
m $18x^2+6x-4$ n $4n^2-9$
o $64y^2-1$ p $15k^2-19k+6$
q $49p^2-14p+1$ r $15x^2-14x+3$
s $25x^2+40x+16$ t $27y^2+6y-8$
u $5p^2-33p-14$ v $10q^2-101q+10$
w $12a^2+25a+12$ x $49p^2-25$

4 a $12+7x+x^2$ b $10-7a+a^2$
c $7-6m-m^2$ d $9-n^2$
e $y^2+9y+20$ f $12x-x^2-35$
g $k^2+19k+90$ h $2a^2+7a+3$
i $19n-6n^2+7$ j $x^2+3xy+2y^2$
k $2n^2+5mn+2m^2$ l $2a^2+ab-3b^2$
m $4p^2-q^2$ n $6x^2-13xy-5y^2$
o $6a^2+13ab+6b^2$ p $81w^2-90wx+25x^2$

Prep quiz 3:07A

1 16 2 49 3 4 4 100
5 $9x^2$ 6 49 7 9 8 4
9 10 10 6

Investigation 3:07

x	y	x^2	y^2	xy	$(x+y)^2$	$x^2+2xy+y^2$	$(x-y)^2$	$x^2-2xy+y^2$
5	3	25	9	15	64	64	4	4
6	1	36	1	6	49	49	25	25
10	4	100	16	40	196	196	36	36

Exercise 3:07A

1 a 4 b 36 c 9 d 100
e $2x$ f $14y$ g $4n$ h $10p$
i q^2 j x^2 k 3 l 9
m 7 n 11 o $4x^2$ p $25n^2$
q $42m$ r $40x$ s $4a$ t $126y$

2 a x^2+6x+9 b $x^2+10x+25$
c x^2+2x+1 d $x^2-12x+36$
e m^2-2m+1 f $n^2-10n+25$
g x^2+4x+4 h $n^2-16n+64$
i $m^2+22m+121$ j $a^2+24a+144$
k $x^2+20x+100$ l $p^2-18p+81$
m $x^2+2xy+y^2$ n $a^2+2am+m^2$
o $x^2+2xt+t^2$ p $a^2-2ab+b^2$
q $k^2-2km+m^2$ r $p^2-2pq+q^2$

3 a $4x^2+12x+9$ b $4x^2+4x+1$
c $9x^2+30x+25$ d $16a^2+8a+1$
e $9a^2+42a+49$ f $49t^2+28t+4$
g $4x^2-4x+1$ h $9a^2-12a+4$
i $25m^2-40m+16$ j $16t^2-56t+49$
k $36q^2-12q+1$ l $81n^2+72n+16$
m $4x^2+4xy+y^2$ n $a^2+6ab+9b^2$
o $9t^2-12xt+4x^2$

Prep quiz 3:07B

1 40 2 40 3 12 4 12 5 24
6 24 7 27 8 27 9 19 10 19

Exercise 3:07B

1 a $x^2 - 16$ b $a^2 - 1$ c $m^2 - 4$
d $n^2 - 49$ e $p^2 - 25$ f $q^2 - 36$
g $x^2 - 9$ h $y^2 - 81$ i $100 - x^2$
j $25 - a^2$ k $64 - x^2$ l $121 - m^2$
m $x^2 - t^2$ n $a^2 - b^2$ o $m^2 - n^2$
p $p^2 - q^2$

2 a $4a^2 - 1$ b $9x^2 - 4$ c $25m^2 - 9$
d $81q^2 - 4$ e $16t^2 - 9$ f $49x^2 - 1$
g $64n^2 - 25$ h $100x^2 - 9$ i $4x^2 - y^2$
j $16a^2 - 9b^2$ k $25p^2 - 4q^2$ l $9m^2 - n^2$
m $4m^2 - 25n^2$ n $4p^2 - 9q^2$ o $x^2 - 25y^2$
p $144x^2 - 25y^2$

Exercise 3:08

1 a $8x - 21$ b $x^2 + x - 2$
c $2x^2 - x - 1$ d $4x - x^2 + 10$
e $9x^2 - 6x + 1$ f $x^2 - 25$
g $6x^2 - 23x + 7$ h $25x^2 - 1$
i $x^2 + 6x + 7$ j $8x$
k $x^2 + 7x - 30$ l $81 - y^2$
m $x^2 - 15x$ n $3x^2 + 9x + 6$
o $x^2 + 2xy + y^2$ p $2x^2 + 5xy + 2y^2$
q $3x$ r $a^2 - 4b^2$
s $2a - 2x$ t $15a^2 + 26a - 21$
u $4m^2 - 20mn + 25n^2$ v $1 - 25y^2$
w $21 - 4x$ x $81x^2 - 64y^2$

2 a $x^2 + 7x + 11$ b $a^2 - 9a + 6$
c $x^2 - 2x + 20$ d $x^2 + 2x + 9$
e $2x^2 + 9x + 11$ f -1
g $12m + 37$ h $-14y - 98$
i $2x^2 + 6x + 5$ j $2a + 5$
k $2x^2 + 8x + 8$ l $2a^2 - 4$
m $5x + 7$ n $y - 17$
o $4x^2 - x - 14$ p $3x^2 + 24x + 49$
q $9x^2 - 10x - 2$ r $10x$
s $p^2 - q^2$ t $2xy + 2y^2$
u $2a^2 + 5ab + 3b^2$ v $2m^2 + 2n^2$
w $3x^2 + 11x + 8$ x $5x^2 + 6x + 1$
y $12xy + 18y^2$ z ab

3 a $3x^2 + 12x + 14$ b $3x^2 + 15x + 20$
c $3a^2 + 1$ d $5x + 7$
e $19a^2 + 13ab - 7b^2$ f $12x^2 + 3x + 12$
g $-4m + 24$ h $4x^2 - 3y^2 + 1$
i $6x^2 + 4xy + 6y^2$ j $-4y^2$

Challenge 3:08

1 $10x^2 + 110x + 385$ 2 $9x^2 + 99x + 330$
3 $11a^2 + 110$ 4 $55m^2 - 55n^2$

Investigation 3:08

Perfect squares

1 a 10 201 b 42 025 c 1 008 016
d 5184 e 9604 f 39 601
g 990 025 h 4489

Difference of two squares

1 a 396 b 840 c 1425 d 12 920
2 a $\sqrt{56}$ b $\sqrt{540}$ c $\sqrt{445}$ d $\sqrt{960}$

Diagnostic test 3

1 a $2a + 3b$ b $2p^2 + 2p$
c $2ab$ d $4a - x - 2$

2 a $56m$ b $30ab$ c $10y^2$ d $-8ny$

3 a $3a$ b $5y$ c $\frac{3c}{2b}$ d $\frac{-1}{3y}$

4 a x b $-\frac{x}{6}$ c $\frac{7a}{15}$ d $\frac{9m}{8}$

5 a $\frac{n}{4}$ b $\frac{10}{ab}$ c $\frac{1}{2}$ d $\frac{6}{5}$

6 a $6m$ b 2 c 12 d $\frac{5a}{2}$

7 a $9x + 63$ b $30a - 12$
c $p^2 + 3p$ d $15a - 6a^2$

8 a $-3x - 6$ b $-2m + 16$
c $-15x - 20$ d $-7 + 2m$

9 a $-x$ b $10n - 7$ c $-a^2 + 6ab$

10 a $\frac{7x+26}{10}$ b $\frac{12a+1}{12}$ c $\frac{5n+11}{12}$

11 a $5(m + 2)$ b $x(x - 3)$
c $3a(2b + 5)$ d $-4(2y + 3)$

12 a $x^2 + 7x + 12$ b $2a^2 - 7a + 3$
c $6 - y - y^2$ d $2x^2 - 5xy - 3y^2$

13 a $x^2 + 4x + 4$ b $a^2 - 14a + 49$
c $4y^2 + 20y + 25$ d $m^2 - 2mn + n^2$

14 a $x^2 - 9$ b $y^2 - 49$
c $4a^2 - 25$ d $x^2 - y^2$

ASSIGNMENT 3A

1 a $7a$ b $18x^2$ c $-4a$
d $2x^2$ e 6 f $\frac{3y}{2}$
g $2x + 3y$ h $6ab^2$ i $2ab$
j $12ab$ k $6a^2 - a$ l $-x - 3y$
m $19 + 5x$ n $12x$ o $4x^2 - x$
p $10x$

2 a $\frac{5x}{6}$ b $\frac{3a}{10}$ c $\frac{5ab}{4}$
d $\frac{2}{3}$ e $\frac{16x}{15}$ f $\frac{13m}{30}$
g $\frac{8n}{7}$ h $\frac{5x+11}{6}$ i $\frac{7a-4}{10}$
j $\frac{8n-7}{18}$

3 a $3(a + 5)$ b $3(2m + 3)$ c $5(3 - y)$
d $x(a - 3)$ e $2x(1 + 3y)$ f $2x(2x - 1)$
g $3b(3a - 2c)$ h $3x(2x - 3 + y)$

4 a $x^2 - 2x$ b $-x + 4$ c $x^2 - 4x + 4$
d $x^2 - 4$ e $x^2 + 4x + 4$ f $4 - 4x + x^2$

5 a $x^2 + x - 2$ b $8x - 3$
c 3 d $2x^2 - 13x - 7$
e $x^2 - 25$ f $9x^2 + 12x + 4$
g $x^2 - x + 2$ h $6 - 5x + x^2$
i $y^2 - x^2$ j $4x^2 - 4xy + y^2$
k $20x + 15$ l $4x^2 + 8x + 4$

ASSIGNMENT 3B

1 a square b rectangle c parallelogram
d rhombus e trapezium f pentagon
g hexagon h octagon i kite
j isosceles triangle
2 a An octagonal prism b Sample answer: 200 mL
3 17
4 a 4 b 10
5 a 40% b 5%
6 a Tasmania; 60% b Victoria; over 90%
c Queensland, just under 3000 per 10 000
d about 50%; between 30% and 40%

ASSIGNMENT 3C

1 a \$958.50 b 40 530
c i 20% ii $\frac{5}{12}$ iii 0·65
2 a 0·875 b 0·068 c $0{\cdot}41\dot{6}$
3 a 2 b 5 c 1 d 2
4 a 8·75 m to 8·85 b 123·445 to 123·455
c 5·5 km to 6·5 km d 3·95°C to 4·05°C
5 a 6 b 35 c 21 d 2
6 a 3 200 000 L b 45 000 000 000 W
c 3 000 000 MB d 15 000 kHz
7 \$2262
8 a 75 kg; \$500
b Volume of sand = 0·8 m^3; Volume of gravel = 1 m^3
9 4 10 18

Chapter 4

Exercise 4:01

1 a even chance b unlikely c impossible
d impossible e certain
2 a 1, 2 b 3, 4, 5, 6 c 2, 4, 6
d 1, 3, 5 e 1, 2, 3, 4, 6 f 1, 2, 3, 4, 5, 6
3 a QS, QC b 5D, 5H, 6D, 6H, 7D, 7H
c JD, JH d 3H, 4H
e JD, JH, QD, QH, KD, KH
f AD, 2D, 3D, 4D, 5D, 6D, 7D, 8D, 9D, 10D, JD, QD, KD
4 a 24 b 28 c 4 d 28 e 40
f 32 g 32 h 12 i 20 j 32
5 a 9 b 8 c 9 d 0 e 91
f 100
6 a Mutually exclusive events are events that have no element in common.
b Non-mutually exclusive events are events that have one or more elements in common.
c 1
d The complement of an event is every element in the sample space that is not in that event.
e Choosing at random means choosing in a way that does not affect the likelihood of outcomes.

7

Outcome	Frequency	Relative frequency (or experimental probability)
two heads	24	$\frac{24}{100}$ or 24%
head and tail	51	$\frac{51}{100}$ or 51%
two tails	25	$\frac{25}{100}$ or 25%
Total:	100	

8

Outcome	Frequency	Relative frequency (or experimental probability)
1	8	$\frac{8}{60}$ or about 13%
2	10	$\frac{10}{60}$ or about 17%
3	9	$\frac{9}{60}$ or about 15%
4	12	$\frac{12}{60}$ or about 20%
5	10	$\frac{10}{60}$ or about 17%
6	11	$\frac{11}{60}$ or about 18%
Total:	60	

9 Four different-coloured sectors, each with an angle of 90° at the centre, should be drawn on the spinner.
10 Answers will vary. A spinner with 4 quadrants could be used, with 'Alan' written in two quadrants and 'Alana' and 'Heather' each written in one quadrant.

Prep quiz 4:02

1 10 2 3 3 $\frac{3}{10}$ 4 $\frac{1}{5}$ 5 $\frac{1}{2}$
6 6 7 $\frac{3}{5}$ 8 $\frac{1}{3}$ 9 $\frac{4}{5}$ 10 $\frac{12}{25}$

Exercise 4:02

1 a $\frac{70}{100}$ (or $\frac{7}{10}$) b $\frac{10}{100}$ (or $\frac{1}{10}$) c $\frac{5}{100}$ (or $\frac{1}{20}$)
d $\frac{30}{100}$ (or $\frac{3}{10}$) e $\frac{15}{100}$ (or $\frac{3}{20}$) f $\frac{85}{100}$ (or $\frac{17}{20}$)
g $\frac{20}{100}$ (or $\frac{1}{5}$) h $\frac{75}{100}$ (or $\frac{3}{4}$)
2 a brown b yellow c $\frac{6}{24}$ (or $\frac{1}{4}$)
d 24
3 faulty: $\frac{5}{100}$ (or $\frac{1}{20}$); good: $\frac{95}{100}$ (or $\frac{19}{20}$)
4 a i $\frac{10}{42}$ (or $\frac{5}{21}$) ii $\frac{5}{42}$
iii $\frac{21}{42}$ (or $\frac{1}{2}$)
b 24%, 12%, 50%

5 a $\frac{18}{100}$ (or $\frac{9}{50}$) b $\frac{35}{100}$ (or $\frac{7}{20}$) c $\frac{65}{100}$ (or $\frac{13}{20}$)
d $\frac{20}{100}$ (or $\frac{1}{5}$)

6 a i $\frac{3}{30}$ (or $\frac{1}{10}$) ii $\frac{13}{30}$
iii $\frac{10}{30}$ (or $\frac{1}{3}$)
b no, but the graph should be similar in shape
c yes

7 a i $\frac{14}{50}$ ii $\frac{5}{50}$ iii $\frac{21}{50}$
b no
c The experimental probabilities of each number should be much closer to the real probabilities (i.e. $16\frac{2}{3}$%).

8 a $\frac{16}{20}$ (or $\frac{4}{5}$ or 80%) b $\frac{1}{20}$ (or 5%)
c $\frac{3}{20}$ (or 15%)

9 a A, C, D, B, E (Answers may vary.)
b (Answers will vary.) One possibility is $P(A) \doteqdot 0{\cdot}01$, $P(B) \doteqdot 0{\cdot}5$, $P(C) \doteqdot 0{\cdot}1$, $P(D) \doteqdot 0{\cdot}9$, $P(E) \doteqdot 0{\cdot}99$.

10 a impossible b even chance c certain
d even chance e certain f even chance

Prep quiz 4:03

1 $\frac{7}{8}$ 2 $\frac{2}{3}$ 3 $\frac{3}{7}$ 4 $\frac{3}{16}$ 5 $\frac{1}{10}$
6 $\frac{1}{4}$ 7 $\frac{1}{3}$ 8 $\frac{2}{3}$ 9 $\frac{5}{26}$ 10 $\frac{3}{10}$

Exercise 4:03

1 a $\frac{1}{6}$ b $\frac{1}{2}$ c $\frac{1}{3}$

2 a $\frac{1}{2}$ b $\frac{1}{5}$ c $\frac{7}{10}$
d $\frac{4}{5}$ e 0 f 1

3 a getting an even number
b getting a head c getting a 6
d drawing a club, diamond or heart
e seeing green or orange
f losing or playing a draw
g choosing a consonant

4 a $\frac{1}{52}$ b $\frac{1}{13}$ c $\frac{1}{2}$ d $\frac{1}{4}$ e $\frac{1}{26}$
f $\frac{2}{13}$ g $\frac{3}{13}$

5 a $\frac{1}{26}$ b $\frac{5}{26}$ c $\frac{1}{13}$ d $\frac{4}{13}$

6 a $\frac{1}{2}$ b $\frac{1}{3}$ c $\frac{1}{6}$ d 1 e 0
f $\frac{5}{6}$

7 a $\frac{1}{6}$ b $\frac{1}{2}$ c $\frac{2}{3}$ d $\frac{1}{3}$

8 a $\frac{1}{4}$ b $\frac{1}{2}$ c $\frac{3}{8}$ d 0

9 a $\frac{13}{25}$ b $\frac{1}{5}$ c $\frac{8}{25}$ d $\frac{8}{25}$

10 a $\frac{3}{5}$ b $\frac{2}{5}$ c $\frac{1}{5}$ d $\frac{3}{5}$ e 1

11 4, no

12 a $\frac{5}{12}$ b $\frac{1}{6}$ c $\frac{1}{12}$ d $\frac{1}{12}$ e $\frac{5}{12}$

13 a 2 b 6 c 8

14 a $\frac{9}{20}$ b $\frac{1}{4}$ c $\frac{7}{10}$ d $\frac{1}{10}$

15 a $\frac{18}{37}$ b $\frac{18}{37}$ c $\frac{1}{37}$ d $\frac{19}{37}$ e $\frac{6}{37}$
f $\frac{11}{37}$ g once every 37 spins
h Lose, because of the wheel's zero slot.

Exercise 4:04

1 a non-mutually exclusive
b mutually exclusive
c non-mutually exclusive

2 a $\frac{53}{100}$ or 53% b $\frac{47}{100}$ or 47% c $\frac{21}{50}$ or 42%
d $\frac{29}{50}$ or 58% e $\frac{9}{50}$ or 18% f $\frac{43}{100}$ or 43%
g $\frac{4}{5}$ or 80% h $\frac{73}{100}$ or 73%

3 a $\frac{1}{2}$ b $\frac{1}{2}$ c $\frac{1}{13}$
d $\frac{12}{13}$ e $\frac{3}{13}$ f $\frac{2}{52}$ or $\frac{1}{26}$
g $\frac{1}{4}$ h 0 i $\frac{6}{52}$ or $\frac{3}{26}$
j $\frac{15}{52}$ k $\frac{1}{13}$ l $\frac{3}{4}$
m $\frac{22}{52}$ or $\frac{11}{26}$ n $\frac{37}{52}$ o $\frac{16}{52}$ or $\frac{4}{13}$
p $\frac{8}{52}$ or $\frac{2}{13}$ q $\frac{23}{52}$

4 a $\frac{1}{2}$ b $\frac{2}{5}$ c $\frac{3}{10}$ d $\frac{2}{5}$
e $\frac{7}{10}$ f $\frac{4}{5}$ g 1 h $\frac{7}{20}$
i $\frac{3}{10}$ j $\frac{2}{5}$ k $\frac{3}{10}$ l $\frac{3}{20}$
m $\frac{3}{5}$ n $\frac{2}{5}$ o $\frac{17}{20}$ p $\frac{3}{20}$

5 a i $\frac{3}{8}$ ii $\frac{3}{8}$
b no c $\frac{3}{4}$ d true
e i $\frac{3}{8}$ ii $\frac{1}{2}$
f yes g false h true

Exercise 4:05

1 a $\frac{18}{100}$ (or 18%) b $\frac{44}{100}$ (or 44%) c $\frac{56}{100}$ (or 56%)
d $\frac{82}{100}$ (or 82%) e $\frac{16}{100}$ (or 16%) f $\frac{2}{100}$ (or 2%)
g $\frac{54}{100}$ (or 54%) h $\frac{28}{100}$ (28%) i $\frac{46}{100}$ (or 46%)

2 a $\frac{11}{60}$ b $\frac{8}{60}$ (or $\frac{2}{15}$) c $\frac{19}{60}$
d $\frac{49}{60}$ e $\frac{41}{60}$ f $\frac{52}{60}$ (or $\frac{26}{30}$)
g 0 (0% chance)

3 a 117 b 35 c 30%
d 47% e 13% f 40%
g 70% h 30%

4 a $\frac{61}{125}$ b $\frac{64}{125}$ c $\frac{29}{125}$
d $\frac{39}{125}$ e $\frac{25}{125}$ (or $\frac{1}{5}$)

5 a $\frac{7}{50}$ b $\frac{2}{50}$ (or $\frac{1}{25}$) c $\frac{5}{50}$ (or $\frac{1}{10}$)
d $\frac{13}{50}$ e $\frac{6}{50}$ (or $\frac{3}{25}$) f 0 (0% chance)

Exercise 4:06

1 a Choosing two counters (with replacement)

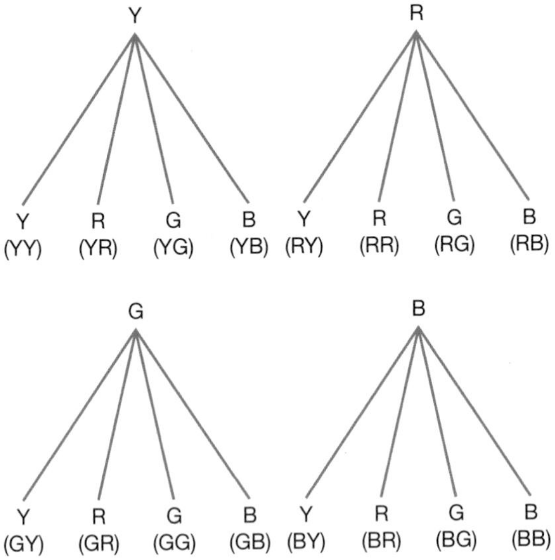

Second choice (with replacement)

First choice	Y	R	G	B
Y	YY	YR	YG	YB
R	RY	RR	RG	RB
G	GY	GR	GG	GB
B	BY	BR	BG	BB

b 16 c 2 d $\frac{2}{16}$

e $\frac{1}{16}$ f $\frac{1}{16}$ g $\frac{15}{16}$

2 a Choosing two counters (without replacement)

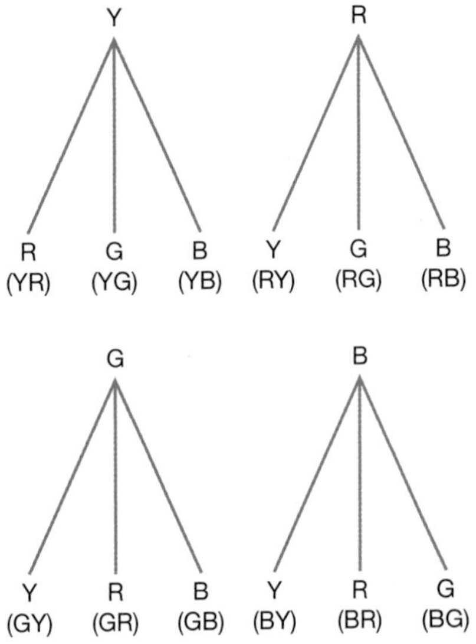

Second choice (without replacement)

First choice	Y	R	G	B
Y		YR	YG	YB
R	RY		RG	RB
G	GY	GR		GB
B	BY	BR	BG	

b 12 c 2 d $\frac{2}{12}$

e $\frac{1}{12}$ f 0 g 1

h

Event	Number of selections	Probability
yellow and red	2	$\frac{2}{12}$
yellow and green	2	$\frac{2}{12}$
yellow and blue	2	$\frac{2}{12}$
2 yellow	0	$\frac{0}{12}$ (or 0)

Event	Number of selections	Probability
red and green	2	$\frac{2}{12}$
red and blue	2	$\frac{2}{12}$
green and blue	2	$\frac{2}{12}$
2 red	0	$\frac{0}{12}$ (or 0)

3 a

Coin

Dice	H	T
1	H1	T1
2	H2	T2
3	H3	T3
4	H4	T4
5	H5	T5
6	H6	T6

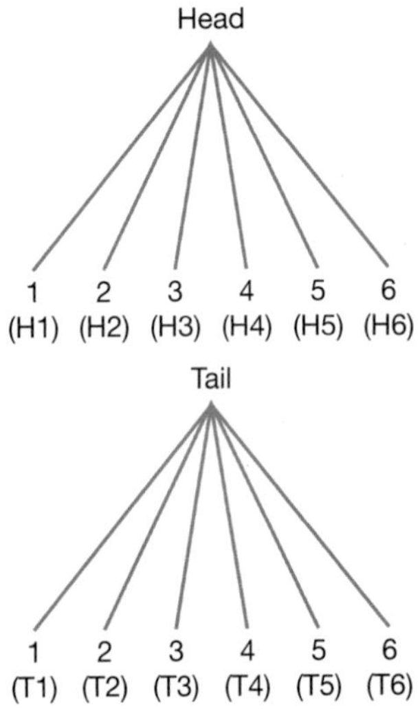

b 12

c i $\frac{1}{12}$ ii $\frac{1}{2}$ iii $\frac{2}{12}$

iv $\frac{4}{12}$ v $\frac{5}{12}$ vi $\frac{10}{12}$

d no

4 a 36 b 11 c $\frac{1}{36}$ d $\frac{1}{36}$ e $\frac{6}{36}$

f $\frac{3}{36}$ g $\frac{3}{36}$ h $\frac{4}{36}$ i $\frac{5}{36}$ j $\frac{5}{36}$

k $\frac{4}{36}$ l $\frac{8}{36}$ m $\frac{15}{36}$ n $\frac{2}{36}$ o $\frac{18}{36}$

p $\frac{30}{36}$ q $\frac{15}{36}$

5 a (3C, 6H), (3C, 7H), (3C, 8D), (3C, 9C), (6H, 3C), (6H, 7H), (6H, 8D), (6H, 9C), (7H, 3C), (7H, 6H), (7H, 8D), (7H, 9C), (8D, 3C), (8D, 6H), (8D, 7H), (8D, 9C), (9C, 3C), (9C, 6H), (9C, 7H)), (9C, 8D)

b 20 c $\frac{2}{20}$ d $\frac{1}{20}$ e $\frac{2}{20}$ f $\frac{2}{20}$

g $\frac{8}{20}$ or $\frac{2}{5}$ h $\frac{8}{20}$ i $\frac{4}{20}$ j $\frac{4}{20}$

k $\frac{2}{20}$ l $\frac{8}{20}$ m $\frac{8}{20}$ n $\frac{16}{20}$ o $\frac{6}{20}$

6 a (3C, 3C), (3C, 6H), (3C, 7H), (3C, 8D), (3C, 9C), (6H, 3C), (6H, 6H), (6H, 7H), (6H, 8D), (6H, 9C), (7H, 3C), (7H, 6H), (7H, 7H), (7H, 8D), (7H, 9C), (8D, 3C), (8D, 6H), (8D, 7H), (8D, 8D), (8D, 9C), (9C, 3C), (9C, 6H), (9C, 7H), (9C, 8D), (9C, 9C)

b 25 c $\frac{2}{25}$ d $\frac{1}{25}$ e $\frac{4}{25}$ f $\frac{2}{25}$

g $\frac{10}{25}$ or $\frac{2}{5}$ h $\frac{8}{25}$ i $\frac{4}{25}$ j $\frac{4}{25}$

k $\frac{3}{25}$ l $\frac{10}{25}$ m $\frac{13}{25}$ n $\frac{21}{25}$ o $\frac{7}{25}$

7 a i $\frac{1}{3}$ ii $\frac{2}{3}$ iii $\frac{1}{3}$ iv $\frac{2}{3}$

v $\frac{2}{3}$ vi $\frac{3}{3}$ or 1

b Knowing that the 2 of hearts has been chosen removes the uncertainty that the 2 will be chosen. The probability of the two-stage event can then be calculated as the possibility of drawing the required card in the second choice to complete the event. In this case the 2 of hearts cannot be chosen as the second choice.

c i $\frac{2}{4}$ ii $\frac{3}{4}$ iii $\frac{1}{4}$ iv $\frac{2}{4}$

v $\frac{3}{4}$ vi $\frac{4}{4}$ or 1

d Knowing that the 2 of hearts has been chosen removes the uncertainty that the 2 will be chosen. The probability of the two-stage event can then be calculated as the possibility of drawing the required card in the second choice to complete the event. In this case the 2 of hearts can be chosen as the second choice.

8 a i 12 ii $\frac{2}{12}$ b i 16 ii $\frac{4}{16}$

9 Answers will vary.

Diagnostic test 4

1 a 1, 2, 3, 4, 5, 6 b head, tail c 1, 3, 5, 7, 9

2 a $\frac{3}{44}$ b $\frac{41}{44}$

c 0. It is possible for me to play worse than ever before and so score more than 109, so the real probability is greater than zero.

3 a $\frac{1}{2}$ b $\frac{5}{6}$ c 0 d $\frac{2}{3}$

4 a $\frac{2}{13}$ b $\frac{3}{26}$ c $\frac{5}{52}$ d $\frac{16}{52}$ or $\frac{13}{26}$

e $\frac{28}{52}$ or $\frac{7}{13}$ f $\frac{24}{52}$ or $\frac{6}{13}$

5 a $\frac{55}{100}$ (or $\frac{11}{20}$), 55% chance

b $\frac{43}{100}$, 43% chance c $\frac{7}{100}$, 7% chance

d $\frac{50}{100}$ (or $\frac{1}{2}$), 50% chance

6 a $\frac{3}{50}$, 6% chance b $\frac{43}{50}$, 86% chance

c $\frac{27}{50}$, 54% chance d $\frac{23}{50}$, 46% chance

ASSIGNMENT 4A

1 a $\frac{1}{6}$ b 0 c $\frac{1}{3}$ d $\frac{1}{2}$ e 1

2 a $\frac{7}{20}$ b $\frac{1}{10}$ c $\frac{13}{20}$

3 a $\frac{2}{5}$ b $\frac{1}{10}$ c $\frac{1}{2}$ d 0

4 a (R1, G1) (R1,Y1) (R1,Y2) (G1, R1) (G1,Y1) (G1,Y2) (Y1, R1) (Y1, G1) (Y1,Y2) (Y2, R1) (Y2, G1) (Y2,Y1)

or

Second choice (without replacement)

First choice	R1	G1	Y1	Y2
R1		RG	RY	RY
G1	GR		GY	GY
Y1	YR	YG		YY
Y2	YR	YG	YY	

or

(without replacement)

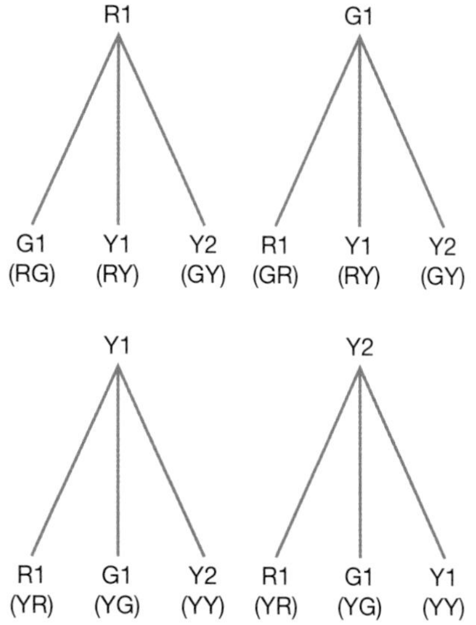

P(the same colour) = $\frac{2}{12}$ or $\frac{1}{6}$

b (R1, R1) (R1, G1) (R1,Y1) (R1,Y2) (G1, R1) (G1, G1) (G1,Y1) (G1,Y2) (Y1, R1) (Y1, G1) (Y1,Y1) (Y1,Y2) (Y2, R1) (Y2, G1) (Y2,Y1) (Y2,Y2)

or

Second choice (with replacement)

First choice	R1	G1	Y1	Y2
R1	RR	RG	RY	RY
G1	GR	GG	GY	GY
Y1	YR	YG	YY	YY
Y2	YR	YG	YY	YY

or

(with replacement)

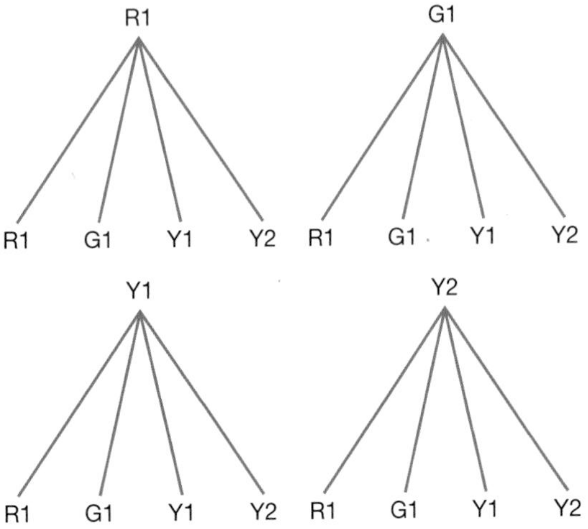

P(the same colour) = $\frac{6}{12}$ or $\frac{1}{2}$

5 a i $\frac{3}{10}$ ii $\frac{1}{4}$

b No; the scores recorded so far are a limited sample. He theoretically could score any result from zero to the maximum 300. (Here the experimental probability is zero.)

6 No; the result of the game depends on the relative strengths of each team. Depending on the type of football, a draw might be much less likely than either team winning.

ASSIGNMENT 4B

1 a midpoint b number line c diagonals
d vertices e hypotenuse f 180°
g 360° h (b) $a° = b°$ i $a = 60°$
j circumference

2 a (1) $3x - 2$ (2) $5x - 4$ (3) $7x + 7$
(4) $4x - 6$ (5) $4x + 10$ (6) $4x - 6$
(7) $2x + 7$ (8) $6x - 6$ (9) $3x + 9$
(10) $6x - 3$ (11) $3x + 13$ (12) $3x - 7$

b (1) $x + 4$ (2) $3x + 8$ (3) $5x - 3$
(4) $2x + 12$ (5) $2x + 6$ (6) $2x + 8$
(7) 9 (8) $4x + 10$ (9) $x - 1$
(10) $4x + 11$ (11) $x + 1$ (12) $x + 13$

c (1) $5x - 7$ (2) $5x + 1$ (3) $7x - 3$
(4) $5x + 7$ (5) $6x + 9$ (6) $4x + 8$
(7) $3x + 3$ (8) $6x - 8$ (9) $4x$
(10) $6x + 11$ (11) $3x + 1$ (12) $4x + 6$

d (1) 6 (2) 20 (3) 16
(4) −64 (5) −16 (6) 4
(7) 20 (8) −32 (9) 96
(10) 224 (11) 8 (12) 1024

3 1 260 000 degrees

4 8 years

5 Estimates should be reasonably close to these.
a 44% b 70% c 87%

ASSIGNMENT 4C

1 a 31 b −54 c −15

2 a \$620 b 80 kg

3 a 17·5% b 16·33%

4 a 0·375 b $1{\cdot}1\dot{6}$ c $\frac{7}{11}$ (or $\frac{63}{99}$)

5 a 10 : 9 b 200 km/h c 2

6 a 6 400 000 b $9{\cdot}5 \times 10^7$ c 2300 kB

7 a $11y$ b $8m - 4p$ c $7a^2 + a$
d $28a$ e $12t^2$ f $420ab$

8 a $4a$ b $4y$ c $-\frac{1}{2n}$
d $\frac{2m}{5}$ (or $\frac{4m}{10}$) e $\frac{9m}{10}$ f $\frac{43a}{30}$
g $\frac{m^2}{20}$ h $1\frac{1}{2}$ i $\frac{x}{2}$

9 a $3x^2 + 7x$ b $42y - 12y^2$ c $-10m + 10$
d $17m - 39$ e $-3a^2$

10 a $4(2m + 3)$ b $2x(2x - 3)$ c $b(12a - 1)$

11 a 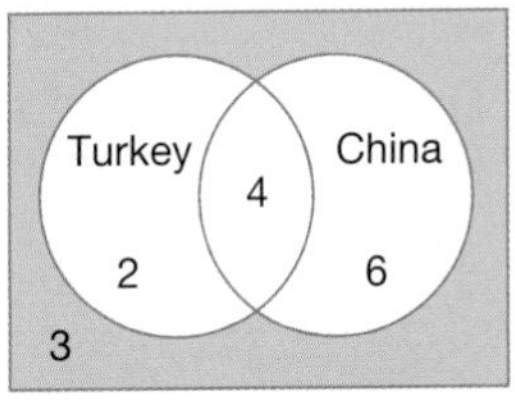 , 4

b 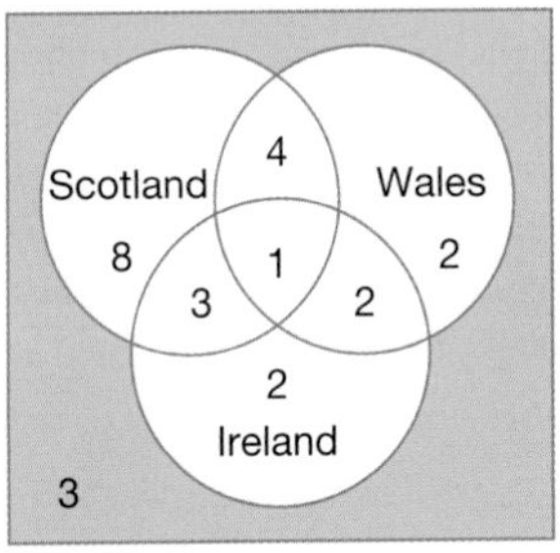 , 3

Chapter 5

Exercise 5:01

1 a $98{\cdot}14\,\text{m}^2$ b $191{\cdot}42\,\text{m}^2$ c $78\,\text{m}^2$

2 a $57{\cdot}1\,\text{m}^2$ b $137{\cdot}16\,\text{m}^2$ c $106\,\text{m}^2$

3 a $31{\cdot}08\,\text{m}^2$ b $5{\cdot}04\,\text{m}^2$ c $158{\cdot}8\,\text{m}^2$

4 a 33·77 cm^2 b 84·82 cm^2 c 103·07 cm^2
5 a 2632·5 mm^2 b 96·3 m^2 c 168·9 m^2
6 a 311·4 m^2 b 115·0 m^2 c 202·4 m^2
7 a 83 cm^2 b 31 cm^2 c 103 cm^2
8 a 8·6 cm^2 b 244·9 cm^2 c 314·2 cm^2
9 a 693·7 m^2 b 22·2 m^2 c 437·7 m^2
10 a i 66·4 m^2 ii 7·98 m^2
b 58·42 m^2 c $5257.80
11 14 m^2
12 a 140 m^2 b $14 000
13 a 112 m^2 b 125·44 m^2 c 128 m^2
d $20 806.40
14 $1494

Investigation 5:01

Laying tiles

1 726 2 117

Laying carpet

1 4·25 m, 2·975 m^2 waste, no joins
2 5·8 m, 8·555 m^2 waste. Yes, there are joins.

Prep quiz 5:02

1 21 cm^2 2 12 cm^2 3 12 cm^2
4 6 5 squares 6 6
7 rectangles 8 opposite faces 9 5
10 13

Exercise 5:02

1 a i 150 cm^2 ii cube iii closed
b i 21 cm^2 ii rectangular prism iii open
c i 27·46 cm^2 ii triangular prism iii closed
d i 62·86 m^2 ii rectangular prism iii closed
e i 36 cm^2 ii triangular prism iii closed
f i 471·96 cm^2 ii triangular prism iii open
2 Area of top and bottom = 140·4 m^2
Area of sides = 25·2 m^2
Area of front and back = 87·36 m^2
Total surface area = 252·96 m^2
3 a 136 cm^2 b 241 cm^2 c 381·72 cm^2
4 a 500 cm^2 b 2350 cm^2 c 12·5 m^2
5 a x = 5 cm; SA = 96 cm^2
b x = 6·24 cm; SA = 452·4 cm^2
c x = 6·40 m; SA = 50·8 m^2
6 253·9 cm^2 (1 dec. pl)
7 30·53 m^2 (1 dec. pl.)
8 Stack B
9 a 12·92 m^2 b 4·4 m c 9·7 m
10 a 648 m^2 b 312·45 m^2 c 295·65 m^2
11 a x = 6·40; SA = 669·43 cm^2
b x = 40·02; SA = 1470·72 m^2
12 $45 945
13 a 4704 cm^2 b 3659 cm^2 c 79·68 cm^2
14 363·1 m^2 (1 dec. pl.)

Prep quiz 5:03

1 8·04 2 372 3 8 cm 4 13 cm
5 6 cm 6 8 cm 7 3·5 cm 8 9 cm
9 5 cm 10 4 cm

Exercise 5:03

1 a 502·65 cm^2 b 376·99 cm^2
c 20·36 m^2 d 917·41 cm^2
2 a i 1658·76 cm^2 ii 760·27 cm^2
iii 2419·03 cm^2
b i 424·87 cm^2 ii 110·84 cm^2
iii 535·71 cm^2
c i 88·22 m^2 ii 215·03 m^2
iii 303·25 m^2
d i 126·67 cm^2 ii 16·08 cm^2
iii 142·75 cm^2
e i 38·68 m^2 ii 73·49 m^2
iii 112·17 m^2
f i 77·41 m^2 ii 30·41 m^2
iii 107·82 m^2
3 a 380 m^2 b 25 m^2 c 15 m^2 d 2500 cm^2
4 Curved surface area = 26·4 m^2
5 3338 cm^2 (nearest cm^2)
6 Cost = $17 436 (nearest dollar)
7 a 139·9 m^2 b $1433.98
8 a 126 m^2 b $8820
9 a SA of 1 L can = 639·3 cm^2;
SA of 2 L can = 1011·6 cm^2
b It is cheaper to sell it in one 2 L can.
10 a 730 cm^2 b 209 cm^2
11 a 1249·8 cm^2 (1 dec. pl.)
b 10 806·93 cm^2 (nearest cm^2)

Exercise 5:04

1 a 18 cm^2 b 22 cm^2 c 26 cm^2
d 24 cm^2
2 a 28 cm^2 b 38 cm^2 c 36 cm^2
3 a 840 cm^2 b 6600 cm^2 c 1194 cm^2
4 a 356 cm^2 b 4980 cm^2 c 3752 cm^2
5 a 31·2 m^2 b 32·0 m^2 c 21·1 m^2
6 a 39·2 m^2 b 14·7 m^2 c 154·7 m^2
7 a 57·12 m^2 b 28·08 m^2
c Three 4 L cans would be needed.
8 76·9 m^2 (1 dec. pl.)
9 $806.40
10 204·5 m^2 (1 dec. pl.)

Investigation 5:04

You would need to calculate the edge length of the equilateral triangle and use this to find the area of the equilateral triangle. You would then need to calculate the area of the octagonal face. Counting the number of octagons and triangles and using the areas already calculated would allow the surface area to be calculated. (Surface area = $4\sqrt{3} + 42$ unit^2)

Prep quiz 5:05

1 11 2 3 3 33 cm^3

4 Multiply the answer to Question 1 by the answer to Question 2.

5 11 6 3 7 33 8 yes

9 yes 10 yes

Exercise 5:05

1 a 4320 cm^3 b 4160 cm^3 c 648 cm^3 d 1155 cm^3 e 960 cm^3

2 a 4934 cm^3 b 1352 cm^3 c 905 cm^3

3 a 292·5 cm^3 b 805·266 cm^3 c 256·932 cm^3

4 a 2293·7 cm^3 b 6090·8 cm^3 c 1022·2 cm^3

5 a 131 m^3 b 15 000 cm^3 c 1·32 m^3

6 a 3435·747 cm^3 b 20·79 m^3 c 5·625 m^3

7 a 13 135·1 cm^3 b 179·5 cm^3 c 1583·7 cm^3

8 a 6232·6 cm^3 b 4672·2 cm^3

9 16 099·1 kg 10 17·7 m^3; 44·25 t

11 1600 kL 12 170 kg

Investigation 5:05

1 a 18 by 12, 20 by 10, 22 by 8, 24 by 6

b

Rectangle	Length (L)	Breadth (B)	Area (A)	$L-B$
1	18	12	216	6
2	20	10	200	10
3	22	8	176	14
4	24	6	144	18

c It increases. d 225 cm^2 e 625 m^2

2 a 4500 cm^3

b 5730 cm^3 (nearest whole number); yes

Diagnostic test 5

1 a 7·14 m^2 b 196·35 cm^2 c 58 m^2

2 a 117·14 m^2 b 36 cm^2 c 666 m^2

3 a 612·6 m^2 b 47·5 m^2 c 15·8 m^2

4 a 400 cm^2 b 704 cm^2 c 351·97 cm^2

5 a 70·518 m^3 b 12 cm^3 c 1008 m^3

6 a 972 m^3 b 19 m^3 c 4 m^3

7 a 400 cm^3 b 768 cm^3 c 324 cm^3

ASSIGNMENT 5A

1 38·43 m^2; $1537.20

2 $60 + 25\sqrt{3} \doteqdot 103{\cdot}3$ cm^2

3 Prism A

4 $8\pi \doteqdot 25{\cdot}1$ m^2

5 104·36 cm^2

6 a 4·47 m^2 (2 dec. pl.) b 0·50 m^3 (2 dec. pl.)

7 a 7·6 units b 139·29 $unit^2$ c 582·13 $unit^2$ d 905·385 $unit^3$

8 a 7163·45 $unit^3$ b 2440 $unit^2$

ASSIGNMENT 5B

1 1800 mL 2 4 3 4 times, 3 times

4 71, 83 or 95; Yes because he is 60 years older than her, so she just adds 60 to her age.

5 a 29 March b 26 April c Hall and Bagnell d Raine and Harris e 8–15 Feb, 15–29 March, 21–28 June

ASSIGNMENT 5C

1 a 18 km/h b $3\frac{1}{3}$ min/km c 20 s/100 m

2 a $\frac{11x}{15}$ b $\frac{-x}{15}$ or $-\frac{x}{15}$ c $\frac{2x^2}{15}$ d $\frac{5}{6}$

3 6 m is between 5·5 m and 6·5 m; 6·0 m is between 5·95 m and 6·05 m; 6·00 m is between 5·995 m and 6·005 m.

4 a 22·5 b 22·51 c 20 d 22·5

5 a $\frac{1}{2}$ b $\frac{9}{20}$ c $\frac{1}{5}$ d $\frac{3}{4}$ e $\frac{1}{4}$

6 a i 57% ii 36% iii 7%

b It would be less than 1%.

c To improve the accuracy you could use a much larger number of trials than 100.

Chapter 6

Exercise 6:01

1 a 2^4 b 3^2 c 5^3 d 7^5 e 10^3 f 9^4 g x^2 h a^4 i n^3 j m^5 k p^6 l y^2 m 4^3 n t^4 o x^5

2 a $2 \times 2 \times 2$ b 4×4 c $6 \times 6 \times 6 \times 6 \times 6$ d $10 \times 10 \times 10 \times 10$ e $7 \times 7 \times 7$ f 3 g $a \times a \times a$ h $x \times x \times x \times x$ i $y \times y$ j $m \times m \times m \times m \times m$ k $n \times n \times n \times n \times n \times n$ l $p \times p \times p$

3 a 32 b 81 c 49 d 121 e 10 000 f 216 g 256 h 78 125 i 32 768 j 59 049 k 16 777 216 l 14 348 907 m 8000 n 27 783 o 455 625 p 592 704

4 a 10^5 b 10^3 c 10^6 d 5^6 e 2^5 f 7^6 g 3^9 h 2^8 i 10^{10}

5 a 10^1 b 10^3 c 10^1 d 5^4 e 7^3 f 3^9 g 2^1 h 5^0 or 1 i 2^6

6 a 10^6 b 10^9 c 10^{12} d 2^{12} e 2^4 f 2^{35} g 3^8 h 5^{15} i 7^8 j $2^6 \times 3^4$ k $7^6 \times 11^8$ l $3^4 \times 2^8$

7 a x^5 b y^6 c m^6 d m^5 e p^{10} f a^2 g y^7 h x^3 i m^7 j $3y^5$ k $3m^6$ l $15x^3$

8 a x^3 b x^4 c x^5 d m^2 e y^3 f m^2 g 1 h 1 i y^6 j $2m^6$

k $2y^8$ l $4x^5$

9 a x^6 b y^8 c a^{15} d 1 e 1
f 1 g y^6 h a^{18} i x^9 j $8x^3$
k $9x^4$ l $625m^8$

10 a $8x^7$ b $5a^3$ c $4m^{10}$ d $8x$ e $5a$
f $4m^2$ g $50y^4$ h $32m^4$ i $32a^9$ j $2y^2$
k 8 l $2a$ m $72x^8$ n $27a^9$ o $108y^7$
p $2x^2$ q $3a^5$ r $3y^5$ s $3a^2$ t $2x^5$
u $2a$

11 a 6 b 6 c 1 d a
e y^3 f m^5 g $8m^6$ h $16n^6$
i $16p^{12}$ j x^5y^3 k a^2b^9 l x^5y^3
m x^3y^4 n a^5b^2 o m^3n^4 p x^4y^6
q $a^2b^2c^2$ r p^3q^9 s $10x^3y^2$ t $28a^3b^5$
u $44a^5b^2$ v $3a^4$ w $-24a^3$ x $2c$
y $22x^2 - 5x^3$ z $12x^2 + 7x + 1$

12 a $30x^6$ b $40a^3$ c $5xy^4$ d $\frac{x^3}{2}$
e $\frac{y}{7}$ f $\frac{10}{x}$ g x^8 h a^{13}
i y^{26} j a^2 k m^2 l n^2
m y^{19} n $8a^{18}$ o b^2 p x^2
q $2a^2$ r $7pq^2$ s $2x^5$ t $6x^6$
u $\frac{xy^3}{16}$

13 a $x^4 - x^2$ b $5a^3 - a^5$
c $5a^3 - a^5$ d $x^3 + xy$
e $7m - m^3$ f $y^3 - xy^2$
g $6a^5 + 9a^3$ h $15x^3 - 5x^2$
i $2m^3n^2 - 2m^5$ j $5x^3 - 3x^2 + 7x$
k $2x^4 + 7x^3 - 14x^2$ l $y^3 - 7y^2 - y$
m $-7x^2$ n $4y^4$
o $-6x^2 + x$

14 a 3^{2x+1} b 5^{y-1} c 2^{4x-2}
d e^{3x+1} e $e^{2x+1} + e^x$ f e^{5x+5}

Exercise 6:02

1 a $\frac{1}{3}$ b $\frac{1}{5}$ c $\frac{1}{2}$ d $\frac{1}{36}$ e $\frac{1}{16}$
f $\frac{1}{1000}$ g $\frac{1}{16}$ h $\frac{1}{10\,000}$ i $\frac{1}{25}$

2 a 11^{-1} b 3^{-1} c 5^{-1} d 7^{-1} e 3^{-3}
f 5^{-4} g 2^{-8} h 7^{-2} i 10^{-2} j 10^{-3}
k 10^{-6} l 10^{-5}

3 a true b false c true d false e false
f false g true h false

4 a 10^{-3} b 10^1 c 10^{-5} d 10^{-3} e 10^{-1}
f 10^{-6} g 10^6 h 10^{-4}

5 a $\frac{1}{a}$ b $\frac{1}{x}$ c $\frac{1}{m}$ d $\frac{1}{y}$ e $\frac{1}{x^3}$
f $\frac{1}{y^2}$ g $\frac{1}{x^4}$ h $\frac{1}{m^6}$ i $\frac{2}{x}$ j $\frac{5}{a^3}$
k $\frac{10}{y^2}$ l $\frac{36}{q^4}$

6 a x^{-1} b x^{-2} c x^{-3} d x^{-4} e $5y^{-2}$
f $3a^{-1}$ g $10m^{-4}$ h $75x^{-3}$ i xy^{-2} j ma^{-2}
k $3ab^{-2}$ l $4xy^{-1}$

7 a 2 b 3 c $1\frac{1}{2}$ d 10
e 4 f 9 g $2\frac{1}{4}$ h $11\frac{1}{9}$

8 a $\frac{1}{x^2}$ b $\frac{1}{a^5}$ c $\frac{3}{x}$
d $\frac{5}{m^2}$ e $\frac{1}{(x+1)^2}$ f $\frac{1}{(3+a)^1}$
g $\frac{1}{(6x)^2}$ or $\frac{1}{36x^2}$ h $\frac{4}{(x+2)^1}$ or $\frac{4}{x+2}$

9 a 0·125 b 0·0625 c 0·04
d 0·015 625 e 0·015 625 f 0·015 625
g 8 h 25 i 400
j 0·064 k 100 000 l 2·56

10 a x b a^3 c m^3
d 1 e $3a$ f $30x^2$
g $5a$ h $30m^2$ i $\frac{1}{x^3}$
j $\frac{2}{a^5}$ k $\frac{8}{y}$ l $\frac{30}{m^5}$

11 a m^5 b x^4 c y^2
d x^4 e $\frac{1}{a^4}$ f $\frac{1}{y^4}$
g $\frac{1}{y^3}$ h $\frac{1}{x^2}$ i $3x^3$
j $\frac{2}{a^4}$ k $\frac{24}{a^5}$ l $2n$

12 a a^6 b $\frac{1}{x^2}$ c $\frac{1}{y^6}$
d m^4 e $\frac{1}{2x^2}$ f $\frac{1}{9x^2}$
g $\frac{25}{x^2}$ h $\frac{49}{x^4}$ i $\frac{1}{abc}$
j $\frac{1}{a^2b^2c^2}$ k $\frac{1}{2a^2b}$ l $\frac{2}{a^2b}$

13 a $\frac{5}{6}$ or $0{\cdot}8\dot{3}$ b $\frac{1}{6}$ or $0{\cdot}1\dot{6}$ c 1
d $\frac{1}{12}$ or $0{\cdot}08\dot{3}$

14 a 3^{2x} b 5^{2y-2} c e^{2x} d e^{3x-1}

Prep quiz 6:03

1 $\sqrt{25} = 5$ 2 $\sqrt{49} = 7$ 3 $\sqrt[3]{8} = 2$
4 $\sqrt[3]{125} = 5$ 5 $n = \frac{1}{2}$ 6 $n = \frac{1}{2}$
7 $n = \frac{1}{2}$ 8 $n = \frac{1}{2}$ 9 $n = \frac{1}{3}$
10 $n = \frac{1}{3}$

Exercise 6:03

1 a $\sqrt{5}$ b $\sqrt{10}$ c $\sqrt{2}$ d $3\sqrt{2}$
e $4\sqrt{3}$ f $7\sqrt{6}$

2 a $3^{\frac{1}{2}}$ b $3\times 2^{\frac{1}{2}}$ c $11^{\frac{1}{3}}$ d $7\times 3^{\frac{1}{2}}$

3 a 2 b 7 c 2 d 2
e 4 f 10 g 12 h 1
i 11 j 2 k 9 l 3

4 a x b a c m d $12x$
e $6y$ f $18n$ g x h y^2
i $2a^3$ j ab^2 k $3x^2y^3$ l $2xy$

5 a $\frac{1}{3}$ b $\frac{1}{5}$ c $\frac{1}{2}$ d 27
e 8 f 32 g 8 h 25
i $\frac{1}{4}$ j 243 k 16 l $\frac{1}{8}$

6 a 15 b 28 c 32 d 9
e 15 f 20 g 3375 h 81
i 3 200 000 j 4 k 32 l 1000

7 a 4 b 2 c 54 d 3
e 1 f $\frac{1}{2}$ g $\frac{1}{2}$ h 4

8 a $9a^2$ b x^4y^8 c $4m^6$ d $\frac{a^2}{b^2}$
e $\frac{8}{x^3}$ f $\frac{y^9}{125}$

Investigation 6:03

- $x^{\frac{1}{2}}, x^1, x^{\frac{3}{2}}, x^2, x^{\frac{5}{2}} \ldots$
  The power of x is increasing by $\frac{1}{2}$ each time.
- $x^{3b} = x^1 \therefore 3b = 1 \therefore b = \frac{1}{3}$
- $\sqrt{8} = \sqrt{2^3} = (2^3)^{\frac{1}{2}} = 2^{\frac{3}{2}} = 2^{\frac{2}{2}} \times 2^{\frac{1}{2}}$
  $= 2\sqrt{2} = (\sqrt{2})^2 \times (\sqrt{2})^1 = (\sqrt{2})^3$
- Some values are: $(x = 4, p = 1, q = 2)$, $(x = 8, p = 1, q = 3)$, $(x = 16, p = 1, q = 4)$

Investigation 6:04

1 a 18 b 180 c 1800
d 40·5 e 405 f 4050
g 62 000 h 620 000 i 6 200 000
j 314·16 k 3141·6
l 31 416. To multiply by 10^n move the decimal point n places to the right.

2 a 0·18 b 0·018 c 0·0018 d 9·685
e 0·9685
f 0·096 85. To divide by 10^n move the decimal point n places to the left.

Exercise 6:04

1 a $2 \times 10^4 = 2 \times 10 \times 10 \times 10 \times 10 = 20\,000$, $2^4 = 2 \times 2 \times 2 \times 2 = 16$
b $5 \times 10^{-2} = 5 \times \frac{1}{10^2} = 5 \times \frac{1}{100} = \frac{5}{100}$, $5^{-2} = \frac{1}{5^2} = \frac{1}{25}$
c $1{\cdot}577\,88 \times 10^{12}$ or 1 577 880 000 000 (taking 1 year = 365·25 days). However, since years that are multiples of 100 are not leap years unless they are multiples of 400, the answer could be 1 577 847 600 000 or $1{\cdot}577\,847\,6 \times 10^{12}$.
d yes (if you are older than 9 years 4 months 8 days)
e $9{\cdot}8 \times 10^{-5}$, 0·0034, $5{\cdot}6 \times 10^{-2}$, 2·04, 6, $5{\cdot}499 \times 10^2$, $3{\cdot}24 \times 10^3$, $1{\cdot}2 \times 10^4$
f $7{\cdot}6 \times 10^{-3}$ cm
g Answers may vary. It would be about 0·5 mm, or 5×10^{-1} mm, or 5×10^{-2} cm.

2 a 21 b 0·21 c 0·21
d 704 e 0·0704 f 0·0704
g 1375 h 0·001 375 i 0·001 375

3 a $4{\cdot}7 \times 10^2$ b $2{\cdot}6 \times 10^3$ c $5{\cdot}3 \times 10^4$
d 7×10^2 e 5×10^4 f 7×10^5
g $6{\cdot}5 \times 10^1$ h $3{\cdot}42 \times 10^2$ i 9×10^1
j $4{\cdot}97 \times 10^3$ k $6{\cdot}35 \times 10^4$ l $2{\cdot}941 \times 10^6$
m $2{\cdot}971 \times 10^2$ n $6{\cdot}93 \times 10^1$ o $4{\cdot}9765 \times 10^3$
p $9{\cdot}31 \times 10^6$ q $6{\cdot}7 \times 10^7$ r $1{\cdot}901 \times 10^5$
s 6×10^5 t $5{\cdot}017 \times 10^5$ u 1×10^5

4 a $7{\cdot}5 \times 10^{-2}$ b $6{\cdot}3 \times 10^{-3}$ c $5{\cdot}9 \times 10^{-1}$
d 8×10^{-2} e 3×10^{-4} f 9×10^{-3}
g 3×10^{-1} h $3{\cdot}01 \times 10^{-2}$ i $5{\cdot}29 \times 10^{-4}$
j $4{\cdot}26 \times 10^{-1}$ k 1×10^{-3} l $9{\cdot}7 \times 10^{-6}$
m 6×10^{-5} n $9{\cdot}07 \times 10^{-4}$ o 4×10^{-9}

5 a 230 b 94 000 c 3700
d 295 e 87·4 f 763 000
g 1075 h 20 000 i 80
j 0·029 k 0·0019 i 0·95
m 0·003 76 n 0·000 463 o 0·0107
p 0·07 q 0·80 r 0·000 005
s 973 000 t 0·0063 u 47 000 000
v 914·2 w 0·010 32 x 100 000 000

Prep quiz 6:05

1 $6{\cdot}9 \times 10^2$ 2 4×10^3 3 $9{\cdot}632 \times 10^2$
4 $7{\cdot}3 \times 10^{-2}$ 5 3×10^{-4} 6 2900
7 800 000 8 0·046 9 0·000 000 5
10 0·814

Exercise 6:05

1 a 63 000 b 0·0014 c 92 500 000

2 a $5{\cdot}6 \times 10^4$ b $4{\cdot}3 \times 10^7$ c $7{\cdot}63 \times 10^5$
d $4{\cdot}0 \times 10^{-4}$ e $2{\cdot}9 \times 10^{-6}$ f $7{\cdot}31 \times 10^{-5}$
g $1{\cdot}5 \times 10^3$ h $2{\cdot}78 \times 10^{-3}$
i $6{\cdot}09 \times 10^6$
j Explanation: $2 \times 10^4 = 20\,000$ whereas $2^4 = 2 \times 2 \times 2 \times 2 = 16$

3 $2{\cdot}9 \times 10^{-6}$, $7{\cdot}31 \times 10^{-5}$, $4{\cdot}0 \times 10^{-4}$, $2{\cdot}78 \times 10^{-3}$, $1{\cdot}5 \times 10^3$, $5{\cdot}6 \times 10^4$, $7{\cdot}63 \times 10^5$, $6{\cdot}09 \times 10^6$, $4{\cdot}3 \times 10^7$

4 a $2{\cdot}1160 \times 10^{14}$ b $5{\cdot}6689 \times 10^{-12}$
c $1{\cdot}6807 \times 10^{-16}$ d $7{\cdot}1538 \times 10^{11}$
e $1{\cdot}6687 \times 10^{14}$ f $1{\cdot}3158 \times 10^{-12}$
g $3{\cdot}9366 \times 10^{12}$ h $4{\cdot}0459 \times 10^{19}$

5 a 318 600 b 0·006 626
c 0·2442 d 0·000 014 44
e 0·008 424 f 771 000
g 86 310 h 0·004 498
i 0·000 188 7

6 a $1{\cdot}394 \times 10^6$, 12 800 km or $1{\cdot}28 \times 10^4$ km
b 5 000 000 km or 5×10^6 km
c 8 min d 2×10^{27} tonnes e 2×10^{38}

Prep quiz 6:06

1 4000 GB 2 7000 MB 3 6000 kB
4 9000 B 5 2000 mm 6 3000 μm
7 5000 nm 8 4 000 000 m 9 8 000 000 μm
10 7 000 000 000 nm

Exercise 6:06

1 a 2 b 4 c 3 d 1
2 a 8×10^3 B b 6×10^3 B
c 4×10^6 B d 8×10^9 B
e $4{\cdot}7 \times 10^{12}$ B f $2{\cdot}4 \times 10^6$ B
g $6{\cdot}15 \times 10^3$ B h $8{\cdot}0 \times 10^9$ B
i $9{\cdot}2 \times 10^{12}$ B j $7{\cdot}70 \times 10^6$ B
k $5{\cdot}15 \times 10^3$ B i $8{\cdot}0 \times 10^9$ B
m $1{\cdot}5 \times 10^{13}$ B n $1{\cdot}03 \times 10^8$ B
o $8{\cdot}52 \times 10^5$ B p $6{\cdot}05 \times 10^{11}$ B
q $8{\cdot}00 \times 10^7$ B r $4{\cdot}0 \times 10^{12}$ B
3 a 8×10^{-3} s b 7×10^{-6} s
c 2×10^{-9} s d 9×10^{-3} s
e $3{\cdot}60 \times 10^{-3}$ s f $8{\cdot}4 \times 10^{-6}$ s
g $7{\cdot}0 \times 10^{-9}$ s h $9{\cdot}56 \times 10^{-3}$ s
i $1{\cdot}25 \times 10^{-9}$ s j $7{\cdot}7 \times 10^{-6}$ s
k $8{\cdot}125 \times 10^{-3}$ s i $8{\cdot}0 \times 10^{-6}$ s
m $1{\cdot}5 \times 10^{-2}$ s n $1{\cdot}03 \times 10^{-4}$ s
o $1{\cdot}852 \times 10^{-6}$ s p $6{\cdot}05 \times 10^{-4}$ s
q $8{\cdot}0 \times 10^{-2}$ s r $2{\cdot}00 \times 10^{-5}$ s
4 Warragamba Dam's capacity is $2{\cdot}031 \times 10^6$ ML or $2{\cdot}031 \times 10^3$ GL or $2{\cdot}031$ TL.
5 a 10^9 or 1 000 000 000
b 10^6 or 1 000 000 c 10^3 or 1000
6 a 10^6 kHz or 1 000 000 kHz
b 10^3 MHz or 1000 MHz
7 73 740 000 bytes

Diagnostic test 6

1 a 9 b 16 c 1000
2 a 3^7 b x^5 c $6m^3n^5$
3 a x^5 b $5a^3$ c $2a^2b$
4 a a^8 b x^{12} c $8a^{12}$
5 a 1 b 5 c 3
6 a $\frac{1}{9}$ b $\frac{1}{5}$ c $\frac{27}{8}$ or $3\frac{3}{8}$
7 a x^4 b $\dfrac{2}{x^2}$ c $\dfrac{9}{x^2}$
8 a 5 b 3 c 2
9 a $12x$ b $7m^3$ c $2x$
10 a $2{\cdot}43 \times 10^2$ b $6{\cdot}7 \times 10^4$ c $9{\cdot}38 \times 10^7$
11 a 130 b 243·1 c 46 300 000
12 a $4{\cdot}3 \times 10^{-2}$ b $5{\cdot}97 \times 10^{-5}$ c 4×10^{-3}
13 a 0·029 b 0·000 093 8 c 0·001 004
14 a $9{\cdot}61 \times 10^{16}$ b $4{\cdot}64 \times 10^7$
c $1{\cdot}4 \times 10^{12}$ d $1{\cdot}2 \times 10^{-3}$
15 a 2.7×10^5 b 2.5×10^4
c 4.3×10^{12} d 1.2×10^{10}
16 a 5×10^6 b 5.0×10^5
c 3×10^{-9} d 5×10^{-6}

ASSIGNMENT 6A

1 a a^5 b $12a^5$ c a^3b^2 d $12a^3b^3$ e 3^5
f a^3 g $7m$ h $4y^4$ i $2a^2b$ j 4^4
k 3^8 l x^6 m a^{11} n m o $2x$
p $\dfrac{a^2}{2}$
2 a 1 b 6 c $125x^9$
d $1000a^6$ e $8x$
3 a $2{\cdot}16 \times 10^4$ b $1{\cdot}25 \times 10^2$ c $7{\cdot}0 \times 10^{-5}$
d $1{\cdot}56 \times 10^{-4}$
4 a 810 000 b 1267 c 0·035
d 0·000 106
5 a 1024 b 531 441 c 145 800 000
d 351 232
6 a 7 b 5 c 8
7 a $3^7 = 2187$ b $10^3 = 1000$ c $2^8 = 256$
8 a m^3 b $72a^{17}$ c 2
9 a $\frac{1}{5}$ b $\frac{1}{16}$ c $\frac{1}{9}$ d $\frac{1}{1000}$
10 a $1{\cdot}3 \times 10^7$ b $5{\cdot}6 \times 10^{-22}$ c $1{\cdot}2 \times 10^{17}$
d $2{\cdot}6 \times 10^{11}$ e $1{\cdot}3 \times 10^{13}$ f $2{\cdot}4 \times 10^7$
g $4{\cdot}1 \times 10^1$ h $2{\cdot}2 \times 10^7$
11 a 8 b 4 c 27 d 100 000
12 a $20x$ b $2x^{-2}$ or $\dfrac{2}{x^2}$ c $6m^2n^3$

ASSIGNMENT 6B

1 16 2 \$96
3 a 3, 6
b i 20 ii 35 iii 405
4 \$30.65
5 a 60 dB b 120 dB
c 10^6 or 1 000 000 d 10^5 or 100 000
e i 4 times ii 64 times iii 32 times

ASSIGNMENT 6C

1 a $\frac{4}{5}$ b $\frac{1}{8}$ c $\frac{1}{500}$ d $\frac{5}{9}$
e $\frac{5}{33}$ f $\frac{31}{45}$
2 a 12 540 b 32%
3 a $a + 6$ b a c $3a$ d $a - 6$
4 a $\dfrac{8a+5}{15}$ b $\dfrac{7y-3}{10}$ c $\dfrac{2p+5}{12}$
5 a $a^2 + 10a + 24$ b $x^2 - 1$
c $m^2 - 8m + 16$ d $6y^2 + 11y - 35$
6 a $\frac{1}{10}$ b $\frac{3}{10}$ c $\frac{7}{10}$
7 a 40 cm² b 48 cm² c 60 cm²
8 a 50 cm³ b 200 cm³

Chapter 7

Exercise 7:01

1 a 66 b 31 c 83 d 1042
e 1·9 f 8·8 g 8 h 4·9
i −13 j −6 k −2 l −3
m 6 n −0·7 o 4·7 p −6
q 3·4 r 0·3 s 5 t 0·1
u 5 v 36 w −14 x 3·52

2 a 5 b 7 c 15 d 24
e 3 f 7 g 1 h −3
i −3 j −3 k −4 l 8

3 a $3\frac{2}{3}$ b $7\frac{3}{4}$ c $89\frac{4}{9}$ d $23\frac{2}{3}$
e 11 f $5\frac{5}{11}$ g $6\frac{2}{3}$ h 6
i 3 j $4\frac{1}{2}$ k $-3\frac{2}{3}$ l $1\frac{1}{5}$
m $-1\frac{3}{7}$ n $-5\frac{2}{3}$ o $4\frac{1}{6}$ p −5
q 1·2 r 6·5 s 1·5 t 3

4 a 7 b 1 c 8 d 6
e 2 f 6 g 4 h 1
i 2 j 9 k no solution l 2

5 a correct b incorrect c correct
d correct e correct f incorrect
g correct h correct i correct
j correct k correct l correct

6 a −2 b $1\frac{1}{2}$ c $1\frac{1}{3}$ d $\frac{1}{4}$ e $-\frac{1}{3}$
f 0 g $1\frac{1}{6}$ h −5 i $4\frac{1}{2}$ j $2\frac{1}{2}$
k $\frac{5}{6}$ l −1 m −4 n $2\frac{1}{6}$ o $2\frac{2}{3}$
p $\frac{3}{4}$ q $1\frac{4}{7}$ r $-\frac{4}{3}$ s −20 t $\frac{2}{3}$
u $4\frac{1}{3}$

Prep quiz 7:02

1 $7x + 28$ 2 $2a - 6$ 3 $20a + 45$
4 $12p - 42$ 5 $-3x + 12$ 6 −5
7 6 8 −9 9 $\frac{1}{2}$ 10 −7

Exercise 7:02

1 a 4 b 1 c 3 d 5 e 6
f 13 g 2 h 5 i −1 j 4
k 2 l 3 m 3 n 8 o 6
p 8 q 1 r 4

2 a $\frac{3}{5}$ b $1\frac{1}{2}$ c $7\frac{3}{4}$ d −1 e 4
f 4 g $\frac{1}{2}$ h $1\frac{7}{10}$ i $1\frac{1}{3}$ j 2
k −2 l 25 m $\frac{5}{7}$ n $5\frac{1}{2}$ o 3
p $1\frac{1}{5}$ q 3 r −12

3 a −4 b 13 c 18 d 4 e 4
f 6 g 2 h 2 i 7 j $4\frac{1}{2}$
k 3 l $2\frac{2}{7}$ m 2 n −5

4 a 1 b 1 c 1 d 2 e 1
f 2 g 2 h 2 i 2 j −46

5 a 2 b 3 c 2 d 2 e 1
f 2 g $-1\frac{3}{8}$ h $3\frac{1}{3}$

Prep quiz 7:03

1 0 2 3 3 −3 4 $3\frac{3}{4}$ 5 $-3\frac{1}{5}$
6 p 7 12 8 $x + 7$ 9 $5m$ 10 $12 - p$

Exercise 7:03

1 a 24 b 20 c 36 d 15 e 12
f 28 g 50 h 18 i $1\frac{3}{5}$ j 8
k 9 l $11\frac{2}{3}$ m 29 n 6 o 1
p 3 q 2 r 6 s $2\frac{3}{4}$ t $1\frac{1}{3}$
u −2 v −22 w $17\frac{2}{3}$

2 a correct b incorrect c correct
d correct e incorrect f incorrect
g correct h correct i correct
j incorrect k correct l incorrect

3 a −12 b $\frac{15}{9}$ c 10 d $\frac{8}{3}$ e $\frac{12}{5}$
f 10 g 3 h $-\frac{1}{7}$ i $\frac{3}{10}$ j $\frac{1}{9}$
k −1 l $\frac{9}{7}$

Prep quiz 7:04

1 2, 4, 6 2 5, 10, 15 3 6
4 60 5 $3x$ 6 a
7 $15x$ 8 $2x + 1$ 9 $4x - 2$
10 $6x - 3$

Exercise 7:04

1 a 6 b 12 c 48 d 12 e 20
f 30 g 8 h 15 i 6 j 30
k 12 l 5 m 24 n 20 o 20
p 8 q 6 r 9

2 a $7\frac{6}{7}$ b $14\frac{3}{7}$ c $4\frac{4}{7}$ d $3\frac{1}{8}$ e $\frac{7}{8}$
f $\frac{4}{11}$ g −62 h $-\frac{1}{13}$ i $-5\frac{4}{5}$

Challenge 7:04

1 a 2 b $\frac{1}{6}$ c $\frac{3}{8}$ d $\frac{3}{11}$ e $\frac{4}{21}$
f −1 g $\frac{1}{7}$ h $3\frac{1}{4}$ i $-4\frac{2}{3}$ j −1
k $-\frac{7}{13}$ l $\frac{16}{31}$

2 a −4 b 2 c 3 d 8 e 3
f 4 g $1\frac{1}{6}$ h $-4\frac{1}{5}$ i $1\frac{2}{3}$ j $1\frac{1}{24}$
k $-\frac{4}{7}$ l $\frac{3}{4}$

Prep quiz 7:05

1 7 2 $x + 3$ 3 $x + y$
4 12 5 $3x$ 6 xy
7 $\$(50 - x)$ 8 $\$5x$ 9 xy
10 $x + 5$ years

Exercise 7:05

1 a $x + 5 = 22$; 17 b $x - 3 = 10$; 13
c $8x = 32$; 4 d $\frac{x}{8} = 7$; 56
e $2x + 6 = 14$; 4 f $3x + 5 = 20$; 5

g $5x - 8 = 22; 6$ h $4(x + 5) = 56; 9$

i $\frac{x}{2} - 5 = 3; 16$

2 a $2x + 3 = 33; 15$ b $4x - 3 = 25; 7$

c $2(x + 3) = 22; 8$ d $\frac{x}{4} - 7 = 1; 32$

e $\frac{x + 4}{3} = 8; 20$

3 a 11 b 7 c 17 d 8

4 a 13 years, 39 years b \$480, \$80

c Anne \$25, Joan \$18 d Jim \$165, Alan \$335

e 40 years

5 a 13 b 19 cm by 13 cm

c 4 kg d 24 km

6 a \$2

b They meet at 2:48 pm when X has travelled 24 km and Y has travelled 16 km.

c The son is 28 years old and his father is 56 years old.

d 3600 litres

7 a Bill is 20 years old and Fred is 45 years old.

b 16 five-cent coins, 34 ten-cent coins

c 12

d small tank 900 L; large tank 1200 L

e 50 km

8 a 200 L/min, 400 L/min

b 25 km c 120 km/h d \$4800

e 9·6 cm by 2·4 cm and 3·2 cm by 0·8 cm

Exercise 7:06

1 a $x \le 0$ b $x \ge -3$ c $x \le -2$

d $x > -2$ e $x > 3$ f $x < 1$

2 The side to the right of $x = 3\frac{1}{2}$.

$9 - 2x < 2$

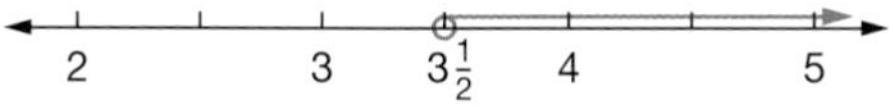

3 a $x < 9$

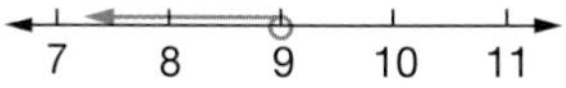

b $y > 2$

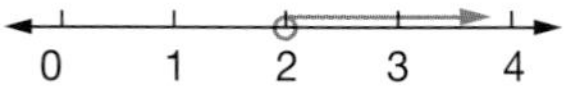

c $m < -2$

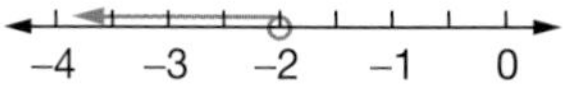

d $m > -5$

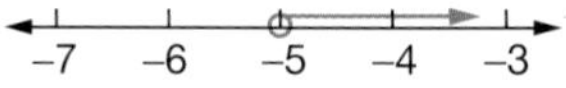

e $p \le -3$

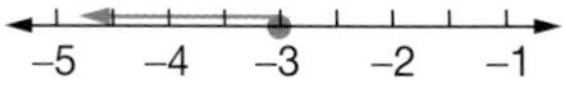

f $m \le 9$

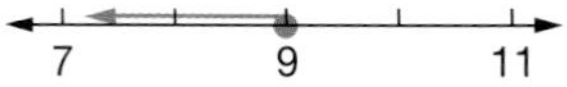

g $y > 5$

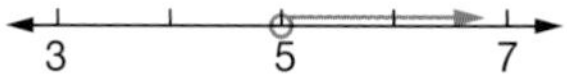

h $m < 7$

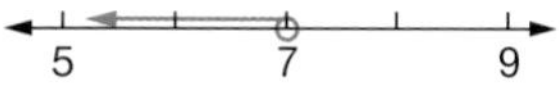

i $x \ge 10$

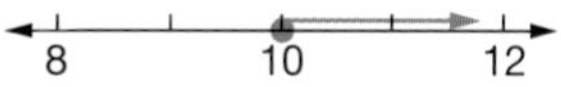

j $m > 18$

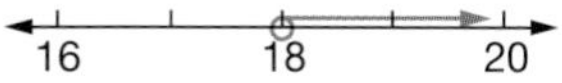

k $p < 5$

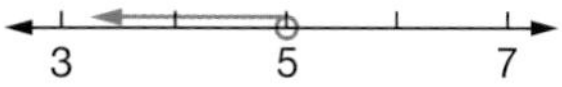

l $x \ge 0$

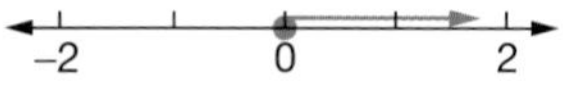

4 a $m > 7$ b $p \le 7$ c $m < 2$

d $y \ge -8\frac{2}{5}$ e $x < 3\frac{3}{4}$ f $x > -2$

g $x < 15$ h $y > 12$ i $m \ge 4$

j $x < -50$ k $x < 6$ l $x > -12$

5 a $m > -8$ b $x < -4$ c $p \ge -4$

d $x > 2$ e $x < -2\frac{1}{2}$ f $x \ge -3\frac{1}{3}$

g $x < -4$ h $x > -3$ i $x \ge -5$

j $x < -6$ k $x < -5$ l $x \le -8$

m $x > -2$ n $x < -6$ o $x < -12$

6 a $x > 3$ b $m < 4$ c $p \ge 3$

d $p \le -1$ e $p \ge 1\frac{1}{5}$ f $x < -3\frac{1}{2}$

g $x \le 4$ h $p \ge 2$ i $y < 1\frac{1}{4}$

j $x < 3$ k $x > 2$ l $x \le 1\frac{1}{2}$

m $x < 4$ n $m > 3$ o $x \le 3\frac{1}{2}$

p $x \ge 4\frac{1}{2}$ q $m > 2\frac{1}{2}$ r $p > 3$

7 a $m < -2$ b $y > -2$ c $x \le -1\frac{1}{2}$

d $x \ge -2$ e $m \le 6$ f $m \ge 8$

g $p > \frac{1}{2}$ h $x > -2$ i $y < -1$

j $x \le -1$ k $y \ge 1$ l $p < -\frac{1}{2}$

m $x \ge -\frac{1}{6}$ n $a \ge 3\frac{3}{4}$ o $x < \frac{1}{6}$

8 a $x > 3$ b $x < 5\frac{1}{2}$ c $m \le 10$

d $a \le 2$ e $b \le -3$ f $m < 0$

g $x < 10$ h $p > 15$ i $x \ge 8$

j $y \ge -1\frac{1}{2}$ k $p < 9$ l $p > 5\frac{1}{2}$

m $x \le 1$ n $x > 6$ o $a \le 8$

p $b < 2\frac{1}{7}$ q $x \ge -18$ r $y < -1\frac{3}{5}$

s $a \le 2\frac{2}{3}$ t $x > -8\frac{1}{2}$ u $x \ge -5$

9 a $3x < 8; x < 2\frac{2}{3}$

b $2x - 4 > 9; x > 6\frac{1}{2}$

c $100 - 4x < 25; x > 18\frac{3}{4}$

d $\frac{94 + 2x}{12} > 16; x > 49$

e $25x - 540 > 2000; x > 101\frac{3}{5}$

Prep quiz 7:07

1 $2ab$ 2 $3ab^2$ 3 $3a + 2b$

4 $4 \times x \times y \times y$ 5 $x \times x + 2 \times x \times y + y \times y$

6 $x \times x + y \times y$ 7 true 8 300

9 8 10 −12

Exercise 7:07

1 a $A = 8{\cdot}64$ b $A = 54$ c $A = 27$
d $A = 12{\cdot}25$ e $A = 44$ f $A = 36{\cdot}3$
g $A = 80$ h $C = 21{\cdot}4$ i $V = 262{\cdot}44$
j $V = 2100{\cdot}84$ k $P = 12{\cdot}4$ l $c = 13$
m $\alpha = 105°$ n $\alpha = 140°$ o $E = 15$

2 a i $C = 100$ ii $C = 0$ iii $C = 40$
b $E = 18{\cdot}75$ c $S = 44{\cdot}7$ d $V = 2011\ \text{cm}^3$

3 a 0·9 b 828 c 36 d 729·6
e −4 f −48 g 189 h 12·48
i 1·61

4 a 7·1 cm b 19·9 cm

5 a 184·4 (1 dec. pl.) b 27·9 (1 dec. pl.)
c $M = 539$, $N = 485$ d 40 117

Prep quiz 7:08

1 $x = 163$ 2 $y = 222$ 3 $x = 49$
4 $x = 370$ 5 $x = 96$ 6 $y = 183$
7 $p = 28$ 8 $m = 54$ 9 $a = 5$
10 $t = 2$

Exercise 7:08

1 a 10 b 15 c 2·4 d 13·2
e 40 f 6 g 6·38 h $26\frac{2}{3}$

2 a 5 b 4 c 4·8 d 15
e 3·6 f 3·75 g 30 h 27

3 a 30 b $3\frac{1}{3}$ c 0·4 d 56
e ±5 f ±3 g ±12 h $\pm\frac{1}{2}$

4 a 2 b 3 c 0 d 12
e 0·6 f 2 g 6 h 0·8

5 a 4 b 25 c 3·1 d 6·8
e 1·6

6 a 3·64 b 0·4 c 13·5 d 13·2
e 100

7 a 3·13 b 1·78 c 1·45 d 7·72
e 37·78

8 a 11·28 cm b 0·92 c 11
d $-1{\cdot}\dot{5}$ e $\frac{15}{8}$ or 1·875

Prep quiz 7:09

1 25 2 a 3 27 4 m
5 5 6 a 7 5 8 m
9 $a = 1$ 10 $x = 8\frac{1}{3}$

Exercise 7:09

1 a $x = p - m$ b $x = m - np$ c $x = pq - n$
d $x = \frac{b}{a}$ e $x = \frac{y}{3}$ f $x = \frac{b+c}{a^2}$
g $x = \frac{b-2d}{a}$ h $x = \frac{b+c}{a}$ i $x = \frac{c-3b}{a}$
j $x = ay$ k $x = \frac{a}{y}$ l $x = by$
m $x = \frac{25}{a}$ n $x = \frac{bc}{a}$ o $x = \frac{pL}{2}$

2 a $x = \frac{a-2y}{2}$ b $x = \frac{p-5t}{5}$
c $x = \frac{y+21}{3}$ d $x = \frac{p+qr}{q}$
e $x = \frac{6a-b}{6}$ f $x = \frac{tv-w}{t}$
g $x = \frac{R-4r}{2r}$ h $x = \frac{p+5qy}{5q}$
i $x = \frac{\pi r^2 - A}{\pi r}$

3 a $y = A - x$ b $x = \frac{P-2B}{2}$
c $d = \frac{C}{\pi}$ d $u = v - at$
e $a = \frac{V-u}{t}$ f $m = \frac{E}{c^2}$
g $D = ST$ h $V = RI$
i $P = \frac{100I}{RT}$ j $R = \frac{P}{I^2}$
k $s = \frac{v^2 - u^2}{2a}$ l $a = \frac{F-p}{c}$
m $n = \frac{P-ma}{a}$ n $p = \frac{x-2aq}{2a}$
o $m = \frac{2K}{V^2}$ p $u = \frac{mv-P}{m}$
q $H = \frac{3V}{A}$ r $h = \frac{3V}{\pi r^2}$
s $h = \frac{S - \pi r^2}{\pi r}$ t $h = \frac{E - \frac{1}{2}mv^2}{mg}$
u $k = \frac{2ab-P}{2a}$ v $a = 2A - b$
w $P = \frac{2A-ha}{h}$ x $r = \frac{q_1 q_2}{F}$
y $d = \frac{T-a}{n-1}$ z $a = \frac{S(r-1)}{r^n - 1}$

Prep quiz 7:10

1 15 2 6 3 13
4 ±3 5 25 6 2 or −8
7 7 8 $3(x + 4)$ 9 $x(x - 2)$
10 $5a(a + 2b)$

Exercise 7:10

1 a $x = \pm\sqrt{\frac{n}{m}}$ b $x = \pm\sqrt{\frac{a}{b}}$
c $x = \pm\sqrt{a+b}$ d $x = \pm\sqrt{k-h}$
e $x = \pm\sqrt{ay}$ f $x = \pm\sqrt{\frac{3m}{n}}$
g $x = \pm\sqrt{L+y^2}$ h $x = \pm\sqrt{\frac{B}{A}}$

2 a $x = \dfrac{c^2}{b}$ b $a = \dfrac{u^2}{3}$

c $a = c^2 + b$ d $a = (c + b)^2$

e $x = \left(\dfrac{P - L}{M}\right)^2$ f $a = \left(\dfrac{M - L}{N}\right)^2$

g $a = \dfrac{L^2 + 1}{3}$ h $a = \dfrac{b - P^2}{2}$

3 a $N = \dfrac{2a}{3}$ b $N = \dfrac{2L - 2a}{3}$

c $N = \dfrac{2x + 6}{3}$ d $N = \dfrac{6L - 2M}{3}$

e $N = 3x - a$ f $N = \dfrac{6x + 1 - 2M}{3}$

g $N = \dfrac{3m - u}{4}$ h $N = \dfrac{a^2 + b^2 + bL}{a}$

4 a $x = \dfrac{b - a}{2}$ b $x = \dfrac{q}{a - p}$

c $x = \dfrac{a - b}{a - 1}$ d $x = \dfrac{n - m}{m - n}$ or -1

e $x = \pm\sqrt{\dfrac{2}{p - q}}$ f $x = \dfrac{L}{A + B + 1}$

g $x = \dfrac{15a}{8}$ h $x = \dfrac{2a}{1 - a}$

i $x = \dfrac{5y}{y - 1}$ j $x = \dfrac{3 - m}{m - 1}$

k $x = \dfrac{a - A}{A - b}$ l $x = \dfrac{Ba + a}{B - 1}$

5

	A	B	C
a	$B = \dfrac{A}{L}$	$X = A + Y$	$t = \dfrac{V - u}{a}$
b	$V = \dfrac{M}{D}$	$S = DT$	$I = \pm\sqrt{\dfrac{P}{R}}$
c	$h = \dfrac{3V}{A}$	$r = \pm\sqrt{\dfrac{3V}{\pi h}}$	$r = \pm\sqrt{\dfrac{s}{4\pi}}$
d	$b = 2M - a$	$y = \dfrac{2A - xh}{h}$	$s = \dfrac{v^2 - u^2}{2a}$
e	$a = \dfrac{x^2 + y^2}{y}$	$h = \dfrac{S}{2\pi r} - r$	$d = \dfrac{2T - 2an}{n(n - 1)}$
f	$c = \dfrac{a^2}{b}$	$X = \dfrac{Y^2}{a^2}$	$a = \dfrac{X^2 + 4b}{4}$
g	$Y = aX^2$	$x = \dfrac{bR^2}{a}$	$b = m^2 n - a$
h	$I = \dfrac{gT^2}{4\pi^2}$	$u = \dfrac{4x^2 t}{A^2}$	$s = \dfrac{v^2 - u^2}{2a}$
i	$a = \dfrac{6y - 3b}{2}$	$X = \dfrac{12Z - 4Y}{3}$	$c = b - 5A$
j	$A = 2x - 3y$	$N = \dfrac{6L + 1}{5}$	$X = \dfrac{a^2}{a - b}$
k	$k = \dfrac{h}{1 - 2h}$	$a = \dfrac{2y}{1 - y}$	$x = \dfrac{3z}{z - 1}$

Exercise 7:11

1 a $17{\cdot}64\,\text{m}^2$ b $1250\,\text{cm}^2$

2 a $A = \pi r^2$ b 7 cm

3 a 149°F b 40°C

4 12 cm

5 a 6·14 m b 2·34 m

6 1·9 cm

7 $P = 2x + D\pi$

a 76·39 m (2 dec. pl.) b 63·66 m (2 dec. pl.)

8 a 7·08 m/s b $4{\cdot}8\,\text{m/s}^2$ c 6·5 s

9 a 2·5 kg b 2·7 m/s

10 60 cm

11 a \$4609 b \$4000 c 14%

12 a $A = \pi(R^2 - r^2)$ b $96{\cdot}8\,\text{cm}^2$

c 3·6 cm d 6·3 cm

13 a $V = \pi r^2 h + \frac{2}{3}\pi r^3$ or $V = \pi r^2(h + \frac{2}{3}r)$

b $145\,\text{m}^3$ c 6·88 m

14 a $5{\cdot}6 \times 10^{-18}$ (2 sig. fig.) b $6{\cdot}2 \times 10^{-22}$ m

15 $3{\cdot}3 \times 10^{-8}$ coulombs (2 sig. fig.)

Diagnostic test 7

1 a $p = 7$ b $m = 12$ c $m = -10$

2 a $x = -4$ b $a = 3$ c $b = -5$

3 a $x = 2$ b $a = 9$ c $x = 2{\cdot}6$

4 a $x = -18$ b $a = 1$ c $m = -14$

5 a $y = 12$ b $m = 12$ c $p = 18$ d $m = 10$

6 a $m = 5$ b $m = 9$ c $p = 7$ d $x = 6\frac{2}{3}$

7 a $m = \frac{5}{2}$ b $x = -2$ c $n = 1$ d $a = \frac{11}{8}$

8 a $a = 12$ b $m = 24$ c $x = -60$ d $y = \frac{19}{6}$

9 a $2a + 7 = 10$ b $\dfrac{a}{3} - 4 = 4$ c $3(a + 6) = 32$

10 a $x + (x + 5) = 57$; 26, 31

b $3x + x + 3x + x = 48$; 6, 18

c $3x + 10 = 2(x + 10)$; 10, 30

11 a 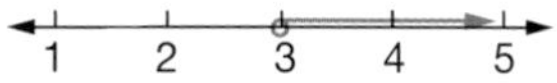

b 

c 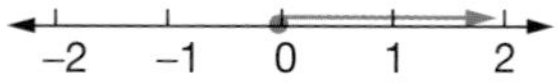

d 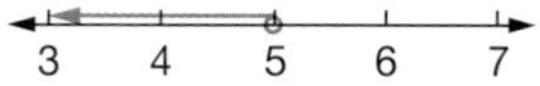

12 a $x > \frac{1}{2}$ b $x < 9\frac{1}{2}$ c $x \geq 5$

13 a $x < -2$ b $x < -63$ c $a < \frac{1}{3}$

14 a 36·2 b 3·7268 c 33·54

15 a 8 b 15·075 c 3·5

16 a $a = \dfrac{x + 2b}{3}$ b $a = \dfrac{V^2 - u^2}{2s}$ c $a = \dfrac{Ah}{D} - b$

17 a $y = \pm\sqrt{\dfrac{x}{a}}$ b $y = \dfrac{A^2 B}{T^2}$ c $y = \dfrac{P}{1 - P}$

ASSIGNMENT 7A

1 a $m = 3$ b $y = -1$ c $m = 3$ d $n = -2$
e $x = 5\frac{1}{2}$ f $x = 1$

2 a $x = -1$ b $a = 6$ c $m = 1\frac{1}{2}$ d $x = -6$
e $n = 11$ f $x = 0$ g $a = \frac{2}{11}$ h $n = -\frac{23}{11}$
i $m = -3$ j $x = -9$

3 a $x = 8$ b $m = 15$ c $x = 9$ d $a = 17$
e $y = 8$ f $p = 3$ g $m = -3$ h $m = -\frac{1}{3}$
i $n = -\frac{16}{5}$ j $x = -13$ k $a = -\frac{70}{3}$ l $q = -\frac{6}{29}$

4 a $m \geq -2$,

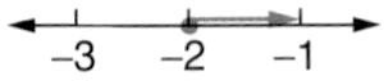

b $x < 4$,

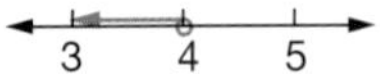

c $n > \frac{2}{5}$,

d $x \leq \frac{3}{2}$,

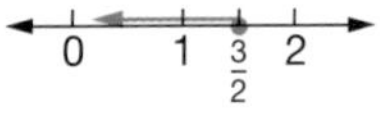

e $y < \frac{3}{2}$,

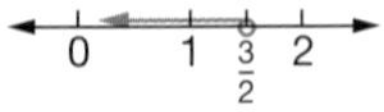

f $n \leq \frac{11}{3}$,

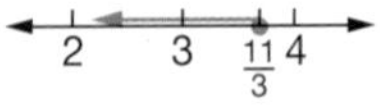

g $x < -4$,

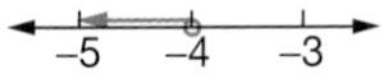

h $x \leq -9$,

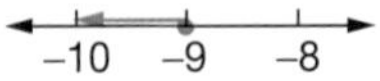

i $a \geq \frac{3}{2}$,

5 a $3x + 7 = 15$, $x = \frac{8}{3}$
b $5(x - 9) = 30$, $x = 15$
c $8x + 10 = 12x - 7$, $x = \frac{17}{4}$
d $x + 4 = 2[(x - 12) + 4]$, ages are 20 and 8
e $12 + x = \frac{3}{2}[2 + x]$, $x = 18$

6 a 66 b 8 c 4·1

7 a $\frac{1}{3}$ b $\frac{-30}{73}$ c $\frac{2}{3}$

8 a $P = \dfrac{100A}{RT}$ b $P = \pm\sqrt{\dfrac{V}{R}}$
c $P = \dfrac{RT^2}{3}$ d $P = \dfrac{Q}{QX + 1}$

9 a $x = \frac{3}{5}$ b $x = 1\frac{2}{3}$ c $x = -1\frac{1}{3}$
d $x = -\frac{2}{15}$ e $x = \frac{13}{22}$ f $p = \frac{5}{8}$

ASSIGNMENT 7B

1

3	1
5	7

2 a $y = 12 - 3x$ b $s = t^2 + 1$

3 a 10 minutes b 55 minutes

4 $\frac{9}{10}$

5 a i 2^{20} ii 2^{30}
b i $2^{20} = 1\,048\,576$ ii $2^{30} = 1\,073\,741\,824$

6 a 60, 80, 100, 120, 140, 160, 180
b $3x$, $4x$, $5x$, $6x$, $7x$, $8x$, $9x$
c 17

ASSIGNMENT 7C

1 a \$115804 b 48·9% (1 dec. pl.)

2 a i $0{\cdot}\dot{3}$ km/min ii 20 km/h
b i 3 min/km ii 18 s

3 a $a^2 + a - 6$ b $a^2 + a - 6$
c $a^2 - 4$ d $a^2 - 4a + 4$

4 a 48% b 23% c 43% d 51%

5 SA of box $A = 3200\,\text{cm}^2$; SA of box $B = 3800\,\text{cm}^2$. Box A uses the least amount.

6 a 10^{10} b 10^{-2} c 10^2 d 10^6

7 a $\frac{1}{16}$ b 2 c 4 d $\frac{1}{4}$

8 a $1{\cdot}15 \times 10^{-12}$ b $5{\cdot}76 \times 10^{12}$

Chapter 8

Exercise 8:01

1 a See page 217. b See page 217.
c See page 217. d commission
e See page 217. f See page 217.
g See page 217. h commission and piece work
i See page 217. j wages and commission

2 a \$997.50 b \$129.20
c \$28.40 d Luke, by \$36.75
e Irene by 40 cents f \$1200.80
g \$883 per week
h i \$824.10 ii \$1464.22
iii \$2663.00 iv \$1115.41
i i \$55 200 ii \$37 806
iii \$63 660 iv \$107 400
j The second salary is greater by \$28.72 per week.
k The second income is higher by \$22.86 per week.

3 a i no ii no iii no
iv (1) \$690 (2) \$1708.90
(3) \$3813.40 (4) \$211.60
b i (1) \$796 (2) \$985
(3) \$1080.55 (4) \$1104.91
ii \$1181
c i \$800 ii \$870 iii \$1142.40
iv \$912.95

4 a \$259.83 b \$576.50 c \$135

5 a \$998.40 b \$1950, \$1220 profit
c \$993.60 d \$777.95, \$19.95

Exercise 8:02

1 a \$408 b \$565.15
c i \$108.60 ii \$181
iii \$167.43 (nearest cent) iv \$253.40
d i \$672 ii \$851.20 iii \$1002.40
iv \$1136.80
e \$295.80 f \$39.20, 1·5 hours

g

No. 53 Name: Tom McSeveny		Time card summary		Whit. Pty Ltd. Rate: $26.20 p/h
Week ending	Number of hours at:			Wage
	normal rates	time-and-a-half	double-time	
21 Jan	35	0	0	$917
28 Jan	35	3	0	$1034.90
4 Feb	35	2	0	$995.60
11 Feb	34	5·5	1	$1159.35
18 Feb	35	7·5	0·5	$1237.95

2 a i $700 ii $987 iii $1046.50 iv $730.10
b $6706.90 c $676.20 d $102 400 e $2532, $58 932 f $1844.80 g $948.95
h i $1000 ii $1340
i $1240, 1.35%
3 a i $296 ii $116.55 iii $493.95 iv $678.49
b i $283.05 ii $432.90 iii $562.40 iv $790.32
c $506.90 d $364.45
e i $4000 ii $5800 iii 3460 iv $7072
4 a $48 246 b $49 210.92 c $52 223.02 d $57 658.44

Exercise 8:03

1 a $200.60 b $595 c $431.95 d $1403.65 e $622.95
2 a i $1381.68 ii $290.15 iii $69.08 iv $936.45
b

Turner, Vicki	Serial No.	Gross Salary or Wage Rate	Super Units		Week Ended	Net Pay	Pay Advice No.
			Entld.	Held			
	6841672	$7209.60	98	98	29/11/13	$936.45	11364

Deductions this week				Pay this week			
Taxation	S'annuation	M'laneous	Total	Normal Pay	Adjustments	Overtime	Gross Earnings
$290.15	$69.08	$86.00	$445.23	$1381.68	–	–	$1381.68

3 a $378.80, 1·8% b $1141.30, 21·3%
c $802.10, 15·3% d $1864.50, 28·1%
4 a $42 568 b $2739.77 c $1027.57
d i $29 400
ii $23 100
iii Answers will differ, but the 'lump sum' option is attractive since you have the money as well.
iv $24 990
e 1333, 1234
5 a $124.57 b $955.06 c $4.98

Exercise 8:04

1 a Nil b $833.53 c $5021.50
d $23 965.02 e $101 758.30
2 a $33 942 b $33 287 c $2866.53
d $199.47
3 $8173.68
4 a $87 006 b $84 910 c $19 363.70
d need to pay $1987.35
5 a $2000 b $1590 c $1320
d $1230 e $1070 f $1455
g $1282.50 h $1134

Prep quiz 8:05

1 $6 2 $3.10 3 $4.35 4 $0.67 5 $5
6 $6.10 7 $8.50 8 $2.50 9 $4.70 10 $2.88

Exercise 8:05

1 a $20 b $3.20 c $17.50
d $9.00 e $8.40 f $11.25
2 a i $0.40 ii $0.30 ii is better buy
b i $0.75 ii $0.80 i is better buy
c i $1.30 ii $1.25 ii is better buy
d i $2.60 ii $2.80 i is better buy
e i $1.30 ii $1.33 i is better buy
f i $4.40 ii $4.20 ii is better buy
3 a $5, $45 b $4, $16 c $8, $92
d $6, $18 e $20, $20 f $7.50, $42.50
g $12, $18 h $21, $7 i $180, $20
j $3, $22 k $27, $18 l $28, $52
4 a $10, 25% b $5, 10% c $25, 25%
d $12, 20% e $18, 50% f $2, 8%
g $3, 12·5% h $12, $33\cdot\dot{3}\%$

5 a $5, $55 b $2, $22
c $10, $110 d $2.50, $27.50
e 80c, $8.80 f $1.20, $13.20
g $5.60, $61.50 h $3.70, $40.70
i $8.30, $91.30 j 55c, $6.05
k 96c, $410.56 l $1.64, $18.04
m 53c, $5.79 n $2.34, $25.76
o $7.20, $79.16

6 a $4 b $7 c $12 d $2.20
e $8.40 f $1.15 g 74c h $1.94
i $7.43 j $4.55 k $2.18 l $13.18
m 86c n $1.99 o $6.13

7

	Cost price	Profit	Selling price
a	$400	$100	$500
b	$240	$60	$300
c	$350	$70	$420
d	$840	$42	$882
e	$750	$250	$1000

8 a (a) 25% (b) 25% (c) 20%
(d) 5% (e) $33\cdot\dot{3}\%$
b (a) 20% (b) 20% (c) $16\cdot\dot{6}\%$
(d) 4·8% (to 1 dec. pl.) (e) 25%

9 a 5 tyres for $55
b 6 ice-creams for $20.40
c 5 litres for $92.50
d 600 mL soft drink for $5.20
e 375 g can for $4.20
f 4 lollies for $4.40
g 375 mL shampoo for $7.65
h 20 kg of potatoes for $25

10 a 600 g for $9.20 b 5 litres for $72
c 1 L bottle for $12.90

11 a $17.60 b $79.05 c $80 discount, 25%
d 30% e $650 f $62
g 11% h $198

12 $72 13 $1338.75

14 a $405 b $459 c $197.60 d $717.72
e $1701.77

15 $0.58

16 a $0.82 b $0.96 c $1.44

17 a $70 b $120 c $180 d $250
e $14 f $26 g $97 h $115
i $12.60 j $37.50 k $215.50 l $1125.80

18 a $10.56 b $5.60 and $9.30
c $20.90, $61.60 and $45.10

19 a $22 b 78·6% c 44%

20 a $38.40 b $21 c $12.47

21 C : SP = 100 : 140 ∴ cost = $220, profit = $88

22 a $300, $330 b $4, $4.40 c $60.50, $66.55

23 The first 'direct buy' price by $9. The second 'sale' price if 1 hour of time and wear and tear on the car is valued at more than $4.40.

24 Robyn's for $130 25 $45.50, 43%

26 9% 27 $14.76

28 The discount price is $40.32 in each case.

29 $104 30 $102.03

31 $457.60 32 $726

33 a $1485 b $1080 c 137.5%

34 a $359.04 b $359.04 c yes
d no e 25·2% f 28%

35 a 18·12% b 31·2544%
c 22·195% d 17·978 156 25%

Exercise 8:06

1 a See page 242. b See page 242.
c See page 242. d See page 242.

2 a $143.80, $56.80 b $1866, $576
c $1138.40, $536.80
d i $874, $144 ii $1019.20, $289.20
iii $1165.60, $435.60 iv $1309.60, $579.60
v $1456, $726 vi $2182, $1452
e $17 180, $2566.70

3 a $200 b $525 c $672 d $216
e $300 f $850 g $2250 h $1132.81

4 a $1200, $5.77 b $3025, $19.39
c $6272, $60.31 d $1116, $7.15
e $2300, $22.12 f $3350, $16.11
g $12 250, $94.23 h $13 632.81, $209.74

5 a $2322 b $10 922 c $303.39

6 a $43 500 b $17 182.50 c $60 682.50
d $1011.38

7 a $1240 b $11 160 c $3839.04
d $14 999.04 e $144.22

8 a $2 b $4.50 c $9.97 d $18.78
e $3 f $42.17 g $18 h $20.79

9 $8.50

10 a $25.38 b $1500.38 c $17.51

11 a $15 900 b $5850 c $1170 d 12%

12 a $11 840 b $15 912.96 c $4072.96
d 8·6%

13 a 17·9% b $9.41 c $3.92

Diagnostic test 8

1 a i $2150 ii $2480
b $234.95

2 a $1017 b $651

3 a $1068.70 b 23%

4 a $74 430 b $71 626 c $1074.39
d $15 899.84 including Medicare
e $265.84 f $66

5 a 50 kg size b 660 mL for $3.75

6 a $7.37 b $59.29 c $2.95 d $19.50

7 a $402.50 b $588, 14% c $32 000

8 a $526.50 b $850

9 a 130% b $3640.90, 72·5%

10 a $5003.20, $2003.20
b i $2583 ii $16 933 iii $705.54
c i $16 400 ii $65 600 iii $25 584
iv $1519.73

ASSIGNMENT 8A

1 a i $672 ii $798
b $635 c $1090 d $2124.40
2 a i 21 kg for $59.60 ii 21 kg pack for $59.60
b $140.64 c $141·82
3 a $52 010 b $8450.25 c $3501.60
4 a $32.89 b $29.60 c no
d approx. 9·1%
5 a 40% b approx. 34%
6 a $2595 b $14 705 c $3749.78
d $236.60 e $21 049.80

ASSIGNMENT 8B

1 a 3 b 10 c 28
2 $3\frac{1}{3}$ m
3 a 10 km b 20 km c 11:30 am
d Bill e 11:30 am f 50 km
g 30 km h 90 km
4 15°
5 a $1800 b $1400 c $37.50

ASSIGNMENT 8C

1 a 0·5 cm b 0·05 cm c 0·0005 m
2 a i 27 ii 0·072
b i 22 ii 5·5
3 a $5\cdot\dot{5}$% b 5·9% c $275; 35%
4 a $x = \frac{y+7}{5}$ b $\frac{m+6}{12}$ c $\frac{m^2}{24}$ d $\frac{3}{2} = 1\frac{1}{2}$
5 $50\cdot0\ \text{cm}^2$
6 a $2\cdot13 \times 10^5$ b $2\cdot15 \times 10^8$
c $5\cdot67 \times 10^{-3}$ d $1\cdot2 \times 10^{-7}$
7 a 56 b 20 c $-6\frac{1}{5}$
8 a $x = \frac{y+7}{5}$ b $x = \frac{c-by}{a}$ c $x = \frac{u^2 - v^2}{2a}$

Chapter 9

Exercise 9:01

1 a 10 b $\sqrt{34}$ c $\sqrt{29}$
2

	a	b	c
BC	4	8	6
AC	5	4	3
AB	$\sqrt{41}$	$\sqrt{52}$	$\sqrt{45}$

3 a $\sqrt{20}$ b $\sqrt{58}$ c $\sqrt{53}$
d $\sqrt{29}$ e $\sqrt{41}$ f $\sqrt{40}$
4 a 5 b 10 c 5 d 10
e 13 f 13 g $\sqrt{20}$ h $\sqrt{5}$
i $\sqrt{89}$ j $\sqrt{17}$ k $\sqrt{26}$ l $\sqrt{2}$
5 a $\sqrt{20}$ units b (−1, 2)
c $\sqrt{106}$ units d (7, 2)
6 a $AB = 5$ units; $BC = \sqrt{50}$ units; $AC = \sqrt{41}$ units
b $AB = \sqrt{13}$ units; $DC = \sqrt{13}$ units
$AD = \sqrt{5}$ units; $BC = \sqrt{5}$ units
c $BD = \sqrt{32}$ units; $AC = 2$ units
d $EF = FG = GH = HE = \sqrt{10}$ units
e 5
f $AB = \sqrt{40}$ units; $BC = \sqrt{40}$ units
Since two sides are equal the triangle is isosceles.
g 13 units

Prep quiz 9:02

1 7 2 1 3 7 4 1 5 7
6 1 7 3 8 1 9 3 10 1

Exercise 9:02

1 a (3, 3) b (−1, −1) c $(1\frac{1}{2}, 0)$
2 a $(2\frac{1}{2}, 2\frac{1}{2})$ b $(3\frac{1}{2}, 7)$ c (−4, 3)
d $(0, -2\frac{1}{2})$ e (−4, −6) f $(4\frac{1}{2}, -5\frac{1}{2})$
g $(\frac{1}{2}, -5)$ h $(-\frac{1}{2}, 3\frac{1}{2})$ i $(-1\frac{1}{2}, -7\frac{1}{2})$
3 a (4, 7) b (3, 7) c (6, 4)
d (−2, 1) e (2, 2) f (1, −2)
g (−4, −8) h (−3, −1) i $(-4, -5\frac{1}{2})$
4 a $(-\frac{1}{2}, -3)$ b $(7\frac{1}{2}, -1)$ c (5, 0)
d $(-\frac{1}{2}, -\frac{1}{2})$ e (−2, −2) f $(5\frac{1}{2}, -5\frac{1}{2})$
g (87, 70) h (70, −26) i (262, 76)
5 a i $(2\frac{1}{2}, 2)$ ii $(2\frac{1}{2}, 2)$ iii yes
iv The diagonals bisect each other.
b (3, 8)
c i (4, 3) ii (4, 3) iii yes
iv The diagonals bisect each other.
6 a $k = 0$ b $d = 15, e = -6$
c (−16, 0) d (7, 2)
7 a C is $(4\frac{1}{2}, 5\frac{1}{2})$; D is (8, 7); E is $(11\frac{1}{2}, 8\frac{1}{2})$
b B is (29, 16); C is (8, 7); E is (22, 13)
8 a AC and BD are the diagonals.
Midpoint of BD is (−4, 2)
Midpoint of AC is (−4, 2)
∴ Diagonals have the same midpoint.
∴ Diagonals bisect each other.
∴ $ABCD$ is a parallelogram.
b Length of both diagonals = $\sqrt{80}$ units.
Midpoint of both diagonals = $(\frac{1}{2}, -1)$
∴ Diagonals bisect each other.
∴ Figure has equal diagonals that bisect each other.
∴ The figure is a rectangle.

Prep quiz 9:03

1 EF 2 A and B 3 C and D
4 E and F 5 B and C 6 D and E
7 F and G 8 up 9 down
10 not at all

Exercise 9:03

1 a positive b positive c negative
d negative e positive f negative

2 a 5 b −5 c $\frac{1}{5}$

3 a $\frac{1}{2}$ b −2 c $\frac{1}{2}$

4 a $-\frac{1}{2}$ b $-\frac{4}{3}$ c $\frac{1}{2}$

5 a $\frac{1}{3}$ b 4 c $\frac{1}{2}$ d $\frac{2}{5}$
e $\frac{1}{6}$ f 3 g $\frac{8}{3}$ h −4
i −1 j $-2\frac{1}{2}$ k −4 l 2

6 a 5 b 2
c i $-\frac{1}{2}$ ii $-\frac{1}{2}$ iii $-\frac{1}{2}$ iv $-\frac{1}{2}$
d If three points lie on the same straight line, then the intervals joining one of the points to the other two must have the same gradients.

Using (−2, 5) and (2, 13), $n = \frac{13-5}{2--2} = 2$

Using (2, 13) and (6, 21), $n = \frac{21-13}{6-2} = 2$

As the intervals joining (2, 13) to the other two points have the same gradient, the points are collinear.

7 a

Line	A	B	C	D
Gradient	2	2	$-\frac{1}{2}$	$-\frac{1}{2}$

b A and B; C and D
c A and B; C and D

8 a

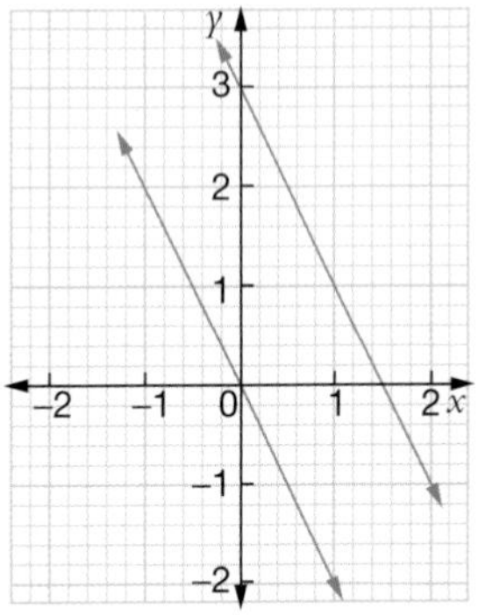

b Yes

9 a i $\frac{1}{4}, \frac{1}{4}$ ii $2\frac{1}{2}, 2\frac{1}{2}$
iii *ABCD* is a parallelogram since it has opposite sides parallel.
b *AB* and *DC* have a gradient of $\frac{2}{7}$ and, hence, are parallel. *AD* and *BC* have a gradient of 1 and, hence, are parallel. Since there are two pairs of parallel sides, *ABCD* is a parallelogram.

10 *AB* and *CD* have a slope of $\frac{1}{4}$ and hence are parallel. *AD* and *BC* have a slope of 4 and hence are parallel. Since there are two pairs of parallel sides, *ABCD* is a parallelogram. Also $AB = AD = \sqrt{153}$ units. Hence, *ABCD* is a parallelogram with a pair of adjacent sides equal. *ABCD* is a rhombus.

Investigation 9:03

1 a C b B c A

2 a 8 m b 5·6 m c 12·8 m

3 a $1\frac{1}{2}$ m b $\frac{1}{2}$ m

4 No, he would need a run of 11·2 m. He could curve the ramp across the slope.

Exercise 9:04

1 a $y = x + 1$

x	0	1	2
y	1	2	3

b $y = 2x$

x	0	1	2
y	0	2	4

c $y = 3x + 1$

x	0	1	2
y	1	4	7

d $y = 6 - 2x$

x	0	1	2
y	6	4	2

e $y = x + 3$

x	0	1	2
y	3	4	5

f $y = 7x + 2$

x	2	3	4
y	16	23	30

g $y = x - 7$

x	0	1	2
y	−7	−6	−5

h $y = 1 - x$

x	0	1	2
y	1	0	−1

i $y = 3$

x	0	1	2
y	3	3	3

2 a

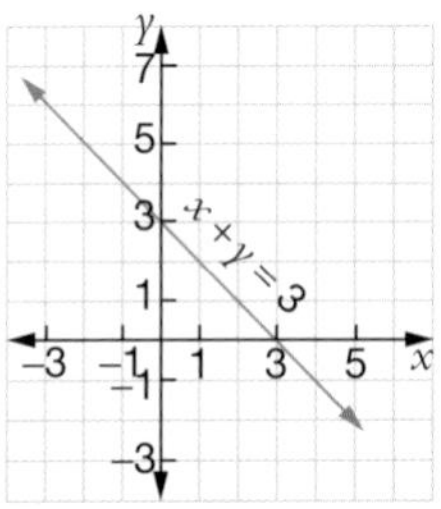

b

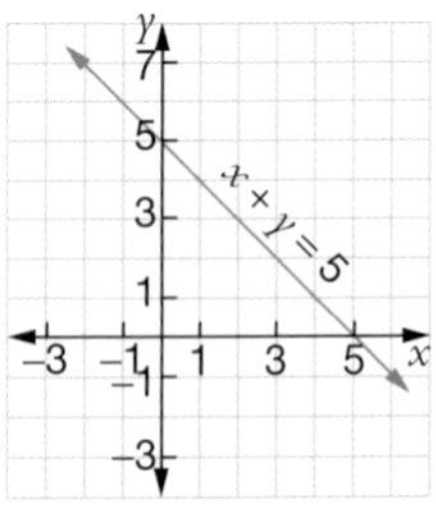

c

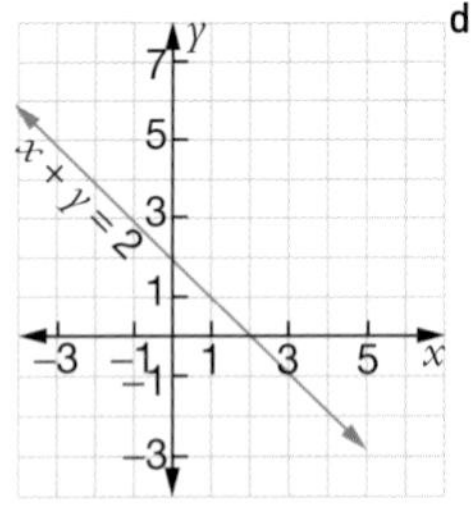

d

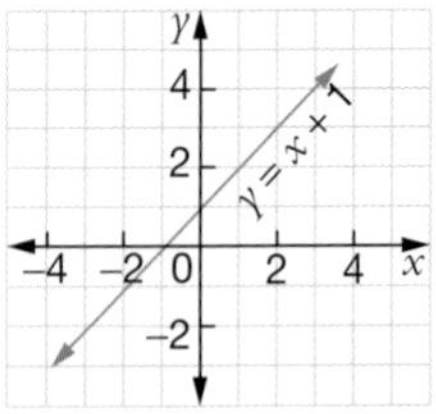

e

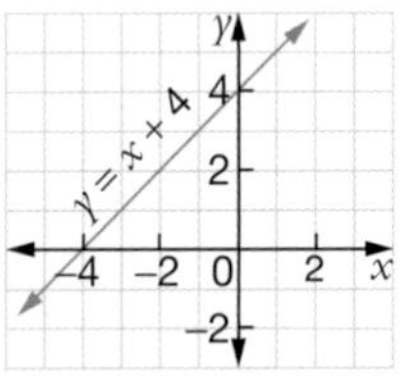

f

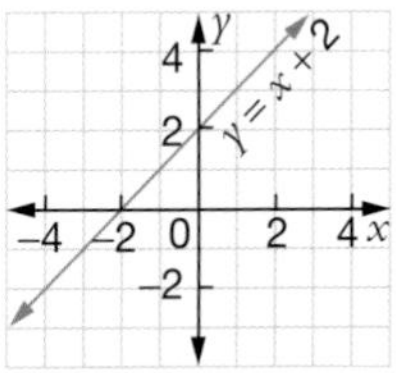

g
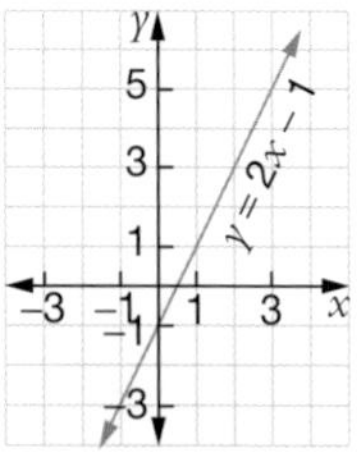

h
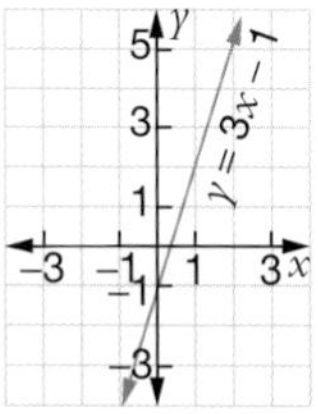

i
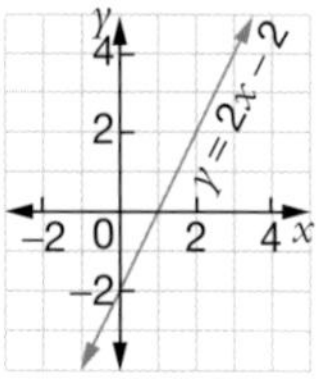

j
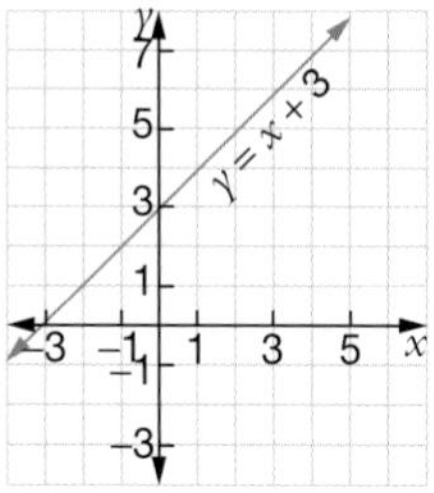

k
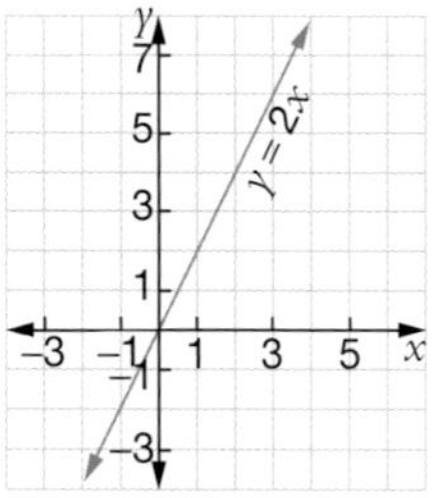

l
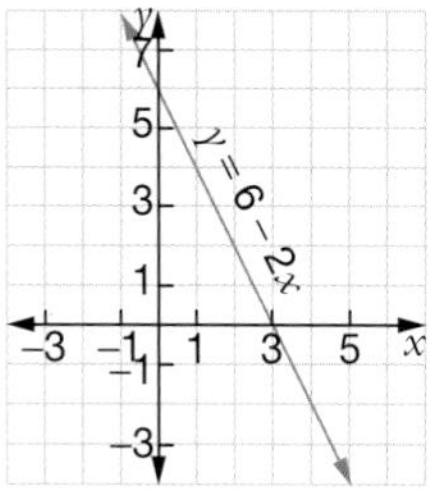

3
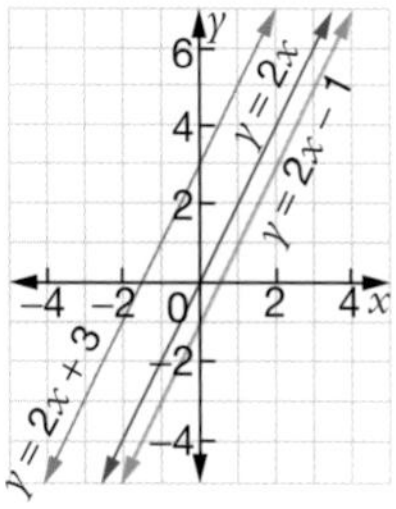

The lines are parallel.

4
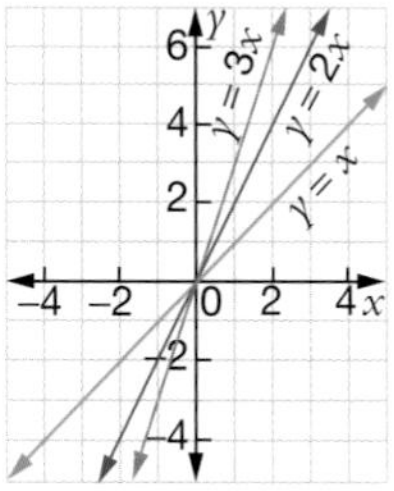

The lines all pass through the origin.

5
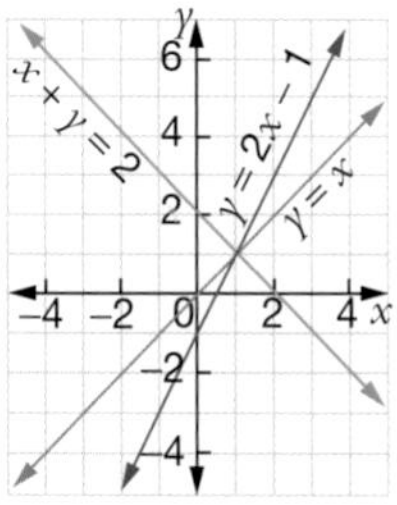

The lines all pass through (1, 1).

6 A, B, D

7 a yes b yes c (7, –2) d (5, 0)

8 a A: $x = -4$, B: $x = -1$, C: $x = 3$, D: $y = 3$, E: $y = 1$, F: $y = -4$

b A: $x = -3$, B: $x = 2$, C: $x = 4$, D: $y = 4$, E: $y = 2$, F: $y = -2$

9 a
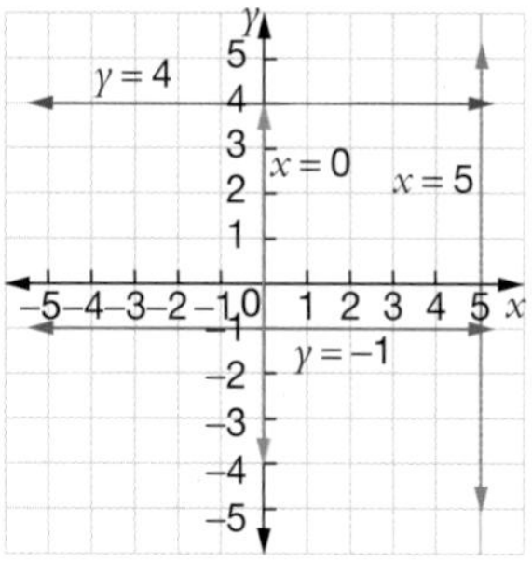

b
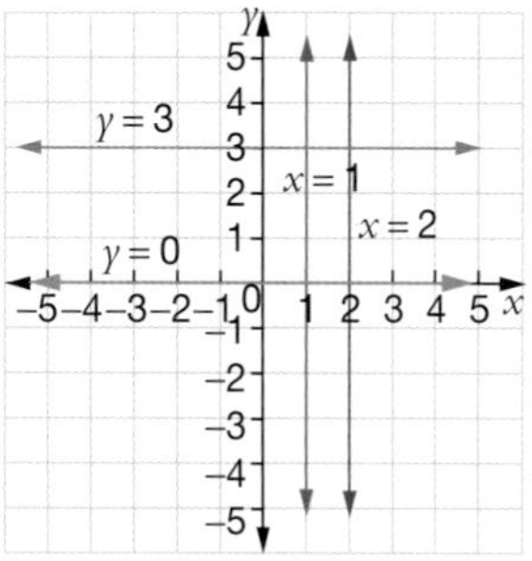

c
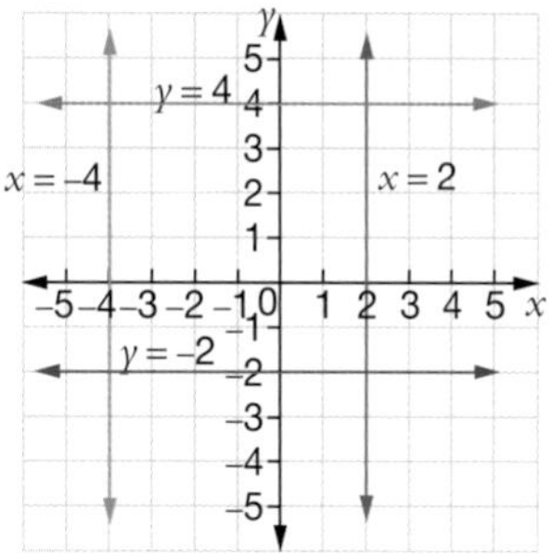

d
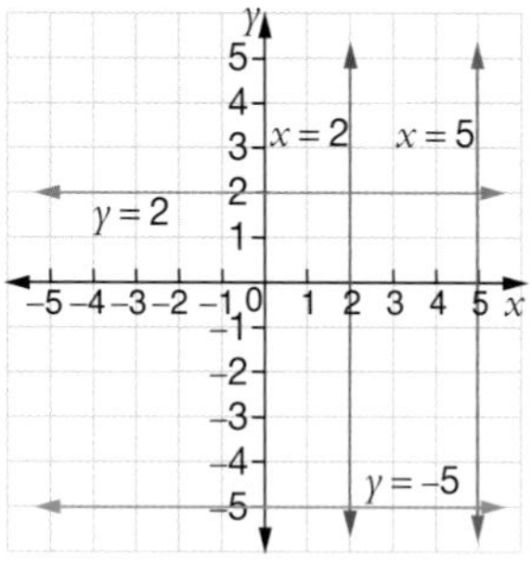

e

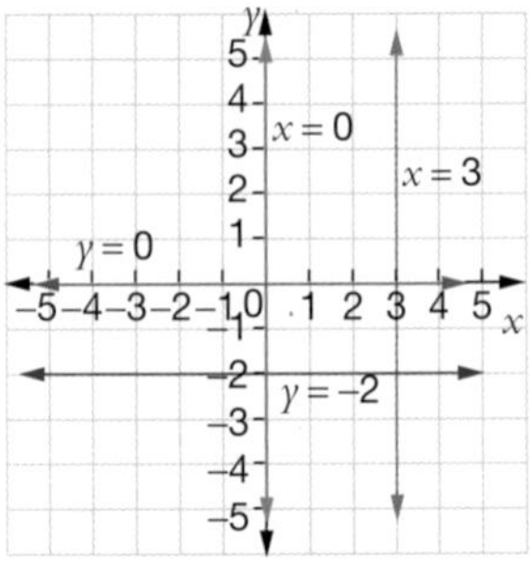

The lines in **a** and **c** enclose square regions.

10 A: $y = x$, B: $y = x - 2$, C: $y = 2x$, D: $x + y = 3$, E: $2x + y = 2$, F: $2x + y = 0$

11 **a** C **b** D **c** A **d** B

12 **a**

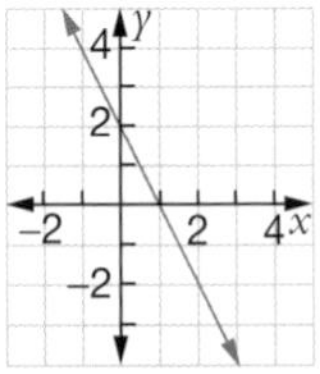

x-intercept is 1
y-intercept is 2

b

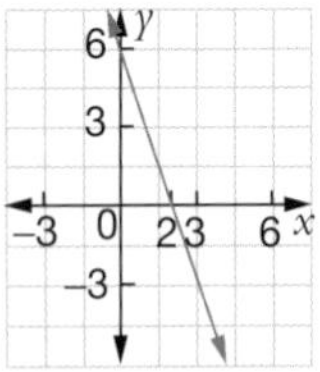

x-intercept is 2
y-intercept is 6

c

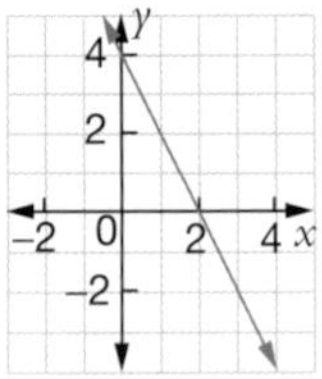

x-intercept is 2
y-intercept is 4

d

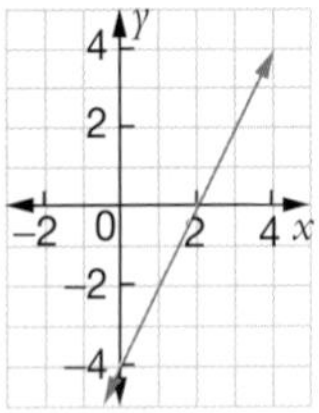

x-intercept is 2
y-intercept is −4

e

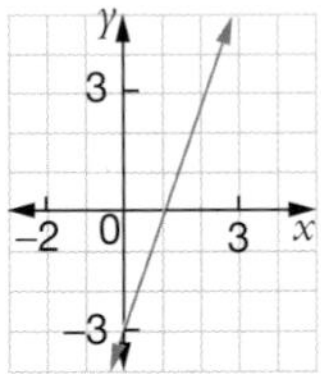

x-intercept is 1
y-intercept is −3

f

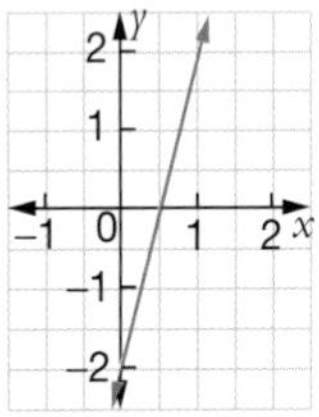

x-intercept is $\frac{1}{2}$
y-intercept is −2

13 **a**

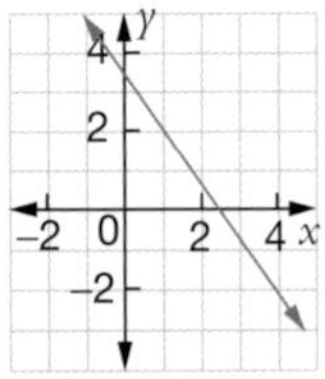

b

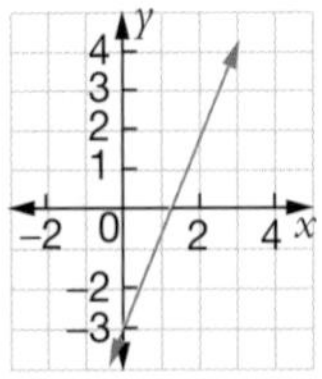

c

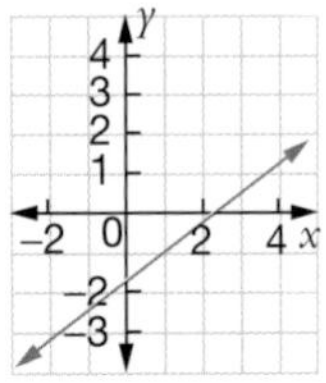

Prep quiz 9:05

1 0 2 b 3 2 4 −1 5 2
6 $\frac{1}{2}$ 7 (0, 2) 8 (0, −1) 9 yes 10 yes

Investigation 9:05

1

Line	Equation	Gradient	y-intercept
A	$y = x + 2$	1	2
B	$y = x - 2$	1	−2
C	$y = \frac{1}{2}x + 1$	$\frac{1}{2}$	1
D	$Y = \frac{1}{2}x - 1$	$\frac{1}{2}$	−1
E	$y = 2x + 2$	2	2
F	$y = 2x - 3$	2	−3

2

Line	Equation	Coefficient of x	Constant
A	$y = x + 2$	1	2
B	$y = x - 2$	1	−2
C	$y = \frac{1}{2}x + 1$	$\frac{1}{2}$	1
D	$y = \frac{1}{2}x - 1$	$\frac{1}{2}$	−1
E	$y = 2x + 2$	2	2
F	$y = 2x - 3$	2	−3

3 The gradient of the line is the same as the coefficient of x. The y-intercept of the line is the same as the constant.

4 $y = -2x + 3$

5 It tells us that m is the gradient and b is the y-intercept.

Exercise 9:05

1 The gradient is stated first.

a 2; 3 **b** 5; 1 **c** 3; 2 **d** 1; 6
e 4; 0 **f** 1; 0 **g** 1; −2 **h** 5; −1
i 6; −4 **j** −2; 3 **k** −1; −2 **l** −3; 1
m $\frac{1}{2}$; 4 **n** $\frac{3}{4}$; −2 **o** $\frac{1}{3}$; 5 **p** −3; 4
q 4; −2 **r** $-\frac{1}{2}$; 3

2 **a** $y = 4x + 9$ **b** $y = -2x + 3$
c $y = 7x - 1$ **d** $y = -5x - 2$
e $y = \frac{1}{2}x + 5$ **f** $y = \frac{2}{3}x - 4$
g $y = 3x + 1$ **h** $y = 2x - 3$
i $y = 5x + \frac{1}{2}$ **j** $y = x + 1\frac{1}{2}$

3 **a** 2; 1; $y = 2x + 1$ **b** $\frac{1}{4}$; 3; $y = \frac{x}{4} + 3$
c $\frac{1}{2}$; 2; $y = \frac{1}{2}x + 2$ **d** $\frac{1}{3}$; 4; $y = \frac{1}{3}x + 4$
e 3; −1; $y = 3x - 1$ **f** −1; −2; $y = -x - 2$
g $-\frac{1}{6}$; $-2\frac{1}{2}$; $y = -\frac{x}{6} - 2\frac{1}{2}$
h $\frac{3}{2}$; 0; $y = \frac{3x}{2}$

4 **a** E **b** B **c** D **d** G **e** F
f A **g** C

5 (In each part the gradient is stated first.)

a 2; 5 b 3; −3 c 2; 4 d 2; −1
e 5; 8 f 6; −12 g 3; −2 h −2; −4
i 2; 7 j −1; 4 k $\frac{1}{2}; 1\frac{1}{2}$ l −3; 5
m −3; 2 n $-\frac{3}{2}; 3$ o $\frac{2}{5}; \frac{1}{5}$

6 a yes b no c yes d yes

7 a $2x - y + 6 = 0; y = 2x - 3$
b $x + y = 3$ and $y = -x + 8$

8 a
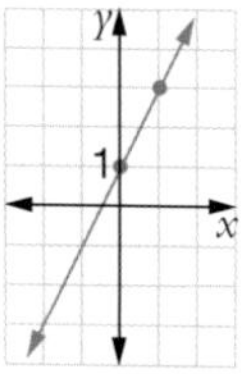

b
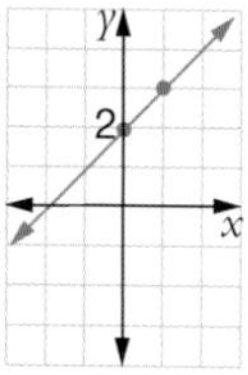

c
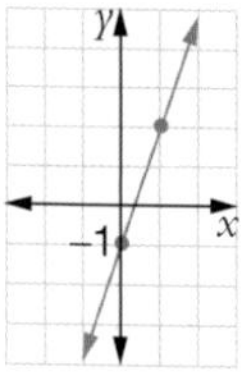

d
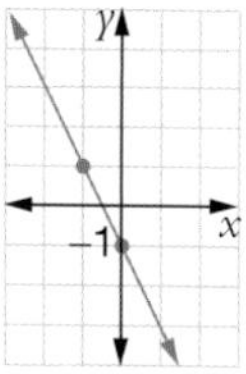

e
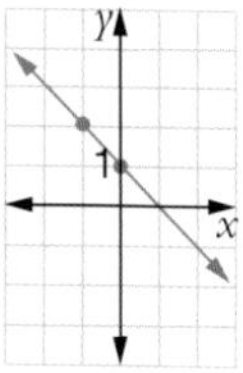

f
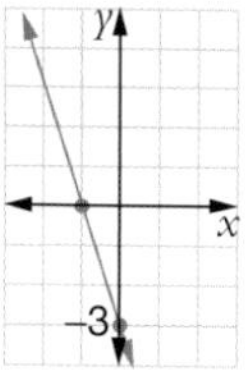

g
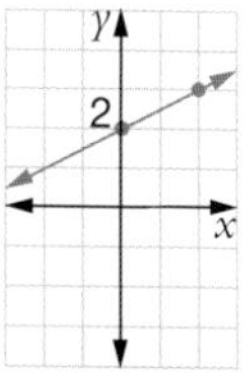

h
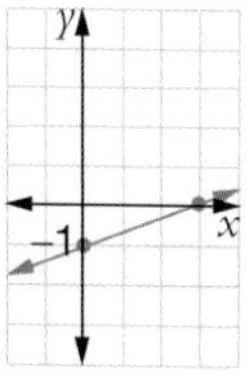

i
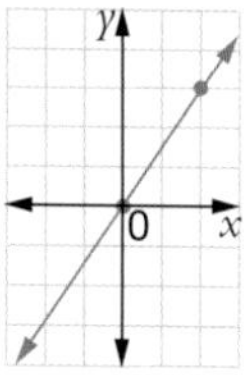

j
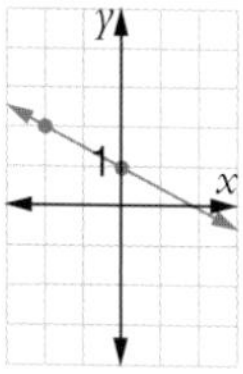

k
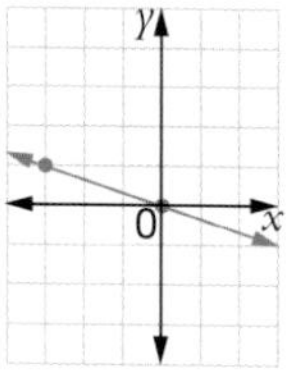

l
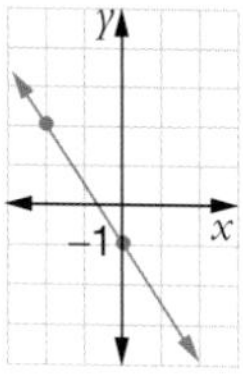

9 a
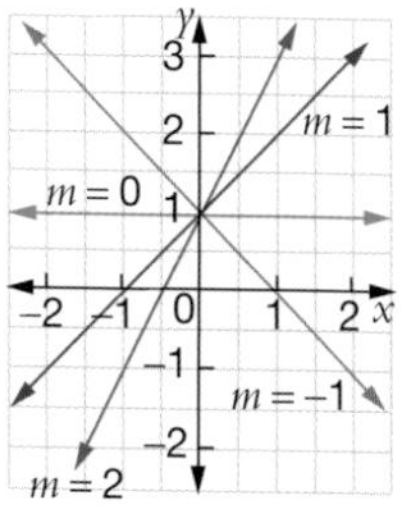

b
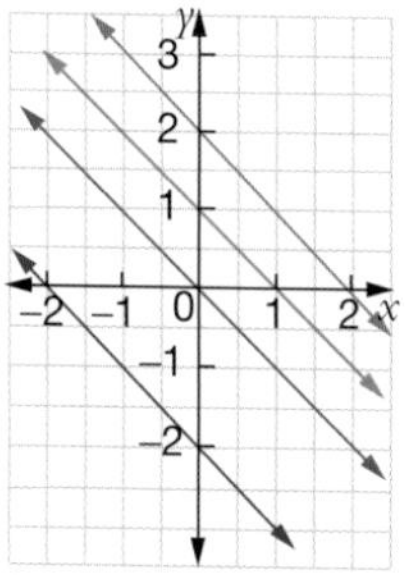

10 a −2 b 2 c $-\frac{1}{2}$ d $\frac{4}{3}$
e 4 f $-\frac{1}{3}$

Prep quiz 9:06

1 3 2 5 3 11 4 0 5 4
6 5 7 1 8 2 9 3 10 0

Exercise 9:06

1 a 1 b 2 c 5 d −5
e −2 f −11

2 a $y = 2x + 1$ b $y = 5x$
c $y = 3x - 4$ d $y = 4x + 10$
e $y = -x + 6$ f $y = -2x + 7$
g $y = -5x + 5$ h $y = \frac{1}{2}x + 3$
i $y = \frac{1}{4}x + 2$ j $y = -\frac{1}{2}x - 3$

3 a $y = 2x - 4$ b $y = -x + 3$
c $y = 3x + 6$ d $y = -3x + 1$
e $y = 3x$ f $y = 4x + 2$
g $y = 4x$ h $y = -2x - 8$
i $y = 2x - 2$ j $y = \frac{1}{2}x + 3\frac{1}{2}$

Exercise 9:07

1 a 4 b 1 c −2 d 5 e $\frac{1}{4}$
f −1 g 3 h 1 i −5 j −3

2 a $y = 4x - 8$ b $y = x + 4$
c $y = -2x + 7$ d $y = 5x + 9$
e $y = \frac{1}{4}x + 1\frac{1}{2}$ f $y = -x + 7$
g $y = 3x$ h $y = x$
i $y = -5x + 3$ j $y = -3x$

3 a $y = 2x + 2$ b $y = -3x + 15$
c $y = 4x + 4$ d $y = 2x + 4, 10 = 2(3) + 4$
e $y = x + 1$

4 a m of $AB = 1$, m of $BC = -3$, m of $AC = -\frac{3}{5}$
b $y = x + 3, y = -3x + 7, y = -\frac{3}{5}x - \frac{1}{5}$
c $3, 7, -\frac{1}{5}$ d $y = 1$ e $m = 0, b = 1$

5 a $y = -2x + 4, -2 = -2(3) + 4$
b Equation of AB is $y = -2x - 2$.
Substitute C (3, −8): $-8 = -2(3) - 2$
∴ C lies on AB
c Equation of line joining (−2, −11) and (3, 4) is $y = 3x - 5$. Substitute (4, 7): $7 = 3(4) - 5$
∴ the points are collinear.

6 a $3x + 7y + 5 = 0$ b $6x - 5y - 8 = 0$
c $470x + 270y + 91 = 0$ d $42x + 138y + 29 = 0$

Exercise 9:08

1 a

x	−3	−2	−1	0	1	2	3
y	10	5	2	1	2	5	10

Graph B

b

x	−3	−2	−1	0	1	2	3
y	8	3	0	−1	0	3	8

Graph C

c

x	−3	−2	−1	0	1	2	3
y	11	6	3	2	3	6	11

Graph A

2

x	−3	−2	−1	0	1	2	3
y	7	2	−1	−2	−1	2	7

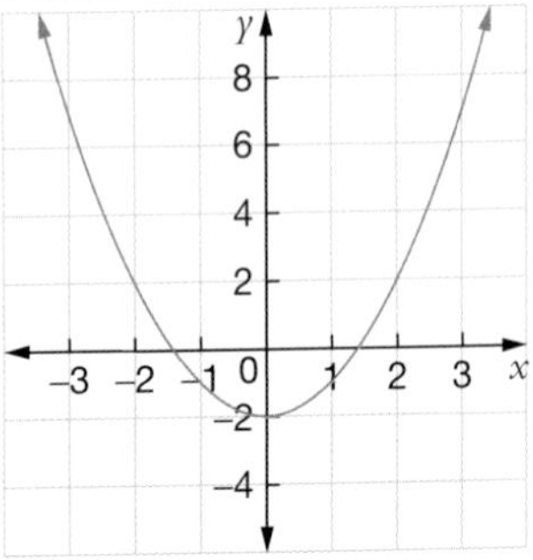

3 a A (0, 2); B (0, 1); C (0,−1)
b yes c yes d yes

4 a

x	−3	−2	−1	0	1	2	3
y	−9	−4	−1	0	−1	−4	−9

Graph E

b

x	−3	−2	−1	0	1	2	3
y	−8	−3	0	1	0	−3	−8

Graph G

c

x	−3	−2	−1	0	1	2	3
y	−11	−6	−3	−2	−3	−6	11

Graph F

5 a E (0,0); F (0,−2); G (0,2)
b yes c yes d yes

6 a B b D c A d C

7 The parabola is concave up if the coefficient of x^2 is positive. It is concave down if the coefficient of x^2 is negative.

8 a

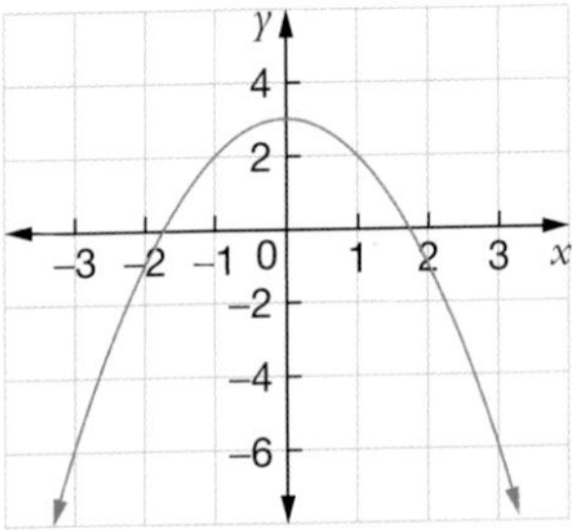

b

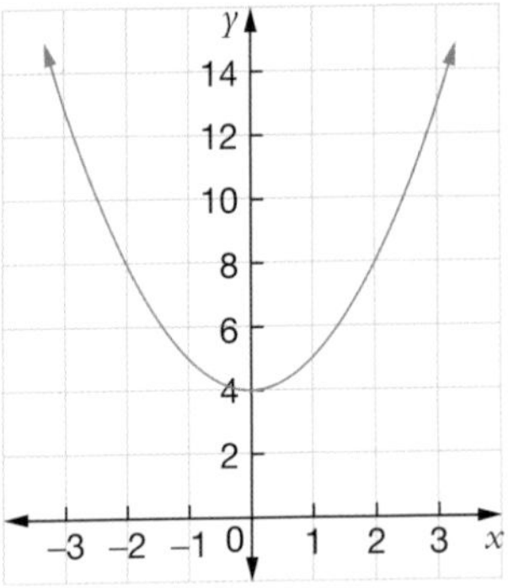

c

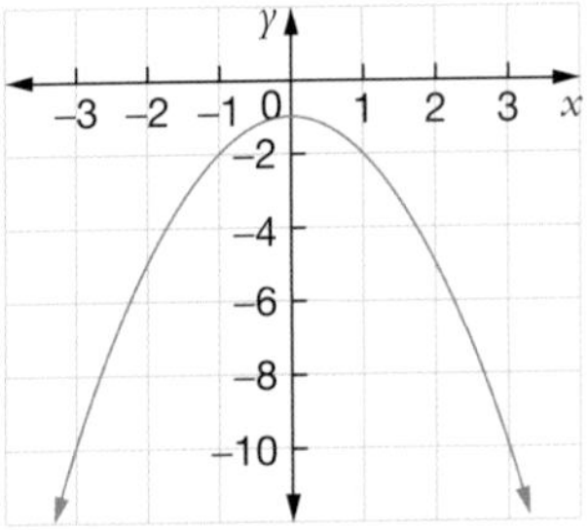

9 a

x	−3	−2	−1	0	1	2	3
y	0·125	0·25	0·5	1	2	4	8

Graph F

b

x	−3	−2	−1	0	1	2	3
y	8	4	1	0·5	−1	0·25	0·125

Graph E

c

x	−3	−2	−1	0	1	2	3
y	−0·125	−0·25	−0·5	−1	−2	−4	−8

Graph H

d

x	−3	−2	−1	0	1	2	3
y	−8	−4	−1	0	−0·5	−0·25	−0·125

Graph G

10 a B b A c D d C

Diagnostic test 9

1 a $\sqrt{45}$ b $\sqrt{61}$ c $\sqrt{34}$

2 a 10 b $\sqrt{13}$ c $\sqrt{17}$

3 a (4, 6) b $(4, 1\frac{1}{2})$ c $(-1, -2\frac{1}{2})$

4 a 1 b −2 c $\frac{1}{2}$

5 a 4 b $-\frac{1}{2}$ c $\frac{2}{3}$

6 a yes b no c yes

7 a

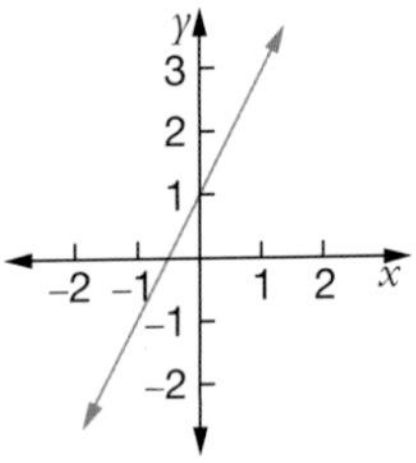

b

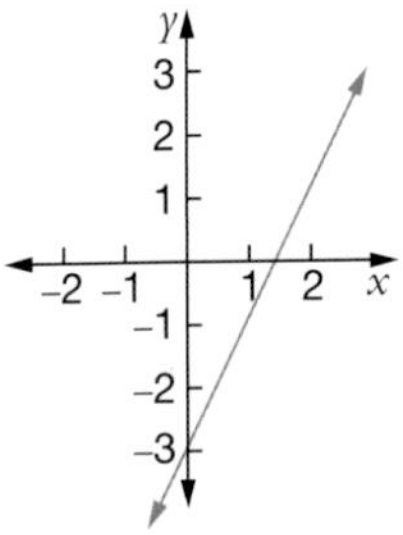

c

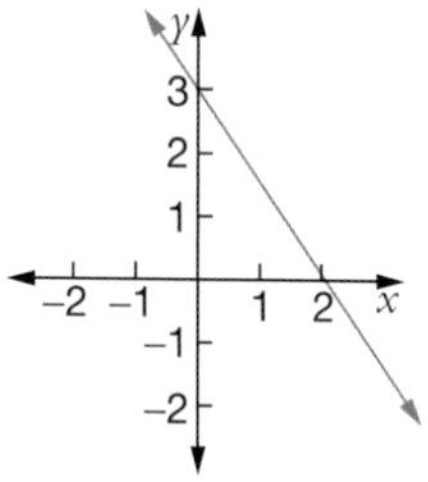

8 a x-int. = $1\frac{1}{2}$, y-int. = −3
  b x-int. = 6, y-int. = 2
  c x-int. = 4, y-int. = 2

9 a

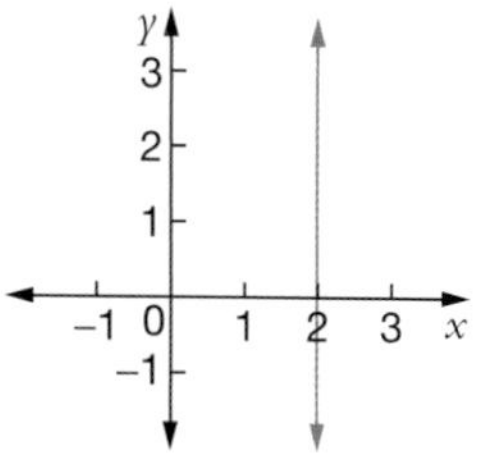

  b

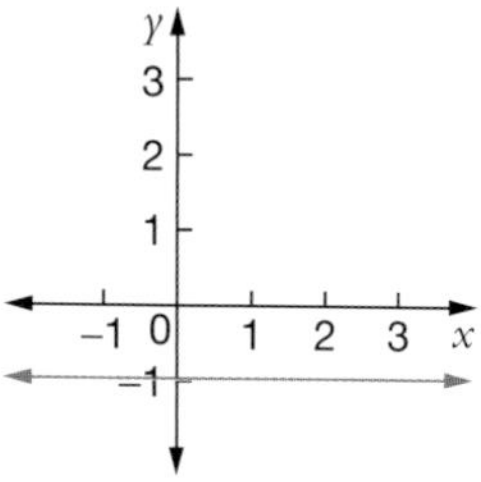

  c

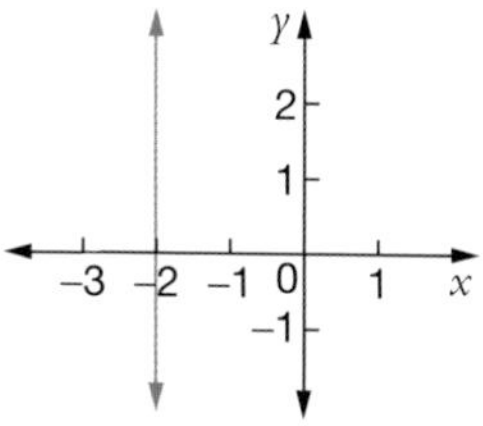

10 a $y = 3x + 2$ b $y = \frac{1}{2}x - 3$
  c $y = 3 - x$
11 a $3x - y + 2 = 0$ b $x - 2y - 6 = 0$
  c $x + y - 3 = 0$
12 a grad. = 2; y-int. = 3 b grad. = −2; y-int. = 3
  c grad. = −1; y-int. = 4
13 a $y = 4x + 6$ b $y = -\frac{2}{3}x + 1$
  c $y = -\frac{5}{2}x - \frac{1}{2}$
14 a $y = 2x + 2$ b $y = -3x + 6$
  c $y = \frac{1}{2}x + 1$
15 a $y = 2x - 1$ b $y = -3x - 1$
  c $y = \frac{4}{3}x$
16 a C b B c A
17 a B b C c A

ASSIGNMENT 9A

1 a $\sqrt{65}$ b $\frac{7}{4}$ c $(4, 1\frac{1}{2})$
2 a 13 b $\frac{12}{5} = 2{\cdot}4$ c $(4\frac{1}{2}, 11)$
3 a $7x - 4y - 22 = 0$
  b $169\frac{1}{2}$
4 a $(0, -3)$; $y = x - 3$ b $y = -\frac{1}{2}x + 6$; 12
  c $y = -2x + 6$
5 $XY = YZ = \sqrt{20}$
  ∴ ΔXYZ is isosceles
  slope of $YZ = 2$
  slope of $YX = -\frac{1}{2}$
  slope of $YZ \times$ slope of $YX = -1$
  ∴ YZ is perpendicular to YX
  ∴ $\Delta XYZ = 90°$
  ∴ ΔXYZ is right-angled and isosceles.
6 $2x - 7y + 22 = 0$
7 If three points are collinear, then the intervals joining one of the points to the other two must have the same gradients.

  Using $A(5, 21)$ and $B(30, 41)$, $m_{BD} = \dfrac{41 - 21}{30 - 5} = \dfrac{4}{5}$

  Using $A(5, 21)$ and $C(100, 97)$, $m_{AC} = \dfrac{97 - 21}{100 - 5} = \dfrac{4}{5}$

  As the intervals joining A to the other two points have the same gradient, the points are collinear.
  Note: This question could also be done by finding the equation of the line through two of the points and then showing that the third point lies on that line.
8 a $(3,6)$; $OB = \sqrt{45}$ b 4·5 units
  c 2·25 unit^2

ASSIGNMENT 9B

1 a 1 b 31, 35, 39, 43, 47, 51, 55, 59 minutes
2 4
3 a 53% b 12 cm c 68%, 46%, 31%, 21%
4 a 6 b 3
5 126 984
6 a

1	2	3	4
3	4	1	2
4	3	2	1
2	1	4	3

  b

1	2	3	4
2	1	4	3
3	4	1	2
4	3	2	1

  Another solution is possible.

ASSIGNMENT 9C

1 a $20a - 25a^2 - 4$ b $25a^2 - 4$
  c $25a^2 - 20a + 4$
2 a 36% b 11% c 38% d 26% e 15%
3 Volume = 6900 cm^3; SA = 2290 cm^2
4 a \$846 b \$93.75; 62·5%
5 a $17\frac{1}{3}$ b $3\frac{1}{11}$
6 a i $\dfrac{1}{a^2}$ ii $\dfrac{6}{a^2}$ iii $\dfrac{1}{36a^2}$
  b i 2 ii $\frac{1}{27}$ iii 13·5

Chapter 10

Prep quiz 10:01

1 1   2 −1   3 −3   4 −11

5 $-2\frac{1}{2}$ 6 −2   7 $-1\frac{1}{2}$ 8 $-4\frac{1}{2}$

9

x	0	1	2
y	−2	1	4

10

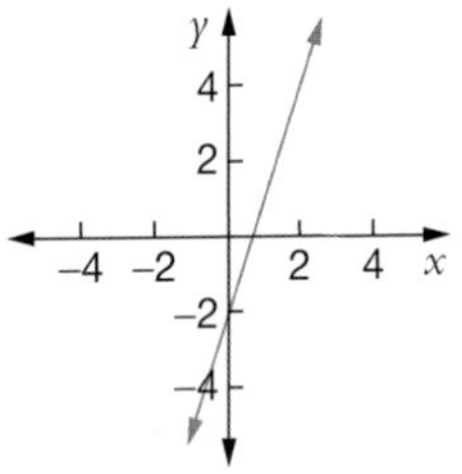

Exercise 10:01

1 a $x = 1, y = 2$ b $x = -2, y = -1$

c $x = -1, y = 2$ d $x = 0, y = 3$

e $x = 4, y = -1$ f $x = 3, y = 0$

g No solution, since the lines are parallel.

h An infinite number of solutions exist, e.g. (−1, 0), (0, 1), $(\frac{1}{2}, 1\frac{1}{2})$. These two equations represent the same line.

2 a $x = 0{\cdot}2, y = 1{\cdot}2$ b $x = -3{\cdot}3, y = -0{\cdot}3$

c $x = 1{\cdot}3, y = -2{\cdot}6$ d $x = 2{\cdot}8, y = -0{\cdot}3$

3 a $x = 2, y = -1$ b $x = 2, y = -1$

c $x = 1, y = -2$ d $x = 2, y = 4$

e $a = -1, b = -2$ f $p = -2, q = 2$

g $a = 1, b = 1$ h $p = 6, q = 2$

4 a

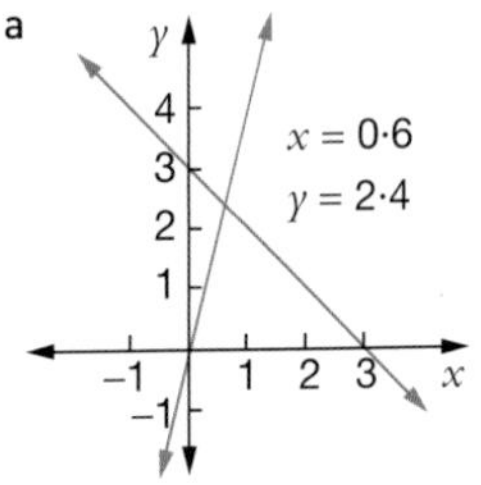

b

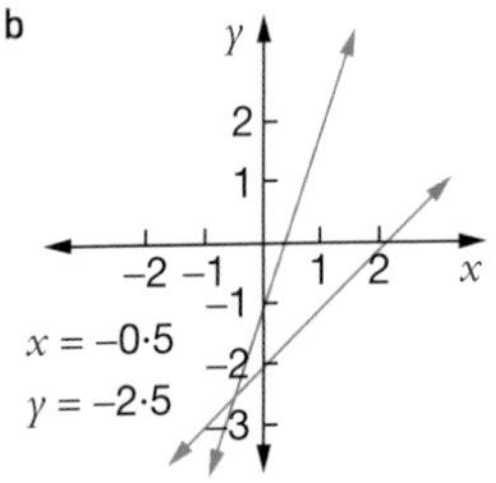

c

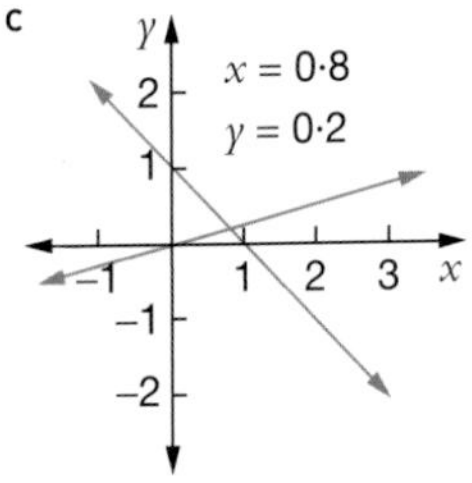

5 a

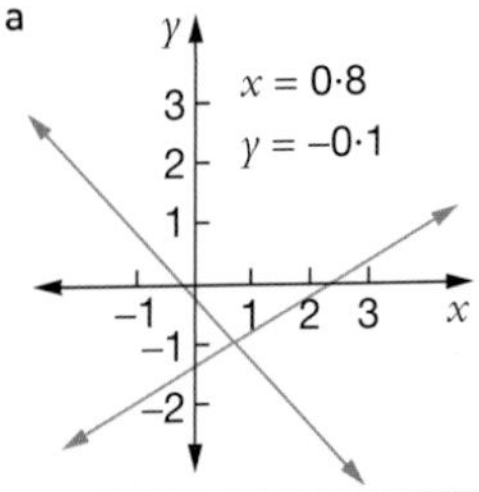

b

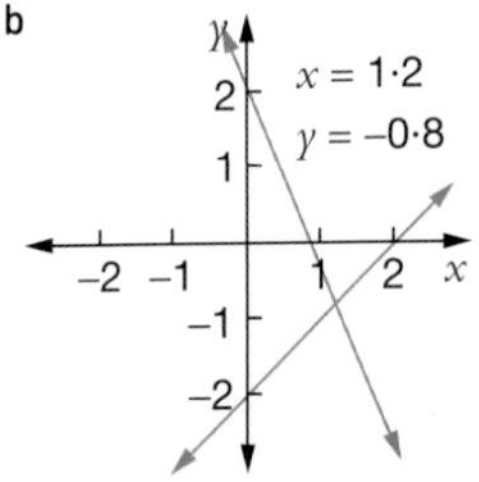

c

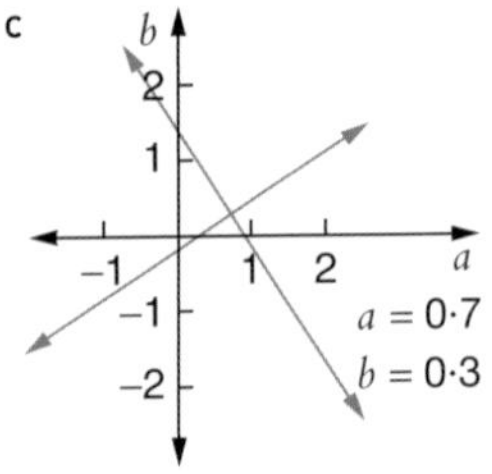

6 The two numbers are 6 and 9.

7 After $2\frac{1}{2}$ hours and 150 km.

8 6 machines, $1080

9

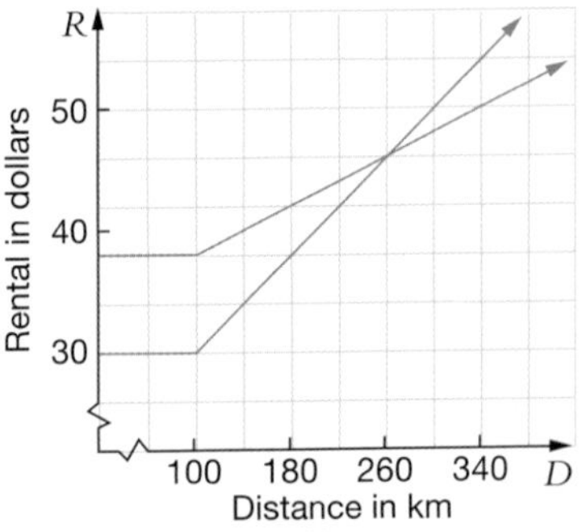

Distance = 260 km

10

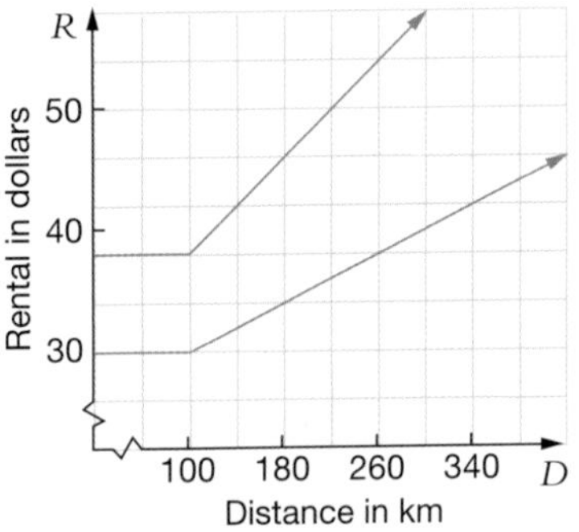

Safety Car Rental is always cheaper.

Exercise 10:02A

1 a $x = -1, y = 4$ b $x = 2, y = 5$

c $x = -2, y = -1$ d $x = 3, y = -2$

e $x = 4, y = 1$ f $x = 4, y = 0$

g $x = 4, y = -2$ h $x = 3, y = 3$

i $x = 6, y = 2$ j $x = 1, y = 5$

2 a $x = 6, y = -1$ b $x = 2\frac{3}{4}, y = \frac{1}{2}$

c $x = -12, y = 10$ d $x = 5, y = 3$

e $x = -2, y = 4$ f $x = 2, y = 3$

g $x = 3, y = 4$ h $x = 5, y = -2$

i $x = -2, y = 4$

3 a $x = \frac{7}{8}, y = \frac{3}{4}$ b $a = -3\frac{2}{3}, b = 17$

c $m = \frac{5}{6}, n = -1\frac{1}{12}$ d $x = \frac{1}{14}, y = -\frac{5}{14}$

4 a $a = 1\frac{1}{16}, b = \frac{3}{8}$ b $x = \frac{12}{17}, y = 1\frac{8}{17}$

c $m = 1\frac{2}{17}, n = \frac{10}{17}$ d $x = -2\frac{1}{3}, y = -4\frac{8}{9}$

Exercise 10:02B

1 a $x=5, y=4$ b $x=5, y=9$
c $x=3, y=1$ d $x=5, y=-1$
e $x=3, y=2$ f $x=1, y=2$
g $x=-2, y=4$ h $x=-8, y=2$
i $x=1\frac{1}{3}, y=7$ j $x=7, y=-1\frac{2}{7}$
k $x=1, y=2\frac{1}{2}$ l $x=2, y=-3\frac{2}{5}$

2 a $x=2, y=1$ b $x=3, y=-8$
c $x=1, y=-4$ d $x=-2, y=-3$
e $x=4, y=6$ f $x=4, y=1$
g $x=3, y=4$ h $x=2\frac{1}{4}, y=\frac{1}{2}$
i $x=4, y=4$ j $x=2, y=1$
k $x=-3, y=5\frac{1}{5}$ l $x=-1, y=-4$

3 a $x=1, y=5$ b $x=2, y=3$
c $x=5, y=-7$ d $x=-2, y=4$
e $x=2, y=3$ f $x=-2\frac{1}{3}, y=1\frac{1}{2}$
g $x=1, y=-2$ h $x=1, y=-8$
i $x=3, y=-5$

4 a $x=4, y=3$ b $x=1, y=5$
c $x=2, y=2$ d $x=3, y=2$
e $x=1, y=-2$ f $x=-2, y=3$
g $x=1, y=-2$ h $x=3, y=1$
i $x=1, y=2$ j $x=0, y=5$
k $x=2, y=9$ l $x=-3, y=2$
m $x=1, y=-1$ n $x=7\frac{8}{11}, y=4\frac{4}{11}$

Exercise 10:03

1 a 7 and 18 b 32 and 65 c 3 and 9
d 11 and 2 e 5 and 22

2 a length = 8 cm, width = 3 cm
b pen = \$1.65, pencil = 35c
c maths 72, science 57
d chocolate \$1.20, drink \$2.50
e Bill = \$1, Jim = 50c

3 a $x=5, y=2$ b $x=3, y=2$
c $x=15, y=30$ d $x=35, y=-35$
e $x=7, y=2$ f $x=4, y=-2$

4 a length = $10\frac{1}{2}$ cm, width = $6\frac{1}{2}$ cm
b box A = $28\frac{1}{3}$ kg, box B = 50 kg
c 36 rows of 45 seats and 12 rows of 40 seats
d 15 seniors and 75 juniors

5 a 8 scarves b 5 weeks

Investigation 10:03

1 34 and 52 2 236 girls, 184 boys
3 23 fours, 6 sixes
4 216 of Company A and 425 of Company B

Diagnostic test 10

1 a $x=-2, y=-1$ b $x=2, y=3$
c $x=-4, y=1$

2 a $x=3, y=1$ b $x=3\frac{2}{5}, y=-1\frac{3}{5}$
c $a=1\frac{3}{7}, b=2\frac{5}{7}$

3 a $x=2, y=1$ b $x=2\frac{3}{5}, y=-\frac{1}{5}$
c $a=2, b=0$

ASSIGNMENT 10A

1 a $x=3, y=0$ b $x=1\frac{1}{3}, y=2\frac{1}{3}$
c $a=1\frac{18}{33}, b=-\frac{6}{33}$ d $a=-2, b=-5\frac{1}{3}$
e $a=1\frac{7}{16}, b=-1\frac{7}{16}$ f $x=\frac{3}{5}, y=-\frac{3}{5}$
g $p=-1, q=3$ h $x=\frac{1}{4}, y=-2$
i $m=1\frac{3}{19}, n=\frac{10}{19}$

2 father is 54 years old, daughter is 18 years old
3 number of adults = 59, number of children = 141
4 share A = \$1.80, share B = \$1.20
5 length = 15 cm, width = 10 cm
6 length = 15 cm width = 5 cm
7 4 km/h

ASSIGNMENT 10B

1 Answers will vary.
a Answers will vary. b overestimate
c Estimate to the nearest metre, then add a few metres to the estimate.

2 1 3 $x = 72$

4 a 3 b 6 c 10 d 28

5 10

6 Dixon-Fly, Wynn-Free, Goad-Back, McCully-Breast with a time of 147·65 seconds.

ASSIGNMENT 10C

1 a 8 b 16 c −16 d −3
e 125 f 6 g 21 h 12·5
i −45 j 1 k $1\frac{9}{20}$ l $\frac{11}{20}$

2 a i 1000 mL (or 1 L) ii 100 mL
b i 54 seconds/lap ii 17 min 35 s
c from 24 500 km up to, but not including, 25 500 km
d 4 650 000
e 6500 MB

3 a $8m^2 - 2m$ b $-32xy$ c $\frac{2}{b}$
d $\frac{3x}{40}$ e $\frac{15x+1}{10}$ f $1\frac{2}{3}$
g $9x - 40$ h $21a$
i $-3 + 4m$ or $4m - 3$

4 a $\frac{19}{100}$ or a 19% chance b $\frac{36}{100}$ or a 36% chance

5 a $p^6 + 5$ b $1\frac{7}{9}$ c 3

6 $2{\cdot}5 \times 10^9$ B

7 a $x = 76$ b $x = -2\frac{3}{5}$ c $y = 8\frac{4}{7}$

8 16% of the cost

Chapter 11

Exercise 11:01

1 a i $\angle L$ ii $\angle M$ iii $\angle N$ iv $\angle O$ v $\angle P$
 b i LP ii ON iii NM iv PO v LM

2 a angles A and D, B and E, C and F; $\Delta ABC \mid\mid\mid \Delta DEF$
 b angles A and F, B and D, C and E; $\Delta ABC \mid\mid\mid \Delta FDE$
 c angles A and Q, B and R, C and S, D and T, E and W; $ABCDE \mid\mid\mid QRSTW$
 d angles A and L, B and M, C and N, D and O, E and P; $ABCDE \mid\mid\mid LMNOP$

3 a AB and DE, BC and EF, AC and DF
 b AB and FD, AC and FE, BC and DE
 c AB and QR, BC and RS, CD and ST, DE and TW, EA and WQ
 d AE and LP, ED and PO, DC and ON, CB and NM, BA and ML

4 a 8 cm b it is tripled c no d no

5 a true b true c false

6 a true
 b i 2 ii 4 iii 3 iv 2·5
 c i 0·75 ii 0·25 iii 0·5 iv 0·625

7 a 2 b 0·5 c 1·5 d $1\frac{1}{3}$
 e 2·5 f 0·6

8 A and B, C and E, D and F

9 a 66 cm, 60 cm, 40 cm, 36 cm
 b 105·6 cm, 96 cm, 64 cm, 57·6 cm
 c 26·4 cm, 24 cm, 16 cm, 14·4 cm
 d 14·85 cm, 13·5 cm, 9 cm, 8·1 cm

10 $RS = 21$, $RQ = 42$, $QP = 33$, $PS = 33$

11 a i 200% ii 50%
 b i 225% ii 75%
 c i 16 cm long 9·6 cm wide
 ii 8 cm long, 4·8 cm wide

Prep quiz 11:02

1 DE 2 DF 3 EF 4 2 5 1·5
6 $\frac{3}{4}$ 7 $1\frac{1}{3}$ 8 $\frac{2}{3}$ 9 $\frac{1}{2}$
10 a 15 cm b 9 cm

Exercise 11:02

1 a $\frac{2}{3}, \frac{3}{2}$ b $\frac{3}{7}, \frac{7}{3}$ c $\frac{2}{3}, \frac{3}{2}$ d $\frac{6}{7}, \frac{7}{6}$

2 a $a = 10, b = 4$ b $x = 5, y = 6$
 c $d = 16, e = 40$

3 a enlargement factor = 3; $x = 12$
 b enlargement factor = 4; $x = 24$
 c enlargement factor = 1·5; $x = 7·5$
 d enlargement factor = 1·6; $x = 14·4$

4 a reduction factor = 0·25; $y = 7·5$
 b reduction factor = $\frac{4}{9}$; $y = 12$
 c reduction factor = $\frac{7}{8}$; $y = 31·5$
 d reduction factor = 0·8; $y = 20$

5 a 36 cm b 10 cm
 c 1·4; 12·6 cm d 12 cm

6 a 1 : 2, $x = 5$ b 1 : 4, $y = 16$ c 3 : 2, $a = 15$
 d 5 : 2, $c = 48$ e 6 : 7, $e = 24$ f 5 : 4, $f = 55$

7 a 7 : 5, $x = 7$, $y = 11·2$ b 5 : 6, $x = 30$, $y = 27·5$
 c 9 : 7, $x = 11·6$, $y = 19·4$ d 7 : 3, $x = 9·3$, $y = 11·7$
 e 7 : 4, $x = 5·1$, $y = 1·7$, $z = 8·8$

Investigation 11:02

1 Photo widths are 14·4 cm and 9·6 cm.
2 There are many combinations possible.

Exercise 11:03A

1 a

Side	AB	AC	BC	DE	DF	EF
Length	40	20	30	80	40	60

 b i 2 ii 2 iii 2
 c true

2 a $AB = 4$ cm, $BC = 3$ cm, $CA = 3·6$ cm; $DE = 6·0$ cm, $EF = 4·5$ cm, $FD = 5·4$ cm
 b i 1·5 ii 1·5 iii 1·5
 c yes

3 a i yes ii 3 iii yes
 b i angles G and D, H and E, I and F; yes
 ii 1·5 iii yes

4 A and C, B and D

5 a J b G c I d F e H

Exercise 11:03B

1 a yes
 b i 2 ii 2 iii 2
 c yes d yes e yes

2 a the ratios are all equal to $\frac{4}{3}$; yes
 b yes c yes

3 a A and B b A and C

4 a H b J c I d F e G

5 a yes b yes

6 a B and C b A and B

7 a yes b yes

8 a A and C b A and B
 c A and C

9 a ΔABC and ΔADE (3 angles equal)
 b ΔABC and ΔEDC (3 angles equal)
 c ΔACD and ΔABE (sides adjacent to equal angles in same ratio)
 d ΔCED and ΔCAB (matching sides in same ratio)
 e ΔABC and ΔEDC (3 angles equal)

Prep quiz 11:04

1 largest 2 smallest 3 true 4 true
5 true 6 DE 7 $\frac{1·5}{2} = \frac{2·25}{3} = \frac{3}{4}$
8 EF 9 ED 10 $\frac{8}{6} = \frac{16}{12} = \frac{20}{15}$

Exercise 11:04

1 a DE, EF, DF

$\therefore \frac{DF}{AC} = \frac{EF}{BC}$

$\therefore \frac{x}{3} = \frac{2\cdot5}{1\cdot5}$

$\therefore x = 3 \times \frac{2\cdot5}{1\cdot5}$

$\therefore x = 5\text{ m}$

b TR, TS, RS

$\therefore \frac{TS}{LN} = \frac{RS}{MN}$

$\therefore \frac{y}{32\cdot6} = \frac{25}{40}$

$\therefore y = 32\cdot6 \times \frac{25}{40}$

$\therefore y = 20\cdot375\text{ m}$

2 a $x = 10\cdot7$ b $y = 10\cdot4$ c $a = 30$ d $y = 40$

3 a $a = 30\cdot8$ b $x = 7\cdot1$ c $x = 5\cdot0$

4 a $x = 4\cdot8$ b $h = 2\cdot4$ c $x = 13\cdot5$ d $x = 7$

5 a $x = 8, y = 5\frac{1}{3}$ b $a = 8, b = 16$

c $a = 40, b = 28\cdot8$ d $x = 28, y = 26\cdot25$

6 a 4·5 m b 4·2 m c 20 m

Prep quiz 11:05

1 100 cm 2 1000 mm 3 2000 cm 4 25 m
5 1 : 100 6 1 : 1000 7 0·6 cm 8 60 cm
9 500 10 4

Exercise 11:05A

1 a 100 b 1000 c 1000
2 a 30 m b 46 m c 23 m
3 a 35 m b 0·5 m c 12 m
4 a 66 mm, 30 mm b 13 200 mm, 6000 mm
c 13·2 m, 6 m
5 a 40 mm, 20 mm
b i 4 mm, 2 mm ii 2 mm, 1 mm
6 a 37 mm b 1 : 100
c i 1600 mm ii 1500 mm
7 a 20 000 cm or 200 m b 380 m
c 1080 m or 1·08 km d about $160 000
e about 94 500 m^2 or 9·45 ha
8 a 4·5 cm b about 122 mm
c 1 : 122 d about 6800 mm or 6·8 m
e about 1220 mm

Exercise 11:05B

1 a 25 cm b 20 cm c 0·3 m
d 17 mm e 167 mm
2 a 16 cm b 32 mm c 14 mm
d 3·2 mm e 5·2 cm
3 a 1 cm b 2 cm c 8 cm
d 8 cm e 3·5 cm f 2 cm
4 a 1 : 100 b 1 : 200 c 1 : 1000 d 1 : 1000
e 1 : 40 f 1 : 4000
5 a 1 m long and 0·5 m wide (i.e. 1 m and 50 cm)
b 0·2 m long and 0·1 m wide (i.e. 20 cm and 10 cm)
c 8 cm long and 4 cm wide
d 4 cm long and 2 cm wide

6 a
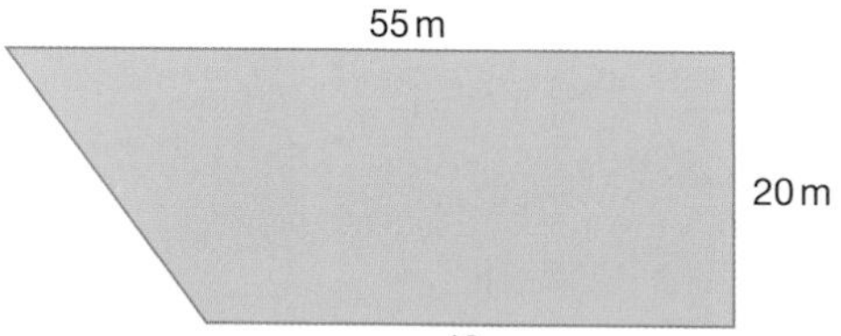

Scale 1 : 1000

b
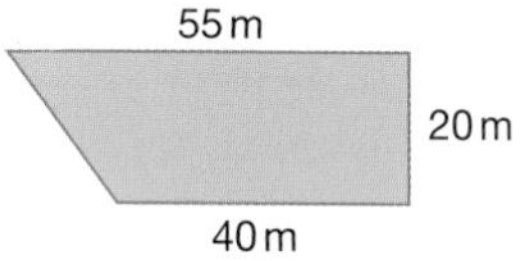

Scale 1 : 2000

c
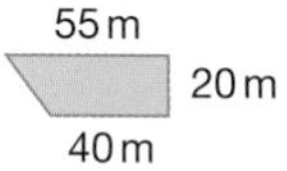

Scale 1 : 5000

7 a 1 : 500 b 1 : 400
c 1 : 1800 (Other answers are possible)

8
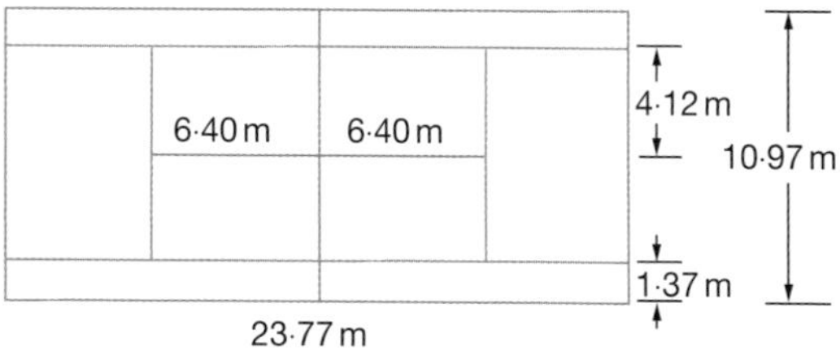

(Measurements are correct to two decimal places.)

9 Scale drawing will show a hand drawn within a 10 cm square.

10 a 215 mm long and 148 mm wide
b 3 m
c 40 cm by 21 cm (or 400 mm by 210 mm)
d 48 mm by 36 mm, sink top is 12 mm long

Diagnostic test 11

1 a no b no c yes d yes
2 a A and H, B and G, C and D
b Factor for H and A is 2 : 1. Factor for B and G is 3:2. Factor for D and C is 3 : 1.
3 a yes b yes c no
4 a 14·4 b 12 c 14·4
5 a yes b no c yes
6 a no b no c no
7 a yes b no c yes
8 a 21 b 25 c 8·8
9 a 110 mm long, 80 mm wide
b 55 mm long, 40 mm wide
c 220 mm long, 160 mm wide
10 a 1 : 4000 b 4 cm c 80 m d 1 : 3

ASSIGNMENT 11A

1 a E b D c F
2 a 18·9 cm by 10·2 cm b 33 cm
3 a $x = 9, y = 15$ b $a = 16, b = 20$
c $a = 32, y = 30$
4 a 23·4 m b $x = 35, y = 81$
5 a 28 cm by 15 cm
b 1 cm : 4 m or 1 : 400; width 3·75 cm

ASSIGNMENT 11B

1 23, 29, 31, 35, 37, 41, 43, 44, 46, 47, 49, 52, 53, 55, 56, 58, 59
2 70·9% (1 dec. pl.)
3 220 g
4 a 2 b 7 c 49 d 24
5 a The percentage change for Australia as a whole.
b i about 1% increase ii about 23% decrease
iii about 32% decrease
c The statistics show an average decrease across Australia in the number of road fatalities of approximately 16%. All states and territories had a reduction in the number of fatalities except WA.

ASSIGNMENT 11C

1 a $3x$ b $3x^5$ c $3x^{-5}$
d $\frac{x^{-5}}{3}$ or $\frac{1}{3}x^{-5}$
2 a 10^3 b 10^{-3} c 10^9 d 10^{-6}
3 a $\frac{9a}{20}$ b $\frac{a}{20}$ c $\frac{a^2}{20}$ d $\frac{5}{4} = 1\frac{1}{4}$
4 a 368·4 cm^2 b 255·3 cm^2
5 a \$1150 b \$54 080
6

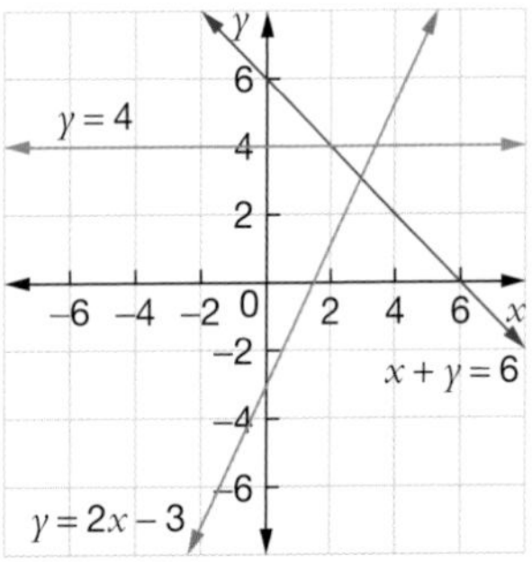

7 a

		Bag B	
		R	W
	R_1	R_1R	R_1W
Bag A	R_2	R_2R	R_2W
	W	WR	WW

b i $\frac{1}{3}$ ii $\frac{1}{6}$ iii $\frac{1}{2}$

Chapter 12

Prep quiz 12:01

1 $3x + 21$ 2 $a^2 - a$ 3 $8p^2 - 12pq$
4 $-15m + 10mn$ 5 $5x$ 6 $2x$
7 $4(n + 2)$ 8 $w(w - 6)$ 9 $b(a + c)$
10 $-3(2y + 3)$

Exercise 12:01

1 a $2(x + 4)$ b $5(2m + 1)$ c $3(3a + 2)$
d $2(2 + 3y)$ e $7(w - 3)$ f $5(3n - 4)$
g $6(2 - 3t)$ h $8(2 - z)$ i $x(x + 5)$
j $a(m + n)$ k $p(6 - p)$ l $a(b - 1)$
2 a $2a(x + 3y)$ b $5m(m + n)$ c $3b(3a + 2c)$
d $2y(2z + 3x)$ e $7t(w - 2t)$ f $5n(3 - 2n)$
g $4p(3 - 2q)$ h $2g(3f - 4h)$ i $xy(x + y)$
j $am(m + n)$ k $6p(1 - p)$ l $bc(a - 1)$
3 a $-2(x + 4)$ b $-5(m - 1)$ c $-3(3a - 4)$
d $-4(1 + 2y)$ e $-w(7w + 1)$ f $-n(m + p)$
g $-4t(3t - 2)$ h $-8y(2x - 3z)$
4 a $x(3 + x - a)$ b $a(x + y + z)$
c $2(2m - 4n + 3p)$ d $5a(b - 3c + 2d)$
e $x(x - 7 + y)$ f $5b(2a - c - 3b)$
5 a $(a + x)(2 + b)$ b $(3 + b)(x + 2)$
c $(a + 3)(a - 2)$ d $(m - 1)(3m + 5)$
e $(2x + 5)(x - 1)$
f $(7 - z)(7 - z)$ or $(7 - z)^2$

Prep quiz 12:02

1 $3(a + 6)$ 2 $x(5 + a)$ 3 $p(q - x)$
4 $3x(a - 3b)$ 5 $x(x - 2)$ 6 $a^2(a + 1)$
7 $3(3 - a)$ 8 $-5(m + 2)$ 9 $(a + 1)(9 + x)$
10 $(x + y)(x - 1)$

Exercise 12:02

1 a $(a + b)(2 + x)$ b $(x + 7)(a + p)$
c $(x - y)(m + n)$ d $(m + n)(x - y)$
e $(2 - x)(a^2 + 7)$ f $(q - 2)(q - 2)$
g $(x + y)(1 + a)$ h $(x - 2)(1 - 3y)$
2 a $(a + b)(p + q)$ b $(3 + x)(a + b)$
c $(m + 3p)(n + 5)$ d $(a + c)(a + b)$
e $(3x + y)(3x - 4)$ f $(3p - 4)(4p + q)$
g $(b + 3)(a + c)$ h $(x + 1)(y + 4)$
i $(a^2 + 1)(a + 1)$ j $(p + r)(q + 5)$
k $(y - 1)(x + 1)$ l $(2 + y)(4a - 1)$
m $(m + 1)(n + 1)$ n $(x + m)(x + y)$
o $(x + w)(x - y)$ p $(x + z)(x + y)$
q $(a + 4)(11 + c)$ r $(a - 1)(a^2 + 1)$
3 a $(y + z)(x - w)$ b $(a + c)(b - d)$
c $(a + 3)(5 - b)$ d $(x - 4)(6 - y)$
e $(y + 2)(11 - x)$ f $(ax - 1)(x - 1)$

Prep quiz 12:03

1 4   2 7   3 11
4 x 5 $3x$ 6 $8x$
7 $x^2 - 4$ 8 $x^2 - 25$ 9 $49 - a^2$
10 $9m^2 - 4n^2$

Exercise 12:03

1 a $(x-2)(x+2)$ b $(a+4)(a-4)$
c $(m+5)(m-5)$ d $(p-9)(p+9)$
e $(y-10)(y+10)$ f $(x-11)(x+11)$
g $(3-x)(3+x)$ h $(1-n)(1+n)$
i $(7-y)(7+y)$ j $(a-b)(a+b)$
k $(x-a)(x+a)$ l $(y+a)(y-a)$
m $(3a-2)(3a+2)$ n $(4x-1)(4x+1)$
o $(5p-3)(5p+3)$ p $(7-2a)(7+2a)$
q $(5p-a)(5p+a)$ r $(m-9n)(m+9n)$
s $(10a-3b)(10a+3b)$ t $(9x+11y)(9x-11y)$

2 a $2(x-4)(x+4)$ b $3(x-6)(x+6)$
c $4(a-5)(a+5)$ d $5(y-2)(y+2)$
e $6(2a-b)(2a+b)$ f $3(x-3y)(x+3y)$
g $8(y-4)(y+4)$ h $5(4p-q)(4p+q)$
i $4(x-4)(x+4)$ j $3(x-1)(x+1)$
k $2(6p-1)(6p+1)$ l $2(1-3x)(1+3x)$
m $2(2a-3m)(2a+3m)$ n $5(5-2a)(5+2a)$
o $2(10x-3y)(10x+3y)$ p $2(7m-2n)(7m+2n)$

Challenge 12:03

Volume (1)	Volume (2)	Volume (3)	Volume (4)
$b \times b \times b$	$(a-b) \times b \times b$	$(a-b) \times a \times b$	$a \times a \times (a-b)$

$\therefore a^3 = b^3 + (ab^2 - b^3) + (a^2b - ab^2) + (a^3 - a^2b)$
$a^3 - b^3 = (a-b)b^2 + (a-b)ab + (a-b)a^2$
$= (a-b)(a^2 + ab + b^2)$

1 $(m-n)(m^2+mn+n^2)$
2 $(x-y)(x^2+xy+y^2)$
3 $(a-2)(a^2+2a+4)$
4 $(m-3)(m^2+3m+9)$
5 $(x-10)(x^2+10x+100)$
6 $(y-5)(y^2+5y+25)$
7 $(4-n)(16+4n+n^2)$
8 $(3-k)(9+3k+k^2)$
9 $(2m-3)(4m^2+6m+9)$
10 $(4x-5y)(16x^2+20xy+25y^2)$
11 $(5x-2y)(25x^2+10xy+4y^2)$
12 $(3m-7n)(9m^2+21mn+49n^2)$

Prep quiz 12:04

1 x^2+5x+6 2 a^2+2a-3 3 $m^2-9m+14$
4 $x^2+10x+25$ 5 a^2-4a+4 6 3, 2
7 4, 5   8 −5, 3   9 4, −1
10 9, −2

Exercise 12:04

1 a $(x+3)(x+1)$ b $(x+2)(x+1)$
c $(x+5)(x+1)$ d $(x+6)(x+1)$
e $(x+5)(x+4)$ f $(x+5)(x+5)$
g $(x+6)(x+6)$ h $(x+7)(x+3)$
i $(x+6)(x+3)$ j $(x+10)(x+4)$
k $(x+6)(x+9)$ l $(x+9)(x+4)$
m $(x-2)(x-2)$ n $(x-6)(x-6)$
o $(x-4)(x-3)$ p $(x-5)(x-4)$
q $(x+3)(x-1)$ r $(x+4)(x-3)$
s $(x+6)(x-2)$ t $(x+10)(x-3)$
u $(x-2)(x+1)$ v $(x-12)(x+2)$
w $(x-10)(x+3)$ x $(x-8)(x+7)$

2 a $(a+4)(a+2)$ b $(m+6)(m+3)$
c $(y+6)(y+7)$ d $(p+3)(p+4)$
e $(x+2)(x+10)$ f $(n+14)(n+3)$
g $(s+18)(x+3)$ h $(a+4)(a+14)$
i $(x-4)(x+1)$ j $(a-4)(a+2)$
k $(p-8)(p+3)$ l $(y+3)(y-2)$
m $(x+8)(x-1)$ n $(q+8)(q-3)$
o $(m+15)(m-3)$ p $(a+21)(a-3)$
q $(y+11)(y-5)$ r $(x-1)(x-1)$
s $(k-3)(k-2)$ t $(x-9)(x-4)$
u $(a-18)(a-4)$ v $(p+6)(p+16)$
w $(q-15)(q+3)$ x $(m-11)(m+7)$

3 a $2(x+2)(x+1)$ b $3(x-3)(x+1)$
c $5(x-4)(x+2)$ d $2(x+4)(x+4)$
e $3(x-11)(x+1)$ f $3(x+3)(x+4)$
g $4(a-5)(a+2)$ h $2(n+3)(n+1)$
i $5(x-4)(x-2)$ j $3(x-3)(x-4)$
k $3(a-9)(a+4)$ l $5(x+10)(x-7)$

Fun spot 12:04

1 The next letter is 'E'. [Each letter is the first letter in the names of the numbers: One, Two, Three etc.]
2 The pilot was the man's daughter.
3 Ask either guard 'Which sack will the other guard tell me has the gold?' Then take the other sack. [Think about it!]

Exercise 12:05

1 a iii b iv c ii d iv

2 a $(2x+1)(x+3)$ b $(3x+2)(x+2)$
c $(2x+3)(x+2)$ d $(2x+1)(x+5)$
e $(3x+2)(x+1)$ f $(2x+5)(x+3)$
g $(x+3)(4x+1)$ h $(5x+2)(x+3)$
i $(2x+3)(x+5)$ j $(2x-1)(x-2)$
k $(3x-2)(x-3)$ l $(5x-2)(x-3)$
m $(x-2)(4x-3)$ n $(5x-3)(2x-3)$
o $(5x-7)(x-3)$ p $(2x+5)(x-2)$
q $(3x-5)(x+3)$ r $(x+3)(4x-1)$
s $(2x+3)(x-2)$ t $(2x+1)(x-3)$
u $(3x-10)(x+3)$ v $(2x+3)(3x-7)$
w $(2x+3)(x-4)$ x $(x+2)(4x-9)$

3 a $(3x+1)(4x+1)$ b $(3a+1)(2a+1)$
c $(3p+2)(2p+1)$ d $(5y-2)(2y-1)$
e $(3x-1)(4x-1)$ f $(3a-2)(3a-5)$
g $(2m+5)(4m-1)$ h $(2n-3)(3n+1)$

i $(7q-2)(3q-2)$ j $(4x-1)(5x+1)$
k $(2m-3)(4m+5)$ l $(6y-5)(3y+2)$
m $(2a+3)(3a-2)$ n $(3k+4)(5k+2)$
o $(2x+3)(4x+3)$ p $(4+a)(1-a)$
q $(2+5m)(1-2m)$ r $(3x+2)(3-x)$
s $(2-3x)(x+3)$ t $(5-7x)(4x+3)$
u $(2-5n)(1+7n)$ v $(3x+4y)(x+2y)$
w $(2x-y)(x-2y)$ x $(5m-7n)(m+n)$

4 a $2(3x-1)(x+2)$ b $2(3a+2)(a-1)$
c $3(2a-3)(a+3)$ d $4(2x-3)(x+3)$
e $2(3x+2)(x+4)$ f $3(2p-1)(2p+3)$
g $5(3q+7)(2q-1)$ h $2(5m-3)(m-4)$
i $5(5a-1)(2a+1)$ j $2(2-5x)(1+x)$
k $3(3-t)(t+4)$ l $3(3+2x)(1+2x)$

5 a $(x+3)(x+5)=x^2+8x+15$;
$(x-3)(x+5)=x^2+2x-15$;
$(x+3)(x-5)=x^2-2x-15$;
$(x-3)(x-5)=x^2-8x+15$;
$(x+1)(x+15)=x^2+16x+15$;
$(x-1)(x+15)=x^2+14x-15$;
$(x+1)(x-15)=x^2-14x-15$;
$(x-1)(x-15)=x^2-16x+15$

b $(x-1)(x+12)=x^2+11x-12$;
$(x-12)(x+1)=x^2-11x-12$;
$(x-3)(x+4)=x^2+x-12$;
$(x-4)(x+3)=x^2-x-12$;
$(x-6)(x+2)=x^2-4x-12$;
$(x-2)(x+6)=x^2+4x-12$

c $(x-1)(x-4)=x^2-5x+4$;
$(x+1)(x+4)=x^2+5x+4$;
$(x-2)(x-3)=x^2-5x+6$;
$(x+2)(x+3)=x^2+5x+6$

d $(5x+1)(x+2)=5x^2+11x+2$;
$(5x+1)(x-2)=5x^2-9x-2$;
$(5x-1)(x+2)=5x^2+9x-2$;
$(5x-1)(x-2)=5x^2-11x+2$

Exercise 12:06

1 a $(x-5)(x-1)$ b $(x-3)(x+3)$
c $(x+2)(y+9)$ d $a(a-9)$
e $(a-3)(a-3)$ f $(2x-1)(2x+1)$
g $(4x-7)(3x+5)$ h $(a-5)(a-8)$
i $5ab(a-2b^2)$ j $(p-q)(p+q)$
k $(p+10)(q-3)$ l $(7x-3)(x+2)$
m $a(a+3-b)$ n $(4-5a)(4+5a)$
o $(1+4a)(1-6a)$ p $(m+n)(4-a)$
q $5y(a-2+3x)$ r $(5x-7)(3x+4)$
s $(xy-1)(xy+1)$ t $(x-8)(x+7)$
u $(2m+3p)(n+2)$ v $(10a-7x)(10a+7x)$
w $(2+x)(1-3x)$ x $(k+8)(k-6)$

2 a $2(1-2x)(1+2x)$ b $5(x-y)(x-2)$
c $2(a-8)(a-3)$ d $3(m-3)(m-3)$
e $(x-1)(x+1)(x^2+1)$ f $(p-4)(p-1)(p+1)$
g $4(x-3)(x+3)$ h $a(a-1)(a+1)$
i $3(a-8)(a-5)$ j $9(1-p)(1+p)$
k $3(k+3)(k-2)$ l $3(2a-3)(4a-1)$

m $a(x+y)(x+3)$ n $(x+y)(x+y+3)$
o $5x(y-2z)(y+2z)$ p $a(3x-2)(2x+3)$
q $(x-y)(x+y+5)$ r $3(x-2)(x-2)$
s $7(3x-2y)(3x+2y)$ t $(a^2+4)(a-2)(a+2)$
u $a(a-4)$ v $(1+p)(1+p^2)$
w $4(2t+3)(t-5)$ x $2(2+x)(2-3x)$

Prep quiz 12:07

1 $\frac{a}{2}$ 2 $\frac{3y}{2x}$ 3 4
4 $\frac{3}{2}$ 5 $3x(2x+3)$ 6 $(x+3)(x+4)$
7 $(x-7)(x+7)$ 8 $3(x+1)^2$ 9 $(x+y)(3+a)$
10 $(2x-1)(x+5)$

Exercise 12:07

1 a $x+2$ b $\frac{2}{x+3}$ c $\frac{4}{x-3}$
d 2 e $\frac{1}{3}$ f $\frac{5}{8}$
g $\frac{1}{2}$ h $\frac{7}{3}$ i $\frac{x+1}{x-1}$
j $x+2$ k $\frac{1}{a-1}$ l $\frac{2y-3}{2}$
m $\frac{a-4}{3-a}$ n $x+1$ o $\frac{x+6}{3}$
p $a-4$ q $x-3$ r $\frac{x-2}{x+1}$
s $\frac{x+1}{x+3}$ t $\frac{m+8}{m-4}$ u $\frac{t+4}{t-3}$
v $\frac{a-x}{a+3}$ w $\frac{x-1}{2x-1}$ x $\frac{2(3a-2)}{2a-1}$

2 a $4x$ b $\frac{y-3}{4}$ c $\frac{10}{21}$
d $\frac{15}{2}$ e $\frac{1}{3}$ f $\frac{3(1+2a)}{5(1-2a)}$
g $\frac{y(2y+3)}{3(y+4)}$ h $\frac{2x+5}{9}$ i $\frac{1}{x+1}$
j $\frac{x-7}{x-5}$ k $\frac{a+3}{a-1}$ l 1
m $\frac{x+3}{x+7}$ n $\frac{m+1}{m+5}$ o $\frac{(a+2)(a-4)}{(a+4)(a-1)}$
p $\frac{x+4}{2}$ q 1 r $\frac{a}{2a-1}$
s 2 t $\frac{(a+b-c)(a-c)}{a+c}$

3 a 6 b $\frac{2}{7}$ c 5
d $\frac{9}{2}$ e $\frac{3}{5(x+1)}$ f 16
g $\frac{m}{2}$ h $\frac{5k}{k-1}$ i $\frac{n-3}{n+2}$
j $\frac{y}{y-7}$ k $\frac{a+1}{a-3}$ l 1

m $\frac{x+2}{x-3}$ n $\frac{p+4}{p-4}$ o $\frac{(n-7)(n-3)}{(n+3)(n+7)}$

p 2 q $3(x-1)$ r 1

s 2 t $\frac{(p+q+r)(p-q)}{p+q}$

Prep quiz 12:08

1 $1\frac{1}{10}$ 2 $1\frac{1}{8}$ 3 $\frac{3}{10}$ 4 $\frac{19}{60}$

5 $\frac{19}{2x}$ 6 $\frac{5}{2a}$ 7 $\frac{13}{6a}$ 8 $\frac{3}{4x}$

9 $\frac{5a}{2x}$ 10 $\frac{7m}{6n}$

Exercise 12:08

1 a $\frac{2x}{(x+1)(x-1)}$ b $\frac{2a+8}{(a+5)(a+3)}$

c $\frac{8}{(y-7)(y+1)}$ d $\frac{5x+19}{(x+3)(x+5)}$

e $\frac{2m-13}{(m+1)(m-2)}$ f $\frac{3t-18}{(t+10)(t+2)}$

g $\frac{7x-4}{(2x-1)(x-1)}$ h $\frac{-3x+31}{(3x+2)(2x+5)}$

i $\frac{59x+1}{(5x-1)(3x+1)}$ j $\frac{13x+21}{2x(x+7)}$

k $\frac{17x-25}{3x(2x+5)}$ l $\frac{1-4a}{2a(2a+1)}$

m $\frac{2x^2+4x}{(x+3)(x+1)}$ n $\frac{-3a}{(2a+1)(4a-1)}$

o $\frac{2x^2+6x+5}{(x+2)(x+1)}$

2 a $\frac{x+3}{(x+1)(x+2)}$ b $\frac{1+x}{x(x+2)}$

c $\frac{x-1}{x(x+3)}$ d $\frac{x+1}{(x-5)(x+2)}$

e $\frac{4x+15}{(x+2)(x+3)}$ f $\frac{5x+2}{(x+1)(x+4)}$

g $\frac{2}{(x+1)(x+3)}$ h $\frac{6x-10}{(x-3)(x+3)(x+1)}$

i $\frac{8x-2}{(x+7)(x-1)(x+1)}$ j $\frac{2x-72}{(x+9)(x+3)(x-1)}$

k $\frac{7x+5}{(2x+1)(x+5)(x+2)}$ l $\frac{-13x-12}{x(2x-1)(3x+2)}$

m $\frac{2x^2+2}{(x+3)(x+1)(x-1)}$ n $\frac{2x+7}{x(x+3)(x+2)}$

3 a $\frac{(1+x)}{x(x+1)}=\frac{1}{x}$ b $\frac{-2}{3(x+3)}$

c $\frac{7}{2(2x+3)}$ d $\frac{3x+8}{(x+1)(x-1)}$

e $\frac{x+5}{2(x-3)(x+3)}$ f $\frac{-1}{x(x+1)(x-1)}$

g $\frac{2x}{(x+1)^2(x-1)}$ h $\frac{2x+7}{(x+3)(x+4)^2}$

i $\frac{6x+22}{(x+2)(x+4)(x+3)}$ j $\frac{6x+14}{(x+3)(x+4)(x+1)}$

k $\frac{-x-1}{(x-2)(x+1)(x-3)}$ l $\frac{x-1}{(x-3)(x+2)(x+1)}$

m $\frac{2}{(x-4)(x-2)}$ n $\frac{x+10}{(2x-1)(x+4)(3x+2)}$

o $\frac{6x+34}{(x-7)(x+7)(x+3)}$ p $\frac{2x-3}{(2x-1)(x+1)(x-1)}$

q $\frac{2x^2-x-5}{(x+2)(x+3)(x-3)}$ r $\frac{-3x-8}{x(x-4)(x+4)}$

s $\frac{7x^2-x-10}{5(x-2)(x+2)^2}$ t $\frac{13x^2-11x+1}{(2x+1)(x-3)(2x-1)}$

Diagnostic test 12

1 a $3(x-4)$ b $a(x+y)$
c $-2(x+3)$ d $x(a+b-c)$

2 a $(a+b)(x+2)$ b $(6+a)(m+n)$
c $(x+1)(y-1)$ d $(a+c)(b+4)$

3 a $(x-5)(x+5)$ b $(a-x)(a+x)$
c $(2-m)(2+m)$ d $(3x-1)(3x+1)$

4 a $(x+3)(x+4)$ b $(x-2)(x-3)$
c $(x-5)(x+2)$ d $(x+5)(x-4)$

5 a $(2x+1)(x+5)$ b $(3x-2)(x-3)$
c $(4x-9)(x+2)$ d $(3x+1)(2x+1)$

6 a $x+2$ b $\frac{6}{7}$ c $\frac{x}{a}$ d $\frac{x+5}{x+2}$

7 a $6x$ b $\frac{a-1}{a-3}$ c $\frac{9}{5}$ d $\frac{x+2}{x-3}$

8 a $\frac{3x+1}{(x+3)(x-1)}$ b $\frac{1}{x(x+2)(x+1)}$

c $\frac{3x+19}{2(x-3)(x+3)}$ d $\frac{-7x-8}{(x+3)(x+4)(x-1)}$

ASSIGNMENT 12A

1 a $(a+4)(a+5)$ b $2(p-2q)$
c $(m-9)(m+5)$ d $(5x^2+1)(x+2)$
e $(2x-1)(2x+1)$ f $xy(x-1)$
g $(3a+1)(2a-5)$ h $(x+6)(x-5)$
i $(3a+5)(a-3)$ j $(x+p)(y+z)$
k $(2x-1)(x+1)$ l $(x^2+2)(x-3)$
m $-5ab(1+2ab)$ n $(x-y)(x+y+2)$
o $(2+3x)(1-3x)$

2 a $2(y-3)(y+3)$ b $3(r+7)(r-4)$
c $2(x+1)(2x^2+3)$ d $2(1-3x)(1+3x)$
e $a(a-8)(a+9)$ f $3(11+a)(1+a)$
g $(x-y)(x+y+1)$ h $x(x-4)$

3 a $\frac{x+12}{x+3}$ b $\frac{5(2x+1)}{x+3}$

c $\frac{5x+13}{(x+2)(x+3)}$ d $\frac{-x^2}{(x-1)(x-2)}$

e $\frac{x-1}{5}$ f $\frac{1}{x-2}$

g $\frac{-2x-3}{(x+2)(x+1)}$ h $\frac{6x-1}{(3x-1)^2}$

i $\frac{1}{3+2x}$ j $\frac{x+2}{5(x-7)}$

ASSIGNMENT 12B

1 a 4 b 6
2 It becomes a left-handed glove.
3 84 : 60 : 36 or 7 : 5 : 3
4 17
5 a 10%
b This would include those who were car passengers ($12\frac{1}{2}$%) as well as those who went by bus ($11\frac{1}{9}$%) and those who went by train (10%). Answer = $33\frac{11}{18}$%
c 23° d 62·5%
6 a Man b Woman c Heart diseases
d Depends on the number of men or women still living.

ASSIGNMENT 12C

1 a $a > 8{\cdot}5$ b $x < -4$ c $m \leq -20$
2 a $16 560 b $5382
3 a 5 b x-int. = 3; y-int. = 4·5 c −2
4 123·552 cm^3
5 $1025; 39%
6 a $1320.50 b $535.55
7 a $y = 3x + 4$ b $y = -2x + 5$ c $y = -2x + 1$
8 a $x = 6, y = -3$ b $x = -1, y = 10$

Chapter 13

Exercise 13:01

1 a BC b DE c KL d PR
e TU f YZ
2 a AB b EF c LM d PQ
e ST f XZ
3 a AC b DF c KM d QR
e SU f XY
4 a AC b AC c $\angle C$ d $\angle C$
5 a $\frac{5}{12}$ b $\frac{8}{6}$ c $\frac{15}{8}$
6 a $\frac{12}{13}$ b $\frac{6}{10}$ c $\frac{8}{17}$
7 a $\frac{9}{15} = \frac{3}{5}$ b $\frac{12}{15} = \frac{4}{5}$ c $\frac{12}{15} = \frac{4}{5}$ d $\frac{12}{9} = \frac{4}{3}$

Prep quiz 13:02

1 opposite 2 hypotenuse 3 adjacent 4 similar
5 change size 6 equal 7 12 cm
8 6 9 9 10 4

Exercise 13:02

1 a

	θ	$\frac{o}{h}$	$\frac{a}{h}$	$\frac{o}{a}$
1	30°	0·5	0·9	0·6
2	30°	0·5	0·9	0·6
3	30°	0·5	0·9	0·6

b The results for $\frac{o}{h}$, $\frac{a}{h}$ and $\frac{o}{a}$ are the same for each triangle.

2 a

	θ	$\frac{o}{h}$	$\frac{a}{h}$	$\frac{o}{a}$
1	50°	0·8	0·7	1·2
2	50°	0·8	0·7	1·2
3	50°	0·8	0·7	1·2

b The results for $\frac{o}{h}$, $\frac{a}{h}$ and $\frac{o}{a}$ are the same for each triangle.

3 a i $\frac{2{\cdot}8}{4{\cdot}9} \doteqdot 0{\cdot}6$ ii $\frac{4}{4{\cdot}9} \doteqdot 0{\cdot}8$ iii $\frac{2{\cdot}8}{4} = 0{\cdot}7$
b i $\frac{5{\cdot}6}{9{\cdot}8} \doteqdot 0{\cdot}6$ ii $\frac{8}{9{\cdot}8} \doteqdot 0{\cdot}8$ iii $\frac{5{\cdot}6}{8} = 0{\cdot}7$
c The results for $\frac{o}{h}$, $\frac{a}{h}$ and $\frac{o}{a}$ are the same for each triangle.
4 a 2 b $x = 6, y = 8$
c i $\frac{3}{5}$ ii $\frac{4}{5}$ iii $\frac{3}{4}$
d i $\frac{6}{10} = \frac{3}{5}$ ii $\frac{8}{10} = \frac{4}{5}$ iii $\frac{6}{8} = \frac{3}{4}$
e The values for each ratio are the same in both triangles.

Exercise 13:03

1 a $\sin\theta = \frac{3}{5}$ b $\sin\theta = \frac{5}{13}$ c $\sin\theta = \frac{24}{25}$
$\cos\theta = \frac{4}{5}$ $\cos\theta = \frac{12}{13}$ $\cos\theta = \frac{7}{25}$
$\tan\theta = \frac{3}{4}$ $\tan\theta = \frac{5}{12}$ $\tan\theta = \frac{24}{7}$
2 a unknown side = 15 b unknown side = 6·708
$\sin\theta = 0{\cdot}600$ $\sin\theta = 0{\cdot}447$
$\cos\theta = 0{\cdot}800$ $\cos\theta = 0{\cdot}894$
$\tan\theta = 0{\cdot}750$ $\tan\theta = 0{\cdot}500$
c unknown side = 2·828
$\sin\theta = 0{\cdot}707$
$\cos\theta = 0{\cdot}707$
$\tan\theta = 1{\cdot}000$
3 a $YZ = 6$, $\tan X = 0{\cdot}750$
b $YZ = 6$, $\tan X = 1{\cdot}2$
c $YZ = 3$, $\tan X = 1{\cdot}5$
4 a $\sin\theta = \frac{3}{5}$ $\cos(90 - \theta) = \frac{3}{5}$
b $\cos\theta = \frac{3}{\sqrt{34}}$ $\sin(90 - \theta) = \frac{3}{\sqrt{34}}$
c $\sin 60° = \frac{\sqrt{12}}{4}$ $\cos 30° = \frac{\sqrt{12}}{4}$
5 a $\sin\theta = \frac{b}{c}$ $\cos(90 - \theta) = \frac{b}{c}$
b $\cos\theta = \frac{a}{c}$ $\sin(90 - \theta) = \frac{a}{c}$

6 a $65°$ b $30°$ c $80°$

7 a i $\frac{3}{5}$ ii $\frac{4}{5}$ iii $\frac{3}{4}$ iv $\frac{3}{4}$

b yes

8 a missing side $= \sqrt{3}$, $\sin 30° = \frac{1}{2}$,

$\cos 30° = \dfrac{\sqrt{3}}{2}$, $\tan 30° = \dfrac{1}{\sqrt{3}}$

b $\sin 30°$, $\tan 30°$, $\cos 30°$

9 a $\cos A = \dfrac{\sqrt{15}}{4}$, $\tan A = \dfrac{1}{\sqrt{15}}$

b $\dfrac{\sqrt{7}}{4}$

10 a i $\dfrac{4}{\sqrt{80}}$ ii $\dfrac{4}{\sqrt{52}}$

b i $\dfrac{\sqrt{175}}{20}$ ii $\dfrac{\sqrt{7}}{4}$

11 a $\tan\theta = \dfrac{3}{4}$ and $\tan\theta = \dfrac{m}{5}$. Hence $\dfrac{m}{5} = \dfrac{3}{4}$ and $m = 3{\cdot}75$.

b $x = \sqrt{20}$, $y = \sqrt{80}$

c i $\frac{3}{5}$ ii $\frac{4}{5}$ iii $4{\cdot}8$

iv $1{\cdot}4$ v $\frac{4{\cdot}8}{5} = 0{\cdot}96$

vi $2 \times \sin\theta \times \cos\theta = 2 \times \frac{3}{5} \times \frac{4}{5}$

$= 0{\cdot}96$

$\sin 2\theta = 0{\cdot}96$ (from v)

$\therefore \sin 2\theta = 2 \times \sin\theta \times \cos\theta$

Exercise 13:04

1 a $16°30'$ b $38°15'$ c $73°54'$
d $305°45'$ e $40°14'$ f $100°40'$
g $12°01'$ h $238°51'$

2 a $17{\cdot}75°$ b $48{\cdot}267°$ c $125{\cdot}717°$
d $88{\cdot}617°$ e $320{\cdot}25°$ f $70{\cdot}9°$
g $241{\cdot}483°$ h $36{\cdot}883°$

3 a $0{\cdot}5000$ b $0{\cdot}8660$ c $0{\cdot}5774$
d $0{\cdot}9455$ e $0{\cdot}5299$ f $1{\cdot}9626$
g $0{\cdot}1219$ h $0{\cdot}0872$

4 a $15°$ b $69°$ c $38°$ d $77°$ e $72°$
f $26°$ g $50°$ h $39°$ i $72°$

5 a $0{\cdot}503$ b $0{\cdot}889$ c $0{\cdot}609$
d $0{\cdot}121$ e $1{\cdot}823$ f $5{\cdot}323$
g $0{\cdot}306$ h $3{\cdot}185$

6 a $36°52'$ b $25°28'$ c $40°10'$
d $78°28'$ e $88°13'$ f $58°34'$
g $52°26'$ h $32°00'$ i $69°28'$

7 a $36{\cdot}87°$ b $25{\cdot}47°$ c $40{\cdot}17°$
d $78{\cdot}46°$ e $88{\cdot}22°$ f $58{\cdot}56°$
g $52{\cdot}43°$ h $32{\cdot}01°$ i $69{\cdot}47°$

8 a $0{\cdot}577, 0{\cdot}5, 0{\cdot}866$ b $1{\cdot}600, 0{\cdot}848, 0{\cdot}530$
c $0{\cdot}537, 0{\cdot}473, 0{\cdot}881$

9 a $0{\cdot}866$ b $0{\cdot}883$ c $1{\cdot}079$

10 a 5 b $5{\cdot}392$ c No, it does not.
d $49{\cdot}5$ (correct to 1 dec. pl.)
e No. Substituting $A = 30°$ shows it is not correct.

Investigation 13:04

1 $BD = 1$, $\angle BAD = 30°$

2 $AD = \sqrt{3}$

3 $\sin 30° = \frac{1}{2}$, $\cos 30° = \dfrac{\sqrt{3}}{2}$, $\tan 30° = \dfrac{1}{\sqrt{3}}$,

$\sin 60° = \dfrac{\sqrt{3}}{2}$, $\cos 60° = \frac{1}{2}$, $\tan 60° = \sqrt{3}$

4 $\angle EDF = \angle EFD$ (base $\angle$s of isosceles Δ)

$\angle EDF + \angle EFD = 90°$ (complementary $\angle$s)

$2 \times \angle EFD = 90°$, $\angle EFD = 45°$

5 $\sqrt{2}$

6 $\sin 45° = \dfrac{1}{\sqrt{2}}$, $\cos 45° = \dfrac{1}{\sqrt{2}}$, $\tan 45° = 1$

Prep quiz 13:05

1 i 2 g 3 h 4 $\dfrac{g}{i}$

5 $\dfrac{h}{i}$ 6 $\dfrac{h}{g}$ 7 $0{\cdot}966$ 8 $0{\cdot}477$

9 $4 \times \tan 25°$ (or $1{\cdot}865$ correct to 3 dec. pl.)

10 $4 \div \tan 25°$ (or $8{\cdot}578$ correct to 3 dec. pl.)

Exercise 13:05

1 a $5{\cdot}9$ b $5{\cdot}1$ c $11{\cdot}1$ d $2{\cdot}5$
e $15{\cdot}9$ f $12{\cdot}1$ g $3{\cdot}8$ h $6{\cdot}2$
i $4{\cdot}6$ j $14{\cdot}4$ k $3{\cdot}8$ l $2{\cdot}1$

2 a $19{\cdot}4$ b $9{\cdot}3$ c $48{\cdot}5$ d $7{\cdot}2$
e $7{\cdot}8$ f $5{\cdot}3$ g $10{\cdot}2$ h $22{\cdot}7$
i $13{\cdot}3$ j $7{\cdot}1$ k $13{\cdot}2$ l $16{\cdot}0$

3 $\angle ACB \doteqdot 63°$, $AC = 7\sin 27° \doteqdot 3{\cdot}178$,
$AB = 7\cos 27° \doteqdot 6{\cdot}237$

4 $5{\cdot}12$ m 5 $5{\cdot}54$ m 6 $13{\cdot}02$ cm

7 1336 m 8 $4{\cdot}06$ m 9 $20{\cdot}57$ m

10 $6{\cdot}15$ cm 11 $2{\cdot}13$ m

12 a $5{\cdot}37$ m b $8{\cdot}45$ m c $4{\cdot}4$ cm d $16{\cdot}9$ cm

13 $15{\cdot}0$ cm 14 $8{\cdot}3$ cm 15 30 cm

16 $20{\cdot}3$ cm 17 $57{\cdot}2$ cm 18 $69{\cdot}3$ cm

19 $300{\cdot}0$ m 20 36 m 21 $5{\cdot}23$ m

22 $54\,m^2$

23 a 1666 m b 200 km/h

24 $15{\cdot}8\,cm^2$

25 a $a\dfrac{\sqrt{3}}{2}$ b $\dfrac{a^2\sqrt{3}}{4}$ c $\dfrac{3a^2\sqrt{3}}{2}$

d i $6\sqrt{3}\ cm^2$ ii $\dfrac{75\sqrt{3}}{2}\ cm^2$ iii $150\sqrt{3}\ cm^2$

Prep quiz 13:06

1 $\frac{5}{13}$ 2 $\frac{12}{13}$ 3 $\frac{15}{8}$ 4 $\frac{15}{17}$

5 $32°$ 6 $12°$ 7 $85°$ 8 $31°20'$

9 $69°29'$ 10 $43°41'$

Exercise 13:06

1 a $24°$ b $49°$ c $44°$ d $53°$ e $34°$
f $46°$ g $32°$ h $35°$ i $49°$

2 a 36°52′ b 45°35′ c 54°19′
d 36°34′ e 36°52′ f 54°17′
3 $\tan x° = \frac{3}{4}$, $\sin x° = \frac{3}{5}$, $\cos x° = \frac{4}{5}$; all give $x = 36°52′$
4 a 27° b 36°28′
5 a 77° b 62°
6 17° 7 7°8′ 8 38°0′
9 34°15′, 55°45′
10 a 33°41′ b 63°26′ c 45°
11 19°45′ 12 59°14′ 13 93°19′
14 a 58° (to the nearest degree)
b 74° (to the nearest degree)

Exercise 13:07

1 68·7 m 2 127 m 3 317 m
4 2·0 m 5 58° 6 3°20′
7 59°36′ 8 14·458 km 9 76 km, 129 km
10 6 km 11 58 km 12 S31°W
13 N16°W, 14·327 km 14 N27°30′E
15 S31°9′E 16 2·448 km
17 a 15·45 m b 16·47 m
18 7·7 cm 19 65° 20 69° and 111°
21 59°29′ 22 5·11 m 23 19°11′, 11·8 cm
24 a $5\sqrt{3}$ b $\sqrt{2}$ c $4\sqrt{3}$
25 a $\frac{100\sqrt{3}}{3}$ cm² b $\frac{20\sqrt{3}}{3}$ m c $9+4\sqrt{3}$ cm
26 68 m 27 74° 28 11 m
29 1558 m, 280 km/h 30 51°

Exercise 13:08

1 a i 3·6 cm ii 6·7 cm iii 7 cm
b i 33°41′ ii 16°36′ iii 31°0′
2 a 11·3 cm b 10·6 cm c 70°32′
d 61°52′ e 69°18′
3 3·4 cm
4 a i 19·3 cm ii 18·7 cm iii 22·8 cm
iv 23·3 cm
b i 34° ii 12°
5 a i 6·93 cm ii 7·55 cm iii 8 cm
iv 8·54 cm
b i 67° ii 54°
6 a 28·40 m b 9°30′
7 999 m 8 415 m
9 a 53°8′ b 57°0′
10 a i 1963 mm ii 3926 mm iii 5194 mm
b 22°

Diagnostic test 13

1 a 3·7321 b 0·3907 c 0·3697 d 1·1204
2 a 0·431 b 1·674 c −0·993 d −0·306
3 a 50°17′ b 47°49′ c 4°4′ d 73°53′
4 a *AB* b *PR* c *YZ*
5 a $\frac{5}{13}$ b $\frac{15}{8}$ c $\frac{3}{5}$
6 a 4·4 b 9·0 c 14·9 d 7·5
7 a 32·0 b 6·4 c 14·3 d 5·7
8 a 38°41′ b 58°2′ c 39°48′ d 50°12′

ASSIGNMENT 13A

1 a 13 b 1·8 c 32
2 a 61°33′ b 55°59′ c 56°9′
3 a 1500 m
b i 975 km ii 1689 km
4 a $h = \frac{a\sqrt{3}}{2}$; $A = \frac{a^2\sqrt{3}}{4}$ cm²
b 344 m
5 $AB = 1848$ mm; $AC = 5190$ mm

ASSIGNMENT 13B

1 a 6
b 168 (120 five-digit numbers and 48 four-digit numbers)
2 *AB* is the line $y = -\frac{2}{3}x + 4$
$C = (3\frac{3}{4}, 1\frac{1}{2})$
∴ Area of $\Delta OBC = 4\frac{1}{2}$ unit²
3 34
4 $\theta = 30°$; $a = 1212$ mm; $b = 2425$ mm
5 $a^2(2\sqrt{3}+6)$ unit²
6 Shop B's discount is equivalent to 7.7% (correct to 1 dec. pl.). Hence shop A offers the best discount.

ASSIGNMENT 13C

1 a $a(a-9)$ b $(a-3)(a+3)$ c $a(a-3)(a+3)$
2 a $\frac{19}{15a}$ b $\frac{17-x}{12}$ c 8
3 a (0, 5) b $(-2\frac{1}{2}, 0)$ c 2
d $-\frac{1}{2}$ e $y = -\frac{1}{2}x + 5$ or $x + 2y - 10 = 0$
f $y = 2x$ g $y = 2\frac{1}{2}$
4 a $x^2 - 2xy + y^2$ b $2a^2 - 9a + 9$
c $a^3 + 1$ d $a^2 + 4a + 4$
e $a^3 + 6a^2 + 12a + 8$
5 a $\frac{1}{a^3}$ b $\frac{2a}{b}$ c $\frac{1}{2a}$ d $\frac{b^3}{a^2}$ e $\frac{1}{2a}$
6 a $x \leq \frac{1}{3}$ b $a \leq -5$ c $x > \frac{6}{7}$
7 a $a = 2, b = -2$ b $x = 2, y = 2$
c $p = -22, q = -18$
8 a $P = \frac{100A}{RT}$ b $P = \pm\sqrt{\frac{V}{R}}$
c $P = \frac{RT^2}{3}$ d $P = \frac{Q}{XQ+1}$

Chapter 14

Exercise 14:01

1 a i 7 ii 5 iii 5 iv 5·714
b i 4 ii 5 iii 7 iv 6·75
c i 6 ii 24 iii 24 iv 22·6
d i 0·8 ii 1·5 iii 1·5 iv 1·5
2 a 6·05 b 64·25 c 7 d 2·71
e 50·24 f 14·78
3 a 181 b 394

4 a mode = 8; mean = 7·68; median = 8

Outcome	Frequency	fx
5	1	5
6	4	24
7	6	42
8	7	56
9	5	45
10	2	20
Total:	25	192

b 14; 11 c 5 d

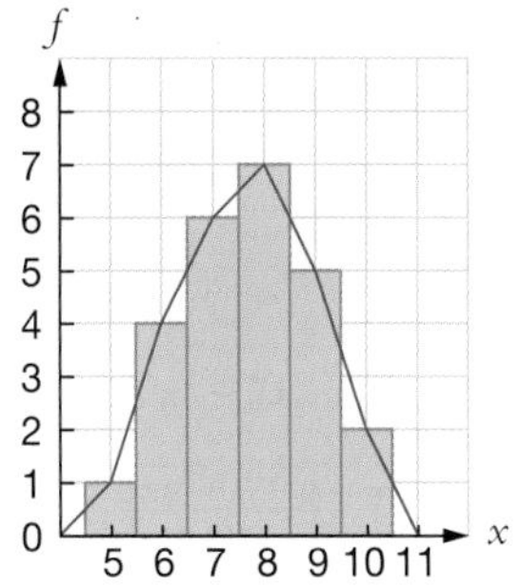

5 a Mazda b no c no

d a column graph or a sector graph

6 a

Children	Frequency	fx
0	4	0
1	6	6
2	9	18
3	5	15
4	3	12
5	0	0
6	1	6
Total:	28	57

b 28 c 57 d 2 e above

7 a i 14 ii 23 and 24

iii 23 iv 23·375

b i 51 ii 53, 63 and 76

iii 63·5 iv 65·29 (2 dec. pl.)

8 a

Class	c.c.	Freq	$f \times c.c.$
64–66	65	25	1625
67–69	68	74	5032
70–72	71	73	5183
73–75	74	24	1776
76–78	77	2	154
	Total:	198	13770

b 66 c 14 d 67–69 e 69·5

f median lies between 67–69 and 70–72

g

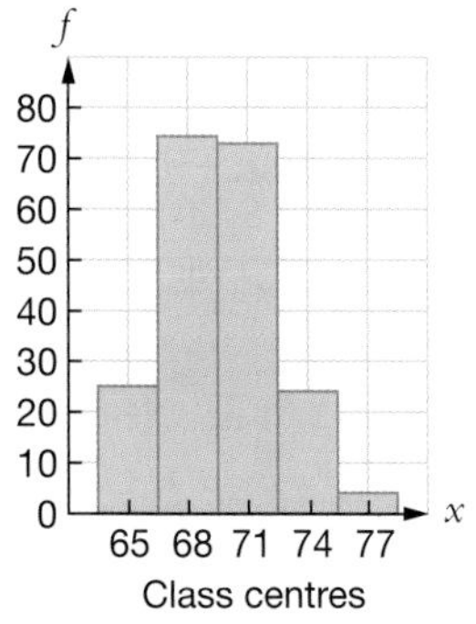

9 a

Number correct	Frequency (f)	fx
9	3	27
10	1	10
11	2	22
12	5	60
13	4	52
14	10	140
15	10	150
16	8	128
17	14	238
18	11	198
19	17	323
20	15	300
Total:	100	1648

b

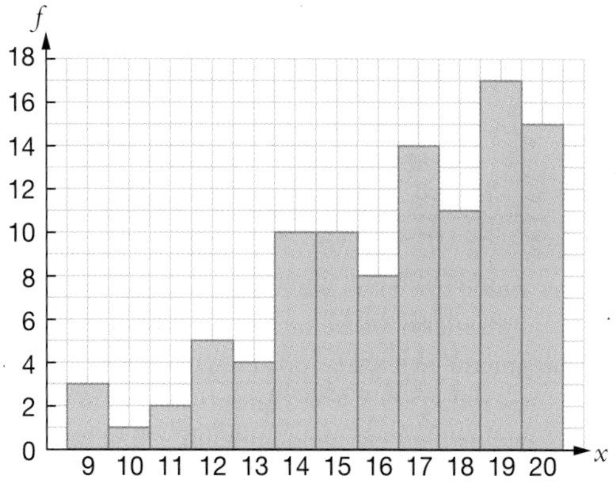

c 16·48 d above

e 2 is the best interval; 5 and 10 give too few classes.

f i

Class	Class centre	f
9–10	9·5	4
11–12	11·5	7
13–14	13·5	14
15–16	15·5	18
17–18	17·5	25
19–20	19·5	32
	Total:	100

ii

Class	Class centre	f
6–10	8	4
11–15	13	31
16–20	18	65
	Total:	100

iii

Class	Class centre	f
1–10	5·5	4
11–20	15·5	96
	Total:	100

Six classes are sufficient to show the characteristics (shape) of the data. As the number of classes is reduced to 3 and then 2, the characteristics (or shape) of the data are lost.

10 a i

Class	f
0–1	1
2–3	0
4–5	2
6–7	2
8–9	1
10–11	3
12–13	1
14–15	2
16–17	2
18–19	3
20–21	4
22–23	2
24–25	2
26–27	2
28–29	3
30–31	3
32–33	2
34–35	2
36–37	1
38–39	2

ii

Class	f
0–4	2
5–9	4
10–14	5
15–19	6
20–24	8
25–29	5
30–34	5
35–39	5

iii

Class	f
0–9	6
10–19	11
20–29	13
30–39	10

b i

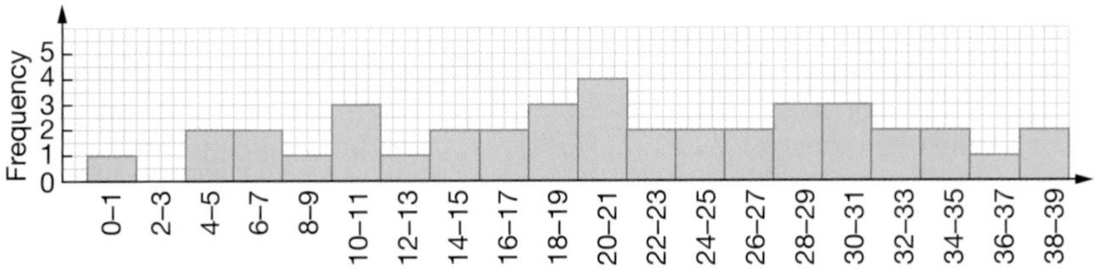

ii

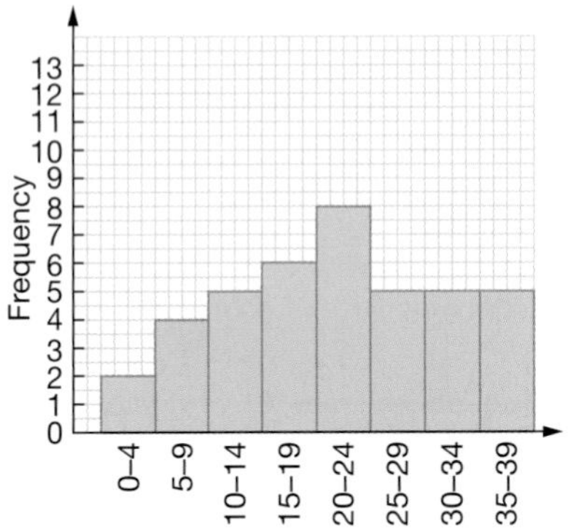

iii

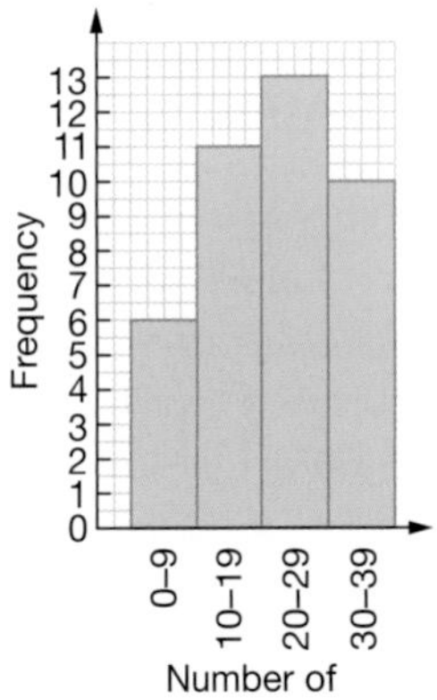

c Answers may vary, but here, a class interval of 5 gives a good view of trends without losing too much detail.

11 a

Leaf (Maths)	Stem	Leaf (English)
	3	9
9 6	4	5 6 8
9 7 5 1	5	1 2 3 9 9 9
8 6 3 2	6	0 1 1 3 6 8
7 7 5 2 0	7	1 2 5 9
7 4 1	8	
7 4	9	

b Maths

i 51 ii 69 iii 69·5

English

i 40 ii 59·5 iii 59·35

c No, actually 75 is a better mark for English than 77 is for Maths compared against the group results.

12 a

Stem	Leaf	Frequency	Class Centre	$f \times c.c.$
$6^{(5)}$	8 8 9 9 9	5	67	335
$7^{(0)}$	0 0 0 0 1 2 2 3 4	9	72	648
$7^{(5)}$	5 5 5 5 6 6 7 7 7 7 8 8	12	77	924
$8^{(0)}$	0 0 0 1 1 1 1 2 3 4 4	11	82	902
$8^{(5)}$	5 8	2	87	174
$9^{(0)}$	0 0 0 1 2 3 3 4	8	92	736
$9^{(5)}$	7 8 9	3	97	291
Total:		50		4010

b modal class is 75–79; mean = 80·2

c median = 78

d median class is 75–79; includes answer to part c

13 Answers will vary due to experimental data.

Exercise 14:02

1 a

Outcome (x)	f	*c.f.*
0	3	3
1	8	11
2	11	22
3	17	39
4	9	48
5	2	50
Total:	50	

b

Outcome (x)	f	*c.f.*
9	1	1
10	13	14
11	22	36
12	30	66
13	21	87
14	13	100
Total:	100	

c

x	f	*c.f.*
0	1	1
1	0	1
2	3	4
3	8	12
4	14	26
5	20	46
6	31	77
7	32	109
8	28	137
9	11	148
10	5	153
Total:	153	

d

x	f	*c.f.*
15	4	4
20	8	12
25	3	15
30	9	24
35	7	31
40	10	41
45	15	56
50	8	64
55	10	74
60	2	76
65	4	80
Total:	80	

2

Score	Frequency	fx	*c.f.*
5	2	10	2
6	3	18	5
7	5	35	10
8	4	32	14
9	4	36	18
10	2	20	20
	Total:	151	

a 7 b 7·55 c 7·5 d 5

3 a 1 b 2 c 7 d 12
e 5 f 20

4 a

Dad
Prog. Total
4
8
14
16
21

b i Adam ii Dad iii Sharon

c 6; 3 times d Dad

e

	Sharon		Adam		Dad		Bron	
	Score	Prog. Total	Score	Prog. Total	Score	Prog. Total	Score	Prog. Total
Round 6	6	28	6	27	7	28	5	24

5

Number (x)	f	fx	*c.f.*
2	3	6	3
3	5	15	8
4	9	36	17
5	12	60	29
6	14	84	43
7	17	119	60
8	15	120	75
9	11	99	86
10	8	80	94
11	4	44	98
12	2	24	100
Total:	100	687	

a mode = 7; mean = 6·87 b 7 c 43

6 a 5th hole

Player's score	Frequency	Cumulative frequency
3	54	54
4	314	368
5	85	453
6	3	456

7th hole

Player's score	Frequency	Cumulative frequency
3	20	20
4	211	231
5	198	429
6	23	452
7	4	456

b i 368 ii 88

c i 429 ii 27

d 5th hole 19%; 7th hole 6%. It indicates that the 5th hole is the more difficult of the two holes.

e

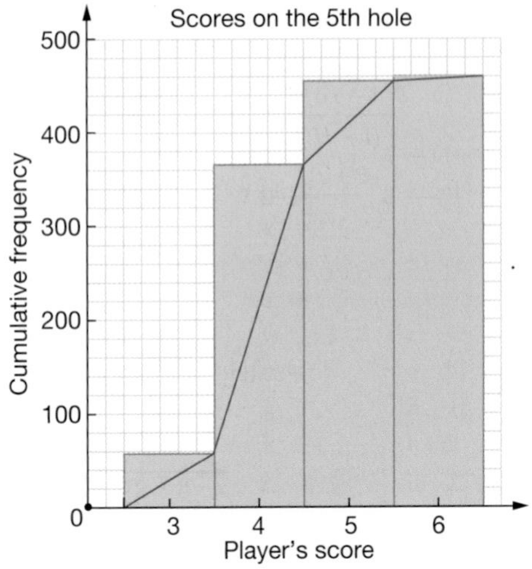

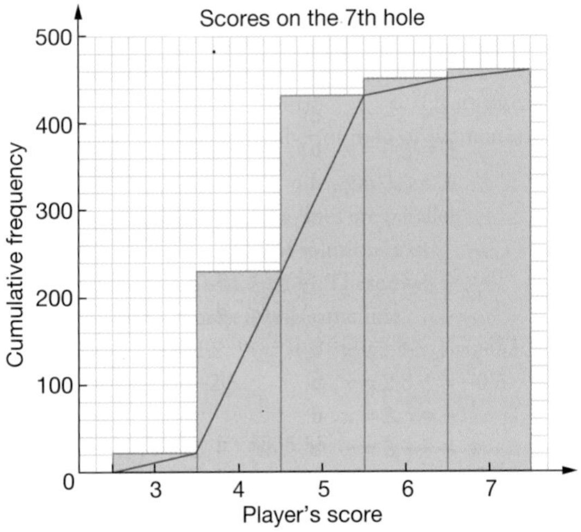

For an easy hole, there would be more golfers with lower scores and fewer with higher scores. The polygon would rise quickly and have a longer horizontal section shaped like '⌐'. For a difficult hole, there would be fewer lower scores and a large number of higher scores. The polygon would remain almost horizontal early and rise quickly for the larger number of higher scores. The polygon be shaped more like '_/'

7

Score	Frequency	Cumu. freq.
68	1	1
69	0	1
70	6	7
71	9	16
72	13	29
73	16	45
74	8	53
75	8	61
76	8	69
77	3	72
78	0	72
79	1	73

a 7 b 16 c 57

8 a 3 b 13 c 7 d 6 e 7 f 5

9 a

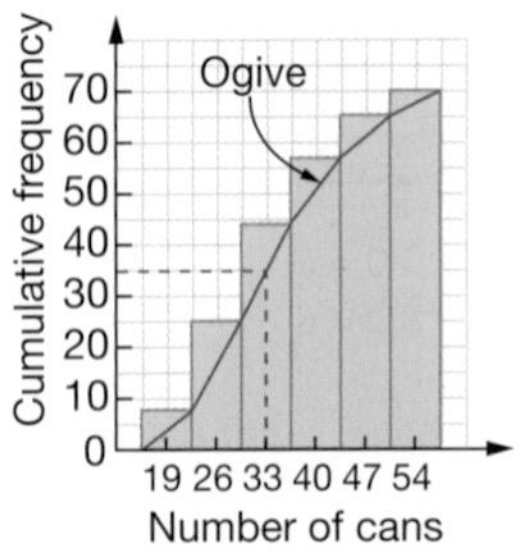

b 30–36

10 a 6–14, 15–23, 24–32, 33–41, 42–50

b

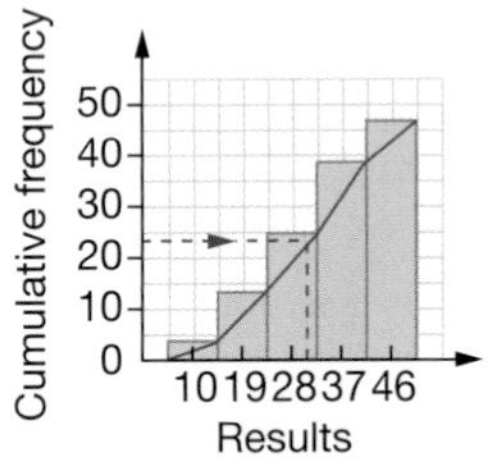

c The median class is 24–32.

11 a 15–19

b

c.c.	2	7	12	17	22	27	32
f	2	4	3	9	4	5	3

c 15–19 d 18

12 a 99 b 61–70 c 50·7 (1 dec. pl.)

d

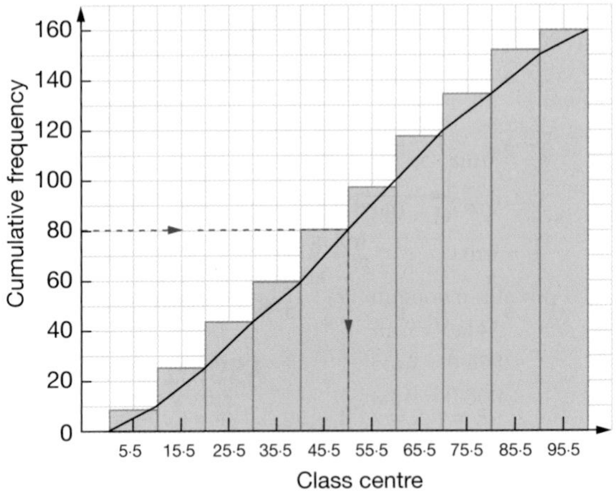

e The median involves two classes: 41–50 and 51–60.

f The median = 50·5

g i 16·25% ii 15% iii 50%

Prep quiz 14:03

1 0 2 1 3 7 4 Set C 5 yes
6 8 7 8 8 8 9 Sets A and D 10 Set C

Exercise 14:03

1 a 3 b 3·5 c 13·5 d 15·5 e 15
2 a 13 b 11 c 15 d 4
3 a 4·5 b 3 c 5·5 d 2·5

4

Score	Freq.	Cumulative freq.
2	1	1
3	3	4
4	6	10
5	10	20
6	10	30
7	4	34
8	4	38
9	2	40

IQR = 2 (using either method)

5 a

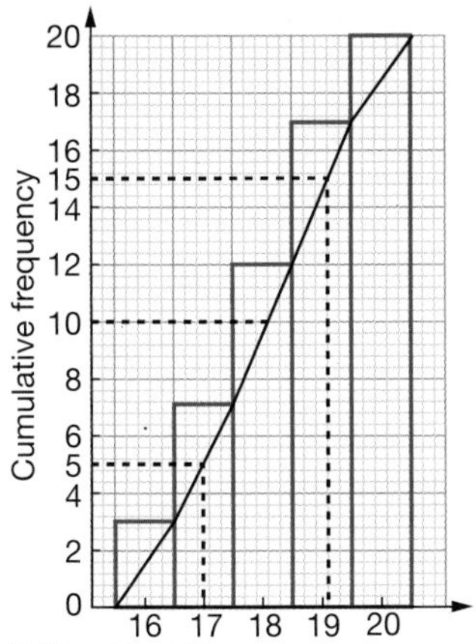

IQR = 19 − 17
= 2

b

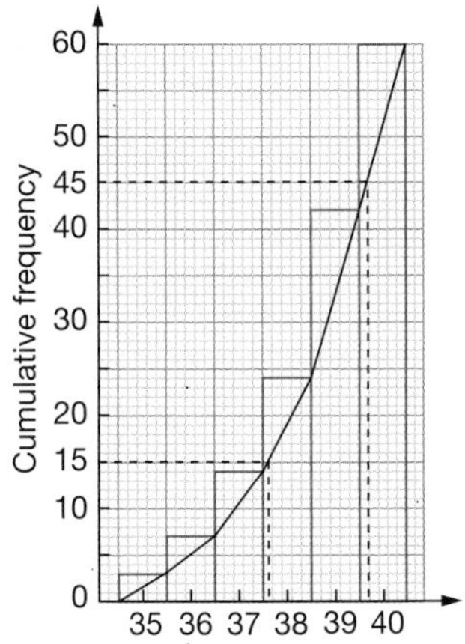

IQR = 40 − 38
= 2

6 a 20 b 4 c 8·5

7 a 4 b 5

8 a 65 b 75 c 10

9 a $Q_1 = 21{\cdot}5$, $Q_2 = 23$, $Q_3 = 25{\cdot}5$, IQR = 4

b $Q_1 = 54{\cdot}5$, $Q_2 = 63{\cdot}5$, $Q_3 = 77$, IQR = 22·5

Exercise 14:04

1	a	i 57	ii 32	iii 12
	b	i 51	ii 20	iii 6
	c	i 52	ii 25	iii 10

2 a (7, 8, 9, 11, 12)

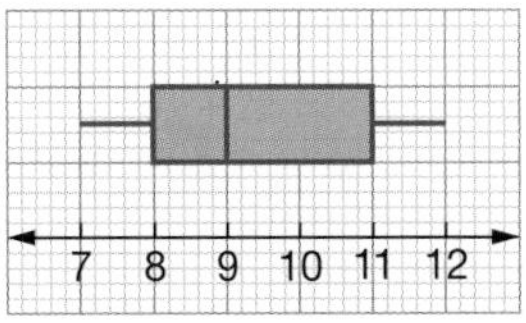

b (16, 25·5, 28, 33·5, 38)

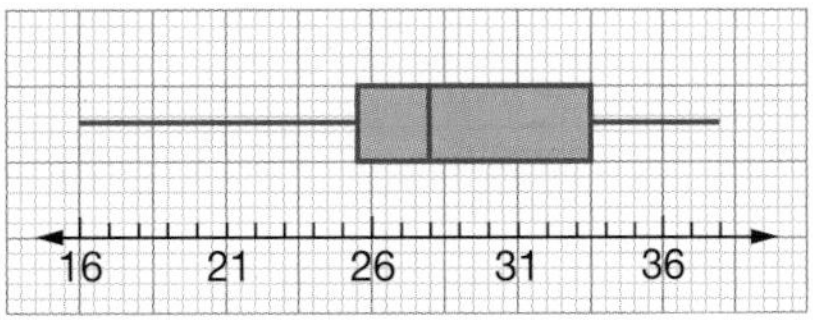

c (14, 32·5, 43, 46, 49)

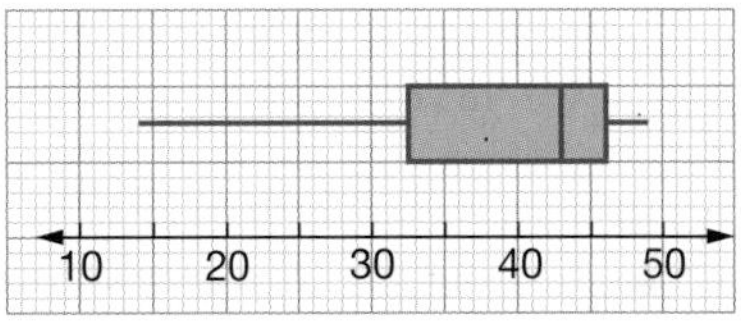

3 a (37, 39·5, 42·5, 44·5, 48)

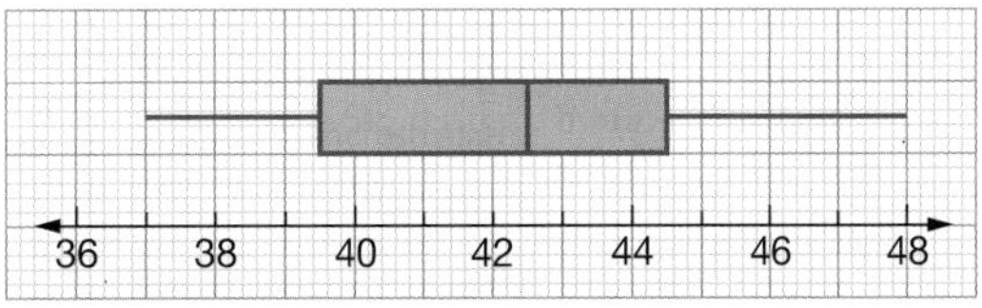

b (59, 71, 76·5, 83, 87)

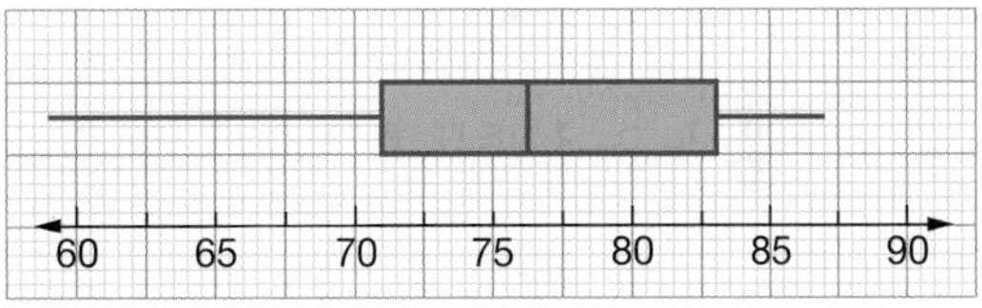

4 a i 25% ii 50%

b i 50% ii 75%

c i 3 ii 4

d Year 10

5 a (17, 20, 20·5, 22, 24)

b

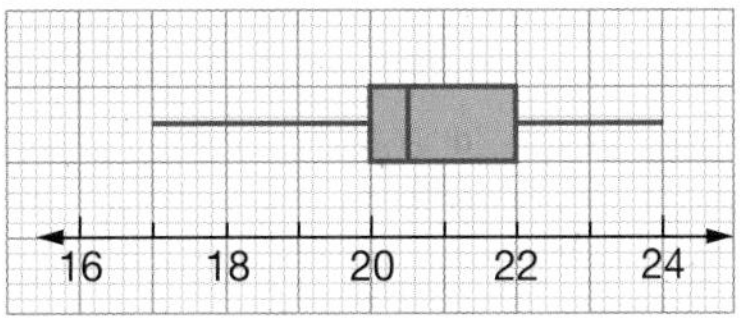

6 a (26, 38·5, 50·5, 68, 82)

b

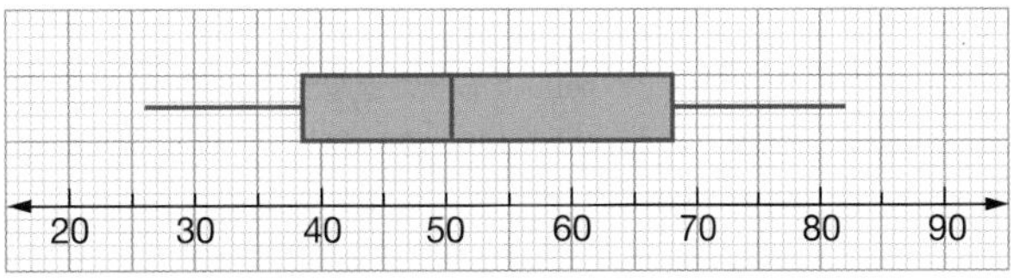

7 a (74, 76, 78, 84, 85) b Ken c Ray

d As the range can be easily affected by an outlier, it is not a good measure of consistency. Ray's lower interquartile range would suggest he is the most consistent player.

8

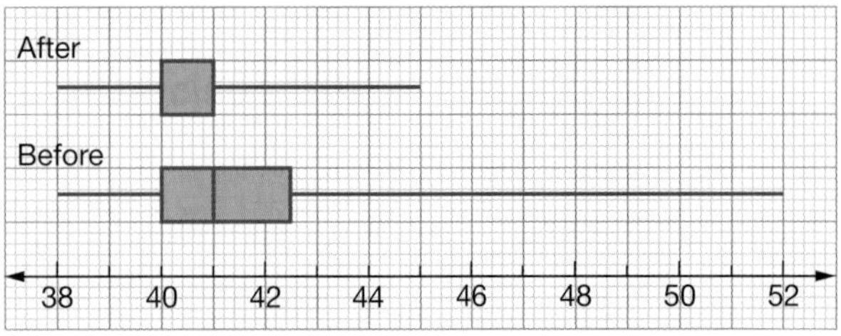

The traffic changes have resulted in more consistent trip times, as indicated by the reduced interquartile range. In fact, 75% of the trip times were less than 41 minutes compared to 50% before the changes. This would suggest that the traffic changes had been effective in reducing the variability in the trip times.

Exercise 14:05

1 a B and D. The skew is caused because of the unevenness of the number of students in each age group. School B has a small senior school, whereas school D has a smaller junior school.

b A

c i A ii B iii C or D iv C

2 a class 1

b i class 2 ii class 2

c class 1: mean = 88·7, range = 16;
class 2: mean = 91·1, range = 19

3 a i negatively skewed
ii positively skewed

b Girls borrow more books than boys.

c Grouped frequency histograms allow a scale to be used to represent large frequencies. If a back-to-back stem-and-leaf plot were used, you would need a large number of leaves in the girls 30–39 column and the boys 1–9 column. This would make the stem-and-leaf plot very wide.

d The distribution would be more uniform. The lowness of the 41–50 column compared to the other columns would make the distribution slightly positively skewed.

4 a Topic 1

b Topic 1 has the smallest spread of scores. It has a lower interquartile range (24·5) than that of Topic 2 (30).

c Topic 1: mean = 61, median = 60
Topic 2: mean = 72, median = 78
The results suggest that the class performed much better on Topic 2. This could be because the class was better prepared or perhaps because the test was easier.

5 a weak swimmer b excellent swimmer

c $43\frac{1}{3}\%$ d 80%

e The program was very successful.

6 a

Test 1	
Score	Frequency
1	5
2	5
3	6
4	5
5	2

Test 2	
Score	Frequency
0	4
1	1
2	10
3	4
4	4

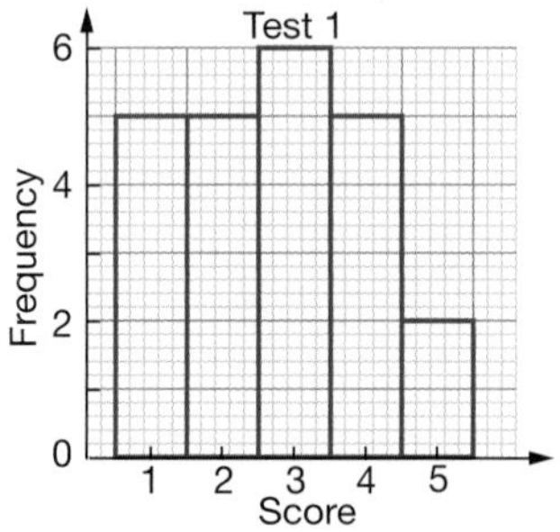

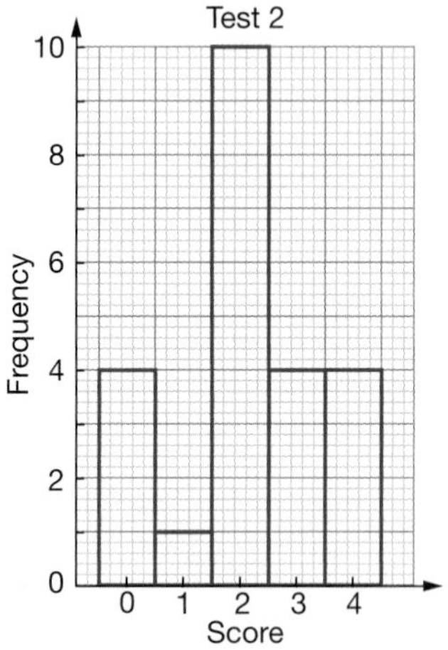

b Test 1 Test 2
Mean = 2·7 Mean = 2·1
Median = 3 Median = 2
Both the mean and median for Test 2 are lower than that of Test 1. This suggests that Test 2 was more difficult than Test 1.

c The interquartile range for Test 1 is 2, whereas for Test 2 it is 1. This would suggest that the scores for Test 1 have a greater spread than those of Test 2.

7 a This shows that the median is 160 cm, the middle half of the scores lie in the range 153 to 168 cm and the 30 heights lie in the range 135 cm to 178 cm.

b Yes. The median class is 160–164 and this contains the median score of the box-and-whiskers graph and it is possible for the middle half of the scores to be in the range 153 cm to 168 cm and the range to be 135 cm to 178 cm.

8 Both brands have the same median, but brand X has a larger interquartile range, a lower minimum and a lower maximum. This would suggest that brand Y will be the best performer.

9 a The data for group 1 is positively skewed, whereas that for group 2 is close to normally distributed. The mean for group 1 would be in the 120s, whereas group 2 is in the 140s. The shape suggests that group 1 is fitter than group 2.

b Group 1: median = 129, IQR = 135 − 127 = 8
Group 2: median = 146, IQR = 154 − 137 = 17
Group 1 has a lower median and its scores are not as spread. Hence group 1 is overall a fitter group than group 2.

10 a The data could be organised into a grouped frequency distribution table using classes of 35–39, 40–44, 45–49 etc. This would give 7 classes. Using class intervals of 30–39, 40–49 etc. would result in only four classes and would not show the differences between the two sets of data. Stem-and-leaf plots would probably not be appropriate because of the number of leaves needed on the 4 stem (40–49) or the $4^{(0)}$ stem (40–44). Either stem-and-leaf plot would probably be too wide. The best way to display the data is a double-column graph with one column for 'before' and another column for 'after'.

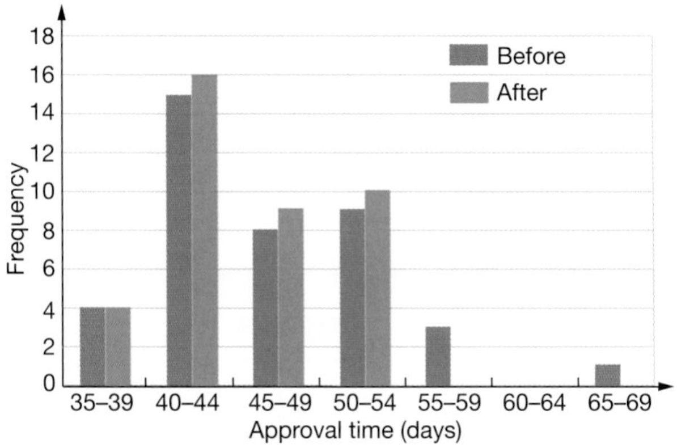

b Either the mean or median could be used as measures of cluster, whereas the interquartile range is probably the best measure of spread to use even though the spread of both sets of data is similar.

c Council's new procedures have reduced the average time taken to approve applications. The median time has been reduced from 45 days to 44 days. The 'after' application times also have a smaller spread than the 'before' times, indicating that the scores are closer to the mean. This would indicate that the new procedures have resulted in more consistent approval times.

Investigation 14:05

1 a 3·8% b 3·3% c 1·2%
2 a 3·3% b 3·5% c 1·4%

3 On the whole, the male population has aged over this period with a decrease in the younger age group and an increase in the older age groups. The same trend is noted in the female population.

4 a i 6·9% ii 9·1%
b 21 101 000

5 The population in 2007 was greater than the population in 1987.

Diagnostic test 14

1 a

Outcome (x)	f	$c.f.$
0	4	4
1	5	9
2	8	17
3	8	25
4	3	28
5	2	30
	30	

b 2 c 25

d

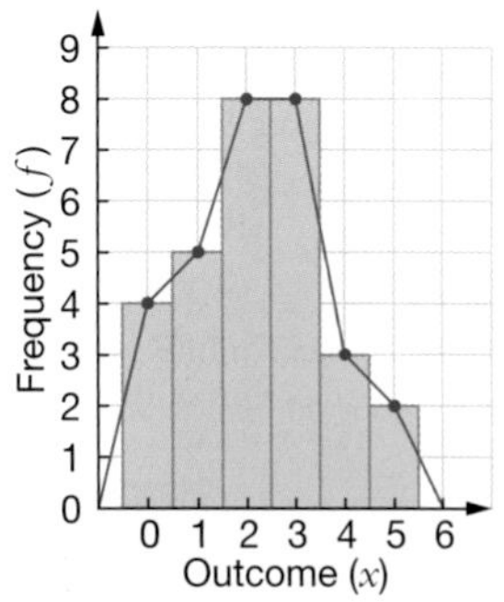

e

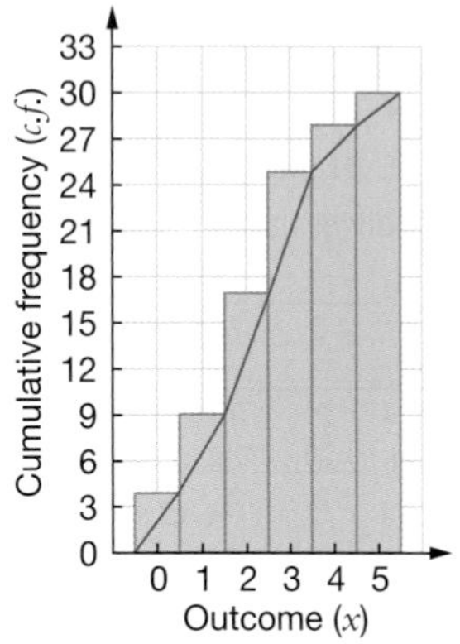

f Range is 5

g Modes are 2 and 3 (bi-modal), median is 2, mean is 2·23 (2 dec. pl.)

2 a 28·23 b 4·36 (2 dec. pl.)

3 **a**

Class	Class centre	Freq.	*c.f.*
0–9	4·5	3	3
10–19	14·5	5	8
20–29	24·5	6	14
30–39	34·5	8	22
40–49	44·5	9	31
50–59	54·5	6	37
60–69	64·5	3	40

b Stem and leaf plot or Ordered stem and leaf plot

Stem	Leaf
0	0 9 4
1	8 7 6 4 1
2	7 6 0 8 5 2
3	1 8 8 7 7 8 3 8
4	5 9 1 3 3 4 3 0 8
5	0 8 2 1 6 3
6	3 9 2

Stem	Leaf
0	0 4 9
1	1 4 6 7 8
2	0 2 5 6 7 8
3	1 3 7 7 8 8 8 8
4	0 1 3 3 3 4 5 8 9
5	0 1 2 3 6 8
6	2 3 9

4 **a** 7 **b** 13 **c** 2

5 **a** 5 **b** 7 **c** 14

6 **a** 7·5

b

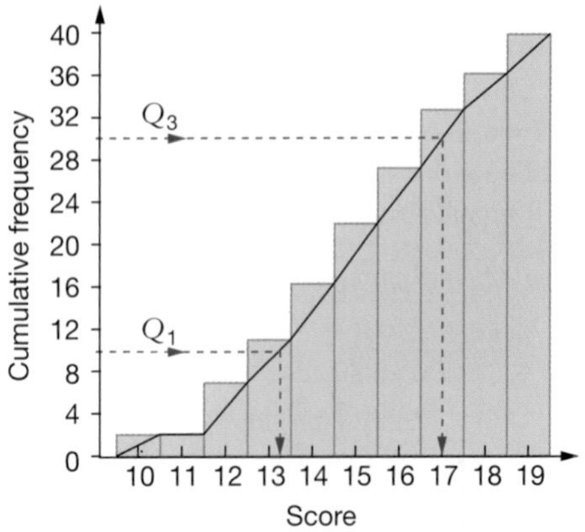

Interquartile range = $Q_3 - Q_1 = 17 - 13 = 4$

c 2·5 **d** 12

7 **a** (1, 3·5, 9·5, 11, 11) **b** (10, 13, 15, 17, 19)

c (20, 28·5, 29·5, 31, 33) **d** (38, 41·5, 46·5, 53·5, 60)

8 **a**

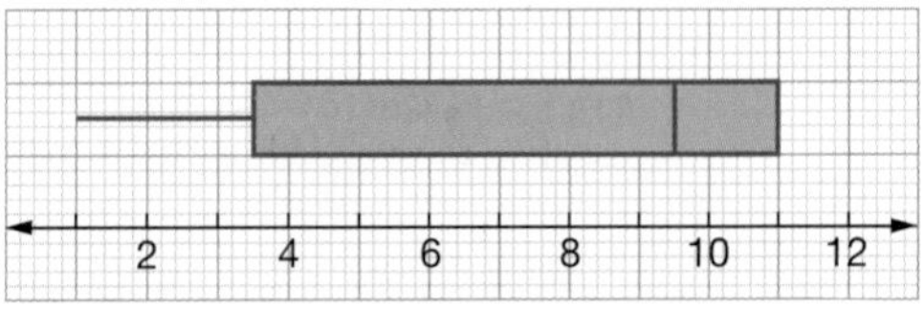

b

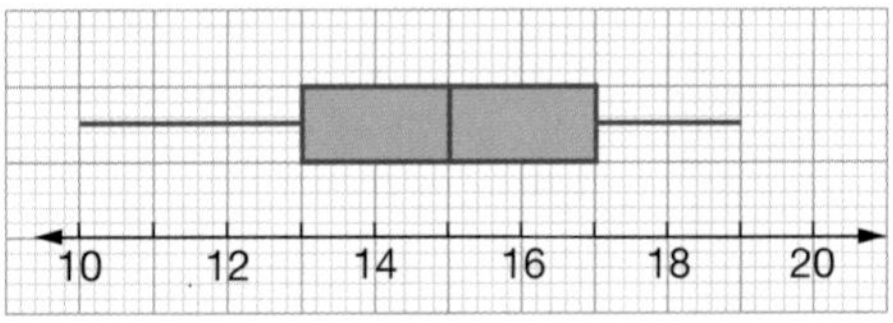

c

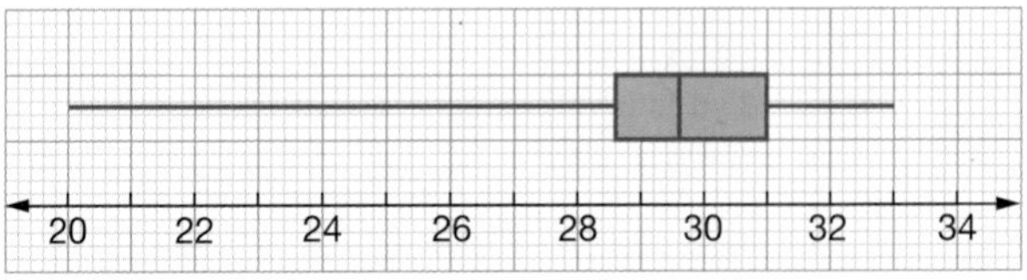

9 **a** 25 **b** range = 60, interquartile range = 22

10 **a**

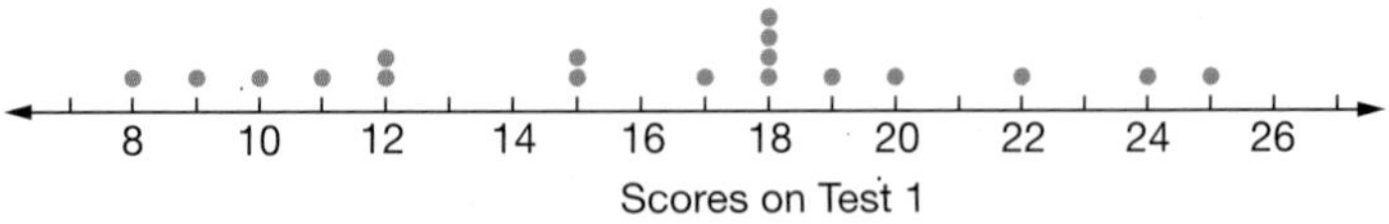

b

Scores		
Test 1 Leaf	Stem	Test 2 Leaf
9 8	0	7 9
9 8 8 8 8 7 5 5 2 2 1 0	1	0 1 2 2 2 2 3 4 5 6 8 9
5 4 2 0	2	0 0 1 3

c

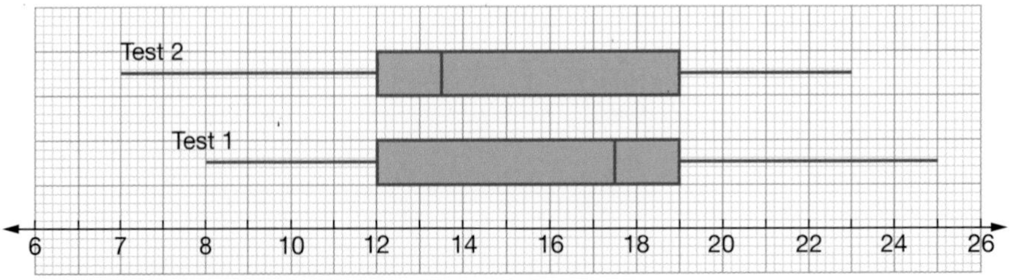

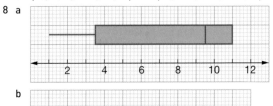

ASSIGNMENT 14A

1 a Yes, 64 is an outlier.

b i 64, 71·5, 73, 76, 81 ii 70, 72, 73, 76 81

c i 4·5 ii 4

d It is positively skewed.

2 a 4 b 43 c 8 d 40 e 72

f 24

g

Class	c.c.	f
30–39	34·5	3
40–49	44·5	5
50–59	54·5	4
60–69	64·5	7
70–79	74·5	8
80–89	84·5	7
90–99	94·5	6

3 Year 4 have clearly performed better. The mean and median are both 66·5 compared to the mean and median for Year 3, which are 49·8 and 48 respectively. Both sets of results have a similar spread, especially if the score of 35 in the Year 4 results is ignored, as it is an outlier. The Year 3 results are positively skewed, whereas the Year 4 results are reasonably symmetric. All of the Year 4 results, with the exception of the outlier, are above the Year 3 mean and median.

4 a i 9 ii 8 iii $9 - 6·5 = 2·5$

iv 1, 6·5, 8, 9, 10

b

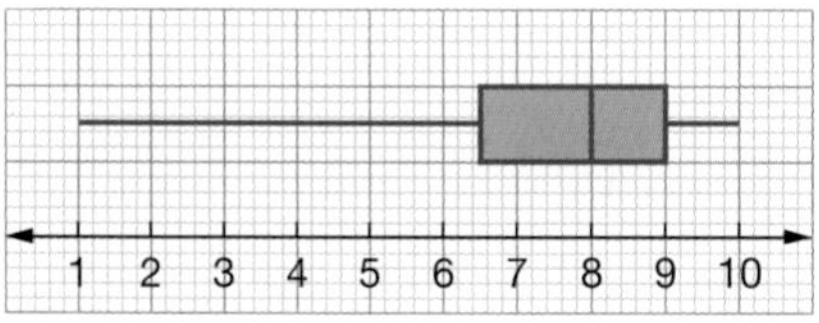

5 a

Class	Class centre (c.c.)	f	c.f.	f × c.c.
10–19	14·5	2	2	29
20–29	24·5	9	11	220·5
30–39	34·5	10	21	345
40–49	44·5	8	29	356
50–59	54·5	16	45	872
60–69	64·5	20	65	1290
70–79	74·5	13	78	968·5
80–89	84·5	14	92	1183
90–99	94·5	7	99	661·5

i Modal class 60–69 ii Mean 59·9 (1 dec. pl.)

b

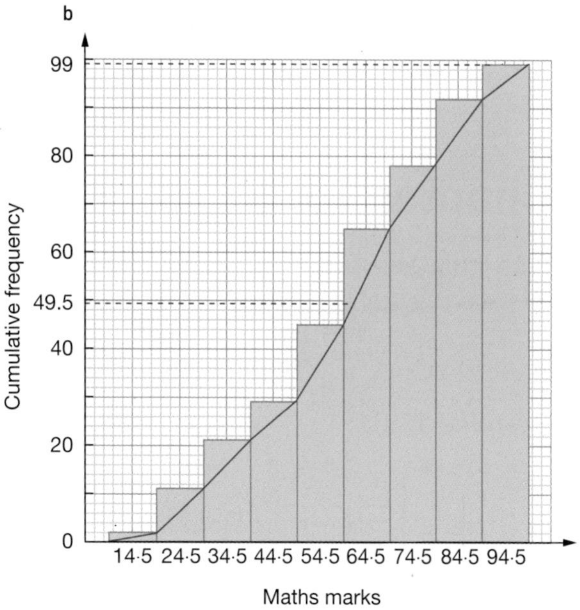

Median class: 60–69

ASSIGNMENT 14B

1 Peter is 52

2 Area = 33·5 cm^2 (1 dec.pl.),
Perimeter = 31·6 cm (1 dec.pl.)

3 40 4 120 minutes

5 The median and mode would not be useful as these are the same as the par of the hole in each case. Calculating the mean for each hole and the percentage of players who scored par or better gives a better indication of the degree of difficulty.

Hole	Par	Mean score	% of players scoring par or better
2	4	4·1	79%
7	5	4·5	94%
11	3	3·3	65%
16	3	3·2	75%

Both the mean and % of players scoring par or better indicate that the degree of difficulty of the hole is 1: Hole 11; 2: Hole 16; 3: Hole 2; 4: Hole 7

6 a E b C c A d D

ASSIGNMENT 14C

1 a 34·6 cm b 32°, 58°, 90°

2 a 160% b 75%

3 a gradient = 2, y-intercept = −3; $y = 2x - 3$

b $y = -\frac{1}{3}x + 4$, (12, 0) c $\left(1\frac{3}{4}, \frac{1}{2}\right)$

4 a $(x + 5)(x - 2)$ b $(a - 8)(a + 7)$

c $(2y - 3)(2y + 3)$ d $(x - 3)(x + a)$

e $(5n - 2)(3n + 1)$

5 a $\dfrac{x+1}{x-2}$ b $x - 3$ c $\dfrac{x+12}{(x-2)(x+2)(x+4)}$

6 a 40% b 41%
c Bag B gives the better chance
7 a $67 998 b $13 949.40 c $1019.97
d Amount owing = $45.37

Chapter 15

Prep quiz 15:01

1 $32 2 $48 3 $80 4 $8
5 1000 g 6 1000 kg 7 60 min 8 10 mm
9 10 000 cm^2 10 1500 mL

Exercise 15:01

1 a 3 km/h b 2 kg/$
c 50c/kg d 1 mL/cm^3
e 40 L/h f $20/h
g $45/day h 7 km/L
i 4 degrees/min j 70 g/cm
k 25 t/block l 120 km/h
m 11 runs/wicket n 3 children/mother
o 7·5 g/cm^3
2 a 15 km b $49 c 16
d $101.40 e 225 f 2010 kJ
g $16 h 7·5 kg i 18 000 000 km
j $800
3 a 60 b 25 000 c 40
d 500 e 180 f 7000
g 6500 h 7·2 i 2
j 490 k 300 000 l 8·5
4 a 1000 b 20 c 40 d 20 e 5
f 40 g 16·$\dot{6}$ h 7 i 50 j 0·5
5 a 6 b 90 c 30 d 5·4 e 0·108
f 38 g 19·2 h 5000 i 20 j 5000
6 27·28 km/h 7 37·6 km/h 8 16·1 km/h
9 3 seconds

Prep quiz 15:02

1 1200 2 7 3 6 4 20
5 200 6 $2.40 7 $6.80 8 $6.40
9 115 10 78 min, 10 s

Exercise 15:02

1 a $A = km$ b 2·5 c 25 d 20
2 a $Y = kx$ b 0·8 c 8 d 65
3 a $H = kd$ b 7·5 c 52·5 cm d 10
4 a $a = kp$ b 8·75 c 7 d 132
5 a $P = 1{\cdot}75m$ b 3·15 c 11·8
6 a $Y = 0{\cdot}5x^2$ b 40·5 c 4
7 a $V = 9{\cdot}8t$ b 29·4 m/s c 1·02 s
8 a 125 m^2 b 14
9 a $5.25 b 12 min, 11 s
10 33·6
11 a $F = \frac{7}{15}cy$ b 4·5 c 42
d 21 e 63
12 a $D = knh$ b $k = \frac{5}{12}$ c 15 m
d 15 m e 22·5 m f 12
13 a 800 b 4 c 40
14 3·2 cm
15 a $D = 4{\cdot}9t^2$ b 78·4 m
16 a $V = 4{\cdot}189r^3$ b 113·103 cm^3 c 10 cm
17 a $T = 2{\cdot}012\sqrt{L}$ b 1·9 s
c 25 cm or 0·25 m

Prep quiz 15:03

1 3 2 1 3 $\frac{1}{2}$ 4 $\frac{5}{3}$ 5 0·25
6 35 7 0·42 8 3·5 9 9 10 2·5

Exercise 15:03

1 a $7 b $k = 7$ c $350 d 14
2 a 120 km b 24 km/h c $k = 24$
d 168 km e 8 h, 20 min
3 a 65
b
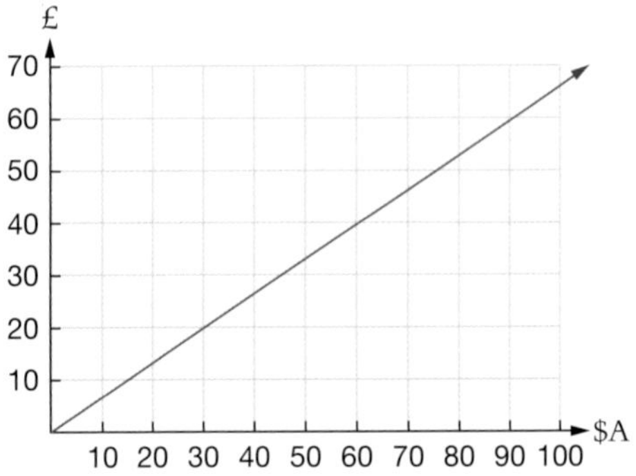

c 0·65 d £325 e $769.23
4 a $90
b
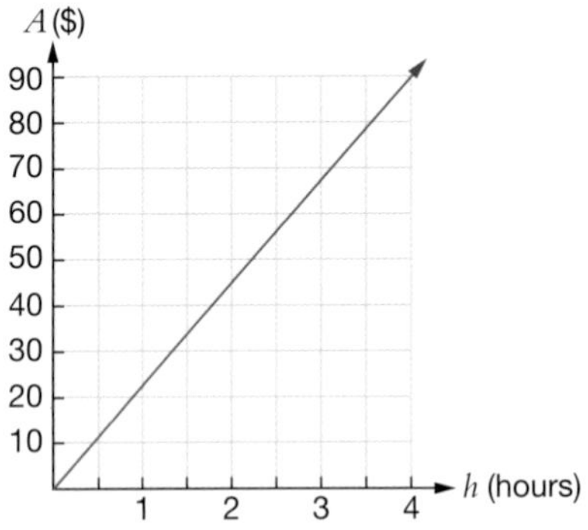

c $A = 22{\cdot}5h$ d 9
5 a $k = 20$

b

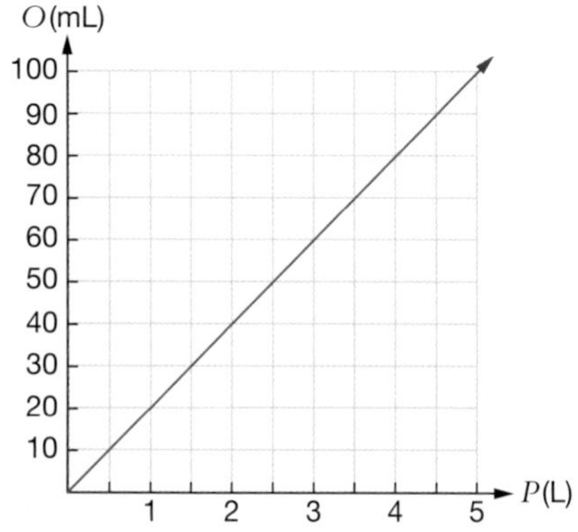

c 1 L   d $K = 50$

e

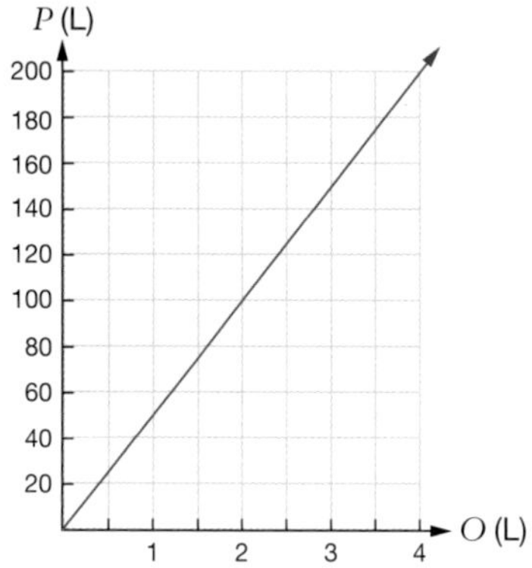

6 a for A, $k = 40$; for B, $k = 50$

b 40 km   c 5 hours   d 60 km/h

Investigation 15:03

1

Time for 4 men	Time for 1 man	Time for 6 men
12 hours	48 hours	8 hours

2

Time for 3 women	Time for 1 woman	Time for 4 women
4 hours	12 hours	3 hours

3

Time for 3 dogs	Time for 1 dog	Time for 9 dogs
6 days	18 days	2 days

4

Time for 3 men	Time for 1 man	Time for 5 men
4 hours	12 hours	2 hours, 24 min

5 a the time increases   b the time decreases

Exercise 15:04

1 a 12 h   b 2 h

2 a 100 min   b 25 min

3 6 days

4 a 5 days

b 53 (answer to the next 'whole' fruit picker)

5 a 1 m/s   b 1·25 m/s   c $3\frac{1}{3}$ minutes

6 a $N = \frac{300}{P}$ b $N = 30$ c $P = 3$

7 a $X = \frac{200}{Y}$ b $Y = 40$ c $X = 40$

8 a $T = \frac{640}{A}$ b 21 min, 20 seconds

c 64 cm^2

9 a $R = \frac{14\,880}{L}$ b 186 times per second

c 31 cm

10 427 units

11 a $X = \frac{6400}{Y^2}$ b 256   c 40

12 a $M = \frac{2\,867\,200\,000}{D^2}$

b 65·82 kg ($D = 6600$ km)

13 5 days

14 4 boys

15 This is a trick question! The Radetsky March would be the same length. The number of musicians and the length of the musical piece are not proportionally related.

Investigation 15:04

1

x	1	2	3	4	6	12
y	12	6	4	3	2	1

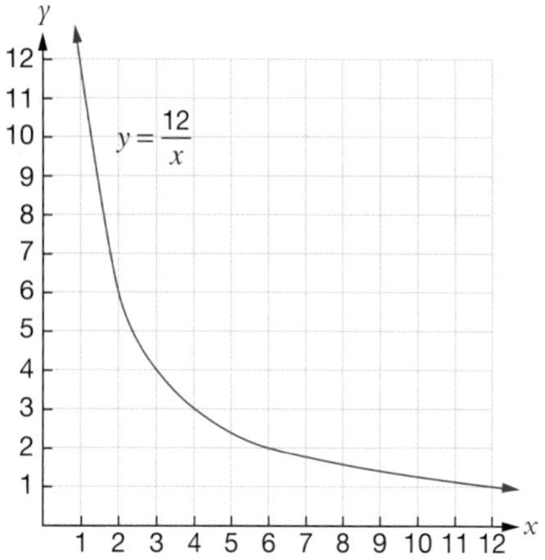

2 a

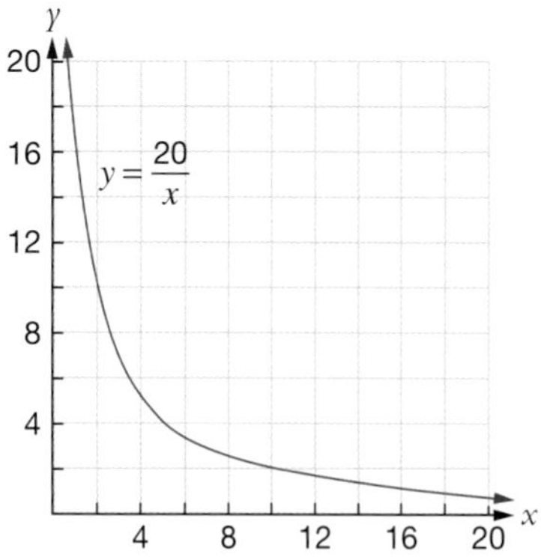

b

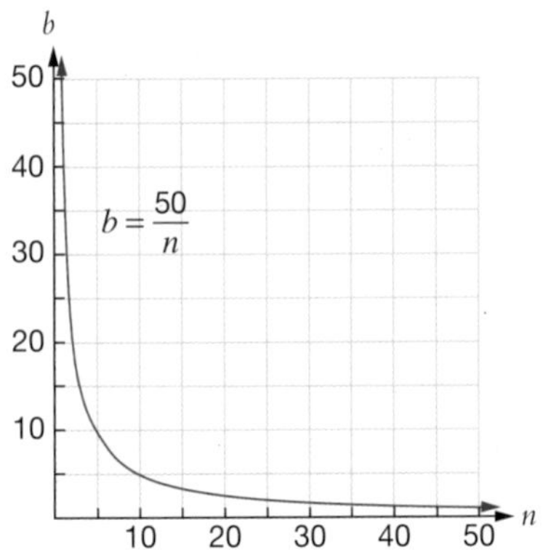

c

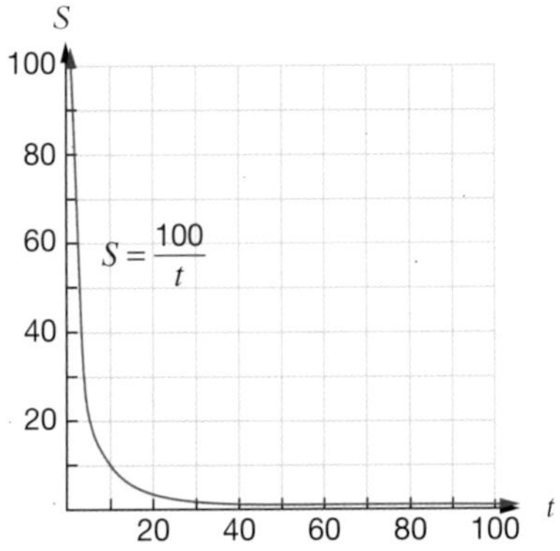

3 a $y = \frac{16}{x}$ b $P = \frac{40}{t}$

Prep quiz 15:05A

1 200 km 2 450 km 3 25 km
4 4 h 5 10 h 6 70 km/h
7 500 km/h 8 A 9 B
10 B

Exercise 15:05A

1 a 30 km b 1:30 pm c 50 km
d 20 km e Yes at 11 am
2 a 5 km b 11:30 am c 60 km
d 11–11:30 am e 5 km/h
3 a 20 km b 20 km c 1 pm
d Increases. The slope of the line becomes steeper.
e 40 km
4 a 5 km b 20 km c 35 km
d increases e 4–5 pm
5 a Bartley b Twice c 1 pm d 150 km
e Bartley travels 200 km, Conway travels 350 km.
6 a Jackson b 75 km/h c increase
d 10–11 am e 125 km
7 a 11:30 am b 35 km

c

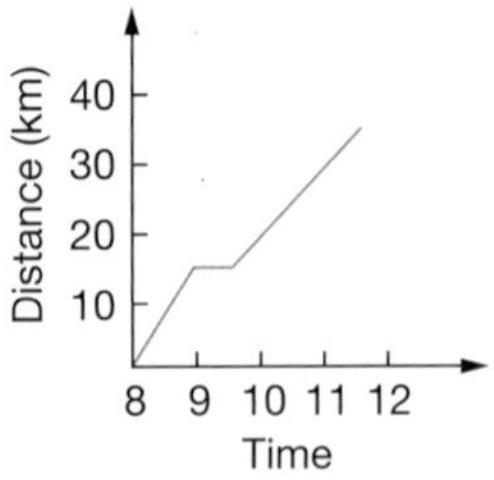

8 a 5:45 pm b 510 km c noon d 4:30 pm

e

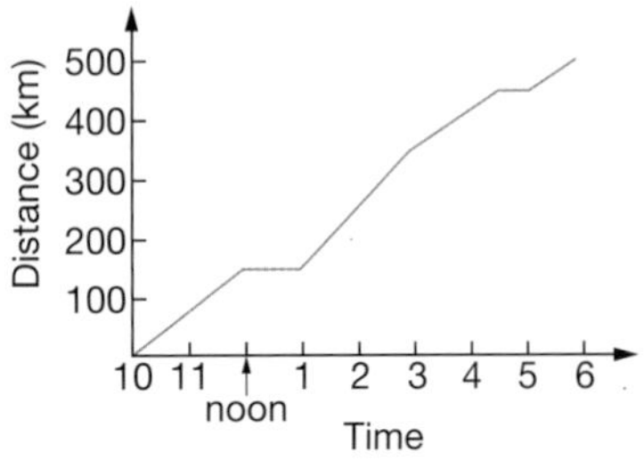

Exercise 15:05B

1 a 15 km/h b 20 km/h
c 10 km/h d 40 km/h
2 a 50 km/h
b faster at point *P* than *Q*
c faster at point *R* than *Q*
d 100 km/h e 50 km/h
3 a 40 km/h b Benny (blue)
c Robyn (purple) d 1:30 pm and 2:15 pm
4 a approximately 67 km/h
b i *A* is less ii *B* is greater
c *F* d *B* and *C*
5 a 30 m/s b 20 m/s c 40 m/s
d decreasing e increasing
6 a i 15·6 m ii 9·1 m
b increases at a decreasing rate
c i 2·4 m/min ii 1·5 m/min

Prep quiz 15:06

1 A 2 B 3 C 4 I 5 II
6 I 7 II 8 Y 9 Z 10 X

Exercise 15:06

1 a E b D c A d C
e F f B
2 C 3 B
4 The tank is empty at the start. It is then filled at a steady rate until the water level is 3 m. This takes 20 mins.
The water level remains at 3 m for 20 mins. The tank is then emptied at a steady rate in 10 mins.
The tank remains empty for 10 mins. This cycle is then repeated.
5 a Jill is resting, then does some exercise requiring a steady application after which she rests, and her pulse rate returns to normal.

b A balloon is blown up by mouth; it remains blown up for a short time until it bursts.

c A car is travelling at a steady rate and then stops. It is stationary for a while with the engine running, after which it starts moving again but fuel is being used at a faster rate—maybe it is going up hill. It then begins to travel at a more economical rate—maybe it is travelling on a flatter surface.

d Sam eats four pieces of pizza before being sick!

6 B

7 I

8 a B b A c C d D

9 a C b D c B d A

10 a III b I c IV

11

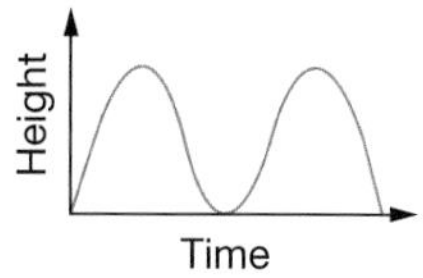

12

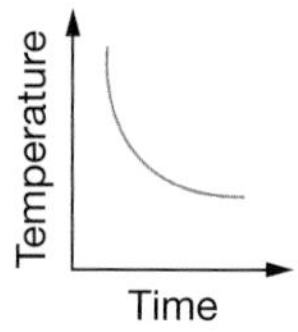

13

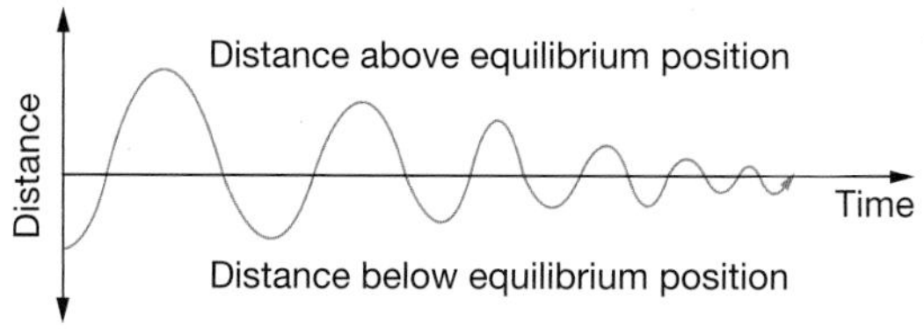

14 a

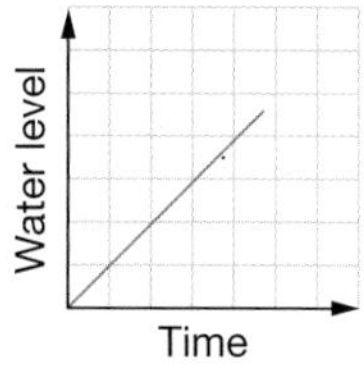

b

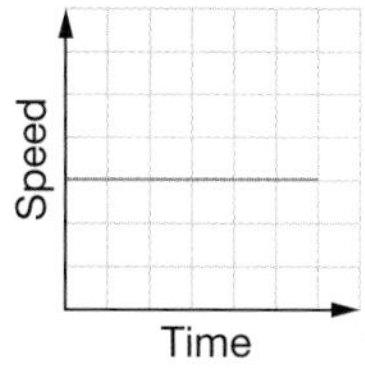

c

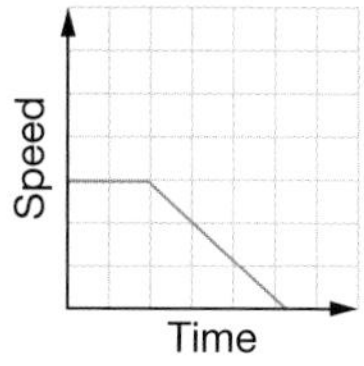

d

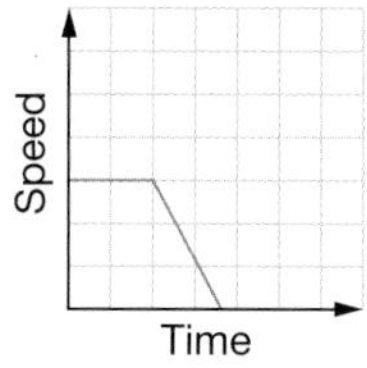

e

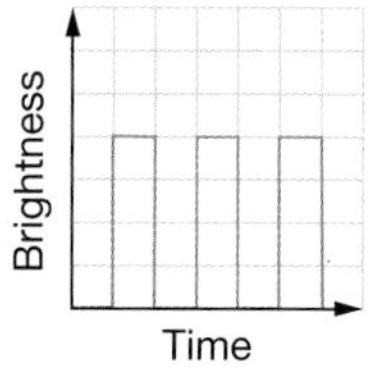

f

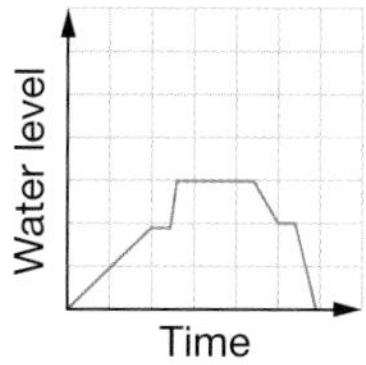

g

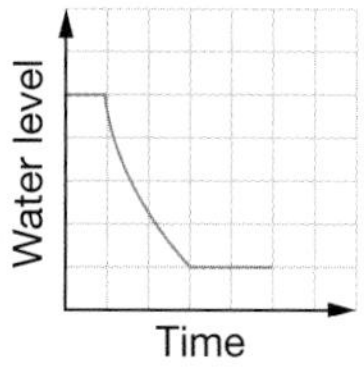

h

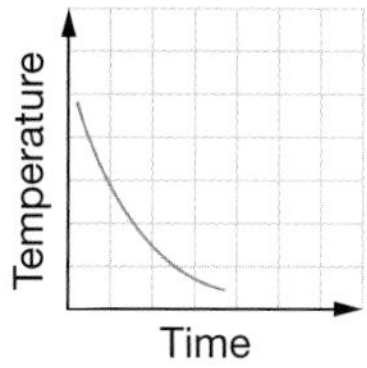

i

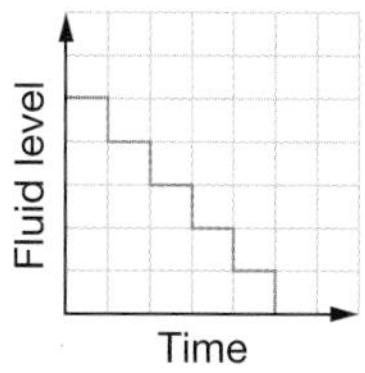

j

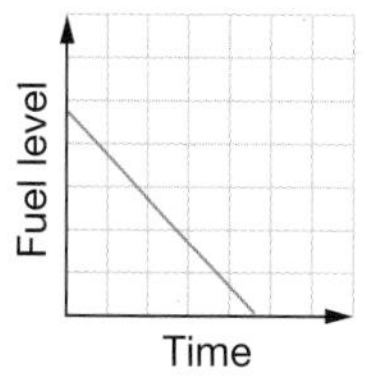

k

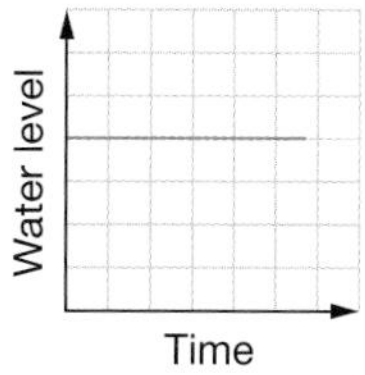

l

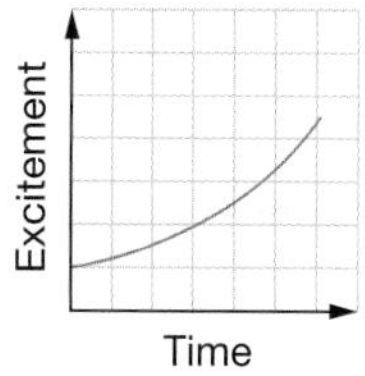

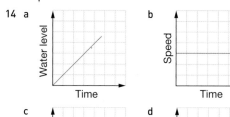

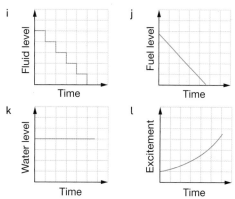

[Your graph for part l might be different, but hopefully it looks like this.]

15

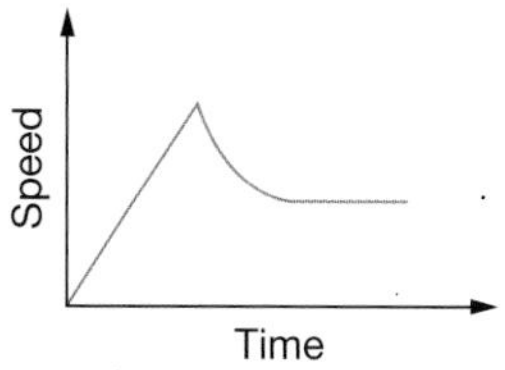

16 a

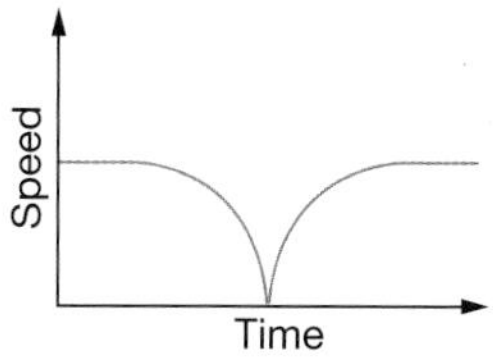

b

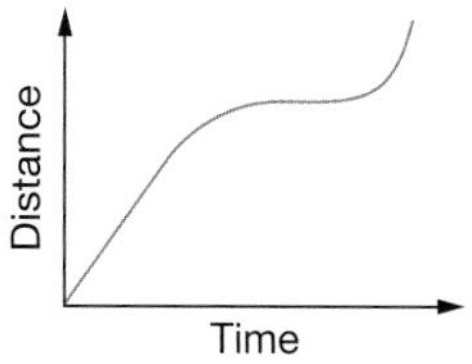

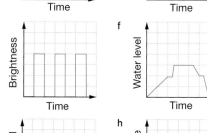

17 a She would turn to the right, as in the picture shown in the question.

b As the difference in steps increases, the radius of the circle decreases.

c The curve of best fit is drawn joining the points.

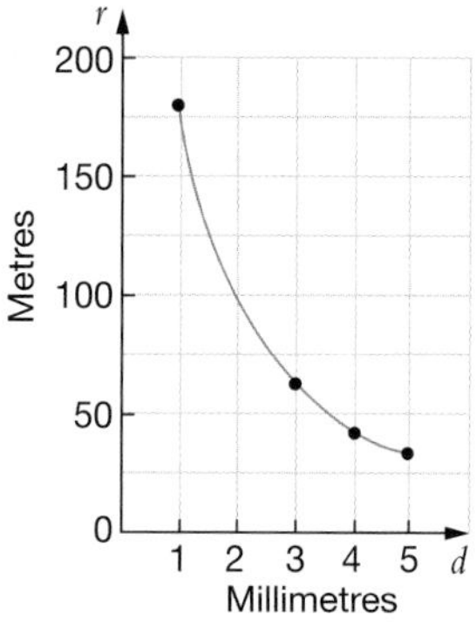

d Since the product of d and t is always 180:

$dr = 180$ or $r = \dfrac{180}{d}$

e When $d = 1{\cdot}5$, $r = \dfrac{180}{1{\cdot}5} = 120$

∴ the radius of the circle would be 120 metres.

f When $d = 0$, $r = \frac{180}{0}$

As $\frac{180}{0}$ cannot exist, there is no circle.

The person walks in a straight line.

18 a 18 000 litres

b

t	0	5	10	20	25	30
V	18 000	12 500	8000	2000	500	0

c

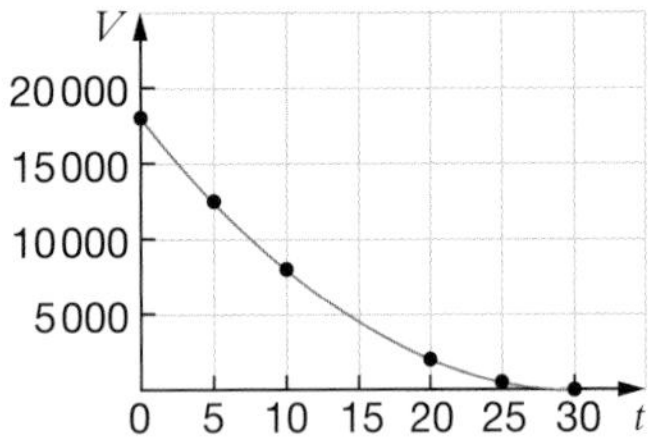

d 9 minutes (approx.)

e No. From the graph the pool drains rapidly at the beginning (perhaps high pressure) but decreases as it nears empty.

Challenge 15:06

v	0 km/h (0 m/s)	30 km/h (8·3 m/s)	60 km/h (16·7 m/s)	80 km/h (22·2 m/s)	100 km/h (27·8 m/s)
d	0 m	18·5 m	57·2 m	94·3 m	140·4 m

1 a yes; approximately 20·2 m/s (72·7 km/h)

b i 65·4 m ii 1·6 m

c i 17·5 m/s ii 11·1 m/s

d i 2·5 m ii 15·9 m

2 Answers will vary.

Diagnostic test 15

1 a 50 b 8 c 24 d 25

2 a 100 b 2 c 15 d 1

3 a direct b indirect c direct d indirect

4 a $k = 5$ b 85 c 34·8

5 a $D = 24T$ b $k = 24$

c 192 km d 9 h, 30 min

6 a $k = 12$ b 264 c 16 h, 40 min

7 a $t = \frac{48}{n}$ b $k = 48$ c 4 hours d 16

8 a $k = 120$ b 2 h, 24 min c 60 km/h

9 a 750 Hz b 37·5 cm

10 a *CD* b *CD* c *AB*

11 a *BC* b *BC* c *CD*

12 a 60 km

b i 10 km/h ii 40 km/h iii 80 km/h

c 12 km/h d 30 km/h, between 2 pm and 3 pm

13 a 2·5 min b 45°C

c 25°C d approx. 75°C

14 a 40 km/h b *Q* c 50 km/h

15 a 60 g b approx. 80°C

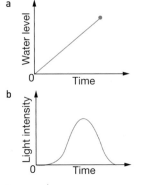

c I d no

16 a

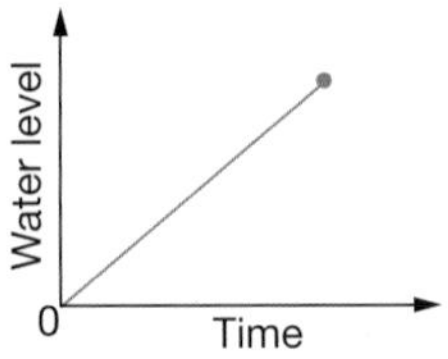

b

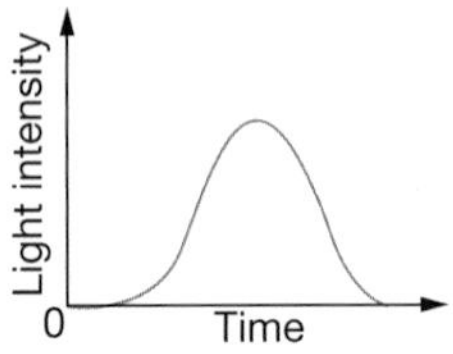

c

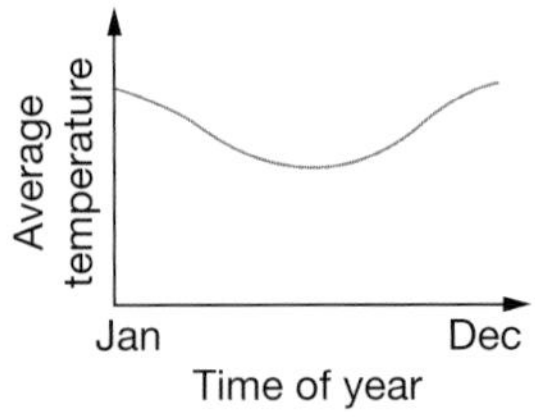

ASSIGNMENT 15A

1 3·6 L/h

2 a 2 min, 45 s b 21·8 km/h

3 a 340 b 470

4 a 34 kg b 104·125 kg

5 a 4·42 cm b 85 cm

6 a 24 days b 48 days

7 a $W = \frac{690}{L}$ b 197·1 kg c 3·83 m

8 a 180 m

b 50 cm; this would be a tight squeeze for most adults.

9

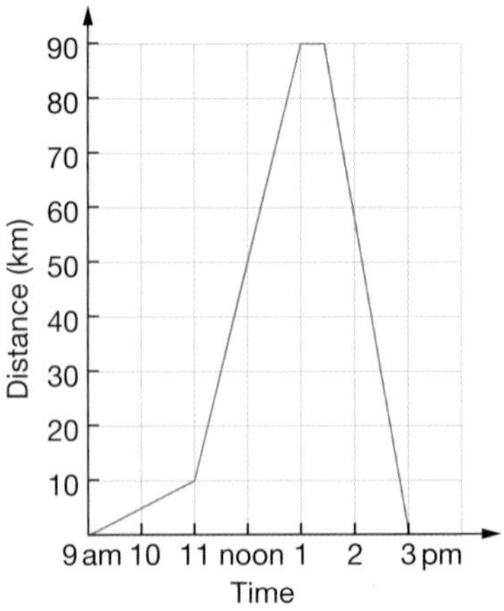

10 Andrew climbs the platform but fails to jump and climbs back down. Helen jumps and is then hauled back to the platform.

ASSIGNMENT 15B

1 a \$2580 b \$280 c 25·5%

2 a 124·7 cm^2 b 593·8 cm^2 c 843·2 cm^2

3 \$545

4 a The first stands for 3 months, the second for 3 years.

b i 5·9 kg ii 10 kg iii 11·7 kg

iv 12·9 kg v 10·6 kg

c 40% d From 4·3 kg to 6·2 kg.

e From about 2·5 kg to 4 kg.

ASSIGNMENT 15C

1 a 18·8 b 47·8

2 1392 m^3, 1 392 000 L

3 a 10 b D is (−2, 3), E is (3, 3) c 5

4 a 10 b 5050 c 15 050 d 512

5 a

Dice B

	Outcome	1	2	3	4	3	3
	6	6, 1	6, 2	6, 3	6, 4	6, 3	6, 3
	2	2, 1	2, 2	2, 3	2, 4	2, 3	2, 3
	3	3, 1	3, 2	3, 3	3, 4	3, 3	3, 3
Dice A	4	4, 1	4, 2	4, 3	4, 4	4, 3	4, 3
	5	5, 1	5, 2	5, 3	5, 4	5, 3	5, 3
	6	6, 1	6, 2	6, 3	6, 4	6, 3	6, 3

b $\frac{21}{36} = \frac{7}{12} \doteqdot 58\%$

c $P(6) = \frac{12}{36}$, $P(4) = \frac{11}{36}$;
6 has more chance of appearing than a 4.

6 a i 48 ii 33 iii 32 iv 26

b

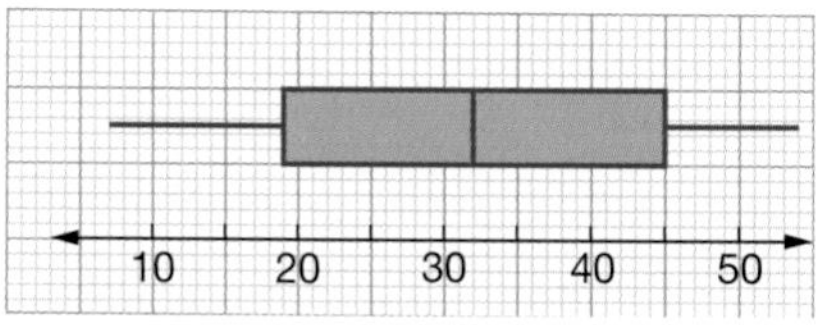